Computer Security

Second Edition

Computer Security
Art and Science

Second Edition

Matt Bishop

with contributions from

Elisabeth Sullivan and Michelle Ruppel

♠♥ Addison-Wesley

Boston • Columbus • New York • San Francisco • Amsterdam • Cape Town
Dubai • London • Madrid • Milan • Munich • Paris • Montreal • Toronto • Delhi • Mexico City
São Paulo • Sydney • Hong Kong • Seoul • Singapore • Taipei • Tokyo

Library of Congress Control Number: 2018950017

ISBN-13: 978-0-321-71233-2
ISBN-10: 0-321-71233-1

1   18

To my dear Holly; our children Heidi, Steven, David, and Caroline; our grandchildren Skyler and Sage; and our friends Seaview, Tinker Belle, Stripe, Baby Windsor, Scout, Fur, Puff, Mouse, Shadow, Fuzzy, Dusty, and the rest of the menagerie.

Contents

Preface

HORTENSIO: Madam, before you touch the instrument
To learn the order of my fingering,
I must begin with rudiments of art
To teach you gamouth in a briefer sort,
More pleasant, pithy and effectual,
Than hath been taught by any of my trade;
And there it is in writing, fairly drawn.
— *The Taming of the Shrew*, III, i, 62–68.

Preface to the Second Edition

Since the first edition of this book was published, the number of computer and information security incidents has increased dramatically, as has their seriousness. In 2010, a computer worm infected the software controlling a particular type of centrifuge used in uranium-enrichment sites [1116, 1137]. In 2013, a security breach at Target, a large chain of stores in the United States, compromised 40 million credit cards [1497, 1745, 2237]. Also in 2013, Yahoo reported that an attack compromised more than 1 billion accounts [779]. In 2017, attackers spread ransomware that crippled computers throughout the world, including computers used in hospitals and telecommunications companies [1881]. Equifax estimated that attackers also compromised the personal data of over 100,000,000 people [176].

These attacks exploit vulnerabilities that have their roots in vulnerabilities of the 1980s, 1970s, and earlier. They seem more complex because systems have become more complex, and thus the vulnerabilities are more obscure and require more complex attacks to exploit. But the principles underlying the attacks, the vulnerabilities, and the failures of the systems have not changed—only the arena in which they are applied has.

Consistent with this philosophy, the second edition continues to focus on the principles underlying the field of computer and information security. Many newer examples show how these principles are applied, or not applied, today; but the principles themselves are as important today as they were in 2002, and earlier. Some have been updated to reflect a deeper understanding of people and systems. Others have been applied in new and interesting ways. But they still ring true.

That said, the landscape of security has evolved greatly in the years since this book was first published. The explosive growth of the World Wide Web, and the consequent explosion in its use, has made security a problem at the forefront of our society. No longer can vulnerabilities, both human and technological, be relegated to the background of our daily lives. It is one of the elements at the forefront, playing a role in everyone's life as one browses the web, uses a camera to take and send pictures, and turns on an oven remotely. We grant access to our personal lives through social media such as Facebook, Twitter, and Instagram, and to our homes through the Internet of Things and our connections to the Internet. To ignore security issues, or consider them simply ancillary details that "someone will fix somehow" or threats unlikely to be realized personally is dangerous at best, and potentially disastrous at worst.

Ultimately, little has changed. The computing ecosystem of our day is badly flawed. Among the manifestations of these technological flaws are that security problems continue to exist, and continue to grow in magnitude of effect. An interesting question to ponder is what might move the paradigm of security away from the cycle of "patch and catch" and "let the buyer beware" to a stable and safer ecosystem.

But we must continue to improve our understanding of, and implementation of, security. Security nihilism—simply giving up and asserting that we cannot make things secure, so why try—means we accept these invasions of our privacy, our society, and our world. Like everything else, security is imperfect, and always will be—meaning we can improve the state of the art. This book is directed towards that goal.

Updated Roadmap

The dependencies of the chapters are the same as in the first edition (see p. xl), with two new chapters added.

Chapter 7, which includes a discussion of denial of service attack models, contains material useful for Chapters 23, 24, 27, and 28. Similarly, Chapter 27 draws on material from the chapters in Part III as well as Chapters 23, 25, 26, and all of Part VIII.

In addition to the suggestions in the preface to the first edition on p. xli about topics for undergraduate classes, the material in Chapter 27 will introduce undergraduates to how attacks occur, how they can be analyzed, and what their effects are. Coupled with current examples drawn from the news, this chapter should prove fascinating to undergraduates.

As for graduate classes, the new material in Chapter 7 will provide students with some background on resilience, a topic increasing in importance. Otherwise, the recommendations are the same as for the first edition (see p. xlii).

Changes to the First Edition

The second edition has extensively revised many examples to apply the concepts to technologies, methodologies, and ideas that have emerged since the first edition was published. Here, the focus is on new material in the chapters; changes to examples are mentioned only when necessary to describe that material. In addition to what is mentioned here, much of the text has been updated.

Chapter 1, "An Overview of Computer Security": This chapter is largely unchanged.

Chapter 2, "Access Control Matrix": Section 2.2.2, "Access Controlled by History" has been changed to use the problem of preventing downloaded programs from accessing the system in unauthorized ways, instead of updating a database. Section 2.4.3, "Principle of Attenuation of Privilege," has been expanded slightly, and exercises added to point out differing forms of the principle.

Chapter 3, "Foundational Results": Definition 3–1 has been updated to make clear that "leaking" refers to a right being added to an element of the access control matrix that did not contain it initially, and an exercise has been added to demonstrate the difference between this definition and the one in the first edition. Section 3.6 discusses comparing security properties of models.

Chapter 4, "Security Policies": Section 4.5.1, "High-Level Policy Languages," now uses Ponder rather than a Java policy constraint language. Section 4.6, "Example: Academic Computer Security Policy," has been updated to reflect changes in the university policy.

Chapter 5, "Confidentiality Policies": Section 5.3.1 discusses principles for declassifying information.

Chapter 6, "Integrity Policies": Section 6.5 presents trust models.

Chapter 7, "Availability Policies": This chapter is new.

Chapter 8, "Hybrid Policies": Section 8.1.3 modifies one of the assumptions of the Chinese Wall model that is unrealistic. Section 8.3.1 expands the discussion of ORCON to include DRM. Section 8.4 adds a discussion of several types of RBAC models.

Chapter 9, "Noninterference and Policy Composition": This chapter adds Section 9.6, which presents side channels in the context of deducibility.

Chapter 10, "Basic Cryptography": This chapter has been extensively revised. The discussion of the DES (Section 10.2.3) has been tightened and the algorithm moved to Appendix F. Discussions of the AES (Section 10.2.5) and elliptic curve cryptography (Section 10.3.3) have been added, and the section on digital signatures moved from Chapter 11 to Section 10.5. Also, the number of digits in the integers used in examples for public key cryptography has been increased from 2 to at least 4, and in many cases more.

Chapter 11, "Key Management": Section 11.4.3 discusses public key infrastructures. Section 11.5.1.4, "Other Approaches," now includes a brief discussion of identity-based encryption.

Chapter 12, "Cipher Techniques": Section 12.1, "Problems," now includes a discussion of type flaw attacks. Section 12.3 discusses authenticated encryption with associated data, and presents the CCM and GCM modes of block ciphers. A new section, Section 12.5.2, discusses the Signal Protocol. Section 12.5.3, "Security at the Transport Layer: TLS and SSL," has been expanded and focuses on TLS rather than SSL. It also discusses cryptographic weaknesses in SSL, such as the POODLE attack, that have led to the use of SSL being strongly discouraged.

Chapter 13, "Authentication": A discussion of graphical passwords has been added as Section 13.3.4. Section 13.4.3 looks at quantifying password strength in terms of entropy. The discussion of biometrics in Section 13.7 has been expanded to reflect their increasing use.

Chapter 14, "Design Principles": The principle of least authority follows the principle of least privilege in Section 14.2.1, and the principle of least astonishment now supersedes the principle of psychological acceptability in Section 14.2.8.

Chapter 15, "Representing Identity": Section 15.5, "Naming and Certificates," now includes a discussion of registration authorities (RAs). Section 15.6.1.3 adds a discussion of the DNS security extensions (DNSSEC). Section 15.7.2 discusses onion routing and Tor in the context of anonymity.

Chapter 16, "Access Control Mechanisms": Section 16.2.6 discusses sets of privileges in Linux and other UNIX-like systems.

Chapter 17, "Information Flow": In contrast to the confidentiality-based context of information flow in the main part of this chapter, Section 17.5 presents information flow in an integrity context. In Section 17.6, the SPI and SNSMG examples of the first edition have been replaced by Android cell phones (Section 17.6.1) and firewalls (Section 17.6.2).

Chapter 18, "Confinement Problem": Section 18.2 has been expanded to include library operating systems (Section 18.2.1.2) and program modification techniques (Section 18.2.2).

Chapter 19, "Introduction to Assurance": Section 19.2.3, which covers agile software development, has been added.

Chapter 20, "Building Systems with Assurance": The example decomposition of Windows 2000 into components has been updated to use Windows 10.

Chapter 21, "Formal Methods": A new section, Section 21.5, discusses functional programming languages, and another new section, 21.6, discusses formally verified products.

Chapter 22, "Evaluating Systems": Sections 22.7, on FIPS 140, and 22.8, on the Common Criteria, have been extensively updated.

Chapter 23, "Malware": Section 23.5 presents botnets, and Sections 23.6.3, 23.6.4, 23.6.5, and 23.6.6 discuss adware and spyware, ransomware, and phishing. While not malware, phishing is a common vector for getting malware onto a system and so it is discussed here.

Chapter 24, "Vulnerability Analysis": Section 24.2.5 reviews several penetration testing frameworks used commercially and based on the Flaw Hypothesis Methodology. Section 24.5 presents the widely used CVE and CWE standards.

Chapter 25, "Auditing": Section 25.3.3, which discusses sanitization, has been expanded.

Chapter 26, "Intrusion Detection": Section 26.3.1 has been expanded to include several widely used machine learning techniques for anomaly detection. Incident response groups are discussed in Section 27.3.

Chapter 27, "Attacks and Responses": This chapter is new.

Chapter 28, "Network Security": The discussion of what firewalls are has been moved to Section 17.6.2, but the discussion of how the Drib configures and uses them remains in this chapter. The Drib added wireless networks, which are discussed in Section 28.3.3.1. Its analysis of using the cloud is in Section 28.3.3.2. The rest of the chapter has been updated to refer to the new material in previous chapters.

Chapter 29, "System Security": This chapter has been updated to refer to the new material in previous chapters.

Chapter 30, "User Security": Section 30.2.2 describes the two-factor authentication procedure used by the Drib. The rest of the chapter has been updated to refer to the new material in previous chapters.

Chapter 31, "Program Security": This chapter has been updated to refer to the new material in previous chapters.

Two new appendices have been added. Appendix F presents the DES and AES algorithms, and Appendix H collects the rules in Chapter 31 for easy reference. In addition, Appendix D examines some hardware enhancements to aid virtualization, and Appendix G contains the full academic security policy discussed in Section 4.6.

Preface to the First Edition[1]

On September 11, 2001, terrorists seized control of four airplanes. Three were flown into buildings, and a fourth crashed, with catastrophic loss of life. In the aftermath, the security and reliability of many aspects of society drew renewed scrutiny. One of these aspects was the widespread use of computers and their interconnecting networks. The issue is not new. In 1988, approximately 5,000 computers throughout the Internet were rendered unusable within 4 hours by a program called a worm [842].[2] While the spread, and the effects, of this program alarmed computer scientists, most people were not worried because the worm did not affect their lives or their ability to do their jobs. In 1993, more users of computer systems were alerted to such dangers when a set of programs called sniffers were placed on many computers run by network service providers and recorded login names and passwords [670].

After an attack on Tsutomu Shimomura's computer system, and the fascinating way Shimomura followed the attacker's trail, which led to his arrest [1736], the public's interest and apprehension were finally aroused. Computers were now vulnerable. Their once reassuring protections were now viewed as flimsy.

Several films explored these concerns. Movies such as *War Games* and *Hackers* provided images of people who can, at will, wander throughout computers and networks, maliciously or frivolously corrupting or destroying information it may have taken millions of dollars to amass. (Reality intruded on *Hackers* when the World Wide Web page set up by MGM/United Artists was quickly altered to present an irreverent commentary on the movie and to suggest that viewers see *The Net* instead. Paramount Pictures denied doing this [869].) Another film, *Sneakers*, presented a picture of those who test the security of computer (and other) systems for their owners and for the government.

Goals

This book has three goals. The first is to show the importance of theory to practice and of practice to theory. All too often, practitioners regard theory as irrelevant and theoreticians think of practice as trivial. In reality, theory and practice are symbiotic. For example, the theory of covert channels, in which the goal is to limit the ability of processes to communicate through shared resources, provides a mechanism for evaluating the effectiveness of mechanisms that confine processes, such as sandboxes and firewalls. Similarly, business practices in the commercial world led to the development of several security policy models such as the Clark-Wilson model and the Chinese Wall model. These models in turn help the designers of security policies better understand and evaluate the mechanisms and procedures needed to secure their sites.

---

[1] Chapter numbers have been updated to correspond to the chapters in the second edition.
[2] Section 23.4 discusses computer worms.

The second goal is to emphasize that computer security and cryptography are different. Although cryptography is an essential component of computer security, it is by no means the only component. Cryptography provides a mechanism for performing specific functions, such as preventing unauthorized people from reading and altering messages on a network. However, unless developers understand the context in which they are using cryptography, and unless the assumptions underlying the protocol and the cryptographic mechanisms apply to the context, the cryptography may not add to the security of the system. The canonical example is the use of cryptography to secure communications between two low-security systems. If only trusted users can access the two systems, cryptography protects messages in transit. But if untrusted users can access either system (through authorized accounts or, more likely, by breaking in), the cryptography is not sufficient to protect the messages. The attackers can read the messages at either endpoint.

The third goal is to demonstrate that computer security is not just a science but also an art. It is an art because no system can be considered secure without an examination of how it is to be used. The definition of a "secure computer" necessitates a statement of requirements and an expression of those requirements in the form of authorized actions and authorized users. (A computer engaged in work at a university may be considered "secure" for the purposes of the work done at the university. When moved to a military installation, that same system may not provide sufficient control to be deemed "secure" for the purposes of the work done at that installation.) How will people, as well as other computers, interact with the computer system? How clear and restrictive an interface can a designer create without rendering the system unusable while trying to prevent unauthorized use or access to the data or resources on the system?

Just as an artist paints his view of the world onto canvas, so does a designer of security features articulate his view of the world of human/machine interaction in the security policy and mechanisms of the system. Two designers may use entirely different designs to achieve the same creation, just as two artists may use different subjects to achieve the same concept.

Computer security is also a science. Its theory is based on mathematical constructions, analyses, and proofs. Its systems are built in accordance with the accepted practices of engineering. It uses inductive and deductive reasoning to examine the security of systems from key axioms and to discover underlying principles. These scientific principles can then be applied to untraditional situations and new theories, policies, and mechanisms.

Philosophy

Key to understanding the problems that exist in computer security is a recognition that the problems are not new. They are old problems, dating from the beginning of computer security (and, in fact, arising from parallel problems in the non-computer world). But the locus has changed as the field of computing has changed. Before the mid-1980s, mainframe and mid-level computers dominated the market, and computer security problems and solutions were phrased in terms of securing files or processes on a single system. With the rise of networking and the Internet, the arena has changed. Workstations and servers, and the networking infrastructure that connects them, now dominate the market. Computer security problems and solutions now focus on a networked environment. However, if the workstations and servers, and the supporting network infrastructure, are viewed as a single system, the models, theories, and problem statements developed for systems before the mid-1980s apply equally well to current systems.

As an example, consider the issue of assurance. In the early period, assurance arose in several ways: formal methods and proofs of correctness, validation of policy to requirements, and acquisition of data and programs from trusted sources, to name a few. Those providing assurance analyzed a single system, the code on it, and the sources (vendors and users) from which the code could be acquired to ensure that either the sources could be trusted or the programs could be confined adequately to do minimal damage. In the later period, the same basic principles and techniques apply, except that the scope of some has been greatly expanded (from a single system and a small set of vendors to the world-wide Internet). The work on proof-carrying code, an exciting development in which the proof that a downloadable program module satisfies a stated policy is incorporated into the program itself, is an example of this expansion.[3] It extends the notion of a proof of consistency with a stated policy. It advances the technology of the earlier period into the later period. But in order to understand it properly, one must understand the ideas underlying the concept of proof-carrying code, and these ideas lie in the earlier period.

As another example, consider Saltzer and Schroeder's principles of secure design.[4] Enunciated in 1975, they promote simplicity, confinement, and understanding. When security mechanisms grow too complex, attackers can evade or bypass them. Many programmers and vendors are learning this when attackers break into their systems and servers. The argument that the principles are old, and somehow outdated, rings hollow when the result of their violation is a non-secure system.

The work from the earlier period is sometimes cast in terms of systems that no longer exist and that differ in many ways from modern systems. This does not vitiate the ideas and concepts, which also underlie the work done today. Once these ideas and concepts are properly understood, applying them in a multiplicity of environments becomes possible. Furthermore, the current mechanisms and technologies will become obsolete and of historical interest themselves as new forms of computing arise, but the underlying principles will live on, to underlie the next generation—indeed the next era—of computing.

The philosophy of this book is that certain key concepts underlie all of computer security, and that the study of all parts of computer security enriches

---

[3] Section 23.9.5.1 discusses proof-carrying code.
[4] Chapter 14 discusses these principles.

the understanding of all parts. Moreover, critical to an understanding of the applications of security-related technologies and methodologies is an understanding of the theory underlying those applications. Advances in the theory of computer protection have illuminated the foundations of security systems. Issues of abstract modeling, and modeling to meet specific environments, lead to systems designed to achieve a specific and rewarding goal. Theorems about composability of policies[5] and the undecidability of the general security question[6] have indicated the limits of what can be done. Much work and effort are continuing to extend the borders of those limits.

Application of these results has improved the quality of the security of the systems being protected. However, the issue is how compatibly the assumptions of the model (and theory) conform to the environment to which the theory is applied. Although our knowledge of how to apply these abstractions is continually increasing, we still have difficulty correctly transposing the relevant information from a realistic setting to one in which analyses can then proceed. Such abstraction often eliminates vital information. The omitted data may pertain to security in non-obvious ways. Without this information, the analysis is flawed.

The practitioner needs to know both the theoretical and practical aspects of the art and science of computer security. The theory demonstrates what is possible. The practical makes known what is feasible. The theoretician needs to understand the constraints under which these theories are used, how their results are translated into practical tools and methods, and how realistic are the assumptions underlying the theories. *Computer Security: Art and Science* tries to meet these needs.

Unfortunately, no single work can cover all aspects of computer security, so this book focuses on those parts that are, in the author's opinion, most fundamental and most pervasive. The mechanisms exemplify the applications of these principles.

Organization

The organization of this book reflects its philosophy. It begins with mathematical fundamentals and principles that provide boundaries within which security can be modeled and analyzed effectively. The mathematics provides a framework for expressing and analyzing the requirements of the security of a system. These policies constrain what is allowed and what is not allowed. Mechanisms provide the ability to implement these policies. The degree to which the mechanisms correctly implement the policies, and indeed the degree to which the policies themselves meet the requirements of the organizations using the system, are questions of assurance. Exploiting failures in policy, in implementation, and in assurance comes next, as well as mechanisms for providing information on the attack. The book concludes with the applications of both theory and policy focused

---

[5]See Chapter 9, "Noninterference and Policy Composition."
[6]See Section 3.2, "Basic Results."

on realistic situations. This natural progression emphasizes the development and application of the principles existent in computer security.

Part I, "Introduction," describes what computer security is all about and explores the problems and challenges to be faced. It sets the context for the remainder of the book.

Part II, "Foundations," deals with basic questions such as how "security" can be clearly and functionally defined, whether or not it is realistic, and whether or not it is decidable. If it is decidable, under what conditions is it decidable, and if not, how must the definition be bounded in order to make it decidable?

Part III, "Policy," probes the relationship between policy and security. The definition of "security" depends on policy. In Part III we examine several types of policies, including the ever-present fundamental questions of trust, analysis of policies, and the use of policies to constrain operations and transitions.

Part IV, "Implementation I: Cryptography," discusses cryptography and its role in security. It focuses on applications and discusses issues such as key management and escrow, key distribution, and how cryptosystems are used in networks. A quick study of authentication completes Part III.

Part V, "Implementation II: Systems," considers how to implement the requirements imposed by policies using system-oriented techniques. Certain design principles are fundamental to effective security mechanisms. Policies define who can act and how they can act, and so identity is a critical aspect of implementation. Mechanisms implementing access control and flow control enforce various aspects of policies.

Part VI, "Assurance," presents methodologies and technologies for ascertaining how well a system, or a product, meets its goals. After setting the background, to explain exactly what "assurance" is, the art of building systems to meet varying levels of assurance is discussed. Formal verification methods play a role. Part VI shows how the progression of standards has enhanced our understanding of assurance techniques.

Part VII, "Special Topics," discusses some miscellaneous aspects of computer security. Malicious logic thwarts many mechanisms. Despite our best efforts at high assurance, systems today are replete with vulnerabilities. Why? How can a system be analyzed to detect vulnerabilities? What models might help us improve the state of the art? Given these security holes, how can we detect attackers who exploit them? A discussion of auditing flows naturally into a discussion of intrusion detection—a detection method for such attacks.

Part VIII, "Practicum," presents examples of how to apply the principles discussed throughout the book. It begins with networks and proceeds to systems, users, and programs. Each chapter states a desired policy and shows how to translate that policy into a set of mechanisms and procedures that support the policy. Part VIII tries to demonstrate that the material covered elsewhere can be, and should be, used in practice.

Each chapter in this book ends with a summary, descriptions of some research issues, and some suggestions for further reading. The summary highlights the important ideas in the chapter. The research issues are current "hot topics" or are topics that may prove to be fertile ground for advancing the state of the art and science of computer security. Interested readers who wish to pursue the topics in any chapter in more depth can go to some of the suggested readings. They expand on the material in the chapter or present other interesting avenues.

Roadmap

This book is both a reference book and a textbook. Its audience is undergraduate and graduate students as well as practitioners. This section offers some suggestions on approaching the book.

Dependencies

Chapter 1 is fundamental to the rest of the book and should be read first. After that, however, the reader need not follow the chapters in order. Some of the dependencies among chapters are as follows.

Chapter 3 depends on Chapter 2 and requires a fair degree of mathematical maturity. Chapter 2, on the other hand, does not. The material in Chapter 3 is for the most part not used elsewhere (although the existence of the first section's key result, the undecidability theorem, is mentioned repeatedly). It can be safely skipped if the interests of the reader lie elsewhere.

The chapters in Part III build on one another. The formalisms in Chapter 5 are called on in Chapters 20 and 21, but nowhere else. Unless the reader intends to delve into the sections on theorem proving and formal mappings, the formalisms may be skipped. The material in Chapter 9 requires a degree of mathematical maturity, and this material is used sparingly elsewhere. Like Chapter 3, Chapter 9 can be skipped by the reader whose interests lie elsewhere.

Chapters 10, 11, and 12 also build on one another in order. A reader who has encountered basic cryptography will have an easier time with the material than one who has not, but the chapters do not demand the level of mathematical experience that Chapters 3 and 9 require. Chapter 13 does not require material from Chapter 11 or Chapter 12, but it does require material from Chapter 10.

Chapter 14 is required for all of Part V. A reader who has studied operating systems at the undergraduate level will have no trouble with Chapter 16. Chapter 15 uses the material in Chapters 10 and 11; Chapter 17 builds on material in Chapters 5, 14, and 16; and Chapter 18 uses material in Chapters 4, 14, and 17.

Chapter 19 relies on information in Chapter 4. Chapter 20 builds on Chapters 5, 14, 16, and 19. Chapter 21 presents highly mathematical concepts and uses material from Chapters 19 and 20. Chapter 22 is based on material in Chapters 5, 19, and 20; it does not require Chapter 21. For all of Part VI, a knowledge of software engineering is very helpful.

Chapter 23 draws on ideas and information in Chapters 5, 6, 10, 14, 16, and 18 (and for Section 23.8, the reader should read Section 3.1). Chapter 24 is self-contained, although it implicitly uses many ideas from assurance. It also assumes a good working knowledge of compilers, operating systems, and in some cases networks. Many of the flaws are drawn from versions of the UNIX operating system, or from Windows systems, and so a working knowledge of either or both systems will make some of the material easier to understand. Chapter 25 uses information from Chapter 4, and Chapter 26 uses material from Chapter 25.

The practicum chapters are self-contained and do not require any material beyond Chapter 1. However, they point out relevant material in other sections that augments the information and (we hope) the reader's understanding of that information.

Background

The material in this book is at the advanced undergraduate level. Throughout, we assume that the reader is familiar with the basics of compilers and computer architecture (such as the use of the program stack) and operating systems. The reader should also be comfortable with modular arithmetic (for the material on cryptography). Some material, such as that on formal methods (Chapter 21) and the mathematical theory of computer security (Chapter 3 and the formal presentation of policy models), requires considerable mathematical maturity. Other specific recommended background is presented in the preceding section. Part IX, the appendices, contains material that will be helpful to readers with backgrounds that lack some of the recommended material.

Examples are drawn from many systems. Many come from the UNIX operating system or variations of it (such as Linux). Others come from the Windows family of systems. Familiarity with these systems will help the reader understand many examples easily and quickly.

Undergraduate Level

An undergraduate class typically focuses on applications of theory and how students can use the material. The specific arrangement and selection of material depends on the focus of the class, but all classes should cover some basic material—notably that in Chapters 1, 10, and 14, as well as the notion of an access control matrix, which is discussed in Sections 2.1 and 2.2.

Presentation of real problems and solutions often engages undergraduate students more effectively than presentation of abstractions. The special topics and the practicum provide a wealth of practical problems and ways to deal with them. This leads naturally to the deeper issues of policy, cryptography, non-cryptographic mechanisms, and assurance. The following are sections appropriate for non-mathematical undergraduate courses in these topics.

- *Policy*: Sections 4.1 through 4.4 describe the notion of policy. The instructor should select one or two examples from Sections 5.1, 5.2.1, 6.2, 6.4, 8.1.1, and 8.2, which describe several policy models informally. Section 8.4 discusses role-based access control.
- *Cryptography*: Key distribution is discussed in Sections 11.1 and 11.2, and a common form of public key infrastructures (called PKIs) is discussed in Section 11.4.2. Section 12.1 points out common errors

in using cryptography. Section 12.4 shows how cryptography is used in networks, and the instructor should use one of the protocols in Section 12.5 as an example. Chapter 13 offers a look at various forms of authentication, including non-cryptographic methods.

- *Non-cryptographic mechanisms*: Identity is the basis for many access control mechanisms. Sections 15.1 through 15.4 discuss identity on a system, and Section 15.6 discusses identity and anonymity on the Web. Sections 16.1 and 16.2 explore two mechanisms for controlling access to files, and Section 16.4 discusses the ring-based mechanism underlying the notion of multiple levels of privilege. If desired, the instructor can cover sandboxes by using Sections 18.1 and 18.2, but because Section 18.2 uses material from Section 4.5, the instructor will need to go over those sections as well.

- *Assurance*: Chapter 19 provides a basic introduction to the often overlooked topic of assurance.

Graduate Level

A typical introductory graduate class can focus more deeply on the subject than can an undergraduate class. Like an undergraduate class, a graduate class should cover Chapters 1, 10, and 14. Also important are the undecidability results in Sections 3.1 and 3.2, which require that Chapter 2 be covered. Beyond that, the instructor can choose from a variety of topics and present them to whatever depth is appropriate. The following are sections suitable for graduate study.

- *Policy models*: Part III covers many common policy models both informally and formally. The formal description is much easier to understand once the informal description is understood, so in all cases both should be covered. The controversy in Section 5.4 is particularly illuminating to students who have not considered the role of policy and the nature of a policy. Chapter 9 is a highly formal discussion of the foundations of policy and is appropriate for students with experience in formal mathematics. Students without such a background will find it quite difficult.

- *Cryptography*: Part IV focuses on the applications of cryptography, not on cryptography's mathematical underpinnings.[7] It discusses areas of interest critical to the use of cryptography, such as key management and some basic cryptographic protocols used in networking.

- *Non-cryptographic mechanisms*: Issues of identity and certification are complex and generally poorly understood. Section 15.5 covers these problems. Combining this with the discussion of identity on the Web

---

[7]The interested reader will find a number of books covering aspects of this subject [440, 787, 788, 914, 1092, 1093, 1318, 1826].

(Section 15.6) raises issues of trust and naming. Chapters 17 and 18 explore issues of information flow and confining that flow.

- *Assurance*: Traditionally, assurance is taught as formal methods, and Chapter 21 serves this purpose. In practice, however, assurance is more often accomplished by using structured processes and techniques and informal but rigorous arguments of justification, mappings, and analysis. Chapter 20 emphasizes these topics. Chapter 22 discusses evaluation standards and relies heavily on the material in Chapters 19 and 20 and some of the ideas in Chapter 21.

- *Miscellaneous Topics*: Section 23.8 presents a proof that the generic problem of determining if a generic program is a computer virus is in fact undecidable. The theory of penetration studies in Section 24.2, and the more formal approach in Section 24.6, illuminate the analysis of systems for vulnerabilities. If the instructor chooses to cover intrusion detection (Chapter 26) in depth, it should be understood that this discussion draws heavily on the material on auditing (Chapter 25).

- *Practicum*: The practicum (Part VIII) ties the material in the earlier part of the book to real-world examples and emphasizes the applications of the theory and methodologies discussed earlier.

Practitioners

Practitioners in the field of computer security will find much to interest them. The table of contents and the index will help them locate specific topics. A more general approach is to start with Chapter 1 and then proceed to Part VIII, the practicum. Each chapter has references to other sections of the text that explain the underpinnings of the material. This will lead the reader to a deeper understanding of the reasons for the policies, settings, configurations, and advice in the practicum. This approach also allows readers to focus on those topics that are of most interest to them.

Register your copy of *Computer Security, Second Edition*, on the InformIT site for convenient access to updates and/or corrections as they become available. To start the registration process, go to informit.com/register and log in or create an account. Enter the product ISBN (9780321712332) and click Submit. Look on the Registered Products tab for an Access Bonus Content link next to this product, and follow that link to access any available bonus materials. If you would like to be notified of exclusive offers on new editions and updates, please check the box to receive email from us.

Acknowledgments

It is not possible to separate those who contributed to the second edition from those who contributed to the first edition, because everything done for the first edition, especially after the first printing, has contributed to the second. So these acknowledgments apply to both editions. That said ...

Special Acknowledgments

Elisabeth Sullivan and Michelle Ruppel contributed the assurance part of this book.

For the first edition, Liz wrote several drafts, all of which reflect her extensive knowledge and experience in that aspect of computer security. I am particularly grateful to her for contributing her real-world knowledge of how assurance is managed. Too often, books recount the mathematics of assurance without recognizing that other aspects are equally important and more widely used. These other aspects shine through in the assurance section, thanks to Liz. As if that were not enough, she made several suggestions that improved the policy part of this book. I will always be grateful for her contribution, her humor, and especially her friendship.

For the second edition, Michelle stepped in to update that part based on her extensive experience and real-world knowledge as a practitioner. She was careful to maintain the tone and style of Liz's writing, and her contributions strengthened the assurance part. I am grateful to her for agreeing to step in, for the exceptional effort she put forth, and the high quality that resulted.

In summary, I am very grateful for their contributions.

Acknowledgments

Many people offered comments, suggestions, and ideas for the second edition. Thanks to Marvin Schaefer, Sean Peisert, Prof. Christian Probst, Carrie Gates, and Richard Ford for their reviews of the various chapters. I appreciate Prof. Ken

Rosen and Prof. Alfred Menezes for their help with Chapter 10, Steven Templeton and Kara Nance for their suggestions on Chapter 27, Karl Levitt for his comments on Chapter 26, and Richard Ford for his many suggestions on Chapter 23. Their advice and suggestions were invaluable in preparing this edition. Of course, any errors in the text are my responsibility, and usually occurred because I did not always follow their advice.

Thanks also to Pasquale Noce, who sent me a thorough analysis of many of the theorems, proving them constructively as opposed to how they were done in the book. He made many other helpful comments and caught some errors.

The students in Peter Reiher's COM SCI 236-80, Computer Security, class at UCLA in the Spring Quarter 2018, and the students in my ECS 153, Computer Security, classes over the past few years at UC Davis used parts of this edition in various stages of preparation. I thank them for their feedback, which also improved the book.

Many others contributed to this book in various ways. Special thanks to Steven Alexander, Amin Alipour, Jim Alves-Foss, Bill Arbaugh, Andrew Arcilla, Alex Aris, Rebecca Bace, Belinda Bashore, Vladimir Berman, Rafael Bhatti, Ziad El Bizri, David Bover, Logan Browne, Terry Brugger, Gordon Burns, Serdar Cabuk, Raymond Centeno, Yang Chen, Yi Chen, HakSoo Choi, Lisa Clark, Michael Clifford, Christopher Clifton, Dan Coming, Kay Connelly, Crispin Cowan, Shayne Czyzewski, Tom Daniels, Dimitri DeFigueiredo, Joseph-Patrick Dib, Till Dörges, Felix Fan, Robert Fourney, Guillermo Francia III, Jeremy Frank, Conny Francke, Martin Gagne, Nina Gholami, Ron Gove, James Hinde, James Hook, Xuxian Jiang, Jesper Johansson, Mark Jones, Calvin Ko, Mark-Neil Ledesma, Ken Levine, Karl Levitt, Luc Longpre, Yunhua Lu, Gary McGraw, Alexander Meau, Nasir Memon, Katherine Moore, Mark Morrissey, Ather Nawaz, Iulian Neamtiu, Dan Nerenburg, Kimberly Nico, Stephen Northcutt, Rafael Obelheiro, Josko Orsulic, Holly Pang, Sean Peisert, Ryan Poling, Sung Park, Ashwini Raina, Jorge Ramos, Brennen Reynolds, Peter Rozental, Christoph Schuba, night SH, David Shambroom, Jonathan Shapiro, Clay Shields, Sriram Srinivasan, Mahesh V. Tripunitara, Vinay Vittal, Tom Walcott, James Walden, Dan Watson, Guido Wedig, Chris Wee, Han Weili, Patrick Wheeler, Paul Williams, Bonnie Xu, Charles Yang, Xiaoduan Ye, Xiaohui Ye, Lara Whelan, John Zachary, Linfeng Zhang, Aleksandr Zingorenko, and to everyone in my and others' computer security classes, who (knowingly or unknowingly) helped me develop and test this material.

The Pearson folks, in particular my editors Laura Lewin and Malobika Chakraborty, and Sheri Replin, were incredibly helpful and patient. Their patience and enthusiasm ensured this second edition was completed, although a bit later than expected. The production people, especially Julie Nahil, Ramya Gangadharan, and Charles Roumeliotis, moved the book smoothly into print, and I thank them for making it as painless as possible. I owe them many thanks. Similarly, for the first edition, the Addison-Wesley folks, Kathleen Billus, Susannah Buzard, Bernie Gaffney, Amy Fleischer, Helen Goldstein, Tom Stone, Asdis Thorsteinsson, and most especially my editor, Peter Gordon, were incredibly patient and helpful, despite fears that this book would never materialize. The fact that it did so is in great measure attributable to their hard work and encouragement. I also thank the production people at Argosy, especially Beatriz Valdés and Craig Kirkpatrick, for their wonderful work.

Dorothy Denning, my advisor in graduate school, guided me through the maze of computer security when I was just beginning. Peter Denning, Barry Leiner, Karl Levitt, Peter Neumann, Marvin Schaefer, Larry Snyder, and several others influenced my approach to the subject. I hope this work reflects in some small way what they gave to me and passes a modicum of it along to my readers.

I also thank my parents, Leonard Bishop and Linda Allen. My father, a writer, gave me some useful tips on writing, which I tried to follow. My mother, a literary agent, helped me understand the process of getting the book published, and supported me throughout.

Finally, I would like to thank my family for their support throughout the writing. My wife Holly, our children Heidi, Steven, David, and Caroline, and grandchildren Skyler and Sage were very patient and understanding and made sure I had time to work on the book. They also provided delightful distractions. To them all, my love and gratitude.

About the Author

Matt Bishop is a professor in the Department of Computer Science at the University of California at Davis. He received his Ph.D. in computer science from Purdue University, where he specialized in computer security, in 1984. He was a systems programmer at Megatest Corporation, a research scientist at the Research Institute of Advanced Computer Science and was on the faculty at Dartmouth College.

His main research area is the analysis of vulnerabilities in computer systems, including modeling them, building tools to detect vulnerabilities, and ameliorating or eliminating them. This includes detecting and handling all types of malicious logic. He works in the areas of network security, the study of denial of service attacks and defenses, policy modeling, software assurance testing, resilience, and formal modeling of access control. He has worked extensively in electronic voting, was one of the members of the RABA study for Maryland, and was one of the two principle investigators of the California Top-to-Bottom Review, which performed a technical review of all electronic voting systems certified in the State of California.

He is active in information assurance education. He was co-chair of the Joint Task Force that developed the *Cybersecurity Curricula 2017: Curriculum Guidelines for Post-Secondary Degree Programs in Cybersecurity*, released in December 2017. He teaches introductory programming, software engineering, operating systems, and (of course) computer security.

Part I

Introduction

Writers say "To write a good book, tell them what you are going to tell them, then tell them, then tell them what you told them." This is the "what we're going to tell you" part.

Chapter 1, "An Overview of Computer Security," presents the underpinnings of computer security and an overview of the important issues to place them in context. It begins with a discussion of what computer security is and how threats are connected to security services. The combination of desired services makes up a policy, and mechanisms enforce the policy. All rely on underlying assumptions, and the systems built on top of these assumptions lead to issues of assurance. Finally, the operational and human factors affect the mechanisms used as well as the policy.

Chapter 1

An Overview of Computer Security

ANTONIO: Whereof what's past is prologue, what to come
In yours and my discharge.
— *The Tempest*, II, i, 257–258.

This chapter presents the basic concepts of computer security. The remainder of this book will elaborate on these concepts in order to reveal the logic underlying the principles of these concepts.

We begin with basic security-related services that protect against threats to the security of the system. The next section discusses security policies that identify the threats and define the requirements for ensuring a secure system. Security mechanisms detect and prevent attacks and recover from those that succeed. Analyzing the security of a system requires an understanding of the mechanisms that enforce the security policy. It also requires a knowledge of the related assumptions and trust, which leads to the threats and the degree to which they may be realized. Such knowledge allows one to design better mechanisms and policies to neutralize these threats. This process leads to risk analysis. Human beings are the weakest link in the security mechanisms of any system. Therefore, policies and procedures must take people into account. This chapter discusses each of these topics.

1.1 The Basic Components

Computer security rests on confidentiality, integrity, and availability. The interpretations of these three aspects vary, as do the contexts in which they arise. The interpretation of an aspect in a given environment is dictated by the needs of the individuals, customs, and laws of the particular organization.

1.1.1   Confidentiality

Confidentiality is the concealment of information or resources. The need for keeping information secret arises from the use of computers in institutions with sensitive information such as government and industry. For example, military and civilian institutions in the government often restrict access to information to those who need that information. The first formal work in computer security was motivated by the military's attempt to implement controls to enforce a "need to know" principle. This principle also applies to industrial firms, which keep their proprietary designs secure lest their competitors try to steal the designs. As a further example, all types of institutions keep some types of personnel records secret.

Access control mechanisms support confidentiality. One access control mechanism for preserving confidentiality is *cryptography*, which transforms data to make it incomprehensible. A *cryptographic key* controls access to the untransformed data, but then the cryptographic key itself becomes another datum to be protected.

EXAMPLE: Enciphering an income tax return will prevent anyone without the key from reading the taxable income on the return. If the owner needs to see the return, it must be deciphered. Only the possessor of the cryptographic key can enter it into a deciphering program. However, if someone else can read the key when it is entered into the program and has access to the enciphered return, the confidentiality of the tax return has been compromised.

Other system-dependent mechanisms can prevent information from being illicitly accessed. Data protected only by these controls can be read when the controls fail or are bypassed. Then the controls' advantage is offset by a corresponding disadvantage. They can protect the secrecy of data more completely than cryptography, but if they fail or are evaded, the data becomes visible.

Confidentiality also applies to the existence of data, which is sometimes more revealing than the data itself. The precise number of people who distrust a politician may be less important than knowing that such a poll was taken by the politician's staff. How a particular government agency harassed citizens in its country may be less important than knowing that such harassment occurred. Access control mechanisms sometimes conceal the mere existence of data, lest the existence itself reveal information that should be protected.

Resource hiding is another important aspect of confidentiality. Organizations often wish to conceal their network configuration as well as what systems they are using. They may not wish others to know about specific equipment (because it could be used without authorization or in inappropriate ways), and a company renting time from a service provider may not want others to know what resources it is using. Access control mechanisms provide these capabilities as well.

All the mechanisms that enforce confidentiality require supporting services from the system. The assumption is that the security services can rely on the kernel, and other agents, to supply correct data. Thus, assumptions and trust underlie confidentiality mechanisms.

1.1.2   Integrity

Integrity refers to the trustworthiness of data or resources, and it is usually phrased in terms of preventing improper or unauthorized change. Integrity includes data integrity (the content of the information) and origin integrity (the source of the data, often called *authentication*). The source of the information may bear on its accuracy and credibility and on the trust that people place in the information.This dichotomy illustrates the principle that the aspect of integrity known as credibility is central to the proper functioning of a system. We will return to this issue when discussing malicious logic.

EXAMPLE: A newspaper may print information obtained from a leak at the White House but attribute it to the wrong source. The information is printed as received (preserving data integrity), but its source is incorrect (corrupting origin integrity).

Integrity mechanisms fall into two classes: *prevention* mechanisms and *detection* mechanisms.

Prevention mechanisms seek to maintain the integrity of the data by blocking any unauthorized attempts to change the data or any attempts to change the data in unauthorized ways. The distinction between these two types of attempts is important. The former occurs when a user tries to change data that she has no authority to change. The latter occurs when a user authorized to make certain changes in the data tries to change the data in other ways. For example, suppose an accounting system is on a computer. Someone breaks into the system and tries to modify the accounting data. Here an unauthorized user has tried to violate the integrity of the accounting database. But if an accountant hired by the firm to maintain its books tries to embezzle money by sending it overseas and hiding the transactions, a user (the accountant) has tried to change data (the accounting data) in unauthorized ways (by not entering the transfer of funds to a Swiss bank account). Adequate authentication and access controls will generally stop the break-in from the outside, but preventing the second type of attempt requires very different controls.

Detection mechanisms do not try to prevent violations of integrity; they simply report that the data's integrity is no longer trustworthy. Detection mechanisms may analyze system events (user or system actions) to detect problems or (more commonly) may analyze the data itself to see if required or expected constraints still hold. The mechanisms may report the actual cause of the integrity violation (a specific part of a file was altered), or they may simply report that the file is now corrupt.

Working with integrity is very different than working with confidentiality. With confidentiality, the data is either compromised or it is not, but integrity includes both the correctness and the trustworthiness of the data. The origin of the data (how and from whom it was obtained), how well the data was protected before it arrived at the current machine, and how well the data is protected on the current machine all affect the integrity of the data. Thus, evaluating integrity is often very difficult, because it relies on assumptions about the source of the data and about trust in that source—two underpinnings of security that are often overlooked.

1.1.3   Availability

Availability refers to the ability to use information or resources. Availability is an important aspect of reliability as well as of system design because an unavailable system is at least as bad as no system at all. The aspect of availability that is relevant to security is that someone may deliberately arrange to deny access to data or to a service by making it unavailable or unusable. System designs usually assume a statistical model to analyze expected patterns of use, and mechanisms ensure availability when that statistical model holds. Someone may be able to manipulate use (or parameters that control use, such as network traffic) so that the assumptions of the statistical model are no longer valid. This means that the mechanisms for keeping the resource or data available are working in an environment for which they were not designed. As a result, they will often fail.

EXAMPLE: Suppose Anne has compromised a bank's secondary system server, which supplies bank account balances. When anyone else asks that server for information, Anne can supply any information she desires. Merchants validate checks by contacting the bank's primary balance server. If a merchant gets no response, the secondary server will be asked to supply the data. Anne's colleague prevents merchants from contacting the primary balance server, so all merchant queries go to the secondary server. Anne will never have a check turned down, regardless of her actual account balance. Notice that if the bank had only one server (the primary one) and that server were unavailable, this scheme would not work. The merchant would be unable to validate the check.

Attempts to block availability, called *denial of service (DoS) attacks*, can be the most difficult to detect, because the analyst must determine if the unusual access patterns are attributable to deliberate manipulation of resources or of environment. Complicating this determination is the nature of statistical models. Even if the model accurately describes the environment, atypical events simply contribute to the nature of the statistics. A deliberate attempt to make a resource unavailable may look like, or be, an atypical event. In some environments, it may not even appear atypical.

1.2   Threats

A *threat* is a potential violation of security. The violation need not actually occur for there to be a threat. The fact that the violation *might* occur means that those actions that could cause it to occur must be guarded against (or prepared for). Those actions are called *attacks*. Those who execute such actions, or cause them to be executed, are called *attackers*.

The three security services—confidentiality, integrity, and availability—counter threats to the security of a system. Shirey [1739] divides threats into four broad classes: *disclosure*, or unauthorized access to information; *deception*, or acceptance of false data; *disruption*, or interruption or prevention of correct operation; and *usurpation*, or unauthorized control of some part of a system. These four broad classes encompass many common threats. Because the threats are ubiquitous, an introductory discussion of each one will present issues that recur throughout the study of computer security.

Snooping or *eavesdropping*, the unauthorized interception of information, is a form of disclosure. It is passive, suggesting simply that some entity is listening to (or reading) communications or browsing through files or system information. *Passive wiretapping* is a form of snooping in which a network is monitored. (It is called "wiretapping" because of the "wires" that compose the network, although the term is used even if no physical wiring is involved.) Confidentiality services seek to counter this threat.

Modification or *alteration*, an unauthorized change of information, covers three classes of threats. The goal may be deception, in which some entity relies on the modified data to determine which action to take, or in which incorrect information is accepted as correct and is released. If the modified data controls the operation of the system, the threats of disruption and usurpation arise. Unlike snooping, modification is active; it results from an entity changing information. *Active wiretapping* is a form of modification in which data moving across a network is altered, new data is injected, or parts of the data are deleted; the term "active" distinguishes it from snooping ("passive" wiretapping). An example is the *man-in-the-middle* attack, in which an intruder reads messages from the sender and sends (possibly modified) versions to the recipient, in hopes that the recipient and sender will not realize the presence of the intermediary. Integrity services seek to counter this threat.

Masquerading or *spoofing*, an impersonation of one entity by another, is a form of both deception and usurpation. It lures a victim into believing that the entity with which it is communicating is a different entity. For example, if a user tries to log into a computer across the Internet but instead reaches another computer that claims to be the desired one, the user has been spoofed. Similarly, if a user tries to read a web page, but an attacker has arranged for the user to be given a different page, another spoof has taken place. This may be a passive attack (in which the user simply accesses the web page), but it is usually an active attack (in which the attacker issues responses dynamically to mislead the user about the web page). Although masquerading is primarily deception, it is often used to usurp control of a system by an attacker impersonating an authorized manager or controller. Integrity services (called "authentication services" in this context) seek to counter this threat.

Some forms of masquerading may be allowed. *Delegation* occurs when one entity authorizes a second entity to perform functions on its behalf. The distinctions between delegation and masquerading are important. If Susan delegates to

Thomas the authority to act on her behalf, she is giving permission for him to perform specific actions as though she were performing them herself. All parties are aware of the delegation. Thomas will not pretend to be Susan; rather, he will say, "I am Thomas and I have authority to do this on Susan's behalf." If asked, Susan will verify this. On the other hand, in a masquerade, Thomas will pretend to be Susan. No other parties (including Susan) will be aware of the masquerade, and Thomas will say, "I am Susan." Should anyone discover that he or she is dealing with Thomas and ask Susan about it, she will deny that she authorized Thomas to act on her behalf. Even though masquerading is a violation of security, delegation is not.

Repudiation of origin, a false denial that an entity sent (or created) something, is a form of deception. For example, suppose a customer sends a letter to a vendor agreeing to pay a large amount of money for a product. The vendor ships the product and then demands payment. The customer denies having ordered the product and, according to a law in the customer's state, is therefore entitled to keep the unsolicited shipment without payment. The customer has repudiated the origin of the letter. If the vendor cannot prove that the letter came from the customer, the attack succeeds. A variant of this is denial by a user that he created specific information or entities such as files. Integrity mechanisms try to cope with this threat.

Denial of receipt, a false denial that an entity received some information or message, is a form of deception. Suppose a customer orders an expensive product, but the vendor demands payment before shipment. The customer pays, and the vendor ships the product. The customer then asks the vendor when he will receive the product. If the customer has already received the product, the question constitutes a denial of receipt attack. The vendor can defend against this attack only by proving that the customer did, despite his denials, receive the product. Integrity and availability mechanisms attempt to guard against these attacks.

Delay, a temporary inhibition of a service, is a form of usurpation, although it can play a supporting role in deception. Typically, delivery of a message or service requires some time t; if an attacker can force the delivery to take more than time t, the attacker has successfully delayed delivery. This requires manipulation of system control structures, such as network components or server components, and hence is a form of usurpation. If an entity is waiting for an authorization message that is delayed, it may query a secondary server for the authorization. Even though the attacker may be unable to masquerade as the primary server, she might be able to masquerade as that secondary server and supply incorrect information. Availability mechanisms can often thwart this threat.

Denial of service, a long-term inhibition of service, is a form of usurpation, although it is often used with other mechanisms to deceive. The attacker prevents a server from providing a service. The denial may occur at the source (by preventing the server from obtaining the resources needed to perform its function), at the destination (by blocking the communications from the server), or along the intermediate path (by discarding messages from either the client or the server, or both). Denial of service poses the same threat as an infinite delay. Availability mechanisms seek to counter this threat.

Denial of service or delay may result from direct attacks or from problems unrelated to security. From our point of view, the cause and result are important; the intention underlying them is not. If delay or denial of service compromises system security, or is part of a sequence of events leading to the compromise of a system, then we view it as an attempt to breach system security. But the attempt may not be deliberate; indeed, it may be a user error, or the product of environmental characteristics, rather than specific actions of an attacker.

1.3   Policy and Mechanism

Critical to our study of security is the distinction between policy and mechanism:

Definition 1–1. A *security policy* is a statement of what is, and what is not, allowed.

Definition 1–2. A *security mechanism* is a method, tool, or procedure for enforcing a security policy.

Mechanisms can be nontechnical, such as requiring proof of identity before changing a password; in fact, policies often require some procedural mechanisms that technology cannot enforce.

As an example, suppose a university's computer science laboratory has a policy that prohibits any student from copying another student's homework files. The computer system provides mechanisms for preventing others from reading a user's files. Anna fails to use these mechanisms to protect her homework files, and Bill copies them. A breach of security has occurred, because Bill has violated the security policy. Anna's failure to protect her files does not authorize Bill to copy them.

In this example, Anna could easily have protected her files. In other environments, such protection may not be easy. For example, the Internet provides only the most rudimentary security mechanisms, which are not adequate to protect information sent over that network. Nevertheless, acts such as the recording of passwords and other sensitive information violate an implicit security policy of most sites (specifically, that passwords are a user's confidential property and cannot be recorded by anyone).

Policies may be presented mathematically, as a list of allowed (secure) and disallowed (nonsecure) states. For our purposes, we will assume that any given policy provides an axiomatic description of secure states and nonsecure states. In practice, policies are rarely so precise; they normally describe in English, or some other natural language, what users and staff are allowed to do. The ambiguity inherent in such a description leads to states that are not classified as "allowed" or "disallowed." For example, consider the homework policy discussed previously. If someone looks through another user's directory without copying homework files, is that a violation of security? The answer depends on site custom, rules, regulations, and laws, all of which are outside our focus and may change over time.

When two different sites communicate or cooperate, the entity they compose has a security policy based on the security policies of the two entities. If those policies are inconsistent, either or both sites must decide what the security policy for the combined site should be. The inconsistency often manifests itself as a security breach. For example, if proprietary documents were given to a university, the policy of confidentiality in the corporation would conflict with the more open policies of most universities. The university and the company must develop a mutual security policy that meets both their needs in order to produce a consistent policy. When the two sites communicate through an independent third party, such as an Internet service provider, the complexity of the situation grows rapidly.

1.3.1 Goals of Security

Given a security policy's specification of "secure" and "nonsecure" actions, security mechanisms can prevent the attack, detect the attack, or recover from the attack. The strategies may be used together or separately.

Prevention means that an attack will fail. For example, if one attempts to break into a host over the Internet and that host is not connected to the Internet, the attack has been prevented. Typically, prevention involves implementation of mechanisms that restrict users to specific actions and that are trusted to be implemented in a correct, unalterable way, so that an attacker cannot defeat the mechanism by changing it. Preventative mechanisms often are very cumbersome and interfere with system use to the point that they hinder normal use of the system. But some simple preventative mechanisms, such as passwords (which aim to prevent unauthorized users from accessing the system), have become widely accepted. Prevention mechanisms can prevent compromise of parts of the system; once in place, the resource protected by the mechanism need not be monitored for security problems, at least in theory.

Detection indicates the effectiveness of preventative measures, and is especially useful when an attack cannot be prevented. Detection mechanisms accept that an attack will occur; the goal is to determine that an attack is under way, or has occurred, and report it. The attack may be monitored, however, to provide data about its nature, severity, and results. Typical detection mechanisms monitor various aspects of the system, looking for actions or information indicating an attack. A good example of such a mechanism is one that gives a warning when a user enters an incorrect password three times. The login may continue, but an error message in a system log reports the unusually high number of mistyped passwords. Detection mechanisms do not prevent compromise of parts of the system, which is a serious drawback. The resource protected by the detection mechanism is continuously or periodically monitored for security problems.

Recovery has two forms. The first is to stop an attack and to assess and repair any damage caused by that attack. As an example, if the attacker deletes a file, one recovery mechanism would be to restore the file from backup media. In practice, recovery is far more complex, because the nature of each attack is unique. Thus, the type and extent of any damage can be difficult to characterize completely. Moreover, the attacker may return, so recovery involves identification and fixing of the vulnerabilities used by the attacker to enter the system. In some cases, retaliation (by attacking the attacker's system or taking legal steps to hold the attacker accountable) is part of recovery. In all these cases, the system's functioning is inhibited by the attack. By definition, recovery requires resumption of correct operation.

In a second form of recovery, the system continues to function correctly while an attack is under way. This type of recovery is quite difficult to implement because of the complexity of computer systems. It draws on techniques of fault tolerance as well as techniques of security and is typically used in safety-critical systems. It differs from the first form of recovery, because at no point does the system function incorrectly. However, the system may disable nonessential functionality. Of course, this type of recovery is often implemented in a weaker form whereby the system detects incorrect functioning automatically and then corrects (or attempts to correct) the error.

1.4   Assumptions and Trust

How do we determine whether a policy correctly describes the required level and type of security for the site? This question lies at the heart of all security, computer and otherwise. Security rests on assumptions specific to the type of security required and the environment in which it is to be employed.

EXAMPLE: Opening a door lock requires a key. The assumption is that the lock is secure against lock picking. This assumption is treated as an axiom and is made because most people would require a key to open a door lock. A good lock picker, however, can open a lock without a key. Hence, in an environment with a skilled, untrustworthy lock picker, the assumption is wrong and the conclusion invalid.

If the lock picker is trustworthy, the assumption is still valid. The term "trustworthy" implies that the lock picker will not pick a lock unless the owner of the lock authorizes the lock picking. This is another example of the role of trust. A well-defined exception to the rules provides a "back door" through which the security mechanism (the locks) can be bypassed. The trust resides in the belief that this back door will not be used except as specified by the policy. If it is used, the trust has been misplaced and the security mechanism (the lock) provides no security.

Like the lock example, a policy consists of a set of axioms that the policy makers believe can be enforced. Designers of policies always make two assumptions. First, the policy correctly and unambiguously partitions the set of system states into "secure" and "nonsecure" states. Second, the security mechanisms prevent the system from entering a "nonsecure" state. If either assumption is erroneous, the system will be nonsecure.

These two assumptions are fundamentally different. The first assumption asserts that the policy is a correct description of what constitutes a "secure" system.

EXAMPLE: A bank's policy may state that officers of the bank are authorized to shift money among accounts. If a bank officer puts $100,000 in his account, has the bank's security been violated? Given the aforementioned policy statement, no, because the officer was authorized to move the money. In the "real world," that action would constitute embezzlement, something any bank would consider a security violation.

The second assumption says that the security policy can be enforced by security mechanisms. These mechanisms are either secure, precise, or broad. Let P be the set of all possible states. Let Q be the set of secure states (as specified by the security policy). Let the security mechanisms restrict the system to some set of states R (thus, $R \subseteq P$). Then we have the following definition.

Definition 1–3. A security mechanism is *secure* if $R \subseteq Q$; it is *precise* if $R = Q$; and it is *broad* if there are states r such that $r \in R$ and $r \notin Q$.

Ideally, the union of all security mechanisms active on a system would produce a single precise mechanism (that is, $R = Q$). In practice, security mechanisms are broad; they allow the system to enter nonsecure states. We will revisit this topic when we explore policy formulation in more detail.

Trusting that mechanisms work requires several assumptions:

- Each mechanism is designed to implement one or more parts of the security policy.
- The union of the mechanisms implements all aspects of the security policy.
- The mechanisms are tamperproof.
- The mechanisms are implemented, installed, and administered correctly.

Because of the importance and complexity of trust and of assumptions, we will revisit this topic repeatedly and in various guises throughout this book.

1.5   Assurance

Trust cannot be quantified precisely. System specification, design, and implementation can provide a basis for determining "how much" to trust a system. This aspect of trust is called *assurance*. It is an attempt to provide a basis for bolstering (or substantiating or specifying) how much one can trust a system.

EXAMPLE: In the United States, aspirin from a nationally known and reputable manufacturer, delivered to the drugstore in a safety-sealed container, and sold with the seal still in place, is considered trustworthy by most people. The bases for that trust are as follows.

- The testing and certification of the drug (aspirin) by the Food and Drug Administration (FDA). The FDA has jurisdiction over many types of medicines and allows medicines to be marketed only if they meet certain clinical standards of usefulness.
- The manufacturing standards of the company and the precautions it takes to ensure that the drug is not contaminated. National and state regulatory commissions and groups ensure that the manufacture of the drug meets specific acceptable standards.
- The safety seal on the bottle. To insert dangerous chemicals into a safety-sealed bottle without damaging the seal is very difficult.

The three technologies (certification, manufacturing standards, and preventative sealing) provide some degree of assurance that the aspirin is not contaminated. The degree of trust the purchaser has in the purity of the aspirin is a result of these three processes.

In the 1980s, drug manufacturers met two of the criteria above, but none used safety seals.[1] A series of "drug scares" arose when a well-known manufacturer's medicines were contaminated after manufacture but before purchase. The manufacturer promptly introduced safety seals to assure its customers that the medicine in the container was the same as when it was shipped from the manufacturing plants.

Assurance in the computer world is similar. It requires specific steps to ensure that the computer will function properly. The sequence of steps includes detailed specifications of the desired (or undesirable) behavior; an analysis of the design of the hardware, software, and other components to show that the system will not violate the specifications; and arguments or proofs that the implementation, operating procedures, and maintenance procedures will produce the desired behavior.

Definition 1–4. A system is said to *satisfy* a specification if the specification correctly states how the system will function.

This definition also applies to design and implementation satisfying a specification.

---

[1] Many used childproof caps, but they prevented only some young children (and some adults) from opening the bottles. They were not designed to protect the medicine from malicious adults.

1.5.1   Specification

A *specification* is a (formal or informal) statement of the desired functioning of the system. It can be highly mathematical, using any of several languages defined for that purpose. It can also be informal, using, for example, English to describe what the system should do under certain conditions. The specification can be low-level, combining program code with logical and temporal relationships to specify ordering of events. The defining quality is a statement of what the system is allowed to do or what it is not allowed to do.

EXAMPLE: A company is purchasing a new computer. They need to trust the system cannot be successfully compromised from the Internet. One of their (English) specifications would read "The system cannot be successfully compromised by an attack over the Internet."

Specifications are used not merely in security but also in systems designed for safety, such as medical technology. They constrain such systems from performing acts that could cause harm. A system that regulates traffic lights must ensure that pairs of lights facing the same way turn red, green, and yellow at the same time and that at most one set of lights facing cross streets at an intersection is green.

A major part of the derivation of specifications is determination of the set of requirements relevant to the system's planned use. Sections 1.6 and 1.7 discuss the relationship of operational and human requirements to security.

1.5.2   Design

The *design* of a system translates the specifications into components that will implement them. The design is said to satisfy the specifications if, under all relevant circumstances, the design will not permit the system to violate those specifications.

EXAMPLE: A design of the computer system for the company mentioned above had no network interface cards, no modem cards, and no network drivers in the kernel. This design satisfied the specification because the system would not connect to the Internet. Hence it could not be successfully attacked over the Internet.

An analyst can determine whether a design satisfies a set of specifications in several ways. If the specifications and designs are expressed in terms of mathematics, the analyst must show that the design formulations are consistent with the specifications. Although much of the work can be done mechanically, a human must still perform some analyses and modify components of the design that violate specifications (or, in some cases, components that cannot be shown to satisfy the specifications). If the specifications and design do not use mathematics, then a convincing and compelling argument should be made. Most often, the specifications are nebulous and the arguments are half-hearted and unconvincing or provide only partial coverage. The design depends on assumptions about what the specifications mean. This leads to vulnerabilities, as we will see.

1.5.3   Implementation

Given a design, the *implementation* creates a system that satisfies that design. If the design also satisfies the specifications, then by transitivity the implementation will also satisfy the specifications.

The difficulty at this step is the complexity of proving that a program correctly implements the design and, in turn, the specifications.

> **Definition 1–5.** A program is *correct* if its implementation performs as specified.

Proofs of correctness require each line of source code to be checked for mathematical correctness. Each line is seen as a function, transforming the input (constrained by preconditions) into some output (constrained by postconditions derived from the function and the preconditions). Each routine is represented by the composition of the functions derived from the lines of code making up the routine. Like those functions, the function corresponding to the routine has inputs and outputs, constrained by preconditions and postconditions, respectively. From the combination of routines, programs can be built and formally verified. One can apply the same techniques to sets of programs and thus verify the correctness of a system.

There are three difficulties in this process. First, the complexity of programs makes their mathematical verification difficult. Aside from the intrinsic difficulties, the program itself has preconditions derived from the environment of the system. These preconditions are often subtle and difficult to specify, but unless the mathematical formalism captures them, the program verification may not be valid because critical assumptions may be wrong. Second, program verification assumes that the programs are compiled correctly, linked and loaded correctly, and executed correctly. Hardware failure, buggy code, and failures in other tools may invalidate the preconditions. A compiler that incorrectly compiles the assignment

```
x := x + 1
```

to the assembly language instructions

```
move contents of x to regA
subtract 1 from contents of regA
move contents of regA to x
```

would invalidate the proof statement that the value of x after the line of code is 1 more than the value of x before the line of code. This would invalidate the proof of correctness. Third, if the verification relies on conditions on the input, the program must reject any inputs that do not meet those conditions. Otherwise, the program is only partially verified.

Because formal proofs of correctness are so time-consuming, *a posteriori* verification techniques known as *testing* have become widespread. During testing, the tester executes the program (or portions of it) on data to determine if the output is what it should be and to understand how likely the program is to contain an error. Testing techniques range from supplying input to ensure that all execution paths are exercised to introducing errors into the program and determining how they affect the output to stating specifications and testing the program to see if it satisfies the specifications. Although these techniques are considerably simpler than the more formal methods, they do not provide the same degree of assurance that formal methods do. Furthermore, testing relies on test procedures and documentation, errors in either of which could invalidate the testing results.

Although assurance techniques do not guarantee correctness or security, they provide a firm basis for assessing what one must trust in order to believe that a system is secure. Their value is in eliminating possible, and common, sources of error and forcing designers to define precisely what the system is to do.

1.6   Operational Issues

Any useful policy and mechanism must balance the benefits of the protection against the cost of designing, implementing, and using the mechanism. This balance can be determined by analyzing the risks of a security breach and the likelihood of it occurring. Such an analysis is, to a degree, subjective, because in very few situations can risks be rigorously quantified. Complicating the analysis are the constraints that laws, customs, and society place on the acceptability of security procedures and mechanisms; indeed, as these factors change, so do security mechanisms and, possibly, security policies.

1.6.1   Cost-Benefit Analysis

Like any factor in a complex system, the benefits of computer security are weighed against their total cost (including the additional costs incurred if the system is compromised). If the data or resources cost less, or are of less value, than their protection, adding security mechanisms and procedures is not cost-effective because the data or resources can be reconstructed more cheaply than the protections themselves. Unfortunately, this is rarely the case.

EXAMPLE: A database provides salary information to a second system that prints checks. If the data in the database is altered, the company could suffer grievous financial loss; hence, even a cursory cost-benefit analysis would show that the strongest possible integrity mechanisms should protect the data in the database.

Now suppose the company has several branch offices, and every day the database downloads a copy of the data to each branch office. The branch offices use the data to recommend salaries for new employees. However, the main office makes the final decision using the original database (not one of the copies). In this case, guarding the integrity of the copies is not particularly important, because branch offices cannot make any financial decisions based on the data in their copies. Hence, the company cannot suffer any financial loss from compromises of the data at the branch offices.

Both of these situations are extreme situations in which the analysis is clear-cut. As an example of a situation in which the analysis is less clear, consider the need for confidentiality of the salaries in the database. The officers of the company must decide the financial cost to the company should the salaries be disclosed, including potential loss from lawsuits (if any); changes in policies, procedures, and personnel; and the effect on future business. These are all business-related judgments, and determining their value is part of what company officers are paid to do.

Overlapping benefits are also a consideration. Suppose the integrity protection mechanism can be augmented very quickly and cheaply to provide confidentiality. Then the cost of providing confidentiality is much lower. This shows that evaluating the cost of a particular security service depends on the mechanism chosen to implement it and on the mechanisms chosen to implement other security services. The cost-benefit analysis should take into account as many mechanisms as possible. Adding security mechanisms to an existing system is often more expensive (and, incidentally, less effective) than designing them into the system in the first place.

1.6.2   Risk Analysis

To determine whether an asset should be protected, and to what level, requires analysis of the potential threats against that asset and the likelihood that they will materialize. The level of protection is a function of the probability of an attack occurring and the effects of the attack should it succeed. If an attack is unlikely, protecting against it typically has a lower priority than protecting against a likely one. If the unlikely attack would cause long delays in the company's production of widgets but the likely attack would be only a nuisance, then more effort should be put into preventing the unlikely attack. The situations between these extreme cases are very subjective.

Let's revisit our company with the salary database that transmits salary information over a network to a second computer that prints employees' checks.

The data is stored on the database system and then moved over the network to the second system. Hence, the risk of unauthorized changes in the data occurs in three places: on the database system, on the network, and on the printing system. If the network is a local (company-wide) one and no wide area networks are accessible, the threat of attackers entering the systems is confined to untrustworthy internal personnel, contractors, and visitors. If, however, the network is connected to the Internet, the risk of geographically distant attackers attempting to intrude is substantial enough to warrant consideration.

This example illustrates some finer points of risk analysis. First, risk is a function of environment. Attackers from a foreign country are not a threat to the company when the computer is not connected to the Internet. If foreign attackers wanted to break into the system, they would need to physically enter the company (and would cease to be "foreign" because they would then be "local"). But if the computer is connected to the Internet, foreign attackers become a threat because they can attack over the Internet. An additional, less tangible issue is the faith in the company. If the company is not able to meet its payroll because it does not know who to pay, the company will lose the faith of its employees. It may be unable to hire anyone, because the people hired would not be sure they would get paid. Investors would not fund the company because of the likelihood of lawsuits by unpaid employees. The risk arises from the environments in which the company functions.

Second, the risks change with time. If a company's network is not connected to the Internet, there seems to be no risk of attacks from other hosts on the Internet. However, despite any policies to the contrary, someone could connect a wi-fi access point to one of the company computers and connect to the Internet through that access point. Should this happen, any risk analysis predicated on isolation from the Internet would no longer be accurate. Although policies can forbid the connection of such a modem and procedures can be put in place to make such connection difficult, unless the responsible parties can guarantee that no such modem will ever be installed, the risks can change.

Third, many risks are quite remote but still exist. In the wi-fi access point example, the company has sought to minimize the risk of an Internet connection. Hence, this risk is "acceptable" but not nonexistent. As a practical matter, one does not worry about acceptable risks; instead, one worries that the risk will become unacceptable.

Finally, the problem of "analysis paralysis" refers to making risk analyses with no effort to act on those analyses. To change the example slightly, suppose the company performs a risk analysis. The executives decide that they are not sure if all risks have been found, so they order a second study to verify the first. They reconcile the studies then wait for some time to act on these analyses. At that point, the security officers raise the objection that the conditions in the workplace are no longer those that held when the original risk analyses were done. The analysis is repeated. But the company cannot decide how to ameliorate the risks, so it waits until a plan of action can be developed, and the process continues. The point is that the company is paralyzed and cannot act on the risks it faces.

1.6.3   Laws and Customs

Laws restrict the availability and use of technology and affect procedural controls. Hence, any policy and any selection of mechanisms must take into account legal considerations.

EXAMPLE: Until the year 2000, the United States controlled the export of strong cryptographic hardware and software (considered munitions under United States law). If a U.S. software company worked with a computer manufacturer in London, the U.S. company could not send cryptographic software to the manufacturer. The U.S. company first would have to obtain a license to export the software from the United States. Any security policy that depended on the London manufacturer's using that cryptographic software would need to take this into account.

EXAMPLE: Suppose the law makes it illegal to read a user's file without the user's permission. An attacker breaks into the system and begins to download users' files. If the system administrators notice this and observe what the attacker is reading, they will be reading the victims' files without permission and therefore violating the law themselves. For this reason, most sites require users to give (implicit or explicit) permission for system administrators to read their files. In some jurisdictions, an explicit exception allows system administrators to access information on their systems without permission in order to protect the quality of service provided or to prevent damage to their systems.

Situations involving the laws of multiple jurisdictions—especially foreign countries—complicate this issue.

EXAMPLE: In the 1990s, the laws involving the use of cryptography in France were very different from those in the United States. The laws of France required companies sending enciphered data out of the country to register their cryptographic keys with the government. Security procedures involving the transmission of enciphered data from a company in the United States to a branch office in France had to take these differences into account.

EXAMPLE: If a policy called for prosecution of attackers and intruders came from Russia to a system in the United States, prosecution would involve asking the United States authorities to extradite the alleged attackers from Russia. This undoubtedly would involve court testimony from company personnel involved in handling the intrusion, possibly trips to Russia, and more court time once the extradition was completed. The cost of prosecuting the attackers might be considerably higher than the company would be willing (or able) to pay.

Laws are not the only constraints on policies and selection of mechanisms. Society distinguishes between *legal* and *acceptable* practices. It may be legal for a company to require all its employees to provide DNA samples for authentication purposes, but it is not socially acceptable. In the United States, requiring the use of Social Security Numbers as passwords is often legal (unless a state law forbids this or the computer is one owned by the U.S. government) but also unacceptable. These practices provide security but at an unacceptable cost, and they encourage users to evade or otherwise overcome the security mechanisms.

The issue that laws and customs raise is a psychological one. A security mechanism that would put users and administrators at legal risk would place a burden on these people that few would be willing to bear; thus, such a mechanism would not be used. An unused mechanism is worse than a nonexistent one, because it gives a false impression that a security service is available. Hence, users may rely on that service to protect their data when in reality their data is unprotected.

1.7   Human Issues

Implementing computer security controls is complex, and in a large organization procedural controls often become vague or cumbersome. Regardless of the strength of the technical controls, if nontechnical considerations affect their implementation and use, the effect on security can be severe. Moreover, if configured or used incorrectly, even the best security control is useless at best and dangerous at worst. Thus, the designers, implementers, and maintainers of security controls are essential to the correct operation of those controls.

1.7.1   Organizational Problems

Security provides no direct financial rewards to the user. It limits losses, but it also requires the expenditure of resources that could be used elsewhere. Unless losses occur, organizations often believe they are wasting money and effort on security. After a loss, the value of these controls suddenly becomes appreciated. Furthermore, security controls often add complexity to otherwise simple operations. For example, if concluding a stock trade takes two minutes without security controls and three minutes with security controls, adding those controls results in a 50% loss of productivity.

Losses occur when security protections are in place, but such losses are expected to be less than they would have been without the security mechanisms. The key question is whether such a loss, combined with the resulting loss in productivity, would be greater than a financial loss or loss of confidence should one of the nonsecured transactions suffer a breach of security.

Compounding this problem is the question of who is responsible for the security of the company's computers. The authority to implement appropriate controls must reside with those who are responsible; the consequence of not doing so is that the people who can most clearly see the need for security measures, and who are responsible for implementing them, will be unable to do so. This is simply sound business practice; responsibility without power causes problems in any organization, just as does power without responsibility.

Once clear chains of responsibility and power have been established, the need for security can compete on equal footing with other needs of the organization. One common problem security managers face is the lack of people trained in the area of computer security. Another problem is that knowledgeable people are overloaded with work. At many organizations, the "security administrator" is also involved in system administration, development, or some other secondary function. In fact, the security aspect of the job is often secondary. The problem is that indications of security problems often are not obvious and require time and skill to spot. Preparation for an attack makes dealing with it less chaotic, but such preparation takes enough time and requires enough attention so that treating it as a secondary aspect of a job means that it will not be performed well, with the expected consequences.

Lack of resources is another common problem. Securing a system requires resources as well as people. It requires time to design a configuration that will provide an adequate level of security, to implement the configuration, and to administer the system. It requires money to purchase products that are needed to build an adequate security system or to pay someone else to design and implement security measures. It requires computer resources to implement and execute the security mechanisms and procedures. It requires training to ensure that employees understand the importance of security, how to use the security tools, how to interpret the results, and how to implement the nontechnical aspects of the security policy.

1.7.2   People Problems

The heart of any security system is people. This is particularly true in computer security, which deals mainly with technological controls that can usually be bypassed by human intervention. For example, a computer system authenticates a user by asking a human for a secret code; if the correct secret code is supplied, the computer assumes that the human is the user, and grants the appropriate access. If an authorized user tells another person his secret code, the unauthorized user can masquerade as the authorized user with small risk of detection.

People who might attack an organization and are not authorized to use that organization's systems are called *outsiders* and can pose a serious threat. Experts agree, however, that a far more dangerous threat comes from disgruntled employees and other *insiders* who are authorized to use the computers. Insiders typically know the organization of the company's systems and what procedures the operators and users follow and often know enough passwords to bypass many security controls that would detect an attack launched by an outsider. Insider misuse of authorized privileges is a very difficult problem to solve.

Untrained personnel also pose a threat to system security. As an example, one operator did not realize that the contents of backup media needed to be verified before the media was stored. When attackers deleted several critical system files, she discovered that none of the backup media could be read.

System administrators who misread the output of security mechanisms, or do not analyze that output, contribute to the probability of successful attacks against their systems. Similarly, administrators who misconfigure security-related features of a system can weaken the site security. Users can also weaken site security by misusing security mechanisms (such as selecting simple passwords that are easy to memorize—and easy to guess).

Lack of technical training is not the only problem. Many successful break-ins have arisen from the art of *social engineering*. If operators will change passwords based on telephone requests, all an attacker needs to do is to determine the name of someone who uses the computer. A common tactic is to pick someone fairly far above the operator (such as a vice president of the company) and to feign an emergency (such as calling at night and saying that a report to the president of the company is due the next morning) so that the operator will be reluctant to refuse the request. Once the password has been changed to one that the attacker knows, he can simply log in as a normal user. Social engineering attacks are remarkably successful and often devastating.

The problem of misconfiguration is aggravated by the complexity of many security-related configuration files. For instance, a typographical error can disable key protection features. Even worse, software does not always work as advertised. One widely used system had a vulnerability that arose when an administrator made too long a list that named systems with access to certain files. Because the list was too long, the system simply assumed that the administrator meant to allow those files to be accessed without restriction on who could access them—exactly the opposite of what was intended.

1.8   Tying It All Together

The considerations discussed above appear to flow linearly from one to the next (see Figure 1–1). Human issues pervade each stage of the cycle. In addition, each stage of the cycle feeds back to the preceding stage, and through that stage to all earlier stages. The operation and maintenance stage is critical to the life cycle. Figure 1–1 breaks it out so as to emphasize the impact it has on all stages. The following example shows the importance of feedback.

EXAMPLE: A major corporation decided to improve its security. It hired consultants, determined the threats, and created a policy. From the policy, the consultants derived several specifications that the security mechanisms had to meet. They then developed a design that would meet the specifications.

During the implementation phase, the company discovered that employees could connect modems to the telephones without being detected. The design required all incoming connections to go through a firewall and had to be modified to divide systems into two classes: systems connected to "the outside," which were

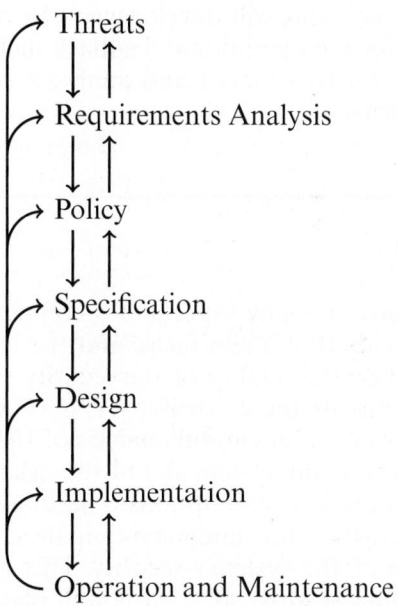

Figure 1–1 The security life cycle.

put outside the firewall, and all other systems, which were put behind the firewall. The design needed other modifications as well.

When the system was deployed, the operation and maintenance phase revealed several unexpected threats. The most serious was that systems were repeatedly misconfigured to allow sensitive data to be sent across the Internet in the clear, because the implementation made using cryptographic software very difficult. Once this problem had been remedied, the company discovered that several "trusted" hosts (those allowed to log in without authentication) were physically outside the control of the company. This violated policy, but for commercial reasons the company needed to continue to use these hosts. The policy element that designated these systems as "trusted" was modified. Finally, the company detected proprietary material being sent to a competitor over electronic mail. This added a threat that the company had earlier discounted. The company did not realize that it needed to worry about insider attacks.

Feedback from operation is critical. Whether or not a program is tested or proved to be secure, operational environments always introduce unexpected problems or difficulties. If the assurance (specification, design, implementation, and testing/proof) phase is done properly, the extra problems and difficulties are minimal. The analysts can handle them, usually easily and quickly. If the assurance phase has been omitted or done poorly, the problems may require a complete reevaluation of the system. If the assurance did not take into account the humans using or administering the system, they may find its operation too complex or cumbersome and will develop ways to circumvent the security controls. The tools used for the operational feedback include auditing, in which the operation of the system is recorded and analyzed so that the analyst can determine what the problems are.

1.9   Summary

Computer security depends on many aspects of a computer system, its use, and its environment. The threats that a site faces, and the level and quality of the countermeasures, depend on the quality of the security services and supporting procedures. The specific mix of these attributes is governed by the site security policy, which is ideally created after careful analysis of the value of the resources on the system or controlled by the system and of the risks involved.

Underlying all this are key assumptions describing what the site and the system accept as true or trustworthy; understanding these assumptions is the key to analyzing the strength of the system's security. This notion of "trust" is the central notion for computer security. If trust is well placed, any system can be made acceptably secure. If it is misplaced, the system cannot be secure in any sense of the word.

Once this is understood, the reason that people consider security to be a relative attribute is plain. Given enough resources, an attacker can often evade the security procedures and mechanisms that are in place. Such a desire is tempered by the cost of the attack, which in some cases can be very expensive. If it is less expensive to regenerate the data than to launch the attack, most attackers will simply regenerate the data.

This chapter has laid the foundation for what follows. All aspects of computer security begin with the nature of threats and the security services that counter them. In future chapters, we will build on these basic concepts.

1.10   Research Issues

Future chapters will explore research issues in the technical realm. However, other, nontechnical issues affect the needs and requirements for technical solutions, and research into these issues helps guide research into technical areas.

A key question is how to quantify risk. The research issue is how to determine the effects of a system's vulnerabilities on its security. For example, if a system can be compromised in any of 50 ways, how can a company compare the costs of the procedures (technical and otherwise) needed to prevent the compromises with the costs of detecting the compromises, countering them, and recovering from them? Many methods assign weights to the various factors, but these methods are ad hoc. A rigorous technique for determining appropriate weights has yet to be found.

The relationships of computer security to the political, social, and economic aspects of the world are not well understood. How does the ubiquity of the Internet change a country's borders? If someone starts at a computer in France, transits networks that cross Switzerland, Germany, Poland, Norway, Sweden, and Finland, and launches an attack on a computer in Russia, who has jurisdiction? How can a country limit the economic damage caused by an attack on its computer networks? How can attacks be traced to their human origins?

This chapter has also raised many technical questions. Research issues arising from them will be explored in future chapters.

1.11   Further Reading

Risk analysis arises in a variety of contexts. Molak [1369] presents essays on risk management and analysis in a variety of fields. Laudan [1141] provides an enjoyable introduction to the subject. Neumann [1444] discusses the risks of technology and recent problems. Software safety (Leveson [1155]) requires an understanding of the risks posed in the environment. Peterson [1518] discusses many programming errors in a readable way. All provide insights into the problems that arise in a variety of environments.

Many authors recount stories of security incidents. The earliest, Parker's wonderful book [1496], discusses motives and personalities as well as technical details. Stoll recounts the technical details of uncovering an espionage ring that began as the result of a 75¢ accounting error [1829, 1831]. Hafner and Markoff describe the same episode in a study of "cyberpunks" [842]. The Internet worm [619, 842, 1600, 1796, 1797] brought the problem of computer security into popular view. Numerous other incidents [723, 842, 1199, 1736, 1763, 1822] have heightened public awareness of the problem.

Several books [249, 442, 707, 1637] discuss computer security for the layperson. These works tend to focus on attacks that are visible or affect the end user (such as pornography, theft of credit card information, and deception). They are worth reading for those who wish to understand the results of failures in computer security. Other books [742, 1687, 1743, 1782, 1930] discuss the impact of computer and information security upon society. Social engineering is also widely discussed [559, 1206, 1244, 1363, 1561].

1.12   Exercises

1. Classify each of the following as a violation of confidentiality, of integrity, of availability, or of some combination thereof.

   a. John copies Mary's homework.

   b. Paul crashes Linda's system.

    c. Carol changes the amount of Angelo's check from $100 to $1,000.

    d. Gina forges Roger's signature on a deed.

    e. Rhonda registers the domain name "Pearson.com" and refuses to let the publishing house buy or use that domain name.

    f. Jonah obtains Peter's credit card number and has the credit card company cancel the card and replace it with another card bearing a different account number.

    g. Henry spoofs Julie's IP address to gain access to her computer.

2. Identify mechanisms for implementing the following. State what policy or policies they might be enforcing.

    a. A password-changing program will reject passwords that are less than five characters long or that are found in the dictionary.

    b. Only students in a computer science class will be given accounts on the department's computer system.

    c. The login program will disallow logins of any students who enter their passwords incorrectly three times.

    d. The permissions of the file containing Carol's homework will prevent Robert from cheating and copying it.

    e. When World Wide Web traffic climbs to more than 80% of the network's capacity, systems will disallow any further communications to or from web servers.

    f. Annie, a systems analyst, will be able to detect a student using a program to scan her system for vulnerabilities.

    g. A program used to submit homework will turn itself off just after the due date.

3. The aphorism "security through obscurity" suggests that hiding information provides some level of security. Give an example of a situation in which hiding information does not add appreciably to the security of a system. Then give an example of a situation in which it does.

4. Give an example of a situation in which a compromise of confidentiality leads to a compromise in integrity.

5. Show that the three security services—confidentiality, integrity, and availability—are sufficient to deal with the threats of disclosure, disruption, deception, and usurpation.

6. In addition to mathematical and informal statements of policy, policies can be implicit (not stated). Why might this be done? Might it occur with informally stated policies? What problems can this cause?

7. For each of the following statements, give an example of a situation in which the statement is true.

    a. Prevention is more important than detection and recovery.

    b. Detection is more important than prevention and recovery.

    c. Recovery is more important than prevention and detection.

8. Is it possible to design and implement a system in which no assumptions about trust are made? Why or why not?

9. Policy restricts the use of electronic mail on a particular system to faculty and staff. Students cannot send or receive electronic mail on that host. Classify the following mechanisms as secure, precise, or broad.

    a. The electronic mail sending and receiving programs are disabled.

    b. As each letter is sent or received, the system looks up the sender (or recipient) in a database. If that party is listed as faculty or staff, the mail is processed. Otherwise, it is rejected. (Assume that the database entries are correct.)

    c. The electronic mail sending programs ask the user if he or she is a student. If so, the mail is refused. The electronic mail receiving programs are disabled.

10. Consider a very high-assurance system developed for the military. The system has a set of specifications, and both the design and implementation have been proven to satisfy the specifications. What questions should school administrators ask when deciding whether to purchase such a system for their school's use?

11. How do laws protecting privacy impact the ability of system administrators to monitor user activity?

12. Computer viruses are programs that, among other actions, can delete files without a user's permission. A U.S. legislator wrote a law banning the deletion of any files from computer disks. What was the problem with this law from a computer security point of view? Specifically, state which security service would have been affected if the law had been passed.

13. Users often bring in programs or download programs from the Internet. Give an example of a site for which the benefits of allowing users to do this outweigh the dangers. Then give an example of a site for which the dangers of allowing users to do this outweigh the benefits.

14. A respected computer scientist has said that no computer can ever be made perfectly secure. Why might she have said this?

15. An organization makes each lead system administrator responsible for the security of the system he or she runs. However, the management determines what programs are to be on the system and how they are to be configured.

    a. Describe the security problem(s) that this division of power would create.
    b. How would you fix them?

16. The president of a large software development company has become concerned about competitors learning proprietary information. He is determined to stop them. Part of his security mechanism is to require all employees to report any contact with employees of the company's competitors, even if it is purely social. Do you believe this will have the desired effect? Why or why not?

17. The police and the public defender share a computer. What security problems does this present? Do you feel it is a reasonable cost-saving measure to have all public agencies share the same (set of) computers?

18. Companies usually restrict the use of electronic mail to company business but do allow minimal use for personal reasons.

    a. How might a company detect excessive personal use of electronic mail, other than by reading it? (*Hint*: Think about the personal use of a company telephone.)
    b. Intuitively, it seems reasonable to ban *all* personal use of electronic mail on company computers. Explain why most companies do not do this.

19. Argue for or against the following proposition. Ciphers that the government cannot cryptanalyze should be outlawed. How would your argument change if such ciphers could be used provided that the users registered the keys with the government?

20. For many years, industries and financial institutions hired people who broke into their systems once those people were released from prison. Now, such a conviction tends to *prevent* such people from being hired. Why you think attitudes on this issue changed? Do you think they changed for the better or for the worse?

21. A graduate student accidentally releases a program that spreads from computer system to computer system. It deletes no files but requires much time to implement the necessary defenses. The graduate student is convicted. Despite demands that he be sent to prison for the maximum time possible (to make an example of him), the judge sentences him to pay a fine and perform community service. What factors do you believe caused the judge to hand down the sentence he did? What would you have done were you the judge, and what extra information would you have needed to make your decision?

Part II

Foundations

How hard is it to determine whether or not a given system satisfies a given security policy? What is the most general system that we can prove to be secure (or nonsecure)? This issue determines the level of abstraction at which we can analyze security. If we can prove that a broad class of systems is secure, then we can prove that a model of a system is secure by determining that it falls into that class. More concretely, we can characterize systems that we can prove to be secure.

In what follows, we use a generic security policy to determine under what conditions we can prove systems to be secure. The results are disappointing and incomplete, and current research focuses on tightening them, but this work lays the theoretical foundation for all that follows, and understanding it is critical to understanding the limits of what we can achieve.

This part of the book presents the underpinnings and theoretical foundations of computer security and several key results.

Chapter 2, "Access Control Matrix," describes a widely used representation of access permissions. The representation is simple enough to capture any access rules and therefore is a useful starting point for deriving theoretical results.

Chapter 3, "Foundational Results," studies the safety question of when security is decidable. It presents three models: the Harrison-Ruzzo-Ullman model, which looks at arbitrary systems; the Take-Grant Protection Model, which looks at a specific system; and the Schematic Protection Model and its descendants, which look at a specific class of systems. It also gives some variants of these and other models, and shows how to compare them.

Chapter 2
Access Control Matrix

> GRANDPRÉ: Description cannot suit itself in words
> To demonstrate the life of such a battle
> In life so lifeless as it shows itself.
> — *The Life of Henry the Fifth*, IV, ii, 53–55.

A *protection system* describes the conditions under which a system is secure. This chapter presents a classical formulation of a protection system. The *access control matrix model* arose both in operating systems research and in database research; it describes allowed accesses using a matrix.

2.1 Protection State

The *state* of a system is the collection of the current values of all memory locations, all secondary storage, and all registers and other components of the system. The subset of this collection that deals with protection is the *protection state* of the system. An *access control matrix* is one tool that can describe the current protection state.

Consider the set of possible protection states P. Some subset Q of P consists of exactly those states in which the system is authorized to reside. So, whenever the system state is in Q, the system is secure. When the current state is in $P - Q$,[1] the system is not secure. Our interest in representing the state is to characterize those states in Q, and our interest in enforcing security is to ensure that the system state is always an element of Q. Characterizing the states in Q is the function of a *security policy*; preventing the system from entering a state in $P - Q$ is the function of a *security mechanism*. Recall from Definition 1–3 that a mechanism that enforces this restriction is *secure*, and if $P = Q$, the mechanism is precise.

The *access control matrix model* is the most precise model used to describe a protection state. It characterizes the rights of each *subject* (active entity, such as a user or a process) with respect to every other entity. The description of elements

---

[1] The notation $P - Q$ means all elements of set P not in set Q.

of the access control matrix *A* form a *specification* against which the current state can be compared. Specifications take many forms, and different specification languages have been created to describe the characteristics of allowable states.

As the system changes, the protection state changes. When a command changes the state of the system, a *state transition* occurs. Very often, constraints on the set of allowed states use these transitions inductively; a set of authorized states is defined, and then a set of operations is allowed on the elements of that set. The result of transforming an authorized state with an operation allowed in that state is an authorized state. By induction, the system will always be in an authorized state. Hence, both states and state transitions are often constrained.

In practice, *any* operation on a real system causes multiple state transitions; the reading, loading, altering, and execution of any datum or instruction causes a transition. We are concerned only with those state transitions that affect the protection state of the system, so only transitions that alter the actions a subject is authorized to take are relevant. For example, a program that resets the value of a local counter variable in a loop to 0 (usually) does not alter the protection state. However, if changing the value of a variable causes the privileges of a process to change, then the process does alter the protection state and needs to be accounted for in the set of transitions.

2.2   Access Control Matrix Model

The simplest framework for describing a protection system is the *access control matrix model*, which describes the rights of subjects over all entities in a matrix. Butler Lampson first proposed this model in 1971 [1132]; Graham and Denning [547, 805] refined it, and we will use their version.

The set of all protected entities (that is, entities that are relevant to the protection state of the system) is called the set of *objects O*. The set of *subjects S* is the set of active objects, such as processes and users. In the access control matrix model, the relationship between these entities is captured by a matrix *A* with *rights* drawn from a set of rights *R* in each entry $A[s, o]$, where $s \in S$, $o \in O$, and $A[s, o] \in R$. The subject *s* has the set of rights $A[s, o]$ over the object *o*. The set of protection states of the system is represented by the triple (S, O, A). For example, Figure 2–1 shows the protection state of a system. Here, process 1, which owns file 1, can read or write file 1 and can read file 2; process 2 can append to file 1 and read file 2, which it owns. Process 1 can communicate with process 2 by writing to it, and process 2 can read from process 1. Each process owns itself and has read, write, and execute rights over itself. Note that the processes themselves are treated as both subjects (rows) and objects (columns). This enables a process to be the target of operations as well as the operator.

Interpretation of the meaning of these rights varies from system to system. Reading from, writing to, and appending to files is usually clear enough, but what does "reading from" a process mean? Depending on the instantiation of the

	file 1	file 2	process 1	process 2
process 1	read, write, own	read	read, write, execute, own	write
process 2	append	read, own	read	read, write, execute, own

Figure 2–1   An access control matrix. The system has two processes and two files. The set of rights is {read, write, execute, append, own}.

model, it could mean that the reader accepts messages from the process being read, or it could mean that the reader simply looks at the state of the process being read (as a debugger does, for example). The meaning of the right may vary depending on the object involved. The point is that the access control matrix model is an *abstract* model of the protection state, and when one talks about the meaning of some particular access control matrix, one must always talk with respect to a particular implementation or system.

The *own* right is a *distinguished* right, which is a right that is treated specially. In most systems, the owner of an object has special privileges: the ability to add and delete rights for other users (and for the owner). In the system shown in Figure 2–1, for example, process 1 could alter the contents of $A[x, \text{file}1]$, where x is any subject.

EXAMPLE: The UNIX system defines the rights *read*, *write*, and *execute*. When a process reads, writes, or executes a file, these terms mean what one would expect. With respect to a directory, however, *read* means to be able to list the contents of the directory; *write* means to be able to create, rename, or delete files or subdirectories in that directory; and *execute* means to be able to access files or subdirectories in that directory. When a process interacts with another process, *read* means to be able to receive signals, *write* means to be able to send signals, and *execute* means to be able to execute the process as a subprocess.

Moreover, the UNIX superuser can access any (local) file regardless of the permissions the owner has granted. In effect, the superuser *owns* all objects on the system. Even in this case however, the interpretation of the rights is constrained. For example, the superuser cannot alter a directory using the system calls and commands that alter files. The superuser must use specific system calls and commands to alter the directory, for example by creating, renaming, and deleting files.

Although the "objects" involved in the access control matrix are normally thought of as files, devices, and processes, they could just as easily be messages sent between processes, or indeed systems themselves. Figure 2–2 shows an example access control matrix for three systems on a local area network (LAN). The rights correspond to various network protocols: *own* (the ability to add servers), *ftp* (the ability to access the system using the File Transfer Protocol, or FTP [1539]),

host names	telegraph	nob	toadflax
telegraph	own	ftp	ftp
nob		ftp, nfs, mail, own	ftp, nfs, mail
toadflax		ftp, mail	ftp, nfs, mail, own

Figure 2–2   Rights on a LAN. The set of rights is {ftp, mail, nfs, own}.

functions	counter	inc_ctr	dec_ctr	manager
inc_ctr	+			
dec_ctr	−			
manager		call	call	call

Figure 2–3   Rights in a program. The set of rights is {+, −, call}.

nfs (the ability to access file systems using the Network File System, or NFS, protocol [142]), and *mail* (the ability to send and receive mail using the Simple Mail Transfer Protocol, or SMTP [1068, 1538]). The subject *telegraph* is a personal computer with an FTP client but no servers, so neither of the other systems can access it, but it can FTP to them. The subject *nob* can access *toadflax* and *nob* itself using an NFS client, and both systems will exchange mail with one another and can *ftp* to each other.

At the micro level, access control matrices can model programming language accesses; in this case, the objects are the variables and the subjects are the procedures (or modules). Consider a program in which events must be synchronized. A module provides functions for incrementing (*inc_ctr*) and decrementing (*dec_ctr*) a counter private to that module. The routine *manager* calls these functions. The access control matrix is shown in Figure 2–3. Note that "+" and "−" are the rights, representing the ability to add and subtract, respectively, and *call* is the ability to invoke a procedure. The routine *manager* can call itself; presumably, it is recursive.

In the examples above, entries in the access control matrix are rights. However, they could as easily have been functions that determined the set of rights at any particular state based on other data, such as a history of prior accesses, the time of day, the rights another subject has over the object, and so forth. A common form of such a function is a locking function used to enforce the Bernstein conditions,[2] so when a process is writing to a file, other processes cannot access the file; but once the writing is done, the processes can access the file once again.

---

[2]The Bernstein conditions ensure that data is consistent. They state that any number of readers may access a datum simultaneously, but if a writer is accessing the datum, no other writers or any reader can access the datum until the current writing is complete [177].

2.2.1   Access Control by Boolean Expression Evaluation

Miller and Baldwin [1347] use an access control matrix to control access to fields in a database. The values are determined by Boolean expressions. Their objects are records and fields; the subjects are users authorized to access the databases. Types of access are defined by the database and are called *verbs*; for example, the Structured Query Language (SQL) would have the verbs *insert* and *update*. Each *rule*, corresponding to a function, is associated with one or more verbs. Whenever a subject attempts to access an object using a right (verb) *r*, the Boolean expression (rule) associated with *r* is evaluated; if it is true, access is allowed while if it is false, access is not allowed.

The Access Restriction Facility (ARF) program exemplifies this approach. It defines subjects as having attributes such as a name, a level, a role, membership in groups, and access to programs, but the user can assign any meaning desired to any attribute. For example,

name	role	group	program
matt	programmer	sys, hack	compilers, editors
holly	artist	user, creative	editors, paint, draw
heidi	chef, gardener	acct, creative	editors, kitchen

Verbs have a default rule, either "closed" (access denied unless explicitly granted; represented by the 0 rule) or "open" (access granted unless explicitly denied; represented by the 1 rule):

verb	default rule
read	1
write	0
paint	0
temperature_control	0

Associated with each object is a set of verbs, and each (object, verb) pair has an associated rule:

name	rules
recipes	write: 'creative' in subject.group
overpass	write: 'artist' in subject.role or 'gardener' in subject.role
.shellrct	write: 'hack' in subject.group and time.hour < 4 and time.hour > 0
oven.dev	temperature_control: 'kitchen' in subject.program and 'chef' in subject.role

The system also provides primitives such as *time* (which corresponds to the current time of day), *date* (the current date), and *temp* (the current temperature). This generates the following access control matrix between midnight and 4 a.m.:

	recipes	overpass	.shellrct	oven.dev
matt	read	read	read, write	
holly	read, write	read, write	read	
heidi	read, write	read, write	read	temperature_control

At other times, the entry *A*[*matt*, .*shellrct*] contains only *read*. The *read* rights in the last row are omitted because, even though the default in general is to allow read access, the default rule for the object *oven. dev* is to deny *read* access:

	recipes	overpass	.shellrct	oven.dev
matt	read	read	read	
holly	read, write	read, write	read	
heidi	read, write	read, write	read	temperature_control

2.2.2   Access Controlled by History

A common problem when running downloaded programs (such as web applets or plug-ins) is that the program may access the system in unauthorized ways, such as deleting or modifying configuration and control files. Abadi and Fournet [3] address this by conditioning access rights of a procedure on the rights of those pieces of code that executed earlier in the process.

They associate a set of rights (the "static rights") with each piece of code and another set of rights (the "current rights") with each process as it executes. When a piece of code runs, the rights of the executing code are the intersection of the code's static rights and the process's current rights.[3] Thus, the specific rights that a process has at any point in time is a function of the pieces of code it has executed and is executing—its history.

EXAMPLE: Consider the following brief program, in which an untrusted routine (*helper_proc*) is loaded and used to find a file to delete:

```
// This routine has no filesystem access rights
// beyond those in a limited, temporary area
procedure helper_proc()
        return sys_kernel_file
```

---

[3]Under some conditions, a piece of code may request that its rights be augmented, but it can only add rights to its set of static rights.

```
// But this has the right to delete files
program main()
        sys_load_file(helper_proc)
        file = helper_proc()
        sys_delete_file(file)
```

The following access control matrix represents the static rights of the program and routine. The file *sys_kernel_file* contains the kernel of the system, and *tmp_file* is a file in the limited, temporary area that *helper_proc* can access:

	sys_kernel_file	tmp_file
main	delete	delete
helper_proc		delete

When the program starts, its current rights are those of *main*:

	sys_kernel_file	tmp_file
main	delete	delete
helper_proc		delete
process (before *helper_proc* loaded)	delete	delete

After *helper_proc* is loaded, the current rights of the process are the intersection of the static rights of *helper_proc* and the current rights of the process:

	sys_kernel_file	tmp_file
main	delete	delete
helper_proc		delete
process (after *helper_proc* loaded)		delete

As *helper_proc* cannot delete system files, neither can the executing process. When it tries to do so, it fails, and a fault of some kind occurs.

2.3   Protection State Transitions

As processes execute operations, the state of the protection system changes. Let the initial state of the system be $X_0 = (S_0, O_0, A_0)$. The set of state transitions is represented as a set of operations $\tau_1, \tau_2, \ldots$. Successive states are represented as $X_1, X_2, \ldots$, where the notation

$$X_i \vdash_{\tau_{i+1}} X_{i+1}$$

means that state transition τ_{i+1} moves the system from state X_i to state X_{i+1}. When a system starts at some state X and, after a series of zero or more state transitions, enters state Y, we can write

$$X \vdash^* Y$$

The representation of the protection system as an access control matrix must also be updated. In the model, sequences of state transitions are represented as single commands, or *transformation procedures*, that update the access control matrix. The commands state which entry in the matrix is to be changed, and how; hence, the commands require parameters. Formally, let c_k be the kth command with formal parameters $p_{k_1}, \ldots, p_{k_m}$. Then the ith transition would be written as

$$X_i \vdash_{c_{i+1}(p_{(i+1)_1}, \ldots, p_{(i+1)_m})} X_{i+1}$$

Note the similarity in notation between the use of the command and the state transition operations. This is deliberate. For every command, there is a sequence of state transition operations that takes the initial state X_i to the resulting state X_{i+1}. Using the command notation allows us to shorten the description of the transformation as well as list the parameters (subjects and objects) that affect the transformation operations.

We now focus on the commands themselves. Following Harrison, Ruzzo, and Ullman [874], we define a set of *primitive commands* that alter the access control matrix. In the following list, the protection state is (S, O, A) before the execution of each command and (S', O', A') after each command. The preconditions state the conditions needed for the primitive command to be executed, and the postconditions state the results.

1. Precondition: $s \notin S$
   Primitive command: **create subject** s
   Postconditions: $S' = S \cup \{s\}, O' = O \cup \{s\}$,
   $(\forall y \in O')[a'[s, y] = \varnothing], (\forall x \in S')[a'[x, s] = \varnothing]$,
   $(\forall x \in S)(\forall y \in O)[a'[x, y] = A[x, y]]$
   This primitive command creates a new subject s. Note that s must not exist as a subject or an object before this command is executed. This operation does not add any rights. It merely modifies the matrix.

2. Precondition: $o \notin O$
   Primitive command: **create object** o
   Postconditions: $S' = S, O' = O \cup \{o\}$,
   $(\forall x \in S')[a'[x, o] = \varnothing]$,
   $(\forall x \in S)(\forall y \in O)[a'[x, y] = A[x, y]]$
   This primitive command creates a new object o. Note that o must not exist before this command is executed. Like **create subject**, this operation does not add any rights. It merely modifies the matrix.

3. Precondition: $s \in S, o \in O, r \in R$
   Primitive command: **enter** r **into** $a[s, o]$
   Postconditions: $S' = S, O' = O, a'[s, o] = a[s, o] \cup \{r\}$,
   $$(\forall x \in S')(\forall y \in O')[(x, y) \neq (s, o) \Rightarrow a'[x, y] = A[x, y]]$$
   This primitive command adds the right r to the cell $a[s, o]$. Note that $a[s, o]$ may already contain the right, in which case the effect of this primitive depends on the instantiation of the model.

4. Precondition: $s \in S, o \in O, r \in R$
   Primitive command: **delete** r **from** $a[s, o]$
   Postconditions: $S' = S, O' = O, a'[s, o] = a[s, o] - \{r\}$,
   $$(\forall x \in S')(\forall y \in O')[(x, y) \neq (s, o) \Rightarrow a'[x, y] = A[x, y]]$$
   This primitive command deletes the right r from the cell $a[s, o]$. Note that $a[s, o]$ need not contain the right, in which case this operation has no effect.

5. Precondition: $s \in S$
   Primitive command: **destroy subject** s
   Postconditions: $S' = S - \{s\}, O' = O - \{s\}$,
   $$(\forall y \in O')[a'[s, y] = \varnothing], (\forall x \in S')[a'[x, s] = \varnothing],$$
   $$a'[s, s] = \varnothing,$$
   $$(\forall x \in S')(\forall y \in O')[a'[x, y] = A[x, y]]$$
   This primitive command deletes the subject s. The column and row for s in A are deleted also.

6. Precondition: $o \in O$
   Primitive command: **destroy object** o
   Postconditions: $S' = S, O' = O - \{o\}$,
   $$(\forall x \in S')[a'[x, o] = \varnothing],$$
   $$(\forall x \in S')(\forall y \in O')[a'[x, y] = A[x, y]]$$
   This primitive command deletes the object o. The column for o in A is deleted also.

These primitive operations can be combined into commands, during which multiple primitive operations may be executed.

EXAMPLE: In the UNIX system, if process p created a file f with owner read (r) and write (w) permission, the command *create·file* capturing the resulting changes in the access control matrix would be

```
command create ·file(p, f)
        create object f;
        enter own into A[p,f];
        enter r into A[p,f];
        enter w into A[p,f];
end
```

Suppose the process p wishes to create a new process q. The following command would capture the resulting changes in the access control matrix:

```
command spawn·process(p,  q)
        create subject q;
        enter own into A[p,q];
        enter r into A[p,q];
        enter w into A[p,q];
        enter r into A[q,p];
        enter w into A[q,p];
end
```

The r and w rights enable the parent and child to signal each other.

The system can update the matrix only by using defined commands; it cannot use the primitive commands directly. Of course, a command may invoke only a single primitive; such a command is called *mono-operational*.

EXAMPLE: The command

```
command make·owner(p,  f)
        enter own into A[p,f];
end
```

is a mono-operational command. It does not delete any existing owner rights. It merely adds p to the set of owners of f. Hence, f may have multiple owners after this command is executed.

2.3.1   Conditional Commands

The execution of some primitives requires that specific preconditions be satisfied. For example, suppose a process p wishes to give another process q the right to read a file f. In some systems, p must own f. The abstract command would be

```
command grant·read·file·A(p,  f,  q)
    if own in A[p,f]
    then
            enter r into A[q,f];
end
```

Any number of conditions may be placed together using **and**. For example, suppose a system has a distinguished right g that allows it to give rights it possesses to another subject. So, if a subject has the rights r and g over an object, it may give any other subject r rights over that object. Then,

```
command grant·read·file·B(p, f, q)
        if r in A[p,f] and g in A[p,f]
        then
                    enter r into A[q,f];
    end
```

Commands with one condition are called *monoconditional*. Commands with two conditions are called *biconditional*. The command *grant·read·file·A* is monoconditional, and the command *grant·read·file·B* is biconditional. Because both have one primitive command, both are mono-operational.

Note that all conditions are joined by **and**, and never by **or**. Because joining conditions with **or** is equivalent to two commands each with one of the conditions, the disjunction is unnecessary and thus is omitted. For example, to achieve the effect of a command equivalent to

```
if own in A[p,f] or g in A[p,f]
then
            enter r into A[q,f];
end
```

define the two commands

```
command grant·read·file·C(p, f, q)
        if own in A[p,f]
        then
                    enter r into A[q,f];
    end
command grant·read·file·D(p, f, q)
        if g in A[p,f]
        then
                    enter r into A[q,f];
    end
```

and then say

```
grant·read·file·C(p, f, q);
grant·read·file·D(p, f, q);
```

Also, the negation of a condition is not permitted—that is, one cannot test for the absence of a right within a command by the condition

```
if r not in A[p,f]
```

This has some interesting consequences, which we will explore in the next chapter.

2.4   Copying, Owning, and the Attenuation of Privilege

Two specific rights are worth discussing. The first augments existing rights and is called the *copy flag*; the second is the *own right*. Both of these rights are related to the principle of attenuation of privilege, which essentially says that a subject may not give away rights it does not possess.

2.4.1   Copy Right

The *copy right* (often called the *grant right*) allows the possessor to grant rights to another. By the principle of attenuation, only those rights the grantor possesses may be copied. Whether the copier must surrender the right, or can simply pass it on, is specific to the system being modeled. This right is often considered a flag attached to other rights; in this case, it is known as the *copy flag*.

EXAMPLE: In the Windows NTFS file system, the copy right corresponds to the "change permission" right.

EXAMPLE: System R was a relational database developed by the IBM Corporation. Its authorization model [651, 822] takes the database tables as objects to be protected. Each table is a separate object, even if the same records are used to construct the table (meaning that two different views of the same records are treated as two separate objects). The users who access the tables are the subjects. The database rights are *read* entries, which define new views on an existing table; *insert*, *delete*, and *update* entries in a table; and *drop* (to delete a table). Associated with each right is a *grant* option; if it is set, the possessor of the privilege can grant it to another. Here, the grant option corresponds to a copy flag.

EXAMPLE: Let *c* be the copy right, and suppose a subject *p* has *r* rights over an object *f*. Then the following command allows *p* to copy *r* over *f* to another subject *q* only if *p* has a copy right over *f*:

```
command grant·r·right(p, f, q)
        if r in A[p, f] and c in A[p, f]
        then
                enter r into A[q, f];
end
```

If *p* does not have *c* rights over *f*, this command will not copy the *r* rights to *q*.

2.4.2   Own Right

The *own right* is a special right that enables possessors to add or delete privileges for themselves. It also allows the possessor to grant rights to others, although to whom they can be granted may be system- or implementation-dependent. The owner of an object is usually the subject that created the object or a subject to which the creator gave ownership.

EXAMPLE: On UNIX and Linux systems, the owner may use the *chown*(1) command to change the permissions that others have over an object. The semantics of delegation of ownership vary among different versions of UNIX and Linux systems. On some versions, the owner cannot give ownership to another user, whereas on other versions, the owner can do so. In this case, the object cannot be later reclaimed. All power passes to the new owner.

Whether a subject can delete an own right depends on the instantiation of the model. Some systems allow an owner to "give away" an object, effectively transferring the *own* right to another subject. Other systems forbid this.

2.4.3   Principle of Attenuation of Privilege

If a subject does not possess a right over an object, it should not be able to give that right to another subject. For example, if Matt cannot read the file *xyzzy*, he should not be able to grant Holly the right to read that file. This is a consequence of the principle of attenuation of privilege.
The principle has several forms; the simplest is [533]:[4]

Principle of Attenuation of Privilege. *A subject may not increase its rights, nor grant rights it does not possess to another subject.*

On most systems, the owner of an object can give other subjects rights over the object whether the owner has those rights enabled or not. At first glance, this appears to violate the principle. In fact, on these systems, the owner can grant itself any right over the object owned. Then the owner can grant that right to another subject. Lastly, the owner can delete the right for itself. So, this apparent exception actually conforms to the principle.

EXAMPLE: Suppose user *matt* owns the file */home/matt/xyz* but does not have *read* permission on it. He can issue the following command to enable anyone to read the file, whether *matt* can read it or not:

```
chmod go+r /home/bishop/xyz
```

If user *holly* tries to execute the same command, the system will reject the command, because *holly* cannot alter the permissions of a file she does not own. If she has *read* permission, she can copy the file and make the copy readable by everyone, thereby achieving the effect of making the contents of the file *at that*

---

[4]See Exercises 8 and 9 for other versions of this privilege.

time world-readable. Of course, should *matt* change the contents of the original file, *holly*'s world-readable version will not reflect those changes.

2.5 Summary

The access control matrix is the primary abstraction mechanism in computer security. In its purest form, it can express any expressible security policy. In practice, it is not used directly because of space requirements; most systems have (at least) thousands of objects and could have thousands of subjects, and the storage requirements would simply be too much. However, its simplicity makes it ideal for theoretical analyses of security problems.

Transitions change the state of the system. They are expressed in terms of commands. A command consists of a possible condition followed by one or more primitive operations. Conditions may involve ownership or the ability to copy a right. The principle of attenuation of privilege constrains a subject from giving a right it does not possess to any other subject.

2.6 Research Issues

The access control matrix is very general. Are there other models, simpler to work with, but equally expressive? Chapter 3, "Foundational Results," explores some of these issues, especially the application of the notion of types to expressive power. Similarly, examining the effects of different types of rules may affect the expressive power of the models.

Database security is an example of a simple application of the access control matrix model. The complexity arises because the elements of the matrix entries are generated by functions with very complex parameter lists. How can one conceal specific entries yet reveal meaningful statistics? How can one conceal some statistics yet reveal others? How can one detect attempts to subvert or circumvent controls?

2.7 Further Reading

The access control matrix is sometimes called an *authorization matrix* in older literature [911].

In 1972, Conway, Maxwell, and Morgan [453], in parallel with Graham and Denning, proposed a protection method for databases equivalent to the access control model. Hartson and Hsiao [877] point out that databases in particular use functions as described above to control access to records and fields; for this reason, entries in the access control matrix for a database are called decision procedures or decision rules. These entries are very similar to the earlier formulary model [910], in which access procedures determine whether to grant access and, if so, provide a mapping to virtual addresses and any required encryption and decryption.

Various enhancements of the access control matrix have been proposed, among them the typed access control matrix [1660] that adds a notion of type to subjects and objects; the augmented typed access control matrix [43] that adds the ability to check for the absence of rights in an element of the matrix; and the attribute-based access control matrix [2092] that augments subjects and objects with arbitrary attributes. Some of these are discussed in Chapter 3, "Foundational Results."

2.8 Exercises

1. Consider a computer system with three users: Alice, Bob, and Cyndy. Alice owns the file *alicerc*, and Bob and Cyndy can read it. Cyndy can read and write the file *bobrc*, which Bob owns, but Alice can only read it. Only Cyndy can read and write the file *cyndyrc*, which she owns. Assume that the owner of each of these files can execute it.

    a. Create the corresponding access control matrix.

    b. Cyndy gives Alice permission to read *cyndyrc*, and Alice removes Bob's ability to read *alicerc*. Show the new access control matrix.

2. Consider the following change in the rules associated with each (object, verb) pair in Miller and Baldwin's model (see Section 2.2.1):

name	rules
recipes	write: 'creative' in subject.group and 'chef' in subject.role
overpass	write: 'artist' in subject.role and 'creative' in subject.group
.shellrct	write: 'hack' in subject.group and (time.hour < 4 or time.hour > 20) and time.hour > 0
oven.dev	temp_ctl: 'kitchen' in subject.program and 'chef' in subject.role

    How does this change the access control matrices shown at the end of that section?

3. Consider a mechanism that *amplifies* rights instead of reducing them. Associate with each (system) routine a *template* of rights. When the routine runs, the rights of the process are augmented by the rights in the associated

template, and when the routine exits, the rights added by the template are deleted. Contrast this with the mechanism described in Section 2.2.2.

    a. What are some of the advantages and disadvantages of the amplification mechanism?

    b. What are some of the advantages and disadvantages of the reducing mechanism?

4. Consider the set of rights {*read, write, execute, append, list, modify, own*}.

    a. Using the syntax in Section 2.3, write a command *delete_all_rights(p, q, o)*. This command causes p to delete all rights the subject q has over an object o.

    b. Modify your command so that the deletion can occur only if p has *modify* rights over o.

    c. Modify your command so that the deletion can occur only if p has *modify* rights over o and q does not have *own* rights over o.

5. Let c be a copy flag and let a computer system have the same rights as in Exercise 4.

    a. Using the syntax in Section 2.3, write a command *copy_all_rights(p, q, s)* that copies all rights that p has over s to q.

    b. Modify your command so that only those rights with an associated copy flag are copied. The new copy should *not* have the copy flag.

    c. In the previous part, what conceptually would be the effect of copying the copy flag along with the right?

6. Suppose Alice has r and w rights over the file *book*. Alice wants to copy r rights to *book* to Bob.

    a. Assuming there is a copy right c, write a command to do this.

    b. Now assume the system supports a copy flag; for example, the right r with the copy flag would be written as rc. In this case, write a command to do the copy.

    c. In the previous part, what happens if the copy flag is *not* copied?

7. Consider a system that allows multiple owners of an object. This system allows an owner to grant rights to other subjects, and to delete them, except that the owner cannot delete another *own* right.

    a. An object o has two owners, p and q. What happens if p deletes all of q's rights to the object? Specifically, does this prevent q from accessing the object?

    b. Assume there are two types of *own* rights, an "original own" own_{orig} and an "added own" own_{add}. The *own* right own_{orig} cannot be copied or added, whereas the own_{add} right enables the possessor to add or delete rights (except for the own_{orig} right). If p has own_{orig} and q has own_{add}, how does your answer to the first part change?

8. Peter Denning [548] formulated the principle of attenuation of privilege as "a procedure cannot access an object passed as a parameter in ways that the caller cannot." Contrast this formulation to that of the Principle of Attenuation of Privilege in Section 2.4.3. In particular, which is the "subject" and which is the "other subject" in the earlier statement?

9. Naftaly Minsky [1353, p. 256] states that "privileges should not be allowed to grow when they are transported from one place in the system to another." Does this differ from the Principle of Attenuation of Privilege as stated in Section 2.4.3? If not, show they are the same; if so, how do they differ?

10. This exercise asks you to consider the consequences of not applying the principle of attenuation of privilege to a computer system.

   a. What are the consequences of not applying the principle at all? In particular, what is the maximal set of rights that subjects within the system can acquire (possibly with the cooperation of other subjects)?

   b. Suppose attenuation of privilege applied only to access rights such as *read* and *write*, but not to rights such as *own* and *grant_rights*. Would this ameliorate the situation discussed in part (a) of this exercise? Why or why not?

   c. Consider a restricted form of attenuation, which works as follows. A subject q is attenuated by the maximal set of rights that q, or any of its ancestors, has. So, for example, if any ancestor of q has r permission over a file f, q can also r f. How does this affect the spread of rights throughout the access control matrix of the system? Develop an example matrix that includes the ancestor right, and illustrate your answer.

Chapter 3
Foundational Results

> MARIA: Ay, but you must confine yourself
> within the modest limits of order.
> — *Twelfth Night*, I, iii, 8–9.

In 1976, Harrison, Ruzzo, and Ullman [874] proved that the security of computer systems was undecidable in the general case and explored some of the limits of this result. In that same year, Jones, Lipton, and Snyder [972] presented a specific system in which security was not only decidable, but decidable in time linear with the size of the system. Minsky [1354] suggested a third model to examine what made the general, abstract case undecidable but at least one specific case decidable. Sandhu [1657] devised a related model extending the decidability results to a large class of systems.

These models explore the most basic question of the art and science of computer security: under what conditions can a generic algorithm determine whether a system is secure? Understanding models and the results derived from them lays the foundations for coping with limits in policy and policy composition as well as applying the theoretical work.

3.1 The General Question

Given a computer system, how can we determine if it is secure? More simply, is there a generic algorithm that allows us to determine whether a computer system is secure? If so, we could simply apply that algorithm to any system; although the algorithm might not tell us where the security problems were, it would tell us whether any existed.

The first question is the definition of "secure." What policy shall define "secure"? For a general result, the definition should be as broad as possible. We use the access control matrix to express our policy. However, we do not provide any special rights such as *copy* or *own*, nor do we apply the principle of attenuation of privilege.

Let R be the set of generic (primitive) rights of the system.

Definition 3–1. When a generic right r is added to an element of the access control matrix that did not contain r initially, that right is said to be *leaked*.[1]

Under this definition, if a system begins with a right r in $A[s, o]$, deletes it, and then adds it back, r has not leaked.

Our policy defines the authorized set of states A to be the set of states in which no command $c(x_1, \ldots, x_n)$ can leak r. This means that no generic rights can be added to the matrix.

We do not distinguish between a *leaking* of rights and an *authorized transfer* of rights. In our model, there is no authorized transfer of rights. (If we wish to allow such a transfer, we designate the subjects involved as "trusted." We then eliminate all trusted subjects from the matrix, because the security mechanisms no longer apply to them.)

Let a computer system begin in protection state s_0.

Definition 3–2. If a system can never leak the right r, the system (including the initial state s_0) is called *safe* with respect to the right r. If the system can leak the right r (enter an unauthorized state), it is called *unsafe with respect to the right r*.

We use these terms rather than *secure* and *nonsecure* because safety refers to the abstract model and security refers to the actual implementation. Thus, a secure system corresponds to a model safe with respect to all rights, but a model safe with respect to all rights does not ensure a secure system.

EXAMPLE: A computer system allows the network administrator to read all network traffic. It disallows all other users from reading this traffic. The system is designed in such a way that the network administrator cannot communicate with other users. Thus, there is no way for the right r of the network administrator over the network device to leak. This system is safe.

Unfortunately, the operating system has a flaw. If a user specifies a certain file name in a file deletion system call, that user can obtain access to any file on the system (bypassing all file system access controls). This is an implementation flaw, not a theoretical one. It also allows the user to read data from the network. So this system is not secure.

The *protection state* of a system consists of the parts of the system state relevant to protection. The *safety question* is: Does there exist an algorithm to

---

[1] Tripunitara and Li [1890] point out that this differs from the definition in Harrison, Ruzzo, and Ullman [874], which defines "leaked" to mean that r is added to any access control matrix entry in which r was not present *in the immediately previous state*. But the proofs in that paper use Definition 3–1. See Exercise 2 for an exploration of the differences when the stated definition in Harrison, Ruzzo, and Ullman is used.

determine whether a given protection system with initial state s_0 is safe with respect to a generic right r?

3.2   Basic Results

The simplest case is a system in which the commands are mono-operational (each consisting of a single primitive operation). In such a system, the following theorem holds.

> **Theorem 3.1.** [874] There exists an algorithm that will determine whether a given mono-operational protection system with initial state s_0 is safe with respect to a generic right r.
>
> **Proof** Because all commands are mono-operational, we can identify each command by the type of primitive operation it invokes. Consider the minimal length sequence of commands $c_1, \ldots, c_k$ needed to leak the right r from the system with initial state s_0.
>
> Because no commands can test for the absence of rights in an access control matrix entry, we can omit the **delete** and **destroy** commands from the analysis. They do not affect the ability of a right to leak.
>
> Now suppose that multiple **create** commands occurred during the sequence of commands, causing a leak. Subsequent commands check only for the presence of rights in an access control matrix element. They distinguish between different elements only by the presence (or lack of presence) of a particular right. Suppose that two subjects s_1 and s_2 are created and the rights in $A[s_1, o_1]$ and $A[s_2, o_2]$ are tested. The same test for $A[s_1, o_1]$ and $A[s_1, o_2] = A[s_1, o_2] \cup A[s_2, o_2]$ will produce the same result. Hence, all **create** commands are unnecessary except possibly the first (if there are no subjects initially), and any commands entering rights into the new subjects are rewritten to enter the new right into the lone created subject. Similarly, any tests for the presence of rights in the new subjects are rewritten to test for the presence of that right in an existing subject (or, if none initially, the first subject created).
>
> Let $|S_0|$ be the number of subjects and $|O_0|$ the number of objects in the initial state. Let n be the number of generic rights. Then, in the worst case, one new subject must be created (one command), and the sequence of commands will enter every right into every element of the access control matrix. After the creation, there are $|S_0| + 1$ subjects and $|O_0| + 1$ objects, and $(|S_0|+1)(|O_0|+1)$ elements. Because there are n generic rights, this leads to $n(|S_0| + 1)(|O_0| + 1)$ commands. Hence, $k \leq n(|S_0| + 1)(|O_0| + 1) + 1$.

By enumerating all possible states we can determine whether the system is safe. Clearly, this may be computationally infeasible, especially if many subjects, objects, and rights are involved, but it is computable (see Exercise 4). Unfortunately, this result does not generalize to all protection systems.

To see this, we express a problem known to be undecidable in terms of the access control matrix model. The halting problem is known to be undecidable, so we develop a mapping between a Turing machine and the access control matrix. Each Turing machine command moves the head and possibly changes the symbols, so we devise commands in the access control matrix model to do the equivalent to the access control matrix.

We now make this intuition rigorous. To begin, let us review the notation for a Turing machine. A Turing machine T consists of a head and an infinite tape divided into cells numbered $1, 2, \ldots$, from left to right. The machine also has a finite set of states K and a finite set of tape symbols M. The distinguished symbol $b \in M$ is a blank and appears on all the cells of the tape at the start of all computations; also, at that time T is in the initial state q_0.

The tape head occupies one square of the tape, and can read and write symbols on that cell of the tape, and can move into the cell to the left (L) or right (R) of the cell it currently occupies. The function $\delta : K \times M \rightarrow K \times M \times \{L, R\}$ describes the action of T. For example, let $p, q \in K$ and $A, B \in M$. Then, if $\delta(p, A) = (q, B, R)$, when T is in state p and the head rests on a cell with symbol A, the tape head changes the symbol in the cell to B, moves right to the next cell (that is, if the head is in cell i, it moves to cell $i+1$), and the Turing machine enters state q. If $\delta(p, A) = (q, B, L)$, then the actions would be the same except the head would move to the left unless it were already in the leftmost square (because the head may never move off the tape).

Let the final state be q_f; if T enters this state, it halts. The *halting problem* is to determine whether an arbitrary Turing machine will enter the state q_f, and is known to be undecidable [638].

Given this, we can now present the following theorem.

Theorem 3.2.   [874] It is undecidable whether a given state of a given protection system is safe for a given generic right.

Proof Proof by contradiction. We show that an arbitrary Turing machine can be reduced to the safety problem, with the Turing machine entering a final state corresponding to the leaking of a given generic right. Then, if the safety problem is decidable, we can determine when the Turing machine halts, showing that the halting problem is decidable, which (as we said above) is false.

First, we construct a map from the states and symbols of T to rights in the access control matrix model. Let the set of generic rights be the symbols in M and a set of distinct symbols each representing an element in K; in other words, the set of tape symbols and states are represented by generic rights, one right for each symbol and one for each state.

The cells of the Turing machine tape are sequentially ordered. We consider only the cells that the head has visited, so suppose T has scanned cells $1, 2, \ldots, n$. To simulate this, we represent each cell as a subject and define a distinguished right called *own* such that s_i owns s_{i+1} for $1 \leq i < k$. If cell i contains the symbol A, then subject s_i has A rights over itself. Furthermore, the subject s_k, which corresponds to the rightmost cell visited, has *endrt* rights over itself; notice that s_{k+1} has not been created in this case. Finally, if the head is in cell j and T is in state p, then subject s_j has p rights over itself also. (To keep the meanings of the rights unambiguous, we require the rights corresponding to the symbols for the tape to be distinct from the rights corresponding to the states.) Figure 3–1 shows an example of this mapping, when the head has visited four cells.

Next, we must translate the Turing machine function δ into access control matrix commands. Suppose that $\delta(p, A) = (q, B, L)$ and the head is not in the leftmost cell. Then, in terms of the access control matrix a, the rights A and p must be replaced by B in the entry $a[s_i, s_i]$ and the right q must be added to $a[s_{i-1}, s_{i-1}]$. The following access control matrix command, in which s_i represents the subject corresponding to the current cell, captures this:

```
command cp,A(si, si-1)
        if own in a[si-1, si] and p in a[si, si] and
        A in a[si, si]
        then
                delete p from a[si, si];
                delete A from a[si, si];
                enter B into a[si, si];
                enter q into a[si-1, si-1];
        end
```

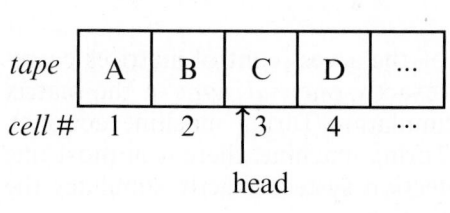

	s_1	s_2	s_3	s_4
s_1	A	*own*		
s_2		B	*own*	
s_3			C,p	*own*
s_4				D,*end*

tape	A	B	C	D	...
cell #	1	2	3	4	...

head

Figure 3–1 The Turing machine (at left) is in state p. The corresponding access control matrix is shown at right.

If the head is in the leftmost cell of the tape, both s_i and s_{i-1} are s_1.

Now consider motion to the right, such as $\delta(p, A) = (q, B, R)$. If the head is not in the rightmost cell k, by the same reasoning as for the left motion, we have

```
command cp,A(si, si+1)
        if own in a[si, si+1] and p in a[si, si] and
        A in a[si, si]
        then
                delete p from a[si, si];
                delete A from a[si, si];
                enter B into a[si, si];
                enter q into a[si+1, si+1];
    end
```

However, if the head is in the rightmost cell k, the command must create a new subject s_{k+1}. Then, to maintain the consistency of the access control matrix, s_k is given *own* rights over the new subject s_{k+1}, s_{k+1} gets *end* rights over itself, and s_k's *end* rights over itself must be removed. At that point, the problem is reduced to the problem of regular right motion. So:

```
command crightmostp,A(sk, sk+1)
        if end in a[sk, sk] and p in a[sk, sk] and
        A in a[sk, sk]
        then
                delete end from a[sk, sk];
                delete p from a[sk, sk];
                delete A from a[sk, sk];
                enter B into a[sk, sk];
                create subject sk+1;
                enter own into a[sk, sk+1];
                enter end into a[sk+1, sk+1];
                enter q into a[sk+1, sk+1];
    end
```

Clearly, only one right in any of the access control matrices corresponds to a state, and there will be exactly one *end* right in the matrix (by the nature of the commands simulating Turing machine actions). Hence, in each configuration of the Turing machine, there is at most one applicable command. Thus, the protection system exactly simulates the Turing machine, given the representation above.

Assume that the Turing machine's initial state is $q_0 \neq q_f$. If the Turing machine enters state q_f, then the protection system has leaked the right q_f; otherwise, the protection system is safe for the generic right q_f. But whether the Turing machine will enter the (halting) state q_f is undecidable, so whether the protection system is safe must be undecidable also.

However, we can generate a list of all unsafe systems.

Theorem 3.3. [533] The set of unsafe systems is recursively enumerable.

Proof See Exercise 6.

Assume that the **create** primitive is disallowed. Clearly, the safety question is decidable (simply enumerate all possible sequences of commands from the given state; as no new subjects or objects are created, at some point no new rights can be added to any element of the access control matrix, so if the leak has not yet occurred, it cannot occur). Thus, it needs only a polynomial amount of space. Hence, we have the following theorem.

Theorem 3.4. [874] For protection systems without the **create** primitives, the question of safety is complete in **P-SPACE**.

Proof Consider a Turing machine bounded in polynomial space. A construction similar to that of Theorem 3.2 reduces that Turing machine in polynomial time to an access control matrix whose size is polynomial in the length of the Turing machine input.

If deleting the **create** primitives makes the safety question decidable, would deleting the **delete** and **destroy** primitives but not the **create** primitive also make the safety question decidable? Such systems are called *monotonic* because they only increase in size and complexity; they cannot decrease. But:

Theorem 3.5. [873] It is undecidable whether a given configuration of a given monotonic protection system is safe for a given generic right.

Restricting the number of conditions in the commands to two does not help:

Theorem 3.6. [873] The safety question for biconditional monotonic protection systems is undecidable.

But if at most one condition per command is allowed:

Theorem 3.7. [873] The safety question for monoconditional monotonic protection systems is decidable.

This can be made somewhat stronger:

Theorem 3.8. [873] The safety question for monoconditional protection systems with **create**, **enter**, and **delete** primitives (but no **destroy** primitive) is decidable.

Thus, the safety question is undecidable for generic protection models but is decidable if the protection system is restricted in some way. Two questions arise. First, given a *particular* system with specific rules for transformation, can we show that the safety question is decidable? Second, what are the weakest restrictions on a protection system that will make the safety question decidable in that system?

3.3   The Take-Grant Protection Model

Can the safety of a particular system, with specific rules, be established (or disproved)? The answer, not surprisingly, is yes. Such a system is the *Take-Grant Protection Model.*

The Take-Grant Protection Model represents a system as a directed graph. Vertices are either subjects (represented by ●) or objects (represented by ○). Vertices that may be either subjects or objects are represented by ⊗. Edges are labeled, and the label indicates the rights that the source vertex has over the destination vertex. Rights are elements of a predefined set R; R contains two distinguished rights: t (for *take*) and g (for *grant*).

As the protection state of the system changes, so does the graph. The protection state (and therefore the graph) changes according to four *graph rewriting rules*:

Take rule: Let **x**, **y**, and **z** be three distinct vertices in a protection graph G_0, and let **x** be a subject. Let there be an edge from **x** to **z** labeled γ with $t \in \gamma$, an edge from **z** to **y** labeled β, and $\alpha \subseteq \beta$. Then the *take* rule defines a new graph G_1 by adding an edge to the protection graph from **x** to **y** labeled α. Graphically,

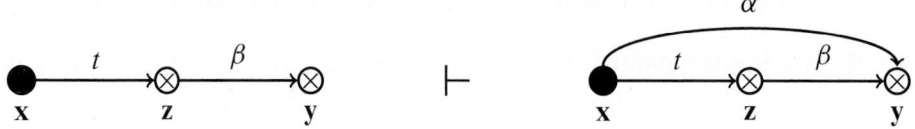

The rule is written "**x** takes (α to **y**) from **z**."

Grant rule: Let **x**, **y**, and **z** be three distinct vertices in a protection graph G_0, and let **z** be a subject. Let there be an edge from **z** to **x** labeled γ with $g \in \gamma$, an edge from **z** to **y** labeled β, and $\alpha \subseteq \beta$. Then the *grant* rule defines a new graph G_1 by adding an edge to the protection graph from **x** to **y** labeled α. Graphically,

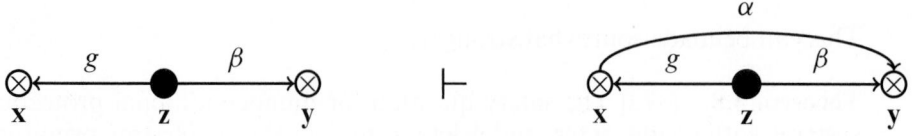

The rule is written "**z** grants (α to **y**) from **x**."

Create rule: Let **x** be any subject in a protection graph G_0 and let $\alpha \subseteq R$. Then the *create* rule defines a new graph G_1 by adding a new vertex **y** to the graph and an edge from **x** to **y** labeled α. Graphically,

The rule is written "**x** creates (α to new vertex) **y**."

Remove rule: Let **x** and **y** be any distinct vertices in a protection graph G_0 such that **x** is a subject. Let there be an edge from **x** to **y** labeled β, and let $\alpha \subseteq \beta$. Then the *remove* rule defines a new graph G_1 by deleting the α labels from β. If β becomes empty as a result, the edge itself is deleted. Graphically,

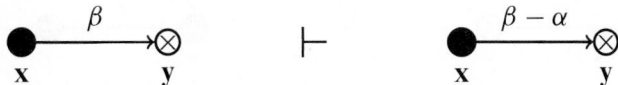

The rule is written "**x** removes (α to) **y**."

Because these rules alter the state of the protection graph, they are called *de jure* ("by law" or "by right") rules.

We demonstrate that one configuration of a protection graph can be derived from another by applying the four rules above in succession. The symbol $\vdash$ means that the graph following it is produced by the action of a graph rewriting rule on the graph preceding it, and the symbol $\vdash^*$ represents a finite number of successive rule applications. Such a sequence of graph rewriting rules is called a *witness*. A witness is often demonstrated by listing the graph rewriting rules that make up the witness (usually with pictures).

A word about notation involving sets of rights will clarify what follows. In a rule such as "vertex **x** grants (β to vertex **y**) to **z**," we tacitly assume that there is a *single* edge labeled β, and not multiple edges each labeled $\beta_1, \ldots, \beta_n$, with $\bigcup_{i=1}^{n} \beta_i = \beta$ [1458].

3.3.1   Sharing of Rights

We first wish to determine if a given right α can be shared—that is, given a protection graph G_0, can a vertex **x** obtain α rights over another vertex **y**? More formally:

> **Definition 3–3.** The predicate *can•share*(α, **x**, **y**, G_0) is true for a set of rights α and two vertices **x** and **y** if and only if there exists a sequence of protection graphs $G_1, \ldots, G_n$ such that $G_0 \vdash^* G_n$ using only *de jure* rules and in G_n there is an edge from **x** to **y** labeled α.

To establish the conditions under which this predicate will hold, we must define a few terms.

Definition 3–4. A *tg-path* is a nonempty sequence $v_0, \ldots, v_n$ of distinct vertices such that for all i, $0 \leq i < n$, v_i is connected to v_{i+1} by an edge (in either direction) with a label containing t or g.

Definition 3–5. Vertices are *tg-connected* if there is a *tg*-path between them.

We can now prove that any two subjects with a *tg*-path of length 1 can share rights. Four such paths are possible. The take and grant rules in the preceding section account for two of them. Lemmata 3.1 and 3.2 cover the other two cases.

Lemma 3.1.

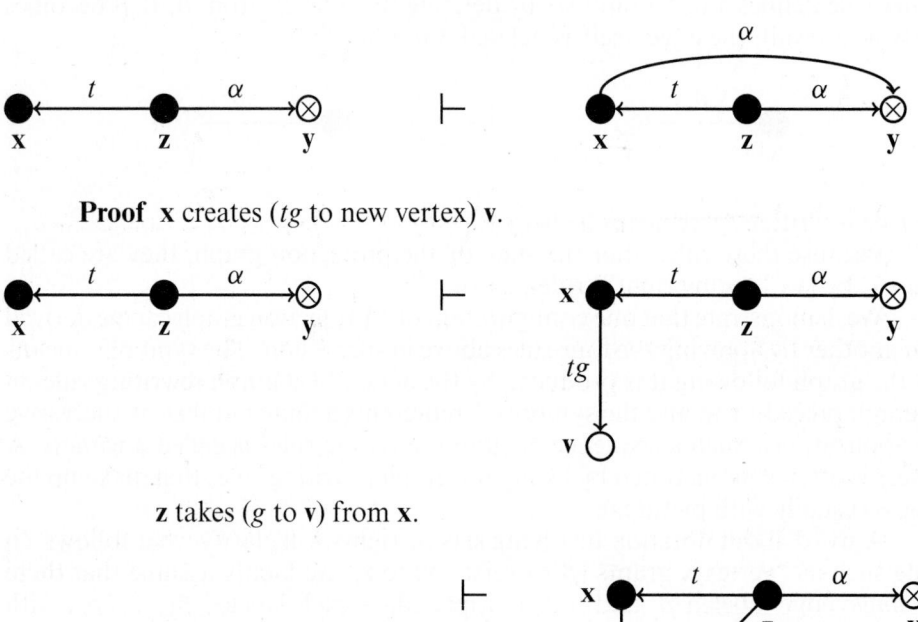

Proof x creates (*tg* to new vertex) **v**.

z takes (*g* to **v**) from **x**.

z grants (α to **y**) to **v**.

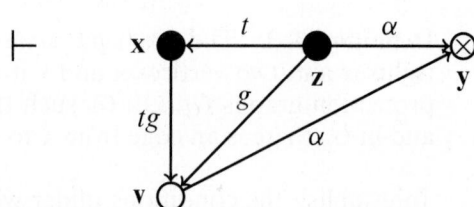

x takes (α to **y**) from **v**.

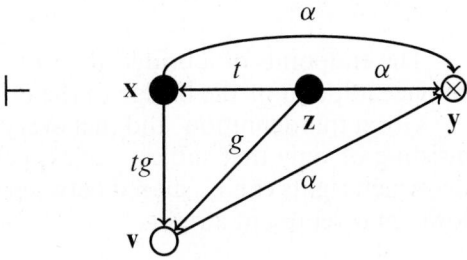

This sequence of rule applications adds an edge labeled α from **x** to **y**.

A similar proof establishes the following lemma.

Lemma 3.2.

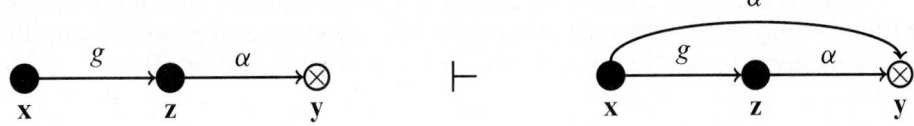

Proof See Exercise 8.

Thus, the take and grant rules are symmetric if the vertices on the *tg*-path between **x** and **y** are subjects. This leads us to the following definition.

Definition 3–6. An *island* is a maximal *tg*-connected subject-only subgraph.

Because an island is a maximal subgraph in which all edges have a label containing *t* or *g*, a straightforward inductive proof shows that any right possessed by any vertex in the island can be shared with any other vertex in the island.

Transferring rights between islands requires that a subject in one island be able to take the right from a vertex in the other island or that a subject be able to grant the right to an intermediate object from which another subject in the second island may take the right. This observation, coupled with the symmetry of take and grant, leads to a characterization of paths between islands along which rights can be transferred. To express it succinctly, we use the following notation. With each *tg*-path, associate one or more words over the alphabet in the obvious way. If the $\{\overrightarrow{t}, \overleftarrow{t}, \overrightarrow{g}, \overleftarrow{g}\}$ path has length 0, then the associated word is the null word ν. The notation t^* means zero or more occurrences of the character *t*, so, for example, t^*g represents the sequence $g, tg, ttg, \ldots$.

Definition 3–7. A *bridge* is a *tg*-path with endpoints v_0 and v_n both subjects and the path's associated word in $\{\overrightarrow{t}*,\ \overleftarrow{t}*,\ \overrightarrow{t}*\overleftarrow{g}\,\overleftarrow{t}*,\ \overrightarrow{t}*\overrightarrow{g}\,\overleftarrow{t}*\}$.

The endpoints of a bridge are both subjects, so the right can be transferred from one endpoint of the bridge to the other.

Given this definition, and that every subject vertex is contained in an island (consisting of only that subject vertex, perhaps), we have established conditions under which rights can be shared between subjects in a protection graph. In what follows, let α represent a right.

Theorem 3.9. [1197] The predicate *subject•can•share*(α, **x**, **y**, G_0) is true if and only if **x** and **y** are both subjects and there is an edge from **x** to **y** in G_0 labeled α, or if the following hold simultaneously:

(a) There is a subject **s** $\in$ G_0 with an **s**-to-**y** edge labeled α.
(b) There exist islands $I_1, \ldots, I_n$ such that **x** is in I_1, **s** is in I_n, and there is a bridge from I_j to I_{j+1} ($1 \leq j < n$).

Objects complicate this result. Because subjects can act but objects cannot, the transfer may begin with a right possessed by an object and conclude with that right being given to another object. The following two definitions help.

Definition 3–8. A vertex **x** *initially spans* to **y** if **x** is a subject and there is a *tg*-path between **x** and **y** with an associated word in $\{\overrightarrow{t}*\overrightarrow{g}\} \cup \{v\}$.

In other words, **x** initially spans to **y** if **x** can grant a right it possesses to **y**.

Definition 3–9. A vertex **x** *terminally spans* to **y** if **x** is a subject and there is a *tg*-path between **x** and **y** with an associated word in $\{\overrightarrow{t}*\} \cup \{v\}$.

In other words, **x** terminally spans to **y** if **x** can take any right that **y** possesses. Note that these two definitions imply that *t* and *g* are not symmetric if either the source or destination vertex of the edge labeled *t* or *g* is an object.

We can now state and prove necessary and sufficient conditions for a right α to be transferred from a vertex **y** to another vertex **x**.

Theorem 3.10. [972] The predicate *can•share*(α, **x**, **y**, G_0) is true if and only if there is an edge from **x** to **y** in G_0 labeled α, or if the following hold simultaneously:

(a) There is a vertex **s** $\in$ G_0 with an **s**-to-**y** edge labeled α.
(b) There exists a subject vertex **x**' such that **x**' = **x** or **x**' initially spans to **x**.

(c) There exists a subject vertex $\mathbf{s}'$ such that $\mathbf{s}' = \mathbf{s}$ or $\mathbf{s}'$ terminally spans to $\mathbf{s}$.

(d) There exist islands $I_1, \ldots, I_n$ such that $\mathbf{x}' \in I_1$, $\mathbf{s}' \in I_n$, and there is a bridge from I_j to I_{j+1} ($1 \leq j < n$).

The idea behind this theorem is simple. Because $\mathbf{s}'$ terminally spans to $\mathbf{s}$, $\mathbf{s}'$ can acquire α rights to $\mathbf{y}$. Given the definition of island, all subjects in I_n can acquire those rights. They can be passed along the bridge to a subject in I_{n-1}, which means that any subject in I_{n-1} can acquire those same rights. This continues until $\mathbf{x}' \in I_1$ acquires those rights. Then, as $\mathbf{x}'$ initially spans to $\mathbf{x}$, $\mathbf{x}'$ can pass the rights to $\mathbf{x}$. Exercise 9 explores a possible alternative representation of this result.

> **Corollary 3.1.** [972] There is an algorithm of complexity $O(|V| + |E|)$ that tests the predicate *can•share*, where V is the set of vertices and E the set of edges, in G_0.

3.3.2 Interpretation of the Model

A model abstracts essential details from a situation to aid in its analysis. For example, the question "Can my competitor access my files?" presumes a knowledge of the rules for sharing files on the computer system (or network). The model must correctly capture these rules to be applicable.

The beauty of the access control matrix model is its malleability; by choosing rights and rules appropriately, an analyst can use it to capture the essence of any situation. The Take-Grant Protection Model presents specific rules and distinguished rights and so can be applied only in specific situations.

The protection state of a system evolves as rules are applied to entities within the system. The question of what states can evolve is thus of interest, because that set of states defines what protection states the (real) system may assume. So, consider the set of states of a particular system that the Take-Grant Protection Model rules can generate. For simplicity, we consider those states arising from a single entity, which (by the take-grant rules above) must be a subject.

> **Theorem 3.11.** [1777] Let G_0 be a protection graph containing exactly one subject vertex and no edges, and let R be a set of rights. Then $G_0 \vdash^* G$ if and only if G is a finite, directed, loop-free graph containing subjects and objects only, with edges labeled from nonempty subsets of R and with at least one subject having no incoming edges.

> **Proof** ($\Rightarrow$) By construction. Assume that G meets the requirements above. Let $\mathbf{x}_1, \ldots, \mathbf{x}_n$ be the set of subjects in G, and without loss of generality let $\mathbf{x}_1$ have no incoming edges. Identify $\mathbf{v}$ with $\mathbf{x}_1$. The graph G' can

be constructed from **v** using the Take-Grant Protection Model rules, as follows:

(a) Perform "**v** creates ($\alpha \cup \{g\}$ to) new x_i" for all x_i, $2 \leq i \leq n$, where α is the union of all labels on the edges going into x_i in G.

(b) For all pairs of vertices x_i and x_j in G with x_i having α rights over x_j, perform "**v** grants (α to x_j) to x_i."

(c) Let β be the set of rights labeling the edge from x_i and x_j in G (note that β may be empty). Perform "**v** removes $((\alpha \cup \{g\}) - \beta$ to) x_j."

The resulting graph G' is the desired graph G.

($\Leftarrow$) Let **v** be the initial subject, and let $G_0 \vdash^* G$. By inspection of the rules, G is finite, loop-free, and a directed graph; furthermore, it consists of subjects and objects only, and all edges are labeled with nonempty subsets of R.

Because no rule allows the deletion of vertices, **v** is in G. Because no rule allows an incoming edge to be added to a vertex without any incoming edges, and **v** has no incoming edges, it cannot be assigned any.

Corollary 3.2.   [1777] A k-component, n-edge protection graph can be constructed from m rule applications, where $2(k-1)+n \leq m \leq 2(k-1)+3n$.

Using the Take-Grant Protection Model, Snyder [1777] showed how some common protection problems could be solved. For example, suppose two processes **p** and **q** communicate through a shared buffer **b** controlled by a trusted entity **s** (for example, an operating system). The configuration in Figure 3–2(a) shows the initial protection state of the system. Because **s** is a trusted entity, the assumption that it has g rights over **p** and **q** is reasonable. To create **b**, and to allow **p** and **q** to communicate through it, **s** does the following:

(a) **s** creates ($\{r, w\}$ to new object) **b**.

(b) **s** grants ($\{r, w\}$ to **b**) to **p**.

(c) **s** grants ($\{r, w\}$ to **b**) to **q**.

This creates the configuration in Figure 3–2(b). The communication channel is two-way; if it is to be one-way, the sender would have write rights and the receiver would have read rights. This configuration also captures the ability of the trusted entity to monitor the communication channel or interfere with it (by altering or creating messages)—a point we will explore in later sections.

3.3.3   Theft in the Take-Grant Protection Model

The proof of the conditions necessary and sufficient for *can•share* requires that all subjects involved in the witness cooperate. This is unrealistic. If Professor Olson does not want any students to read her grade file, the notion of "sharing" fails

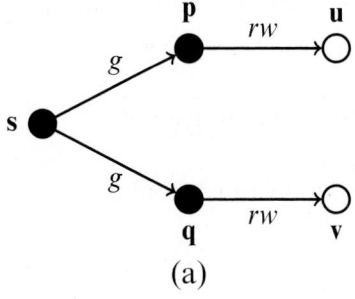
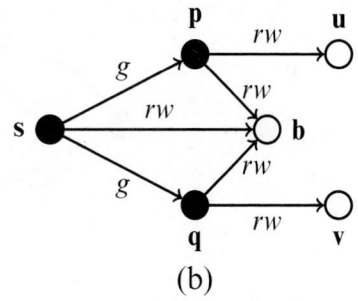

Figure 3–2   (a) The initial state of the system: s, a trusted entity, can grant rights to untrusted processes p and q. Each process p and q controls its own private information (here represented by files u and v). (b) The trusted entity has created a buffer b shared by the untrusted processes.

to capture the unwillingness to grant access. This leads to a notion of *stealing*, in which no owner of any right over an object grants that right to another.

> **Definition 3–10.** Let G_0 be a protection graph, let **x** and **y** be distinct vertices in G_0, and let $\alpha \in R$. The predicate *can•steal*$(\alpha, \mathbf{x}, \mathbf{y}, G_0)$ is true when there is no edge from **x** to **y** labeled α in G_0 and there exists a sequence of protection graphs $G_1, \ldots, G_n$ for which the following hold simultaneously:
>
> (a) There is an edge from **x** to **y** labeled α in G_n.
> (b) There is a sequence of rule applications $\rho_1, \ldots, \rho_n$ such that $G_{i-1} \vdash G_i$ using ρ_i.
> (c) For all vertices **v** and **w** in G_{i-1}, $1 \leq i < n$, if there is an edge from **v** to **y** in G_0 labeled α, then ρ_i is not of the form "**v** grants (α to **y**) to **w**."

Part (c) also excludes sequences of rules at least one of which is a grant rule that culminate in α to **y** being granted to **z**. Specifically, this excludes the sequence of rules for $i = 1, \ldots, n$, "vertex **x** grants (α_i to vertex **y**) to **z**," where $\bigcup_{i=1}^{n} \alpha_i = \alpha$ [1458].

This definition disallows owners of the α right to **y** from transferring that right. It does not disallow those owners from transferring other rights. Consider Figure 3–3. The given witness exhibits *can•steal*$(\alpha, \mathbf{s}, \mathbf{w}, G_0)$. In step (1), the owner of the α right to **w** grants other rights (specifically, t rights to **v**) to a different subject, **s**. Without this step, the theft cannot occur. The definition only forbids grants of the rights to be stolen. Other rights may be granted. One justification for this formulation is the ability of attackers to trick others into surrendering rights. While the owner of the target right would be unlikely to grant that right, the owner might grant other rights. This models the Trojan horse (see Section 23.2), in which the owner of the rights is unaware she is giving them away.

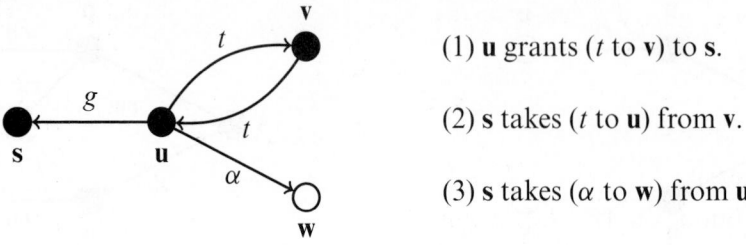

(1) **u** grants (*t* to **v**) to **s**.

(2) **s** takes (*t* to **u**) from **v**.

(3) **s** takes (*α* to **w**) from **u**.

Figure 3–3 The take-grant rules to the right of the graph are a witness to a theft in that graph in which the owner, u, of the stolen right, α, grants other rights to another subject (*t* rights to v are granted to s).

Making the target of the theft a subject complicates this situation. According to Definition 3–10, the target may give away any rights as well. In this case, the owner is acting as a moderator between the target and the source and must restrain the transfer of the right through it. This models the case of mandatory access controls.

Theorem 3.12. [1777] The predicate *can•steal*(*alpha*, **x**, **y**, G_0) is true if and only if the following hold simultaneously:

(a) There is no edge from **x** to **y** labeled *α* in G_0.
(b) There exists a subject vertex **x′** such that **x′** = **x** or **x′** initially spans to **x**.
(c) There exists a vertex **s** with an edge labeled *α* to **y** in G_0 and for which *can•share*(*t*, **x**, **s**, G_0) holds.

Proof (⇒) Assume that the three conditions above hold. If **x** is a subject, then **x** need merely obtain *t* rights to **s** and then use the take rule to obtain *α* rights to **y**. By definition, this satisfies *can•steal*(*α*, **x**, **y**, G_0).
　　Suppose **x** is an object. Then by Theorem 3.10, because *can•share*(*t*, **x**, **s**, G_0) holds, there exists a subject vertex **x′** that *tg*-initially spans to **x** and for which the predicate *can•share*(*t*, **x′**, **s**, G_0) is true. Without loss of generality, assume that the *tg*-initial span is of length 1 and that **x′** has *t* rights over **s** in G_0. If **x′** does not have an edge labeled *α* to **y** in G_0, then **x′** takes *α* rights to **y** and grants those rights to **x**, satisfying the definition. If **x′** has an edge labeled *α* to **y** in G_0, then **x′** will create a "surrogate" to which it can give *t* rights to **s**:

1. **x′** creates (*g* to new subject) **x″**.
2. **x′** grants (*t* to **s**) to **x″**.
3. **x′** grants (*g* to **x**) to **x″**.

Now $\mathbf{x}''$ has t rights over $\mathbf{s}$ and g rights over $\mathbf{x}$, so the rule applications

1. $\mathbf{x}''$ takes (α to $\mathbf{y}$) from $\mathbf{s}$.
2. $\mathbf{x}''$ grants (α to $\mathbf{y}$) to $\mathbf{x}$.

satisfy the definition. Hence, *can•steal*(α, $\mathbf{x}$, $\mathbf{y}$, G_0) holds if the three conditions in the theorem hold.

($\Leftarrow$) Assume that *can•steal*(α, $\mathbf{x}$, $\mathbf{y}$, G_0) holds. Then condition (a) of the theorem holds directly from Definition 3–10.

Condition (a) of Definition 3–10 implies *can•share*(α, $\mathbf{x}$, $\mathbf{y}$, G_0). From condition (b) of Theorem 3.10, we immediately obtain condition (a) of this theorem.

Condition (a) of Theorem 3.10 ensures that the vertex $\mathbf{s}$ in condition (3.12) of this theorem exists.

We must show that *can•share*(t, $\mathbf{x}$, $\mathbf{s}$, G_0) holds. Let ρ be a sequence of rule applications. Consider the minimal length sequence of rule applications deriving G_n from G_0. Let i be the least index such that $G_{i-1} \vdash_{\rho_i} G_i$ and such that there is an edge labeled α from some vertex $\mathbf{p}$ to $\mathbf{y}$ in G_i but not in G_{i-1}. Then G_i is the first graph in which an edge labeled α to $\mathbf{y}$ is added.

Obviously, ρ_i is not a remove rule. It cannot be a create rule, because $\mathbf{y}$ already existed. By condition (c) of Definition 3–10, and the choice of i ensuring that all vertices with α rights to $\mathbf{y}$ in G_i are also in G_0, ρ_i cannot be a grant rule. Hence, ρ_i must be a take rule of the form

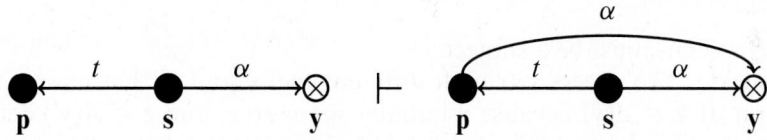

for some vertex $\mathbf{s}$ in G_0. From this, *can•share*(t, $\mathbf{p}$, $\mathbf{s}$, G_0) holds. By condition (c) of Theorem 3.10, there is a subject $\mathbf{s}'$ such that $\mathbf{s}' = s$ or $\mathbf{s}'$ terminally spans to $\mathbf{s}$, and by condition (d), there exists a sequence of islands $I_1, \ldots, I_n$ such that $\mathbf{x}' \in I_1$ and $\mathbf{s}' \in I_n$.

If $\mathbf{s}$ is an object (and thus $\mathbf{s}' \neq \mathbf{s}$), consider two cases. If $\mathbf{s}'$ and $\mathbf{p}$ are in the same island, then take $\mathbf{p} = \mathbf{s}'$. If they are in different islands, the derivation cannot be of minimal length; choose $\mathbf{s}'$ in the same island to exhibit a shorter one. From this, the conditions of Theorem 3.10 have been met, and *can•share*(t, $\mathbf{x}$, $\mathbf{s}$, G_0) holds.

If $\mathbf{s}$ is a subject ($\mathbf{s}' = \mathbf{s}$), then $\mathbf{p} \in I_n$, and we must show that $\mathbf{p} \in G_0$ for Theorem 3.10 to hold. If $\mathbf{p} \notin G_0$, then there is a subject $\mathbf{q}$ in one of the islands such that *can•share*(t, $\mathbf{q}$, $\mathbf{s}$, G_0) holds. (To see this, note that $\mathbf{s} \in G_0$ and that none of the *de jure* rules adds new labels to incoming edges on existing vertices.) Because $\mathbf{s}$ is an owner of the α right to $\mathbf{y}$ in G_0, we must derive a witness for this sharing in which **s** does not grant (α to **q**). If **s** and **q** are distinct, replace each rule application of the form

> **s** grants (α to **y**) to **q**

with the sequence

> **p** takes (α to **y**) from **s**
> **p** takes (g to **q**) from **s**
> **p** grants (α to **y**) to **q**

thereby transferring the right (α to **y**) to **q** without **s** granting. If **s** = **q**, then the first rule application in this sequence suffices.

Hence, there exists a witness to *can•share*(t, **x**, **s**, G_0) in which **s** does not grant (α to **y**). This completes the proof.

3.3.4 Conspiracy

The notion of theft introduced the issue of cooperation: which subjects are actors in a transfer of rights, and which are not? This raises the issue of the number of actors necessary to transfer a right. More formally, what is the minimum number of actors required to witness a given predicate *can•share*(α, **x**, **y**, G_0)?

Consider a subject vertex **y**. Then **y** can share rights from any vertex to which it terminally spans and can pass those rights to any vertex to which it initially spans.

> **Definition 3–11.** The *access set* $A(\mathbf{y})$ *with focus* **y** is the set of vertices **y**, all vertices **x** to which **y** initially spans, and all vertices **x′** to which **y** terminally spans.

Of course, a focus must be a subject.

Consider two access sets with different foci **y** and **y′** that have a vertex **z** in common. If **z** $\in A(\mathbf{y})$ because **y** initially spans to **z**, and **z** $\in A(\mathbf{y'})$ because **y′** initially spans to **z**, by the definition of initial span, no rights can be transferred between **y** and **y′** through **z**. A similar result holds if both **y** and **y′** terminally span to **z**. However, if one focus initially spans to **z** and the other terminally spans to **z**, rights can be transferred through **z**. Because we care about the transfer of rights, we identify a set of vertices that can be removed from the graph without affecting transfers:

> **Definition 3–12.** The *deletion set* $\delta(\mathbf{y}, \mathbf{y'})$ contains all vertices **z** in the set $A(\mathbf{y}) \cap A(\mathbf{y'})$ for which (a) **y** initially spans to **z** and **y′** terminally spans to **z**, (b) **y** terminally spans to **z** and **y′** initially spans to **z**, (c) **z** = **y**, or (d) **z** = **y′**.

Given the deletion set, we construct an undirected graph, called the *conspiracy graph* and represented by H, from G_0:

1. For each subject vertex **x** in G_0, there is a corresponding vertex $h(\mathbf{x})$ in H with the same label.
2. If $\delta(\mathbf{y}, \mathbf{y'}) \neq \varnothing$ in G_0, there is an edge between $h(\mathbf{y})$ and $h(\mathbf{y'})$ in H.

The conspiracy graph represents the paths along which subjects can transfer rights. The paths are unidirectional because the rights can be transmitted in either direction. Furthermore, each vertex in H represents an access set focus in G_0.

EXAMPLE: In Figure 3–4, the access sets are:

$$A(\mathbf{x}) = \{\mathbf{x}, \mathbf{a}\} \quad A(\mathbf{c}) = \{\mathbf{c}, \mathbf{b}, \mathbf{d}\} \quad A(\mathbf{y}) = \{\mathbf{y}\} \quad A(\mathbf{h}) = \{\mathbf{h}, \mathbf{f}, \mathbf{i}\}$$
$$A(\mathbf{b}) = \{\mathbf{b}, \mathbf{a}\} \quad A(\mathbf{d}) = \{\mathbf{d}\} \quad A(\mathbf{f}) = \{\mathbf{f}, \mathbf{y}\} \quad A(\mathbf{e}) = \{\mathbf{e}, \mathbf{d}, \mathbf{i}, \mathbf{j}\}$$

The vertex $\mathbf{z}$ is not in $A(\mathbf{e})$ because the path from $\mathbf{e}$ to $\mathbf{z}$ is neither a terminal nor an initial span. For the same reason, the vertex $\mathbf{y}$ is not in $A(\mathbf{h})$. Using these sets gives the following nonempty deletion sets:

$$\delta(\mathbf{x}, \mathbf{b}) = \{\mathbf{a}\} \quad \delta(\mathbf{c}, \mathbf{d}) = \{\mathbf{d}\} \quad \delta(\mathbf{y}, \mathbf{f}) = \{\mathbf{y}\}$$
$$\delta(\mathbf{b}, \mathbf{c}) = \{\mathbf{b}\} \quad \delta(\mathbf{c}, \mathbf{e}) = \{\mathbf{d}\} \quad \delta(\mathbf{h}, \mathbf{f}) = \{\mathbf{f}\}$$
$$\delta(\mathbf{d}, \mathbf{e}) = \{\mathbf{d}\}$$

Although $A(\mathbf{e}) \cap A(\mathbf{h}) = \{\mathbf{i}\}$, the vertex $\mathbf{i}$ is in $A(\mathbf{e})$ because $\mathbf{e}$ initially spans to $\mathbf{i}$, and $\mathbf{i}$ is in $A(\mathbf{h})$ because $\mathbf{h}$ initially spans to $\mathbf{i}$. Hence, $\delta(\mathbf{e}, \mathbf{h}) = \varnothing$ and there is no edge between $h(\mathbf{e})$ and $h(\mathbf{h})$ in G_0.

The conspiracy graph exhibits the paths along which rights can be transmitted. Let the set $I(\mathbf{p})$ contain the vertex $h(\mathbf{p})$ and the set of all vertices $h(\mathbf{p}')$ such that $\mathbf{p}'$ initially spans to $\mathbf{p}$; let the set $T(\mathbf{q})$ contain the vertex $h(\mathbf{q})$ and the set of all vertices $h(\mathbf{q}')$ such that $\mathbf{q}'$ terminally spans to $\mathbf{q}$. Then:

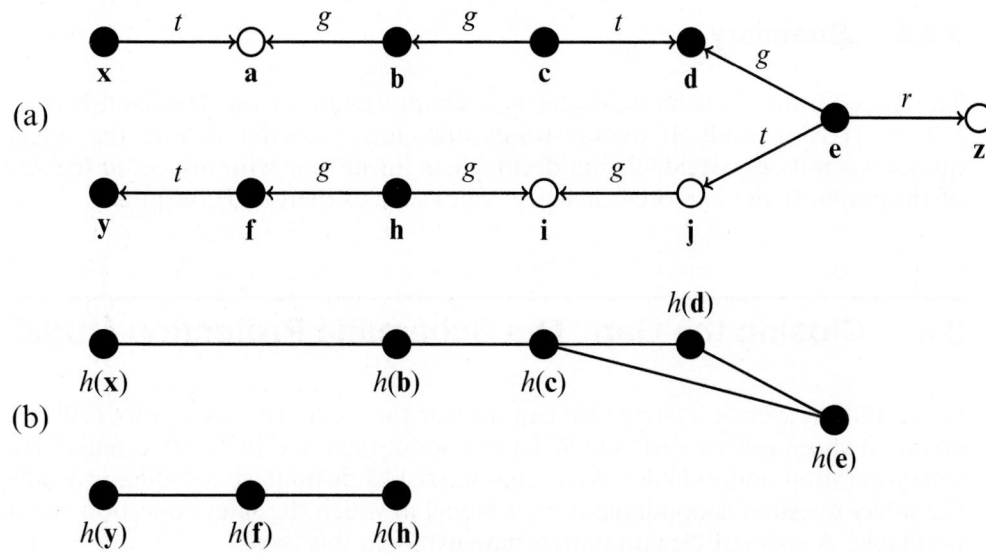

Figure 3–4   (a) A take-grant protection graph. (b) The corresponding conspiracy graph.

Theorem 3.13. [1777] *can•share*(α, **x**, **y**, G_0) is true if and only if there is a path from some $h(\mathbf{p}) \in I(\mathbf{x})$ to some $h(\mathbf{q}) \in T(\mathbf{y})$.

Furthermore:

Theorem 3.14. [1777] Let n be the number of vertices on a shortest path between $h(\mathbf{p})$ and $h(\mathbf{q})$, with **p** and **q** as in Theorem 3.13. Then n conspirators are necessary and sufficient to produce a witness to *can•share*(α, **x**, **y**, G_0).

EXAMPLE: In Figure 3–4, the shortest path between $h(\mathbf{e})$ and $h(\mathbf{x})$ has four vertices ($h(\mathbf{x})$, $h(\mathbf{b})$, $h(\mathbf{c})$, and $h(\mathbf{e})$), so four conspirators are necessary and sufficient to witness *can•share*(r, **x**, **z**, G_0). Such a witness is

1. **e** grants (r to **z**) to **d**.
2. **c** takes (r to **z**) from **d**.
3. **c** grants (r to **z**) to **b**.
4. **b** grants (r to **z**) to **a**.
5. **x** takes (r to **z**) from **a**.

and the conspirators are **e**, **c**, **b**, and **x**. To see that this is minimal, note that both **x** and **b** must act to transfer the right through **a**, **e** must act to transfer the right to another vertex, and in order to pass the right from **d** to **b**, **c** must act.

3.3.5   Summary

The Take-Grant Protection Model is a counterpoint to the Harrison-Ruzzo-Ullman (HRU) result. It demonstrates that, for a specific system, the safety question is not only decidable but decidable in linear time with respect to the size of the graph. It also explores ancillary issues such as theft and conspiracy.

3.4   Closing the Gap: The Schematic Protection Model

Given that in specific systems we can answer the safety question, why can't we answer it about generic systems? What is it about the HRU model that makes the safety question undecidable? What characteristics distinguish a model in which the safety question is decidable from a model in which the safety question is not decidable? A series of elegant papers have explored this issue.

The first paper introduced a model called the Schematic Send-Receive (SSR) Protection Model [1656]. The Schematic Protection Model (SPM) [1657] generalizes these results.

The key notion of the Schematic Protection Model, also called the SPM, is the *protection type*. This is a label for an entity that determines how control rights affect that entity. For example, if the Take-Grant Protection Model is viewed as an instance of a scheme under the SPM, the protection types are *subject* and *object* because the control rights *take*, *grant*, *create*, and *remove* affect subject entities differently than they do object entities. Moreover, under SPM, the protection type of an entity is set when the entity is created, and cannot change thereafter.

In SPM, a *ticket* is a description of a single right. An entity has a set of tickets (called a *domain*) that describe what rights it has over another entity. A ticket consists of an *entity name* and a *right symbol*; for example, the ticket X/r allows the possessor of the ticket to apply the right r to the entity X. Although a ticket may contain only one right, if an entity has multiple tickets X/r, X/s, and X/t, we abbreviate them by writing X/rst.

Rights are partitioned into a set of inert rights (RI) and control rights (RC). Applying an inert right does not alter the protection state of the system. For example, reading a file does not modify which entities have access to the document, so *read* is an inert right. But in the Take-Grant Protection Model, applying the take rule does change the protection state of the system (it gives a subject a new right over an object). Hence, the *take* right is a control right. SPM ignores the effect of applying inert rights, but not the effect of applying control rights.

The attribute c is a copy flag; every right r has an associated copyable right rc. A ticket with the copy flag can be copied to another domain. The notation $r:c$ means r or rc, with the understanding that all occurrences of $r:c$ are read as r or all are read as rc.

We partition the set of types T into a subject set TS and an object set TO. The type of an entity X is written $\tau(X)$. The type of a ticket $X/r:c$ is $\tau(X/r:c)$, which is the same as $\tau(X)/r:c$. More formally, let E be the set of entities; then $\tau : E \to T$ and $\tau : E \times R \to T \times R$.

The manipulation of rights is controlled by two relationships: a *link predicate* and a *filter function*. Intuitively, the link predicate determines whether the source and target of the transfer are "connected" (in a mathematical sense), and the filter function determines whether the transfer is authorized.

3.4.1   Link Predicate

A link predicate is a relation between two subjects. It is local in the sense that its evaluation depends only on the tickets that the two subjects possess. Formally:

> **Definition 3–13.** Let $dom(X)$ be the set of tickets that X possesses. A link predicate $link_i(X, Y)$ is a conjunction or disjunction (but not a negation) of the following terms, for any right $z \in RC$:
>
> 1. $X/z \in dom(X)$
> 2. $X/z \in dom(Y)$
> 3. $Y/z \in dom(X)$

4. $\mathbf{Y}/z \in dom(\mathbf{Y})$

5. **true**

A finite set of link predicates $\{link_i \mid i = 1, \ldots, n\}$ is called a *scheme*. If only one link predicate is defined, we omit the subscript i.

EXAMPLE: The link predicate corresponding to the Take-Grant Protection Model rules *take* and *grant* is

$$link(\mathbf{X}, \mathbf{Y}) = \mathbf{Y}/g \in dom(\mathbf{X}) \vee \mathbf{X}/t \in dom(\mathbf{Y})$$

Here, $\mathbf{X}$ and $\mathbf{Y}$ are connected if $\mathbf{X}$ has g rights over $\mathbf{Y}$ or $\mathbf{Y}$ has t rights over $\mathbf{X}$, which corresponds to the model in the preceding section.

EXAMPLE: The link predicate

$$link(\mathbf{X}, \mathbf{Y}) = \mathbf{X}/b \in dom(\mathbf{X})$$

connects $\mathbf{X}$ to every other entity $\mathbf{Y}$ provided that $\mathbf{X}$ has b rights over itself. With respect to networks, b would correspond to a broadcast right. However, $\mathbf{X}$ does not yet have the right to broadcast to all $\mathbf{Y}$ because predicates do not endow the ability to exercise that right. Similarly, the predicate

$$link(\mathbf{X}, \mathbf{Y}) = \mathbf{Y}/p \in dom(\mathbf{Y})$$

corresponds to a *pull* connection between all entities $\mathbf{X}$ and $\mathbf{Y}$. Again, this is not sufficient for $\mathbf{Y}$ to exercise the pull right, but it is necessary.

EXAMPLE: The universal link depends on no entity's rights:

$$link(\mathbf{X}, \mathbf{Y}) = \text{true}$$

This link holds even when $\mathbf{X}$ and $\mathbf{Y}$ have no tickets that refer to each other.

3.4.2 Filter Function

A filter function imposes conditions on when transfer of tickets can occur. Specifically, a filter function is a function $f_i : TS \times TS \rightarrow 2^{T \times R}$ that has as its range the set of copyable tickets. For a copy to occur, the ticket to be copied must be in the range of the appropriate filter function.

Combining this requirement with the others, a ticket $X/r{:}c$ can be copied from $dom(\mathbf{Y})$ to $dom(\mathbf{Z})$ if and only if, for some i, the following are true:

1. $\mathbf{X}/rc \in dom(\mathbf{Y})$
2. $link_i(\mathbf{Y}, \mathbf{Z})$
3. $\tau(\mathbf{X})/r{:}c \in f_i(\tau(\mathbf{Y}), \tau(\mathbf{Z}))$

One filter function is defined for each link predicate. As with the link predicates, if there is only one filter function, we omit the subscripts.

EXAMPLE: Let $f(\tau(\mathbf{Y}), \tau(\mathbf{Z})) = T \times R$. Then any ticket is transferable, assuming that the other two conditions are met. However, if $f(\tau(\mathbf{Y}), \tau(\mathbf{Z})) = T \times RI$, then only inert rights are transferable; and if $f(\tau(\mathbf{Y}), \tau(\mathbf{Z})) = \varnothing$, no rights can be copied.

3.4.3   Putting It All Together

Let us take stock of these terms by considering two examples: an owner-based policy and the Take-Grant Protection Model.

In an owner-based policy, a subject $\mathbf{U}$ can authorize another subject $\mathbf{V}$ to access an object $\mathbf{F}$ if and only if $\mathbf{U}$ owns $\mathbf{F}$. Here, the set of subjects is the set of users and the set of objects is the set of files. View these as types. Then:

$$TS = \{user\}, TO = \{file\}$$

In this model, ownership is best viewed as copy attributes—that is, if $\mathbf{U}$ owns $\mathbf{F}$, all its tickets for $\mathbf{F}$ are copyable. Under this interpretation, the set of control rights is empty because no rights are required to alter the state of the protection graph. All rights are inert. For our example, assume that the r (read), w (write), a (append), and x (execute) rights are defined. Then:

$$RC = \varnothing, RI = \{r{:}c, w{:}c, a{:}c, x{:}c\}$$

Because the owner can give the right to any other subject, there is a connection between each pair of subjects and the link predicate is always true:

$$link(\mathbf{U}, \mathbf{V}) = \textbf{true}$$

Finally, tickets can be copied across these connections:

$$f(user, user) = \{file/r, file/w, file/a, file/x\}$$

EXAMPLE: Suppose a user Peter wishes to give another user Paul execute permissions over a file called *doom*. Then $\tau(\text{Peter}) = user$, $\tau(doom) = file$, and $doom/xc \in dom(\text{Peter})$. Because any user can give rights away to any other user, all users are "connected" in that sense, so $link(\text{Peter, Paul}) = $ **true**. Finally, because $\tau(doom) = file$, and $\tau(\text{Paul}) = user$, we have $\tau(doom)/xc \in f(\tau(\text{Peter}), \tau(\text{Paul}))$. Thus, Peter can copy the ticket $doom/x$ to Paul.

The Take-Grant Protection Model can be formulated as an instance of SPM. The set of subjects and objects in the Take-Grant model corresponds to the set of subjects and objects in SPM:

$$TS = \{subject\}, TO = \{object\}$$

The control rights are t (take) and g (grant), because applying them changes the protection state of the graph. All other rights are inert; for our example, we will take them to be r (read) and w (write). All rights can be copied (in fact, the Take-Grant Protection Model implicitly assumes this), so:

$$RC = \{tc, gc\}, RI = \{rc, wc\}$$

Rights can be transferred along edges labeled t or g, meaning that one vertex on the edge has take or grant rights over the other. Let **p** and **q** be subjects. Then the link predicate is

$$link(\mathbf{p}, \mathbf{q}) = \mathbf{p}/t \in dom(\mathbf{q}) \vee \mathbf{q}/g \in dom(\mathbf{p})$$

Finally, any right can be transferred, so the filter function is simply

$$f(subject, subject) = \{subject, object\} \times \{tc, gc, rc, wc\}$$

We now explore how the transfer of tickets occurs in SPM.

3.4.4   Demand and Create Operations

The *demand function* $d : TS \rightarrow 2^{T \times R}$ authorizes a subject to demand a right from another entity. Let a and b be types. Then $a/r:c \in d(b)$ means that every subject of type b can demand a ticket $\mathbf{X}/r:c$ for all $\mathbf{X}$ such that $\tau(\mathbf{X}) = a$. This is a generalization of the take rule in the Take-Grant model. The take rule refers to an individual subject. The demand function refers to all subjects of a particular type (here, of type b).

EXAMPLE: In the owner-based policy, no user can force another to give rights; hence, the range of the demand function is empty: $d(user) = \varnothing$. In the Take-Grant Protection Model, there is also no demand function. Although the *take* right is similar, to treat it as the demand right would require the creation of additional types to distinguish between those vertices directly connected by take edges to subjects and all other vertices. This complicates the system unnecessarily. Hence, $d(subject) = \varnothing$.

Sandhu [1658] has demonstrated that a sophisticated construction eliminates the need for the demand operation. Thus, although the demand rule is present in SPM, that rule is omitted from the models that followed SPM.

Creating a new entity requires handling not only the type of the new entity but also the tickets added by the creation. The type of the new entity is specified by the relation *can-create* (*cc*): $cc \subseteq TS \times T$; a subject of type a can create entities of type b if and only if $cc(a, b)$ holds.

In practice, the rule of *acyclic creates* limits the membership in this relation. Represent the types as vertices, and let a directed edge go from a to b if $cc(a, b)$. The relation cc is acyclic if this graph has no loops except possibly a loop from one vertex to itself (the loop is not considered a cycle in this context). Figure 3–5 gives an example of both cyclic and acyclic *can-create* relations. The rationale for this rule is to eliminate recursion in cc; if a subject of type a can create a subject of type b, none of the descendents of the subject can create a subject of type a. This simplifies the analysis without unduly limiting the applicability of the model.

Let **A** be a subject of type $a = \tau(\mathbf{A})$ and let **B** be an entity of type $b = \tau(\mathbf{B})$. The *create-rule* $cr(a, b)$ specifies the tickets introduced when a subject of type a creates an entity of type b.

If **B** is an object, the rule specifies the tickets for **B** to be placed in $dom(\mathbf{A})$ as a result of the creation. Only inert tickets can be created, so $cr(a, b) \in \{b/r: c \mid r \in RI\}$, and **A** gets **B**/$r$:$c$ if and only if b/r:$c \in cr(a, b)$.

If **B** is a subject, the rule also specifies that the tickets for **A** be placed in $dom(\mathbf{B})$ as a result of the creation. Assume that types a and b are distinct. Let $cr_p(a, b)$ be the set of tickets the creation adds to $dom(\mathbf{A})$, and let $cr_c(a, b)$ be the set of tickets the creation adds to $dom(\mathbf{B})$. Then **A** gets the ticket **B**/r:c if b/r:$c \in$

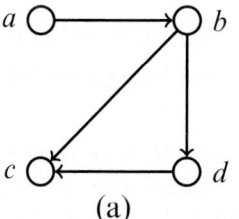
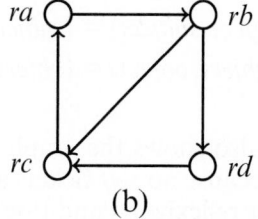

Figure 3–5 The rule of acyclic creates. (a) The *can-create* relation *cc* = {(a, b), (b, c), (b, d), (d, c)}. Because there are no cycles in the graph, *cc* satisfies the rule of acyclic creates. (b) Same as (a), except that the *can-create* relation is *cc'* = *cc* ∪ {(c, a)}, which creates a cycle; hence, *cc'* does not follow the rule of acyclic creates.

$cr_p(a, b)$ and **B** gets the ticket **A**/r:c if a/r:$c \in cr_c(a, b)$. We write $cr(a, b) = \{a/r$:
$c, b/r$:$c \mid r$:$c \in R\}$. If the types a and b are not distinct, then do the types refer to
the creator or the created? To avoid this ambiguity, if $a = b$, we define $self/r$:c to
be tickets for the creator and a/r:c to be tickets for the created, and we say that
$cr(a, a) = \{a/r$:$c, self/r$:$c \mid r$:$c \in R\}$. $cr_p(a, b)$ and $cr_c(a, b)$ are subsets of $cr(a, a)$,
as before.

Recall that the principle of attenuation of privilege (see Section 2.4.3) states
that no entity may have more rights than its creator. The *attenuating create-rule*
captures this notion:

Definition 3–14. A *create-rule* $cr(a, a) = cr_p(a, b) \mid cr_c(a, b)$ is *attenuating* if:

1. $cr_c(a, b) \subseteq cr_p(a, b)$ and
2. a/r:$c \in cr_c(a, b) \Rightarrow self/r$:$c \in cr_p(a, b)$.

A scheme is *attenuating* if, for all types a such that $cc(a, a)$, then $cr(a, a)$
is attenuating. If the graph for cc is constructed as above and has no loops, the
scheme is attenuating.

EXAMPLE: The *can-create* relation for the owner-based policy says that users can
create files; hence, $cc(user) = \{file\}$. The creator of the file can give itself any inert
rights over the file; hence, $cr(user, file) = \{file/r$:$c \mid r \in RI\}$. Figure 3–6 shows the
graph that this *can-create* relation induces; it is clearly acyclic and loop-free, so
the scheme is attenuating.

In the Take-Grant Protection Model, a subject can create either a subject or
an object; hence, $cc = \{(subject, subject), (subject, object)\}$. A subject can give itself
any rights over the vertices it creates, but it does not give the created subject any
rights (although the creator may subsequently apply the grant rule to do so). Hence,
$cr_c(a, b) = \varnothing$ and $cr_p(a, b) = \{subject/tc, subject/gc, subject/rc, subject/wc\}$, so:

$$cr(subject, subject) = \{subject/tc, subject/gc, subject/rc, subject/wc\} \mid \varnothing$$
$$cr(subject, object) = \{object/tc, object/gc, object/rc, object/wc\}$$

Figure 3–6 also shows the graph that this cc induces. It, too, is acyclic, but not
loop-free. Because no *self* tickets are provided (the Take-Grant Protection Model
rules are not reflexive), condition (2) of Definition 3–14 fails and the scheme is
not attenuating.

Only *dom*(**A**) and *dom*(**B**) are affected by *create-rule*; no other entity has its
domain changed. Thus, the *create-rule* is local; this means that creation has only
a local impact on the state of the system and again mimics real systems.

(a)   (b)

Figure 3–6 Graph (a) corresponds to the *cc* for the owner-based policy. Graph (b) corresponds to the Take-Grant Protection Model. Both are acyclic; graph (a) is loop-free, but graph (b) contains a loop from one vertex to that same vertex.

3.4.5   Safety Analysis

The goal of this model is to identify types of policies that have tractable safety analyses. Our approach will be to derive a *maximal state* in which any additional entities or rights do not affect the safety analysis. We then analyze this state.

First, we introduce a *flow function* that captures the flow of tickets around a particular state of the system being modeled.

> **Definition 3–15.** A *legal transition* is a change in state caused by an operation that is authorized. A *history* is a sequence of legal transitions. A *derivable* state is a state obtainable by beginning at some initial state and applying a history.

In simpler terms, a system begins at an initial state. An authorized operation (such as the copying of a ticket) causes a legal transition. Suppose a sequence of legal transitions moves the system into a (final) state. Then that sequence forms a history, and the final state is derivable from the history and the initial state.

We represent states by a superscript h. The set of subjects in state h is SUB^h, the set of entities is ENT^h, and the *link* and *dom* relations in the context of state h are $link_i^h$ and dom^h.

> **Definition 3–16.** If there are two entities $\mathbf{X}$ and $\mathbf{Y}$, and either
>
> (a) for some i, $link_i^h(\mathbf{X}, \mathbf{Y})$ or
>
> (b) there is a sequence of subjects $\mathbf{X}_0, \ldots, \mathbf{X}_n$ such that $link_i^h(\mathbf{X}, \mathbf{X}_0)$, $link_i^h(\mathbf{X}_n, \mathbf{Y})$, and for $k = 1, \ldots, n$, $link_i^h(\mathbf{X}_{k-1}, \mathbf{X}_k)$
>
> then there is a *path^h* from $\mathbf{X}$ to $\mathbf{Y}$.

In other words, a *path^h* from $\mathbf{X}$ to $\mathbf{Y}$ means that either a single link or a sequence of links connects $\mathbf{X}$ and $\mathbf{Y}$. We write this as $path^h(\mathbf{X}, \mathbf{Y})$. Multiple *path^h*s may connect **X** and **Y**; in that case, we enumerate them as *path$_j^h$*(**X**, **Y**), $j = 1, \ldots, m$.

The following algorithm defines the set of the tickets that can flow over a *path^h* from **X** to **Y**. This set is called the *capacity*, or *cap*(*path^h*(**X**, **Y**)).

1. If *link$_i^h$*(**X**, **Y**), then *cap*(*path^h*(**X**, **Y**)) = $f_i(\tau(\mathbf{X}), \tau(\mathbf{Y}))$.

2. Otherwise, *cap*(*path^h*(**X**, **Y**)) = $\{\tau(\mathbf{Y})/r{:}c \mid \tau(\mathbf{Y})/rc \in f_0(\tau(\mathbf{X}), \tau(\mathbf{X}_0)) \wedge$
   $[(\forall k = 1, \ldots, n)\ \tau(\mathbf{Y})/rc \in f_k(\tau(\mathbf{X}_{k-1}), \tau(\mathbf{X}_k))] \wedge \tau(\mathbf{Y})/r{:}c \in f_n(\tau(\mathbf{X}_n),$
   $\tau(\mathbf{Y}))\}$.

In this set, the tickets for all but the final link must be copyable. If they are, any tickets in the last link will be in the capacity, whether or not they are copyable.

Now we can define the flow function as the union (sum) of all the capacities between two entities.

> **Definition 3–17.** Let there be m *path^h*s between subjects **X** and **Y** in state h. The *flow function flow^h* : $SUB^h \times SUB^h \to 2^{T \times R}$ is defined as *flow^h*(**X**, **Y**) = *cap*(*path$_0^h$*(**X**, **Y**)) $\cup \ldots \cup$ *cap*(*path$_m^h$*(**X**, **Y**)).

Sandhu [1657] has shown that the flow function requires $O(|T \times R||SUB^h|^3)$, and hence the computation's time complexity is polynomial in the number of subjects in the system.

This definition allows us to sharpen our intuition of what a "maximal state" is (and will ultimately enable us to define that state formally). Intuitively, a maximal state maximizes flow between all pairs of subjects. Call the maximal state $*$ and the flow function corresponding to this state *flow**; then if a ticket is in *flow**(**X**, **Y**), there exists a sequence of operations that can copy the ticket from **X** to **Y**. This brings up two questions. First, is a maximal state unique? Second, does every system have a maximal state?

We first formally define the notion of maximal state using a relation named $\le_0$.

> **Definition 3–18.** The relation $g \le_0 h$ is true if and only if, for all pairs of subjects **X** and **Y** in SUB^0, *flow^g*(**X**, **Y**) $\subseteq$ *flow^h*(**X**, **Y**). If $g \le_0 h$ and $h \le_0 g$, g and h are equivalent.

In other words, the relation $\le_0$ induces a set of equivalence classes on the set of derivable states.

> **Definition 3–19.** For a given system, a state m is maximal if and only if $h \le_0 m$ for every derivable state h.

In a maximal state, the flow function contains all the tickets that can be transferred from one subject to another. Hence, all maximal states are in the same equivalence class and thus are equivalent. This answers our first question.

To show that every system has a maximal state, we first show that for any state in a finite collection of derivable states, there is a maximal state.

Lemma 3.3. Given an arbitrary finite collection H of derivable states, there exists a derivable state m such that, for all $h \in H$, $h \leq_0 m$.

Proof By induction on $|H|$.

Basis. Take $H = \varnothing$ and m to be the initial state. The claim is trivially true.

Induction Hypothesis. The claim holds when $|H| = n$.

Induction Step. Let $|H'| = n + 1$, where $H' = G \cup \{h\}$; thus, $|G| = n$. Choose $g \in G$ such that, for every state $x \in G$, $x \leq_0 g$; such a state's existence is guaranteed by the induction hypothesis.
    Consider the states g and h, defined above. Each of these states is established by a history. Let M be an interleaving of these histories that preserves the relative order of transitions with respect to g and h, and with only the first create operation of duplicate create operations in the two histories. Let M attain state m. If either $path^g(\mathbf{X}, \mathbf{Y})$ for $\mathbf{X}, \mathbf{Y} \in SUB^g$ or $path^h(\mathbf{X}, \mathbf{Y})$ for $\mathbf{X}, \mathbf{Y} \in SUB^h$, then $path^m(\mathbf{X}, \mathbf{Y})$, as g and h are ancestor states of m and SPM is monotonic. Thus, $g \leq_0 m$ and $h \leq_0 m$, so m is a maximal state in H'. This concludes the induction step and the proof.

Take one state from each equivalence class of derivable states. To see that this is finite, consider each pair of subjects in SUB^0. The flow function's range is $2^{T \times R}$, so that function can take on at most $2^{|T \times R|}$ values. Given that there are $|SUB^0|^2$ pairs of subjects in the initial state, there can be at most $2^{|T \times R|}|SUB^0|^2$ distinct equivalence classes.

Theorem 3.15. There exists a maximal state $*$ for every system.

Proof Take K to be the collection of derivable states that contains exactly one state from each equivalence class of derivable states. From above, this set is finite. The theorem follows from Lemma 3.3.

In this model, the safety question now becomes: *Is it possible to have a derivable state with $\mathbf{X}/r:c$ in dom($\mathbf{A}$), or does there exist a subject $\mathbf{X}$ with ticket $\mathbf{X}/rc$ in the initial state or which can demand $\mathbf{X}/rc$ and $\tau(\mathbf{X})/r:c$ in flow*$(\mathbf{B}, \mathbf{A})$?*
    To answer this question, we need to construct a maximal state and test. Generally, this will require the creation of new subjects. In the general case, this is undecidable. But in special cases, this question is decidable. We now consider an important case—that of acyclic attenuating schemes—and determine how to construct the maximal state.
    Consider a state h. Intuitively, generating a maximal state m from h will require all three types of operations (create, demand, and copy). Define u to be a state corresponding to h but with a minimal number of new entities created such

that *m* can be derived from *u* without any create operations. (That is, begin in state *h*. Use create operations to create as few new entities as possible such that state *m* can be derived from the new state after the entities are created. The state after the entities are created, but before any other operations occur, is *u*.) For example, if in the history from *h* to *m*, subject **X** creates two entities of type *y*, in *u* there would be only one entity of type *y*. That entity would act as a surrogate for the two entities that **X** created. Because *m* can be derived from *u* in polynomial time, if *u* can be created by adding to *h* a finite number of subjects, the safety question is decidable in polynomial time for such a system.

We now make this formal.

Definition 3–20. [1657, p. 425] Given any initial state 0 of an acyclic attenuating scheme, the *fully unfolded state u* is the state derived by the following algorithm.

```
(* delete any loops so it's loop-free *)
cc′ = cc − { (a, a) | a ∈ TS }
(* mark all subjects as unfolded *)
folded = ∅
for X ∈ SUB⁰ do
        folded = folded ∪ { X }
(* if anything is folded, it has to be unfolded *)
while folded ≠ ∅ do begin
    (* subject X is going to be unfolded *)
    folded = folded − { X }
    (* for each type X can create, create one entity of *)
    (* that type and mark it as folded; this will force *)
    (* the new entity to be unfolded *)
    for y ∈ TS do begin
      if cc′(τ(X), y) then
        X creates Y of type y
        (* system is in state g here *)
        if Y ∈ SUBᵍ then
          folded = folded ∪ { Y }
    end
end
(* now account for the loops; the system is in state h
   here *)
for X ∈ SUBʰ do
    if cc(τ(X), τ(X)) then
        X creates Y of type τ(X)
(* currently in desired state u *)
```

The **while** loop will terminate because the system is acyclic and attenuating, hence the types of the created entities must all be different—and *TS* is a finite set.

Definition 3–21. Given any initial state of an acyclic attenuating scheme, for every derivable state h define the *surrogate function* $\sigma : ENT^h \to ENT^u$ by

$$\sigma(X) = \begin{cases} X & \text{if } X \in ENT^0 \\ \sigma(Y) & \text{if } Y \text{ creates } X \text{ and } \tau(Y) = \tau(X) \\ \tau(X)-\text{surrogate of } \sigma(Y) & \text{if } Y \text{ creates } X \text{ and } \tau(Y) \neq \tau(X) \end{cases}$$

It is easy to show that $\tau(\sigma(A)) = \tau(A)$.

If $\tau(X) = \tau(Y)$, then $\sigma(X) = \sigma(Y)$. If $\tau(X) \neq \tau(Y)$, then in the construction of u, $\sigma(X)$ creates $\sigma(Y)$ (see the **while** loop of Definition 3–20). Also, in this construction, $\sigma(X)$ creates entities X' of type $\tau(X') = \tau(\sigma(X))$ (see the last **for** loop of Definition 3–20). So, by Definition 3–14, we have the following lemma.

Lemma 3.4. For a system with an acyclic attenuating scheme, if X creates Y, then tickets that would be introduced by pretending that $\sigma(X)$ creates $\sigma(Y)$ are in $dom^u(\sigma(X))$ and $dom^u(\sigma(Y))$.

Now, let H be a legal history that derives a state h from the initial state of an acyclic attenuating system. Without loss of generality, we may assume that H's operations are ordered such that all create operations come first, followed by all demand operations, followed by all copy operations. Replace the transitions in H as follows, while preserving their relative order:

1. Delete all create operations.
2. Replace "X demands $Y/r:c$" with "$\sigma(X)$ demands $\sigma(Y))/r:c$."
3. Replace "Z copies $X/r:c$ from Y" with "$\sigma(Z)$ copies $\sigma(X)/r:c$ from $\sigma(Y)$."

Call the new history G. Then:

Lemma 3.5. Every transition in G is legal, and if $X/r:c \in dom^h(Y)$, then $\sigma(X)/r:c \in dom^g(\sigma(Y))$.

Proof By induction on the number of copy operations in H.

Basis. Assume that H consists only of create and demand operations. Then G consists only of demand operations. By construction, and because σ preserves type, every demand operation in G is legal. Furthermore, $X/r:c$ can appear in $dom^h(Y)$ in one of three ways. If $X/r:c \in dom^0(Y)$, then $X, Y \in ENT^0$ and $\sigma(X)/r:c \in dom^g(\sigma(Y))$ trivially holds. If a create operation in H put $X/r:c \in dom^h(Y)$, $\sigma(X)/r:c \in dom^g(\sigma(Y))$ by Lemma 3.4. And if a demand operation put $X/r:c \in dom^h(Y)$, then $\sigma(X)/r:c \in dom^g(\sigma(Y))$ follows from the corresponding demand operation in G. This establishes both parts of the claim.

Induction Hypothesis. Assume that the claim holds for all histories with k copy operations, and consider a history H with $k + 1$ copy operations. Let H' be the initial sequence of H composed of k copy operations, and let h' be the state derived from H'.

Induction Step. Let G' be the sequence of modified operations corresponding to H'. By the induction hypothesis, G' is a legal history. Let g' be the state derived from G'. Suppose the final operation of H is "$\mathbf{Z}$ copies $\mathbf{X}/r\text{:}c$ from $\mathbf{Y}$." By construction of G, the final operation of G is "$\sigma(\mathbf{Z})$ copies $\sigma(\mathbf{X})/r\text{:}c$ from $\sigma(\mathbf{Y})$." Now, h differs from h' by at most $\mathbf{X}/r\text{:}c \in dom^h(\mathbf{Z})$. However, the construction causes the final operation of G to be $\sigma(\mathbf{X})/r\text{:}c \in dom^h(\sigma(\mathbf{Z}))$, proving the second part of the claim.

     Because H' is legal, for H to be legal the following conditions must hold:

1. $\mathbf{X}/rc \in dom^{h'}(\mathbf{Y})$
2. $link_i^{h'}(\mathbf{Y}, \mathbf{Z})$
3. $\tau(\mathbf{X}/r\text{:}c) \in f_i(\tau(\mathbf{Y}), \tau(\mathbf{Z}))$

The induction hypothesis, the first two conditions above, and $\mathbf{X}/r : c \in dom^{h'}(\mathbf{Y})$ mean that $\sigma(\mathbf{X})/rc \in dom^{g'}(\sigma(\mathbf{Y}))$ and $link_i^{g'}(\sigma(\mathbf{Y}), \sigma(\mathbf{Z}))$. Because σ preserves type, the third condition and the induction hypothesis imply $\tau(\sigma(\mathbf{X})/r : c) \in f_i(\tau(\sigma(\mathbf{Y})), \tau(\sigma(\mathbf{Z})))$. G' is legal, by the induction hypothesis; so, by these conditions, G is legal. This establishes the lemma.

Corollary 3.3. For every i, if $link_i^h(\mathbf{X}, \mathbf{Y})$, then $link_i^g(\sigma(\mathbf{X}), \sigma(\mathbf{Y}))$.

We can now present the following theorem.

Theorem 3.16. For a system with an acyclic attenuating scheme, for every history H that derives h from the initial state, there exists a history G without create operations that derives g from the fully unfolded state u such that

$$(\forall\, \mathbf{X}, \mathbf{Y} \in SUB^h)[\, flow^h(\mathbf{X}, \mathbf{Y}) \subseteq flow^g(\sigma(\mathbf{X}), \sigma(\mathbf{Y}))]$$

Proof It suffices to show that for every $path^h$ from $\mathbf{X}$ to $\mathbf{Y}$ there is a $path^g$ from $\sigma(\mathbf{X})$ to $\sigma(\mathbf{Y})$ for which $cap(path^h(\mathbf{X}, \mathbf{Y})) = cap(path^g(\sigma(\mathbf{X}), \sigma(\mathbf{Y})))$. Induct on the number of links.

Basis. Let the length of the $path^h$ from $\mathbf{X}$ to $\mathbf{Y}$ be 1. By Definition 3–16, $link_i^h(\mathbf{X}, \mathbf{Y})$. So, by Corollary 3.3, $link_i^g(\sigma(\mathbf{X}), \sigma(\mathbf{Y}))$. Then $cap(path^h(\mathbf{X}, \mathbf{Y})) = cap(path^g(\sigma(\mathbf{X}), \sigma(\mathbf{Y})))$ as σ preserves type, verifying the claim.

Induction Hypothesis. Assume that the claim holds for every *path^h* of length k.

Induction Step. Consider a *path^h* from **X** to **Y** of length $k + 1$. Then there exists an entity **Z** with a *path^h* from **X** to **Z** of length k, and $link_j^h(\mathbf{Z}, \mathbf{Y})$. By the induction hypothesis, there is a *path^g* from $\sigma(\mathbf{X})$ to $\sigma(\mathbf{Z})$ with the same capacity as the *path^h* from **X** to **Z**. By Corollary 3.3, we have $link_j^g(\sigma(\mathbf{Z}), \sigma(\mathbf{Y}))$. Because σ preserves type, there is a *path^g* from **X** to **Y** with $cap(path^h(\mathbf{X}, \mathbf{Y})) = cap(path^g(\sigma(\mathbf{X}), \sigma(\mathbf{Y})))$, proving the induction step and therefore the theorem.

Thus, any history derived from an initial state u can be simulated by a corresponding history applied to the fully unfolded state v derived from u. The maximal state corresponding to v is #u; the history deriving this state has no creates. From Theorem 3.16, for every history that derives h from the initial state,

$$(\forall \, \mathbf{X}, \mathbf{Y} \in SUB^h)[\, flow^h(\mathbf{X}, \mathbf{Y}) \subseteq flow^{\#u}(\sigma(\mathbf{X}), \sigma(\mathbf{Y}))]$$

For $\mathbf{X} \in SUB^0$, $\sigma(\mathbf{X}) = \mathbf{X}$; therefore, $(\forall \, \mathbf{X}, \mathbf{Y} \in SUB^0)[\, flow^h(\mathbf{X}, \mathbf{Y}) \subseteq flow^{\#u}$ $(\mathbf{X}, \mathbf{Y})]$. This demonstrates the following corollary.

Corollary 3.4. The state #u is a maximal state for a system with an acyclic attenuating scheme.

Not only is #u derivable from u, it is derivable in time polynomial with respect to $|SUB^u|$ (and therefore to $|SUB^0|$). Moreover, the straightforward algorithm for computing $flow^{\#u}$ will be exponential in $|TS|$ in the worst case. This means that for acyclic attenuating schemes, the safety question is decidable.

The situation for cyclic schemes is different. Sandhu has shown that, in general, safety in schemes with cycles of length 2 or greater in *can-create* is undecidable. But with cycles of length 1, safety is decidable [1661]. Thus, the dividing line between decidability and undecidability in SPM is whether the scheme is an acyclic attenuating one.

3.5 Expressive Power and the Models

The HRU and SPM models present different aspects of the answer to the safety question. The obvious issue is the relationship between these models. For example, if SPM and HRU are equivalent, then SPM provides a more specific answer to the safety question than the HRU analysis does (that is, safety in acyclic attenuating schemes is decidable). If HRU can describe some systems that SPM cannot, then SPM's answer applies only to a limited set of systems. This bears some examination.

3.5.1   Brief Comparison of HRU and SPM

Sandhu [1651] has used SPM to represent multilevel security models, integrity models, and the Take-Grant Protection Model, so SPM subsumes those models. But the HRU model is central to safety analysis problems, and we explore its relationship to SPM in more detail.

How does SPM compare with the HRU model? If the two models are equivalent, then any safety analysis of SPM also applies to HRU and SPM offers some significant advantages over HRU for such analyses.

First, SPM is a higher-level model than HRU. This allows policies to be expressed very succinctly and at a more abstract level than in the access control matrix model. Hence, safety analyses can focus on the limits of the model and not on the details of representation. By way of contrast, safety analyses using the HRU model usually require a detailed mapping of the policy to the model, followed by an analysis.

However, the HRU model allows rights to be revoked and entities to be deleted (the **delete**, **destroy subject**, and **destroy object** rules). The SPM model has no revocation rule. The justification is exactly the same as for the Take-Grant Protection Model analyses that ignore that model's remove rule: what is removed can be replaced. So, in some sense, comparing HRU and SPM directly is unfair. A better comparison is one between SPM and a monotonic HRU scheme, in which there are no revocation rules, and we will use that model for further comparison.

In terms of comprehensiveness, HRU allows multiconditional commands. For example, suppose a system has a *parent* right, similar to the *create* right but requiring two subjects to have those rights over one another. Then either subject can execute a *multicreate* command that creates a new object and gives both subjects *r* rights over the new object. The multicreate command would be:

```
command multicreate(s₀, s₁, o)
        if p in a[s₀,s₁] and p in a[s₁,s₀]
        then
                create object o;
                enter r into a[s₀,o];
                enter r into a[s₁,o];
end
```

However, SPM cannot express this command easily because the *can-create* function allows creators to have at most one type. If s_0 and s_1 have different types, SPM has no mechanism for creating o. This suggests that SPM is less expressive than HRU.

3.5.2   Extending SPM

Ammann and Sandhu [42, 1651, 1659] revisited the notion of creation in SPM. Implicit in all models discussed so far is the assumption of a single parent. This assumption is not common in nature. (Consider humans, who have two parents.) It is more common in computer science, but (as we shall see) changing paradigms often simplifies solutions.

Consider two users, Anna and Bill, who must cooperate to perform a task but who do not trust each other. This problem of mutual suspicion is one of the oldest problems in security [805] and arises in multiuser computing systems. The usual solution is for Anna to define a proxy and give it only those rights she wishes Bill to have and for Bill to define a proxy similarly. Then Anna gives Bill's proxy the privileges to invoke Anna's proxy, and Bill gives Anna's proxy similar privileges. Working indirectly, the two proxies can work together and perform the task. Multiple indirection is disallowed (or else Anna's proxy could give her rights to Bill's proxy to a third party). Hence, the way the proxies use rights must be restricted, leading to a complex set of rights and manipulations.

Multiple parenting simplifies this model. Anna and Bill jointly create a proxy. Each then gives the proxy only those rights needed to perform the task. Neither parent is allowed to copy rights from the proxy. At this point, the copy operation must embody all restrictions on the manipulation of proxy rights and abilities, which is simpler than restricting the particular application of rights (as must be done in the preceding solution).

The Extended Schematic Protection Model (or ESPM) adds multiple parenting to SPM. The *joint creation* operation includes the SPM creation operation as a special case. The *can-create* function becomes

$$cc \subseteq TS \times \ldots \times TS \times T$$

The *create rules* for the parents in a joint creation operation can allow the parents to get one another's rights to the child as well as their own, but this is equivalent to a creation rule in which parent rights are not copied, followed by applications of the copy rule. For simplicity, we require that each parent be given tickets only for its own rights over the new child, and not for rights of other parents.

Let $X_1, \ldots, X_n$ be the n subject parents and let Y be the created entity. We represent the sets of rights with $R_{1,i}, R_{2,i}, R_3, R_{4,i} \subseteq R$ for $i = 1, \ldots, n$. Each creation rule has i components, each of which provides the tickets to the ith parent and the child; for example, the ith rule is

$$cr_{P_i}(\tau(X_1), \ldots, \tau(X_n), \tau(Y)) = Y/R_{1,i} \cup X_i/R_{2,i}$$

The child also has a rule of the form

$$cr_C(\tau(X_1), \ldots, \tau(X_n), \tau(Y)) = Y/R_3 \cup X_1/R_{4,1} \cup \ldots \cup X_n/R_{4,n}$$

These rules are analogous to the single-parent creation rules, but with one for each parent.

EXAMPLE: To expand on this concept, let's revisit Anna's and Bill's situation. Anna and Bill are equals, so for modeling purposes they have the same type a. The proxy is of type p; because the proxy has delegated authority, a and p may be different. We model the rights that proxy has by the right $x \in R$. Thus:

$$cc(a, a) = p$$
$$cr_{Anna}(a, a, p) = cr_{Bill}(a, a, p) = \varnothing$$
$$cr_{proxy}(a, a, p) = \text{Anna}/x \cup \text{Bill}/x$$

Then the proxy can use the right x to transfer whatever set of privileges the proxy requires.

Considering two-parent joint creation operations is sufficient for modeling purposes. To demonstrate this, we show how the two-parent joint creation operation can implement a three-parent joint creation operation.

Let $\mathbf{P}_1$, $\mathbf{P}_2$, and $\mathbf{P}_3$ be three subjects; they will create a (child) entity $\mathbf{C}$. With a three-parent joint creation operation, *can-create* will be

$$cc(\tau(\mathbf{P}_1), \tau(\mathbf{P}_2), \tau(\mathbf{P}_3)) = Z \subseteq T$$

and the type of the child is $\tau(\mathbf{C}) \in T$. The creation rules are

$$cr_{\mathbf{P}_1}(\tau(\mathbf{P}_1), \tau(\mathbf{P}_2), \tau(\mathbf{P}_3), \tau(\mathbf{C})) = \mathbf{C}/R_{1,1} \cup \mathbf{P}_1/R_{2,1}$$
$$cr_{\mathbf{P}_2}(\tau(\mathbf{P}_1), \tau(\mathbf{P}_2), \tau(\mathbf{P}_3), \tau(\mathbf{C})) = \mathbf{C}/R_{1,2} \cup \mathbf{P}_2/R_{2,2}$$
$$cr_{\mathbf{P}_3}(\tau(\mathbf{P}_1), \tau(\mathbf{P}_2), \tau(\mathbf{P}_3), \tau(\mathbf{C})) = \mathbf{C}/R_{1,3} \cup \mathbf{P}_3/R_{2,3}$$
$$cr_{\mathbf{C}}(\tau(\mathbf{P}_1), \tau(\mathbf{P}_2), \tau(\mathbf{P}_3), \tau(\mathbf{C})) = \mathbf{C}/R_3 \cup \mathbf{P}_1/R_{4,1} \cup \mathbf{P}_2/R_{4,2} \cup \mathbf{P}_3/R_{4,3}$$

Our demonstration requires that we use the two-parent joint creation rule, not the three-parent rule. At the end of the demonstration, the parents and the child should have exactly the same tickets for one another. We will create additional entities and types, but they cannot interact with any other entities (in effect, they do not exist for the rest of the entities). Finally, if the creation fails, the parents get no new tickets.

For convenience, and to simplify the notation, we assume that the parents and child are all of different types.

Define four new entities $\mathbf{A}_1$, $\mathbf{A}_2$, $\mathbf{A}_3$, and $\mathbf{S}$; each $\mathbf{A}_i$, of type $a_i = \tau(\mathbf{A}_i)$, will act as an agent for the corresponding parent $\mathbf{P}_i$, and $\mathbf{S}$, of type $s = \tau(\mathbf{S})$, will act as an agent for the child. Let the type t represent parentage—that is, an entity with the ticket $\mathbf{X}/t$ has $\mathbf{X}$ as a parent. Again, without loss of generality, we assume that a_1, a_2, a_3, s, and t are all new types.

During the construction, each agent will act as a surrogate for its parent; this agent obtains tickets on behalf of the parent, and only after the child is created does the agent give the parent the ticket. That way, if the construction fails, the parent has no new tickets.

Augment the *can-create* rules as follows:

$$cc(p_1) = a_1$$
$$cc(p_2, a_1) = a_2$$
$$cc(p_3, a_2) = a_3$$
$$cc(a_3) = s$$
$$cc(s) = c$$

These rules enable the parents to create the agents. The final agent can create the agent for the child, which subsequently creates the child. Note that the second agent has two parents ($\mathbf{P}_2$ and $\mathbf{A}_1$), as does the third agent ($\mathbf{P}_3$ and $\mathbf{A}_2$); these rules are the two-parent joint creation operation.

On creation, the create rules dictate the new tickets given to the parent and the child. The following rules augment the existing rules:

$$cr_{\mathbf{P}}(p_1, a_1) = \varnothing \qquad\qquad cr_{\mathbf{C}}(p_1, a_1) = p_1/Rtc$$
$$cr_{\mathbf{P}_{first}}(p_2, a_1, a_2) = \varnothing$$
$$cr_{\mathbf{P}_{second}}(p_2, a_1, a_2) = \varnothing \quad cr_{\mathbf{C}}(p_2, a_1, a_2) = p_2/Rtc \cup a_1/tc$$
$$cr_{\mathbf{P}_{first}}(p_3, a_2, a_3) = \varnothing$$
$$cr_{\mathbf{P}_{second}}(p_3, a_2, a_3) = \varnothing \quad cr_{\mathbf{C}}(p_3, a_2, a_3) = p_3/Rtc \cup a_2/tc$$
$$cr_{\mathbf{P}}(a_3, s) = \varnothing \qquad\qquad cr_{\mathbf{C}}(a_3, s) = a_3/tc$$
$$cr_{\mathbf{P}}(s, c) = \mathbf{C}/Rtc \qquad\qquad cr_{\mathbf{C}}(s, c) = c/R_3t$$

Here, $cr_{\mathbf{P}_{first}}$ and $cr_{\mathbf{P}_{second}}$ indicate the tickets given to the first and second parents, respectively.

The link predicates indicate over which links rights can flow; essentially, no tickets can flow to the parents until the child is created. The following links restrain flow to the parents by requiring each agent to have its own "parent" right:

$$link_1(\mathbf{A}_2, \mathbf{A}_1) = \mathbf{A}_1/t \in dom(\mathbf{A}_2) \wedge \mathbf{A}_2/t \in dom(\mathbf{A}_2)$$
$$link_1(\mathbf{A}_3, \mathbf{A}_2) = \mathbf{A}_2/t \in dom(\mathbf{A}_3) \wedge \mathbf{A}_3/t \in dom(\mathbf{A}_3)$$
$$link_2(\mathbf{S}, \mathbf{A}_3) = \mathbf{A}_3/t \in dom(\mathbf{S}) \wedge \mathbf{C}/t \in dom(\mathbf{C})$$
$$link_3(\mathbf{A}_1, \mathbf{C}) = \mathbf{C}/t \in dom(\mathbf{A}_1)$$
$$link_3(\mathbf{A}_2, \mathbf{C}) = \mathbf{C}/t \in dom(\mathbf{A}_2)$$
$$link_3(\mathbf{A}_3, \mathbf{C}) = \mathbf{C}/t \in dom(\mathbf{A}_3)$$
$$link_4(\mathbf{A}_1, \mathbf{P}_1) = \mathbf{P}_1/t \in dom(\mathbf{A}_1) \wedge \mathbf{A}_1/t \in dom(\mathbf{A}_1)$$
$$link_4(\mathbf{A}_2, \mathbf{P}_2) = \mathbf{P}_2/t \in dom(\mathbf{A}_2) \wedge \mathbf{A}_2/t \in dom(\mathbf{A}_2)$$
$$link_4(\mathbf{A}_3, \mathbf{P}_3) = \mathbf{P}_3/t \in dom(\mathbf{A}_3) \wedge \mathbf{A}_3/t \in dom(\mathbf{A}_3)$$

The filter functions dictate which tickets are copied from one entity to another:

$$f_1(a_2, a_1) = a_1/t \cup c/Rtc$$
$$f_1(a_3, a_2) = a_2/t \cup c/Rtc$$
$$f_2(s, a_3) = a_3/t \cup c/Rtc$$
$$f_3(a_1, c) = p_1/R_{4,1}$$
$$f_3(a_2, c) = p_2/R_{4,2}$$
$$f_3(a_3, c) = p_3/R_{4,3}$$
$$f_4(a_1, p_1) = c/R_{1,1} \cup p_1/R_{2,1}$$
$$f_4(a_2, p_2) = c/R_{1,2} \cup p_2/R_{2,2}$$
$$f_4(a_3, p_3) = c/R_{1,3} \cup p_3/R_{2,3}$$

Now we begin the construction. The creations proceed in the obvious order; after all are completed, we have

- P_1 has no relevant tickets.
- P_2 has no relevant tickets.
- P_3 has no relevant tickets.
- A_1 has P_1/Rtc.
- A_2 has $P_2/Rtc \cup A_1/tc$.
- A_3 has $P_3/Rtc \cup A_2/tc$.
- S has $A_3/tc \cup C/Rtc$.
- C has C/R_3t.

We now apply the links and filter functions to copy rights. The only link predicate that is true is $link_2(S, A_3)$, so we apply f_2; then A_3's set of tickets changes, as follows:

- A_3 has $P_3/Rtc \cup A_2/tc \cup A_3/t \cup C/Rtc$.

Now $link_1(A_3, A_2)$ is true, so applying f_1 yields

- A_2 has $P_2/Rtc \cup A_1/tc \cup A_2/t \cup C/Rtc$.

Now $link_1(A_2, A_1)$ is true, so applying f_1 again yields

- A_1 has $P_1/Rtc \cup A_1/t \cup C/Rtc$.

At this point, all $link_3$s in this construction hold, so

- C has $C/R_3 \cup P_1/R_{4,1} \cup P_2/R_{4,2} \cup P_3/R_{4,3}$.

Then the filter functions associated with $link_4$, all of which are also true, finish the construction:

- $\mathbf{P}_1$ has $\mathbf{C}/R_{1,1} \cup \mathbf{P}_1/R_{2,1}$.
- $\mathbf{P}_2$ has $\mathbf{C}/R_{1,2} \cup \mathbf{P}_2/R_{2,2}$.
- $\mathbf{P}_3$ has $\mathbf{C}/R_{1,3} \cup \mathbf{P}_3/R_{2,3}$.

This completes the construction. As required, it adds no tickets to $\mathbf{P}_1, \mathbf{P}_2, \mathbf{P}_3$, and $\mathbf{C}$ except those that would be added by the three-parent joint creation operation. The intermediate entities, being of unique types, can have no effect on other entities. Finally, if the creation of $\mathbf{C}$ fails, no tickets can be added to $\mathbf{P}_1, \mathbf{P}_2$, and $\mathbf{P}_3$ because none of the link predicates in this construction is true; hence, no filter functions apply.

Generalizing this construction to n parents leads to the following theorem.

Theorem 3.17. [1651] The two-parent joint creation operation can implement an n-parent joint creation operation with a fixed number of additional types and rights, and augmentations to the link predicates and filter functions.

A logical question is the relationship between ESPM and HRU; Ammann and Sandhu show that the following theorem holds.

Theorem 3.18. [1651] The monotonic ESPM model and the monotonic HRU model are equivalent.

Furthermore, the safety analysis is similar to that of SPM; the only difference is in the definition of the state function σ. The corresponding function σ' takes the joint creation operation into account; given this, the nature of the unfolding algorithm is roughly analogous to that of SPM. This leads to the equivalent of Theorem 3.16.

Theorem 3.19. [1651] For an ESPM system with an acyclic attenuating scheme, for every history H that derives h from the initial state there exists a history G without create operations that derives g from the fully unfolded state u such that

$$(\forall \mathbf{X}, \mathbf{Y} \in SUB^h)[\, flow^h(\mathbf{X}, \mathbf{Y}) \subseteq flow^g(\sigma'(\mathbf{X}), \sigma'(\mathbf{Y}))]$$

Because the proof is analogous to that of Theorem 3.16, we omit it.

What is the benefit of this alternative representation? If SPM and ESPM model the same systems, the addition of n-parent joint creation operations is not at all interesting. But if ESPM can represent systems that SPM cannot, the addition is very interesting. More generally, how can we compare different models?

3.5.3   Simulation and Expressiveness

Ammann, Sandhu, and Lipton [44] use a graph-based representation to compare different models. An abstract machine represents an access control model; as usual, that machine has a set of states and a set of transformations for moving from one state to another. A directed graph represents a state of this machine. A vertex is an entity; it has an associated type that is static. Each edge corresponds to a right and, like a vertex, has a static type determined on creation. The source of the edge has some right(s) over the target. The allowed operations are as follows:

1. *Initial state operations*, which simply create the graph in a particular state;
2. *Node creation operations*, which add new vertices and edges with those vertices as targets; and
3. *Edge adding operations*, which add new edges between existing vertices.

As an example, we simulate the three-parent joint creation operation with two-parent joint creation operations. As before, nodes P_1, P_2, and P_3 are the parents; they create a new node C of type c with edges of type e. First, P_1 creates A_1, which is of type a, and an edge from P_1 to A_1 of type e'. Both a and e' are used only in this construction.

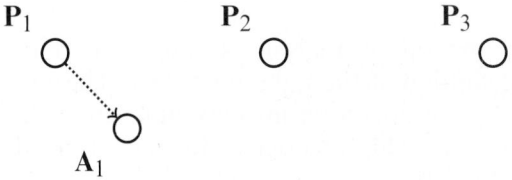

Then A_1 and P_2 create a new node A_2, which is of type a, and A_2 and P_3 create a new node A_3, with type a, and edges of type e' as indicated:

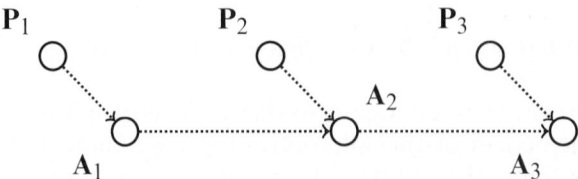

Next, A_3 creates a new node S, which is of type a, which in turn creates a new node C, of type c:

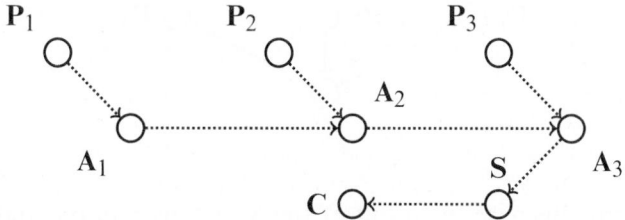

Finally, an edge adding operation depending on the presence of edges $P_1 \rightarrow A_1$, $A_1 \rightarrow A_2$, $A_2 \rightarrow A_3$, $A_3 \rightarrow S$, and $S \rightarrow C$ adds an edge of type e from P_1 to C. An edge adding operation depending on the presence of edges $P_2 \rightarrow A_2$, $A_2 \rightarrow A_3$, $A_3 \rightarrow S$, and $S \rightarrow C$ adds an edge of type e from P_2 to C. A last edge adding operation depending on the presence of edges $P_3 \rightarrow A_3$, $A_3 \rightarrow S$, and $S \rightarrow C$ adds an edge of type e from P_3 to C:

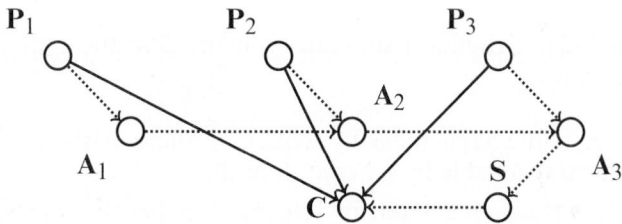

This completes the simulation. Exercise 14 suggests a simpler simulation.

The formal definition of *simulation* relies on two other notions: a *scheme* and a *correspondence* between schemes.

Definition 3–22. A *scheme* is an abstract finite-state machine that defines finite sets of node types, edge types, initial state operations, node creation operations, and edge adding operations. A *model* is a set of schemes.

Definition 3–23. Let $NT(X)$ and $ET(X)$ be the sets of node types and edge types, respectively, in scheme X. Then scheme A and scheme B correspond if and only if the graph defining the state in scheme A is identical to the subgraph obtained by taking the state in scheme B and deleting all nodes not in $NT(A)$ and all edges not in $ET(A)$.

Consider the simulation of a scheme SC_3 with a three-parent joint creation operation by a scheme SC_2 with a two-parent joint creation operation, as was done earlier. After the three-parent joint creation operation, the SC_3 state would be as follows:

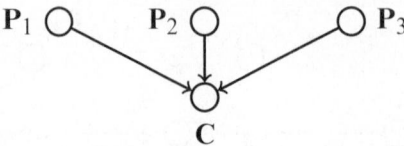

Contrasting this with the result of the SC_2 construction, and the fact that the types a and e' do not exist in SC_3, this state in SC_3 clearly corresponds to the state resulting from the construction in SC_2.

Intuitively, scheme A simulates scheme B if every state reachable by A corresponds to a state reachable by B. Because A may have more edge types and node types than B, simulation implies that if A can enter a state a, either there is a corresponding state reachable by B or, if not, A can transition to another state a' from a and there is a state reachable by B that corresponds to a'. The last condition means that if scheme A has a halting state, then scheme B must have a corresponding halting state; otherwise, the simulation is incorrect.

Definition 3–24. Scheme A simulates scheme B if and only if both of the following are true:

(a) For every state b reachable by scheme B, there exists some corresponding state a reachable by scheme A; and

(b) For every state a reachable by scheme A, either the corresponding state b is reachable by scheme B or there exists a successor state a' reachable by scheme A that corresponds to a state reachable by scheme B.

Now we can contrast the expressive power of models.

Definition 3–25. If there is a scheme in model MA that no scheme in model MB can simulate, then model MB is *less expressive than* model MA. If every scheme in model MA can be simulated by a scheme in model MB, then model MB is *as expressive as* model MA. If MA is as expressive as MB and MB is as expressive as MA, the models are *equivalent*.

EXAMPLE: Consider a model M with one scheme A that defines three nodes called X_1, X_2, and X_3 and a two-parent joint creation operation. A has one node type and one edge type. The two-parent joint creation operation creates a new node and adds edges from both parents to the child. A has no edge adding operations. A's initial state is simply X_1, X_2, and X_3, with no edges. Now, consider a model N

with one scheme B that is the same as scheme A except that scheme B has a one-parent creation operation instead of a two-parent joint creation operation. Both A and B begin at the identical initial state. Which, if either, is more expressive?

Clearly, scheme A can simulate scheme B by having the two parents be the same node. Hence model M is as expressive as model N.

How might scheme B simulate the creation operation of scheme A? Suppose X_1 and X_2 jointly create a new node Y in scheme A; then there are edges from X_1 and X_2 to Y, but no edge from X_3 to Y. Scheme B can use its single-parent creation operation to create a node Y with parent X_1. However, an edge adding operation must allow the edge from X_2 to Y to be added. Consider what this edge adding operation must allow. Because there is only one type of node, and one type of edge, the edge adding operation must allow an edge to be added between any two nodes.

Because edges can be added only by using the two-parent joint creation operation in scheme A, all nodes in scheme A have even numbers of incoming edges. But given the edge adding rule in scheme B, because we can add an edge from X_2 to Y, we can also add an edge from X_3 to Y. Thus, there is a state in scheme B containing a node with three incoming edges. Scheme A cannot enter this state. Furthermore, because there is no remove rule and only one edge type, scheme B cannot transition from this state to a state in which Y has an even number of incoming edges. Hence, scheme B has reached a state not corresponding to any state in scheme A, and from which no state corresponding to a state in scheme A can be reached. Thus, scheme B cannot simulate scheme A, and so model N is less expressive than model M.

Given these definitions, Ammann, Lipton, and Sandhu prove the following theorem.

Theorem 3.20. [44] Monotonic single-parent models are less expressive than monotonic multiparent models.

Proof Begin with scheme A in the preceding example. We show by contradiction that this scheme cannot be simulated by any monotonic scheme B with only a single-parent creation operation. (The example does not show this because we are removing the requirement that scheme B begin in the same initial state as scheme A.)

Consider a scheme B that simulates scheme A. Let nodes X_1 and X_2 in A create node Y_1 with edges from X_1 and X_2 to Y_1. Then in scheme B there is a node W that creates Y_1 with a single incoming edge from W. The simulation must also use edge adding operations to add edges from X_1 to Y_1 and from X_2 to Y_1 (assuming that $W \neq X_1$ and $W \neq X_2$).

Let W invoke the single-parent creation operation twice more to create nodes Y_2 and Y_3 and use the edge adding rules to add edges from X_1 to Y_1, Y_2, and Y_3 and from X_2 to Y_1, Y_2, and Y_3. The resulting state clearly corresponds to a state in scheme A.

Because scheme A has exactly one node type, $\mathbf{Y}_1$, $\mathbf{Y}_2$, and $\mathbf{Y}_3$ are indistinguishable as far as the application of the node creation and edge adding rules is concerned. So proceed as in the example above: in scheme A, let $\mathbf{Y}_1$ and $\mathbf{Y}_2$ create $\mathbf{Z}$. In the simulation, without loss of generality, let $\mathbf{Y}_1$ create $\mathbf{Z}$ using a single-parent creation operation. Then scheme B uses an edge adding operation to add an edge from $\mathbf{Y}_2$ to $\mathbf{Z}$—but that same edge adding rule can be used to add one more edge into $\mathbf{Z}$ from $\mathbf{Y}_3$. Thus, there are three edges coming into $\mathbf{Z}$, which (as we saw earlier) is a state that scheme A cannot reach, and from which no future state in scheme B that corresponds to a state in scheme A can be reached. Hence, scheme B does not simulate scheme A, which contradicts the hypothesis.

Thus, no such scheme B can exist.

This theorem answers the question posed earlier: because ESPM has a multiparent joint creation operation and SPM has a single-parent creation operation, ESPM is indeed more expressive than SPM.

3.5.4   Typed Access Matrix Model

The strengths of SPM and ESPM appear to derive from the notion of "types." In particular, monotonic ESPM and monotonic HRU are equivalent, but the safety properties of ESPM are considerably stronger than those of HRU. Sandhu expanded the access control matrix model by adding a notion of "type" and revisited the HRU results. This model, called the *Typed Access Matrix (TAM) Model* [1660], has safety properties similar to those of ESPM and supports the notion that types are critical to the safety problem's analysis.

TAM augments the definitions used in the access control matrix model by adding types.

Definition 3–26. There is a finite set of types T, containing a subset of types *TS* for subjects.

The type of an entity is fixed when the entity is created (or in the initial state) and remains fixed throughout the lifetime of the model. The notion of *protection state* is similarly augmented.

Definition 3–27. The *protection state* of a system is (S, O, τ, A), where S is the set of subjects, O is the set of objects, A is the access control matrix, and $\tau : O \rightarrow T$ is a type function that specifies the type of each object. If $x \in S$, then $\tau(x) \in TS$, and if $x \in O$, then $\tau(x) \in T - TS$.

The TAM primitive operations are the same as for the access control matrix model, except that the create operations are augmented with types.

1. Precondition: $s \notin S$
   Primitive command: **create subject** s **of type** ts

Postconditions: $S' = S \cup \{s\}, O' = O \cup \{s\},$
$(\forall y \in O')[\tau'(y) = \tau(y)], \tau'(s) = ts,$
$(\forall y \in O')[a'[s, y] = \varnothing], (\forall x \in S')[a'[x, s] = \varnothing],$
$(\forall x \in S)(\forall y \in O)[a'[x, y] = a[x, y]]$

In other words, this primitive command creates a new subject s. Note that s must not exist as a subject *or* *object* before this command is executed.

2. Precondition: $o \notin O$

Primitive command: **create object** o **of type** to

Postconditions: $S' = S, O' = O \cup \{o\},$
$(\forall y \in O')[\tau'(y) = \tau(y)], \tau'(o) = to,$
$(\forall x \in S')[a'[x, s] = \varnothing],$
$(\forall x \in S)(\forall y \in O)[a'[x, y] = a[x, y]]$

In other words, this primitive command creates a new object o. Note that o must not exist before this command is executed.

These primitive operations are combined into commands defined as in the access control matrix model. Commands with conditions are called *conditional commands*; commands without conditions are called *unconditional commands*.

Finally, we define the models explicitly.

Definition 3–28. A *TAM authorization scheme* consists of a finite set of rights R, a finite set of types T, and a finite collection of commands. A *TAM system* is specified by a TAM authorization scheme and an initial state.

Definition 3–29. The *Monotonic Typed Access Matrix (MTAM) Model* is the TAM Model without the **delete**, **destroy subject**, and **destroy object** primitive operations.

Definition 3–30. Let $\alpha(x_1 : t_1, \ldots, x_k : t_k)$ be a creating command, where $x_1, \ldots, x_k \in O$ and $\tau(x_1) = t_1, \ldots, \tau(x_k) = t_k$. Then t_i is a child type in $\alpha(x_1 : t_1, \ldots, x_k : t_k)$ if any of **create subject** x_i **of type** t_i or **create object** x_i **of type** t_i occurs in the body of $\alpha(x_1 : t_1, \ldots, x_k : t_k)$. Otherwise, t_i is a parent type in $\alpha(x_1 : t_1, \ldots, x_k : t_k)$.

From this, we can define the notion of acyclic creations.

Definition 3–31. The *creation graph* of an MTAM scheme is a directed graph with vertex set V and an edge from $u \in V$ to $v \in V$ if and only if there is a creating command in which u is a parent type and v is a child type. If the creation graph is acyclic, the MTAM system is said to be *acyclic*; otherwise, the MTAM system is said to be *cyclic*.

As an example, consider the following command, where s and p are subjects and f is an object:

```
command cry•havoc(s:u, p:u, f:v, q:w)
        create subject p of type u;
        create object f of type v;
        enter own into a[s, p];
        enter r into a[q, p];
        enter own into a[p, f];
        enter r into a[p, f];
        enter w into a[p, f];
end
```

Here, u and v are child types and u and w are parent types. Note that u is both a parent type and a child type. The creation graph corresponding to the MTAM scheme with the single command *cry•havoc* has the edges (u, u), (u, w), (v, u), and (v, w). Thus, this MTAM scheme is cyclic. Were the **create subject** p **of type** u deleted from the command, however, u would no longer be a child type, and the resulting MTAM scheme would be acyclic.

Sandhu has proven the following theorem.

Theorem 3.21.   [1660] Safety is decidable for systems with acyclic MTAM schemes.

The proof is similar in spirit to the proof of Theorem 3.16.

Furthermore, because MTAM subsumes monotonic mono-operational HRU systems, a complexity result follows automatically:

Theorem 3.22.   [1660] Safety is NP-hard for systems with acyclic MTAM schemes.

However, Sandhu has also developed a surprising result. If all MTAM commands are limited to three parameters, the resulting model (called "ternary MTAM") is equivalent in expressive power to MTAM. Further:

Theorem 3.23.   [1660] Safety for the acyclic ternary MTAM model is decidable in time polynomial in the size of the initial access control matrix.

3.6   Comparing Security Properties of Models

A more general question is whether two models have the same security properties. So far, the safety question has been the security property of interest. But in many cases, other questions such as bounds on determining safety or the notion of confinement, in which one determines what actions a specific subject can take (see Chapter 18), are also of interest. The previous section showed ESPM is more expressive than SPM; but can one express in ESPM all the security properties that SPM can express? That states correspond does not ensure they have the same security properties. The specific transformation used to compare the models does.

This section presents a general theory of comparison. We then use it to compare TAM and a variant, the Augmented Typed Matrix Model.

3.6.1   Comparing Schemes and Security Properties

Tripunitara and Li [1889] examined the question of whether two access control models have the same security properties. They view access requests as *queries* that ask whether a subject has the right to perform an action on an object. To do this, we examine an alternate definition of "scheme."

> **Definition 3–32.** Let Σ be a set of states, Q a set of queries, $e : \Sigma \times Q \to$ *{true, false}* the *entailment relation*, and T a set of state transition rules. Then the system (Σ, Q, e, T) is an *access control scheme*.

Suppose a subject requests access to an object. This request corresponds to a query $q \in Q$. If the access is allowed in the state $\sigma \in \Sigma$, then $e(\sigma, q) =$ *true*; otherwise, $e(\sigma, q) =$ *false*. As before, $\tau \in T$ is a relation defining a state transition, and we would write τ changing the system from state $\sigma_0 \in \Sigma$ to $\sigma_1 \in \Sigma$ as $\sigma_0 \vdash \sigma_1$. However, in this type of analysis, we want to know if τ *allows* the state to change from σ_0 to σ_1; if so, we write $\sigma_0 \mapsto_\tau \sigma_1$ to emphasize we are looking at *permissions* and not the results of the transition. Similarly, if τ allows a sequence of changes that would take the system from state σ_0 to $\sigma_n \in \Sigma$, then we write $\sigma_0 \mapsto_\tau^* \sigma_n$, and we say σ_n is τ-reachable from σ_0.

EXAMPLE: The Take-Grant Protection Model is an example of an access control scheme. In it:

- Σ is the set of all possible protection graphs.
- Q is the set of queries {*can•share*(α, v_1, v_2, G_0) | $\alpha \in R$, $v_1, v_2 \in G_0$}, where v_1 and v_2 are vertices and G_0 the initial protection graph.
- e is defined as $e(\sigma_0, q) =$ *true* if q holds and $e(\sigma_0, q) =$ *false* otherwise.
- T is the set composed of sequences of take, grant, create, and remove rules.

We use this structure to frame the question of whether a scheme has a particular security property:

> **Definition 3–33.** Let (Σ, Q, e, T) be an access control scheme. Then a *security analysis instance* is a tuple (σ, q, τ, Π), where $\sigma \in \Sigma$, $q \in Q$, $\tau \in T$, and Π is one of the quantifiers $\forall$ or $\exists$.

If Π is $\exists$, then the security analysis instance is called *existential*, and asks whether there exists a state σ' such that $\sigma \mapsto_\tau^* \sigma'$ and $e(\sigma', q) = true$. Similarly, if Π is $\forall$, then the security analysis instance is called *universal*, and asks whether for every state σ' such that $\sigma \mapsto_\tau^* \sigma'$, $e(\sigma', q) = true$.

EXAMPLE: The safety question is an example of a security analysis instance. In the Take-Grant Protection Model, the state σ_0 is G_0, the query q is *can•share*(r, **x**, **y**, G_0), the state transition τ is a sequence of take-grant rules, and Π is the existential quantifier $\exists$. Then the security analysis instance examines whether **x** has r rights over **y** in the graph with initial state G_0.

The next definition generalizes this to a number of queries.

Definition 3–34. Let (Σ, Q, e, T) be an access control scheme. Then a *compositional security analysis instance* is a tuple $(\sigma, \phi, \tau, \Pi)$, where σ, τ, and Π are as in Definition 3–33, and ϕ is a propositional logic formula of queries drawn from Q.

The comparison of two models requires that one be mapped onto another.

Definition 3–35. Let $A = (\Sigma^A, Q^A, e^A, T^A)$ and $B = (\Sigma^B, Q^B, e^B, T^B)$ be two access control schemes. A *mapping* from A to B is a function $f : (\Sigma^A \times T^A) \cup Q^A \to (\Sigma^B \times T^B) \cup Q^B$.

The idea here is that each query in A corresponds to a query in B, and each state and state transition pair in A corresponds to a state and state transition pair in B. We now formalize the notion of preserving security properties in two ways, first for security analysis instances and then for compositional security analysis instances.

Definition 3–36. Let f be a mapping from A to B. The *image of a security analysis instance* $(\sigma^A, q^A, \tau^A, \Pi)$ *under* f is $(\sigma^B, q^B, \tau^B, \Pi)$, where $f((\sigma^A, \tau^A)) = (\sigma^B, \tau^B)$ and $f(q^A) = q^B$. The mapping f is *security-preserving* if every security analysis instance in A is true if and only if its image is true.

This definition says that given a security instance analysis in B and a mapping f from A to B, one can solve the security analysis instance in A. However, because of the focus on individual queries, it does not cover composition of queries. The next definition does so. For notational convenience, let $f(\phi^A) = \phi^B$ be shorthand for replacing every query q^A in ϕ^A with $f(q^B)$.

Definition 3–37. Let f be a mapping from A to B. The *image of a compositional security analysis instance* $(\sigma^A, \phi^A, \tau^A, \Pi)$ *under* f is $(\sigma^B, \phi^B, \tau^B, \Pi)$, where $f((\sigma^A, \tau^A)) = (\sigma^B, \tau^B)$ and $f(\phi^A) = \phi^B$. The mapping f is *strongly security-preserving* if every compositional security analysis instance in A is true if and only if its image is true.

Our interest is in mappings that preserve security properties. Consider two models with a map between them. Security properties deal with answers to queries about states and transitions; so, given two corresponding states and two corresponding sequences of state transitions, corresponding queries must give the same answer. The next definition formalizes this notion.

Definition 3–38. Let $A = (\Sigma^A, Q^A, e^A, T^A)$ and $B = (\Sigma^B, Q^B, e^B, T^B)$ be two access control schemes and let f be a mapping from A to B. The states σ^A and σ^B are *equivalent under the mapping f* when $e^A(\sigma^A, q^A) = e^B(\sigma^B, q^B)$. The mapping f is a *state-matching reduction* if, for every $\sigma^A \in \Sigma^A$ and $\tau^A \in T^A$, $(\sigma^B, \tau^B) = f((\sigma^A, \tau^A))$ has the following properties:

1. For every state σ'^A in scheme A such that $\sigma^A \mapsto_\tau^* \sigma'^A$, there is a state σ'^B in scheme B such that $\sigma^B \mapsto_\tau^* \sigma'^B$, and σ'^A and σ'^B are equivalent under the mapping f.

2. For every state σ'^B in scheme B such that $\sigma^B \mapsto_\tau^* \sigma'^B$, there is a state σ'^A in scheme A such that $\sigma^A \mapsto_\tau^* \sigma'^A$, and σ'^A and σ'^B are equivalent under the mapping f.

This definition says that, for every sequence of states and transitions in model A, there exists a corresponding sequence of states and transitions in B, and *vice versa*. The sequences need not be the same number of steps, and indeed the intermediate states and transitions need not correspond. But the initial and terminal states must be equivalent. In other words, for every reachable state in one model, a matching state in the other model gives the same answer for every query—as we desire.

We now show this definition precisely characterizes maps that are strongly security-preserving.

Theorem 3.24. [1889] A mapping f from scheme A to scheme B is strongly security-preserving if and only if f is a state-matching reduction.

Proof ($\Rightarrow$) Let f be a state-matching reduction from A to B. Let $(\sigma^A, \phi^A, \tau^A, \Pi)$ be a compositional security analysis instance in A and $(\sigma^B, \phi^B, \tau^B, \Pi)$ be a compositional security analysis instance in B. We must show that $(\sigma^A, \phi^A, \tau^A, \Pi)$ is true if and only if $(\sigma^B, \phi^B, \tau^B, \Pi)$ is true.

We first consider existential compositional security analysis, that is, where Π is $\exists$. Assume there is a τ^A-reachable state σ'^A from σ^A in which ϕ^A

is true. By the first property of Definition 3–38, there exists a state σ'^B that corresponds to σ'^A in which ϕ^B holds. This means that $(\sigma^B, \phi^B, \tau^B, \Pi)$ is true. A similar argument, but using the second property in Definition 3–38 rather than the first, shows that if there is a τ^B-reachable state σ'^B from σ^B in which ϕ^B is true, then $(\sigma^A, \phi^A, \tau^A, \Pi)$ is true.

Next, consider universal compositional security analysis, that is, where Π is $\forall$. Assume there is a τ^A-reachable state σ'^A from σ^A in which ϕ^A is false. By the first property of Definition 3–38, there exists a state σ'^B that corresponds to σ'^A in which ϕ^B is also false. This means that $(\sigma^B, \phi^B, \tau^B, \Pi)$ is false. Similarly, by the second property of Definition 3–38, if a compositional security instance in B is false, the corresponding instance in A is false.

($\Leftarrow$) Let f be a mapping from A to B that is not a state-matching reduction. Then there are $\sigma^A \in \Sigma^A$ and $\tau^A \in T^A$ such that $f((\sigma^A, \tau^A)) = (\sigma^B, \tau^B)$ that violate at least one of the properties in Definition 3–38.

Assume the first does not hold, and let σ^A and σ^B be corresponding states in instances in A and B, respectively. There is a τ^A-reachable state σ'^A from σ^A such that no state τ^B-reachable from σ^B is equivalent to σ'^B. We now generate a query ϕ^A, and corresponding query ϕ^B, for which the existential compositional security analysis instance in A is true but in B is false. To construct ϕ^A, begin with ϕ^A being empty. Then, examine each query q^A in Q^A. If $e(\sigma'^A, q^A)$ is true, conjoin q^A to ϕ^A. If not, conjoin $\neg q^A$ to ϕ^A. From this construction, $e(\sigma'^A, \phi^A)$ is true; but for $\phi^B = f(\phi^A)$ and all states σ'^B τ^B-reachable from σ^B, $e(\sigma'^B, \phi^B)$ is false. Thus by Definition 3–37, f is not strongly security-preserving.

A similar argument shows that, when the second does not hold, f is not strongly security-preserving.

We can now define "expressive power" in terms of state-matching reductions.

Definition 3–39. If access control model MA has a scheme that cannot be mapped into a scheme in access control model MB using a state-matching reduction, then model MB is *less expressive than* model MA. If every scheme in model MA can be mapped into a scheme in model MB using a state-matching reduction, then model MB is *as expressive as* model MA. If MA is as expressive as MB, and MB is as expressive as MA, the models are *equivalent*.

Contrast this with Definition 3–25, which defines simulation in monotonic schemes. Definition 3–39 does not assume monotonicity; in the language of state-matching reductions, a query may initially be true, but then at a later time be false. This is not possible in a monotonic scheme.

Simulation may be defined in other ways as well. For example, Sandhu and Ganta [1662] use a definition that requires the simulating model to grant access when the simulated model grants access, but the simulating model need not deny access when the simulated model does. This is suitable for safety analysis, but does not preserve other security properties.

It is to those more general policies we now turn.

3.6.2 Augmented Typed Access Matrix Model

The Augmented Typed Access Matrix Model (ATAM) [43] adds the ability to test for the *absence* of rights to TAM. As an example, consider the following command, where s is a subject and f is an object:

```
command add•right(s:u, f:v)
        if own in a[s,f] and r not in a[s,f]
        then
                    enter r into a[s,f]
end
```

This adds the right for s to $r f$ if s owns f and does not have the r right over f. Under ATAM, the expression "r **not in** $a[s,f]$" is true if $r \notin a[s,f]$. But such a test is disallowed by the semantics of TAM.

An interesting question is how the augmentation of TAM affects its use in answering the safety question. Sandhu and Gupta demonstrate that TAM and ATAM are equivalent in that sense by developing a mapping from ATAM to TAM [1662]. But a more general question, that of whether there is a mapping that will preserve security properties, shows a difference—there is no mapping from ATAM to TAM that is strongly security-preserving.

Consider TAM as an access control model. Let S, O, R, and T be the set of subjects, objects, rights, and types, respectively, and let S_σ, O_σ, R_σ, T_σ, and a_σ be the subjects, objects, rights, types, and access control matrix for state σ, respectively. The function $t : S_\sigma \cup O_\sigma \rightarrow T_\sigma$ gives the type of each subject or object in state σ. Then, a state $\sigma \in \Sigma$ is defined as $\sigma = (S_\sigma, O_\sigma, a_\sigma, R_\sigma, T_\sigma, t)$. A state transition rule is simply a command, so T is the set of possible commands. The TAM model allows queries of the form "is $r \in a[s,o]$?" and for state $\sigma \in \Sigma$, $e(\sigma, r \in a[s,o]) = true$ if and only if all of $s \in S_\sigma$, $o \in O_\sigma$, $r \in R_\sigma$, and $r \in a_\sigma[s,o]$ are true.

The access control model of ATAM is the same as that of TAM, except that an additional type of query is allowed. ATAM also allows queries of the form "is $r \notin a[s,o]$?" and the function $e(\sigma, r \notin a[s,o]) = true$ is defined appropriately.

Theorem 3.25. [1889] A state-matching reduction from ATAM to TAM does not exist.

Proof By contradiction. Assume f is a state-matching reduction from ATAM to TAM. We consider a simple ATAM scheme. The initial state σ_0 is empty (no subjects or objects). All entities are of the same type t, and there is only one right r. The state transition rule consists of two commands. The first creates a subject:

```
command make•subj(s:t)
        create subject s of type t;
end
```

The second adds a right to an access control matrix entry:

```
command add•right(x:t, y:t)
        enter r into a[x,y];
end
```

Queries in ATAM take one of two forms. Write $q_{i,j} = r \in a[s_i, s_j]$ for a query about whether an element of the access control matrix contains the right r, and $\widehat{q_{i,j}} = r \notin a[s_i, s_j]$ for a query about whether a right r is not in the element of the access control matrix.

For convenience, we use a superscript T to designate components of the TAM system. So, for example, the initial state of the TAM system is written $\sigma_0^T = f(\sigma_0)$, and the state transition rule is written $\tau^T = f(\tau)$.

Two observations will prove useful. First, by Definition 3–38, how f maps queries does not depend on the initial state or state transitions of a model. Second, for two distinct queries p and q in ATAM, if $p \neq q$ in ATAM, then $p^T \neq q^T$ in TAM.

Consider the corresponding command schema τ^T in TAM. As commands execute, they can change the value of a query. A query in TAM is of the form $r \in a[x, y]$. We can determine an upper bound m on the number of queries that such a command can change the value of; in the worst case, simply count the number of **enter** primitive operations in each command, and take m to be the maximum. Note m does not depend on the query, but on σ^T and τ^T. Choose some $n > m$.

Consider the state σ_k in ATAM such that $\sigma_0 \mapsto_\tau^* \sigma_k$ and $e(\sigma_k, \neg q_{1,1} \wedge \widehat{q_{1,1}} \wedge \cdots \wedge \neg q_{n,n} \wedge \widehat{q_{n,n}}) = true$. This means that $e(\sigma_k, q_{i,j}) = false$ and $e(\sigma_k, \widehat{q_{i,j}}) = true$ for all i,j such that $1 \leq i \leq n$ and $1 \leq j \leq n$. In other words, no query that asks if a right r is in an access control matrix element is true, and all queries that ask if a right r is not in an access control element are true. To construct such a state from σ_0, simply execute the *make•subj* command n times, once for each of $s_1, \ldots, s_n$.

As f is a state-matching reduction, there is a state σ_k^T in TAM that causes the corresponding queries to be answered in the same way. Consider the sequence of state transitions $\sigma_0^T \mapsto_{\tau T} \sigma_1^T \mapsto_{\tau T} \ldots \mapsto_{\tau T}^* \sigma_k^T$. Choose the first state σ_C^T that satisfies $e(\sigma_C^T, q_{i,j}^T \vee \widehat{q_{i,j}}^T) = true$ for all i, j such that $1 \leq i \leq n$ and $1 \leq j \leq n$. Such a state exists, as σ_k^T is such a state.

As σ_0^T is *not* such a state, there also exists a state σ_{C-1}^T for which $e(\sigma_{C-1}^T, \neg q_{v,w}^T \wedge \neg \widehat{q_{v,w}}^T) = true$, where $1 \leq v \leq n$ and $1 \leq w \leq n$. Now, a state σ in ATAM for which $e(\sigma, \neg q_{v,w}^T \wedge \neg \widehat{q_{v,w}}^T) = true$ is one in which either s_v or s_w (or both) do not exist. Thus, in that state, one of the following two compositional queries also holds:

1. $Q_1 = \neg q_{v,1} \wedge \neg \widehat{q_{v,1}} \wedge \neg q_{v,2} \wedge \neg \widehat{q_{v,2}} \wedge \ldots \wedge \neg q_{v,n} \wedge \neg \widehat{q_{v,n}} \wedge \neg q_{1,v} \wedge \neg \widehat{q_{1,v}} \wedge \neg q_{2,v} \wedge \neg \widehat{q_{2,v}} \wedge \ldots \wedge \neg q_{n,v} \wedge \neg \widehat{q_{n,v}}$
2. $Q_2 = \neg q_{w,1} \wedge \neg \widehat{q_{w,1}} \wedge \neg q_{w,2} \wedge \neg \widehat{q_{w,2}} \wedge \ldots \wedge \neg q_{w,n} \wedge \neg \widehat{q_{w,n}} \wedge \neg q_{1,w} \wedge \neg \widehat{q_{1,w}} \wedge \neg q_{2,w} \wedge \neg \widehat{q_{2,w}} \wedge \ldots \wedge \neg q_{n,w} \wedge \neg \widehat{q_{n,w}}$

Therefore, in TAM, $e(\sigma_{C-1}^T, Q_1^T \vee Q_2^T) = true$.

Now, consider what happens in the state transition from σ_{C-1}^T to σ_C^T. The command must change the values of at least n queries in Q_1^T or Q_2^T from false to true. But we showed above that each command can change at most m queries from false to true, and $m < n$.

Thus, no such state-matching reduction exists.

This shows that ATAM can express security properties that TAM cannot. Therefore, ATAM is more expressive than TAM, in the sense of Definition 3–39.

3.7   Summary

The safety problem is a rich problem that has led to the development of several models and analysis techniques. Some of these models are useful in other contexts. These models provide insights into the boundary line between decidability and undecidability, which speaks to the degree of generality of analysis. Ultimately, however, security (the analogue of safety) is analyzed for a system or for a class of systems, and the models help us understand when such analysis is tractable and when it is not.

The notions of "expressiveness" deal both with the safety question, and more generally with security properties, of models. This notion allows us to compare the models to determine which models encompass other models, and to compare the security properties of models.

3.8   Research Issues

The critical research issue is the characterization of the class of models for which the safety question is decidable. The SRM results state sufficiency but not necessity. A set of characteristics that are both necessary and sufficient would show exactly what causes the safety problem to become undecidable, which is an open issue.

Related questions involve the expressive power of the various models. The models allow policies to be expressed more succinctly than in the access control matrix model. Can these more sophisticated models express the same set of policies that the access control matrix model can express? Are there other models that are easy to work with yet allow all protection states of interest to be expressed?

3.9   Further Reading

Tripunitara and Li [1888, 1890] discuss different meanings of "safety" and critique the HRU result. Fischer and Kühnhauser [682] discuss efficiently checking safety of an HRU model.

Soshi, Maekawa, and Okamoto [1792] present the Dynamic-Typed Access Matrix Model, which is essentially TAM except that the types of objects can change dynamically. They show that, under certain restrictions, the safety problem in this model is decidable; with additional restrictions, it becomes NP-hard. Zhang, Li, and Nalla [2092] examine the safety question for an access control matrix model that associates attributes with objects.

Biskup [234] presents some variants on the Take-Grant Protection Model. Shahriari and Jalili [1721] apply a variant of the Take-Grant Protection Model to analyze network vulnerabilities. Conrad, Alves-Foss, and Lee [448] embed uncertainty in the application of Take-Grant by using a Monte Carlo simulation to model the relevant parameters.

Budd [309] analyzes safety properties of grammatical protection schemes, which he and Lipton defined earlier [1196]. Motwani, Panigraphy, Saraswat, and Venkatasubramanian [1389] generalize these schemes.

Sandhu has presented interesting work on the representation of models, and has unified many of them with his transform model [1652, 1663, 1664].

Amthor, Kühnhauser, and Pölck [48] examine heuristics for analyzing safety problems, presenting a heuristic algorithm to analyze safety. Kleiner and Newcomb [1067] develop an alternate model of access control that focuses on the commands rather than the entities, and use a first-order temporal logic to study decidability and other safety properties of that model. Koch, Mancini, and Parisi-Presicce [1083] use a graphical representation of security policies to study conditions under which safety of those policies is decidable.

Several extensions to the access control matrix model have been studied. Zhang and Li [2092] study safety of the attribute-based access control matrix model, in which each entity is augmented with metadata called attributes. Soshi, Maekawa, and Okamoto [1792] modify TAM to allow the type of an entity to change dynamically, and develop conditions under which safety in this Dynamic Typed Access Matrix (DTAM) model is decidable.

Amthor, Kühnhauser, and Pölck [47] map SELinux security policy mechanisms onto the HRU model, providing a way to analyze safety and other properties of that system. Li and Tripunitara [1166] examine the decidability of safety in an alternate model of access control, the Graham-Denning model [805].

3.10 Exercises

1. The proof of Theorem 3.1 states the following: Suppose two subjects s_1 and s_2 are created and the rights in $A[s_1, o_1]$ and $A[s_2, o_2]$ are tested. The same test for $A[s_1, o_1]$ and $A[s_1, o_2] = A[s_1, o_2] \cup A[s_2, o_2]$ will produce the same result. Justify this statement. Would it be true if one could test for the absence of rights as well as for the presence of rights?

2. The proof of Theorem 3.1 states that we can omit the **delete** and **destroy** commands as they do not affect the ability of a right to leak when no command can test for the absence of rights. Justify this statement. If such tests were allowed, would **delete** and **destroy** commands affect the ability of a right to leak?

3. Suppose "leaked" were defined to mean adding a generic right r to an element of the access control matrix that does not contain it. This means that a right leaks if the right was present initially, then deleted, and then added back. Note the difference between this definition and Definition 3–1, in which generic right r is said to be leaked when it is added to an element of the access control matrix that did not contain r in the initial state. This differs from Definition 3–1 because if $A[s, o]$ contains r in the initial state, a later transition deletes r from that element, and a succeeding transition enters r in $A[s, o]$, then the right is said to leak, whereas under Definition 3–1, it is not leaked.

   a. Is it true that the **delete** and **destroy** commands do not affect the ability of a right to leak? Why or why not?

   Now we consider how to modify the proof to show that Theorem 3.1 still holds. As in the proof of the theorem, we can identify each command by the type of primitive operation it invokes. Consider the minimal length sequence of commands $c_1, \ldots, c_k$ needed to leak the right r from the system with initial state σ_0. Assume the last command c_k leaks r into $A[s_i, o_i]$, and look at the first **create** command in the sequence. Five cases exist, and if in all cases k is bounded, the claim holds. The following are the cases:

b. Suppose there is no such **create** command. Show that $k \leq n|S_0||O_0|$.

c. Suppose the command is **create subject** s, where $s \in S_0$. Show that $k \leq n|S_0||O_0| + 2$.

d. Suppose the command is **create subject** s, where $s \notin S_0$. Show that $k \leq n(|S_0| + 1)(|O_0| + 1) + 2$.

e. Suppose the command is **create object** o, where $o \in O_0$. Show that $k \leq n(|S_0| + 1)(|O_0| + 1) + 4$.

f. Suppose the command is **create object** o, where $o \notin O_0$. Show $k \leq n(|S_0| + 1)(|O_0| + 2) + 4$.

From [1890].

4. Assume "leaked" is defined as in Exercise 3. How does this affect the proof of Theorem 3.2?

5. Someone asks, "Since the Harrison-Ruzzo-Ullman result says that the security question is undecidable, why do we waste our time trying to figure out how secure the UNIX operating system is?" Please give an answer justifying the analysis of the security of the UNIX system (or any system, for that matter) in light of the HRU result.

6. Prove Theorem 3.3. (*Hint*: Use a diagonalization argument to test each system as the set of protection systems is enumerated. Whenever a protection system leaks a right, add it to the list of unsafe protection systems.)

7. Prove or disprove: The claim of Lemma 3.1 holds when **x** is an object.

8. Prove Lemma 3.2.

9. Prove or give a counterexample: The predicate *can•share*$(\alpha, \mathbf{x}, \mathbf{y}, G_0)$ is true if and only if there is an edge from **x** to **y** in G_0 labeled α, or if the following hold simultaneously.

a. There is a vertex with an **s**-to-**y** edge labeled α.

b. There is a subject vertex $\mathbf{x}'$ such that $\mathbf{x}' = \mathbf{x}$ or $\mathbf{x}'$ initially spans to **x**.

c. There is a subject vertex $\mathbf{x}'$ such that $\mathbf{s}' = \mathbf{s}$ or $\mathbf{s}'$ terminally spans to **s**.

d. There is a sequence of subjects $\mathbf{x}_1, \ldots, \mathbf{x}_n$ with $\mathbf{x}_1 = \mathbf{x}'$, $\mathbf{x}_n = \mathbf{s}'$, and $\mathbf{x}_i$ and $\mathbf{x}_{i+1}$ $(1 \leq i < n)$ being connected by an edge labeled t, an edge labeled g, or a bridge.

10. Reverse the edge between **d** and **e** in Figure 3–4(a) so there is an edge labeled g from **d** to **e**. Is *can•share*$(r, \mathbf{x}, \mathbf{z}, G_0)$ still true? If so, please show a witness; if not, please prove it does not hold.

11. The Take-Grant Protection Model provides two rights, *take* and *grant*, that enable the transfer of other rights. SPM's *demand* right, in many ways

analogous to *take*, was shown to be unnecessary. Could *take* similarly be dropped from the Take-Grant Protection Model?

12. The discussion of acyclic creates imposes constraints on the types of created subjects but not on the types of created objects. Why not?

13. Consider the construction of the three-parent joint creation operation from the two-parent joint creation operation shown in Section 3.5.2. In [44], $cr_C(s, c) = c/R_3$ and $link_2(\mathbf{S}, \mathbf{A}_3) = \mathbf{A}_3/t \in dom(\mathbf{S})$. Why is this not sufficient to derive the three-parent joint creation operation from the two-parent joint creation operation?

14. The simulation of three-parent creation by two-parent creation using the Ammann, Lipton, and Sandhu scheme mimics the simulation using SPM. Present a simpler, more direct simulation using the Ammann, Lipton, and Sandhu scheme that requires only five operations.

15. In Theorem 3.25, show that for two distinct queries p and q in ATAM, if $p \neq q$ in ATAM, then $p^T \neq q^T$ in TAM. (*Hint*: Show that, if this is false, then there is a state σ such that $\sigma_0 \mapsto^*_\tau \sigma$ and $e(\sigma, p \wedge \neg q) = true$.)

Part III

Policy

S ecurity analysts organize the needs of a site in order to define a security policy. From this policy, analysts develop and implement mechanisms for enforcing the policy. The mechanisms may be procedural, technical, or physical. Part III describes the notion of policy and how it can be expressed and formalized, and how different types of policies affect accesses.

Chapter 4, "Security Policies," presents the abstract notion of a security policy and some ways to represent policies. Policy languages abstract some of the common elements of policies and allow expression of policies both at abstract levels and in terms of the properties of the particular systems under consideration.

Chapter 5, "Confidentiality Policies," discusses policies designed primarily for confidentiality. Many government organizations, especially the military, must keep information secret, as described by these policies. Chapter 5 focuses on the Bell-LaPadula security policy.

Chapter 6, "Integrity Policies," discusses policies designed primarily for integrity. Banks, insurance companies, and other commercial and industrial firms worry more about data and programs being corrupted than about them being read, and use these policies.

Chapter 7, "Availability Policies," considers policies that govern the ability to access resources, and the quality of service that defines "access." With the growth of the Internet and the sharing of systems on a wide scale, especially as epitomized by the idea of "cloud computing," the ability to access resources as intended is critical for computing.

Chapter 8, "Hybrid Policies," presents policies that are hybrids of confidentiality and integrity security policies. One comes from the world of stock brokerage, and another from medical systems. Other types of policy models discussed here are originator controlled models and role-based models.

Chapter 9, "Noninterference and Policy Composition," discusses the noninterference and nondeducibility models of security policies and the composition of security policies in general.

Chapter 4
Security Policies

A security policy defines "secure" for a system or a set of systems. Security policies can be informal or highly mathematical in nature. After defining a security policy precisely, we expand on the nature of "trust" and its relationship to security policies. We also discuss different types of policy models.

4.1   The Nature of Security Policies

Consider a computer system to be a finite-state automaton with a set of transition functions that change state. Then:

Definition 4–1. A *security policy* is a statement that partitions the states of the system into a set of *authorized*, or *secure*, states and a set of *unauthorized*, or *nonsecure*, states.

A security policy sets the context in which we can define a secure system. What is secure under one policy may not be secure under a different policy. More precisely:

Definition 4–2. A *secure system* is a system that starts in an authorized state and cannot enter an unauthorized state.

Consider the finite-state machine in Figure 4–1. It consists of four states and five transitions. The security policy partitions the states into a set of authorized states $A = \{s_1, s_2\}$ and a set of unauthorized states $UA = \{s_3, s_4\}$. This system

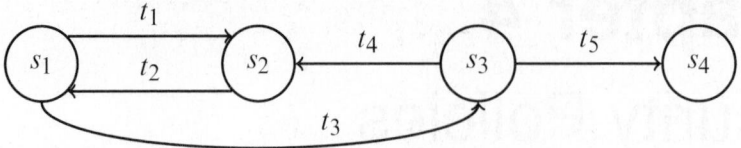

Figure 4–1   A simple finite-state machine.

is not secure, because regardless of which authorized state it starts in, it can enter an unauthorized state. However, if the edge from s_1 to s_3 were not present, the system would be secure, because it could not enter an unauthorized state from an authorized state.

> **Definition 4–3.** A *breach of security* occurs when a system enters an unauthorized state.

We informally discussed the three basic properties relevant to security in Section 1.1. We now define them precisely.

> **Definition 4–4.** Let X be a set of entities and let I be some information. Then I has the property of *confidentiality* with respect to X if no member of X can obtain information about I.

Confidentiality implies that information must not be disclosed to some set of entities. It may be disclosed to others. The membership of set X is often implicit—for example, when we speak of a document that is confidential. Some entity has access to the document. All entities not authorized to have such access make up the set X.

> **Definition 4–5.** Let X be a set of entities and let I be some information or a resource. Then I has the property of *integrity* with respect to X if all members of X trust I.

This definition is deceptively simple. In addition to trusting the information itself, the members of X also trust that the conveyance and storage of I do not change the information or its trustworthiness (this aspect is sometimes called *data integrity*). If I is information about the origin of something, or about an identity, the members of X trust that the information is correct and unchanged (this aspect is sometimes called *origin integrity* or, more commonly, *authentication*). Also, I may be a resource rather than information. In that case, integrity means that the resource functions correctly (meeting its specifications). This aspect is called *assurance* and will be discussed in Part VI, "Assurance." As with confidentiality, the membership of X is often implicit.

Definition 4–6. Let X be a set of entities and let I be a resource. Then I has the property of *availability* with respect to X if all members of X can access I.

The exact definition of "access" in Definition 4–6 varies depending on the needs of the members of X, the nature of the resource, and the use to which the resource is put. If a book-selling server takes up to 1 hour to service a request to purchase a book, that may meet the client's requirements for "availability." If a server of medical information takes up to 1 hour to service a request for information regarding an allergy to an anesthetic, that will not meet an emergency room's requirements for "availability."

A security policy considers all relevant aspects of confidentiality, integrity, and availability. With respect to confidentiality, it identifies those states in which information leaks to those not authorized to receive it. This includes the leakage of rights and the illicit transmission of information without leakage of rights, called *information flow*. Also, the policy must handle changes of authorization, so it includes a temporal element. For example, a contractor working for a company may be authorized to access proprietary information during the lifetime of a nondisclosure agreement, but when that nondisclosure agreement expires, the contractor can no longer access that information. This aspect of the security policy is often called a *confidentiality policy*.

With respect to integrity, a security policy identifies authorized ways in which information may be altered and entities authorized to alter it. Authorization may derive from a variety of relationships, and external influences may constrain it; for example, in many transactions, a principle called *separation of duties* forbids an entity from completing the transaction on its own. Those parts of the security policy that describe the conditions and manner in which data can be altered are called the *integrity policy*.

With respect to availability, a security policy describes what services must be provided. It may present parameters within which the services will be accessible—for example, that a browser may download web pages but not Java applets. It may require a level of service—for example, that a server will provide authentication data within 1 minute of the request being made. This relates directly to issues of quality of service.

The statement of a security policy may formally state the desired properties of the system. If the system is to be provably secure, the formal statement will allow the designers and implementers to prove that those desired properties hold. If a formal proof is unnecessary or infeasible, analysts can test that the desired properties hold for some set of inputs. Later chapters will discuss both these topics in detail.

In practice, a less formal type of security policy defines the set of authorized states. Typically, the security policy assumes that the reader understands the context in which the policy is issued—in particular, the laws, organizational policies, and other environmental factors. The security policy then describes conduct, actions, and authorizations defining "authorized users" and "authorized use."

EXAMPLE: A university disallows cheating, which is defined to include copying another student's homework assignment (with or without permission). A computer science class requires the students to do their homework on the department's computer. One student notices that a second student has not read-protected the file containing her homework and copies it. Has either student (or have both students) breached security?

The second student has not, despite her failure to protect her homework. The security policy requires no action to prevent files from being read. Although she may have been too trusting, the policy does not ban this; hence, the second student has not breached security.

The first student has breached security. The security policy disallows the copying of homework, and the student has done exactly that. Whether the security policy specifically states that "files containing homework shall not be copied" or simply says that "users are bound by the rules of the university" is irrelevant; in the latter case, one of those rules bans cheating. If the security policy is silent on such matters, the most reasonable interpretation is that the policy disallows actions that the university disallows, because the computer science department is part of the university.

The retort that the first user could copy the files, and therefore the action is allowed, confuses *mechanism* with *policy*. The distinction is sharp:

Definition 4–7. A *security mechanism* is an entity or procedure that enforces some part of the security policy.

EXAMPLE: In the preceding example, the policy is the statement that no student may copy another student's homework. One mechanism is the file access controls; if the second student had set permissions to prevent the first student from reading the file containing her homework, the first student could not have copied that file.

EXAMPLE: Another site's security policy states that information relating to a particular product is proprietary and is not to leave the control of the company. The company stores its backup tapes in a vault in the town's bank (this is common practice in case the computer installation is completely destroyed). The company must ensure that only authorized employees have access to the backup tapes even when the tapes are stored off-site; hence, the bank's controls on access to the vault, and the procedures used to transport the tapes to and from the bank, are considered security mechanisms. Note that these mechanisms are not technical controls built into the computer. Procedural, or operational, controls also can be security mechanisms.

Security policies are often implicit rather than explicit. This causes confusion, especially when the policy is defined in terms of the mechanisms. This definition may be ambiguous—for example, if some mechanisms prevent a specific action and others allow it. Such policies lead to confusion, and sites should avoid them.

EXAMPLE: The UNIX operating system, initially developed for a small research group, had mechanisms sufficient to prevent users from accidentally damaging one another's files; for example, the user *ken* could not delete the user *dmr*'s files (unless *dmr* had set the files and the containing directories to allow this). The implied security policy for this friendly environment was "do not delete or corrupt another's files, and any file not protected may be read."

When the UNIX operating system moved into academic institutions and commercial and government environments, the previous security policy became inadequate; for example, some files had to be protected from individual users (rather than from groups of users). Not surprisingly, the security mechanisms were inadequate for those environments.

The difference between a policy and an abstract description of that policy is crucial to the analysis that follows.

Definition 4–8. A *policy model* is a model that represents a particular policy or class of policies.

A model abstracts details relevant for analysis. Analyses rarely discuss particular policies; they usually focus on *specific characteristics* of policies, because many policies exhibit these characteristics, and the more policies with those characteristics, the more useful the analysis. By the HRU result (see Theorem 3.2), no single nontrivial analysis can cover all policies, but restricting the class of security policies sufficiently allows meaningful analysis of that class of policies.

4.2   Types of Security Policies

Each site has its own requirements for the levels of confidentiality, integrity, and availability, and the site policy states these needs for that particular site.

Definition 4–9. A *military security policy* (also called a *governmental security policy*) is a security policy developed primarily to provide confidentiality.

The name comes from the military's need to keep some information secret, such as the date that a troop ship will sail. Although integrity and availability are important, organizations using this class of policies can overcome the loss of either—for example, by using orders not sent through a computer network. But the compromise of confidentiality would be catastrophic, because an opponent would be able to plan countermeasures (and the organization may not know of the compromise).

Confidentiality is one of the factors of privacy, an issue recognized in the laws of many government entities (such as the Privacy Act of the United States [1702, 2205] and similar legislation of the European Union [2198, 2199]). Aside from constraining what information a government entity can legally obtain from individuals, such acts place constraints on the disclosure and use of that information. Unauthorized disclosure can result in penalties that include jail or fines; also, such disclosure undermines the authority and respect that individuals have for the government and inhibits them from disclosing that type of information to the agencies so compromised.

Definition 4–10. A *commercial security policy* is a security policy developed primarily to provide integrity.

The name comes from the need of commercial firms to prevent tampering with their data, because they could not survive such compromises. For example, if the confidentiality of a bank's computer is compromised, a customer's account balance may be revealed. This would certainly embarrass the bank and possibly cause the customer to take her business elsewhere. But the loss to the bank's "bottom line" would be minor. However, if the integrity of the computer holding the accounts were compromised, the balances in the customers' accounts could be altered, with financially ruinous effects.

Some integrity policies use the notion of a transaction. Like database specifications, they require that actions occur in such a way as to leave the database in a consistent state. These policies, called *transaction-oriented integrity security policies*, are critical to organizations that require consistency of databases.

EXAMPLE: When a customer moves money from one account to another, the bank uses a well-formed transaction. This transaction has two distinct parts: money is first debited to the original account and then credited to the second account. Unless both parts of the transaction are completed, the customer will lose the money. With a well-formed transaction, if the transaction is interrupted, the state of the database is still consistent—either as it was before the transaction began or as it would have been when the transaction ended. Hence, part of the bank's security policy is that all transactions must be well-formed.

The role of trust in these policies highlights their difference. Confidentiality policies place no trust in objects; so far as the policy is concerned, the object could be a factually correct report or a tale taken from *Aesop's Fables*. The policy statement dictates whether that object can be disclosed. It says nothing about whether the object should be believed.

Integrity policies, to the contrary, indicate how much the object can be trusted. Given that this level of trust is correct, the policy dictates what a subject can do with that object. But the crucial question is how the level of trust is assigned. For example, if a site obtains a new version of a program, should that program have high integrity (that is, the site trusts the new version of that program) or low integrity (that is, the site does not yet trust the new program), or should the level of trust be somewhere in between (because the vendor supplied the program, but it has not been tested at the local site as thoroughly as the old version)? This makes integrity policies considerably more nebulous than confidentiality policies. The assignment of a level of confidentiality is based on what the classifier wants others to know, but the assignment of a level of integrity is based on what the classifier subjectively believes to be true about the trustworthiness of the information.

Two other terms describe policies related to security needs. Because they appear elsewhere, we define them now.

Definition 4–11. A *confidentiality policy* is a security policy dealing only with confidentiality.

Definition 4–12. An *integrity policy* is a security policy dealing only with integrity.

Both confidentiality policies and military policies deal with confidentiality. However, a confidentiality policy does not deal with integrity at all, whereas a military policy may. A similar distinction holds for integrity policies and commercial policies.

4.3   The Role of Trust

The role of trust is crucial to understanding the nature of computer security. This book presents theories and mechanisms for analyzing and enhancing computer security, but any theories or mechanisms rest on certain assumptions. When someone understands the assumptions her security policies, mechanisms, and procedures rest on, she will have a very good understanding of how effective those policies, mechanisms, and procedures are. Let us examine the consequences of this maxim.

A system administrator receives a security patch for her computer's operating system. She installs it. Has she improved the security of her system? She has indeed, given the correctness of certain assumptions:

- She is assuming that the patch came from the vendor and was not tampered with in transit, rather than from an attacker trying to trick her into installing a bogus patch that would actually open security holes. Winkler [2011] describes a penetration test in which this technique enabled attackers to gain direct access to the computer systems of the target.

- She is assuming that the vendor tested the patch thoroughly. Vendors are often under considerable pressure to issue patches quickly and sometimes test them only against a particular attack. The vulnerability may be deeper, however, and other attacks may succeed. When someone released an exploit of one vendor's operating system code, the vendor released a correcting patch in 24 hours. Unfortunately, the patch opened a second hole, one that was far easier to exploit. The next patch (released 48 hours later) fixed both problems correctly.

- She is assuming that the vendor's test environment corresponds to her environment. Otherwise, the patch may not work as expected. As an example, a vendor's patch once enabled the host's personal firewall, causing it to block incoming connections by default. This prevented many programs from functioning. The host had to be reconfigured to allow the programs to continue to function [2253]. This assumption also covers possible conflicts between different patches, such as patches from different vendors of software that the system is using.

- She is assuming that the patch is installed correctly. Some patches are simple to install, because they are simply executable files. Others are complex, requiring the system administrator to reconfigure network-oriented properties, add a user, modify the contents of a registry, give rights to some set of users, and then reboot the system. An error in any of these steps could prevent the patch from correcting the problems, as could an inconsistency between the environments in which the patch was developed and in which the patch is applied. Furthermore, the patch may claim to require specific privileges, when in reality the privileges are unnecessary and in fact dangerous.

These assumptions are fairly high-level, but invalidating any of them makes the patch a potential security problem.

Assumptions arise also at a much lower level. Consider formal verification (see Chapter 21), an oft-touted panacea for security problems. The important aspect is that formal verification provides a formal mathematical proof that a given program P is correct—that is, given any set of inputs i, j, k, the program P will produce the output x that its specification requires. This level of assurance is greater than most existing programs provide, and hence makes P a desirable program. Suppose a security-related program S has been formally verified for the operating system O. What assumptions would be made when it was installed?

- The formal verification of S is correct—that is, the proof has no errors. Because formal verification relies on automated theorem provers or other formal methods as well as human analysis, the theorem provers must be programmed correctly.

- The assumptions made in the formal verification of S are correct; specifically, the preconditions hold in the environment in which the program is to be executed. These preconditions are typically fed to the theorem provers as well as the program S. An implicit aspect of this assumption is that the version of O in the environment in which the program is to be executed is the same as the version of O used to verify S.

- The program will be transformed into an executable whose actions correspond to those indicated by the source code; in other words, the compiler, linker, loader, and any libraries are correct. An experiment with one version of the UNIX operating system demonstrated how devastating a rigged compiler could be [1875]. Some attack tools replace libraries with others that perform additional functions, thereby increasing security risks [307, 353, 418].

- The hardware will execute the program as intended. A program that relies on floating-point calculations would yield incorrect results on some computer CPU chips, regardless of any formal verification of the program, owing to a flaw in these chips [431]. Similarly, a program that relies on inputs from hardware assumes that specific conditions cause those inputs.

The point is that *any* security policy, mechanism, or procedure is based on assumptions that, if incorrect, destroy the superstructure on which it is built. Analysts and designers (and users) must bear this in mind, because unless they understand what the security policy, mechanism, or procedure is based on, they jump from an unwarranted assumption to an erroneous conclusion.

4.4 Types of Access Control

A security policy may use two types of access controls, alone or in combination. In one, access control is left to the discretion of the owner. In the other, the operating system controls access, and the owner cannot override the controls.

The first type is based on user identity and is the most widely known.

Definition 4–13. If an individual user can set an access control mechanism to allow or deny access to an object, that mechanism is a *discretionary access control* (DAC), also called an *identity-based access control* (IBAC).

Discretionary access controls base access rights on the identity of the subject and the identity of the object involved. Identity is the key; the owner of the object constrains who can access it by allowing only particular subjects to have access. The owner states the constraint in terms of the identity of the subject, or the owner of the object.

EXAMPLE: Suppose a child keeps a diary. The child controls access to the diary, because she can allow someone to read it (grant read access) or not allow someone to read it (deny read access). The child allows her mother to read it, but no one else. This is a discretionary access control because access to the diary is based on the identity of the subject (mom) requesting read access to the object (the diary).

The second type of access control is based on fiat, and identity is irrelevant:

Definition 4–14. When a system mechanism controls access to an object and an individual user cannot alter that access, the control is a *mandatory access control* (MAC), occasionally called a *rule-based access control*.

The operating system enforces mandatory access controls. Neither the subject nor the owner of the object can determine whether access is granted. Typically, the system mechanism will check attributes associated with both the subject and the object to determine whether the subject should be allowed to access the object. Rules describe the conditions under which access is allowed.

EXAMPLE: The law allows a court to access driving records without an owner's permission. This is a mandatory control, because the owner of the record has no control over the court's access to the information.

Definition 4–15. An *originator controlled access control* (ORCON or ORGCON) bases access on the creator of an object (or the information it contains).

The goal of this control is to allow the originator of the file (or of the information it contains) to control the dissemination of the information. The owner of the file has no control over who may access the file. Section 8.3 discusses this type of control in detail.

EXAMPLE: Bit Twiddlers, Inc., a company famous for its embedded systems, contracts with Microhackers Ltd., a company equally famous for its microcoding abilities. The contract requires Microhackers to develop a new microcode language for a particular processor designed to be used in high-performance embedded systems. Bit Twiddlers gives Microhackers a copy of its specifications for the processor. The terms of the contract require Microhackers to obtain permission before it gives any information about the processor to its subcontractors. This is an originator controlled access mechanism because, even though Microhackers owns the file containing the specifications, it may not allow anyone to access that information unless the creator of that information, Bit Twiddlers, gives permission.

4.5   Policy Languages

A *policy language* is a language for representing a security policy. High-level policy languages express policy constraints on entities using abstractions. Low-level policy languages express constraints in terms of input or invocation options to programs existing on the systems.

4.5.1   High-Level Policy Languages

A policy is independent of the mechanisms. It describes constraints placed on entities and actions in a system. A high-level policy language is an unambiguous expression of policy. Such precision requires a mathematical or programmatic formulation of policy; common English is not precise enough.

One such language is Ponder [496, 1222, 1885], a declarative language for specifying security and management policies. It provides support for several different types of policies: authorization policies, delegation policies, information filtering policies, obligation policies, and refrain policies.

EXAMPLE: In Ponder, entities are organized into hierarchical domains. Let network administrators be users in the domain */NetAdmins*, developers for network infrastructure be in the domain */NetDevelopers*, and network engineers be in the domain */NetEngineers*. Network engineer trainees are a subdomain, */NetEngineers/Trainees*. The routers in a local area network are in the domain */localnetwork/routers*, and that network also has a testbed for net routers, the domain */localnetwork/testbed/routers*.

Authorization policy specifications, enforced by controllers associated with the objects that are the targets of actions, fall into two classes. The first defines allowed actions and the second disallowed actions. The following states that network administrators can enable and disable routers on the local network; they can also reconfigure them, and cause them to dump the configuration:

```
inst auth+ switchAdmin {
        subject /NetAdmins;
        target  /localnetwork/routers;
        action  enable(), disable(), reconfig(),
                dumpconfig();
}
```

However, network engineer trainees cannot run performance tests on these routers during the day:

```
inst auth- testOps {
      subject /NetEngineers/trainees;
      target  /localnetwork/routers;
      action  testperformance();
      when    Time.between("0800", "1700");
}
```

Delegation policy specifications describe the delegation of rights. Here, the network engineers are delegated the authority to enable, disable, and reconfigure routers in the testbed. The delegation comes from the network administrators, and is good for 8 hours:

```
inst deleg+ (switchAdmin) delegSwitchAdmin {
    grantee  /NetEngineers;
    target   /localnetwork/testNetwork/routers;
    action   enable(), disable(), reconfig();
    valid    Time.duration(8);
}
```

The key item in this policy specification is "grantee," which designates the subjects (or subject domain) being delegated the authorization to carry out actions in the relevant authorization policy. The above specification delegates authorizations from the policy switchAdmin shown above. Only the authorization for actions enable, disable. and reconfig are delegated. When a delegation under this policy occurs, it is valid for 8 hours, after which it is automatically revoked.

Information filtering policy specifications control the dissemination of information. They differ from authorization policies in that the operation is performed first, and then the policy is applied to determine whether the results should be (possibly transformed and then) returned to the subject. Thus, the policy

```
inst auth+ switchOpsFilter {
    subject  /NetAdmins;
    target   /localnetwork/routers;
    action   dumpconfig(what)
             { in partial = "config"; } // default filter
             if (Time.between("2000", "0500"))
                 { in partial = "all"; }
}
```

says that network administrators can dump everything from the local network routers between 8:00 p.m. and 5:00 a.m., and the configuration information from the routers on the local network at any time.

Refrain policy specifications are similar to the authorization denial policy specifications, except that they are enforced by the subjects, not the target controllers. The following specification says that network engineers cannot send test results to nework developers while those tests are in progress (presumably because it might cause them to take actions that would affect the testing):

```
inst refrain testSwitchOps {
    subject  s=/NetEngineers;
    target   /NetDevelopers;
    action   sendTestResults();
    when     s.teststate="in progress"
}
```

The name s represents the domain of network engineers. The when constraint holds when the state of the test is "in progress," and when that constraint holds, the policy specification requires that the network engineers refrain from taking the action sendTestResults with the network developers as the target.

Finally, the *obligation* policy specification requires that specific actions be taken when certain events occur. For example, consider what happens when three consecutive login attempts to a network administrator's account fail:

```
inst oblig loginFailure {
    on       loginfail(userid, 3);
    subject  s=/NetAdmins/SecAdmins;
    target   t=/NetAdmins/users ^ (userid);
    do       t.disable() -> s.log(userid);
}
```

On the third failure (loginfail(userid, 3)), the network security administrators (who are a subset of the network administrators) will disable the account (t.disable), and then make a log entry into the log using an operation in the network security administrator's domain (s.log(userid)).

As an example of how Ponder can be used, consider a policy requiring separation of duty in the issuance of checks. The policy, which is to be enforced dynamically, requires that two different members of the */Accounting* domain approve the check. The Ponder policy specification for this is:

```
inst auth+ separationOfDuty {
    subject  s=/Accountants;
    target   t=checks;
    action   approve(), issue();
    when     s.id <> t.issuerid;
}
```

Here, the when constraint requires that the userid associated with the check issuance (t.userid) cannot be the accountant who approves the issuance (s.id).

In addition to these specifications, Ponder allows the grouping of policies for easy organization, and the use of roles. Role inheritance and role hierarchies are also supported, as are representations of management structure and classes of policies. Its flexibility and use of domains of subjects and objects make it able to express a variety of policies.

Another policy specification language, the *domain-type enforcement language* (DTEL) [111] grew from an observation of Boebert and Kain [252] that access could be based on types; they confine their work to the types "data" and "instructions." This observation served as the basis for a firewall [1877] and for other secure system components. DTEL uses implementation-level constructs to express constraints in terms of language types, but not as arguments or input to specific system commands. Hence, it combines elements of low-level and high-level languages. Because it describes configurations in the abstract, it is a high-level policy language.

EXAMPLE: DTEL associates a type with each object and a domain with each subject. The constructs of the language constrain the actions that a member of a domain can perform on an object of a specific type. For example, a subject cannot execute a text file, but it can execute an object file.

Consider a policy that restricts all users from writing to system binaries. Only subjects in the administrative domain can alter system binaries. A user can enter this domain only after rigorous authentication checks. In the UNIX world, this can be described using four distinct subject domains:

- *d_user*, the domain for ordinary users
- *d_admin*, the domain for administrative users (who can alter system binaries)
- *d_login*, the domain for the authentication processes that comply with the domain-type enforcement
- *d_daemon*, the domain for system daemons (including those that spawn login)

The *login* program (in the *d_login* domain) controls access between *d_user* and *d_admin*. The system begins in the *d_daemon* domain because the *init* process lies there (and *init* spawns the *login* process whenever anyone tries to log in).

We consider these five object types:

- *t_sysbin*, for executable files
- *t_readable*, for readable files
- *t_writable*, for writable files
- *t_dte*, for data used by the domain-type enforcement mechanisms
- *t_generic*, for data generated from user processes

For our purposes, consider these types to be partitions. In practice, objects can be both readable and writable; we ignore this for purposes of exposition. DTEL represents this as

```
type t_readable, t_writable, t_sysbin, t_dte, t_generic;
```

Characterize each domain as a sequence. The first component is a list of the programs that begin in this domain. The other elements of the sequence consist of a set of rights, an arrow, and a type. Each element describes the set of rights that members of the domain have over the named type.

EXAMPLE: Consider the *d_daemon* domain. When the *init* program begins, it starts in this domain. It can create (c), read (r), write (w), and do a directory search (d) of any object of type *t_writable*. It can read, search, and execute (x) any object of type *t_sysbin*. It can read and search anything of type *t_generic*, *t_readable*, or *t_dte*. Finally, when the *init* program invokes the *login* program, the *login* program transitions into the *d_login* domain automatically (auto). Putting this together, we have

```
domain d_daemon = (/sbin/init),
                  (crwd->t_writable),
                  (rd->t_generic, t_readable, t_dte),
                  (rxd->t_sysbin),
                  (auto->d_login);
```

An important observation is that, even if a subject in the domain *d_daemon* is compromised, the attacker cannot alter system binaries (files of type *t_sysbin*), because that domain has no write rights over files of that type. This implements separation of privilege (see Section 14.2.6) and was a motive behind the development of this policy.

EXAMPLE: As a second example, the policy requires that only administrative subjects (domain *d_admin*) be able to write system executables (of type *t_sysbin*). The administrator uses an ordinary UNIX command interpreter. Subjects in *d_admin* can read, write, execute, and search objects of types *t_readable*, *t_writable*, *t_dte*, and *t_sysbin*. If the type is not specified at creation, the new object is assigned the *t_generic* type. Finally, a subject in this domain can suspend processes executing in the *d_daemon* domain using the *sigtstp* signal. This means

```
domain d_admin = (/usr/bin/sh, /usr/bin/csh,
                  /usr/bin/ksh),
                 (crwxd->t_generic),
                 (rwxd->t_readable, t_writable, t_dte,
                  t_sysbin),
                 (sigtstp->d_daemon);
```

The user domain must be constrained similarly. Here, users can write only objects of type *t_writable*, can execute only objects of type *t_sysbin*, can create only objects of type *t_writable* or *t_generic*, and can read and search all domains named.

```
domain d_user = (/usr/bin/sh, /usr/bin/csh, /usr/bin/ksh),
                (crwxd->t_generic),
                (rxd->t_sysbin),
                (crwd->t_writable),
                (rd->t_readable, t_dte);
```

Because no user commands imply a transition out of the domain, the final component is empty.

The *d_login* domain controls access to the *d_user* and *d_admin* domains. Because this is its only function, no subject in that domain should be able to execute another program. It also is authorized to change the user ID (hence, it has the right *setauth*). Access to the domain is to be restricted to the login program. In other words,

```
domain d_login = (/usr/bin/login),
                 (crwd->t_writable),
                 (rd->t_readable, t_generic, t_dte),
                 setauth,
                 (exec->d_user, d_admin);
```

Initially, the system starts in the *d_daemon* state:

```
initial_domain = d_daemon;
```

A series of assign statements sets the initial types of objects. For example,

```
assign -r t_generic /;
assign -r t_writable /usr/var, /dev, /tmp;
assign -r t_readable /etc;
assign -r -s t_dte /dte;
assign -r -s t_sysbin /sbin, /bin, /usr/bin, /usr/sbin
```

The -r flag means that the type is applied recursively; the -s flag means that the type is bound to the name, so if the object is deleted and a new object is created with the same name, the new object will have the same type as the deleted object. The assign lines are processed in order, with the longest path name taking precedence. So, everything on the system without a type assigned by the last four lines is of type *t_generic* (because of the first line).

If a user process tries to alter a system binary, the enforcement mechanisms will check to determine if something in the domain *d_user* is authorized to write to an object of type *t_sysbin*. Because the domain description does not allow this, the request is refused.

Now augment the policy above to prevent users from modifying system logs. Define a new type *t_log* for the log files. Only subjects in the *d_admin* domain, and in a new domain *d_log*, can alter the log files. The set of domains would be extended as follows:

```
type t_readable, t_writable, t_sysbin, t_dte, t_generic,
     t_log;
domain d_daemon = (/sbin/init),
                  (crwd->t_writable),
```

```
                    (rxd->t_sysbin),
                    (rd->t_generic, t_dte, t_readable),
                    (auto->d_login, d_log);
    domain d_log = (/usr/sbin/syslogd),
                    (crwd->t_log),
                    (rwd->t_writable),
                    (rd->t_generic, t_readable);
    assign -r t_log /usr/var/log;
    assign t_writable /usr/var/log/wtmp, /usr/var/log/utmp;
```

If a process in the domain *d_daemon* invokes the *syslogd* process, the *syslogd* process enters the *d_log* domain. It can now manipulate system logs and can read and write writable logs but cannot access system executables. If a user tries to manipulate a log object, the request is denied. The *d_user* domain gives its subjects no rights over *t_log* objects.

4.5.2   Low-Level Policy Languages

A low-level policy language is simply a set of inputs or arguments to commands that set, or check, constraints on a system.

EXAMPLE: The UNIX-based windowing system X11 provides a language for controlling access to the console (on which X11 displays its images). The language consists of a command, *xhost*, and a syntax for instructing the command to allow access based on host name (IP address). For example,

```
xhost +groucho -chico
```

sets the system so that connections from the host *groucho* are allowed but connections from *chico* are not.

EXAMPLE: File system scanning programs check conformance of a file system with a stated policy. The policy consists of a database with desired settings. Each scanning program uses its own little language to describe the settings desired.
    One such program, *tripwire* [1053], assumes a policy of constancy. It records an initial state (the state of the system when the program is first run). On subsequent runs, it reports files whose settings have changed.
    The policy language consists of two files. The first, the *tw.config* file, contains a description of the attributes to be checked. The second, the database, contains the values of the attributes from a previous execution. The database is kept in a readable format but is very difficult to edit (for example, times of modification are kept using base 64 digits). Hence, to enforce conformance with a specific policy, an auditor must ensure that the system is in the desired state initially and set up the *tw.config* file to ignore the attributes not relevant to the policy.

The attributes that *tripwire* can check are protection, file type, number of links, file size, file owner, file group, and times of creation, last access, and last modification. *Tripwire* also allows the cryptographic checksumming of the contents of the file. An example *tripwire* configuration file looks like

```
/usr/mab/tripwire-1.1  +gimnpsu012345678-a
```

This line states that all attributes are to be recorded, including all nine cryptographic checksums, but that the time of last access (the "a") is to be ignored (the "-"). This applies to the directory and to all files and subdirectories contained in it. After *tripwire* is executed, the database entry for a *README* file might be

```
/usr/mab/tripwire-1.1/README 0 ..../. 100600 45763 1 917
10 33242 .gtPvf .gtPvY .gtPvY 0 .ZD4ccOWr8i21ZKaI..LUOr3
.0fwo5:hf4e4.8TAqd0V4ubv ?...... ...9b3
1M4GX01xbGIX0oVuGo1h15z3 ?:Y9jfa04rdzM1q:eqt1APgHk
?.Eb9yo.2zkEh1XKovX1:d0wF0kfAvC
?1M4GX01xbGIX2947jdyrior38h15z3 0
```

Clearly, administrators are not expected to edit the database to set attributes properly. Hence, if the administrator wishes to check conformance with a particular *policy* (as opposed to looking for changes), the administrator must ensure that the system files conform to that policy and that the configuration file reflects the attributes relevant to the policy.

EXAMPLE: The RIACS file system checker [215] was designed with different goals. It emphasized the ability to set policy and then check for conformance. It uses a database file and records fixed attributes (with one exception—the cryptographic checksum). The property relevant to this discussion is that the database entries are easy to understand and edit:

```
/etc/pac 0755 1 root root 16384 12 22341 Jan 12, 1987 at
         12:47:54
```

The attribute values follow the file name and are permissions, number of links, owner and group, size (in bytes), checksum, and date and time of last modification. After generating such a file, the analyst can change the values as appropriate (and replace those that are irrelevant with a wild card "*"). On the next run, the file system state is compared with these values.

4.6   Example: Academic Computer Security Policy

Security policies can have few details, or many. The explicitness of a security policy depends on the environment in which it exists. A research lab or office environment may have an unwritten policy. A bank needs a very explicit policy. In practice, policies begin as generic statements of constraints on the members of the organization. These statements are derived from an analysis of threats, as described in Chapter 1, "An Overview of Computer Security." As questions (or incidents) arise, the policy is refined to cover specifics. As an example, we present part of an academic security policy that focuses on electronic communications. The full electronic communications policy is presented in Appendix G, "Example Academic Security Policy."

4.6.1   General University Electronic Communications Policy

The University of California consists of 10 campuses, each headed by a Chancellor and a Provost. Overseeing all the campuses is the University of California Office of the President (UCOP). UCOP issues policies that apply to all campuses, and each campus then implements the policy consistent with directions from UCOP.

The basic electronic communications policy (see Section G.2), issued by UCOP and last revised on August 18, 2013, begins with a statement of the importance of electronic communications, which includes email, voice, and video as well as other means of electronic communications. It then states the purposes of the policy and to whom the policy applies. Interestingly, the policy applies to electronic communication records in electronic form, and cautions explicitly that it does not apply to printed copies of those records or communications.

As noted above, this policy applies to the University of California system, but not to the U.S. Department of Energy laboratories that the University manages, or to users who are agents or employees of the Department of Energy. It gives general guidelines for implementation of the policy by the campuses, for example "procedures shall include information on ... authorized users, procedures for restricting or denying use of its electronic communications services, adjudication of complaints, network monitoring practices, ..."[1] It also points out that certain abuses not only violate the policy but also the law, and that violators of the policy may be subject to University disciplinary procedures as well as legal penalties.

The next section discusses the allowable uses of University electronic communications resources. The policy emphasizes the desire of the University not to deal with the contents of electronic communications, and that all communications relating to the administration of the University are public records under the California Public Records Act. Other communications may also be public records. It then identifies the allowable users—University faculty, staff, students, and others associated with the University, and others authorized by the Chancellor or UCOP, or who are participating in programs sponsored by the University.

---

[1] See Section G.2.2.D.2.

Allowable uses are more complex. Basically, electronic communications cannot be used for commercial purposes such as endorsements, for illegal activities, for running personal businesses, or for any purpose that violates University or campus policies or rules. Users cannot claim to represent the University unless they are properly authorized to do so, and may not interfere with others' use or put an "excessive strain" on electronic communications resources. This rules out using those resources for spamming and denial of service attacks, for example. Incidental personal use is allowed providing that it does not interfere with other uses of electronic communications resources; but, as noted above, those communications may be examined to determine if they are public records within the meaning of the Public Records Act. Further, anonymous communications are also allowed subject to campus guidelines, but the use of false identities is forbidden. The section concludes with an admonition to respect intellectual property laws, and that in accordance with the U.S. Digital Millenium Copyright Act, the University may suspend or terminate accounts of users who repeatedly violate copyright laws.

The policy then discusses the privacy and confidentiality of electronic communications. Privacy of electronic communications is respected in the same way as for paper communications. The policy forbids the reading or disclosing of these communications without permission of the holder, except in specific enumerated circumstances:

- when required by law;
- when there is reliable evidence that the law or University policies are being violated;
- when not doing so may result in significant harm, loss of significant evidence of violations of law or University policy, or significant liability to the University or the members of its community; and
- when not doing so would seriously hamper the administrative or teaching obligations of the University.

In general, access without consent of the holder requires written permission of a senior administrator (such as a Vice Chancellor or Senior Vice President, Business and Finance) designated to give this permission. Exceptions are in response to a subpoena or search warrant. If immediate access is require to deal with an emergency, approval must be obtained as soon as possible after the access. Further, in any of these circumstances, those affected by the disclosure must be notified of the action and the reasons for the action, as soon as possible.

This section then discusses privacy protections and the laws and other University policies that apply. It also notes that privacy has some limits, specifically that some electronic communications may constitute public records and therefore may become public, that electronic communications may be captured on backups, and that during the course of system monitoring to ensure reliability and security, system and network administrators may see electronic communications; however, they are instructed to respect the privacy of those communications. If, during the course of their normal work, they come across "improper governmental activity (including violations of law or University policy)," they may report it consistent with the University's Whistleblower Policy.[2]

The penultimate section covers security. This section describes the security services and practices, such as permitting routine monitoring, the need to maintain authentication, authorization, and other mechanisms commensurate with University policies. Recovery and audit mechanisms are to be used to ensure reliability and detect security problems.

The policy concludes with some comments on the retention of electronic communications.

Appendix A, "Definitions,"[3] raises an interesting point in its definition of "Electronic Communications," which it defines as "[a]ny transfer of signals, writings, images, sounds, data or intelligence that is, created, sent, forwarded, replied to, transmitted, distributed, broadcast, stored, held, copied, downloaded, displayed, viewed, read, or printed by one or several electronic communications systems." When read in conjunction with the definition of "Transactional Information," which includes email headers, senders, and recipients, this appears to encompass the network packets used to carry the email from one host to another. The policy states explicitly that transmissions are monitored for security and reliability purposes, resolving an ambiguity in an earlier version of the policy [2151]. But this illustrates a problem with policies expressed in natural languages. The language is often imprecise. This motivates the use of more mathematical languages, such as DTEL, for specifying policies.

4.6.1.1   Attachment: User Advisories

Because a policy can be confusing to ordinary users, UCOP has added an attachment designed for the general University community.[4] This advisory reiterates the main points of the Electronic Communication Policy, and adds some cautions. For example, it reminds readers that in general what is forbidden in the physical world is also forbidden in the digital world.

It also encourages users of electronic communications to think of others. In particular, it suggests treating electronic communications like any other form of communication, and showing others the same courtesy and consideration in both environments. It points out that laws governing the privacy of electronic communications are not as mature as laws governing privacy in other areas (the example given is telephonic communications), so users should assume a lesser degree of privacy—and, if broadcasting a message or posting to a website, assume little to no privacy. Also, it reviews various government and University policies applying to personal information and student and University records.

Finally, the advisory states limits on what the University provides. The University does not provide routine encryption of electronic communications,

---

[2] See Section G.2.4.C.2.b.
[3] See Section G.2.7.
[4] See Section G.3.

but users can use various technologies to do so. Similarly, the University does not routinely provide authentication mechanisms for electronic communication, and the advisory notes it is easy to falsify the sender of a message (although it is a violation of University policy to do so). Electronic communications are backed up for reliability purposes, but the University does not guarantee that these backups will be available to users, or even be maintained for any given time.

4.6.2   Implementation at UC Davis

UC Davis describes the implementation of the Electronic Communications Policy in the Policy and Procedure Manual, Section 310–23, "Electronic Communications—Allowable Use."[5] It is augmented by an additional exhibit, the "Acceptable Use Policy."[6]

The goal of electronic communication is to support the University's mission of teaching, research, and community service. The policy emphasizes that they incorporate the UC Davis Principles of Community: that people have inherent dignity, the right of freedom of expression, the obligation to respect and be courteous to others, and to cherish the differences that makes the community so rich. This means that users must respect the rights of others when using electronic communication resources. Using these resources in pursuit of education, university business, or university-related activities is encouraged.

The policy identifies the allowed users more specifically than the Electronic Communications Policy, specifically UCD students, staff, faculty, and other academic appointees and affiliated people; the latter must be sponsored by a department and must fill out a temporary affiliate form. It further covers people leaving UCD; email may be forwarded, provided that the recipient agrees to return to the department any email pertaining to University business.

The allowable uses section goes into details specific to the UC Davis campus; for example, only Chancellor-approved charitable activities may use electronic communication resources. Using them in a way that creates a hostile educational or work environment (for example, for harassment) or that violates obscenity laws is forbidden. Beyond these restrictions, it reiterates that incidental personal use is permitted under the conditions given in the Electronic Communications Policy.

The policy details unacceptable conduct. Users must respect copyrights and license agreements, and the integrity of electronic communication resources. Thus, creating computer worms or viruses is strictly forbidden unless (a) it is done as part of an academic research or instruction program supervised by academic personnel and (b) it does not compromise the University's electronic communication resources. Users are required to protect passwords for University

---

[5]See Section G.4.
[6]See Section G.1.

resources, and must comply with all laws and University policies pertinent to electronic communications.

This interpretation adds campus-specific requirements and procedures to the university's policy. The local augmentation amplifies the system policy; it does not contradict it or limit it. Indeed, what would happen if the campus policy conflicted with the system's policy? In general, the higher (system-wide) policy would prevail. The advantage of leaving implementation to the campuses is that they can take into account local variations and customs, as well as any peculiarities in the way the administration and the Academic Senate govern that campus.

4.7   Security and Precision

Chapter 1 presented definitions of security and precision in terms of states of systems. Can one devise a generic procedure for developing a mechanism that is both secure and precise? Jones and Lipton [971] explored this question for confidentiality policies; similar results hold for integrity policies. For this analysis, they view programs as abstract functions.

Definition 4–16. Let p be a function $p : I_1 \times \ldots \times I_n \to R$. Then P is a program implementing p with n inputs $i_k \in I_k, 1 \leq k \leq n$, and one output $r \in R$.

The observability postulate makes one assumption of what follows explicit.

Axiom 4.1 (Observability Postulate). *The output of a function $p(i_1, \ldots, i_n)$ encodes all available information about $i_1, \ldots, i_n$.*

Consider a program that does not alter information on the system, but merely provides a "view" of its inputs. Confidentiality policies seek to control what views are available; hence the relevant question is whether the value of $p(i_1, \ldots, i_n)$ contains any information that it should not contain.

This postulate is needed because information can be transmitted by modulating shared resources such as runtime, file space used, and other channels such as covert channels (see Chapter 18) and side channels (see Section 9.6). Even though these channels are not intended to be used for sending information, that they are shared enables violation of confidentiality policies. From an abstract point of view, covert channels are part of the output (result) of the program's execution, and hence the postulate is appropriate. But as a matter of implementation, these channels may be observable even when the program's output is not.

EXAMPLE: Consider a program that asks for a user name and a password. If the user name is illegal, or is not associated with the password, the program prints "Bad." If the user name has the given password, it prints "Good." The inputs are the user name, the password, and the database of associations, so the inputs are in the set of all strings. The output is in the set { "Bad", "Good" }.

If the user name is illegal, the program does not access the password database (because there can be no valid password for the user), and it immediately prints "Bad." But if the user name is valid, the program must access the password database, which takes a noticeable amount of time. This means that the time that the computation takes is an output of the function. So the observability postulate says that analysts must consider the delay in computing the response as an output of the computation. This makes sense. If the program immediately prints "Bad," the observer concludes that the user name is unknown. If a delay occurs before the program prints "Bad," the observer concludes that the user is known but the password is incorrect.

Let E be the set of outputs from a program p that indicate errors.

Definition 4–17. Let p be a function $p : I_1 \times \ldots \times I_n \to R$. A *protection mechanism* m is a function $m : I_1 \times \ldots \times I_n \to R \cup E$ for which, when $i_k \in I_k, 1 \leq k \leq n$, either

(a) $m(i_1, \ldots, i_n) = p(i_1, \ldots, i_n)$ or
(b) $m(i_1, \ldots, i_n) \in E$.

Informally, this definition says that every legal input to m produces either the same value as for p or an error message. The set of output values from p that are excluded as outputs from m are the set of outputs that would impart confidential information.

EXAMPLE: Continuing the example above, E might contain the messages "Password Database Missing" and "Password Database Locked." Then, if the program could not access the password database, it would print one of those messages (and case [b] of the definition would apply); otherwise, it would print "Good" or "Bad" and case (a) would apply.

Now we define a confidentiality policy.

Definition 4–18. A *confidentiality policy* for the program $p : I_1 \times \ldots \times I_n \to R$ is a function $c : I_1 \times \ldots \times I_n \to A$, where $A \subseteq I_1 \times \ldots \times I_n$.

In this definition, A corresponds to the set of inputs that may be revealed. The complement of A with respect to $I_1 \times \ldots \times I_n$ corresponds to the confidential inputs. In some sense, the function c filters out inputs that are to be kept confidential. For all inputs $I_1, \ldots, I_n$, the symbol $\nu \in I_i$ means that no input from I_i is given.

The next definition captures how well a security mechanism conforms to a stated confidentiality policy.

Definition 4–19. Let $c : I_1 \times \ldots \times I_n \rightarrow A$ be a confidentiality policy for a program p. Let $m : I_1 \times \ldots \times I_n \rightarrow R \cup E$ be a security mechanism for the same program p. Then the mechanism m is secure if and only if there is a function $m' : A \rightarrow R \cup E$ such that, for all $i_k \in I_k, 1 \leq k \leq n$, $m(i_1, \ldots, i_n) = m'(c(i_1, \ldots, i_n))$.

In other words, given any set of inputs, the protection mechanism m returns values consistent with the stated confidentiality policy c. Here, the term "secure" is a synonym for "confidential." We can derive analogous results for integrity policies.

EXAMPLE: If $c(i_1, \ldots, i_n)$ is a constant vector, the policy's intent is to deny the observer any information, because the output does not vary with the inputs. But if $c(i_1, \ldots, i_n) = (i_1, \ldots, i_n)$, and $m' = m$, then the policy's intent is to allow the observer full access to the information. As an intermediate policy, if $c(i_1, \ldots, i_n) = (i_1, v, \ldots, v)$, then the policy's intent is to allow the observer information about the first input but no information about other inputs.

The distinguished policy *allow* : $I_1 \times \ldots \times I_n \rightarrow A$ generates a selective permutation of its inputs. By "selective," we mean that it may omit inputs. Hence, the function $c(i_1, \ldots, i_n) = i_1$ is an example of *allow*, because its output is a permutation of some of its inputs. More generally, for $k \leq n$,

$$allow(i_1, \ldots, i_n) = (i'_1, \ldots, i'_k)$$

where $i'_1, \ldots, i'_k$ is a permutation of any k of $i_1, \ldots, i_n$.

EXAMPLE: Revisit the program that checks user name and password association. Let U be the set of potential user names, P the set of potential passwords, and D the set of authentication databases. As a function, $auth : U \times P \times D' \rightarrow \{T, F\}$. T and F represent true and false, respectively. Then for $u \in U, p \in P$, and $d \in D$, $auth(u, p, d) = T$ if and only if the pair $(u, p) \in d$. Under the policy $allow(i_1, i_2, i_3) = (i_1, i_2, v)$, there is no function $auth'$ such that

$$auth'(allow(u, p, d)) = auth'(u, p, v) = auth(u, p, d)$$

for all d because $auth'$ has no access to elements of D. So $auth$ is not secure as an enforcement mechanism.

EXAMPLE: Consider a program q with k nonnegative integer inputs; it computes a single nonnegative integer. A Minsky machine [1352] can simulate this program by starting with the input $i_j \in I_j$ in register j (for $1 \leq j \leq k$). The output may disclose information about one or more inputs. For example, if the program is to return the third input as its output, it is disclosing information. Fenton [664] examines these functions to determine if the output contains confidential information.

The observability postulate does not hold for the program q above, because q ignores runtime. The computation may take more time for certain inputs, revealing information about them. This is an example of a *covert channel* (see Section 18.3). It also illustrates the need for precise modeling. The policy does not consider runtime as an output when, in reality, it is an output.

As an extreme example, consider the following program:

```
if x = null then halt;
```

Fenton does not define what happens if x is not **null**. If an error message is printed, the resulting mechanism may not be secure. To see this, consider the program

```
y := 0;
if x = 0 then begin
          y := 1;
          halt;
end;
halt;
```

Here, the value of y is the error message. It indicates whether or not the value of x is 0 when the program terminates. If the security policy says that information about x is not to be revealed, then this mechanism is not secure.

A secure mechanism ensures that the policy is obeyed. However, it may also disallow actions that do not violate the policy. In that sense, a secure mechanism may be overly restrictive. The notion of *precision* measures the degree of overrestrictiveness.

Definition 4–20. Let m_1 and m_2 be two distinct protection mechanisms for the program p under the policy c. Then m_1 is *as precise as* m_2 ($m_1 \approx m_2$) provided that, for all inputs $(i_1, \ldots, i_n)$, if $m_2(i_1, \ldots, i_n) = p(i_1, \ldots, i_n)$, then $m_1(i_1, \ldots, i_n) = p(i_1, \ldots, i_n)$. We say that m_1 is *more precise than* m_2 ($m_1 \sim m_2$) if there is an input $(i'_1, \ldots, i'_n)$ such that $m_1(i'_1, \ldots, i'_n) = p(i'_1, \ldots, i'_n)$ and $m_2(i'_1, \ldots, i'_n) \neq p(i'_1, \ldots, i'_n)$.

An obvious question is whether or not two protection mechanisms can be combined to form a new mechanism that is as precise as the two original ones. To answer this, we need to define "combines," which we formalize by the notion of "union."

Definition 4–21. Let m_1 and m_2 be protection mechanisms for the program p. Then their union $m_3 = m_1 \cup m_2$ is defined as

$$m_3(i_1, \ldots, i_n) = \begin{cases} p(i_1, \ldots, i_n) & \text{when } m_1(i_1, \ldots, i_n) = p(i_1, \ldots, i_n) \text{ or} \\ & \quad m_2(i_1, \ldots, i_n) = p(i_1, \ldots, i_n) \\ m_1(i_1, \ldots, i_n) & \text{otherwise.} \end{cases}$$

This definition says that for inputs on which m_1 or m_2 returns the same value as p, their union does also. Otherwise, that mechanism returns the same value as m_1. From this definition and the definitions of *secure* and *precise*, we have:

Theorem 4.1. Let m_1 and m_2 be secure protection mechanisms for a program p and policy c. Then $m_1 \cup m_2$ is also a secure protection mechanism for p and c. Furthermore, $m_1 \cup m_2 \approx m_1$ and $m_1 \cup m_2 \approx m_2$.

Generalizing, we have:

Theorem 4.2. For any program p and security policy c, there exists a precise, secure mechanism m^* such that, for all secure mechanisms m associated with p and c, $m^* \approx m$.

Proof Immediate by induction on the number of secure mechanisms associated with p and c.

This "maximally precise" mechanism m^* is the mechanism that ensures security while minimizing the number of denials of legitimate actions. If there is an effective procedure for determining this mechanism, we can develop mechanisms that are both secure and precise. Unfortunately,

Theorem 4.3. There is no effective procedure that determines a maximally precise, secure mechanism for any policy and program.

Proof Let the policy c be the constant function—that is, no information about any of the inputs is allowed in the output. Let p be a program that computes the value of some total function $T(x)$ and assigns it to the variable z. We may without loss of generality take $T(0) = 0$.

Let q be a program of the following form:

```
p;
if z = 0 then y := 1 else y := 2;
halt;
```

Now, consider the value of the protection mechanism $m(0)$. From the above program, either $m(0) = 1$ (if p, and hence q, completes) or it is undefined (if p halts before the "if" statement). As the policy c is the constant function, m must also be constant.

If, for all inputs x, $T(x) = 0$, then $m(x) = 1$ (because m is secure). So, assume there is an input x' for which $T(x') \neq 0$. Then, either $m(x') = 2$ (again, because m is secure) or is undefined (if p halts before the assignment). From the definition of T, as $T(0) = 0$, so $m(0) = 1$. But this means m has different values for different inputs, and so is not a constant function. Thus, $m(0) = 1$ if and only if $T(x) = 0$ for all x.

If we can effectively determine m, we can effectively determine whether $T(x) = 0$ for all x. But this is clearly equivalent to solving the halting problem.

There is no general procedure for devising a mechanism that conforms exactly to a specific security policy and yet allows all actions that the policy allows. It may be possible to do so in specific cases, especially when a mechanism defines a policy, but there is no general way to devise a precise and secure mechanism.

4.8   Summary

Security policies define "security" for a system or site. They may be implied policies defined by the common consensus of the community, or they may be informal policies whose interpretations are defined by the community. Both of these types of policies are usually ambiguous and do not precisely define "security." A policy may be formal, in which case ambiguities arise either from the use of natural languages such as English or from the failure to cover specific areas.

Formal mathematical models of policies enable analysts to deduce a rigorous definition of "security" but do little to improve the average user's understanding of what "security" means for a site. The average user is not mathematically sophisticated enough to read and interpret the mathematics.

Trust underlies all policies and enforcement mechanisms. Policies themselves make assumptions about the way systems, software, hardware, and people behave. At a lower level, security mechanisms and procedures also make such assumptions. Even when rigorous methodologies (such as formal mathematical models or formal verification) are applied, the methodologies themselves simply push the assumptions, and therefore the trust, to a lower level. Understanding the assumptions and the trust involved in any policies and mechanisms deepens one's understanding of the security of a system.

This brief overview of policy, and of policy expression, lays the foundation for understanding the more detailed policy models used in practice.

4.9   Research Issues

The critical issue in security policy research is the expression of policy in an easily understood yet precise form. The development of policy languages focuses on supplying mathematical rigor that is intelligible to humans. A good policy language allows not only the expression of policy and its maintenance over time but also the analysis of a system to determine if it conforms to that policy.

The latter may require that the policy language be compiled into an enforcement program (to enforce the stated policy, as DTEL does) or into a verification program (to verify that the stated policy is enforced, as *tripwire* does). Balancing enforcement with requirements is also an important area of research, particularly in real-time environments.

The underlying role of trust is another crucial issue in policy research. Development of methodologies for exposing underlying assumptions and for analyzing the effects of trust and the results of belief is an interesting area of formal mathematics as well as a guide to understanding the safety and security of systems. Design and implementation of tools to aid in this work are difficult problems on which research will continue for a long time to come.

4.10   Further Reading

Much of security analysis involves definition and refinement of security policies. Wood [2021] has published a book of templates for policies, and includes several example policies. That book justifies each part and allows readers to develop policies by selecting the appropriate parts from a large set of possibilities. Essays by Bailey [115] and Abrams and Bailey [8] discuss management of security issues and explain why different members of an organization interpret the same policy differently. Sterne's wonderful paper [1823] discusses the nature of policy in general. Schneider [1682] characterizes security policies that can be enforced by monitoring the execution of (components of) systems.

Jajodia and his colleagues [958] present a "little language" for expressing authorization policies. They show that their language can express many aspects of existing policies and argue that it allows elements of these policies to be combined into authorization schemes. Some policy languages target specific environments such as distributed infrastructure management [25], cognitive radios [626], the release of information requiring the approval of several domains [1585, 1873], user privacy [26], network routing policies [1832], web services [49], firewall configurations [132, 1542], and describing attacks [614, 1331, 1554]. Ponder is flexible enough to be used to describe policy for mobile agents [1374] and for differentiated services [1225]; extensions to it include Ponder2, designed for autonomous pervasive environments [1907], and PonderFlow, for OpenFlow environments [137]. Others such as KAoS [1914, 1915], PDL [1202], PMAC [24], and Rei [986] are general enough to use in many different settings.

Fraser and Badger [719] have used DTEL to enforce many policies. Cholvy and Cuppens [409] describe a method of checking policies for consistency and determining how they apply to given situations. Similar techniques have been used for firewall configurations [1200, 2070, 2085].

The extensible markup language XML is the basis for several policy languages such as XACML [1589], and various extensions [66, 195, 1274] apply those languages to particular domains. Nordbotten's tutorial [1459] discusses several XML-based standards.

Son, Chaney, and Thomlinson [1788] discuss enforcement of partial security policies in real-time databases to balance real-time requirements with security. Their idea of "partial security policies" has applications in other environments. Zurko and Simon [1754, 2112] present an alternative focus for policies.

4.11   Exercises

1. In Figure 4–1, suppose that edge t_3 went from s_1 to s_4. Would the resulting system be secure?

2. Revisit the example of one student copying another student's homework assignment. Describe three other ways the first student could copy the second student's homework assignment, even assuming that the file access control mechanisms are set to deny him permission to read the file.

3. A noted computer security expert has said that without integrity, no system can provide confidentiality.

   a. Assume the system provides no integrity controls. Do you agree with the noted computer security expert? Justify your answer.

   b. Now suppose the system has no confidentiality controls. Can this system provide integrity without confidentiality? Again, justify your answer.

4. A cryptographer once claimed that security mechanisms other than cryptography were unnecessary because cryptography could provide any desired level of confidentiality and integrity. Ignoring availability, either justify or refute the cryptographer's claim.

5. Classify each of the following as an example of a mandatory, discretionary, or originator controlled policy, or a combination thereof. Justify your answers.

   a. The file access control mechanisms of the UNIX operating system

   b. A system in which no memorandum can be distributed without the creator's consent

   c. A military facility in which only generals can enter a particular room

   d. A university registrar's office, in which a faculty member can see the grades of a particular student provided that the student has given written permission for the faculty member to see them

6. Write a Ponder instance authorization to allow a professor to read an assignment submitted to a drop box between 7:00 a.m. and noon.

7. Use DTEL to create a domain *d_guest* composed of processes executing the restricted shell */usr/bin/restsh*. These processes cannot create any files. They can read and execute any object of type *t_sysbin*. They can read and search any object of type *t_guest*.

8. When using *tripwire*, system administrators typically exclude a check for the time of last access (the a).

   a. Why?

   b. Suppose a system administrator wanted to know if the file */usr/mab/ tripwire-1.1/PRIVATE* has been accessed in the past day. How could the administrator arrange to do this without *tripwire* indicating whether other files had been accessed?

9. Consider the UC Davis policy on reading electronic mail. A research group wants to obtain raw data from a network that carries all network traffic to the Department of Political Science.

   a. Discuss the impact of the electronic mail policy on the collection of such data.

   b. How would you change the policy to allow the collection of this data without abandoning the principle that electronic mail should be protected?

10. Prove Theorem 4.1. Show all elements of your proof.

11. Expand the proof of Theorem 4.2 to show the statement, and the proof, of the induction.

Chapter 5
Confidentiality Policies

SHEPHERD: Sir, there lies such secrets in this fardel
and box which none must know but the king;
and which he shall know within this hour, if I
may come to the speech of him.
— *The Winter's Tale*, IV, iv, 785–788.

Confidentiality policies emphasize the protection of confidentiality. The importance of these policies lies in part in what they provide, and in part in their role in the development of the concept of security. This chapter explores one such policy—the Bell-LaPadula Model—and the controversy it engendered.

5.1 Goals of Confidentiality Policies

A confidentiality policy, also called an *information flow policy*, prevents the unauthorized disclosure of information. Unauthorized alteration of information is secondary. For example, the navy must keep confidential the date on which a troop ship will sail. If the date is changed, the redundancy in the systems and paperwork should catch that change. But if the enemy knows the date of sailing, the ship could be sunk. Because of extensive redundancy in military communications channels, availability is also less of a problem.

The term "governmental" covers several requirements that protect citizens' privacy. In the United States, the Privacy Act requires that certain personal data be kept confidential. Income tax returns are legally confidential and are available only to the Internal Revenue Service or to legal authorities with a court order. The principle of "executive privilege" and the system of nonmilitary classifications suggest that the people working in the government need to limit the distribution of certain documents and information. Governmental models represent the policies that satisfy these requirements.

5.2   The Bell-LaPadula Model

The Bell-LaPadula Model [149, 150] corresponds to military-style classifications. It has influenced the development of many other models and indeed much of the development of computer security technologies.

5.2.1   Informal Description

The simplest type of confidentiality classification is a set of *security clearances* arranged in a linear (total) ordering (see Figure 5–1). These clearances represent sensitivity levels. The higher the security clearance, the more sensitive the information (and the greater the need to keep it confidential). A subject has a *security clearance*. In the figure, Claire's security clearance is C (for CONFIDENTIAL), and Thomas's is TS (for TOP SECRET). An object has a *security classification*; the security classification of the electronic mail files is S (for SECRET), and that of the telephone list files is UC (for UNCLASSIFIED). (When we refer to both subject clearances and object classifications, we use the term "classification.") The goal of the Bell-LaPadula security model is to prevent information flowing from objects at a security classification higher than a subject's clearance to that subject.

The Bell-LaPadula security model combines mandatory and discretionary access controls. In what follows, "S has discretionary read (or write) access to O" means that the access control matrix entry for S and O corresponding to the discretionary access control component contains a read (or write) right. In other words, were the mandatory controls not present, S would be able to read (or write) O.

Let $L(S) = l_s$ be the security clearance of subject S, and let $L(O) = l_o$ be the security classification of object O. For all security classifications $l_i, i = 0, ..., k-1$, $l_i < l_{i+1}$:

Simple Security Condition, Preliminary Version: S can read O if and only if $l_o \leq l_s$ and S has discretionary read access to O.

TOP SECRET (TS)	Tamara, Thomas	Personnel Files
SECRET (S)	Sally, Samuel	Electronic Mail Files
CONFIDENTIAL (C)	Claire, Clarence	Activity Log Files
UNCLASSIFIED (UC)	Ulaley, Ursula	Telephone List Files

Figure 5–1   At the left is the basic confidentiality classification system. The four security levels are arranged with the most sensitive at the top and the least sensitive at the bottom. In the middle are individuals grouped by their security clearances, and at the right is a set of documents grouped by their security levels.

In Figure 5–1, for example, Claire and Clarence cannot read personnel files, but Tamara and Sally can read the activity log files (and, in fact, Tamara can read any of the files, given her clearance), assuming that the discretionary access controls allow it.

Should Tamara decide to copy the contents of the personnel files into the activity log files and set the discretionary access permissions appropriately, Claire could then read the personnel files. Thus, for all practical purposes, Claire could read the files at a higher level of security. A second property prevents this:

*-Property (Star Property), Preliminary Version: *S* can write *O* if and only if $l_o \geq l_s$ and *S* has discretionary write access to *O*.

Because the activity log files are classified C and Tamara has a clearance of TS, she cannot write to the activity log files.

If both the simple security condition, preliminary version, and the *-property, preliminary version, hold, call the system a *secure system*. A straightforward induction establishes the following theorem.

> **Theorem 5.1.** *Basic Security Theorem, Preliminary Version:* Let *S* be a system with a secure initial state s_0, and let *T* be a set of state transformations. If every element of *T* preserves the simple security condition, preliminary version, and the *-property, preliminary version, then every state $s_i, i \geq 0$, is secure.

Expand the model by adding a set of categories to each security classification. Each category describes a kind of information. Objects placed in multiple categories have the kinds of information in all of those categories. These categories arise from the "need to know" principle, which states that no subject should be able to read objects unless reading them is necessary for that subject to perform its functions. The sets of categories to which a person may have access is simply the power set of the set of categories. For example, if the categories are NUC, EUR, and US, someone can have access to any of the following sets of categories: ∅ (none), { NUC }, { EUR }, { US }, { NUC, EUR }, { NUC, US }, { EUR, US }, and { NUC, EUR, US }. These sets of categories form a lattice under the operation ⊆ (subset of); see Figure 5–2. (Appendix A, "Lattices," discusses the mathematical nature of lattices.)

Each security clearance or classification and category forms a *security level*.[1] As before, we say that subjects *have clearance at* (or *are cleared into*, or *are in*) a security level and that objects are at the level of (or are in) a security level. For example, William may be cleared into the level (SECRET, { EUR }) and George

---

[1] This terminology is not fully agreed upon. Some call security levels "compartments." However, other use this term as a synonym for "categories." We follow the terminology of the unified exposition [150].

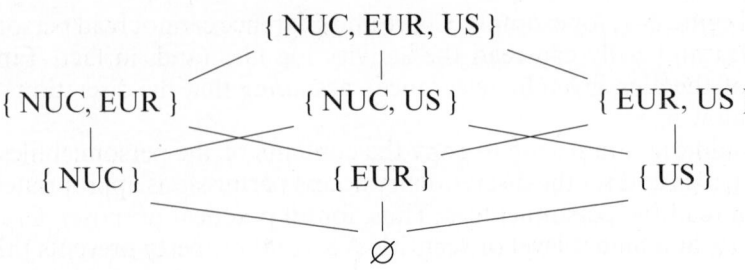

Figure 5–2 Lattice generated by the categories NUC, EUR, and US. The lines represent the ordering relation induced by ⊆.

into the level (TOP SECRET, { NUC, US }). A document may be classified as (CONFIDENTIAL, { EUR }).

Security levels change access. Because categories are based on a "need to know," someone with access to the category set { NUC, US } presumably has no need to access items in the category EUR. Hence, read access should be denied, even if the security clearance of the subject is higher than the security classification of the object. But if the desired object is in any security level with category sets ∅, { NUC }, { US }, or { NUC, US } and the subject's security clearance is no less than the document's security classification, access should be granted because the subject is cleared into the same category set as the object. This suggests a new relation for capturing the combination of security classification and category set. Define the relation *dom* (dominates) as follows.

Definition 5–1. The security level (L, C) dominates the security level (L', C'), written $(L, C)\,dom(L', C')$, if and only if $L' \leq L$ and $C' \subseteq C$.

We write $(L, C)\,\neg dom(L', C')$ when $(L, C)\,dom(L', C')$ is false. This relation also induces a lattice on the set of security levels [534].

EXAMPLE: George is cleared into security level (SECRET, { NUC, EUR }), DocA is classified as (CONFIDENTIAL, { NUC }), DocB is classified as (SECRET, { EUR, US }), and DocC is classified as (SECRET, { EUR }). Then:

- George *dom* DocA as CONFIDENTIAL ≤ SECRET and { NUC } ⊆ { NUC, EUR }
- George ¬*dom* DocB as { EUR, US } ⊄ { NUC, EUR }
- George *dom* DocC as SECRET ≤ SECRET and { EUR } ⊆ { NUC, EUR }

Let $C(S)$ be the category set of subject S, and let $C(O)$ be the category set of object O. The simple security condition, preliminary version, is modified in the obvious way:

Simple Security Condition: S can read O if and only if $S\,dom\,O$ and S has discretionary read access to O.

In the previous example, George can read DocA and DocC but not DocB (again, assuming that the discretionary access controls allow such access).

Suppose Paul is cleared into security level (SECRET, { EUR, US, NUC }) and has discretionary read access to DocB. Paul can read DocB; were he to copy its contents to DocA and set its access permissions accordingly, George could then read DocB. The modified *-property prevents this:

*-Property: S can write to O if and only if $O\,dom\,S$ and S has discretionary write access to O.

DocA *dom* Paul is false (because $C(Paul) \not\subseteq C(DocA)$), so Paul cannot write to DocA.

The simple security condition is often described as "no reads up" and the *-property as "no writes down."

Redefine a *secure system* to be a system in which both the simple security property and the *-property hold. The analogue to the Basic Security Theorem, preliminary version, can also be established by induction.

> **Theorem 5.2.** *Basic Security Theorem:* Let S be a system with a secure initial state s_0, and let T be a set of state transformations. If every element of T preserves the simple security condition and the *-property, then every state $s_i, i \geq 0$, is secure.

At times, a subject must communicate with another subject at a lower level. This requires the higher-level subject to write into a lower-level object that the lower-level subject can read.

EXAMPLE: A colonel with (SECRET, { NUC, EUR }) clearance needs to send a message to a major with (SECRET, { EUR }) clearance. The colonel must write a document that has at most the (SECRET, { EUR }) classification. But this violates the *-property, because (SECRET, { NUC, EUR }) *dom* (SECRET, { EUR }).

The model provides a mechanism for allowing this type of communication. A subject has a *maximum security level* and a *current security level*. The maximum security level must dominate the current security level. A subject may (effectively) decrease its security level from the maximum in order to communicate with entities at lower security levels.

EXAMPLE: The colonel's maximum security level is (SECRET, { NUC, EUR }). She changes her current security level to (SECRET, { EUR }). This is valid, because the maximum security level dominates the current security level. She can then create the document at the major's clearance level and send it to him.

How this policy is instantiated in different environments depends on the requirements of each environment. The conventional use is to define "read" as "allowing information to flow from the object being read to the subject reading," and "write" as "allowing information to flow from the subject writing to the object being written." Thus, "read" usually includes "execute" (because by monitoring the instructions executed, one can determine the contents of portions of the file) and "write" includes "append" (as the information is placed in the file, it does not overwrite what is already in the file, however). Other actions may be included as appropriate; however, those who instantiate the model must understand exactly what those actions are. Chapter 9, "Noninterference and Policy Composition," and Chapter 18, "Confinement Problem," will discuss this subject in considerably more detail.

5.2.2   Example: Trusted Solaris

Trusted Solaris [2140, 2241, 2244–2246] is based on a noninterference policy model (see Chapter 9), which appears as a Bell-LaPadula model for user and process interactions. The mandatory access control policy is based on labels of subjects and objects.

Labels consist of a classification and a set of categories. The security administrator defines the set of valid labels. A *sensitivity label* of a subject and an object is used for mandatory access control. A *clearance* is the least upper bound of all the sensitivity labels of a subject; the clearance need not be a valid label, though. All system objects that are available to users have the distinguished label ADMIN_LOW, which any other label dominates; the privileged administrative objects such as logs and configuration files have the distinguished label ADMIN_HIGH, which dominates any other label.

Each subject S has a controlling user U_S. In addition to a clearance and a sensitivity label S_L, a subject also has an attribute *privileged*(S, P) indicating whether S can override or bypass part of a security policy P, and another attribute *asserted*(S, P) indicating whether S is currently asserting *privileged*(S, P).

The model defines six rules. In the following, a named object O has sensitivity label O_L, and C_L is the clearance of subject S. The policy elements involved are P_1, which is "change S_L," P_2, which is "change O_L," P_3, which is "override O's mandatory read access contol," and P_4, which is "override O's mandatory write access control."

- If $\neg$*privileged*(S, P_1), then no sequence of operations can change S_L to a value that it has not previously assumed.
- If $\neg$*privileged*(S, P_1), then *asserted*(S, P_1) is always false.

- If $\neg privileged(S, \text{change } S_L)$, then no value of S_L can be outside the clearance of U_S.
- For all subjects S and named objects O, if $\neg privileged(S, P_2)$, then no sequence of operations can change O_L to a value that it has not previously assumed.
- For all subjects S and named objects O, if $\neg privileged(S, P_3)$, then write access to O is granted only if $S_L \text{ dom } O_L$. This is the instantiation of the Bell-LaPadula simple security condition.
- For all subjects S and named objects O, if $\neg privileged(S, P_4)$, then read access to O is granted only if $O_L \text{ dom } S_L$ and $C_L \text{ dom } O_L$. This is the instantiation of the Bell-LaPadula *-property.

When a user logs into a Trusted Solaris system, the system determines whether the user's session is to be a single-level session. Each account is assigned a label range; the upper bound of the range is the user's clearance and the lower bound is the user's minimum label. If the two are the same, the user is given a single level session with that label. If not, the user is asked whether the session is to be a single-level or multilevel session, and if the latter the user can specify the session clearance (which must not be dominated by the user's minimum label, and must be dominated by the user's clearance). During a multilevel session, the user can change to any label in the range from the user's minimum label to the session clearance. This is helpful when a single user will define several workspaces, each with its own sensitivity level. Of course, the session clearance must dominate the sensitivity labels of all workspaces used during that session.

Unlike in the Bell-LaPadula model, writing is allowed only when the labels of the subject and the object are equal, or when the file is in a special *downgraded directory* that the administrator can create. In that case, the following must all be true for a subject S with sensitivity label S_L and clearance C_L to write to a file O with sensitivity label O_L, which is in a directory D with sensitivity label D_L:

- $S_L \text{ dom } D_L$;
- S has discretionary read and search access to D;
- $O_L \text{ dom } S_L$ and $O_L \neq S_L$;
- S has discretionary write access to O; and
- $C_L \text{ dom } O_L$.

Note that the subject cannot read the object.

EXAMPLE: A process has clearance C_L and label S_L, a file has sensitivity label F_L, and the file is in a directory with sensitivity label D_L. The process has discretionary access to read and write the file and to read and search the directory. If $S_L \text{ dom } F_L$, then the process can read the file. If $S_L = F_L$, then the process can write the file.

If the administrator creates a special case to allow writing up, as $S_L \, dom \, D_L$, $F_L \, dom \, S_L$, $F_L \neq S_L$, and $C_L \, dom \, F_L$, then the process can write the file. Note that, as $S_L \neg dom \, F_L$, the process cannot read the file in this case.

In all cases, the discretionary access controls must allow the accesses shown for the process to be able to read or write the file.

When a process creates a file, the file is given the process's label.

5.2.2.1   Directories and Labels

Suppose a process tries to create a file at level L_2 in a directory that contains a file with label L_1 ($L_1 \, dom \, L_2$). The create will fail, and now the process knows that an "invisible" file at a level it does not dominate exists in this directory. Two mechanisms have been developed to handle this situation.

Trusted Solaris uses a *multilevel directory* (MLD) to hold files of different sensitivity levels [2244, 2246]. Initially, all home directories and many directories for spool and temporary files are MLDs, and new directories can be created as MLDs. An MLD contains directories at single sensitivity levels called *single-level directories* or SLDs. These in turn contain ordinary UNIX directories, files, and file system objects. If a process creates a file in an MLD and no SLD with the corresponding label exists, that SLD will be created.

MLDs allow two types of file references. The first, a regular reference, simply names a file in the directory. The operating system automatically maps that name into a name in the SLD with the same sensitivity label as the process.[2] The second, a reference using adornment, enables the process to name a file in a specific SLD by giving the full ("adorned") name of the MLD and identifying the specific SLD in it. This enables a process, for example, to list all SLDs in an MLD with the same sensitivity label as the process.

EXAMPLE: A process references an MLD by its name, for example *mydir*. This was a transparent reference; an adorned reference, giving the actual directory name, would have the prefix ".MLD" (that is, .MLD.*mydir*).

Suppose that the MLD contained three SLDs, with distinct labels L_1, L_2, and L_3. The SLDs would be called .SLD.1, .SLD.2, and .SLD.3, respectively.

If process p had sensitivity label L_2, p could read, write, create, and delete objects in the SLD with label L_2 (that is, .SLD.2), because they are at the same level. Whenever p referred to a file in *mydir*, Trusted Solaris translated the path name to refer to the file in .MLD.*mydir*/.SLD.2.

To read a file f in .SLD.3 (which has label L_3), p specified the name of the file to be read. Thus, it would have opened the file .MLD.*mydir*/.SLD.3/f. If p had specified the unadorned name, *mydir*/f, that would have been translated into the file name .MLD.*mydir*/.SLD.1/f, which would have referred to a different file.

---

[2]If necessary, for example when creating the file, the system would create the SLD.

The information that a process obtained about an MLD depends on the particular system call used.

EXAMPLE: When a process executed the system call

```
res = mldstat("/tmp", &stbuf)
```

the structure *stbuf* was filled with information about the MLD /tmp. But if it executed the system call

```
res = stat("/tmp", &stbuf)
```

then that structure would be filled with information about the SLD in /tmp corresponding to the sensitivity label of the process, and not its containing MLD /tmp.

Of course, the mandatory and discretionary permissions must be set appropriately so the calls can be made.

An alternate technique, called *labeled zones* (or, more simply, *zones*), provides a different method of handling directories. Solaris Trusted Extensions, which support non-Trusted Solaris systems, uses this technique, as do other multilevel secure systems [649, 2241].

A *zone* is a virtual environment tied to a unique label. It provides isolation among processes, because by default each process can only access objects within its zone. A distinguished *global zone* encompasses everything on the system, and thus has the label ADMIN_HIGH. Only administrators can access this zone.

A zone has a unique root directory. When this is mounted, all objects within the file system have the zone's label. Other file systems can be imported, or mounted, from another zone. They retain their original label. Before the import, the kernel checks the relationships between the two zone's labels.

- If the import is to be read-only, the importing zone's label must dominate the label of the zone of the file system being imported. This enforces the simple security property.
- If the import is to be read-write, the zone labels must be equal. As each zone has a unique label, the zones are the same; thus, no import is needed.

Labels are checked only at the time of import. Because of the nature of zones, this ensures that a process can access an object only when the multilevel security constraints allow.

Imported file systems have names distinct from files in the importing zone. In Solaris Trusted Extensions, an imported file system is mounted at the directory "*/zone/label.*" Executables from system areas, which are in the global zone, are mounted using a special loopback option that makes them appear to be at

ADMIN_LOW. This same option is used to mount file systems read-only when that system is mounted in a zone the label of which dominates that of the file system.

EXAMPLE: Figure 5–3 shows a Solaris Trusted Extensions system global zone, at level ADMIN_HIGH, containing three other labeled zones, labeled L_1, L_2, and L_3. Each zone has a root directory with an export and zone subdirectories. As L_1 *dom* L_2, L_1's zone subdirectory itself has a subdirectory L_2 upon which the contents of L_2's export subdirectory is mounted. This enables a process in L_1 to read files with L_2's classification that L_1 has discretionary permission to read. Further, to allow access to system executables, configuration files, and other necessary system elements, the system directories are mounted as subdirectories under L_1's root directory using the loopback option. A process in L_1 can only read a file in zone L_2 if that file is in the export subdirectory and discretionary permissions are set appropriately. As L_3 *dom* L_2, the L_3 zone is structured similarly. As L_1 and L_3 are disjoint (that is, neither dominates the other), they do not share any files.

In addition, each zone has system directories imported from the global zone. These are mounted at the level ADMIN_LOW, and thus can only be read.

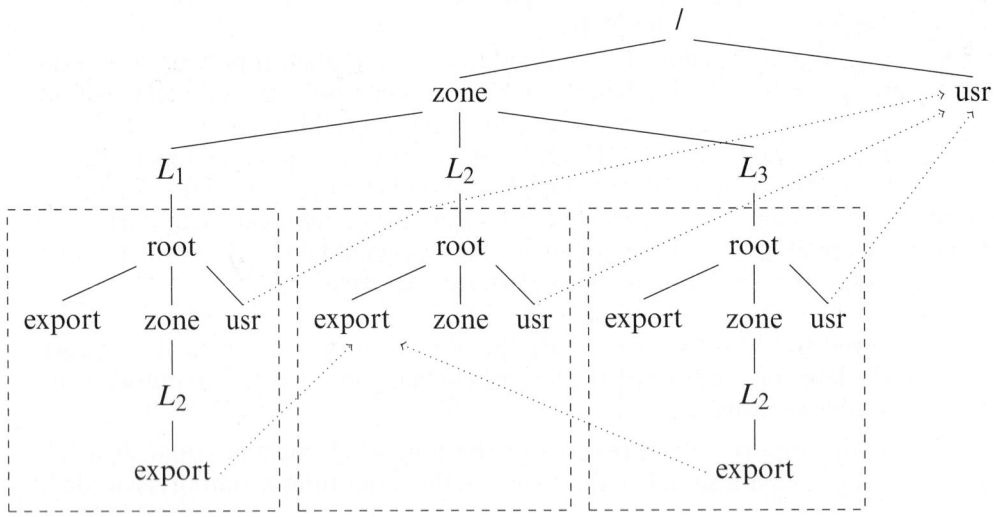

Figure 5–3 An example Solaris Trusted Extensions file system. Three labeled zones (L_1, L_2, and L_3) are configured to make their export subdirectories visible. Only zones whose labels dominate L_2 can see those directories. Further, the system directories such as /usr are mounted in each zone so processes can execute system programs. The solid lines are normal mounts; the dotted lines are loopback mounts.

5.2.3   Formal Model

Let S be the set of subjects of a system and let O be the set of objects. Let P be the set of rights $\underline{r}$ for read, $\underline{a}$ for write, $\underline{w}$ for read/write, and $\underline{e}$ for empty.[3] Let M be a set of possible access control matrices for the system. Let C be the set of classifications (or clearances), let K be the set of categories, and let $L = C \times K$ be the set of security levels. Finally, let F be the set of 3-tuples (f_s, f_o, f_c), where f_s and f_c associate with each subject maximum and current security levels, respectively, and f_o associates with each object a security level. The relation *dom* from Definition 5–1 is defined here in the obvious way.

The system objects may be organized as a set of hierarchies (trees and single nodes). Let H represent the set of hierarchy functions $h : O \rightarrow \mathcal{P}(O)$.[4] These functions have two properties. Let $o_i, o_j, o_k \in O$. Then:

- If $o_i \neq o_j$, then $h(o_i) \cap h(o_j) = \varnothing$.
- There is no set $\{ o_1, o_2, ..., o_k \} \subseteq O$ such that $o_{i+1} \in h(o_i)$ for each $i = 1, ..., k$, and $o_{k+1} = o_1$.

(See Exercise 5.)

A state $v \in V$ of a system is a 4-tuple (b, m, f, h), where $b \in \mathcal{P}(S \times O \times P)$ indicates which subjects have access to which objects, and what those access rights are; $m \in M$ is the access control matrix for the current state; $f \in F$ is the 3-tuple indicating the current subject and object clearances and categories; and $h \in H$ is the hierarchy of objects for the current state. The difference between b and m is that the rights in m may be unusable because of differences in security levels; b contains the set of rights that may be exercised, and m contains the set of discretionary rights.

R denotes the set of requests for access. The form of the requests affects the instantiation, not the formal model, and is not discussed further here. Four outcomes of each request are possible: $\underline{y}$ for yes (allowed), $\underline{n}$ for no (not allowed), $\underline{i}$ for illegal request, and $\underline{o}$ for error (multiple outcomes are possible). D denotes the set of outcomes. The set $W \subseteq R \times D \times V \times V$ is the set of actions of the system. This notation means that an entity issues a request in R, and a decision in D occurs, moving the system from one state in V to another (possibly different) state in V. Given these definitions, we can now define the history of a system as it executes.

Let N be the set of positive integers. These integers represent times. Let $X = R^N$ be a set whose elements x are sequences of requests, let $Y = D^N$ be a set whose

---

[3] The right called "empty" here is called "execute" in Bell and LaPadula [150]. However, they define "execute" as "neither observation nor alteration" (and note that it differs from the notion of "execute" that most systems implement). For clarity, we changed the $\underline{e}$ right's name to the more descriptive "empty."

[4] $\mathcal{P}(O)$ is the power set of O—that is, the set of all possible subsets of O.

elements y are sequences of decisions, and let $Z = V^N$ be a set whose elements z are sequences of states. The ith components of x, y, and z are represented as x_i, y_i, and z_i, respectively. The interpretation is that for some $t \in N$, the system is in state $z_{t-1} \in V$; a subject makes request $x_t \in R$, the system makes a decision $y_t \in D$, and as a result the system transitions into a (possibly new) state $z_t \in V$.

A system is represented as an initial state and a sequence of requests, decisions, and states. In formal terms, $\Sigma(R, D, W, z_0) \subseteq X \times Y \times Z$ represents the system, and z_0 is the initial state of the system. $(x, y, z) \in \Sigma(R, D, W, z_0)$ if and only if $(x_t, y_t, z_t, z_{t-1}) \in W$ for all $t \in N$. (x, y, z) is an *appearance* of $\Sigma(R, D, W, z_0)$.

EXAMPLE: Consider a system with two levels (HIGH and LOW), one category (ALL), one subject s, one object o, and two rights, read ($\underline{r}$) and write ($\underline{w}$). Then:

$$S = \{ s \}, O = \{ o \}, P = \{ \underline{r}, \underline{w} \}, C = \{ \text{HIGH}, \text{LOW} \}, K = \{ \text{ALL} \}$$

For every function $f \in F$, $f_c(s)$ is either (LOW, { ALL }) or (HIGH, { ALL }), and $f_o(o)$ is either (LOW, { ALL }) or (HIGH, { ALL }). Now, suppose $b_1 = \{ (s, o, \underline{r}) \}$, $m_1 \in M$ gives s read access over o, and for $f_1 \in F$, $f_{c,1}(s) = (\text{HIGH}, \{ \text{ALL} \})$ and $f_{o,1}(o) = (\text{LOW}, \{ \text{ALL} \})$. This describes a state of the system in which s has read rights to o, so $v_0 = (b_1, m_1, f_1) \in V$.

Now suppose $S = \{ s, s' \}$, $f_{s,1}(s') = (\text{LOW}, \{ \text{ALL} \})$, and m_1 gives s' write access over o as well as giving s read access over o. Because s' has not yet written o, b_1 is unchanged. Take $z_0 = (b_1, m_1, f_1)$ and consider the system $\Sigma(R, D, W, z_0)$. If s' makes the request r_1 to write to o, the system will decide $d_1 = \underline{y}$ (yes), and will transition to the state $v_1 = (b_2, m_1, f_1) \in V$, where $b_2 = \{ (s, o, \underline{r}), (s', o, \underline{w}) \}$. In this case, $x = (r_1)$, $y = (\underline{y})$, and $z = (v_0, v_1)$.

The next request r_2 is for s to write to o; however, this is disallowed ($d_2 = \underline{n}$, or no). The resulting state is the same as the preceding one. Now $x = (r_1, r_2)$, $y = (\underline{y}, \underline{n})$, and $z = (v_0, v_1, v_2)$, where $v_2 = v_1$.

5.2.3.1   Basic Security Theorem

The Basic Security Theorem combines the simple security condition, the *-property, and a discretionary security property. We now formalize these three properties.

Formally, the simple security condition is:

Definition 5–2. $(s, o, p) \in S \times O \times P$ satisfies the *simple security condition* relative to f (written *ssc rel f*) if and only if one of the following holds:

(a) $p = \underline{e}$ or $p = \underline{a}$

(b) $p = \underline{r}$ or $p = \underline{w}$, and $f_s(s)\, dom\, f_o(o)$

This definition says that, to satisfy the simple security condition, either s cannot read o or the security level of s must dominate that of o. A state (b, m, f, h) satisfies the simple security condition if all elements of b satisfy *ssc rel f*. A system satisfies the simple security condition if all its states satisfy the simple security condition.

Let $s \in S$ and $p_1, \ldots, p_n \in R$. Define $b(s : p_1, \ldots, p_n)$ to be the set of all objects that s has $p_1, \ldots, p_n$ access to:

$$b(s : p_1, \ldots, p_n) = \{ o \mid o \in O \wedge [(s, o, p_1) \in b \vee \ldots \vee (s, o, p_n) \in b] \}$$

If a subject can write to an object, the object's classification must dominate the subject's clearance ("write up"); if the subject can also read the object, the subject's clearance must be the same as the object's classification ("equality for read"). More formally:

Definition 5–3. A state (b, m, f, h) satisfies the **-property* if and only if, for each $s \in S$, the following hold:

(a) $b(s : \underline{a}) \neq \varnothing \Rightarrow [\forall o \in b(s : \underline{a})[f_o(o) \, dom \, f_c(s)]]$
(b) $b(s : \underline{w}) \neq \varnothing \Rightarrow [\forall o \in b(s : \underline{w})[f_o(o) = f_c(s)]]$
(c) $b(s : \underline{r}) \neq \varnothing \Rightarrow [\forall o \in b(s : \underline{r})[f_c(s) \, dom \, f_o(o)]]$

This prevents a higher level subject from writing information where a lower-level subject can (then) read it. A system satisfies the *-property if all its states satisfy the *-property. In many systems, only a subset S' of subjects satisfy the *-property; in this case, we say that the *-property is satisfied relative to $S' \subseteq S$.

Definition 5–4. A state (b, m, f, h) satisfies the *discretionary security property* (*ds-property*) if and only if, for each triple $(s, o, p) \in b$, $p \in m[s, o]$.

The access control matrix allows the controller of an object to condition access based on identity. The model therefore supports both mandatory and discretionary controls, and defines "secure" in terms of both. A system satisfies the discretionary security property if all its states satisfy the discretionary security property.

Definition 5–5. A system is *secure* if it satisfies the simple security condition, the *-property, and the discretionary security property.

The notion of an *action*, or a request and decision that moves the system from one state to another, must also be formalized, as follows.

Definition 5–6. $(r, d, v, v') \in R \times D \times V \times V$ is an *action* of $\Sigma(R, D, W, z_0)$ if and only if there is an $(x, y, z) \in \Sigma(R, D, W, z_0)$ and a $t \in N$ such that $(r, d, v, v') = (x_t, y_t, z_t, z_{t-1})$.

Thus, an action is a request/decision pair that occurs during the execution of the system.

We now can establish conditions under which the three properties hold.

Theorem 5.3. $\Sigma(R, D, W, z_0)$ satisfies the simple security condition for any secure state z_0 if and only if, for every action $(r, d, (b, m, f, h), (b', m', f', h'))$, W satisfies the following:

(a) Every $(s, o, p) \in b - b'$ satisfies *ssc rel f*.
(b) Every $(s, o, p) \in b'$ that does not satisfy *ssc rel f* is not in b.

Proof Let $(x, y, z) \in \Sigma(R, D, W, z_0)$ and write $z_t = (b_t, m_t, f_t, h_t)$ for $t \in N$.

($\Rightarrow$) By contradiction. Without loss of generality, take $b = b_t$ and $b' = b_{t-1}$. Assume that $\Sigma(R, D, W, z_0)$ satisfies the simple security condition for some secure state z_0, and that either some $(s, o, p) \in b - b' = b_t - b_{t-1}$ does not satisfy *ssc rel f_t* or some $(s, o, p) \in b' = b_{t-1}$ that does not satisfy *ssc rel f_t* is in $b = b_t$. If the former, there is some $(s, o, p) \in b_t$ that does not satisfy *ssc rel f_t*, because $b_t - b_{t-1} \subseteq b_t$. If the latter, there is some $(s, o, p) \in b_{t-1}$ that does not satisfy *ssc rel f_t* but that is in b_t. In either case, there is some $(s, o, p) \in b_t$ that does not satisfy the simple security condition relative to f_t, which means that $\Sigma(R, D, W, z_0)$ does not satisfy the simple security condition for some secure state z_0, contradicting the hypothesis.

($\Leftarrow$) By induction on t.

Basis. $z_0 = (b_0, m_0, f_0, h_0)$ is secure, by the hypothesis of the claim.

Induction Hypothesis. $z_{i-1} = (b_{i-1}, m_{i-1}, f_{i-1}, h_{i-1})$ is secure, for $i < t$.

Induction Step. Let $(x_t, y_t, z_t, z_{t-1}) \in W$. By (a), every $(s, o, p) \in b_t - b_{t-1}$ satisfies *ssc rel f_t*. Let $\overline{b_{t-1}} = \{ (s, o, p) | (s, o, p) \in b_{t-1} \wedge (s, o, p)$ does not satisfy *ssc rel f_t* $\}$. By (b), $b_t \cap \overline{b_{t-1}} = \varnothing$; so, $\overline{b_{t-1}} \cap (b_t \cap b_{t-1}) = (\overline{b_{t-1}} \cap b_t) \cap b_{t-1} = \varnothing$. This means that if $(s, o, p) \in b_t \cap b_{t-1}$, then $(s, o, p) \notin \overline{b_{t-1}}$ and so (s, o, p) satisfies *ssc rel f_t*. Hence, if $(s, o, p) \in b_t$, then either $(s, o, p) \in b_t \cap b_{t-1}$ or $(s, o, p) \in b_t - b_{t-1}$. In the first case, the induction hypothesis ensures that (s, o, p) satisfies the simple security condition. In the second case, (a) ensures that (s, o, p) satisfies the simple security condition. Hence, $z_t = (b_t, m_t, f_t, h_t)$ is secure. This completes the proof.

Theorem 5.4. $\Sigma(R, D, W, z_0)$ satisfies the *-property relative to $S' \subseteq S$ for any secure state z_0 if and only if, for every action $(r, d, (b, m, f, h), (b', m', f', h'))$, W satisfies the following for every $s \in S'$:

(a) Every $(s, o, p) \in b - b'$ satisfies the *-property with respect to S'.
(b) Every $(s, o, p) \in b'$ that does not satisfy the *-property with respect to S' is not in b.

Proof See Exercise 7.

Theorem 5.5. $\Sigma(R, D, W, z_0)$ satisfies the ds-property for any secure state z_0 if and only if, for every action $(r, d, (b, m, f, h), (b', m', f', h'))$, W satisfies the following:

(a) Every $(s, o, p) \in b - b'$ satisfies the ds-property.
(b) Every $(s, o, p) \in b'$ that does not satisfy the ds-property is not in b.

Proof See Exercise 8.

Theorems 5.3, 5.4, and 5.5 combine to give us the Basic Security Theorem:

Theorem 5.6. *Basic Security Theorem:* $\Sigma(R, D, W, z_0)$ is a secure system if z_0 is a secure state and W satisfies the conditions of Theorems 5.3, 5.4, and 5.5.

Proof Immediate from Theorems 5.3, 5.4, and 5.5.

5.2.3.2   Rules of Transformation

A *rule* is a function $\rho : R \times V \to D \times V$. Intuitively, a rule takes a state and a request, and determines if the request meets the conditions of the rule (the decision). If so, it moves the system to a (possibly different) state. The idea is that a rule captures the means by which a system may transition from one state to another.

Of course, the rules affect the security of a system. For example, a rule that changes all read rights so that a subject has the ability to read objects with classifications higher than the subject's clearance may move the system from a secure state to a nonsecure state. In this section we develop constraints that rules must meet to preserve security, and we give an example rule.

Definition 5–7. A rule ρ is *ssc-preserving* if, for all $(r, v) \in R \times V$ and v satisfying *ssc rel* f, $\rho(r, v) = (d, v')$ means that v' satisfies *ssc rel* f'.

Similar definitions hold for the *-property and the ds-property. If a rule is ssc-preserving, *-property-preserving, and ds-property-preserving, the rule is said to be *security-preserving*.

We define a relation with respect to a set of rules $\omega = \{ \rho_1, ..., \rho_m \}$ in such a way that each type of request is handled by at most one rule; this eliminates ambiguity and ensures that the mapping from $R \times V$ to $D \times V$ is one-to-one.

Definition 5–8. Let $\omega = \{ \rho_1, ..., \rho_m \}$ be a set of rules. For request $r \in R$, decision $d \in D$, and states $v, v' \in V$, $(r, d, v, v') \in W(\omega)$ if and only if $d \neq \underline{i}$ and there is a unique integer i, $1 \leq i \leq m$, such that $\rho_i(r, v') = (d, v)$.

This definition says that if the request is legal and there is only one rule that will change the state of the system from v to v', the corresponding action is in $W(\omega)$.

The next theorem presents conditions under which a set of rules preserves the simple security condition.

Theorem 5.7. Let ω be a set of ssc-preserving rules, and let z_0 be a state satisfying the simple security condition. Then $\Sigma(R, D, W, z_0)$ satisfies the simple security condition.

Proof By contradiction. Let $(x, y, z) \in \Sigma(R, D, W(\omega), z_0)$ be a state that does not satisfy the simple security property. Without loss of generality, choose $t \in N$ such that (x_t, y_t, z_t) is the first appearance of $\Sigma(R, D, W(\omega), z_0)$ that does not satisfy the simple security property. Because $(x_t, y_t, z_t, z_{t-1}) \in W(\omega)$, there is a unique rule $\rho \in \omega$ such that $\rho(x_t, z_{t-1}) = (y_t, z_t)$, and $y_t \neq \underline{i}$. Because ρ is ssc-preserving, and z_{t-1} satisfies the simple security condition, by Definition 5–7, z_t must meet the simple security condition. This contradicts our choice of t, and the assumption that (x, y, z) does not meet the simple security property. Hence, the theorem is proved.

When does adding a state preserve the simple security property?

Theorem 5.8. Let $v = (b, m, f, h)$ satisfy the simple security condition. Let $(s, o, p) \notin b$, $b' = b \cup \{ (s, o, p) \}$, and $v' = (b', m, f, h)$. Then v' satisfies the simple security condition if and only if either of the following conditions is true:

(a) Either $p = \underline{e}$ or $p = \underline{a}$.
(b) Either $p = \underline{r}$ or $p = \underline{w}$, and $f_s(s) \, dom \, f_o(o)$.

Proof For (a), the theorem follows from Definition 5–2 and v' satisfying *ssc rel f*. For (b), if v' satisfies the simple security condition, then, by definition, $f_s(s) \, dom \, f_o(o)$. Moreover, if $f_s(s) \, dom \, f_o(o)$, then $(s, o, p) \in b'$ satisfies *ssc rel f*; hence, v' is secure.

Similar theorems hold for the *-property:

Theorem 5.9. Let ω be a set of *-property-preserving rules, and let z_0 be a state satisfying the *-property. Then $\Sigma(R, D, W, z_0)$ satisfies the *-property.

Proof See Exercise 8.

Theorem 5.10. Let $v = (b, m, f, h)$ satisfy the *-property. Let $(s, o, p) \in b$, $b' = b \cup \{ (s, o, p) \}$, and $v' = (b', m, f, h)$. Then v' satisfies the *-property if and only if one of the following conditions holds:

(a) $p = \underline{a}$ and $f_o(o) \, dom \, f_c(s)$
(b) $p = \underline{w}$ and $f_o(o) = f_c(s)$
(c) $p = \underline{r}$ and $f_c(s) \, dom \, f_o(o)$

Proof If v' satisfies the *-property, then the claim follows immediately from Definition 5–3. Conversely, assume that condition (a) holds. Let $(s', o', p') \in b'$. If $(s', o', p') \in b$, the assumption that v satisfies the *-property means that v' also satisfies the *-property. Otherwise, $(s', o', p') = (s, o, p)$ and, by condition (a), the *-property holds. The proof for each of the other two conditions is similar. Thus, v' satisfies the *-property.

Theorem 5.11. Let ω be a set of ds-property-preserving rules, and let z_0 be a state satisfying the ds-property. Then $\Sigma(R, D, W(\omega), z_0)$ satisfies the ds-property.

Proof See Exercise 8.

Theorem 5.12. Let $v = (b, m, f, h)$ satisfy the ds-property. Let $(s, o, p) \notin b$, $b' = b \cup \{ (s, o, p) \}$, and $v' = (b', m, f, h)$. Then v' satisfies the ds-property if and only if $p \in m[s, o]$.

Proof If v' satisfies the ds-property, then the claim follows immediately from Definition 5–4. Conversely, assume that $p \in m[s, o]$. Because $(s', o', p') \in b'$, the ds-property holds for v'. Thus, v' satisfies the ds-property.

Finally, we present the following theorem.

Theorem 5.13. Let ρ be a rule and $\rho(r, v) = (d, v')$, where $v = (b, m, f, h)$ and $v' = (b', m', f', h')$. Then:

(a) If $b' \subseteq b, f' = f$, and v satisfies the simple security condition, then v' satisfies the simple security condition.
(b) If $b' \subseteq b, f' = f$, and v satisfies the *-property, then v' satisfies the *-property.
(c) If $b' \subseteq b, m[s, o] \subseteq m'[s, o]$ for all $s \in S$ and $o \in O$, and v satisfies the ds-property, then v' satisfies the ds-property.

Proof Suppose that v satisfies the simple security property. Because $b' \subseteq b$, $(s, o, \underline{r}) \in b'$ implies $(s, o, \underline{r}) \in b$, and $(s, o, \underline{w}) \in b'$ implies $(s, o, \underline{w}) \in b$. So

$f_s(s) \, dom f_o(o)$. But $f' = f$. Thus, $f'_s(s) \, dom f'_o(o)$. So v' satisfies the simple security condition.

The proofs of the other two parts are analogous.

5.2.4   Example Model Instantiation: Multics

We now examine the modeling of specific actions. The Multics system [150, 1477] has 11 rules affecting the rights on the system. These rules are divided into five groups. Let the set Q contain the set of request operations (such as *get*, *give*, and so forth). Then:

- $R^{(1)} = Q \times S \times O \times M$. This is the set of requests to request and release access. The rules are *get-read*, *get-append*, *get-execute*, *get-write*, and *release-read/execute/write/append*. These rules differ in the conditions necessary for the subject to be able to request the desired right. The rule *get-read* is discussed in more detail in Section 5.2.4.1.

- $R^{(2)} = S \times Q \times S \times O \times M$. This is the set of requests to give access to and remove access from a different subject. The rules are *give-read/execute/write/append* and *rescind-read/execute/write/append*. Again, the rules differ in the conditions needed to acquire and delete the rights, but within each rule, the right being added or removed does not affect the conditions. Whether the right is being added or deleted does affect them. The rule *give-read/execute/write/append* is discussed in more detail in Section 5.2.4.2.

- $R^{(3)} = Q \times S \times O \times L$. This is the set of requests to create and reclassify objects. It contains the *create-object* and *change-object-security-level* rules. The object's security level is either assigned (*create-object*) or changed (*change-object-security-level*).

- $R^{(4)} = S \times O$. This is the set of requests to remove objects. It contains only the rule *delete-object-group*, which deletes an object and all objects beneath it in the hierarchy.

- $R^{(5)} = S \times L$. This is the set of requests to change a subject's security level. It contains only the rule *change-subject-current-security-level*, which changes a subject's current security level (not the maximum security level).

Then, the set of requests is $R = R^{(1)} \cup R^{(2)} \cup R^{(3)} \cup R^{(4)} \cup R^{(5)}$.

The Multics system includes the notion of trusted users. The system does not enforce the *-property for this set of subjects $S_T \subseteq S$; however, members of S_T are trusted not to violate that property.

For each rule ρ, define $\Delta(\rho)$ as the domain of the request (that is, whether or not the components of the request form a valid operand for the rule).

We next consider two rules in order to demonstrate how to prove that the rules preserve the simple security property, the *-property, and the discretionary security property.

5.2.4.1   The *get-read* Rule

The *get-read* rule enables a subject s to request the right to read an object o. Represent this request as $\rho = (get, s, o, \underline{r}) \in R^{(1)}$, and let the current state of the system be $v = (b, m, f, h)$. Then *get-read* is the rule $\rho_1(r, v)$:

> **if** $(r \notin \Delta(\rho_1))$ **then** $\rho_1(r, v) = (\underline{i}, v)$;
> **else if** $(f_s(s) \, dom \, f_o(o)$ **and** $(s \in S_T$ **or** $f_c(s) \, dom \, f_o(o))$ **and** $r \in m[s, o])$
>   **then** $\rho_1(r, v) = (\underline{y}, b \cup \{ (s, o, \underline{r}) \}, m, f, h))$;
> **else** $\rho_1(r, v) = (\underline{n}, v)$;

The first **if** tests the parameters of the request; if any of them are incorrect, the decision is "illegal" and the system state remains unchanged. The second **if** checks three conditions. The simple security property for the maximum security level of the subject and the classification of the object must hold. Either the subject making the request must be trusted, or the *-property must hold for the *current* security level of the subject (this allows trusted subjects to read information from objects above their current security levels but at or below their maximum security levels; they are trusted not to reveal the information inappropriately). Finally, the discretionary security property must hold. If these three conditions hold, so does the Basic Security Theorem. The decision is "yes" and the system state is updated to reflect the new access. Otherwise, the decision is "no" and the system state remains unchanged.

We now show that if the current state of the system satisfies the simple security condition, the *-property, and the ds-property, then after the *get-read* rule is applied, the state of the system also satisfies those three conditions.

> **Theorem 5.14.** The *get-read* rule ρ_1 preserves the simple security condition, the *-property, and the ds-property.

> **Proof** Let v satisfy the simple security condition, the *-property, and the ds-property. Let $\rho_1(r, v) = (d, v')$. Either $v' = v$ or $v' = (b \cup \{ (s_2, o, \underline{r}) \}, m, f, h)$, by the *get-read* rule. In the former case, because v satisfies the simple security condition, the *-property, and the ds-property, so does v'. So let $v' = (b \cup (s_2, o, \underline{r}), m, f, h)$.
>   Consider the simple security condition. From the choice of v', either $b' - b = \varnothing$ or $b' - b = \{ (s_2, o, \underline{r}) \}$. If $b' - b = \varnothing$, then $\{ (s_2, o, \underline{r}) \} \in b$, so $v = v'$, proving that v' satisfies the simple security condition. Otherwise, because the *get-read* rule requires that $f_s(s) \, dom \, f_o(o)$, Theorem 5.8 says that v' satisfies the simple security condition.

Consider the *-property. From the definition of the *get-read* rule, either $s \in S_T$ or $f_c(s) \, dom \, f_o(o)$. If $s \in S_T$, then s is trusted and the *-property holds by the definition of S_T. Otherwise, by Theorem 5.10, because $f_c(s) \, dom \, f_o(o)$, v' satisfies the *-property.

Finally, consider the ds-property. The condition in the *get-read* rule requires that $\underline{r} \in m[s, o]$ and $b' - b = \varnothing$ or $b' - b = \{ (s_2, o, \underline{r}) \}$. If $b' - b = \varnothing$, then $\{ (s_2, o, \underline{r}) \} \in b$, so $v = v'$, proving that v' satisfies the ds-property. Otherwise, $\{ (s_2, o, \underline{r}) \} \notin b$, which meets the conditions of Theorem 5.12. From that theorem, v' satisfies the ds-property.

Hence, the *get-read* rule preserves the security of the system.

5.2.4.2   The *give-read* Rule

The *give-read* rule[5] enables a subject s to give subject s_2 the (discretionary) right to read an object o. Conceptually, a subject can give another subject read access to an object if the giver can alter (write to) the parent of the object. If the parent is the root of the hierarchy containing the object, or if the object itself is the root of the hierarchy, the subject must be specially authorized to grant access.

Some terms simplify the definitions and proofs. Define *root(o)* as the root object of the hierarchy h containing o, and define *parent(o)* as the parent of o in h. If the subject is specially authorized to grant access to the object in the situation just mentioned, the predicate *canallow(s, o, v)* is true. Finally, define $m \wedge m[s, o] \leftarrow \underline{r}$ as the access control matrix m with the right $\underline{r}$ added to entry $m[s, o]$.

Represent the *give-read* request as $r = (s_1, give, s_2, o, \underline{r}) \in R^{(2)}$, and let the current state of the system be $v = (b, m, f, h)$. Then, *give-read* is the rule $\rho_6(r, v)$:

> **if** $(r \notin \Delta(\rho_6))$ **then** $\rho_6(\underline{i}, v) = (\underline{i}, v)$;
> **else if** ([$o \neq root(o)$ **and** $parent(o) \neq root(o)$ **and** $parent(o) \in b(s_1 : \underline{w})$]
>   **or** [$parent(o) = root(o)$ **and** $canallow(s_1, o, v)$]
>   **or** [$o = root(o)$ **and** $canallow(s_1, root(o), v)$])
>   **then** $\rho_6(r, v) = (\underline{y}, (b, m \wedge m[s_2, o] \leftarrow \underline{r}, f, h))$;
> **else** $\rho_6(r, v) = (\underline{n}, v)$;

The first **if** tests the parameters of the request; if any of them are incorrect, the decision is "illegal" and the system state remains unchanged. The second **if** checks several conditions. If neither the object nor its parent is the root of the hierarchy containing the object, then s_1 must have write rights to the parent. If the object or its parent is the root of the hierarchy, then s_1 must have special permission to give s_2 the read right to o. The decision is "yes" and the access

---

[5] Actually, the rule is *give-read/execute/write/append*. The generalization is left as an exercise for the reader.

control matrix is updated to reflect the new access. Otherwise, the decision is "no" and the system state remains unchanged.

We now show that if the current state of the system satisfies the simple security condition, the *-property, and the ds-property, then after the *give-read* rule is applied, the state of the system also satisfies those three conditions.

Theorem 5.15. The *give-read* rule ρ_6 preserves the simple security condition, the *-property, and the ds-property.

Proof Let v satisfy the simple security condition, the *-property, and the ds-property. Let $\rho_6(r, v) = (d, v')$. Either $v' = v$ or $v' = (b, m \wedge m[s, o] \leftarrow \underline{r}, f, h)$, by the *give-read* rule. In the former case, because v satisfies the simple security condition, the *-property, and the ds-property, so does v'. So, let $v' = (b, m \wedge m[s, o] \leftarrow \underline{r}, f, h)$.

Here, $b' = b$, $f' = f$, and $m[x, y] = m'[x, y]$ for all $x \in S$ and $y \in O$ such that $x \neq s$ and $y \neq o$. In that case, $m[s, o] \subseteq m'[s, o]$. Hence, by Theorem 5.13, v' satisfies the simple security condition, the *-property, and the ds-property.

Hence, the *get-read* rule preserves the security of the system.

5.3   Tranquility

The *principle of tranquility* states that subjects and objects may not change their security levels once they have been instantiated. Suppose that security levels of objects can be changed, and consider the effects on a system with one category and two security clearances, HIGH and LOW. If an object's security classification is raised from LOW to HIGH, then any subjects cleared to only LOW can no longer read that object. Similarly, if an object's classification is dropped from HIGH to LOW, any subject can now read that object.

Both situations violate fundamental restrictions. Raising the classification of an object means that information that was available is no longer available; lowering the classification means that information previously considered restricted is now available to all.

Raising the classification of an object blocks further access to that object by some subjects. The model does not define how to determine the appropriate classification of information. It merely describes how to manipulate an object containing the information once that object has been assigned a classification. Information in an object with a particular classification is assumed to be known to all who can access that object, and so raising its classification will not achieve the desired goal (preventing access to the information). The information has already been accessed.

EXAMPLE: In 1978, James Bamford requested documents about the U.S. Department of Justice's investigation of illegal wiretapping by the U.S. National Security Agency. After some delay, the Department of Justice provided 250 pages of newly declassified information, over the National Security Agency's objections. Two years later, the National Security Agency prevailed upon a different U.S. Attorney General to retroactively classify the pages, thereby raising their classification. Despite a demand that he return the pages and not publish information in them, Mr. Bamford did so in his book *The Puzzle Palace*. He was not prosecuted [7].

Lowering the classification level is another matter entirely and is known as the *declassification problem*. In essence, the LOW subjects either have, or have had, access to HIGH information, in violation of the simple security condition. Because this makes information available to subjects who did not have access to it before, it is in effect a "write down" that violates the *-property. The typical solution is to define a set of trusted entities or subjects that will remove all sensitive information from the HIGH object before its classification is changed to LOW. How those entities are defined depends on policy.

EXAMPLE: In some systems, the owners of each object are trusted to determine how to release it. The JFlow language [1407] is an extension to Java that uses labels consisting of a set of owners and, for each owner, a list of "readers" that each trusts. The set of readers that *all* owners of an object trusts is called the *effective reader set*, and consists of those subjects with the ability to access (read) the information. By adding readers to its own list, an owner can effectively declassify the information in the object.

The tranquility principle actually has two forms:

Definition 5–9. The *principle of strong tranquility* states that security levels do not change during the lifetime of the system.

Strong tranquility eliminates the need for trusted declassifiers, because no declassification can occur. Moreover, no raising of security levels can occur. This eliminates the problems discussed above. However, stong tranquility is also inflexible and in practice is usually too strong a requirement.

Definition 5–10. The *principle of weak tranquility* states that security levels do not change in a way that violates the rules of a given security policy.

Weak tranquility moderates the restriction to allow harmless changes of security levels. It is more flexible, because it allows changes, but it disallows any violations of the security policy (in the context of the Bell-LaPadula Model, the simple security condition and *-property).

EXAMPLE: In Trusted Solaris, the security administrator must provide specific authorization for a user to be able to change the MAC label of a file [2244]. The authorizations are "downgrade file label" and "upgrade file label." If the user is not the owner of the file whose label is to be changed, the additional authorization "act as file owner" is required.

5.3.1   Declassification Principles

Sabelfeld and Sands [1635] present some principles for declassification. Although intended to describe information flow in programs,[6] these principles apply equally well to systems. Those parts of the security policy governing declassification are called the *declassification policy*, and in the context of these principles, "secure" means that the classification of information only changes to a lower level in accordance with the declassification policy.

The *principle of semantic consistency* says that, as long as the semantics of the parts of the system not involved in declassification do not change, those parts of the system may be altered without affecting the security of the system. Thus, changing a component in the system that does not do declassification will not cause the classification of information to be lowered. The requirement that the semantics not change eliminates possible "leaking" due to semantic incompatibilities. For example, the notion of *delimited release* allows information to be declassified and released only through specific channels, called *escape hatches* [1633]. Semantic consistency requires that the inputs to, or function of, the escape hatches not be changed by changes to other parts of the system. Otherwise, an attacker may be able to obtain information that is not covered by the declassification policy due to the changes.

Now consider a system that releases information not covered by the declassification policy. The declassification mechanisms must not conceal these leaks of information. This *principle of occlusion* says that a declassification operation cannot conceal the *improper* lowering of security levels. As an example, the property of *robust declassification* [1412, 2080] states that an attacker cannot use declassification channels (such as the escape hatches) to obtain information that was not properly declassified. A system that meets this property also satisfies the principle of occlusion, because the declassification mechanisms do not conceal that information, it can be leaked. Information may still leak, of course, but the ability to detect this fact is unrelated to declassification.

The *principle of conservativity* simply says that, absent any declassification, the system is secure. The basis for this principle is the observation that a system in which classifications of information never change to a lower level is secure under the above definition. Similarly, when declassification is performed in an authorized manner by authorized subjects, the system remains secure—the *principle of monotonicity of release*. Put another way, declassifying information in accord with the declassification policy does not make the system less secure. In essence, a system with no declassification provides a baseline against which the same system, but

---

[6]See Chapter 17.

with a declassification policy, can be measured. This view treats declassification as exceptions to the security policy (although authorized ones). A government agency that never declassifies any information might be considered secure; should it declassify information, though, there is the potential for information that should remain confidential to be declassified by accident—making the system nonsecure. Thus, in some sense, declassification creates a potential "hole" in the system security policy, and weakens the system.

Tranquility plays an important role in the Bell-LaPadula Model, because it highlights the trust assumptions in the model. It raises other problems in the context of integrity that we will revisit in the next chapter.

5.4   The Controversy over the Bell-LaPadula Model

The Bell-LaPadula Model became the target of inquiries into the foundations of computer security. The controversy led to a reexamination of security models and a deeper appreciation of the complexity of modeling real systems.

5.4.1   McLean's †-Property and the Basic Security Theorem

In a 1985 paper [1296], McLean argued that the "value of the [Basic Security Theorem] is much overrated since there is a great deal more to security than it captures. Further, what is captured by the [Basic Security Theorem] is so trivial that it is hard to imagine a realistic security model for which it does not hold" [1296, p. 67]. The basis for McLean's argument was that, given assumptions known to be nonsecure, the Basic Security Theorem could prove a nonsecure system to be secure. He defined a complement to the *-property:

> **Definition 5–11.** A state (b, m, f, h) satisfies the *†-property* if and only if, for each $s \in S$, the following hold:
>
> (a) $b(s : \underline{a}) \neq \varnothing \Rightarrow [\forall o \in b(s : \underline{a})[f_c(o) \, dom \, f_o(s)]]$
> (b) $b(s : \underline{w}) \neq \varnothing \Rightarrow [\forall o \in b(s : \underline{w})[f_c(o) = f_o(s)]]$
> (c) $b(s : \underline{r}) \neq \varnothing \Rightarrow [\forall o \in b(s : \underline{r})[f_c(o) \, dom \, f_c(c)]]$

In other words, the †-property holds for a subject s and an object o if, whenever s has $\underline{w}$ rights over o, the clearance of s dominates the classification of o. This is exactly the reverse of the *-property, which holds that the classification of o would dominate the clearance of s. A state satisfies the †-property if and only if, for every triplet (s, o, p), where the right p involves writing (that is, $p = \underline{a}$ or $p = \underline{w}$), the †-property holds for s and o.

McLean then proved the analogue to Theorem 5.4:

Theorem 5.16. $\Sigma(R, D, W, z_0)$ satisfies the †-property relative to $S' \subseteq S$ for any secure state z_0 if and only if, for every action $(r, d, (b, m, f, h), (b', m', f', h'))$, W satisfies the following for every $s \in S'$:

(a) Every $(s, o, p) \in b - b'$ satisfies the †-property with respect to S'.
(b) Every $(s, o, p) \in b'$ that does not satisfy the †-property with respect to S' is not in b.

Proof See Exercise 5, with "*-property" replaced by "†-property."

From this theorem, and from Theorems 5.3 and 5.5, the analogue to the Basic Security Theorem follows.

Theorem 5.17. *McLean's Basic Security Theorem:* $\Sigma(R, D, W, z_0)$ is a secure system if and only if z_0 is a secure state and W satisfies the conditions of Theorems 5.3, 5.16, and 5.5.

However, the system $\Sigma(R, D, W, z_0)$ is clearly nonsecure, because a subject with HIGH clearance can write information to an object with LOW classification. Information can flow down, from HIGH to LOW. This violates the basic notion of security in the confidentiality policy.

Consider the role of the Basic Security Theorem in the Bell-LaPadula Model. The goal of the model is to demonstrate that specific rules, such as the *get-read* rule, preserve security. But what is security? The model defines that term using the Basic Security Theorem: an instantiation of the model is secure if and only if the initial state satisfies the simple security condition, the *-property, and the ds-property, and the transition rules preserve those properties. In essence, the theorems are assertions about the three properties.

The rules describe the changes in a *particular* system instantiating the model. Showing that the system is secure, as defined by the analogue of Definition 5–3, requires proving that the rules preserve the three properties. Given that they do, McLean's Basic Security Theorem asserts that reachable states of the system will also satisfy the three properties. The system will remain secure, given that it starts in a secure state.

LaPadula pointed out that McLean's statement does not reflect the assumptions of the Basic Security Theorem [1138]. Specifically, the Bell-LaPadula Model assumes that a transition rule introduces no changes that violate security, but does *not* assume that any *existing* accesses that violate security are eliminated. The rules instantiating the model do no elimination (see the *get-read* rule, Section 5.2.4.1, as an example).

Furthermore, the *nature* of the rules is irrelevant to the model. The model accepts a definition of "secure" as axiomatic. The specific *policy* defines "security" and is an instantiation of the model. The Bell-LaPadula Model uses a military definition of security: information may not flow from a dominating entity to a dominated entity. The *-property captures this requirement. But McLean's variant uses a different definition: rather than meet the *-property, his policy requires that information not flow from a dominated entity to a dominating entity. This is not a confidentiality policy. Hence, a system satisfying McLean's policy will not satisfy a confidentiality policy.

However, the sets of properties in both policies (the confidentiality policy and McLean's variant) are inductive, and both Basic Security Theorems hold. The properties may not make sense in a real system, but this is irrelevant to the model. It is very relevant to the *interpretation* of the model, however. The confidentiality policy requires that information not flow from a dominating subject to a dominated object. McLean substitutes a policy that allows this. These are alternative instantiations of the model.

McLean makes these points by stating problems that are central to the use of any security model. The model must abstract the notion of security that the system is to support. For example, McLean's variant of the confidentiality policy does not provide a correct definition of security for military purposes. An analyst examining a system could not use this variant to show that the system implemented a confidentiality classification scheme. The Basic Security Theorem, and indeed all theorems, fail to capture this, because the definition of "security" is axiomatic. The analyst must establish an appropriate definition. All the Basic Security Theorem requires is that the definition of security be inductive.

McLean's second observation asks whether an analyst can prove that the system being modeled meets the definition of "security." Again, this is beyond the province of the model. The model makes claims based on hypotheses. The issue is whether the hypotheses hold for a real system.

5.4.2   McLean's System Z and More Questions

In a second paper [1297], McLean sharpened his critique. System transitions can alter any system component, including b, f, m, and h, as long as the new state does not violate security. McLean used this property to demonstrate a system, called System Z, that satisfies the model but is not a confidentiality security policy. From this, he concluded that the Bell-LaPadula Model is inadequate for modeling systems with confidentiality security policies.

System Z has the weak tranquility property and supports exactly one action. When a subject requests any type of access to any object, the system downgrades all subjects and objects to the lowest security level, adds access permission to the access control matrix, and allows the access.

Let System Z's initial state satisfy the simple security condition, the *-property, and the ds-property. It can be shown that successive states of System Z also satisfy those properties and hence System Z meets the requirements of the Basic Security Theorem. However, with respect to the confidentiality security policy requirements, the system clearly is not secure, because all entities are downgraded.

McLean reformulated the notion of a secure action. He defined an alternative version of the simple security condition, the *-property, and the ds-property. Intuitively, an action satisfies these properties if, given a state that satisfies the properties, the action transforms the system into a (possibly different) state that satisfies these properties, and *eliminates any accesses present in the transformed state that would violate the property in the initial state*. From this, he shows:

Theorem 5.18. $\Sigma(R, D, W, z_0)$ is a secure system if z_0 is a secure state and each action in W satisfies the alternative versions of the simple security condition, the *-property, and the ds-property.

Proof See [1297].

Under this reformulation, System Z is not secure because this rule is not secure. Specifically, consider an instantiation of System Z with two security clearances, (HIGH, { ALL }) and (LOW, { ALL }) (LOW < HIGH). The initial state has a subject s and an object o. Take $f_c(s) = $ (LOW, { ALL }), $f_o(o) = $ (HIGH, { ALL }), $m[s, o] = \{ \underline{w} \}$, and $b = \{ (s, o, \underline{w}) \}$. When s requests read access to o, the rule transforms the system into a state wherein $f'_o(o) = $ (LOW, { ALL }), $(s, o, \underline{r}) \in b'$, and $m'[s, o] = \{ \underline{r}, \underline{w} \}$. However, because $(s, o, \underline{r}) \in b' - b$ and $f_o(o) \, dom \, f_s(s)$, an illegal access has been added. Yet, under the traditional Bell-LaPadula formulation, in the final state $f'_c(s) = f'_o(o)$, so the read access is legal and the state is secure, hence the system is secure.

McLean's conclusion is that proving that states are secure is insufficient to prove the security of a system. One must consider both states and transitions.

Bell [148] responded by exploring the fundamental nature of modeling. Modeling in the physical sciences abstracts a physical phenomenon to its fundamental properties. For example, Newtonian mathematics coupled with Kepler's laws of planetary motion provide an abstract description of how planets move. When observers noted that Uranus did not follow those laws, they calculated the existence of another, trans-Uranean planet. Adams and Lavoisier, observing independently, confirmed its existence. Refinements arise when the theories cannot adequately account for observed phenomena. For example, the precession of Mercury's orbit suggested another planet between Mercury and the sun. But none was found.[7] Einstein's theory of general relativity, which modified the theory of how planets move, explained the precession, and observations confirmed his theory.

Modeling in the foundations of mathematics begins with a set of axioms. The model demonstrates the consistency of the axioms. A model consisting of points, lines, planes, and the axioms of Euclidean geometry can demonstrate the

---

[7]Observers reported seeing this planet, called Vulcan, in the mid-1800s. The sighting was never officially confirmed, and the refinements discussed above explained the precession adequately. Willy Ley's book [1160] relates the charming history of this episode.

consistency of those axioms. Attempts to prove the inconsistency of a geometry created without the Fifth Postulate[8] failed; eventually, Riemann replaced the plane with a sphere, replaced lines with great circles, and using that model demonstrated the consistency of the axioms (which became known as "Riemannian geometry"). Gödel demonstrated that consistency cannot be proved using only axioms within a system (hence Riemannian geometry assumes the consistency of Euclidean geometry, which in turn assumes the consistency of another axiomatizable system, and so forth). So this type of modeling has natural limits.

The Bell-LaPadula Model was developed as a model of existing phenomena, namely the existing classification scheme. Bell pointed out that McLean's work presumed a purely mathematical model, with axioms that differ from the existing classification scheme.

In the physical science sense of modeling, the Bell-LaPadula Model is a tool for demonstrating certain properties of rules. Whether the properties of System Z are desirable is an issue the model cannot answer. If no rules should change security compartments of entities, the system should enforce the principle of strong tranquility. System Z clearly violates this principle, and hence would be considered not secure. (The principle of tranquility adds requirements to state transitions, so given that principle, the Bell-LaPadula Model actually constrains both states and state transitions.)

In the foundations of mathematics sense, Bell pointed out that the two models (the original Bell-LaPadula Model and McLean's variant) define security differently. Hence, that System Z is not secure under one model, but secure under the other, is not surprising. As an example, consider the following definitions of a prime number.

> **Definition 5–12.** A *prime number* is an integer $n > 1$ that has only 1 and itself as divisors.

> **Definition 5–13.** A *prime number* is an integer $n > 0$ that has only 1 and itself as divisors.

Both definitions, from a mathematical point of view, are acceptable and consistent with the laws of mathematics. So, is the integer 1 prime? By Definition 5–12, no; by Definition 5–13, yes. Neither answer is "right" or "wrong" in an absolute sense.[9]

---

[8] The Fifth Postulate of Euclid states that given a line and a point, there is exactly one line that can be drawn through that point parallel to the existing line. Attempts to prove this postulate failed. In the 1800s, Riemann and Lobachevsky demonstrated the axiomatic nature of the postulate by developing geometries in which the postulate does not hold [1451].

[9] By convention, mathematicians use Definition 5–12. The integer 1 is neither prime nor composite.

5.5   Summary

The influence of the Bell-LaPadula Model permeates all policy modeling in computer security. It was the first mathematical model to capture attributes of a real system in its rules. It formed the basis for several standards, including the Department of Defense's Trusted Computer System Evaluation Criteria (the TCSEC or the "Orange Book," discussed in Chapter 22) [2239]. Even in controversy, the model spurred further studies in the foundations of computer security.

Other models of confidentiality arise in practical contexts. They may not form lattices. In this case, they can be embedded into a lattice model. Still other confidentiality models are not multilevel in the sense of Bell-LaPadula. These models include integrity issues, and Chapter 8, "Hybrid Policies," discusses several.

Confidentiality models may be viewed as models constraining the way information moves about a system. The notions of noninterference and nondeducibility provide an alternative view that in some ways matches reality better than the Bell-LaPadula Model; Chapter 9, "Noninterference and Policy Composition," discusses these models.

McLean's questions and observations about the Bell-LaPadula Model raised issues about the foundations of computer security, and Bell and LaPadula's responses fueled interest in those issues.

5.6   Research Issues

Research issues in confidentiality arise in the application of multilevel security models. One critical issue is the inclusion of declassification within the model (as opposed to being an exception, allowed by a trusted user such as the system security officer). A second such issue is how to abstract the details of the system being modeled to a form about which results can be proved; databases and multilevel networks are often the targets of this. A third issue is the relationship of different formulations of the model. What is their expressive power? Which allows the most accurate description of the system being modeled?

Another issue is that of models of information flow. The confidentiality models usually speak in terms of channels designed to move information (such as reading and writing). But information can flow along other channels. How to integrate these channels into models, and how to show that models correctly capture them, are critical research issues.

Determining what information is safe to declassify, and how to do so without inadvertently making other confidential data available in some form, is also a critical problem. Research in this area usually focuses on information flow in programs, but much of this work can be generalized to systems.

Yet another issue is how to apply confidentiality policies to a collection of systems implementing slightly different variations of the policy and with different security interfaces. How can the systems be merged to meet the policy? How does one derive the wrapper specifications needed to allow the systems to connect securely, and how does one validate that the resulting policy is "close enough" to the desired policy in practice?

5.7   Further Reading

The developers of the ADEPT-50 system presented a formal model of the security controls that predated the Bell-LaPadula Model [1184, 1992]. Landwehr [1133] explored aspects of formal models for computer security. Denning and her colleagues used the Bell-LaPadula Model in SeaView [540, 543], a database designed with security features. The model forms the basis for several other models, including the database model of Jajodia and Sandhu [959], the military message system model of Landwehr and his colleagues [1136], and the MLS-PCA model for avionics [1995]. The latter are excellent examples of how models are applied in practice.

Dion [572] extended the Bell-LaPadula Model to allow system designers and implementers to use that model more easily. Sidhu and Gasser [1747] designed a local area network to handle multiple security levels. Watson [1981] applies the model to workflows in clouds.

Feiertag, Levitt, and Robinson [655] developed a multilevel model that has several differences from the Bell-LaPadula Model. Taylor [1862] elegantly compares them. Smith and Winslett [1767] use a mandatory model to model databases that differ from the Bell-LaPadula Model. Gambel [733] discusses efforts to apply a confidentiality policy similar to Bell-LaPadula to a system developed from off-the-shelf components, none of which implemented the policy precisely.

Irvine and Volpano [947] cast multilevel security in terms of a type subsystem for a polymorphic programming language.

Myers [1408] summarizes the utility of information flow security policies for programming. Papers by Myers and Liskov [1409, 1411] give more detail on the decentralized label model and its implications. Chong and Myers [410] also consider requirements for declassification and erasing together. Askarov and Sabelfeld [86] present a policy unifying declassification, key release, and encryption policies. Matos [1260] discusses the declassification problems introduced by mobile code. Many papers discuss the nontechnical aspects of declassification. David [505] discusses problems of declassification faced by the U.S. government, and also discusses the history of declassification in the U.S. government's observation of the earth from space [506].

Foley and Jacob discuss computer-supported collaborative working confidentiality policies in the guise of specification [696]. Wiemer discusses policy models in the context of sharing information with foreign governments [2004].

In addition to Solaris, other systems such as SE-Linux, FreeBSD [1982], and databases such as DB2 for z/OS [1398] implement multilevel security.

5.8 Exercises

1. Why is it meaningless to have compartments at the UNCLASSIFIED level (such as (UNCLASSIFIED, { NUC }) and (UNCLASSIFIED, { EUR }))?

2. Given the security levels TOP SECRET, SECRET, CONFIDENTIAL, and UNCLASSIFIED (ordered from highest to lowest), and the categories A, B, and C, specify what type of access (read, write, both, or neither) is allowed in each of the following situations. Assume that discretionary access controls allow anyone access unless otherwise specified.

   a. Paul, cleared for (TOP SECRET, { A, C }), wants to access a document classified (SECRET, { B, C }).

   b. Anna, cleared for (CONFIDENTIAL, { C }), wants to access a document classified (CONFIDENTIAL, { B }).

   c. Jesse, cleared for (SECRET, { C }), wants to access a document classified (CONFIDENTIAL, { C }).

   d. Sammi, cleared for (TOP SECRET, { A, C }), wants to access a document classified (CONFIDENTIAL, { A }).

   e. Robin, who has no clearances (and so works at the UNCLASSIFIED level), wants to access a document classified (CONFIDENTIAL, { B }).

3. What does Trusted Solaris placing system executables at ADMIN_LOW prevent? Why is this important?

4. Administrative files containing information that users are not to read or write have labels of ADMIN_HIGH in Trusted Solaris.

   a. Why does this prevent users from reading the files?

   b. Why does this prevent users from writing the files?

5. Prove that the two properties of the hierarchy function (see Section 5.2.3) allow only trees and single nodes as organizations of objects.

6. Declassification effectively violates the *-property of the Bell-LaPadula Model. Would raising the classification of an object violate any properties of the model? Why or why not?

7. Prove Theorem 5.4. (*Hint*: Proceed along lines similar to the proof of Theorem 5.3.)

8. Prove Theorem 5.5.

9. Consider Theorem 5.6. Would the theorem hold if the requirement that z_0 be a secure state were eliminated? Justify your answer.

10. Prove Theorems 5.9 and 5.11.

11. Consider McLean's reformulation of the simple security condition, the *-property, and the ds-property (see page 164).

   a. Does this eliminate the need to place constraints on the initial state of the system in order to prove that the system is secure?

   b. Why do you believe Bell and LaPadula did not use this formulation?

Chapter 6
Integrity Policies

> ISABELLA: Some one with child by him? My cousin Juliet?
> LUCIO: Is she your cousin?
> ISABELLA: Adoptedly; as school-maids change their names
> By vain, though apt affection.
> — *Measure for Measure*, I, iv, 45–48.

An inventory control system may function correctly if the data it manages is released; but it cannot function correctly if the data can be randomly changed. So integrity, rather than confidentiality, is key. These policies are important because many commercial and industrial firms are more concerned with accuracy than disclosure. This chapter discusses the major integrity security policies and explores their design.

6.1 Goals

Commercial requirements differ from military requirements in their emphasis on preserving data integrity. Lipner [1193] identifies five commercial requirements:

1. Users will not write their own programs, but will use existing production programs and databases.
2. Programmers will develop and test programs on a nonproduction system; if they need access to actual data, they will be given production data via a special process, but will use it on their development system.
3. A special process must be followed to install a program from the development system onto the production system.
4. The special process in requirement 3 must be controlled and audited.
5. The managers and auditors must have access to both the system state and the system logs that are generated.

These requirements suggest several principles of operation.

First comes *separation of duty*. The principle of separation of duty states that if two or more steps are required to perform a critical function, at least two different people should perform the steps. Moving a program from the development system to the production system is an example of a critical function. Suppose one of the application programmers made an invalid assumption while developing the program. Part of the installation procedure is for the installer to certify that the program works "correctly," that is, as required. The error is more likely to be caught if the installer is a different person (or set of people) than the developer. Similarly, if the developer wishes to subvert the production data with a corrupt program, the certifier either must not detect the code to do the corruption, or must be in league with the developer.

Next comes *separation of function*. Developers do not develop new programs on production systems because of the potential threat to production data. Similarly, the developers do not process production data on the development systems. Depending on the sensitivity of the data, the developers and testers may receive sanitized production data. Further, the development environment must be as similar as possible to the actual production environment.

Last comes *auditing*. Commercial systems emphasize recovery and accountability. Auditing is the process of analyzing systems to determine what actions took place and who performed them. Hence, commercial systems must allow extensive auditing and thus have extensive logging (the basis for most auditing). Logging and auditing are especially important when programs move from the development system to the production system, since the integrity mechanisms typically do not constrain the certifier. Auditing is, in many senses, external to the model.

Even when disclosure is at issue, the needs of a commercial environment differ from those of a military environment. In a military environment, clearance to access specific categories and security levels brings the ability to access information in those compartments. Commercial firms rarely grant access on the basis of "clearance"; if a particular individual needs to know specific information, he or she will be given it. While this can be modeled using the Bell-LaPadula Model, it requires a large number of categories and security levels, increasing the complexity of the modeling. More difficult is the issue of controlling this proliferation of categories and security levels. In a military environment, creation of security levels and categories is centralized. In commercial firms, this creation would usually be decentralized. The former allows tight control on the number of compartments, whereas the latter allows no such control.

More insidious is the problem of information aggregation. Commercial firms usually allow a limited amount of (innocuous) information to become public, but keep a large amount of (sensitive) information confidential. By aggregating the innocuous information, one can often deduce much sensitive information. Preventing this requires the model to track what questions have been asked, and this complicates the model enormously. Certainly the Bell-LaPadula Model lacks this ability.

6.2   The Biba Model

In 1977, Biba [196] studied the nature of the integrity of systems. He proposed three policies, one of which was the mathematical dual of the Bell-LaPadula Model.

A system consists of a set S of subjects, a set O of objects, and a set I of integrity levels.[1] The levels are ordered. The relation $< \subseteq I \times I$ holds when the second integrity level dominates the first. The relation $\leq \subseteq I \times I$ holds when the second integrity level either dominates or is the same as the first. The function $min : I \times I \rightarrow I$ gives the lesser of the two integrity levels (with respect to $\leq$). The function $i : S \cup O \rightarrow I$ returns the integrity level of an object or a subject. The relation $\underline{r} \subseteq S \times O$ defines the ability of a subject to read an object; the relation $\underline{w} \subseteq S \times O$ defines the ability of a subject to write to an object; and the relation $\underline{x} \subseteq S \times S$ defines the ability of a subject to invoke (execute) another subject.

Some comments on the meaning of "integrity level" will provide intuition behind the constructions to follow. The higher the level, the more confidence one has that a program will execute correctly (or detect problems with its inputs and stop executing). Data at a higher level is more accurate and/or reliable (with respect to some metric) than data at a lower level. Again, this model implicitly incorporates the notion of "trust"; in fact, the term "trustworthiness" is used as a measure of integrity level. For example, a process at a level higher than that of an object is considered more "trustworthy" than that object.

Integrity labels, in general, are not also security labels. They are assigned and maintained separately, because the reasons behind the labels are different. Security labels primarily limit the flow of information; integrity labels primarily inhibit the modification of information. They may overlap, however, with surprising results (see Exercise 3).

Biba tests his policies against the notion of an information transfer path:

Definition 6–1. An *information transfer path* is a sequence of objects $o_1, \ldots, o_{n+1}$ and a corresponding sequence of subjects $s_1, \ldots, s_n$ such that $s_i \underline{r} o_i$ and $s_i \underline{w} o_{i+1}$ for all i, $1 \leq i \leq n$.

Intuitively, data in the object o_1 can be transferred into the object o_{n+1} along an information flow path by a succession of reads and writes.

---

[1] The original model did not include categories and compartments. The changes required to add them are straightforward.

6.2.1   Low-Water-Mark Policy

Whenever a subject accesses an object, the low-water-mark policy [196] changes the integrity level of the subject to the lower of the subject and the object. Specifically:

1. $s \in S$ can write to $o \in O$ if and only if $i(o) \leq i(s)$.
2. If $s \in S$ reads $o \in O$, then $i'(s) = min(i(s), i(o))$, where $i'(s)$ is the subject's integrity level after the read.
3. $s_1 \in S$ can execute $s_2 \in S$ if and only if $i(s_2) \leq i(s_1)$.

The first rule prevents writing from one level to a higher level. This prevents a subject from writing to a more highly trusted object. Intuitively, if a subject were to alter a more trusted object, it could implant incorrect or false data (because the subject is less trusted than the object). In some sense, the trustworthiness of the object would drop to that of the subject. Hence, such writing is disallowed.

The second rule causes a subject's integrity level to drop whenever it reads an object at a lower integrity level. The idea is that the subject is relying on data less trustworthy than itself. Hence, its trustworthiness drops to the lesser trustworthy level. This prevents the data from "contaminating" the subject or its actions.

The third rule allows a subject to execute another subject provided the second is not at a higher integrity level. Otherwise, the less trusted invoker could control the execution of the invoked subject, corrupting it even though it is more trustworthy.

This policy constrains any information transfer path:

Theorem 6.1. [196] If there is an information transfer path from object $o_1 \in O$ to object $o_{n+1} \in O$, then enforcement of the low-water-mark policy requires that $i(o_{n+1}) \leq i(o_1)$ for all $n > 1$.

Proof If an information transfer path exists between o_1 and o_{n+1}, then Definition 6–1 gives a sequence of subjects and objects identifying the entities on the path. Without loss of generality, assume that each read and write was performed in the order of the indices of the vertices. By induction, for any $1 \leq k \leq n$, $i(s_k) = min\{i(o_j) \mid 1 \leq j \leq k\}$ after k reads. As the nth write succeeds, by rule 1, $i(o_{n+1}) \leq i(s_n)$. Thus, by transitivity, $i(o_{n+1}) \leq i(o_1)$.

This policy prevents direct modifications that would lower integrity labels. It also prevents indirect modification by lowering the integrity label of a subject that reads from an object with a lower integrity level.

The problem with this policy is that, in practice, the subjects change integrity levels. In particular, the level of a subject is nonincreasing, which means that it will soon be unable to access objects at a high integrity level. An alternative policy is to decrease object integrity levels rather than subject integrity levels, but this policy has the property of downgrading object integrity levels to the lowest level.

6.2.2 Ring Policy

The ring policy [196] ignores the issue of indirect modification and focuses on direct modification only. This solves the problems described above. The rules are as follows:

1. Any subject may read any object, regardless of integrity levels.
2. $s \in S$ can write to $o \in O$ if and only if $i(o) \leq i(s)$.
3. $s_1 \in S$ can execute $s_2 \in S$ if and only if $i(s_2) \leq i(s_1)$.

The difference between this policy and the low-water-mark policy is simply that any subject can read any object.

6.2.3 Biba's Model (Strict Integrity Policy)

The strict integrity policy model [196] is the dual of the Bell-LaPadula Model, and is most commonly called "Biba's model." Its rules are as follows:

1. $s \in S$ can read $o \in O$ if and only if $i(s) \leq i(o)$.
2. $s \in S$ can write to $o \in O$ if and only if $i(o) \leq i(s)$.
3. $s_1 \in S$ can execute $s_2 \in S$ if and only if $i(s_2) \leq i(s_1)$.

Given these rules, Theorem 6.1 still holds, but its proof changes (see Exercise 1). Note that rules 1 and 2 imply that if both read and write are allowed, $i(s) = i(o)$.

Like the low-water-mark policy, this policy prevents indirect as well as direct modification of entities without authorization. By replacing the notion of "integrity level" with "integrity compartments," and adding the notion of discretionary controls, one obtains the full dual of Bell-LaPadula. Indeed, the rules require "no reads down" and "no writes up"—the exact opposite of the simple security condition and the *-property of the Bell-LaPadula Model.

EXAMPLE: Pozzo and Gray [1543, 1544] implemented Biba's strict integrity model on the distributed operating system LOCUS [1533]. Their goal was to limit execution domains for each program to prevent untrusted software from altering data or other software. Their approach was to make the level of trust in software and data explicit. They have different classes of executable programs. Their *credibility ratings* (Biba's integrity levels) assign a measure of trustworthiness on a scale from 0 (untrusted) to n (highly trusted), depending on the source of the software. Trusted file systems contain only executable files with the same credibility level. Associated with each user (process) is a risk level that starts out set to the highest credibility level at which that user can execute. Users may execute programs with credibility levels at least as great as the user's risk level. To execute programs at a lower credibility level, a user must use the *run-untrusted* command. This acknowledges the risk that the user is taking.

EXAMPLE: The FreeBSD system's implementation of the Biba model [2185] uses integers for both parts of an integrity label. The integrity level consists of a *grade*, the values of which are linearly ordered, and a *compartment*, the set of which is not ordered. A grade is represented by an integer value between 0 and 65,535 inclusive, with higher grades having higher numbers. A category is represented by an integer value between 0 and 255 inclusive. The labels are written as "biba/100:29+64+130," meaning the label has integrity grade 100 and is in integrity categories 29, 64, and 130. FreeBSD defines three distinguished labels: "biba/low," which is the lowest label; "biba/high," which is the highest label; and "biba/equal," which is equal to all labels.

    Objects have a single label. Like the Trusted Solaris implementation of the Bell-LaPadula model, subjects have three. The first is the label at which the subject is currently; the other two represent the low and high labels of a range. These are written as biba/*currentlabel*(*lowlabel-highlabel*). The subject can change its current label to any label within that range. So, a subject with label biba/75:29+64(50:29-150:29+64+130+150) can read but not write to an object with label biba/100:29+64+130 as the object's label dominates the subject's label. If the subject changes its label to biba/100:29+64+130, it will be able to read from and write to the object.

6.3   Lipner's Integrity Matrix Model

Lipner returned to the Bell-LaPadula Model and combined it with the Biba model to create a model [1193] that conformed more accurately to the requirements of a commercial policy. For clarity, we consider the Bell-LaPadula aspects of Lipner's model first, and then combine those aspects with Biba's model.

6.3.1   Lipner's Use of the Bell-LaPadula Model

Lipner provides two security levels, in the following order (higher to lower):

- Audit Manager (AM): system audit and management functions are at this level.
- System Low (SL): any process can read information at this level.

He similarly defined five categories:

- Development (D): production programs under development and testing, but not yet in production use
- Production Code (PC): production processes and programs
- Production Data (PD): data covered by the integrity policy
- System Development (SD): system programs under development, but not yet in production use
- Software Tools (T): programs provided on the production system not related to the sensitive or protected data

Lipner then assigned users to security levels based on their jobs. Ordinary users will use production code to modify production data; hence, their clearance is (SL, { PC, PD }). Application developers need access to tools for developing their programs, and to a category for the programs that are being developed (the categories should be separate). Hence, application programmers have (SL, { D, T }) clearance. System programmers develop system programs and, like application programmers, use tools to do so; hence, system programmers should have clearance (SL, { SD, T }). System managers and auditors need system high clearance, because they must be able to access all logs; their clearance is (AM, { D, PC, PD, SD, T }). Finally, the system controllers must have the ability to downgrade code once it is certified for production, so other entities cannot write to it; thus, the clearance for this type of user is (SL, { D, PC, PD, SD, T }) with the ability to downgrade programs. These security levels are summarized in Figure 6–1.

The system objects are assigned to security levels based on who should access them. Objects that might be altered have two categories: that of the data itself and that of the program that may alter it. For example, an ordinary user needs to execute production code; hence, that user must be able to read production code. Placing production code in the level (SL, { PC }) allows such access by the simple security property of the Bell-LaPadula Model. Because an ordinary user needs to alter production data, the *-property dictates that production data be in (SL, { PC, PD }). Similar reasoning supplies the levels in Figure 6–2.

Users	Clearance
Ordinary users	(SL, { PC, PD })
Application developers	(SL, { D, T })
System programmers	(SL, { SD, T })
System managers and auditors	(AM, { D, PC, PD, SD, T })
System controllers	(SL, { D, PC, PD, SD, T }) and downgrade privilege

Figure 6–1 Security levels for subjects.

Objects	Class
Development code/test data	(SL, { D, T })
Production code	(SL, { PC })
Production data	(SL, { PC, PD })
Software tools	(SL, { T })
System programs	(SL, { ∅ })
System programs in modification	(SL, { SD, T })
System and application logs	(AM, { *appropriate categories* })

Figure 6–2   Security levels for objects.

All logs are append-only. By the *-property, their classes must dominate those of the subjects that write to them. Hence, each log will have its own categories, but the simplest way to prevent their being compromised is to put them at a higher security level.

We now examine this model in light of the requirements in Section 6.1.

1. Because users do not have execute access to category T, they cannot write their own programs, so requirement 1 is met.

2. Application programmers and system programmers do not have read or write access to category PD, and hence cannot access production data. If they do require production data to test their programs, the data must be downgraded from PD to D, and cannot be upgraded (because the model has no upgrade privilege). The downgrading requires intervention of system control users, which is a special process within the meaning of requirement 2. Thus, requirement 2 is satisfied.

3. The process of installing a program requires the downgrade privilege (specifically, changing the category of the program from D to PC), which belongs only to the system control users; hence, only those users can install applications or system programs. The use of the downgrade privilege satisfies requirement 3's need for a special process.

4. The control part of requirement 4 is met by allowing only system control users to have the downgrade privilege; the auditing part is met by requiring all downgrading to be logged.

5. Finally, the placement of system management and audit users in AM ensures that they have access both to the system state and to system logs, so the model meets requirement 5.

Thus, the model meets all requirements. However, it allows little flexibility in special-purpose software. For example, a program for repairing an inconsistent or erroneous production database cannot be application-level software. To remedy these problems, Lipner integrates his model with Biba's model.

6.3.2   Lipner's Full Model

Lipner then augmented the security classifications with three integrity classifications (highest to lowest) [1193]:

- System Program (ISP): the classifications for system programs
- Operational (IO): the classifications for production programs and development software
- System Low (ISL): the classifications at which users log in

Two integrity categories distinguish between production and development software and data:

- Development (ID): development entities
- Production (IP): production entities

The security category T (tools) allowed application developers and system programmers to use the same programs without being able to alter those programs. The new integrity categories now distinguish between development and production, so they serve the purpose of the security tools category, which is eliminated from the model. We can also collapse production code and production data into a single category. This gives us the following security categories:

- Production (SP): production code and data
- Development (SD): same as (previous) security category Development (D)
- System Development (SSD): same as (previous) security category System Development (SD)

The security clearances of all classes of users remain equivalent to those of the model without integrity levels and categories. The integrity classes are chosen to allow modification of data and programs as appropriate. For example, ordinary users should be able to modify production data, so users of that class must have write access to integrity category IP. Figure 6–3 shows the integrity classes and categories of the classes of users.

The final step is to select integrity classes for objects. Consider the objects Production Code and Production Data. Ordinary users must be able to write the latter but not the former. By placing Production Data in integrity class (ISL, { IP }) and Production Code in class (IO, { IP }), an ordinary user cannot alter production code but can alter production data. Similar analysis leads to the levels in Figure 6–4.

The repair class of users has the same integrity and security clearance as that of production data, and so can read and write that data. It can also read

Users	Security clearance	Integrity clearance
Ordinary users	(SL, { SP })	(ISL, { IP })
Application developers	(SL, { SD })	(ISL, { ID })
System programmers	(SL, { SSD })	(ISL, { ID })
System controllers	(SL, { SP, SD }) and downgrade privilege	(ISP, { IP, ID })
System managers and auditors	(AM, { SP, SD, SSD })	(ISL, { IP, ID })
Repair	(SL, { SP })	(ISL, { IP })

Figure 6–3   Security and integrity levels for subjects.

Objects	Security level	Integrity level
Development code/test data	(SL, { SD })	(ISL, { IP })
Production code	(SL, { SP })	(IO, { IP })
Production data	(SL, { SP })	(ISL, { IP })
Software tools	(SL, { $\varnothing$ })	(IO, { ID })
System programs	(SL, { $\varnothing$ })	(ISP, { IP, ID })
System programs in modification	(SL, { SSD, })	(ISL, { ID })
System and application logs	(AM, { *appropriate categories* })	(ISL, { $\varnothing$ })
Repair	(SL, { SP })	(ISL, { IP })

Figure 6–4   Security and integrity levels for objects.

production code (same security classification and (IO, { IP }) *dom* (ISL, { IP }), system programs (SL, { SP }) *dom* (SL, { $\varnothing$ }) and (ISP, { IP, ID }) *dom* (ISL, { IP }), and repair objects (same security classes and same integrity classes); it can write, but not read, the system and application logs (as (AM, { SP }) *dom* (SL, { SP }) and (ISL, { IP }) *dom* (ISL, { $\varnothing$ }). It cannot access development code/test data (since the security categories are disjoint), system programs in modification (since the integrity categories are disjoint), or software tools (again, since the integrity categories are disjoint). Thus, the repair function works as needed.

The reader should verify that this model meets Lipner's requirements for commercial models (see Exercise 8).

6.3.3   Comparison with Biba

Lipner's model demonstrates that the Bell-LaPadula Model can meet many commercial requirements, even though it was designed for a very different purpose. The resiliency of that model is part of its attractiveness; however, fundamentally, the Bell-LaPadula Model restricts the flow of information. Lipner notes this, suggesting that combining his model with Biba's may be the most effective.

6.4 Clark-Wilson Integrity Model

In 1987, David Clark and David Wilson developed an integrity model [423] radically different from previous models. This model uses transactions as the basic operation, which models many commercial systems more realistically than previous models.

One main concern of a commercial environment, as discussed above, is the integrity of the data in the system and of the actions performed on that data. The data is said to be *in a consistent state* (or *consistent*) if it satisfies given properties. For example, let D be the amount of money deposited so far today, W the amount of money withdrawn so far today, YB the amount of money in all accounts at the end of yesterday, and TB the amount of money in all accounts so far today. Then the consistency property is

$$D + YB - W = TB$$

Before and after each action, the consistency conditions must hold. A *well-formed transaction* is a series of operations that transition the system from one consistent state to another consistent state. For example, if a depositor transfers money from one account to another, the transaction is the transfer; two operations, the deduction from the first account and the addition to the second account, make up this transaction. Each operation may leave the data in an inconsistent state, but the well-formed transaction must preserve consistency.

The second feature of a commercial environment relevant to an integrity policy is the integrity of the transactions themselves. Who examines and certifies that the transactions are performed correctly? For example, when a company receives an invoice, the purchasing office requires several steps to pay for it. First, someone must have requested a service, and determined the account that would pay for the service. Next, someone must validate the invoice (was the service being billed for actually performed?). The account authorized to pay for the service must be debited, and the check must be written and signed. If one person performs all these steps, that person could easily pay phony invoices; however, if at least two different people perform these steps, both must conspire to defraud the company. Requiring more than one person to handle this process is an example of the principle of separation of duty.

Computer-based transactions are no different. Someone must certify that the transactions are implemented correctly. The principle of separation of duty requires that the certifier and the implementors be different people. In order for the transaction to corrupt the data (either by illicitly changing the data or by leaving the data in an inconsistent state), two different people must either make similar mistakes or collude to certify the well-formed transaction as correct.

6.4.1   The Model

The Clark-Wilson model defines data constrained by its integrity controls as *constrained data items*, or CDIs. Data not subject to the integrity controls are called *unconstrained data items*, or UDIs. For example, in a bank, the balances of accounts are CDIs since their integrity is crucial to the operation of the bank, whereas the gifts selected by the account holders when their accounts were opened would be UDIs, because their integrity is not crucial to the operation of the bank. The set of CDIs and the set of UDIs partition the set of all data in the system being modeled.

A set of *integrity constraints* (similar in spirit to the consistency constraints discussed above) constrain the values of the CDIs. In the bank example, the consistency constraint presented earlier would also be an integrity constraint.

The model also defines two sets of procedures. *Integrity verification procedures*, or IVPs, test that the CDIs conform to the integrity constraints at the time the IVPs are run. In this case, the system is said to be in a *valid state*. *Transformation procedures*, or TPs, change the state of the data in the system from one valid state to another; TPs implement well-formed transactions.

Return to the example of bank accounts. The balances in the accounts are CDIs; checking that the accounts are balanced, as described above, is an IVP. Depositing money, withdrawing money, and transferring money between accounts are TPs. To ensure that the accounts are managed correctly, a bank examiner must certify that the bank is using proper procedures to check that the accounts are balanced, to deposit money, to withdraw money, and to transfer money. Furthermore, those procedures may apply only to deposit and checking accounts; they might not apply to other types of accounts, such as petty cash. The Clark-Wilson model captures these requirements in two *certification rules*:

Certification rule 1 (CR1): When any IVP is run, it must ensure that all CDIs are in a valid state.

Certification rule 2 (CR2): For some associated set of CDIs, a TP must transform those CDIs in a valid state into a (possibly different) valid state.

CR2 defines as *certified* a relation that associates a set of CDIs with a particular TP. Let C be the certified relation. Then, in the bank example,

$$(\text{balance}, \text{account}_1), (\text{balance}, \text{account}_2), \ldots, (\text{balance}, \text{account}_n) \in C$$

CR2 implies that a TP may corrupt a CDI if it is not certified to work on that CDI. For example, the TP that invests money in the bank's stock portfolio would corrupt account balances even if the TP were certified to work on the portfolio, because the actions of the TP make no sense on the bank accounts. Hence, the system must prevent TPs from operating on CDIs for which they have not been certified. This leads to the following *enforcement rule*:

Enforcement rule 1 (CR1): The system must maintain the *certified* relations, and must ensure that only TPs certified to run on a CDI manipulate that CDI.

Specifically, ER1 says that if a TP f operates on a CDI o, then $(f, o) \in C$. However, in a bank, a janitor is not allowed to balance customer accounts. This restriction implies that the model must account for the person performing the TP, or user. The Clark-Wilson model uses an enforcement rule for this:

Enforcement rule 2 (CR2): The system must associate a user with each TP and set of CDIs. The TP may access those CDIs on behalf of the associated user. If the user is not associated with a particular TP and CDI, then the TP cannot access that CDI on behalf of that user.

This defines a set of triples (*user, TP, {CDIset}*) to capture the association of users, TPs, and CDIs. Call this relation *allowed A*. Of course, these relations must be certified:

Certification rule 3 (CR3): The *allowed* relations must meet the requirements imposed by the principle of separation of duty.

Because the model represents users, it must ensure that the identification of a user with the system's corresponding user identification code is correct. This suggests:

Enforcement rule 3 (CR3): The system must authenticate each user attempting to execute a TP.

An interesting observation is that the model does not require authentication when a user logs into the system, because the user may manipulate only UDIs. But if the user tries to manipulate a CDI, the user can do so only through a TP; this requires the user to be certified as allowed (per ER2), which requires authentication of the user (per ER3).

Most transaction-based systems log each transaction so that an auditor can review the transactions. The Clark-Wilson model considers the log simply as a CDI, and every TP appends to the log; no TP can overwrite the log. This leads to:

Certification rule 4 (CR4): All TPs must append enough information to reconstruct the operation to an append-only CDI.

When information enters a system, it need not be trusted or constrained. For example, when one deposits money into an automated teller machine (ATM), one need not enter the correct amount. However, when the ATM is opened and the cash or checks counted, the bank personnel will detect the discrepancy and fix it before they enter the deposit amount into one's account. This is an example of a UDI (the stated deposit amount) being checked, fixed if necessary, and certified as correct before being transformed into a CDI (the deposit amount added to one's account). The Clark-Wilson model covers this situation with certification rule 5:

Certification rule 5 (CR5): Any TP that takes as input a UDI may perform only valid transformations, or no transformations, for all possible values of the UDI. The transformation either rejects the UDI or transforms it into a CDI.

The final rule enforces the separation of duty needed to maintain the integrity of the relations in rules ER2 and ER3. If a user could create a TP and associate some set of entities and herself with that TP (as in ER3), she could have the TP perform unauthorized acts that violate integrity constraints. The final enforcement rule prevents this:

Enforcement rule 4 (CR4): Only the certifier of a TP may change the list of entities associated with that TP. No certifier of a TP, or of an entity associated with that TP, may ever have execute permission with respect to that entity.

This rule requires that all possible values of the UDI be known, and that the TP be implemented so as to be able to handle them. This issue arises again in both vulnerabilities analysis and secure programming.

This model contributed two new ideas to integrity models. First, it captured the way most commercial firms work with data. The firms do not classify data using a multilevel scheme, and they enforce separation of duty. Second, the notion of certification is distinct from the notion of enforcement, and each has its own set of rules. Assuming correct design and implementation, a system with a policy following the Clark-Wilson model will ensure that the enforcement rules are obeyed. But the certification rules require outside intervention, and the process of certification is typically complex and prone to error or to incompleteness (because the certifiers make assumptions about what can be trusted). This is a weakness in some sense, but it makes explicit assumptions that other models do not.

6.4.1.1   A UNIX Approximation to Clark-Wilson

Polk describes an implementation of Clark-Wilson under the UNIX operating system [1529]. He first defines "phantom" users that correspond to locked accounts. No real user may assume the identity of a phantom user.

Now consider the triple (*user, TP, {CDIset}*). For each TP, define a phantom user to be the owner. Place that phantom user into the group that owns each of the CDIs in the CDI set. Place all real users authorized to execute the TP on the CDIs in the CDI set into the group owner of the TP. The TPs are setuid to the

TP owner,[2] and are executable by the group owner. The CDIs are owned either by *root* or by a phantom user.

EXAMPLE: Suppose access to each CDI is constrained by user only—that is, in the triple, *TP* can be any TP. In this case, the CDI is owned by a group containing all users who can modify the CDI.

EXAMPLE: Now, suppose access to each CDI is constrained by TP only—that is, in the triple, *user* can be any user. In this case, the CDIs allow access to the owner, a phantom user *u*. Then each TP allowed to access the CDI is owned by *u*, setuid to *u*, and world-executable.

Polk points out three problems. Two different users cannot use the same TP to access two different CDIs. This requires two separate copies of the TP, one for each user and associated CDI. Secondly, this greatly increases the number of setuid programs, which increases the threat of improperly granted privileges. Proper design and assignment to groups minimizes this problem. Finally, the superuser can assume the identity of any phantom user. Without radically changing the nature of the *root* account, this problem cannot be overcome.

6.4.2 Comparison with the Requirements

We now consider whether the Clark-Wilson model meets the five requirements in Section 6.1. We assume that production programs correspond to TPs and that production data (and databases) are CDIs.

1. If users are not allowed to perform certifications of TPs, but instead only "trusted personnel" are, then CR5 and ER4 enforce this requirement. Because ordinary users cannot create certified TPs, they cannot write programs to access production databases. They must use existing TPs and CDIs—that is, production programs and production databases.

2. This requirement is largely procedural, because no set of technical controls can prevent a programmer from developing and testing programs on production systems. (The standard procedural control is to omit interpreters and compilers from production systems.) However, the notion of providing production data via a special process corresponds to using a TP to sanitize, or simply provide, production data to a test system.

3. Installing a program from a development system onto a production system requires a TP to do the installation and "trusted personnel" to do the certification.

---

[2]That is, the TPs execute with the rights of the TP owner, and not of the user executing the TP.

4. CR4 provides the auditing (logging) of program installation. ER3 authenticates the "trusted personnel" doing the installation. CR5 and ER4 control the installation procedure (the new program being a UDI before certification and a CDI, as well as a TP in the context of other rules, after certification).

5. Finally, because the log is simply a CDI, management and auditors can have access to the system logs through appropriate TPs. Similarly, they also have access to the system state.

Thus, the Clark-Wilson model meets Lipner's requirements.

6.4.3   Comparison with Other Models

The contributions of the Clark-Wilson model are many. We compare it with the Biba model to highlight these new features.

Recall that the Biba model attaches integrity levels to objects and subjects. In the broadest sense, so does the Clark-Wilson model, but unlike the Biba model, each object has two levels: constrained or high (the CDIs) and unconstrained or low (the UDIs). Similarly, subjects have two levels: certified (the TPs) and uncertified (all other procedures). Given this similarity, can the Clark-Wilson model be expressed fully using the Biba model?

The critical distinction between the two models lies in the certification rules. The Biba model has none; it asserts that "trusted" subjects exist to ensure that the actions of a system obey the rules of the model. No mechanism or procedure is provided to verify the trusted entities or their actions. But the Clark-Wilson model provides explicit requirements that entities and actions must meet; in other words, the method of upgrading an entity is itself a TP that a security officer has certified. This underlies the assumptions being made and allows for the upgrading of entities within the constructs of the model (see ER4 and CR5). As with the Bell-LaPadula Model, if the Biba model does not have tranquility, trusted entities must change the objects' integrity levels, and the method of upgrading need not be certified.

Handling changes in integrity levels is critical in systems that receive input from uncontrolled sources. For example, the Biba model requires that a trusted entity, such as a security officer, pass on every input sent to a process running at an integrity level higher than that of the input. This is not practical. However, the Clark-Wilson model requires that a trusted entity (again, perhaps a security officer) certify the method of upgrading data to a higher integrity level. Thus, the trusted entity would not certify each data item being upgraded; it would only need to certify the method for upgrading data, and the data items could be upgraded. This is quite practical.

Can the Clark-Wilson model emulate the Biba model? The relations described in ER2 capture the ability of subjects to act on objects. By choosing TPs appropriately, the emulation succeeds (although the certification rules constrain trusted subjects in the emulation, whereas the Biba model imposes no such constraints). The details of the construction are left as an exercise for the reader (see Exercise 12).

6.5   Trust Models

Integrity models deal with changes to entities. They state conditions under which the changes preserve those properties that define "integrity." However, they do not deal with the confidence one can have in the initial values or settings of that entity. Put another way, integrity models deal with the *preservation* of trustworthiness, but not with the *initial* evaluation of whether the contents can be trusted.

Trust models, on the other hand, deal with exactly that problem. They provide information about the credibility of data and entities. Because trust is subjective, trust models typically express the trustworthiness of one entity in terms of another. Interestingly, the term "trust" is difficult to define, and much work treats it as axiomatic.

We use the following definition:

> **Definition 6–2.** [734] Anna *trusts* Bernard if Anna believes, with a level of subjective probability, that Bernard will perform a particular action, both before the action can be monitored (or independently of the capacity of being able to monitor it) and in a context in which it affects Anna's own action.

This defines trust in terms of actors, but it also can apply to the credibility of information. Asking whether the data is "trusted" is really asking if a reader of the data believes to some level of subjective probability that the entity providing the data obtained it accurately and without error, and is providing it accurately and without error. Hence, in the above definition, the reader is Anna, the provider is Bernard, and the "particular action" is that of gathering and providing the data.

This definition captures three important points about trust [6]. First, it includes the subjective nature of trust. Second, it captures the idea that trust springs from belief in that which we do not, or cannot, monitor. Third, the actions of those we trust affects our own actions. This also leads to the notion of transitivity of trust.

> **Definition 6–3.** *Transitivity of trust* means that, if a subject Anna trusts a second subject Bernard, and Bernard trusts a third subject Charlene, then Anna trusts Charlene.

In practice, trust is not absolute, so whether trust is transitive depends on Anna's assessment of Bernard's judgment. This leads to the notion of *conditional transitivity of trust* [6], which says that Anna can trust Charlene when:

- Bernard recommends Charlene to Anna;
- Anna trusts Bernard's recommendations;

- Anna can make judgments about Bernard's recommendations; and
- Based on Bernard's recommendation, Anna may trust Charlene less than Bernard does.

If Anna establishes trust in Charlene based on her observations and other interactions, the trust is *direct*. If it is established based on Anna's acceptance of Bernard's recommendation of Charlene, then the trust is *indirect*. Indirect trust may take a path involving many intermediate entities. This is called *trust propagation* because the trust propagates among many entities.

Castelfranchi and Falcone [362] argue that trust is a cognitive property, so only agents with goals and beliefs can trust another agent. This requires the trusting agent, Anna, to estimate risk and then decide, based on her willingness to accept (or not accept) the risk, whether to rely on the one to be trusted, Bernard. This estimation arises from social and technological sources, as well as Anna's observations and her taking into account recommendations. They identify several belief types:

- *Competence belief*: Anna believes Bernard to be competent to aid Anna in reaching her goal.
- *Disposition belief*: Anna believes that Bernard will actually carry out what Anna needs to reach her goal.
- *Dependence belief*: Anna believes she needs what Bernard will do, depends on what Bernard will do, or that it is better for Anna to rely on Bernard than not to rely on him.
- *Fulfillment belief*: Anna believes the goal will be achieved.
- *Willingness belief*: Anna believes that Bernard has decided to take the action she desires.
- *Persistence belief*: Anna believes that Bernard will not change his mind before carrying out the desired action.
- *Self-confidence belief*: Anna believes that Bernard knows that he can take the desired action.

Parsons et al. [1498] provide a set of schemes to evaluate arguments about trust. Trust coming from experience will be based either on Anna's personal experience about Bernard ("direct experience") or on her observation of evidence leading her to conclude Bernard is reliable ("indirect experience"). Trust coming from validation requires that, due to his particular knowledge ("expert opinion"), position ("authority"), or reputation ("reputation"), Bernard be considered an expert in the domain of the goals or actions that Anna wants Bernard to perform to reach that goal. Trust can also come from Anna's observations about Bernard's character ("moral nature") or her belief that Bernard's being untrustworthy would be to Bernard's disadvantage ("social standing"). Finally, Anna can trust Bernard because of factors strictly external to any knowledge of Bernard, for example that most people from Bernard's community are trustworthy ("majority behavior"), that not trusting Bernard poses an unacceptable risk ("prudence"), or that it best serves Anna's current interests ("pragmatism").

These humanistic traits have analogues in the technological world, but ultimately the trust models frame the technology to provide evidence to support the evaluation of arguments about trust. By using a set of predetermined belief rules, much of the trust analysis can be automated. However, the automation is an attempt to mimic the way the relevant authority, whatever that may be, would evaluate the arguments based on the belief types to determine the appropriate level of trust.

Trust management systems provide a mechanism for instantiating trust models. They use a language to express relationships about trust, often involving assertions or claims about the properties of trust in the model. They also have an evaluation mechanism or engine that takes data and the trust relationships (called the *query*), and provides a measure of the trust in an entity, or determines whether an entity should be trusted or an action taken. The result of the evaluation is rarely complete trust or complete distrust; more often, it is somewhere between.

We distinguish between two basic types of trust models: policy-based models and recommendation-based models.

6.5.1 Policy-Based Trust Management

Policy-based trust models use credentials to instantiate policy rules that determine whether to trust an entity, resource, or information. The credentials themselves are information, so they too may be input to these rules. Trusted third parties often vouch for these credentials. For example, Kerberos (see Section 11.2.2) allows users to verify identity, effectively producing an identity credential. Similarly, certificates (see Section 11.4) encode information about identity and other attributes of the entity, and are often used as credentials. Complicating this is that many agents are automated, particularly web-based agents, and they act on behalf of users to access services and take other actions. In order to do so, they must decide which servers to use and which actions to perform. Thus, trust models generally assume that the agents will act autonomously.

The statement of policies requires a language in which to express those policies. The differing goals of trust models have led to different languages. Some, particularly those intended for the Semantic Web, include negotiation protocols; others simply supply a language to express the rules. The expressiveness of a language determines the range of policies it can express. Usability of the language speaks to the ease of users defining polices in that language, as well as the ability to analyze policies. The languages should also be easily mapped into enforcement mechanisms, so the policies they describe can be enforced.

EXAMPLE: The Keynote trust management system [245] is based on Policy-Maker [246], but is extended to support applications that use public keys. It is designed for simplicity, expressivity, and to be extensible. Its basic units are the assertion and the action environment.

Assertions are either policy assertions or credential assertions. Policy assertions make statements about policy; credential assertions make statements about credentials, and these assertions describe the actions allowed to possessors of the stated credentials. An action environment is a set of attributes that describe an action associated with a set of credentials. An evaluator takes a set of policy assertions describing a local policy, a set of credentials, and an action environment, and determines whether a proposed action is consistent with the local policy by applying the assertions to the action environment.

An assertion is composed of a set of fields listed in Figure 6–5. The "KeyNote-Version" must appear first if it present; similarly, the "Signature" field must come last, if present. If the value of the `Authorizer` field is "POLICY", the assertion is a policy assertion. If that value is a credential, the assertion is a credential assertion. The evaluator returns a result from a set of values called the Compliance Values.

As an example, consider an email domain [244]. The following policy authorizes the holder of credential `mastercred` for all actions:

```
Authorizer: "POLICY"
Licensees: "mastercred"
```

When the evaluator evaluates this policy and the credential assertion

```
KeyNote-Version: 2
Local-Constants: Alice="cred1234", Bob="credABCD"
Authorizer: "authcred"
Licensees: Alice || Bob
Conditions: (app_domain == "RFC822-EMAIL") &&
            (address ˜= "ˆ.*@keynote\\.ucdavis\\.edu$")
Signature: "signed"
```

Field	Meaning
Authorizer	Principal making the assertion
Comment	Annotation describing something about the assertion
Conditions	Conditions under which Authorizer trusts Licensee to perform action
KeyNote-Version	Version of KeyNote used for writing assertions
Licensees	Principals authorized by the assertion
Local-Contents	Adds or changes attributes in the current assertion
Signature	Encoded digital signature of Authorizer

Figure 6–5 KeyNote fields and their meanings.

the evaluator enables the entity with the credential identified by "authcred" to trust the holders of either credential "cred1234" or credential "credABCD" to issue credentials for users in the email domain (app_domain == "RFC822-EMAIL") when the address involved ends in "@keynote.ucdavis.edu". So Alice and Bob might be issuers of certificates for members of that domain, and the holder of the credential "authcred" will trust them for those certificates. The evaluator's Compliance Values are { _MIN_TRUST, _MAX_TRUST }. If the action environment is

```
_ACTION_AUTHORIZERS=Alice
app_domain = "RFC822-EMAIL"
address = "snoopy@keynote.ucdavis.edu"
```

then the action satisfies the policy and the evaluator would return _MAX_TRUST (meaning it is trusted because it satisfies the assertions). Conversely, the action environment

```
_ACTION_AUTHORIZERS=Bob
app_domain = "RFC822-EMAIL"
address = "opus@admin.ucdavis.edu"
```

does not satisfy the policy, and the evaluator returns _MIN_TRUST (meaning it is an untrusted action).

As a second example, consider separation of duty for a company's invoicing system. The policy delegates authority for payment of invoices to the entity with credential fundmgrcred:

```
Authorizer: "POLICY"
Licensee: "fundmgecred"
Conditions: (app_domain == "INVOICE" && @dollars < 10000)
```

To implement the separation of duty requirement, the following credential assertion requires at least two signatures on any expenditure:

```
KeyNote-Version: 2
Comment: This credential specifies a spending policy
Authorizer: "authcred"
Licensees: 2-of("cred1", "cred2", "cred3", "cred4",
            "cred5")
Conditions: (app_domain=="INVOICE") # note nested clauses
            -> { (@dollars) < 2500) -> _MAX_TRUST;
                (@dollars < 7500) -> "ApproveAndLog";
              };
Signature: "signed"
```

This says that the authorizer with credential "`authcred`" (probably a financial officer of the company) allows any two people with any of the five listed credentials to approve payment of invoices under $7,500, but the approval of any invoice for $2,500 or more will be logged. So in this context, the Compliance Value set is { "Reject", "ApproveAndLog", "Approve" }. Thus, if the action environment is

```
_ACTION_AUTHORIZERS = "cred1,cred4"
app_domain = "INVOICE"
dollars = "1000"
```

then the evaluator returns "`Approve`" because it satisfies the policy. This assertion

```
_ACTION_AUTHORIZERS = "cred1,cred2"
app_domain = "INVOICE"
dollars = "3541"
```

causes the evaluator to return "`ApproveandLog`". And these assertions

```
_ACTION_AUTHORIZERS = "cred1"
app_domain = "INVOICE"
dollars = "1500"
```

and

```
_ACTION_AUTHORIZERS = "cred1,cred5"
app_domain = "INVOICE"
dollars = "8000"
```

cause the evaluator to return "`Reject`".

The simplicity of the KeyNote language allows it to be used in a wide variety of environments. This makes KeyNote very powerful, allowing the delegation of trust as needed. By changing the evaluation engine, the assertions may be augmented to express arbitrary conditions. Indeed, KeyNote's predecessor, PolicyMaker, allowed assertions to be arbitrary programs, so it supported both the syntax used in KeyNote and a much more general tool.

Ponder (see Section 4.5.1) can be used to express trust relationships. Rei [986] is a language for expressing trust in a pervasive computing environment, and KAoS [1915] focuses on grid computing and web services. Cassandra [144] is a trust management system tailored for electronic health records.

6.5.2   Reputation-Based Trust Management

Reputation-based models use past behavior, especially during interactions, and information gleaned from other sources to determine whether to trust an entity. This may include recommendations from other entities.

Abdul-Rahman and Hailes [6] base trust on the recommendations of other entities. They distinguish between direct trust relationships (where Amy trusts Boris) and recommender trust relationships (where Amy trusts Boris to make recommendations about another entity). Trust categories refine the nature of the trust; for example, Amy may trust Boris to recommend trustworthy web services, but not to vouch for another entity's identity. Each entity maintains its own list of relationships.

Trust is computed based on the protocol flow through the system. The direct and recommender trust values have specific semantics. For example, Abdul-Rahman and Hailes use for direct trust the values -1 as representing untrust-worthy, the integers from 1 to 4 inclusive representing the lowest trust level to completely trustworthy, and 0 as the inability to make trust judgments. For recommender trust values, the integers -1 and 0 represent the same as for direct trust and the meaning of the integers 1 to 4 inclusive represent how close the judgment of the recommender is to the entity being recommended to. Together with an agent's identification and trust category, this forms a *reputation*. Formally, a *recommendation* is trust information that contains one or more reputations.

EXAMPLE: Suppose Amy wants to get Boris's recommendation about Danny, specifically about his ability to write a program, because Amy needs to hire a good programmer. Amy knows Boris and trusts his recommendations with (recommender) trust value 2 (his judgment is somewhat close to hers). She sends Boris a request for a recommendation about Danny's programming abilities. Boris does not know Danny, so he sends a similar request to Carole, who does know Danny. Carole believes Danny is an above average programmer, so she replies to Boris with a recommendation of 3 (more trustworthy than most programmers). Bob adds his own name to the end of the recommendation and forwards it to Amy.

Amy can now compute a trust value for the path used to find out about Danny using the following formula:

$$t(T, P) = tv(T) \prod_{i=1}^{n} \frac{tv(R_i)}{4} = 3 \times \frac{2}{4} \times \frac{3}{4} = 1.125 \tag{6.1}$$

where T is the entity about which information is sought (in this example, Danny), P the path taken (here, the path nodes are Boris and Carole), $tv(x)$ the trust value of x, and t the overall trust in the path.

The metrics or evaluating recommendations are critical; they are also poorly understood. The previous formula, for example, "was derived largely by intuition" [6, p. 57]. The advantage to a simple formula is that it is easily understood; the disadvantage is that the recommendation score is very coarse.

Recommendation systems use many different types of metrics. Statistical models are common, as are belief models (in which the probabilities involved may not sum up to 1, due to uncertainties of belief) and fuzzy models (in which reasoning involves degrees of trustworthiness, rather than being trustworthy or not trustworthy). Previous experience with interactions can also be factored in.

EXAMPLE: The PeerTrust recommendation system [2036] uses a trust metric based on complaints as feedback. Let $u \in P$ be a node in a peer-to-peer network P; let $p(v, t) \in P$ be the node that u interacts with in transaction t. Let $S(u, t)$ be the amount of satisfaction u gets from $p(u, t)$. Let $I(u)$ be the total number of transactions that u performs. Then the trust value of u is computed by the formula

$$T(u) = \sum_{t=1}^{I(u)} S(u, t) Cr(p(u, t))$$

$Cr(v)$ is the credibility of node v's feedback. One of the proposed measures for it is

$$Cr(v) = \sum_{t=1}^{I(v)} S(v, i) \frac{T(p(v, t))}{\sum_{x=1} I(v) T(p(v, x))}$$

The credibility of v therefore depends on its prior trust values.

6.6 Summary

Integrity models are gaining in variety and popularity. The problems they address arise from industries in which environments vary wildly. They take into account concepts (such as separation of privilege) from beyond the scope of confidentiality security policies. This area will continue to increase in importance as more and more commercial firms develop models or policies to help them protect their data.

Although the policy and reputation trust models are presented separately, trust management systems can combine them. The SULTAN system [810] does this using four components. The specification editor and the analysis tool provide policy-based analyses, and the risk and monitoring services feed information about experience back into the system.

Underlying most trust models is some form of logic. Various logics such as fuzzy logics and belief logics incorporate the lack of certainty in general trust and enable reasoning about trust in the framework of that logic. The result is very similar to reputation models, in that one obtains various metrics for trust.

6.7 Research Issues

Central to the maintenance of integrity is an understanding of how trust affects integrity. A logic for analyzing trust in a model or in a system would help analysts understand the role of trust. The problem of constructing such a logic that captures realistic environments is an open question.

The development of realistic integrity models is also an open research question, as are the analysis of a system to derive models and the generation of mechanisms to enforce them. Although these issues arise in all modeling, integrity models are particularly susceptible to failures to capture the underlying processes and entities on which systems are built.

Models for analyzing software and systems to determine whether they conform to desired integrity properties is another critical area, and much of the research on "secure programming" is relevant here. In particular, has the integrity of a piece of software, or of data on which that software relies, been compromised? In the most general form, this question is undecidable; in particular cases, with software that exhibits specific properties, this question is decidable.

The quantification of trust is an open problem. Part of the problem is an understanding of exactly what "trust" means, as it depends not only on environment but also on the psychological, organizational, and sociological forces in the system being modeled. Even when the entities involved are automated, a human or group of humans must provide the judgment on which the trust metrics are based. Perhaps this is why policy-based models are seen as more definitive—the rules of the policy give a straightforward answer, whereas reputation-based trust modeling requires feedback to be effective. But how to evaluate and integrate that feedback to produce results deemed to be accurate is another complex, and open, problem.

6.8   Further Reading

Nash and Poland discuss realistic situations in which mechanisms are unable to enforce the principle of separation of duty [1425]. Other studies of this principle include its use in role-based access control [1111, 1167, 1754], databases [1463], and multilevel security [1463]. Notargiacomo, Blaustein, and McCollum [1461] present a generalization of Clark-Wilson suitable for trusted database management systems that includes dynamic separation of duty. Foley [695] presents two formal definitions of integrity and uses them to reason about separation of duty and other mechanisms.

Integrity requirements arise in many contexts. The SELinux example policy has been analyzed with respect to certain of the Clark-Wilson rules [954]. Saltman [1640] and Neumann [1446] provide an informative survey of the requirements for secure electronic voting, and other papers discuss models that provide integrity in voting [16, 389–391, 1321, 1595]. Chaum's classic paper on electronic payment [386] raises issues of confidentiality and shows that integrity and anonymity can coexist; Bitcoin [1419] used his, and other, ideas to develop a widely used instantiation of digital cash [1420]. Integrity in databases is crucial to their correctness [93, 754, 812, 1966]. The analysis of trust in software is also an issue of integrity [46, 101, 1379].

Chalmers compares commercial policies with governmental ones [372]. Lee [1148] discusses an alternative to Lipner's use of mandatory access controls for implementing commercial policies. Another integrity model considers the acceptance of all parties to the contents of a document [1958].

Trust modeling and management has become more important as the Internet and the use of automated agents have grown. Several surveys examine trust in various environments like the web [83, 384, 809, 968], for providing online services [975], for distributed systems [1163], and for social networks [1118, 1439, 1961]. Other trust models include REFEREE [416], which provides trust management for web applications, and Appleseed [2105], which proposes trust metrics on the Semantic Web. KeyNote has been used to manage policy efficiently in an Internet protocol [247]. Studies of metrics provide guidance on their effectiveness in various environments [781, 782, 997]. The transfer of trust in information integrity protocols has also been explored [1753].

6.9   Exercises

1. Prove Theorem 6.1 for the strict integrity policy of Biba's model.

2. Give an example that demonstrates that the integrity level of subjects decreases in Biba's low-water-mark policy. Under what conditions will the integrity level remain unchanged?

3. Suppose a system used the same labels for integrity levels and categories as for subject levels and categories. Under what conditions could one subject read an object? Write to an object?

4. In Pozzo and Gray's modification of LOCUS, what would be the effect of omitting the *run-untrusted* command? Do you think this enhances or degrades security?

5. Explain why the system controllers in Lipner's model need a clearance of (SL, { D, PC, PD, SD, T }).

6. Construct an access control matrix for the subjects and objects of Lipner's commercial model. The matrix will have entries for *r* (read) and *w* (write) rights. Show that this matrix is consistent with the requirements listed in Section 6.1.

7. Show how separation of duty is incorporated into Lipner's model.

8. Verify that Lipner's integrity matrix model (Section 6.3) meets Lipner's requirements for commercial models (Section 6.1).

9. In the Clark-Wilson model, must the TPs be executed serially, or can they be executed in parallel? If the former, why? If the latter, what constraints must be placed on their execution?

10. Prove that applying a sequence of transformation procedures to a system in a valid state results in the system being in a (possibly different) valid state.

11. The relations *certified* (see ER1) and *allowed* (see ER2) can be collapsed into a single relation. Please do so and state the new relation. Why doesn't the Clark-Wilson model do this?

12. Show that the enforcement rules of the Clark-Wilson model can emulate the Biba model.

13. One version of Polk's implementation of Clark-Wilson on UNIX systems requires transaction procedures to distinguish users in order to determine which CDIs the user may manipulate. This exercise asks you to explore the implementation issues in some detail.

    a. Polk suggests using multiple copies of a single TP. Show, with examples, *exactly* how to set this up.

    b. Polk suggests that wrappers (programs that perform checks and then invoke the appropriate TPs) could be used. Discuss, with examples, *exactly* how to set this up. In particular, what checks would the wrapper need to perform?

    c. An alternative implementation would be to combine the TPs and wrappers into a single program. This new program would be a version of the TP that would perform the checks and then transform the CDIs. How difficult would such a combination be to implement? What would be its advantages and disadvantages compared with multiple copies of a single TP? Compared with the use of wrappers?

14. In KeyNote, write an assertion that would allow the second action environment in the example on page 193 to satisfy the policy. For your assertion, the evaluator is to return _MAX_TRUST.

15. Consider the KeyNote example for the company's invoicing system. The assertion requires two signatures on any invoice under $10,000. If the invoice is under $500, the chief financial officer believes this is unnecessary; one signature should suffice. Write a KeyNote assertion that says only one signature is needed if the amount of the invoice is under $500.

16. Return to Amy's problem of finding out if Danny is a good programmer in the first example of Section 6.5.2. Amy does not know Carole, so she asks Boris for a recommendation about Carole's recommendation. Boris wants to assign a (recommender) trust level of 3 to this. How would this change the computation of Amy's trust value for the path used to find out about Danny?

17. SULTAN uses separate modules to consider both policy-based and reputation-based trust metrics. Devise a generic architecture of a trust management system that integrates the two types of metrics. How do the reputation trust values affect the evaluation of the policy rules, and how do the results of evaluating the policy rules change the reputation trust values?

18. The text states that whether or not the integrity of a generic piece of software, or of generic data on which that generic software relies, has been compromised is undecidable. Prove that this is indeed the case.

Chapter 7
Availability Policies

> LADY MACBETH: Alack, I am afraid they have awak'd,
> And 'tis not done. Th' attempt and not the deed
> Confounds us. Hark! I laid their daggers ready;
> He could not miss 'em.
> — *Macbeth*, II, ii, 10–13.

Confidentiality and integrity policies describe what can be done once a resource or information is accessed. Availability policies describe when, and for how long, the resource can be accessed. Violations of these policies may occur unintentionally or deliberately.

7.1   Goals of Availability Policies

An availability policy ensures that a resource can be accessed in some way in a timely fashion. This is often expressed in terms of "quality of service." As an example, a commercial website selling merchandise will need to display details of items for customer requests in a matter of seconds or, at worst, a minute. The goal of the customer is to see what the website is selling, and the goal of the site is to make information available to the customer. However, the site does not want customers to alter prices displayed on the website, so there is no availability for altering information. As another example, a website enabling students to upload homework must allow some alterations (students must be able to upload their homework, possibly multiple times per assignment) quickly and no access for the students to read other students' assignments. As these examples show, an availability policy defines the type of access and what a "timely fashion" means. These depend on the nature of the resource and the goals of the accessing entity.

When a resource or service is not available, a denial of service occurs. This problem is closely related to the problems of safety and liveness. A denial of service that results from the service giving incorrect responses means the service is not performing the functions that the client is expecting; this is a safety property.

Similarly, a denial of service that prevents users from accessing the service is a liveness problem. But other problems can cause a denial of service, such as assignment of inadequate resources to a process.

The difference between the mechanisms used to support availability in general, and availability as a security requirement, lies in the assumptions underlying the failures. In the general case, lack of accessibility can be modeled using an average case model, in which this condition occurs following a (known or unknown) statistical model. The failures occur naturally. For example, the failure rates of disk drives depends upon many factors such as the age, the manufacturer, and environment [1526] and can be statistically modeled, although the precise model to be used is unclear [1693]. But the mechanisms used to support availability as a security requirement use a worst-case model, in which an adversary deliberately tries to make the resource or information unavailable. Because attackers induce this condition, models used in computer security describe failures that are nonrandom, and indeed may well be nonstatistical.

7.2   Deadlock

Perhaps the simplest form of availability is that of disallowing deadlocks.

> **Definition 7–1.** A *deadlock* is a state in which some set of processes block, each waiting for another process in the set to take some action.

Deadlock can occur if four conditions hold simultaneously:

1. The resource is not shared (*mutual exclusion*).
2. An entity must hold the resource and block, waiting until another resource becomes available (*hold and wait*).
3. A resource being held cannot be released (*no preemption*).
4. A set of entities must be holding resources such that each entity is waiting for a resource held by another entity in the set (*circular wait*).

There are three approaches to handling deadlock: preventing it, avoiding it, or detecting and recovering from it.

EXAMPLE: Preventing deadlock requires that the system prevent at least one of the above conditions from holding. Early methods required a process to request and obtain all resources necessary to complete its task before starting. An alternative method was to require the process to relinquish all resources when it needed a new one; then it would simply request the new one and all the resources it just released. These invalidated the hold and wait condition, but both have many disadvantages. Linearly ordering resource types breaks the circular wait condition. In this scheme, each resource type r_i is assigned a number i. In order to acquire resources of type r_a, the process must first release all resources with a lower or equal number. It can reacquire them by adding them to the request for r_a. Mutual exclusion is necessary for some resources, as is not preempting their use.

Dijkstra's Banker's Algorithm is an example of a deadlock avoidance technique. A system can be in either a *safe state*, in which deadlock cannot occur, or an *unsafe state*, which may (but need not) lead to deadlock. Initially, each process states the maximum number and type of resources it will need to complete. A process needing a resource requests it from the resource manager. That manager applies the Banker's Algorithm to determine whether granting the request will place the system in an unsafe state; if so, the process blocks until the request can be satisfied. The algorithm guarantees that all requests will be satisfied in a finite time. Further, the processes must release allocated resources in a finite time. But the term "finite" is indefinite; it could be a very long time, but not infinite. These and other considerations, such as the difficulty of knowing the maximum number and type of resources a process will use, mean that the algorithm is not used in practice.

Deadlock detection techniques allow deadlocks to occur, but detect them and then recover from them. Resource graphs represent processes and resources as nodes, requests as directed edges from a process node to a resource node, and an assignment as a directed edge from a resource node to a process node. When cycles occur, the property of circular wait holds and the processes are deadlocked. Recovery techniques include simply terminating one of the processes, or suspending it and releasing its resources; either of these methods breaks the cycle. Some systems such as distributed databases periodically capture their current state as a checkpoint, and when deadlock occurs they roll back to the most recent checkpoint. Other systems assume deadlocks are infrequent, and rely on the user to detect them and initiate recovery (usually by terminating a process).

Deadlock is a specific example of a situation in which a process is denied service, such as access to a resource. It is usually not due to an attack. A process can acquire multiple resources needed by other processes, and then not release them. In this situation, the process is not blocked (although the others are), so it is not a deadlock.

Denial of service models generalize this problem to include attacks.

7.3   Denial of Service Models

A basic requirement for the use of systems and networks is access. The access must occur in a time frame suitable for the type of access and the use to which the accessed resource, and any associated data, will be put.

Definition 7–2. [772] A *denial of service* occurs when a group of authorized users of a service makes that service unavailable to a (disjoint) group of authorized users for a period of time exceeding a defined maximum waiting time.

The term "authorized user" here must be read expansively. If a user is not authorized, then in theory access control mechanisms that protect the server will block the unauthorized users from accessing the server. But in practice, the access control mechanisms may be ineffective. An intruder may compromise a user's account to gain access to a server. The policy controlling access to a network server may be unworkable, such as one stating that only customers interested in the products sold may access the server—but the access control mechanisms could not tell whether a remote user accessing the server was interested in the products, or trying to block access by others. Hence the first "group of authorized users" is simply the group of users with access to the service, whether the security policy grants them access or not.

Underlying all models and mechanisms is the assumption that, in the absence of other processes, there are sufficient resources to enable a process requesting those resources to proceed. If those resources cannot be allocated to the process, then the security problem is one of inadequate resources, a management problem not dealt with here.

Denial of service models have two essential components. The first is a *waiting time policy*. This controls the time between a request for a resource and the allocation of that resource to the requesting process. A denial of service occurs when the bound set by this policy is exceeded. The environment in which the request is made influences the policy. The acceptable waiting time for a pacemaker to take action affecting a patient's heart beating is considerably different than the acceptable waiting time for a purchase from an Internet website to be acknowledged.

The second is a *user agreement* that establishes constraints a process ("user") must meet in order to ensure service. These are designed to ensure that a process will receive service within the waiting time. For example, a user agreement for parallel processes accessing a mutually exclusive resource would be that, once a process acquires the resource, it must (eventually) release that resource and when released, there are enough unallocated resources to enable a process waiting for those resources to proceed.

When combined, these two components ensure that a process meets the conditions needed to receive the resources it needs and not create a denial of service. It will receive those resources after an acceptable waiting time. Thus, the process can proceed and not itself be denied service.

Two types of models, constraint-based models and state-based models, formalize these notions.

7.3.1   Constraint-Based Model

Some models of denial of service rely on the enforcement of constraints to ensure availability. The Yu-Gligor model of denial of service [2065] has two parts, a *user agreement* and a *finite waiting time* policy. The former focuses on undesirable invocation sequences, and the latter on the sharing policies and mechanisms.

7.3.1.1   User Agreement

The goal of the user agreement is to describe the properties that the users of the server must meet. It is not a part of the specification of a service because it involves actions taken that do not involve the particular service. For example, user interaction with multiple services requires an agreement covering those services. An enforcement mechanism is necessary because users may not follow the agreement, and indeed may be unaware of it. The deadlock avoidance technique is an example of this.

> **Definition 7–3.** [2065] A *user agreement* is a set of constraints designed to prevent denial of service.

Let S_{seq} be the set of sequences of all possible invocations of a service, and U_{seq} the set of sequences of all possible invocations by a user. The set $U_{i,seq}$ is the subset of U_{seq} that user U_i can invoke. The use of a service involves commands to consume a resource produced or controlled by that service. This means there are two types of operations. Let C be the set of operations that user U_i performs to consume the service, and let P be the set of operations that produce the resources consumed by user U_i. As resources must be produced before they can be consumed, there is a partial ordering of operations. The partial order relation $p < c$ means that operation p must precede operation c. Call A_i the set of allowed operations for user U_i. Then the set R_i is the set of relations between every pair of allowed operations for that user.

EXAMPLE: Consider the problem of a mutually exclusive resource, in which only one process at a time may use the resource. The operations here are $C = \{acquire\}$ and $P = \{release\}$. Each process may execute both operations; hence, for two processes p_1 and p_2, $A_i = \{acquire_i, release_i\}$ for $i = 1, 2$. Given that a process must acquire the resource before it can release the resource, $R_i = \{(acquire_i < release_i\}$ for $i = 1, 2$.

Next, let $U_i(k)$ represent the initial subsequence of U_i of length k and let $n_o(U_i(k))$ be the number of times operation o occurs in $U_i(k)$. Then $U_i(k)$ is said to be *safe* if the following two conditions hold:

- if $o \in U_{i,seq}$, then $o \in A_i$; and
- for all k, if $(o_1 < o_2) \in R_i$, then $n_{o_1}(U_i(k)) \geq n_{o_2}(U_i(k))$.

This simply says that if operation o is in the sequence of commands that user U_i executes, it is an allowed operation, and that if one operation must precede a second, the number of times the first operation is executed must be at least as great as the number of times the second operation is executed.

Now consider the resources of all services. Let $s \in S_{seq}$ be a possible invocation sequence of a service. Operations in s may block, waiting for the service to become available, to process a response, or for some other reason. Call this condition c the service condition. Let $o_i^*(c)$ represent an operation o_i that is blocked waiting for condition c to become true. Once execution resumes, let $o_i(c)$ represent the operation. An important point is that once c becomes true, $o_i^*(c)$ may not resume immediately because another operation waiting on the condition may proceed first. Let $s(0)$ be the initial subsequence of s up to the blocked operation $o_i^*(c)$, and let $s(k)$ be the subsequence of operations in s between the $k - 1$st and kth time condition c becomes true after $o_i^*(c)$. The notation $p_i^*(c) \xrightarrow{s(k)} o_i(c)$ means that o_i is blocked waiting on condition c at the end of $s(0)$ and resumed operation at the end of $s(k)$. Then S_{seq} is said to be *live* if, for every $o_i^*(c)$ there is a set of subsequences $s(0), \ldots, s(k)$ such that it is an initial subsequence of some $s \in S_{seq}$ and $o_i^*(c) \xrightarrow{s(k)} o_i(c)$.

EXAMPLE: Return to the mutually exclusive resource of the previous example, and consider the sequence $(acquire_i, release_i, acquire_i, acquire_i, release_i)$. The operations $acquire_i$ and $release_i$ are both in A_i, and the relation $acquire_i < release_i$ is in R_i. Take $o_1 = acquire_i$ and $o_2 = release_i$. The subsequences $U_i(k)$, and the corresponding $n_o(k)$s, are:

$U_i(1) = (acquire_i)$, so $n_{o_1}(U_i(1)) = 1$, and $n_{o_2}(U_i(1)) = 0$
$U_i(2) = (acquire_i, release_i)$, so $n_{o_1}(U_i(2)) = 1$, and $n_{o_2}(U_i(2)) = 1$
$U_i(3) = (acquire_i, release_i, acquire_i)$, so $n_{o_1}(U_i(3)) = 2$,
  and $n_{o_2}(U_i(3)) = 1$
$U_i(4) = (acquire_i, release_i, acquire_i, acquire_i)$, so $n_{o_1}(U_i(4)) = 3$,
  and $n_{o_2}(U_i(4)) = 1$
$U_i(5) = (acquire_i, release_i, acquire_i, acquire_i, release_i)$, so $n_{o_1}(U_i(5)) = 3$,
  and $n_{o_2}(U_i(5)) = 2$

Thus, for all $k = 1, \ldots, 5$, $n_{o_1}(U_i(k)) \geq n_{o_2}(U_i(k))$. Hence the sequence is safe.

Next, let the service condition c be true whenever the resource can be allocated, that is, initially and whenever a $release_i$ operation is performed. The sequence

$$(acquire_1, acquire_2^*(c), release_1, release_2, \ldots, acquire_k, acquire_{k+1}^*(c),$$
$$release_k, release_{k+1}, \ldots)$$

is a live sequence because $acquire_k^*(c) \xrightarrow{s(1)} acquire_{k+1}(c)$ for all $k \geq 1$. Here, $acquire_{k+1}(c)$ occurs between $release_k$ and $release_{k+1}$.

Temporal logic provides a mechanism for expressing user agreements. It specifies the allowed operations, their order, and the invocation sequence that users external to the service must obey. In the examples that follow, □ means "henceforth" (that is, the predicate is true and will remain true), and ◇ means "eventually" (that is, the predicate is either true now or will become true in the future).[1]

EXAMPLE: Return to the example of acquiring and releasing a resource type. Here, the user agreement must ensure that, once a process is blocked, waiting on an *acquire* operation, a sufficient number of *release* operations will occur to release sufficient resources of that type to allow the blocked process to proceed:

service resource_allocator

user agreement

$in(acquire) \rightsquigarrow ((\Box\Diamond(\#active\_release > 0) \lor (free \geq acquire.n))$

This says that, when a process issues an *acquire* operation, then at some later time, at least one *release* operation will occur, and there will be sufficient resources released so the blocked process can acquire the desired number of resources.

7.3.1.2   Finite Waiting Time Policy

The goal of a finite waiting time policy is to ensure no user is excluded from using the resource in question. It consists of three parts.

The *fairness policy* prevents starvation. It ensures that the process using a resource will not be blocked indefinitely if the process is given opportunities to make progress. Thus, under a fairness policy, if two processes are vying for a single resource that must be acquired and released, one process cannot acquire and release the resource in such a way that the other process has no chance to acquire the resource.

The *simultaneity policy* ensures progress by providing the opportunities the process needs to use the resource. This complements the fairness policy by providing all processes with opportunities to make progress. The fairness policy then assures that the process will be able to take advantage of some of those opportunities.

The *user agreement* has been discussed in the previous section. It can be satisfied either by applying the service invocation constraints to ensure that the sequence of invocations is in S_{seq} (and thus the users obey the user agreements) or

---

[1] See Appendix E for more about predicate and temporal logic.

by enforcing the individual user agreements, which will ensure that the sequences of user invocations are controlled before the actual invocations occur.

If all three parts hold, then no process will wait an indefinite time before accessing the resource. However, if at least one of these parts does not hold, then the finite waiting time is not guaranteed, and a process may wait indefinitely.

Specifying the parts of a finite waiting time policy is done as part of the service specification.

EXAMPLE: Again using the example of acquiring and releasing a resource type, this section of a service specification covers the finite waiting time policy.

> **sharing policies**
> > **fairness**
> > > 1. $(at(acquire) \wedge \Box\Diamond((free \geq acquire.n) \wedge (\#active = 0))) \leadsto$
> > > $after(acquire)$
> > > 2. $(at(release) \wedge \Box\Diamond(\#active = 0)) \leadsto after(release)$
> > **simultaneity**
> > > 1. $(in(acquire) \wedge (\Box\Diamond(free \geq acquire.n)) \wedge (\Box\Diamond(\#active = 0))) \leadsto$
> > > $((free \geq acquire.n) \wedge (\#active = 0))$
> > > 2. $(in(release) \wedge \Box\Diamond(\#active\_release > 0)) \leadsto (free \geq acquire.n)$

In the "fairness" section, the first line says that, when an *acquire* operation occurs, at some point in the future (and possibly when it occurs), if there are sufficient resources free to satisfy the *acquire* request, and there are no other active operations, then the process will acquire the resources. The second line says that when a *release* operation occurs, and at some point in the future there are no other active operations, the resource will be released. Both relate to a process not blocking forever when there are opportunities to progress.

In the "simultaneity" section, the first condition says that whenever a process blocks at an *acquire* operation, the conditions that enough resources are available to satisfy the request and that there are no active operations will be true infinitely often, and at some point both will be true simultaneously. The second condition says that if a process blocks at an *acquire* operation, and in the future some other processes release their resources, eventually enough resources will be available to satisfy the request. These two conditions deal with a process's ability to make progress.

Combined with the user agreement specification above, these ensure that the process will not block indefinitely on an *acquire* or *release* operation.

7.3.1.3   Service Specification

The service specification consists of interface operations, private operations not available outside the service, resource and concurrency constraints, and the finite waiting time policy. Thus, it depends on what the service is, and how it is to be invoked.

EXAMPLE: The interface operations of the resource allocation service define the entry points to the service. In what follows, process *id* currently holds *own*[*id*] units of the resource, and can acquire *quota*[*id*] units at most. There are *free* units of the resource in total.

> **interface operations**
>   acquire(*n*: *units*)
>   **exception conditions**: *quota*[*id*] < *own*[*id*] + *n*
>   **effects**: *free*$'$ = *free* − *n*
>   *own*[*id*]$'$ = *own*[*id*] + *n*
>   release(*n*: *units*)
>   **exception conditions**: *n* > *own*[*id*]
>   **effects**: *free*$'$ = *free* + *n*
>   *own*[*id*]$'$ = *own*[*id*] − *n*

A process may invoke the *acquire* operation to acquire some number of units, but no more than the maximum it is allowed (*quota*[*id*]); if it tries to, an exception occurs. Similarly, if it attempts to release more units than it has (*own*[*id*]) by invoking the *release* operation, an exception occurs.

The resource constraint section defines the conditions that must hold throughout the operation of the service:

> **resource constraints**
>
> 1. $\Box$((*free* ≥ 0) ∧ (*free* ≤ *size*))
> 2. ($\forall$ *id*) [$\Box$((*own*[*id*] ≥ 0) ∧ (*own*[*id*] ≤ *quota*[*id*]))]
> 3. (*free* = *N*) ⇒ ((*free* = *N*) UNTIL (*after*(acquire) ∨ *after*(release)))
> 4. ($\forall$) [*id* (*own*[*id*] = *M*) ⇒ ((*own*[*id*] = *M*) UNTIL (*after*(acquire) ∨ *after*(release)))]

Constraint 1 says that the number of available units of the resource must always be non-negative and less than the total number of resource units (*size*). Constraint 2 says that a process must have a non-negative number of units assigned, and the number of units assigned must be no greater than the maximum the process is allowed to have. Constraint 3 says that the number of unallocated resource units does not change until a successful *acquire* or *release* operation occurs. The last constraint says that the number of resources a process has does not change until a successful *acquire* or *release* operation occurs. Taken together, these constrain both the assignment of resources in general and the assignment to a particular process.

The concurrency constraints enforce mutual exclusion, so only one process at a time may invoke the service:

> **concurrency constraints**
>
> 1. $\Box$((#*active* ≤ 1)
> 2. (#*active* = 1) $\leadsto$ (#*active* = 0)

The first constraint says that at most one process may use the service at a time; the second says that when a process uses the service, it will eventually end its use of the service.

Combined with the sharing policies discussed above, these policies ensure that no denial of service occurs when the user agreement is enforced.

The service specification policies and the user agreements prevent denial of service if they are enforced. But they do not prevent a long wait time; rather they merely ensure that the wait time is finite. A state-based model considers this problem.

7.3.2   State-Based Modes

Millen's state transition model [1338] is similar to the Yu-Gligor model in the previous section. It allows a maximum waiting time to be specified. The model is based upon a resource allocation system and a denial of service protection base that enforces its policies.

7.3.2.1   Model of a Resource Allocation System

Let R be a set of resource types, and assume the number of each is constant. Each resource type $r \in R$ has some fixed number of units, called the *capacity* $c(r)$, and a *maximum holding time* $m(r)$ that a process can hold a resource.

Let P be a set of processes. A process can be in one of two states, *running* or *sleeping*. When a process is allocated a resource, it is running. Multiple processes may be running at a time. An upper bound limits the amount of time a process can run without being interrupted, if only by the scheduler. So, for example, if the system uses a round robin scheduler with a quantum of q, then the process will be suspended after q units of time have passed. If the CPU is considered a resource, then $m(CPU) = q$.

The function $A : P \times R \to \mathbb{N}$ is the current allocation of resources of type r to process p. It can be represented as a matrix. The notation $A_p(r)$ is a vector of the number of units of each resource type currently allocated to p. As no more than $c(r_i)$ resources of type r_i exist, no more than $c(r_i)$ units of the resource can be allocated at any time. Thus:

(R1)   The system cannot allocate more instances of a resource type than it has. So

$$(\forall r_i \in R) \left[\sum_{p \in P} A_p(r_i) \leq c(r_i) \right]$$

The function $T : P \to \mathbb{N}$ represents the system time when the resource assignment to the process was last changed. Its range is the number of time units at which the change occurred. It can be represented as a vector, each element corresponding to a process's associated time.

Next come the requirements of the process with respect to resources. The function $Q^S : P \times R \to \mathbb{N}$ is the required allocation matrix for resources to processes. $Q_p^S(p, r)$ is the number of resources r beyond that which it is holding that p will need simultaneously. As with A, the notation $Q_p^S(r)$ means that process p will require up to $Q_p^S(r)$ additional units of resource r. Similarly, the function $Q^T : P \times R \to \mathbb{N}$ is a matrix the entries of which show how much longer the process needs the resources allocated. Like T, each entry is measured in time units and so all values are nonnegative.

Given this, let *running(p)* be true if process p is executing, and false otherwise. Then p has all the resources it requires to proceed. Thus:

(R2) A currently running process must not require additional resources to run:

$$running(p) \Rightarrow Q_p^S = \mathbf{0}$$

The predicate *asleep(p)* is true when the process is not executing. This might be because it needs resources (that is, $Q_p^S \neq \mathbf{0}$) or because it is blocked for a reason unrelated to resource allocation.

(A, T, Q^S, Q^T) defines the current state of a system.

A state transition is represented as $(A, T, Q^S, Q^T) \to (A', T', Q^{S\prime}, Q^{T\prime})$. For our purposes, state transitions occur as a result of allocation and deallocation of resources (that is, changes to A), or changes in resource requirements (changes to Q^S or Q^T). The former may occur at any time the process involved is not running (i.e., *running(p)* = false), and the latter just before the process enters the nonrunning state.

There are three types of transitions of interest:

- A *deactivation transition* is a transition *running(p)* $\to$ *asleep'(p)*. The process ceases to execute.
- An *activation transition* is a transition *asleep(p)* $\to$ *running'(p)*. The process begins or resumes execution.
- A *reallocation transition* is a transition in which a process p has resources allocated or deallocated. It can only occur when *asleep(p)*.

Consider a reallocation transition. A process must block for its resource allocation to change. If a process is running both before and after the transition, the reallocation cannot affect that process. Thus:

(R3) Resource reallocation does not affect the allocations of a running process. So

$$(running(p) \wedge running'(p)) \Rightarrow (A_p' = A_p)$$

A process makes progress when it runs for some period of time. This execution must occur between changes in the allocation of resources. However,

T is changed only when a process blocks for resource allocation or deallocation. Thus:

(R4) The time $T(p)$ associated with a process p changes only when resources are allocated to, or deallocated from, p. So

$$(A'_p(\text{CPU}) = A_p(\text{CPU})) \Rightarrow (T'(p) = T(p))$$

As a process can block for a variety of reasons, the difference in successive time values indicates the time between changes in the allocation of resources to a process, and not actual execution time. Further, as time runs forward, the values in the vector are monotonically increasing between changes in the allocation of the CPU:

(R5) Updates in a time vector increase the value of the element being updated. So

$$(A'_p(\text{CPU}) \neq A_p(\text{CPU})) \Rightarrow (T'(p) > T(p))$$

When a process's resource allocation changes, the values in the allocation matrix Q^S must be updated. If the process updates the elements in the matrix during its activation transition, then resources that are allocated may not be properly accounted for, especially if the process does not immediately resume execution after the change. This constraint requires that the system update the matrix before the process resumes execution.

(R6) When a process p is reallocated resources, the allocation matrix elements are updated before the process resumes execution. So

$$asleep(p) \Rightarrow Q_p^{S'} = Q_p^S + A_p - A'_p$$

(R7) The time that the process needs the resources does not change. So

$$asleep(p) \Rightarrow Q_p^{T'} = Q^T$$

Finally, when a deactivation transition occurs, a process may or may not change its resource requirements. But it will surrender the CPU.

(R8) When a process ceases to execute, the only resource it must surrender is the CPU. So

$$(running(p) \wedge asleep'(p)) \Rightarrow A'_p(r) = \begin{cases} A_p(r) - 1 & \text{if } r = \text{CPU} \\ A_p(r) & \text{otherwise} \end{cases}$$

A resource allocation system is a system in a state (A, T, Q^S, Q^T) satisfying (R1) and (R2) and with state transitions being constrained to meet (R3)–(R8).

7.3.2.2 Denial of Service Protection Base

In addition to the constraints on the resource allocation system, the denial of service protection base further constrains resource allocation to meet a specific policy.

> **Definition 7–4.** [1338] A *denial of service protection base* (DPB) is a mechanism that is tamperproof, cannot be prevented from operating, and guarantees authorized access to the resources it controls.

A DPB has four parts: a resource allocation system, a resource monitor, a waiting time policy, and a user agreement.

A *resource monitor* controls the allocation and deallocation of resources, and their timing. For example, it may require that a process never be allocated more than the total number of resources of each type, and that the process will be assigned the resources it needs before some maximum time.

(D1) Q_p^S is called *feasible* if $(\forall i)\,[Q_p^S(r_i) + A_p(r_i) \leq c(r_i)] \wedge Q_p^S(\text{CPU}) \leq 1$.

(D2) T_p is called *feasible* if $(\forall i)\,[T_p(r_i) \leq max(r_i)]$, where $max(r_i)$ is the maximum time a process must wait for its needed allocation of resources of type i.

A user agreement adds a (possibly empty) set of additional constraints on the resource monitor. In this model, the constraints apply to changes in allocation of resources when a process transitions from a running state to a state in which it is not running.

A waiting time policy describes how long a process can wait for resources. Several such policies are possible. Section 7.3.1.2 presents a finite waiting time policy in the context of the Yu-Gligor model. In this model the waiting time policy is expressed in terms of transitions. Let $\sigma = (A, T, Q^S, Q^T)$. Then a finite waiting time policy is

$$(\forall p, \sigma)(\exists \sigma')\,[running'(p) \wedge T'(p) \geq T(p)]$$

This says that for every process p and every state σ, there is a successor state in which p is executing and resources have been allocated to p. A maximum waiting time policy is

$$(\exists M)(\forall p, \sigma)(\exists \sigma')\,[running'(p) \wedge 0 < T'(p) - T(p) \leq M]$$

Other policies are possible.

In addition to these parts, a DPB must satisfy two constraints:

- Each process that satisfies the user agreement constraints will progress in a way that satisfies the waiting time policy.

- No resource other than the CPU is deallocated from a process unless that resource is no longer needed:

$$(\forall i)r_i \neq \text{CPU} \wedge A_p(r_i) \neq 0 \wedge A'_p(r_i) = 0 \Rightarrow Q^T_p(r_i) = 0$$

EXAMPLE: A DPB is designed to prevent denial of service attacks. The system running it has only one CPU, and there is a maximum waiting time policy in place. The user agreement has three parts:

(C1) The resource allocation and time requirements of the processes satisfy (D1) and (D2).

(C2) A process in a running state executes for at least a minimum amount of time before it transitions to a nonrunning state.

(C3) If the process requires a resource type, then the time it needs that resource for when it enters a nonrunning state is the difference between the time it needed that resource for when it entered the previous running state and the time slice for which it just ran. More precisely,

$$Q^T_p \neq \mathbf{0} \wedge running(p) \wedge asleep'(p) \Rightarrow$$

$$(\forall r \in R)[Q^T_p(r) \leq max(0, max_r Q^T_p(r) - (T'(p) - T(p)))]$$

Consider a system with n processes and a round robin scheduling algorithm with quantum q. Initially, no process has any resources. The resource monitor selects a process p to give resources to; when that process has the resources it needs, it executes until its associated time vector $Q^T_p = \mathbf{0}$ or the monitor concludes p does not satisfy (C1).

First, we show that no resource r_i is deallocated from a process p that satisfies (C1) until $Q^T_p(r_i) = 0$. Before a process p is selected, no resources are allocated to any process. Thus, the next process that satisfies (C1) is selected. It is activated and runs until the process enters the *asleep* state or q. The former means the process has completed. When the latter occurs, the monitor simply gives the process p another quantum of execution time. This repeats until $Q^T_p = \mathbf{0}$, at which point the process needs no more resources.

Let $m(r_i)$ be the the maximum time that any process will hold resources of type r_i. Take $M = max_r m(r)$. Because p meets (C1), M is also an upper bound for all elements of Q^T_p. Take d to be the lesser of q and the minimum amount of time before the process transitions to a nonrunning state; by (C2), such a minimum exists. By (C3), at the end of each quantum, $m(r_i)$ is reduced by d. Thus, after $\lfloor \frac{M}{d} + 1 \rfloor$ quanta, every element of Q^T_p must be 0. Thus, no resources are deallocated until $(\forall i)Q^T_p(r_i) = 0$, as claimed.

Next, we show that there is a maximum time for each round robin cycle. Let t_a be the time between the resource monitor beginning the cycle and the time when it has allocated the required resources to the favored process p. Then the resource monitor allocates the CPU resource to p; call this time t_{CPU}. It does this between each quantum. When the process completes, the resource monitor deallocates the resources given to p; this takes time t_d. Thus, as p satisfies (C1), the time needed to run p and deallocate all resources is $t_a + \lfloor \frac{M}{d} + 1 \rfloor (q + t_{CPU}) + t_d$. So the maximum time the cycle will take is $(t_a + \lfloor \frac{M}{d} + 1 \rfloor (q + t_{CPU}) + t_d) n$. Thus, there is a maximum time for each round robin cycle.

These two results will prevent a denial of service.

7.4   Example: Availability and Network Flooding

The SYN flood is the most common type of flooding attack. It is based on the initiation of a connection using the TCP protocol (see Figure 7–1) [615]. The attacker sends the SYN packet to the target, which replies with a SYN/ACK message. But the target fails to receive the ACK packet. As a result, the resources used to hold information about the (pending) connection are held for a period of time before they are released.

The attacker can suppress the sending of the ACK in a number of ways. First, the SYN packet might contain the (spoofed) source address of a nonexistent or nonresponsive host, so the host either never receives the SYN/ACK packet or never responds to it. The attacker could also use the IP address of a system under the attacker's control, so the attacker can block the ACK packet from being sent. This is particularly attractive if the attacker controls a large number of systems such as a botnet (see Section 23.5). If the packets come from multiple sources but have the same destination, the attack is a *distributed denial of service* attack.

In what follows, the term "legitimate handshake" refers to a connection attempt that is not part of a SYN flood. If the client in a legitimate handshake receives the SYN/ACK packet from the server, it will respond with the appropriate ACK to complete the handshake and begin the connection. The term "attack handshake," on the other hand, refers to a connection attempt that is part of a

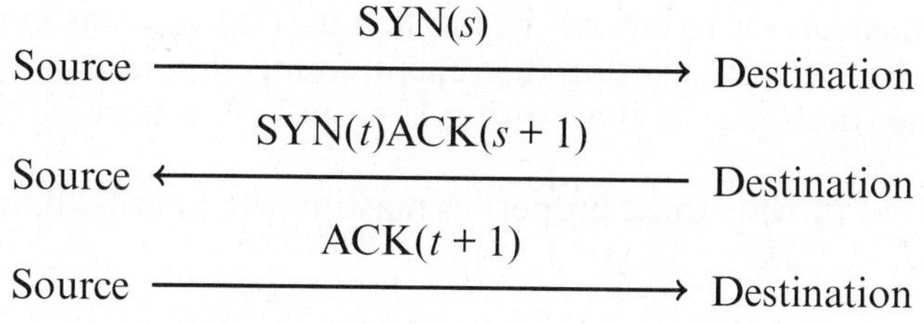

Source $\xrightarrow{\text{SYN}(s)}$ Destination

Source $\xleftarrow{\text{SYN}(t)\text{ACK}(s+1)}$ Destination

Source $\xrightarrow{\text{ACK}(t+1)}$ Destination

Figure 7–1 The TCP three-way handshake. The SYN packet is a TCP packet with sequence number s (or t) and the SYN flag set. Likewise, the ACK packet is a TCP packet with acknowledgment number $s + 1$ (or $t + 1$) and the ACK flag set. The middle message is a single TCP packet with both SYN and ACK flags set.

SYN flood. The client in an attack handshake will never send an ACK packet to complete the handshake. When the first step in the handshake completes, the server has a "pending connection" and once the handshake completes, the server opens a connection. A critical observation is that the server cannot distinguish between a legitimate handshake and an attack handshake. Both follow the same steps. The only difference lies in whether the third part of the handshake is sent (and received).

7.4.1   Analysis

There are two aspects of SYN flooding. The first is the consumption of bandwidth. If the flooding is more than the capacity of the physical network medium, or of intermediate nodes, legitimate handshakes may be unable to reach the target. The second is the use of resources—specifically, memory space—on the target. If the flooding absorbs all the memory allocated for half-open connections, then the target will discard the SYN packets from legitimate handshake attempts.

Placing the SYN flood attack in the context of the models of denial of service illuminates why the attack works, and how countermeasures compensate for it. The key observation is that the waiting time policy has a maximum wait time, which is the time that the sending process will wait for a SYN/ACK message from the receiver. Specifically, the fairness policy component must assure that a process waiting for the resources will acquire them. But this does not hold; indeed, the point of the attack is to ensure this does not happen. In terms of the Yu-Gligor model, the finite wait time does not hold; in terms of the Millen model, requirement (D2) does not hold. Further, the (implicit) user agreement that traffic from one client will not prevent that of other clients from reaching the server, and that once begun the client will complete the three-way TCP handshake, is also violated. So in both models, the user agreements are violated.

Countermeasures thus focus on ensuring the resources needed for the legitimate handshake to complete are available, and every legitimate client gets access to the server. But the focus of the countermeasures differ. Some manipulate the opening of the connections at the end point; others control which packets, or the rate at which packets, are sent to the destination. In the latter case, the goal of the countermeasures is to ensure the implicit user agreements are enforced. In the former, if the focus is ensuring that client connection attempts will succeed after some time, the focus is the waiting time policy; otherwise, it is the user agreement.

Methods to provide these properties may involve intermediate systems, the server, or both.

7.4.2   Intermediate Systems

This approach tries to reduce the consumption of resources on the target by using routers to divert or eliminate illegitimate traffic. The key observation here is that the SYN flood is handled before it reaches the firewall, at the infrastructure level. The goal is to have only legitimate handshakes reach the destinaton system.

EXAMPLE: Cisco routers can use "TCP intercept mode" to implement this approach [2126]. When the router sees a SYN packet coming from the Internet, it does not forward the packet to its destination. Instead, the router responds, and tries to establish the connection. If the SYN packet is part of a legitimate handshake and a connection is established, the router establishes a connection with the intended destination and merges the two connections. If the SYN packet is part of an attack handshake, the router never sees a following ACK packet, and times the pending connection out without ever contacting the putative destination. The router uses short timeouts to ensure it does not run out of space for pending connections. The TCP intercept feature may be set either on a per-host basis or for all hosts on the Internet.

An alternative is to have a system monitor the network traffic and track the state of the three-way handshake.

EXAMPLE: Synkill [1695] is an active monitor that analyzes packets being sent to some set of systems to be protected. It classifies IP addresses as never seen (*null*), not flooding (*good*), flooding (*bad*), or unknown (*new*). Initially, a set of IP addresses may be put into these classes. As synkill monitors the network, it adds addresses to each class.

When synkill sees an SYN packet, it checks the IP address. If that address is *bad*, synkill immediately sends an RST to the destination. This terminates the pending connection. If the IP address is *good*, synkill ignores the packet. If the IP address has not yet been seen, it is classified as *new*. A subsequent ACK or RST packet from the new address will cause the address to be added to the list of *good* addresses, because its behavior is correct, but if no such packet is seen for a specified expiry period, the new address is assumed to be attempting a SYN flood and is moved into the *bad* set of IP addresses, and an RST is sent to the destination.

If no traffic from a *good* address is observed during a different time interval, called the *staleness time*, the address is deleted from the list of *good* addresses.

Experiments showed that the effects of using synkill enabled legitimate connections to be completed. Delays grew as the rate of SYN packets from different IP addresses grew, but the developers concluded that the delays were acceptable given a powerful enough computer running synkill.

A third method is to place the intermediate systems as near to the probable sources of the attack.

EXAMPLE: D-WARD [1355] is a defense against denial of service attacks that relies on routers close to the sources (as opposed to the target networks), reducing the congestion throughout the network and providing accurate blocking of attack traffic without interfering with legitimate traffic. It is placed at the gateway of networks, and examines packets leaving the network and entering the Internet.

D-WARD has three components. The *observation component* has a set of legitimate internal addresses. It monitors packets leaving the network over intervals of time, and gathers statistics on them. Any packets that have addresses that are not legitimate are discarded. During each interval, it tracks the number of simultaneous connections to each remote host; an unusually large number may indicate an attack on a remote host from a system on the network. It also examines connections where there is a large amount of outgoing traffic but little response traffic. For some protocols, this indicates that the remote host is overwhelmed. It then aggregates traffic statistics to each remote address, and classifies the flows as attack, suspicious, or normal. If the statistics match a legitimate traffic model, the flow is normal; if not, it is attack. Once the statistics of the flow begin to match a legitimate traffic model (indicating the attack has ended), the flow becomes suspicious, and remains so for a period of time. If the flow remains suspicious and not attack, then after that time it becomes normal.

When an attack is detected, the *rate-limiting component* limits the amount of packets that can be sent. This reduces the volume of traffic from the network to the remote host. Unlike many systems, D-WARD bases how it limits the rate upon its best guess of the amount of traffic the remote host can handle. When the flow becomes normal, D-WARD raises the rate limit until the sending rate is as before.

The *traffic-policing component* obtains information from both the observation and the rate-limiting components, and based on that decides whether to drop packets. For example, packets for normal connections are always forwarded. Packets for the other flows may be forwarded provided doing so does not exceed the flow's rate limit.

D-Ward was deployed on systems in a research laboratory for 4 months. A large number of false alerts occurred during the first month. Tuning the D-WARD parameters significantly reduced this number, and eliminated user complaints about network problems.

The problem with these techniques is that they simply push the focus of the attack back from the firewall onto infrastructure systems. They do not solve the problem, but depending on how the intermediate systems are distributed, they may ameliorate it sufficiently to allow legitimate connections to reach their destinations.

7.4.3 TCP State and Memory Allocations

This approach springs from the way in which most TCP servers are implemented. When a SYN packet is received, the server creates an entry in a data structure of pending connections and then sends the SYN/ACK packet. The entry remains until either a corresponding ACK is received or a timeout occurs. In the former case, the connection is completed; in the latter case, a new entry for the next SYN packet is created. Under a SYN flood, the pending connections in the data structure never move to the connected state. As these time out, new SYNs create new entries to continue the cycle.

The data structure contains the state of the pending connection. This information typically includes the source IP address, a sequence number, and other (internal) information. When the client replies with an ACK packet to complete the handshake, the server uses this information to verify that the ACK packet corresponds to the initial SYN packet. The SYN flood succeeds because the space allocated to hold this state information is filled *before* any three-way handshakes are completed. Legitimate handshakes cannot obtain space in the data structure. However, if legitimate handshakes can be assured space, to some level of probability, then legitimate handshakes have a probability of successfully completing even in the face of a denial of service attack.

Several techniques are used to make availability of space more likely [615]. One is to reduce the space used to store connection information.

EXAMPLE: The SYN cache technique allocates space for each pending connection, but the space is much less than for a full connection [1150]. The FreeBSD system implements this approach [2185]. On initialization, a hash table (the *syncache*) is created. When a SYN packet arrives, the system generates a hash value from the packet header and uses that hash to determine which bucket to store the pending connection information in. If the bucket is full, the oldest element is dropped. The system stores enough information to be able to send a SYN/ACK, which it does. If the remote host returns the appropriate ACK, the system removes the pending connection entry from the hash table. It then uses this to create a connection, storing the data associated with it in a different table. If an RST comes in, the system searches the syncache for a corresponding entry and deletes it. If there is no response, another SYN/ACK is sent after a short time interval. This is repeated for a fixed number of times, and if there are no responses, the pending connection is deleted from the table.

A second approach is to push the tracking of state to the client. For example, if the state can be encoded in the initial sequence number of the ACK, the server can re-derive the information from information in the client's ACK packet. Then no state needs to be kept on the server system. This approach is called the SYN cookie approach [183]. The FreeBSD system also uses this technique [2185].

EXAMPLE: When a SYN packet arrives, the kernel generates a number called a *syncookie*. The system then sends a SYN/ACK to the remote host with the cookie as the ACK sequence number. If a corresponding ACK packet is received, the data in that packet enables the cookie to be recomputed and compared to the sequence number in the ACK. If they match, a connection is built; if not, the packet is ignored.

FreeBSD systems can use the SYN cookie technique to augment the use of the SYN cache. In this configuration, if a pending connection cannot be inserted into the syncache (for example, because there are too many incoming connections), the system will use the SYN cookie technique.

The syncookie is constructed using a cryptographic hash function to hash data from the source and destination addresses and ports, flags, a sequence number, and one of two pieces of information generated by the FreeBSD system that are changed every 15 seconds. The cookie consists of 24 bits from the hash augmented by some control information, bringing it to 32 bits to form the cookie. This construction makes the cookie much harder to guess than an ordinary sequence number.

Combining the SYN cookie and SYN cache techniques overcomes one of the problems of the SYN cache defense, that of the syncache being full. Should that happen, the next handshake will either cause an existing entry to be dropped, potentially interrupting a legitimate handshake, or the incoming handshake will be ignored. SYN cookies introduce other problems. The construction of the cookie omits certain fields from the initial SYN packet that can provide parameters to make the connection more efficient. Further, an attacker can attempt to forge an ACK with a valid cookie as the sequence number. This would require a large number of packets (see Exercise 1), and the attacker could not tell from the connection whether she succeeded.

A third technique assumes that there is a fixed amount of space for the state of pending connections. A SYN flood causes attack handshakes to fill this space. After some constant amount of time (usually 75 seconds), the server deletes the state information associated with the attack handshake. This is called the "timeout" of the pending connection. This approach simply varies the times before the timeouts depending on the amount of space available for new pending connections. As the amount of available space decreases, so does the amount of time before the system begins to time out connections. This approach is called *adaptive timeout*.

EXAMPLE: Freedman [722] modified the kernel of a SunOS system to provide adaptive time-outs of pending connections. First, he shortened the timeout period for pending connections from 75 to 15 seconds. He then modified the formula for queuing pending connections. Suppose a process allows up to b pending connections on a given port. Let a be the number of completed connections that the process has not begun using.[2] Let p be the number of pending connections. Let c be a tunable parameter. When $a + p > cb$, the current SYN message is dropped.

Adaptive timeouts run the risk of blocking legitimate handshakes as well as attack handshakes, so the parameters must be chosen carefully.

These techniques improve the ability of systems to continue to be available during flooding attacks. The first two techniques change the allocation of space for pending connections by trading the space used to store the state information

---

[2]Specifically, the number of connections that have completed the TCP three-way handshake but are awaiting an *accept* system call from the process.

of pending connections for extra computations to validate the states of incoming ACKs. The third method times out pending connections quickly to make more space available for the incoming handshakes.

7.4.4   Other Flooding Attacks

An attacker can use a relay to create flooding. A reflector attack is one in which an attacker uses other systems to relay (reflect) attacks against a victim. An amplification attack has the attacker send a small amount of traffic to another system, which in turn sends much more traffic to the victim. One such attack amplifies the number of packets received from the attacker.

EXAMPLE: The Smurf attack is a classic amplification attack. It relies on the router forwarding ICMP packets to all hosts on its network. The attacker sends an ICMP packet to the router with the destination address set to the broadcast address of the network (the last octet of the IP address is always 255). The router then sends a copy of the packet to each host on the network. By sending a steady stream of such packets, the attacker achieves the effect of sending that stream to all hosts on that network even though there is really only one stream of ICMP packets.

The countermeasure is to block the router from forwarding external ICMP packets that have the broadcast address as the destination.

A second attack amplifies the size of the packet that the attacker sent.

EXAMPLE: A DNS amplification attack [2149] exploits DNS resolvers that are configured to accept queries from any host rather than only hosts on their own network. The attacker sends a packet with the source address set to that of the victim. This packet contains a query that will cause the DNS resolver to send a large amount of information to the victim. For example, a zone transfer query results in the source being sent all the resource records for that zone. A query is typically small; the records for the zone may comprise a large amount of data. Thus, one small query results in a large amount of data being sent to the victim. The data will be sent in multiple packets, each larger than the query packet.

A reflector attack hides the identity of the host from which the attack originates. The attack appears to come from the reflector system or systems. If these systems are scattered throughout the Internet, then they can easily overwhelm the victim, especially if the attack is an amplification attack. The key is that the attacker must send a message that causes the reflector to forward traffic to the victim—and if the message causes the reflector to create much more traffic than the size of the message, or the number of packets in the message, the attack will be more effective.

An interesting class of denial of service attacks send packets to the target in pulses, each pulse being large enough to cause the target to miss incoming packets. This pulsing denial-of-service attack [1221] may only degrade the target's performance, but if that drops below the stated quality of service, this is a denial of service attack. This attack induces three anomalies in the traffic. When the attack floods the victim, the ratio of the incoming TCP packets to the outgoing ACKs increases dramatically, because the rate of incoming packets is much higher than the system can send ACKs. When the attacker reduces the number of packets it sends to the victim, the number of ACKs will drop; coupling this with an analysis of the distribution of the incoming packet interarrival time, which will be anomalous, this indicates a pulsing denial of service attack. The Vanguard detection scheme uses these characteristics to detect this attack [1220].

7.5   Summary

Availability policies speak to the ability to access systems, data, and other resources. With respect to security, availability policies deal with malicious processes that attempt to deny service to other processes.

Models of denial of service present conditions under which availability is not guaranteed. They have two key components. A waiting time policy describes the length of time a process can wait before a denial of service occurs. This can be presented as a maximum waiting time, a finite waiting time, or some other policy. A user agreement consists of constraints on the processes using the resource to ensure they will receive service within the waiting time, and not prevent other processes from receiving services. The Yu-Gligor model presents these components as constraints. The Millen model uses constraints on state transitions to ensure availability.

Networks provide examples of the instantiation of these models. The SYN flood attack exploits the opening handshake to establish a TCP connection by beginning but not completing the handshake. This violates the waiting time policies with respect to nonattack connection establishment. Countermeasures seek to ensure that the waiting time policy is met, for example by winnowing out attacks at an intermediate host or by limiting the amount of state, or not keeping state, at the server system. Once the handshake completes, a connection is then established.

Reflector and amplification attacks hide the source of the attack. Amplification attacks also cause the reflector to send much more traffic to the victim than the reflector received from the attacker.

7.6   Research Issues

Characterizing the effects of denial of service attacks, and hence lack of availability, leads to two types of models. The first type is statistical or numerical and requires metrics appropriate for the environment being studied. How to develop these metrics, and demonstrate they adequately capture the quantification sought, is an area of active research. The second type of model is formal, examining the causes of the lack of availability and developing requirements to prevent those conditions from arising.

Preventing and recovering from denial of service attacks in networks is also an area of active work. The way in which they are launched, the intermediaries used to amplify or reflect the attacks, and vulnerabilities in both system and infrastructure systems all must be considered. Bandwidth consumption leads to distributed detection and remediation to prevent the consumption from growing too great. How to do this is complex because of the multiplicity of entities on the Internet, and that different rules and laws may control what they can (or are willing) to do. This makes infrastructure defenses that depend upon components in different organizations or jurisdictions a legal and political problem as well as a technical one.

The nature of wireless environments exacerbate the problem. Enabling wireless networks to function in the face of jamming or other attacks is growing in importance as the Internet of Things also grows, because many such devices communicate with their controller or with one another using wireless protocols and mechanisms. With vehicular networks, where autonomous automobiles communicate with one another to avoid crashes, an effective denial of service could be catastrophic for the occupants of the car and others nearby. Availability of the network components and end points thus is critical, meaning how a lack of availability is handled is equally critical.

When a previously unavailable system becomes available, service is restored to an acceptable degree but possibly not to the desired degree. Resilience is an aspect that describes this recovery. A resilient system is one that can recover to the desired degree when a failure occurs. The security aspects of resilience are based on availability or lack of availability, and deal with recovery. Resilience in confidentiality inverts the problem: how does one recover from the leaking of information, which is now widely available, when that information should be available only to a small set of entities? Given the leaking of secret corporate, government, and personal information, this question is a fertile area for research.

7.7 Further Reading

Chang [382] and Peng et al. [1511] provide tutorials on network-based denial of service attacks and countermeasures. Schneider [1681] uses a state machine representation to describe protocols for different models of failure, and how to tolerate these faults.

The quantification of lack of availability requires the development of metrics. Mirkovic et al. [1356] develop a series of metrics from network traces to characterize quality of service, and hence availability, at multiple network layers.

Data from SETI@home [964] enabled researchers to develop a method to find sets of hosts with similar statistical properties with respect to availability. This is essential to understand when a statistical model of availability can be applied to analyze availability, and when a new model must be developed. Ford et al. [698] use data from Google's storage infrastructure to characterize the availability of cloud-based storage systems. Xie and Yu [2035] use statistical mechanisms in traffic patterns and document accesses to detect denial of service attacks on websites. Availability of a software system has also been studied [1891], as has the quantification of resilience of ad hoc networks to denial of service attacks [1].

PacketScore [1057] is a filtering mechanism that scores incoming packets based on a variety of attributes, and uses that information to build a dynamic model of incoming traffic. It then discards packets that exceed certain thresholds that include a consideration of system load. The Nozzle [1838] uses a set of layers that filter incoming traffic based on each layer's policy and on the level of congestion at that layer.

Various network architectures can inhibit the effectiveness of denial of service attacks. The Traffic Validation Architecture [2044] puts a capability[3] into the SYN/ACK packet, and all subsequent packets must include that capability to be passed on to the destination. Other architectures use puzzles to limit the ability of attackers to flood [774]. This can be done at the initiation of a TCP connection [1970, 1978] or at the IP level [663]. It can also be done at intermediate filtering nodes [1235]. An approach based on the Cognitive Packet Network infrastructure [758] has also been proposed.

Different models present different ways to think about lack of availability. Meadows [1310] proposes developing protocols that are resistant to denial of service attacks, and formalizes the principles for this. Aura et al. analyze attempts to disable links within a network to isolate portions of that network [98]. Myers and Liskov's model of decentralized labeling for confidentiality and integrity [1409] has been extended to availability [2090]. A fault tree–based model has been applied in practice [238]. Taxonomies are derived from defenses and attacks [399, 1802].

7.8 Exercises

1. Calculate the number of packets an attacker will need to generate and send to have a 0.5 probability of creating a syncookie that works.

2. Consider an availability method that requires a client to present the solution to a puzzle in order for the server to accept packets from it. Under the Yu-Gligor constraint model, would the focus for this enforcement mechanism be a waiting time policy, a user agreement, or both? Why?

---

[3]See Section 16.2.

3. Consider countermeasures for the SYN flood attack that are present on intermediate systems and are designed to allow only legitimate handshakes reach the destination system (see Section 7.4.2). Is the focus of this type of countermeasure the waiting time policy, the user agreements, or both? Why?

4. Describe a mechanism that protects availability in a distributed system. The mechanisms you identify must enable the protected services to provide correct responses as well as allow access to the service.

5. The problem of resilience in confidentiality poses an availability problem in which availability is to be *reduced* and not expanded. Discuss how this might be done, and what the implications of each proposed method are.

6. The "right to be forgotten" is a legal principle in the European Union [2119]. It provides that, under certain circumstances, an individual can have data about them removed from Internet search engines. This right is not recognized in many countries. Given that, how does the right to be forgotten affect availability?

Chapter 8
Hybrid Policies

> JULIET: Come, vial.
> What if this mixture do not work at all?
> Shall I be marry'd then tomorrow morning?
> No, no! this shall forbid it, lie thou there.
> — *The Tragedy of Romeo and Juliet*, IV, iii, 20–22.

Few organizations limit their security objectives to confidentiality, integrity, or availability only; most desire all, in some mixture. This chapter presents two such models. The Chinese Wall model is derived from the British laws concerning conflict of interest. The Clinical Information Systems security model is derived from medical ethics and laws about dissemination of patient data. Break-the-glass models examine cases in which the planned access control must be overridden due to exceptional circumstances. Two other models present alternative views of information management. Originator controlled access control lets the creator determine (or assign) who should access the data and how. Role-based access control formalizes the more common notion of "groups" of users.

8.1 Chinese Wall Model

The Chinese Wall model [292] is a model of a security policy that refers equally to confidentiality and integrity. It describes policies that involve a conflict of interest in business, and is as important to those situations as the Bell-LaPadula Model is to the military. For example, British law requires the use of a policy similar to this, and correct implementation of portions of the model provides a defense in cases involving certain criminal charges [2157, 2215]. The environment of a stock exchange or investment house is the most natural environment for this model. In this context, the goal of the model is to prevent a conflict of interest in which a trader represents two clients, and the best interests of the clients conflict, so the trader could help one gain at the expense of the other.

8.1.1   Informal Description

Consider the database of an investment house. It consists of companies' records about investment and other data that investors are likely to request. Analysts use these records to guide the companies' investments, as well as those of individuals. Suppose Anthony counsels National Bank in its investments. If he also counsels City Bank in its investments, he has a potential conflict of interest, because the two banks' investments may come into conflict. Hence, Anthony cannot counsel both banks.

The following definitions capture this:

Definition 8–1. The *objects* of the database are items of information related to a company.

Definition 8–2. A *company dataset* (CD) contains objects related to a single company.

Definition 8–3. A *conflict of interest class* (COI) contains the datasets of companies in competition.

Let *COI(O)* represent the COI class that contains object O, and let *CD(O)* be the company dataset that contains object O. The model assumes that each object belongs to exactly one COI class.

Anthony has access to the objects in the CD of National Bank. Because the CD of City Bank is in the same COI class as that of National Bank, Anthony cannot gain access to the objects in City Bank's CD. Thus, this structure of the database provides the required ability. (See Figure 8–1.)

This implies a temporal element. Suppose Anthony first worked on National Bank's portfolio and was then transferred to City Bank's portfolio. Even

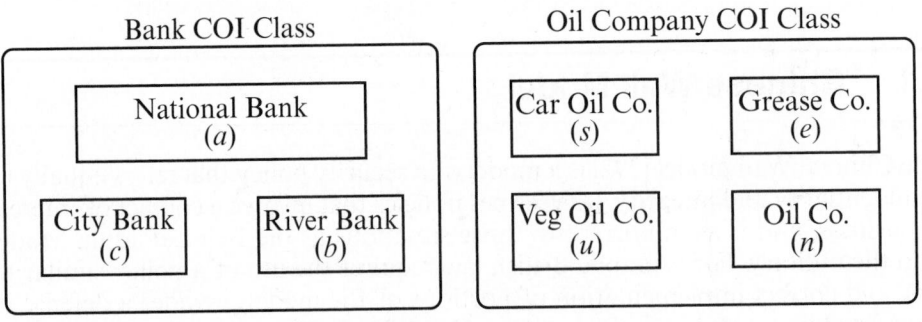

Figure 8–1   The Chinese Wall model database. It has two COI classes. The one for banks contains three CDs. The other one, for oil companies, contains four CDs. Susan may have access to no more than one CD in each COI, so she could access City Bank's CD and Veg Oil Co.'s CD, but not City Bank's CD and National Bank's CD.

though he is working only on one CD in the bank COI class at a time, much of the information he learned from National Bank's portfolio will be current. Hence, he can guide City Bank's investments using information about National Bank— a conflict of interest. This leads to the following rule, where $PR(S)$ is the set of objects that S has read.

CW-Simple Security Condition, Preliminary Version: S can read O if and only if either of the following is true:

1. There is an object O' such that S has accessed O' and $CD(O') = CD(O)$.
2. For all objects O', $O' \in PR(S) \Rightarrow COI(O') \neq COI(O)$.

Initially, $PR(S) = \varnothing$, and the initial read request is assumed to be granted. Given these assumptions, in the situation above, National Bank's COI class and City Bank's COI class are the same, so the second part of the CW-simple security condition applies, and Anthony cannot access an object in the former, having already accessed an object in the latter.

Two immediate consequences of this rule affect subject rights. First, once a subject reads any object in a COI class, the only other objects in that COI class that the subject can read are in the same CD as the read object. So, if Susan accesses some information in City Bank's CD, she cannot later access information in National Bank's CD.

Second, the minimum number of subjects needed to access every object in a COI class is the same as the number of CDs in that COI class. If the oil company COI class has four CDs, then at least four analysts are needed to access all information in the COI class. Thus, any trading house must have at least four analysts to access all information in that COI class without creating a conflict of interest.

In practice, companies have information they can release publicly, such as annual stockholders' reports and filings before government commissions. The Chinese Wall model should not consider this information restricted, because it is available to all. Hence, the model distinguishes between sanitized data and unsanitized data; the latter falls under the CW-simple security condition, preliminary version, whereas the former does not.

This means that sanitized objects must reside in a COI class with a single CD consisting only of sanitized objects. (See Exercise 1.)

The CW-simple security condition can be reformulated to include this notion.

CW-Simple Security Condition: S can read O if and only if any of the following is true:

1. There is an object O' such that S has accessed O' and $CD(O') = CD(O)$.
2. For all objects O', $O' \in PR(S) \Rightarrow COI(O') \neq COI(O)$.
3. O is a sanitized object.

Suppose Anthony and Susan work in the same trading house. Anthony can read objects in National Bank's CD, and Susan can read objects in City Bank's CD. Both can read objects in Veg Oil's CD. If Anthony can also write to objects in Veg Oil's CD, then he can read information from objects in National Bank's CD and write to objects in Veg Oil's CD, and then Susan can read that information; so, Susan can indirectly obtain information from National Bank's CD, causing a conflict of interest. The CW-simple security condition must be augmented to prevent this.

CW-*-Property: A subject S may write to an object O if and only if both of the following conditions hold:

1. The CW-simple security condition permits S to read O.
2. For all unsanitized objects O', S can read $O' \Rightarrow CD(O') = CD(O)$.

In the example above, Anthony can read objects in both National Bank's CD and Veg Oil's CD. Thus, condition 1 is met. However, assuming that National Bank's CD contains unsanitized objects (a reasonable assumption), then because Anthony can read those objects, condition 2 is false. Hence, Anthony cannot write to objects in Veg Oil's CD.

8.1.2   Formal Model

Let S be a set of subjects, O a set of objects, and $L = C \times D$ a set of labels. Define projection functions $l_1 : O \rightarrow C$ and $l_2 : O \rightarrow D$. C corresponds to the set of COI classes, and D to the set of CDs, in the informal exposition above. The access matrix entry for $s \in S$ and $o \in O$ is $H(s, o)$; that element is *true* if s has read o, and is *false* otherwise. (Note that H is *not* an access control matrix, because it does not reflect the allowed accesses, but merely the read accesses that have occurred.) Finally, $R(s, o)$ represents s's request to read o.

The model's first assumption is that a CD does not span two COI classes. Hence, if two objects are in the same CD, they are in the same COI class.

Axiom 8.1. For all $o, o' \in O$, if $l_2(o) = l_2(o')$, then $l_1(o) = l_1(o')$.

The contrapositive is as follows:

Lemma 8.1. For all $o, o' \in O$, if $l_1(o) \neq l_1(o')$, then $l_2(o) \neq l_2(o')$.

So two objects in different COI classes are also in different CDs.

Axiom 8.2. A subject s can read an object o if and only if, for all $o' \in O$ such that $H(s, o') = true$, either $l_1(o') \neq l_1(o)$ or $l_2(o') = l_2(o)$.

This axiom is the CW-simple security condition: a subject can read an object if and only if it has not read objects in other datasets in the object's COI class, or if it has read objects in the object's CD. However, this rule must also hold initially for the state to be secure. So, the simplest state for which the CW-simple security condition holds is that state in which no accesses have occurred; and in that state, any requests for access should be granted. The next two axioms state this formally.

Axiom 8.3. $H(s, o) = \textit{false}$ for all $s \in S$, and $o \in O$ is an initially secure state.

Axiom 8.4. If for some $s \in S$ and for all $o \in O$, $H(s, o) = \textit{false}$, then any request $R(s, o)$ is granted.

The following theorem shows that a subject can only read the objects in a single dataset in a COI class.

Theorem 8.1. Suppose a subject $s \in S$ has read an object $o \in O$. If s can read $o' \in O$, $o' \neq o$, then $l_1(o') \neq l_1(o)$ or $l_2(o') = l_2(o)$.

Proof By contradiction. Because s has read o, $H(s, o) = \textit{true}$. Suppose s reads o'; then $H(s, o) = \textit{true}$. By hypothesis, $l_1(o') = l_1(o)$ and $l_2(o') \neq l_2(o)$. Summarizing this:

$$H(s, o) = \textit{true} \wedge H(s, o') = \textit{true} \wedge l_1(o') = l_1(o) \wedge l_2(o') \neq l_2(o)$$

Without loss of generality, assume that s read o first. Then $H(s, o) = \textit{true}$ when s read o'; by Axiom 8.2, either $l_1(o') \neq l_1(o)$ or $l_2(o') = l_2(o)$. This leads to

$$(l_1(o') \neq l_1(o) \vee l_2(o') = l_2(o)) \wedge (l_1(o') = l_1(o) \wedge l_2(o') \neq l_2(o))$$

which is equivalent to

$$(l_1(o') \neq l_1(o) \wedge l_1(o') = l_1(o) \wedge l_2(o') \neq l_2(o)) \vee (l_2(o') = l_2(o) \wedge l_1(o')$$
$$= l_1(o) \wedge l_2(o') \neq l_2(o))$$

However, because $l_1(o') \neq l_1(o) \wedge l_1(o') = l_1(o)$ is false, and $l_2(o') = l_2(o) \wedge l_2(o') \neq l_2(o)$ is also false, this expression is false, contradicting the hypothesis. ∎

From this, it follows that a subject can access at most one CD in each COI class.

Lemma 8.2. Suppose a subject $s \in S$ can read an object $o \in O$. Then s can read no o' for which $l_1(o') = l_1(o)$ and $l_2(o') \neq l_2(o)$.

Proof Initially, s has read no object, so by Axioms 8.3 and 8.4, access will be granted for any object o. This proves the lemma for the trivial case. Now, consider another object o'. By Theorem 8.1, if s can read $o' \in O$, $o' \neq o$, then $l_1(o') \neq l_1(o)$ or $l_2(o') = l_2(o)$. Conversely, if $l_1(o') = l_1(o)$ and $l_2(o') \neq l_2(o)$, s cannot read o', proving the lemma in the general case.

Suppose a single COI class has n CDs. Then at least n subjects are needed to access every object. The following theorem establishes this requirement.

Theorem 8.2. Let $c \in C$ and $d \in D$. Suppose there are n objects $o_i \in O$, $1 \leq i \leq n$, for which $l_1(o_i) = c$ for $1 \leq i \leq n$, and $l_2(o_i) \neq l_2(o_j)$, $1 \leq i, j \leq n$, $i \neq j$. Then for all such o, there is an $s \in S$ that can read o if and only if $n \leq |S|$.

Proof By Axiom 8.2, if any subject s can read an $o \in O$, it cannot read any other $o' \in O$. Because there are n such o, there must be at least n subjects to meet the conditions of the theorem.

We next add the notion of sanitizing data. Let $v(o)$ be the sanitized version of object o; so, for example, if $v(o) = o$, the object contains only public information. All sanitized objects are in a special CD in a COI containing no other CD.

Axiom 8.5. $l_1(o) = l_1(v(o))$ if and only if $l_2(o) = l_2(v(o))$.

Writing is allowed only if information cannot leak indirectly between two subjects; for example, the object cannot be used as a kind of mailbox. The next axiom captures this constraint.

Axiom 8.6. A subject $s \neq S$ can write to an object $o \neq O$ if and only if the following conditions hold simultaneously.

1. $H(s, o) = true$.
2. There is no $o' \neq O$ with $H(s, o') = true$, $l_2(o) \neq l_2(o')$, $l_2(o) \neq l_2(v(o))$, $l_2(o') = l_2(v(o))$ and s can read o'.

The next definition captures the notion of "information flow" by stating that information can flow from one object to another if a subject can access both objects.

Definition 8–4. Information may *flow* from $o \in O$ to $o' \in O$ if there exists a subject $s \in S$ such that $H(s, o) = true$ and $H(s, o') = true$. This is written (o, o').

Information flows even if the access is read-only, because then s can act on information contained in both objects, so in some sense information has flowed between them into a third entity (the subject).

The next theorem shows that unsanitized information is confined to its CD, but sanitized information may flow freely about the system.

Theorem 8.3. For any given system, the set of all information flows is the set

$$\{(o, o') \mid o \in O \land o' \in O \land l_2(o) = l_2(o') \lor l_2(o) = l_2(v(o))\}$$

Proof The set

$$F = \{(o, o') \mid o \in O \land o' \in O \land \exists s \in S \text{ such that } (H(s, o)$$
$$= true \land H(s, o') = true)\}$$

is the set of all information flows in the system, by Definition 8–4. Let F^* be its transitive closure, which is the set of all information flows that may occur as the system changes state.

The rules banning write access constrain which of these flows will be allowed. The set of flows that Axiom 8.6 excludes are those in the set

$$X = \{(o, o') \mid o \in O \land o' \in O \land l_2(o) \neq l_2(o') \land l_2(o) \neq l_2(v(o))\}$$

The remaining information flows are

$$F^* - X = \{(o, o') \mid o \in O \land o' \in O \land \neg(l_2(o) \neq l2(o') \land l_2(o) \neq l_2(v(o)))\}$$

which, by propositional logic, is equivalent to

$$F^* - X = \{(o, o') \mid o \in O \land o' \in O \land (l_2(o) = l_2(o') \lor l_2(o) = l_2(v(o)))\}$$

establishing the result.

8.1.3   Aggressive Chinese Wall Model

Lin [1179, 1180] observed that a basic assumption of the Chinese Wall model was unrealistic. Specifically, the COI classes in the model are actually related to business classes. Consider the COIs in Figure 8–1. It assumes that all banks are in competition, and no bank competes with an oil company. But this partition does not reflect the situation in which oil companies invest their earnings in companies that will support them, which places them in competition with banks; so the oil company spans both COIs. Similarly, one bank may be a savings bank only, another a brokerage house. As those two serve different functions, they do not compete.

More precisely, Lin noted that the Chinese Wall model assumes one can partition the set of objects O into COIs, and thence into CDs [1181]. Define the conflict of interest relation (CIR) to be the relation induced by a COI, so that for $o_1, o_2 \in O$, if o_1 and o_2 are in the same COI, then $(o_1, o_2) \in$ CIR. This is reflexive, symmetric, and transitive. Thus, CIR forms an equivalence relation, and partitions the objects so that no object belongs to more than one class.

The problem is that in practice, CIR does not partition the objects, and hence is not an equivalence class. For example, in practice, a company is not in conflict with itself, so it is not reflexive, and $(o, o) \notin$ CIR. It also is not transitive. Consider a bank B that does both savings and investments. A large computer company C has its own private savings unit, to enable employees to bank on the premises. An oil company G does investments. Thus, $(C, B) \in$ CIR and $(B, G) \in$ CIR. However, the computer company and the oil company have no common interests, and hence $(C, G) \notin$ CIR.

Hence the assumption that O can be decomposed into partitions is false.

Lin [1179] developed a mathematical basis for a version of the Chinese Wall model that defined COI classes not based on business classes. This model, the *Aggressive Chinese Wall Security Model*, defines a relation that is similar to CIR, but is both reflexive and transitive.

> **Definition 8–5.** The *generalized conflict of interest relation* (GCIR) is the reflexive, transitive closure of the relation CIR.

To create GCIR, first for all objects $o \in O$, add (o, o) to CIR. Then take the transitive closure of the result. As GCIR is reflexive, symmetric, and transitive, it defines the equivalence classes that the Chinese Wall model uses to create the COI classes. Intuitively, $(o, o') \in$ CIR if there is a direct information flow path between o and o'. GCIR generalizes this to $(o, o') \in$ GCIR if and only if there is an *indirect* information flow path between o and o'.

If one now replaces the notion of conflict of interest classes induced by CIR to generalized conflict of interest classes induced by GCIR, then the theorems given above still hold.

8.1.4   Bell-LaPadula and Chinese Wall Models

The Bell-LaPadula Model and the Chinese Wall model are fundamentally different. Subjects in the Chinese Wall model have no associated security labels, whereas subjects in the Bell-LaPadula Model do have such labels. Furthermore, the Bell-LaPadula Model has no notion of "access history," but this notion is central to the Chinese Wall model's controls.

To emulate the Chinese Wall model using Bell-LaPadula, we assign a security category to each (COI, CD) pair. We define two security levels, S (for *sanitized*) and U (for *unsanitized*). By assumption, $S \, dom \, U$. Figure 8–2 illustrates this mapping for the system in Figure 8–1. Each object is transformed into two objects, one sanitized and one unsanitized.

Each subject in the Chinese Wall model is then assigned clearance for the compartments that do not contain multiple categories corresponding to CDs in

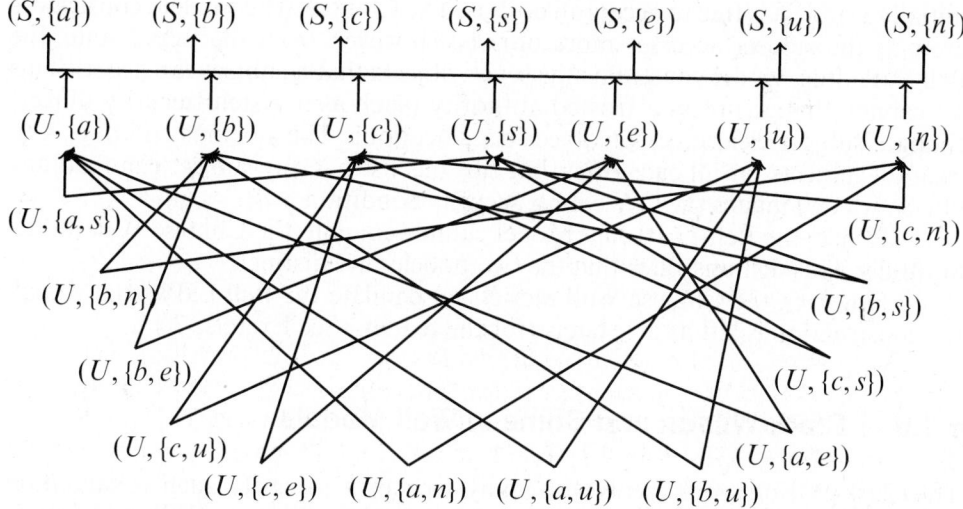

Figure 8–2 The relevant parts of the Bell-LaPadula lattice induced by the transformation applied to the system in Figure 8–1. For example, a subject with security clearance in class (U, {a, s}) can read objects with labels (U, {a}) and (U, {s}). The Bell-LaPadula Model defines other compartments (such as (U, {a, b})), but because these would allow access to different CDs in the same COI class, the Chinese Wall model requires that compartment to be empty.

the same COI class. For example, if Susan can read the National Bank and Veg Oil CDs, her processes would have clearance for compartment (U, {a, n}). There are three possible clearances from the bank COI class, and four possible clearances from the oil company COI class, combining to give 12 possible clearances for subjects. Of course, all subjects can read all sanitized data.

The CW-simple security condition clearly holds. The CW-*-property also holds, because the Bell-LaPadula *-property ensures that the category of input objects is a subset of the category of output objects. Hence, input objects are either sanitized or in the same category (that is, the same CD) as that of the subject.

This construction shows that at any time the Bell-LaPadula Model can capture the state of a system using the Chinese Wall model. But the Bell-LaPadula Model cannot capture changes over time. For example, suppose Susan falls ill, and Anna needs to access one of the datasets to which Susan has access. How can the system know if Anna is allowed to access that dataset? The Chinese Wall model tracks the history of accesses, from which Anna's ability to access the CD can be determined. But if the corresponding category is not in Anna's clearances, the Bell-LaPadula Model does not retain the history needed to determine whether her accessing the category would violate the Chinese Wall constraints.

A second, more serious problem arises when one considers that subjects in the Chinese Wall model may choose which CDs to access; in other words, initially a subject is free to access all objects. The Chinese Wall model's constraints grow as the subject accesses more objects. However, from the initial state, the Bell-LaPadula Model constrains the set of objects that a subject can access. This set cannot change unless a trusted authority (such as a system security officer) changes subject clearances or object classifications. The obvious solution is to clear all subjects for all categories, but this means that any subject can read any object, which violates the CW-simple security condition.

Hence, the Bell-LaPadula Model cannot emulate the Chinese Wall model faithfully. This demonstrates that the two policies are distinct.

However, the Chinese Wall model can emulate the Bell-LaPadula Model; the construction is left as an exercise for the reader. (See Exercise 3.)

8.1.5   Clark-Wilson and Chinese Wall Models

The Clark-Wilson model deals with many aspects of integrity, such as validation and verification, as well as access control. Because the Chinese Wall model deals exclusively with access control, it cannot emulate the Clark-Wilson model fully. So, we consider only the access control aspects of the Clark-Wilson model.

The representation of access control in the Clark-Wilson model is the second enforcement rule, ER2. That rule associates users with transformation procedures and constrained data items on which they can operate. If one takes the usual view that "subject" and "process" are interchangeable, then a single person could use multiple processes to access objects in multiple CDs in the same COI class. Because the Chinese Wall model would view processes independently of who was executing them, no constraints would be violated. However, by requiring that a "subject" be a specific individual and including all processes executing on that subject's behalf, the Chinese Wall model is consistent with the Clark-Wilson model.

8.2   Clinical Information Systems Security Policy

Medical records require policies that combine confidentiality and integrity, but in a very different way than for brokerage firms. Conflicts of interest among doctors treating patients are not normally a problem. Patient confidentiality, authentication of both records and the personnel making entries in those records, and assurance that the records have not been changed erroneously are critical. Anderson [57] presents a model for such policies that illuminates the combination of confidentiality and integrity to protect patient privacy and record integrity.

Anderson defines three types of entities in the policy.

Definition 8–6. A *patient* is the subject of medical records, or an agent for that person who can give consent for the person to be treated.

Definition 8–7. *Personal health information* is information about a patient's health or treatment enabling that patient to be identified.

In more common parlance, the "personal health information" is contained in a medical record. We will refer to "medical records" throughout, under the assumption that all personal health information is kept in the medical records.

Definition 8–8. A *clinician* is a health-care professional who has access to personal health information while performing his or her job.

The policy also assumes that personal health information concerns one individual at a time. Strictly speaking, this is not true. For example, obstetrics/gynecology records contain information about both the father and the mother. In these cases, special rules come into play, and the policy does not cover them.

The policy is guided by principles similar to the certification and enforcement rules of the Clark-Wilson model. These principles are derived from the medical ethics of several medical societies, and from the experience and advice of practicing clinicians.[1]

The first set of principles deals with access to the medical records themselves. It requires a list of those who can read the records, and a list of those who can append to the records. Auditors are given access to copies of the records, so the auditors cannot alter the original records in any way. Clinicians by whom the patient has consented to be treated can also read and append to the medical records. Because clinicians often work in medical groups, consent may apply to a set of clinicians. The notion of groups abstracts this set well. Thus:

Access Principle 1: Each medical record has an access control list naming the individuals or groups who may read and append information to the record. The system must restrict access to those identified on the access control list.

Medical ethics require that only clinicians and the patient have access to the patient's medical record. Hence:

Access Principle 2: One of the clinicians on the access control list (called the *responsible clinician*) must have the right to add other clinicians to the access control list.

Because the patient must consent to treatment, the patient has the right to know when his or her medical record is accessed or altered. Furthermore, if a clinician who is unfamiliar to the patient accesses the record, the patient should be notified of the leakage of information. This leads to another access principle:

Access Principle 3: The responsible clinician must notify the patient of the names on the access control list whenever the patient's medical record is opened. Except for situations given in statutes, or in cases of emergency, the responsible clinician must obtain the patient's consent.

---

[1] The principles are numbered differently in Anderson's paper.

Erroneous information should be corrected, not deleted, to facilitate auditing of the records. Auditing also requires that all accesses be recorded, along with the date and time of each access and the name of each person accessing the record.

Access Principle 4: The name of the clinician, the date, and the time of the access of a medical record must be recorded. Similar information must be kept for deletions.

The next set of principles concern record creation and information deletion. When a new medical record is created, the clinician creating the record should have access, as should the patient. Typically, the record is created as a result of a referral. The referring clinician needs access to obtain the results of the referral, and so is included on the new record's access control list.

Creation Principle: A clinician may open a record, with the clinician and the patient on the access control list. If the record is opened as a result of a referral, the referring clinician may also be on the access control list.

How long the medical records are kept varies with the circumstances. Normally, medical records can be discarded after 8 years, but in some cases—notably cancer cases—the records are kept longer.

Deletion Principle: Clinical information cannot be deleted from a medical record until the appropriate time has passed.

Containment protects information, so a control must ensure that data copied from one record to another is not available to a new, wider audience. Thus, information from a record can be given only to those on the record's access control list.

Confinement Principle: Information from one medical record may be appended to a different medical record if and only if the access control list of the second record is a subset of the access control list of the first.

A clinician may have access to many records, possibly in the role of an advisor to a medical insurance company or department. If this clinician were corrupt, or could be corrupted or blackmailed, the secrecy of a large number of medical records would be compromised. Patient notification of the addition limits this threat.

Aggregation Principle: Measures for preventing the aggregation of patient data must be effective. In particular, a patient must be notified if anyone is to be added to the access control list for the patient's record and if that person has access to a large number of medical records.

Finally, systems must implement mechanisms for enforcing these principles.

Enforcement Principle: Any computer system that handles medical records must have a subsystem that enforces the preceding principles. The effectiveness of this enforcement must be subject to evaluation by independent auditors.

Anderson developed guidelines for a clinical computer system based on his model [54].

8.2.1   Bell-LaPadula and Clark-Wilson Models

Anderson notes that the Confinement Principle imposes a lattice structure on the entities in this model, much as the Bell-LaPadula Model imposes a lattice structure on its entities. Hence, the Bell-LaPadula protection model is a subset of the Clinical Information Systems security model. But the Bell-LaPadula Model focuses on the subjects accessing the objects (because there are more subjects than security labels), whereas the Clinical Information Systems model focuses on the objects being accessed by the subjects (because there are more patients, and medical records, than clinicians). This difference does not matter in traditional military applications, but it might aid detection of "insiders" in specific fields such as intelligence.

The Clark-Wilson model provides a framework for the Clinical Information Systems model. Take the constrained data items to be the medical records and their associated access control lists. The transaction procedures are the functions that update the medical records and their access control lists. The integrity verification procedures certify several items:

- A person identified as a clinician is a clinician (to the level of assurance required by the system).
- A clinician validates, or has validated, information in the medical record.
- When someone (the patient and/or a clinician) is to be notified of an event, such notification occurs.
- When someone (the patient and/or a clinician) must give consent, the operation cannot proceed until the consent is obtained.

Finally, the requirement of auditing (Clark-Wilson certification rule CR4) is met by making all records append-only, and notifying the patient whenever the access control list changes.

8.3   Originator Controlled Access Control

Mandatory and discretionary access controls (MACs and DACs) do not handle environments in which the originators of documents retain control over them even after those documents are disseminated. Graubart [813] developed a policy called ORGCON or ORCON (for "ORiginator CONtrolled") in which a subject can give another subject rights to an object only with the approval of the creator of that object.

EXAMPLE: The Secretary of Defense of the United States drafts a proposed policy document and distributes it to her aides for comment. The aides are not allowed to distribute the document any further without permission from the secretary. The secretary controls dissemination; hence, the policy is ORCON. The trust in this policy is that the aides will not release the document illicitly—that is, without the permission of the secretary.

In practice, a single author does not control dissemination; instead, the organization on whose behalf the document was created does. Hence, objects will be marked as ORCON on behalf of the relevant organization. The controller disseminating the object is called the *originator*, and the ones who receive copies of the objects are the *owners* of those objects.

Suppose a subject $s \in S$ marks an object $o \in O$ as ORCON on behalf of organization X. Organization X allows o to be disclosed to subjects acting on behalf of a second organization, Y, subject to the following restrictions:

1. The object o cannot be released to subjects acting on behalf of other organizations without X's permission.
2. Any copies of o must have the same restrictions placed on it.

Discretionary access controls are insufficient for this purpose, because the owner of an object can set any permissions desired. Thus, X cannot enforce condition 2.

Mandatory access controls are theoretically sufficient for this purpose, but in practice have a serious drawback. Associate a separate category C containing o, X, and Y and nothing else. If a subject $y \in Y$ wishes to read o, $x \in X$ makes a copy o' of o. The copy o' is in C, so unless $z \in Z$ is also in category C, y cannot give z access to o'. This demonstrates adequacy.

Suppose a member w of an organization W wants to provide access to a document d to members of organization Y, but the document is not to be shared with members of organization X or Z. So, d cannot be in category C because if it were, members $x \in X$ and $z \in Z$ could access d. Another category containing d, W, and Y must be created. Multiplying this by several thousand possible relationships and documents creates an unacceptably large number of categories.

A second problem with mandatory access controls arises from the abstraction. Organizations that use categories grant access to individuals on a "need to know" basis. There is a formal, written policy determining who needs the access based on common characteristics and restrictions. These restrictions are applied at a very high level (national, corporate, organizational, and so forth). This requires a central clearinghouse for categories. The creation of categories to enforce ORCON implies local control of categories rather than central control, and a set of rules dictating who has access to each compartment.

ORCON abstracts none of this. ORCON is a decentralized system of access control in which each originator determines who needs access to the data. No centralized set of rules controls access to data; access is at the complete discretion of the originator. Hence, the MAC representation of ORCON is not suitable.

A solution is to combine features of the MAC and DAC models. The rules are as follows:

1. The owner of an object cannot change the access controls of the object.
2. When an object is copied, the access control restrictions of that source are copied and bound to the target of the copy.
3. The creator (originator) can alter the access control restrictions on a per-subject and per-object basis.

The first two rules are from mandatory access controls. They say that the system controls all accesses, and no one may alter the rules governing access to those objects. The third rule is discretionary and gives the originator power to determine who can access the object. Hence, this hybrid scheme is neither MAC nor DAC.

The critical observation here is that the access controls associated with the object are under the control of the *originator* and not the owner of the object. Possession equates to only some control. The owner of the object may determine to whom he or she gives access, but only if the originator allows the access. The owner may not override the originator.

8.3.1 Digital Rights Management

The owner of content, such as a movie or a book, may wish to control its distribution. When the content is given to a purchaser, the owner of the content may not want the purchaser to distribute it further without permission. The ORCON model describes this situation.

Definition 8–9. *Digital rights management* (DRM) is the persistent control of digital content.

This issue arises most often when dealing with copyrights. DRM technology controls what the recipient of a copyrighted work can, and cannot, do with that work.

EXAMPLE: A movie studio produces a new movie. It wishes to sell copies of the movie over the web. If the studio simply allowed people to purchase and download the movie from the studio's website, the purchaser could then redistribute it freely. To prevent this, the studio uses a DRM scheme. That scheme does not prevent the owner from further distributing the movie; however, the people to whom the owner distributes the movie cannot play it.

A DRM scheme has several elements [1968]. The basic ones are as follows:

- The *content* is the information being protected. It may be simple (as a single movie or book) or composite (in which several pieces of content, from different sources and with different rights, are combined).
- The *license* is the token that describes the uses to which the content may be put.
- A *grant* is that part of a license that gives specific authorizations to one or more entities. It may also include conditions that constrain the use of the grant.
- The *issuer* is the entity that issues the license. It may be the creator or a distributor.
- A *principal* is an identification of an entity. It is typically used in a license to identify to whom the license applies.
- A *device* is a mechanism used to view the content. It manages the licenses, principals, and any copies of the resource.

EXAMPLE: In the previous example, the content is the movie itself. The license is the token binding the playing of that movie to the specific copy that is downloaded. It includes a grant allowing the movie to be played on some set of equipment, with the condition that geographically the equipment be located within a particular country. The issuer is the movie studio or its authorized distributor. The principal is the user who downloaded the movie.

DRM schemes provide relationships among these elements. These relationships must satisfy three basic properties [1086]:

1. The system must implement controls on the use of the content. These controls constrain what clients can do with the content, so for example simply distributing the content encrypted and providing the keys to those authorized to see the content is insufficient (see Exercise 7).
2. The rules that constrain the users of the content must be associated with the content itself, and not the users.
3. The controls and rules must persist throughout the life of the content, even when the content is distributed in unauthorized ways or to unauthorized recipients.

EXAMPLE: Some music on Apple's iTunes store is protected by a DRM system called FairPlay.[2] The scheme is based upon cryptographic licensing of the system and the user.

---

[2]In 2007, Apple made some music available without DRM for a higher price. It subsequently incorporated this feature into music on the Apple cloud.

The user must authorize that particular system to play music. The iTunes program provides this capability. It first generates a globally unique number for the computer system and sends that to Apple's servers. The servers then add it to the list of systems authorized to play music for that user. At most five computer systems can be authorized per user; when the limit is reached, further authorizations are denied.

Suppose Sage purchases a song from iTunes. The song file is enciphered with the AES cipher (see Section 10.2.5) using a master key, which is in turn locked by a randomly generated user key from iTunes. iTunes then sends the user key to the Apple servers, which store it for future use. The key is encrypted on both the Apple server and on the local computer.

When Sage plays the song, iTunes first decrypts the user key, and then uses that to decipher the master key. It can then use the master key to decipher the song file and play it. Note that iTunes need not contact the Apple servers for authorization to play the song.

When Sage authorizes a new system, the Apple server sends that system all the user keys stored on the server so it can immediately play the music controlled by FairPlay. When she deauthorizes a system, it deletes all the locally stored user keys and notifies Apple to delete its global unique ID from the list of authorized computers.

When the content is protected, it can only be used on an authorized system. If the content is copied to an unauthorized system, the user keys will not be available and so the content cannot be used.

Conditions for use and for further distribution are stated using a *rights expression language*. Vendors often develop their own proprietary language to meet their needs. Other languages provide ways to express a wide variety of policies [1968, 1969].

EXAMPLE: Microsoft's PlayReady DRM [2187, 2188] uses a different model than Apple's FairPlay. It provides finer-grained control over use. The content is first enciphered using the AES algorithm (see Section 10.2.5). The cryptographic key is made available to a license server, and the content is made available for distribution to clients. To play the content, the PlayReady client downloads the content and requests a license from a PlayReady license server. The license server authenticates the client and, if successful, returns a license. The client then checks the constraints in the license, and if they allow playback, the client uses the license key to decipher the content and play it.

The client's request for a license includes both an identifier for the content to be played and the client's public key (see Section 10.3). The license server authenticates the client and verifies both the user and client are authorized to play the content. It then constructs a license containing the content key and usage constraints, enciphers this using the client's public key, and sends it to the client. The client then decrypts the license with its private key.

The rights expression language supports several different types of constraints. Temporal constraints allow the content to be viewed over a specific period of time, enabling the renting of the content. They also allow a validity period, after which the license must be renewed; this allows subscription-based services. Purchasing constraints allow the consumer to buy content, and the language provides means to express constraints on copying, transferring, or converting the content. Some applications, such as for streaming live television content, require constraints based on geographical location and on availability (as for example when a sporting event is not to be available near where the game is played). PlayReady supports these constraints, too [2189].

Some DRM technologies create unanticipated problems, especially when the software implementing the DRM modifies system programs or the kernel without the user's understanding of the effects of such modification. The example of Sony's DRM mechanism on page 778 serves as a warning of how not to implement DRM.

8.4   Role-Based Access Control

The ability, or need, to access information may depend on one's job functions.

EXAMPLE: Allison is the bookkeeper for the Department of Mathematics. She is responsible for balancing the books and keeping track of all accounting for that department. She has access to all departmental accounts. She moves to the university's Office of Admissions to become the head accountant (with a substantial raise). Because she is no longer the bookkeeper for the Department of Mathematics, she no longer has access to those accounts. When that department hires Sally as its new bookkeeper, she will acquire full access to all those accounts. Access to the accounts is a function of the job of bookkeeper, and is not tied to any particular individual.

This suggests associating access with the particular job of the user [668].

Definition 8–10. A *role* is a collection of job functions. Each role r is authorized to perform one or more transactions (actions in support of a job function). The set of authorized transactions for r is written *trans*(r).

Definition 8–11. The *active role of a subject s*, written *actr*(s), is the role that s is currently performing.

Definition 8–12. The *authorized roles of a subject s*, written *authr*(s), is the set of roles that s is authorized to assume.

Definition 8–13. The predicate *canexec(s, t)* is true if and only if the subject *s* can execute the transaction *t* at the current time.

Three rules reflect the ability of a subject to execute a transaction.

Axiom 8.7. Let S be the set of subjects and T the set of transactions. The *rule of role assignment* is

$$(\forall s \in S)(\forall t \in T)[canexec(s, t) \rightarrow actr(s) \neq \varnothing]$$

This axiom simply says that if a subject can execute any transaction, then that subject has an active role. This binds the notion of execution of a transaction to the role rather than to the user.

Axiom 8.8. Let S be the set of subjects. Then the *rule of role authorization* is

$$(\forall s \in S)[actr(s) \subseteq authr(s)]$$

This rule means that the subject must be authorized to assume its active role. It cannot assume an unauthorized role. Without this axiom, any subject could assume any role, and hence execute any transaction.

Axiom 8.9. Let S be the set of subjects and T the set of transactions. The *rule of transaction authorization* is

$$(\forall s \in S)(\forall t \in T)[canexec(s, t) \rightarrow t \in trans(actr(s))]$$

This rule says that a subject cannot execute a transaction for which its current role is not authorized.

The forms of these axioms restrict the transactions that can be performed. They do not ensure that the allowed transactions can be executed. This suggests that role-based access control (RBAC) is a form of mandatory access control. The axioms state rules that must be satisfied before a transaction can be executed. Discretionary access control mechanisms may further restrict transactions.

EXAMPLE: Some roles subsume others. For example, a trainer can perform all actions of a trainee, as well as others. One can view this as containment. This suggests a hierarchy of roles, in this case the trainer role containing the trainee role. As another example, many operations are common to a large number of roles. Instead of specifying the operation once for each role, one specifies it for a role containing all other roles. Granting access to a role R implies that access is granted for all roles contained in R. This simplifies the use of the RBAC model (and of its implementation).

If role r_i contains role r_j, we write $r_i > r_j$. Using our notation, the implications of containment of roles may be expressed as

$$(\forall s \in S)[r_i \in authr(s) \land r_i > r_j \to r_j \in authr(s)]$$

EXAMPLE: RBAC can model the separation of duty rule [1111]. Our goal is to specify separation of duty centrally; then it can be imposed on roles through containment, as discussed in the preceding example. The key is to recognize that the users in some roles cannot enter other roles. That is, for two roles r_1 and r_2 bound by separation of duty (so the same individual cannot assume both roles)

$$(\forall s \in S)[r_1 \in authr(s) \to r_2 \notin authr(s)]$$

Capturing the notion of mutual exclusion requires a new predicate.

Definition 8–14. Let r be a role, and let s be a subject such that $r \in auth(s)$. Then the *mutually exclusive authorization* set $meauth(r)$ is the set of roles that s cannot assume because of the separation of duty requirement.

Putting this definition together with the above example, the principle of separation of duty can be summarized as [1111]

$$(\forall r_1, r_2 \in R)[r_2 \in meauth(r_1) \to [(\forall s \in S)[r_1 \in authr(s) \to r_2 \notin authr(s)]]]$$

Sandhu et al. [1655] have developed a family of models for RBAC. $RBAC_0$ is the basic model. $RBAC_1$ adds role hierarchies; $RBAC_2$ adds constraints; and $RBAC_3$ adds both hierarchies and constraints by combining $RBAC_1$ and $RBAC_2$.

$RBAC_0$ has four entities. *Users* are principals, and *roles* are job functions. A *permission* is an access right. A *session* is a user interaction with the system during which the user may enter any role that she is authorized to assume. A user may be in multiple roles at one time. More formally:

Definition 8–15. $RBAC_0$ has the following components:

- A set of users U, a set of roles R, a set of permissions P, and a set of sessions S
- A relation $PA \subseteq P \times R$ mapping permissions to roles
- A relation $UA \subseteq U \times R$ mapping users to roles
- A function $user : S \to U$ mapping each session $s \in S$ to a user $u \in U$
- A function $roles : S \to 2^R$ mapping each session $s \in S$ to a set of roles $roles(s) \subseteq \{r \in R | (user(s), r) \in UA\}$, where s has the permissions $\bigcup_{r \in roles(s)} \{p \in P | (p, r) \in PA\}$

The last means that when a user assumes role *r* during session *s*, *r* and hence the user assuming *r* acquires a set of permissions associated with *r*.

RBAC$_1$ adds role hierarchies. A hierarchy is a means for structuring roles using containment, and each role is less powerful than those higher in the hierarchy. Each interior role contains the job functions, and hence permissions, of its subordinate roles. Formally:

> **Definition 8–16.** RBAC$_1$ makes the following changes to the definition of RBAC$_0$:
>
> - Add a partial order $RH \subseteq R \times R$ called the role hierarchy
> - Change the function *roles* : $S \rightarrow 2^R$ to map each session $s \in S$ to a set of roles $roles(s) \subseteq \{r \in R | (\exists r' \geq r)(user(s), r') \in UA\}$, where *s* has the permissions $\bigcup_{r \in roles(s)} \{p \in P | (\exists r'' \geq r)(p, r'') \in PA\}$, and for $r_1, r_2 \in R$, $r_1 \geq r_2$ means $(r_2, r_1) \in RH$.

The last means that when user *u* assumes a role *r* with subordinate roles, *u* can establish a session with any combination of the subordinate roles, and that session receives the permissions it would acquire in RBAC$_0$, plus any permissions that subordinate roles have. So, in effect, the user gets the permissions assigned to the role assumed, as well as the permissions of all roles subordinate to that role.

Role hierarchies can limit the inheritance of permissions through *private roles*. Figure 8–3 shows a hierarchy where the employees report to line management. But employees in this organization have the right to air grievances to an ombudsman who does not answer to line management, and indeed will not report to them. In this case, the ombudsman role is private with respect to the line management.

RBAC$_2$ is based on RBAC$_0$, but adds constraints on the values that the components can assume. For example, two roles may be mutually exclusive; this constrains the values that can be in the sets *UA* and *PA*. Another example is to constrain the function *roles* to allow a user to be in exactly one role at a time. Formally:

> **Definition 8–17.** RBAC$_2$ adds to the RBAC$_0$ model constraints that determine allowable values for the relations and functions.

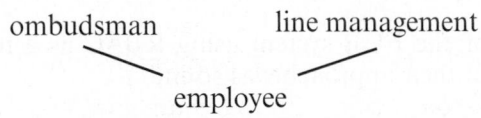

Figure 8–3 An example of a private role.

$RBAC_3$ combines all three models. One can think of it as adding hierarchies to $RBAC_2$:

Definition 8–18. $RBAC_3$ combines the $RBAC_1$ and $RBAC_2$ models, providing both role hierarchies and constraints that determine allowable values for the relations and functions.

An interesting use for RBAC is to manage the role assignments and privilege assignments—in essence, have the model manage its own components. To do this, a set of administrative roles AR and a set of administrative permissions AP are disjoint from the ordinary roles R and permissions P. Constraints allow nonadministrative permissions to be assigned to nonadministrative roles only, and administrative permissions to be assigned to administrative roles only. The ARBAC97 and the ARBAC02 models [1471, 1654] extend $RBAC_3$ to cover role-based administration of roles for RBAC.

EXAMPLE: Dresdner Bank developed an enterprise-wide role-based access control system called FUB to manage access rights based upon a combination of job function and position within the bank [1674]. When an employee launches an application, the application transmits a request contains identifying information for both the user and the application to the FUB. The FUB returns the appropriate profile that contains the rights for that application and that employee role.

Dresdner Bank has 65 official positions such as Clerk, Branch Manager, and Member of the Board of Directors. There are 368 job functions. A role is defined by the position and job function, but only about 1300 roles are in use. The Human Resources Department creates the roles and the users, and assigns users to roles. Thus, when a user leaves, part of the exit processing by the Human Resources Department is to delete the user's assignment to roles. The Application Administrator assigns access rights to an application. These rights are represented by numbers the meaning of which is known only to the Application Administrator. The Application Administrator then passes the numbers to the FUB administrator, who assigns the roles that can access the application using the numbers.

In the definition of roles, the positions form a partial order. Thus, one role is superior to another when the first role's job function is higher than the second's, and the job functions are the same. An alternative approach is to have the job functions be ordered hierarchically, for example by saying that the function auditor includes the functions of an accountant. In this context, the positions could be ignored, and the hierarchy based solely on the partial ordering of job functions.

The analysis of the FUB system using RBAC as a model increased the bank's confidence that their approach was sound.

A problem that often arises in practice is defining useful roles and determining the permissions they need. This process is called *role engineering* [472].

A similar, often more complex, problem arises when two organizations that both use RBAC merge, as the roles each defines are rarely compatible with the roles the other defines—yet many job functions will overlap. Role mining is the process of analyzing existing role and user permission to determine an optimal assignment of permissions to roles. This is an NP-complete problem in theory, but in practice near-optimal, or even optimal, solutions can be produced [637, 714, 1210, 1916, 1917, 2088].

8.5 Break-the-Glass Policies

Sometimes security requirements conflict. Consider a health-care policy that controls access to medical records. In an emergency, doctors may need to override restrictions to get immediate access to a patient's medical record, for example if the patient is unconscious and unable to give consent. Povey [1540] proposed a control to handle this situation:

> **Definition 8–19.** A *break-the-glass* policy allows access controls to be overridden in a controlled manner.

The term comes from "breaking-the-glass" to activate an emergency alarm. These policies are added to standard access control policies, and enable them to be overridden. The overriding is logged for future analysis.

Break-the-glass schemes are invoked when a user attempts to access information and the access is denied. The system either informs the user of the break-the-glass option, or the user knows about it through external sources. In either case, the user can override the denial. Should she do so, the system immediately notifies those whom it is supposed to notify, and logs the notification and the user's actions [671].

EXAMPLE: The Rumpole policy [1252] implements a break-the-glass policy. *Evidential rules* define how evidence is assembled to create the context in which a break-the-glass request is made. *Break-glass rules* define permissions, which may include constraints such as imposing an obligation to justify the need for the break-the-glass action at a later time. *Grant policies* define how the break-glass rules are combined to determine whether to grant the override.

Rumpole's enforcement model consists of a policy decision point and an enforcement point. A break-the-glass request consists of a subject, the desired action, the resource, and obligations that the subject will accept should the override be granted. The decision point grants the request unconditionally, denies the request, or returns the request with a set of obligations that the subject must accept for the break-the-glass request to be granted. The subject then sends a new request with the new obligations.

8.6   Summary

The goal of this chapter was to show that policies typically combine features of both integrity and confidentiality policies. The Chinese Wall model accurately captures requirements of a particular business (brokering) under particular conditions (the British law). The Clinical Information Systems model does the same thing for medical records. Both models are grounded in current business and clinical practice.

ORCON and RBAC take a different approach, focusing on which entities *will* access the data rather than on which entities *should* access the data. ORCON allows the author (individual or corporate) to control access to the document; RBAC restricts access to individuals performing specific functions. The latter approach can be fruitfully applied to many of the models discussed earlier.

Break-the-glass policies provide conditions under which normal access control rules are to be violated. They are useful in cases where unanticipated situations requiring human intervention may occur.

8.7   Research Issues

Policies for survivable systems, which continue functioning in the face of massive failures, are critical to the secure and correct functioning of many types of banking, medical, and governmental systems. Of particular interest is how to enable such systems to reconfigure themselves to continue to work with a limited or changed set of components.

ORCON provides controls that are different from DAC and MAC. Are other controls distinct enough to be useful in situations where DAC, MAC, and ORCON don't work? How can integrity and consistency be integrated into the model?

Most DRM schemes are developed for the specific organization that wants to use DRM. The multiplicity of these systems inhibits acceptance. For example, a consumer who wishes to buy several digital movies and books from four movie studios and three publishers may have to use seven different DRM schemes, each with its own user interface. Thus, the development of interoperable DRM schemes is an area of active research. Another area is the usability of DRM mechanisms, because they must balance this with the protection of the rights of the content owners. This also introduces privacy concerns, another fertile area of research.

Integrating roles into models appears straightforward: just use roles instead of users. But the issues are more subtle, because if an individual can change roles, information may flow in ways that should be disallowed. The issue of integrating roles into existing models, as well as defining new models using roles, is an area that requires much research.

8.8   Further Reading

Meadows [1306] discusses moving the Chinese Wall into a multilevel security context. Atluri, Chun, and Mazzoleni [94] apply it to develop a model for decentralized workflows.

Mišić and Mišić present an implementation of the CISSP model for wireless sensor networks [1357].

Roberts [1599] discusses the tension between ORCON and the principle that information should be made public. He proposes decentralizing the notion of "originator" in ORCON to enable recipients of the information to weigh the benefits and drawbacks of releasing the information.

McCollum, Messing, and Notargiacomo [1276] have suggested an interesting variation of ORCON, called "Owner-Retained Access Control." Unlike ORCON, this model keeps a list of the originators and owners. Like ORCON, the intersection of all sets controls access. Sandhu [1660] expresses ORCON using the typed access matrix model (see Section 3.5.4). Related to ORCON, but different, are attribution models [229, 422, 936, 1586].

Li, Tripunitara, and Bizri [1167] examine the computational complexity of enforcing static separation of duty policies. Chandramouli [379] provides a framework for implementing many access control policies in CORBA and discusses an RBAC policy as an example. He also presents a little language for describing policies of interest. Several papers discuss languages to constrain role-based authorizations [28, 474, 1754, 1779].

Various other forms of access control policies exist. Among them are purpose-based access control [331, 332], task-based access control (TBAC) [1872], task-role-based access control (T-RBAC) [1470], temporal role-based access control (TRBAC) [186], generalized temporal role-based access control (GTR-BAC) [978], spatial role-based access control [863], coalition-based access control (CBAC) [434], organization-based access control (ORBAC) [622], team-based access control (TMAC) [37], and—most generally—attribute-based access control [843, 2069]. These policies typically focus on some aspect of the entities involved, the environment or organization of those entities, or some other characteristic of the entities.

Architectures and standards for DRM [961, 1621] have been developed to provide interoperability of DRM policies and mechanisms. Mohanty [1368] combines watermarking and encryption to provide DRM from the source of the content. Lan and Lewis examine the usability of the Microsoft Rights

Management application [1120]. The societal implications of DRM have also been explored [59, 117, 1110, 1250, 1648]. Bellovin [161] discusses several security implications of DRM mechanisms.

8.9 Exercises

1. Why must sanitized objects be in a single company dataset in their own conflict of interest class, and not in the company dataset corresponding to the institution producing the sanitized object?

2. Devise an algorithm that generates an access control matrix A for any given history matrix H of the Chinese Wall model.

3. Develop a construction to show that a system implementing the Chinese Wall model can support the Bell-LaPadula Model.

4. Call a relation an *anti-equivalence relation* if its complement is an equivalence relation. This question asks you to look at CIR and its complement, called IAR.

   a. Show that IAR is reflexive.

   b. Show that IAR is symmetric.

   c. If CIR is anti-transitive (that is, $(x, y) \in \text{CIR}, (y, z) \in \text{CIR} \Rightarrow (x, z) \notin \text{CIR}$), is IAR transitive?

   d. More generally, assuming CIR is not transitive, is IAR transitive?

5. Show that the Clinical Information System model's principles implement the Clark-Wilson enforcement and certification rules.

6. Consider using mandatory access controls and compartments to implement an ORCON control. Assume that there are k different organizations. Organization i will produce $n(i, j)$ documents to be shared with organization j.

   a. How many compartments are needed to allow any organization to share a document with any other organization?

   b. Now assume that organization i will need to share $n_m(i, i_1, \ldots, i_m)$ documents with organizations $i_1, \ldots, i_m$. How many compartments will be needed?

7. A publisher wishes to implement a DRM scheme for its digital books. Please explain why enciphering the contents of the books, and then distributing the appropriate cryptographic keys, is insufficient to provide a digital rights management scheme.

8. Someone once observed that "the difference between roles and groups is that a user can shift into and out of roles, whereas that user has a group identity (or identities) that are fixed throughout the session."

    a. Consider a system such as a Berkeley-based UNIX system, in which users have secondary group identities that remain fixed during their login sessions. What are the advantages of roles with the same administrative functions as the groups?

    b. Consider a system such as a System V-based UNIX system, in which a process can have exactly one group identity. To change groups, users must execute the *newgrp* command. Do these groups differ from roles? Why or why not?

9. The Rumpole policy requires the user to resubmit a request for break-the-glass access if the policy decision point returns a new set of obligations that the subject must accept. Why does the policy decision point simply check the obligations and, if they are a subset of the obligations in the request, grant the request?

10. With the exception of the break-the-glass policy model, the models in this chapter do not discuss availability. What unstated assumptions about that service are they making?

11. A physician who is addicted to a painkilling medicine can prescribe the medication for herself. Please show how RBAC in general, and Definition 8–14 specifically, can be used to govern the dispensing of prescription drugs to prevent a physician from prescribing medicine for herself.

Chapter 9
Noninterference and Policy Composition

> GONERIL: Combine together against the enemy,
> For those domestic poor particulars
> Are not to question here.
> — *The Tragedy of King Lear*, V, i, 29–31.

Organizations usually have multiple policy-making units. If two different branches of an organization have conflicting policy needs, or even different policy needs, what policy should the organization as a whole adopt? If one of the policies requires six levels of security, and another three, how can they be composed into a coherent whole—or can they? The answers to these general questions come from information flow models that abstract the essence of security policies. Introduced in 1982, these models focus on each process's view of the system to ensure that no high-level information is visible, or can be deduced, by a low-level process. We begin by reviewing the problem and introducing the notions of noninterference and unwinding. We then expand with variations of noninterference called "nondeducibility" and "restrictiveness." We conclude by studying the composition of security policies using these models and side channel attacks.

9.1 The Problem

Return to the Bell-LaPadula Model for a moment. That model forbids reading of higher-level objects (the simple security condition) and writing to lower-level objects (the *-property). However, writing can take many forms.

EXAMPLE: Suppose two users are sharing a single system. The users are separated, each one having a virtual machine, and they cannot communicate directly with one another. However, the CPU is shared on the basis of load. If user Matt (cleared for SECRET) runs a CPU-intensive program, and user Holly (cleared for CONFIDENTIAL) does not, Matt's program will dominate the CPU. This provides a *covert channel* through which Matt and Holly can communicate. They agree on a time interval and a starting time (say, beginning at noon, with intervals of 1 minute). To transmit a 1 bit, Matt runs his program in the interval; to transmit a 0 bit, Matt does not. Every minute, Holly tries to execute a program, and if the program runs, then Matt's program does not have the CPU and the bit is 0; if the program does not run in that interval, Matt's program has the CPU and the transmitted bit is 1. Although not "writing" in the traditional sense, information is flowing from Matt to Holly in violation of the Bell-LaPadula Model's constraints.

This example demonstrates the difficulty of separating policy from mechanism. In the abstract, the CPU is transmitting information from one user to another. This violates the *-property, but it is not writing in any traditional sense of the word, because no operation that alters bits on the disk has occurred. So, either the model is insufficient to prevent Matt and Holly from communicating, or the system is improperly abstracted and a more comprehensive definition of "write" is needed. This is one problem, and in what follows, exploring it will lead to the notions of noninterference and nondeducibility.

9.1.1   Composition of Bell-LaPadula Models

The techniques of modular decomposition and bottom-up programming are widely used throughout the disciplines of computer science, including computer security. Many standards require secure components to be connected to create a secure distributed or networked system. An obvious question is whether or not the composition of two secure systems is itself secure. For our purposes, we assume that the implementation of those systems is precise with respect to the security policy, and we confine ourselves to the issue of composition of security policies. If their composition is not secure, then the composed system is not secure.

Consider two systems with policies that match the Bell-LaPadula Model. These policies can be represented as lattices. The composed system is therefore the composition of the lattices. The relevant issue is the relationship among the labels (security levels and categories). If they are the same, the composition is simply the lattice itself. If they differ, the new lattice must reflect the relationship among the compartments.

EXAMPLE: Consider two systems with policies modeled by the Bell-LaPadula Model. One system, *windsor*, has two security levels, LOW and HIGH, and two categories, EAST and WEST. The other system, *scout*, has three security levels, LOW, S, and TS, and two categories, EAST and SOUTH. Figure 9–1 shows the lattices of these two systems. We are told that the two EAST categories have the same meaning, as do the two LOW security levels. So the relevant issues are (1) how S and TS compare with HIGH and (2) how SOUTH compares with EAST and WEST. Assume that HIGH corresponds to a level between S and TS, and that

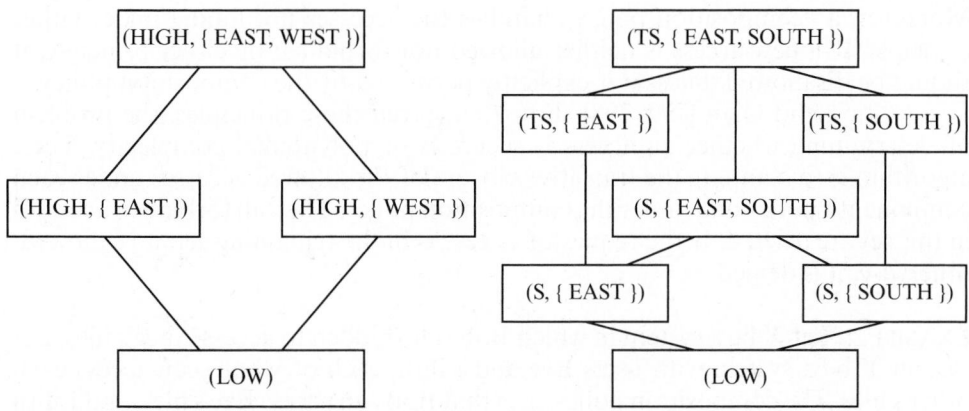

Figure 9–1 The lattice on the left corresponds to the policy of system *windsor* and the one on the right represents system *scout*.

SOUTH is a category disjoint from EAST and WEST. Then the composed lattice has four security levels (LOW, S, HIGH, and TS) and three categories (EAST, WEST, and SOUTH). Drawing the resulting lattice is left as an exercise for the reader.

The security policy of the composite system in the preceding example is a composition of the two security policies of the component systems. If we can change the policies that the components must meet, then composing multiple secure systems to produce a single secure system becomes trivial. However, if we must compose two components that meet a particular policy and show that the resulting composition also meets that same policy, the problem becomes quite difficult. We will explore this surprising fact at length throughout the rest of this chapter.

An interesting question is how to compose systems with different policies to produce a secure policy. Under these conditions, the notion of "security" is not clear: which policy dominates? Gong and Qian [797, 798] suggest the following guiding principles.

Axiom 9.1 (Principle of Autonomy). Any access allowed by the security policy of a component must be allowed by the composition of the components.

Axiom 9.2 (Principle of Security). Any access forbidden by the security policy of a component must be forbidden by the composition of the components.

The composite system therefore satisfies the security policies of its components because the policies of the components take precedence over the composite.

Moreover, a "composition policy" handles the accesses not falling under either principle. If a new access is neither allowed nor forbidden by either principle, it should be disallowed unless it is explicitly permitted by the composition policy.[1]

Gong and Qian [797, 798] show that, given these principles, the problem of determining whether an access is secure is of polynomial complexity. Their algorithm is to compute the transitive closure of the allowed accesses under each component's policy and under the composition policy. Then all forbidden accesses in this set are deleted. If the requested access is in the remaining set, it is allowed; otherwise, it is denied.

EXAMPLE: Let X be a system in which Bob is forbidden to access Alice's files. Let system Y be a system with users Eve and Lilith, each of whom can access each other's files. The composition policy says that Bob can access Eve's files, and Lilith can access Alice's files. The question is, can Bob access Lilith's files?

We write (a, b) to indicate that a can access b's files and we write $AS(x)$ to denote the access set of x:

$$AS(X) = \varnothing$$
$$AS(Y) = \{(\text{Eve, Lilith}), (\text{Lilith, Eve})\}$$
$$AS(X \cup Y) = \{(\text{Bob, Eve}), (\text{Lilith, Alice}), (\text{Eve, Lilith}), (\text{Lilith, Eve})\}$$

The transitive closure of the last set is

$$AS(X \cup Y)^+ = \{(\text{Bob, Eve}), (\text{Bob, Lilith}), (\text{Bob, Alice}), (\text{Eve, Lilith}),$$
$$(\text{Eve, Alice}), (\text{Lilith, Eve})\}$$

Deleting accesses that conflict with the access policies of the components yields

$$AS(X \cup Y)^- = \{(\text{Bob, Eve}), (\text{Bob, Lilith}), (\text{Eve, Lilith}), (\text{Eve, Alice}),$$
$$(\text{Lilith, Eve})\}$$

So Bob can access Lilith's files.

The dropping of the accesses that violate components' restrictions after the transitive closure has been computed eliminates accesses that are allowed by the composition policy but forbidden by the components. This is dictated by the principle of security. Without it, Bob could read Alice's files in the composition but not within the component.

Determining the minimum set of accesses that the composition policy must forbid in order to enforce both principles is generally in NP.

---

[1] This differs from Gong and Qian's approach, in which they allow the access unless the composition policy explicitly forbids it, but follows the Principle of Fail-Safe Defaults (see Section 14.2.2).

9.2 Deterministic Noninterference

The example above suggests an alternative view of security phrased in terms of *interference*. In essence, a system is secure if groups of subjects cannot interfere with one another. In the first example in Section 9.1, the "interference" would be Matt's interfering with Holly's acquiring the CPU for her process. Intuitively, this notion is more inclusive than "writing" and enables us to express policies and models more simply. Gougen and Meseguer [780] used this approach to define security policies.

To begin, we view a system as a state machine consisting of a set $\Sigma = \{\sigma_0, \sigma_1, \ldots\}$ of states, a set $S = \{s_0, s_1, \ldots\}$ of subjects, a set $O = \{o_1, \ldots\}$ of outputs, and a set $Z = \{z_1, \ldots\}$ of commands. For notational convenience, we define a set of state transition commands $C = S \times Z$, because in what follows the clearance of the subject executing the command affects the actual command that is performed.

> **Definition 9–1.** A *state transition function* $T : C \times \Sigma \rightarrow \Sigma$ describes the effect of executing command c when in state σ, and an output function $P : C \times S \rightarrow O$ describes the output of the machine on executing command c in state σ. Initially, the system is in state σ_0.

We do not define any inputs, because either they select the specific commands to be executed or they can be encoded in the set of state transition commands. If the number x is to be input, we simply define a command that corresponds to reading x. We can encode the initial state as a command; the system begins at the empty state (and the first command moves it to σ_0). This notation simplifies the abstract system.

In this system, the state transition commands produce outputs. The outputs are therefore functions of the transition commands, and thus are functions of the inputs and the initial state. We have also assumed that the system is deterministic, since the state transition functions are functions, and time is not considered. We will relax this restriction later.

EXAMPLE: Consider a machine with two bits of state information, H and L (for "high" and "low," respectively). The machine has two commands, $xor0$ and $xor1$, which exclusive-or both bits with 0 and 1, respectively. There are two users: Holly (who can read high and low information) and Lucy (who can read only low information). The system keeps two bits of state (H, L). For future reference, this will be called the *two-bit machine*. For this example, the operation affects both state bits regardless of whether Holly or Lucy executes the instruction. (This is not a requirement of the two-bit machine and will be varied later on.)

Let the set $\Sigma = \{(0, 0), (0, 1), (1, 0), (1, 1)\}$, the set $S = \{\text{Holly}, \text{Lucy}\}$, and the set $C = \{xor0, xor1\}$. Figure 9–2 shows the result of the state transition function. The output function for Holly is both bits; for Lucy, it is the L bit only.

| Commands | Input states (H, L) | | | |
	$(0, 0)$	$(0, 1)$	$(1, 0)$	$(1, 1)$
$xor0$	$(0, 0)$	$(0, 1)$	$(1, 0)$	$(1, 1)$
$xor1$	$(1, 1)$	$(1, 0)$	$(0, 1)$	$(0, 0)$

Figure 9–2   State transition function.

Next, let us relate outputs to state. Two observations will make the formulation straightforward. First, T is inductive in the first argument as $T(c_0, \sigma_0) = \sigma_1$ and $T(c_{i+1}, \sigma_{i+1}) = T(c_{i+1}, T(c_i, \sigma_i))$. This gives us the notion of applying a sequence of commands to an initial state, so let C^* be the set of sequences of commands in C—that is, C^* is the transitive closure of C under composition. Then $T^* : C^* \times S \to S$, where

$$c_s = c_0, \ldots, c_n \Rightarrow T^*(c_s, \sigma_i) = T(c_n, T(c_{n-1}, \ldots, T(c_0, \sigma_i) \ldots))$$

Second, the output function P is also inductive in the second argument. This allows us to define a similar function $P^* : C^* \times S \to O$, which gives the sequence of outputs resulting from a sequence of commands to a system beginning at an initial state.

Given the assumptions above, the outputs provide a record of the system's functioning. The problem is that some subjects are restricted in the outputs (and actions) they can see. In the first example in Section 9.1, Holly should not have seen Matt's outputs, but Matt could see any outputs from Holly. We make this notion rigorous.

> **Definition 9–2.** Let $T^*(c_s, \sigma_i)$ be a sequence of state transitions for a system. Let $P^*(c_s, \sigma_i)$ be the corresponding outputs. Then $proj(s, c_s, \sigma_i)$ is the set of outputs in $P^*(c_s, \sigma_i)$ that subject s is authorized to see, in the same order as those outputs appear in $P^*(c_s, \sigma_i)$.

In this definition, each command may produce some output, but subjects with insufficient clearance may not be able to see that output, lest they deduce information about the previous state of the system. The function $proj(s, c_s, \sigma_i)$ is simply the list of outputs resulting from removing the outputs that s is not authorized to see.

This captures the notion that s may not see all outputs because the security policy may restrict s's access to them. However, s may not have knowledge of all commands, either, and so we need a corresponding definition for them.

> **Definition 9–3.** Let $G \subseteq S$ be a group of subjects, and let $A \subseteq Z$ be a set of commands. Define $\pi_G(c_s)$ as the subsequence of c_s obtained by deleting all elements (s, z) in c_s with $s \in G$. Define $\pi_A(c_s)$ as the subsequence of c_s

obtained by deleting all elements (s, z) in c_s with $z \in A$. Define $\pi_{G,A}(c_s)$ as the subsequence of c_s obtained by deleting all elements (s, z) in c_s such that both $s \in G$ and $z \in A$.

This purge function π captures the notion that certain command executions must be invisible to some subjects. Applying the purge function to an output string generates the output string corresponding to those commands that the subject is allowed to see. For a specific system, the desired protection domains would dictate the membership of G and A.

EXAMPLE: In the two-bit machine, let $\sigma_0 = (0, 1)$. Holly applies the command *xor0*, Lucy the command *xor1*, and Holly the command *xor1* to the state machine. The commands affect both state bits, and both bits are output after each command. We take c_s to be the sequence (Holly, *xor0*), (Lucy, *xor1*), (Holly, *xor1*). The output is 011001 (where bits are written sequentially, the H bit being first in each pair).

$$proj(\text{Holly}, c_s, \sigma_0) = 011001$$

$$proj(\text{Lucy}, c_s, \sigma_0) = 101$$

$$\pi_{\text{Lucy}}(c_s) = \pi_{\text{Lucy},xor1}(c_s) = (\text{Holly}, xor0), (\text{Holly}, xor1)$$

$$\pi_{\text{Holly}}(c_s) = (\text{Lucy}, xor1)$$

$$\pi_{\text{Lucy},xor0}(c_s) = (\text{Holly}, xor0), (\text{Lucy}, xor1), (\text{Holly}, xor1)$$

$$\pi_{\text{Holly},xor0}(c_s) = \pi_{xor0}(cs) = (\text{Lucy}, xor1), (\text{Holly}, xor1)$$

$$\pi_{\text{Holly},xor1}(c_s) = (\text{Holly}, xor0), (\text{Lucy}, xor1)$$

$$\pi_{xor1}(c_s) = (\text{Holly}, xor0)$$

Intuitively, if the set of outputs that any user can see corresponds to the set of inputs that that user can see, then the system is secure. The following definition formalizes this as "noninterference."

Definition 9–4. Let $G, G' \subseteq S$ be distinct groups of subjects and let $A \subseteq Z$ be a set of commands. Users in G executing commands in A *are noninterfering with* users in G' (written $A, G : | G'$) if and only if, for all sequences c_s with elements in C^*, and for all $s \in G'$, $proj(s, c_s, \sigma_i) = proj(s, \pi_{G,A}(c_s), \sigma_i)$.

If either A or G is not present, we handle it in the obvious way.

EXAMPLE: Consider the sequence $c_s = (\text{Holly}, xor0), (\text{Lucy}, xor1), (\text{Holly}, xor1)$ in the two-bit machine with operations affecting both state bits and both bits being output after each command. Take $G = \{\text{Holly}\}$, $G' = \{\text{Lucy}\}$, and $A = Z$.

Then $\pi_{\text{Holly}}(c_s) = (\text{Lucy}, xor1)$, so $proj(\text{Lucy}, \pi_{\text{Holly}}(c_s), \sigma_0) = 1$. This means that the statement $\{\text{Holly}\} :| \{\text{Lucy}\}$ is false, because $proj(\text{Lucy}, c_s, \sigma_0) = 101 \neq proj(\text{Lucy}, \pi_{\text{Holly}}(cs), \sigma_0)$. Intuitively, this makes sense, because commands issued to change the H bit also affect the L bit.

EXAMPLE: Modify the set of commands above so that Holly can alter only the H bit and Lucy only the L bit. Consider the sequence $c_s = (\text{Holly}, xor0), (\text{Lucy}, xor1), (\text{Holly}, xor1)$. Given an initial state of $(0, 0)$, the output is $0_H 1_L 1_H$, where the subscripts indicate the security level of the output. Take $G = \{\text{Holly}\}$, $G' = \{\text{Lucy}\}$, and $A = Z$; so $\pi_{\text{Holly}}(c_s) = (\text{Lucy}, xor1)$ and $proj(\text{Lucy}, \pi_{\text{Holly}}(c_s), \sigma_0) = 1$. Now we have $proj(\text{Lucy}, c_s, \sigma_0) = 101 = proj(\text{Lucy}, \pi_{\text{Holly}}(cs), \sigma_0)$, and $\{\text{Holly}\} :| \{\text{Lucy}\}$ holds. Again, intuition suggests that it should, because no action that Holly takes has an effect on the part of the system that Lucy can observe.

We can now formulate an alternative definition of a security policy. By Definition 4–1, a security policy describes states in which forbidden interferences do not occur (authorized states). Viewed in this light [780], we have:

Definition 9–5. A *security policy* is a set of noninterference assertions.

The set of noninterference relations defined in Definition 9–4 characterizes the security policy completely. An alternative, less common but more elegant approach begins with the notion of a security policy and characterizes noninterference in terms of that definition [1625].

Consider a system X as a set of protection domains $D = \{d_1, \ldots, d_n\}$. Associated with X are states, commands, subjects, and transition commands. Whenever a transition command c is executed, the domain in which it is executed is written $dom(c)$.

Definition 9–5A. Let r be a reflexive relation on $D \times D$. Then r defines a security policy.

The relation r defines how information can flow. If $d_i r d_j$, then information can flow from domain d_i to domain d_j. Otherwise, it cannot. Because information can flow within a protection domain, $d_i r d_i$. Note that this definition says nothing about the content of the security policy; it merely defines what a "policy" is.

We can define a function π' analogous to the π in Definition 9–3, but the commands in A and the subjects in G and G' are now part of the protection domains, so we express π' in terms of protection domains.

Definition 9–3A. Let $d \in D$, $c \in C$, and $c_s \in C^*$. Then $\pi'_d(\nu) = \nu$, where ν is the empty sequence. If $dom(c)rd$, then $\pi'_d(c_s c) = \pi'_d(c_s)c$. Otherwise, $\pi'_d(c_s c) = \pi'_d(c_s)$.

This says that if executing c will interfere with protection domain d, then c will be "visible." Otherwise, the resulting command sequence has the same effect as if c were not executed.

Given this definition, defining noninterference security is immediate.

Definition 9–4A. Let a system consist of a set of domains D. Then it is *noninterference-secure with respect to the policy* r if $P^*(c, T^*(c_s, \sigma_0)) = P^*(c, T^*(\pi'_d(c_s), \sigma_0))$.

Rather than defining a projection function (as in Definition 9–2), consider the set of states related by an equivalence relation with respect to a domain of a command.

Definition 9–2A. Let $c \in C$ and $dom(c) \in D$, and let $\sim^{dom(c)}$ be an equivalence relation on the states of a system X. Then $\sim^{dom(c)}$ is *output-consistent* if $\sigma_a \sim^{dom(c)} \sigma_b \Rightarrow P(c, \sigma_a) = P(c, \sigma_b)$.

In other words, two states are output-consistent if, for the subjects in $dom(c)$, the projections of the outputs for both states after c is applied are the same. This immediately leads to the following lemma.

Lemma 9.1. Let $T^*(c_s, \sigma_0) \sim^d T^*(\pi_d(c_s), \sigma_0)$ for $c \in C$. Then, if $\sim^d$ is output-consistent, X is *noninterference-secure with respect to the policy* r.

Proof Take $d = dom(c)$ for some $c \in C$. Applying Definition 9–2A to the hypothesis of this claim, $P^*(c, T^*(c_s, \sigma_0)) = P^*(c, T^*(\pi'_{dom(c)}(c_s), \sigma_0))$. But this is the definition of noninterference-secure with respect to r (see Definition 9–4A).

Contrasting this approach with the more common first approach illuminates the importance of the security policy. In the first approach, the security policy was defined in terms of noninterference, but it arose from the conditions that caused the particular set of subjects G and the commands A. So, in some sense, Definition 9–5 is circular. The second approach eliminates this circularity, because noninterference is characterized in terms of a defined security policy. However, the second approach obscures the relationship among subjects, commands, and noninterference requirements because of the abstraction of "protection domains." The notion of outputs characterizing commands is crucial, because information flow is defined in terms of outputs. So both characterizations have their places.

9.2.1   Unwinding Theorem

The unwinding theorem links the security of sequences of state transition commands to the security of the individual state transition commands. The name comes from "unwinding" the sequence of commands. This theorem is central to the analysis of systems using noninterference, because it reduces the problem of proving that a system design is multilevel-secure to proving that if the system design matches the specifications from which certain lemmata are derived, then the design is mathematically certain to provide multilevel-security correctly.[2]

We follow Rushby's treatment [1625]. The next two definitions provide the necessary background.

> **Definition 9–6.** Let r be a policy. Then a system X *locally respects* r if $dom(c)$ being noninterfering with $d \in D$ implies $\sigma_a \sim^d T(c, \sigma_a)$.

If the command c does not have any effect on domain d under policy r, then the result of applying c to the current state should appear to have no effect with respect to domain d. When this is true, the system locally respects r.

> **Definition 9–7.** Let r be a policy and $d \in D$. If $\sigma_a \sim^d \sigma_b \Rightarrow T(c, \sigma_a) \sim^d T(c, \sigma_b)$, the system X is *transition-consistent* under policy r.

Transition consistency simply means that states remain equivalent with respect to d for all commands c.

> **Theorem 9.1** (Unwinding Theorem). Let r be a policy, and let X be a system that is output-consistent, transition-consistent, and locally respects r. Then X is *noninterference-secure with respect to the policy r*.

> **Proof** The goal is to establish that $\sigma_a \sim^d \sigma_b \Rightarrow T^*(c_s, \sigma_a) \sim^d T^*(\pi'_d(c_s), \sigma_b)$. We do this by induction on the length of c_s.

> *Basis.* If $c_s = \nu$, $T^*(c_s, \sigma_a) = \sigma_a$ and $\pi'_d(\nu) = \nu$. The claim follows immediately.

> *Induction Hypothesis.* Let $c_s = c_1 \ldots c_n$. Then $\sigma_a \sim^d \sigma_b \Rightarrow T^*(c_s, \sigma_a) \sim^d T^*(\pi'_d(c_s), \sigma_b)$.

> *Induction Step.* Consider $c_s c_{n+1}$. We assume $\sigma_a \sim^d \sigma_b$. We must show the consequent. We consider two distinct cases for $T^*(\pi'_d(c_s c_{n+1}), \sigma_b)$.

> 1. If $(dom(c_{n+1}), d) \in r$, by definition of T^* and Definition 9–3A,

> $$T^*(\pi'_d(c_s c_{n+1}), \sigma_b) = T^*(\pi'_d(c_s)c_{n+1}, \sigma_b) = T(c_{n+1}, T^*(\pi'_d(c_s), \sigma_b))$$

---

[2]This says nothing about the implementation of that design, of course. See Part VI, "Assurance."

As X is transition-consistent, if $\sigma_a \sim^d \sigma_b$, then $T(c_{n+1}, \sigma_a) \sim^d T(c_{n+1}, \sigma_b)$. From this and the induction hypothesis,

$$T(c_{n+1}, T^*(c_s, \sigma_a)) \sim^d T(c_{n+1}, T * (\pi'_d(cs), sb))$$

Substituting for the right side from the previous equality,

$$T(c_{n+1}, T^*(c_s, \sigma_a)) \sim^d T^*(\pi'_d(c_s c_{n+1}), \sigma_b)$$

From the definition of T^*, this becomes

$$T^*(c_s c_{n+1}, \sigma_a) \sim^d T * (\pi'_d(c_s c_{n+1}), \sigma_b)$$

proving the hypothesis.

2. If $(dom(c_{n+1}), d) \notin r$, by Definition 9–3A,

$$T^*(\pi'_d(c_s c_{n+1}), \sigma_b) = T^*(\pi'_d(c_s), \sigma_b)$$

From the induction hypothesis, this means

$$T^*(c_s, \sigma_a) \sim^d T^*(\pi'_d(c_s c_{n+1}), \sigma_b)$$

As X locally respects r, $\sigma \sim^d T(c_{n+1}, \sigma)$ for any s. Then $T(c_{n+1}, \sigma_a) \sim^d \sigma_a$, so

$$T(c_{n+1}, T^*(c_s, \sigma_a)) \sim^d T^*(c_s, \sigma_a)$$

Substituting back, this becomes

$$T(c_{n+1}, T^*(c_s, \sigma_a)) \sim^d T^*(\pi'_d(c_s c_{n+1}), \sigma_b)$$

verifying the hypotheses.

In either case, then, the hypothesis holds, completing the induction step. Having completed the induction, take $\sigma_a = \sigma_b = \sigma_0$. Then, by Lemma 9.1, if $\sim^d$ is output-consistent, X is *noninterference-secure with respect to the policy r*.

The significance of Theorem 9.1 is that it provides a basis for analyzing systems that purport to enforce a noninterference policy. Essentially, one establishes the conditions of the theorem for a particular set of commands and states with respect to some policy and a set of protection domains. Then noninterference security with respect to r follows.

9.2.2   Access Control Matrix Interpretation

Rushby presented a simple example of the use of the unwinding theorem [1625]. The goal is to apply the theorem to a system with a static access control matrix. Our question is whether or not the given conditions are sufficient to provide noninterference security.

   We begin with a model of the system. As usual, it is composed of subjects and objects. The objects are locations in memory containing some data. The access control matrix controls the reading and writing of the data. The system is in a particular state; the state encapsulates the values in the access control matrix.

   Specifically, let $L = \{1_1, \ldots, l_m\}$ be the set of objects (locations) in memory or on disk. Let $V = v_1, \ldots, v_n$ be the set of values that the objects may assume. As usual, the set of states is $\Sigma = \{\sigma_1, \ldots, \sigma_k\}$. The set $D = \{d_1, \ldots, d_j\}$ is the set of protection domains. We also define three functions for convenience:

1. $value : L \times \Sigma \rightarrow V$ returns the value stored in the given object when the system is in the given state.
2. $read : D \rightarrow \mathcal{P}(V)$ returns the set of objects that can be observed under the named domain.[3]
3. $write : D \rightarrow \mathcal{P}(V)$ returns the set of objects that can be written under the named domain.

   Let s be a subject in the protection domain d, and let o be an object. The functions represent the access control matrix A because the entry corresponding to $A[s, o]$ contains "read" if $o \in read(d)$ and contains "write" if $o \in write(d)$. This also leads to a natural interpretation of the equivalence relation in Definition 9–2A—namely, that two states are equivalent with respect to a given protection domain if and only if the values of all objects that can be read under that protection domain are the same. Symbolically,

$$[\sigma_a \sim^{dom(c)} \sigma_b] \Leftrightarrow [\forall l_i \in read(d)[value(l_i, \sigma_a) \neq value(l_i, T(c, \sigma_a))]]$$

   The system X enforces the relevant access control policy r when the following three conditions are met:

1. The output of some command c being executed within the protection domain $dom(c)$ depends only on the values for which subjects in $dom(c)$ have *read* access:

$$\sigma_a \sim^{dom(c)} \sigma_b \Rightarrow P(c, \sigma_a) = P(c, \sigma_b)$$

---

[3]$\mathcal{P}(V)$ denotes the power set of V.

2. If command c changes the value in object l_i, then c can only use values in objects in the set $read(dom(c))$ to determine the new value:

$$[\sigma_a \sim^{dom(c)} \sigma_b \text{ and } (value(l_i, T(c, \sigma_a)) \neq value(l_i, \sigma_a) \text{ or}$$
$$value(l_i, T(c, \sigma_b)) \neq value(l_i, \sigma_b))] \Rightarrow value(l_i, T(c, \sigma_a))$$
$$= value(l_i, T(c, \sigma_b))$$

The second part of the disjunction ensures that if $l_i \in read(dom(c))$, the values in l_i after c is applied to state σ_a and state σ_b may differ.

3. If command c changes the value in object l_i, then $dom(c)$ provides the subject executing c with write access to l_i:

$$value(l_i, T(c, \sigma_a)) \neq value(l_i, \sigma_a) \Rightarrow l_i \in write(dom(c))$$

These requirements are standard for access control mechanisms (in particular, note that they are independent of any particular security policy, although such a policy must exist). We now augment our system with two more requirements for some security policy r.

4. Let $u, v \in D$. Then $urv \Rightarrow read(u) \subseteq read(v)$.

This requirement says that if u can interfere with v, then every object that can be read in protection domain u can also be read in protection domain v. This follows from the need of v to read information from something in u. Given this, if an object that could not be read in u could be read in v, but some other object in u could be read in v, information could flow from the first object to the second and hence out of domain u.

5. $l_i \in read(u)$ and $l_i \in write(v) \Rightarrow vru$.

This simply says that if a subject can read an object in domain v, and another subject can read that object in domain u, then domain v can interfere with domain u.

Theorem 9.2. Let X be a system satisfying the five conditions above. Then X is *noninterference-secure with respect to the policy r.*

Proof Taking the equivalence relation to be $\sim^d$ in Definition 9–2A, condition 1 and the definition of "output-consistent" are the same.

We use proof by contradiction to show that X locally respects r. Assume that $(dom(c), d) \in r$ but that $\sigma_a \sim^d T(c, \sigma_a)$ does not hold. By the interpretation of $\sim^d$, this means that there is some object whose value is changed by c:

$$\exists(l_i \in read(d))[value(l_i, \sigma_a) \neq value(l_i, T(c, \sigma_a))]$$

By condition 3, $l_i \in write(dom(c))$. Combining this with the selection of l_i, both parts of condition 5 hold. By that condition, $(dom(c), d) \in r$. This contradicts the hypothesis, so $\sigma_a \sim^d T(c, \sigma_a)$ must hold and X locally respects r.

We next consider transition consistency. Assume that $\sigma_a \sim^d \sigma_b$; we must show that $value(l_i, T(c, \sigma_a)) = value(l_i, T(c, \sigma_b))$ for $l_i \in read(d)$. We consider three cases, each dealing with the change that c makes in l_i in states σ_a and σ_b:

1. Let $value(l_i, T(c, \sigma_a)) \neq value(l_i, \sigma_a)$. By condition 3, $l_i \in write(dom(c))$. Because $l_i \in read(d)$, condition 5 yields $(dom(c), d) \in r$. By condition 4, $read(dom(c)) \subseteq read(d)$. Because $\sigma_a \sim^d \sigma_b$, $\sigma_a \sim^{dom(c)} \sigma_b$. Condition 2 then yields the desired result.
2. If $value(l_i, T(c, \sigma_b)) \neq value(l_i, \sigma_b)$, an argument similar to case 1 yields the desired result.
3. Let $value(l_i, T(c, \sigma_a)) = value(l_i, \sigma_a)$ and $value(l_i, T(c, \sigma_b)) = value(l_i, \sigma_b)$. The interpretation of $\sigma_a \sim^d \sigma_b$ is that $value(l_i, \sigma_a) = value(l_i, \sigma_b)$ for $l_i \in read(d)$. The result follows immediately.

In all three cases, X is transition-consistent.

Under the stated conditions, X is output-consistent, locally respects r, and is transition-consistent. By the unwinding theorem (Theorem 9.1), then, X is noninterference-secure with respect to the policy r.

All that remains is to verify that the five conditions hold for the system being modeled.

9.2.3   Security Policies That Change over Time

We now extend the preceding noninterference analysis to include policies that are not static. As an example of such a policy, consider an access control matrix for a discretionary access control mechanism. Subjects may revoke permissions, or add permissions, over objects they own. The analysis above assumes that the matrix will be constant; in practice, the matrix rarely is.

EXAMPLE: Let w be the sequence of elements of C leading up to the current state. Let $cando(w, s, z)$ be true if the subject s has permission to execute the command z in the current state. We condition noninterference for the system on $cando$. In the current state, if $cando(w, \text{Holly}, \text{"read } f\text{"})$ is false, then Holly cannot interfere with any other user by reading file f.

We now generalize the notion of noninterference to handle this case. First, we must define a function analogous to $\pi_{G,A}(w)$.

Definition 9–8. Let $G \subseteq S$ be a group of subjects and let $A \subseteq Z$ be a set of commands. Let p be a predicate defined over elements of C^*. Let $cs = c_1, \ldots, c_n \in C^*$. Let ν represent the empty sequence. Then $\pi''(\nu) = \nu$, and $\pi''(c_1, \ldots, c_n) = (c'_1, \ldots, c'_n)$, where $c'_i = \nu$ if $p(c'_1, \ldots, c'_{i-1})$ and $c_i = (s, z)$ with $s \in G$ and $z \in A$, and $c'_i = c_i$ otherwise.

The essence of the definition lies in the use of the predicate. Informally, $\pi''(c_s)$ is c_s; however, when the predicate p is true and an element of c_s involves a subject in G and a command in A, the corresponding element of c_s is replaced by ν. This deletes that element. From this, the extension to noninterference is straightforward.

Definition 9–9. Let $G, G' \subseteq S$ be groups of subjects and let $A \subseteq Z$ be a set of commands. Let p be a predicate defined over elements of C^*. Users in G executing commands in A are *noninterfering with* users in G' under the condition p (written $A, G :| G'$ **if** p) if and only if $proj(s, c_s, \sigma_i) = proj(s, \pi''(c_s), \sigma_i)$ for all sequences $c_s \in C^*$ and all $s \in G$.

EXAMPLE: Return to the discretionary access control example. A very simple security policy based on noninterference is

$$\forall(s \in S)\forall(z \in Z)[\{z\}, \{s\} :| S \text{ if } \neg cando(w, s, z)]$$

This says that if a subject cannot execute the command in any state, that subject cannot use that command to interfere with any subject in the system.

EXAMPLE: Goguen and Meseguer [780] amplify this policy by considering systems in which rights can be passed to other users. Define the command $pass(s, z)$, $s \in S$ and $z \in Z$, to grant to s the right to execute command z. Let $w_n = v_1 \ldots v_n$ be a sequence of n elements, $v_i \in C^*$; then $prev(w_n) = w_{n-1}$ and $last(w_n) = v_n$. Our policy will say that no subject s can use z to interfere if, in the previous state, s did not have the right to z, and no subject having that right gave it to s:

$$\{z\}, \{s\} :| S \text{ if } [\neg cando(prev(w), s, z) \wedge [cando(prev(w), s',$$

$$pass(s, z)) \Rightarrow \neg last(w) = (s', pass(s, z))]]$$

Suppose the user $s_1 \in S$ has the right to execute $pass(s_2, z)$, $s_2 \in S$, $z \in Z$, so for all sequences w, $cando(w, s_1, pass(s_2, z))$ is true. Initially, s_2 does not have the right to execute z; thus, $cando(\nu, s_2, z)$ is true. Now, let $z' \in Z$ be such that (s_3, z'), $s_3 \in S$, is noninterfering with (s_2, z); in other words, for each w_n with $v_n = (s_3, z')$,

$cando(w_n, s_2, z) = cando(w_{n-1}, s_2, z)$. Then this policy says that for all $s \in S$:

$$proj(s, ((s_2, z), (s_1, pass(s_2, z)), (s_3, z'), (s_2, z)), \sigma_i) =$$

$$proj(s, ((s_1, pass(s_2, z)), (s_3, z'), (s_2, z)), \sigma_i)$$

So s_2's first execution of z does not affect any subject's observation of the system.

9.2.4   Composition of Deterministic Noninterference-Secure Systems

As noted earlier, Gougen and Meseguer [780] assume that the output is a function of the input. This implies determinism, because a nondeterministic mapping (that is, one with two or more elements of the range corresponding to one element of the domain) is not a function. It also implies uninterruptibility, because differences in timing of interrupts can result in differences in state, and hence in output. For example, suppose a user enters a command to delete a file. This appears to take some time, so the user interrupts the command. If the interrupt occurs before the deletion, the system will be in a different state than if the interrupt occurs after the deletion (but before the command can terminate properly).

McCullough [1280] has examined the implications of the determinism for composing systems. Consider composing the following systems. Systems *louie* and *dewey* compute at the LOW level. System *hughie* computes at the HIGH level. The composed system has one output buffer, b_L, which anyone can read. It also has one input buffer, b_H, which receives input from a HIGH source. Three buffers connect the three systems. Buffer b_{LH} connects *louie* to *hughie*, and buffer b_{DH} connects *dewey* to *hughie*. *dewey* and *louie* write to these buffers, and *hughie* reads from them. Both *dewey* and *louie* can write to the third buffer, b_{LDH}, from which *hughie* can read.

Figure 9–3 summarizes this composition. Note that all three systems are noninterference-secure. *hughie* never outputs anything, so its inputs clearly do not interfere with its (nonexistent) outputs. Similarly, neither *dewey* nor *louie* input anything, so their (nonexistent) inputs do not interfere with their outputs.

If all buffers are of finite capacity, and blocking sends and receives are used, the system is not

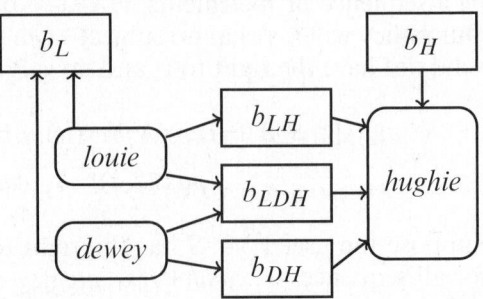

Figure 9–3   Composition of systems.

noninterference-secure. Without loss of generality, assume that buffers b_{DH} and b_{LH} have capacity 1. *louie* cycles through the following algorithm:

1. *louie* sends a message to b_{LH}. This fills the buffer.
2. *louie* sends a second message to b_{LH}.
3. *louie* sends a 0 to buffer b_L.
4. *louie* sends a message to b_{LDH} to signal *hughie* that *louie* has completed a cycle.

dewey follows the same algorithm, but uses b_{DH} for b_{LH} and writes a 1 to b_L. *hughie* reads a bit from b_H, receives a message from b_{LH} (if the bit read from b_H is 0) or from b_{DH} (if the bit read from b_H is 1), and finally does a receive on b_{LDH} (to wait for the buffer to be filled).

Suppose *hughie* reads a 0 from b_H. It reads a message from b_{LH}. At that point, *louie*'s second message can go into the buffer and *louie* completes step 2. *louie* then writes a 0 into b_L. *dewey*, meanwhile, is blocked at step 1 and so cannot write anything to b_L. A similar argument shows that if *hughie* reads a 1 from b_H, a 1 will appear in the buffer b_L. Hence, a HIGH input is copied to a LOW output.

So, even though the systems are noninterference-secure, their composition is not. Exercise 4 examines the influence of the requirement that buffers be finite and of the use of blocking sends and receives.

9.3 Nondeducibility

Gougen and Meseguer [780] characterize security in terms of state transitions. If state transitions caused by high-level commands interfere with a sequence of transitions caused by low-level commands, then the system is not noninterference-secure. But their definition skirts the intent of what a secure system is to provide. The point of security, in the Bell-LaPadula sense, is to restrict the flow of information from a high-level entity to a low-level entity. That is, given a set of low-level outputs, no low-level subject should be able to deduce anything about the high-level outputs. Sutherland [1842] reconsidered this issue in these terms.

Consider a system as a "black box" with two sets of inputs, one classified HIGH and the other LOW. It also has two outputs, again, one HIGH and the other LOW. This is merely a reformulation of the state machine model, because the inputs drive the commands used to create state transitions and generate output. However, the difference in view allows a more intuitive definition of security.

If an observer cleared only for LOW can take a sequence of LOW inputs and LOW outputs, and from them deduce information about the HIGH inputs or outputs, then information has leaked from HIGH to LOW. The difference between this notion and that of noninterference is subtle.

EXAMPLE: Revisit the two-bit system. When operations are executed by HIGH, only the HIGH state bit changes, and the same is true for LOW. Let $\sigma_0 = (0, 0)$. The commands are (Holly, $xor1$), (Lucy, $xor0$), (Lucy, $xor1$), (Lucy, $xor0$), (Holly, $xor1$), and (Lucy, $xor0$), and both bits are output after each command. So, the output string (which includes the initial state) is 00101011110101, the even-numbered bits being LOW and the odd-numbered bits being HIGH.

These functions are not noninterference-secure with respect to Lucy. Because Lucy is cleared only for LOW, she sees the output string as 0001111. But deleting the HIGH commands would produce the string 00111 for Lucy, which is different (and thereby violates Definition 9–4).

However, given the string 00111, Lucy cannot deduce what instructions were deleted because they do not affect the values in the output string; the deletions only affect its length. Hence, this version of the two-bit system is secure with respect to the property described above.

We now formalize this notion of "secure." In what follows, it suffices to consider the LOW user deducing information about the HIGH inputs, because the HIGH inputs and LOW inputs define the HIGH outputs.[4]

> **Definition 9–10.** An *event system* is a 4-tuple (E, I, O, T), where E is a set of events, $I \subseteq E$ is a set of input events, $O \subseteq E$ is a set of output events, and T is the set of all possible finite sequences of events that are legal within the system. The set E is also partitioned into H, the set of HIGH events, and L, the set of LOW events.

The sets of HIGH inputs and outputs are $H \cap I$ and $H \cap O$, respectively; the sets of LOW inputs and outputs are $L \cap I$ and $L \cap O$. Let T_{LOW} contain the set of all possible finite sequences of LOW events that are legal within the system.

Define a projection function $\pi_L : T \rightarrow T_{LOW}$ that deletes all HIGH inputs from a given trace. Then a LOW observer should be unable to deduce anything about the set of HIGH inputs from a trace $t_{LOW} \in T_{LOW}$. In other words, given any such t_{LOW}, the trace $t \in T$ that produced t_{LOW} is equally likely to be any trace such that $\pi(t) = t_{LOW}$. More formally:

> **Definition 9–11.** A system is *deducibly secure* if, for every trace $t_{LOW} \in T_{LOW}$, the corresponding set of high-level traces contains every possible trace $t \in T$ for which $\pi_L(t) = t_{LOW}$.

EXAMPLE: Consider the two-bit machine in Section 9.2, and assume that $xor0$ and $xor1$ apply to both the HIGH and LOW bits and that both bits are output

---

[4]When outputs contain HIGH information that is not a function of the inputs, high-level outputs need to be protected [841]. Such systems are not common, so we explicitly exclude them from this analysis.

after each command. For notational convenience, the first input at each level is the initial state; successive inputs of 0 and 1 correspond to $xor0$ and $xor1$, respectively. The first two inputs will be at the HIGH and LOW levels.

The sequence of inputs $1_H 010_H 10$ occurs (where a subscript H indicates a HIGH input and unsubscripted numbers indicate a LOW input). Then the output will be 1001011010 (where the odd-numbered bits are LOW and the even bits HIGH). Lucy will see this as 01100. She knows that the first input was 0, the second was 1, and the third is not visible. However, the result is to leave the 1 unchanged; knowing the operation of the system, Lucy deduces that the HIGH input was 0 (because $1 \, xor \, 0 = 1$ and $1 \, xor \, 1 = 0$). Hence, this system is not deducibly secure.

Now assume that the $xor0$ and $xor1$ apply only to the LOW or HIGH bits depending on whether the user executing them is at the LOW or HIGH state, respectively. Then the output sequence of the inputs above is 1011111011; Lucy will see this as 01101. However, she can deduce nothing about the HIGH inputs; any of the input sequences $0_H 010_H 10$, $01_H 0101_H 10$, $1_H 010_H 10$, or $1_H 011_H 10$ could have produced the LOW output sequence. Hence, this system is deducibly secure.

9.3.1   Composition of Deducibly Secure Systems

In general, systems that are deducibly secure are not composable [1280]. However, the following modification eliminates the problem that arose during composition of noninterference-secure systems.

> **Definition 9–12.** *Strong noninterference* is the property of deducible security augmented by the requirement that no HIGH-level output occurs unless a HIGH-level input causes it.

EXAMPLE: The two-bit machine that applies operations only to the state bit with the appropriate level, and outputs both HIGH and LOW state bits after each operation, does not meet the strong noninterference property even though it is deducibly secure. But if it only outputs the bit at the level of the operation, it will meet the strong noninterference property.

Weber[5] has shown that systems meeting the strong noninterference property are composable. But this property is too restrictive, in the sense that it forbids systems that are obviously secure.

---

[5]See [1280, p. 183].

EXAMPLE: A system takes LOW inputs and emits them as HIGH outputs. This is clearly deducibly secure, because the LOW user sees no outputs (at either the HIGH or LOW level). However, it does not meet the requirement of strong noninterference, because there are no HIGH inputs [1280].

9.4   Generalized Noninterference

The preceding discussion of noninterference tacitly assumed that the systems involved were deterministic. Specifically, input and output were synchronous. Output depended only on commands triggered by input, and input was processed one datum at a time. This does not model real systems, where asynchronous events (inputs and commands) are the rule rather than the exception.

McCullough [1279, 1280] generalized noninterference to include nondeterministic systems; such systems that meet the noninterference property are said to meet the *generalized noninterference-secure property*. McCullough also pointed out that noninterference security is more robust than nondeducible security. Minor changes of assumptions can affect whether or not a system is nondeducibly secure. The following example illustrates this point.

EXAMPLE: Consider a system with two levels (HIGH and LOW), two users (Holly, who is cleared for HIGH, and Lucy, who is at the LOW level), and one text file at the HIGH level. This file has a fixed size, and the special text symbol ✧ marks those locations that are empty (unused). Holly can edit the file. Lucy can execute a program that does the following (where char_in_file[n] returns the nth character in the file):

```
while true do begin
        n = read_integer_from_user;
        if n > file_length or char_in_file[n] == ✧ then
                print random_character;
        else
                print char_in_file[n];
    end;
```

This system is not noninterference-secure, because the HIGH inputs (the changes that Holly makes to the text file) affect the LOW outputs. However, the system is deducibly secure if Lucy cannot deduce the contents of the file from the program outputs. If the output of the program is meaningful (for example, "This book is interesting") or can be made meaningful (for example, "Thqs book ir interexting"), then the system is not nondeducibly secure; otherwise, it is. This sensitivity to assumption requires that deducible security be carefully defined in terms of allowed inferences, and that assumptions be made explicit.

9.4.1   Composition of Generalized Noninterference Systems

Composing systems that meet the generalized noninterference-secure property does not necessarily produce systems that meet this property. McCullough's demonstration [1280] provides insight into both the nature of generalized non-restrictiveness and the characteristics that make it noncomposable.

Consider a machine *cat*, which has two levels, HIGH and LOW, of inputs and outputs (see Figure 9–4). Inputs may come from the right or left, and outputs may go to the right or left. The machine accepts HIGH inputs. The HIGH inputs are output on the right, and after some number of inputs, the machine emits two LOW outputs, the first a *stop_count* output and the second a 0 or a 1, the former if an even number of HIGH inputs and outputs occur, and the latter if an odd number of HIGH inputs and outputs occur. Finally, *cat* processes each input and generates either a HIGH or LOW output before the next input is received.

The machine *cat* is noninterference-secure. If there is an even number of HIGH inputs, the output could be 0 (meaning an even number of outputs) or 1 (meaning an odd number of outputs). If there is an odd number of HIGH inputs, the output could be 0 (meaning an odd number of outputs) or 1 (meaning an even number of outputs). So the high-level inputs do not affect the output, as required.

Now define a machine *dog* to work like *cat*, with the following changes:

- Its HIGH outputs are to the left.
- Its LOW outputs of 0 or 1 are to the right.
- *stop_count* is an input from the left, causing *dog* to emit the 0 or 1.

This machine is summarized in Figure 9–5.

As with *cat*, *dog* is noninterference-secure. When *stop_count* arrives, there may or may not be inputs for which there are not yet corresponding outputs. Hence, the high-level inputs do not affect the low-level output, just as for the machine *cat*.

Compose these two noninterference-secure machines (see Figure 9–6). We require that once an output is transmitted from *cat* to *dog* (or vice versa), it arrives. However, the *stop_count* message may arrive at *dog* before all input

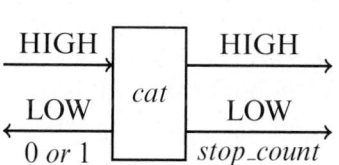

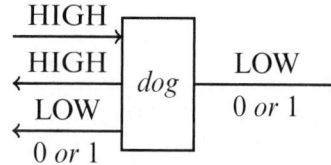

Figure 9–5 The machine *dog*. Here, *stop_count* is an input that stops counting.

Figure 9–4 The machine *cat*. Its HIGH input is copied to the HIGH output.

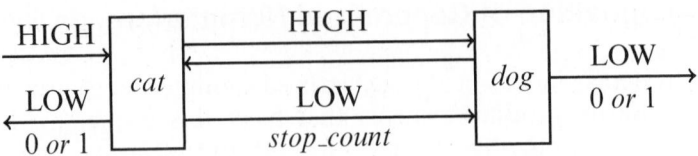

Figure 9–6 The composite machine *catdog*. Both *cat* and *dog* are noninterference-secure, but the composite machine is not.

messages have generated corresponding outputs. Suppose *cat* emits 0 and *dog* emits 1. Then an even number of HIGH inputs and outputs have occurred on *cat*, and an odd number on *dog*. Because every HIGH input on *cat* is sent to *dog*, and vice versa, several scenarios arise:

1. *cat* has received an odd number of inputs and generated an odd number of outputs, and *dog* has received an odd number of inputs and generated an even number of outputs. However, because *dog* has sent an even number of outputs to *cat*, *cat* must have had at least one input from the left.

2. *cat* has received an odd number of inputs and generated an odd number of outputs, and *dog* has received an even number of inputs and generated an odd number of outputs. But then an input message from *cat* has not arrived at *dog*, which contradicts our assumption.

3. *cat* has received an even number of inputs and generated an even number of outputs, and *dog* has received an even number of inputs and generated an odd number of outputs. However, because *dog* has sent an odd number of outputs to *cat*, *cat* must have had at least one input from the left.

4. *cat* has received an even number of inputs and generated an even number of outputs, and *dog* has received an odd number of inputs and generated an even number of outputs. But then an input message from *dog* has not arrived at *cat*, which contradicts our assumption.

So, if the composite machine *catdog* emits a 0 to the left and a 1 to the right, it must have received at least one input from the left. A similar result holds if *catdog* emits a 1 to the left and a 0 to the right. It can also be shown (see Exercise 8) that if there are no HIGH inputs, the outputs from both sides will be the same. Thus, the HIGH inputs affect the LOW outputs, and so the machine *catdog* is not noninterference-secure.

Zakinthinos and Lee [2075] proved some interesting results related to the composition of noninterference-secure systems. They center their results on the absence of feedback. Intuitively, once information flows from one component to another, no information flows from the second component back to the first.

Definition 9–13. Consider a system with n distinct components. Components c_i and c_j are *connected* if any output of c_i is an input to c_j. If for all c_i connected to c_j, c_j is not connected to any c_i, then the system is a *feedback-free* system.

In other words, for all pairs of components, information can flow in only one direction. Zakinthinos and Lee prove the following theorem.

Theorem 9.3. A feedback-free system composed of noninterference-secure systems is itself noninterference-secure.

Proof See [2075].

Feedback can be allowed under specific conditions. If at least one low-level input or output occurs before any high-level output is translated into a high-level input, then noninterference is preserved.

Lemma 9.2. A noninterference-secure system can feed a HIGH output o to a HIGH input i if the arrival of o (at the input of the next component) is delayed until *after* the next LOW input or output.

Proof See [2075].

This lemma leads to the following theorem.

Theorem 9.4. A system with feedback as described in Lemma 9.2 and composed of noninterference-secure systems is itself noninterference-secure.

Proof See [2075].

9.5   Restrictiveness

The problem with the preceding composition is the need for a machine to act the same way whether a LOW input is preceded by a HIGH input, a LOW input, or no input. The machine *dog* does not meet this criterion. If the first message to *dog* is *stop_count*, *dog* emits a 0. If a HIGH input precedes *stop_count*, *dog* may emit either a 0 or a 1. McCullough used a state model to capture the criteria [1280].

9.5.1   State Machine Model

Assume a state machine of the type discussed in Section 9.2. Let the machine have two levels, LOW and HIGH.

Now consider such a system with the following properties:

1. For every input i_k and state σ_j, there is an element $c_m \in C^*$ such that $T^*(c_m, \sigma_j) = \sigma_n$, where $\sigma_n \neq \sigma_j$.
2. There exists an equivalence relation $\equiv$ such that:
   a. If the system is in state σ_i and a sequence of HIGH inputs causes a transition from σ_i to σ_j, then $\sigma_i \equiv \sigma_j$.
   b. If $\sigma_i \equiv \sigma_j$ and a sequence of LOW inputs $i_1, \ldots, i_n$ causes a system in state σ_i to transition to state σ_i', then there is a state σ_j' such that $\sigma_i' \equiv \sigma_j'$ and the inputs $i_1, \ldots, i_n$ cause a system in state σ_j to transition to state σ_j'.

3. Let $\sigma_i \equiv \sigma_j$. If a sequence of HIGH outputs $o_1, \ldots, o_n$ indicates a system in state σ_i transitioned to state σ_i', then for some state σ_j' with $\sigma_j' \equiv \sigma_i'$, a sequence of HIGH outputs $o_1', \ldots, o_m'$ indicates a system in state σ_j transitioned to state σ_j'.
4. Let $\sigma_i \equiv \sigma_j$, let c and d be HIGH output sequences, and let e be a LOW output. If the output sequence ced indicates that a system in state σ_i transitions to state σ_i', then there are HIGH output sequences c' and d' and a state σ_j' such that $c'ed'$ indicates that a system in state σ_j transitions to state σ_j'.

Property 1 says that T^* is a total function and that inputs and commands always move the system to a different state.

Property 2 defines an equivalence relation between two states. The equivalence relation holds if the LOW projections of both states are the same. The first part of this property says that two states are equivalent if either is reachable from the other using *only* HIGH commands. The second part concerns two different states with the same LOW projection. The states resulting from giving the same LOW commands to the two equivalent, original states have the same LOW projections. Taken together, the two parts of property 2 say that if two states are equivalent, HIGH commands do not affect the LOW projection of the states (which is, of course, the same). Only LOW commands affect the LOW projections.

Property 3 says that HIGH outputs do not indicate changes in the LOW projections of states. Property 4 states that intermingled LOW and HIGH outputs cause changes in the LOW state that reflect the LOW outputs only. Assume that two states have the same LOW projection. If there is an output sequence leading from one of these states to a third state, then there is another output sequence leading from the other state to a fourth state, and the third and fourth states have the same LOW projection. Hence, the LOW outputs indicate nothing about the

HIGH state of the system; only the LOW state is visible, and regardless of the output sequence, the LOW projections of the two results are the same.

Definition 9–14. A system is *restrictive* if it meets the four properties above.

9.5.2 Composition of Restrictive Systems

Intuitively, the problem with composition of generalized noninterference-secure systems is that a HIGH output followed by a LOW output may not have the same effect as the LOW input, as we have seen. However, by properties 3 and 4, a restrictive system does not have this problem. Thus, the composition of restrictive systems should be restrictive.

Consider the following composition. Let M_1 and M_2 be two systems, and let the outputs of M_1 be acceptable as inputs to M_2. Let μ_{1i} ($1 \leq i \leq n_1$) be the states of M_1 and let μ_{2i} ($1 \leq i \leq n_2$) be the states of M_2. The states of the composite machine are pairs of the states of each component. Let e be an event causing a transition. Then e causes the composite machine to change state from (μ_{1a}, μ_{2a}) to (μ_{1b}, μ_{2b}) if any of the following conditions holds:

1. When M_1 is in state μ_{1a} and e occurs, M_1 transitions to state μ_{1b}; e is not an event for M_2; and $\mu_{2a} = \mu_{2b}$.

2. When M_2 is in state μ_{2a} and e occurs, M_2 transitions to state μ_{2b}; e is not an event for M_1; and $\mu_{1a} = \mu_{1b}$.

3. When M_1 is in state μ_{1a} and e occurs, M_1 transitions to state μ_{1b}; when M_2 is in state μ_{2a} and e occurs, M_2 transitions to state μ_{2b}; and e is an input to one machine and an output from the other.

Intuitively, these conditions state that an event causing a transition in the composite system must cause a transition in at least one of the components. Furthermore, if the transition occurs in exactly one of the components, the event must not cause a transition in the other component system when it is not connected to the composite system.

Definition 9–15. $(\sigma_a, \sigma_b) \equiv_C (\sigma_c, \sigma_d)$ if and only if $\sigma_a \equiv \sigma_c$ and $\sigma_b \equiv \sigma_d$.

The equivalence relation $\equiv_C$ corresponds to the equivalence relation in property 2 for the composite system.

From these, we can show:

Theorem 9.5. The system resulting from the composition of two restrictive systems is itself restrictive.

Proof See Exercise 9.

9.6   Side Channels and Deducibility

An interesting use of nondeducibility arises from side channels.

> **Definition 9–16.** A *side channel* is a set of characteristics of a system from which an adversary can deduce confidential information about the system or a computation.

In a side channel attack, consider the information to be derived as HIGH, and the information obtained from the set of characteristics of the system to be LOW. Then the attack deduces HIGH values from only the LOW values. So the attack works on systems that are not deducibly secure.

EXAMPLE: Kocher's timing attacks on cryptosystems illustrate this [1084]. Kocher notes that the instructions executed by implementations of cryptosystems depend on the setting of bits in the key. For example, the algorithm in Figure 9–7 implements a fast modular exponentiation function. If a bit is 1, two multiplications occur; otherwise, one multiplication occurs. The extra multiplication takes extra time. Kocher determines bits of the confidential exponent by measuring computation time

Kocher's attack derives information about the computation from the characteristic of time. As a cryptographic key is confidential, this is a side channel attack.

This is an example of a *passive side channel attack*, because results are derived only from observations. The adversary simply monitors the system, and can record and analyze the observations offline if needed. In an *active side channel attack*, the adversary disrupts the system in some way, causing it to react to the disruption. The adversary measures the reaction, and from that deduces the desired information.

```
x := 1; atmp := a;
for i := 0 to k-1 do begin
        if z_i = 1 then
                x := (x * atmp) mod n;
        atmp := (atmp * atmp) mod n;
end;
result := x;
```

Figure 9–7   A fast modular exponentiation routine. This routine computes $x = a^z \bmod n$. The bits of z are $z_{k-1} \ldots z_0$.

EXAMPLE: One active attack derives information about the computation from the characteristic of memory accesses in a chip core [2048]. The Intel x86 processor has several cores. Each core has two levels of caches (L1 and L2), and the chip itself has a third cache (L3 or LLC). The caches are hierarchical, so if there is a cache miss on the L1 cache, the core goes to the L2 cache; if that misses, L3 is checked, and if that is a miss, a memory fetch occurs. The processors used here have inclusive caches, so the L3 cache has copies of all data in the lower level caches. Finally, assume pages are shared among processes. This setup enables the attack.

In the first phase, the adversary flushes a set of bytes (a *line*) from the cache—this is the disruption. This clears the data from all three levels of caches. The second phase consists of the adversary waiting so that the victim has a chance to access that memory line. The adversary, in the third phase, reloads the line. If the victim did so already, the time required will be short as the data will be fetched from the L3 cache. Otherwise, a memory fetch will be necessary, increasing the time needed for the reload.

The researchers used this technique to trace the execution of GnuPG, and were able to derive the bits of a 2,048-bit private key with a maximum of 190 bits incorrect. Interestingly, when they experimented using a virtual machine rather than a physical one, the rate of errors climbed; for example, on one system, the average went from 1.41 erroneous bits to 26.55 bits, and on another from 25.12 bits to 66.12. This emphasized how important the environment is to a side channel attack. The virtual machines add processing, and therefore use of the caches, to handle the virtualization, affecting the results.

Standaert et al. [1814] propose a model of side channels that is illuminating. Although their model is aimed specifically at recovering cryptographic keys, it works equally well for any targeted information.

Definition 9–17. A *primitive* is the instantiation of a computation. A *device* is the system on which the computation is performed. The output of the side channel is called a *physical observable*. The *leakage function* captures the characteristics of the side channel and the mechanisms to monitor the resulting physical observables. An *implementation function* is the instantiation of both the device and the leakage function. The *side channel adversary* is an algorithm that can query the implementation to get outputs from the leakage function.

This model has two implications for side channel attacks. First, devices on which primitives are executed have characteristics that are affected by those computations. The leakage function captures this effect. Secondly, an adversary must have access sufficient to obtain the outputs of the leakage function and to analyze them to determine the effects of the computation on the output. That in turn means the adversary must experiment to determine that effect.

EXAMPLE: In the first example, Kocher divided the outputs of the leakage function into two parts. The *signal* was the variations in output due to the bit in the exponent being derived, and the *noise* was the variations in output due to other effects such as imprecision in measurements and timing variations due to other causes. He uses statistical analysis to determine how many readings (samples) are necessary to derive the bits of the exponent.

In the second example, the leakage function was affected by the noise produced by the virtual machines. Data from the use of the physical machines also differed; the experimenters concluded this was due to one chip using more advanced optimizations than the other, and thus producing more noise.

Other side channels include acoustics [760], power [458, 620, 1240, 1326, 1378, 1549], and electromagnetic radiation emissions [1924].

EXAMPLE: In 1985, van Eck reported on a study that decoded electromagnetic radiation from CRT video display units [1922]. The radiation produced by the device radiates as a broadband harmonic, and thus can be easily captured. The key problem is that the TV receiver on which the images are reconstructed does not receive the synchronization signals necessary to stabilize the picture, so if the frequencies in the video display unit do not match the those of the TV receiver, the picture is unstable and hard to read. van Eck notes that an extension can easily be built that will capture the synchronization signals, thus overcoming this problem.

van Eck used a black-and-white TV, a directional antenna, and an antenna amplifier to capture the electromagnetic radiation. He then used a device containing two oscillators to generate the image for the TV, one for the horizontal and one for the vertical synchronization signals. He noted that the two synchronization frequencies are related by the number of display lines on the screen, so only the oscillator generating the horizontal synchronization signal need be adjusted. As a result, using his special equipment, he was able to reconstruct the pictures on video display units in buildings.

A similar experiment took place in 2007. California Secretary of State Debra Bowen tested electronic voting systems certified for use in California. During the test of one system, the testers found that enabling audio so the ballot was read to the voter (as would be necessary for a visually impaired voter) produced interference with sound from a radio positioned nearby [2201]. This leads to an attack that violates voters' privacy, and is an example of a side channel consisting of electromagnetic radiation.

9.7   Summary

Noninterference is an alternative formulation of security policy models. It asserts that a strict separation of subjects requires that *all* channels, not merely those designed to transmit information, must be closed. The various definitions of noninterference, generalized noninterference, nondeducibility, and restrictiveness are attempts to determine under what conditions different systems with the same security policy can be composed to produce a secure system.

When policies of component systems differ, the issue becomes one of reconciling policies or establishing a systemwide definition of "security" and then demonstrating that the composition meets the definition. The composite system should reflect the principles of security and autonomy. Although establishing whether a particular action is to be allowed is easy, optimizing the checking of accesses is not. Reconciling disparate policies also can be a complex matter, involving technical analysis and politics to determine what the managers of the autonomous components will allow.

9.8   Research Issues

Whenever a result is shown to be in NP, approximating the desired result using an approach of polynomial complexity becomes an attractive area of research. How can one approximate the minimum set of accesses that the composite policy must forbid in order to enforce both the principles of autonomy and security?

Models of noninterference, nondeducibility, generalized noninterference, and restrictiveness assume a static protection system, although some basic work on protection systems that change over time has been done for noninterference. How would the composability of these properties, and the results regarding containment of information flow, change if the protection system were dynamic? How does nondeterminism affect these systems? Generalized noninterference deals with nondeterministic systems, but do those results carry into nondeducibility and restrictiveness? What effects would the analogous results have?

Finally, suppose that a system is nondeducibly secure, but there are two possible sets of HIGH actions that correspond to the LOW trace. The probability of one set having occurred is 0.99; the probability of the other set having occurred is 0.01. Although the system is nondeducibly secure by the definition (because the LOW user cannot determine which of the two possible sets was executed), it is very likely that the first set was executed. This demonstrates that the nondeducible security model does not handle probability; neither do the other models. Incorporating this sense of "probable" is a viable research area.

9.9   Further Reading

Security policy composition arises in the cloud [71, 1851, 2108], distributed systems [371, 1963], federated databases [311, 1473, 1880], government [979, 1424], and other networks [568] because of the interconnections among multiple organizations. Gligor, Gavrila, and Ferraiolo [778] discuss composition policies with a focus on separation of duty. McDaniel and Prakash [1281] examine the complexity of reconciling multiple security policies.

Studies of information flow include work on all of the models described in this chapter. Graham-Cumming [806] discusses noninterference in the context of the language CSP to illustrate its use. Allen [35] compares noninterference and nondeducibility using CSP. Roscoe, Woodcock, and Wulf [1606] develop an approach using process algebra to specify security properties and show how to verify noninterference using it. McLean [1298] argues that a trace-based analysis of noninterference offers some advantages over the traditional state-based analysis technique because it allows a more abstract analysis that is valid unless the user interface changes. However, Bevier and Young [190] counter that a state machine model can provide a better link to verification and specification work, and should be pursued. Van der Meyden and Zhang [1919] compare the different frameworks and compare the semantic models underlying each. Researchers have studied whether, and how, software implements noninterference properties [198, 1117, 1632, 1634].

The results in this section assert that if components meet certain security requirements, then their composition meets those requirements. The most pessimistic properties of connections are assumed. McDermid and Shi [1282] argue that a more realistic approach is to assert that if components meet certain internal security requirements, and their connections meet certain external security requirements, then the entire system is secure. As an example, McLean [1299] developed a model, separability, that can be applied to systems where low-level events cannot affect high-level events. For those systems, separability is simpler than restrictiveness, and provides the same assurances of security of composability. McLean also noted that security properties can be defined by sets of sets of traces [1299]. Clarkson and Schneider [428] extended this idea to develop security policies as sets of trace properties.

Johnson and Thayer [969] have developed another definition of security, called "forward correctibility," that is also composable. It has some advantages over the restrictiveness property. Millen [1339] has developed and proved a version of the unwinding theorem for this model. Mantel [1246] generalized Johnson's and Thayer's results to apply to other forms of composition, and developed a variant of forward correctability that also enables composition without restricting high-level outputs.

Gray [815] discusses the application of probability theory to these models; it has since been extended to include reactive systems including cryptographic computational primitives [108]. Focardi and Gorrieri [693] agree, pointing out that the issue of nondeterminism is closely related.

An interesting application of noninterference and nondeducibility is to cyber-physical systems; they have been used to analyze controllers of vehicles [1231] and a simple power distribution network [732].

9.10 Exercises

1. Draw the lattice described in the first example in Section 9.1.1.

2. The system *plugh* has users Skyler, Matt, and David. Skyler cannot access David's files, and neither Skyler nor David can access Matt's files. The system *xyzzy* has users Holly, Sage, and Heidi. Sage cannot access either Holly's or Heidi's files. The composition policy says that Matt and Holly can access one another's files, and Skyler can access Sage's files. Apply the Principles of Autonomy and Security to determine who can read whose files in the composition of *xyzzy* and *plugh*.

3. Consider the two-bit machine in Section 9.2. Suppose Lucy applies the command *xor*0, then Holly the command *xor*0, then Holly the command *xor*0, and finally Lucy the command *xor*1.

   a. Assuming a command affects both the HIGH and LOW bits, give the values of $proj(\text{Holly}, c_s, \sigma_0)$, $proj(\text{Lucy}, c_s, \sigma_0)$, $\pi_{\text{Lucy}}(c_s)$, $\pi_{\text{Holly}}(c_s)$, $\pi_{\text{Lucy}, xor0}(c_s)$, $\pi_{\text{Holly}, xor0}(c_s)$, $\pi_{\text{Holly}, xor1}(c_s)$, and $\pi_{xor1}(c_s)$.

   b. Assuming a command affects only the bit at the level of the user, give the values of the functions above.

4. Consider the systems *louie* and *dewey* in Section 9.2.4.

   a. Suppose the sends and receives for the buffers are nonblocking. Is the composition of *hughie, dewey*, and *louie* still noninterference-secure? Justify your answer.

   b. Suppose all buffers are unbounded. Is the composition of *hughie, dewey*, and *louie* still noninterference-secure? Justify your answer.

5. Modify the two-bit system in the first example in Section 9.3 as follows. Whenever a HIGH operation is performed, the HIGH state bit is output. Whenever a LOW operation is performed, the LOW state bit is output. The initial state is not output (in contrast to the example). Is this version of the two-bit system noninterference-secure with respect to Lucy? Why or why not?

6. In the second example in Section 9.3, Lucy sees the output sequence as 011011. Given that she knows the low-level input sequence, list all possible input sequences that match the known low-level input sequence and produce the desired output.

7. Prove that a system that meets the definition of generalized noninterference security also meets the definition of deducible security.

8. Suppose composite machine *catdog* (see Section 9.4.1) receives no HIGH inputs. Show it emits the same value from the left and the right.

9. Prove Theorem 9.5.

10. In composite machine *catdog* (see Section 9.4.1), suppose *cat* can accept a number of inputs before processing them—that is, *cat*'s input buffer has a capacity greater than 1. This machine now emits the same value from the left and the right. Is it still true that the composite machine has received no inputs from the left? (From [1458].)

11. Consider again the algorithm in Figure 9–7. The power used is another side channel for most instantiations of this algorithm. Explain how this side channel works. How might you add sufficient noise to it to render it unusable?

Part IV

Implementation I: Cryptography

Cryptography provides many mechanisms on which security techniques and technologies are built. Part IV reviews the basics of cryptography and its use in computer security.

Chapter 10, "Basic Cryptography," reviews the principle elements of cryptosystems. It presents some symmetric ciphers, public key ciphers, cryptographic hash functions, and digital signatures. This material is the basis for Chapters 11, 12, and 13.

Chapter 11, "Key Management," discusses the basics of managing cryptographic keys. Authentication and key exchange protocols are often combined, so this chapter includes authentication protocols that provide the ability to generate a common cryptographic key for future use. Generating keys is an intricate subject, full of traps for the unwary, and some basic principles and techniques improve the strength of the keys generated. Distributing fixed keys throughout the infrastructure leads to protocols for public key interchange, including certificates and key escrow and recovery protocols.

Chapter 12, "Cipher Techniques," builds on the previous two chapters to present cryptographic protocols used in practice. It includes a discussion of stream and block ciphers and presents three Internet protocols as examples of how protocols work.

Chapter 13, "Authentication," discusses authentication in a single system (although the system may be a remote one). As networking authentication protocols increase in importance, and as smart cards and other hardware become more common, the use of passwords as the sole authenticators is being deprecated. However, many of the protocols and mechanisms require a PIN or other authentication data. This shifts the problem of authentication to a new level. Even there, the systems require the principles of how to choose a good password and how to identify oneself to the device or system from which the protocol is launched.

Chapter 10
Basic Cryptography

YORK: Then, York, be still awhile, till time do serve:
Watch thou and wake when others be asleep,
To pry into the secrets of the state;
— *The Second Part of King Henry the Sixth*, I, i, 249–260.

Cryptography is a deep mathematical subject. Because this book focuses on system security, we consider cryptography as a supporting tool. Viewed in this context, the reader needs only a brief overview of the major points of cryptography relevant to that use. This chapter provides such an overview.

Cryptographic protocols provide a cornerstone for secure communication. These protocols are built on ideas presented in this chapter and are discussed at length in later chapters.

10.1   Cryptography

The word *cryptography* comes from two Greek words meaning "secret writing" and is the art and science of concealing meaning. *Cryptanalysis* is the breaking of codes. The basic component of cryptography is a *cryptosystem*.

Definition 10–1. A *cryptosystem* is a 5-tuple $(\mathcal{E}, \mathcal{D}, \mathcal{M}, \mathcal{K}, \mathcal{C})$, where $\mathcal{M}$ is the set of *plaintexts*, $\mathcal{K}$ the set of *keys*, $\mathcal{C}$ is the set of *ciphertexts*, $\mathcal{E} : \mathcal{M} \times \mathcal{K} \to \mathcal{C}$ is the set of *enciphering functions*, and $\mathcal{D} : \mathcal{C} \times \mathcal{K} \to \mathcal{M}$ is the set of *deciphering functions*.

EXAMPLE: In the latter days of the Roman Republic, Julius Caesar was preparing to invade Italy. His confidential communications with his secret allies in Rome were enciphered using a cipher in which the letters are shifted by 3 (so this type of cipher is called a *shift cipher* or a *Caesar cipher*). For example, the letter "A" becomes "D," "B" becomes "E," and so forth, ending with "Z" becoming "C."

So the word "HELLO" is enciphered as "KHOOR." Informally, this cipher is a cryptosystem with

$$\mathcal{M} = \{\text{all sequences of Roman letters}\}$$
$$\mathcal{K} = \{i \mid i \text{ an integer such that } 0 \le i \le 25\}$$
$$\mathcal{E} = \{E_k \mid k \in \mathcal{K} \text{ and } \forall(m = m_1 \ldots m_n \in \mathcal{M})[E_k(m_i) = (m_i + k) \bmod 26]\}$$

Representing each letter by its position in the alphabet (with "A" in position 0), "HELLO" is 7 4 11 11 14; if $k = 3$, the ciphertext is 10 7 14 14 17, or "KHOOR."

$$\mathcal{D} = \{D_k \mid k \in \mathcal{K} \text{ and } \forall(c = c_1 \ldots c_n \in \mathcal{C})[D_k(c_i) = (26 + c_l - k) \bmod 26]\}$$

Each D_k simply inverts the corresponding E_k. We also have

$$\mathcal{C} = \mathcal{M}$$

because $\mathcal{E}$ is clearly a set of onto functions.

The primary goal of cryptography is to keep enciphered information secret, thereby countering the threat of disclosure (see Section 1.2). Cryptography can also be used to provide integrity of both data and origin, thereby countering the threats of modification and masquerading. It can also provide nonrepudiation, countering the threat of repudiation of origin. Thus, it is a remarkably powerful mechanism that computer security techniques rely on heavily.

Cryptosystems are based on two types of transformations [1725]. The first, *onfusion*, replaces parts of the plaintext message with other data, to hide the original content. The second, *diffusion*, scrambles the plaintext message so that the original content is spread throughout the message. These increase the difficulty of uncovering the original plaintext message.

10.1.1   Overview of Cryptanalysis

Cryptanalysis is the analysis of cryptosystems in order to decipher the messages. *Kerckhoff's Principle* says that the security of a cryptosystem cannot rely on an adversary's not knowing the algorithms for encryption and decryption [1826]. Thus, standard cryptographic practice is to assume that she knows the algorithms used to encipher and decipher, and the set of possible keys, but not the specific cryptographic key (in other words, she knows $\mathcal{K}$, $\mathcal{D}$, and $\mathcal{E}$).

An adversary may use three types of attacks:

- In a *ciphertext only* attack, the adversary has only the ciphertext. Her goal is to find the corresponding plaintext. If possible, she may try to find the key, too.

- In a *known plaintext* attack, the adversary has the ciphertext and the plaintext that was enciphered. Her goal is to find the key that was used.
- In a *chosen plaintext* attack, the adversary may ask that specific plaintexts be enciphered. She is given the corresponding ciphertexts. Her goal is to find the key that was used.

A good cryptosystem protects against all three.

Attacks use both mathematics and statistics. The mathematical methods examine the assumptions of the problems upon which the security of the ciphers rests. The statistical methods make assumptions about the statistics of the plaintext language and examine the ciphertext to correlate its properties with those assumptions. Those assumptions are collectively called a *model* of the language. Common models of language are 1-gram models (reflecting frequence of individual letters), 2-gram models (reflecting frequencies of pairs of letters), Markov models, and word models.

10.2   Symmetric Cryptosystems

Symmetric cryptosystems (also called *single key* or *secret key* cryptosystems) are cryptosystems that use the same key for encipherment and decipherment. In these systems, for all $c \in C$ and $k \in K$, there is a $D_k \in D$ such that $D_k(E_k(m)) = m$.

EXAMPLE: The shift cipher discussed earlier had a key of 3, so the enciphering function was E_3. To decipher "KHOOR," we used the same key in the decipherment function D_3. Hence, the shift cipher is a symmetric cipher.

There are two basic types of symmetric ciphers: *transposition* ciphers that diffuse the data in the plaintext and *substitution* ciphers that replace the data in the plaintext.

10.2.1   Transposition Ciphers

A *transposition cipher* rearranges the characters in the plaintext to form the ciphertext. The letters are not changed. Thus, each encryption key $k \in K$ indicates a permutation algorithm. The set of encryption functions E is simply the set of permutations of m, and the set of decryption functions D is the set of inverse permutations.

EXAMPLE: The *rail fence cipher* is composed by writing the plaintext in two rows, proceeding down, then across, and reading the ciphertext across, then down. For example, the plaintext "HELLO, WORLD" would be written as

```
HLOOL
ELWRD
```

resulting in the ciphertext "HLOOLELWRD."

Mathematically, the key to a transposition cipher is a permutation function. Because the permutation does not alter the frequency of plaintext characters, a transposition cipher can be detected by comparing character frequencies with a model of the language. If, for example, character frequencies for 1-grams match those of a model of English, but 2-gram frequencies do not match the model, then the text is probably a transposition cipher.

Attacking a transposition cipher requires rearranging the letters of the ciphertext. This process, called *anagramming*, uses tables of *n*-gram frequencies to identify common *n*-grams. The cryptanalyst arranges the letters in such a way that the characters in the ciphertext form some *n*-grams with highest frequency. This process is repeated, using different *n*-grams, until the transposition pattern is found.

EXAMPLE: Consider the ciphertext "HLOOLELWRD." According to Konheim's digram table [1092, p. 19], the digram "HE" occurs with frequency 0.0305 in English. Of the other possible digrams beginning with "H," the frequency of "HO" is the next highest, at 0.0043, and the digrams "HL," "HW," "HR," and "HD" have frequencies of less than 0.0010. Furthermore, the frequency of "WH" is 0.0026, and the digrams "EH," "LH," "OH," "RH," and "DH" occur with frequencies of 0.0002 or less. This suggests that "E" follows "H." We arrange the letters so that each letter in the first block of five letters (from '"H" up to but not including the "E") is adjacent to the corresponding letter in the second block of five letters, as follows:

```
HE
LL
OW
OR
LD
```

Reading the letters across and down produces "HELLOWORLD." Note that the shape of the arrangement is different from that in the previous example. However, the two arrangements are equivalent, leading to the correct solution.

10.2.2   Substitution Ciphers

A *substitution cipher* changes characters in the plaintext to produce the ciphertext.

EXAMPLE: The shift cipher discussed earlier had a key of 3, altering each letter in the plaintext by mapping it into the letter three characters later in the alphabet (and circling back to the beginning of the alphabet if needed). This is a substitution cipher.

A shift cipher is susceptible to a statistical ciphertext-only attack.

Figure 10–1 presents a character-based, or 1-gram, model of English text; others are 2-gram models (reflecting frequencies of pairs of letters), Markov models, and word models. In what follows, we use the 1-gram model and assume that the characters are chosen independently of one another.

EXAMPLE: Consider the ciphertext "KHOOR ZRUOG." We first compute the frequency of each letter in the ciphertext:

| G | 0.1 | H | 0.1 | K | 0.1 | O | 0.3 | R | 0.2 | U | 0.1 |
| Z | 0.1 | | | | | | | | | | |

We now apply the character-based model. Let $\phi(i)$ be the correlation of the frequency of each letter in the ciphertext with the character frequencies in English (see Figure 10–1). Let $\phi(c)$ be the frequency of character c (expressed as a fraction). The formula for this correlation for this ciphertext (with all arithmetic being mod 26) is

$$\varphi(i) = \sum_{0 \leq c \leq 25} \phi(c)p(c - i) = 0.1p(6 - i) + 0.1p(7 - i) + 0.1p(10 - i)$$
$$+0.3p(14 - i) + 0.2p(17 - i) + 0.1p(20 - i) + 0.1p(25 - i)$$

This correlation should be a maximum when the key k translates the ciphertext into English. Figure 10–2 shows the values of this function for the values of i. Trying the most likely key first, we obtain as plaintext "EBIIL TLOIA" when $i = 6$, "AXEEH PHKEW" when $i = 10$, "HELLO WORLD" when $i = 3$, and "WTAAD LDGAS" when $i = 14$.

The example above emphasizes the statistical nature of this attack. The statistics indicated that the key was most likely 6, when in fact the correct key was 3. So the attacker must test the results. The statistics simply reduce the number of trials in most cases. Only three trials were needed, as opposed to 13 (the expected number of trials if the keys were simply tried in order).

a	0.07984	h	0.06384	n	0.06876	t	0.09058
b	0.01511	i	0.07000	o	0.07691	u	0.02844
c	0.02504	j	0.00131	p	0.01741	v	0.01056
d	0.04260	k	0.00741	q	0.00107	w	0.02304
e	0.12452	l	0.03961	r	0.05912	x	0.00159
f	0.02262	m	0.02629	s	0.06333	y	0.02028
g	0.02013					z	0.00057

Figure 10–1   Table of character frequencies in the English language

i	$\varphi(i)$	i	$\varphi(i)$	i	$\varphi(i)$	i	$\varphi(i)$
0	0.0469	7	0.0461	13	0.0505	19	0.0312
1	0.0393	8	0.0194	14	0.0561	20	0.0287
2	0.0396	9	0.0286	15	0.0215	21	0.0526
3	0.0586	10	0.0631	16	0.0306	22	0.0398
4	0.0259	11	0.0280	17	0.0386	23	0.0338
5	0.0165	12	0.0318	18	0.0317	24	0.0320
6	0.0676					25	0.0443

Figure 10–2   The value of $\varphi(i)$ for $0 \leq i \leq 25$ using the model in Figure 10–1.

EXAMPLE: Using Konheim's model of single-character frequencies [1092, p. 16], the most likely keys (in order) are $i = 6$, $i = 10$, $i = 14$, and $i = 3$. Konheim's frequencies are different than Denning's, and this accounts for the change in the third most probable key.

A variant of the shift cipher, called an *affine cipher*, uses a multiplier in addition to the shift. Exercise 4 examines this cipher.

10.2.2.1   Vigenère Cipher

The shift cipher maps every character into another character in one alphabet. Such a cipher is a *monoalphabetic* cipher. As noted above, it preserves the statistics of the underlying message, which a cryptanalyst can use to decipher the message.

A *polyalphabetic* cipher uses multiple alphabets to generate the ciphertest, thereby obscuring the statistics. The Vigenère cipher is such a cryptosystem. In it, the key is a sequence of letters. The key letters are applied to successive plaintext characters, and when the end of the key is reached, the key starts over. The length of the key is called the *period* of the cipher. Figure 10–3 shows a *tableau*, or table, to implement this cipher efficiently. Because this requires several different key letters, this type of cipher is called *polyalphabetic*.

EXAMPLE: The first line of a limerick is enciphered using the key "BENCH," as follows:

```
Key         B ENCHBENC HBENC HBENCH BENCHBENCH
Plaintext   A LIMERICK PACKS LAUGHS ANATOMICAL
Ciphertext  B PVOLSMPM WBGXU SBYTJZ BRNVVNMPCS
```

For many years, the Vigenère cipher was considered unbreakable. Then a Prussian cavalry officer, Major Kasiski, noticed that repetitions occur when characters of the key appear over the same characters in the ciphertext. The

```
  A B C D E F G H I J K L M N O P Q R S T U V W X Y Z
A A B C D E F G H I J K L M N O P Q R S T U V W X Y Z
B B C D E F G H I J K L M N O P Q R S T U V W X Y Z A
C C D E F G H I J K L M N O P Q R S T U V W X Y Z A B
D D E F G H I J K L M N O P Q R S T U V W X Y Z A B C
E E F G H I J K L M N O P Q R S T U V W X Y Z A B C D
F F G H I J K L M N O P Q R S T U V W X Y Z A B C D E
G G H I J K L M N O P Q R S T U V W X Y Z A B C D E F
H H I J K L M N O P Q R S T U V W X Y Z A B C D E F G
I I J K L M N O P Q R S T U V W X Y Z A B C D E F G H
J J K L M N O P Q R S T U V W X Y Z A B C D E F G H I
K K L M N O P Q R S T U V W X Y Z A B C D E F G H I J
L L M N O P Q R S T U V W X Y Z A B C D E F G H I J K
M M N O P Q R S T U V W X Y Z A B C D E F G H I J K L
N N O P Q R S T U V W X Y Z A B C D E F G H I J K L M
O O P Q R S T U V W X Y Z A B C D E F G H I J K L M N
P P Q R S T U V W X Y Z A B C D E F G H I J K L M N O
Q Q R S T U V W X Y Z A B C D E F G H I J K L M N O P
R R S T U V W X Y Z A B C D E F G H I J K L M N O P Q
S S T U V W X Y Z A B C D E F G H I J K L M N O P Q R
T T U V W X Y Z A B C D E F G H I J K L M N O P Q R S
U U V W X Y Z A B C D E F G H I J K L M N O P Q R S T
V V W X Y Z A B C D E F G H I J K L M N O P Q R S T U
W W X Y Z A B C D E F G H I J K L M N O P Q R S T U V
X X Y Z A B C D E F G H I J K L M N O P Q R S T U V W
Y Y Z A B C D E F G H I J K L M N O P Q R S T U V W X
Z Z A B C D E F G H I J K L M N O P Q R S T U V W X Y
```

Figure 10–3 The Vigenère tableau.

number of characters between the repetitions is a multiple of the period. From this observation, he developed an effective attack.

EXAMPLE: Let the message be "THE BOY HAS THE BAG" and let the key be "VIG." Then

Key	VIGVIGVIGVIGVIG
Plaintext	THEBOYHASTHEBAG
Ciphertext	OPKWWECIYOPKWIM

In the ciphertext, the string "OPKW" appears twice. Both are caused by the key sequence "VIGV" enciphering the same ciphertext, "THEB." The ciphertext repetitions are nine characters apart. As Figure 10–4 shows, the lower this value, the less variation in the characters of the ciphertext and, from our models of English, the longer the period of the cipher.

Period	Expected IC	Period	Expected IC	Period	Expected IC
1	0.0660	7	0.0420	50	0.0386
2	0.0520	8	0.0415	60	0.0385
3	0.0473	9	0.0411	70	0.0384
4	0.0450	10	0.0408	80	0.0384
5	0.0436	20	0.3940	90	0.0383
6	0.0427	30	0.0389	99	0.0383
		40	0.0387		

Figure 10–4   Indices of coincidences for different periods.

The first step in the Kasiski method is to determine the length of the key. The *index of coincidence* (IC) measures the differences in the frequencies of the letters in the ciphertext. It is defined as the probability that two letters randomly chosen from the ciphertext will be the same. The lower this value, the less variation in the characters of the ciphertext and, from our models of English, the longer the period of the cipher.

Let F_c be the frequency of cipher character c, and let N be the length of the ciphertext. Then the index of coincidence IC can be shown to be (see Exercise 6)

$$IC = \frac{1}{N(N-1)} \sum_{i=0}^{25} F_i(F_i - 1)$$

We examine the ciphertext for multiple repetitions and tabulate their length and the number of characters between successive repetitions. The period is likely to be a factor of the number of characters between these repetitions. From the repetitions, we establish the probable period, using the index of coincidence to check our deduction. We then tabulate the characters for each key letter separately and solve each as a shift cipher.

EXAMPLE: Consider the Vigenère cipher

```
ADQYS MIUSB OXKKT MIBHK IZOOO EQOOG IFBAG KAUMF
VVTAA CIDTW MOCIO EQOOG BMBFV ZGGWP CIEKQ HSNEW
VECNE DLAAV RWKXS VNSVP HCEUT QOIOF MEGJS WTPCH
AJMOC HIUIX
```

Could this be a shift cipher (which is a Vigenère cipher with a key length of 1)? We find that the index of coincidence is 0.0433, which indicates a key of around length 5. So we assume that the key is of length greater than 1, and apply the Kasiski method. Repetitions of length 2 are likely coincidental, so we look for repetitions of length 3 or more:

Letters	Start	End	Gap length	Gap length factors
OEQOOG	24	54	30	2, 3, 5
MOC	50	122	72	2, 2, 2, 3, 3

The longest repetition is six characters long; this is unlikely to be a coincidence. The gap between the repetitions is 30. The next longest repetition, "MOC," is three characters long and has a gap of 72. The greatest common divisor of 30 and 72 is 6. So let us try 6.

To verify that this is reasonable, we compute the index of coincidence for each alphabet. We first arrange the message into six rows, one for each alphabet:

```
A  I  K  H  O  I  A  T  T  O  B  G  E  E  E  R  N  E  O  S  A  I
D  U  K  K  E  F  U  A  W  E  M  G  K  W  D  W  S  U  F  W  J  U
Q  S  T  I  Q  B  M  A  M  Q  B  W  Q  V  L  K  V  T  M  T  M  I
Y  B  M  Z  O  A  F  C  O  O  F  P  H  E  A  X  P  Q  E  P  O  X
S  O  I  O  O  G  V  I  C  O  V  C  S  C  A  S  H  O  G  C  C
M  X  B  O  G  K  V  D  I  G  Z  I  N  N  V  V  C  I  J  H  H
```

We then compute the indices of coincidence for these alphabets:

Alphabet #1: IC = 0.0692   Alphabet #4: IC = 0.0562
Alphabet #2: IC = 0.0779   Alphabet #5: IC = 0.1238
Alphabet #3: IC = 0.0779   Alphabet #6: IC = 0.0429

All indices of coincidence indicate a single alphabet except for the indices of coincidence associated with alphabets #4 (period between 1 and 2) and #6 (period between 5 and 6). Given the statistical nature of the measure, we will assume that these are skewed by the distribution of characters and proceed on the assumption that there are 6 alphabets, and hence a key of length 6.

Counting characters in each column (alphabet) yields

Row	A	B	C	D	E	F	G	H	I	J	K	L	M	N	O	P	Q	R	S	T	U	V	W	X	Y	Z
#1	3	1	0	0	4	0	1	1	3	0	1	0	0	1	3	0	0	1	1	2	0	0	0	0	0	0
#2	1	0	0	2	2	2	1	0	0	1	3	0	1	0	0	0	0	1	0	4	0	4	0	0	0	0
#3	1	2	0	0	0	0	0	0	2	0	1	1	4	0	0	0	4	0	1	3	0	2	1	0	0	0
#4	2	1	1	0	2	2	0	1	0	0	0	0	1	0	4	3	1	0	0	0	0	0	0	2	1	1
#5	1	0	5	0	0	0	2	1	2	0	0	0	0	0	5	0	0	0	3	0	0	2	0	0	0	0
#6	0	1	1	1	0	0	2	2	3	1	1	0	1	2	1	0	0	0	0	0	0	3	0	1	0	1

An unshifted alphabet has the following characteristics ("L" meaning low frequency, "M" meaning moderate frequency, and "H" meaning high frequency):

H M M M H M M H H M M M M H H M L H H H M L L L L L

We now compare the frequency counts in the six alphabets above with the frequency count of the unshifted alphabet. The first alphabet matches the characteristics of the unshifted alphabet (note the values for "A," "E," and "I" in particular). Given the gap between "B" and "I," the third alphabet seems to be shifted with "I" mapping to "A." A similar gap occurs in the sixth alphabet between "O" and "V," suggesting that "V" maps to "A." Substituting into the ciphertext (lowercase letters are plaintext) produces

```
aDiYS riUkB OckKl MIghK aZOto EiOOl iFtAG paUeF
VatAs CIitW eOCno EiOOl bMtFV egGoP CneKi HSseW
nECse DdAAa rWcXS anSnP HheUl QOnoF eEGos WlPCm
aJeOC miUaX
```

In the last line, the group "aJe" suggests the word "are." Taking this as a hypothesis, the second alphabet maps "A" into "S." Substituting back produces

```
aliYS rickB Ocksl MIghs aZOto miOOl intAG paceF
Vatis CIite eOCno miOOl butFV egooP Cnesi HSsee
nECse ldAAa recXS ananP Hhecl QOnon eEGos elPCm
areOC micaX
```

The last block suggests "mical," because "al" is a common ending for adjectives. This means that the fourth alphabet maps "O" into "A," and the cipher becomes

```
alimS rickp Ocksl aIghs anOto micOl intoG pacet
Vatis qIite ecCno micOl buttV egood Cnesi vSsee
nsCse ldoAa reclS anand Hhecl eOnon esGos eldCm
arecC mical
```

In English, a "Q" is always followed by a "U," so the "I" in the second group of the second line must map to "U." The fifth alphabet maps "M" to "A." The cipher is solved:

```
alime rickp acksl aughs anato mical intos pacet
hatis quite econo mical butth egood onesi vesee
nsose ldoma recle anand thecl eanon essos eldom
areco mical
```

With proper spacing, capitalization, and punctuation, we have

> A limerick packs laughs anatomical
> Into space that is quite economical.
> But the good ones I've seen
> So seldom are clean,
> And the clean ones so seldom are comical.

The key is "ASIMOV."

The Vigenère cipher is easy to break by hand. However, the principles of attack hold for more complex ciphers that can be implemented only by computer. A good example is the encipherments that several older versions of WordPerfect used [171, 173]. These allowed a user to encipher a file with a password. Unfortunately, certain fields in the enciphered file contained information internal to WordPerfect, and these fields could be predicted. This allowed an attacker to derive the password used to encipher the file, and from that the plaintext file itself.

10.2.2.2   One-Time Pad

Repetitions provide a means for the cryptanalyst to attack the Vigenère cipher. The *one-time pad* is a variant of the Vigenère cipher with a key that is at least as long as the message and is chosen at random, so it does not repeat. Technically, it is a threshold scheme (see Section 16.3.2), and is provably impossible to break [240] (see also Section C.3.3, "Perfect Secrecy").

The weakness of the one-time pad is that the key must never be used more than once.

EXAMPLE: In 1943, the U.S. Army's Signal Intelligence Service began to examine messages sent from Soviet agents in the United States to Moscow. These messages were encoded using a complex cipher that was based on a one-time pad, which in this context was a set of pages of random number groups. This in theory made the messages unbreakable. But sometimes the manufacturers of these pads reused pages. Taking advantage of this duplication, cryptanalysts in the Signal Intelligence Service and, later, the U.S. National Security Agency, were able to decipher many of the messages sent between 1943 and 1980, providing insight into Soviet espionage of that time.

10.2.3   Data Encryption Standard

The Data Encryption Standard (DES) [2146] is one of the most important symmetric cryptosystems in the history of cryptography. It provided the impetus for many advances in the field and laid the theoretical and practical groundwork for many other ciphers. While analyzing it, researchers developed differential and linear cryptanalysis. Cryptographers developed other ciphers to avoid real, or perceived, weaknesses; cryptanalysts broke many of these ciphers and found weaknesses in others. Many of the features of the DES are used in other ciphers. Hence, even though it is used infrequently, it is well worth understanding.

In 1973, the U.S. National Bureau of Standards (NBS)[1] invited the submission of proposals for a cryptographic system, in an effort to develop a commercial standard that could also be used for unclassified government communications. The requirements included that the algorithm be made public, available to all to use freely, efficient, and economic to implement. They received no suitable proposals. In 1974, the NBS issued another invitation. At the time, IBM was developing a cryptosystem for use in the commercial world [1903]. IBM submitted this algorithm, LUCIFER [1791], to the NBS, which requested the U.S. National Security Agency's help in evaluating the algorithm. It modified the algorithm in several ways, published the modified algorithm, and held two workshops to evaluate the cryptosystem. The modified cryptosystem was adopted as a standard in 1976 [1684].

10.2.3.1   Structure

The DES is bit-oriented, unlike the other ciphers we have seen. It uses both transposition and substitution and for that reason is sometimes referred to as a *product cipher*. Its input, output, and key are each 64 bits long. The sets of 64 bits are referred to as *blocks*. Thus, M, K, and C are sets of all combinations of 64 bits, $\mathcal{E}$ the DES encryption algorithm, and $\mathcal{D}$ the DES decryption algorithm.

The cipher consists of 16 *rounds*, or iterations. Each round uses a separate key of 48 bits. These *round keys* are generated from the key block by dropping the parity bits (reducing the effective key size to 56 bits), permuting the bits, and extracting 48 bits. A different set of 48 bits is extracted for each of the 16 rounds. If the order in which the round keys is used is reversed, the input is deciphered.

The rounds are executed sequentially, the input of one round being the output of the previous round. The right half of the input, and the round key, are run through a function f that produces 32 bits of output; that output is then xor'ed into the left half, and the resulting left and right halves are swapped.

The function f provides the strength of the DES. The right half of the input (32 bits) is expanded to 48 bits, and this is xor'ed with the round key. The resulting 48 bits are split into eight sets of six bits each, and each set is put through a substitution table called the S-box. Each S-box produces four bits of output. They are catenated into a single 32-bit quantity, which is permuted. The resulting 32 bits constitute the output of the f function.

Section F.1 describes the algorithm in detail, and presents the tables involved.

---

[1]The name was later changed to the National Institute of Standards and Technology (NIST).

10.2.3.2   Analysis of the DES

When the DES was first announced, it was criticized as too weak. First, Diffie and Hellman [565] argued that a key length of 56 bits was simply too short, and they designed a machine that could break a DES-enciphered message in a matter of days. Although their machine was beyond the technology of the time, they estimated that it could soon be built for about \$20,000,000. Second, the reasons for many of the decisions in the design of the DES—most notably, those involving the S-boxes—were classified. Many speculated that the classification hid "trapdoors," or ways to invert the cipher without knowing the key.

Some properties of the DES were worrisome. First, it had 4 weak keys (keys that were their own inverses) and 12 semiweak keys (keys whose inverses were other keys). Second, let $\overline{k}$, $\overline{m}$, and $\overline{c}$ be the complement of the key k, the plaintext m, and the ciphertext c, respectively. Let $DES_k(m)$ be the encipherment of plaintext m under key k. Then the *complementation property* states that

$$DES_k(m) = c \Rightarrow DES_{\overline{k}}(\overline{m}) = \overline{c}$$

Third, some of the S-boxes exhibited irregular properties. The distribution of odd and even numbers was nonrandom, raising concerns that the DES did not randomize the input sufficiently. Several output bits of the fourth S-box seemed to depend on some of the output bits of the third S-box. This again suggested that there was a structure to the S-boxes, and because some of the design decisions underlying the S-boxes were unknown, the reasons for the structure were unknown. The structure made hardware implementation of the DES simpler [1904]. It distributed the dependence of each output bit on each input bit rapidly, so that after five rounds each output bit depended on every key and input bit [1327]. It could have been needed to prevent the cipher from being broken easily. It also could enable a trapdoor to allow the cipher to be broken easily. There was considerable speculation that the NSA had weakened the algorithm, although a congressional investigation did not reflect this [140].

In 1990, a breakthrough in cryptanalysis answered many of these questions. Biham and Shamir applied a technique called *differential cryptanalysis* to the DES [204, 206, 207]. This technique required them to generate 2^{47} pairs of chosen plaintext and ciphertext, considerably fewer than the trial-and-error approach others had used. During the development of this technique, they found several properties of the DES that appeared to answer some of the questions that had been raised.

First, for a known plaintext attack, the initial version of differential cryptanalysis requires 2^{56} plaintext and ciphertext pairs for a 15-round version of the DES. For the full 16 rounds, 2^{58} known plaintext and ciphertext pairs are needed, which is more than sufficient for a trial-and-error approach. (Matsui subsequently improved this using a variant attack called *linear cryptanalysis* [1261, 1262]; this attack requires 2^{43} known plaintext and ciphertext pairs on average.) Second, small changes in the S-boxes weakened the cipher, reducing the required number of chosen plaintext and ciphertext pairs. Third, making every bit of the round keys independent for an effective key length of $16 \times 48 = 768$ bits did not make the DES resistant to differential cryptanalysis, which suggests that the designers of the DES knew about differential analysis. Coppersmith later confirmed this [459].

10.2.3.3   DES and Modes

The DES is used in several modes [2147]. Using it directly is called *electronic codebook* (ECB) mode, and is very rare. Modes in which it can be used to generate a pseudo-one-time pad are *cipher feedback* (CFB) mode (see Section 12.2.1.2) and *output feedback* (OFB) mode (see Section 12.2.1.1). Its most common modes of use are *cipher block chaining* (CBC) mode (see Section 12.2.2), *encrypt-decrypt-encrypt* (EDE) mode, and *triple DES* mode (the EDE and triple DES modes are described in Section 12.2.2.1).

10.2.3.4   Retirement of the DES

In 1998, a design for a computer system and software that could break any DES-enciphered message in a few days was published [625]. This design complemented several challenges to break specific DES messages. Those challenges had been solved using computers distributed throughout the Internet. By 1999, it was clear that the DES no longer provided the same level of security as it had 10 years earlier, and the search was on for a new, stronger cipher to fill the needs that the DES no longer filled. In 2001, the Advanced Encryption Standard was announced (see Section 10.2.5), and in 2005, NIST officially withdrew the DES [138]. Triple DES mode remains the only approved implementation [127].

10.2.4   Other Modern Symmetric Ciphers

Several algorithms were proposed to overcome the weaknesses found in the DES. NewDES (which, despite its name, is not a variant of DES but a new algorithm) has a block size of 64 bits and a key length of 120 bits [1703]. However, it can be broken using an attack similar to differential cryptanalysis [1023]. FEAL has a block size of 64 bits and a key size of 64 bits [1364, 1735]. FEAL-4 (FEAL with 4 rounds) and FEAL-8 (FEAL with 8 rounds) fell to differential cryptanalysis with 20 [1404] and 10,000 [770] chosen plaintexts, respectively. Biham and Shamir broke FEAL-N, which uses N rounds, for $N < 32$ by differential cryptanalysis more quickly than by trial-and-error [206]. It was proposed that the key be lengthened to 128 bits, but the 128-bit key proved as easy to break as FEAL-N with the original 64-bit key. REDOC-II [485] has an 80-bit block and a 160-bit key. It has 10 rounds, and although a single round was successfully cryptanalyzed [205], the use of 10 rounds appears to withstand differential cryptanalysis.

LOKI89 [304], proposed as an alternative to the DES, was vulnerable to differential cryptanalysis [206]. Its successor, LOKI91 [302], uses a 64-bit key and a 64-bit block size. Linear cryptanalysis fails to break this cipher [1883].

LOKI97 [303] uses a 128-bit block size and a 256-bit key schedule, but is believed to be vulnerable to both linear and differential cryptanalysis [1075]. Khufu [1323] has a block size of 64 bits and a key size of 512 bits. When used with 24 or 32 rounds, it resists chosen plaintext attacks. Its S-boxes are computed from the keys. Khafre [1323], similar in design to Khufu, uses fixed S-boxes, but it has been broken [206].

IDEA is an 8-round cipher that uses 64-bit blocks and 128-bit keys [1124]. It uses three operations: exclusive or, addition modulo 2^{16}, and multiplication modulo $2^{16} + 1$. It appears to withstand known attacks [881, 1125] but variants with fewer than the full 8 rounds have been broken [203, 532]. It is used in commercial software—notably, in the electronic mail program PGP (and not the GNU software GPG) [1213]—but is patented and requires licensing for use in commercial software.

Schneier developed Blowfish [1683] as an alternative to the DES, unencumbered by patents. It appears to be secure against linear cryptanalysis [1418], but has been superseded by Twofish [1690, 1691], a finalist for the Advanced Encryption Standard (AES), the successor to the DES (see Section 10.2.5). Other ciphers that were finalists for the AES were Serpent [199], RC6 [1597], and MARS [328]. These were extensively analyzed as part of that competition [201, 365, 950, 1021, 1022, 1737].

10.2.5   Advanced Encryption Standard

In 1997, the U.S. National Institute of Standards and Technology (NIST) announced a competition to select the successor to the DES. Like the DES, the chosen algorithm had to be available for royalty-free use. Unlike the DES, it was to encipher 128 bit blocks and use keys of 128, 192, and 256 bits. Initially, 21 cryptosystems were submitted. The developers presented the cryptosysytems in two workshops, and then selected Twofish, Serpent, RC6, MARS, and Rijndael. After a third workshop, NIST announced that Rijndael was selected to be the Advanced Encryption Standard [2116].

10.2.5.1   Structure

Like the DES, the AES is a bit-oriented product cipher. Unlike the DES, the AES can use keys of 128, 192, or 256 bits and operates on 128 bits of input, producing 128 bits of output. The number of rounds in the AES depends upon the key length—10 rounds if the key is 128 bits, 12 rounds if the key is 192 bits, and 14 rounds if the key is 256 bits. Thus, $\mathcal{M}$ and $\mathcal{C}$ are sets of all combinations of 128 bits and $\mathcal{K}$ is the set of all combinations of 128, 192, or 256 bits, depending on the key length chosen. $\mathcal{E}$ is the AES encryption algorithm for the key length selected, and $\mathcal{D}$ the corresponding AES decryption algorithm.

The AES maintains a state array that initially consists of the input. Each round transforms the state array, and the contents of the array at the end of the last round is the output.

Associated with each round is a round key. If the AES is n rounds, there will be n round keys. The original key is divided into 4-byte words.[2] The *RotWord* transformation rotates the word by 1 byte; the *SubWord* transformation changes the bytes by applying an S-box. The result is xor'ed with a bit string, and then with the corresponding word of the previous round (or the initial key, if this is the first round key). Each round key consists of 4, 6, or or 8 words depending on the length of the original key.

To begin the encryption, the transformation *AddRoundKey* combines the supplied key with the state array. Next come a series of rounds, each of which (except the last) consists of four operations. First, the *SubBytes* transformation substitutes new values for each byte in the state array using an S-box. Then, the *ShiftRows* transformation cyclically shifts rows. The *MixColumns* transformation alters each column independently, and then the *AddRoundKey* transformation xors the state with the round key. The last round omits the *MixColumns* transformation. The contents of the resulting state array is the output.

Decryption is accomplished in a similar fashion. The round key schedule is reversed, and three of the four transformations are changed. In each round, the *InvShiftRows* transformation, which is the inverse of the *ShiftRows* transformation used in encryption, shifts the rows of the state array. The *InvSubBytes* transformation reverses the *SubBytes* transformation using an S-box that is the inverse of the one associated with *SubBytes*. Then the *AddRoundKey* transformation xors in the appropriate round key, and the *InvMixColumns* transformation, again the inverse of the *MixColumns* transformation, reverses the *MixColumns* transformation. The final round omits the *InvMixColumns* transformation.

An alternate expression of the decryption algorithm notes that *InvShiftRows* and *InvSubBytes* commute with respect to (functional) composition, and that *InvMixColumns* is linear with respect to the column input. Given these, the *Equivalent Inverse Cipher* algorithm exchanges the order of the *InvShiftRows* and *InvSubBytes* transformations, applies *InvMixColumns* to all round keys except the initial key and the final round key, and then exchanges the order of the *InvMixColumns* and *AddRoundKey* transformations. This provides a more efficient structure for decryption, paralleling the structure of encryption.

Section F.2 describes the algorithm in detail, including the tables and transformations involved.

10.2.5.2   Analysis of the AES

The designers constructed the AES to withstand the attacks to which the DES showed weakness [490]. As with the DES, the selection of the values in the S-box is critical. Unlike the DES, the developers described the design principles underlying the choice of S-box. The first is nonlinearity, so the output of the transformation is not a linear function of the input. The second is algebraic complexity, so the inverse of each byte is obtained, and this is remapped with an affine transformation. The result is that no input to the S-box is ever mapped either to itself or to its bitwise complement.

---

[2]A "byte" in this context is 8 bits, regardless of the underlying architecture.

The designers also took care that the AES transformation diffused the input bits rapidly. After 2 successive rounds, every bit in the state array depends on every bit in the state array from 2 rounds ago. As several attacks trace the dispersion of bits through 6 rounds, and then examine their propagation over 2 more rounds, providing a minimum of 10 rounds makes such attacks infeasible.

The generation of the round keys also hinders several known attacks. These attacks, in which the adversary either knows some key bits or can deduce relationships among the bits of different but similar keys, become more difficult as the length of the key increases. So, increasing the number of rounds with the key length adds complexity that hinders these attacks. In addition, the round key generation uses a different constant for each round, eliminating some symmetries, and also uses the S-box, so the round keys are nonlinear with respect to the original keys.

The AES has been studied for potential weaknesses, both during the competition and after. No weak or semiweak keys have been identified [2116]. Further, its design inhibits differential and linear cryptanalysis attacks [576], as well as many other attacks [200, 202, 1021, 1074, 1950]. Some of these attacks are effective against various forms of *reduced-round AES*, which are versions of the AES that use a smaller number of rounds. The effectiveness of these attacks is measured in the number of chosen (or known) plaintext/ciphertext pairs, the number of encryptions, and the memory used. For example, one recent chosen plaintext attack [596] can break 7-round AES-128, AES-192, and AES-256 with 2^{116} plaintexts, encryptions, and memory, 8-round AES-192 with 2^{113} plaintexts, 2^{129} memory, and 2^{172} encryptions, and 8-round AES-256 with 2^{113} plaintexts, 2^{129} memory, and 2^{196} encryptions. Other attacks require fewer chosen plaintexts but more encryptions. One attack on 7-round AES-192 requires about $2^{91.2}$ chosen plaintexts and $2^{139.2}$ encryptions, and on 8-round AES-256, $2^{89.1}$ chosen plaintexts and $2^{229.7}$ memory [1211]. Others target 9-round AES, breaking the 192-bit key version with 2^{67} chosen plaintexts and $2^{143.33}$ encryptions [803], and the 256-bit key version with 2^{59} chosen plaintexts and 2^{119} encrptions [1780]. Of course, the complexity of these attacks increases dramatically when applied to the full AES rather than a reduced-round variant. Certain unexpected algebraic structures within the AES have suggested other possible attacks, as has the possibility of combining different attacks, but the effectiveness of these ideas is still being evaluated [996].

10.2.5.3 AES Modes

The modes of operation described for the DES have been extended to include the AES, and a new *counter* mode (CTR) [603] has been added (see Section 12.2.1.1). The AES is not used in EDE or "Triple AES" mode, because the extended block size makes those modes unnecessary [323]. Numerous other modes have also been recommended.

The design of the AES, which uses basic operations such as xor and is oriented towards 8-bit bytes, allows high-performance implementations in both hardware and software on a wide variety of processors [624, 659, 738, 1474, 1815].

Indeed, some vendors have created special instructions to support AES encryption and decryption [832, 833, 1242].

Like the DES, the AES has spurred studies in cryptanalysis. One effect of these studies is a deeper understanding of how block ciphers work, how to cryptanalyze them, and how to design them to resist attacks. Other effects of these studies remain to be seen.

10.3   Public Key Cryptography

In 1976, Diffie and Hellman [564] proposed a new type of cryptography that distinguished between encipherment and decipherment keys. One of the keys would be publicly known; the other would be kept private by its owner. Symmetric cryptography requires the sender and recipient to share a common key. Public key cryptography does not. If the encipherment key is public, to send a secret message simply encipher the message with the recipient's public key. Then send it. The recipient can decipher it using his private key. Chapter 11, "Key Management," discusses how to make public keys available to others.

Interestingly, James Ellis, a cryptographer working for the British government's Communications-Electronics Security Group, developed the concept of public key cryptography (which he called "non-secret encryption") in a January 1970 report. Two of his colleagues found practical implementations. This work remained classified until 1997 [629].

Because one key is public, and its complementary key must remain secret, a public key cryptosystem must meet the following three conditions:

- It must be computationally easy to encipher or decipher a message given the appropriate key.
- It must be computationally infeasible to derive the private key from the public key.
- It must be computationally infeasible to determine the private key from a chosen plaintext attack.

The first system to meet these requirements generates a shared session key (see Section 11.2.3.1).

Public key systems are based on hard problems. The first type uses NP-complete problems that have special cases that are easy to solve. The system transforms that simpler problem into the more general problem. The information to do this is called "trapdoor information." If an adversary finds that information, the problem can be transformed back into the simpler one, and the adversary can break the system.

EXAMPLE: An early public key cipher was based on the knapsack problem. Given a set of numbers $A = \{a_1, \ldots, a_n\}$ and an integer C, find a subset of

A whose integers add exactly to *C*. This problem is NP-complete. However, if the a_i are chosen so that each $a_i > a_{i-1} + \cdots + a_1$, then the knapsack is called *superincreasing* and can easily be solved. Merkle and Hellman [1324] developed trapdoor information allowing them to construct a trapdoor knapsack from a superincreasing one.

In 1982, Shamir developed a polynomial-time method for determining trapdoor information [1723], thereby breaking the knapsack cipher. In 1984, Brickell extended this by showing how to break a cipher consisting of iterated knapsacks [293].

A second type is based on hard mathematical problems such as finding the factors of a very large number. The RSA cryptosystem (see Section 10.3.2) provides confidentiality, authentication, and integrity using a problem related to factoring.

An important comment about the examples in this section is necessary.

In the examples that follow, we will use small numbers for pedagogical purposes. In practice, the numbers would be much larger, and often the encipherment schemes will use additional techniques to prevent the success of attacks such as precomputation (see Section 12.1.1) and changing the order of the ciphertext blocks (see Section 12.1.2).

10.3.1 El Gamal

The El Gamal cryptosystem [627] provides message secrecy. It is based on the discrete logarithm problem.

> **Definition 10–2.** Let *n*, *g*, and *b* be integers with $0 \leq a < n$ and $0 \leq b < n$. The *discrete logarithm problem* is to find an integer *k* such that $0 \leq k < n$ and $a = g^k \bmod n$.

Choose a prime number *p* with $p - 1$ having at least one large factor. Choose some *g* such that $1 < g < p$; *g* is called a *generator*, because repeatedly adding *g* to itself, and reducing mod *p*, will generate all integers between 0 and $p - 1$ inclusive. Next, select an integer k_{priv} such that $1 < k_{priv} < p - 1$, and take $y = g^{k_{priv}} \bmod p$. Then k_{priv} will be the private key and the triplet $K_{pub} = (p, g, y)$ will be the public key.

EXAMPLE: Alice chooses $p = 262643$, a prime number; $p - 1 = 262642 = 2 \times 131321$ has at least one large factor, so her choice is suitable. She chooses $g = 9563$ and the public key $k_{priv} = 3632$. Then

$$y = g^{k_{priv}} \bmod p = 9563^{3632} \bmod 262643 = 27459$$

so the public key is $K_{pub} = (p, g, y) = (262643, 9563, 27459)$.

To encipher a message m, choose a random integer k that is relatively prime to $p - 1$. Compute the following:

$$c_1 = g^k \bmod p$$
$$c_2 = my^k \bmod p$$

The ciphertext is then $c = (c_1, c_2)$.

EXAMPLE: Represent each plaintext character by a number between 00 (A) and 25 (Z); 26 represents a blank. Bob wants to send Alice the message "PUPPIESARESMALL." Using the representation above, with three characters per block, the plaintext is 152015 150804 180017 041812 001111. He uses Alice's public key (above) to encipher the message character by character, choosing a different random integer k for each block:

$$k = 5 \Rightarrow c_{1,1} = 9563^5 \bmod 262643 = 15653$$
$$c_{1,2} = (152015)27459^5 \bmod 262643 = 923$$
$$k = 3230 \Rightarrow c_{2,1} = 9563^{3230} \bmod 262643 = 46495$$
$$c_{2,2} = (150804)27459^{3230} \bmod 262643 = 109351$$
$$k = 9921 \Rightarrow c_{3,1} = 9563^{9921} \bmod 262643 = 176489$$
$$c_{3,2} = (180017)27459^{9921} \bmod 262643 = 208811$$
$$k = 176 \Rightarrow c_{4,1} = 9563^{88247} \bmod 262643 = 88247$$
$$c_{4,2} = (041812)27459^{176} \bmod 262643 = 144749$$
$$k = 28119 \Rightarrow c_{5,1} = 9563^{28119} \bmod 262643 = 152432$$
$$c_{5,2} = (001111)27459^{28119} \bmod 262643 = 5198$$

or (15653, 923), (46495, 109351), (176489, 208811), (88247, 144749), (152432, 5198).

Decipherment is straightforward. Simply compute

$$m = c_2 c_1^{-k_{priv}} \bmod p$$

EXAMPLE: Alice receives Bob's ciphertext, and proceeds to decipher it:

$$(923)15653^{-3632} \bmod 262643 = 152015$$
$$(109351)46495^{-3632} \bmod 262643 = 150804$$
$$(208811)176489^{-3632} \bmod 262643 = 180017$$

$$(144749)88247^{-3632} \bmod 262643 = 41812$$
$$(5198)152432^{-3632} \bmod 262643 = 1111$$

Translating this into characters, this is PUP PIE SAR ESM ALL, or PUPPIESARESMALL, which was indeed what Bob sent.

The El Gamal cryptosystem provides strength comparable to other cryptosystems but uses a shorter key. It also introduces randomness into the cipher, so the same letter enciphered twice produces two different ciphertexts. This prevents attacks that depend upon repetition. However, care must be taken; if a random integer k is used twice, an attacker who obtains the plaintext for one message can easily decipher the other (see Exercise 10). Also, notice that c_2 is a linear function of m, so an attacker can forge messages that are multiples of previously enciphered messages. As an example, if (c_1, c_2) is the ciphertext of message m, (c_1, nc_2) is the ciphertext corresponding to nm. Protocols using El Gamal must prevent an attacker from being able to forge this type of message.

Network security protocols often use El Gamal due to its shorter key length. See Section 12.5.3 for an example. It can also be used for authentication (see Section 10.5.2.2).

10.3.2   RSA

The RSA cryptosystem was first described publicly in 1978 [1598]. Unknown at the time was the work of Clifford Cocks in 1973, where he developed a similar cryptosystem. This work was classified, and only became public in the late 1990s [629].

RSA is an exponentiation cipher. Choose two large prime numbers p and q, and let $n = pq$. The totient $\phi(n)$ of n is the number of numbers less than n with no factors in common with n. It can be shown that $\phi(n) = (p - 1)(q - 1)$ (see Exercise 12).

EXAMPLE: Let $n = 10$. The numbers that are less than 10 and are relatively prime to (have no factors in common with) n are 1, 3, 7, and 9. Hence, $\phi(10) = 4$. Similarly, if $n = 21$, the numbers that are relatively prime to n are 1, 2, 4, 5, 8, 10, 11, 13, 16, 17, 19, and 20. So $\phi(21) = 12$.

Choose an integer $e < n$ that is relatively prime to $\phi(n)$. Find a second integer d such that $ed \bmod \phi(n) = 1$. The public key is (e, n), and the private key is d.

Let m be a message. Then

$$c = m^e \bmod n$$

and

$$m = c^d \bmod n$$

Exercise 13 shows why this works.

When implementing this cipher, two issues are the computation of the modular exponentiation and finding two large primes. Exercise 19 shows how to compute the modular exponentiation quickly. Large prime numbers are found by generating large random numbers and then testing them for primality [291, 1607, 1826, 1955].

EXAMPLE: Let $p = 181$ and $q = 1451$. Then $n = 262631$ and $\phi(n) = 261000$. Alice chooses $e = 154993$, so her private key is $d = 95857$. As in the El Gamal example, Bob wants to send Alice the message "PUPPIESARESMALL," so he encodes it the same way, giving the plaintext 152015 150804 180017 041812 001111. Using Alice's public key, the ciphertext is

$$152015^{154993} \bmod 262631 = 220160$$
$$150804^{154993} \bmod 262631 = 135824$$
$$180017^{154993} \bmod 262631 = 252355$$
$$041812^{154993} \bmod 262631 = 245799$$
$$001111^{154993} \bmod 262631 = 070707$$

or 220160 135824 252355 245799 070707.

In addition to confidentiality, RSA can provide data and origin authentication; this is used in digital signatures (see Section 10.5.2.1). If Alice enciphers her message using her private key, anyone can read it, but if anyone alters it, the (altered) ciphertext cannot be deciphered correctly.

EXAMPLE: Suppose Alice wishes to send Bob the same message in such a way that Bob will be sure that Alice sent it. She enciphers the message with her private key and sends it to Bob. As indicated above, the plaintext is represented as 152015 150804 180017 041812 001111. Using Alice's private key, the ciphertext is

$$152015^{95857} \bmod 262631 = 072798$$
$$150804^{95857} \bmod 262631 = 259757$$
$$180017^{95857} \bmod 262631 = 256449$$
$$041812^{95857} \bmod 262631 = 089234$$
$$001111^{95857} \bmod 262631 = 037974$$

or 072798 259757 256449 089234 037974. In addition to origin authenticity, Bob can be sure that no letters were altered.

Providing both confidentiality and authentication requires enciphering with the sender's private key and the recipient's public key.

EXAMPLE: Suppose Alice wishes to send Bob the message "PUPPIESARE-SMALL" in confidence and authenticated. Again, assume that Alice's private key is 95857. Take Bob's public key to be 45593 (making his private key 235457). The plaintext is represented as 152015 150804 180017 041812 001111. The encipherment is

$$(152015^{95857} \bmod 262631)^{45593} \bmod 262631 = 249123$$
$$(150804^{95857} \bmod 262631)^{45593} \bmod 262631 = 166008$$
$$(180017^{95857} \bmod 262631)^{45593} \bmod 262631 = 146608$$
$$(041812^{95857} \bmod 262631)^{45593} \bmod 262631 = 092311$$
$$(001111^{95857} \bmod 262631)^{45593} \bmod 262631 = 096768$$

or 249123 166008 146608 092311 096768.

The recipient uses the recipient's private key to decipher the message and the sender's public key to authenticate it. Bob receives the ciphertext above, 249123 166008 146608 092311 096768. The decipherment is

$$(249123^{235457} \bmod 262631)^{154993} \bmod 262631 = 152012$$
$$(166008^{235457} \bmod 262631)^{154993} \bmod 262631 = 150804$$
$$(146608^{235457} \bmod 262631)^{154993} \bmod 262631 = 180017$$
$$(092311^{235457} \bmod 262631)^{154993} \bmod 262631 = 041812$$
$$(096768^{235457} \bmod 262631)^{154993} \bmod 262631 = 001111$$

or 152015 150804 180017 041812 001111. This corresponds to the message Alice sent.

The use of a public key system provides a technical type of nonrepudiation of origin. The message is deciphered using Alice's public key. Because the public key is the inverse of the private key, only the private key could have enciphered the message. Because Alice is the only one who knows this private key, only she could have enciphered the message. The underlying assumption is that Alice's private key has not been compromised, and that the public key bearing her name really does belong to her.

In practice, no one would use blocks of the size presented here. The issue is that, even if n is very large, if one character per block is enciphered, RSA can be broken using the techniques used to break symmetric substitution ciphers (see Sections 10.2.2 and 12.1.3). Furthermore, although no individual block can be altered without detection (because the attacker presumably does not have access to the private key), an attacker can rearrange blocks and change the meaning of the message.

EXAMPLE: A general sends a message to headquarters asking if the attack is on. Headquarters replies with the message "ON" enciphered using an RSA cipher with a 2,048-bit modulus, but each letter is enciphered separately. An attacker intercepts the message and swaps the order of the blocks. When the general deciphers the message, it will read "NO," the opposite of the original plaintext.

Moreover, if the attacker knows that headquarters will send one of two messages (here, "NO" or "ON"), the attacker can use a technique called "forward search" or "precomputation" to break the cipher (see Section 12.1.1). For this reason, plaintext is usually padded with random data to make up a block. This can eliminate the problem of forward searching, because the set of possible plaintexts becomes too large to precompute feasibly.

A different general sends the same request as in the example above. Again, headquarters replies with the message "ON" enciphered using an RSA cipher with a 2,048-bit modulus. Each letter is enciphered separately, but the first 10 bits of each block contain the number of the block, the next 8 bits contain the character, and the remaining 2,030 bits contain random data. If the attacker rearranges the blocks, the general will detect that block 2 arrived before block 1 (as a result of the number in the first 10 bits) and rearrange them. The attacker also cannot precompute the blocks to determine which contains "O," because she would have to compute 2^{2030} blocks, which is computationally infeasible.

10.3.3   Elliptic Curve Ciphers

Miller [1351] and Koblitz [1082] proposed a public key scheme based on *elliptic curves*. This scheme can be applied to any scheme that depends on the discrete logarithm problem. Here, we show a version of El Gamal using elliptic cryptography.

> **Definition 10–3.** An *elliptic curve* is an equation of the form $y^2 = x^3 + ax + b$.

Figure 10–5 shows the plot of the curve $y^2 = x^3 + 4x + 10$. Consider two points on the curve, P_1 and P_2. If $P_1 \neq P_2$, draw a line through them. If $P_1 = P_2$, then draw a tangent to the curve at P_1. Suppose that line intersects the curve at a third point, $P_3 = (x_3, y_3)$. Take $P_4 = (x_3, -y_3)$. We define P_4 to be the sum of P_1 and P_2. Otherwise, the line is vertical, so take $P_1 = (x, y)$ and treat ∞ as another point of intersection with the curve. The third point of intersection is $P_2 = (x, -y)$, so given the above definition of addition, we have $P_1 + \infty = (x, y) = P_1$. Hence the point at ∞ is the identity in addition. It is also its own inverse.

More precisely, let $P_1 = (x_1, y_1)$ and $P_2 = (x_2, y_2)$. Define

$$m = \begin{cases} \dfrac{y_2 - y_1}{x_2 - x_1} & \text{when } P_1 \neq P_2 \\[2ex] \dfrac{3x_1^2 + a}{2y_1} & \text{otherwise} \end{cases}$$

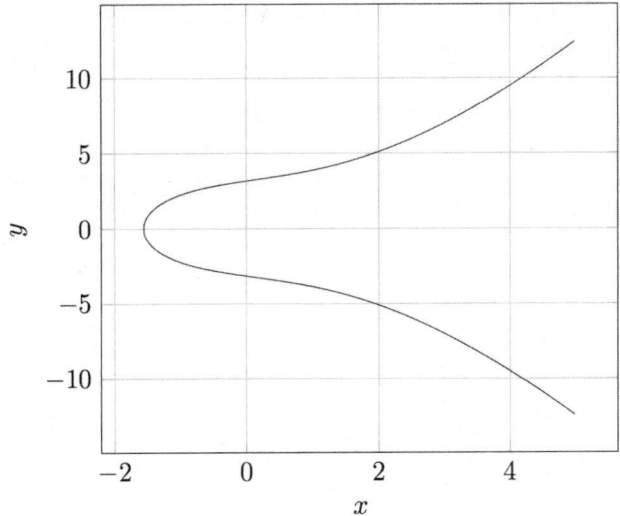

Figure 10–5 Plot of the elliptic curve $y^2 = x^3 + 4x + 10$.

Then $P_3 = P_1 + P_2$, where

$$x_3 = m^2 - x_1 - x_2$$
$$y_3 = m(x_1 - x_3) - y_1$$

Also, if $P_4 = -P_3$, then $x_4 = x_3$ and $y_4 = -y_3$.

This can be turned into a cryptosystem using modular arithmetic, where the modulus used is a prime number p. Thus, the curve of interest is of the form

$$y^2 = x^3 + ax + b \bmod p$$

with p a prime number and $4a^3 + 27b^2 \neq 0$.[3] Suppose we add a point P to itself n times. Call the result Q, so $Q = nP$. If n is large, it is generally very hard to compute from Q and P. This is the basis for the security of the cryptosystem.

Thus, an elliptic curve cryptosystem has four parameters: (a, b, p, P). The private key is a randomly chosen integer $k<p$; in practice, one chooses this number to be less than the number of (integer) points on the curve. The corresponding

---

[3] More generally, elliptic curves can be over any finite field. When the size of the finite field is a power of 2, the equation has the form $y^2 + xy = x^3 + ax^2 + b$; the rules for addition are also slightly different.

public key is $K = kP$. In the following examples, we shall use the shorthand $(x, y) \bmod p$ to mean $(x \bmod p, y \bmod p)$. Also, $a^{-1} \bmod p$ is the value x that satisfies the equation $ax \bmod p = 1$ (see Section B.3).

To use the elliptic curve version of El Gamal, choose a point P on the curve, and a private key k_{priv}. Then compute $Q = k_{priv}P$. Using the elliptic curve above, this means that the public key is (P, Q, a, p). To encipher a message m, it is first expressed as a point on the elliptic curve. The sender then selects a random number k and computes

$$c_1 = kP$$

$$c_2 = m + kQ$$

and sends those to the recipient. To decipher the message, the recipient computes

$$m = c_2 - k_{priv}c_1$$

EXAMPLE: Alice and Bob now decide to use the elliptic curve version of El Gamal to encipher their messages. They use the same elliptic curve and point as in the previous example. Bob chooses a random number $k_{Bob} = 1847$ as his private key. He then computes his public key $K_{Bob} = k_{Bob}P = 1847(1002, 493) \bmod 2503 = (460, 2083)$.

Alice wants to send Bob the message $m = (18, 1394)$. To encipher it, she chooses a random number $k = 717$, computes

$$c_1 = kP = 717(1002, 493) \bmod 2503 = (2134, 419)$$

$$c_2 = m + kK_{Bob} = (18, 1394) + 717(460, 2083) \bmod 2503 = (221, 1253)$$

and sends c_1 and c_2 to Bob.

To decipher the message, Bob computes

$$k_{Bob}c_1 = 1847(2134, 419) \bmod 2503 = (652, 1943)$$

and uses this to compute

$$m = c_2 - c_1 = (221, 1253) - (652, 1943) \bmod 2503 = (18, 1394)$$

thereby recovering the plaintext message.

The generation of elliptic curves suitable for cryptography is a complex question. In particular, it requires a careful selection of parameters. For example, when $b = 0$ and $p \bmod 4 = 3$, or when $a = 0$ and $p \bmod 3 = 2$, the discrete log problem underlying elliptic curve cryptography becomes significantly easier to solve. Thus, choosing these parameters weakens the cryptosystem. Ways to generate elliptic curves are being studied [440]. Several parameter sets have been recommended for use. The U.S. NIST recommends curves P-192, P-224, P-256, P-384, or P-521 for elliptic curves using a prime modulus, and degree 163, 233, 283, 409, or 571 binary fields [2148]. Certicom recommends these as well, except that the degree 233 binary field is replaced by a degree 239 binary field [2231]. These curves are widely used. Some questions have been raised about the strength of these curves [181]. Other proposed curves include those of the Brainpool standard [1203], Curve1174 [182], Curve25519 [180], and several others [271].

The advantage to using elliptic curves over other forms of public key cryptography is that the keys can be shorter, and hence the computation time is shorter. As an example, elliptic curve cryptography with a key length of 256 to 383 bits provides a level of security comparable to RSA with a modulus of 3,072 bits [126]. Koblitz, Koblitz, and Menezes [1081] review how elliptic curve cryptography became widely accepted, with a discussion of it and RSA.

10.4   Cryptographic Checksums

Suppose Alice wants to send Bob a message of n bits. She wants Bob to be able to verify that the message he receives is the same one that was sent. So she applies a mathematical function, called a *checksum function*, to generate a smaller set of k bits from the original n bits. This smaller set is called the *checksum* or *message digest*. Alice then sends Bob both the message and the associated checksum. When Bob gets the message, he recomputes the checksum and compares it with the one Alice sent. If they match, he assumes that the message has not been changed; if they do not match, then either the message or the checksum has changed, and so they cannot be trusted to be what Alice sent him.

Of course, an adversary can change the message and alter the checksum to correspond to the message. For the moment, assume this will not happen; we will relax this assumption in Section 10.5.

EXAMPLE: The parity bit in the ASCII representation is often used as a single-bit checksum. If *odd parity* is used, the sum of the 1 bits in the ASCII representation of the character, and the parity bit, is odd. Assume that Alice sends Bob the letter "A." In ASCII, the representation of "A" using odd parity is $p1000001$ in binary, where p represents the parity bit. Because two bits are set, the parity bit is 1 for odd parity.

When Bob gets the message 11000001, he counts the 1 bits in the message. Because this number is odd, Bob believes that the message has arrived unchanged.

To minimize the probability that a change to either the message or the checksum will be detected, the checksum function must satisfy specific properties.

> **Definition 10–4.** A *cryptographic checksum function* (also called a *strong hash function* or a *strong one-way function*) $h : A \to B$ is a function that has the following properties:
>
> 1. For any $x \in A$, $h(x)$ is easy to compute.
> 2. For any $y \in B$, it is computationally infeasible to find $x \in A$ such that $h(x) = y$.
> 3. It is computationally infeasible to find $x, x' \in A$ such that $x \neq x'$ and $h(x) = h(x')$. (Such a pair is called a *collision*.)

The third requirement is often stated as:

> $3'$. Given any $x \in A$, it is computationally infeasible to find another $x' \in A$ such that $x \neq x'$ and $h(x) = h(x')$.

However, properties 3 and $3'$ are subtly different. It is considerably harder to find an x' meeting the conditions in property $3'$ than it is to find a pair x and x' meeting the conditions in property 3. To explain why, we need to examine some basics of cryptographic checksum functions.

Given that the checksum contains fewer bits than the message, several messages must produce the same checksum. Ideally, the hashes of all possible messages will be evenly distributed over the set of possible checksums. Furthermore, the checksum that any given message produces can be determined only by computing the checksum. Such a checksum function acts as a random function.

The size of the output of the cryptographic checksum is an important consideration owing to a mathematical principle called the *pigeonhole principle*.

> **Definition 10–5.** The *pigeonhole principle* states that if there are n containers for $n + 1$ objects, at least one container will hold two objects.

To understand its application here, consider a cryptographic checksum function that computes hashes of three bits and a set of files each of which contains five bits. This yields $2^3 = 8$ possible hashes for $2^5 = 32$ files. Hence, at least four different files correspond to the same hash.

Now assume that a cryptographic checksum function computes hashes of 128 bits. The probability of finding a message corresponding to a given hash is 2^{-128}, but the probability of finding two messages with the same hash (that is, with the value of neither message being constrained) is 2^{-64} (see Exercise 24).

Definition 10–6. A *keyed* cryptographic checksum function requires a cryptographic key as part of the computation. A *keyless* cryptographic checksum does not.

Many keyless hash functions have been developed. The best known are MD4 [1593] and MD5 [1594] (128-bit checksums), RIPEMD-160 [575] (160-bit checksum), HAVAL [2096] (128-, 160-, 192-, 224-, and 256-bit checksums), and the Secure Hash Algorithm family of hash functions [2214] (SHA-1, SHA-224, SHA-256, SHA-384, SHA-512). Dobbertin devised a method for generating collisions in MD4 [574] and MD5 [573]. Wang and Yu used a differential attack to find collisions in MD4 and MD5 very quickly [1972]; their attack also works on HAVAL-128, RIPEMD, and the original version of SHA (now called SHA-0) [2213]. Various techniques for finding collisions have found collisions in several SHA hash functions, all on versions with a reduced number of steps (such as 58-step SHA-1 [1971], 70-step SHA-1 [516], 24-step SHA-2, SHA-256, and SHA-512 [1649], and 38-step SHA-256 [1317]).

In 2012, the U.S. NIST selected the Keccak hash function as SHA-3 [2229]. The design of Keccak prevents many of the collision-finding attacks that succeeded in previous hash functions [491]. In 2013, however, a different kind of attack succeeded with 3-round Keccak-384 and Keccak-512, and 5-round Keccak-256 [571]. Only the future will tell whether SHA-3 continues to be as robust as is believed.

10.4.1 HMAC

HMAC is a generic term for an algorithm that uses a keyless hash function and a cryptographic key to produce a keyed hash function [1102]. This mechanism enables Alice to validate that data Bob sent to her is unchanged in transit. Without the key, anyone could change the data and recompute the message authentication code, and Alice would be none the wiser.

The need for HMAC arose because keyed hash functions are derived from cryptographic algorithms. Many countries restrict the import and export of software that implements such algorithms. They do not restrict software implementing keyless hash functions, because such functions cannot be used to conceal information. Hence, HMAC builds on a keyless hash function using a cryptographic key to create a keyed hash function.

Let h be a keyless hash function that hashes data in blocks of b bytes to produce a hash l bytes long. Let k be a cryptographic key. We assume that the length of k is no greater than b; if it is, use h to hash it to produce a new key of length b. Let k' be the key k padded with bytes containing 0 to make b bytes. Let *ipad* be a sequence of bytes containing the bits 00110110 and repeated b times; let *opad* be a similar sequence with the bits 01011100. The HMAC-*h* function with key *k* for message *m* is

$$\text{HMAC-}h(k, m) = h(k' \oplus opad \,||\, h(k' \oplus ipad||m))$$

where $\oplus$ is exclusive or and $||$ is concatenation.

Bellare, Canetti, and Krawczyk [155] analyze the security of HMAC and conclude that the strength of HMAC depends on the strength of the hash function *h*. Emphasizing this, attacks on HMAC-MD4, HMAC-MD5, HMAC-SHA-0, and HMAC-SHA-1 have been developed, some of which recover partial [451, 1054] or full keys [710, 1965]. Bellare [154] extends the analysis by explaining under what conditions HMAC is secure.

Various HMAC functions are used in Internet security protocols (see Chapter 12).

10.5   Digital Signatures

As electronic commerce grows, so does the need for a provably high degree of authentication and integrity. Think of Alice's signature on a contract with Bob. Bob not only has to know that Alice is the other signer and is signing it; he also must be able to prove to a disinterested third party (called a *judge*) that Alice signed it and that the contract he presents has not been altered since Alice signed it. Such a construct plays a large role in managing cryptographic keys as well. This construct is called a *digital signature*.

> **Definition 10–7.** A *digital signature* is a construct that authenticates both the origin and contents of a message in a manner that is provable to a disinterested third party.

The "proof" requirement introduces a subtlety. Let *m* be a message. Suppose Alice and Bob share a secret key *k*. Alice sends Bob the message and its encipherment using *k*. Is this a digital signature?

First, Alice has authenticated the contents of the message, because Bob deciphers the enciphered message and can check that the message matches the deciphered one. Because only Bob and Alice know *k*, and Bob knows that he did not send the message, he concludes that it has come from Alice. He has authenticated the message origin and integrity. However, based on the mathematics alone, Bob cannot prove that he did not create the message, because he knows the key used to create it. Hence, this is not a digital signature.

Public key cryptography solves this problem. Let d_{Alice} and e_{Alice} be Alice's private and public keys, respectively. Alice sends Bob the message and its encipherment using d_{Alice}. As before, Bob can authenticate the origin and contents of the message, but in this situation a judge can determine that Alice signed the message, because only Alice knows the private key with which the message was signed. The judge merely obtains Alice's public key e_{Alice} and uses that to decipher the enciphered message. If the result is the original message, Alice signed it. This is in fact a digital signature.

A digital signature provides the service of nonrepudiation. If Alice claims she never sent the message, the judge points out that the originator signed the message with her private key, which only she knew. Alice at that point may claim that her private key was stolen, or that her identity was incorrectly bound in the certificate (see Chapter 15, "Representing Identity"). The notion of "nonrepudiation" provided here is strictly technical. In fact, Alice's key might have been stolen, and she might not have realized this before seeing the digital signature. Such a claim would require ancillary evidence, and a court or other legal agency would need to handle it. For the purposes of this section, we consider the service of nonrepudiation to be the inability to deny that one's cryptographic key was used to produce the digital signature.

10.5.1 Symmetric Key Signatures

All secret key digital signature schemes rely on a trusted third party. The judge must trust the third party. Merkle's scheme is typical [1322].

Let Cathy be the trusted third party. Alice shares a cryptographic key k_{Alice} with Cathy. Likewise, Bob shares k_{Bob} with Cathy. When Alice wants to send Bob a contract m, she enciphers the message using k_{Alice} and sends it to Bob. Bob sends it to Cathy, who deciphers the message using k_{Alice}, enciphers it with k_{Bob}, and returns this to Bob. He can now decipher it. To verify that Alice sent the message, the judge has Cathy decipher the enciphered message Alice sent and the enciphered message Bob received from Cathy using Alice's and Bob's keys. If they match, the sending is verified; if not, one of them is a forgery.

10.5.2 Public Key Signatures

In our earlier example, we had Alice encipher the message with her private key to produce a digital signature. We now examine two specific systems.

10.5.2.1 RSA Digital Signatures

Section 10.3.2 discussed the RSA system. We observe that using it to authenticate a message produces a digital signature. However, we also observe that the strength of the system relies on the protocol describing how RSA is used as well as on the RSA cryptosystem itself.

First, suppose that Alice wants to trick Bob into signing a message m. She computes two other messages m_1 and m_2 such that $m_1 m_2 \bmod n_{Bob} = m$. She has Bob sign m_1 and m_2. Alice then multiplies the two signatures together mod n_{Bob}, giving Bob's signature on m (see Exercise 13). The defense is to not sign random documents and, when signing, never sign the document itself; sign a cryptographic hash of the document [1684].

EXAMPLE: Let $n_{Alice} = 262631$, $e_{Alice} = 154993$, $d_{Alice} = 95857$, $n_{Bob} = 288329$, $e_{Bob} = 22579$, and $d_{Bob} = 138091$. Alice and Bob have many possible contracts, each represented by three letters, from which they are to select and sign one.

Alice first asks Bob to sign the sequence 225536, so she can validate his signature. Bob computes

$$225536^{138091} \bmod 288329 = 271316$$

Alice then asks Bob to sign contract "AYE" (002404):

$$002404^{138091} \bmod 288329 = 182665$$

Alice now computes

$$(002404)(225536) \bmod 288329 = 130024$$

She then claims that Bob agreed to contract "NAY" (130024). She presents the signature

$$(271316)(182665) \bmod 288329 = 218646$$

Judge Janice is called, and she computes

$$218646^{22579} \bmod 288329 = 130024$$

Naturally, Janice concludes that Bob is lying, because his public key deciphers the signature. So Alice has successfully tricked Bob.

Enciphering a message and then signing it creates a second problem [60]. Suppose Alice is sending Bob her signature on a confidential contract m. She enciphers it first, then signs it:

$$c = \left(m^{e_{Bob}} \bmod n_{Bob} \right)^{d_{Alice}} \bmod n_{Alice}$$

She then sends the result to Bob. However, Bob wants to claim that Alice sent him the contract M. Bob computes a number r such that $M^r \bmod n_{Bob} = m$. He then republishes his public key as (re_{Bob}, n_{Bob}). Note that the modulus does not change. Now, he claims that Alice sent him M. The judge verifies this using his current public key. The simplest way to fix this is to require all users to use the same exponent but vary the moduli.

EXAMPLE: Smarting from Alice's trick, Bob seeks revenge. He and Alice agree to sign the contract "LUR" (112017). Alice first enciphers it, then signs it:

$$(112017^{22579} \bmod 288329)^{95857} \bmod 262631 = 42390$$

She sends it to Bob. Bob, however, wants the contract to be "EWM" (042212). He computes an r such that $042212^r \bmod 288329 = 112017$; one such r is $r = 9175$. He then computes a new public key $re_{Bob} \bmod \phi(n_{Bob}) = (9175)(22579) \bmod 287184 = 102661$. He replaces his current public key with (102661, 288329), and resets his private key to 161245. He now claims that Alice sent him contract "EWM," signed by her.

Judge Janice is called. She takes the message 42390 and deciphers it:

$$(42390^{154993} \bmod 262631)^{161245} \bmod 288329 = 042212$$

She concludes that Bob is correct.

This attack will not work if one signs first and then enciphers. The reason is that Bob cannot access the information needed to construct a new public key, because he would need to alter Alice's public key (see Exercise 27).

However, signing first and then enciphering enables the recipient to decipher the signed message, re-encrypt it using a third party's public key, and then forward it to the third party. The third party then cannot tell if the original sender sent it directly to him. This is the *surreptitious forwarding attack*. Several solutions to providing enciphered, authenticated messages have been proposed [510, 1101]. One simple solution is to embed the signer's and recipient's names in the signed message. Another is to sign the message, encrypt it, and sign the result; a variant is to encrypt the message, then sign that, and then encrypt the result.

10.5.2.2 El Gamal Digital Signature

This scheme is based on the El Gamal cryptosystem presented in Section 10.3.1. Recall that the generator g is chosen so that $1 < g < p$, where p is a prime number with $p - 1$ having a large factor; the private key d is chosen so that $1 < d < p - 1$; and the public key is (p, g, y), where $y = g^d \bmod p$.

Suppose Alice wants to send Bob a signed contract m. She chooses a number k that is less than, and relatively prime to, $p - 1$ and has not been used before. She computes $a = g^k \bmod p$ and then uses the Extended Euclidean Algorithm (see Appendix B) to find b such that

$$m = (da + kb) \bmod p - 1$$

The pair (a, b) is the signature.

To verify the signature, check that

$$y^a a^b \bmod p = g^m \bmod p$$

EXAMPLE: Alice and Bob decide to use the El Gamal digital signature scheme. As before, Alice chooses $p = 262643$, $g = 9563$, and $d_{Alice} = 3632$, yielding $y = 27459$. She wants to send Bob the signed contract "PUP" (152015). She chooses $k = 601$, which is relatively prime to $p - 1 = 262643$. She computes

$$a = 9563^{601} \bmod 262643 = 202897$$

and then uses the Extended Euclidean Algorithm to solve for b:

$$152015 = (3632 \times 202897 + 601 \times b) \bmod 262642$$

This yields $b = 225835$. She sends Bob the message $m = 152015$ and the signature (202897, 225835).

Bob obtains the message and wants to verify the signature. He computes

$$y^a a^b \bmod p = 27459^{202897} 202897^{225835} \bmod 262643 = 157499$$

and

$$g^m \bmod p = 9563^{152015} \bmod 262643 = 157499$$

Because the two match, Alice signed the message.

If someone learns k, the corresponding message m, and the signature (a, b), then she can use the Extended Euclidean Algorithm to recover d, Alice's private key.

EXAMPLE: Bob happens to learn that Alice signed the last message using $k = 601$. He immediately solves the following equation for d:

$$m = (da + kb) \bmod p - 1 \Rightarrow 152015 = (202897 \times d + 601 \times 225835) \bmod 262642$$

which yields $d = 3632$. This is Alice's private key.

10.5.2.3   El Gamal Digital Signature Using Elliptic Curve Cryptography

An elliptic curve version of the El Gamal digital signature is also used. Represent the message by an integer m. Choose a point P on the elliptic curve $y^2 = x^3 + ax + b \bmod p$, where p is a large prime. Let n be the number of integer points on the curve. Choose a private key k_{priv} and compute $Q = k_{priv}P$; the corresponding public key is (P, Q, a, p).

To digitally sign, choose a random integer k such that $1 \leq k < n$, and compute

$$R = kP$$
$$s = k^{-1}(m - k_{priv}x) \bmod n$$

where x is the first component of R. The digital signature is then (m, R, s).

To validate the signature, the recipient computes

$$V_1 = xQ + sR$$
$$V_2 = mP$$

If $V_1 = V_2$, then the signature is verified. Otherwise, the signature does not correspond to either the message, the private key used to sign the message, or both.

EXAMPLE: Alice and Bob decide to use the El Gamal digital signature scheme with elliptic curve cryptography. As in Section 10.3.3, they choose the elliptic curve $y^2 = x^3 + 4x + 14 \bmod 2503$ and the point $P = (1002, 493)$. This curve has $n = 2477$ integer points on it. Again, Bob chooses $k_{Bob} = 1847$, and so $Q = k_{Bob}P = 1847$ $(1002, 493) \bmod 2503 = (460, 2083)$.

Bob wishes to digitally sign the message $m = 379$ and send it to Alice. He first chooses a number $k = 877$ that is relatively prime to $p = 2503$. He then computes

$$R = kP = 877(1002, 493) = (1014, 788)$$
$$s = k^{-1}(m - k_{priv}x) \bmod n = 877^{-1}(379 - 1847 \times 1014) \bmod 2477 = 2367$$

and sends $(m, R, s) = (379, (1014, 788), 2367)$.

When Alice receives the message and digital signature, she computes

$$V_1 = xQ + sR = 1014(460, 2083) + 2367(1014, 788) = (535, 1015)$$
$$V_2 = mP = 379(1002, 493) = (535, 1015)$$

As $V_1 = V_2$, the digital signature checks.

10.6 Summary

For our purposes, three aspects of cryptography require study. Symmetric cryptography uses a single key shared by all involved. Public key cryptography uses two keys, one shared and the other private. Both types of cryptosystems can provide secrecy and origin authentication (although symmetric cryptography requires a trusted third party to provide both). Cryptographic hash functions may or may not use a secret key and provide data authentication.

All cryptosystems are based on substitution (of some quantity for another) and permutation (scrambling of some quantity). Cryptanalysis, the breaking of ciphers, uses statistical approaches (such as the Kasiski method and differential cryptanalysis) and mathematical approaches (such as attacks on the RSA method). As techniques of cryptanalysis improve, our understanding of encipherment methods also improves and ciphers become harder to break. The same holds for cryptographic checksum functions. However, as computing power increases, key length must also increase. A 56-bit key was deemed secure by many in 1976; it is clearly not secure now.

10.7   Research Issues

Cryptography is an exciting area of research, and all aspects of it are being studied. New secret key ciphers incorporate techniques for defeating differential and linear cryptanalysis. New public key ciphers use simple instances of *NP*-hard problems as their bases, and they cast those instances into the more general framework of the *NP*-hard problem. Other public key ciphers revisit well-studied, difficult symmetric problems (such as factoring) and use them so that mathematically breaking the cipher is equivalent to solving the hard problem. Still others are built on the notion of randomness (in the sense of unpredictability).

Cryptanalytic techniques are also improving. From the development of differential cryptanalysis came linear cryptanalysis. The use of *NP*-hard problems leads to an analysis of the problem underlying the cipher to reduce it to the simpler, solvable case. The use of symmetric mathematical problems leads to the application of advanced technology to make the specific problem computable; for example, advances in technology have increased the sizes of numbers that can be factored, which in turn lead to the use of larger primes as the basis for ciphers such as RSA.

Advances in both cryptography and cryptanalysis lead to a notion of "provable security." The issue is to prove under what conditions a cipher is unbreakable. Then, if the conditions are met, perfect secrecy is obtained. Similar issues arise with cryptographic protocols (some of which the next chapters will explore). This leads to the area of assurance and serves as an excellent test base for many assurance techniques.

A weak point of the use of cryptography is that the ciphertext must be decrypted for operations such as searching. Homomorphic cryptosystems allow operations to be performed on the ciphertexts, and the result is the same as the operations being applied to the plaintext and then enciphered. Fully homomorphic encryption allows arbitrary functions to be computed. Current schemes are computationally expensive. Making them quicker, and developing somewhat homomorphic encryption schemes that allow only a certain number of operations to be performed, are topics under active study.

Digital signatures provide the assurance needed to accept documents as legally binding: a judge can determine whether specific parties signed them (to the limits of the protocols). If an attacker could forge a digital signature, the judge could reach incorrect conclusions. Research in both compromising of digital signature schemes and development of more secure schemes is examining how to minimize this threat.

10.8 Further Reading

Cryptography is a vast, rich subject. Kahn's book *The Codebreakers* [988, 990] is required reading for anyone interested in this field. Other excellent historical books set the context for codebreaking during World War II [310, 989, 1613]. Helen Fouché Gaines presents techniques for cryptanalysis of many symmetric ciphers using traditional, pencil-and-paper analysis [731]. Sinkov applies basic mathematics to many of these symmetric ciphers [1759]. Schneier describes many old, and new, algorithms in a clear, easy-to-understand manner [1684]; his book is excellent for implementers. The underpinnings of these algorithms, and others, lie in statistics and mathematics. For symmetric cryptography, Konheim's book [1092] is superb once the reader has mastered his notation. Unlike other books, it focuses on cryptanalysis of symmetric ciphers using statistical attacks.

A number of books [914, 1093, 1248, 1486, 1887] discuss modern cryptography and its applications. Spillman's book [1803] is an excellent introduction. Menezes, Van Oorschot, and Vanstone's book [1318] is a valuable reference. Goldreich's two-volume series on the foundations of cryptography [787, 788] focuses on the underlying mathematics and formalisms of cryptography. Ferguson, Schneier, and Kohno [667] discuss the applications of cryptography to designing protocols.

Digital signature protocols abound. One standard, the DSS [2148], uses a variant of El Gamal; others, especially those associated with the ITU's X.500 series of recommendations, recommend (but do not require) RSA. Gran [808] discusses digital signatures in general and presents many case studies. Hammond [859] places digital signatures in the context of law and policy.

Several homomorphic encryption schemes have been proposed. Fully homomorphic encryption schemes [761, 762, 1921] are expensive in terms of both space and computation. Naehrig et al. [1415] point out that many applications require only a limited number of operations. Several such schemes exist [262, 1488]. Bosch et al. survey provably secure searchable encryption schemes [272]; Poh et al. explore the underlying structure of searchable symmetric encryption schemes [1528].

Zheng [2095] demonstrated a cryptographic primitive called *signcryption* that acts both as a digital signature and an encrypting public key. Schemes based on El Gamal [2095], elliptic cryptography, and identity-based cryptosystems have since been developed.

10.9   Exercises

1. A cryptographer once stated that cryptography could provide complete security, and that any other computer security controls were unnecessary. Why is he wrong? (*Hint*: Think of an implementation of a cryptosystem, and ask what aspect(s) of the implementation can cryptography not protect.)

2. Decipher the following ciphertext, which was enciphered using the Caesar cipher: TEBKFKQEBZLROPBLCERJXKBSBKQP.

3. If one-time pads are provably secure, why are they so rarely used in practice?

4. An affine cipher has the form $c = (am + b) \bmod n$. Suppose m is an integer between 0 and 25, each integer representing a letter.

   a. Let $n = 26$, $a = 3$, and $b = 123$. What is the ciphertext corresponding to the phrase THIS IS A CIPHER MESSAGE.

   b. A requirement for a cipher is that every plaintext letter corresponds to a different ciphertext letter. If a and b are not relatively prime to n, does the affine cipher meet this property? Either prove it does or present a counterexample.

5. Let k be the encipherment key for a Caesar cipher. The decipherment key differs; it is $26 - k$. One of the characteristics of a public key system is that the encipherment and decipherment keys are different. Why then is the Caesar cipher a classical cryptosystem, not a public key cryptosystem? Be specific.

6. The index of coincidence was defined as "the probability that two randomly chosen letters from the ciphertext will be the same." Derive the formula in Section 10.2.2.1 for the index of coincidence from this definition.

7. The following message was enciphered with a Vigenère cipher. Find the key and decipher it.

```
TSMVM MPPCW CZUGX HPECP RFAUE IOBQW PPIMS FXIPC
TSQPK SZNUL OPACR DDPKT SLVFW ELTKR GHIZS FNIDF
ARMUE NOSKR GDIPH WSGVL EDMCM SMWKP IYOJS TLVFA
HPBJI RAQIW HLDGA IYOUX
```

8. Prove that two users who perform a Diffie-Hellman key exchange will have the same shared key.

9. Prove the decipherment equation of the El Gamal cipher (see p. 308) correctly recovers the message m from ciphertext (c_1, c_2) that was enciphered using the encipherment equation of the El Gamal cipher (see p. 308).

10. Alice enciphers messages m and m' using the El Gamal cipher. Unfortunately, she uses the same random integer k. Eve intercepts the ciphers C and c' corresponding to the two messages, respectively. She learns m through various sources. But she only has the ciphertext c' corresponding to m'. Show how she can get m'.

11. In the example enciphering "HELLO WORLD" using the RSA cipher (the second example in Section 10.3.2), the modulus was chosen as 77, even though the magnitude of the cleartext blocks is at most 25. What problems in transmission and/or representation might this cause?

12. Prove the following:

   a. If p is a prime, $\phi(p) = p - 1$.
   b. If p and q are two distinct primes, $\phi(pq) = (p - 1)(q - 1)$.

13. Euler's generalization of Fermat's Little Theorem says that, for integers a and n such that a and n are relatively prime, $a^{\phi(n)}$ mod $n = 1$. Use this to show that deciphering of an enciphered message produces the original message with the RSA cryptosystem. Does enciphering of a deciphered message produce the original message also?

14. Alice and Bob are creating RSA public keys. They select different moduli n_{Alice} and n_{Bob}. Unknown to both, n_{Alice} and n_{Bob} have a common factor.

   a. How could Eve determine that n_{Alice} and n_{Bob} have a common factor without factoring those moduli?
   b. Having determined that factor, show how Eve can now obtain the private keys of both Alice and Bob.

15. Consider the RSA cipher with $p = 5$ and $q = 7$. Show that $d = e$ for all choices of public key e and private key d.

16. Consider the RSA cryptosystem. Show that the ciphertexts corresponding to the messages 0, 1 and $n - 1$ are the messages themselves. Are there other messages that produce the same ciphertext as plaintext?

17. It is often said that breaking RSA is equivalent to factoring the modulus, n.

   a. Prove that if n can be factored, one can determine the private key d from the modulus n and the public key e.
   b. Show that it is not necessary to factor n in order to determine the private key d from the modulus n and the public key e. (*Hint*: Look closely at the equation for computing the private key from n and e.)

18. Prove the fundamental laws of modular arithmetic:

    a. $(a + b) \bmod n = (a \bmod n + b \bmod n) \bmod n$
    b. $ab \bmod n = ((a \bmod n)(b \bmod n)) \bmod n$

19. Consider the problem of computing $152015^{154993} \bmod 262631$.

    a. The naive way is to multiply 152015 by itself 154993 times, then divide by 262631. This produces very large intermediate numbers. How can this exponentiation be done in such a way that no intermediate value is greater than or equal to 262631?

    b. The number of multiplications is still prohibitively large. Consider an alternate approach:

```
function modexp(a, b, n : integer)
begin
         var result := 1;

         while b > 0 do begin
                 if b mod 2 = 1 then
                         result = (result * a) mod n
                 b = b / 2
                 a = (a * a) mod n
         end

         return result
end
```

    If this function is called as modexp(152015, 154993, 262631), how many multiplications are required to compute the result?

20. Consider the public keys (e_1, n_1) and (e_2, n_2) of two RSA cryptosystems.

    a. You have discovered that n_1 and n_2 have a common factor but do not know what it is. How would you find it?

    b. You have intercepted a message c enciphered using the first public key. You also know the common factor of n_1 and n_2. Show how to decrypt c.

21. Suppose Alice and Bob have RSA public keys in a file on a server. They communicate regularly using authenticated, confidential messages. Eve wants to read the messages but is unable to crack the RSA private keys of Alice and Bob. However, she is able to break into the server and alter the file containing Alice's and Bob's public keys.

    a. How should Eve alter that file so that she can read confidential messages sent between Alice and Bob, and forge messages from either?

    b. How might Alice and/or Bob detect Eve's subversion of the public keys?

22. Is the identity function, which outputs its own input, a good cryptographic checksum function? Why or why not?

23. Is the UNIX *sum* program, which exclusive ors all words in its input to generate a one-word output, a good cryptographic checksum function? Why or why not?

24. Assume that a cryptographic checksum function computes hashes of 128 bits. Prove that the probability is 0.5 that at least one collision will occur after hashing (2^{64}) randomly selected messages.

25. The example involving the DES-MAC cryptographic hash function stated that a birthday attack would find collisions given 2^{32} messages. Alice wants to take advantage of this to swindle Bob. She draws up two contracts, one that Bob has agreed to sign and the other that Bob would not sign. She needs to generate a version of each that has the same checksum. Suggest how she might do this. (*Hint*: Adding blank spaces, or inserting a character followed by a backspace, will not affect the meaning of either contract.)

26. Consider an RSA digital signature scheme (see Section 10.5.2.1). Alice tricks Bob into signing messages m_1 and m_2 such that $m = m_1 m_2 \bmod n_{Bob}$. Prove that Alice can forge Bob's signature on m.

27. Return to the example on page 321. Bob and Alice agree to sign the contract "G" (06). This time, Alice signs the message first and then enciphers the result. Show that the attack Bob used when Alice enciphered the message and then signed it will now fail.

Chapter 11
Key Management

Key management refers to the distribution of cryptographic keys; the mechanisms used to bind an identity to a key; and the generation, maintenance, and revoking of such keys. We assume that identities correctly define principals—that is, a key bound to the identity "Bob" is really Bob's key. Alice did not impersonate Bob's identity to obtain it. Chapter 15, "Representing Identity," discusses the problem of identifiers naming principals; Chapter 13, "Authentication," discusses a principal authenticating herself to a single system. This chapter assumes that authentication has been completed and that identity is assigned. The problem is to propagate that authentication to other principals and systems.

We first discuss authentication and key distribution. Next comes key generation and the binding of an identity to a key using certificates. We then discuss key storage and revocation. We conclude with digital signatures.

A word about notation. The statement

$$X \rightarrow Y : \{m\}k$$

means that entity X sends entity Y a message m enciphered with key k. Subscripts to keys indicate to whom the keys belong, and are written where multiple keys are in use. For example, k_{Alice} and k_{Bob} refer to keys belonging to Alice and Bob, respectively. If Alice and Bob share a key, that key will be written as $k_{Alice,Bob}$ when the sharers are not immediately clear from the context. In general, k represents a secret key (for a symmetric cryptosystem), e a public key, and d a private key (for a public key cryptosystem). If multiple messages are listed sequentially, they are concatenated and sent. The operator $a \parallel b$ means that the bit sequences a and b are concatenated.

11.1   Session and Interchange Keys

We distinguish between a *session key* and an *interchange key* [1949].

> **Definition 11–1.** An *interchange key* is a cryptographic key associated with a principal to a communication. A *session key* is a cryptographic key associated with the communication itself.

This distinction reflects the difference between a communication and a user involved in that communication. Alice has a cryptographic key used specifically to exchange information with Bob. This key does not change over interactions with Bob. However, if Alice communicates twice with Bob (and "communication" can be using, for example, an email or a web browser), she does not want to use the same key to encipher the messages. This limits the amount of data enciphered by a single key and reduces the likelihood of an eavesdropper being able to break the cipher. It also hinders the effectiveness of replay attacks. Instead, she will generate a key for that single session. That key enciphers the data, and it is discarded when the session ends. Hence, the name of the key is a "session key."

Session keys also prevent forward searches (see Section 12.1.1). A forward search attack occurs when the set of plaintext messages is small. The adversary enciphers all plaintexts using the target's public key. When ciphertext is intercepted, it is compared with the precomputed texts. This quickly gives the corresponding plaintext. A randomly generated session key, used once, would prevent this attack. (See Exercise 2 for another approach.)

EXAMPLE: Suppose Alice is a client of Bob's stockbrokering firm. She needs to send Bob one of two messages: BUY or SELL. The attacker, Cathy, enciphers both messages with Bob's public key. When Alice sends her message, Cathy compares it with her messages and sees which one it matches.

An interchange key is associated with a principal. Alice can use the key she shares with Bob to convince Bob that the sender is Alice. She uses this key for all sessions. It changes independently of session initiation and termination.

11.2   Key Exchange

The goal of key exchange is to enable Alice to communicate secretly with Bob, and vice versa, using a shared cryptographic key. Solutions to this problem must meet the following criteria:

- The key that Alice and Bob are to share cannot be transmitted in the clear. Either it must be enciphered when sent, or Alice and Bob must derive it without an exchange of data from which the key can be derived. Alice and Bob can exchange data, but a third party cannot derive the key from the data exchanged.

- Alice and Bob may decide to trust a third party (called "Cathy" here).
- The cryptosystems and protocols are publicly known. The only secret data is to be the cryptographic keys involved.

Symmetric cryptosystems and public key cryptosystems use different protocols.

11.2.1   Symmetric Cryptographic Key Exchange

Suppose Alice and Bob wish to communicate. If they share a common key, they can use a symmetric cryptosystem. But how do they agree on a common key? If Alice sends one to Bob, Eve the eavesdropper will see it and be able to read the traffic between them.

To avoid this bootstrapping problem, symmetric protocols rely on a trusted third party, Cathy. Alice and Cathy share a secret key, and Bob and Cathy share a (different) secret key. The goal is to provide a secret key that Alice and Bob share. The following simple protocol provides a starting point [1684]:

1. Alice $\rightarrow$ Cathy : {request for session key to Bob}k_{Alice}
2. Cathy $\rightarrow$ Alice : {$k_{session}$}k_{Alice} || {$k_{session}$}k_{Bob}
3. Alice $\rightarrow$ Bob : {$k_{session}$}k_{Bob}

Bob now deciphers the message and uses $k_{session}$ to communicate with Alice.

This particular protocol is the basis for many more sophisticated protocols. However, it can be compromised. Assume that Alice sends Bob a message (such as "Deposit $500 in Dan's bank account today") enciphered under $k_{session}$. If an adversary "Eve" records the third message in the exchange above, and the message enciphered under $k_{session}$, she can send Bob the message {$k_{session}$}k_{Bob} followed by the message enciphered under $k_{session}$. Bob will not know that this is a repeat of an earlier message.

Avoiding problems such as this replay attack adds considerable complexity. Key exchange protocols typically add, at a minimum, some sort of defense against replay attack. In the process of the exchange, they also may provide authentication.

11.2.1.1   Needham-Schroeder Protocol

One of the best-known symmetric key exchange and authentication protocols is the Needham-Schroeder protocol [1435].

1. Alice $\rightarrow$ Cathy : {Alice || Bob || r_1}
2. Cathy $\rightarrow$ Alice : {Alice || Bob || r_1 || $k_{session}$ || {Alice ||
$$k_{session}\}k_{Bob}\}k_{Alice}$$

3. Alice $\rightarrow$ Bob : {Alice $\|$ $k_{session}$}k_{Bob}

4. Bob $\rightarrow$ Alice : {r_2}$k_{session}$

5. Alice $\rightarrow$ Bob : {$r_2 - 1$}$k_{session}$

In this protocol, r_1 and r_2 are two numbers generated at random, except that they cannot repeat between different protocol exchanges. These numbers are called *nonces*. So if Alice begins the protocol anew, her r_1 in the first exchange will not have been used there before. The basis for the security of this protocol is that both Alice and Bob trust Cathy.

When Bob receives the third message and deciphers it, he sees that the message names Alice. Since he could decipher the message, the message was enciphered using a key he shares only with Cathy. Because he trusts Cathy not to have shared the key k_{Bob} with anyone else, the message must have been enciphered by Cathy. This means that Cathy is vouching that she generated $k_{session}$ so Bob could communicate with Alice. So Bob trusts that Cathy sent the message to Alice, and that Alice forwarded it to him.

However, if Eve recorded the message, she could have replayed it to Bob. In that case, Eve would not have known the session key, so Bob sets out to verify that his unknown recipient does know it. He sends a random message enciphered by $k_{session}$ to Alice. If Eve intercepts the message, she will not know what to return; should she send anything, the odds of her randomly selecting a message that is correct are very low and Bob will detect the attempted replay. But if Alice is indeed initiating the communication, when she gets the message she can decipher it (because she knows $k_{session}$), apply some fixed function to the random data (here, decrement it by 1), encipher the result, and return it to Bob. Then Bob will be sure he is talking to Alice.

Alice needs to convince herself that she is talking to Bob. When she receives the second message from Cathy, she deciphers it and checks that Alice, Bob, and r_1 are present. This tells her that Cathy sent the second message (because it was enciphered with k_{Alice}, which only she and Cathy know) and that it was a response to the first message (because r_1 is in both the first and second messages). She obtains the session key and forwards the rest to Bob. She knows that only Bob has $k_{session}$, because only she and Bob can read the messages containing that key. So when she receives messages enciphered with that key, she will be sure that she is talking to Bob.

The Needham-Schroeder protocol assumes that all cryptographic keys are secure. In practice, session keys will be generated pseudorandomly. Depending on the algorithm used, it may be possible to predict such keys. Denning and Sacco [545] assumed that Eve could obtain a session key and subvert the authentication. After the previous steps, the following exchange takes place:

1. Eve $\rightarrow$ Bob : {Alice $\|$ $k_{session}$}k_{Bob}

2. Bob $\rightarrow$ Alice : {r_3}$k_{session}$ [intercepted by Eve]

3. Eve $\rightarrow$ Bob : {$r_3 - 1$}$k_{session}$

Now Bob thinks he is talking to Alice. He is really talking to Eve.

Denning and Sacco suggest using timestamps to enable Bob to detect this replay. Applying their method to the Needham-Schroeder protocol yields

1. Alice → Cathy : {Alice ∥ Bob ∥ r_1}
2. Cathy → Alice : {Alice ∥ Bob ∥ r_1 ∥ $k_{session}$ ∥ {Alice ∥ t ∥
$$k_{session}\}k_{Bob}\}k_{Alice}$$
3. Alice → Bob : {Alice ∥ t ∥ $k_{session}$}k_{Bob}
4. Bob → Alice : {r_2}$k_{session}$
5. Alice → Bob : {$r_2 - 1$}$k_{session}$

where t is a timestamp. When Bob gets the message in step 3, he rejects it if the timestamp is too old ("too old" being determined from the system in use). This modification requires synchronized clocks. Denning and Sacco note that a principal with a slow clock is vulnerable to a replay attack. Gong [795] adds that a party with a fast clock is also vulnerable, and simply resetting the clock does not eliminate the vulnerability.

11.2.1.2   Otway-Rees Protocol

The Otway-Rees protocol [1481] corrects these problems[1] by avoiding the use of timestamps.

1. Alice → Bob : {n ∥ Alice ∥ Bob ∥ {r_1 ∥ n ∥ Alice ∥ Bob}k_{Alice}}
2. Bob → Cathy : {n ∥ Alice ∥ Bob ∥ {r_1 ∥ n ∥ Alice ∥ Bob}k_{Alice} ∥
$$\{r_2 \parallel n \parallel \text{Alice} \parallel \text{Bob}\}k_{Bob}\}$$
3. Cathy → Bob : {n ∥ {r_2 ∥ $k_{session}$}k_{Alice} ∥ {r_2 ∥ $k_{session}$}k_{Bob}}
4. Bob → Alice : {n ∥ {r_1 ∥ $k_{session}$}k_{Alice}}

The purpose of the integer n is to associate all messages with a particular exchange. Again, consider the elements of the protocol.

When Alice receives the fourth message from Bob, she checks that the n agrees with the n in the first message that she sent to Bob. If so, she knows that this is part of the exchange. She also trusts that Cathy generated the session key because only Cathy and Alice know k_{Alice}, and the random number r_1 agrees with what Alice put in the enciphered portion of the message. Combining these factors, Alice is now convinced that she is talking to Bob.

When Bob receives the message from Cathy, he determines that the n corresponds to the one he received from Alice and sent to Cathy. He deciphers that portion of the message enciphered with his key, and checks that r_2 is what he sent. He then knows that Cathy sent the reply, and that it applies to the exchange with Alice.

---

[1] Needham and Schroeder also supply a modification [1436]; see Exercise 12.

Because no timestamps are used, the synchronization of the system clocks is irrelevant. Now suppose Eve acquired an old session key and the message in 3. She forwards that message to Alice. Alice immediately rejects it if she has no ongoing key exchanges with Bob. If she does, and n does not match, she rejects Eve's message. The only way Eve could impersonate Bob is if she acquired $k_{session}$ for an ongoing exchange, recorded the third message, and resent the relevant portion to Alice before Bob could do so. In that case, however, Eve could simply listen to the traffic, and no replay would be involved.

Unless implemented carefully, this protocol, and many others, are vulnerable to an attack called a *type flaw attack* (see Section 12.1.4).

11.2.1.3   Bellare-Rogaway Protocol

The Bellare-Rogaway protocol takes a very different approach [159]. They note that, although authentication and symmetric key exchange are often considered together, they are really different problems. So their protocol only provides symmetric key exchange and not authentication. Rather than have one of the parties interact with the trusted server directly and send the results to the other party, this protocol has the trusted server send to both parties. In this protocol, h_{user} represents a keyed hash function that uses *user*'s interchange key.

1. Alice → Bob : {Alice ∥ Bob ∥ r_1}
2. Bob → Cathy : {Alice ∥ Bob ∥ r_1 ∥ r_2}
3. Cathy → Bob : {{$k_{session}$}k_{Bob} ∥ h_{Bob}(Alice ∥ Bob ∥ r_1 ∥ {$k_{session}$}k_{Bob})}
4. Cathy → Alice : {{$k_{session}$}k_{Alice} ∥ h_{Alice}(Alice ∥ Bob ∥ r_1 ∥ {$k_{session}$}k_{Alice})}

When Bob receives the first message, he computes the value of the cryptographic hash function using his name, Alice's name, his nonce r_1, and the enciphered session key in the message. If it agrees with the hash Cathy sent, he then uses his interchange key to decipher the session key. Alice obtains the same session key in a similar way.

If Eve obtains only the message in step 3 (or step 4), she will need to know the appropriate interchange key, which by assumption she does not. If she has obtained a previously used session key and recorded the corresponding message, there are two possibilities. If the protocol has begun, both Alice and Bob have generated new nonces. So when either computes the appropriate hash, the hash will be incorrect because the wrong nonce is used. Hence the message will be discarded. If the protocol has not begun, Alice and Bob will discard the replayed message.

The simplicity of this protocol is remarkable, and it has been proved to be secure, in the sense that Eve cannot obtain a current session key from the messages in the protocol or by impersonating Alice or Bob [157, 159]. It is an excellent example of how changing one's view slightly—here by considering authentication and symmetric key exchange separately—can affect security mechanisms.

11.2.2 Kerberos

Kerberos [1441, 1442, 1821] uses the Needham-Schroeder protocol as modified by Denning and Sacco. A client, Alice, wants to use a server S. Kerberos requires her to use two servers to obtain a credential that will authenticate her to S. First, Alice must authenticate herself to the Kerberos system; then she must obtain a *ticket* to use S (see the next paragraph). This separates authentication of the user to the issuer of tickets and the vouching of identity to S. In practice, though, the authentication server and the ticket-granting server are the same system, known as the *key distribution center*.

The basis of Kerberos is a credential known as the *ticket*. Suppose Alice wants to use the ticket-granting service Barnum. The ticket for this contains

$$T_{Alice,Barnum} = \text{Barnum} \parallel \{\text{Alice} \parallel \text{Alice address} \parallel \text{valid time} \parallel$$
$$k_{Alice,Barnum}\}k_{Barnum}$$

In this ticket, k_{Barnum} is the key that Barnum shares with the authentication server, and $k_{Alice,Barnum}$ is the session key that Alice and Barnum will share. The valid time is the time interval during which the ticket is valid, which is typically several hours. The ticket is the issuer's voucher for the identity of the requester of the service.

The *authenticator* contains the identity of the sender of a ticket and is used when Alice wants to show Barnum that the party sending the ticket is the same as the party to whom the ticket was issued. It contains

$$A_{Alice,Barnum} = \{\text{Alice} \parallel \text{generation time} \parallel k_t\}k_{Alice,Barnum}$$

where $k_{Alice,Barnum}$ is the session key that Alice and Barnum share, k_t is an alternative session key, and the authenticator was created at generation time. Alice generates an authenticator whenever she sends a ticket. She sends both the ticket and the authenticator in the same message.

Alice's goal is to print a file using the service Gutenberg. The authentication server is Cerberus and the ticket-granting server is Barnum. The Kerberos protocol proceeds as follows:

1. Alice → Cerberus : Alice ∥ Barnum
2. Cerberus → Alice : $\{k_{Alice,Barnum}\}k_{Alice} \parallel T_{Alice,Barnum}$

At this point, Alice deciphers the first part of the message to obtain the key she will use to communicate with Barnum. Kerberos uses the user's password as the key, so if Alice enters her password incorrectly, the decipherment of the session key will fail. These steps occur only at login; once Alice has the ticket for the ticket-granting server Barnum, she caches it and uses it:

3. Alice → Barnum : Gutenberg ∥ $A_{Alice,Barnum} \parallel T_{Alice,Barnum}$
4. Barnum → Alice : Alice ∥ $\{k_{Alice,Gutenberg}\}k_{Alice,Barnum} \parallel T_{Alice,Gutenberg}$

5. Alice $\rightarrow$ Gutenberg : $A_{Alice,Gutenberg} \parallel T_{Alice,Gutenberg}$

6. Gutenberg $\rightarrow$ Alice : $\{t + 1\}k_{Alice,Gutenberg}$

In these steps, Alice first constructs an authenticator and sends it, with the ticket and the name of the server, to Barnum. Barnum validates the request by comparing the data in the authenticator with the data in the ticket. Because the ticket is enciphered using the key Barnum shares with Cerberus, he knows that it came from a trusted source. He then generates an appropriate session key and sends Alice a ticket to pass on to Gutenberg. Step 5 repeats step 3, except that the name of the service is not given (because Gutenberg is the desired service). Step 6 is optional; Alice may ask that Gutenberg send it to confirm the request. If it is sent, t is the timestamp.

Bellovin and Merritt [165] discuss several potential problems with the Kerberos protocol. In particular, Kerberos relies on clocks being synchronized to prevent replay attacks [1129]. If the clocks are not synchronized, and if old tickets and authenticators are not cached, replay is possible. In Kerberos 5, authenticators are valid for five minutes, so tickets and authenticators can be replayed within that interval. Also, because the tickets have some fixed fields, a dictionary attack can be used to determine keys shared by services or users and the ticket-granting service or the authentication service, much as the WordPerfect cipher was broken (see the end of Section 10.2.2.1). Researchers at Purdue University used this technique to show that the session keys generated by Kerberos 4 were weak; they reported deciphering tickets, and finding session keys, within minutes [579]. Yu, Hartman, and Raeburn [2067] showed a flaw in Kerberos 4 that enabled an attacker to impersonate any principal. As a result, the MIT Kerberos Team announced that Kerberos 4 had reached the end of its life in 2006 [1359].

The Kerberos Version 5 protocol has been formally analyzed [330] and shown to provide the claimed authentication and secrecy properties. It supports intra-organizational communication, called "cross-realm operation" [1442]. To do this, the two realms must share an inter-realm key. Cervesato et al. [369] note that this requires the intermediate ticket-granting servers to be trusted. Sakane et al. [1639] present six requirements for cross-realm operation in large-scale industrial systems that deal with this, and other, threats.

11.2.3   Public Key Cryptographic Key Exchange and Authentication

Conceptually, public key cryptography makes exchanging keys very easy. Alice simply uses Bob's public key to encipher a session key she generates:

Alice $\rightarrow$ Bob : $\{k_{session}\}e_{Bob}$

where e_{Bob} is Bob's public key. Bob deciphers the message and obtains the session key $k_{session}$. Now he and Alice can communicate securely, using a symmetric cryptosystem.

As attractive as this protocol is, it has a similar flaw to our original symmetric key exchange protocol. Eve can forge such a message. Bob does not know who the message comes from.

One obvious fix is to sign the session key:

$$\text{Alice} \rightarrow \text{Bob} : \{\text{Alice} \parallel \{k_{session}\}d_{Alice}\}e_{Bob}$$

where d_{Alice} is Alice's private key. When Bob gets the message, he uses his private key to decipher the message. He sees the key is from Alice. Bob then uses her public key to obtain the session key. Schneier [1684] points out that Alice could also include a message enciphered with $k_{session}$.

These protocols assume that Alice has Bob's public key e_{Bob}. If not, she must get it from a public server, Peter. With a bit of ingenuity, Eve can arrange to read Bob's messages to Alice, and vice versa.

1. Alice → Peter : {send me Bob's public key}   [intercepted by Eve]
2. Eve → Peter : {send me Bob's public key}
3. Peter → Eve : e_{Bob}
4. Eve → Alice : e_{Eve}
5. Alice → Bob : $\{k_{session}\}e_{Eve}$ [intercepted by Eve]
6. Eve → Bob : $\{k_{session}\}e_{Bob}$

Eve now has the session key and can read any traffic between Alice and Bob. This is called a *man-in-the-middle attack* and illustrates the importance of identification and authentication in key exchange protocols. The man-in-the-middle attack works because there is no binding of identity to a public key. When presented with a public key purportedly belonging to Bob, Alice has no way to verify that the public key in fact belongs to Bob. This issue extends beyond key exchange and authentication. To resolve it, we need to look at the management of cryptographic keys.

11.2.3.1 Diffie-Hellman

The Diffie-Hellman scheme [564] was the first public key cryptosystem proposed, and it is still in use today. A pair of users use this algorithm to generate a common key. It is based on the discrete logarithm problem. This problem is to find a value of d such that $n = g^d \mod p$ for a given n, g, and prime p (see Section 10.3.1). Although solutions are known for small values of p, the difficulty increases exponentially as p increases [1128].

In this cryptosystem, all users share a common modulus p and a g other than 0, 1, or $p - 1$. Each user chooses a private key d and computes a public key e. When two users want to communicate, each enciphers the other's public key using their own private key, and uses the result as the shared secret key S.

EXAMPLE: Alice and Bob have chosen $p = 121001$ and $g = 6981$. They choose their private keys to be $d_{Alice} = 526784$ and $d_{Bob} = 5596$. Their public keys are

$$e_{Alice} = 6981^{26874} \bmod 121001 = 22258$$

and

$$e_{Bob} = 6981^{5596} \bmod 121001 = 112706$$

Suppose Bob wishes to send Alice a message. He computes a shared secret key by enciphering Alice's public key using his private key:

$$S_{Bob,Alice} = (e_{Alice})^{d_{Bob}} \bmod p = 22258^{5596} \bmod 121001 = 78618$$

Then he enciphers his message using this key (and any desired secret key cryptosystem). When Alice gets the message, she computes the key she shares with Bob as

$$S_{Alice,Bob} = (e_{Bob})^{d_{Alice}} \bmod p = 112706^{26874} \bmod 121001 = 78618$$

and can decipher the message. The mathematical properties of modular exponentiation ensure that for any two users A and B, $S_{A,B} = S_{B,A}$ (see Exercise 8).

Because the users share a common secret key S, the Diffie-Hellman scheme is an example of a *symmetric key exchange protocol*. Under the assumption that solving the discrete logarithm problem is computationally infeasible, deriving a private key from the corresponding public key is also computationally infeasible. In practice, p must be very large (hundreds of bits) for this assumption to be met.

This key exchange algorithm has a version based on elliptic curves.

EXAMPLE: Alice and Bob have chosen the elliptic curve $y^2 = x^3 + 4x + 14$ mod 2503 and the point $P = (1002, 493)$ to begin the elliptic curve version of Diffie-Hellman. This curve has 2428 (integer) points on it. Each chooses a private key, and in practice selects a number between 1 and 2476 inclusive. Suppose Alice chooses $d_{Alice} = 1379$ and Bob chooses $d_{Bob} = 2011$. Alice derives her public key by multiplying P and her private key, so

$$e_{Alice} = d_{Alice}P \bmod p = 1379(1002, 493) \bmod 2503 = (1041, 1659)$$

Similarly, Bob computes his public key as

$$e_{Bob} = d_{Bob}P \bmod p = 2011(1002, 493) \bmod 2503 = (629, 548)$$

Now they decide they wish to communicate. They exchange public keys. Then Bob computes

$$d_{Bob}e_{Alice} \bmod p = 2011(1041, 1659) \bmod 2503 = (2075, 2458)$$

Similarly, Alice computes

$$d_{Alice}e_{Bob} \bmod p = 1379(629, 548) \bmod 2503 = (2075, 2458)$$

They now share a common key.

11.3 Key Generation

The secrecy that cryptosystems provide resides in the selection of the crypto-graphic key. If an attacker can determine someone else's key, the attacker can read all traffic enciphered using that key or can use that key to impersonate its owner. Hence, generating keys that are difficult to guess or to determine from available information is critical.

This raises the issue of randomness. Given a set $\mathcal{K}$ of potential keys, the probability of a key being guessed is at a minimum when the key is selected at random from the elements of $\mathcal{K}$. The problem of selecting such a key is equivalent to generating a random number between 0 and $|\mathcal{K}| - 1$, inclusive (see Exercise 1). Typically, many keys are required, so a sequence of random numbers is needed.

Definition 11–2. A *sequence of cryptographically random numbers* is a sequence of numbers $x_1, x_2, \ldots$ such that for any positive integer k, an observer cannot predict x_k even if $x_1, \ldots, x_{k-1}$ are known.

A random number generator requires a physical source of randomness, such as background radiation or some other quantifiable physical phenomenon. For example, in 1955 the RAND Corporation published a table of one million random digits obtained from measuring random pulses [1869]. Other mechanisms use electromagnetic phenomena [22, 652, 1985] or characteristics of the physical computing environment such as disk latency [511,611,839,960,1692]. Characteristics of the external environment may affect the quality of these generators [1793].

Because mechanisms for doing this are often not available, computers use algorithms to generate sequences of numbers that act as though they were random.

Definition 11–3. A *sequence of cryptographically pseudorandom numbers* is a sequence of numbers generated by an algorithm that is intended to simulate a sequence of cryptographically random numbers.

When we say "random numbers" and "pseudorandom numbers" without any further qualification, we mean cryptographically random and pseudorandom numbers.

Creating such generators is difficult [1494]. A common method of generating pseudorandom numbers is by a linear congruential generator

$$x_k = (ax_{k-1} + b) \bmod n$$

where a and b are parameters, n is the period of the sequence, and a, b, and n are relatively prime. Reeds [1575] and Boyer [280, 281] show how to determine a and b given some numbers from the sequence. The obvious generalization, a polynomial congruential generator

$$x_k = (a_j x_{k-1}^j + \ldots + a_1 x_1 + a_0) \bmod n$$

has also been broken [1100].

The best software pseudorandom number generators are mixing functions.

Definition 11–4. [611] A *strong mixing function* is a function of two or more inputs that produces an output each bit of which depends on some nonlinear function of all the bits of the input.

The Advanced Encryption Standard (AES) (see Section 10.2.5) is an example of a strong mixing function. The AES takes 256, 320, or 384 bits of input (128 message bits and 128, 192, or 256 key bits) and produces 128 output bits. The dependence of the output bits on the input bits is complex and nonlinear. The Secure Hash Algorithm (SHA) family of hash functions are also strong mixing functions, producing up to 512 output bits from an arbitrary set of input bits.

The initial input to the mixing function must be unpredictable and irreproducible. Random numbers are best, but if they cannot be obtained, lots of data obtained from highly variable sources often suffices.

EXAMPLE: On a multiuser UNIX system, the status of the processes is highly variable. An attacker is unlikely to reproduce the state at a future time. So the command

```
( date ; ps gaux ) | sha512
```

would produce acceptable pseudorandom data. In this command, *ps gaux* lists all information about all processes on the system. The date is added simply for more information about the state.

Biometrics can also be used to produce random sequences. This technique is based upon the fact that physical variations (such as those caused by heat) cause randomness in the least significant digits of the collected biometric data.

For example, data gathered from brain signals and galvanic skin responses passed statistical and complexity tests for randomness [1849].

More commonly, biometrics are used to generate cryptographic keys that are tied to individuals. These keys need to be chosen in such a way that an adversary is unlikely to be able to determine them, but must be able to be regenerated consistently.

To generate a key from biometric data, that data is first represented as a bit string, the *feature descriptor*. The feature descriptor is then transformed in some way, such as using error-correcting codes [507], a lattice mapping [2094], or a secret sharing scheme such as Shamir's (see Section 16.3.2) [1372]. The cryptographic key is then generated from this transformed data.

Methods have been developed for generating cryptographic keys from many features, for example faces [396, 1867], handwritten signatures [725], and voice [351, 1372].

Generating cryptographic keys from biometrics requires care in choosing both the biometric and the method for measuring that biometric. If two measurements of the same biometric feature of a principal are made, the variation must be small enough so that the measurements are statistically indistinguishable; similarly, if two measurements of the same biometric feature of two different principals are made, the variation must be large enough so that the measurements are statistically distinguishable. This constrains the choice of features used for biometrics.

If a cryptographic key generated from biometrics is compromised, it must be replaced with a different key. One way to enable this is to introduce random data into the generation, for example by distorting the biometric measurement in some way [729, 1569]. Then, if the key is compromised, the random data is changed.

11.4   Cryptographic Key Infrastructures

Because symmetric cryptosystems use shared keys, it is not possible to bind an identity to a key. Instead, two parties need to agree on a shared key. Section 11.2, "Key Exchange," presents protocols that do this.

Public key cryptosystems use two keys, one of which is to be available to all. The association between the cryptographic key and the principal is critical, because it determines the public key used to encipher messages for secrecy. If the binding is erroneous, someone other than the intended recipient could read the message.

For purposes of this discussion, we assume that the principal is identified by a name of some acceptable sort (Chapter 15, "Representing Identity," discusses this issue in more detail) and has been authenticated to the entity that generates the cryptographic keys. The question is how some (possibly different) principal can bind the public key to the representation of identity.

An obvious idea is for the originator to sign the public key with her private key, but this merely pushes the problem to another level, because the recipient would only know that whoever generated the public key also signed it. No identity is present.

Kohnfelder [1087] suggests creating a message containing a representation of identity, the corresponding public key, and having a trusted authority sign it. A timestamp t is also added:

$$C_{Alice} = \{e_{Alice} \parallel \text{Alice} \parallel t\}d_{Cathy}$$

This type of structure is called a *certificate*.

> **Definition 11–5.** A *certificate* is a token that binds an identity to a cryptographic key.

When Bob wants to communicate with Alice, he obtains Alice's certificate C_{Alice}. Assuming that he knows the trusted authority Cathy's public key, he can decipher the certificate. He first checks the timestamp t to see when the certificate was issued. From this, he can determine whether the certificate is too old to be trusted. The public key in the certificate belongs to the subject named in the certificate, so Bob now has Alice's public key. He knows that Cathy signed the certificate and therefore that Cathy is vouching to some degree that the public key belongs to Alice. If he trusts Cathy to make such a determination, he accepts the public key as valid and belonging to Alice.

One immediate problem is that Bob must know Cathy's public key to validate the certificate. Two approaches deal with this problem. The first, by Merkle, eliminates Cathy's signature; the second structures certificates into signature chains.

11.4.1   Merkle's Tree Authentication Scheme

Merkle [1322] notes that public keys and associated identities can be kept as data in a file. Changing any of these changes the file. This reduces the problem of substituting faked keys or identities to a data integrity problem. Cryptographic hash functions create checksums that reveal changes to files. Merkle uses them to protect the file.

Let Y_i be an identifier and its associated public key, and let $Y_1, \ldots, Y_n$ be stored in a file. Define a function $f : D \times D \to D$, where D is a set of bit strings. Let $h : \mathbb{N} \times \mathbb{N} \to D$ be a cryptographic hash function:

$$h(i,j) = \begin{cases} f\left(h\left(i, \left\lfloor \frac{i+j}{2} \right\rfloor\right), h\left(\left\lfloor \frac{i+j}{2} \right\rfloor + 1, j\right)\right) & \text{if } i < j \\ f(Y_i, Y_j) & \text{otherwise} \end{cases}$$

The hash of the entire file (called the *root*) is $h(1, n)$. Drawn as a diagram, the recursion creates a tree structure of the hashes (see Figure 11–1).

EXAMPLE: Suppose a user wants to validate Y_3 in Figure 11–1. The user does this by recomputing $h(1, 4)$, the hash for the entire file. This requires computing each of the intermediate nodes on the path from Y_3 to the root, $h(1, 4)$. To do so, the user needs to know the right child of $h(3, 4)$ and the left child of $h(1, 4)$. Thus

$$h(3, 3) = f(Y_3, Y_3)$$
$$h(3, 4) = f(h(3, 3), h(4, 4))$$
$$h(1, 4) = f(h(1, 2), h(3, 4))$$

This means that either the hashes or the certificates themselves must be available. For efficiency, the hashes would be precomputed.

Under Merkle's scheme, the ancillary hashes needed to validate a certificate are called the *authentication path*. In the example above, the authentication path of Y_3 is Y_3, $h(4, 4)$, and $h(1, 2)$. The authentication path forms the certificate C_3.

Merkle's scheme requires only that the root value be known and that the file be publicly available. If any identity and public key pair is compromised, then the root value will be incorrect and this will be detected during validation. However, if anyone changes their public key, the root value must be recomputed and redistributed.

Merkle's scheme is important because it examines certificate hierarchies and suggests a mechanism that does not use public key signatures to create certificates. However, the need to have the file available so the root value can be recomputed at will makes this scheme impractical for networks involving large numbers of certificates on widely separated systems.

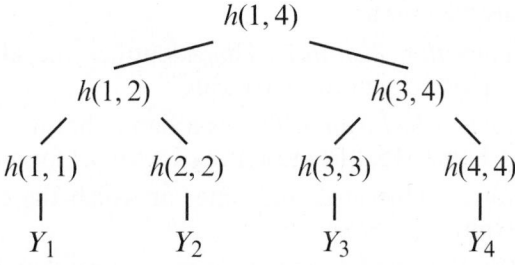

Figure 11–1 A representation of the recursion involved in Merkle's scheme for a file with four identity and public key pairs. The hash of the file is $h(1, 4)$, and this is known to all parties.

11.4.2   Certificate Signature Chains

The usual form of a certificate is for the issuer to encipher a hash of the identity of the subject (to whom the certificate is issued), the public key, and information such as time of issue or expiration using the issuer's private key. To validate the certificate, a user uses the issuer's public key to decipher the hash and check the data in the certificate. The user trying to validate the certificate must obtain the issuer's public key. If the issuer has a certificate, the user can get that key from the issuer's certificate. This pushes the problem to another level: how can the issuer's certificate be validated?

Two approaches to this problem are to construct a tree-like hierarchy, with the public key of the root known out of band, or to allow an arbitrary arrangement of certifiers and rely on each individual's knowledge of the certifiers. First, we examine X.509, which describes certificates in general. We then look at the PGP certificate structure.

11.4.2.1   X.509: Certificate Signature Chains

The ITU standard X.509 [2176] is the basis for many other protocols. It defines certificate formats and certificate validation in a generic context. Soon after its original issue in 1988, I'Anson and Mitchell [939] found problems with both the protocols and the certificate structure. These problems were corrected in the 1993 version, referred to as X.509v3. Based on experiences using X.509 certificates in privacy-enhanced electronic mail (see Section 12.5.1), other fields were added.

The X.509v3 certificate has the following components [457, 2176]:

1. *Version.* Each successive version of the X.509 certificate has new fields added. If fields 8, 9, and 10 (see below) are present, this field must be 3; if fields 8 and 9 are present, this field is either 2 or 3; and if none of fields 8, 9, and 10 are present, the version number can be 1, 2, or 3.

2. *Serial number.* This must be unique among the certificates issued by this issuer. In other words, the pair (*issuer's Distinguished Name, serial number*) must be unique.

3. *Signature algorithm identifier.* This identifies the algorithm, and any parameters, used to sign the certificate.

4. *Issuer's Distinguished Name.* This is a name that uniquely identifies the issuer. See Chapter 15, "Representing Identity," for a discussion.

5. *Validity interval.* This gives the times at which the certificate becomes valid and expires.

6. *Subject's Distinguished Name.* This is a name that uniquely identifies the subject to whom the certificate is issued. See Section 15.5 for a discussion.

7. *Subject's public key information.* This identifies the algorithm, its parameters, and the subject's public key.

8. *Issuer's unique identifier.* Under some circumstances, issuer Distinguished Names may be recycled (for example, when the Distinguished Name refers to a role, or when a company closes and a second company with the same Distinguished Name opens). This field allows the issuer to disambiguate among entities with the same issuer name.

9. *Subject's unique identifier.* This field is like field 8, but for the subject.

10. *Extensions.* These define certain extensions in the areas of key and policy information, certificate path constraints, and issuer and subject information. Each extension is a triplet, the first field being the extension identifier, the second a flag indicating whether the extension is critical or not, and the third being the value.

11. *Signature.* This field identifies the algorithm and parameters used to sign the certificate, followed by the signature (an enciphered hash of fields 1 to 10) itself.

To validate the certificate, the user obtains the issuer's public key for the particular signature algorithm (field 3) and deciphers the signature (field 11). The user then uses the information in the signature field (field 11) to recompute the hash value from the other fields. If it matches the deciphered signature, the signature is valid if the issuer's public key is correct. The user then checks the period of validity (field 5) to ensure that the certificate is current.

Definition 11–6. A *certificate authority* (CA) is an entity that issues certificates.

If all certificates have a common issuer, then the issuer's public key can be distributed out of band. However, this is infeasible. For example, it is highly unlikely that France and the United States could agree on a single issuer for their organizations' and citizens' certificates. This suggests multiple issuers, which complicates the process of validation.

Suppose Alice has a certificate from her local CA, Cathy. She wants to communicate with Bob, whose local CA is Dan. The problem is for Alice and Bob to validate each other's certificates.

Let $X \ll Y \gg$ represent the certificate that the CA X issues for the subject Y. Bob's certificate is Dan$\ll$Bob$\gg$. If Cathy has issued a certificate to Dan, Dan has a certificate Cathy$\ll$Dan$\gg$; similarly, if Dan has issued a certificate to Cathy, Cathy has a certificate Dan$\ll$Cathy$\gg$. In this case, Dan and Cathy are said to be cross-certified.

Definition 11–7. Two CAs are *cross-certified* if each has issued a certificate for the other.

Because Alice has Cathy's (trusted) public key, she can obtain Cathy≪Dan≫ and form the signature chain

Cathy≪Dan≫ Dan≪Bob≫

Because Alice can validate Dan's certificate, she can use the public key in that certificate to validate Bob's certificate. Similarly, Bob can acquire Dan≪Cathy≫ and validate Alice's certificate:

Dan≪Cathy≫ Cathy≪Alice≫

Signature chains can be of arbitrary length. The only requirement is that each certificate can be validated by the one before it in the chain. (X.509 suggests organizing CAs into a hierarchy to minimize the lengths of certificate signature chains, but this is not a requirement.)

Certificates can be revoked or canceled. A list of such certificates enables a user to detect, and reject, invalidated certificates. Section 11.5.2 discusses this.

11.4.2.2   PGP Certificate Signature Chains

PGP is an encipherment program widely used to provide privacy for electronic mail throughout the Internet, and to sign files digitally. It uses a certificate-based key management infrastructure for users' public keys. Its certificates and key management structure differ from X.509's in several ways. Here, we describe OpenPGP's structure [340], but much of this discussion also applies to other versions of PGP.

An OpenPGP certificate is composed of *packets*. A packet is a record with a tag describing its purpose. A certificate contains a public key packet followed by zero or more signature packets. An OpenPGP public key packet has the following structure:

1. *Version*. This is either 3 or 4. Version 3 is compatible with all versions of PGP; Version 4 is not compatible with old (Version 2.6) versions of PGP.

2. *Time of creation*. This specifies when the certificate was created.

3. *Validity period* (Version 3 only). This gives the number of days that the certificate is valid. If it is 0, the certificate does not expire.

4. *Public key algorithm and parameters*. This identifies the algorithm used and gives the parameters for the cryptosystem used. Version 3 packets contain the modulus for RSA (see Section 10.3.2). Version 4 packets contain the parameters appropriate for the cryptosystem used.

5. *Public key*. This gives the public key. Version 3 packets contain the exponent for RSA. Version 4 packets contain the public key for the cryptosystem identified in field 4.

The information in an OpenPGP signature packet is different for the two versions. Version 3 contains the following:

1. *Version*. This is 3.
2. *Signature type*. This describes the specific purpose of the signature and encodes a level of trust (see Section 15.5.3, "Trust"). For example, signature type 0x11 says that the signer has not verified that the public key belongs to the named subject.
3. *Creation time*. This specifies the time at which the fields following were hashed.
4. *Key identifier of the signer*. This specifies the key used to generate the signature.
5. *Public key algorithm*. This identifies the algorithm used to generate the signature.
6. *Hash algorithm*. This identifies the algorithm used to hash the signature before signing.
7. *Part of signed hash value*. After the data is hashed, field 3 is given the time at which the hash was computed, and that field is hashed and appended to the previous hash. The first two bytes are placed into this field. The idea is that the signature can be rejected immediately if the first two bytes hashed during the validation do not match this field.
8. *Signature*. This contains the encipherment of the hash using the signer's private key.

A Version 4 signature packet is considerably more complex, but as a Version 3 signature packet does, it binds a signature to an identifier and data. The interested reader is referred to the OpenPGP specifications [340].

PGP certificates differ from X.509 certificates in several important ways. Unlike X.509, a single key may have multiple signatures. (All Version 4 PGP keys are signed by the owner; this is called *self-signing*.) Also unlike X.509, a notion of "trust" is embedded in each signature, and the signatures for a single key may have different levels of trust. The users of the certificates can determine the level of trust for each signature and act accordingly.

EXAMPLE: Suppose Alice needs to communicate with Bob. She obtains Bob's public key PGP certificate, Ellen,Fred,Giselle,Bob≪Bob≫ (where the X.509 notation is extended in the obvious way). Alice knows none of the signers, so she gets Giselle's PGP certificate, Henry,Irene,Giselle≪Giselle≫, from a certificate server. She knows Henry vaguely, so she obtains his certificate, Ellen,Henry≪Henry≫, and verifies Giselle's certificate. She notes that Henry's signature is at the "casual" trust level, so she decides to look elsewhere for confirmation. She obtains Ellen's certificate, Jack,Ellen≪Ellen≫, and immediately recognizes Jack as her husband. She has his certificate and uses it to validate Ellen's certificate. She notes that his signature is at the "positive" trust level, so she accepts

Ellen's certificate as valid and uses it to validate Bob's. She notes that Ellen signed the certificate with "positive" trust also, so she concludes that the certificate, and the public key it contains, are trustworthy.

In the example above, Alice followed two signature chains:

Henry≪Henry≫ Henry≪Giselle≫ Giselle≪Bob≫

and

Jack≪Ellen≫ Ellen≪Bob≫

The unchecked signatures have been dropped. The trust levels affected how Alice checked the certificate.

A subtle distinction arises here between X.509 and PGP certificates. X.509 certificates include an element of trust, but the trust is not indicated in the certificate. PGP certificates indicate the level of trust, but the same level of trust may have different meanings to different signers. Chapter 15 will examine this issue in considerable detail.

11.4.3   Public Key Infrastructures

The deployment and management of public keys is complex because of the different requirements of various protocols. Several such infrastructures are in place, such as the PGP Certificate Servers and the commercial certificate issuers for web browsers.

> **Definition 11–8.** A *public key infrastructure* (PKI) is an infrastructure that manages public keys and certificate authorities.

Let us examine the Internet X.509 public key infrastructure [457].

11.4.3.1   The Internet X.509 PKI

The Internet X.509 PKI has two basic types of certificates:

- An *end entity certificate* is one issued to entities not authorized to issue certificates.
- A *certificate authority certificate* (called a *CA certificate*) is one issued to a CA. A *self-issued certificate* has the issuer and subject as the same entity. A *self-signed certificate* is a self-issued certificate in which the public key in the certificate can be used to validate the certificate's digital signature; these are useful to provide a public key that begins a certificate chain.

Such a CA is known as a *trust anchor*. A *cross-certificate* is a certificate issued by one CA to another CA, and is intended to describe a trust relationship between the CAs.

When a user wants to obtain a certificate, she first registers with a CA. The CA may delegate the registration task to another entity, called the *registration authority* (RA). In either case, the registering entity is responsible for verifying the identity of the user as required by the CA's policy. The user then initializes her set of keys, obtaining the public key of the CA and generating its public and private keys. The CA then issues the appropriate certificate containing the user's identity and public key, as discussed in Section 11.4.2.1, sends it to the user, and stores it in a certificate repository.

Certificate extensions are either critical or noncritical, as noted earlier. An application supporting Internet certificates must reject a certificate containing an unrecognized critical extension, or one that the application cannot process. The application may ignore any unrecognized noncritical extension, but must process those it recognizes.

All conforming CAs must support the following extensions; they may support others.

- The *authority key identifier* extension, which must be noncritical, identifies the public key that can be used to validate the digital signature of the certificate. This is necessary if the issuer has multiple key pairs used to sign certificates. If the certificate is self-signed, this extension can be omitted; otherwise, it must be present.

- The *subject key identifier* extension, which must be noncritical, contains the same value as the authority key field. If the subject of the certificate is a CA, then this field must be present.

- The *key usage* extension, which should be critical, describes the purposes for which the public key can be used. These purposes include enciphering cryptographic keys (such as session keys), enciphering data, validating digital signatures of certificates, validating digital signatures other than on certificates, signing certificates, and so forth.

- The *basic constraints* extension, which must be critical if the certificate is used to validate the digital signatures of certificates and may be either critical or noncritical otherwise, identifies whether the subject is a CA and, if the public key can be used to verify a certificate's digital signature, the number of intermediate certificates that may follow this one in a certificate chain and that are not self-signed certificates.

- The *certificate policies* extension, when present on an end-entity certificate, says under what policy the certificate is issued, and what the certificate may be used for. When present on a CA certificate, this extension limits the set of policies on any certificate chain that includes this certificate.

The presence of these extensions simplifies processing and eliminates some earlier constraints on the Internet PKI. If the first one were not present, the validator would need to try different keys of the issuing CA to determine whether the certificate was valid. In earlier versions of the Internet PKI, the specific key used to sign the certificate often indicated which policy applied to the certificate. Now, the key identifiers and the certificate policy extensions do this explicitly. The key usage extension makes clear what the public key in the certificate is to be used for. Before, this was either embedded in the issuer's policy, or the public key was assumed to be valid for all purposes. Finally, the basic constraints extension limits the length of the certificate subchain beginning at the certificate and extending to the end point, not including self-signed certificates.

All conforming applications that process these certificates must recognize the following extensions:

- The key usage, certificate policies, and basic constraints extensions.
- The *subject alternative name* extension, which must be critical, provides another name for the subject, such as an email address, an IP address, and so forth. If present, the issuing CA must verify that this is another name for the subject of the certificate.
- The *name constraints* extension is in CA certificates only. It constrains what names are allowed in the subject field and subject alternative name extension of certificates following it in the certificate chain, unless those certificates are self-signed. It does not apply to self-signed certificates.
- The *policy constraints* extension, which must be critical, controls when the policy for the certificate chain containing this certificate must be explicit or when the policy in the issuer of a certificate in the chain can no longer be the same as the policy of the subject, even if the certificate says that it is.
- The *extended key usage* extension allows the issuer to specify uses of the public key beyond those given in the key usage extension, for example using the public key to sign downloadable executable code.
- The *inhibit anyPolicy* extension, which must be critical, enables a wildcard (*anyPolicy*) to match policies only if it occurs in an intermediate self-signed certificate in a certificate chain.

These extensions also add flexibility and control. The subject alternative name allows multiple subject names in a certificate; earlier versions did not allow this. The name constraints, policy constraints, and inhibit anyPolicy extensions control the policies that apply to the use of the certificate and the meaning of the subject names. The extended key usage field allows the public key to be used for purposes beyond the ones identified in the key usage extension.

11.4.3.2   Problems with PKIs

The heart of any PKI is trust. Ultimately, problems with PKIs are problems with the trust reposed in the infrastructure.

Consider the nature of a certificate. The issuer is binding the identity of a subject to a public key, so the issuer claims with some degree of confidence that the identity belongs to the principal claiming that identity. The degree of confidence of the identity depends entirely on the CA or its delegate (usually the registration authority). Section 15.5 explores this issue in depth.

The understanding of the CA's policies is also critical. If an end entity uses a certificate, that entity trusts that the CA is the appropriate CA for the policy that embodies the use of the certificate. Failure to validate this may result in accepting or rejecting a certificate inappropriately.

A common source of confusion is the belief that a certificate embodies authorization of some kind. It does not. An authorization may be associated with an identity, but that is external to the PKI.

Trust in implementation also abounds. For example, the CA's systems containing the private keys used to sign the certificates must protect those keys. If an adversary can obtain those private keys, it can issue certificates in the name of the CA, or revoke existing certificates issued by that CA.

One final, critical assumption is that no two certificates will have the same public (and hence private) key. If Alice discovers Bob's certificate has the same public key as hers, she knows Bob's private key, violating a key assumption in the use of public key cryptosystems. A study of certificates throughout the Internet shows this problem has arisen in practice [1151, 1152].

11.5   Storing and Revoking Keys

Key storage arises when a user needs to protect a cryptographic key in a way other than by remembering it. If the key is public, of course, any certificate-based mechanism will suffice, because the goal is to protect the key's integrity. But secret keys (for symmetric cryptosystems) and private keys (for public key cryptosystems) must have their confidentiality protected as well.

11.5.1   Key Storage

Protecting cryptographic keys sounds simple: just put the key into a file, and use operating system access control mechanisms to protect it. Unfortunately, as discussed in Chapter 24, operating system access control mechanisms can often be evaded or defeated, or may not apply to some users. On a single-user system, this consideration is irrelevant, because no one else will have access to the system while the key is on the system. On a multiuser system, other users have access to the system. On a networked system, an attacker could trick the owner into downloading a program that would send keystrokes and files to the attacker, thereby revealing the confidential cryptographic key. We consider these systems.

On such systems, enciphering the file containing the keys will not work, either. When the user enters the key to decipher the file, the key and the contents of the file will reside in memory at some point; this is potentially visible to other users on a multiuser system. The keystrokes used to decipher the file could be recorded and replayed at a later date. Either will compromise the key.

A feasible solution is to put the key onto one or more physical devices, such as a special terminal, ROM, or smart card [536, 618, 1265]. The key never enters the computer's memory. Instead, to encipher a message, the user inserts the smart card into a special device that can read from, and write to, the computer. The computer sends it the message to be protected, and the device uses the key on the smart card to encipher the message and send it back to the computer. At no point is the cryptographic key present on the computer.

A variant relies on the observation that if the smart card is stolen, the thief has the cryptographic key. Instead of having it on one card, the key is split over multiple devices (two cards, a card and the physical card reader, and so on.) Now, if a thief steals one of the cards, the stolen card is useless because it does not contain the entire key.

11.5.1.1   Key Escrow

As the previous discussion implies, keys can belong to roles.

EXAMPLE: The UNIX superuser password, like the Windows Administrator password, refers to the role of system administrator. In the absence of other password management techniques (see Chapter 13) all people who take those roles need to know the password.

A reasonable concern is how one recovers the key if it is lost, or if the people who know it are unable or unwilling to reveal it. Three alternatives arise: either the key or the cryptosystem can be weak, or a copy of the key can be placed somewhere.

> **Definition 11–9.** A *key escrow system* is a system in which a third party can recover a cryptographic key.

The contexts in which key escrow arises are business (recovery of backup keys, for example) and law enforcement (recovery of keys used to encipher communications to which an authority requires access, such as enciphered letters or telephone messages). Beth et al. [188] identify five desirable properties or goals.

1. The escrow system should not depend on the encipherment algorithm. The escrow techniques should work regardless of how the messages are enciphered.
2. Privacy protection mechanisms must work from one end to the other and be part of the user interface. This protects the user's privacy unless the escrowed keys are used, and then only those who have the escrowed keys can access the messages.

3. Requirements (legal or business) must map to the key exchange protocol. This prevents a user from enciphering a message and then entering it directly into the communications channel, bypassing the escrow system.

4. A system supporting key escrow must require that all parties authenticate themselves. In particular, if a principal uses the escrowed keys, the system must ensure that the principal is authenticated not only by name but also by the time and place of the principal and by any equipment used in the interception and the decipherment. This protects against unauthorized parties using escrowed keys.

5. If the message is to be observable for a limited time, the key escrow system must ensure that the keys are valid for that interval exactly (no more and no less).

Key escrow systems consist of a user security component, a key escrow component, and a data recovery component [541]. The user security component does the encryption and decryption as well as supports the key escrow component. The key escrow component manages the storage and use of the data recovery keys. The data recovery component does the data recovery.

The most famous key escrow system was the one that the U.S. government's Clipper chip supports.

11.5.1.2   Key Escrow System and the Clipper Chip

Although the Clipper chip was the best-known component of the U.S. government's Escrowed Encryption Standard (EES) [2152], the system itself was a set of interlocking components designed to balance the need for law enforcement access to enciphered traffic against citizens' right to privacy. How well the system achieves this balance was left for the reader to decide in light of his or her philosophies. This section focuses on the technical components only [538, 546].

The key escrow hardware components consisted of a chip called "Clipper," which was used to prepare the per-message escrow information, and a device called the Key Escrow Decrypt Processor (KEDP). The chip was placed into the user security component of each device and was numbered uniquely (this number is called a UID, for "Unique Identifier for Device"). The KEDP was available to agencies authorized to read messages. In addition, a special facility created the escrow devices and programs the chips, and the key used to access messages was split and the parts given to two different escrow agencies.

Each user security component contained a unique device key k_{unique} and a nonunique family key k_{family} in addition to the UID. The user security component used a symmetric cipher called Skipjack [2230]. Skipjack accepts 64-bit blocks as input and enciphers them into 64-bit output blocks using an 80-bit key. (The details of Skipjack were classified until 1998 [2195].) In addition to the enciphered message, the user security component generated a Law Enforcement Access Field (LEAF) of 128 bits, containing

$$\{UID \parallel \{k_{session}\}k_{unique} \parallel hash\}k_{family}$$

where *hash* was a 16-bit authenticator generated from the session key and an initialization vector [242]. This was transmitted with the message.

The user component chip was programmed in a secure facility. Two escrow agents, one from each of the two key escrow agencies, were present. In addition, a set of family key components had been generated.

Each escrow agent independently supplied a random seed and key number. The family key components were combined to form k_{family}, and the key numbers were combined to make a key component enciphering key k_{comp}. The random seeds were mixed with additional random data to generate a sequence of keys k_{unique} for the chips being created. Each chip was imprinted with the UID, the k_{unique} for that chip, and a copy of k_{family}.

When k_{unique} was created, the key generator created two additional key components k_{u_1} and k_{u_2}, where $k_{u_1} \oplus k_{u_2} = k_{unique}$. These components were enciphered under the key component k_{comp}. The first escrow agent was given $\{k_{u_1}\}k_{comp}$, and the second was given $\{k_{u_2}\}k_{comp}$. The escrow agents took these encrypted key components to their respective agencies.

When Alice obtained legal authorization to read a message, she first ran the LEAF through the KEDP. The KEDP knew k_{family}, so it could validate the contents of the LEAF and obtain the UID for the sending device. Alice took the authorization and the UID to each of the two escrow agencies. They verified that the authorization was valid (using whatever procedures were appropriate), and each brought its encrypted key component and the corresponding key numbers. The components, LEAF, and key numbers were loaded onto the KEDP. The KEDP used the key numbers to generate k_{comp}, uses k_{comp} to obtain k_{u_1} and k_{u_2}, and exclusive-ors k_{u_1} and k_{u_2} to obtain k_{unique}. The KEDP then extracted the appropriate 80 bits of the LEAF and deciphered them to obtain the session key $k_{session}$. Because that key enciphered the message, the message can now be read.

Blaze pointed out an interesting way to defeat the key escrowing [242]. He noticed that the hash component of the LEAF was only 16 bits long. This means that out of the 2^{128} possible LEAFs, 2^{112} will have a valid checksum. Of these, only one has the actual session key and UID. An attacker could generate a LEAF with a valid checksum but an incorrect session key and UID, thereby defeating the decipherment efforts of the party authorized to obtain the session key. Blaze ran some experiments, and found that the expected time to generate such a LEAF was 42 minutes. Although too slow for telephonic applications, it was very feasible for an application such as electronic mail. Denning and Smid [546] also had pointed out that deployed devices would have countermeasures, such as a counter of the number of times an invalid LEAF was presented, that would defeat Blaze's trial-and-error method.

The Encrypted Key Escrow system met the first four goals of a key escrow system (see Section 11.5.1.1). Unfortunately, it failed on the fifth. The problem was that k_{unique} was fixed for each unit, so if an authority obtained that key, he can read any message enciphered by the device, with or without authorization.

11.5.1.3   The Yaksha Security System

Ganesan [735] developed a key escrow system meeting the five requirements. This system, Yaksha, is based on the RSA cryptosystem and a central server. The central server will generate session keys, which it can provide on demand to appropriate authorities (or which it can destroy).

In this system, each user has two private keys derived from the original RSA key. Let n_{Alice} be Alice's modulus. The first private key, d_{AliceA}, is known only to Alice; the second, d_{AliceY}, is known only to the Yaksha server. The keys are related:

$$d_{AliceA}d_{AliceY} \bmod \phi(n_{Alice}) = d_{Alice}$$

Alice's public key is e_{Alice} and is available to all. Bob has similar keys d_{BobB}, d_{BobY}, and e_{Bob}.

When Alice wishes to communicate with Bob, she sends a message to Yaksha asking for a session key. The Yaksha server generates a random session key $k_{session}$. The server then sends Alice

$$C_{Alice} = (k_{session})^{d_{AliceY}e_{Alice}} \bmod n_{Alice}$$

Alice can determine the session key as

$$(C_{Alice})^{d_{AliceA}} \bmod a_{Alice} = k_{session}$$

Similarly, Bob, who receives an analogous message, can recover the session key. The Yaksha server can archive the session key, or delete it, as needed.

This scheme eliminates the problem of an authority acquiring an escrow key and being able to read multiple sessions. Because the session key is random and not reused (a nonce), only the message that it enciphered can be read. This satisfies goal 5. Goal 1 is met if the focus is on the message enciphering algorithms, because the Yaksha system is tied to an RSA interchange with the server. The other requirements can be implemented, if a supporting infrastructure is available; certainly, interaction with the Yaksha server requires authentication.

11.5.1.4   Other Approaches

The fifth goal relies on "time." Both the EES and Yaksha interpret "time" as "sessions." Others have explored basing escrow systems on the length of time needed to solve some difficult problem. For example, Beth et al. [188] present an escrow system in which the secret key used to generate the session key is not given to the escrow authority, but a related key is. To find the actual key from the related key, the authority must solve an instance of the discrete log problem. Techniques such as this assume that the difficulty of solving a particular problem is relatively constant. With advances in technology, such assumptions must be examined carefully.

Bellare and Rivest [158] have proposed a technique called "translucent cryptography," in which some fraction f of the messages Alice sends to Bob can be read. Their proposal relies on a cryptographic technique called "oblivious transfer," in which a message is received with a given probability [156]. This is not a key escrow system, because the keys are not available, but it does serve the ends of such a system in that the messages can be read with a specified probability. The puzzle is the value to which f must be set.

Identity-based encryption uses as a public key a publicly known identifier, for example an identifier that uniquely names the user. First proposed by Shamir [1724], such a scheme requires a trusted third party to use (or provide to the requester to use) a secret to compute the private keys, because if no secret were used, anyone could derive a private key from a public key. Such a scheme also provides an effective escrow system, because given a message enciphered with a public key, the trusted third party can use the secret to derive the corresponding private key and read the message.

Shamir identified two additional properties that public key cryptosystems must meet in order to be suitable for identity-based encryption:

1. Private keys can be easily computed from public keys and a secret s.
2. It is computationally infeasible to compute a private key from a public key without knowing s.

He then showed that the RSA cryptosystem cannot meet both these conditions at the same time. In 2001, Cocks [430] and Boneh and Franklin [260, 261] independently developed identity-based encryption schemes. Boneh and Franklin's method provides key escrow in the way that Shamir's scheme does, and they further showed how to augment their system to provide a "global escrow" key to decrypt any ciphertext encrypted using the public keys of their system.

11.5.2   Key Revocation

Certificate formats contain a key expiration date. If a key becomes invalid before that date, it must be revoked. Typically, this means that the key is compromised, or that the binding between the subject and the key has changed.

We distinguish this from an expired certificate. An expired certificate has reached a predesignated period after which it is no longer valid. That the lifetime has been exceeded is the only reason. A revoked certificate has been canceled at the request of the owner or issuer for some reason other than expiration.

There are two problems with revoking a public key. The first is to ensure that the revocation is correct—in other words, to ensure that the entity revoking the key is authorized to do so. The second is to ensure timeliness of the revocation throughout the infrastructure. This second problem depends on reliable and highly connected servers and is a function of the infrastructure as well as of the locations of the certificates and the principals who have copies of those certificates. Ideally, notice of the revocation will be sent to all parties when received, but invariably there will be a time lag.

The Internet X.509 PKI uses lists of certificates.

> **Definition 11–10.** A *certificate revocation list* is a list of certificates that are no longer valid.

A certificate revocation list contains the serial numbers of the revoked certificates and the dates on which they were revoked. It also contains the name of the issuer, the date on which the list was issued, and when the next list is expected to be issued. The issuer also signs the list [457, 2176]. Under X.509, only the issuer of a certificate can revoke it.

To minimize the time lag, the Internet X.509 PKI also supports an online revocation system [1665]. When validating a certificate, the system can use the Online Certificate Status Protocol (OCSP) to determine whether the certificate has been revoked. The request includes the certificate's serial number, the hash of its issuer name, the hash of its issuer's public key, and an identification of the hash algorithm. The server will respond that the certificate is "good," "revoked," or "unknown" (meaning the responder does not know about the certificate being requested). This method is particularly useful when time is critical, for example during stock trades.

PGP allows signers of certificates to revoke their signatures as well as allowing owners of certificates, and their designees, to revoke the entire certificates. The certificate revocation is placed into a PGP packet and is signed just like a regular PGP certificate. A special flag marks it as a revocation message.

Boneh and Franklin [260, 261] point out that identity-based encryption provides a simple key revocation mechanism, provided the lifetime of the key is known when it is generated. Simply add some extra data that depends upon the time—for example, the current year or month—to the public key. Then the corresponding private key is valid only until the extra information expires, for example at the end of the year or the month. This revokes the key at that time by causing it to expire.

11.6 Summary

Cryptographic infrastructure provides the mechanisms needed to use cryptography. The infrastructure sees to the distribution of keys and the security of the procedures and mechanisms implementing cryptographic algorithms and protocols.

Key exchange and authentication protocols, although distinct in principle, are often combined because the first step in most communications is to prove identity. Exchanging a session key in the process saves another exchange. Both public key and symmetric cryptosystems can provide authentication and key exchange, provided that the appropriate infrastructure is present.

A key element of such an infrastructure is a mechanism for binding cryptographic keys to identity. This mechanism leads to the distinction between session keys (generated once per session, and associated with that session) and interchange keys (generated once per principal, and associated with that principal). It also leads to certification, in which a representation of identity, along with other information such as expiration time, is cryptographically signed and distributed as a unit. The name of the signer (issuer) is included so that the certificate can be verified.

The mechanism used to sign certificates and other documents is a digital signature. A disinterested third party, called a judge, must be able to confirm or disprove that the (alleged) sender computed the digital signature of the (alleged) signed message.

Session keys require pseudorandom number generation. Of the many algorithms in use, the best are mixing algorithms in which every bit of the output depends on every bit of the input, and no bit can be predicted even if all previous bits are known.

The management of keys involves storing them and revoking them, both of which involve system issues as well as cryptographic ones. Another aspect is the idea of key recovery. Under some circumstances (such as the key holder dying, or a legal order), a principal may need to obtain a key to read enciphered information. Key escrow systems provide this capability, but must meet strict requirements to ensure that they do not permit unauthorized and unlimited access to messages.

11.7   Research Issues

All issues discussed in this chapter are under active study. In particular, the design and deployment of public key infrastructures are critical as electronic commerce becomes more common. Unless technical mechanisms are sufficiently robust to support legal enforcement, electronic commerce will not be accepted. Key management mechanisms, in particular, must mimic the noncomputer world's procedures and processes, because they could be used to replace those processes.

Authentication protocols are critical to network use, and it is seductively easy to believe they are correct when they are not. Researchers are creating and testing various logics of authentication to prove protocols correct, or to prove them incorrect and fix them. The results of applying such logics must be interpreted in light of the environment in which the authentication protocol is used. For example, a proof that protocol X authenticates a user is misleading if that user keeps his private key in a file that anyone can read. The integration of system information, and of assumptions, into logics, as well as the development of new logics, are prime topics for research.

Key escrow defeats the confidentiality aspect of cryptographic protocols. Development is actively under way to minimize the threat of unauthorized users accessing escrow and recovery systems. Both symmetric and public key cryptographic methods, as well as more esoteric methods relying on techniques such as oblivious transfer, are under study. Researchers are also proposing systems that allow decipherment to some degree of probability rather than within some period of time.

11.8   Further Reading

When a user joins a Kerberos system, the user's password, or cryptographic key, must be set up on the Kerberos authentication server. This may be difficult when Kerberos is used over the Internet. The PKINIT protocol uses public key cryptography to replace the password [585, 2099–2101]; the current version of PKINIT fixes a problem that allowed a man-in-the-middle attack [368].

Dodis, Ostrovsky, Reyzin, and Smith [577] formalize the notion of "closeness" for biometric data. Ballard, Kamara, and Reiter [120] identify several subtleties in using biometric data to generate cryptographic keys in practice.

Ellison explores methods of binding an identity to a public key without using certificates [631]. Identity-based encryption provides this ability, as a user's public key is typically derived from certain aspects of that user's identity. Al-Riyami and Paterson [30] develop a scheme in which the trusted third party and a user use their own secrets to generate the private key; this prevents the third party from obtaining the user's private key. Alternate schemes assume slightly different security models and infrastructures [112, 1122]. Dent [553] compares these schemes with one another, and with traditional PKI-based schemes.

The Internet Key Exchange Protocol Version 2 [1012] deals with key exchange and authentication on the Internet. Several key exchange protocols are based on symmetric cryptosystems [325, 1440]. Protocols based on public key methods abound (see, for example, [1229, 1435, 1479, 1860, 2017, 2018, 2107]). Quantum key exchange offers still more key distribution methods [170, 290, 1864], but is prohibitively expensive.

Several papers discuss issues in public key infrastructure, including interoperation [899, 933, 934, 1489, 1617], organization [1157, 1208], requirements [81, 1604], and models [456, 1333, 1514, 1530, 1668]. The Resource Public Key Infrastructure (RPKI) [1154] uses the Internet X.509 PKI to support secure distribution of routing information. Several books [14, 413, 925] discuss many aspects of public key infrastructures. Ellison and Schneier [633] present often overlooked risks in using PKIs.

Several key escrow schemes explore different ways to control access. Burmester et al. [322] present a nonidentity-based protocol with a limited time span. Clark [421] and Walker et al. [1960] discuss the relationship between key recovery and key escrow. Others have proposed enhancements and extensions to various Internet protocols for key recovery [118, 1253, 1584, 1742].

The Skipjack cryptosystem has been studied extensively [200, 1523]. The lessons drawn from the nontechnical aspects of the proposed U.S. key escrow system have spurred an examination of the nontechnical aspects of key escrow in general [243, 727, 1329, 1678, 1810].

11.9   Exercises

1. The problem of selecting a cryptographic key is equivalent to generating a random number between 0 and $|\mathcal{K}| - 1$, inclusive. However, certain issues may complicate this process. This exercise asks you to examine them.

   a. The DES has 16 keys with undesirable properties (the weak and semi-weak keys). These keys cannot be used safely. Describe how to map the selection of a key for the DES into the problem of generating random numbers.

   b. RSA requires that prime numbers be generated. The usual technique is to generate a large random number and test it for primality. Assuming that you have an algorithm P that tests for primality in a "reasonable" time,[2] and assuming that you have a random number generator, how would you generate such a prime number efficiently?

2. Consider the case of Alice and her stockbroker, Bob, in the example in Section 11.1. Instead of BUY and SELL, Alice will send Bob one of 50 messages $m_1, \ldots, m_{50}$, where $m_i = i$ for $1 \le i \le 50$. Bob's RSA public key is (37, 77). The attacker Eve intercepts the ciphertext 39. Without computing Bob's private key, determine which message Alice sent to Bob.

3. Consider the Otway-Rees protocol. Assume that each enciphered message is simply the bits corresponding to the components of the message concatenated together. So, for example, in the first message, one must know the names "Alice" and "Bob," and the length of the random numbers r_1 and n, to be able to parse the portion of the first message that is enciphered with k_{Alice}. The separate parts of the enciphered message have no indicators; the recipient is expected to determine them.

   a. Consider Alice when all four steps of the protocol have been completed. How does Alice know that steps 2 and 3 have taken place?

   b. Massicotte asks us to assume that an adversary Edgar is impersonating Bob, and has sufficient control over the exchange so that he receives the

---

[2] In practice, a number is tested for primality by applying a series of probabilistic tests on the chosen number until the probability of that number being composite is sufficiently low. See, for example, Wagstaff [1955] and Stinson [1826].

messages intended for Bob. Bob never sees them. What components of the protocol does Edgar know—that is, does he know r_1, r_2, n, or $k_{session}$, or the names of "Alice" and "Bob"? How?

c. Given this, in step 4 of the protocol, how might Edgar provide Alice with a session key that he knows?

d. How might someone fix this?

4. Consider the following authentication protocol, which uses a symmetric cryptosystem. Alice generates a random message r, enciphers it with the key k she shares with Bob, and sends the enciphered message $\{r\}k$ to Bob. Bob deciphers it and sends $\{r+1\}k$ back to Alice. Alice deciphers the message and compares it with r. If the difference is 1, she knows that her correspondent shares the same key k and is therefore Bob. If not, she assumes that her correspondent does not share the key k and so is not Bob. Does this protocol authenticate Bob to Alice? Why or why not?

5. Needham and Schroeder suggest the following variant of their protocol:

   1. Alice → Bob : Alice
   2. Bob → Alice : $\{Alice \parallel rand_3\}k_{Bob}$
   3. Alice → Cathy : $\{Alice \parallel Bob \parallel rand_1 \parallel \{Alice \parallel rand_3\}k_{Bob}\}$
   4. Cathy → Alice : $\{Alice, Bob \parallel rand_1 \parallel k_{session} \parallel \{Alice \parallel rand_3 \parallel$
   $$k_{session}\}k_{Bob}\}k_{Alice}$$
   5. Alice → Bob : $\{Alice \parallel rand_3 \parallel k_{session}\}k_{Bob}$
   6. Bob → Alice : $\{rand_2\}k_{session}$
   7. Alice → Bob : $\{rand_2 - 1\}k_{session}$

   Show that this protocol solves the problem of replay as a result of stolen session keys.

6. What purpose would a random biometric-based cryptographic key be used for? A biometric-based cryptographic key that is associated with an individual?

7. Modify Kohnfelder's scheme (see page 344) to allow a principal to issue its own certificate. Identify one or more problems other principals might have in relying on such a certificate. In particular, under what conditions would this solve the problem of an impostor spoofing the sender?

8. A developer is trying to enable a program to validate the contents of memory locations in a specific part of memory have not been corrupted. She decides to use a Merkle tree authentication scheme in which the memory locations are the leaves.

   a. Describe the structure of the tree. In particular, what would the interior nodes contain? How would it be organized to enable fast validation of the contents of a memory location?

   b. If the program accessing the memory makes a change to the contents of one of the memory locations, what steps must it take to ensure the contents are not considered corrupt in the future? How would it do these steps?

   c. The developer is concerned that an adversary might change data in the sensitive memory locations. Ideally, she could place all data into protected, secure memory locations. Unfortunately, that memory is expensive. What is the minimum number of nodes that she must place into protected, secure memory to ensure she will detect any unexpected changes to the memory locations under consideration?

9. The original version of the Internet PKI [1033] was organized as a tree. The root, the Internet Policy Registration Authority (IPRA), operated under the auspices of the Internet Society. It only gave certificates to Policy Certification Authorities (PCAs), which in turn issued certificates for Certificate Authorities (CAs). Certificates in this PKI did not have any extension fields.

   a. A PCA forms the root of a subtree that complies with a single certification policy. All subordinate CAs agree to follow that PCA's policy. The PCA must file a digitally signed copy of a document stating the policy with the IPRA; this document was immutable. Among other things, this policy must describe technical and procedural measures that the PCA will take to protect the generation and storage of its public and private keys as well as any information it gathers about the CAs it certifies. Discuss the advantages and disadvantages of embedding a description of these measures in an immutable policy document. How would you ameliorate the disadvantages?

   b. A single PCA could support many different policies. Each policy would be associated with a different certificate. The subject name for all these certificates would be that of the PCA. What information would a verifier need to determine which policy applied to a given PCA certificate? What field of the certificate would be critical here?

   c. A CA was bound by a name subordination rule, which said the subject names in certificates that CAs issued must be subordinate to the issuer name (that is, a CA can only certify entities in the name tree of which it is a root). How would this requirement be implemented in the Internet X.509 PKI?

   d. The document specifying the original version of the Internet PKI stated that the privacy-enhanced electronic mail (PEM) implementations "must provide a user with the ability to display a full certification path for any certificate employed in PEM upon demand" [1033, p. 26]. Such a requirement was unusual because it specified a requirement upon the user interface of an application that used the Internet PKI and not the implementation of the PKI iteslf. Why was this requirement put into the standard?

10. An X.509 certificate revocation list contains a field specifying when the next such list is expected to be issued. Why is that field present?

11. After a Kerberos principal is authenticated to a server, the server must determine if the principal is authorized to use the service. One implementation of Kerberos had the ticket-granting service perform the authorization check, and not issue a ticket if the principal was not authorized to use the service.

    a. Under what conditions might an organization prefer to use the ticket-granting server as an authorization server?

    b. Under what conditions would it prefer to leave authorization in the hands of each server?

12. Show that, under the Yaksha security scheme, Alice can obtain the session key by computing

$$(C_{Alice})^{d_{AliceA}} \bmod n_{Alice}$$

13. Rather than a key escrow system, various governments have proposed requiring "backdoors" to be designed into implementations of cryptosystems so that law enforcement officers could access the information being enciphered and deciphered under appropriate legal constraints. With such backdoors, law enforcement could detect and thwart many criminal actions.

    a. Suppose the government of Sylvania decides to require all cryptographic software and hardware manufactured within it borders to have such backdoors. Would its traditional enemy, Freedonia, be likely to require the same type of backdoors to be put into all such equipment made in Freedonia? If not, what are the implications for the effectiveness of Sylvania's efforts to thwart crime that involved use of cryptographic equipment?

    b. Now consider only Sylvania. If backdoors are put into all cryptographic implementation, law enforcement would also use that equipment. What could criminals then do to anticipate efforts of law enforcement?

    c. If law enforcement were allowed to buy cryptographic implementations that did not have such backdoors, might these implementations leak to the general public? Why or why not? If they did, what would be the result with respect to the goals of the requirements?

Chapter 12
Cipher Techniques

> IAGO: So will I turn her virtue into pitch,
> And out of her own goodness make the net
> That shall enmesh them all.
> — *The Tragedy of Othello*, II, iii, 361–363.

Cryptographic systems are sensitive to environment. Using cryptosystems over a network introduces many problems. This chapter presents examples of these problems and discusses techniques for dealing with them. First comes a description of stream and block ciphers, followed by a review of the organization of the network layers. We then present several network protocols to show how these techniques are used in practice.

The key point of this chapter is that the strength of a cryptosystem depends in part on how it is used. A mathematically strong cryptosystem is vulnerable when implemented or used incorrectly.

12.1   Problems

The use of a cipher without consideration of the environment in which it is to be used may not provide the security that the user expects. Three examples will make this point clear.

12.1.1   Precomputing the Possible Messages

Simmons discusses the use of a "forward search" to decipher messages enciphered for confidentiality using a public key cryptosystem [1752]. His approach is to focus on the entropy (uncertainty) in the message. To use an example from Section 11.1, Cathy knows that Alice will send one of two messages—BUY or SELL—to Bob. The uncertainty is which one Alice will send. So Cathy enciphers both messages with Bob's public key. When Alice sends the message, Cathy intercepts it and compares the ciphertext with the two she computed. From this, she knows which message Alice sent.

Simmons's point is that if the plaintext corresponding to intercepted ciphertext is drawn from a (relatively) small set of possible plaintexts, the cryptanalyst can encipher the set of possible plaintexts and simply search that set for the intercepted ciphertext. Simmons demonstrates that the size of the set of possible plaintexts may not be obvious. As an example, he uses digitized sound. The initial calculations suggest that the number of possible plaintexts for each block is 2^{32}. Using forward search on such a set is clearly impractical, but after some analysis of the redundancy in human speech, Simmons reduces the number of potential plaintexts to about 100,000. This number is small enough so that forward searches become a threat.

This attack is similar to attacks to derive the cryptographic key of symmetric ciphers based on chosen plaintext (see, for example, Hellman's time-memory tradeoff attack [893]). However, Simmons's attack is for public key cryptosystems and does not reveal the private key. It only reveals the plaintext message.

12.1.2 Misordered Blocks

Denning [533] points out that in certain cases, parts of a ciphertext message can be deleted, replayed, or reordered.

EXAMPLE: Consider RSA. As in the example on page 310, take $p = 181$ and $q = 1451$. Then $n = 262631$ and $\phi(n) = 261000$. Bob chooses $e = 45593$, so his private key $d = 235457$. In this cryptosystem, each plaintext character is represented by a number from 00 ("A") to 25 ("Z"), and the message characters are in groups of three.

Alice wants to send Bob the message "TOM NOT ANN" (191412 131419 001313). She enciphers this message using his public key, obtaining 193459 029062 081227, and sends the message. Cathy intercepts it and rearranges the ciphertext: 081227 029062 193459. When Bob receives it, he deciphers the message and obtains "ANN NOT TOM," the opposite of what Alice sent.

Even if Alice digitally signed each part, Bob could not detect this attack. The problem is that the parts are not bound to one another. Because each part is independent, there is no way to tell when one part is replaced or added, or when parts are rearranged.

One solution is to generate a cryptographic checksum of the entire message (see Section 10.4) and sign that value. A second solution is to include a sequence number in each block before encrypting it.

12.1.3 Statistical Regularities

The independence of parts of ciphertext can give information relating to the structure of the enciphered message, even if the message itself is unintelligible.

The regularity arises when each part is enciphered separately, such that the same plaintext always produces the same ciphertext. This type of encipherment is called *codebook mode* or *electronic codebook mode* (ECB), because each part is effectively looked up in a list of plaintext-ciphertext pairs. For example, if the word "INCOME" is enciphered as one block, all occurrences of the word produce the same ciphertext:

EXAMPLE: Consider a banking database with two records:

```
MEMBER: HOLLY INCOME $100,000
MEMBER: HEIDI INCOME $100,000
```

Suppose the encipherment of this data under a block cipher is

```
ABCQZRME GHQMRSIB CTXUVYSS RMGRPFQN
ABCQZRME ORMPABRZ CTXUVYSS RMGRPFQN
```

If an attacker determines who these records refer to, and that "CTXUVYSS" is the encipherment of the "INCOME" keyword, he will know that Holly and Heidi have the same income.

Figure 12–3 on page 376 shows the regularity when an image is enciphered.

12.1.4   Type Flaw Attacks

A type flaw attack occurs when an attacker exploits the assumption that components of messages have a particular meaning. As an example, consider the Otway-Rees protocol described in Section 11.2.1. Assume an adversary Ichabod can intercept messages for the trusted third party Cathy. In the following, the messages to and from Ichabod appear to Bob to be to and from Cathy:

1. Alice → Bob : $num \parallel$ Alice $\parallel$ Bob $\parallel \{rand_1 \parallel num \parallel$ Alice $\parallel$ Bob$\}k_{Alice}$
2. Bob → Ichabod : $num \parallel$ Alice $\parallel$ Bob $\parallel$
   $\{rand_1 \parallel num \parallel$ Alice $\parallel$ Bob$\}k_{Alice} \parallel$
   $\{rand_2 \parallel num \parallel$ Alice $\parallel$ Bob$\}k_{Bob}$
3. Ichabod → Bob : $num \parallel \{rand_1 \parallel num \parallel$ Alice $\parallel$ Bob$\}k_{Alice} \parallel$
   $\{rand_2 \parallel num \parallel$ Alice $\parallel$ Bob$\}k_{Bob}$
4. Bob → Alice : $num \parallel \{rand_1 \parallel num \parallel$ Alice $\parallel$ Bob$\}k_{Alice}$

In step 3, Bob expects a message in which the two encrypted parts consist of a nonce followed by a session key. But Ichabod simply replays the message he received from Bob, who interprets the part following the nonce $rand_2$ as the session key. He then sends the first encrypted part to Alice, who makes the same assumption. But Alice and Bob's assumptions are incorrect. So now Alice and Bob communicate using the shared secret key $num \parallel$ Alice $\parallel$ Bob—which Ichabod knows [282, 1205].

In practice, many of these attacks can be foiled by tagging components of cryptographic messages with the type of the entity or entities being sent [884].

Meadows [1311] has pointed out that under certain conditions it is possible to confuse the tag with data. Li and Wang [1174] examine the underlying reasons that a protocol is vulnerable to this attack.

12.1.5   Summary

Despite the use of sophisticated cryptosystems and random keys, cipher systems may provide inadequate security if not used carefully. The protocols directing how these cipher systems are used, and the ancillary information that the protocols add to messages and sessions, overcome these problems. This emphasizes that ciphers and codes are not enough. The methods, or protocols, for their use also affect the security of systems.

12.2   Stream and Block Ciphers

Some ciphers divide a message into a sequence of parts, or blocks, and encipher each block with the same key.

> **Definition 12–1.** Let E be an encryption algorithm, and let $E_k(b)$ be the encryption of message b with key k. Let a message $m = b_1b_2\ldots$, where each b_i is of a fixed length. Then a *block cipher* is a cipher for which $E_k(m) = E_k(b_1)E_k(b_2)\ldots$.

EXAMPLE: The AES is a block cipher. It breaks the message into 128-bit blocks and uses the same key to encipher each block.

Other ciphers use a nonrepeating stream of key elements to encipher characters of a message.

> **Definition 12–2.** Let E be an encryption algorithm, and let $E_k(b)$ be the encryption of message b with key k. Let a message $m = b_1b_2\ldots$, where each b_i is of a fixed length, and let $k = k_1k_2\ldots$ be the bits in k. Then a *stream cipher* is a cipher for which $E_k(m) = E_{k_1}(b_1)E_{k_2}(b_2)\ldots$.

If the key stream k of a stream cipher repeats itself, it is a *periodic cipher*.

EXAMPLE: The Vigenère cipher (see Section 10.2.2.1) is a stream cipher. Take b_i to be a character of the message and k_i to be a character of the key. This cipher is periodic, because the key is of finite length, and should the key be shorter than the message, the key is repeated.

The one-time pad (see Section 10.2.2.2) is also a stream cipher but is not periodic, because the key stream never repeats.

12.2.1   Stream Ciphers

The one-time pad is a cipher that can be proven secure (see Section 10.2.2.2, "One-Time Pad"). Bit-oriented ciphers implement the one-time pad by exclusive-or'ing each bit of the key with one bit of the message. For example, if the message is 00101 and the key is 10010, the ciphertext is $0 \oplus 1 \parallel 0 \oplus 0 \parallel 1 \oplus 0 \parallel 0 \oplus 1 \parallel 1 \oplus 0$ or 10111. But how can one generate a random, infinitely long key?

12.2.1.1   Synchronous Stream Ciphers

To simulate a random, infinitely long key, synchronous stream ciphers generate bits from a source other than the message itself. The simplest such cipher extracts bits from a register to use as the key. The contents of the register change on the basis of the current contents of the register.

> **Definition 12–3.** An *n-stage linear feedback shift register* (LFSR) consists of an *n*-bit *register* $r = r_0 \ldots r_{n-1}$ and an *n*-bit *tap sequence* $t = t_0 \ldots t_{n-1}$. To obtain a key bit, r_{n-1} is used, the register is shifted one bit to the right, and the new bit $r_0 t_0 \oplus \ldots \oplus r_{n-1} t_{n-1}$ is inserted.

EXAMPLE: Let the tap sequence for a four-stage LFSR be 1001, and let the initial value of the register be 0010. The key bits extracted, and the values in the register, are

current register	key	new bit	new register
0010	0	$01 \oplus 00 \oplus 10 \oplus 01 = 0 \oplus 0 \oplus 0 \oplus 0 = 0$	0001
0001	1	$01 \oplus 00 \oplus 00 \oplus 11 = 0 \oplus 0 \oplus 0 \oplus 1 = 1$	1000
1000	0	$11 \oplus 00 \oplus 00 \oplus 01 = 1 \oplus 0 \oplus 0 \oplus 0 = 1$	1100
1100	0	$11 \oplus 10 \oplus 00 \oplus 01 = 1 \oplus 0 \oplus 0 \oplus 0 = 1$	1110
1110	0	$11 \oplus 10 \oplus 10 \oplus 01 = 1 \oplus 0 \oplus 0 \oplus 0 = 1$	1111
1111	1	$11 \oplus 10 \oplus 10 \oplus 11 = 1 \oplus 0 \oplus 0 \oplus 1 = 0$	0111
0111	1	$01 \oplus 10 \oplus 10 \oplus 11 = 0 \oplus 0 \oplus 0 \oplus 1 = 1$	1011
1011	1	$11 \oplus 00 \oplus 10 \oplus 11 = 1 \oplus 0 \oplus 0 \oplus 1 = 0$	0101
0101	1	$01 \oplus 10 \oplus 00 \oplus 11 = 0 \oplus 0 \oplus 0 \oplus 1 = 1$	1010
1010	0	$11 \oplus 00 \oplus 10 \oplus 01 = 1 \oplus 0 \oplus 0 \oplus 0 = 1$	1101
1101	1	$11 \oplus 10 \oplus 00 \oplus 11 = 1 \oplus 0 \oplus 0 \oplus 1 = 0$	0110
0110	0	$01 \oplus 10 \oplus 10 \oplus 01 = 0 \oplus 0 \oplus 0 \oplus 0 = 0$	0011
0011	1	$01 \oplus 00 \oplus 10 \oplus 11 = 0 \oplus 0 \oplus 0 \oplus 1 = 1$	1001
1001	1	$11 \oplus 00 \oplus 00 \oplus 11 = 1 \oplus 0 \oplus 0 \oplus 1 = 0$	0100
0100	0	$01 \oplus 10 \oplus 00 \oplus 01 = 0 \oplus 0 \oplus 0 \oplus 0 = 0$	0010
0010	0	$01 \oplus 00 \oplus 10 \oplus 01 = 0 \oplus 0 \oplus 0 \oplus 0 = 0$	0001

and the cycle repeats. The key stream that this LFSR produces has a period of 15 and is 010001111010110.

The LFSR method is an attempt to simulate a one-time pad by generating a long key sequence from a little information. As with any such attempt, if the key is shorter than the message, breaking part of the ciphertext gives the cryptanalyst information about other parts of the ciphertext. For an LFSR, a known plaintext attack can reveal parts of the key sequence. If the known plaintext is of length $2n$, the tap sequence for an n-stage LFSR can be determined completely.

Nonlinear feedback shift registers do not use tap sequences; instead, the new bit is a function of the current register bits.

Definition 12–4. An *n-stage nonlinear feedback shift register* (NLFSR) consists of an n-bit register $r = r_0 \ldots r_{n-1}$. To obtain a key bit, r_{n-1} is used, the register is shifted one bit to the right, and the new bit is set to $f(r_0, \ldots, r_{n-1})$, where f is any function of n inputs.

EXAMPLE: Let the function f for a four-stage NLFSR be $f(r_0, r_1, r_2, r_3) = (r_0 \text{ and } r_2)$ or r_3, and let the initial value of the register be 1100. The key bits extracted, and the values in the register, are

current register	key	new bit	new register
1100	0	$f(1, 1, 0, 0) = (1 \text{ and } 0)$ or $0 = 0$	0110
0110	0	$f(0, 1, 1, 0) = (0 \text{ and } 1)$ or $0 = 0$	0011
0011	1	$f(0, 0, 1, 1) = (0 \text{ and } 1)$ or $1 = 1$	1001
1001	1	$f(1, 0, 0, 1) = (1 \text{ and } 0)$ or $0 = 0$	0100
0100	0	$f(0, 1, 0, 0) = (0 \text{ and } 0)$ or $0 = 0$	0010
0010	0	$f(0, 0, 1, 0) = (0 \text{ and } 1)$ or $0 = 0$	0001
0001	1	$f(0, 0, 0, 1) = (0 \text{ and } 0)$ or $1 = 1$	1000
1000	0	$f(1, 0, 0, 0) = (1 \text{ and } 0)$ or $0 = 0$	0100
0100	0	$f(0, 1, 0, 0) = (0 \text{ and } 1)$ or $0 = 0$	0010
0010	0	$f(0, 0, 1, 0) = (0 \text{ and } 1)$ or $0 = 0$	0001

and the cycle repeats. The key stream that this NLFSR produces has a period of 4 (with an initial nonrepeating sequence of length 4) and is $0011\overline{0010}\ldots$ (the overstruck part repeats indefinitely).

NLFSRs are not common because there is no body of theory about how to build NLFSRs with long periods. By contrast, it is known how to design n-stage LFSRs with a period of $2^n - 1$, and that period is maximal.

A second technique for eliminating linearity is called *output feedback mode*. Let E be an encryption function. Define k as a cryptographic key, and define r as a register. To obtain a bit for the key, compute $E_k(r)$ and put that value into the register. The rightmost bit of the result is exclusive-or'ed with one bit of the message. The process is repeated until the message is enciphered. The key k and the initial value in r are the keys for this method. This method differs from the NLFSR in that the register is never shifted. It is repeatedly enciphered.

A variant of output feedback mode is called the *counter method*. Instead of using a register r, simply use a counter that is incremented or otherwise transformed for every encipherment, so that the value of the counter is unique for each encryption. The initial value of the counter replaces r as part of the key. This method enables one to generate the ith bit of the key without generating the bits $0, \ldots, i - 1$. If the initial counter value is i_0 and the value is incremented for each encryption, set the register to $i + i_0$. By way of contrast, in output feedback mode, one must generate all the preceding key bits.

12.2.1.2   Self-Synchronous Stream Ciphers

Self-synchronous ciphers obtain the key from the message itself. The simplest self-synchronous cipher is called an *autokey* cipher and uses the message itself for the key.

EXAMPLE: The following is an autokey version of the Vigenère cipher, with the key drawn from the plaintext:

```
key          XTHEBOYHASTHEBA
plaintext    THEBOYHASTHEBAG
ciphertext   QALFPNFHSLALFCT
```

Contrast this with the example on page 295. The key there is "VIG" and the resulting ciphertext contains a three-character repetition.

The problem with this cipher is the selection of the key. Unlike a one-time pad, any statistical regularities in the plaintext show up in the key. For example, the last two letters of the ciphertext associated with the plaintext word "THE" are always "AL," because "H" is enciphered with the key letter "T" and "E" is enciphered with the key letter "H." Furthermore, if the analyst can guess any letter of the plaintext, she can determine all successive plaintext letters.

An alternative is to use the ciphertext as the key stream. A good cipher will produce pseudorandom ciphertext, which approximates a random one-time pad better than a message with nonrandom characteristics (such as a meaningful English sentence).

EXAMPLE: The following is an autokey version of the Vigenère cipher, with the key drawn from the ciphertext:

```
key          XQXBCQOVVNGNRTT
plaintext    THEBOYHASTHECAT
ciphertext   QXBCQOVVNGNRTTM
```

This eliminates the repetition ("ALF") in the preceding example.

This type of autokey cipher is weak, because plaintext can be deduced from the ciphertext. For example, consider the first two characters of the ciphertext, "QX." The "X" is the ciphertext resulting from enciphering some letter with the key "Q." Deciphering, the unknown letter is "H." Continuing in this fashion, the analyst can reconstruct all of the plaintext except for the first letter.

A variant of the autokey method, *cipher feedback mode*, uses a shift register. Let E be an encipherment function. Define k as a cryptographic key and r as a register. To obtain a bit for the key, compute $E_k(r)$. The rightmost bit of the result is exclusive-or'ed with one bit of the message, and the other bits of the result are discarded. The resulting ciphertext is fed back into the leftmost bit of the register, which is right shifted one bit. (See Figure 12–1.)

Cipher feedback mode has a *self-healing property*. If a bit is corrupted in transmission of the ciphertext, the next n bits will be deciphered incorrectly. But after n uncorrupted bits have been received, the shift register will be reinitialized to the value used for encipherment and the ciphertext will decipher properly from that point on.

As in the counter method, one can decipher parts of messages enciphered in cipher feedback mode without deciphering the entire message. Let the shift register contain n bits. The analyst obtains the previous n bits of ciphertext. This is the value in the shift register before the bit under consideration was enciphered. The decipherment can then continue from that bit on.

12.2.2   Block Ciphers

Block ciphers encipher and decipher multiple bits at once using the same key. Errors in transmitting one block generally do not affect other blocks, but as each block is enciphered independently, using the same key, identical plaintext blocks produce identical ciphertext blocks. This allows the analyst to search for data by determining what the encipherment of a specific plaintext block is.

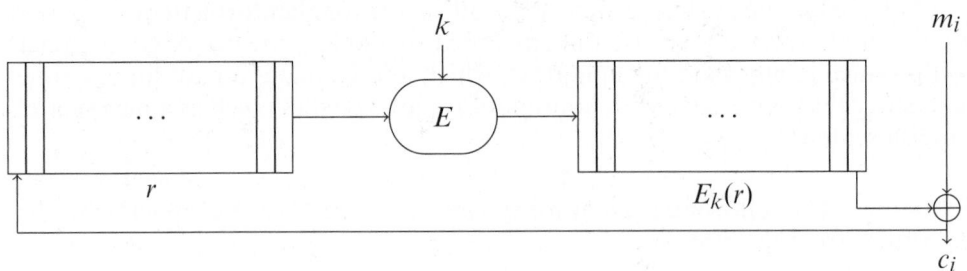

Figure 12–1 Diagram of cipher feedback mode. The register r is enciphered with key k and algorithm E. The rightmost bit of the result is exclusive-or'ed with one bit of the plaintext m_i to produce the ciphertext bit c_i. The register r is right-shifted one bit, and c_i is fed back into the leftmost bit of r.

To prevent this type of attack, some information related to the block's position is inserted into the plaintext block before it is enciphered. The information can be bits from the preceding ciphertext block [658] or a sequence number [1037]. The disadvantage is that the effective block size is reduced, because fewer message bits are present in a block.

Cipher block chaining does not require the extra information to occupy bit spaces, so every bit in the block is part of the message. The CBC mode is an iterative mode in which a block of ciphertext depends not only on its input but also on the preceding ciphertext block. Before a plaintext block is enciphered, that block is exclusive-or'ed with the preceding ciphertext block. In addition to the key, this technique requires an *initialization vector* with which to exclusive-or the initial plaintext block. Taking E_k to be the encipherment algorithm with key k, and I to be the initialization vector, the cipher block chaining technique is

$$c_0 = E_k(m_0 \oplus I)$$

$$c_i = E_k(m_i \oplus c_{i-1}) \text{ for } i > 0$$

Figure 12–2 shows this mode, and Figure 12–3 visually compares the effect of enciphering an image without and with cipher block chaining.

Like cipher feedback mode, CBC mode has the *self-healing property*. If one block of ciphertext is altered, the error propagates for at most two blocks. Figure 12–4 shows how a corrupted block affects others.

12.2.2.1   Multiple Encryption

Other approaches involve multiple encryption. Using two keys k and k' of length n to encipher a message as $c = E_{k'}(E_k(m))$ looks attractive because it has an effective key length of $2n$, whereas the keys to E are of length n. However, Merkle and Hellman [1325] have shown that this encryption technique can be broken using 2^{n+1} encryptions, rather than the expected 2^{2n} (see Exercise 3).

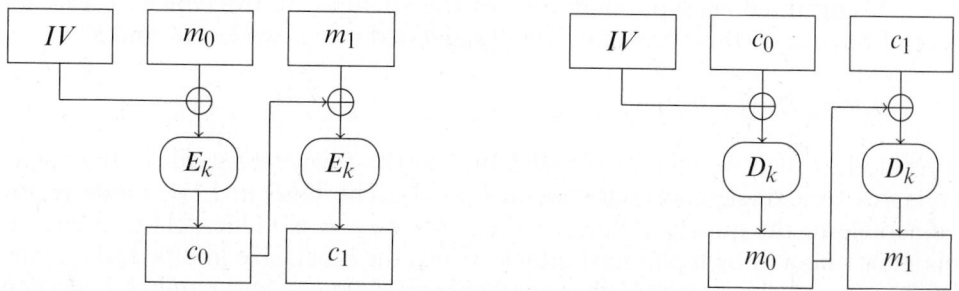

Figure 12–2 Cipher block chaining mode. The left diagram shows encipherment; each ciphertext is "fed back" into the cipher stream. The right diagram shows decipherment.

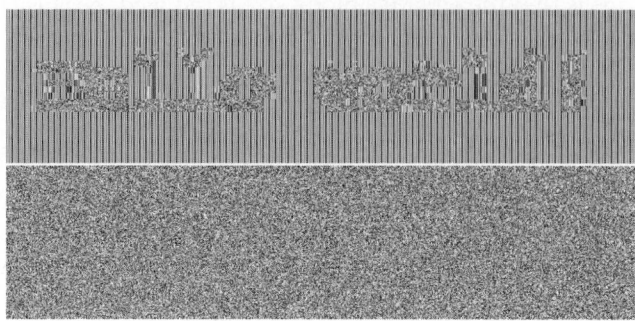

Figure 12–3 The middle image is the top image encrypted using AES-128 in ECB mode. The bottom image is the top image encrypted using AES-128 in CBC mode. CBC mode combines the previous ciphertext block with the current plaintext block and encrypts the result obscuring the regularity in the top image.

Incorrect ciphertext:	ef7c4cb2b4ce6f3b	f6266e3a97af0e2c
	746ab9a6308f4256	33e60b451b09603d
Corresponding plaintext:	efca61e19f4836f1	3231333336353837
	3231343336353837	3231343336353837
The real plaintext:	3231343336353837	3231343336353837
	3231343336353837	3231343336353837

Figure 12–4 Example of the self-healing property. The ciphertext at the top was stored incorrectly (the underlined "4c" should be "4b"). Its decipherment is shown next, with the incorrect octets underlined. The plaintext enciphered with the DES to create the ciphertext is shown at the bottom.

Using three encryptions improves the strength of the cipher. There are several ways to do this. Tuchman [1902] suggested using two keys k and k':

$$c = E_k(D_{k'}(E_k(m)))$$

This mode, called *two-key Triple DES* or *Encrypt-Decypt-Encrypt* (EDE) mode, collapses to a single encryption when $k = k'$. The DES in EDE mode is not vulnerable to the attack outlined earlier. However, it is vulnerable to a chosen plaintext and a known plaintext attack. If b is the block size in bits, and n is the key length, the chosen plaintext attack takes $\mathcal{O}(2^n)$ space, and requires 2^n chosen plaintexts [1325]. The known plaintext attack requires p known plaintexts, and takes $\mathcal{O}(2^{n+b}/p)$ time and $\mathcal{O}(p)$ memory [1923]. Two-key Triple DES was widely used in the financial community, but it is no longer approved for use in the U.S. government [126].

Another way is to use three independent keys, so the third key is different than the first key. This version is called *three-key Triple DES*. Breaking this using a chosen plaintext attack using p plaintexts requires $\mathcal{O}(2^{n+1}p + 2^{n+b+1}/p)$ time and $\mathcal{O}(2^n/p)$ memory [1215]. This also holds if the middle decryption is turned into an encryption.

12.3   Authenticated Encryption

Authenticated encryption [776, 777, 1602] transforms a message in such a way that confidentiality, integrity, and authentication are simultaneously provided. A variant, authenticated encryption with associated data (AEAD), also provides integrity and authentication for an unencrypted portion of the message. This is useful when the message has a header that must be cleartext because it contains information necessary to forward or decrypt the encrypted part of the message, and validate the entire message. Two examples of this type of encryption are Counter with CBC-MAC (CCM) mode and Galois Counter Mode (GCM). In both cases, the message consists of two parts: the part to be encrypted and authenticated (called the *message*) and the part to be authenticated but not encrypted (called the *associated data*). Either may be omitted, in which case they are treated as having length 0.

12.3.1   Counter with CBC-MAC Mode

Counter with CBC-MAC Mode (CCM) [2001] is an example of AEAD defined for block ciphers with block size 128 bits such as the AES. Each block is made up of 16 octets (sets of 8 bits).

It has two parameters. l_A is the size of the authentication field, and may be any of 4, 6, 8, 10, 12, 14, or 16 octets. l_M is the size of the message length, and may take up between 2 and 8 octets inclusive. In addition, it requires a nonce of $15 - l_M$ octets.

Let k be the key, n a nonce, M the message, and A the additional data that is to be authenticated but not encrypted. The mode proceeds in three phases.

Phase 1 is the computation of the authentication field T. The procedure prepends a set of blocks B_i to the message. The first block, B_0, contains information about the cipher.

- Octet 0 contains flags. Bits 0 through 2 contain $l_M - 1$; bits 3 through 5 contain $\frac{l_A - 2}{2}$; bit 6 contains 1 if there is associated data and 0 if not; and bit 7 is reserved, and always 0.
- Octets $1 \ldots 15 - l_M$ contain the nonce n.
- Octets $16 - l_M \ldots 15$ contain the length of the message in octets.

When there is associated data, the next octets contain information about its length l_A. The number of octets needed depends on l_A as follows. The value of l_A is stored with the most significant byte first.

- If $0 < l_A < 2^{16} - 2^8$, the first two octets contain l_A.
- If $2^{16} - 2^8 \leq l_A < 2^{32}$, the first octet is 0xff, the second is 0xfe, and the next four octets contain l_A.
- If $2^{32} \leq l_A < 2^{64}$, the first and second octets are both 0xff, and the other six octets contain l_A

Block B_0 and these octets are prepended to the associated data A, and the result is split into 16-octet blocks, padding the last block with zeros if needed. Then the message is split into blocks, with padding of zeros added to the last block if needed, and the result appended to the previous part. This results in a sequence of blocks $B_0, \ldots, B_m$.

The CBC-MAC is computed from these blocks:

$$x_1 = E_k(B_0)$$
$$x_{i+1} = E_k(x_i \oplus B_i) \text{ for } i = 1, \ldots, m$$

The MAC T is then the first l_A bytes of x_{m+1}.

Phase 2 is encryption. The message is encrypted using counter mode. Let b_0 be a block with the following content:

- Octet 0 contains flags. Bits 0 through 2 contain $l_M - 1$ and all other bits are 0.
- Octets $1 \ldots 15 - l_M$ contain the nonce n.
- Octets $16 - l_M \ldots 15$ contain the ith counter's value.

Then the key blocks S_i are computed by

$$S_i = E_k(A_i)$$

Let the message M be composed of z blocks $M_1 \ldots M_z$. To encrypt the message, compute

$$C_i = M_i \oplus S_i \text{ for } i = 1, \ldots, z$$

Note that S_0 is not used to encrypt the message. Instead, let s_A be the first l_A bytes of S_0. The authentication value U is then computed as:

$$U = T \oplus s_A$$

In phase 3, the sender constructs $C = C_1 \ldots C_z$, and then sends $C \parallel U$. Decryption and validation is carried out by reversing the process.

An important requirement of the use of CCM is what to do should validation fail. In that case, the recipient must reveal only that the computed T is incorrect, and not anything more. In particular the recipient must not reveal the incorrect value of T or any part of the decrypted message.

Jonsson has shown that the security and privacy CCM provides are similar to that of other modes [974]; Fouque et al. have extended those results [711]. Bellare, Rogaway, and Wagner point out several limitations of CCM mode [160], among them CCM needing the length of both the message and the associated data before it can encrypt, and that the nonce length may not provide adequate security when nonces are chosen randomly. They propose an alternate mode, EAX, that solves these problems [160].

12.3.2   Galois Counter Mode

The Galois Counter Mode (GCM) [604, 1264, 1289, 1934] is a widely used method of AEAD that can be implemented efficiently in hardware, enabling its use when encrypted data is to be exchanged at high speeds. Further, if an encrypted authenticated message is changed, a new authentication value can be computed with cost proportional to the number of changed bits. It also allows the use of an initialization vector (called a "nonce") of any length.

To provide authenticated encryption, GCM has four parameters. A secret key k is used by the underlying block cipher. A nonce IV may be up to 2^{64} bits long; for efficiency reasons, 96 bits are recommended. The plaintext message M may be up to $2^{39} - 256$ bits long; the ciphertext C will have the same number of bits. The associated data A may be up to 2^{64} bits long. The authentication value is T, and it is t bits long.

In what follows, the message M is composed of 128-bit blocks $M_0 \ldots M_n$, where M_n may not be a complete block; call its length in bits u (that is, $0 < u \leq 128$). The ciphertext C is similarly composed of 128-bit blocks $C_0 \ldots C_n$, and the number of bits matches the number of bits in M. Similarly, the associated data A is composed of 128-bit blocks $A_0 \ldots A_m$, where A_m may not be a complete block; call its length in bits v (that is, $0 < v \leq 128$).

For this mode, multiplication (written $X \cdot Y$) is performed in the field $GF(2^{128})$. Figure 12–5 shows the algorithm.

First, we show the hash function $GHASH(H, A, C)$. It is computed iteratively, as shown below, and X_{m+n+1} is its value.

1. $X_0 = 0$.
2. For $i = 1, \ldots, m - 1$, $X_i = (X_{i-1} \oplus A_i) \cdot H$.
3. $X_m = (X_{m-1} \oplus A_m) \cdot H$, where A_m is right-padded with zeros to make it a block.
4. For $i = m + 1, \ldots, m + n - 1$, $X_i = (X_{i-1} \oplus C_i) \cdot H$.

```
/* multiply X and X to produce Z in GF(2^128) */
function GFmultiply(X, Y: integer)
begin
        Z := 0
        V := X;
        for i := 0 to 127 do begin
                if Y_i = 1 then Z := Z ⊕ V;
                V := rightshift(V, 1);
                if V_127 = 1 then V := V ⊕ R;
        end
        return Z;
end
```

Figure 12–5 Multiplication in the field $GF(2^{128})$. Here, Y_i is the *i*th *leftmost* bit, and V_{127} is the leftmost bit of *V*. All of X, Y, and Z are 128-bit numbers. The distinguished value *R* is 11100001 followed by 120 zero bits, and *rightshift(X, n)* shifts the bits making up *X* n bits to the right, bringing in 0 bits from the left. Adapted from [1289].

5. $X_{m+n} = (X_{m+n-1} \oplus C_n) \cdot H$, where C_n is right-padded with zeros to make it a block.

6. $X_{m+n+1} = (X_{m+n} \oplus (l_A || l_C)) \cdot H$, where l_A and l_C are the lengths of the associated data and ciphertext in bits, respectively, *left*-padded with zeros to form 64 bits each.

To perform the authenticated encryption, the following steps are performed in the order indicated:

1. $H = E_k(0^{128})$, where 0^{128} is the block with all bits 0.

2. If the length of the *IV* is 96, set $Y_0 = IV || 0^{31}1$, where $0^{31}1$ is 31 0 bits followed by a 1 bit. Otherwise, set $Y_0 = GHASH(H, v, IV)$, where v is empty (length 0 bits).

3. For $i = 1, \ldots, n$, divide Y_{i-1} into two parts, a right part I_{i-1} and a left part L_{i-1}. I_{i-1} is the rightmost 32 bits, and it is treated as an unsigned 32-bit integer. Compute $I_i = I_{i-1} + 1 \bmod 2^{32}$, and set $Y_i = L_{i-1} || I_i$.

4. For $i = 1, \ldots, n-1$, $C_i = M_i \oplus E_k(Y_i)$.

5. Let $MSB_u(X)$ be the u most significant bits (leftmost bits) of X. Then $C_n = M_n \oplus MSB_u(E_k(Y_n))$.

6. The authentication value $T = MSB_t(GHASH(H, A, C) \oplus E_k(Y_0))$. This is sometimes called the *GMAC*.

The tag and ciphertext are then sent.

To verify the message, the receiver performs the same operations as encryption, but in the order 1, 2, 6, 3, 4, and 5. When the authentication value is computed (step 6 in the encryption, 3 here), it is then compared to the one that was sent. If they match, the ciphertext is then decrypted; otherwise, the system returns a failure and the ciphertext is discarded.

The security of GCM depends on certain properties. If the nonce is reused, part of H can be obtained [980]. If the length of the authentication value is too short, forgeries can occur and from that, H can be determined [666], enabling undetectable forgeries. A number of researchers have studied whether particular values of H (called "weak keys") make forging messages easier than when nonweak values of H are used [861, 1546, 1631, 2047].

Both GCM encryption and authentication have been proven to be secure [952, 1290]. An ancillary result is that restricting the length of the nonce to 96 bits produces a stronger AEAD cipher than when the length of the nonce is unrestricted.

12.4   Networks and Cryptography

Before we discuss Internet protocols, a review of the relevant properties of networks is in order. The ISO/OSI model [1859] provides an abstract representation of networks suitable for our purposes. Recall that the ISO/OSI model is composed of a series of layers (see Figure 12–6). Each host, conceptually, has a principal at each layer that communicates with a peer on other hosts. These principals communicate with principals at the same layer on other hosts. Layer 1, 2, and 3 principals interact only with similar principals at neighboring (directly connected) hosts. Principals at layers 4, 5, 6, and 7 interact only with similar principals at the other end of the communication. (For convenience, "host" refers to the appropriate principal in the following discussion.)

Each host in the network is connected to some set of other hosts. They exchange messages with those hosts. If host *nob* wants to send a message to host *windsor*, *nob* determines which of its immediate neighbors is closest to *windsor* (using an appropriate routing protocol) and forwards the message to it. That host, *baton*, determines which of its neighbors is closest to *windsor* and forwards the message to it. This process continues until a host, *sunapee*, receives the message and determines that *windsor* is an immediate neighbor. The message is forwarded to *windsor*, its endpoint.

> **Definition 12–5.** Let hosts $C_0, \ldots, C_n$ be such that C_i and C_{i+1} are directly connected, for $0 \leq i < n$. A communications protocol that has C_0 and C_n as its endpoints is called an *end-to-end protocol*. A communications protocol that has C_j and C_{j+1} as its endpoints is called a *link protocol*.

The difference between an end-to-end protocol and a link protocol is that the intermediate hosts play no part in an end-to-end protocol other than

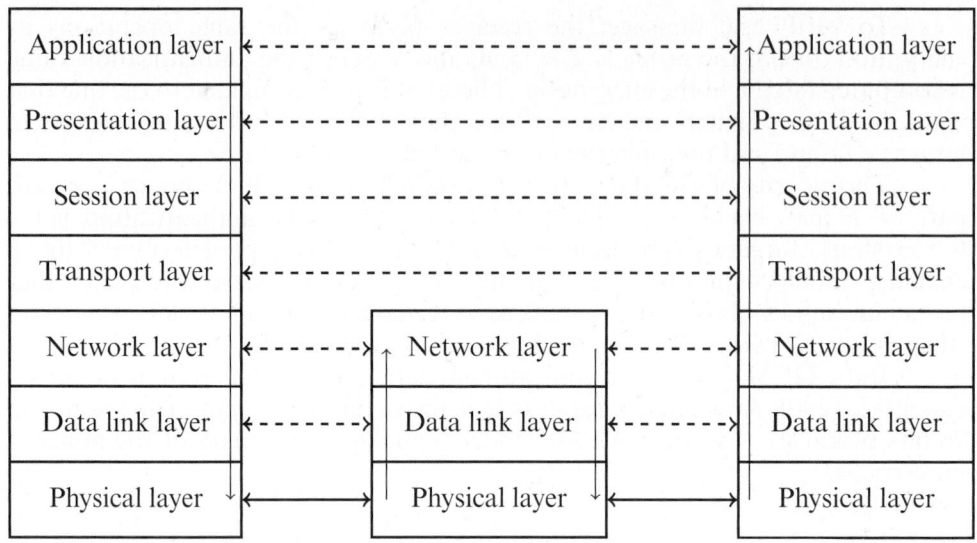

Figure 12–6 The ISO/OSI model. The dashed arrows indicate peer-to-peer communication. For example, the transport layers are communicating with each other. The solid arrows indicate the actual flow of bits. For example, the transport layer invokes network layer routines on the local host, which invoke data link layer routines, which put the bits onto the network. The physical layer passes the bits to the next "hop," or host, on the path. When the message reaches the destination, it is passed up to the appropriate level.

forwarding messages. On the other hand, a link protocol describes how each pair of intermediate hosts processes each message.

EXAMPLE: The *ssh* protocol [2058, 2059] is an applications layer protocol that allows users to obtain a virtual terminal on a remote host. Thus, it is an end-to-end protocol. IP is a network layer protocol that guides messages from a host to one of its immediate neighbors. Thus, it is a link protocol.

The protocols involved can be cryptographic protocols. If the cryptographic processing is done only at the source and at the destination, the protocol is an end-to-end protocol. If cryptographic processing occurs at each host along the path from source to destination, the protocol is a link protocol. When encryption is used with either protocol, we use the terms *end-to-end encryption* and *link encryption*, respectively.

EXAMPLE: The messages between the *ssh* client and server are enciphered at the client and the server only [2059]. The protocol uses end-to-end encryption. The PPP Encryption Control Protocol [1328] enciphers messages between intermediate hosts. When a host gets the message, it deciphers the message, determines which neighbor to send it to, reenciphers the message using the key appropriate for that neighbor, and sends it to that neighbor. This protocol uses link encryption.

In link encryption, each host shares a cryptographic key with its neighbor. (If public key cryptography is used, each host has its neighbor's public key. Link encryption based on public keys is rare.) The keys may be set on a per-host basis or a per-host-pair basis. Consider a network with four hosts called *windsor*, *stripe*, *facer*, and *seaview*. Each host is directly connected to the other three. With keys distributed on a per-host basis, each host has its own key, making four keys in all. Each host has the keys for the other three neighbors, as well as its own. All hosts use the same key to communicate with *windsor*. With keys distributed on a per-host-pair basis, each host has one key per possible connection, making six keys in all. Unlike the per-host situation, in the per-host-pair case, each host uses a different key to communicate with *windsor*. The message is deciphered at each intermediate host, reenciphered for the next hop, and forwarded. Attackers monitoring the network medium will not be able to read the messages, but attackers at the intermediate hosts will be able to do so.

In end-to-end encryption, each host shares a cryptographic key with each destination. (Again, if the encryption is based on public key cryptography, each host has—or can obtain—the public key of each destination.) As with link encryption, the keys may be selected on a per-host or per-host-pair basis. The sending host enciphers the message and forwards it to the first intermediate host. The intermediate host forwards it to the next host, and the process continues until the message reaches its destination. The destination host then deciphers it. The message is enciphered throughout its journey. Neither attackers monitoring the network nor attackers on the intermediate hosts can read the message. However, attackers can read the routing information used to forward the message.

These differences affect a form of cryptanalysis known as *traffic analysis*. A cryptanalyst can sometimes deduce information not from the content of the message but from the sender and recipient. For example, during the Allied invasion of Normandy in World War II, the Germans deduced which vessels were the command ships by observing which ships were sending and receiving the most signals. The content of the signals was not relevant; their source and destination were. Similar deductions can reveal information in the electronic world.

EXAMPLE: ARS&C is an engineering firm developing the next generation of network protocols. Each employee of ARS&C has his or her own workstation. All network traffic is enciphered using end-to-end encryption. A competitor of the company appears to be obtaining proprietary data. ARS&C has hired Alice to figure out who is leaking the information.

Alice begins by monitoring all network traffic. She notices that the workstations are grouped into three different divisions: corporate management, sales, and engineering. The leaks are coming from the engineering systems. She looks at the sources and destinations of all connections to and from the engineering systems and notices that the connections from corporate management center on three systems: *curly*, *larry*, and *moe*. The connections from *larry* always occur between midnight and four in the morning; those from the other two occur during the day. Alice then looks at the events of the days on which the connections take place. The connections from *curly* and *moe* occur on the days of management reviews and are invariably to the *ftp* or *www* port. The connections from *larry* are more infrequent and are to the *ssh* port. A few days after each connection from *larry*, the competitor seems to have acquired new proprietary information.

From this analysis, Alice suggests that the host *larry* is somehow involved in the problem. She needs to check the systems that *larry* connects to and see if the proprietary data is on those systems. At no time has Alice read any of the traffic, because it is encrypted; but from the traffic analysis, she has determined the system involved in the compromise.

12.5   Example Protocols

Several Internet protocols illustrate different facets of cryptographic techniques. This section examines three such protocols, each at a different layer. PEM is a privacy-enhanced electronic mail protocol at the applications layer and demonstrates the considerations needed when designing such a protocol. Its techniques are similar to those of PGP, a widely used security-enhanced electronic mail protocol. The instant messaging protocol Signal provides security for real-time communications. TLS provides transport layer security. Application layer protocols such as HTTP can use TLS to ensure secure connections. IPsec provides security mechanisms at the network, or IP, layer.

12.5.1   Secure Electronic Mail: PEM and OpenPGP

Electronic mail is a widely used mechanism for communication over the Internet. It is also a good example of how practical considerations affect the design of security-related protocols. We begin by describing the state of electronic mail and then show how security services can be added.

Figure 12–7 shows a typical network mail service. The *user agent* (UA) interacts directly with the sender. When the message is composed, the UA hands it to the *message transport*, or *transfer*, *agent* (MTA). The MTA transfers the message to its destination host, or to another MTA, which in turn transfers the message further. At the destination host, the MTA invokes a user agent to deliver the message.

An attacker can read electronic mail at any of the computers on which MTAs handling the message reside, as well as on the network itself. An attacker

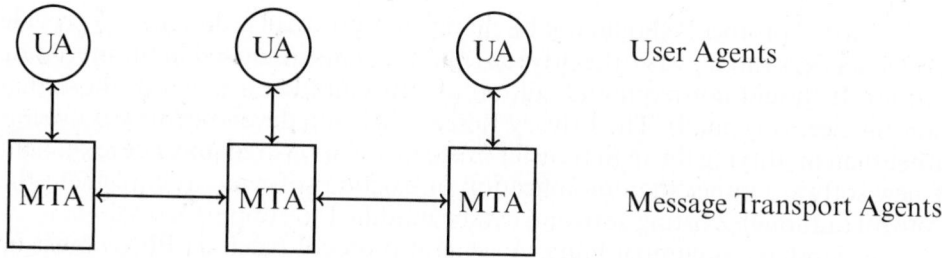

Figure 12–7   Message handling system. The user composes mail on the UA (user agent). When she sends it, the message is passed to the MTA (message transport, or transfer, agent). The MTA passes the message to other MTAs, until it reaches the MTA associated with the destination host. That host transfers it to the appropriate UA for delivery.

could also modify the message without the recipient detecting the change. Because authentication mechanisms are minimal and easily evaded, a sender could forge a letter from another and inject it into the message handling system at any MTA, from which it would be forwarded to the destination. Finally, a sender could deny having sent a letter, and the recipient could not prove otherwise to a disinterested party. These four types of attacks (violation of confidentiality, authentication, message integrity, and nonrepudiation) make electronic mail nonsecure.

In 1985, the Internet Research Task Force on Privacy (also called the Privacy Research Group) began studying the problem of enhancing the privacy of electronic mail. The goal of this study was to develop electronic mail protocols that would provide the following services:

1. Confidentiality, by making the message unreadable except to the sender and recipient(s)
2. Origin authentication, by identifying the sender precisely
3. Data integrity, by ensuring that any changes in the message are easy to detect
4. Nonrepudiation of origin (if possible)

The protocols were christened Privacy-enhanced Electronic Mail (or PEM).

A second protocol, called Pretty Good Privacy (PGP), provides similar features. Because the design of PEM is well-documented and illustrates many of the considerations that influenced PGP, we begin with PEM and then discuss a widely used version of PGP, called OpenPGP.

12.5.1.1   Design Principles

Creating a viable protocol requires the developers to consider several design aspects. Otherwise, acceptance and use of the protocol will be very limited.

Related protocols should not be changed. A protocol is designed to provide specific services (in this case, the privacy enhancements discussed in the preceding section). It should not require alteration of other protocols (such as those that transmit electronic mail). The Privacy Research Group developed new protocols rather than modifying the mail transfer protocols. This also requires development of new software rather than modification of existing software to implement the protocol (although existing software can be modified to support it).

A corollary is compatibility. A general protocol (such as PEM) must be compatible with as many other protocols and programs as possible. The protocols must work with a wide range of software, including software in all environments that connect to the Internet.

Another important principle is independence. The privacy enhancements should be available if desired but should not be mandatory. If a new protocol provides specific services, the user should be able to use the services desired, which may (or may not) be all the ones that the protocol provides. For example, a sender might care about sender authentication but not confidentiality. This also enables some users to send privacy-enhanced electronic mail, and others to send unprotected electronic mail, on the same system. Recipients can also read either type of mail.

Finally, two parties should be able to use the protocol to communicate without prearrangement. Arranging a communications key out of band (such as in person or over the telephone) can be time-consuming and prone to error. Furthermore, callers must authenticate themselves to the recipients. This is difficult and is another error-prone operation.

To summarize, the design goals of PEM were:

1. Not to redesign existing mail system or protocols
2. To be compatible with a range of MTAs, UAs, and other computers
3. To make privacy enhancements available separately, so they are not required
4. To enable two parties to use the protocol to communicate without prearrangement

12.5.1.2   Basic Design

PEM defines two types of keys. The message to be sent is enciphered with a *data encipherment key* (DEK), corresponding to a session key. This key is generated randomly and is used only once. It must be sent to the recipient, so it is enciphered with an *interchange key*. The interchange keys of the sender and recipient must be obtained in some way other than through the message.

This requires several assumptions. First, the interchange key must be available to the respective parties. If symmetric ciphers are used, the keys must be exchanged out of band—for example, by telephone or courier. If public keys are used, the sender needs to obtain the certificate of the recipient.

If Alice wants to send a confidential message to Bob, she obtains Bob's interchange key k_{Bob}. She generates a random DEK $k_{session}$ and enciphers the message m. She then enciphers the DEK using the interchange key. She sends both to Bob:

$$\text{Alice} \rightarrow \text{Bob} : \{m\}k_{session}\{k_{session}\}k_{Bob}$$

Bob can then decipher the session key and from it obtain the message.

If Alice wants to send an authenticated, integrity-checked message to Bob, she first computes a cryptographic hash $h(m)$ of the message, possibly using a random session key (if the hash function requires one). The value that the hash function computes is called a *message integrity check* (MIC). She then enciphers the MIC (and the session key, if one was used) with her interchange key k_{Alice} and sends it to Bob:

$$\text{Alice} \rightarrow \text{Bob} : m\{h(m)\}k_{Alice}$$

Bob uses Alice's interchange key to decipher the MIC, recomputes it from m, and compares the two. If they do not match, either the message or the value of the hash has been changed. In either case, the message cannot be trusted.

To send an enciphered, authenticated, integrity-checked message, combine the operations discussed above, as follows:

$$\text{Alice} \rightarrow \text{Bob} : \{m\}k_{session}\{h(m)\}k_{Alice}\{k_{session}\}k_{Bob}$$

The nonrepudiation service comes from the use of public key cryptography. If Alice's interchange key is her private key, a third party can verify that she signed the message by deciphering it with her public key. Alice cannot refute that her private key was used to sign the message. (She can dispute that she signed it by claiming her private key was compromised. Preventing this is beyond the scope of the cryptographic protocols. In this context, "nonrepudiation" refers only to the inability to deny that the private key was used to sign the message.)

12.5.1.3   Other Considerations

When the interchange keys are for public key cryptosystems, PEM suggests the use of a certificate-based key management scheme (see Section 15.5, "Naming and Certificates"). However, it is not a requirement.

When PEM was designed, a major problem was the specification of Internet electronic mail [477, 1538]. Among the restrictions placed on it, the requirements that the letter contain only ASCII characters and that the lines be of limited length were the most onerous. Related to this is the difference among character sets. A letter typed on an ASCII-based system would be unreadable on a non-ASCII-based system.

A three-step encoding procedure overcame these problems.

1. The local representations of the characters making up the letter were changed into a canonical format. This format satisfied the requirements of RFC 822-compliant mailers (specifically, all characters were seven-bit ASCII characters, lines were less than 1,000 characters long, and lines ended with a carriage return followed by a newline[1] [477]).

2. The message integrity check was computed and enciphered with the sender's interchange key. If confidentiality were required, the message would be enciphered as described above.

3. The message was treated as a stream of bits. Every set of six bits was mapped into a character, and after every 64 characters,[2] a newline was inserted.

The resulting ASCII message had PEM headers (indicating algorithms and key) prepended. PEM headers and body were surrounded by lines indicating the start and end of the PEM message.

If the recipient had PEM-compliant software, she could read the message. Otherwise, she could not. If the message were authenticated and integrity-checked (but not encrypted), she should be able to read the message even if she did not have PEM-compliant software (remember that one of the design goals was compatibility with existing mail programs). The special mode MIC-CLEAR handled this case. In this mode, the message check was computed and added, but the message was not transformed into the representation of step 3. On receipt, the authentication and message integrity check might have failed because some MTAs added blank lines, changed the end-of-line character, or deleted terminating white space from lines. Although this did not alter the meaning of the message, it did change the content. Hence, PEM-compliant software would report that the message had been altered in transit. But people could use normal mail reading programs to read the letter. (Whether they should trust it was another matter. Given that the PEM software had reported changes, the recipients should have at least verified the contents in some way before trusting the letter.)

12.5.1.4   OpenPGP and PEM

Philip Zimmermann developed PGP independently of the development of PEM. A variant of PGP, called OpenPGP [340], was subsequently developed as a proposed Internet standard.

The structure of a PGP message is a sequence of packets of message characteristics, such as keying material and signatures, and the message itself. The

---

[1]The dot stuffing convention (so that a line containing a single "." was not seen as a message terminator) was not used (see Section 4.3.2.2 of RFC 1421 [1189]).

[2]The character set is drawn from parts of the international alphabet IA5 common to most other alphabets.

message is stored in a literal data packet, and the first byte indicates whether the data is binary or text. That is followed by the file name, a date, and then the message itself. An end of line in a text message is stored as a carriage return followed by a newline; these are translated to the local form when the message is processed.

For reasons stated earlier, the user may request that messages be "armored" or sent as ASCII text; this is common when the message contains binary data. The data is translated into a canonical form, and appropriate OpenPGP headers (such as a version line) are prepended. A checksum (represented in the canonical form) and a trailing line are added.

The supported ciphers are also different, as Table 12–1 shows. There are two reasons. Initially, the developers of PGP wanted an alternative to the DES cipher, so they included IDEA. Later, PGP became very widely used, and the OpenPGP standard was developed. It continues to evolve. PEM, however, was not widely used, and hence it has not been updated since 1993. Thus, it lacks many of the later ciphers that OpenPGP includes.

Finally, PGP uses a different, nonhierarchical certificate management scheme described in Sections 11.4.2.2 and 15.5.

12.5.1.5 Summary

PEM demonstrates how system factors influence the use of cryptographic protocols. While central to the design and implementation of PEM systems, the cryptographic protocols require a supporting infrastructure. The need for compatibility guides many design choices for this infrastructure. The environment of development also affects the infrastructure.

12.5.2 Instant Messaging

Instant messaging has begun to supplant some uses of electronic mail because it is designed to enable two or more parties to engage in a real-time dialogue. Thus, for these applications, security and authentication are as important as they are for email.

Table 12–1 **Comparison of ciphers used by PEM and OpenPGP. Both are extensible, so other ciphers can be added.**

Cryptosystem	OpenPGP	PEM
Interchange	RSA, El-Gamal	RSA, DES-ECB
Data encryption	IDEA, DES-EDE, CAST5, Blowfish, Twofish, AES-123, AES-192, AES-256	DES-CBC
Hash	MD5, SHA-1, RIPE-MD/160, SHA256, SHA384, SHA512, SHA224	MD2, MD5

The *Signal Protocol* [441, 1254, 1516, 2252] is designed to provide these services. It also provides perfect forward secrecy, so the compromise of a key will not enable an adversary to read previously sent messages.

The protocol has three steps. First, the clients register with the messaging server. The registration involves cryptographic keys and a representation of identity. The second step occurs when two clients wish to communicate; they must set up a session. Once the session is established, they exchange messages.

The cryptographic protocol uses several different keys. Several public keys are associated with each client.

- A long-term *identity key pair IK* generated when the client program is installed. This is a Curve25519 key [180] (see page 315).
- A medium-term *signed pre-key pair SPK* generated when the client program is installed, and that is changed periodically. It too is a Curve25519 pair.
- An ephemeral *one-time pre-key pair OPK* that is obtained from a list of Curve25519 key pairs. These are generated when the client is installed; when they run out, new ones are generated.

Whenever a public key is sent, it is encoded into a byte sequence. We omit an explicit representation of this to simplify the exposition.

Associated with each session are:

- The *message key*, an 80-byte key used to encrypt messages. It consists of three parts: a 32-byte key for AES-256 encryption, a 32-byte value for the HMAC-SHA256 cryptographic checksum, and 16 bytes for an initialization vector.
- The *chain key* is a 32-byte value that is used to generate the message keys.
- The *root key* is another 32-byte value used to generate the chain keys.

Several cryptographic functions and hashes are also used. As noted previously, public keys are Diffie-Hellman keys obtained using the elliptic curve Curve25519; this cipher is represented here as ECDH. Symmetric keys are produced using two methods. The first is an application of HMAC_SHA256. The second uses an HMAC-based key derivation function (HKDF) [1103]. This has two stages. The first stage takes keying material s (a nonsecret salt; if omitted, this is treated as all 0 bits) and x (other material) and produces a fixed-length pseudorandom key k:

$$k = \text{HMAC\_SHA256}(s, x)$$

Along with other information, this pseudorandom key is then given to a second stage that expands the key to the desired length:

$$\text{HDKF\_Extend, L}(k, info) = T(1) \parallel T(2) \parallel \ldots$$

where *info* is a string of characters such as "WhisperGroup," L is the number of octets to output, and

$$T(i) = \begin{cases} empty\ string & \text{if } i = 0 \\ \text{HMAC\_SHA256}(k, T(i-1) \parallel info \parallel i) & \text{if } i > 0 \end{cases}$$

The result, $\text{HKDF}(s, x)$, is the first L octets of the output of HDKF_Extend.

We now describe each of the steps. In what follows, Alice wishes to communicate with Bob. The messaging server is W. Public keys have the superscript *pub*, and private keys the superscript *priv*.

12.5.2.1 Registration Step

Alice generates her identity key pair $(IK_{Alice}^{pub}, IK_{Alice}^{priv})$; her pre-key pair $(SPK_{Alice}^{pub}, SPK_{Alice}^{priv})$; and a set of one-time pre-key pairs $(OPK_{Alice,1}^{pub}, OPK_{Alice,1}^{priv})$, $(OPK_{Alice,2}^{pub}, OPK_{Alice,2}^{priv}), \ldots$. She signs her public pre-key $SSPK_{Alice} = sign(IK_{Alice}^{priv}, SPK_{Alice}^{pub})$. Then she sends her identity public key, her pre-key public key, her signed pre-key, and her set of one-time pre-key public keys to the server:

R1. Alice $\rightarrow W$: $IK_{Alice}^{pub}, SPK_{Alice}^{pub}, SSPK_{Alice}, OPK_{Alice,1}^{pub}, OPK_{Alice,2}^{pub}, \cdots$

This is called the *pre-key bundle*. This completes Alice's registration. Bob registers with the server similarly.

12.5.2.2 Session Setup and Initial Message

Alice now wants to establish a session with Bob. She first requests Bob's key bundle from the server. The server sends it. If Bob's set of one-time pre-keys are all used, no such pre-keys are included:

S1. Alice $\rightarrow W$: *message requesting Bob's pre-key bundle*

S2. $W \rightarrow$ Alice $IK_{Bob}^{pub}, SPK_{Bob}^{pub}, SSPK_{Bob}, OPK_{Bob,i}^{pub}$

Alice verifies $SSPK_{Bob}$ is in fact the signature for SPK_{Bob}^{pub}. If the verification fails, the setup stops. If the verification succeeds, Alice generates another ephemeral Curve25519 key pair $(EK_{Alice}^{pub}, EK_{Alice}^{priv})$. She then computes a master secret:

$$master\_secret = \text{ECDH}(IK_{Alice}^{priv}), SPK_{Bob}^{pub}) \parallel \text{ECDH}(EK_{Alice}^{priv}, IK_{Bob}^{pub}) \parallel$$
$$\text{ECDH}(EK_{Alice}^{priv}, SPK_{Bob}^{pub}) \parallel \text{ECDH}(EK_{Alice}^{priv}, OPK_{Bob,i}^{pub})$$

If no one-time pre-key is sent, the last encryption is omitted. Alice then deletes EK_{Alice}^{priv} and the intermediate values used to compute the *master_secret*. She uses the master secret to compute the root and chain keys. Let 0^{256} be 256 bits of all 0s and F be 256 bits of all 1s. Then Alice computes $HKDF(0^{256}, F||master\_secret)$. The first 32 bytes are the root key k_r, and the next 32 bytes are the first chain key k_c.

Finally, Alice creates associated data consisting of $A = IK_{Alice}^{pub} \parallel IK_{Bob}^{pub}$; she may append additional information if desired.

12.5.2.3 Sending Messages

Alice now completes the session setup by sending her first message to Bob. Alice creates a message key k_m derived from the chain key k_c:

$$k_m = HMAC\_SHA256(k_c, 1)$$

She uses this as the key to an AEAD encryption scheme that encrypts the message using the AEC-256 algorithm in CBC mode and authenticates the message and associated data using the HMAC-SHA256 algorithm.

Alice then sends Bob a message containing IK_{Alice}^{pub}, a new ephemeral Curve25519 public key EK_{Alice}^{pub}, an indicator of which of Bob's one-time pre-keys was used, and the results of the AEAD encryption.

When Bob receives the message, he calculates the master secret using his own private keys and the public keys Alice has sent. He deletes the $(OPK_{Bob,i}^{pub}, OPK_{Bob,i}^{priv})$ pair and then computes the root and chain keys. Note he can be offline when Alice's message arrives because the information to decipher and validate the message is contained in the header.

At this point, Alice and Bob begin to exchange messages. When Alice sends messages before she receives Bob's reply to any of them, she uses a *Hash Ratchet* to change the message key for each message. Call the message key used to encipher the last message sent $k_{m,i}$, and the chain key that was used to create it $k_{c,i}$. Then the next message is enciphered using the message key $k_{m,i+1} = HMAC\_SHA256(k_{c,i}, 1)$, and the chain key is advanced as $k_{c,i+1} = HMAC\_SHA256(k_{c,i}, 2)$.

Once Alice receives a reply from Bob, she enters the second phase of the double ratchet. In this phase, she computes a new chain key and root key using her current root key k_r, her ephemeral key EK_{Alice}^{priv}, and the ephemeral key in the header of the received message EK_{Bob}^{pub}:

$$HKDF(k_r, ECDH(EK_{Bob}^{pub}, EK_{Alice}^{priv}))$$

The first 32 octets form the new chain key, and the next 32 octets the new root key.

12.5.2.4   Summary

Key management for instant messaging protocols is more complex than that for electronic mail because of the nature of the application. Much of the derivation and manipulation of keys is to provide perfect forward secrecy, to ensure that previously transmitted messages remain secret. As a result, the Signal Protocol provides many security services that protect the secrecy and privacy of messages. That protocol is widely used in these services, including Signal and WhatsApp.

12.5.3   Security at the Transport Layer: TLS and SSL

The Transport Layer Security (TLS) protocol [563] is a standard designed to provide privacy, data integrity, and (if desired) authentication in WWW browsers and servers. It is similar to an older protocol, version 3 of the Secure Socket Layer (SSL) [724], developed by Netscape Corporation for the same purpose. Because the use of SSL is deprecated, we will focus on version 1.2 of TLS, and point out the differences between it and SSL.

TLS works in terms of *connections* and *sessions* between clients and servers.

Definition 12–6. A *TLS session* is an association between two peers. A *TLS connection* is the set of mechanisms used to transport data in a TLS session.

A single session may have many connections. Two peers may have many sessions active at the same time, but this is not common.

Each party keeps information related to a session with each peer. The data associated with a session includes the following information:

- A session identifier that uniquely identifies the session
- The peer's X.509v3 certificate (which is empty if no such certificate is needed)
- A compression method used to reduce the volume of data
- A cipher specification that includes all the relevant parameters for generating the keys, for the cipher, and for the message authentication code (MAC)[3]
- A "master secret" of 48 bits shared with the peer
- A flag indicating whether this session can be used to start new connections

A connection describes how data is sent to, and received from, the peer. Each party keeps information related to a connection. Each peer has its own

---

[3]This is another term for a message integrity check (MIC); we use the TLS protocol specification term here for consistency.

parameters. The key with which the client enciphers data is (probably) not the same as the key with which the server enciphers data. The information associated with the connection includes the following:

- Whether this is a server or a client
- Random data for the server and client
- The server and client write keys, which each uses to encipher data
- The server and client write MAC keys, which each uses to compute a MAC
- The initialization vectors for the ciphers, if needed
- The server and client sequence numbers

TLS consists of two layers supported by numerous cryptographic mechanisms. We begin by describing the mechanisms, then the lower layer, and finally the upper layer.

12.5.3.1   Supporting Cryptographic Mechanisms

During the setup negotiations, the peers determine a cryptographic mechanism for providing confidentiality and message and origin integrity. Interchange keys are used to establish a session key. Because all parts of TLS use cryptographic mechanisms, we discuss them first.

The initial phase of session setup uses a public key cryptosystem to exchange keys. The messages are enciphered using a classical cipher and are checksummed using a cryptographic checksum. Initially, the handshake protocol assumes no interchange cipher, no classical cipher, and no checksum. The handshake protocol then negotiates the selection of these mechanisms.

TLS uses three basic interchange ciphers. If the interchange cipher is RSA, the server must provide an RSA certificate for key exchange. The server may request that the client provide either an RSA or DSS certificate for signatures.

Three types of Diffie-Hellman ciphers serve as interchange ciphers. "Diffie-Hellman" denotes a cipher system in which the certificate contains the cipher parameters and is signed by an appropriate certification authority. "Ephemeral Diffie-Hellman" refers to a cipher system in which a DSS or RSA certificate is used to sign the parameters to the Diffie-Hellman cipher. This implies that the parameters will not be used again (or else they would have been in a certificate) and so are "ephemeral." "Anonymous Diffie-Hellman" refers to use of Diffie-Hellman without either party being authenticated. This cipher is vulnerable to attacks, and its use is "strongly discouraged" according to the TLS specification.

Elliptic curve versions of Diffie-Hellman ciphers also serve as interchange ciphers in TLS. However, the anonymous version is not supported.

TLS derives its master secret, keys, and initialization vectors using a pseudorandom function *PRF* that generates as many bits as needed for those quantities. Let *hash* be a hash function and *seed* be a public and random quantity. Define

$$A(i) = \begin{cases} seed & i = 0 \\ \text{HMAC\_}hash(secret, A(i-1)) & i > 0 \end{cases}$$

The hash expansion function P_*hash* generates any desired number of bits from a given hash function *hash* and a parameter *x*:

$$\begin{aligned} \text{P\_}hash(x, seed) = \ & \text{HMAC\_}hash(x \parallel A(1) \parallel seed) \parallel \\ & \text{HMAC\_}hash(x \parallel A(2) \parallel seed) \parallel \\ & \text{HMAC\_}hash(x \parallel A(3) \parallel seed) \parallel \dots \end{aligned}$$

The hash expansion function is the basis for *PRF*, which also includes an ASCII string as a label:

$$PRF(x, label, seed) = \text{P\_}hash(secret, label \parallel seed)$$

TLSv1.2 implementations should use SHA-256 as the *hash* function.

Then the 48-bit secret *master* is computed from the *premaster* secret by

$$master = PRF(premaster, \text{``master secret''}, r_1 \parallel r_2)$$

(with any excess bits discarded). Then the key block is computed by

$$key\_block = PRF(master, \text{``key expansion''}, r_1 \parallel r_2)$$

where "master secret" and "key expansion" are the ASCII strings without the quotation marks. When enough bits for the keys have been generated, the bits are divided into six parts. The first two parts are the client and server keys used for computing MACs, the next two parts are the client and server keys used to encipher the messages, and the last two parts are the client and server initialization vectors. The last two may be omitted if the ciphers being used do not require them.

When TLS enciphers a block at the record layer (see Section 12.5.3.2), it uses the cryptosystem negotiated during the initialization of the session. The cryptosystem may be a stream cipher or a block cipher. If it is the former, the blocks are enciphered sequentially, with the state of the stream at the end of one block carrying over to the next block. If it is the latter, the block is padded to the block size by adding bytes after the MAC. The padding is arranged so that the length of the padding is added just before the cipher block boundary.

Before TLS sends a block, it computes a MAC using the following:

$$hash(MAC\_ws, seq \parallel TLS\_comp \parallel TLS\_vers \parallel TLS\_len \parallel block)$$

where *MAC_ws* is the MAC write key, *seq* is the sequence number of the block, *TLS_comp*, *TLS_vers*, and *TLS_len* are the message type, version of TLS, and length of the block, respectively, and *block* is the data.

12.5.3.2   Lower Layer: TLS Record Protocol

The TLS record protocol provides a basis for secure communication. The protocol to be secured runs on top of it. For example, TLS adds security to HTTP by taking HTTP messages and applying the steps listed below to each message. However, the TLS record protocol need not handle retransmissions or unreliable delivery, because it runs on top of TCP. TCP handles the transport layer functions such as retransmissions and reliable delivery.

The TLS record protocol provides both confidentiality and message integrity for the records being sent. It accepts messages from the higher layer. Each message is split, if needed, into multiple parts. The TLS record protocol can transport a block of at most $2^{14} = 16,384$ bytes. The following steps are applied to each block, and the blocks are reassembled at the end.

The block is compressed. The MAC of the (compressed) block is computed as described earlier, and the compressed block and MAC are enciphered.[4] Finally, the TLS record header is prepended. The header contains the message type, the major version number, the minor version number, and the length of the block. Figure 12–8 shows these steps.

If the MAC and enciphering key have not been selected (which happens when the record layer carries messages for the handshake protocol; see Section 12.5.3.3), the encipherment algorithm is the identity transformation and no MAC is used. (In other words, the record layer does neither encipherment nor computation of the MAC.)

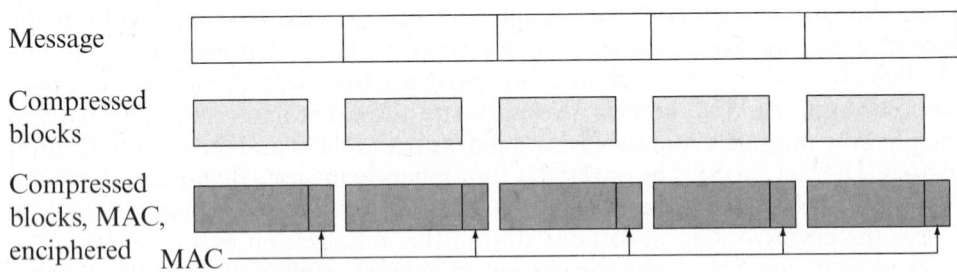

Figure 12–8   TLS record layer. The message is split into blocks. Each block is compressed, has a MAC added, and is enciphered.

---

[4]During the handshake described in Section 12.5.3.3, the peers may use an extension to negotiate encrypting first, then generating a MAC of the encrypted data [838].

12.5.3.3   Upper Layer: TLS Handshake Protocol

The TLS handshake protocol sets up the parameters for the TLS record protocol. It consists of four rounds that enable the peers to agree on keys, ciphers, and MAC algorithms. The exact sequence depends on the level of security desired. For clarity, in the following discussion we assume that the client and server use RSA as the interchange cryptosystem and AES-128 for the session cryptosystem.

The first round creates the TLS connection between the client C and the server S. If the server initiates the handshake, it sends an empty *server_hello* message, and the client begins the protocol. The client can initiate the handshake by sending the message without the server's request:

> 1. $C \rightarrow S$: *version* $\|$ r_1 $\|$ *session_id* $\|$ *cipher_list* $\|$ *compression_list* $\|$ *extension_list*

where *version* is the version of TLS that the client uses and r_1 is a nonce composed of a timestamp and a set of 28 random bytes. The *session_id* is either empty (meaning a new session) or the session identification number of an existing session (meaning that parameters are to be updated). The *cipher_list* is a list of ciphers that the client understands, in order of preference, and the *compression_list* identifies the compression algorithms that the client understands, again in order of preference. The client may also include a list of extensions such as encrypt-then-MAC after *compression_list*.

The server responds with its own message:

> 2. $S \rightarrow C$: *version* $\|$ r_2 $\|$ *session_id* $\|$ *cipher* $\|$ *compression* $\|$ *extension_list*

which indicates the selection of the parameters for the connection. Here, *version* is the highest version of TLS that both the client and server understand, the *cipher* and *compression* fields identify the cipher and compression algorithms, *session_id* identifies the session (if the corresponding field in the client's message was empty, this is the identification number of the new session), and r_2 is a nonce (timestamp and 28 random bytes) that the server generated. If the client included a list of extensions, the server may also append a list of extensions that it supports; this list must be a subset of the extensions that the client included in its list. This ends the first round.

The server authenticates itself in the second round. (If the server is not going to authenticate itself, it sends the final message in this round—message 6—immediately.) First, it sends the client its X.509v3 certificate *server_cert*:[5]

> 3. $S \rightarrow C$: *cert_chain*

---

[5] If the client is not using RSA, the server sends a certificate appropriate for the cryptosystem in use.

The *cert_chain* is a sequence of certificates. The first one must be the server's certificate. Each other certificate in the chain validates the certificate immediately before it.

If the certificate does not contain enough information to allow the premaster secret to be exchanged, the server sends an additional message to set the parameters. For example, if Diffie-Hellman with an RSA certificate is used, the message would be

4. $S \rightarrow C : p \parallel g \parallel public\_key \parallel \{hash(r_1 \parallel r_2 \parallel p \parallel g \parallel public\_key)\}k_S$

The first three parameters are the prime number, generator, and public key for the Diffie-Hellman cryptosystem in use. A digital signature of those parameters, prefixed by the random data r_1 and r_2 from the first two messages to prevent replay, is then appended. Other cryptosystems have other parameters, and hence other formats for this message.

If the server is not anonymous, it may request a certificate from the client:

5. $S \rightarrow C : cert\_type \parallel signature\_algorithms \parallel good\_cert\_authorities$

where *cert_type* identifies the type of certificate that the server will accept (by cryptosystem used), *signature_algorithm* the list of hash and signature algorithm pairs that the server can use, in order of preference, and *good_cert_authorities* the certification authorities that the server will accept. The server then sends a message ending the second round:

6. $S \rightarrow C : server\_hello\_done$

Next, the client validates the server's certificate (if any) and the parameters (again, if any were sent). If the server requested a certificate, the client obliges or replies with an alert indicating that it has no certificate:

7. $C \rightarrow S : client\_cert$

The client next sends a message to begin the key exchange. Since our peers are using RSA, the appropriate public key is used to encipher the 2-byte version number from the *first* message and 46 additional random bytes to produce a "premaster secret" *premaster*. The server and client will use this to generate a shared master secret:[6]

8. $C \rightarrow S : encrypted\_premaster$

Both parties now compute the master secret *master* from *pre*, as discussed above.

---

[6]If Diffie-Hellman is used, and a Diffie-Hellman certificate was sent, this message is empty; otherwise, it contains the client's public value.

If the client certificate can be used to sign messages, then the server sends a validation to the client. The message is simply all previous messages put together and digitally signed:

9. $C \rightarrow S$: *digitally_signed(messages)*

Then, the client tells the server to begin using the cipher specified (using a "change cipher spec" message; see Section 12.5.3.4). The client updates its session and connection information to reflect the cipher it uses. It then sends an acknowledgement:

10. $C \rightarrow S$: *change_cipher_spec*
11. $C \rightarrow S$: *PRF(master* || "client finished" || *hash(messages))*

where *master* is the master secret and *messages* are all messages previously sent during the handshake protocol. The server replies with a similar acknowledgement:

12. $S \rightarrow C$: *change_cipher_spec*
13. $S \rightarrow C$: *PRF(master* || "server finished" || *hash(messages))*

The handshake is now complete.

12.5.3.4   Upper Layer: TLS Change Cipher Spec Protocol

The change cipher spec protocol is a single byte with value 1. It is sent after new cipher parameters have been negotiated (or renegotiated). The new parameters are considered "pending" because the old parameters are in use. When this protocol message is received, the "pending" parameters become the parameters in use.

12.5.3.5   Upper Layer: TLS Alert Protocol

The alert protocol signals that an unusual condition exists. A *close_notify alert* signals that the sender will not send any more messages over the connection. All pending data is delivered, but any new messages are ignored.

All other alerts are *error alerts*. Errors are either *warnings* or *fatal errors*. In the latter case, as soon as the error is sent or received, the connection is torn down. The cause of the error and its type (warning or fatal) are independent; however, some errors are always fatal.

12.5.3.6   Upper Layer: Heartbeat Extension

The goal of the Heartbeat protocol extension [1708] is to enable a peer to verify that its peer is responsive. It consists of two messages. Both messages have four fields. The first consists of a value indicating that the message is a request; that is followed by the length of the data in the message, and then data of that length. The last field consists of random data. The total length cannot exceed 2^{14} bytes.

When a heartbeat message is received, the recipient ignores the fourth field. If the second field is too large, the message is discarded. Otherwise, the recipient returns a new heartbeat message containing the same payload, and a first field indicating this is a response. The padding may of course be different.

A client or server indicates its ability to respond to heartbeat messages in the extensions list of the handshake. Once a heartbeat message is sent, no more should be sent until a response is received. Finally, a heartbeat message should never be sent during the initial handshake.

An error in one implementation of the Heartbeat extension shows the need for checking inputs carefully, as discussed in Chapter 31. In this implementation [600], the size of the payload as specified in the second field was not validated against the actual length of the packet payload. Thus, an attacker could put a payload length much larger than that of the actual payload. The recipient would load the heartbeat message into the buffer it used for all incoming messages, and then copy out the number of bytes in the payload length. This meant that the contents of the response message, data that was previously in the buffer and not in the request message's payload, would be sent to the requester. That extra data often contained sensitive information such as cryptographic keys or other private data. The vulnerability was simple to fix, but many popular websites were vulnerable until they fixed the problem.

12.5.3.7   Upper Layer: Application Data Protocol

This protocol simply passes data from the application layer to the TLS Record Protocol layer. The record protocol transports the data to the peer using the current compression and cipher algorithms.

12.5.3.8   Differences between SSL Version 3 and TLS Version 1.2

SSLv3 differs from TLS in four ways.

First, the master secret is computed differently. SSL computes the master secret, and the key block, as follows:

$$
\begin{aligned}
master = \ &MD5(premaster \parallel SHA(\text{`A'} \parallel premaster \parallel r_1 \parallel r_2)) \parallel \\
&MD5(premaster \parallel SHA(\text{`BB'} \parallel premaster \parallel r_1 \parallel r_2)) \parallel \\
&MD5(premaster \parallel SHA(\text{`CCC'} \parallel premaster \parallel r_1 \parallel r_2))
\end{aligned}
$$

where *premaster* is the shared data and r_1 and r_2 are shared random numbers. The client and server MAC write keys, client and server write keys, and client and server initialization vectors (if needed) are computed similarly, by generating a key block with enough bits to produce all six quantities:

$$
\begin{aligned}
key\_block = \ &MD5(master \parallel SHA(\text{`A'} \parallel master \parallel r_1 \parallel r_2)) \parallel \\
&MD5(master \parallel SHA(\text{`BB'} \parallel master \parallel r_1 \parallel r_2)) \parallel \\
&MD5(master \parallel SHA(\text{`CCC'} \parallel master \parallel r_1 \parallel r_2)) \parallel \ \dots
\end{aligned}
$$

Then the keys are derived from the key block in the same way as for TLS.

Second, when the record layer computes a MAC for each block, the MAC is

$$hash(MAC\_ws \parallel opad \parallel$$
$$hash(MAC\_ws \parallel ipad \parallel seq \parallel SSL\_comp \parallel SSL\_len \parallel block))$$

where *hash* is the particular hash function used (MD5 or SHA), *MAC_ws* is the MAC write key of the entity, *ipad* and *opad* are the *ipad* and *opad* from HMAC (see Section 10.4.1), *seq* is the sequence number, *SSL_comp* is the message type (taken from the higher layer protocol), *SSL_len* is the length of the block, and *block* is the block itself.

Third, the last few messages of the handshake are different. Specifically, the verification message is

$$9'. \quad C \rightarrow S : hash(master \parallel opad \parallel hash(messages \parallel master \parallel ipad))$$

Here, *master* is the master secret computed from *premaster* sent in the previous step, *ipad* and *opad* are as defined for the HMAC, and *messages* is the concatenation of messages 1 through 8.

The two finishing messages are also different. After the client sends a "change cipher spec" message, it sends a "finish message":

$$11'. \quad C \rightarrow S : hash(master \parallel opad \parallel$$
$$hash(messages \parallel 0x434C4E54 \parallel master \parallel ipad))$$

The server responds with a "change cipher spec" message telling the client to use the ciphers that the server specified, and it updates its session and connection information accordingly. It then sends its "finish" message:

$$13'. \quad S \rightarrow C : hash(master \parallel$$
$$opad \parallel hash(messages \parallel 0x53525652 \parallel master \parallel ipad))$$

In both the client's and the server's "finish" message, the quantities are as for message 9, except that *messages* includes message 9.

Finally, the set of ciphers allowed is different. For example, SSL (and earlier versions of TLS) allows the use of RC4, but given the weaknesses found in it [34, 691], its use is deprecated.

SSL also supports a set of ciphers for the Fortezza cryptographic token [2158, 2159] used by the U.S. Department of Defense.

12.5.3.9   Problems with SSL

The use of SSL is deprecated for a variety of reasons. One attack in particular is nefarious enough to warrant not using SSL: the POODLE attack [1370].

The Padding Oracle On Downgraded Legacy Encryption (POODLE) attack is based on the use of CBC encryption. The problem is that, when SSL pads its messages to achieve a block size, all but the last byte of the padding are random, and cannot be checked on decryption. This allows the attacker to obtain information even if the information is enciphered with a scheme that uses CBC encryption.

The padding works as follows: suppose the message ends in a full block. SSL will add an additional block of padding, and the last byte of that padding will be the number of bytes of random padding. So, if the block size is b, then the last byte of that block will contain $b - 1$. The other bytes of this last block will be random bytes. Similarly, if the last block has $b - 1$ bytes, then the padding byte will be the 0 byte (as there are no other padding bytes).

When a peer received an incoming ciphertext record $c_1, \ldots, c_n$, that entity decrypts it to $m_1, \ldots, m_n$ by $m_i = D_k(c_i) \oplus c_{i-1}$, with c_0 being the initialization vector. It then removes the padding at the end, and computes and checks the MAC by computing it over the remaining bytes. Now, replace c_n with some earlier block $c_j, j \neq n$. Then, if the last byte of c_j contains the same value as the last byte of c_n, then the same number of padding bytes will be discarded as in the unaltered message, and the message will be accepted as valid. This allows an attacker to figure out the contents of one byte of the message.

By artfully arranging for the HTTP messages to end with a known number of padding bytes, and for sensitive information to be aligned on a particular byte, an attacker can use a man-in-the-middle attack to read bytes of the message. If the server rejects the message, the attacker tries again. The server is expected to accept the changed message in 1 out of 256 tries.

This attack eliminates one cipher suite in SSL. The other uses RC4, which—as noted above—is very weak; indeed, it was removed from the set of allowed TLS ciphers [1534]. As a result, SSL has been deprecated, and whenever possible is being disabled.

TLS does not suffer from this problem because the padding bytes are not random; *all* are set to the length of the padding. Further, TLS implementations must check this padding for validity before accepting the message.

12.5.3.10   Summary

TLS provides a transport mechanism that supports confidentiality and integrity. It supports a variety of ciphers and MACs. Any higher-level application protocol can use this protocol, and it is the basis for many Internet security mechanisms.

12.5.4   Security at the Network Layer: IPsec

IPsec version 3 (called "IPsec" here) is a collection of protocols and mechanisms that provide confidentiality, authentication, message integrity, and replay detection at the IP layer [1036]. Because cryptography forms the basis for these services, the protocols also include a key management scheme, which we will not discuss here.

Conceptually, think of messages being sent between two hosts as following a path between the hosts. The path also passes through other intermediate hosts. IPsec mechanisms protect all messages sent along a path. If the IPsec mechanisms reside on an intermediate host (for example, a firewall or gateway), that host is called a *security gateway.*

IPsec has two modes. *Transport mode* encapsulates the IP packet data area (which is the upper layer packet) in an IPsec envelope, and then uses IP to send the IPsec-wrapped packet. The IP header is not protected. *Tunnel mode* encapsulates an entire IP packet in an IPsec envelope and then forwards it using IP. Here, the IP header of the encapsulated packet is protected. (Figure 12–9 illustrates these modes.) Transport mode is used when both endpoints support IPsec. Tunnel mode is used when either or both endpoints do not support IPsec but two intermediate hosts do.

EXAMPLE: Secure Corp. and Guards Inc. wish to exchange confidential information about a pending fraud case. The hosts *main.secure.com* and *fraud.guards.com* both support IPsec. The messages between the systems are encapsulated using transport mode at the sender and processed into cleartext at the receiver.

Red Dog LLC is a third corporation that needs access to the data. The data is to be sent to *gotcha.reddog.com*. Red Dog's systems do not support IPsec, with one exception. That exception is the host *firewall.reddog.com* that is connected to both Red Dog's internal network and the Internet. Because none of Red Dog's other hosts is connected to the Internet, all traffic to *gotcha* from Secure Corp. must pass through *firewall.reddog.com*. So *main.secure.com* uses tunnel mode to send its IPsec packets to Red Dog. When the packets arrive at the firewall, the IPsec information is removed and validated, and the enclosed IP packet is forwarded to *gotcha*. In this context, *firewall.reddog.com* is a security gateway.

Two protocols provide message security. The *authentication header* (AH) *protocol* provides message integrity and origin authentication and can provide anti-replay services. The *encapsulating security payload* (ESP) *protocol* provides confidentiality and can provide the same services as those provided by the AH

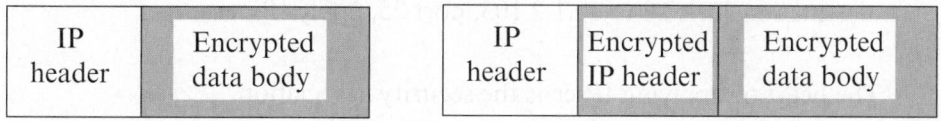

Figure 12–9 The packet on the left is in transport mode, because the body of the packet is encrypted but its header is not. The packet on the right is in tunnel mode, because the packet header and the packet body are both encrypted. The unencrypted IP header is used to deliver the encrypted packet to a system on which it can be decrypted and forwarded.

protocol. Both protocols are based on cryptography, with key management supplied by the Internet Key Exchange (IKE) protocol (although other key exchange protocols, including manual keying, may be used). IPsec requires that ESP be implemented, and AH may or may not be implemented.

12.5.4.1   IPsec Architecture

IPsec mechanisms use one or more security policy databases (SPDs) to determine how to handle messages. Each entry specifies an action associated with the packet. Legal actions are discarding the message, applying security services to the message, and forwarding the message with no change. The action taken depends on information in the IP and transport layer headers.

When a packet arrives, the IPsec mechanism selects the appropriate SPD. The SPD determines which entry applies on the basis of the attributes of the packet. These attributes include the source and destination port and address, the transport layer protocol involved, and other data.

EXAMPLE: An SPD has two entries for destination addresses 10.1.2.3 to 10.1.2.103. The first applies to packets with destination port 25. The second applies to packets transporting the protocol HTTP. If a packet arrives with destination address 10.1.2.50, and its destination port is 25, the first entry applies; if its destination port is 80, the second entry applies.

Entries are checked in order. If one has a different policy for securing electronic mail depending on its destination, the more specific entries are placed where they will be searched first. If no entry matches the incoming packet, it is discarded.

EXAMPLE: In the example above, the administrator wants to discard SMTP packets coming from host 192.168.2.9 and forward packets from host 192.168.19.7 without applying IPsec services. Assuming that the SPD entries are searched from first to last, the SPD would have these three entries:

> source 192.168.2.9, destination 10.1.2.3 to 10.1.2.103, port 25, discard
> source 192.168.19.7, destination 10.1.2.3 to 10.1.2.103, port 25, bypass
> destination 10.1.2.3 to 10.1.2.103, port 25, apply IPsec

The heart of applying IPsec is the security association.

Definition 12–7. A *security association* (SA) is an association between peers for security services. The security association is unidirectional.

A security association is a set of security enhancements to a channel along which packets are sent. It defines the security protocol that is to be applied to packets sent over that association. It is uniquely identified by the Security Parameters Index (SPI) and, possibly, the protocol (ESP or AH). If multicast is supported, the SPI is assigned by the group key server or controller.

Each SA uses either ESP or AH, but not both. If both are required, two SAs are created. Similarly, if IPsec is to provide security between two peers in both directions, two SAs are needed.

When IPsec services are to be applied, the SPD entry identifies an entry in an SA database (SAD) based on the SPD entries and the packet such as remote IP addresses, local IP addresses, and the protocol. An SAD entry consists of a set of selectors and the corresponding SA.

EXAMPLE: Continuing the example above, focus on the case in which IPsec is to be applied. The SPD entry for 10.1.2.101 could take the selector for the SAD from the packet (so the selector might be the SA with the destination address 10.1.2.101) or from the SPD entry (so the selector might be the SA with the destination addresses in the range 10.1.2.3 to 10.1.2.103).

Each SAD entry contains information about the SA. The fields include the following:

- The SPI is used to construct the ESP and AH headers for outgoing packets and to identify a particular SA for incoming packets.
- The AH algorithm identifier, keys, and other parameters are used when the SA uses the AH protocol.
- The ESP encipherment algorithm identifier, keys, and other parameters are used when the SA uses the confidentiality service of the ESP protocol.
- The ESP integrity algorithm identifier, keys, and parameters are used when the SA uses the authentication and data integrity services of the ESP protocol.
- The lifetime of the SA is either the time at which the SA must be deleted and a new one formed or a count of the maximum number of bytes allowed over this SA.
- The IPsec protocol mode is tunnel mode, transport mode, or a wildcard. If it is a wildcard, either protocol mode is acceptable. Security gateways need to support only tunnel mode, but host implementations must support both modes.

An additional field checks for replay in inbound packets:

- The anti-replay window field is used to detect replay (see Section 12.5.4.2). If the SA does not use the antirieplay feature, this field is not used.

Outbound packets have sequence numbers, the generation of which is controlled by two fields:

- The sequence number counter generates the AH or ESP sequence number.
- The sequence counter overflow field stops further traffic over the SA if the sequence counter overflows.

The entries in the SAD are processed in order. When inbound traffic arrives, the SAD is searched for a match on the SPI, source, and destination addresses. If there is no match, the SAD is searched for a match on the SPI and destination address. If there is still no match, the SAD is searched using either just the SPI or both the SPI and protocol, whichever is appropriate. If there is no match, the packet is discarded. Otherwise, the entry identifies the SA that the packet is associated with and enables the replay check (if desired). If the packet is to be forwarded, the SPD determines the relevant services, the appropriate services are supplied, and the packet is forwarded.

In some situations, multiple SAs may protect packets.

Definition 12–8. A *security association bundle* (*SA bundle*) is a sequence of security associations that the IPsec mechanisms apply to packets.

Tunnel mode SAs can be nested. This is called *iterated tunneling* and occurs when multiple hosts build tunnels through which they send traffic. The endpoints may be the same, although support for iterated tunneling is required only when at least one endpoint of the two tunnels is different. The tunnels may be entirely nested.

EXAMPLE: Return to Secure Corp. and Red Dog LLC. The fraud group within Secure has a host, *frauds*, that has IPsec mechanisms. The Red Dog fraud group has a new system, *equity*, that also has IPsec mechanisms. Both Secure's gateway to the Internet, *gateway*, and Red Dog's gateway to the Internet, *firewall*, have IPsec mechanisms. Because the data is so sensitive, the fraud groups decide that they need to protect their data within each company. The SA between the gateways is not enough.

The data transfer now has two SAs. The first goes from *gateway.secure.com* to *firewall.reddog.com* and is in tunnel mode. The second, also in tunnel mode, begins at *frauds.secure.com*, tunnels through the SA from *gateway.secure.com* to *firewall.reddog.com*, and terminates at *equity.reddog.com*.

Iteration of transport mode SAs occurs when both the AH and ESP protocols are used. This is called *transport adjacency*, and when it is used, application of the ESP protocol should *precede* application of the AH protocol. The idea is that the ESP protocol protects the higher-layer (transport) protocol and the AH protocol protects the IP packet. Were the AH protocol to be applied first, the ESP protocol would not protect the IP packet headers.

Transport layer protocol headers and data	IP header from *frauds*	ESP from *frauds*	AH from *frauds*	IP header from *frauds*	ESP from *gateway*	AH from *gateway*	IP header from *gateway*

Figure 12–10 An IPsec-protected packet going through nested tunnels. The filled rectangles represent headers. The leftmost IP header and the following data constitute the original packet. The IPsec mechanisms add the ESP, AH, and IP headers of *frauds* and forward the packet to *gateway*. This is the first SA and is in tunnel mode. The host *gateway* adds the ESP, AH, and IP headers shown, putting the packet into the second tunnel mode SA.

It is instructive to examine the appearance of the packets in the example above. Figure 12–10 shows the packet layout as it travels between the two companies. Notice that the packet generated by *frauds* is encapsulated in another IP packet with the IPsec services applied to the inner packet. Both headers identify *equity* as the destination. When the packet arrives at *gateway*, the original IP header is (probably) not visible to *gateway*. In this case, the SAD and SPD use a special identifier to indicate that the source is obscured (see Exercise 9). The appropriate SA directs the packet to be encapsulated and forwarded to *firewall*, so the added IP header identifies *firewall* as the destination IP address. When the packet arrives at *firewall*, it uses the incoming packet's destination IP address (*firewall*), security protocol, and SPI to locate the SA. This bundle tells *firewall* to authenticate and decrypt the contents of the packet. The inner IP packet is then used to look up the appropriate action in the SPD, which (in this case) is to bypass IPsec. The packet is then forwarded to *equity*, which repeats the processing. The innermost IP packet is then forwarded to *equity* and processed.

We now examine the AH and ESP protocols.

12.5.4.2   Authentication Header Protocol

The goal of the authentication header (AH) protocol [1034] is to provide origin authentication, message integrity, and protection against replay, if desired. It protects static fields of the IP packet header as well as the contents of the packet.

The important parameters included in the AH header are an indication of the length of the header, the SPI of the SA under which this protocol is applied, a sequence number used to prevent replay, and an Integrity Value Check (IVC)[7] padded to a multiple of 32 bits (for IPv4) or 64 bits (for IPv6).

The AH protocol has two steps. The first checks that replay is not occurring. The second checks the authentication data.

---

[7]This is another term for a message integrity check (MIC); we use the AH protocol specification term here for consistency.

When a packet is sent, the sender assumes that anti-replay is used unless it is told otherwise. If anti-replay is used, the sender first checks that the sequence number will not cycle; if it would, a new SA must be created. Whether anti-replay is enabled or not, it adds 1 to the current sequence number. The sender then calculates the IVC of the packet. The IVC includes all fields in the IP header that will not change in transit or that can be predicted (such as the destination field), the AH header (with the IVC field set to 0 for this computation), and any encapsulated or higher-layer data. Mutable fields in the IP header (such as the type of service, flags, fragment offset, time to live, and header checksum fields) are set to 0 for this computation. If an extended sequence number is used, the IVC uses all 64 bits of the number even though the AH header only contains the low-order 32 bits.

When a packet arrives, the IPsec mechanism determines if the packet contains an authentication header. If so, it uses the SPI and (possibly) the destination address to find the associated SA in the SAD. If no such SA exists, the packet is discarded. Otherwise, the key, IVC algorithm, and anti-replay settings are obtained from the SAD entry.

If the anti-replay service is desired, a "sliding window" mechanism checks that the packet is new. Think of the SA as operating on a stream of packets. Conceptually, the window contains slots for at least 32 packets (64 should be the default). Each slot has the sequence number of the packet for that slot. When a packet arrives, the mechanism checks that the packet's sequence number is at least that of the leftmost slot in the window. If not, the packet is discarded. The IVC of the packet is then verified, and if it is incorrect, the packet is discarded. Otherwise, if the packet's sequence number lies within the window, but the slot with that sequence number is occupied, the packet is discarded. If the slot is empty, the packet is inserted into the slot. Finally, if the packet lies to the right of the window, the window is advanced to create a slot for the packet. The packet is then placed in that slot, which is the rightmost slot in the window.

If the anti-replay service is not used, the IVC is verified. The IVC is computed in the same way as the sender (that is, appropriate fields are replaced by zeros) and is compared with the IVC in the AH. If the two differ, the packet is discarded.

The cryptosystems that implementations of the AH protocol must support change over time and are documented in Internet RFCs. As of October 2017, RFC 8221 contains this information.

12.5.4.3   Encapsulating Security Payload Protocol

The goal of the encapsulating security payload (ESP) protocol [1035] is to provide confidentiality, origin authentication and message integrity (here called "integrity" for brevity), protection against replay if desired, and a limited form of traffic flow confidentiality. It protects only the transport data or encapsulated IP data; it does not protect the IP header.

The important parameters included in the ESP header are the SPI of the SA under which this protocol is applied, a sequence number used to prevent replay, a generic "payload data" field, padding, the length of the padding, and an optional authentication data field.

The data in the payload data field depends on the ESP services enabled. For example, if an SA needs to resynchronize a cryptographic algorithm used in chaining mode, the sender could include an initialization vector here. As more algorithms for the ESP are defined, they may specify data to be included in this field.

Because the ESP protocol begins enciphering with the payload data field and protects both header fields and data, the IPsec mechanism may need to pad the packet in order to have the number of bits or bytes required by the cryptographic algorithm. The padding field allows for this adjustment. The padding length field contains the number of padding bytes; no more than 255 bytes of padding are allowed.

At least one of the confidentiality and integrity services must be selected. Furthermore, because packets may not arrive in order, any synchronization material must be carried in the payload field. Otherwise, the packets that follow a missing packet may be unintelligible.

When a packet is sent, the sender adds an ESP header, including any required padding, to the payload (either the transport data or an encapsulated IP packet). This includes a sequence number. As with the AH, this can be used for an anti-replay service that is enabled by default. If anti-replay is used, the sequence number is handled as it is for the AH.

The sender then enciphers the result (except for the SPI and sequence numbers). If integrity is desired, the integrity check is computed as for the AH protocol, except that it is over the ESP header and payload, excluding the IVC field, after the encryption. It does not include the IP header that encapsulates the ESP header and payload. The relevant SA dictates the cryptographic keys and algorithms that are used.

When a packet arrives, the IPsec mechanism determines if the packet contains an ESP header. If so, it uses the SPI and (possibly) the protocol and destination address to find the associated SA in the SAD. If no such SA exists, the packet is discarded. Otherwise, the SA parameters are obtained from the SAD entry.

If the integrity service is used, the anti-replay feature and the ICV verification proceed as for the AH, again except that only the ESP and the payload are used. Because the authentication data is inserted after encipherment, it is not enciphered and so can be used directly.

If the confidentiality service is used, the IPsec mechanisms decipher the enciphered portion of the ESP header. Any padding is processed, and the payload is deciphered. If the SA specifies transport mode, the IP header and payload are treated as the original IP packet. If the SA specifies tunnel mode, the encapsulated IP packet is treated as the original IP packet.

If the cryptosystem used combines confidentiality and integrity, then the above two steps are combined. The anti-replay feature (if used) is performed first; then the integrity check and decryption occur simultaneously. At that point, processing proceeds as above.

Typical implementations of public key cryptosystems are far slower than implementations of classical cryptosystems. Hence, implementations of ESP assume a classical cryptosystem, although this is not required.

The cryptosystems that implementations of the ESP protocol must support change over time and are documented in Internet RFCs. As of October 2017, RFC 8221 contains this information.

12.5.5   Conclusion

Each of the three protocols adds security to network communications. The "best" protocol to use depends on a variety of factors.

To what do the requisite security services apply? If they are specific to one particular application, such as remote logins, then using a program with application layer security is appropriate. When a program that requires security services is used in an environment that does not supply those services, or that the user does not trust to supply the requisite services, the application should supply its own security.

If more generic services are needed, lower-layer security protocols can supply security services to multiple applications and can do so whether or not the application has its own mechanisms for security services. Transport layer protocols such as TLS are end-to-end security mechanisms. They are appropriate when the intermediate hosts are not trusted, when the end hosts support the transport protocol, and when the application uses a connection-oriented (transport) protocol. Network layer mechanisms such as IPsec may provide security services on either an end-to-end or a link basis. They are appropriate when securing connectionless channels or when the infrastructure supports the network layer security mechanisms.

The application layer security protocol PEM provides security services for electronic mail messages. Consider using TLS for this goal. TLS does not authenticate the message *to the recipient*; it merely authenticates the transport connection. Specifically, if Alice sends Bob a message, PEM will authenticate that Alice composed the message and that Bob received it unaltered (and possibly that the message was kept confidential). TLS can authenticate that Alice sent the message to Bob, that it arrived as sent, and possibly that it was confidential in transit. TLS does not verify that Alice composed the message or that the message was confidential and unchanged on Alice's system or Bob's system. In other words, TLS secures the connection; PEM secures the electronic mail (the contents of the connection). Similarly, IPsec protects the packets and their contents in transit, but authentication is of the hosts and not of Alice or Bob.

12.6   Summary

If one uses a cryptosystem without considering the protocols directing its use, the security service that the cryptosystem is to provide can be deficient.

Precomputation attacks, assumptions about message sizes, message formats, and statistical attacks can all compromise messages.

Stream and block ciphers have different orientations (bits and blocks, respectively) that affect solutions to these problems. Stream ciphers emulate a one-time pad either through an externally keyed source (such as an LFSR, which generates a stream of key bits from an initial seed) or internally (such as the autokey ciphers or through feedback modes). Block ciphers emulate "codebooks" in which a set of bits maps to a different set of bits. (In practice, the mapping is algorithmic.)

Over a network, cryptographic protocols and cryptosystems are the basis for many security services, including confidentiality, authentication, integrity, and nonrepudiation. These services can be provided at different layers, depending on the assumptions about the network and the needs of the servers and clients.

12.7   Research Issues

Cryptographic protocols are the foundation of many security mechanisms and are sensitive to the assumptions inherent in their environments. As with authentication protocols, a critical area of research is to verify that protocols provide the services they claim to provide. Another area is to determine what assumptions are relevant to the protocol. For example, is a trusted server required? How could one modify the protocol so it would work without such a server (or prove that the protocol cannot work)?

Designing protocols for the Internet, or for any large, heterogeneous internet, requires flexibility without sacrificing security. The problem is as much political as technical. When several suitable protocols can solve a particular problem, different sites will try different protocols. During this process, some protocols will prove inadequate, others will need modification, and some will work. The resulting protocols may coexist or may be combined. Determining which protocol is the "best" is an open research topic.

The interaction of different layers of the network (the "network stack") with respect to both the protocols and implementations is another area of study.

12.8   Further Reading

Garrett [751], Barr [128], Seberry and Pieprzyk [1705], and Denning [533] discuss the theory of linear feedback shift registers. Schneier [1684] presents a variant called Feedback Carry Shift Registers. Beker and Piper [147] discuss stream ciphers. Rueppel analyzes design criteria for stream ciphers [1619]. Several papers [460, 1048, 1499] discuss the cryptanalysis of stream ciphers, and several others [691, 790, 791, 1267–1269, 1358, 1520, 1755, 2027, 2028] discuss the strength of particular stream ciphers.

Bellovin [162] discusses security problems in many Internet protocols; Kent [1032] provides a different perspective. S/MIME [1564, 1565] provides confidentiality, authentication, integrity, and nonrepudiation to sending and receiving MIME data in email. Whitten and Tygar [2002] discuss usability problems with PGP clients; Ruoti and colleagues revisited this 15 years later [1624]. They also discuss user interface characteristics affecting the usability of secure email systems [1623]. Zurko and Simon [2112] compare usability issues with the certificate management interfaces of PGP and PEM. Garfinkel and his colleagues [744, 745] and Ruoti and colleagues [1622] examine other user interfaces to encrypted email. McGregor et al. examine the use of PGP by journalists in their collaborative investigation of leaked documents [1288].

Research into secure messaging has identified establshing trust, securing conversations, and protecting privacy during transmission as key challenges [1910]. Herzberg and Leibowitz [896] examine the user interfaces of several instant messaging applications.

Rescorla [1581] presents an in-depth description of SSL and TLS. The security of SSL and TLS have been analyzed in several ways [1360, 1381, 1953, 2049]. Turner [1906] reviews the history of TLS briefly. The next version of TLS, version 1.3, is under development, and its security is being extensively analyzed [110, 476, 584, 955]. Downgrade attacks such as FREAK [189] and Logjam [19] take advantage of the presence of export-controlled ciphers in SSL. Naylor and his colleagues [1427] discuss the performance impact of TLS and SSL when used with HTTP.

Oppliger [1475], Kaufman et al. [1013], and Doraswamy and Harkins [583] present overviews of IPsec version 2; Stallings [1809], discusses IPsec version 3. Frankel and Krishnan [715] give an overview of the RFCs that define the current version of IPsec and its supporting cryptographic infrastructure. Bellovin [164] discusses the cryptographic security of IPsec. Hamed, Al-Shaer, and Marreo [857] study the verification of IPsec security policies. Aura et al. [97] study reconciling multiple IPsec policies. Yin and Wang [2056] introduce the context of an application into the IPsec policy model.

Bishop [220] examines the Network Time Protocol (NTPv2). The application layer protocol SSH, developed by Ylönen [2058, 2059], provides secure remote logins and connections. Vixie [1938] and Bellovin [163] discuss issues related to the Directory Name Services, and the protocol DNSSEC [73–76, 1480, 2031] adds several security services to DNS.

The electronic commerce protocol SET [2154, 2226–2228] uses dual digital signatures to tie components of messages together in such a way that neither the messages nor their association can be repudiated. Ford and Baum [699] discuss SET and the supporting infrastructure. SET has been modeled and analyzed, and minor problems found [152, 153, 298, 1015, 1620]. The 3-D Secure protocol, used to authenticate online transactions, has several problems [1402]. Ghosh [763] provides a balanced view of the dangers of Internet commerce using the Web; others [891, 1417] discuss developing e-commerce services and sites.

12.9 Exercises

1. Let the function f for a four-stage NLFSR be $f(r_0, \ldots, r_{n-1}) = (r_0$ and $r_1)$ or r_3, and let the initial value of the register be 1001. Derive the initial sequence and cycle.

2. An n-stage LFSR produces a sequence with a period of length at most $2^n - 1$, but the register has n bits and thus may assume 2^n values. Why can the length of the period never be 2^n? Which register value is excluded from the cycle, and why?

3. Consider double encryption, where $c = E_{k'}(E_k(m))$ and the keys k and k' are each n bits long. Assume that each encipherment takes one time unit. A cryptanalyst will use a known plaintext attack to determine the key from two messages m_0 and m_1 and their corresponding ciphertexts c_0 and c_1.

   a. The cryptanalyst computes $E_x(m_0)$ for each possible key x and stores each in a table. How many bits of memory does the table require? How many time units does it take to compute the entry?

   b. The cryptanalyst computes $y = D_{x'}(c_0)$, where D is the decipherment function corresponding to E, for each possible key x', and then checks the table to see if y is in it. If so, (x, x') is a candidate for the key pair. How should the table be organized to allow the cryptographer to find a match for y in time $O(1)$? How many time units will pass before a match must occur?

   c. How can the cryptographer confirm that (x, x') is in fact the desired key pair?

   d. What are the maximum amounts of time and memory needed for the attack? What are the expected amounts of time and memory?

4. A network consists of n hosts. Assuming that cryptographic keys are distributed on a per-host-pair basis, compute how many different keys are required.

5. One cryptographic checksum is computed by applying the DES in CBC mode to the message or file and using the last n bits of the final enciphered block as the checksum. (This is a keyed hash; the parties must agree on the key and the initialization vector used.) Analyze this hash function. In particular, how difficult is it to find two different messages that hash to the same value? How difficult is it to generate a second message that produces the same hash value as the first message?

6. A variant of the autokey cipher is to pick a well-known book and use its text, starting at some agreed-upon location. For example, the plaintext THEBO YHAST HECAT might be enciphered as the phrase AVARI ANTOF THEAU, with the sender and recipient agreeing that the first sentence in Exercise 6 of Chapter 12 in this book is the initial key. Describe a problem with this approach that could lead to a successful decipherment.

7. Unlike PEM, PGP requires the user to set a flag to indicate whether the file being protected is text or binary data. Explain why such a flag is necessary. Why does PEM not require such a flag?

8. The TLS protocol has several layers. Why was the protocol split into different layers, rather than just using one layer?

9. Redraw Figure 12–10 assuming that the SA between *frauds* and *equity* is a transport mode SA rather than a tunnel mode SA.

10. When the IVC for the AH protocol is computed, why are mutable fields set to 0 rather than omitted?

11. Section 12.5.5 discusses the use of TLS to provide confidentiality, authentication, and integrity security services for electronic mail and suggests that PEM is more appropriate. Consider a remote login protocol in the same context. In answering the following questions, please state *explicitly* any assumptions that you make.

   a. One goal of the protocol is to provide user authentication from the client to the server. Which layer (application, transport, or network) would be most appropriate for providing this service? Why?

   b. Another goal of the protocol is to provide host authentication between the client and the server, so the client knows which server it is communicating with, and vice versa. At which layer should these services be provided, and why?

   c. Assume that the remote login protocol is connection-oriented. Which layer should supply message integrity and confidentiality services, and why?

   d. Assume that the remote login protocol may use either a connection-oriented or a connectionless protocol (depending on various network factors determined when the client contacts the server). Which layer should supply message integrity and confidentiality services, and why?

Chapter 13
Authentication

ANTIPHOLUS OF SYRACUSE: To me she speaks; she moves me for her theme!
What, was I married to her in my dream?
Or sleep I now and think I hear all this?
What error drives our eyes and ears amiss?
Until I know this sure uncertainty,
I'll entertain the offer'd fallacy
— *The Comedy of Errors*, II, ii, 185–190.

Authentication is the binding of an identity to a principal. Network-based authentication mechanisms require a principal to authenticate to a single system, either local or remote. The authentication is then propagated. This chapter explores the question of authentication to a single system.

13.1 Authentication Basics

Subjects act on behalf of some other, external entity. The identity of that entity controls the actions that its associated subjects may take. Hence, the subjects must bind to the identity of that external entity.

Definition 13–1. *Authentication* is the binding of an identity to a subject.

The external entity must provide information to enable the system to confirm its identity. This information comes from one (or more) of the following:

1. What the entity knows (such as passwords or secret information)
2. What the entity has (such as a badge or card)
3. What the entity is (such as fingerprints or retinal characteristics)
4. Where the entity is (such as in front of a particular terminal)

The authentication process consists of obtaining the authentication information from an entity, analyzing the data, and determining if it is associated with that entity. This means that the computer must store some information about the entity. It also suggests that mechanisms for managing the data are required. We represent these requirements in an *authentication system* [221] consisting of five components:

1. The set A of authentication information is the set of specific information with which entities prove their identities.
2. The set C of complementary information is the set of information that the system stores and uses to validate the authentication information.
3. The set F of complementation functions that generate the complementary information from the authentication information. That is, for $f \in F$, $f : A \rightarrow C$.
4. The set L of authentication functions that verify identity. That is, for $l \in L, l : A \times C \rightarrow \{\textbf{true}, \textbf{false}\}$.
5. The set S of selection functions that enable an entity to create or alter the authentication and complementary information.

EXAMPLE: A user authenticates himself by entering a password, which the system compares with the cleartext passwords stored online. Here, A is the set of strings making up acceptable passwords, $C = A$, $F = \{I\}$, and $L = \{\textbf{eq}\}$, where I is the identity function and **eq** is **true** if its arguments are the same and **false** if they are not.

13.2 Passwords

Passwords are an example of an authentication mechanism based on what people know: the user supplies a password, and the computer validates it. If the password is the one associated with the user, that user's identity is authenticated. If not, the password is rejected and the authentication fails.

Definition 13–2. A *password* is information associated with an entity that confirms the entity's identity.

The simplest password is some sequence of characters. In this case, the *password space* is the set of all sequences of characters that can be passwords.

EXAMPLE: Suppose an installation requires each user to choose a sequence of 10 digits as a password. Then A has 10^{10} elements (from "0000000000" to "9999999999").

The set of complementary information may contain more, or fewer, elements than A, depending on the nature of the complementation function. Originally, most systems stored passwords in protected files. However, the contents of such files might be accidentally exposed. Morris and Thompson [1380] recount an amusing example in which a Multics system editor swapped pointers to the temporary files being used to edit the password file and the message of the day file (printed whenever a user logged in); the result was that whenever a user logged in, the cleartext password file was printed. The solution is to use a one-way hash function to hash the password into a complement [2006].

EXAMPLE: The original UNIX password mechanism does not store the passwords online in the clear. Instead, one of 4,096 functions hashes the password into an 11-character string, and two characters identifying the function used are prepended [1380]. The 13-character string is then stored in a file.

A UNIX password is composed of up to eight ASCII characters; for implementation reasons, the ASCII NUL (0) character is disallowed. Hence, A is the set of strings of up to eight characters, each chosen from a set of 127 possible characters.[1] A contains approximately 6.9×10^{16} passwords. However, the set C contains strings of exactly 13 characters chosen from an alphabet of 64 characters. C contains approximately 3.0×10^{23} strings.

The UNIX hashing functions $f \in \mathcal{F}$ are based upon a permutation of the Data Encryption Standard. $\mathcal{F}$ consists of 4,096 such functions f_i, $0 \le i < 4,096$.

The UNIX authentication functions in $(\mathcal{L})$ are *login*, *su*, and other programs that confirm a user's password during execution. This system supplies the proper element of C; that information may not be available to the user. Some of these functions may be accessible over a network—for example, through the telnet or FTP protocols.

The selection functions in (S) are programs such as *passwd* and *nispasswd*, which change the password associated with an entity.

Versions of UNIX and Linux now allow much longer passwords. For example, FreeBSD 10 (a variant of the UNIX operating system) allows passwords of up to 128 characters [709]. Also, the hash functions in $\mathcal{F}$ are MD5, Blowfish, SHA-256, SHA-512, an extended form of the original UNIX hashing functions (see Exercise 10), and a hash algorithm compatible with the Microsoft Windows NT scheme. The binary hashed output of these functions is translated into printable strings, the precise encoding used varying with the hash algorithm selected.

The goal of an authentication system is to ensure that entities are correctly identified. If one entity can guess another's password, then the guesser can impersonate the other. The authentication model provides a systematic way to analyze this problem. The goal is to find an $a \in A$ such that, for $f \in \mathcal{F}$,

---

[1] In practice, some characters (such as the delete character) have special meanings and are rarely used.

$f(a) = c \in C$ and c is associated with a particular entity (or any entity). Because one can determine whether a is associated with an entity only by computing $f(a)$ or by authenticating via $l(a)$, we have two approaches for protecting the passwords, often used simultaneously:

1. Hide enough information so that one of a, c, or f cannot be found.
2. Prevent access to the authentication functions $\mathcal{L}$.

EXAMPLE: Many UNIX systems make the files containing complementation information readable only by *root*. These schemes, which use shadow password files, make the set of complements c in actual use unknown. Hence, there is insufficient information to determine whether or not $f(a)$ is associated with a user. Similarly, other systems make the set of complementation functions $\mathcal{F}$ unknown; again, the computation of the value $f(a)$ is not possible. This is an example of the first approach.

As an example of the second approach, consider a site that does not allow the *root* user to log in from a network. The *login* functions exist but always fail. Hence, one cannot test authentication of *root* with access to these functions over a network.

13.3   Password Selection

The goal of password selection schemes is to make the difficulty of guessing the password as great as possible without compromising the ability of the user to use that password. Several schemes designed to meet this criterion have been proposed, and we examine the most common ones here.

13.3.1   Random Selection of Passwords

In this scheme, passwords are generated randomly from some set of characters and some set of lengths. This minimizes the chances of an attacker guessing a password.

Theorem 13.1. Let the expected time required to guess a password be T. Then T is a maximum when the selection of any of a set of possible passwords is equiprobable.

Proof See Exercise 1.

Theorem 13.1 guides random selection of passwords in the abstract. In practice, several other factors mediate the result. For example, passwords selected at random include very short passwords. Attackers try short passwords as initial guesses (because there are few enough of them so that all can be tried). This suggests that certain classes of passwords should be eliminated from the space of legal passwords P. The danger, of course, is that by eliminating those classes, the size of P becomes small enough for an exhaustive search.

Complicating these considerations is the quality of the random (or pseudo-random) number generator. If the period of the password generator is too small, the size of P allows every potential password to be tested. This situation can be obvious, although more often it is not.

EXAMPLE: Morris and Thompson [1380] tell about a PDP-11 system that randomly generated passwords composed of eight capital letters and digits, so to all appearances, $|P| = (26 + 10)^8 = 36^8$. Testing a password took 0.00156 seconds, so trying all possible passwords would require 140 years. The attacker noticed that the pseudorandom number generator used on the PDP-11 had a period of $2^{16} - 1$ (because the PDP-11 is a 16-bit machine). This meant that there were only $2^{16} - 1 = 65,535$ possible passwords. Trying all of them would take about 102 seconds. It actually took less than 41 seconds to find all the passwords.

Human factors also play a role in this problem. Psychological studies have shown that humans can repeat with perfect accuracy about eight meaningful items, such as digits, letters, or words [109, 455, 1348]. If random passwords are eight characters long, humans can remember one such password. So a person who is assigned two random passwords must write them down—and indeed, studies have shown this to be the case [14]. Although most authorities consider this to be poor practice, the vulnerabilities of written passwords depend on where a written password is kept. If it is kept in a visible or easily accessed place (such as taped to a terminal or a keyboard or pinned to a bulletin board), writing down the password indeed compromises system security. However, if wallets and purses are rarely stolen by thieves with access to the computer systems, writing a password down and keeping it in a wallet or purse is often acceptable.

Michele Crabb describes a clever method of obscuring the written password [473]. Let X be the set of all strings over some alphabet. A site chooses some simple transformation algorithm $t : X \rightarrow A$. Elements of X are distributed on pieces of paper. Before being used as passwords, they must be transformed by applying t. Typically, t is very simple; it must be memorized, and it must be changed periodically.

EXAMPLE: The transformation algorithm is: "Capitalize the third letter in the word, and append the digit 2." The word on the paper is "Swqgle3". The password will be "SwQgle32".

This scheme is most often used when system administrators need to remember many different passwords to access many different systems. Then, even if the paper is lost, the systems will not be compromised.

With computers, this method can use any transformation, including encryption [756].

13.3.2   Pronounceable and Other Computer-Generated Passwords

A compromise between using random, unmemorizable passwords and writing passwords down is to use pronounceable passwords. Gasser [752] did a detailed study of such passwords for the Multics system and concluded that they were viable on that system.

Pronounceable passwords are based on the unit of sound called a phoneme. In English, phonemes for constructing passwords are represented by the character sequences *cv*, *vc*, *cvc*, or *vcv*, where *v* is a vowel and *c* a consonant.

EXAMPLE: The passwords "helgoret" and "juttelon" are pronounceable passwords; "przbqxdf" and "zxrptglfn" are not.

The advantage of pronounceable passwords is that fewer phonemes need to be used to reach some limit, so that the user must memorize "chunks" of characters rather than the individual characters themselves. In effect, each phoneme is mapped into a distinct character, and the number of such characters is the number of legal phonemes. In general, this means that the number of pronounceable passwords of length n is considerably lower than the number of random passwords of length n. Hence, an offline dictionary attack is expected to take less time for pronounceable passwords than for random passwords.

Assume that passwords are to be at most 8 characters long. Were these passwords generated at random from a set of 96 printable characters, there would be 7.23×10^{15} possible passwords. But if there are 440 possible phonemes, generating passwords with up to 6 phonemes produces approximately the same number of possible passwords. One can easily generalize this from phonemes to words, with similar results. One way to alleviate this problem is through *key crunching* [811].

Definition 13–3. Let n and k be two integers, with $n \geq k$. *Key crunching* is the hashing of a string of length n or less to another string of length k or less.

Cryptographic hash functions such as the ones in Section 10.4 are used for key crunching.

Pronounceable password mechanisms often suffer from a "smallest bucket" problem [736]. The probabilities of the particular phonemes, and hence the passwords, are not uniform, either because users reject certain generated passwords as unpronounceable (or impossible for that particular user to remember) or because the phonemes are not equiprobable in the chosen natural language. So the generated passwords tend to cluster into "buckets" of unequal distribution. If an attacker can find a "bucket" containing an unusually large number of passwords, the search space is reduced dramatically. Similarly, if an attacker can find a bucket with an unusually small number of passwords that users might be likely to select, the search space again is reduced dramatically. Indeed, Ganesan and Davies [736] examined two pronounceable password schemes and found the distribution of passwords into the buckets to be nonuniform.

13.3.3   User Selection of Passwords

Psychological studies have shown that people can remember items (such as passwords) better when they create them. This *generation effect* [557, 1762] means that user-created passwords will be more memorable than computer-generated ones. Countering this advantage is that users tend to select familiar passwords such as dictionary words, as discussed above. Thus, when users can select passwords, the selection mechanism should constrain what passwords users are allowed to select. This technique, called *proactive password selection* [222], enables users to propose passwords they can remember, but rejects any that are deemed too easy to guess. It has several variations; the most widely used are text-based passwords.

The set of passwords that are easy to guess is derived from experience coupled with specific site information and prior studies [905, 1380, 1798]. Klein [231, 1063] took 13,892 password hashes and used a set of dictionaries to guess passwords. He found that 8% of the guessed passwords were dictionary words, 4% were commonly used names, and 3% were user or account names. He also found that 17.5% of the passwords had a length of under 6, 34.7% were of length 6, 24.4% were of length 7, and 23.4% were of length 8 (the maximum length allowed).

Later studies [301, 308, 1313, 2041] have produced similar results. Unlike Klein's, these studies did not guess passwords, using instead user surveys or publicly disclosed passwords. Nevertheless, they are illuminating. For example, Bryant and Campbell [308] found 68.8% of the passwords were between six and nine characters long, and 18.6% were longer. Further, alphanumeric passwords dominate. Other studies confirm this.

Some categories of passwords that researchers have found easy to guess are any of the following:

1. Account names
2. User names
3. Computer names
4. Dictionary words
5. Patterns from the keyboard
6. Letters, digits, or letters and digits only
7. Passwords used in the past

8. Passwords with too many characters in common with the previous (current) password

9. Variants such as replacing letters with control characters, "a" with "2" or "4", "e" with "3", "h" with "4", "i" with "1", "l" with "1", "o" with "0", "s" with "5" or "$", and "z" with "5"

Additionally, passwords that are short are easily found (the length of "short" depends on the current technology).

EXAMPLE: The strings "hello" and "mycomputer" are poor passwords because they violate criteria 4. The strings "qwertyuiop[" and "311t3$p32k" are also poor as the first is the top row of letters from a U.S. keyboard (violating criterion 5), and the second is the word "elitespeak" modified as in criterion 9.

Good passwords can be constructed in several ways. Perhaps the best way is to pick a verse from an obscure text or poem (or an obscure verse from a well-known poem) and select the characters for the string from its letters. An experiment showed passwords generated in this way were more resistant to guessing than passwords generated in other ways [1114].

EXAMPLE: Few people can recite the third verse of "The Star-Spangled Banner" (the national anthem of the United States):

And where is that band who so vauntingly swore
That the havoc of war and the battle's confusion
A home and a country should leave us no more?
Their blood has wiped out their foul footsteps' pollution.
No refuge could save the hireling and slave
From the terror of flight, or the gloom of the grave:
And the star-spangled banner in triumph doth wave
O'er the land of the free and the home of the brave

Choose the second letter of each word of length 4 or greater of the first four lines, alternating case, and add punctuation from the end of the lines followed by a "+" and the initials of the author of the poem: "WtBvStHbChCsLm?TbWtF.+FSK". This is also a password that is hard to guess. But see Exercise 5.

Definition 13–4. A *proactive password checker* is software that enforces specific restrictions on the selection of new passwords. These restrictions are called the *password policy.*

A proactive password checker must meet several criteria [231]:

1. It must always be invoked. Otherwise, users could bypass the proactive mechanism.

2. It must be able to reject any password in a set of easily guessed passwords (such as in the list above).

3. It must discriminate on a per-user and a per-site basis. Passwords suitable at one organization may be very poor at another.

4. It should have a pattern-matching facility. Many common passwords, such as "aaaaa", are not in dictionaries but are easily guessed. A pattern-matching language makes detecting these patterns simple.

5. It should be able to execute subprograms and accept or reject passwords based on the results. This allows the program to handle spellings that are not in dictionaries. It also allows administrators to extend the password filtering in unanticipated ways.

6. The tests should be easy to set up, so administrators do not erroneously allow easily guessed passwords to be accepted.

EXAMPLE: The proactive password checker OPUS [1799] addresses the sizes of dictionaries. Its goal is to find a compact representation for very large dictionaries. Bloom filters provide the mechanism. Each word in the dictionary is run through a hash function that produces an integer h_i of size less than some parameter n. This is repeated for k different hash functions, producing k integers $h_1, \ldots, h_k$. The OPUS dictionary is represented as a bit vector of length n. To put the word into the OPUS dictionary, bits $h_1, \ldots, h_k$ are set.

When a user proposes a new password, that word is run through the same hash functions. Call the output $h'_1, \ldots, h'_k$. If any of the bits $h'_1, \ldots, h'_k$ are not set in the OPUS dictionary, the word is not in the OPUS dictionary and is accepted. If all are set, then to some degree of probability the word is in a dictionary fed to OPUS and should be rejected.

EXAMPLE: Ganesan and Davies [736] propose a similar approach. They generate a Markov model of the dictionary, extract information about trigrams, and normalize the results. Given a proposed password, they test to see if the word was generated by the Markov model extracted from the dictionary. If so, it is deemed too easy to guess and is rejected.

Both these methods are excellent techniques for reducing the space required to represent a dictionary. However, they do not meet all the requirements of a proactive password checker and should be seen as part of such a program rather than as sufficient on their own.

EXAMPLE: A "little language" designed for proactive password checking [223] is based on these requirements. The language includes functions for checking whether or not words are in a dictionary (a task that could easily use the techniques of OPUS or Ganesan and Davies). It also included pattern matching and the ability to run subprograms, as well as the ability to compare passwords against previously chosen passwords.

The language contains pattern matching capabilities. If the variable *gecos* contained the string then the expression

```
setpat "$gecos" "^\([\^,]*\), \(.*\)$" name office
```

matches the pattern with the value of *gecos* (obtained by prefixing a "$" to the variable name). The strings matched by the subpatterns in "\(" and "\)" are assigned to the variables *name* and *office* (so *name* is "Matt Bishop" and *office* is "2209 Watershed Science"). Equality and inequality operators work as string operators. All integers are translated to strings before any operations take place. In addition, functions check whether words are in a file or in the output of programs.

A logical extension of passwords is the passphrase.

Definition 13–5. A *passphrase* is a password composed of multiple words and, possibly, other characters.

Given advances in computing power, passwords that were once deemed secure are now easily discoverable. A passphrase increases the length of passwords while allowing the user to pick something that is easier to remember. Passphrases may come from known texts, or from the user's own imagery.

EXAMPLE: Continuing with "The Star Spangled Banner," one might generate a passphrase from the third and sixth line: "A home and a country should leave us no more? From the terror of flight, or the gloom of the grave." Another example comes from the comic *xkcd* [1401], where the passphrase "correct horse battery staple" has as a memory aid a horse looking at something and saying "That's a battery staple" and someone saying "Correct!"

The memorability of user-selected passwords and passphrases is a good example of how environment affects security. Given the ubiquity of web servers that require passwords, people will reuse passwords. One study [688] found that the average user has between six and seven passwords, and each is shared among about four sites; the researchers obtained this information from users who opted in to a component of a browser that recorded information including statistics about their web passwords (but *not* the password itself). The question is how people select these passwords.

Ana Maria de Alvaré [514] observed that users are unlikely to change a password until they find the password has been compromised; she also found they construct passwords that are as short as the password changing mechanism will allow.

Passphrases appear no harder to remember than passwords. Keith et al. [1018] conducted an experiment with three groups, one of which received no guidance about password selection, one of which had to select passwords that were at least 7 characters long, and one of which needed to pick a passphrase of at least 15 characters; the latter two groups' selections also had to have an uppercase letter, a lowercase letter, and a nonletter. They then monitored login attempts to a course website over the term, and found no significant difference in the login failure rates after correcting for typographical errors. However, there were significantly more typographical errors among the users with passphrases. Later work [1019] showed that if passphrases consisted of text such as found in normal documents (called "word processing mode" or WPM), the rate of typographical errors dropped. Of course, one potential problem is that users may choose words from a small set when creating passphrases.

One widely used method for keeping track of passwords is to encipher them and store them using a password wallet.

Definition 13–6. A *password wallet* or *password manager* is a mechanism that encrypts a set of a user's passwords.

The wallet allows users to store multiple passwords in a repository that is itself encrypted using a single cryptographic key, so the users need only remember that key (sometimes called a *master key*). The advantage is that the master key can be quite complex, as that is the only password the user need remember. But there are two disadvantages: accessibility and cascading disclosure.

The user must have access to the password wallet whenever she needs a password. The widespread use of portable computing on cellular telephones, tablets, and laptops has ameliorated this availability problem, but absent such devices the user needs access to the system or systems where the wallet is stored. Further, if the user's master password is discovered, for example because it is easy to guess or the system with the password wallet is compromised, then *all* passwords in the wallet are also disclosed.

13.3.4 Graphical Passwords

These schemes require a user to draw something to authenticate. The system encodes this drawing in some way and compares it to a stored encoding of an initial drawing made by that user. If the two match, the user is successfully authenticated. Here, A is the set of all possible graphical elements, C the stored representation of the graphical elements, and F the set of functions that compare the graphical elements to the complementary information.

Biddle, Chiasson, and van Oorschot [197] categorize these schemes based on how the user is expected to remember the password.

Recall-based systems require users to recall and draw a secret picture. The selection functions $s \in S$ typically supply a grid for the users to draw their picture. The picture can be a continuous stroke or several disconnected strokes. The system encodes this as a sequence of coordinates. When a user logs in and supplies the password, the entered password is encoded and the result compared to the stored encoding. Some systems require an exact match; others require that the entered drawing be "close enough" to the stored one.

Recognition-based systems require users to recognize a set of images. Typically, a user is presented with a collection of images and must select one or more images from that set. These systems use images of faces, art images, and pictures of all kinds. Then the user must select those images (or a subset of them) from sets of images presented when authentication is required. A variation is to require the images to be selected in the order users first chose them in.

Cued-recall systems require users to remember and identify specific locations within an image. The system assigns the user an image, and the user initializes his password by selecting some number of places or points in the image. To authenticate, the user simply selects the same set when presented with the image. The effectiveness of this scheme depends in part upon how the system determines when the points selected are close enough to the initial points.

The expectation is that the set of possible graphical elements $|\mathcal{A}|$ in each of the schemes is sufficiently large to inhibit guessing attacks. However, just as with text-based passwords, the graphical elements are often selected from a much smaller space. For example, users often draw or select patterns of some kind in recall-based systems, and select prominent features or points in cued-based systems, so searching based on common patterns is often fruitful, just as searching for common words and patterns is often fruitful in text-based passwords. Recognition-based systems suffer from a similar problem; for example, when the images are faces, user selection is influenced by race and gender [197].

Human factors play a large role in the effectiveness of graphical passwords. Stobert and Biddle [1827] studied the memorability of graphical passwords and found that users could remember recognition-based graphical passwords the best but slow login times hindered their usability. They proposed a scheme that combined recall-based and recognition-based schemes and found it more effective than either individual scheme. A different experiment used a cued-recall system that presented image components in different ways when the password was created. The distribution of passwords changed depending on the order of component presentation [1879]. As the security depends on the distribution of passwords this means that presentation must be considered when users are selecting cued-recall-based passwords.

13.4 Attacking Passwords

Guessing passwords requires either the set of complementation functions and complementary information or access to the authentication functions. In both approaches, the goal of the defenders is to maximize the time needed to guess the password. A generalization of Anderson's Formula [51] provides the fundamental basis.

Let P be the probability that an attacker guesses a password in a specified period of time. Let G be the number of guesses that can be tested in one time unit. Let T be the number of time units during which guessing occurs. Let N be the number of possible passwords. Then $P \geq \frac{TG}{N}$.

EXAMPLE: Let R be the number of bytes per minute that can be sent over a communication line, let E be the number of characters exchanged when logging in, let S be the length of the password, and let A be the number of characters in the alphabet from which the characters of the password are drawn. The number of possible passwords is $N = A^S$, and the number of guesses per minute is $G = \frac{R}{E}$. If the period of guessing extends M months, this time in minutes is $T = 4.32 \times 10^4 M$. Then

$$P \geq \frac{4.32 \times 10^4 M}{A^S} \frac{R}{E}$$

or $A^S \geq \frac{4.32 \times 10^4 MR}{PE}$, the original statement of Anderson's Formula.

EXAMPLE: Let passwords be composed of characters drawn from an alphabet of 96 characters. Assume that 5×10^8 guesses can be tested each second. We wish the probability of a successful guess to be 0.001 over a 365-day period. What is the minimum password length that will give us this probability?

From the formulas above, we want $N \geq \frac{TG}{P} = \frac{(365 \times 24 \times 60 \times 60)(5 \times 10^8)}{0.001} \approx$ 1.58×10^{19}. Thus, we must choose an integer S such that

$$\sum_{i=0}^{S} 96^i \geq N = 1.58 \times 10^{19}$$

This holds when $S \geq 10$. So, to meet the desired conditions, passwords of at least length 10 must be required.

Several assumptions underlie these examples. First, the time required to test a password is constant. Second, all passwords are equally likely to be selected. The first assumption is reasonable, because the algorithms used to validate passwords are independent of the password's length, or the variation is negligible. The second assumption usually does not hold, leading attackers to focus on those passwords they expect users to select. This leads to dictionary attacks.

Definition 13–7. A *dictionary attack* is the guessing of a password by repeated trial and error.

The name of this attack comes from the list of words (a "dictionary") used for guesses. The dictionary may be a set of strings in random order or (more usually) a set of strings in decreasing order of probability of selection.

13.4.1   OffLine Dictionary Attacks

This version assumes the sets $\mathcal{F}$ of complementation functions and $\mathcal{C}$ of complementary information is known to the attacker.

> **Definition 13–8.** In an *offline dictionary attack*, the attacker takes each guess g and computes $f(g)$ for each $f \in \mathcal{F}$. If $f(g)$ corresponds to the complementary information for entity E, then g authenticates E under f.

EXAMPLE: Attackers who obtain a UNIX system's password file can use the (known) complementation functions to test guesses. (Many programs automate this process [2057].) This is an offline attack. But the attackers need access to the system to obtain the complementation data in the password file. To gain access, they may try to guess a password using the authentication function. They use a known account name (such as *root*) and guess possible passwords by trying to log in. This is an online attack.

The issue of efficiency controls how well an authentication system withstands dictionary attacks. Precomputation speeds up offline dictionary attacks. One method is due to Martin Hellman [893], and was originally designed to find DES keys.

Let $f \in \mathcal{F}$ be the complementation function. Choose m passwords $sp_i \in \mathcal{A}$. Let $r : \mathcal{C} \to \mathcal{A}$ be a function that transforms an element of $\mathcal{C}$ into an element of $\mathcal{A}$ (r is called the *reduction function*). For each password, let $xp_{i,0} = sp_i$, and compute $xp_{i,j} = f(r(xp_{i,j-1}))$ for $j = 1, \ldots, t$. Let $ep_i = xp_{i,t}$. The pairs (sp_i, ep_i) are then stored in a table T, and the intermediate values discarded. Figure 13–1a shows this process, and Figure 13–1b shows the stored table.

An attacker wants to determine the password p that has the complementary information $c = f(p)$. First, the attacker looks at the ep_i in the table. If there is an i such that $ep_i = c$, then p is the value in the next-to-last column in Figure 13–1a because that value was used to produce ep_i. To find it, the attacker reconstructs

$$sp_1 \to xp_{1,1} = f(sp_1) \to xp_{1,2} = f(r(xp_{1,1})) \to \cdots \to ep_1 = f(r(xp_{1,t-1})) \quad (sp_1, ep_1)$$

$$sp_2 \to xp_{2,1} = f(sp_2) \to xp_{2,2} = f(r(xp_{2,1})) \to \cdots \to ep_2 = f(r(xp_{2,t-1})) \quad (sp_2, ep_2)$$

$$\vdots \qquad \vdots \qquad \vdots \qquad \vdots \qquad \vdots \qquad \vdots$$

$$sp_m \to xp_{m,1} = f(sp_m) \to xp_{m,2} = f(r(xp_{m,1})) \to \cdots \to ep_m = f(r(xp_{m,t-1})) \quad (sp_m, ep_m)$$

(a)   (b)

Figure 13–1 Search tables: (a) the computation process; (b) what is stored.

the chain of hashes leading up to ep_i. If c does not match any of the ep_i, then the attacker computes $f(p)$ and compares it to the ep_i. On a match, p is in the second-to-last column; to find it, the attacker reconstructs that chain. The process iterates until the password is found or until the password is determined not to be in the table.

Rivest [533, p. 100] suggested a simple optimization. Rather than choose the endpoints based on a parameter t, choose them based on a property of the value of the endpoints, for example that the first n bits are 1, that is expected to hold after t iterations. Then, given a hash, iterate the complementation function (and reduction function) until an endpoint is generated. This produces variable-length chains.

One problem with these tables lies in *collisions*. When the computation of two chains produces the same value at any intermediate point, the chains merge. *Rainbow tables* [1469] allow collisions without merging. To do this, multiple reduction functions are used. So for each password, $xp_{i,j} = f(r_i(xp_{i,j-1}))$ for $j = 1, \ldots, t$. This allows collisions, but in order for two chains to merge, the collisions must occur for the same value j in both chains.

13.4.1.1   Salting

If an offline dictionary attack is aimed at finding *any* user's password (as opposed to *a particular* user's password), a technique known as *salting* increases the amount of work required [1380]. Salting makes the choice of complementation function a function of randomly selected data. Ideally, the random data is different for each user. Then, to determine if the string s is the password for any of a set of n users, the attacker must perform n complementations, each of which generates a different complement. Thus, salting increases the work by the order of the number of users.

EXAMPLE: Linux and UNIX-like systems use salts that are generated when the password is selected. As an example, FreeBSD 10 defines three schemes.

In the *traditional* scheme, the salt is a 12-bit integer chosen at random. The specific complementation function depends on the salt. The E table in the DES (see Figure F–3a) is perturbed in one of $2^{12} = 4,096$ possible ways—if bit i in the salt is set, table entries i and $i + 24$ are exchanged [1380]—and the message of all 0 bits is enciphered using the password as a key. The result of the encipherment is then enciphered with the password, iterating this procedure until 25 encipherments have occurred. The resulting 64 bits are mapped into 11 characters chosen from a set of 64 characters. The salt is split into two sets of 6 bits, and those sets are mapped to printable characters using the same alphabet. The 11-character representation of output is appended to the 2-character representation of the salt. The authentication function is chosen on the basis of the salt also; hence, the salt must be available to all programs that need to verify passwords.

In the *extended* scheme, the system stores a salt of 24 bits and a count of 24 bits, and the password can be any length. The password is transformed into a DES key by enciphering the first 8 bytes with itself using the DES; the result is xor'ed with the next 8 bytes of the password, and the result is enciphered with itself. This continues until all characters of the password have been used. Next, the salt is used to perturb the E-table as in the traditional scheme. The result of the password transformation is used as the key to encipher the message of all 0 bits, as in the traditional scheme, but the encipherment iterates the number of times indicated by count, rather than 25. The result is then transformed into a printable string, using the same technique as in the traditional algorithm.

In the *modular* scheme, one of five algorithms is used: MD5, Blowfish, SHA256, SHA-512, and the scheme used in Windows NT. The salts in these cases are treated as character strings and combined with the password during the hashing. The advantage to these schemes over the traditional one is that the password can be any length, and the length of the salt depends on the algorithm used (for example, SHA-256 and SHA-512 allow a salt of at most 16 characters).

In all cases, the salt and password hash are stored as a string. To determine which scheme is used, the system looks at the first characters of the stored string. If the first character is "_", then the extended scheme is being used. If it is "$", the following characters up to the next "$" indicate which algorithm of the modular scheme is to be used. Otherwise, the traditional scheme is used.

13.4.2   OnLine Dictionary Attacks

If either the complementary information or the complementation functions are unavailable, the authentication functions $l \in \mathcal{L}$ may be used.

> **Definition 13–9.** In an *online dictionary attack*, the attacker supplies the guess g to an authentication function $l \in \mathcal{L}$. If l returns **true**, g is the correct password.

Although using the authentication functions that systems provide for authorized users to log in sounds difficult, the patience of some attackers is amazing. One group of attackers guessed passwords in this manner for more than two weeks before gaining access to one target system.

Unlike an offline dictionary attack, this attack cannot be prevented, because the authentication functions must be available to enable legitimate users to access the system. The computer has no way of distinguishing between authorized and unauthorized users except by knowledge of the password.

Defending against such attacks requires that the authentication functions be made difficult for attackers to use, or that the authentication functions be made to react in unusual ways. Several types of techniques are common.

Backoff techniques increase the time between interactions as the number of interactions increases. One such technique, exponential backoff, begins when a user attempts to authenticate and fails. Let x be a parameter selected by the system administrator. The system waits $x^0 = 1$ second before reprompting for the name and authentication data. If the user fails again, the system reprompts after $x^1 = x$

seconds. After n failures, the system waits x^{n-1} seconds. Other backoff techniques use arithmetic series rather than geometric series (reprompting immediately, then waiting x seconds, then waiting $2x$ seconds, and so forth).

EXAMPLE: If a user fails to supply a valid name and the corresponding password in three tries, FreeBSD 9.0 applies a linear backoff scheme. It adds a five-second delay in prompting for every attempt beyond the third try.

On the Web, this approach is infeasible as one can simply disconnect from the site and then reconnect. Instead, websites use CAPTCHAs,[2] which are visual or audio tests that are easy for humans to solve, but difficult for humans to solve [1946]. The test may require the user to type a sequence of characters presented on a grainy background with the characters positioned at various angles. It may have the user identify specific objects in a set of images with complex or cluttered backgrounds. Concerns about the ease of use of CAPTCHAs, especially audio CAPTCHAs, have been raised [326, 2042], and several services exist that will solve CAPTCHAs on request [1388].

An alternate approach is *disconnection*. After some number of failed authentication attempts, the connection is broken and the user must reestablish it. This technique is most effective when connection setup requires a substantial amount of time, such as redialing a telephone number. It is less effective when connections are quick, such as over a network.

EXAMPLE: If a user fails to supply a valid name and the corresponding password in 10 tries, FreeBSD 9.0 breaks the connection.

Disabling also thwarts online dictionary attacks. If n consecutive attempts to log in to an account fail, the account is disabled until a security manager can reenable it. This prevents an attacker from trying too many passwords. It also alerts security personnel to an attempted attack. They can take appropriate action to counter the threat.

One should consider carefully whether to disable accounts and which accounts to disable. A (possibly apocryphal) story concerns one of the first UNIX vendors to implement account disabling. No accounts were exempt from the rule that three failed logins disabled the account. An attacker broke into a user account, and then attempted to log in as *root* three times. The system disabled that account. The system administrators had to reboot the system to regain *root* access.

EXAMPLE: Linux systems and Windows 7, 8, and 10 systems have the ability to disable accounts after failed logins. Typically, the Linux *root* account cannot be disabled. The Windows *administrator* account can be locked out (the equivalent of "disabled" in this context) from network logins, but not from local logins.

---

[2]The acronym stands for "Completely Automated Public Turing tests to tell Computers and Humans Apart."

Jailing gives the unauthenticated user access to a limited part of the system in order to gull that user into believing that he or she has full access. The jail then records the attacker's actions. This technique is used to determine what the attacker wants or simply to waste the attacker's time.

EXAMPLE: An attacker was breaking into the computers of AT&T Bell Laboratories. Bill Cheswick detected the attack and simulated a slow computer system. He fed the attacker bogus files and watched what the attacker did. He concluded that keeping the jail was not an effective way to discover the attacker's goals [402].

One form of the jailing technique is to plant bogus data on a running system, so that after breaking in the attacker will grab the data. (This technique, called *honeypots*, is often used in intrusion detection. See Section 27.3.2.1, "Containment Phase.") Clifford Stoll used this technique to help trap an attacker who penetrated computers at the Lawrence Berkeley Laboratory. The time required to download the bogus file was sufficient to allow an international team to trace the attacker through the international telephone system [1829, 1831].

13.4.3   Password Strength

How well the password selection schemes work to produce passwords that are difficult to guess requires an examination of selected passwords. Some data sets come from users or system administrators who cooperate with the researchers performing the study; others come from data sets gathered by attackers who compromise the passwords in some way and distribute them, or are themselves compromised.

A NIST report [324] uses the standard definition of entropy (see Appendix C) and defines two additional types of entropy.

Definition 13–10. *Guessing entropy* is the expected amount of work to guess the password of a selected user.

Definition 13–11. Given a set of passwords, *min-entropy* is the expected amount of work to guess any single password in the set.

Computing these requires that the distribution of passwords be known.

EXAMPLE: Suppose passwords are randomly assigned. Each password is composed of 8 characters drawn from a set of 94 characters each of which is equally likely to be chosen. Then the entropy of each password is $lg\,94^8 \approx lg(6.1 \times 10^{15}) \approx$ 52.4. As any password in the set of possible passwords is equally likely to be assigned, the guessing entropy and min-entropy are the same.

When users select passwords, the password policy controlling the selection affects the entropy of the passwords.

EXAMPLE: The NIST report considers three scenarios: one where users can select any password, one in which users can select any password not in a dictionary, and one in which users must include a mixture of case and nonalphabetic characters in their password. Following various studies [1699, 1728], they assume:

1. The entropy of the first character is 4 bits.

2. The entropy of the next seven characters (2–8) is 2 bits per character.

3. The entropy of the next twelve characters (9–20) is 1.5 bits per character.

4. The entropy of all subsequent characters is 1 bit per character.

5. If the password policy is that of the second scenario, up to 6 bits are added to the computed entropy.

6. If the password policy is that of the last scenario, 6 bits are added to the computed entropy.

Under these assumptions, the guessing entropies of an 8-character password under each of the three scenarios are 18, 24, and 30 bits respectively (contrast that to 52.4 bits for a random password), and for a 16-character password, the guessing entropies are 30, 32, and 38 bits respectively (and for a random password of that length, the guessing entropy is 105.4 bits).

Computing the min-entropy is much more difficult because, as noted, users often select easy to guess passwords. So the NIST report provides a password policy that will ensure at least 10 bits of min-entropy. That policy disallows:

1. Detectable permutations of user names; or

2. Passwords matching a list of at least 50,000 common passwords, ignoring case.

They note that requiring users to choose passwords of at least 15 characters will probably produce a min-entropy of at least 10.

Unfortunately, there is no way to convert Shannon entropy into guessing entropy [1929]; indeed, Weir et al. [1989] show experimentally that these metrics do not reflect the strength of passwords in practice. Bonneau [264] presents alternate metrics including one based on the attacker's desired success rate. He validated this metric using a study of anonymized statistical data gathered from 70,000,000 Yahoo! passwords.[3]

Florêncio and Herley [688] gathered data about passwords used to access websites. For privacy reasons, they did not record passwords. Instead, they

---

[3] The passwords themselves were *not* collected, and Yahoo!'s legal team approved the data gathering and analysis [264].

divided the set of characters into four alphabets: lowercase letters ("a" to "z," 26 characters), uppercase letters ("A" to "Z," 26 characters), digits ("0" to "9," 10 characters), and other (22 special characters). Let the number of characters in the *alphabets* used be α and the password length be L. They calculated the password strength as $\log_2 \alpha^L$. When they applied their metric to passwords used at various websties, they noted that the more important the service provided to the user, the stronger the password seemed to be; passwords for the New York Times websites, for example, averaged a strength of 37.86, whereas passwords for employees accessing a corporate website had an average strength of 51.36.

Kelley et al. used an alternate approach [1020]. They used Mechanical Turk to create a study that required users to select a password that conformed to one of seven policies, and then use it again several days later to obtain a small payment. Users were given one of two scenarios, the first involving a password protecting low value information (an online survey), and the second a password protecting high value information (email). The passwords had to conform to a policy chosen from seven possible policies, such as "passwords must have at least 16 characters" or "passwords must have at least 8 characters, including mixed case letters, a symbol, and a digit; it may not contain a dictionary word." They collected 12,000 passwords. Next, they defined *guess numbers* as the number of guesses required to guess a specific password for a specific algorithm. Thus, each password had a guess number for the brute-force algorithm based on a Markov model [2093] and another guess number of a heuristic algorithm [1990]. They found that the best password policy changed as more guesses were made; ultimately, requiring passwords to be at least 16 characters long had the greatest guessing number.

Password meters provide an estimate of password strength [348, 363]. When users change passwords, the presence of a password meter matters more than the meter's design, and their influence depends on the context in which the password will be used; if the user considers the account iportant, the password chosen will be stronger than when the meter is not present [617].

13.5 Password Aging

Guessing passwords requires that access to the sets of complements and complementation functions or the set of authentication functions be obtained. If none of these have changed by the time the password is guessed, then the attacker can use the password to access the system.

Consider the last sentence's conditional clause. The techniques discussed in Section 13.3 attempt to negate the part saying "the password is guessed" by making that task difficult. The other part of the conditional clause, "if none of these have changed," provides a different approach: ensure that, by the time a password is guessed, it is no longer valid.

Definition 13–12. *Password aging* is the requirement that a password be changed after some period of time has passed or after some event has occurred.

Assume that the expected time to guess a password is 90 days. Then changing the password more frequently than every 90 days will, in theory, reduce the probability that an attacker can guess a password that is still being used. In practice, aging by itself ensures little, because the estimated time to guess a password is an average; it balances those passwords that can be easily guessed against those that cannot. If users can choose passwords that are easy to guess, the estimation of the expected time must look for a minimum, not an average. Hence, password aging works best in conjunction with other mechanisms such as the ones discussed in this chapter.

There are problems involved in implementing password aging. The first is forcing users to change to a different password. The second is providing notice of the need to change and a user-friendly method of changing passwords.

Password aging is useless if a user can simply change the current password to the same thing. One technique to prevent this is to record the *n* previous passwords. When a user changes a password, the proposed password is compared with these *n* previous ones. If there is a match, the proposed password is rejected. The problem with this mechanism is that users can change passwords *n* times very quickly, and then change them back to the original passwords. This defeats the goal of password aging.

An alternate approach is based on time. In this implementation, the user must change the password to one other than the current password. The password cannot be changed for a minimum period of time. This prevents the rapid cycling of passwords. However, it also prevents the user from changing the password should it be compromised within that time period.

EXAMPLE: UNIX and UNIX-like systems use the time period method to age passwords (when password aging is turned on). They record the time of the last change, the minimum time before which the password can be changed again, and the time by which the password must be changed. Different systems use different formats. Linux systems record the information in terms of days since January 1, 1970; FreeBSD 10 systems record it in terms of seconds since midnight of that epoch.

If passwords are selected by users, the manner in which users are reminded to change their passwords is crucial. Users must be given time to think of good passwords or must have their password choices checked. Grampp and Morris [807] point out that, although there is no formal statistical evidence to support it, they have found that the easiest passwords to guess are on systems that do not give adequate notice of upcoming password expirations. A study by Tam et al. [1854] found that sending a warning message one day before the password expired was optimal.

EXAMPLE: Most System V-based UNIX systems give no warnings or reminders before passwords expire. Instead, when users try to log in, they are told that their passwords have expired. Before they can complete the logins, they must change their passwords as part of the login process. Linux systems, on the other hand, give warning messages every time a user logs in within some period of time before the password expires. The default period of time is two weeks, but can be changed by the system administrator.

In this vein, a further weakness of password aging is how users select the next password. A study by Zhang, Monrose, and Reiter [2093] found that people who were given previous passwords for an account with password aging were able to guess the current password 41% of the time. Further, passwords for 17% of the accounts were guessed in no more than five tries. Chiasson and van Oorschot [404] show that the optimal benefit from password aging is to reduce the attacker's expectation of success during the interval between password changes from 1 (certain success when passwords are not aged) to 0.632 for each period. They conclude that password aging's effectiveness is offset by the user interaction issues.

13.5.1 One-Time Passwords

The ultimate form of password aging occurs when a password is valid for exactly one use.

> **Definition 13–13.** A *one-time password* is a password that is invalidated as soon as it is used.

The problems in any one-time password scheme are the generation of random (or pseudorandom) passwords and the synchronization of the user and the system. The former problem is solved by using a cryptographic hash function or enciphering function such as HMAC-SHA-1, and the latter either by having the system inform the user which password it expects—for example, by numbering all the user's passwords and having the system provide the number of the one-time password it expects—or synchronizing based on time or a counter.

EXAMPLE: S/Key [852, 853] implements a one-time password scheme. It uses a technique first suggested by Lamport [1130] to generate the passwords. Let h be a one-way hash function (S/Key uses MD4 or MD5, depending on the version). Then the user chooses an initial seed k, and the key generator calculates

$$h(k) = k_1, h(k_1) = k_2, \ldots, h(k_{n-1}) = k_n$$

The passwords, in the order they are used, are

$$p_1 = k_n, p_2 = k_{n-1}, \ldots, p_{n-1} = k_2, p_n = k_1$$

Suppose an attacker intercepts p_i. Because $p_i = k_{n-i+1}, p_{i+1} = k_{n-i}$, and $h(k_{n-i}) = k_{n-i+1}$, the attacker would need to invert h, or launch a dictionary attack on h, in order to determine the next password. Because h is a one-way function, it cannot be inverted. Furthermore, for MD4 and MD5, dictionary attacks are not a threat provided the seeds are chosen randomly, an assumption we (and the authors of S/Key) make implicitly.

The S/Key system takes the seed the user enters and generates a list of n passwords. The implementation presents each password as a sequence of six short words (but the internal representation is an integer). The user can generate a numbered list of these sequences. S/Key initializes a database, called the *skeykeys* file, with the number of the next password to be supplied and the hexadecimal representation of the last password correctly supplied.

The protocol proceeds as follows:

1. User Matt supplies his name to the server.

2. The server replies with the number i stored in the *skeykeys* file.

3. Matt supplies the corresponding password p_i.

4. The server computes $h(p_i) = h(k_{n-i+1}) = k_{n-i+2} = p_{i+1}$ and compares the result with the stored password. If they match, the authentication succeeds. S/Key updates the number in the *skeykeys* file to $i-1$ and stores p_i in the file. If the authentication fails, the *skeykeys* file is left unchanged.

When a user has used all passwords of a particular sequence of passwords, that user's entry in the *skeykeys* file must be reinitialized. This requires the user to reregister with the S/Key program.

OPIE [1285] is a widely used implementation of S/Key.

EXAMPLE: Two other one-time password schemes use a counter rather than iterated hash functions. The *HMAC-Based One-Time Password Algorithm* (HOTP) [1390] uses the HMAC-SHA-1 cryptographic hash function to hash a shared secret key k and an 8-byte counter c that is synchronized between the user and the system. In addition, $d \geq 6$ is a system parameter. The algorithm works as follows:

1. Compute $h = \text{HMAC-SHA-1}(k, c)$. The output $h = h_0 \ldots h_{19}$ is 20 bytes long.

2. Let b be the number represented by the low order 4 bits of h_{19}. Then let p be the low-order 31 bits of $h_b h_{b+1} h_{b+2} h_{b+3}$.

3. $\text{HOTP}(k, c) = p \bmod 10^d$.

Each time the algorithm is used to authenticate, the client's counter is incremented. However, the server's counter is incremented only on a successful authentication. This may result in the counters being out of sync. So HOTP defines a parameter s on the server. The server then calculates the next s values, and checks to see if any match. If so, the counters can be resynchronized.

The *Time-Based One-Time Password Algorithm* (TOTP) [1391] uses a time-based value for the counter in HOTP. It defines an initial counter time t_0 and a time step parameter x. The time t used as the counter is $\frac{t-t_0}{x}$, so the counter value is the same for x time units. TOTP also may use the HMAC-SHA-256 or HMAC-SHA-512 hash functions instead of the HMAC-SHA-1 hash function required for HOTP. Clock drift poses a problem, because it will make the client and server times out of sync, and hence TOTP will fail. TOTP defines a parameter s that is the number of intervals of size x preceding and following the current interval. If an authentication request fails, TOTP can then try s time values preceding the current time, and s values following it; on a match, the clocks can be resynchronized.

One-time passwords are considerably simpler with hardware support because the passwords need not be printed on paper or some other medium.

13.6   Challenge-Response

Passwords have the fundamental problem that they are reusable. If an attacker sees a password, she can later replay the password. The system cannot distinguish between the attacker and the legitimate user, and allows access. An alternative is to authenticate in such a way that the transmitted password changes each time. Then, if an attacker replays a previously used password, the system will reject it.

Definition 13–14. Let user U desire to authenticate himself to system S. Let U and S have an agreed-on secret function f. A *challenge-response* authentication system is one in which S sends a random message m (the challenge) to U, and U replies with the transformation $r = f(m)$ (the response). S validates r by computing it separately.

Challenge-response algorithms are similar to the IFF (identification—friend or foe) techniques that military airplanes use to identify allies and enemies.

13.6.1   Pass Algorithms

Definition 13–15. Let there be a challenge-response authentication system in which the function f is the secret. Then f is called a *pass algorithm*.

Under this definition, no cryptographic keys or other secret information may be input to f. The algorithm computing f is itself the secret.

EXAMPLE: Haskett [879] suggests using this scheme in combination with a standard password scheme. After the user supplies a reusable password, a second prompt is given (Haskett points out that this could be the same as the system's standard prompt, to confuse attackers). At this point, the user must enter some string based on an algorithm. For example, if the prompt "abcdefg" were given, the appropriate response could be "bdf"; if the prompt were "ageksido," the appropriate response could be "gkio" (the algorithm is every other letter beginning with the second). Or, to use Haskett's example, the pass algorithm can alter a fixed password. In this case, at the prompt, the user would enter "wucsmfxymap" if the terminal were on a dial-in line, "acdflmq" if it were in a semi-secure area, and "cfm" if it were in a secure area. Here, "cfm" is the expected password; the location dictates how many random characters surround each of the letters.

13.6.2   Hardware-Supported Challenge-Response Procedures

Hardware support comes in two forms: a program for a general-purpose computer and special-purpose hardware support. Both perform the same functions.

The first type of hardware device, informally called a *token*, provides mechanisms for hashing or enciphering information. With this type of device, the system sends a challenge. The user enters it into the device. The device returns the appropriate response. Some devices require the user to enter a personal identification number or password, which is used as a cryptographic key or is combined with the challenge to produce the response.

The second type of hardware device is temporally based. Every 60 seconds, it displays a different number. The numbers range from 0 to $10^n - 1$, inclusive. A similar device is attached to the computer. It knows what number the device for each registered user should display. To authenticate, the user provides his login name. The system requests a password. The user then enters the number shown on the hardware device, followed by a fixed (reusable) password. The system validates that the number is the one expected for the user at that time and that the reusable portion of the password is correct.

EXAMPLE: The RSA SecurID 700 and 800 Hybrid Authenticator tokens [2210, 2211] use a system based on time. Every minute, the token outputs a six-digit number. A set of six bars indicates how long until the number changes; every 10 seconds, one of the bars disappears. In addition to the features described above, the password is invalidated once a login succeeds. (See Exercise 12.)

13.6.3   Challenge-Response and Dictionary Attacks

Whether or not a challenge-response technique is vulnerable to a offline dictionary attack depends on the nature of the challenge and the response. In general, if the attacker knows the challenge and the response, a dictionary attack proceeds as for a reusable password system.

EXAMPLE: Suppose a user is authenticating herself using a challenge-response system. The system generates a random challenge r, and the user returns the value $E_k(r)$ of r enciphered using the key k. Then the attacker knows both r and $E_k(r)$ and can try different values of k until the encipherment of r matches $E_k(r)$.

In practice, it is not necessary to know the value of r. Most challenges are composed of random data combined with public data that an attacker can determine.

EXAMPLE: In the authentication system Kerberos [1821], an authentication server enciphers data consisting of a name, a timestamp, some random data, and a cryptographic key. An attacker does not see the original data sent to the server. By knowing the form and contents of part of the data sent back, the attacker can try cryptographic keys until the known parts of the enciphered data decipher correctly. From this, she can derive the cryptographic key to be used in future communications. Researchers at Purdue University combined this with a weakness in key generation to compromise Kerberos Version 4 [579].

Bellovin and Merritt [166] propose a technique, called *encrypted key exchange* (EKE), that defeats offline dictionary attacks. Basically, it ensures that random challenges are never sent in the clear. Because the challenges are random, and unknown to the attacker, the attacker cannot verify when she has correctly deciphered them. Hence, the offline dictionary attack is infeasible.

The protocol assumes that Alice shares a secret password with Bob.

1. Alice uses the shared password s to encipher a randomly selected public key p for a public key system. Alice then forwards this key, along with her name, to Bob.

2. Bob determines the public key using the shared password, generates a random secret key k, enciphers it with p, enciphers the result with s, and sends it to Alice.

3. Alice deciphers the message to get k. Now both Bob and Alice share a randomly generated secret key. At this point, the challenge-response phase of the protocol begins.

Alice generates a random challenge r_A, enciphers it using k, and sends $E_k(r_A)$ to Bob.

4. Bob uses k to decipher r_A. He then generates a random challenge r_B and enciphers both with k to produce $E_k(r_A r_B)$. He sends this to Alice.

5. Alice deciphers the message, validates r_A, and determines r_B. She enciphers it using k and sends the message $E_k(r_B)$ back to Bob.

6. Bob deciphers the message and verifies r_B.

At this point, both Alice and Bob know that they are sharing the same random key k. To see that this system is immune to offline dictionary attacks, look at each exchange. Because the data sent in each exchange is randomly selected and never visible to the attacker in plaintext form, the attacker cannot know when she has correctly deciphered the message.

13.7 Biometrics

Identification by physical characteristics is as old as humanity. Recognizing people by their voices or appearance, and impersonating people by assuming their appearance, was widely known in classical times. Efforts to find physical characteristics that uniquely identify people include the Bertillion cranial maps, fingerprints, and DNA sampling. Using such a feature to identify people for a computer would ideally eliminate errors in authentication.

Biometrics is the automated measurement of biological or behavioral features that identify a person [1343]. When a user is given an account, the system administration takes a set of measurements that identify that user to an acceptable degree of error. Whenever the user accesses the system, the biometric authentication mechanism verifies the identity. Lawton [1143] points out that this is considerably easier than identifying the user because no searching is required. A comparison to the known data for the claimed user's identity will either verify or reject the claim. Characteristics used are fingerprints, voice characteristics, eyes, facial features, keystroke dynamics, and other personal attributes [957].

Because biometrics are measurements of the characteristics of the individual, people are tempted to believe that attackers cannot pose as authorized users on systems that use biometrics. Several assumptions underlie this belief [1567, 1686].

1. The biometric data is initialized properly. This means that the biometric data is that of the person whose identity it is bound to. If, for example, Ann's fingerprint is listed as being Penny's, then the biometric device will incorrectly identify Ann as Penny.

2. The biometric device is accurate in the environment in which it is used. For example, if a fingerprint scanner is under observation, having it scan a mask of another person's finger would be detected. But if it is not under observation, such a trick might not be detected and the unauthorized user might gain access.

3. The methods and algorithms by which the input biometric is compared to the stored biometrics only return a successful match when the two biometrics belong to the same person. The problem here is that most biometrics vary between measurements. The comparison must take these variations into account. If the algorithm requires too precise a match, the biometric validator might return a false negative. Conversely, if the

algorithm accepts too large a variance, the validator might return a false positive. Either of these situations compromises security.

4. The stored biometric data and the software validating the biometric input has not been corrupted. If the former has been, Ann's stored biometric data may be replaced with Penny's, so Penny is incorrectly identified as Ann. Corrupting the software can cause it to return a match when there is no match, or vice versa.

5. The transmission from the biometric device to the computer's analysis process is tamperproof. Otherwise, one could corrupt the transmission, causing a variety of security problems.

6. The transmission from the biometric device to the computer's analysis process is not a replay. Otherwise, one could record a legitimate authentication and replay it later to gain access.

If any of these assumptions do not hold, then an attacker can authenticate as someone else. Thus, biometric mechanisms must ensure these assumptions are satisfied to the greatest possible degree. Exercise 13 explores these in more detail.

We now briefly explore some commonly used biometrics.

13.7.1 Fingerprints

Fingerprints can be measured in a variety of ways, and new ones are being developed. Two examples will show how they work.

Optical devices use cameras. The finger is placed onto a clear, lighted surface, usually a prism. The prism is illuminated, and the light reflects off the surface where the fingerprint rests to a camera. The fingerprint ridges obscure the rays from the light source, causing the ridges to appear as dark parts of the image [916]. Feature extraction methods then build a representation of the fingerprint that can be stored.

A capacitative technique uses the differences in electrical charges of the whorls on the finger to detect those parts of the finger touching a chip and those raised. The data is converted into a graph in which ridges are represented by vertices and vertices corresponding to adjacent ridges are connected. Each vertex has a number approximating the length of the corresponding ridge. At this point, determining matches becomes a problem of graph matching [949]. This problem is similar to the classical graph isomorphism problem, but because of imprecision in measurements, the graph generated from the fingerprint may have different numbers of edges and vertices. Thus, the matching algorithm is an approximation.

EXAMPLE: Apple's Touch ID system on iPhones, iPads, and some laptops uses a capacitative system to gather data from the finger pressing on the home button [2114].

A technique that uses finger vein biometrics captures an image of the finger using an infrared camera. This shows the veins and shades produced by other internal structures such as bones and muscles. An image of the attributes is then extracted. One way is to use an adaptive technique that determines the threshold for the light parts of the image (veins, etc.), clarifying the image. Then various noise reduction algorithms remove irregularities, and the resulting image is translated into the storage form. Experiments show this method achieves a very high identification rate, with few false recognitions [1399]. Another method locates the valley-like structures in the image (the veins), and compares the number of matching pixels in the image with the number of pixels in the patterns. This method also shows a low error rate in experiments [1789].

Like other authentication mechanisms, fingerprints can be spoofed [1920], leading to the development of countermeasures [1249].

13.7.2 Voices

Authentication by voice, also called *speaker verification* or *speaker recognition*, involves recognition of a speaker's voice characteristics [343] or verbal information verification [1170, 1171]. The former uses statistical techniques to test the hypothesis that the speaker's identity is as claimed. The system is first trained on fixed passphrases or phonemes that can be combined. To authenticate, either the speaker says the passphrase or repeats a word (or set of words) composed of the learned phonemes. Verbal information verification deals with the contents of utterances. The system asks a set of questions such as "What is your mother's maiden name?" and "In which city were you born?" It then checks that the answers spoken are the same as the answers recorded in its database. The key difference is that speaker verification techniques are speaker-dependent, but verbal information verification techniques are speaker-independent, relying only on the content of the answers [1172].

Voice recognition systems are particularly vulnerable to replay attacks in which an adversary records, and later replays, the authorized user's voice. One detection method, designed for mobile phones, uses the difference in time that a voice reaches two microphones in the phone. The user says a passphrase that contains phonemes that produce known differences in time based on the placement of the phone and the user's voice. Experiments show the differences are not the same when the speech is replayed [2091].

13.7.3 Eyes

Authentication by eye characteristics uses the iris and the retina. Patterns within the iris are unique for each person. So one verification approach is to compare the patterns statistically and ask whether the differences are random [503, 504, 2005]. Retinal scans rely on the uniqueness of the patterns made by blood vessels at the back of the eye. This requires a laser beaming onto the retina, which is highly intrusive [1251]. This method is typically used only in the most secure facilities [1143].

The availability of eye tracking devices has led to the study of eye motion as an authentication mechanism. The device tracks specific features of the eyes, such as statistics about the pupil size, the speed of eye motion and the length of time of lack of motion, and the steadiness of the gaze. The more features used in the analysis, the more accurate the identification, and using all features enabled attackers to be detected quickly (over 90% in 40 seconds), with few false negatives [612]. A variant of eye motion uses eye gestures, in which the user moves her eyes in a particular way and that motion is compared to a predetermined shape [518].

13.7.4   Faces

Face recognition consists of several steps. First, the face is located. If the user places her face in a predetermined position (for example, by resting her chin on a support), the problem becomes somewhat easier. However, facial features such as hair and glasses may make the recognition harder. Techniques for doing this include the use of neural networks [1178, 1614] and templates [2074]. The resulting image is then compared with the relevant image in the database. The correlation is affected by the differences in the lighting between the current image and the reference image, by distortion, by "noise," and by the view of the face. The correlation mechanism must be "trained." An alternative approach is to focus on the facial features such as the distance between the nose and the chin, and the angle of the line drawn from one to the other [1645].

Techniques have been developed to detect spoofing attacks on facial recognition systems, called "presentation attacks" [1557]. An interesting problem is that many of the data sets used to train facial recognition systems are biased, resulting in higher error rates for those whom the data set is biased against [315, 768].

13.7.5   Keystrokes

Keystroke dynamics requires a signature based on keystroke intervals, keystroke pressure, keystroke duration, and where the key is struck (on the edge or in the middle). This signature is believed to be unique in the same way that written signatures are unique [982, 1502]. Keystroke recognition can be both static and dynamic. Static recognition is done once, at authentication time, and usually involves typing a fixed, known string [67, 1373]. Once authentication has been completed, an attacker can capture the connection (or take over the terminal) without detection. Dynamic recognition is done throughout the session, so the aforementioned attack is not feasible. However, the signature must be chosen so that variations within an individual's session do not cause the authentication to fail. For example, keystroke intervals may vary widely, and the dynamic recognition mechanism must take this into account. The statistics gathered from a user's typing are then run through statistical tests (which may discard some data as invalid, depending on the technique used) that account for acceptable variance in the data [835].

13.7.6 Combinations

Several researchers have combined some of the techniques described above to improve the accuracy of biometric authentication. Lumini and Nanni [1217] provide an overview of techniques used to do this. Dieckmann, Plankensteiner, and Wagner [562] combined voice sounds and lip motion with the facial image. Duc et al. [592] describe a "supervisor module" for melding voice and face recognition with a success rate of 99.5%. Lu et al. [1209] combined mouse and eye movement. The results of experiments involving fusions of biometric characteristics indicate that a higher degree of accuracy can be attained than when only a single characteristic is used.

13.8 Location

Denning and MacDoran [544] suggest an innovative approach to authentication. They reason that if a user claims to be Anna, who is at that moment working in a bank in California but is also logging in from Russia at the same time, the user is impersonating Anna. Their scheme is based on the Global Positioning System (GPS), which can pinpoint a location to within a few meters. The physical location of an entity is described by a location signature derived from the GPS satellites. Each location (to within a few meters) and time (to within a few milliseconds) is unique, and hence form a location signature. This signature is transmitted to authenticate the user. The host also has a location signature sensor (LSS) and obtains a similar signature for the user. If the signatures disagree, the authentication fails.

If the LSS is stolen, the thief would have to log in from an authorized geographic location. Because the signature is generated from GPS data, which changes with respect to time, location, and a variety of vagaries resulting from the nature of the electromagnetic waves used to establish position, any such signature would be unique and could not be forged. Moreover, if intercepted, it could not be replayed except within the window of temporal uniqueness.

This technique can also restrict the locations from which an authorized user can access the system.

EXAMPLE: Suppose Anna is an employee of a bank in California. The bank uses location-based authentication to verify logins. Anna's LSS is stolen, and the thief takes it to New York. From there, the thief tries to access the bank's computer.

Anna's LSS generates a signature and transmits it to the bank. The bank's LSS determines that Anna's LSS is in New York and is supplying a correct signature. However, Anna is not authorized to access the bank's computer from New York, so the authentication is rejected. If the thief tries to forge a message indicating that Anna is connecting from inside California, the host's LSS would report that Anna was at a different location and would reject the connection.

An interesting point is that the authentication can be done continuously. The LSS simply intermingles signature data with the transmitted data, and the host checks it. If the connection were hijacked, the data from the LSS would be lost.

A mobile phone or other mobile computer may be used as an LSS [2089].

13.9 Multifactor Authentication

Authentication methods can be combined, or multiple methods can be used. Multifactor authentication uses two different forms of authentication to validate identity.

EXAMPLE: A mechanism that asks first for a password and then requires the user to enter a sequence of numbers sent to a smartphone is multifactor as it uses what the entity knows (the password) and what the entity has (the smartphone). A mechanism that asks for a password and then the answer to a question is not multifactor, as it uses only what the entity knows.

The widespread use of cell phones and other portable computing media, coupled with the growth of attacks on authentication systems, has encouraged the use of two-factor authentication. For example, many banks, particularly in Europe and Asia, use multifactor authentication [1052]. More commonly, many social networking web providers are encouraging users to adopt it.

EXAMPLE: Google provides a two-factor authentication protocol (called "2-Step Verification") [825, 2162]. After a user supplies a login name and password, Google sends a six-digit code to a prearranged phone number or Google's mobile app. The user retrieves this code and enters it on the web page. If the number matches what was sent, authentication succeeds.

This method requires that the user have two factors. If the phone number is used, the user must have immediate access to the phone. This is usually a cell phone, which most people carry with them; but it can be any phone. Google can send the code by voice or text. When sent to the app, the user must have the device with the app.

Techniques using multiple methods assign one or more authentication methods to each entity. The entity must authenticate using the specific method, or methods, chosen. The specific authentication methods vary from system to system, but in all cases the multiple layers of authentication require an attacker to know more, or possess more, than is required to spoof a single layer.

EXAMPLE: Some versions of the UNIX operating system provide a mechanism called *pluggable authentication modules* (PAM) [1646]. When a program authenticates a user, it invokes a library routine, *pam_authenticate*, that accesses a set of configuration files. These files are in the directory */etc/pam.d*. Each file in that directory has the same name as the program to which it applies. For example, the library routine will access the file */etc/pam.d/ftpd* when called from the program *ftpd*. That file contains a sequence of lines describing the authentication modules to be invoked and how their results are to be handled.

```
auth   sufficient   /usr/lib/security/pam_ftp.so
auth   required     /usr/lib/security/pam_unix_auth.so \
                    use_first_pass
auth   required     /usr/lib/security/pam_listfile.so \
                    onerr=succeed item=user sense=deny \
                    file=/etc/ftpusers
```

The first field describes the nature of the line. All checks that the PAM library function will make relate to authentication of a user. The first entry invokes the module */usr/lib/security/pam_ftp.so*. This module obtains the user's name and password. If the name is "anonymous," the password is assumed to be the user's email address. In this case, the module succeeds. If the user's name is not "anonymous," the variable *PAM_AUTHTOK* is set to the entered password, the variable *PAM_RUSER* is set to the entered user name, and the module fails.

If the module succeeds, the library returns to the caller, indicating success (because of the "sufficient" in the second field). If it fails, the next two entries will be used (because of the "required" in their second fields). The second entry invokes a module that performs the standard UNIX password authentication. The argument "use_first_pass" means that the password is in the variable *PAM_AUTHTOK*. If the module fails, the failure is recorded, but the next line is invoked anyway. Then the third entry is invoked. Its module looks in the file */etc/ftpusers* for the user name in the variable *PAM_RUSER* (because of "item=user"). If found, the module fails ("sense=deny"). If an error occurs (for example, because the file does not exist), the module succeeds ("onerr=succeed"). If both of the modules in the last two lines succeed, the user is authenticated. If not, the user's authentication fails.

The second field controls the calling of the modules. The entries are processed in the order in which they appear. If the second field is "sufficient" and the module succeeds, authentication is completed. If the second field is "required," failure of the module makes authentication fail, but all required modules are invoked before the failure is reported. To make the PAM library routine return immediately after the failure of a module, the second field must be set to "requisite." Finally, an "optional" field indicates that if all other modules fail (whether they precede or follow this entry), the module in this entry is invoked.

The idea of invoking successive modules is called *stacking*. The variables *PAM_AUTHTOK* and *PAM_RUSER* (and some others) enable stacked modules to communicate with one another. (The option "use_first_pass" in entry 2 is an example of this.) The caller need know nothing about how the administrator has set up authentication. Because the order in which the PAM modules are called can change, the caller can make no assumptions about how the modules work. The authentication is in effect hidden from the program.

Modules can control access to resources on the basis of factors other than authentication. The following file, *letc/pam.d/login*, corresponds to standard UNIX authentication and resource checking at login time:

```
auth       required   /usr/lib/security/pam_unix_auth.so
account    required   /usr/lib/security/pam_unix_acct.so
password   required   /usr/lib/security/pam_unix_passwd.so
session    required   /usr/lib/security/pam_unix_session.so
```

The first entry performs the standard password authentication. The second line controls access on the basis of such factors as time of day, and the fourth line does so on the basis of the resources available for the session. The third entry is invoked when the user changes the password.

13.10 Summary

Authentication consists of an entity, the user, trying to convince a different entity, the *verifier*, of the user's identity. The user does so by claiming to know some information, to possess something, to have some particular set of physical characteristics, or to be in a specific location. The verifier has some method of validating the claim, possibly with auxiliary equipment.

Passwords are the most basic authentication mechanism. They are vulnerable to guessing unless precautions ensure that there is a large enough set of possible passwords and that each potential password in the set is equally likely to be selected. Challenge-response techniques allow the system to vary the password and are less vulnerable to compromise because the password is never transmitted in the clear. One-time passwords, an example of this technique, are particularly effective against guessing attacks because even if a password is guessed, it may not be reused.

Some forms of authentication require hardware support. A cryptographic key is embedded in the device. The verifier transmits a challenge. The user computes a response using the hardware device and transmits it to the verifier. The verifier then validates the signature.

Biometrics measures physical characteristics of the user. These characteristics are sent to the verifier, which validates them. Critical to the successful use of biometric measurements is the understanding that they are simply passwords (although very complex ones) and must be protected in the same way that passwords must be protected.

Location requires the verifier to determine the location of the user. If the location is not as it should be, the verifier rejects the claim.

In practice, some combination of these methods is used. The specific methods, and their ordering, depend on the resources available to the verifier and the user, the strength of the authentication required, and external factors such as laws and customs.

13.11 Research Issues

Because of human factors such as writing passwords down or choosing passwords that are easy to remember, much research focuses on making authentication schemes difficult to break but easy to use. Using noncharacter password schemes (such as graphical motion) appears to be promising. Research into techniques and the psychology underlying them may improve this situation. Further, given the multiplicity of passwords, storing them in a form that a user can easily access but that an attacker cannot access is another important issue.

Authentication protocols involve passwords, often as cryptographic keys. Protocols that prevent offline dictionary attacks make attacks of authentication schemes more difficult. Research into provably secure protocols, which cannot be broken, and into probabilistic authentication protocols (such as zero-knowledge proofs) will harden authentication even more. Considerable effort is being made to minimize the time and storage requirements of these protocols, as well as to maximize their robustness in the face of attacks.

Methods of authentication not requiring traditional text-based passwords require that usability and memorability be balanced with accuracy. Human factors are critical in this.

Biometrics enables systems to authenticate users based on physical characteristics. Because fingerprints uniquely identify people, they should make excellent authenticators. Research into mechanisms for recording biometric data under varying conditions is critical to the success of authentication using biometrics. For example, if voiceprints are used, the mechanisms must correctly identify an individual even if that individual has a bad cold.

Single system sign-on is a mechanism whereby a user logs on once and has access to all systems and resources within the organizational unit. This requires compatibility among a wide variety of authentication mechanisms, and development of mechanisms for integrating a wide variety of systems into a single sign-on organization is an area of active research.

13.12   Further Reading

Discussions of the strength of the UNIX password scheme provide insight into how gracefully authentication schemes age. Bishop [218] and Feldmeier and Karn [660] discuss attacks on the UNIX scheme. Su and Bishop use a Connection Machine in a dictionary attack [1840]; Kedem and Ishihara use a PixelFlow SIMD computer [1017]. Leong and Tham [1153] discuss specific password-cracking hardware. Weir et al. [1990] presents a probabilistic attack on passwords that draws on previously disclosed passwords.

Narayanan and Shmatikov [1421] observed that the distribution of letters in easy-to-remember passwords is likely to be the same as for the language of the passwords, and using that observation reduced the search time in rainbow tables considerably.

Dell'Amico, Michiardi, and Roudier [529] compare methods of guessing user-chosen passwords and conclude that the most effective techniques depend on the set from which passwords are drawn. Inglestat and Sasse [944] state that password policies should focus on principles of human-computer interaction to help users select passwords for specific contexts of use, rather than applying a blanket requirement to maximize password strength. In particular, studies of passwords generally conflate two models, the first being that of a user who chooses passwords randomly and the second being the efficiency of offline attacks; this combination ignores many other threats such as phishing (see Section 23.6.6) [266]. One study concluded that offline dictionary attacks occur much less often than widely believed [690]. Florêncio and Herley [689] examined the password policies of 75 websites, and concluded that the policies were independent of the security needs of the website. van Oorschot and Herley [1924] discuss factors affecting password policies and argue that passwords will not disappear any time soon, contrary to conventional wisdom. Bonneau et al. [265] present a framework to compare authentication schemes used on the Web, and found that other schemes do not provide all the benefits of passwords, supporting Herley and van Oorschott's conclusion.

Smith [1770] proposed using word association to authenticate users. One study [2113] had users provide 20 personal questions and answers; to authenticate, they had to answer five questions randomly chosen from these; as noted above, if the answers are publicly known, this scheme fails. Bunnell et al. [313] used 40 questions, evenly divided between fact and opinion.

An interesting version of authentication by what you know is *whom you know* [287]. This technique mimics people being identified through mutual acquaintances in societies.

Other biometric characteristics used for user authentication include palm prints [2087], wearables [241], mouse dynamics [1583, 1731], touch-screen patterns [519], and electrocardiogram data [831]. Cell phones have numerous sensors that biometric authenticators can use [1319, 1926]. Some work examines metrics for evaluating biometric's security [1568]. Jain, Nandakumar, and Ross [956] provide a good review of biometric research.

Honan [920] points out that what one organization may display on the Web, another may use to authenticate users. This is a problem in social networks, where information used to authenticate or validate users is available on multiple websites but with differing degrees of privacy [946]. This results in the unintentional leaking of information on one site that is used to authenticate on another site, for example when resetting a password [2083].

Peisert, Talbot, and Kroeger [1510] present four principles of authentication. These principles acknowledge the fact that humans are able to infer from context much about an identity, whereas computers cannot.

13.13 Exercises

1. Prove Theorem 13.1.

2. A system allows the user to choose a password with a length of one to eight characters, inclusive. Assume that 10,000 passwords can be tested per second. The system administrators want to expire passwords once they have a probability of 0.10 of having been guessed. Determine the expected time to meet this probability under each of the following conditions.

   a. Password characters may be any ASCII characters from 1 to 127, inclusive.

   b. Password characters may be any alphanumeric characters ("A" through "Z," "a" through "z," and "0" through "9").

   c. Password characters must be digits.

3. Anderson's Formula assumes that all passwords are equally likely to be chosen. Generalize the formula to handle cases in which the probability of the ith string in a set of possible passwords is p_i.

4. Classify the following proposed passwords as good choices or poor choices, and justify your reasoning:

   a. Mary

   b. go2work

   c. cat&dog

   d. 3.1515pi

5. The strings used as examples of good passwords are constructed to make them difficult to guess. Yet the particular good passwords in this chapter should not be used as passwords. Why not?

6. If password aging is based on previous passwords, why should those previous passwords not be stored in the clear on disk?

7. Why should salts be chosen at random?

8. Does using passwords with salts make attacking a specific account more difficult than using passwords without salts? Explain why or why not.

9. Show that a system using an EKE scheme is vulnerable to an online dictionary attack.

10. The designers of the UNIX password algorithm used a 12-bit salt to perturb the first and third sets of 12 entries in the E-table of the UNIX hashing function (the DES). Consider a system with 2^{24} users. Assume that each user is assigned a salt from a uniform random distribution and that anyone can read the password hashes and salts for the users.

    a. What is the expected time to find all users' passwords using a dictionary attack?

    b. Assume that eight more characters were added to the password and that the DES algorithm was changed so as to use all 16 password characters. What would be the expected time to find all users' passwords using a dictionary attack?

    c. Assume that the passwords were eight characters long but that the salt length was increased to 24 bits. Again, the salts (and the corresponding algorithms) are known to all users. What would be the expected time to find all users' passwords using a dictionary attack?

11. The example describing S/Key stated that "for MD4 and MD5, dictionary attacks are not a threat provided the seeds are chosen randomly." Why? How realistic is this assumption?

12. Why should a time-based authentication system invalidate the current password on a successful authentication?

13. A computer system uses biometrics to authenticate users. Discuss ways in which an attacker might try to spoof the system under each of the following conditions:

    a. The biometric hardware is directly connected to the system, and the authentication software is loaded onto the system.

    b. The biometric hardware is on a stand-alone computer connected to the system, and the authentication software on the stand-alone computer sends a "yes" or "no" to the system indicating whether or not the user has been authenticated.

14. What complications arise in dynamic keystroke monitoring as a biometric authentication mechanism when the user's keystrokes are sent over the Internet? In particular, what characteristics of the keystroke sequences are valid, and which ones are distorted by the network?

15. PAM can be used to provide authorization as well as authentication. Design a set of modules for the PAM scheme that implements the Chinese Wall model.

Part V

Implementation II: Systems

Part V discusses noncryptographic implementation mechanisms. It focuses on the sharing of rights and information.

Chapter 14, "Design Principles," presents eight basic design principles for security mechanisms. These principles underlie computer security mechanisms and apply to some extent to the policies that the mechanisms enforce.

Chapter 15, "Representing Identity," discusses the representation of identity within a system. Identities include group and role representation of users, as well as the privileges they have or acquire.

Chapter 16, "Access Control Mechanisms," presents the basic access control mechanisms and the various ways in which they are organized. These mechanisms can be discretionary or mandatory, and sometimes even based on the originator of a document.

Chapter 17, "Information Flow," discusses mechanisms for analyzing and controlling the flow of information throughout a system. Both runtime mechanisms and compiler-based mechanisms allow such flows to be restricted.

Chapter 18, "Confinement Problem," discusses the problem of containing data for authorized uses only. It presents sandboxes and covert channels.

Chapter 14
Design Principles

> FALSTAFF: If I had a thousand sons, the
> first human principle I would teach them should
> be, to forswear thin potations and to addict
> themselves to sack.
> — *The Second Part of King Henry the Fourth*, IV, iii, 133–136.

Specific design principles underlie the design and implementation of mechanisms for supporting security policies. These principles build on the ideas of simplicity and restriction. This chapter discusses those basic ideas and design principles.

14.1 Underlying Ideas

Saltzer and Schroeder [1644] describe eight principles for the design and implementation of security mechanisms; Saltzer and Kaashoek [1643] later refined them. The principles draw on the ideas of simplicity and restriction.

Simplicity makes designs and mechanisms easy to understand. More importantly, simple designs lead to fewer problems, and those that occur are usually easier to deal with. Minimizing the interaction of system components minimizes the number of sanity checks on data being transmitted from one component to another.

EXAMPLE: The program *sendmail* reads configuration data from a binary file. System administrators generated the binary file by "freezing," or compiling, a text version of the configuration file. This created three interfaces: the mechanism used to edit the text file, the mechanism used to freeze the file, and the mechanism *sendmail* used to read the frozen file. The second interface required manual intervention and was often overlooked. To minimize this problem, *sendmail* checked that the frozen file was newer than the text file. If not, it warned the user to update the frozen configuration file.

The security problem lies in the assumptions that *sendmail* made. For example, the compiler would check that a particular option had an integer value. However, *sendmail* would not recheck this; it assumed that the compiler had done the checking. Errors in the compiler checks, or *sendmail*'s assumptions being inconsistent with those of the compiler, could produce security problems. If the compiler allowed the default UID to be a user name (say, daemon with a UID of 1), but *sendmail* assumed that it was an integer UID, then *sendmail* would scan the string "daemon" as though it were an integer. Most input routines would recognize that this string is not an integer and would default the return value to 0. Thus, *sendmail* would deliver mail with the root UID rather than with the desired daemon UID.

Simplicity also reduces the potential for inconsistencies within a policy or set of policies.

EXAMPLE: A college rule requires any teaching assistant who becomes aware of cheating to report it. A different rule ensures the privacy of student files. A TA contacts a student, pointing out that some files for a program were not submitted. The student tells the TA that the files are in the student's directory, and asks the TA to get the files. The TA does so, and while looking for the files notices two sets, one with names beginning with "x" and the other set not. Unsure of which set to use, the TA takes the first set. The comments show that they were written by a second student. The TA gets the second set, and the comments show that they were written by the first student. On comparing the two sets, the TA notes that they are identical except for the names in the comments. Although concerned about a possible countercharge for violation of privacy, the TA reports the student for cheating. As expected, the student charges the TA with violating his privacy by reading the first set of files. The rules conflict. Which charge or charges should be sustained?

Restriction minimizes the power of an entity. The entity can access only information it needs.

EXAMPLE: Government officials are denied access to information for which they have no need (the "need to know" policy). They cannot communicate that which they do not know.

Entities can communicate with other entities only when necessary, and in as few (and narrow) ways as possible.

EXAMPLE: All communications with prisoners are monitored. Prisoners can communicate with people on a list (given to the prison warden) through personal visits or mail, both of which are monitored to prevent the prisoners from receiving contraband such as files for cutting through prison bars or weapons to help them break out. The only exception to the monitoring policy is when prisoners meet with their attorneys. Such communications are privileged and so cannot be monitored.

"Communication" is used in its widest possible sense, including that of imparting information by not communicating.

EXAMPLE: Bernstein and Woodward, the reporters who broke the Watergate scandal, describe an attempt to receive information from a source without the source's directly answering the question. They suggested a scheme in which the source would hang up if the information was inaccurate and remain on the line if the information was accurate. The source remained on the line, confirming the information [178].

14.2   Principles of Secure Design

The principles of secure design discussed in this section express common-sense applications of simplicity and restriction in terms of computing. We will discuss detailed applications of these principles throughout the remainder of Part V and in Part VIII, "Practicum." However, this chapter mentions specific examples.

14.2.1   Principle of Least Privilege

This principle restricts how privileges are granted.

> **Definition 14–1.** The *principle of least privilege* states that a subject should be given only those privileges that it needs in order to complete its task.

If a subject does not need an access right, the subject should not have that right. Furthermore, the *function* of the subject (as opposed to its identity) should control the assignment of rights. If a specific action requires that a subject's access rights be augmented, those extra rights should be relinquished *immediately* on completion of the action. This is the analogue of the "need to know" rule: if the subject does not need access to an object to perform its task, it should not have the right to access that object. More precisely, if a subject needs to append to an object, but not to alter the information already contained in the object, it should be given append rights and not write rights.

In practice, most systems do not have the granularity of privileges and permissions required to apply this principle precisely. The designers of security mechanisms then apply this principle as best they can. In such systems, the consequences of security problems are often more severe than the consequences for systems that adhere to this principle.

EXAMPLE: The UNIX operating system does not apply access controls to the user *root*. That user can terminate any process and read, write, or delete any file. Thus, users who create backups can also delete files. The administrator account on Windows has the same powers.

This principle requires that processes should be confined to as small a protection domain as possible.

EXAMPLE: A mail server accepts mail from the Internet and copies the messages into a spool directory; a local server will complete delivery. The mail server needs the rights to access the appropriate network port, to create files in the spool directory, and to alter those files (so it can copy the message into the file, rewrite the delivery address if needed, and add the appropriate "Received" lines). It should surrender the right to access the file as soon as it has finished writing the file into the spool directory, because it does not need to access that file again. The server should not be able to access any user's files, or any files other than its own configuration files.

14.2.1.1   Principle of Least Authority

Closely related to the principle of least privilege is the principle of least authority [1349]. The two are often treated as meaning the same. However, some authors make a distinction between "permission" and "authority." They treat permission as determining what actions a process can take on objects directly, and authority as determining that effects a process may have on an object, either directly (as with permission) or indirectly through its interactions with other processes or subsystems.

Miller and Shapiro [1349] give a good example from the Take-Grant Protection Model. In that model, the rights would represent actions that subjects could take over objects, and so represent permissions. But the *de facto* rules of that model, which govern information transfer, show how information can flow from a subject to an object that is not directly connected to the subject. Hence the subject does not have permission to write information into the object, but it does have permission to pass the information to a second subject, and that subject can write the information into the object.[1]

> **Definition 14–2.** The *principle of least authority* states that a subject should be given only the authority that it needs in order to complete its task.

If one reads the principle of least privilege as speaking to *permissions*, then this principle is somewhat different. But if it speaks to *authority*, the two are the same.

14.2.2   Principle of Fail-Safe Defaults

This principle restricts how privileges are initialized when a subject or object is created.

---

[1] This is the *find* rule described by Bishop and Snyder [213, 233].

Definition 14–3. The *principle of fail-safe defaults* states that, unless a subject is given explicit access to an object, it should be denied access to that object.

This principle requires that the default access to an object is *none*. Whenever access, privileges, or some security-related attribute is not *explicitly* granted, it should be denied. Moreover, if the subject is unable to complete its action or task, it should undo those changes it made to the security state of the system before it terminates. This way, even if the program fails, the system is still safe.

EXAMPLE: If the mail server is unable to create a file in the spool directory, it should close the network connection, issue an error message, and stop. It should not try to store the message elsewhere or to expand its privileges to save the message in another location, because an attacker could use that ability to overwrite other files or fill up other disks (a denial of service attack). The protections on the mail spool directory itself should allow create and write access only to the mail server and read and delete access only to the local server. No other user should have access to the directory.

In practice, most systems will allow an administrator access to the mail spool directory. By the principle of least privilege, that administrator should be able to access only the subjects and objects involved in mail queueing and delivery. As we have seen, this constraint minimizes the threats if that administrator's account is compromised. The mail system can be damaged or destroyed, but nothing else can be.

Because many users do not change default access control permissions, this rule applies to the default settings for both the system and for users.

14.2.3   Principle of Economy of Mechanism

This principle simplifies the design and implementation of security mechanisms.

Definition 14–4. The *principle of economy of mechanism* states that security mechanisms should be as simple as possible.

If a design and an implementation are simple, fewer possibilities exist for errors. The checking and testing process is less complex, because fewer components and cases need to be tested. Complex mechanisms often make assumptions about the system and environment in which they run. If these assumptions are incorrect, security problems may result.

EXAMPLE: The *ident* protocol [1807] sends the user name associated with a process that has a TCP connection to a remote host. A mechanism on host *nob* that allows access based on the results of an *ident* protocol result makes the assumption that the originating host is trustworthy. If host *toadflax* decides to attack host *nob*, it can connect and then send any identity it chooses in response to the *ident* request. This is an example of a mechanism making an incorrect assumption about the environment (specifically, that host *toadflax* can be trusted).

Interfaces to other modules are particularly suspect, because modules often make implicit assumptions about input or output parameters or the current system state; should any of these assumptions be wrong, the module's actions may produce unexpected and erroneous results. Interaction with external entities, such as other programs, systems, or humans, amplifies this problem.

EXAMPLE: The *finger* protocol transmits information about a user or system [2106]. Many client implementations assume that the server's response is well-formed. However, if an attacker were to create a server that generated an infinite stream of characters, and a *finger* client were to connect to it, the client would print all the characters. As a result, log files and disks could be filled up, resulting in a denial of service attack on the querying host. This is an example of incorrect assumptions about the input to the client.

14.2.4   Principle of Complete Mediation

This principle restricts the caching of information, which often leads to simpler implementations of mechanisms.

> **Definition 14–5.** The *principle of complete mediation* requires that all accesses to objects be checked to ensure that they are allowed.

Whenever a subject attempts to read an object, the operating system should mediate the action. First, it determines if the subject is allowed to read the object. If so, it provides the resources for the read to occur. If the subject tries to read the object again, the system should check that the subject is still allowed to read the object. Most systems would not make the second check. They would cache the results of the first check and base the second access on the cached results.

EXAMPLE: When a UNIX process tries to read a file, the operating system determines if the process is allowed to read the file. If so, the process receives a file descriptor encoding the allowed access. Whenever the process wants to read the file, it presents the file descriptor to the kernel. The kernel then allows the access.

If the owner of the file disallows the process permission to read the file after the file descriptor is issued, the kernel still allows access. This scheme violates the principle of complete mediation, because the second access is not checked. The cached value is used, resulting in the denial of access being ineffective.

The mediator should check that the request comes from the claimed source (authenticity) and that it has not been tampered with (integrity). After those are validated, the access should be granted if, and only if, the access is authorized. Failure to check authenticity and integrity can cause security problems.

EXAMPLE: The Domain Name Service (DNS) caches information mapping host names into IP addresses. If an attacker is able to "poison" the cache by implanting records associating a bogus IP address with a name, one host will route connections to another host incorrectly. Section 15.6.1.2 discusses this in more detail.

14.2.5   Principle of Open Design

This principle suggests that security should not depend solely on secrecy.

> **Definition 14–6.** The *principle of open design* states that the security of a mechanism should not depend on the secrecy of its design or implementation.

Designers and implementers of a program must not depend on secrecy of the details of their design and implementation to ensure security. Others can ferret out such details either through technical means, such as disassembly and analysis, or through nontechnical means, such as searching through garbage receptacles for source code listings (called "dumpster-diving"). If the strength of the program's security depends on the ignorance of the user, a knowledgeable user can defeat that security mechanism. The term "security through obscurity" captures this concept exactly.

This is especially true of cryptographic software and systems. Because cryptography is a highly mathematical subject, companies that market cryptographic software or use cryptography to protect user data frequently keep their algorithms secret. Experience has shown that such secrecy adds little if anything to the security of the system. Worse, it gives an aura of strength that is all too often lacking in the actual implementation of the system.

Keeping cryptographic keys and passwords secret does not violate this principle, because a key is not an algorithm. However, keeping the enciphering and deciphering algorithms secret would violate it.

Issues of proprietary software and trade secrets complicate the application of this principle. In some cases, companies may not want their designs made public, lest their competitors use them. The principle then requires that the design and implementation be available to people barred from disclosing it outside the company.

EXAMPLE: The Content Scrambling System (CSS) is a cryptographic algorithm that protects DVD movie disks from unauthorized copying. The DVD disk has an authentication key, a disk key, and a title key. The title key is enciphered with the disk key. A block on the DVD contains several copies of the disk key, each enciphered by a different player key, and a checksum of the disk key. When a DVD is inserted into a DVD player, the algorithm reads the authentication key and then authenticates the device (presumably to verify it is allowed to read the following keys). It then deciphers the disk keys using the DVD player's unique key. When it finds a deciphered key with the correct hash, it uses that key to decipher the title key, and it uses the title key to decipher the movie [1824]. (Figure 14–1 shows the layout of the keys.)

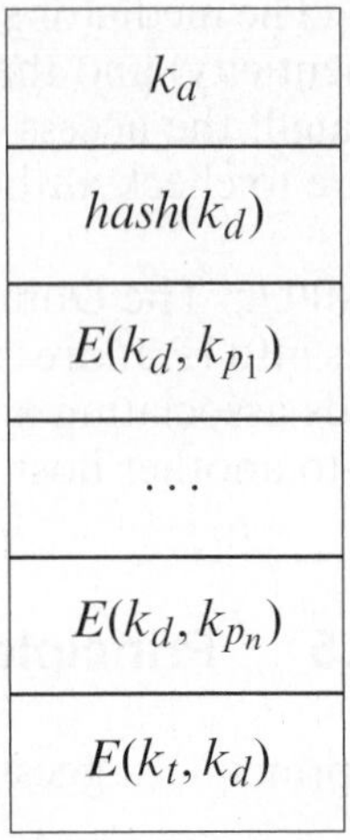

The authentication and disk keys are not located in the file containing the movie, so if one copies the file, one still needs the DVD disk in the DVD player to be able to play the movie.

In 1999, a group in Norway acquired a (software) DVD playing program that had an unenciphered key. They also derived an algorithm completely compatible with the CSS algorithm from the software. This enabled them to decipher any DVD movie file. Software that could perform these functions rapidly became available throughout the Internet, much to the discomfort of the DVD Copyright Control Association, which promptly sued to prevent the code from being made public [643, 1465]. As if to emphasize the problems of providing security by concealing algorithms, the plaintiff's lawyers filed a declaration containing the source code of an implementation of the CSS algorithm. When they realized this, they requested that the declaration be sealed from public view. By then, the declaration—with the source code—had been posted on several Internet sites, including one that had more than 21,000 downloads of the declaration before the court sealed it [1278].

k_a
$hash(k_d)$
$E(k_d, k_{p_1})$
$\cdots$
$E(k_d, k_{p_n})$
$E(k_t, k_d)$

Figure 14–1 DVD key layout. k_a is the authentication key, k_t the title key, k_d the disk key, and k_{p_i} the key for DVD player i.

14.2.5.1   Minimize Secrets

The principle of open design implies that the designer should minimize secrets. Secrets can leak no matter how confidential one thinks they are—and mistakes do occur that sometimes reveal them, as in the above example. Protecting the confidentiality of a few secrets is typically simpler than protecting the confidentiality of many secrets.

This rule also suggests that designers should plan for the compromise of any secrets. When a secret is compromised, it should be simple and quick to restore the system to a state where the (formerly) secret data has no value. Minimizing the number of secrets reduces the number of these contingency plans, simplifying management.

14.2.6   Principle of Separation of Privilege

This principle is restrictive because it limits access to system entities.

> **Definition 14–7.** The *principle of separation of privilege* states that a system should not grant permission based on a single condition.

This principle is equivalent to the separation of duty principle discussed in Section 6.1. Company checks for more than $75,000 must be signed by two officers of the company. If either does not sign, the check is not valid. The two conditions are the signatures of both officers.

Similarly, systems and programs granting access to resources should do so only when more than one condition is met. This provides a fine-grained control over the resource as well as additional assurance that the access is authorized.

EXAMPLE: On Berkeley-based versions of the UNIX operating system, the program *su*, which enables users to change from their accounts to the *root* account, requires two conditions to be met. The first condition is that the user knows the *root* password. The second condition is that the user is in the *wheel* group (the group with GID 0). Meeting either condition is not sufficient to acquire *root* access; meeting both conditions is required.

14.2.7   Principle of Least Common Mechanism

This principle is restrictive because it limits sharing.

> **Definition 14–8.** The *principle of least common mechanism* states that mechanisms used to access resources should not be shared.

Sharing resources provides a channel along which information can be transmitted, and so such sharing should be minimized. In practice, if the operating system provides support for virtual machines, the operating system will enforce this privilege automatically to some degree (see Chapter 18, "Confinement Problem"). Otherwise, it will provide some support (such as a virtual memory space) but not complete support (because the file system will appear as shared among several processes).

EXAMPLE: A website provides electronic commerce services for a major company. Attackers want to deprive the company of the revenue it obtains from that website. They flood the site with messages and tie up the electronic commerce services. Legitimate customers are unable to access the website and, as a result, take their business elsewhere.

Here, the sharing of the Internet with the attackers' sites caused the attack to succeed. The appropriate countermeasure would be to restrict the attackers' access to the segment of the Internet connected to the website. Techniques for doing this include proxy servers such as the Purdue SYN intermediary [1695] or traffic throttling (see Section 7.4, "Availability and Network Flooding"). The former targets suspect connections; the latter reduces the load on the relevant segment of the network indiscriminately.

Minimizing the number of shared mechanisms also reduces the scope of an attack that compromises such a mechanism. If all versions of an operating system use the same program, then compromising that single program enables attackers to compromise any system of that type. But if the systems each use a slightly different version of the program, then compromise becomes more difficult.

EXAMPLE: Attack tools assume an underlying structure or configuration of a system or program. In order to invalidate this assumption, researchers have studied how to inject artificial diversity effectively into programs and systems. Then the attack tools will not work properly.

Object code obfuscation tools scramble the flow of execution and the placement of data in memory. For example, many attacks target the return address for function calls, which is stored on a stack and thus in a predictable location. Adding a layer of indirection requires changing the function call and return sequence. Then an attempt to overwrite the return address will change the index into the table instead. By appropriately constraining that value and obscuring how the actual return addresses are stored, the attacker will be unlikely to guess the actual location of the return address, defeating this class of attacks [381]. Other techniques randomize the order of variables and functions in memory or introduce random gaps between formerly contiguous areas of storage, and locations of memory regions. This renders ineffective attack tools that rely on the memory layout of the program [193].

14.2.8   Principle of Least Astonishment

This principle recognizes the human element in computer security.

> **Definition 14–9.** The *principle of least astonishment* states that security mechanisms should be designed so that users understand the reason that the mechanism works the way it does and that using the mechanism is simple.

This principle requires security mechanisms to use a model that the target audience (users and system administrators, typically) can easily understand. If the audience's mental model is too different than that used by the designers and implementers, then their confusion may undermine the security mechanisms.

Thus, configuring and executing a program should be as easy and as intuitive as possible, and any output should be clear, direct, and useful. If security-related software is too complicated to configure, system administrators may unintentionally set up the software in a nonsecure manner. Similarly, security-related user programs must be easy to use and must output understandable messages. If a user is changing a password, and the proposed password is rejected, the password changing program should state why it was rejected rather than giving a cryptic error message. If a configuration file has an incorrect parameter, the error message should describe the proper parameter.

EXAMPLE: The *ssh* program [131, 2058] allows a user to set up a public key mechanism for enciphering communications between systems. The installation and configuration mechanisms for the UNIX version allow one to arrange that the public key be stored locally without any password protection. In this case, one need not supply a password to connect to the remote system, but will still obtain the enciphered connection. This mechanism satisfies the principle of least astonishment.

On the other hand, security requires that the messages impart no unnecessary information.

EXAMPLE: When a user supplies the wrong password during login, the system should reject the attempt with a message stating that the login failed. If it were to say that the password was incorrect, the user would know that the account name was legitimate. If the "user" were really an unauthorized attacker, she would then know the name of an account for which she could try to guess a password.

Balancing the needs of security and the mental models of users requires that the designers and implementers take into account the environment in which the security mechanisms are used.

EXAMPLE: A mainframe system allows users to place passwords on files. Accessing the files requires that the program supply the password. Although this mechanism violates the principle as stated, it is considered sufficiently minimal to be acceptable. On an interactive system, where the pattern of file accesses is more frequent and more transient, this requirement would be too great a burden to be acceptable.

14.2.8.1   Psychological Acceptability

The principle of least astonishment is similar to one of Saltzer's and Schroeder's original principles, the *principle of psychological acceptability*. That principle stated that that security mechanisms should not make the resource more difficult to access than if the security mechanisms were not present. The difference between that principle and the principle of least astonishment is that the former expressed an ideal, whereas the latter recognizes that security mechanisms may add additional steps to accessing the resource. The question is whether those additional steps are unnecessarily difficult to take to the particular population of users of the system.

14.3   Summary

The design principles discussed in this chapter are fundamental to the design and implementation of security mechanisms. They encompass not only technical details but also human interaction. Several principles come from nontechnical environments, such as the principle of least privilege. Each principle involves the restriction of privilege according to some criterion, or the minimization of complexity to make the mechanisms less likely to fail.

14.4   Research Issues

These principles pervade all research touching on the design and implementation of secure systems. The principle of least privilege raises the issue of granularity of privilege. Is a "write" privilege sufficient, or should it be fragmented—for example, into "write" and "write at the end" or "append," or into the ability to write to specific blocks? How does the multiplicity of rights affect system administration and security management? How does it affect architecture and performance? How does it affect the user interface and the user's model of the system?

Least common mechanism problems arise when dealing with denial of service attacks, because such attacks exploit shared media. The principle of least common mechanism plays a role in handling covert channels, which are discussed further in Chapter 18.

Separation of privilege arises in the creation of user and system roles. How much power should administrative accounts have? How should they work together? These issues arise in role-based access control, which is discussed in Section 8.4.

The principle of complete mediation runs counter to the philosophy of caching. One caches data to keep from having to retrieve the information when it is next needed, but complete mediation requires the retrieval of access permissions. How are these conflicting forces balanced in practice?

Research in software and systems design and implementation studies the application of the principle of economy of mechanism. How can interfaces be made simple and consistent? How can the various design paradigms lead to better-crafted, simpler software and systems?

Whether "open source" software (software the source of which is publicly available) is more secure than other software is a complex question. Analysts can check open source software for security problems more easily than they can software for which no source is available. Knowing that one's coding will be available for public scrutiny should encourage programmers to write better, tighter code. On the other hand, attackers can also look at the source code for security flaws, and various pressures (such as time to market) weigh against careful coding. Furthermore, the debate ignores security problems introduced by misconfigured software, or software used incorrectly.

Experimental data for the debate about the efficacy of open source software is lacking. An interesting research project would be to design an experiment that would provide evidence either for or against the proposition that if source code for software is available, then that software has (or causes) fewer security problems than software for which source code is not available. Part of the research would be to determine how to make this question precise, what metrics and statistical techniques should be used to analyze the data, and how the data should be collected.

An understanding of people's world views, and mental models of how computers and security should work, are the basis for applying the principle of least astonishment. The user interface of many security mechanisms, and the details that users must master, differ from their real-world counterparts for a variety of reasons. Thus, understanding how to communicate security issues to people, and tailoring mechanisms to interpret user commands properly, is an area of active research in both the security and human factors communities.

14.5 Further Reading

Many papers discuss the application of these principles to security mechanisms. Succeeding chapters will present references for this aspect of the principles. Other papers present different sets of principles. These papers are generally specializations or alternative views of the principles in this chapter, tailored for particular environments. Abadi and Needham [4] and Anderson and Needham [60] discuss principles for the design of cryptographic protocols; Syverson discusses their limits [1847], and Moore [1377] and Abadi [2] describe problems in cryptographic protocols. Wood [2019, 2020] discusses principles for secure systems design with an emphasis on groupware. Shapiro and Hardy elaborate on a set of principles underlying the design of the operating system EROS [1729]. Bonyun [268] focuses on architectural principles. Landwehr and Goldschlag [1135] consider Internet security. Other examples are for authentication protocols used in the infrastructure of the power grid [1049], for designing privacy constraints into systems [367], and for computer forensics [1506].

Principles for interacting with people are also under study. Yee discusses principles for user interfaces for secure systems [2051]. Peisert et al. [1510] identify principles of authentication that correspond to physical validation of identity. Stajano and Wilson [1808] present some principles underlying successful computer scams, and from them derive principles for protecting people. Motiee et al. [1387] examine user considerations about the use of the principle of least privilege.

14.6 Exercises

1. The PostScript language [18] describes page layout for printers. Among its features is the ability to request that the interpreter execute commands on the host system.

   a. Describe a danger that this feature presents when the language interpreter is running with administrative or root privileges.

   b. Explain how the principle of least privilege could be used to ameliorate this danger.

2. A common technique for inhibiting password guessing is to disable an account after three consecutive failed login attempts (see Section 13.4.2).

   a. Discuss how this technique might prevent legitimate users from accessing the system. Why is this action a violation of the principle of least common mechanism?

   b. One can argue that this is an example of fail-safe defaults, because by blocking access to an account under attack, the system is defaulting to a known, safe state. Do you agree or disagree with this argument? Justify your answer.

3. Kernighan and Plauger [1041] argue a minimalist philosophy of tool building. Their thesis is that each program should perform exactly one task, and more complex programs should be formed by combining simpler programs. Discuss how this philosophy fits in with the principle of economy of mechanism. In particular, how does the advantage of the simplicity of each component of a software system offset the disadvantage of a multiplicity of interfaces among the various components?

4. Design an experiment to determine the performance impact of checking access permissions for each file access (as opposed to once at the file's opening). If you have access to a system on which you can modify the file access mechanism, run your experiment and determine the impact.

5. A company publishes the design of its security software product in a manual that accompanies the executable software.

   a. In what ways does this satisfy the principle of open design? In what ways does it not?

   b. Given that the design is known, what advantages does keeping the source code unavailable give the company and those who purchase the software? What disadvantages does it cause?

6. Assume that processes on a system share no resources. Is it possible for one process to block another process's access to a resource? Why or why not? From your answer, argue that denial of service attacks are possible or impossible.

7. Given that the Internet is a shared network, discuss whether preventing denial of service attacks is inherently possible or not possible. Do systems connected to the Internet violate the principle of least common mechanism?

8. A program called *lsu* [219] gives access to role accounts. The user's access rights are checked, and the user is required to enter her password. If access rules allow the change and the user's password is correct, *lsu* allows the change. Given that Mary uses *lsu* from her account, why does *lsu* require her to enter her password? Name the principles involved, and why they require this.

9. Recall the S/Key one-time password algorithm discussed in Section 13.5.1. When a user prints a list of S/Key passwords for future use, the system encodes each hash value as a set of six short words and prints them. Why does it not merely print out the hash values?

10. The program *su* enables a UNIX user to access another user's account. Unless the first user is the superuser, *su* requires that the password of the second user be given. A (possibly apocryphal) version of *su* would ask for the user's password and, if it could not determine if the password was correct because the password file could not be opened, *immediately* grant superuser access so that the user could fix the problem. Discuss which of the design principles this approach meets, and which ones it violates.

11. Among the design principles Yee [2051] identifies is the *principle of expected ability*, which says that the interface must not lead the user to believe it is possible to do something that cannot be done. Which of the design principles in this chapter support this principle?

Chapter 15
Representing Identity

> AEMELIA: Most mighty duke, behold a man much wrong'd.
> All gather to see them.
> ADRIANA: I see two husbands, or mine eyes deceive me!
> DUKE SOLINUS: One of these men is Genius to the other;
> And so of these, which is the natural man,
> And which the spirit? Who deciphers them?
> DROMIO OF SYRACUSE: I, sir, am Dromio: command him away.
> DROMIO OF EPHESUS: I, sir, am Dromio: pray, let me stay.
> — *The Comedy of Errors*, V, i, 332–338.

The theme of identity runs throughout humanity's experience, and computers are no exception. In computer science, an identity is the basis for assignment of privileges and is integral in the designation of a protection domain. This chapter discusses the many different types of identity and the contexts in which they arise. It begins with the identity of a principal on a system, first singly and then as defined by function. Designation of identity for certificates follows, as does identity on a network with respect to both individual processes and individual hosts. The chapter concludes with the notion of an anonymous user.

15.1 What Is Identity?

Identity is simply a computer's representation of an entity.

Definition 15–1. A *principal* is a unique entity. An *identity* specifies a principal.

Authentication binds a principal to a representation of identity internal to the computer. Each system has its own way of expressing this representation, but all decisions of access and resource allocation assume that the binding is correct.

Identities are used for several purposes. The two main ones are for accountability and for access control. Accountability requires an identity that tracks principals across actions and changes of other identities, so that the principal taking any action can be unambiguously identified. Access control requires an identity that the access control mechanisms can use to determine if a specific access (or type of access) should be allowed.

Accountability is tied to logging and auditing. It requires an unambiguous identification of the principal involved. On many systems, this is not possible. Instead, the logged identity maps to a user account, to a group, or to a role.

Most systems base access rights on the identity of the principal executing the process. That is, all processes executed by user *bishop* have some set of rights. All processes executed by user *holly* have a set of rights that may differ from those that *bishop*'s processes have. However, a process may have fewer rights than the principal executing it, and in fact there are substantial reasons to reduce privileges. Chapter 16, "Access Control Mechanisms," discusses this topic in more depth.

15.2   Files and Objects

The identity of a file or other entity (here called an "object") depends on the system that contains the object.

Local systems identify objects by assigning names. The name may be intended for human use (such as a file name), for process use (such as a file descriptor or handle), or for kernel use (such as a file allocation table entry). Each name may have different semantics.

EXAMPLE: The UNIX operating system offers four different types of file names. The *device number* and *inode* uniquely identify a file. The inode contains file attribute information such as access control permissions and ownership information, and identifies the specific disk blocks that contain the file's data. Processes read files using a *file descriptor* that abstracts the inode into a representation that the process can read from, write to, and so forth. Once created, the file descriptor cannot be rebound to a different file. Processes (and users) can also use *file names* that identify files by describing their positions in the file hierarchy. UNIX file names may be *absolute path names* that describe the locations of files with respect to the root of the UNIX file hierarchy, or *relative path names* that describe the locations of files with respect to the directory in which the current process is executing.

The semantics of the names differ in important ways. Most critically, when a process or user operates on a file, the kernel maps the file name to an inode using an iterative procedure. It obtains the inode of the first directory in the path,[1] opens it, and within that directory locates the inode number of the next component in the path. This continues until the file's inode number is found. Two references to the same file name will reference different file objects when the file is deleted after the first reference and a new file, with the same name as the deleted file, is created. This can create problems with programs (see Section 31.5.3.3, "Race Conditions in File Accesses").

However, when a file descriptor is created, it refers to a specific object. Regardless of how the file is manipulated, the inode that the file descriptor refers to remains present until the file descriptor is closed, which breaks the association between the descriptor and the inode.

If the object resides on a different system, the name must encode the location of the object.

EXAMPLE: A *uniform resource locator* (URL) identifies an object by its location and the protocol needed to access it. The object with the URL *http://abccorp.com/pub/README* specifies that the named object can be accessed by using the HTTP protocol to request the object */pub/README* from the host *abccorp.com*. The URL does not say that the object is located on that host. Indeed, the host may construct the object to respond to the request, or it may forward the request to another host, or it may be invalid.

One file may have multiple names. The semantics of the system determine the effects of each name. For example, some systems define "deleting a file" to mean removing the given file name. The file object itself will not be deleted until all its names (or all names meeting certain conditions) have been deleted. Section 30.3.1.3, "File Deletion," discusses this issue further.

15.3 Users

In general, a *user* is an identity tied to a single entity. Specific systems may add additional constraints. Systems represent user identity in a number of different ways. Indeed, the same system may use different representations of identity in different contexts.

---

[1] If the path is an absolute path name, the first directory in the path is the root directory, which has a well-known inode number (typically 0, 1, or 2). If the path is a relative path name, the first directory has the same inode number as the directory in which the process executes.

EXAMPLE: Versions of the UNIX operating system usually represent user identity as an integer between 0 and some large integer (usually 65,535). This integer is called the *user identification number*, or UID. Principals (called *users*) may also be assigned *login names*. Each login name corresponds to a single UID (although one UID may have many different login names).

When the kernel deals with user identity, it uses the UID; for example, the superuser is any user whose UID is 0 regardless of that user's name. However, when a user logs in, she provides her identity as her login name. Similarly, all logging uses the login name rather than the numeric UID.

The same principal may have many different identities. Typically each identity serves a particular function.

EXAMPLE: Versions of the UNIX operating system provide several types of user identities [1294]. Because a user is a subject, and a process executes on behalf of a user, the various identities are associated with processes. The *real* UID is the user identity at initial login, but it can be changed. The *effective* UID is the user identity used for access control. For example, if only UID 22 can read a particular file, and a process's real UID is 22 and its effective UID is 35, the user will not be able to read the file. If the process's real UID were 35 and its effective UID were 22, access would be granted.

A special class of programs, called *setuid programs* [747], create processes with the effective UID being that of the owner of the program rather than that of the user executing the program. The resulting process has the access rights of the owner of the program rather than those of the user executing the program.

In an effort to limit the need for special privileges, UNIX systems provide a *saved* UID. Whenever the effective UID changes, the saved UID is set to the value of the effective UID *before* the change. The user can switch among the real, effective, and saved UIDs. This allows the process to be given *root* privileges, use them for a limited time (effective UID of 0), drop them (saved UID of 0, nonzero effective UID), and reacquire them later.

Traditionally, the real UID was used to track the original UID of the process. However, the superuser can change it. To provide an unalterable means of recording the original real UID of the process, many UNIX systems provide an *audit* or *login* UID. This UID is assigned at login and cannot be changed.[2]

Where disambiguation of two users with the same identification is required, additional information is needed. On a network, for example, the host name or domain name may be attached to the identity.

EXAMPLE: Kerberos key distribution centers (see Section 11.2.2) can interoperate. Each one forms the basis of a "realm" (essentially a domain controlled by the Kerberos key distribution center). Kerberos users are then identified by both name and realm. For example "anne@realm1.com" refers to the user

---

[2]Interestingly, some systems allow *root* to change the audit UID after assignment.

"anne" in the realm "realm1.com," and she is presumably different than the user "anne@realm2.com" ("anne" in the realm "realm2.com").

15.4   Groups and Roles

An "entity" may be a set of individual entities referred to by a single identifier. The members of the set must be distinguishable, but the set may have an identity separate from any of its elements.

Principals often need to share access to files. Most systems allow principals to be grouped into sets called, logically enough, *groups*. Groups are essentially a shorthand tool for assigning rights to a set of principals simultaneously.

Two implementations of groups provide different abilities and therefore are based on different models. The first simply uses a group as an alias for a set of principals. Principals are assigned to groups, and they stay in those groups for the lifetimes of their sessions. The second model allows principals to change from one group to another. After each change, the rights belonging to the principal as a member of the previous group are discarded and the rights of the new group are added. The difference lies in the representations of identity. In the former model, the identity assigned to a principal remains static; it is the principal identity and the set of identities of each group that the principal is a part of. This identity does not change throughout the lifetime of the session. In the latter model, the identity of the principal is the identity of the user and the set of identities of each group of which the principal is currently a member. It is dynamic, and should the principal change from one group to another, the identity of that principal also changes. In practice, one discusses "user identity" and "group identity."

EXAMPLE: UNIX users are assigned membership to a group when they log in [1294]. Each process has two identities, a "user identification" and a "group identification." On older UNIX systems, each principal can be in only one group at a time. The command *newgrp*(1) changes this identity. The principal can change to any group of which he is a member. On other UNIX systems, each principal can be in several groups at a time. On login, the user is placed into all groups of which he is a member.

Membership in a group is often based on some set of attributes, for example membership in an organization, a particular medical condition, or access to particular sets of equipment or data. A commonly used attribute is a person's job because the job requirements dictate the rights that someone needs to do the job.

More precisely, a *role* is a type of group that ties membership to function. When a principal assumes a role, the principal is given certain rights that belong to that role. When the principal leaves the role, those rights are removed. The rights given are consistent with the functionality that the principal needs to perform the tasks expected of members of the role.

EXAMPLE: On the DG/UX system, a multilevel secure system, system administration privileges belong to the *sysadmin* role, not the *root* user [2186]. That user's rights are restricted. The *sysuser* user can assume the *sysadmin* role to administer the host, or the *netadmin* role to administer the network. Several such roles are defined.

15.5   Naming and Certificates

Chapter 11 described certificates as a mechanism for binding cryptographic keys to identifiers. The identifier corresponds to a principal; it must uniquely identify the principal to avoid confusion.

Suppose the principals are people. The identifiers cannot be names, because many different people may have the same name. (How many people named "John Smith" or "Pierre LeBlanc" are there?) The identifiers must include ancillary information to distinguish the "Matt Bishop" who teaches at UC Davis from a different person named "Matt Bishop" who works at Microsoft Corporation.

EXAMPLE: The X.509v4 public-key certificates use identifiers called *Distinguished Names* [2032, 2176]. A Distinguished Name identifies a principal. It consists of a series of fields, each with a key and a value. When written as strings, the fields are separated by "/" and the key and value by "=".[3] To use our earlier example, the "Matt Bishop" who teaches at the University of California might have the Distinguished Name

```
/O=University of California/OU=Davis campus/
OU=Department of Computer Science/CN=Matt Bishop/
```

(where the key "O" means organization, "OU" means organizational unit, and "CN" means common name) and the "Matt Bishop" who works at Microsoft might have the Distinguished Name

```
/O=Microsoft Corporation/OU=Quality Assurance/
CN=Matt Bishop/
```

Although the names are the same, the individuals, and hence the Distinguished Names, are different.

Certification authorities (CAs) vouch, at some level, for the identity of the principal to which the certificate is issued. Every CA has two policies controlling how it issues certificates.

---

[3] When compiled into a binary format, in many cases the key is implied by the data structure.

Definition 15–2. A *CA authentication policy* describes the level of authentication required to identify the principal to whom the certificate is to be issued.

Definition 15–3. A *CA issuance policy* describes the principals to whom the CA will issue certificates.

The difference between these two policies is that the first simply establishes the level of proof of identity needed for the CA to accept the principal's claim of identity whereas the second answers the question, "Given the identity of the principal, will the CA issue a certificate?"

EXAMPLE: In 1996, Verisign Corporation ran several CAs. Each had its own policies of issuance and authentication for certificates [746].
  Individuals obtained certificates (called "Digital IDs") from one of three CAs.[4] The class 1 CA authenticated the individual's electronic mail address. This CA provided a certificate for sending and receiving electronic mail securely. The class 2 CA required that the individual supply his real name and address, which was verified through an online database. This CA provided a certificate suitable for online purchasing and was (roughly) equivalent to the level of authentication for a credit card. The class 3 CA required a background check from an investigative service. The certificate from this CA provided a higher level of assurance of identity than the other two certificates. All three CAs had the same issuance policy: that certificates were issued to individuals. A fourth CA provided certificates to web servers. This CA had the same issuance policy as the class 3 CA. Consumers who did business with the website had a high degree of assurance that the website was whom it claimed to be.

In many cases, a CA delegates to a third party, the *registration authority* (RA), the checking of data to be put into the certificate, such as identity. When the RA determines that the CA's requirements for issuing a certificate are met, the RA instructs the CA to issue the certificate. CAs can issue certificates to other organizations. The hierarchical certificate-based key management architecture demonstrates how such an organization can lead to a simple hierarchical structure of policies [1033].

EXAMPLE: The infrastructure organizes CAs into a hierarchical, tree-based structure. Each node in the tree corresponds to a CA. Consider a node that is the root of a subtree. The CAs under that root are constrained by the policies of that root; the subordinate nodes may issue certificates with more restrictive policies, but not with more liberal policies.
  The root of the tree is the *Internet Policy Registration Authority* (IPRA). It sets policies that all subordinate CAs must follow, and it certifies other CAs

---

[4]Actually, a single CA issued multiple types of certificates. Conceptually, the single organization is acting as though it were multiple CAs.

called *policy certification authorities* (PCAs). Each PCA has its own issuance and authentication policies, but those policies must not conflict with the policies set by the IPRA. The PCAs issue certificates to ordinary CAs, which can then issue certificates to organizations or individuals. The IPRA and PCAs do not issue certificates to individuals or organizations. All CAs, PCAs, and the IPRA have unique Distinguished Names.

The elegance of this approach is twofold. Because all PCA policies are public, on receiving a certificate one can determine how much trust to place in the identity in the certificate (authentication policy) as well as the requirements that the holder had to meet to have the certificate issued (issuance policy).

To understand how this works, suppose the University of Valmont wishes to establish a CA for both students and staff. The requirements for certification for these groups are different. Students must present valid registration cards to obtain certificates. These certificates would be considered low-assurance certificates (because of the nature of the registration process) and so would be signed using the university's low-assurance certificate. This certificate, in turn, is signed by a PCA that requires its subordinate CAs to make a good-faith effort to verify the identities of those to whom it issues certificates. But the university requires staff members to present proof of employment and fingerprints, which are compared with the fingerprints obtained when each employee was hired. This provides a high level of assurance of identity, and so the University of Valmont signs these certificates with its high-assurance certificate, obtained from a different PCA that requires the use of biometrics for verification of identity.

The certificates for student John and professor Marsha are both signed by the same organization, but they are signed using different cryptographic keys. John's certificate is signed by the key corresponding to a low-assurance certificate (because the first PCA signed it), and Marsha's certificate is signed by the key corresponding to a high-assurance certificate (because the second PCA signed it). By checking the policies of each of the PCAs, and (possibly) the CA, the recipient of one of these certificates can tell what the policies of issuance and assurance are. (A potential conflict arises because the CA has the same Distinguished Name for two different types of policies. Section 15.5.1 discusses this topic further.)

As another example of how the certificates encode policy, note that Marsha's certificate implicitly identifies her as being affiliated with the University of Valmont. This type of certificate is called an *organizational certificate*. The Internet infrastructure defines a second type of certificate, a *residential certificate*, that identifies the principal's residential address. Marsha has one of these, issued by the post office, and identifying her as a citizen residing in the city of Valmont:

```
/C=US/SP=Louisiana/L=Valmont/PA=27 Russell Blvd./
   CN=Marsha/
```

Here, "C" is the country code, "SP" is the province or state name, "L" is the locality (city, town, or village), and "PA" is the street address.

The principals need not be people or organizations; they can be roles.

EXAMPLE: A company wishes to have its comptroller authorized to digitally sign documents. To this end, it issues a certificate to the role:

```
/O=Hodgepodge Corporation/
OU=Office of Big Money/RN=Comptroller/
```

Even if the current comptroller leaves and a new one is hired, the same certificate can be used. Here, "Comptroller" is a role (and the use of the "RN" key, for "Role Name," reflects this).

The identifiers in a certificate need not be formal Distinguished Names. The certificates used with PGP, for example, allow the subject to provide any identifier he or she wishes. The convention is to use a name and an electronic mail address [340], but this permits a high level of ambiguity, especially when mail addresses change frequently. This leads directly to conflicts; how can a CA ensure that the certificate it issues does not conflict with another?

15.5.1 Conflicts

Both X.509 and PGP are silent about certificate conflicts. They assume that the CAs will prevent conflicts. The CA's Distinguished Name is in the certificate, so if no two CAs have the same Distinguished Name and each CA requires that principals be identified uniquely among the set of principals certified by that CA, no conflicts will arise.

The PEM certification hierarchy uses the same approach: the IPRA requires that each PCA have a unique Distinguished Name, and no PCA may certify two CAs with the same Distinguished Name. But in practice, there may be conflicts. For example, suppose John A. Smith and John B. Smith, Jr. both live at the same address. John B. Smith, Jr. applies for a certificate, based on his residence, from the post office, which issues one:

```
/C=US/SP=Maine/L=Portland/PA=1 First Ave./
CN=John Smith/
```

His father, John A. Smith, applies to the Quick Certificate Company for a residential certificate. His Distinguished Name would be identical to his son's, but the Quick Certificate Company would have no way to know this because there is no central repository of certificates. The PEM infrastructure deals with this problem in two ways. First, it requires that all CA Distinguished Names be "superior" to the Distinguished Name of the principal.

EXAMPLE: In the University of Valmont case, if Marsha's certificate were

```
/C=US/O=University of Valmont/
OU=Computer Science Department/CN=Marsha/
```

then the University of Valmont's CA would be either

```
/C=US/O=University of Valmont/
OU=Computer Science Department/
```

if the issuer were the Computer Science Department, or

```
/C=US/O=University of Valmont/
```

if the issuer were the university itself. The University of New York, with a Distinguished Name of

```
/C=US/O=University of New York/
```

could not issue a certificate to Marsha as an employee of the University of Valmont, because its Distinguished Name is not superior to that of Marsha.

This works for organizational certificates, since each organization can be its own CA, or can empower subordinate units to be their own CAs. However, it is unrealistic to expect that only one entity will issue residential certificates. This immediately leads to a conflict.

EXAMPLE: Suppose Heidi Smith's daughter is named Heidi O. Smith (the mother has no middle name). Heidi O. Smith needs a residential certificate to apply for college. She goes to the post office and obtains one with the following Distinguished Name:

```
/C=US/SP=California/L=San Rafael/
PA=1 Forbes Ave./CN=Heidi Smith/
```

Because CA Distinguished Names are superior to those of the principals, the post office must have a Distinguished Name that is one of the following:

```
/C=US/
/C=US/SP=California/
/C=US/SP=California/L=San Rafael/
/C=US/SP=California/L=San Rafael/PA=1 Forbes Ave./
```

Heidi's mother must fill out a financial aid package and needs a certificate to sign it. Because the line at the post office is too long, she goes to Quick and Cheap Certs, Inc. and obtains a residential certificate from them:

```
/C=US/SP=California/L=San Rafael/PA=1 Forbes Ave.
  /CN=Heidi Smith/
```

But by the same rule, the Distinguished Name that Quick and Cheap Certs, Inc. uses in the certificate could be the same name as that of the post office.

The PEM infrastructure contains an explicit exception that allows multiple residential CAs to have the same Distinguished Name. But this issue also arises when the same CA wishes to issue certificates under two different policies, and hence under two different PCAs. Because the CA uses the same Distinguished Name for all its certificates, how does one determine under which policy a certificate was issued?

EXAMPLE: John's certificate was issued under a low-assurance policy. He uses it to sign a letter to Eve. When Eve gets John's certificate, she validates it. She cannot determine whether the high-assurance authentication policy or the low-assurance authentication policy was used.

The PEM infrastructure handles these conflicts with a Distinguished Name conflict detection database. Before a PCA may issue a certificate to a CA, it must determine if a conflict exists. It sends a query to the database containing the following information:

- A hash value computed on a canonical representation of the CA's Distinguished Name
- The CA's public key in the certificate
- The Distinguished Name of the PCA

If the first two fields conflict with any other entry in the database, the IPRA returns the conflicting entry. (The two PCAs must then resolve the conflict.) Otherwise, the information is entered into a new record and a timestamp is added.

This mechanism does not ensure uniqueness of Distinguished Names. It *does* ensure uniqueness of the pair (Distinguished Name, public key), and therein lies the answer to the above-mentioned conflicts. In the residential certificate example, the post office and Quick and Cheap Certs, Inc. have different public keys, so the CA for the certificates could be determined at validation time. In the University of Valmont example, the different public keys used to sign the certificate would indicate under which policy the university issued the certificate.

15.5.2   The Meaning of the Identity

The authentication policy defines the way in which principals prove their identities. Each CA has its own requirements (although they may be constrained by contractual requirements, such as with PCAs). All rely on nonelectronic proofs of identity, such as biometrics (fingerprints), documents (driver's license, passports), or personal knowledge. If any of these means can be compromised, the CA may issue the certificate in good faith to the wrong person.

This hearkens back to the issue of trust. Ignoring the trust required for cryptography to work, the certificate is the binding of an *external* identity to a cryptographic key and a Distinguished Name. If the issuer can be fooled, all who rely on that certificate may also be fooled.

With the erosion of privacy in many societies comes the need for anonymity. This conflicts with the notion of a certificate binding an identity to a Distinguished Name and a public key. The conflict arises when the anonymous principal needs to send a set of integrity-checked, confidential electronic messages to a recipient and to ensure that the recipient realizes that all of the messages have come from the same source (but the recipient cannot know what the source is).

EXAMPLE: A government plans to require all citizens with a specific gene to register, because anecdotal evidence suggests that people with that gene commit crimes slightly more often than other people. The government plans to make the law without publicity, because aside from the civil liberties issues, there is no reputable scientific evidence to back up the belief. A government employee decides to alert the media. She realizes that the government will promptly deny the plan and change its approach to getting the law passed. She feels that she will be fired (or charged with a crime) if the government determines who she is, and would therefore be unable to reveal any changes in the plan. So she decides to publicize the plans anonymously.

Anonymous, or *persona*, certificates supply the requisite anonymity. A CA issues a persona certificate under a policy that makes the Distinguished Name of the principal meaningless. For example, a persona certificate with a principal Distinguished Name of

```
/C=US/O=House of Representatives/CN=Jessica Rabbit/
```

does not imply that the certificate was issued to someone named Jessica Rabbit. PGP certificates can have any name to identify the principal, and can innately provide anonymity in this sense.

EXAMPLE: Continuing, our heroine obtains a persona certificate and sends a copy of the government's plan to the media, using electronic mail, as described above. The government denies the plan and secretly changes its strategy. It has some employees leak verifiably false information so that if the original whistleblower sends another message, it is less likely to be believed. But she does, and she uses the same certificate to authenticate the message. Now the media can check that the two messages came from the same source (or at least were signed with the same certificate), whereas the false messages were signed by different certificates.

15.5.3   Trust

The goal of certificates is to bind the correct identity to the public key. When a user obtains a certificate, the issuer of that certificate is vouching, to some degree of certainty, that the identity corresponds to the principal owning the public key. The critical question is the degree of that assurance.

X.509v4, and the PEM certification hierarchy, define the degree of certainty in the policy of the CA that issues the certificate. If a CA requires a passport as identification, then the degree of certainty is high; if it requires an unsworn statement of identity, the degree of certainty is low. But even high-assurance CAs can be fooled. In the case of the passport, passports can be stolen or forged. So the level of trust in an identity is not quantifiable. Rather, it is an estimate based on the policy of the CA, the rigor with which that policy is followed, and the assumptions that the policy makes.

EXAMPLE: Consider the CA that requires a passport to issue a certificate. The certificate will have as its DN the name in the passport, the name of the country issuing the passport, and the passport number. There are several points of trust in this policy. First, the CA assumes that the passport is not forged and that the name has not been altered. Second, the CA assumes that the country issuing the passport issued it to the person named in the passport. Third, the CA assumes that the individual presenting the passport is the individual to whom the passport was issued.[5] Fourth, the users of the certificate assume that the CA has actually checked the passport and the individual using the passport to obtain a certificate.

PGP certificates include a series of signature fields (see Section 11.4.2.2), each of which contains a level of trust of the identity in the certificate.[6] The OpenPGP specification defines four levels [340]:

- Generic certification of a user name and a public key packet; this makes no assertions about the correctness of the name.
- Persona certification of a user name and a public key; the signer has done no verification that the user name correctly identifies the principal.
- Casual certification of a user name and a public key; the signer has done some verification that the user name correctly identifies the principal.
- Positive certification of a user name and a public key; the signer has done substantial verification that the user name correctly identifies the principal.

Even here, though, the trust is not quantifiable. What exactly do "some verification" and "substantial verification" mean? The OpenPGP specification does not define them, preferring to leave their definitions to the signer, so the same terms can imply different levels of assurance to different signers.

EXAMPLE: At a university, "substantial verification" may mean having a student identification card and a matching driver's license. The university's CA would sign the student's PGP certificate with level 4 trust. But at a high-security government installation that requires background checks before certificates are signed, the university's "substantial verification" would most likely be considered level 2 trust, "no verification."

---

[5] Passport photographs are notoriously poor, making visual identification questionable unless conditions are optimal.

[6] This is encoded in the signature type field of the signature.

The point is that knowing the policy, or the trust level with which the certificate is signed, is not enough to evaluate how likely it is that the identity identifies the correct principal. Knowing how the CA or signer interprets the policy and enforces its requirements is also required.

EXAMPLE: On March 22, 2001, Verisign, Inc. and Microsoft Corporation [2247] reported that Verisign had issued two certificates to someone claiming to be a representative of Microsoft Corporation. The individual was not. Both companies took steps to cancel the certificates and prevent them from being used.

If the CA delegates the validation of identity (and other information) to a registration authority (RA), then the CA trusts that the RA abides by the policy of the CA, and is not otherwise compromised. The delegation means that the CA is still ultimately responsible for the certificates it issues.

EXAMPLE: A user account on a registration authority for the certificate authority Comodo was compromised. The attacker used the RA to generate requests for certificates for Google, Yahoo, Skype, and other major Internet sites. The compromise was detected within hours, and the fraudulently issued certificates were immediately revoked [446, 851]. The compromised account was deactivated immediately.

15.6   Identity on the Web

Certificates are not ubiquitous on the Internet. Several other means attach identity to information, even though the binding may be very transient.

The Internet requires every host to have an address. The address may be fixed or may change, and without cryptography the binding is weak. Many servers send information about the state of the client's interaction, so that when the client reconnects, the server can resume the transaction or glean information about previous transactions.

15.6.1   Host Identity

Host identity is intimately bound to networking. A host not connected to *any* network can have any name, because the name is used only locally. A host connected to a network can have many names or one name, depending on how the interface to the network is structured and the context in which the name is used.

The ISO/OSI model [1859] provides a context for the issue of naming. Figure 12–6 shows the layers of the ISO/OSI model. Each host, conceptually, has a principal at each layer that communicates with a peer on other hosts. These principals communicate with principals at the same layer on other hosts. Each principal on an individual host can have different names (also called "addresses") at each layer. All names identify the same host, but each one refers to a particular context in which the host functions.

EXAMPLE: A computer has an Ethernet (media access control layer, or MAC) address of 00:05:02:6B:A8:21, an IP address of 192.168.35.89, and a host name of *cherry.orchard.net*. At the data link level, the system is known by its Ethernet address. At the network level, it is known by its IP address. At the application level, it is known by its host name. The system is also on an AppleTalk network, with an AppleTalk address of network 51, node 235. Other systems on the AppleTalk network identify the host by that name.

Shoch [1740] suggests that a "name" identifies a principal and an "address" identifies where that principal is located. In the context of host identification, the "address" indicates where on a network (and, sometimes, the specific network) the host is located. A "name" indicates in what domain the host resides, and corresponds to a particular address. Although Shoch's terminology is instructive in many contexts, in this context a location identifies a principal just as well as a name. We do not distinguish between the two in the context of identification.

If an attacker is able to spoof the identity of another host, all protocols that rely on that identity are relying on a faulty premise and are therefore being spoofed. When a host has a sequence of names, each relying on the preceding name, then an attacker spoofing the first identity can compromise all the other identities. For example, the host identity is based on the IP identity. Similarly, the IP identity is based on the Ethernet identity. If an attacker can alter entries in databases containing the mapping of a lower-level identity to a higher-level identity, the attacker can spoof one host by routing traffic to another.

15.6.1.1   Static and Dynamic Identifiers

An identifier can be either static or dynamic. A *static identifier* does not change over time; a *dynamic identifier* changes either as a result of an event (such as a connection to a network) or over time.

Databases contain mappings between different names. The best known of these is the Domain Name Service (DNS) [1365, 1366], which associates host names and IP addresses. In the absence of cryptographic authentication of hosts, the consistency of the DNS is used to provide weak authentication.

EXAMPLE: The DNS contains *forward records*, which map host names into IP addresses, and *reverse records*, which map IP addresses into names. A reverse domain lookup occurs when a process extracts the IP address of its remote peer, determines the associated host name (perhaps using the DNS), and then obtains the set of IP addresses associated with that host name (again, possibly using the DNS). If the IP address obtained from the peer matches any of the IP addresses associated with that host name, then the host name is accepted as the one obtained in the first lookup. Otherwise, the host name is rejected as untrusted.

The belief in the trustworthiness of the host name in this case relies on the integrity of the DNS database. Section 15.6.1.2, "Security Issues with the Domain Name Service," examines this issue.

Floating identifiers are assigned to principals for a limited time. Typically, a server maintains a pool of identifiers. A client contacts the server using an identifier agreed on between the two (the *local identifier*). The server transmits an identifier that the client can use in other contexts (the *global identifier*) and notifies any intermediate hosts (such as gateways) of the association between the local and global identifiers.

EXAMPLE: Bootless University provides a network to which students can hook up laptops. Rather than assign each student laptop an IP address, the university has created a DHCP server [589, 590] for this network. When a student connects her laptop to the network, the laptop transmits its MAC address to the server. The server responds with an unused IP address belonging to the network. The laptop accepts that IP address and uses it to communicate on the Internet.

A gateway can translate between a local address and a global address.

EXAMPLE: The Zerbche company has 500 computers on a local area network, but only 256 Internet addresses. The internal network assigns as (fixed) local addresses the IP addresses 10.1.x.y, where x and y reflect internal configuration details not relevant here. A gateway connects the internal network to the Internet.

When a user at host 10.1.3.241 wants to access the Internet, it forwards its packets to the gateway. The gateway assigns a legitimate IP address to the internal, local address; say that IP address is 101.43.21.241. The gateway then rewrites the source address of each packet, changing 10.1.3.241 to 101.43.21.241, and puts the packets out on the Internet. When the gateway receives packets destined for host 101.43.21.241, it checks its internal table, rewrites those addresses as 10.1.3.241, and forwards them to the internal network, and the packets go to their destination. This translation is invisible to either end of the communication, and enables up to some number of hosts on the internal network to communicate with hosts on the Internet. The Network Address Translation protocol (NAT) [1806] is used on the Internet to perform this function.

In the absence of cryptography, authentication using dynamic naming is different from authentication using static naming. The primary problem is that the association of the identity with a principal varies over time, so any authentication based on the name must also account for the time. For example, if the DNS record entries corresponding to the dynamic name are not updated whenever the name is reassigned, the reverse domain lookup method of authentication fails.[7]

---

[7]This failure does not necessarily mean that the DNS has been compromised. Some systems store the forward and reverse lookup information in separate files. Updating the forward lookup information file does not change the reverse lookup information file. Unless the latter is updated also, the stated problem occurs.

The contrast between static and dynamic naming in authentication is worth noting in light of the different properties described in Chapter 13, "Authentication." The reverse domain lookup technique of authentication corresponds to checking a property of a principal (what it is) with static naming, because the name is bound permanently to the principal. But that technique corresponds to checking a possession of a principal (what it has) with dynamic naming, because the principal will relinquish that name at some point.

15.6.1.2   Security Issues with the Domain Name Service

Understanding the centrality of trust in the databases that record associations of identity with principals is critical to understanding the accuracy of the identity. The DNS provides an example of this. The belief in the trustworthiness of the host name in this case relies on the integrity of the DNS database. If the association between a host name and an IP address can be corrupted, the identifier in question will be associated with the wrong host.

Several attacks on the DNS have been discussed [91, 163, 493, 1694]. The goal of these attacks is to cause a victim to associate incorrectly a particular IP address with a host name. They assume the attacker is able to control the responses from an authoritative domain name server. "Control" means that the attacker has control over the name server or can intercept queries to that server and return its own responses.

The attacker can change the records associating the IP address with the host name, so that a query for one returns an incorrect answer for the other. A second technique, known as "cache poisoning," relies on the ability of a server to add extra DNS records to the answer to a query. In this case, the extra records added give incorrect association information. Schuba [1694] uses this to demonstrate how the reverse name lookup can be compromised. The attacker connects to the victim. The victim queries the DNS for the host name associated with the IP address. The attacker ensures that two records are returned: a record with the bogus host name associated with the IP address, and the reverse record. The DNS protocol allows this piggybacking to enable the client to cache records. The cache is checked before any records are requested from the server, so this may save a network request. The third technique ("ask me") is similar: the attacker prepares a request that the victim must resolve by querying the attacker. When the victim queries the attacker, the attacker returns the answer, along with two records for the mapping that he is trying to spoof (one for the forward mapping, one for the reverse). The last corrupts the paths among the client and DNS hosts to ensure the resolution uses a corrupt DNS server.

Judicious use of cryptographically based techniques coupled with careful administration of DNS servers can effectively limit the ability of attackers to use these attacks. The Domain Name System Security Extensions do exactly this.

15.6.1.3   DNS Security Extensions

In 1999, several security extensions were proposed to augment the DNS protocols [606–610]. These extensions, collectively called the Domain Name System Security

Extensions (DNSSEC), were revised in 2005 [73–75]. These extensions provide integrity—specifically, both origin and data integrity—to DNS information.

The DNS organizes information into *resource records* (RRs). For example, a CNAME RR defines the canonical name for a host. DNSSEC defines a signature resource record (RRSIG RR), a public key resource record (DNSKEY RR), and a resource record for the name of the next hostname (NSEC RR). DNSSEC associates a digital signature with sets of resource records in the RRSIG resource record. Each DNS server has an associated public key, made available in the DNSKEY RR. When a resolver requests authenticated data from a DNS name server, the DNS server sends the desired set of resource records, and the RRSIG record containing the digital signature of the earlier records. The resolver can verify the signature using the associated public key, querying for it if needed. It can then verify the DNS name server's address in a similar manner.

The NSEC resource record serves a different function: it allows verifying that a particular host name does not correspond to an IP address. The resolver requests a record corresponding to a host name. The server responds with an NSEC record showing the *next* valid host name in a sorted order. This tells the resolver that the name being queried for does not exist in that domain. It is an authoritative statement that no host with that name exists.

Unfortunately, this allows an attacker to derive the names of all hosts in the domain by repeatedly sending queries for host names that have no corresponding addresses. The NSEC3 resource record contains similar information, but the host names are replaced with a cryptographic hash of the real host names [1142]. The attacker can therefore not glean legitimate names from the contents of the NSEC3 record. This resource record is incompatible with earlier implementations, and so an additional protocol determines which type of record is to be sent.

DNSSEC, if properly implemented, makes both the spoofing and cache poisoning attacks immediately detectable. It is also designed to minimize overhead. For example, it does not define a public key infrastructure. Thus, if a private key is compromised, an attacker can use that key to launch spoofing and cache poisoning attacks from the compromised domain. There is no key revocation mechanism. But the same effect can be achieved by simply replacing the public key and private key. Those who request the new key will validate the records. Those who do not will determine something is wrong, because the resource records being sent will appear to have an invalid signature.

The security of the DNS is critical to the security of the Internet's infrastructure. DNSSEC provides substantial improvements to the current level of trust required for that security.

15.6.2   State and Cookies

Many Internet applications require that the client or server maintain state to simplify the transaction process [133].

Definition 15–4. A *cookie* is a token that contains information about the state of a transaction on a network.

Although the transaction can be any client-server interaction, the term "cookie" is most widely used in reference to interactions between web browsers and clients. These cookies minimize the storage requirements of the servers and put the burden of maintaining required information on the client. The cookies consist of several values.

- The *name* (or *key*) and *value* are encoded into the cookie and represent the state. The interpretation is that the *name* has an associated *value*.
- The *expires* field indicates when the cookie is valid. Expired cookies are discarded; they are not to be given out. If this field is not present, the cookie will be deleted at the end of the session.
- The *domain* states the domain for which the cookie is intended. It consists of the last *n* fields of the domain name of a server. The cookie will be sent to servers in that domain. For example, domain=.adv.com specifies that the cookie is to be sent to any requesting server in the *adv.com* domain. A domain field must have at least one embedded "." in it; this prevents a server from sending over a cookie ending in ".com" and then requesting all cookies for the domain ".com."

   There is no requirement that a cookie be sent from a host in the domain. This can be used to track certain types of accesses, as discussed below.
- The *path* further restricts the dissemination of the cookie. When a web server requests a cookie, it provides a domain (its own). Cookies that match that domain may be sent to the server. If the server specifies a path, the path must be the leading substring of the path specified in the cookie.
- If the *secure* field is set, the cookie will be sent only over secured connections (that is, to HTTPS or HTTP over TLS).

EXAMPLE: Caroline logs in to a web server, *www.books.com*, used to sell books. She selects two books to buy and adds them to her "shopping cart." The web server sends her a cookie with name "bought" and value "BK=234&BK=8763." The domain for the cookie is ".books.com." The expiration field is omitted. When Caroline goes to the page to pay for the books, the server asks for the cookie "bought" belonging to the domain ".books.com." From the value of the cookie, the server sees that Caroline wants to buy books numbered 234 and 8763. Had Caroline terminated the session (by exiting her browser, for example), the cookie would be deleted and no record would exist of the books she thought about purchasing.

The restriction of sending cookies to hosts in the cookie's domain prevents one web server from requesting cookies sent by a second web server. However, a web server can send cookies marked for the domain of a second server. When the user accesses the second web server, that server can request the cookies marked for its domain but sent by the first server.

EXAMPLE: When Caroline accesses the web server to buy books, that server sends her a cookie with name "id," value "books.com," and domain "adv.com." Several advertisements at the *www.books.com* website take Caroline to the server *www.adv.com*. When Caroline follows one of those links to that server, the server requests her cookies for that domain. Caroline's browser sends the cookie. From this, *www.adv.com* can determine the website from which Caroline obtained the cookie.

Caroline need not even follow the advertisement. Most such advertisements are images, and the *www.books.com* server does not have those images online. Instead, the web page contains a pointer to some other server, such as *www.adv.com*. When Caroline's browser pulls the *www.books.com* web page over, that page contains an instruction for her browser to contact *www.adv.com* to get the advertising image. When that is done, *www.adv.com* can request the cookie that *www.books.com* had sent over.

Cookies can contain authentication information, both user related and host related. Using cookies for authentication treats them as tokens supplied by the browser to validate (or state and validate) an identity. Depending on the sensitivity of the interactions with the server, protecting the confidentiality of these cookies may be critical. Exercise 1 explores this topic in more detail.

15.7   Anonymity on the Web

Identification on the Internet arises from associating a particular host with a connection or message. The recipient can determine the origin from the incoming packet. If only one person is using the originating host, and the address is not spoofed, someone could guess the identity of the sender with a high degree of accuracy.

An *anonymizer* is a site that hides the origins of connections. It functions as a proxy server—that is, it operates on behalf of another entity. A user connects to the anonymizer and tells it the destination. The anonymizer makes the connection, so the destination host sees only the anonymizer. The anonymizer forwards traffic in both directions.

The destination believes it is communicating with the anonymizer because all traffic will have the anonymizer's address in it. However, the anonymizer is merely a go-between and merely passes information between the destination and the origin.

Anonymizers work primarily on electronic mail and HTTP traffic, although the same principles apply to any type of network messages.

15.7.1 Email Anonymizers

Electronic mail anonymizers are conceptually simple and demonstrate the techniques used and the privacy issues that arise. The story of the Finnish anonymizer *anon.penet.fi* is worth recounting, because it was the first widely used anonymizer. Its demise points out the problems in both using and running anonymizers.

EXAMPLE: The host *anon.penet.fi* offered an anonymous electronic mail service. One would send a letter to it, naming another destination (either an individual or a USENET news group). The anonymizer would strip off the headers, assign an anonymous ID (*anon374*, for example) to the letter, and record the sender and the associated anonymous ID in a database. The letter would then be delivered to its destination, as though user *anon374* at *anon.penet.fi* had sent it. The recipients could not tell the original sender from the letter. They would reply to the letter by sending the reply to *anon374* at *anon.penet.fi*. This letter would be anonymized in the same way the original letter was anonymized, and would then be forwarded to the real electronic mail address corresponding to *anon374*.

This exchange is not truly anonymous. Even though the end parties do not know who each other are, the anonymizer knows who both are.

Definition 15–5. A *pseudo-anonymous* (or *pseudonymous*) *remailer* is a remailer that replaces the originating electronic mail addresses (and associated data) of messages it receives before it forwards them, but keeps mappings of the anonymous identities and the associated origins.

The problem is that the binding between the anonymous address and the real address is known somewhere. If that point can be made to reveal the association, anonymity ceases to exist.

EXAMPLE: The association between the anonymous ID and the electronic mail address of the sender was *anon.penet.fi*'s undoing [894]. Some material, claimed to be child pronography, was circulated through the site. A Finnish court directed the owner of the site to reveal the database so the plaintiffs could determine the electronic mail address of the sender, thereby ending the anonymity. Although the owner appealed the order, he subsequently shut down the site.

The association can be obscured by using a sequence of pseudo-anonymous remailers. Tracing the origin then requires the trackers to obtain information from several sites. But the chain must exist if replies are to be sent back to the original sender. Eliminating that requirement allows true anonymity.

Definition 15–6. [785] A *Cypherpunk* (or *type 1*) *remailer* is a remailer that deletes the header of an incoming message and forwards the remainder to its destination.

Unlike a pseudo-anonymous remailer, no record of the association between the originating address and the remailer address is kept. Thus, one cannot trace the message by mapping the remailer's user name to an electronic mail address.

Cypherpunk remailers are typically used in a chain, and messages sent through them are always enciphered [834]. Figure 15–1 shows how this works. Bob composes a message to Alice and then uses PGP to encipher it twice. The first encipherment is for the destination "remailer 2." The resulting message is then enciphered for delivery to remailer 1. Bob then mails the message to remailer 1. It deciphers the message, sees that it is to be sent to remailer 2, and forwards it. Remailer 2 receives the message, deciphers it, and forwards the message to Alice. Because there is no record of who sent the message to remailer 1, it cannot be tied back to Bob's electronic mail address. Because remailer 2 received the message from remailer 1, it cannot associate any real electronic mail address with the destination address (Alice). This illustrates the reason for using chains of Cypherpunk remailers. Were only one remailer used, it could associate the real sender with the real recipients. Although two remailers, or any number of remailers, could cooperate to do the same thing, in practice such cooperation is very difficult to achieve. Again, the issue of trust in the remailers is central to the success of Cypherpunk remailers.

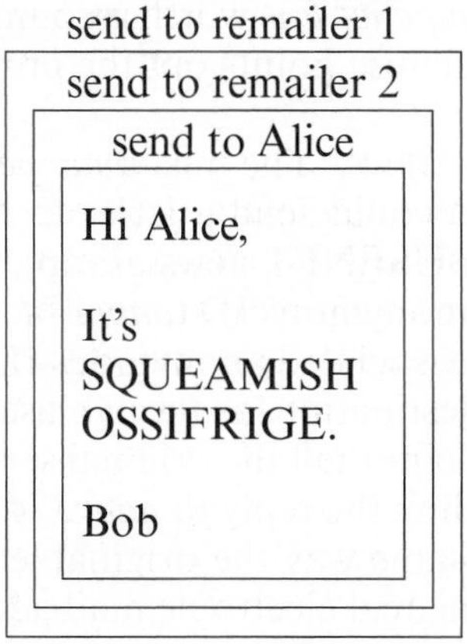

Figure 15–1 A message sent to a Cypherpunk remailer. Remailer 1 forwards the message to remailer 2, and remailer 2 sends it to Alice.

But there is still a weakness. Suppose an attacker could monitor all traffic between the source and the destination but the remailers themselves remained uncompromised. Then the attacker could view traffic into and out of a remailer but could not see the association of incoming traffic with outgoing traffic. The goal of the attacker would be to reconstruct this association [785, 834].

Obviously, reconstructing this association from cleartext messages is simple: just compare the bodies of incoming messages with those of outgoing messages. The envelope for the current remailer will be deleted; otherwise, the bodies will be the same. This is the reason to encipher all messages going through a Cypherpunk remailer. In the following discussion, we assume that all such messages are enciphered. The attacks all involve traffic analysis.

If a remailer immediately forwards a message after receiving it, and before any other message arrives (or if processing is guaranteed to occur in order of arrival), then the attacker can determine the association. One approach to obscuring this is to hold messages for random intervals of time; however, unless the interval is greater than the average interarrival time, the delay does not help. (Some remailers allow the sender to specify the length of the interval.)

A second approach is to randomize the order of processing of the incoming messages; implicit in this approach is a delay to allow such reordering. Cypherpunk remailers that do this keep a pool of incoming messages. No messages are sent out until the pool contains a fixed number, call it n, of messages. When the nth message arrives, one of the messages in the pool is selected and sent. This protects the associations against passive attacks. However, an active attacker can send enough messages to the remailer so that all $n - 1$ messages in the pool are sent (see Exercise 2).

A third approach deals with message size. As a message moves through its chain of remailers, each remailer strips off an outside envelope. Thus, the size of the message decreases. The attacker can use this by recording the sizes of messages entering and leaving the remailer. No outbound message can be associated with an inbound message of lesser or equal size. Furthermore, the size of the envelope can be estimated well enough to estimate how much the message would shrink by, thus eliminating more possible associations. To limit this threat, some remailers allow users to append junk to the message and instruct the remailer to delete it. Again, this reduces message size; it does not increase it.

The final attack is also active. The attacker replays the messages many times to the first remailer, which forwards them. The attacker monitors the outbound traffic and looks for a bump in the amount of traffic from the remailer corresponding to the messages sent into the remailer. This associates the outbound path with the inbound path. To prevent this attack, remailers cannot forward the same message more than once.

A second type of remailer, based on ideas from Chaum's paper [393] (which uses the term "mix" to describe the obscuring of information), does not suffer from these problems.

> **Definition 15–7.** [785] A *Mixmaster* (or *type 2*) *remailer* is a Cypherpunk remailer that handles only enciphered messages and that pads or fragments messages to a fixed size before sending them.

This hinders the attacks described above. The contents of the incoming and outgoing messages cannot be matched, because everything is enciphered. Traffic analysis based on size is not possible, because all messages (incoming and outgoing) are of the same size. All messages are uniquely numbered, so replay attacks are not possible. Message fragments are not reassembled until the message reaches the last remailer in the chain, so reordering attacks are more difficult. Figure 15–2 shows what a Mixmaster message looks like. Special software is used to construct the messages, whereas Cypherpunk remailers can accept messages constructed by hand.

In practice, messages sent through Mixmaster remailers are untraceable unless the remailers themselves are compromised. In that case, one could track

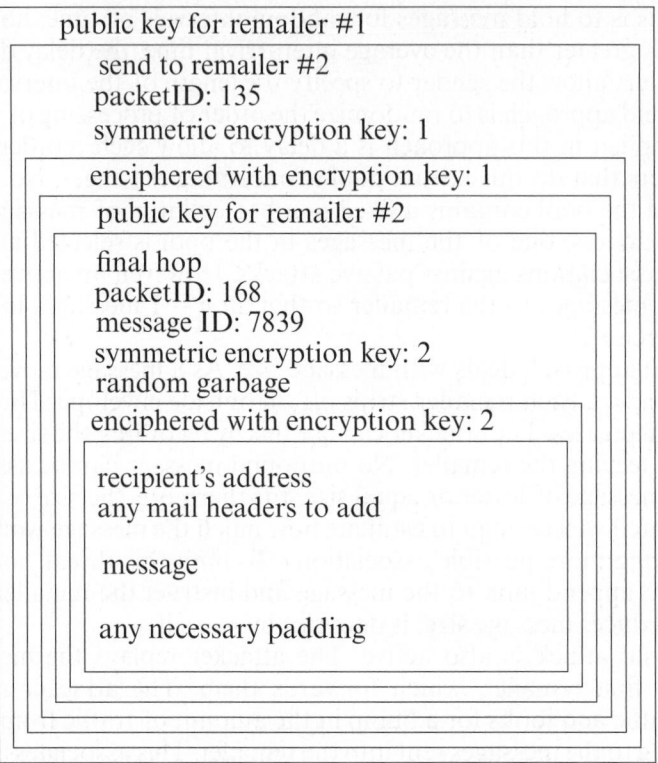

Figure 15–2   A Mixmaster message. This is a fragment of a multipart message sent through two remailers. Messages are enciphered using both a public key and symmetric key algorithm, and random garbage is added as well as padding. The recipient's address is visible only to the last remailer.

packet and message IDs and make associations as desired. The point is that anonymity assumes that the remailers can be trusted not to disclose associations. The Mixmaster technique minimizes the threat of compromised remailers, because all remailers must track origin, packet, and message IDs, and the final remailer must also track destination address, packet, and message IDs for the sender to be associated with a received message. This technique is not foolproof; if only one message is sent over the network, an attacker can easily determine the sender and receiver, for example. But it substantially adds to the difficulty of matching an anonymous letter to a sender.

The Mixmaster remailer BABEL [834] adds the ability to reply without knowing the identity of, or even the actual email address of, the sender. Mixminion [497] provides an alternate approach to managing replies by treating reply messages as new messages, so one cannot determine if an email is a reply. These techniques can be generalized to routing [789, 1848], and hence to any protocol.

15.7.2   Onion Routing

Onion routing is a technique that hides a route from not only observers but also from the nodes along the route. Each node in the path, except the first, is aware only of its predecessor and successor in the route. Typically, the first node will select the route, although provisions exist for intermediate nodes changing a route.

> **Definition 15–8.** [789] *Onion routing* is a method of routing that ensures each node in the route knows only the two adjacent nodes in the route.

Suppose a client wishes to communicate with a server, but in such a way as to remain anonymous. The client chooses a proxy that will perform the routing. The message will be routed through a set of routers, each of which will forward the message to the next router. At the end of this route, the final router will forward the message to the server. Associated with each router is a public key pair, with the public key available to all proxies.

The heart of the onion route is the onion:

$$\{expires||nexthop||E_F||k_F||E_B||k_B||payload\}pub_r$$

Here, pub_r is the public key of the router (or terminal proxy) this message will be forwarded to; E_F and E_B identify encryption algorithms to be used when sending messages forward to the server and backwards to the client, respectively, with k_F and k_B being the corresponding keys; *nexthop* is the router or proxy to which the message is to be forwarded; *expires* is an expiration time for which the payload is to be saved; and *payload* is the data associated with the message. Note the *payload* may itself be a message of this form, or it may be the data that the terminal proxy is to forward to the server. Each router has a table that stores a virtual circuit number associated with a route, the forward and backwards keys and algorithms, the onion, and the next router to which messages along this route are to be forwarded. If this router is the last one, the forwarding entry (and *nexthop* in the packet) are both set to **NULL**.

To create a route, the proxy first determines the path that the message is to follow. The proxy can define this route exactly, or can define it loosely, in which case each router is free to route messages to the next hop over other routes, thereby adding routers to the path. The proxy creates an onion encapsulating the route, embeds it in a *create* message, along with a virtual circuit identification number, and forwards it to the next router on the path. This router deciphers the onion using its private key ("peels the onion") and checks to see if this is a replay by comparing the result to entries in the table. If it is, the message is discarded. If not, the router assigns a virtual circuit identification number to this route, sees what the virtual circuit number on the incoming message was, and enters the pair into a table. It also stores the keys and encryption algorithm identifiers for this route in the table. It then generates a new *create* message and puts its assigned virtual circuit identification number and the "peeled" onion into this message. The resulting message is smaller than the one received, so the payload (the "peeled" onion) is padded to match the size of the original incoming message, and then is forwarded to the next hop.

To send a message, the client proxy simply applies the decryption algorithms corresponding to each backwards encryption algorithm along the route. So, for example, if the route begins at W, and goes through X and Y to Z, the message m would be transformed to

$$d_X(k_X, d_Y(k_Y, d_Z(k_Z, m)))$$

where d_I is the decryption algorithm corresponding to the encryption algorithm E_B for router I. It then puts this into a data message with the appropriate virtual circuit identifier and sends it to X. X enciphers the message, producing

$$d_Y(k_Y, d_Z(k_Z, m))$$

and forwards that in a data message with the virtual circuit number it assigned to this route (adding padding if necessary to ensure the size of the message is the same as the original). This continues until the message reaches Z. At that point, m is known and is forwarded through the server's proxy.

To reply, the server sends a message m' to the server's proxy. That enciphers it with its encrypting algorithm and key, adds padding if necessary, and forwards it to the next hop. This process iterates until the message containing m' arrives at the client's proxy. That proxy has the keys used along the route, so it can decipher the message and deliver it.

A virtual circuit can be eliminated in two ways. If the client or server wish to destroy the virtual circuit, it sends a *destroy* message along the circuit. As each router receives the message, it replaces the original virtual circuit number with the one it assigned and forwards the message to the next hop. It then deletes the entry corresponding to the virtual circuit identified in the destroy message. The payload for this message is empty, but padded and enciphered appropriately.

If the client's proxy is compromised, the attacker can see all messages and the routes taken, and from that may be able to deduce the server. If the server's proxy is compromised, the attacker can see all messages sent to the server, but cannot deduce the client from the routing information because the only visible router is the hop preceding the server's proxy. If a router in the path is compromised, no traffic can be read due to the encryption; only the previous and next routers can be determined.

If an attacker is able to see all traffic moving on the network, however, then by watching the flow of messages she could deduce which clients and servers were communicating. One approach would be to match client and server message sizes. Preventing this means all messages sent through the onion network must be the same size; this is achieved by fragmenting and padding messages to a fixed size. A second approach is to observe the flow of messages. Defeating this requires that all onion routers be used equally. This leads to the observation that the onion network requires meaningless messages to be sent among the routers, to obscure the flow of any real messages.

An early implementation of onion routing dealt with web browsing [1848]. This led to the development of the onion router Tor, which modified the original design.

EXAMPLE: Tor [570] is a widely used onion router. It connects clients and servers through streams that run over virtual circuits established among onion routers (ORs). Each OR has an identity key and an onion key. The identity key is used to sign information about the router. The onion key is used to read requests to set up circuits, and is changed periodically. All virtual circuits are over TLS connections, and TLS establishes a third key for this.

Tor's basic message unit is the *cell*. Each cell is 512 bytes long and is either a control or a relay cell. If the cell header contains a command, the cell is a control cell that directs the recipient to take some action, such as create or destroy a circuit. Otherwise, the cell is a relay cell that deals with an established circuit. Figure 15–3 shows some of the Tor commands.

All cell headers also have a virtual circuit number. A virtual circuit is set up over TLS connections. Several circuits may use the same TLS connections; this reduces the overhead imposed by cryptography and network latencies. Similarly, streams move data over virtual circuits, and several streams may be multiplexed over a single virtual circuit.

Setting up a virtual circuit requires the client's onion proxy (OP_c) to know where the ORs it may use are. Tor uses directory services for this. A group of well-known ORs track information about available ORs, such as the keys, address, and exit policy associated with each OR. Other ORs periodically upload information about the state of the onion network. When an OP_c wants to set up a route, it contacts one of these directory servers and from the information it receives, it chooses a path.

Command	Type	Action
create	command	set up a new circuit
created	command	acknowledge that a new circuit has been created
destroy	command	tear down a circuit
data	relay	cell contains message data
begin	relay	opens a stream
connected	relay	relay begin succeeded
extend	relay	extend the existing circuit by a hop
extended	relay	relay extend succeeded
end	relay	close stream cleanly
teardown	relay	close broken stream

Figure 15–3 Tor command and relay commands.

Tor uses a route with three ORs, namely the entry OR_1, the middle OR_2, and the exit OR_3. OR_1 communicates with the client's onion proxy OP_c, and OR_3 with the server (OP_s).

Let $RSA(x)$ denote the encipherment of message x using the onion key of the destination OR; let g and p be as in the Diffie-Hellman cryptosystem (see Section 11.2.3.1). Let $x_1, \ldots, x_n$ and $y_1, \ldots, y_n$ be generated randomly, and let $k_i = g^{x_i y_i} \bmod p$; the forward and backwards keys are extracted from this. Also, let $h(x)$ be a cryptographic hash of message x.

The following protocol creates a virtual circuit between OP_c and OP_s:

1. $OP_c \rightarrow OR_1$: {create $\|$ c_1 $\|$ $RSA(g^{x_1})$}
2. $OR_1 \rightarrow OP_c$: {created $\|$ c_1 $\|$ g^{y_1} $\|$ $h(k_1)$}
3. $OP_c \rightarrow OR_1$: {relay $\|$ c_1 $\|$ {extend $\|$ OR_2 $\|$ $RSA(g^{x_2})$}}
4. $OR_1 \rightarrow OR_2$: {create $\|$ c_2 $\|$ $RSA(g^{x_2})$}
5. $OR_2 \rightarrow OR_1$: {created $\|$ c_2 $\|$ g^{y_2} $\|$ $h(k_2)$}
6. $OR_1 \rightarrow OP_c$: {relay $\|$ c_1 $\|$ {extended $\|$ g^{y_2} $\|$ $h(k_2)$}}
7. $OP_c \rightarrow OR_1$: {relay $\|$ c_1 $\|$ {extend $\|$ OR_3 $\|$ $RSA(g^{x_3})$}}
8. $OR_1 \rightarrow OR_2$: {relay $\|$ c_2 $\|$ {extend $\|$ OR_3 $\|$ $RSA(g^{x_3})$}}
9. $OR_2 \rightarrow OR_3$: {create $\|$ c_3 $\|$ $RSA(g^{x_3})$}
10. $OR_3 \rightarrow OR_2$: {created $\|$ c_3 $\|$ g^{y_3} $\|$ $h(k_3)$}
11. $OR_2 \rightarrow OR_1$: {relay $\|$ c_2 $\|$ {extended $\|$ g^{y_3} $\|$ $h(k_3)$}}
12. $OR_1 \rightarrow OP_c$: {relay $\|$ c_1 $\|$ {extended $\|$ g^{y_3} $\|$ $h(k_3)$}}

At this point, OP_c has the keys for OR_1, OR_2, and OR_3. Call the forward keys f_1, f_2, and f_3 respectively.

When the client wants to send a message m to the server, it sends the message to OP_c. OP_c then enciphers the message using AES-128 in counter mode, to produce

$$\{\{\{m\}f_3\}f_2\}f_1$$

and puts this into a relay data cell. It then sends the cell to OR_1, which deciphers the cell, determines the next hop by looking up the circuit number in its table, puts the payload into another relay data cell, and forwards it. OR_2 does the same, forwarding the result to OR_3. OR_3 deciphers the cell, and then either carries out what the payload requests (for example, opening a TCP connection to the server) or forwards the payload to the server.

To reply, the server sends a reply r to OR_3, which enciphers it with its backwards key, embeds it in a relay data packet, and forwards it to OR_2. OR_2 uses the circuit number to determine where the next hop is, enciphers the cell with its backwards key, and sends the result to OR_1. OR_1 acts similarly, and sends the result to OP_c. As OP_c has all the backwards keys associated with the routers on the route, it can decipher the message and forward it to the client.

One problem with onion routing is getting to it. A government or other entity that wishes to determine who is using such a network can look for traffic between a client and a known entry router. One approach to limiting this threat is to have entry routers that are not listed publicly but are available to those who wish to use them.

EXAMPLE: Tor deals with this problem through the use of *bridge relays*, or *bridges* for short. These are entry routers that are not listed in the Tor directories of entry points. Instead, users who wish to use them can go to a specific web page, or send an email to a specific address. Once the user obtains a set of bridges, they can be added to the Tor network settings, and then Tor will use the bridge as an entry router.

Governments and other entities that wish to prevent the use of onion routing can also look at packets being sent from a client and determine they are intended for an onion router. This requires examining the packet contents and looking for particular structures. A counter to this is to obfuscate the traffic, so it does not appear to have the structures being checked for. When the packet reaches the entry point, it is then deobfuscated, and handled normally.

EXAMPLE: Tor provides this capability with *pluggable transports*. These modules transform the traffic to make misidentification easy. Tests have shown that, for example, a pluggable transport that uses format-transforming encryption has allowed the experimenters to access URLs that are otherwise censored [605].

15.7.2.1 Anonymity for Better or Worse

Anonymity provides a shield to protect people from having to associate their identities with some data. Is this desirable?

The easiest way to answer this is to ask what the purpose of anonymity is. Anonymity is power, because it allows one to make statements without fear of reprisals. One can even deny having made the statements when questioned, and with true anonymity, the denial cannot be disproved.

Anonymity allows one to shape the course of debate by implication. Alexander Hamilton, James Madison, and John Jay deliberately used the name "Publius" to hide their authorship of the Federalist Papers. Aside from hiding the authors' identity, the "Publius" pseudonym was chosen because the Roman Publius was seen as a model governor. The pseudonym implied that the authors stood for responsible political philosophy and legislation [858]. The discussion of the Federalist Papers focused on their content, not on the personalities of their authors.

Anonymity allows whistleblowers considerable protection. Those who criticize the powerholders often fall into disfavor, even when their criticism is valid, and the powerholders take action. Galileo promulgated the theory that the Earth circles the Sun and was brought before the Inquisition [892]. Ernest Fitzgerald exposed cost overruns on the U.S. Air Force C-54 airplane and was removed from his position. After several court victories, he was reinstated [327]. Contrast this with the anonymous sources that spoke with Bernstein and Woodward during the Watergate scandal. The reporters combined those anonymous sources (especially one called "Deep Throat"[8]) with public records to uncover a pattern of activity that ultimately led to impeachment charges against President Richard Nixon, his resignation, and criminal indictments and convictions of many government officials. No action could be taken against the sources, because their identities were unknown [178, 179].

Whether these are benefits or drawbacks depends on whether one is the powerholder under attack or the person attacking the powerholder. In many societies, questioning of authority is considered desirable and beneficial to the society, and in such cases the need for anonymity outweighs the problems, especially when the powerholders will strike back at the critics. In other societies, those who hold power are considered to be more experienced and knowledgeable and are trusted to act in the best interests of the society. In those societies, anonymous criticism would be considered destabilizing and inimical to the best interests of the social order. The reader must decide how anonymity affects the society of which he or she is a part.

Just as anonymity is a tool with which powerholders can be attacked, the powerholders can use it to attack those they consider to be adversaries. Franz Kafka's book *The Trial* [985], which describes a trial in which the accused does not know the (anonymous) judges, is considered a masterpiece of existential literature. However, as dissidents in many countries have found, anonymous judges are not always fictional. In the United States during the period when Martin Dies and Joseph McCarthy held sway, anonymous accusers cost many people their livelihoods, and in some cases their lives (see, for example, Donner [582] and Nizer [1457]).

Anonymity also protects privacy. From this perspective, as we move through a society, parts of that society gather information about us. Grocery stores can record what we purchase, bookstores can record what books we buy, and libraries can record what books we read. Individually, each datum seems unimportant, but when the data is correlated, the conclusions that can be drawn are frighteningly complete. Credit bureaus do this to a degree already, by obtaining information from a variety of credit sources and amalgamating them into a single credit report that includes income, loans, and revolving credit accounts such as credit cards.

This poses three risks to individuals. First, incorrect conclusions can come from data interpreted incorrectly. For example, suppose one visits websites looking for information on a proscribed narcotic. One conclusion is that the individual is looking for information on making or obtaining such a drug for illicit purposes, but this conclusion could be wrong. The individual could be a high school student assigned to write a report on dangerous drugs. The individual

---

[8]Deep Throat was actually W. Mark Felt, at the time an Associate Director of the U.S. Federal Bureau of Investigation [2023]. He was identified in 2005. Had his identity been known at the time of the Watergate scandal, he would have suffered severe consequences.

could be a doctor seeking information on the effects of the use of the drug, for treating a patient. Or the individual could simply be curious. There is insufficient information to draw any of these conclusions.

Second, erroneous information can cause great harm. The best examples of this are cases of "identity theft," in which one person impersonates another, using a faked driver's license, Social Security card, or passport to obtain credit in another's name [539, 1512]. The credit reporting agencies will amalgamate the information under the real person's records, and when the thief defaults, the victim will have to clear himself. Identity theft also occurs in other arenas such as social networks [208], where the goal is to gain the confidence of a victim by impersonating another.

Third, the right to privacy inherent in many societies includes what Brandeis called the "right to be let alone—the most comprehensive of rights and the right most valued by civilized men" [288]. Anonymity serves as a shield behind which one can go about one's business and be let alone. No central, or distributed, authority can tie information obtained about an anonymous entity back to an individual. Without the right to anonymity, protecting one's privacy becomes problematic. Stalkers can locate people and harass them; indeed, in one case a stalker murdered an actress [104]. On the Web, one may have to accept cookies that can be used to construct a profile of the visitor. Organizations that use cookies for this purpose generally adopt an "opt-out" approach, in which a user must request that no information be gathered, rather than an "opt-in" approach, in which a user must expressly give permission for the information to be gathered. If the user is anonymous, no meaningful profile can be constructed. Furthermore, the information gathered cannot be matched with information in credit records and other data banks. The ability to prevent others from gathering information about you without your consent is an example of the right to privacy.

Anonymity for personal protection has its disadvantages, too. Jeremy Bentham's panopticon introduced the notion of perpetual and complete monitoring to prevent crime and protect citizens. The idea that governments should be able to detect crimes as they happen and intervene, or establish that a crime has been committed and act to apprehend the perpetrators, is attractive because of the sense of security it gives citizens. But many, including the Founding Fathers of the United States, regarded this as too high a price to be paid. As Benjamin Franklin wrote, "They that can give up essential liberty to obtain a little temporary safety deserve neither liberty nor safety" [135].

Perhaps the only conclusion one can draw is that, like all freedoms and all powers, anonymity can be used for good or for evil. The right to remain anonymous entails a responsibility to use that right wisely.

15.8 Summary

Every access control mechanism is based on an identity of some sort. An identity may have many different representations (for example, as an integer and as a string). A principal may have many different identities. One certificate may identify the principal by its role, another by its job, and a third by its address. A host on the Internet has multiple addresses, each of which is an identity.

Identities are bound to principals, and the strength and accuracy of that binding determines how systems act when presented with the identity. Unfortunately, trust cannot be measured in absolute terms except for complete trust and no trust. Reality dictates a continuum, not discrete values. Understanding how an identity is bound to a principal provides insight into the trustworthiness of that identity.

Anonymity allows a principal to interact with others without revealing his or her true identity. Anonymity comes in two forms: pseudo-anonymity, in which an intermediary knows the true identity (and can relay messages without revealing that identity); and true anonymity, in which no one knows the true identity. The use of anonymity entails a responsibility to use it wisely.

15.9　Research Issues

Identification is an area of ongoing research, both in the sense of determining who a principal is and in the sense of determining how to identify that principal uniquely. The ubiquity of the World Wide Web complicates this issue, because different organizations may have the same name. If so, which one can use its name for its identifier?

The issue of naming—in particular, how to represent relationships among principals—is a deep one. One goal is to enable an observer to draw conclusions about relationships from the identities; the PEM hierarchy's use of subordinate Distinguished Names is an example of this. Another issue is delegation—in particular, how one can identify a principal acting on behalf of another. How can one use naming mechanisms to describe such a relationship, and how can one affirm that the claimed relationship is correct?

A name is an attribute of an entity used to identify the entity. As noted in this chapter, an entity may have many names, or many names may refer to the same entity. Other attributes may identify the entity. For example, a role is an attribute, as is the CPU type, web browser, and domain for systems, the location and type of business of commercial firms, and facial figures and DNA of people. Research into managing attributes deals with access control as well as authentication, and is growing in importance.

Anonymity is another important area of research. Designing remailers and other tools to anonymize the senders of messages, and to prevent messages from being traced back to their origins, is of interest.

Anonymity is also an important factor in payment of money over the Internet. Digital cash is analogous to physical cash; once spent, there is nothing that ties it to a particular individual. As commercial firms and organizations sell products over the Internet, digital cash provides a simple way for individuals to purchase items just as they would purchase items from a grocery store. The protocols involved must deal with the need for untraceability, as well as preventing the digital cash from being spent twice (thereby defrauding the repository that issued the cash). Implementing protocols that handle all situations correctly is another area of research.

15.10   Further Reading

Representation of identity varies from system to system. Bishop [219] discusses implementation of role accounts using standard UNIX account mechanisms. Faden [648] describes an implementation for Solaris. McNutt [1302] presents requirements and procedures for implementing roles to manage UNIX systems. Sandhu and Ahn [1653] extend the UNIX group semantics to include hierarchies.

Ellison explores methods of identifying a principal through relationships to others [631] and the meaning of a name [632]. Rivest and Lampson developed a simple infrastructure, SDSI, that simply uses public keys as principals, and ignores any notion of "individual" [1596]; others combine this with a simple PKI to produce an authorization system [424, 1164]. Ellison and Dohrmann analyze establishing identity using SDSI in a group collaboration [630]. Park et al. presents an extension of persona certificates that separate the verification of ownership of a private key from the verification of the contents of the certificate [1495].

Saltzer [1642] lucidly discusses the issues and principles that affect naming on the Internet. Several RFCs discuss schemes for naming hosts and other principals on the Internet and the issues that implementing them raise [623, 867, 1069, 1070, 1149, 1330, 1608, 2081]. An "attribute certificate" [1493, 2176] binds attributes to a principal, and many studies have looked at the use of, and management of, attribute information [227, 229, 370, 936, 1190, 2061].

Several cryptographic protocols allow information to be broadcast anonymously. The best-known such algorithm is Chaum's "Dining Cryptographers Problem" [387], in which the goal is to determine if one of the dining cryptographers paid for the meal (without revealing which one), or someone else did. Waidner and Pfitzmann [1957] point out that Chaum's solution could be disrupted if one of the cryptographers lies, and present an algorithm (called "The Dining Cryptographers in the Disco") to detect it. Golle and Juels [793] present an alternate solution that handles other attacks as well.

Chaum [393] first described digital cash. Okamoto and Ohta [1472] list desirable properties for digital cash systems and present a protocol that meets them. Other protocols include Brands's protocol [289], electronic checks [388,392], endorsed e-cash [342], CAFE [258], NetCash [1314], NetCard [58], and BitCoins [1419]. Smart cards can carry digital cash [56, 114] and banks and other financial institutions have taken advantage. Some such schemes have been compromised [1403]. Callas and other panelists [339] discuss the actual systems deployed. Von Solms and Naccache note that the untraceability of digital cash makes solving certain crimes more difficult [1947].

Bacard [105] discusses the basics of anonymous remailers. Mazières and Kaashoek [1273] describe a type 1 remailer in operation. Naessens, De Decker, and Demuynck add accountability to anonymous email [1416], but this requires the use of a trusted third party to determine when deanonymization is appropriate. Several attacks on mixes such as Tor, and appropriate countermeasures, have been studied [963, 1119, 1188, 1712, 2103]. Alsabah and Goldberg [38] examine several proposed improvements to the security of Tor.

15.11   Exercises

1. When discussing the nature of identity, Section 15.1 refers to a "principal" rather than a "user." What type of entity other than a user might an identity refer to? Why might such an entity be more important for accountability than an individual user?

2. Most operating systems define two types of names. A *direct alias* (name or link) identifies the specific entry in a file allocation table (such as an inode), and an *indirect alias* is itself a file containing the path name of a second file. When one opens an indirect alias for certain actions (such as reading or writing), the operating system instead opens the file named in the indirect alias. Specific commands operate on the indirect alias itself (as opposed to the file it names).

   a. Can indirect aliases ever loop? That is, can there exist a chain of indirect aliases $i_1, \ldots, i_n$ such that $i_1 = i_n$? If so, how would the system detect such loops? What should it do when one is discovered?

   b. Can a loop with direct aliases occur?

   c. The text points out the difference between a file name and a file descriptor. How does the introduction of indirect aliases complicate the resolution of an alias to a device number and inode?

   d. On some systems, a direct alias cannot refer to an inode on a different device. Suppose the system were altered to allow a device number to be included in the alias, so a direct alias could refer to a file on another device. What complications might arise? Do indirect aliases, which can reference files on other devices, have the same complications?

3. On versions of the UNIX and Linux operating systems, some programs determine rights by the effective UID, and others by the user name.

   a. Suppose two different user accounts have the same UID. What problems might this cause? What, if any, are the benefits?

   b. Suppose two different users have the same login name. What problems might this cause? What, if any, are the benefits?

4. Give reasons why *root* should not be able to change the audit UID on a UNIX system, and give reasons why it should. Which reasons sound more persuasive to you?

5. What problems might the failure to quantify the levels of trust in an OpenPGP certificate pose?

6. The website *www.widget.com* requires users to supply a user name and a password. This information is encoded into a cookie and sent back to the browser. Whenever the user connects to the web server, the cookie is sent. This means that the user need only supply a password at the beginning of the session. Whenever the server requests reauthentication, the client simply sends the cookie. The name of the cookie is "identif."

   a. Assume that the password is kept in the clear in the cookie. What should the settings of the secure and expires fields be? Why?

   b. Assume that the name and password are hashed and that the hash is stored in the cookie. What information must the server store to determine the user name associated with the cookie?

   c. Is the cookie storing state or acting as an authentication token, or both? Justify your answer.

7. Recall that DNSSEC associates a digital signature with sets of resource records.

   a. How does this solve the problem of cache poisoning?

   b. What assumption(s) underlie the claim that DNSSEC solves cache poisoning attacks?

8. Assume that a Cypherpunk remailer reorders messages. It has a pool of $n-1$ messages at all times. When the nth message arrives, one of the n messages is selected at random and forwarded. An attacker floods the server with enough messages to force the $n-1$ messages in the original pool to be sent.

   a. Assuming that the message to be sent is chosen according to a uniform random distribution, what is the expected number of messages that the attacker would have to send to achieve this goal?

   b. How can the attacker determine when all the messages originally in the pool have been sent?

9. Consider a scheme that allows a recipient to reply to a message from a chain of Cypherpunk remailers. Assume that encipherment is used throughout the chain.

   a. Bob selects a chain of remailers for the return path. He creates a set of keys and enciphers them so that only the key for the current remailer is visible to that remailer. Design a technique by which he could accomplish this. Describe how he would include this data in his message.

   b. How should Alice's mailer handle the processing of the return address information?

   c. When Bob receives the reply, what does it contain? How can he obtain the cleartext reply?

Chapter 16
Access Control Mechanisms

> CASSIO: Why, no. The day had broke
> Before we parted. I ha' made bold, Iago,
> To send in to your wife. My suit to her
> Is that she will to virtuous Desdemona
> Procure me some accéss.
> — *The Tragedy of Othello*, III, i, 32–36.

Recall the access control matrix discussed in Chapter 2. As in the theoretical model, an implementation of the array and the commands to manipulate it provide a mechanism that the system can use to control access to objects. Unfortunately, there are several problems with a straightforward implementation. On a typical system, the number of subjects and objects will be very large. Most entries in the matrix will be either blank (indicating no access) or the same (because implementations often provide a default setting). Also, the creation and deletion of subjects and objects will require the matrix to be managed carefully, adding to the complexity of this code.

Instead, several optimizations enable systems to use more convenient, and in some cases simpler, versions of the access control matrix. *Access control lists* and *capabilities* are variants based on the access control matrix that eliminate many of the problems mentioned above. Various organizations of these mechanisms lead to powerful controls, such as the ring-based mechanism of Multics. A third mechanism, *locks and keys*, is based on cryptography and provides a powerful alternative. A fourth mechanism uses access control lists to implement an ORCON-like control.

16.1   Access Control Lists

An obvious variant of the access control matrix is to store each column with the object it represents. Thus, each object has associated with it a set of pairs, with each pair containing a subject and a set of rights. The named subject can access the associated object using any of those rights. More formally:

> **Definition 16–1.** Let S be the set of subjects, and R the set of rights, of a system. An *access control list* (ACL) l is a set of pairs $l = \{(s, r) \mid s \in S, r \subseteq R\}$. Let *acl* be a function that determines the access control list l associated with a particular object o. The interpretation of the access control list $acl(o) = \{(s_i, r_i) \mid 1 \leq i \leq n\}$ is that subject s_i may access o using any right in r_i.

EXAMPLE: Consider the access control matrix in Figure 2–1, on page 33. The set of subjects is process 1 and process 2, and the set of objects is file 1, file 2, process 1, and process 2. The corresponding access control lists are

acl(file 1) = { (process 1, { read, write, own }), (process 2, { append }) }
acl(file 2) = { (process 1, { read }), (process 2, { read, own }) }
acl(process 1) = { (process 1, { read, write, execute, own }), (process 2,
{ read }) }
acl(process 2) = { (process 1, { write }), (process 2, { read, write, execute,
own }) }

Each subject and object has an associated ACL. Thus, process 1 owns file 1, and can read from or write to it; process 2 can only append to file 1. Similarly, both processes can read file 2, which process 2 owns. Both processes can read from process 1; both processes can write to process 2. The exact meanings of "read" and "write" depend on the instantiation of the rights.

One issue is the matter of default permission. If a subject is not named in the ACL, it has no rights over the associated object. On a system with many subjects, the ACL may be very large. If many subjects have the same right over the file, one could define a "wildcard" to match any unnamed subjects, and give them default rights (see Section 16.1.2.3).

16.1.1 Abbreviations of Access Control Lists

Some systems abbreviate access control lists. The basis for file access control in the UNIX operating system is of this variety. UNIX systems divide the set of users into three classes: the *owner* of the file, the *group owner* of the file, and all *other* users (sometimes called the *world*). Each class has a separate set of rights.

EXAMPLE: UNIX systems provide read (r), write (w), and execute (x) rights. User *bishop* creates a file in the group *vulner*. Initially, *bishop* requests that he be able to read from and write to the file, that members of the group be allowed to read from the file, and that no one else have access to the file. Then the permissions would be rw for owner, r for group, and none for other.

UNIX permissions are represented as three triplets. The first is the owner rights, the second, group rights, and the third, other rights. Within each triplet, the first position is *r* if read access is allowed or – if it is not; the second position is *w* if write access is allowed or – if it is not; and the third position is *x* if execute access is allowed or – if it is not. The permissions for *bishop*'s file would be *rw–r–––––*.

An interesting topic is how UNIX systems assign group ownership. Traditionally, UNIX systems assign the effective principal group ID of the creating process. But in some cases this is not appropriate. For instance, suppose the line printer program works by using group permissions; say its group is *lpdaemon*. Then, when a user copies a file into the spool directory, *lpdaemon* must own the spool file. The simplest way to enforce this requirement is to make the spool directory group owned by *lpdaemon* and to have the group ownership inherited by all files created in that directory. Most systems—notably, Solaris and Linux systems—augment the semantics of file protection modes by setting the setgid bit on the directory when any files created in the directory are to inherit the group ownership of the containing directory.

Abbreviations of access control lists, such as those supported by the UNIX operating system, suffer from a loss of granularity. Suppose a UNIX system has five users. Anne wants to allow Beth to read her file, Caroline to write to it, Della to read and write to it, and Elizabeth to execute it. Because there are only three sets of permissions and five desired arrangements of rights (including Alice), three triplets are insufficient to allow all desired modes of access. Hence, Alice must compromise, and either give someone more rights than she desires or give someone fewer rights. Similarly, traditional UNIX access control does not allow one to say "everybody but user Fran"; to do this, one must create a group of all users except Fran. Such an arrangement is cumbersome, the more so because only a system administrator can create groups.

Many systems augment abbreviations of ACLs with full-blown ACLs. This scheme uses the abbreviations of ACLs as the default permission controls; the explicit ACL overrides the defaults as needed. The exact method varies.

EXAMPLE: Many Linux systems, MacOS X, and the FreeBSD system define two sets of permissions: minimal ACLs and extended ACLs. Minimal ACLs correspond to the standard UNIX permissions; extended ACLs augment these with full access control lists.

The minimal ACL has three entries corresponding to the owner, group owner, and other (everyone else). They are represented as

owner entry	`user::rwx`
group owner entry	`group::rwx`
other entry	`other::rwx`

where `rwx` contains `r`, `w`, or `x` in appropriate combinations. They correspond to the standard Linux and UNIX file permissions.

The extended ACL defines rights for named users and groups. Each entry is similar to those for the minimal ACL, except that the second part of the entry contains the name of the user or group to which the entry applies. For example, the entry `user:skyler:rwx` means the user *skyler* has read, write, and execute permissions; the entry `user:sage:r` means the user *sage* has read permissions; and the entry `group:child:rx` means that members of the group *child* have read and execute permission.

The extended ACL entries are interpreted in light of a "mask entry." This mask is applied only when extended ACLs are present, and it is applied to the group owner entry and any named group and user entries. Such a subject has a right if the right exists in both the extended ACL entry and the mask. The mask is not applied to the owner rights or the other (world) rights.

To determine whether a subject can access an object using a particular right, the applicable rights are determined using the following algorithm. The steps are executed in the order shown, and the algorithm stops as soon as the applicable rights are determined.

1. If the subject is the owner, the owner entry gives the set of applicable rights.

2. If the subject is named in a named user entry, the set of applicable rights is the set of rights in that entry that are also in the mask.

3. If the subject is in the group owner, the set of applicable rights is the set of rights in that entry that are also in the mask.

4. If the subject is in one or more of the named groups, the set of applicable rights is the union of the rights of all such entries that are also in the mask.

5. The other entry gives the applicable rights.

The access is allowed if the particular right is in the set of applicable rights.

As a specific example, consider the following representation of a system's access control permissions for the file *xyzzy*, owned by user *heidi* and group *family*. The group *child* has three users, *skyler*, *sage*, and *steven*. The user *sage* is also a member of the group *family*.

```
user::rw-
user:skyler:rwx
group::rw-
group:child:r-
mask::rw-
other::r-
```

Here, *heidi* can read and write the file (from the owner rights), and another user *mike* can read it (other rights).

Because *skyler* is in a named user entry, his rights are those of the entry that also appear in the mask. So, *skyler* can read and write the file, but not execute it as execute is not in the user mask. Note that the named user entry is used, even though *skyler* is also in the group *child*.

But *sage* is in the group owner, *family*. So, the group owner rights combined with the mask apply. Thus, *sage* can read and write the file.

Finally, *steven* is in the group *child* and not in the group owner *family*, so the named group entry for *child* applies. As read is the only right in both the named group entry and the mask, *steven* can read the file.

16.1.2   Creation and Maintenance of Access Control Lists

Specific implementations of ACLs differ in details. Some of the issues are as follows:

- Which subjects can modify an object's ACL?
- If there is a privileged user (such as *root* in the UNIX system or *administrator* in Windows systems), do the ACLs apply to that user?
- Does the ACL support groups or wildcards (that is, can users be grouped into sets based on a system notion of "group" or on pattern matching)?
- How are contradictory access control permissions handled? If one entry grants read privileges only and another grants write privileges only, which right does the subject have over the object?
- If a default setting is allowed, do the ACL permissions modify it, or is the default used only when the subject is not explicitly mentioned in the ACL?

Because these issues are critical to the correct use of ACLs on a system, we will explore them in more detail.

16.1.2.1   Which Subjects Can Modify an Object's ACL?

When an ACL is created, rights are instantiated. Chief among these rights is the one we will call *own*. Possessors of the *own* right can modify the ACL.

Creating an object also creates its ACL, with some initial value (possibly empty, but more usually the creator is initially given all rights, including *own*, over the new object). By convention, the subject with *own* rights is allowed to modify the ACL. However, some systems allow anyone with access to manipulate the rights.

EXAMPLE: The relational database System R [822] contains sets of *n*-tuples making up the records, and each element of each *n*-tuple has attributes. These *n*-tuples are stored as tables, with the records as the rows and the attributes as the columns. Each table defines a relation.

The rights for manipulating a table (relation) include *read* (for reading rows, querying using the relation, or defining views), *update* (for writing to a table), *insert* (for adding rows), *delete* (for deleting rows), and *drop* (for deleting tables). Each right has a modifier, called the *grant* option, which if set allows the possessor to give the right to another. Any user with access to a table can give rights to any other user, provided the right has the *grant* option. Hence, possession of access (and a *grant* option associated with each right), not ownership, controls the transfer of rights.

16.1.2.2   Do the ACLs Apply to a Privileged User?

Many systems have users with extra privileges. The two best known are the *root* superuser on UNIX systems and the *administrator* user on Windows systems. Typically, ACLs (or their degenerate forms) are applied in a limited fashion to such users.

EXAMPLE: Solaris UNIX systems use both the abbreviations of ACLs standard to UNIX systems and a full-blown ACL [2235]. The abbreviations of ACLs are ignored when *root* is the subject, but the full ACLs apply even to *root*.

16.1.2.3   Does the ACL Support Groups and Wildcards?

In its classic form, ACLs do not support groups or wildcards. In practice, systems support one or the other (or both) to limit the size of the ACL and to make manipulation of the lists easier. A group can either refine the characteristics of the processes to be allowed access or be a synonym for a set of users (the members of the group).

EXAMPLE: IBM's version of the UNIX operating system, called AIX, uses an ACL (called "extended permissions") to augment the traditional UNIX abbreviations of ACLs (called "base permissions") [726]. Unlike traditional ACLs, the AIX ACL allows one to specify permissions to be added or deleted from the user's set. The specific algorithm is:

1. Determine what set S of permissions the user has from the base permissions.

2. If extended permissions are disabled, stop. The set S is the user's set of permissions.

3. Get the next entry in the extended permissions. If there are no more, stop. The set S is the user's set of permissions.

4. If the entry has the same user and group as the process requesting access, determine if the entry denies access. If so, stop. Access is denied.

5. Modify S as dictated by the permissions in the entry.

6. Go to 3.

As a specific example, consider the following representation of an AIX system's access control permissions for the file *xyzzy*:

```
attributes:
base permissions
    owner(bishop):    rw-
    group(sys):       r--
    others:           ---
extended permissions enabled
    specify        rw-  u:holly
    permit         -w-  u:heidi, g=sys
    permit         rw-  u:matt
    deny           -w-  u:holly, g=faculty
```

Initially, the group *sys* had read permission only on the file. The second line of the extended permissions adds write permission for processes with UID *heidi* and GID *sys*. The first line of the extended permissions gives processes with UID *holly* read and write access, except when the GID of the process is *faculty*, in which case the process cannot write to the object (see the fourth line of the extended permissions).

EXAMPLE: The UNICOS 7.0 operating system provided ACLs similar to those of AIX, but allowed wildcards [2248]. For example,

```
holly : maceranch : r
```

meant that a process with UID *holly* and GID *maceranch* could read the object with which the ACL was associated. The ACL entry

```
holly : * : r
```

meant that a process with UID *holly* could access the object regardless of the group that the process was in. And the entry

```
* : maceranch : r
```

meant that any process with GID *maceranch* could read the object.

16.1.2.4   Conflicts

A conflict arises when two access control list entries in the same ACL give different permissions to the subject. The system can allow access if any entry would give access, deny access if any entry would deny access, or apply the first entry that matches the subject.

EXAMPLE: If any entry in an AIX ACL denies access, the subject is denied access regardless of the location of that entry. Otherwise, if any entry has granted access, the subject is granted access. This is an example of denial taking precedence.

EXAMPLE: Cisco routers apply the first ACL entry that matches the incoming packet [2216]. If none applies, the incoming packet is discarded. This is an example of the third approach, with a default rule of deny.

16.1.2.5   ACLs and Default Permissions

When ACLs and abbreviations of ACLs or default access rights coexist (as on many UNIX systems), there are two ways to determine access rights. The first is to apply the appropriate ACL entry, if one exists, and to apply the default permissions or abbreviations of ACLs otherwise. The second way is to augment the default permissions or abbreviations of ACLs with those in the appropriate ACL entry.

EXAMPLE: The AIX extended permissions fall into the second category, because they modify the base permissions.

EXAMPLE: If a packet entering a Cisco router is destined for a host on a network behind the router, but the router has no access list entry that allows the packet to be forwarded, the packet is discarded. This is an example of the first method, because the default permission is deny.

16.1.3   Revocation of Rights

Revocation, or the prevention of a subject's accessing an object, requires that the subject's rights be deleted from the object's ACL.

Preventing a subject from accessing an object is simple. The entry for the subject is deleted from the object's ACL. If only specific rights are to be deleted, they are removed from the relevant subject's entry in the ACL.

If ownership does not control the giving of rights, revocation is more complex.

EXAMPLE: Return to System R. Suppose Anna has given Peter *update* rights over a relation *T* but now wishes to revoke them. System R holds that after the revoking, the protection state of the system should be as it was before Anna gave Peter any rights. Specifically, if Peter gave Mary *update* rights, when Anna revokes Peter's *update* rights, Mary's *update* rights should be revoked unless someone other than Peter has also given her *update* rights.

To implement this, System R defines a relation called *Sysauth*. The attributes of this relation are (*User, Table, Grantor, Read, Insert, Delete, Drop, Update*). The values of the attributes corresponding to the rights are timestamps indicating when the right was given (except for *Update*, which we will deal with later). For example, if Anna gave Peter *read* rights over the relation *Reports* at time 10, Michelle gave them to Mary at time 15, and Peter gave them to Mary at time 20, the table would be:

User	Table	Grantor	Read
Peter	Reports	Anna	10
Mary	Reports	Michelle	15
Mary	Reports	Peter	20

If Anna revokes Peter's *read* rights, and Mary obtained her *read* rights from Peter after Anna gave them to Peter, her *read* rights would also be revoked. Peter can no longer read *Reports*, and had Michelle not given Mary the right, Mary would not be able to read *Reports* either. But deleting Ann's permissions to Peter, and thus Peter's to Mary, leaves an entry for Mary—namely, the one from Michelle:

User	Table	Grantor	Read
Mary	Reports	Michelle	15

So Mary can still read *Reports*.

The *update* right has a value of *All*, *Some*, or *None*. These values refer to the set of rows that can be changed. If the value is *Some*, a second relation called *Syscolauth* records the columns that the subject can update. This table also records times, and revocation proceeds as for the other columns.

16.1.4   Example: NTFS and Access Control Lists

Microsoft Corporation's Windows operating systems support the NTFS file system. The NTFS file system provides a set of rights, called *basic permissions*, that apply to objects (files and directories, called "folders" in Windows and NTFS terminology). In the ACLs, each entry contains the user or group, the right, and whether the right is allowed or denied.

Windows applies the idea of inheritance to permissions. By default, when an object is created, it inherits the permissions of its parent folder. A user can change these permissions, and when a folder's permissions are changed, so are the corresponding permissions of all subfolders and files in those folders.

EXAMPLE: A project manager creates a directory called *Project* on the network drive *N:*. Initially, *Project* has the same permissions as the root directory of the network drive, *N:*. She then changes the permissions of *Project* to allow any member of the group *projdoer* to modify the folder.

Tom, a member of *projdoer*, creates a folder called *Design* in *Project*. That file inherits its initial permissions from *Project*. Tom then turns off *delete* permission for the group for *Design*. Now, whenever a new folder is created in *Design*, the group *Delete* permission will be turned off.

A subject can have the following permissions over each NTFS object (file or folder):

- *full control*: the subject has all rights to the file, including the right to take ownership of it.
- *modify*: the subject has all rights to the object except for the right to take ownership of it.
- *read & execute*: if the object is a file, the subject can read and execute it; if the object is a folder, the subject can list the files in the folder and subfolders.
- *list folder contents*: this applies only to objects that are folders, and is just like read and execute except that it is not inherited by files in the folder or in subfolders.
- *read*: if the object is a file, the subject can view its contents; if the object is a folder, the user can view the contents of the folder and the attributes of those contents.
- *write*: if the object is a file, the subject can write data to it; if the object is a folder, the subject can create new files and subfolders in it.

If the subject has none of these rights over the object, then it cannot access the object.

The basic permissions are aggregated into another set of rights called *special permissions*:

- *traverse folder/execute file*: if the object is a folder, the subject can access its subfolders whether or not the subject has explicit permission to read the contents of the folder; if a file, the subject can execute the file.
- *list folders/read data*: if the object is a folder, the subject can list its contents; if the object is a file, the subject can read the file.
- *read attributes*: the subject can read the basic attributes of the object.
- *read extended attributes*: the subject can read the extended attributes of the object.
- *create files/write data*: if the object is a folder, the subject can create files in it; if the object is a file, the subject can write data to it.
- *create folders/append data*: if the object is a folder, the subject can create subfolders in it; if the object is a file, the subject can append data to it.
- *write attributes*: the subject can write the basic attributes of the object.
- *write extended attributes*: the subject can write the extended attributes of the object.
- *delete subfolders and files*: the subject can delete subfolders and files within the (folder) object, whether or not it has permission to delete the individual subfolders and files.

- *delete*: the subject can delete the object, unless it is a nonempty folder and the subject does *not* have the *delete subfolders and files* permission on the object.

- *read permissions*: the subject can read the basic and special permissions for the object.

- *change permissions*: the subject can change the basic and special permissions for the object.

- *take ownership*: the subject can make itself the owner of the object.

- *synchronize*: the subject can synchronize the (offline) object.

When a user accesses a file, Windows 10 first examines the file's ACL. If the user is not present in the ACL, and is not a member of any group listed in the ACL, access is denied. Otherwise, if any ACL entry denies the user access, Windows 10 denies the access (this is an explicit denial, which is calculated first). If access is not explicitly denied, and the user is named in the ACL (as either a user or a member of a group), the user has the union of the set of rights from each ACL entry in which the user is named.

EXAMPLE: Suppose Paul, Quentin, and Regina use a Windows 10 system. Paul and Quentin are in the group *students*. Quentin and Regina are in the group *staff*. The directory *e:\stuff* has its access control list set to (*staff, create files/write data, allow*), (*Quentin, delete subfolders and files, allow*), (*students, delete subfolders and files, deny*). Under this list, the first entry enables Regina to create subfolders or files in *e:\stuff*. The third entry disallows all members of the group *students* from deleting subfolders and files in *e:\stuff*. The second entry would allow Quentin to delete these, except that Quentin is in the *students* group, and in Windows 10 an explicit deny (as given in the third entry) overrides any grants of permission. Hence, Quentin cannot delete them.

Now, let Regina create a subdirectory *plugh* in *e:\stuff*. She then disallows Paul's *delete subfolders and files* access, but wants Quentin to have *delete subfolders and files* access. She takes the following steps:

1. Create *e:\stuff\plugh*; it inherits from *e:\stuff* the ACL (*staff, create files/write data, allow*), (*Quentin, delete subfolders and files, allow*), (*students, delete subfolders and files, deny*).

2. Delete the last entry in the ACL; from the second entry, this gives Quentin *delete subfolders and files* access.

3. Add the entry (Paul, *delete subfolders and files, deny*) to the ACL.

The last step is superfluous, because Windows 10 denies access by default, but it is safer to add it anyway, lest the group *students* be given rights. If that should happen, Paul would get those rights unless the (Paul, *delete subfolders and files, deny*) entry were present.

16.2   Capabilities

Conceptually, a capability is like the row of an access control matrix. Each subject has associated with it a set of pairs, with each pair containing an object and a set of rights. The subject associated with this list can access the named object in any of the ways indicated by the named rights. More formally:

> **Definition 16–2.** Let O be the set of objects, and R the set of rights, of a system. A *capability list* c is a set of pairs $c = \{(o, r) \mid o \in O, r \subseteq R\}$. Let *cap* be a function that determines the capability list c associated with a particular subject s. The interpretation of the capability list $cap(s) = \{(o_i, r_i) \mid 1 \leq i \leq n\}$ is that subject s may access o_i using any right in r_i.

We abbreviate "capability list" as C-List.

EXAMPLE: Again, consider the access control matrix in Figure 2–1, on page 33. The set of subjects is process 1 and process 2. The corresponding capability lists are

cap(process 1) = { (file 1, { read, write, own }), (file 2, { read }),
(process 1, {read, write, execute, own }), (process 2, { write }) }

cap(process 2) = { (file 1, { append }), (file 2, { read, own }),
(process 1,{ read }), (process 2, { read, write, execute, own }) }

Each subject has an associated C-List. Thus, process 1 owns file 1, and can read or write to it; process 1 can read file 2; process 1 can read, write to, or execute itself and owns itself; and process 1 can write to process 2. Similarly, process 2 can append to file 1; process 2 owns file 2 and can read it; process 2 can read process 1; and process 2 can read, write to, or execute itself and owns itself.

Capabilities encapsulate object identity. When a process uses a capability to access an object, the operating system examines the capability to determine both the object and the access to which the process is entitled. This reflects how capabilities for memory management work; the location of the object in memory is encapsulated in the capability. Without the capability, the process cannot identify the object in a way that will give it the desired access.

EXAMPLE: To open a UNIX file, a process gives the file name to the kernel. The kernel obtains the file's inode number by resolving the name through the file hierarchy. Once the inode is obtained, the system determines if the requested access should be granted using the access control permissions. If the access is granted, the operating system returns a capability called a *file descriptor*. The capability is tightly bound to the file object, so even if the file is deleted and a new file with the same name is created, the file descriptor still refers to the previous file.

The "codewords" of Iliffe [943] are similar to capabilities. Dennis and Van Horn [552] first suggested "capabilities" as a way to control access to objects in memory or secondary storage. Fabry generalized this idea to implement capability-based addressing [647].

The architecture of capabilities is more interesting than that of access control lists. The access control list and the process identity are under the control of the operating system. In the absence of flaws, user processes can change them only by invoking the operating system services. However, a process must identify a capability in order to use it, so the process must have some control over the capabilities. If the process can forge a capability and then use it, access controls fail.

16.2.1 Implementation of Capabilities

Three mechanisms are used to protect capabilities: tags, protected memory, and cryptography.

A *tagged* architecture has a set of bits associated with each hardware word. The tag has two states: *set* and *unset*. If the tag is set, an ordinary process can read but not modify the word. If the tag is unset, an ordinary process can read and modify the word. Further, an ordinary process cannot change the state of the tag; the processor must be in a privileged mode to do so.

EXAMPLE: The B5700 [1478] used a tagged architecture (although it did not use capabilities as protection mechanisms). The tag field consisted of three bits and indicated how the architecture was to treat the word (pointer, descriptor, type, and so on).

More common is to use the protection bits associated with paging or segmentation. All capabilities are stored in a page (segment) that the process can read but not alter. This requires no special-purpose hardware other than that used by the memory management scheme. But the process must reference capabilities indirectly, usually through pointers, rather than directly.

EXAMPLE: The CAP system [1437] did not allow processes to modify the segment in which instructions lay. It also stored capabilities in this segment. A fence register separated instructions and capabilities.

EXAMPLE: The Extremely Reliable Operating System (EROS) is a capability-based system that stores its capabilities in *capability pages*. These pages are protected with a tag indicating their type, so only the kernel can access them [1729, 1730].

A third alternative is to use cryptography. The goal of tags and memory protection is to prevent the capabilities from being altered. This is akin to integrity checking. Cryptographic checksums are another mechanism for checking the integrity of information. Each capability has a cryptographic checksum associated with it, and the checksum is digitally enciphered using a cryptosystem whose key is known to the operating system.

When the process presents a capability to the operating system, the system first recomputes the cryptographic checksum associated with the capability. It then either enciphers the checksum using the cryptographic key and compares it with the one stored in the capability, or deciphers the checksum provided with the capability and compares it with the computed checksum. If they match, the capability is unaltered. If not, the capability is rejected.

EXAMPLE: The Amoeba system is a distributed system that uses capabilities to name objects [1858]. On creation, a capability corresponding to the object is returned. To use the object, the program presents the corresponding capability. The capability encodes the name of the object (24 bits), the server that created it (48 bits), and the rights (8 bits) in a 128-bit quantity. Initially, all rights are turned on.

The last 48 bits are used as a check field. This is a random number selected at creation time. (Because the capability is given to the owner of the object, the owner can freely modify the rights without danger.) The number is stored in a table corresponding to the server that created the object, so whenever the capability is presented to that server, it verifies that the random number is correct. An attacker would need to know the random number in order to be able to forge a capability. However, as Tanenbaum notes, the system is vulnerable if a capability is disclosed.

16.2.2   Copying and Amplifying Capabilities

The ability to copy capabilities implies the ability to give rights. To prevent processes from indiscriminately giving away rights, a *copy flag* is associated with capabilities. A process cannot copy a capability to another process unless the copy flag is set. If the process does copy the capability, the copy flag may be turned off (at the discretion of either the process or the kernel).

EXAMPLE: Amoeba uses an interesting scheme. It does not control copying rights. However, the uses to which those copied rights can be put are restricted.

Suppose user *matt* wishes to allow user *holly* to read an object he owns. He passes his capability for that object to the server and requests a restricted capability for reading. The server creates a new capability for the object but with only the *read* right turned on. The rights field now is all 0s except for the read bit, which is a 1. This is xor'ed with the random check and input to a cryptographic hash function. The output is the new random number for this capability. The restricted capability is then passed back to *matt*, who gives it to *holly*.

When *holly* uses the capability, the server notes that at least one bit in the rights field is 0. It takes the rights field, xors it with the random number of the original capability (stored in its tables), and hashes the result. If the resulting hash matches the random number in the capability, the capability is valid; otherwise, it is not.

Amplification is the increasing of privileges. The idea of modular programming, and especially of abstract data types, requires that the rights a process has over an object be amplified.

To understand why, consider the following abstract data type for a counter:

```
module counter;
        procedure entry increment(var ctr: integer);
        begin
                ctr := ctr + 1;
        end;
        function entry getval(ctr: integer);
        begin
                getval := ctr;
        end;
        procedure entry clear(var ctr: integer);
        begin
                ctr := 0;
        end;
    end.
```

Suppose x is declared to be a counter. The rules of abstract data types allow that object to be accessed *only* by the *counter* module. So, initially the capability for x would contain the right to invoke the *counter* module only. But when the object is passed to the counter module, the process must now be able to read and write to that object. Hence, the capability must be amplified temporarily while the module *counter* is active.

EXAMPLE: The seminal system HYDRA [433, 2030] used amplification templates to amplify a process's rights. Associated with each procedure in the module is a template that adds rights to the capabilities as needed. For example, the template for the *getval* procedure would add read rights while the procedure was active. The template for the *increment* procedure would add read and write rights.

EXAMPLE: The Intel iAPX 432 system [991, 2168] implements a similar mechanism in hardware. Its "access descriptors" correspond to capabilities. Three bits in the capability control various system functions. One of these bits controls amplification of rights. When an abstract data type module is constructed, the permission bits of the type control object (which defines the data type) are set to the permissions that the procedure needs. When the procedure is called, the system checks the amplification bit. If it is set, the rights in the type control object are or'ed with the rights in the descriptor of the object being passed. This combination defines the rights available to the procedure.

16.2.3   Revocation of Rights

In a capability system, revoking access to an object requires that all the capabilities granting access to that object be revoked. Conceptually, each process could be checked, and the capabilities deleted. The cost of such an operation would be unacceptable, however, so alternative methods are used.

The simplest mechanism is indirection [1574]. Define one or more *global object tables*. In this scheme, each object has a corresponding entry in a table. Capabilities do not name the object directly; they name the entry in the table corresponding to the object.

This scheme has several advantages. First, to revoke capabilities, the entry in the global object table is invalidated. Then any references will obtain an invalid table entry and will be rejected. Second, if only some of the capabilities are to be revoked, the object can have multiple entries, each corresponding to a different set of rights or a different group of users.

EXAMPLE: Amoeba uses essentially this scheme. To revoke a capability, the owner of the object requests that the server change the random number and issue a new capability. This invalidates all existing capabilities.

An alternative revocation mechanism uses abstract data type managers. Included with each abstract data type is a revocation procedure. When access is to be revoked, the type manager simply disallows further accesses by the subject whose rights are being revoked. This does not affect alternative methods of accessing the objects underlying the abstract data types. For example, access to a file may be revoked, but this technique would not block access to the underlying segments through an alternative type manager. The SCP3 system used this technique [2015].

16.2.4   Limits of Capabilities

Boebert [250] credits Neumann and his colleagues [1450] with a demonstration of the importance of controlling the copying of capabilities. Without such restrictions, a capability system cannot enforce the *-property of the Bell-LaPadula Model (see Chapter 5).

Suppose capabilities can be copied into one's C-List. Let Heidi be cleared for HIGH information, and Lou only for LOW information. The file "lough" has LOW classification. Lou asks for a capability to read and write to the file "lough" and obtains it (call the capability "rw*lough"). Lou stores the capability in the file "lough." Now, Heidi requests a capability to read "lough" (call it "r*lough"); by the simple security condition, this is granted. Heidi uses this to read "lough," thereby obtaining the capability "rw*lough." She can now write to a LOW object, even though she has HIGH clearance. This violates the *-property. (See Figure 16–1.)

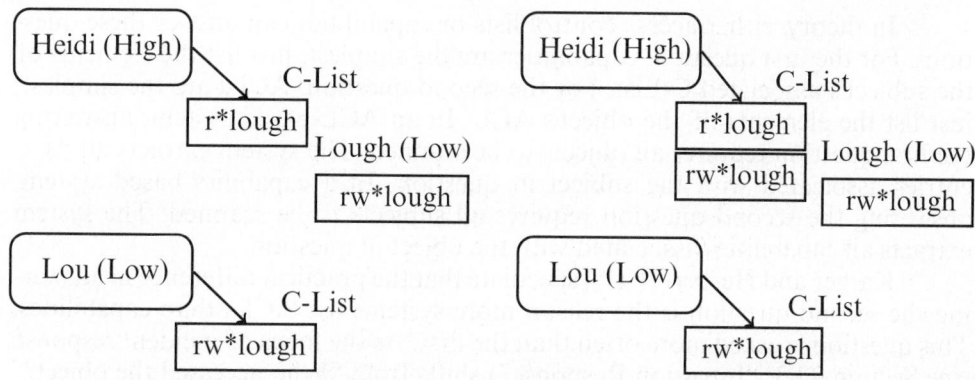

Figure 16–1 Copying and reading capabilities. The left diagram shows the capability rw*lough copied into the file lough. In the right diagram, Heidi has read the contents of the file lough and added the capability it contains to her C-List.

Kain and Landwehr [993] present two ways to handle this problem. Their first technique assigns a security classification to the capability itself. When the capability is created, its compartment is the same as the requesting process, and the capability contains read, read and write, or write rights depending on whether its compartment dominates, is the same as, or is dominated by that of the object to which the capability refers. Similar rules apply when a capability is copied. So, in Boebert's example, because the capability "rw*lough" is copied to HIGH, and because the destination (HIGH level) dominates the source ("lough," at the LOW level), the resulting capability has only the right to read.

Their second solution uses a technique from Karger and Herbert [1007], although in a different context. Before a capability is passed to another process, the kernel evaluates the capability to determine if passing it to the subject violates any security properties. In Boebert's example, the *-property is violated, so Heidi's request to obtain "rw*lough" would be denied.

A simpler approach is to distinguish between the "copy capability" right and the "read" right. The Take-Grant Protection Model (see Section 3.3) uses this difference to resolve Boebert's example. That Heidi could *read* the capability did not mean that she could *acquire* (take or copy) it. Heidi would be able to read the capability but could not add it to her C-List.

16.2.5   Comparison with Access Control Lists

Two questions underlie the use of access controls:

- Given a subject, what objects can it access, and how?
- Given an object, what subjects can access it, and how?

In theory, either access control lists or capabilities can answer these questions. For the first question, capabilities are the simplest; just list the elements of the subject's associated C-List. For the second question, ACLs are the simplest; just list the elements of the object's ACL. In an ACL-based system, answering the first question requires all objects to be scanned. The system extracts all ACL entries associated with the subject in question. In a capability-based system, answering the second question requires all subjects to be scanned. The system extracts all capabilities associated with the object in question.

Karger and Herbert [1007] speculate that the practical difference in answering the second question is the reason more systems use ACLs than capabilities. This question is asked more often than the first. As the focus of incident response (see Section 27.3, "Intrusion Response") shifts from "Who accessed the object?" to include "What else did that subject access?" capability-based systems may become more common.

16.2.6 Privileges

Many UNIX-like systems define specific sets of *privileges* that processes may possess. These privileges can be used to override restrictions on access, or (by removing them) restrict access further. These are not capabilities in the sense of Definition 16–2 because no particular object is associated with the right. The right applies to all objects.

Privileges enable fine-grained restrictions on processes, in accordance with the principle of least privilege. Typically, processes have at least three sets of privileges:

- The *bounding* set, which is the set of all privileges that the process may assert
- The *effective* set, which is the set of current privileges that the process may assert
- The *saved* set, which is a set of rights, typically used to save rights for some future purpose

The effective set and the saved set are both subsets of the bounding set.

EXAMPLE: The effective and saved UIDs in many versions of the UNIX operating system (see page 474) are an implementation of the effective and saved sets. The effective set is the set of privileges belonging to the user with the effective UID. When a user changes identity using, for example, the *setuid* system call, the current effective UID becomes the saved UID, and the new UID becomes the effective UID. Now, the new effective UID defines the privileges in the effective set, and the previous effective UID defines the privileges in the saved set.

In the previous example, the privileges are implicit because the UIDs define them. Some systems have explicit privileges that augment the ones defined by user, group, and role identities.

EXAMPLE: Trusted Solaris defines a number of privileges that override file system and process access controls [2156, 2245]. For example, the privilege PRIV_FILE_MAC_WRITE allows a process to write to a file when mandatory access controls would normally prevent the write. Similarly, PRIV_FILE_DAC_READ allows a process to read a file when the associated permission bits (or ACL) would prevent the read.

Privileges are grouped into types. File system privileges override restrictions imposed on file systems, such as mandatory and discretionary access controls. Process privileges enable processes to perform process-related actions that would normally be prevented. The management of these privileges shows how they can be used to "bracket" sections of code that need extra privileges.

Associated with each executable file are an *allowed set* (*AS*) of privileges, which says what privileges will be assigned to the process created by executing the file, and a *forced set* (*FS*) of privileges that the process must have when it begins execution. The forced set is a subset of the allowed set.

Trusted Solaris processes have four sets of privileges:

- The *inheritable set* (*IS*) contains those privileges inherited from the parent process.
- The *permitted set* (*PS*) contains all the privileges that the process may assert, which is defined as $(FS \cup IS) \cap AS$.
- The *effective set* (*ES*) contains the privileges the program requires for the current task. Initially, $ES = PS$.
- The *saved set* (*SS*) contains privileges inherited from the parent process and allowed for use; that is, $SS = IS \cap AS$.

Here, the permitted set corresponds to the bounding set.

A programmer can use this structure to bracket effective privileges, so they are present only when needed. This limits the time and use to which a privilege can be put, enforcing the principle of least privilege. For example, if a process needs to read a file at a particular point in its execution, the privileges PRIV_FILE_MAC_READ and PRIV_FILE_DAC_READ would be in the permitted and effective sets when the program begins. The programmer would then delete the privileges from the effective set, ensuring they could not be used yet. Then, just before the program needs to read the file, the process would reset its effective set to include those two privileges (it can do so because they are in the permitted set). After the read, it would then remove those privileges from the effective set.

Once the program no longer needs to read the file at any point in the future, it can remove the privileges from its permitted set. Then, it cannot add them back, even if (for example) it is compromised.

Linux capabilities work similarly [854].

An alternate approach is to use capabilities to confine processes. This follows the philosophy of viewing capabilities as limiting the privileges of subjects, because the subject can only do what its capabilities allow.

EXAMPLE: Capsicum, described in more detail on page 589, is a framework designed with this philosophy [1983]. It first appeared in FreeBSD 9. It changes the notion of file descriptor to include not only the descriptor but a set of capabilities associated with that file descriptor.

When a process enters capability mode, it invokes a library that spawns a new process that executes a run-time linker that augments its capabilities with those delegated from the application. That linker then loads other libraries and links them with the application binary, which it then executes. The executing application can query the library for delegated capabilities as needed.

As an example, the program *tcpdump* captures network traffic matching one or more supplied patterns. Because the ability to read the network requires privileges acquired when the program starts, it can enter capability mode directly after those privileges. This constrains access to the rest of the system. Two additional changes were required. The first blocked access to the (inherited) standard input file descriptor; this prevented *tcpdump* from reading input from a keyboard. The second changed the DNS resolution method, which no longer worked as the resolver required access to the file system, which capability mode disallowed. The solution was to switch to a lightweight resolver that sent DNS queries to a daemon that did the actual resolution. The communication channel was set up before entering capability mode, and thus the process inherited the required access to the daemon.

16.3 Locks and Keys

The locks and keys technique combines features of access control lists and capabilities. A piece of information (the lock) is associated with the object and a second piece of information (the key) is associated with those subjects authorized to access the object and the manner in which they are allowed to access the object. When a subject tries to access an object, the subject's set of keys is checked. If the subject has a key corresponding to any of the object's locks, access of the appropriate type is granted.

The difference between locks and keys and the other access control mechanisms is the dynamic nature of the former. An access control list is static in the sense that all changes to it are manual; a user or process must interact with the list to make the change. Locks and keys, on the other hand, may change in response to system constraints, general instructions about how entries are to be added, and any factors other than a manual change.

Gifford [769] suggests a cryptographic implementation of locks and keys. The object o is enciphered with a cryptographic key. The subject has a deciphering key. To access the object, the subject deciphers it. Gifford points out that this provides a simple way to allow n subjects to access the data (called *or-access*). Simply encipher n copies of the data using n different keys, one per subject. The object o is then represented as o', where

$$o' = (E_1(o), \ldots, E_n(o))$$

The system can easily deny access except on the request of n subjects (called *and-access*). Simply iterate the cipher using n different keys, one per subject:

$$o' = E_1(\ldots(E_n(o))\ldots)$$

EXAMPLE: The IBM 370 system [992] assigns each process an access key and assigns each page a storage key and a fetch bit. If the fetch bit is cleared, only read accesses are allowed. If the fetch bit is not set, and the access key matches the storage key of a particular page, the process can write to that page. If the fetch bit is set and the access key is 0 (which occurs in nonuser mode), the process can write to any page. If the access key is neither 0 nor the same as the storage key, the process cannot access the page.

EXAMPLE: Cisco routers have a mechanism called *dynamic access control lists* that is a lock and key mechanism [2216]. Consider a router that transfers packets between the Internet and an internal network. We want to limit external access to the (internal) server with address 10.1.2.3 to weekdays between 9:00 a.m. and 5:00 p.m. Our router's IP address is 10.1.1.1. The following is the relevant portion of the dynamic access control list:

```
access-list 100 permit tcp any host 10.1.1.1 eq telnet
access-list 100 dynamic test timeout 180 permit ip
   any host
        10.1.2.3 time-range my-time
time-range my-time
        periodic weekdays 9:00 to 17:00
line vty 0 2
        login local
        autocommand access-enable host timeout 10
```

The first line tells the router to accept packets coming to it over the Internet and going to the *telnet* port. (The binding of the access control list to the Internet connection is not shown.) The user will enter a name and a password, and if they match a pair in the configuration file, the connection will close and the router will add an access control list entry for that remote host to access the server 10.1.2.3 over any IP protocol. After 180 minutes, the access control list entry will be discarded even if there are connections at that time (this effectively terminates the connections). The access control entry is valid only between 9:00 a.m. and 5:00 p.m. on weekdays (the "time-range" block). Furthermore, any host matching this new entry is to be allowed access; if no packets from that host are received within a 10-minute interval, the access control entry is to be deleted (the "line" block).

16.3.1   Type Checking

Type checking restricts access on the basis of the types of the subject and object. It is a form of locks and keys access control, the pieces of information being the type. Systems use type checking in areas other than security.

EXAMPLE: UNIX-like systems use type checking to protect the integrity of their file systems. Under the UNIX model, all file system objects are files, but the kernel disallows the use of *write* to change the directory. Instead, users must call specific system calls to create and delete entities in the directory. This allows the kernel to ensure that all writing to the directory file will create entries of the correct format. The kernel disallows certain operations, such as *write*, to file system objects of type *directory*.

The simplest case of type checking is distinguishing instructions from data. The operation *execute* can be performed only on instructions, and the operations *read* and *write* can be performed only on data. Many systems and processors such as the PDP-11 [2203], the Intel Itanium 64 and IA-32 [2179, 2180], the AMD64 [2117], and the ARM11 [78] provide features to enforce this distinction.

EXAMPLE: One form of a type of attack called *buffer overflow* (see Section 24.3.1, "Two Security Flaws") involves overwriting of a buffer stored on a memory stack and changing of the return address on the stack to the location of the buffer. When the input routine executes a return to the caller, the return address is popped from the stack and placed in the program counter. The contents of the buffer are then executed as instructions.

Some vendors have tried to eliminate this type of attack by marking the memory in which the stack resides as data. The systems cannot execute data, and therefore the program terminates right after the return address is popped and placed into the program counter.

Like pages, files can be either "executable" or "data."

EXAMPLE: Boebert, Young, Kain, and Hansohn [253] propose labeling of subjects and objects in Logical Coprocessor Kernel or LOCK (formerly Secure Ada

Target or SAT) [253, 846, 1670, 1671], a system designed to meet the highest level of security under the Department of Defense criteria [2239]. Once compiled, programs have the label "data" and cannot be executed until a sequence of specific, auditable events changes the label to "executable." After that, the program cannot be modified.

Strictly enforced type checking is a powerful protection mechanism. The DTEL policy language discussed in Section 4.5.1, and the supporting domain and type enforcement (DTE) mechanism, are a good example. Walker et al. [1959] discuss the implementation of DTE using DTEL at length for the UNIX operating system. The Sidewinder firewall uses a similar approach.

EXAMPLE: Like DTEL, Sidewinder [1877] assigns each subject a domain and each object a type. The *domain definition table* defines how domains may interact with types. For instance, packets coming from inside the firewall are assigned one type, and packets from the outside are assigned a second type. This separates the two.

Suppose that an attacker outside the firewall is able to embed in a legal packet a second, fake packet and that this fake packet contains an IP source address that is inside the firewall. The attacker sends the packet to the Sidewinder firewall and then sends a second packet to overwrite the part of the first packet before the fake packet. If there were no typing, the firewall could confuse the fake packet, which came from outside, with a legitimate packet originating from inside the firewall. However, because Sidewinder types outside packets differently than those originating behind the firewall, the fake packet will have the type "outside" even though the source address is from the inside. Thus, it will not be forwarded to the inside.

16.3.2   Sharing Secrets

A question related to the locks and keys access methods is how to construct a control that will allow any three out of ten people to gain access to a file.

EXAMPLE: An organization prepares for its managers being incapacitated by deciding that three senior managers must agree that a manager is incapacitated before her system account can be accessed by anyone else. However, the organization realizes that any particular group of three senior managers might not all be available when needed. So, the organization chooses ten senior managers and schedules them so that at least three are always available. Assuming that any three agree a manager is incapacitated, they can grant access to her account. But if only two believe she is incapacitated, they can do nothing until they have convinced a third manager.

Each manager in the organization takes her passwords and secondary authentication information and places them in a file. The files are enciphered and sent to many different computers. The decryption key must be broken up and the parts distributed in such a way that exactly three of the recipients can reassemble the original key.

This implements the principle of separation of privilege (see Section 14.2.6). A threshold scheme provides this capability.

> **Definition 16–3.** A (t, n)-*threshold scheme* is a cryptographic scheme in which a datum is divided into n parts, any t of which are sufficient to determine the original datum. The n parts are called *shadows*.

The previous example requires a (3, 10)-threshold scheme to protect the decryption key (datum). The locks and keys scheme can solve this problem using a combination of or-access and and-access mechanisms, but the number of representations of the datum grows rapidly (see Exercise 7). An alternative is to use a cryptographic method designed to share secrets.

Shamir [1722] based a secret sharing algorithm on Lagrange interpolating polymonials. He selects a polynomial of degree $t - 1$ and sets the constant to the secret value. The shadows are the polynomial evaluated at an arbitrary point. By the laws of polynomial arithmetic, because the polynomial is of degree $t - 1$, at least t values are needed to rederive the polynomial.

Let $P(x) = (a_{t-1}x^{t-1} + \ldots + a_1 x + a_0) \bmod p$. The number we wish to share is S. Choose p to be greater than both S and n. Choose $a_0 = S$; note that $P(0) = S$. Choose $a_1, \ldots, a_{t-1}$ arbitrarily. Then choose $P(1), \ldots, P(n)$ as the n shadows.

EXAMPLE: We wish to share the secret key $S = 7$ using a (3, 5)-threshold scheme. We choose $p = 11$, $a_2 = 5$, $a_1 = 3$, and $a_0 = S = 7$. Thus, $P(x) = (5x^2 + 3x + 7) \bmod 11$. The five shadows are

$$P(1) = (5(1)^2 + 3(1) + 7) \bmod 11 = (5 + 3 + 7) \bmod 11 = 15 \bmod 11 = 4$$
$$P(2) = (5(2)^2 + 3(2) + 7) \bmod 11 = (20 + 6 + 7) \bmod 11 = 33 \bmod 11 = 0$$
$$P(3) = (5(3)^2 + 3(3) + 7) \bmod 11 = (45 + 9 + 7) \bmod 11 = 61 \bmod 11 = 6$$
$$P(4) = (5(4)^2 + 3(4) + 7) \bmod 11 = (80 + 12 + 7) \bmod 11$$
$$= 101 \bmod 11 = 2$$
$$P(5) = (5(5)^2 + 3(5) + 7) \bmod 11 = (125 + 15 + 7) \bmod 11$$
$$= 147 \bmod 11 = 4$$

We give each shadow to a different person.

To recover the polynomial, we interpolate any t shadows. Let $P(x_i) = k_i$. The formula for the interpolated polynomial is

$$P(x) = \sum_{s=1}^{t} k_s \prod_{j=1, j \neq s}^{t} \frac{x - x_j}{x_s - x_j} \bmod p$$

EXAMPLE: The people holding shadows 1, 2, and 5 decide to recompute the secret. Take $x_1 = 1$, $x_2 = 2$, and $x_3 = 5$; from the previous example, this yields $k_1 = 4$, $k_2 = 0$, and $k_3 = 4$. Recall that $p = 11$. Applying the formula above, we have

$$P(x) = \left[4\frac{(x-2)(x-5)}{(1-2)(1-5)} + 0\frac{(x-1)(x-5)}{(2-1)(2-5)} + 4\frac{(x-1)(x-2)}{(5-1)(5-2)} \right] \bmod 11$$

which yields

$$P(x) = [(x-2)(x-5) + 4(x-1)(x-2)] \bmod 11 = 5x^2 + 3x + 7 \bmod 11$$

So the secret is $P(0) = 7$.

To protect a file using a secret sharing scheme, the system first enciphers the file. The cryptographic key then becomes the secret to be shared. If necessary, the key may be split into blocks of appropriate size, and each set of blocks shared using a secret sharing scheme. In theory, someone could share the contents of the file itself using a secret sharing scheme, but unless the file is very small, the benefits of sharing are outweighed by the problem of each user managing his or her own shadows for the file.

16.4 Ring-Based Access Control

The Multics system [461, 1477] generalizes the notion of a supervisor and user state with a protection mechanism called *ring-based access control*. To understand its simplicity and elegance, one must realize that files and memory are treated the same from the protection point of view. For example, a procedure may occupy a segment of the disk. When invoked, the segment is mapped into memory and executed. Data occupies other segments on disk, and when accessed, they are mapped into memory and accessed. In other words, there is no conceptual difference between a segment of memory and a segment on a disk.

Segments are of two kinds: data and procedure. A segment could have r (read) rights, w (write) rights, e (execute) rights, and a (append) rights associated with it. These rights are contained in access control lists, which constrain access on a per-user basis. So all procedures that user *bishop* executes would have the rights associated with that user, *bishop*.

In addition, the Multics system defines a sequence of *protection rings* (or *rings*, for short) numbered from 0 to 63.[1] The kernel resides in ring 0. The higher the ring number, the lower the privileges of the segments in that ring. We also say that "a procedure executes in ring r" because the ring is associated with the individual segment, not with the entire process.

---

[1] In fact, the system as implemented had eight rings [1478, p. 141].

Subject to the access constraints noted in the following lists, procedures can "cross" ring boundaries. In some cases, the crossing causes a "ring-crossing fault" that traps to the kernel. At that point, a mechanism called the Gatekeeper checks arguments and access and performs other functions that constrain ring crossings. In other cases, no ring-crossing fault is induced, and access is permitted if the access modes allow.

A *gate* is simply an entry point (like the "public" designators of object-oriented languages). Gates are specially declared within programs, and the compiler and linker generate special code to make these entry points available to other procedures.

Assume that a procedure executing in ring r wants to access a data segment. Associated with each data segment is a pair of ring numbers called an *access bracket* (a_1, a_2), with $a_1 \leq a_2$. Assume that the data segment's permissions allow the desired access. The ring numbering adds an extra constraint:

- $r \leq a_1$: access permitted
- $a_1 < r \leq a_2$: r and e access permitted; w and a access denied
- $a_2 < r$: all accesses denied

Assume that the same procedure, again executing in ring r, wants to access a procedure segment. Each procedure segment has an access bracket, just like a data segment. A procedure segment may also have a *call bracket* (c_1, c_2), with $c_1 \leq c_2$. By convention, when a call bracket is present, $c_1 = a_2$, leading to an alternative notation of (a_1, a_2, a_3), where (a_1, a_2) is the access bracket and (a_2, a_3) is the call bracket (that is, $c_2 = a_3$). The rules for access differ slightly from those for accessing a data segment:

- $r < a_1$: access permitted, but a ring-crossing fault occurs
- $a_1 \leq r \leq a_2$: all accesses permitted and no fault occurs
- $a_2 < r \leq a_3$: access permitted if made through a valid gate
- $a_3 < r$: all accesses denied

EXAMPLE: Assume that a data segment has the access bracket (2, 4) and *heidi* has rw rights over the segment. If *heidi*'s procedure executes in ring 1, and tries to read the data, the read succeeds. If *heidi*'s procedure executes in ring 3, any reads succeed and any writes fail. If *heidi*'s procedure executes in ring 5, all accesses fail.

EXAMPLE: Assume that a procedure segment has the bracket (2, 4, 6)—that is, its access bracket is (2, 4) and its call bracket is (4, 6). *heidi*'s procedure calls that procedure. If *heidi*'s procedure executes in ring 1, a ring-crossing fault occurs, but the call succeeds (unless the Gatekeeper blocks the call). If *heidi*'s procedure executes in ring 3, the call succeeds and no ring-crossing fault occurs. If *heidi*'s procedure executes in ring 5 and calls the procedure segment through a valid gate, the call succeeds; otherwise, it fails. If *heidi*'s procedure executes in ring 7, the call fails.

The reason for the brackets shows how practical details complicate ideal solutions. Conceptually, the access bracket should contain one ring. However, consider a procedure embodying a service routine (such as "access file"). Then procedures in other rings accessing that routine would cause a large number of ring crossings. The operating system would need to handle these crossings, increasing the overhead. But if the procedures were within the service routine's access bracket, no ring-crossing faults would occur. Hence, the access bracket minimizes operating system overhead in this context.

A similar situation arises with different classes of users. Suppose a service routine lies in ring *a*. Some users need to invoke this routine. Others are allowed to invoke it in specific ways—for example, to access some system resource in a particular manner. Still others should not invoke it at all. The access bracket handles the first and third sets of users, but the second set cannot be handled with an access bracket. However, with a call bracket, the second set can access the service routine and be forced to use predefined entry points (the gates). Hence, the need for call brackets.

Variants of the ring mechanism have been used by other systems. The Intel Itanium architecture, for example, provides four levels of privilege, level 0 being the most privileged and level 3 the least [2180]. Contrast this with the more traditional two levels (user and supervisor) and the influence of the rings of Multics is clear.

16.5   Propagated Access Control Lists

The Propagated Access Control List (PACL) mechanism [2003] provides the creator of an object with control over who can access the object. It is an implementation that is ideal for the ORCON policy (see Section 8.3). The creator (originator) is kept with the PACL, and only the creator can change the PACL. When a subject reads an object, the PACL of the object is associated with the subject. When a subject creates an object, the PACL of the subject is associated with the object.

The notation $PACL_{subject}$ means that *subject* is the originator of the PACL. Only *subject* can change that PACL. The notation PACL(*entity*) is the PACL associated with *entity*.

EXAMPLE: Ann creates the file *dates*. Ann wants to control who can read the file. The file's PACL is the PACL associated with Ann: PACL(*dates*) = $PACL_{Ann}$.

Let the PACL of an object o be PACL(o) = PACL$_s$. When another subject s' reads o, PACL(o) must augment PACL(s'). Otherwise, s' could create another subject o', and copy the data from o to o'. Then s would have no control over the data in o, defeating the purpose of using PACLs.

Hence, an object can have PACLs associated with two creators. If so, both creators control access to the object. Only subjects common to both PACLs can access the object. Otherwise, one creator would not control access to the data it expects to control. The default is to deny access unless both creators allow it.

EXAMPLE: Ann allows Betty, Dorothy, and Elisabeth access to the file *dates*. Before Betty reads *dates*, her PACL is PACL$_{Betty}$. After Betty reads dates, her PACL changes to PACL$_{Betty}$ ∩ PACL($dates$) = PACL$_{Betty}$ ∩ PACL$_{Ann}$. Write this as PACL$_{Betty,Ann}$.

Betty creates the file *datescopy*. The system assigns Betty's PACL to *datescopy*. Hence, PACL($datescopy$) = PACL$_{Betty,Ann}$.

If PACL$_{Betty}$ allows Cherisse and Dorothy access to objects, Dorothy will be able to access *datescopy* but Cherisse and Elisabeth will not. Because Dorothy is in both PACL$_{Ann}$ and PACL$_{Betty}$, both originators of *datescopy* agree that Dorothy can access the data in that file. So Dorothy is in PACL$_{Betty,Ann}$. Because Cherisse is not in PACL$_{Ann}$, and because Elisabeth is not in PACL$_{Betty}$, one originator of *datescopy* does not want them to have access to the data in *datescopy*. Hence, neither of them is in PACL$_{Betty,Ann}$.

Discretionary access controls can augment PACLs. They restrict access, but they cannot allow access to subjects excluded by the PACL.

EXAMPLE: Betty does not want Dorothy to be able to read the file *datescopy*. However, Dorothy is allowed access by PACL$_{Betty,Ann}$. Betty, being the owner of the file, can change the access control list associated with the file (but not the PACL). So Betty sets the access control list to deny access to Dorothy.

This example illustrates the distinction between the PACL mechanism and the ACL mechanism. A PACL is associated with data, whereas an ACL is associated with an object. The PACL follows the information as it flows around the system, but an ACL stays with each object. In the example, Cherisse cannot access the information in *dates* because of the setting of PACL($dates$), and cannot access the information in any derivative of *dates* because PACL($dates$) propagates with the information. The copiers of the information cannot change this.

Were the files protected by ACLs instead of PACLs, the ACL would not be copied with the information. So, Cherisse would not be able to read dates, but Betty could copy that file and set the ACL so that Cherisse could read it. Ann would not control the information; she would have to trust those with access to dates not to give access to others.

16.6   Summary

Access control mechanisms implement controls on subjects and objects. Access control lists bind the data controlling access to the object. Capability lists bind that data to the subject. Locks and keys distribute the data between the subject and the object. All are particularly well-suited for discretionary access controls, because usually the owners of the objects determine who gets access. If the controller of access is the operating system, then these mechanisms also can implement mandatory access controls.

Ring-based mechanisms generalize the notion of "supervisor" and "user" mode. They are particularly well-suited for mandatory access controls, because the operating system enforces the barriers to ring crossings. However, the brackets must be chosen judiciously.

Propagated access control lists are associated with information rather than with the objects that contain the information. This makes them particularly suitable for implementing originator controlled policies.

16.7   Research Issues

Access control mechanisms provide ways of enforcing stated policies. How can these mechanisms work together to enforce policies? What limits do their natures impose on their use?

As an example, PACLs were created to provide a mechanism for enforcing ORCON policies. How can this mechanism be implemented in a manner that prevents users from compromising the system? Could other mechanisms enforce ORCON policies and be easier to implement?

Language-based techniques are seeing a resurgence. These techniques assert that compilers should add access-checking code to the programs. This technique is particularly well-suited for mobile code, where the operating systems may enforce different access control policies. The implications of the differences in policy between what a mobile program needs in order to perform its task, and how the system on which it is run limits its access, are under active study.

Proofs that the mechanisms supply security services sufficient to meet the goals of a system are another research issue. The method of noninterference and its related properties, discussed in Chapter 9, "Noninterference and Policy Composition," provide a basis for such proofs. Alternative techniques may be simpler and may take into account specific system details.

Finally, new or modified mechanisms may provide better control for particular policies or systems. This is also an area of research.

16.8   Further Reading

Saltzer [1641] describes the use of access control lists in Multics. Kramer [1098] describes their incorporation into the Linus system. Stiegler [1825] describes structures used to implement ACLs. Riechmann and Hauck [1587] discuss extensions.

In addition to the systems described in this chapter, several others, both abstract and real, use capabilities [794, 876, 1942]. Klein [1062] describes how to emulate capabilities using setuid programs in traditional UNIX systems. EROS is a descendant of the KeyKOS system, which implemented capabilities [259, 868, 1556]. CapROS [2125], a successor to EROS, and the seL4 microkernel [1064] use capabilities. Ko [1080] developed a model of the ring bracket mechanism and demonstrated that it can enforce either the Bell-LaPadula confidentiality policy or the Biba integrity policy, but not both.

Blakley [239], Asmuth and Bloom [88], and others [1962] discuss other secret sharing schemes. Simmons discusses several generalizations [1749–1751]. Others discuss several forms of cheating and how to compensate for them [294, 1177, 1884].

16.9   Exercises

1. In general, ACLs use "owners" (users) rather than individual processes. Why?

2. Alice can read and write to the file x, can read the file y, and can execute the file z. Bob can read x, can read and write to y, and cannot access z.

   a. Write a set of access control lists for this situation. Which list is associated with which file?

   b. Write a set of capability lists for this situation. With what is each list associated?

3. Revoking an individual's access to a particular file is easy when an access control list is used. How hard is it to revoke a user's access to a particular set of files, but not to all files? Compare and contrast this with the problem of revocation using capabilities.

4. Explain why some UNIX-based systems with ACLs do not allow *root* to alter the ACL. What problems might this create?

5. The second example in Section 16.2 asserts that UNIX file descriptors are in fact capabilities. Please explain in detail why this is true. (*Hint*: How are file descriptors used?)

6. Suppose a user wishes to edit the file *xyzzy* in a capability-based system. How can he be sure that the editor cannot access any other file? Could this be done in an ACL-based system? If so, how? If not, why not?

7. Consider implementing secret sharing using the locks and keys or-access and and-access controls. Let each encipherment operation take one unit of time, and let each enciphered datum take one unit of space. Under each of the following conditions, how much time and space are needed to store a datum so that t out of n people can reconstruct the datum?

   a. For $t = 3$ and $n = 10$
   b. For $t = 5$ and $n = 10$
   c. For general t and n (That is, give the general formulae for space and time.)

8. Consider Multics procedures p and q. Procedure p is executing and needs to invoke procedure q. Procedure q's access bracket is (5, 6) and its call bracket is (6, 9). Assume that q's access control list gives p full (read, write, append, and execute) rights to q. In which ring(s) must p execute for the following to happen?

   a. p can invoke q, but a ring-crossing fault occurs.
   b. p can invoke q provided that a valid gate is used as an entry point.
   c. p cannot invoke q.
   d. p can invoke q without any ring-crossing fault occurring, but not necessarily through a valid gate.

9. Consider Multics procedure p and data segment d. Procedure p is executing and needs to access segment d. Segment d's access bracket is (5, 6). Assume that d's access control list gives p full (read, write, append, and execute) rights to d. In which ring(s) must p execute for the following to happen?

   a. p can read, write to, and append to d.
   b. p can read d but not write to or append to d.
   c. p cannot access d.

10. Consider ownership as a right that allows the changing of capabilities (or access control lists). How might you implement this right using capabilities? How might you implement it using access control lists? Contrast these implementations of capability lists and access control lists with PACLs.

Chapter 17
Information Flow

> BOTTOM: Masters, I am to discourse wonders: but
> ask me not what; for if I tell you, I am no true
> Athenian. I will tell you every thing, right as it
> fell out.
> — *A Midsummer Night's Dream*, IV, ii, 30–33.

Although access controls can constrain the rights of a user, they cannot constrain the flow of information through a system. In particular, when a system has a security policy regulating information flow, the system must ensure that the information flows do not violate the constraints of the policy. Both compile-time mechanisms and runtime mechanisms support the checking of information flows. Several systems implementing these mechanisms demonstrate their effectiveness.

17.1 Basics and Background

Information flow policies define the way information moves throughout a system. Typically, these policies are designed to preserve confidentiality of data or integrity of data. In the former, the policy's goal is to prevent information from flowing to a user not authorized to receive it. In the latter, information may flow only to processes that are no more trustworthy than the data.

Any confidentiality and integrity policy embodies an information flow policy.

EXAMPLE: The Bell-LaPadula Model (see Section 5.2) describes a lattice-based information flow policy. Given two compartments *A* and *B*, information can flow from an object in *A* to a subject in *B* if and only if *B* dominates *A*. Similarly, Biba's Strict Integrity Model (see Section 6.2.3) also describes a lattice-based information flow policy. Given two compartments *A* and *B*, information can flow from an object in *A* to a subject in *B* if and only if *A* dominates *B*.

Let x be a variable in a program. Represent the information flow class of x by $\underline{x}$.

EXAMPLE: Consider a system that uses the Bell-LaPadula Model. The variable x, which holds data in the compartment (TS, { NUC, EUR }), is set to 3. Then $x = 3$ and $\underline{x} = (\text{TS}, \{\text{NUC}, \text{EUR}\})$.

17.1.1   Entropy-Based Analysis

We now define precisely the notion of information flow. Intuitively, information flows from an object x to an object y if the application of a sequence of commands c causes the information initially in x to affect the information in y. We use the notion of entropy, or uncertainty (see Appendix C, "Entropy and Uncertainty"), to formalize this concept.

Let c be a sequence of commands taking a system from state s to another state t. Let x and y be objects in the system. We assume that x exists when the system is in state s and has the value x_s. We require that y exist in state t and have the value y_t. In addition, if y exists in state s, it has value y_s.

> **Definition 17–1.** The command sequence c causes a *flow of information* from x to y if $H(x_s \mid y_t) < H(x_s \mid y_s)$. If y does not exist in s, then $H(x_s \mid y_s) = H(x_s)$.

This definition states that information flows from the variable x to the variable y if the value of y after the commands allows one to deduce information about the value of x before the commands were run.

This definition views information flow in terms of the information that the value of y allows one to deduce about the value in x. For example, the statement

```
y := x;
```

reveals the value of x in the initial state, so $H(x_s \mid y_t) = 0$ (because given the value y_t, there is no uncertainty in the value of x_s). The statement

```
y := x / z;
```

reveals some information about x_s, but not as much as the first statement.

The result of the sequence c must reveal information about the initial value of x for information to flow. The sequence

```
tmp := x;
y := tmp;
```

has information flowing from x to y because the (unknown) value of x at the beginning of the sequence is revealed when the value of y is determined at the end of the sequence. However, no information flow occurs from *tmp* to *x*, because the initial value of *tmp* cannot be determined at the end of the sequence.

EXAMPLE: Consider the statement

```
x := y + z;
```

Let y take any of the integer values from 0 to 7, inclusive, with equal probability, and let z take the value 1 with probability 0.5 and the values 2 and 3 with probability 0.25 each. Let s be the state before this operation is executed, and let t be the state immediately after it is executed. Then $H(y_s) = H(y_t) = 3$ and $H(z_s) = H(z_t) = 1.5$. Once the value of x_t is known, y_s can assume at most three values, so $H(y_s \mid x_t) < \lg 3 \approx 1.58$. Thus, information flows from y to x. Similar results hold for $H(z_s \mid x_t)$; see Exercise 1.

EXAMPLE: Consider a program in which x and y are integers that may be either 0 or 1. The statement

```
if x = 1 then y := 0;
else y := 1;
```

does not explicitly assign the value of x to y.

Assume that x is equally likely to be 0 or 1. Then $H(x_s) = 1$. But $H(x_s \mid y_t) = 0$, because if y is 0, x is 1, and vice versa. Hence, $H(x_s \mid y_t) = 0 < H(x_s \mid y_s) = H(x_s) = 1$. Thus, information flows from x to y.

> **Definition 17–2.** An *implicit flow of information* occurs when information flows from x to y without an explicit assignment of the form y := f(x), where f(x) is an arithmetic expression with the variable x.

The flow of information occurs, not because of an assignment of the value of x, but because of a flow of control, or other behavior, based on the value of x. This demonstrates that analyzing programs for assignments to detect information flows is not enough. To detect all flows of information, implicit flows must be examined.

17.1.2   Information Flow Models and Mechanisms

An information flow policy is a security policy that describes the authorized paths along which that information can flow. Part III, "Policy," discussed several models of information flow, including the Bell-LaPadula Model, nonlattice and nontransitive models of information flow, and nondeducibility and noninterference. Each model associates a label, representing a security class, with information and with entities containing that information. Each model has rules about the conditions under which information can move throughout the system.

In this chapter, we use the notation $\underline{x} \leq \underline{y}$ to mean that information can flow from an element of class $\underline{x}$ to an element of class $\underline{y}$. Equivalently, this says that information with a label placing it in class $\underline{x}$ can flow into class y.

Earlier chapters usually assumed that the models of information flow policies were lattices. We first consider nonlattice information flow policies and how their structures affect the analysis of information flow. We then turn to compiler-based information flow mechanisms and runtime mechanisms. We conclude with a look at flow controls in practice.

17.2   Nonlattice Information Flow Policies

Denning [534] identifies two requirements for information flow policies. Both are intuitive. Information should be able to flow freely among members of a single class, providing reflexivity. If members of one class can read information from a second class, they can save the information in objects belonging to the first class. Then, if members of a third class can read information from the first class, they can read the contents of those objects and, effectively, read information from the second class. This produces transitivity. The Bell-LaPadula Model exhibits both characteristics. For example, Cathy *dom* Betty, and Betty *dom* Anne, then Cathy *dom* Anne.

However, in some circumstances, transitivity is undesirable.

EXAMPLE: Betty is a confidante of Anne, and Cathy is a confidante of Betty. Hence, information can flow from Anne to Betty, and from Betty to Cathy. Anne confides to Betty that she is having an affair with Cathy's significant other. Needless to say, it is not desirable that this information flow directly from Anne to Cathy.

If information flow throughout a system is not transitive, then Denning's lattice model of information flow cannot represent the system. But such systems exist, as just pointed out. Lattices may not even model transitive systems.

EXAMPLE: Two faculty members are co-principle investigators of a grant. Graduate students report to both faculty members, and graduate students supervise undergraduate students on the project. The faculty members have equal power, neither being able to overrule the other. Clearly, information flows from the undergraduates to the graduates, and then on to the faculty members, so the system is transitive. But the graduate students have no single least upper bound, because both faculty members dominate them and there is no entity that dominates both faculty members. Hence, the information flow relations in this system do not form a lattice.

We generalize the notion of a confidentiality policy. An *information flow policy I* is a triple $I = (SC_I, \leq_I, join_I)$, where SC_I is a set of security classes, $\leq_I$ is an ordering relation on the elements of SC_I, and $join_I$ combines two elements of SC_I.

EXAMPLE: Denning's lattice model for the Bell-LaPadula Model has SC_I as the set of security compartments, $\leq_I$ as the relation *dom*, and $join_I$ as the relation least upper bound.

We now present a model of information flow that does not require transitivity and apply it to two cases in which the information flow relations do not form a lattice. In the first case, the relations are transitive; in the second, they are not.

17.2.1   Confinement Flow Model

Foley [694] presented a model of confinement flow. Assume that an object can change security classes; for example, if the data stored in a variable changes, the security class of the variable becomes that of the data. Associate with each object x a security class $\underline{x}$.

> **Definition 17–3.**   [694] The *confinement flow model* is a 4-tuple $(I, O, confine, \rightarrow)$ in which $I = (SC_I, \leq_I, join_I)$ is a lattice-based information flow policy; O is a set of entities; $\rightarrow: O \times O$ is a relation with $(a, b) \in \rightarrow$ if and only if information can flow from a to b; and, for each $a \in O$, $confine(a) = (\underline{a}_L, \underline{a}_U) \in SC_I \times SC_I$, with $\underline{a}_L \leq_I \underline{a}_U$, and the interpretation that for $a \in O$, if $\underline{x} \leq \underline{a}_U$, information can flow from x to a, and if $\underline{a}_L \leq \underline{x}$, information can flow from a to x.

This means that $\underline{a}_L$ is the lowest classification of information allowed to flow out of a, and $\underline{a}_U$ is the highest classification of information allowed to flow into a.

The security requirement for an information flow model requires that if information can flow from a to b, then b dominates a under the ordering relation of the lattice. For the confinement flow model, this becomes

$$(\forall a, b \in O)[a \rightarrow b \Rightarrow \underline{a}_L \leq_I \underline{b}_U]$$

EXAMPLE: Let $a, b, c \in O$. Define

> $confine(a) = [\text{CONFIDENTIAL}, \text{CONFIDENTIAL}]$
> $confine(b) = [\text{SECRET}, \text{SECRET}]$
> $confine(c) = [\text{TOPSECRET}, \text{TOPSECRET}]$

The possible information flows are $a \rightarrow b$, $a \rightarrow c$, $b \rightarrow a$, $b \rightarrow c$, $c \rightarrow a$, and $c \rightarrow b$. If only secure flows (those meeting the security requirement of the confinement flow model) are allowed, then $a \rightarrow b$, $a \rightarrow c$, and $b \rightarrow c$ are the legal flows (because $\underline{a}_L \leq_I \underline{b}_U$, $\underline{a}_L \leq_I \underline{c}_U$, and $\underline{b}_L \leq_I \underline{c}_U$). Thus, transitivity holds.

Now consider x, y, and z. These three variables can assume values of different classifications:

$$confine(x) = [\text{CONFIDENTIAL}, \text{CONFIDENTIAL}]$$
$$confine(y) = [\text{SECRET}, \text{SECRET}]$$
$$confine(z) = [\text{CONFIDENTIAL}, \text{TOPSECRET}]$$

The possible information flows are $x \rightarrow y$, $x \rightarrow z$, $y \rightarrow x$, $y \rightarrow z$, $z \rightarrow x$, and $z \rightarrow y$. If only secure flows are allowed, then $x \rightarrow y$, $x \rightarrow z$, $y \rightarrow z$, and $z \rightarrow x$ are the legal flows. But information cannot legally flow from y to x, because $\underline{y}_L \leq_I \underline{x}_U$ is false. Hence, transitivity fails.

This model exhibits weak tranquility. It also binds intervals of security classes, rather than a single security class (as in the Bell-LaPadula Model). The lattice of security classes induces a second lattice on these intervals (see Exercise 2).

17.2.2   Transitive Nonlattice Information Flow Policies

Consider a company in which line managers report income to two different superiors—a business manager and an auditor. The auditor and the business manager are independent. Thus, information flows from the workers to the line managers, and from the line managers to the business manager and the auditor. This model is reflexive (because information can flow freely among entities in the same class) and transitive (because information can flow from the workers to the business manager and auditor). However, there is no way to combine the auditor and the business manager, because there is no "superior" in this system. Hence, the information flow relations do not form a lattice. Figure 17–1 captures this situation.

Definition 17–4. A *quasi-ordered set* $Q = (S_Q, \leq_Q)$ is a set S_Q and a relation $\leq_Q$ defined on S_Q such that the relation is both reflexive and transitive.

The company described here forms a quasi-ordered set. Handling the information flow now becomes a matter of defining a lattice that includes the quasi-ordered set. For all $x \in S_Q$, let $f(x) = \{y \mid y \in S_Q \wedge y \leq_Q x\}$. Define the set $S_{QP} = \{f(x) \mid x \in S_Q\}$ and the relation $\leq_{QP} = \{(x, y) \mid x, y \in S_{QP} \wedge x \subseteq y\}$. Then S_{QP} is a partially ordered set under $\leq_{QP}$. f preserves ordering, so $x \leq_Q y$ if and only if $f(x) \leq_{QP} f(y)$.

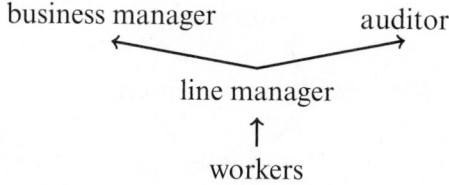

Figure 17–1 An example of a nonlattice information flow policy. Because the business manager and the auditor are independent, they have no least upper bound. Hence, the structure is not a lattice.

Assume S_{QP} is finite. Then Denning [535] shows how to turn a partially ordered set into a lattice.

1. Let $S'_{QP} = \{S_Q, \varnothing\} \cup S_{QP}$.
2. Define $ub(x, y) = \{z \mid z \in S'_{QP} \land x \cup y \subseteq z\}$ (here, ub stands for "upper bound," which contains all sets containing all elements of both x and y). Then define $lub(x, y) = \cap ub(x, y)$. If this is not in S'_{QP}, add it, and repeat this step until every pair of elements has an upper bound.
3. Define the lower bound $lb(x, y)$, and the greatest lower bound $glb(x, y)$ similarly, and ensure that every pair of elements has a lower bound.

The structure $(S'_{QP}, \leq_{QP})$ is now a lattice.

At this point, the information flow policy simply emulates that of the containing lattice.

17.2.3 Nontransitive Information Flow Policies

Foley [694] has considered the problem of modeling nontransitive systems. He defines a procedure for building lattices from such systems. His procedure adds entities and relations to the model, but the procedure keeps the nontransitive relationships of the original entities and relations intact.

EXAMPLE: A government agency has the policy shown in Figure 17–2. It involves three types of entities: public relations officers (PRO), who need to know more than they can say publicly; analysts (A); and spymasters (S). The accesses of the three types of entities are confined to certain types of data, as follows:

$confine$(PRO) = [public, analysis]
$confine$(A) = [analysis, top-level]
$confine$(S) = [covert, top-level]

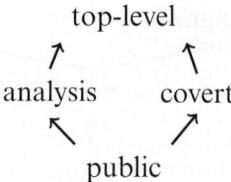

Figure 17–2 An example of a government agency information flow policy. Public information is available to all. All other types of information are restricted, with analysis data and covert data (about secret missions) being distinct types of data. Top-level data is synthesized from both covert and analysis data.

According to the confinement flow model, PRO $\leq$ A, A $\leq$ PRO, PRO $\leq$ S, A $\leq$ S, and S $\leq$ A. But data cannot flow to the public relations officers; S $\leq$ A and A $\leq$ PRO do *not* imply S $\leq$ PRO. The system is not transitive.

Government (and private) agencies often use procedures to insulate public relations officers from data that is not to be leaked. Although the agency may trust the public relations officers, people make mistakes, and what the officers don't know, they cannot accidentally blurt out. So the example is realistic.

> **Definition 17–5.** Let $R = (SC_R, \leq_R, join_R)$ represent a reflexive information flow policy. A *dual mapping* $(l_R(x), h_R(x))$ maps R to an ordered set $P = (S_P, \leq_P)$:
> $l_R : SC_R \rightarrow S_P$ with $l_R(x) = \{x\}$
> $h_R : SC_R \rightarrow S_P$ with $h_R(x) = \{y \mid y \in S_P \wedge y \leq_R x\}$

The relation $\leq_P$ indicates "subset," and the elements in S_P are the set of subsets of SC_R. The dual mapping is called *order preserving* if and only if

$$(\forall a, b \in SC_R)[a \leq_R b \Leftrightarrow l_R(a) \leq_P h_R(b)]$$

The set S_P formed by the dual mapping of a reflexive information flow policy is a (possibly improper) subset of the power set of SC_R. It is a partially ordered set. Denning's procedure, as previously discussed, can transform this into a lattice. Hence, without loss of generality, we can assume that the set $P = (S_P, \leq_P)$ is a lattice.

An order-preserving dual mapping preserves the ordering relation under the transformation. It also preserves nonorderings and hence nontransitivity. We now have:

> **Theorem 17.1.** A dual mapping from a reflexive information flow policy R to an ordered set P is order preserving.

Proof Let $R = (SC_R, \leq_R, join_R)$ be an information flow policy and let $P = (S_P, \leq_P)$ be an ordered set. Let $(l_R(x), h_R(x))$ be the dual mapping from R to S_P. Let $a, b \in SC_R$.

($\Rightarrow$) Let $a \leq_R b$. By Definition 17–5, $a \in l_R(a)$ and $a \in h_R(b)$. Thus, $l_R(a) \in h_R(b)$, or $l_R(a) \leq_P h_R(b)$, as claimed.

($\Leftarrow$) Let $l_R(a) \leq_P h_R(b)$. By Definition 17–5, $l_R(a) \in h_R(b)$. Because $l_R(a) = \{a\}$, this means that $a \in h_R(b)$. Thus, $a \in S_P$ and $a \leq_R b$, as claimed.

This completes the proof.

We can now interpret the information flow policy requirements. Let

$$confine(x) = [\underline{x_L}, \underline{x_U}]$$

and consider class y. Then information can flow from x to an element of y if and only if $\underline{x_L} \leq_R y$, or $l_R(\underline{x_L}) \subseteq h_R(y)$. Information can flow from an element of y to x if and only if $y \leq_R \underline{x_U}$, or $l_R(\underline{y}) \subseteq h_R(\underline{x_U})$.

EXAMPLE: Return to the government agency with the policy shown in Figure 17–2 and the entity types discussed in the preceding example. Call this policy R. We have the following flow relationships among the security classes:

> public $\leq_R$ public
> public $\leq_R$ analysis   analysis $\leq_R$ analysis
> public $\leq_R$ covert   covert $\leq_R$ covert
> public $\leq_R$ top-level   covert $\leq_R$ top-level
> analysis $\leq_R$ top-level   top-level $\leq_R$ top-level

The dual mapping elements l_R and h_R are

> $l_R(\text{public}) = \{\text{public}\}$ $h_R(\text{public}) = \{\text{public}\}$
> $l_R(\text{analysis}) = \{\text{analysis}\}$ $h_R(\text{analysis}) = \{\text{public, analysis}\}$
> $l_R(\text{covert}) = \{\text{covert}\}$ $h_R(\text{covert}) = \{\text{public, covert}\}$
> $l_R(\text{top-level}) = \{\text{top-level}\}$ $h_R(\text{top-level}) = \{\text{public, analysis, covert, top-level}\}$

Let p, a, and s be entities of the types PRO, A, and S, respectively. In terms of P, they are confined as follows:

> $confine(p) = [\{\text{public}\}, \{\text{public, analysis}\}]$
> $confine(a) = [\{\text{analysis}\}, \{\text{public, analysis, covert, top-level}\}]$
> $confine(s) = [\{\text{covert}\}, \{\text{public, analysis, covert, top-level}\}]$

Thus

> $p \rightarrow a$ because {public} $\subseteq$ {public, analysis, covert, top-level}
> $a \rightarrow p$ because {analysis} $\subseteq$ {public, analysis}
> $p \rightarrow s$ because {public} $\subseteq$ {public, analysis, covert, top-level}
> $a \rightarrow s$ because {analysis} $\subseteq$ {public, analysis, covert, top-level}
> $s \rightarrow a$ because {covert} $\subseteq$ {public, analysis, covert, top-level}

However, because {covert} $\not\subseteq$ {public, analysis}, information cannot flow from s to p, reflecting the lack of transitivity of the system.

Nonlattice policies can be embedded into lattices. Hence, analysis of information flows may proceed without loss of generality under the assumption that the information flow model is a lattice.

17.3   Static Mechanisms

Compiler-based mechanisms check that information flows throughout a program are authorized. The mechanisms determine if the information flows in a program *could* violate a given information flow policy. This determination is not precise, in that secure paths of information flow may be marked as violating the policy; but it is secure, in that no unauthorized path along which information may flow will be undetected.

> **Definition 17–6.** A set of statements is *certified* with respect to an information flow policy if the information flow within that set of statements does not violate the policy.

EXAMPLE: Consider the program statement

```
if x = 1 then y := a;
else y := b;
```

By the rules discussed earlier, information flows from x and a to y or from x and b to y, so if the policy says that $\underline{a} \leq \underline{y}$, $\underline{b} \leq \underline{y}$, and $\underline{x} \leq \underline{y}$, then the information flow is secure. But if $\underline{a} \leq \underline{y}$ only when some other variable $z = 1$, the compiler-based mechanism must determine whether $z = 1$ before certifying the statement. Typically, this is infeasible. Hence, the compiler-based mechanism would not certify the statement.

The mechanisms described here follow those developed by Denning and Denning [533, 542].

17.3.1   Declarations

For our discussion, we assume that the allowed flows are supplied to the checking mechanisms through some external means, such as from a file. The specifications of allowed flows involve security classes of language constructs. The program involves variables, so some language construct must relate variables to security classes. One way is to assign each variable to exactly one security class. We opt for a more liberal approach, in which the language constructs specify the set of classes from which information may flow into the variable. For example,

> x: **integer class** { A, B }

states that x is an integer variable and that data from security classes A and B may flow into x. Note that the classes are statically, not dynamically, assigned. Viewing the security classes as a lattice, this means that x's class must be at least the least upper bound of classes A and B—that is, $lub\{A, B\} \leq \underline{x}$.

Two distinguished classes, *Low* and *High*, represent the greatest lower bound and least upper bound, respectively, of the lattice. All constants are of class *Low*.

Information can be passed into or out of a procedure through parameters. We classify parameters as *input parameters* (through which data is passed into the procedure), *output parameters* (through which data is passed out of the procedure), and *input/output parameters* (through which data is passed into and out of the procedure).

```
(* input parameters are named i_s; output parameters, o_s; *)
(* and input/output parameters, io_s, with s a subscript *)
procedure something(i_1, ..., i_k; var o_1, ..., o_m, io_1, ..., io_n);
var l_1, ..., l_j;          (* local variables *)
begin
        S;                  (* body of procedure *)
end;
```

The class of an input parameter is simply the class of the actual argument:

> i_s: **type class** { i_s }

We assume that any output-only parameter is initialized in the procedure. Because information can flow from any input parameter to any output parameter, the declaration of an output parameter must capture this:

> o_s: **type class** { i_1, ..., i_k, io_1, ..., io_n }

The input/output parameters are like output parameters, except that the initial value (as input) affects the allowed security classes:

$$io_s: \textbf{type class } \{ i_1, \ldots, i_k, io_1, \ldots, io_n \}$$

EXAMPLE: Consider the following procedure for adding two numbers:

```
procedure sum(x: integer class { x };
        var out: integer class { x, out });
begin
        out := out + x;
end;
```

Here, we require that $\underline{x} \leq \underline{out}$ and $\underline{out} \leq \underline{out}$ (the latter holding because $\leq$ is reflexive).

The declarations presented so far deal only with basic types, such as integers, characters, floating point numbers, and so forth. Nonscalar types, such as arrays, records (structures), and variant records (unions) also contain information. The rules for information flow classes for these data types are built on the scalar types.

Consider the array

```
a: array 1 .. 100 of integer;
```

First, look at information flows out of an element $a[i]$ of the array. In this case, information flows from $a[i]$ and from i, the latter by virtue of the index indicating which element of the array to use. Information flows into $a[i]$ affect only the value in $a[i]$, and so do not affect the information in i. Thus, for information flows from $a[i]$, the class involved is $lub\{\underline{a[i]}, \underline{i}\}$; for information flows into $a[i]$, the class involved is $\underline{a[i]}$.

17.3.2   Program Statements

A program consists of several types of statements. Typically, they are classified as follows:

1. Assignment statements
2. Compound statements
3. Conditional statements
4. Iterative statements
5. Goto statements

6. Procedure calls
7. Function calls
8. Input/output statements

We consider each of these types of statements separately, with two exceptions. Function calls can be modeled as procedure calls by treating the return value of the function as an output parameter of the procedure. Input/output statements can be modeled as assignment statements in which the value is assigned to (or assigned from) the input source or output destination, such as a file. Hence, we do not consider function calls and input/output statements separately.

17.3.2.1 Assignment Statements

An assignment statement has the form

$$y := f(x_1, \ldots, x_n)$$

where y and x_1, ..., x_n are variables and f is some function of those variables. Information flows from each of the x_i's to y. Hence, the requirement for the information flow to be secure is

- $lub\{\underline{x_1}, \ldots, \underline{x_n}\} \leq \underline{y}$

EXAMPLE: Consider the statement

$$x := y + z;$$

Then the requirement for the information flow to be secure is $lub\{\underline{y}, \underline{z}\} \leq \underline{x}$.

17.3.2.2 Compound Statements

A compound statement has the form

```
begin
        S₁;
        ...
        Sₙ;
end;
```

where each of the S_i's is a statement. If the information flow in each of the statements is secure, then the information flow in the compound statement is secure. Hence, the requirements for the information flow to be secure are

- $S_1, \ldots, S_n$ secure

EXAMPLE: Consider the statements

```
begin
        x := y + z;
        a := b * c - x;
end;
```

Then the requirements for the information flow to be secure are $lub\{y, z\} \leq \underline{x}$ for S_1 and $lub\{\underline{b}, \underline{c}, \underline{x}\} \leq \underline{a}$ for S_2. So, the requirements for secure information flow for the block are $lub\{\underline{y}, \underline{z}\} \leq \underline{x}$ and $lub\{\underline{b}, \underline{c}, \underline{x}\} \leq \underline{a}$.

17.3.2.3   Conditional Statements

A conditional statement has the form

```
if f(x1, ..., xn) then
             S1;
else
             S2;
end;
```

where $x_1, \ldots, x_n$ are variables and f is some (boolean) function of those variables. Either S_1 or S_2 may be executed, depending on the value of f, so both must be secure. As discussed earlier, the selection of either S_1 or S_2 imparts information about the values of the variables $x_1, \ldots, x_n$, so information must be able to flow from those variables to any targets of assignments in S_1 and S_2. This is possible if and only if the lowest class of the targets dominates the highest class of the variables $x_1, \ldots, x_n$. Thus, the requirements for the information flow to be secure are

- S_1 and S_2 secure
- $lub\{\underline{x_1}, \ldots, \underline{x_n}\} \leq glb\{\underline{y} \mid y$ is the target of an assignment in S_1 and $S_2\}$

As a degenerate case, if statement S_2 is empty, it is trivially secure and has no assignments.

EXAMPLE: Consider the statements

```
if x + y < z then
             a := b;
else
             d := b * c - x;
end;
```

Then the requirements for the information flow to be secure are $\underline{b} \leq \underline{a}$ for S_1 and $lub\{\underline{b}, \underline{c}, \underline{x}\} \leq \underline{d}$ for S_2. But the statement that is executed depends on the values of x, y, and z. Hence, information also flows from x, y, and z to d and a. So, the requirements are $\underline{b} \leq \underline{a}$, $lub\{\underline{b}, \underline{c}, \underline{x}\} \leq \underline{d}$, and $lub\{\underline{x}, \underline{y}, \underline{z}\} \leq glb\{\underline{a}, \underline{d}\}$.

17.3.2.4   Iterative Statements

An iterative statement has the form

```
while f(x₁, ..., xₙ) do
        S;
```

where $x_1, \ldots, x_n$ are variables and f is some (boolean) function of those variables. Aside from the repetition, this is a conditional statement, so the requirements for information flow to be secure for a conditional statement apply here.

To handle the repetition, first note that the number of repetitions causes information to flow only through assignments to variables in S. The number of repetitions is controlled by the values in the variables $x_1, \ldots, x_n$, so information flows from those variables to the targets of assignments in S—but this is detected by the requirements for information flow of conditional statements.

However, if the program never leaves the iterative statement, statements after the loop will never be executed. In this case, information has flowed from the variables $x_1, \ldots, x_n$ by the absence of execution. Hence, secure information flow also requires that the loop terminate.

Thus, the requirements for the information flow to be secure are

- Iterative statement terminates
- S secure
- $lub\{\underline{x}_1, \ldots, \underline{x}_n\} \leq glb\{\underline{y} \mid y$ is the target of an assignment in $S\}$

EXAMPLE: Consider the statements

```
while i < n do
begin
        a[i] := b[i];
        i := i + 1;
end;
```

This loop terminates. If $n \leq i$ initially, the loop is never entered. If $i < n$, i is incremented by a positive integer, 1, and so increases, at each iteration. Hence, after $n - i$ iterations, $n = i$, and the loop terminates.

Now consider the compound statement that makes up the body of the loop. The first statement is secure if $\underline{i} \leq \underline{a[i]}$ and $\underline{b[i]} \leq \underline{a[i]}$; the second statement is secure because $\underline{i} \leq \underline{i}$. Hence, the compound statement is secure if $lub\{\underline{i}, \underline{b[i]}\} \leq \underline{a[i]}$.

Finally, $a[i]$ and i are targets of assignments in the body of the loop. Hence, information flows into them from the variables in the expression in the while statement. So, $lub\{i, n\} \leq glb\{a[i], i\}$. Putting these together, the requirement for the information flow to be secure is $lub\{i, n, b[i]\} \leq glb\{a[i], i\}$ (see Exercise 5).

17.3.2.5   Goto Statements

A goto statement contains no assignments, so no explicit flows of information occur. Implicit flows may occur; analysis detects these flows.

Definition 17–7. A *basic block* is a sequence of statements in a program that has one entry point and one exit point.

EXAMPLE: Consider the following code fragment:

```
procedure transmatrix(x: array [1..10][1..10] of integer
   class { x }; var y: array [1..10][1..10] of integer
   class { y } );
var i, j: integer class { tmp };
begin
      i := 1;                                  (* b₁ *)
```
```
12:    if i > 10 goto 17;                      (* b₂ *)
```
```
          j := 1;                              (* b₃ *)
```
```
14:          if j > 10 then goto 16;           (* b₄ *)
```
```
             x[i][j] := y[j][i];              (* b₅ *)
             j := j + 1;
             goto 14;
```
```
16:          i := i + 1;                       (* b₆ *)
             goto 12;
```
```
17:                                            (* b₇ *)
end;
```

There are seven basic blocks, labeled b_1 through b_7 and separated by lines. The second and fourth blocks have two ways to arrive at the entry—either from a jump to the label or from the previous line. They also have two ways to exit—either by the branch or by falling through to the next line. The fifth block has three lines and always ends with a branch. The sixth block has two lines and can be entered either from a jump to the label or from the previous line. The last block is always entered by a jump.

Control within a basic block flows from the first line to the last. Analyzing the flow of control within a program is therefore equivalent to analyzing the flow of control among the program's basic blocks. Figure 17–3 shows the flow of control among the basic blocks of the body of the procedure *transmatrix*.

When a basic block has two exit paths, the block reveals information implicitly by the path along which control flows. When these paths converge later in the program, the (implicit) information flow derived from the exit path from the basic block becomes either explicit (through an assignment) or irrelevant. Hence, the class of the expression that causes a particular execution path to be selected affects the required classes of the blocks along the path up to the block at which the divergent paths converge.

Definition 17–8. An *immediate forward dominator* of a basic block b (written *IFD*(b)) is the first block that lies on all paths of execution that pass through b.

EXAMPLE: In the procedure *transmatrix*, the immediate forward dominators of each block are $IFD(b_1) = b_2$, $IFD(b_2) = b_7$, $IFD(b_3) = b_4$, $IFD(b_4) = b_6$, $IFD(b_5) = b_4$, and $IFD(b_6) = b_2$.

To compute the information flow requirement for the set of blocks along the path, simply apply the logic for the conditional statement. Each block along the path is taken because of the value of an expression. Information flows from the variables of the expression into the set of variables assigned in the blocks. Let B_i

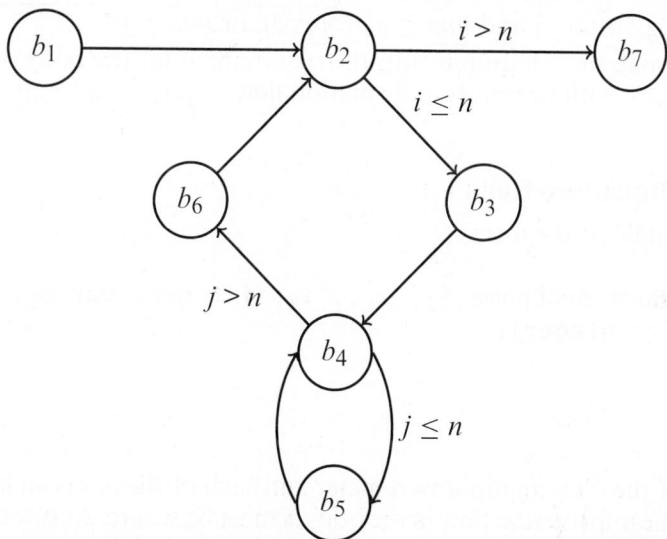

Figure 17–3 The control flow graph of the procedure *transmatrix*. The basic blocks are labeled b_1 through b_7. The conditions under which branches are taken are shown over the edges corresponding to the branches.

be the set of blocks along an execution path from b_i to $IFD(b_i)$, but excluding these endpoints (see Exercise 6). Let $x_{i1}, \ldots, x_{in}$ be the set of variables in the expression that selects the execution path containing the blocks in B_i. The requirements for the program's information flows to be secure are

- All statements in each basic block are secure.
- $lub\{\underline{x_{i1}}, \ldots, \underline{x_{in}}\} \leq glb\{\underline{y} \mid y$ is the target of an assignment in $B_i\}$.

EXAMPLE: Consider the body of the procedure *transmatrix*. We first state requirements for information flow within each basic block:

b_1: $Low \leq \underline{i} \Rightarrow$ secure
b_3: $Low \leq \underline{j} \Rightarrow$ secure
b_5: $lub\{\underline{x[i][j]}, \underline{i}, \underline{j}\} \leq \underline{y[j][i]} \wedge \underline{j} \leq \underline{j} \Rightarrow lub\{\underline{x[i][j]}, \underline{i}, \underline{j}\} \leq \underline{y[j][i]}$
b_6: $lub\{Low, \underline{i}\} \leq \underline{i} \Rightarrow$ secure

The conditions for b_1, b_3, and b_6 are by definition satisfied. The requirement for b_5 to be secure is, for $i = 1, \ldots, n$ and $j = 1, \ldots, n$, $lub\{\underline{x[i][j]}, \underline{i}, \underline{j}\} \leq \underline{y[j][i]}$. By the declarations, this is true when $lub\{\underline{x}, \underline{tmp}\} \leq \underline{y}$.

In this procedure, $B_2 = \{b_3, b_4, b_5, b_6\}$ and $B_4 = \{b_5\}$. Thus, in B_2, statements assign values to i, j, and $y[j][i]$. In B_4, statements assign values to j and $y[j][i]$. The expression controlling which basic blocks in B_2 are executed is $i \leq 10$; the expression controlling which basic blocks in B_4 are executed is $j \leq 10$. Secure information flow requires that $\underline{i} \leq glb\{\underline{i}, \underline{j}, \underline{y[j][i]}\}$ and $\underline{j} \leq glb\{\underline{j}, \underline{y[j][i]}\}$. In other words, $\underline{tmp} \leq glb\{\underline{tmp}, \underline{y}\}$ and $\underline{tmp} \leq glb\{\underline{tmp}, \underline{y}\}$, or $\underline{tmp} \leq \underline{y}$.

Combining these requirements, the requirement for the body of the procedure to be secure with respect to information flow is $lub\{\underline{x}, \underline{tmp}\} \leq \underline{y}$.

17.3.2.6 Procedure Calls

A procedure call has the form

```
procedure procname(i₁, ..., iₘ: integer; var o₁, ..., oₙ:
        integer);
begin
        S;
end;
```

where each of the i_j's is an input parameter and each of the o_j's is an input/output parameter. The information flow in the body S must be secure. As discussed earlier, information flow relationships may also exist between the input parameters and the output parameters. If so, these relationships are necessary for S to be secure. The actual parameters (those variables supplied in the call to the procedure) must also satisfy these relationships for the call to be secure. Let $x_1, \ldots, x_m$ and $y_1, \ldots, y_n$ be the actual input and input/output parameters, respectively. The requirements for the information flow to be secure are

- S secure
- For $j = 1, \ldots, m$ and $k = 1, \ldots, n$, if $\underline{i_j} \leq \underline{o_k}$ then $\underline{x_j} \leq \underline{y_k}$
- For $j = 1, \ldots, n$ and $k = 1, \ldots, n$, if $\underline{o_j} \leq \underline{o_k}$ then $\underline{y_j} \leq \underline{y_k}$

EXAMPLE: Consider the procedure *transmatrix* from the preceding section. The body of the procedure is secure with respect to information flow when $lub\{\underline{x}, \underline{tmp}\} \leq \underline{y}$. This indicates that the formal parameters x and y have the information flow relationship $\underline{x} \leq \underline{y}$. Now, suppose a program contains the call

```
transmatrix(a, b)
```

The second condition asserts that this call is secure with respect to information flow if and only if $\underline{a} \leq \underline{b}$.

17.3.3 Exceptions and Infinite Loops

Exceptions can cause information to flow.

EXAMPLE: Consider the following procedure [533, p. 306], which copies the (approximate) value of x to y:

```
procedure copy(x: integer class { x };
                    var y: integer class Low);
var    sum: integer class { x };
       z: integer class Low;
begin
       z := 0;
       sum := 0;
       y := 0;
       while z = 0 do begin
               sum := sum + x;
               y := y + 1;
       end
end
```

When *sum* overflows, a trap occurs. If the trap is not handled, the procedure exits. The value of x is $\frac{MAXINT}{y}$, where $MAXINT$ is the largest representable integer on the system. At no point, however, is the flow relationship $\underline{x} \leq \underline{y}$ checked.

If exceptions are handled explicitly, the compiler can detect problems such as this. Denning again supplies such a solution.

EXAMPLE: Suppose the system ignores all exceptions unless the programmer specifically handles them. Ignoring the exception in the preceding example would cause the program to loop indefinitely. So, the programmer would want the loop to terminate when the exception occurs. The following line does this:

```
on overflowexception sum do z := 1;
```

This line causes information to flow from *sum* to *z*, meaning that $\underline{sum} \leq \underline{z}$. Because $\underline{z}$ is *Low* and $\underline{sum}$ is $\{x\}$, this is incorrect and the procedure is not secure with respect to information flow.

Denning also notes that infinite loops can cause information to flow in unexpected ways.

EXAMPLE: The following procedure copies data from x to y. It assumes that x and y are either 0 or 1.

```
procedure copy(x: integer 0..1 class { x };
          var y: integer 0..1 class Low);
begin
        y := 0;
        while x = 0 do
              (* nothing *);
        y := 1;
end.
```

If x is 0 initially, the procedure does not terminate. If x is 1, it does terminate, with y being 1. At no time is there an explicit flow from x to y. This is an example of a *covert channel*, which we will discuss in detail in Chapter 18.

17.3.4   Concurrency

Of the many concurrency control mechanisms that are available, we choose to study information flow using semaphores [566]. Their operation is simple, and they can be used to express many higher-level constructs [297, 1748, 1857]. The specific semaphore constructs are

```
wait(x):     if x = 0 then block until x > 0; x := x - 1;
signal(x):   x := x + 1;
```

where x is a semaphore. As usual, the wait and the signal are indivisible; once either one has started, no other instruction will execute until the wait or signal finishes.

Reitman and his colleagues [62, 1578] point out that concurrent mechanisms add information flows when values common to multiple processes cause specific actions. For example, in the block

```
begin
        wait(sem);
        x := x + 1;
end;
```

the program blocks at the *wait* if *sem* is 0, and executes the next statement when *sem* is nonzero. The earlier certification requirement for compound statements is not sufficient because of the implied flow between *sem* and *x*. The certification requirements must take flows among local and shared variables (semaphores) into account.

Let the block be

```
begin
        S₁;
        ...
        Sₙ;
end;
```

Assume that each of the statements $S_1, \ldots, S_n$ is certified. Semaphores in the *signal* do not affect information flow in the program in which the *signal* occurs, because the *signal* statement does not block. But following a *wait* statement, which may block, information implicitly flows from the semaphore in the *wait* to the targets of successive assignments.

Let statement S_i be a *wait* statement, and let *shared*(S_i) be the set of shared variables that are read (so information flows from them). Let $g(S_i)$ be the greatest lower bound of the targets of assignments following S_i. A requirement that the block be secure is that $shared(S_i) \leq g(S_i)$. Thus, the requirements for certification of a compound statement with concurrent constructs are

- $S_1, \ldots, S_n$ secure
- For $i = 1, \ldots, n, shared(S_i) \leq g(S_i)$

EXAMPLE: Consider the statements

```
begin
        x := y + z;
        wait(sem);
        a := b * c - x;
end;
```

The requirements that the information flow be secure are $lub\{\underline{y}, \underline{z}\} \leq \underline{x}$ for S_1 and $lub\{\underline{b}, \underline{c}, \underline{x}\} \leq \underline{a}$ for S_2. Information flows implicitly from *sem* to a, so $\underline{sem} \leq \underline{a}$. The requirements for certification are $lub\{\underline{y}, \underline{z}\} \leq \underline{x}$, $lub\{\underline{b}, \underline{c}, \underline{x}\} \leq \underline{a}$, and $\underline{sem} \leq \underline{a}$.

Loops are handled similarly. The only difference is in the last requirement, because after completion of one iteration of the loop, control may return to the beginning of the loop. Hence, a semaphore may affect assignments that precede the *wait* statement in which the semaphore is used. This simplifies the last condition in the compound statement requirement considerably. Information must be able to flow from all shared variables named in the loop to the targets of all assignments. Let *shared*(S_i) be the set of shared variables read, and let $t_1, \ldots, t_m$ be the targets of assignments in the loop. Then the certification conditions for the iterative statement

```
while f(x₁,  ..., xₙ) do
        S;
```

are

- Iterative statement terminates
- S secure
- $lub\{\underline{x_1}, \ldots, \underline{x_n}\} \leq glb\{\underline{t_1}, \ldots, \underline{t_m}\}$
- $lub\{\underline{shared(S_1)}, \ldots, \underline{shared(S_n)}\} \leq glb\{\underline{t_1}, \ldots, \underline{t_m}\}$

EXAMPLE: Consider the statements

```
while i < n do
begin
        a[i] := item;
        wait(sem);
        i := i + 1;
end;
```

This loop terminates. If $n \leq i$ initially, the loop is never entered. If $i < n$, i is incremented by a positive integer, 1, and so increases, at each iteration. Hence, after $n - i$ iterations, $n = i$, and the loop terminates.

Now consider the compound statement that makes up the body of the loop. The first statement is secure if $\underline{i} \leq \underline{a[i]}$ and $\underline{item} \leq \underline{a[i]}$. The third statement is secure because $\underline{i} \leq \underline{i}$. The second statement induces an implicit flow, so $\underline{sem} \leq \underline{a[i]}$ and $\underline{sem} \leq \underline{i}$. The requirements are thus $\underline{i} \leq \underline{a[i]}$, $\underline{item} \leq \underline{a[i]}$, $\underline{sem} \leq \underline{a[i]}$, and $\underline{sem} \leq \underline{i}$.

Finally, concurrent statements have no information flow among them per se. Any such flows occur because of semaphores and involve compound statements. The certification conditions for the concurrent statement

```
cobegin
        S₁;
        ...
        Sₙ;
coend;
```

are

- $S_1, \ldots, S_n$ secure

EXAMPLE: Consider the statements

```
cobegin
        x := y + z;
        a := b * c - y;
coend;
```

The requirements that the information flow be secure are $lub\{\underline{y}, \underline{z}\} \leq \underline{x}$ for S_1 and $lub\{\underline{b}, \underline{c}, \underline{y}\} \leq \underline{a}$ for S_2. The requirement for certification is simply that both of these requirements hold.

17.3.5 Soundness

Denning and Denning [542], Andrews and Reitman [62], and others build their argument for security on the intuition that combining secure information flows produces a secure information flow, for some security policy. However, they never formally prove this intuition. Volpano, Irvine, and Smith [1945] express the semantics of the aforementioned information on flow analysis as a set of types, and equate certification that a certain flow can occur to the correct use of types. In this context, checking for valid information flows is equivalent to checking that variable and expression types conform to the semantics imposed by the security policy.

Let x and y be two variables in the program. Let x's label dominate y's label. A set of information flow rules is *sound* if the value in x cannot affect the value in y during the execution of the program. (The astute reader will note that this is a form of noninterference; see Chapter 9.) Volpano, Irvine, and Smith use language-based techniques to prove that, given a type system equivalent to the certification rules discussed previously, all programs without type errors have that noninterference property. Hence, the information flow certification rules of the Dennings and of Andrews and Reitman are sound.

17.4   Dynamic Mechanisms

The goal of an execution-based mechanism is to prevent an information flow that violates policy. Checking the flow requirements of explicit flows achieves this result for statements involving explicit flows. Before the assignment

$$y := f(x_1, \ldots, x_n)$$

is executed, the execution-based mechanism verifies that

$$lub\{\underline{x}_1, \ldots, \underline{x}_n\} \leq \underline{y}$$

If the condition is true, the assignment proceeds. If not, it fails. A naïve approach, then, is to check information flow conditions whenever an explicit flow occurs.

Implicit flows complicate checking, because dynamic analysis follows the flow of control. Thus, information flow paths not taken are ignored.

EXAMPLE: Let x and y be variables. The requirement for certification for a particular statement y *op* x is that $\underline{x} \leq \underline{y}$. The conditional statement

```
if x = 1 then y := a;
```

causes a flow from x to y. Now, suppose that when $x \neq 1$, $\underline{x} = High$ and $\underline{y} = Low$. If flows were verified only when explicit, and $x \neq 1$, the implicit flow would not be checked. The statement may be incorrectly certified as complying with the information flow policy.

Fenton explored this problem using a special abstract machine.

17.4.1   Fenton's Data Mark Machine

Fenton [664] created an abstract machine called the *Data Mark Machine* to study handling of implicit flows at execution time. Each variable in this machine had an associated security class, or tag. Fenton also included a tag for the program counter (PC).

The inclusion of the PC allowed Fenton to treat implicit flows as explicit flows, because branches are merely assignments to the PC. He defined the semantics of the Data Mark Machine. In the following discussion, *skip* means that the instruction is not executed, *push*(x, $\underline{x}$) means to push the variable x and its security class $\underline{x}$ onto the program stack, and *pop*(x, $\underline{x}$) means to pop the top value and security class off the program stack and assign them to x and $\underline{x}$, respectively.

Fenton defined five instructions. The relationships between execution of the instructions and the classes of the variables are as follows:

1. The increment instruction

   ```
   x := x + 1
   ```

   is equivalent to

   ```
   if PC ≤ x then x := x + 1
   else skip
   ```

2. The conditional instruction

   ```
   if x = 0 then goto n
   else x := x - 1
   ```

   is equivalent to

   ```
   if x = 0 then { push(PC, PC); PC = lub{PC, x}; PC := n; }
   else          { if PC ≤ x then { x := x - 1; }
                   else skip }
   ```

   This branches, and pushes the PC and its security class onto the program stack. As is customary, the PC is incremented so that when it is popped, the instruction following the *if* statement is executed. This captures the PC containing information from x (specifically, that x is 0) while following the goto.

3. The return

   ```
   return
   ```

   is equivalent to

   ```
   pop(PC, PC);
   ```

   This returns control to the statement following the last if statement. Because the flow of control would have arrived at this statement, the PC no longer contains information about x, and the old class can be restored.

4. The branch instruction

```
if' x = 0 then goto n
else x := x - 1
```

is equivalent to

```
if' x = 0 then { if x ≤ PC then { PC := n; } else skip }
else              { if PC ≤ x then { x := x - 1; }
                    else skip }
```

This branches without saving the PC on the stack. If the branch occurs, the PC is in a higher security class than the conditional variable x, so adding information from x to the PC does not change the PC's security class.

5. The halt instruction

```
halt
```

is equivalent to

```
if stack empty then halt execution
```

The program stack being empty ensures that the user cannot obtain information by looking at the program stack after the program has halted (for example, to determine which *if* statement was last taken).

EXAMPLE: (From [533, p. 290]) Consider the following program, in which x initially contains 0 or 1:

```
1. if x = 0 then goto 4 else x := x - 1
2. if z = 0 then goto 6 else z := z - 1
3. halt
4. z := z + 1
5. return
6. y := y + 1
7. return
```

This program copies the value of x to y. Suppose that $x = 1$ initially. The following table shows the contents of memory, the security class of the PC at each step, and the corresponding certification check:

x	y	z	PC	$\underline{PC}$	stack	certification check
1	0	0	1	*Low*	—	
0	0	0	2	*Low*	—	$Low \leq \underline{x}$
0	0	0	6	$\underline{x}$	(3, *Low*)	
0	1	0	7	$\underline{x}$	(3, *Low*)	$\underline{PC \leq y}$
0	1	0	3	*Low*	—	

Fenton's machine handles errors by ignoring them. Suppose that, in this program, $y \leq x$. Then at the fifth step, the certification check fails (because $\underline{PC} = \underline{x}$). So, the assignment is skipped, and at the end $y = 0$ regardless of the value of x. But if the machine reports errors, the error message informing the user of the failure of the certification check means that the program has attempted to execute step 6. It could do so only if it had taken the branch in step 2, meaning that $z = 0$. If $z = 0$, then the *else* branch of statement 1 could not have been taken, meaning that $x = 0$ initially.

To prevent this type of deduction, Fenton's machine continues executing in the face of errors, but ignores the statement that would cause the violation. This satisfies the requirements. Aborting the program, or creating an exception visible to the user, would also cause information to flow against policy.

The problem with reporting of errors is that a user with lower clearance than the information causing the error can deduce the information from knowing that there has been an error. If the error is logged in such a way that the entries in the log, and the action of logging, are visible only to those who have adequate clearance, then no violation of policy occurs. But if the clearance of the user is sufficiently high, then the user can see the error without a violation of policy. Thus, the error can be logged for the system administrator (or other appropriate user), even if it cannot be displayed to the user who is running the program. Similar comments apply to any exception action, such as abnormal termination.

17.4.2   Variable Classes

The classes of the variables in the examples above are fixed. Fenton's machine alters the class of the PC as the program runs. This suggests a notion of dynamic classes, wherein a variable can change its class. For explicit assignments, the change is straightforward. When the assignment

```
y := f(x1, ..., xn)
```

occurs, y's class is changed to $lub\{\underline{x}_1, \ldots, \underline{x}_n\}$. Again, implicit flows complicate matters.

EXAMPLE: (From [533, p. 285]) Consider the following program (which is the same as the program in the example for the Data Mark Machine):

```
procedure copy(x : integer class { x };
            var y : integer class { y });
var z : integer class variable { Low };
begin
        y := 0;
        z := 0;
        if x = 0 then z := 1;
        if z = 0 then y := 1;
end;
```

In this program, z is variable and initially *Low*. It changes when something is assigned to z. Flows are certified whenever anything is assigned to y. Suppose $\underline{y} < \underline{x}$.

If $x = 0$ initially, the first statement checks that $Low \leq \underline{y}$ (trivially true). The second statement sets z to 0 and $\underline{z}$ to *Low*. The third statement changes z to 1 and $\underline{z}$ to $lub\{Low, \underline{x}\} = \underline{x}$. The fourth statement is skipped (because $z = 1$). Hence, y is set to 0 on exit.

If $x = 1$ initially, the first statement checks that $Low \leq \underline{y}$ (again, trivially true). The second statement sets z to 0 and $\underline{z}$ to *Low*. The third statement is skipped (because $x = 1$). The fourth statement assigns 1 to y and checks that $lub\{Low, \underline{z}\} = Low \leq \underline{y}$ (again, trivially true). Hence, y is set to 1 on exit.

Information has therefore flowed from x to y even though $\underline{y} < \underline{x}$. The program violates the policy but is nevertheless certified.

Fenton's Data Mark Machine would detect this violation (see Exercise 7).

Denning [534] suggests an alternative approach. She raises the class of the targets of assignments in the conditionals and verifies the information flow requirements, even when the branch is not taken. Her method would raise $\underline{z}$ to $\underline{x}$ in the third statement (even when the conditional is false). The certification check at the fourth statement then would fail, because $lub\{Low, \underline{z}\} = \underline{x} \leq \underline{y}$ is false.

Denning [533, p. 285] credits Lampson with another mechanism. Lampson suggested changing classes only when explicit flows occur. But all flows force certification checks. For example, when $x = 0$, the third statement sets $\underline{z}$ to *Low* and then verifies $\underline{x} \leq \underline{z}$ (which is true if and only if $\underline{x} = Low$).

17.5   Integrity Mechanisms

The previous analyses used confidentiality constraints to control the flow of information; the constraints were based on a multilevel security policy such as Bell-LaPadula. The analyses are equally effective when the constraints are intended to protect integrity, for example when they are based on a multilevel integrity policy such as Biba.

As a multilevel integrity policy model is the mathematical dual of the corresponding multilevel security policy model, the constraints on information flow are simply the duals of the security-based constraints used in Sections 17.3 and 17.4.

Consider the integrity constraint for information flow in an assignment statement

```
y := f(x₁, ..., xₙ)
```

where y and $x_1, \ldots, x_n$ are variables and f is some function of those variables. As before, information flows from each of the x_i's to y. Thus, if y has a higher integrity level than any of the x_i's, information from those x_i's would taint the integrity of y. Hence, the requirement for the integrity of y to be preserved is

- $glb\{\underline{x}_1, \ldots, \underline{x}_n\} \geq \underline{y}$

Similarly, a conditional statement of the form

```
if f(x1, ..., xn) then
        S1;
else
        S2;
end;
```

where $x_1, \ldots, x_n$ are variables and f is some (boolean) function of those variables is handled similarly. Either S_1 or S_2 may be executed, depending on the value of f, so both must satisfy integrity constraints. As discussed earlier, the selection of either S_1 or S_2 imparts information about the values of the variables $x_1, \ldots, x_n$, so information must be able to flow from those variables to any targets of assignments in S_1 and S_2. This is possible if and only if the lowest class of the variables $x_1, \ldots, x_n$ dominates the highest integrity class of the targets. Thus, the requirements for the information flow to be secure are

- S_1 and S_2 satisfy integrity constraints.
- $glb\{\underline{x}_1, \ldots, \underline{x}_n\} \geq lub\{\underline{y} \mid y$ is the target of an assignment in S_1 and $S_2\}$.

As a degenerate case, if statement S_2 is empty, it has no assignments.

Dynamic information flow is handled similarly. We leave the development of an integrity version of Fenton's Data Mark Machine as an exercise to the reader (see Exercise 9).

17.6   Example Information Flow Controls

Like the program-based information flow mechanisms discussed in this chapter, both special-purpose and general-purpose computer systems have information flow controls at the system level. File access controls, integrity controls, and other types of access controls are mechanisms that attempt to inhibit the flow of information within a system, or between systems.

The first example follows a line of research that examines privacy in information flow on cell phones. The second example describes firewalls, which act to control information flow between (or among) networks.

17.6.1   Privacy and Android Cell Phones

Cell phones are becoming ubiquitous and more powerful. Users can augment the usual telephone functionality with millions of commercial and free applications (*apps*) available for all brands. Many of the free apps use advertising libraries to fetch advertising content, monitor clicks, and display the advertisements using the WebView subsystem. Other products offer information or services or tailor their in-app advertising to the habits, locations, and other personal characteristics of the user.

Because of the complexity of the permissions structure of cell phones, apps often are given permission to access all data and resources on the cell phone. Further, the advertising (and other) libraries are part of the app, so they have the same privilege. Thus, any web page downloaded and displayed will execute any Javascript (or other) code with the privileges of the app. This violates the principle of least privilege. It also means that the app can use the resources of the phone to gather information it does not need, and send that information to unknown parties. This puts the privacy of the user at risk, and possibly others whose data is stored on the phone [284, 1397].

This is an information flow problem, because the confidential information in the phone is flowing to an untrusted destination. Thus, tools have been developed to analyze the flow of information in apps. Here, we focus on the Android operating system because it has been extensively studied and is widely used on a variety of cell phones.

Android is based on the Linux system. The executables are in a bytecode format called Dalvik executables (DEX). The apps are event driven, and use system libraries to carry out much of their functionality; for example, a native OpenGL library manages the graphics and another, Webkit, handles web browsing. These libraries are considered part of the underlying Android system and so are considered trusted. Each app executes within a virtual machine, the Dalvik VM interpreter. A subsystem called Binder controls interprocess communication, which is communication between the Dalvik VMs of the processes.

The analysis uses a two-level security model. The higher level is called *untainted* (U) and the lower level, *tainted* (T). This model has no security categories, so the levels form a linear ordering, with $U > T$. It is effectively a two-level version of the Bell-LaPadula Model.

TaintDroid [634, 635] is an example of a dynamic Android information flow analysis tool. It considers Android native libraries as trusted; those that communicate information externally, such as a library that sends a message, are also designated as *taint sinks*. Objects are tagged as U or T and the tags are propagated throughout the execution of the app. The interpreters are augmented to handle the tags. When an app communicates with another app, for example by accessing shared objects, the tag is also communicated; so Binder also is augmented to handle tags. When an untrusted app invokes a library that is a taint sink, the taint tag of the data being sent is recorded.

The bytecode defines several operations, and the tags are modified according to the information flow rules described in section 17.3. To handle native libraries, TaintDroid assigns taint tags to the external variables that the native code accesses; it also assigns a taint tag to the returned value. The value assigned depends upon knowledge of what the native code does; this is determined in a variety of ways, including heuristics.

The interprocess communication mechanism sends messages composed of one or more variables. Keeping track of the taint tags requires a trade-off between precision and performance. If the entire message has one tag, the variables tagged U will be subsumed and when the message is received it will have a T tag. But if each byte in the message has its own tag, the performance suffers by a factor of approximately 2. TaintDroid compromises by grouping tags of variables with the same tag into a structure with a starting address and a size. Thus, two variables that are adjacent in the message take up a single entry in the structure.

Files have a single taint tag that is updated when the file is written and propagated into the appropriate variables when the file is read. As with interprocess communication, this can lead to imprecision, but saves on memory usage and minimizes performance impact. On the other hand, Android databases are queried, and so the information retrieved can have taint values assigned based on the database query responder. So the databases are not assigned a single taint value.

Finally, the information obtained from the cell phone's sensors may be sensitive, and if so should be tagged as T. TaintDroid determines these tags based on characteristics of the information. For example, data obtained from the microphone or camera would be considered privacy sensitive, and hence tagged T, as would the phone number and various cell phone and device identifiers.

Enck and his colleagues conducted two studies to determine the effectiveness of TaintDroid. The first study [634], conducted in 2010, selected 30 popular apps out of a set of 358 apps that required permission to access the Internet, and any of the cell phone location, camera, or microphone. The apps could also access cell phone information. In this set of apps, TaintDroid flagged 105 network connections as accessing data labeled T. Two of them sent cell phone identification information such as the phone number to a server; of the nine that sent device identifiers, two did not notify the user that they would do so. Fifteen apps sent location information to third parties, and none indicated they would do so. TaintDroid correctly identified all these messages. It had no false positives.

Two years later, the researchers revisited the 30 apps [635]. Only 18 of them ran on the current version of Android, and of those 18, only 3 apps still sent location information to third parties. However, 8 exposed device identification information (3 that did so in 2010, and 5 new ones) without consent. They also found two new flows that could reveal tainted information, because of the changes they made to TaintDroid. Again, no false positives were observed.

Other dynamic analysis tools provide mechanisms for app creators to constrain information flow. For example, DroidDisintegrator [1892] extends the techniques used in TaintDroid to enable app developers to do this. Jia et al. [967] implement information flow constraints that allow multiple security and integrity compartments.

Like other dynamic information flow analysis tools, TaintDroid detects flows that occur during execution, so if a different set of inputs and conditions would cause the apps to take a different execution path, those information flows will not be examined unless they also occur in the current execution. Static information flow analysis tools such as AndroidLeaks [766], Amandroid [1987], FlowDroid [84], Epicc [1468], and CHEX [1212] implement the information flow rules in Section 17.3, but each in a different way. All suffer from the limitations of static analysis in being overly conservative.

AppAudit [2033] seeks to have the best of both static and dynamic analysis by combining them. It examines the code statically. It looks for a potential path from a *source* API that accesses sensitive information and a *sink* API that sends data out of the device. If there is a path from a function to a source API and a sink API, that function is labeled as *suspicious*. Complicating the detection of suspicious functions are the callback functions that notify a listener that some event occurred (such as a computation completing). As many *trigger* APIs may register callback functions, the static analyzer cannot determine which callback function will be heard. So, AppAudit treats those functions that call a trigger API as invoking all possible callback functions of the registered type. This can result in identifying potential flows that will never be realized, so AppAudit then dynamically executes suspicious functions to determine if sensitive data could be leaked. In tests, AppAudit reported no information flow paths that could not be taken, and the information flow paths it missed depended on the contents of a text message.

17.6.2   Firewalls

Firewalls are systems that sit between networks, usually an organization's internal network and some other external network such as the Internet. The firewall controls access between the networks. The advantage of firewalls is that they can filter network traffic *before* it reaches the target host. They can also redirect network connections as appropriate, or throttle traffic to limit the amount of traffic that flows into (or out of) the internal network.

> **Definition 17–9.** A *firewall* is a host that mediates access to a network, allowing and disallowing certain types of access on the basis of a configured security policy.

EXAMPLE: A company wishes to prevent any variants of the worm Conficker [85, 1144] from entering its networks. Conficker is a worm that connects to a botnet (the *Conficker botnet*) and can then be used for a variety of purposes, including downloading other malware and controlling the infected system. Conficker spreads through a vulnerability in the Microsoft Windows Service server [1145, 1332], so a firewall can be configured to examine packets that are targeting that service to determine if they contain any variant of Conficker.

Once Conficker is resident, it generates a list of domain names and tries to contact the botnet at those hosts. Every Conficker worm will generate the same set of domain names, and it changes every three hours. The generation sequence, and hence set of domains, is known. So the firewall can also be configured to block outgoing traffic to those domains, neutralizing the "botnet" aspect of conficker.

There are two basic types of firewalls. The first accepts or rejects messages on the basis of packet header information, such as destination addresses or ports.

Definition 17–10. A *filtering firewall* performs access control on the basis of attributes of the packet headers, such as destination addresses, source addresses, and options.

Routers and other infrastructure systems are typical examples of filtering firewalls. They allow connections through the firewall, usually on the basis of source and destination addresses and ports. Access control lists provide a natural mechanism for representing these policies.

This contrasts with the second type of firewall, which never allows such a direct connection. Instead, special agents called *proxies* control the flow of information through the firewall.

Definition 17–11. A *proxy* is an intermediate agent or server that acts on behalf of an endpoint without allowing a direct connection between the two endpoints. A *proxy* (or *application level*) *firewall* uses proxies to perform access control.

A proxy firewall adds to a filtering firewall the ability to base access on content, either at the packet level or at a higher level of abstraction. Thus, a proxy firewall can base access control on the contents of packets and messages, as well as on attributes of the packet headers.

EXAMPLE: A company wishes to check all incoming electronic mail for computer viruses. It implements a mail proxy at the firewall between the Internet and the company intranet. The proxy has a virus scanning program (see Chapter 23). When mail arrives at the firewall, the proxy mail daemon accepts the mail. It then runs the virus scanner. If the scanner reports that there are no viruses in the mail or in any associated attachments, the proxy forwards the mail to the desired recipient. If the virus scanner reports that the mail or an attachment contains a virus, the mail is discarded (or some other appropriate action is taken). The fact that the electronic mail message is reassembled at the firewall by a mail agent acting on behalf of the mail agent at the ultimate destination makes this a proxy firewall.

EXAMPLE: Because Java applets usually come from untrusted sources, many organizations want to block the applets from entering their internal networks. A simple method of doing this is to block the applets at a firewall. When an HTTP connection is made through the firewall, the firewall creates a proxy to reassemble the packets and determine if they contain a Java applet. The proxy then may use one of three approaches to block the applet.

First, it can rewrite the HTML tag to something other than "<applet>". When the page is delivered to the browser, the browser will not recognize the applet and will not run it. This method requires the firewall to determine that the connection is indeed an HTTP connection and to parse the HTML in that connection. Both are nontrivial tasks.

The second approach is to look for incoming files with the hexadecimal sequence "CA FE BA BE". All Java class files must contain this four-byte signature in order to be properly recognized and interpreted. If this sequence is found, the file is immediately discarded. The danger here is a false positive. Because ActiveX and Javascript code are different, this approach cannot block those types of applets.

The third approach is to block based on file name, but this is far more problematic because the names do not necessarily represent the contents of the file. Many browsers require Java class files to end in ".class". The firewall can block these applets. However, more recent browsers allow Java class files to be combined into archives. The names of these archives often end in ".zip". This is a popular format among users of MS-DOS and Windows, so it is not realistic to block all such files.

Martin, Rajagopalan, and Rubin [1258] conclude that the situation is rather bleak for stopping Java applets at the firewall.

A variant of the application-level firewall assembles enough of a packet to determine whether it should be forwarded.

Definition 17–12. A *stateful* firewall is a firewall that keeps track of the state of each connection.

Although no proxies are involved, a stateful firewall can examine the contents of connections, even when the data in question is spread over several packets. For example, a connection to port 25 typically indicates electronic mail, as that is the standard port for the SMTP (email) protocol. A packet filtering firewall would not detect that, for example, HTTP messages were being sent to a host on the internal network if those messages were being sent to port 25 on that host. A stateful firewall would detect that the messages were not messages associated with the SMTP protocol and block them.

Organizations typically partition their network into several parts, with firewalls between parts to prevent information from leaking. A common arrangement is to have two different internal networks, one accessible to the public and the other not (see Figure 17–4).

Definition 17–13. The DMZ^1 is a portion of a network that separates a purely internal network from an external network.

When information moves from the Internet to the internal network, confidentiality is not at issue. However, integrity is. So there are firewalls between the Internet and the DMZ, and between the DMZ and the internal network. These must not accept messages that will cause servers to work incorrectly or to crash. When information moves from the internal network to the Internet, confidentiality and integrity are both at issue. The firewalls must ensure that no confidential information goes to the Internet. The arrangement and configuration of the firewalls provide the supporting access control mechanisms used to implement the policy.

In addition to controlling information flow, a different point of view is to use the firewall as an audit mechanism. In this role, the firewall analyzes the packets that transit it. The firewall can then base actions on this analysis, leading to traffic shaping (in which percentages of bandwidth are reserved for specific types of traffic), changes in access permissions due to the amount and nature of the traffic, and other controls.

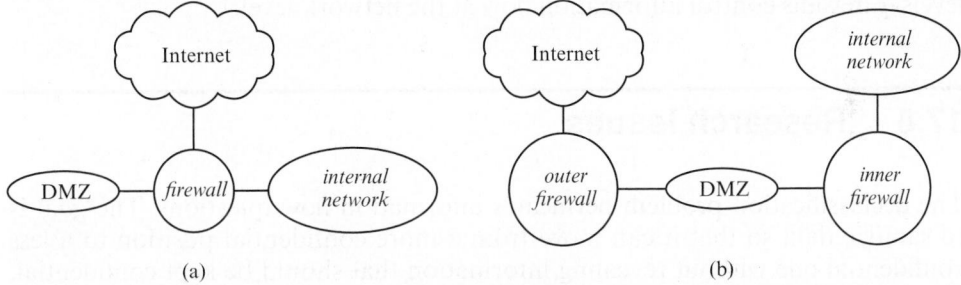

Figure 17–4 This figure shows two different common configurations for using firewalls to protect company internal networks. In both cases, the subnets labeled "DMZ" provide limited public access to various servers. In (a), the firewall is dual-homed and routes messages to the internal network or the DMZ as appropriate. In (b), the outer firewall sits between the Internet and the internal network. The inner firewall sits between the DMZ and the subnets that are not to be accessed by the public.

---

[1] "DMZ" stands for "demilitarized zone." The acronym is always used in this context.

17.7   Summary

Two aspects of information flow are the amount of information flowing and the way in which it flows. Given the value of one variable, entropy measures the amount of information that one can deduce about a second variable. The flow can be explicit, as in the assignment of the value of one variable to another, or implicit, as in the antecedent of a conditional statement depending on the conditional expression.

Traditionally, models of information flow policies form lattices. Should the models not form lattices, they can be embedded in lattice structures. Hence, analysis of information flow assumes a lattice model.

A compiler-based mechanism assesses the flow of information in a program with respect to a given information flow policy. The mechanism either certifies that the program meets the policy or shows that it fails to meet the policy. It has been shown that if a set of statements meet the information flow policy, their combination (using higher-level language programming constructs) meets the information flow policy.

Dynamic mechanisms check flows at runtime. Unlike static mechanisms, dynamic mechanisms either allow the flow to occur (if the flow satisfies the information flow policy) or report or block it (if the flow violates the policy). Classifications of information may be static or dynamic.

The Android information flow analysis tools are examples of mechanisms that provide information flow controls at the program and program statement levels. Firewalls control information flow at the network level.

17.8   Research Issues

The declassification problem permeates information flow questions. The goal is to sanitize data so that it can move from a more confidential position to a less confidential one without revealing information that should be kept confidential. In the integrity sense, the goal is to accredit data as being more trustworthy than its current level. These problems arise in governmental and commercial systems. Augmenting existing models to handle this problem is complex, as suggested in Chapters 5 and 6.

Automated analysis of programs for information flows introduces problems of specification and proof. The primary problem is correct specification of the desired flows. Other problems include the user interface to such a tool (especially if the analysts are programmers and not experts in information flow or program proving methodologies); what assumptions are implicitly made; and how well the model captures the system being analyzed. In some cases, models introduce flows with no counterparts in the existing system. Detecting these flows is critical to a correct and meaningful analysis.

The cascade problem involves aggregation of authorized information flows to produce an unauthorized flow. It arises in networks of systems. The problem of removing such cascades is *NP*-complete. Efforts to approximate the solution must take into account the environment in which the problem arises.

17.9   Further Reading

The Decentralized Label Model [1409, 1410] allows one to specify information flow policies on a per-entity basis. Formal models sometimes lead to reports of flows not present in the system; Eckmann [613] discusses these reports, as well as approaches to eliminating them. Austin and Flanagan [99] present the permissive-upgrade strategy to reduce the number of false positives in information flow analysis. Guttmann [840] draws lessons from the failure of an information flow analysis technique.

Akella, Tang, and McMillin [29] analyze information flow in cyber-physical systems, which requires taking the physical components, and thereby their physics, into account. Web browsers provide a fertile ground for the application of information flow for detecting attacks [517, 848, 1943].

Sabelfeld and Myers [1632] survey methods of information flow control based on programming languages. Schwartz et al. [1701] consider the benefits and drawbacks of dynamic taint analysis and forward symbolic execution. Russo and Sabelfeld [1629] consider the trade-off between static and dynamic flow analysis. Information flow analysis techniques and tools have been developed for many languages, including Java [134, 378, 759, 1407], JavaScript [417, 560, 888], and others [1169, 1292, 1531].

The cascade problem is identified in the Trusted Network Interpretation [2242]. Numerous studies of this problem describe analyses and approaches [681, 708, 1342, 1715, 1716]; the problem of correcting it with minimum cost is *NP*-complete [923].

The Security Pipeline Interface (SPI) [912] adds a processor between a host and destination (such as a disk), and the processor ensures that only information flows allowed by policy occur. It is similar to a firewall, but at the host level. The Secure Network Server Mail Guard [1467, 1768] is in essence a firewall between classified and unclassified networks, filtering all traffic between the two and blocking or sanitizing the messages as appropriate. Keromytis and Prevelakis [1042] provide a detailed overview of firewalls.

Many books and papers describe firewalls and the design of network infrastructures that use them. Cheswick, Bellovin, and Rubin [403] cover the basics of firewalls, and Lodin and Schuba [1204] describe their use. Schuba and Spafford [1696] have created a reference model for firewalls. Kamara et al. [995] analyze vulnerabilities in firewalls. Several papers discuss tools and analysis methods for configuring and managing firewalls [31, 132, 397, 1200, 1271, 1911,

2024, 2070, 2085]. Mansmann, Göbel, and Cheswick [1245] consider visualizing firewall configurations as an aid to network administration.

A multithreaded or distributed environment adds to the complexity of constraints on information flow [692, 1766, 1899]. Some architectural characteristics can be used to enforce these constraints [495, 948, 1004].

17.10   Exercises

1. Revisit the example for x := y + z in Section 17.1.1. Assume that x does not exist in state s. Confirm that information flows from y and z to x by computing $H(y_s \mid |x_t)$, $H(y_s)$, $H(z_s \mid x_t)$, and $H(z_s)$ and showing that $H(y_s \mid x_t) < H(y_s)$ and $H(z_s \mid x_t) < H(z_s)$.

2. Let $L = (S_L, \leq_L)$ be a lattice. Define:

   a. $S_{IL} = \{[a, b] \mid a, b \in S_L \wedge a \leq_L b\}$

   b. $\leq_{IL} = ([a_1, b_1], [a_2, b_2]) \mid a_1 \leq_L a_2 \wedge b_1 \leq_L b_2$

   c. $lub_{IL}([a_1, b_1], [a_2, b_2]) = (lub_L(a_1, a_2), lub_L(b_1, b_2))$

   d. $glb_{IL}([a_1, b_1], [a_2, b_2]) = (glb_L(a_1, a_2), glb_L(b_1, b_2))$

   Prove that the structure $IL = (S_{IL}, \leq_{IL})$ is a lattice.

3. Prove or disprove that the set P formed by the dual mapping of a reflexive information flow policy (as discussed in Definition 17–5) is a lattice.

4. Extend the semantics of the information flow security mechanism in Section 17.3.1 for records (structures).

5. Why can we omit the requirement $lub\{i, b[i]\} \leq a[i]$ from the requirements for secure information flow in the example for iterative statements (see Section 17.3.2.4)?

6. In the flow certification requirement for the goto statement in Section 17.3.2.5, the set of blocks along an execution path from b_i to $IFD(b_i)$ excludes these endpoints. Why are they excluded?

7. Prove that Fenton's Data Mark Machine described in Section 17.4.1 would detect the violation of policy in the execution time certification of the *copy* procedure.

8. Using integrity labels rather than security labels, redo the analysis of information flow in Sections 17.3.1 and Section 17.3.2.

9. Using integrity labels rather than security labels, define an "Integrity Fenton Data Mark Machine." Analyze the program in the example on page 565.

10. Section 17.6.1 says that enabling advertising libraries and the apps that invoke them to execute in the same environment, with the same privileges, violates the principle of least privilege (see Section 14.2.1).

    a. Explain why. How might the principle be enforced?

    b. On the Web, the protocol, host, and port in a URL define an "'origin." The *same origin policy* allows scripts in a web page to access data in a second web page only if they have the same origin. Older versions of the Android's WebView component treated every object with the protocol *file://* (that is, the URL begins with that string) as though it had the same origin, violating the same origin policy. So any JavaScript embedded in HTML in a local file can, if loaded into WebView, access resources with the same permissions as the app. Why is this dangerous?

11. A common organization of a network provides a DMZ to which the public has controlled access. For each of Saltzer and Schroeder's other design principles [1641] (see Chapter 14), explain whether, and if so how, the principle is relevant to the creation and use of the DMZ.

12. A *science DMZ* [500, 1505] is a set of network design patterns that, among other capabilities, enable scientists to transfer large amounts of data at high speed. You have been asked to design the interface between a science DMZ and a high-speed public network that has enough bandwidth to support the data transfer speeds that the scientists require. As it is a public network, it is untrusted, whereas the science DMZ is trusted. The scientists use the regular Internet for other purposes, such as email and web browsing.

    a. Given the science DMZ is connected to a special-purpose public network used *only* for high-speed data transfer, what are the threats that should concern you?

    b. You have been instructed that, for security reasons, you must put a firewall at the interface. What type of firewall—filtering or proxy—would be most appropriate there? Why?

    c. As noted in Chapter 16 on page 527, some routers can have their access control lists reprogrammed dynamically. Would this be better than a firewall for handling the threats you identified? Why or why not?

Chapter 18
Confinement Problem

> TROILUS: This is the monstruosity in love, lady; that
> the will is infinite and the execution confin'd; that
> the desire is boundless and the act a slave to limit.
> — *Troilus and Cressida*, III, ii, 82–84.

When a program executes, it interacts with its environment. The security policy allows some interactions and disallows others. The confinement problem deals with prevention of processes from taking disallowed actions. Beginning with Lampson's characterization of this problem, this chapter continues with a discussion of methods for confinement such as virtual machines and sandboxes. It concludes with a discussion of covert channels. This chapter focuses on confinement. Chapter 23, "Malware," discusses tools and techniques used to breach confinement.

18.1 The Confinement Problem

Consider a client and a server. When the client issues a request to the server, the client sends the server some data. The server then uses the data to perform some function and returns a result (or no result) to the client. Access control affects the function of the server in two ways.

1. The server must ensure that the resources it accesses on behalf of the client include only those resources that the client is authorized to access.
2. The server must ensure that it does not reveal the client's data to any other entity not authorized to see the client's data.

The first requirement represents the goal of the service provider. That goal is to prevent the client from sending messages to the server that cause it to access, alter, transmit, or consume resources that the client is not authorized to access, alter, transmit, or consume. The second requirement represents the goal of the service user. That goal is to prevent the server from transmitting confidential information to the service provider. In both cases, the server must be confined to accessing only a specific set of resources.

EXAMPLE: A server balances accounts for subscribers. The subscribers use a client to transmit the register entries, the current bank balance, and those withdrawals and deposits that have cleared the bank to the server. The server returns the list of outstanding checks and deposits and any discrepancy between the register balance and the bank balance. Subscribers pay a fee for each use.

The service provider requires that the server correctly record who used the service each time it is used. Otherwise, the service provider cannot bill for the use of the service. The threat is that someone may use the service without being detected (and therefore without being charged) or that the user may impersonate another subscriber (resulting in the wrong subscriber being charged). The service provider also does not want the server to transmit billing records or any other unauthorized information to the client. The server should send only the information it derived from the data that the client sent. So the server must be confined to operating only on the data it is sent.

The subscriber expects certain security services from the server. The server must correctly log the user's invocation so that the user is not charged incorrectly. (This matches the need of the service provider.) The server must not record or transmit the data that the subscriber sends to it because the subscriber's data is confidential to the subscriber and is not relevant to the service provider. So the server must be confined to keeping the data to itself and to sending the results only to the subscriber. Lampson [1131] calls this the confinement problem.

> **Definition 18–1.** The *confinement problem* is the problem of preventing a server from leaking information that the user of the service considers confidential.

One characteristic of processes that do not leak information comes from the observation that a process must store data for later retrieval (the leaking). A process that does not store information cannot leak it. However, in the extreme, such processes also cannot perform any computations, because an analyst could observe the flow of control (or state of the process) and from that flow deduce information about the inputs. This leads to the observation that a process that cannot be observed and cannot communicate with other processes cannot leak information. Lampson calls this *total isolation*.

In practice, achieving total isolation is difficult. The processes to be confined usually share resources such as CPUs, networks, and disk storage with other, unconfined processes. The unconfined processes can transmit information over those shared resources.

> **Definition 18–2.** A *covert channel* is a path of communication that was not designed to be used for communication.

The difference between a covert channel and a side channel (see Section 9.6) lies in the way the sender and receiver interact. With a covert channel, the sender and receiver cooperate to transmit information from the sender to the receiver. With a side channel, the receiver extracts information from a characteristic or attribute, and there is no active sender cooperating with the receiver.

EXAMPLE: Process p is to be confined such that it cannot communicate with process q. However, processes p and q share a file system. In order for process p to send a message to process q, it creates a file called *send* in a directory that both processes can read. Just before process q is to read the information, q deletes the *send* file. Process p then transmits a bit by creating a file named *0bit* or *1bit*, as appropriate. When q detects either file, it records the bit and deletes the file. This continues until p creates a file called *end*, at which point the communication ceases.

Confinement is transitive. Assume that a process p is confined to prevent leakage. If it invokes a second process q, then q must be similarly confined or q could leak the information that p passes.

Definition 18–3. The *rule of transitive confinement* states that if a confined process invokes a second process, the second process must be as confined as the caller.

Confinement is a mechanism for enforcing the principle of least privilege (see Section 14.2.1). A properly confined process cannot transmit data to a second process unless the transmission is needed to complete their task. The problem is that the confined process needs access to the data to be transmitted and so the confinement must be on the transmission, not on the data access. To complicate matters, the process may have to transmit some information to the second process. In this case, the confinement mechanism must distinguish between transmission of authorized data and transmission of unauthorized data.

The combination of these problems illustrates the difficulty of preventing leakage. The dilemma is that modern computers are designed to share resources, and yet by the act of sharing they create channels of communication along which information can be leaked.

Lipner [1192] examines the problem from a policy and modeling aspect. He considers two types of covert channels. The first involves the use of storage to transmit information. If a model correctly describes *all* ways in which information can be stored and read, then the model abstracts both legitimate and covert channels along which information can flow. The model constrains all accesses to storage. The only accesses allowed are those authorized by the policy, so the flows of information are legitimate. However, if the model does not capture all such flows, then unauthorized flows, or covert channels, arise.

Lipner then notes that all processes can obtain at least a rough idea of time. This makes time a communication channel. A program can "read" time by checking the system clock or (alternatively) by counting the number of instructions it has executed during a period of wall clock time. A program can "write" time by executing a set number of instructions and stopping, allowing another process to execute. This shared channel cannot be made exclusive unless a process does not share the computer with another process, which suggests isolation as a remedy.

A good example of this is the side channel (see Section 9.6), which is a form of covert channel. A side channel attack does not require a sender desiring to transmit information. Instead, the sender is passive; the recipient derives information about the sender from a covert channel. Like a covert channel, a side channel requires the recipient to be able to observe some characteristic of the sender. So, techniques used to analyze, limit, and close covert channels also defend against the exploitation of side channels.

We explore the mechanism of isolation first. Then we examine covert channels in more detail and discuss other approaches to analyzing them, including techniques for identifying covert channels and isolating them.

18.2   Isolation

Systems isolate processes in two ways [1744]. In the first, the process is executed in a controlled environment. In the second, when the process is generated, it is altered so that the actions of the process will satisfy an isolation policy. The first provides interfaces that mediate access to the resources of the underlying computer. The second transforms the source code, ancillary libraries, or executable before it is executed.

18.2.1   Controlled Environment

A controlled environment is an environment that constrains process execution in such a way that it can only interact with other entities in a manner that preserves its isolation. One way to do this is to ensure the hardware on which the process runs is disconnected from all other systems.

EXAMPLE: Supervisory control and data acquisition (SCADA) systems control industrial processes such as refining oil, generating and distributing power and water, and treating waste and sewage. The first generation of SCADA systems used serial protocols and were not connected to other systems and networks. Hence external attackers could not compromise those systems and, through them, the processes they controlled. Thus, they had no computer security defenses; their developers focused on detecting malfunctions. The second generation used serial networks connected to computers that were not connected to the Internet, and the current third generation uses TCP/IP and runs on networks connected to the Internet. Attackers could attempt to compromise these systems, and indeed have done so since 1998 [335, 376].

As another example, electronic voting systems record voters' votes, and make them available in some fashion to be tallied to obtain election results. The integrity of these systems is paramount to ensuring the election results are accurate. Physical isolation is one component of ensuring this. For example, Section 19205 of the U.S. state of California's Election Code [2123] requires that no part of a voting system can be connected to the Internet at any time, receive or transmit wireless messages at any time, or transmit or receive election data over an external network if sent between a polling place, satellite location, or counting center. The intent is to prevent any attacks on those systems from the Internet, or any other external network (including the public telephone system).

Virtual machines provide another type of environment that constrains process execution.

18.2.1.1 Virtual Machines

Definition 18–4. A *virtual machine* is a program that simulates the hardware of a (possibly abstract) computer system.

A virtual machine uses a special operating system called a *virtual machine monitor* or *hypervisor* to provide a virtual machine on which conventional operating systems can run. A *type-1 hypervisor* runs directly on the system; a *type-2 hypervisor* is a program that runs on another operating system. Appendix D discusses virtual machines in more detail.

The primary advantage of a virtual machine is that existing operating systems do not need to be modified. They run on the hypervisor. The hypervisor enforces the desired security policy. This is transparent to the user. The hypervisor functions as a security kernel.

In terms of policy, a hypervisor deals with subjects (the subjects being the virtual machines). Even if one virtual machine is running hundreds of processes, the hypervisor knows only about the virtual machine. Thus, it can apply security checks to its subjects, and those controls apply to the processes that those subjects are running. This satisfies the rule of transitive confinement.

EXAMPLE: Karger and colleagues at Digital Equipment Corporation developed a virtual machine monitor (VMM) for the DEC VAX [1010]. The monitor is a security kernel and can run either the VMS or the Ultrix operating system. The VMM runs on the native VAX hardware and is invoked whenever the virtual machine executes a privileged instruction. Its structure is typical of virtual machines designed to provide security.

The VAX has four levels of privilege: user, supervisor, executive, and kernel modes. In order to provide a compatible virtual machine, the virtual machines must also have four levels of privilege. However, the kernel mode allows a process to access privileged instructions on the VAX hardware directly. Only the VMM is allowed to do this. The virtual machines cannot access kernel mode. The solution is to provide virtual modes. These modes are VM user (corresponding to user mode), VM supervisor mode, and VM executive and VM kernel modes (both actually executive mode).[1]

The VMM subjects are users and virtual machines. VMM has a basic, flat file system for its own use and partitions the remaining disk space among the virtual machines. Those machines may use any file structure they desire, and each virtual machine has its own set of file systems. Each subject and object has a multilevel security and integrity label, and the security and integrity levels form an access class. Two entities have the same access class if and only if their security and integrity labels are the same, and one entity dominates another if and only if both the security and integrity classes dominate.

An integral component of the VMM is an auditing mechanism. This mechanism records actions for later analysis.

EXAMPLE: The Xen 3.0 hypervisor [125] uses a different approach when run on the Intel® virtualization technology [2046].[2] The processor supports two modes, VMX root operation and VMX nonroot operation. Fully virtualized domains called *hardware-based virtual machines* (HVMs) support unmodified guest operating systems; these run in VMX nonroot operation mode. The Xen hypervisor runs in VMX root operation mode.

When a guest operating system executes a privileged instruction, the operation can only be executed as a VMX root operation. Thus, control transfers to the Xen hypervisor; this is a *VM exit*. The hypervisor determines whether to execute the instruction. After it does so and updates the HVM appropriately, it returns control to the guest operating system. This is called a *VM entry*.

Here there are eight levels of privilege. Four rings exist in the VMX nonroot operation mode, and four more in the VMX root operation mode. This avoids the need to overload one of the rings, as the DEC VMM architecture does.

Because virtual machines provide the same interface for communication with other virtual machines that computers provide, those channels of communication can be controlled or severed. As mentioned earlier, if a single host runs multiple virtual machines, those virtual machines share the physical resources of the host on which they run. They may also share logical resources, depending on how the virtualizing kernel is implemented. This provides a fertile ground for covert channels, a subject explored in Section 18.3.

A *container* is similar to a virtual machine. Unlike a virtual machine, all containers share the same kernel, and execute instructions natively; thus, a container does not emulate the instructions of another hardware architecture. Each container contains the libraries and applications needed to execute the program or programs it contains, and isolates its contents from other containers.

---

[1] Appendix D discusses this approach in more detail.

[2] Section D.2.1 discusses this architecture.

EXAMPLE: Docker [254, 445, 591] is a container widely used in Linux systems. It contains all libraries, programs, and other data for the software being contained. Thus, it provides an ideal development environment that can be moved from one system to another. The container software itself runs as a daemon that launches containers, monitors them so it can take supporting actions, and controls their levels of isolation.

The isolation is enforced using features of the Linux kernel. For example, containers have a reduced set of capabilities, their own namespace, and their own file system. They can also be configured to restrict resource usage among its processes. The Docker daemon also controls access of the containers to the network, and containers can have different levels of network access set when they start. Each container is assigned its own IP address, and the *root* user of the container is different than the *root* user of the system.

18.2.1.2 Library Operating Systems

Virtual machines provide isolation by presenting the process with a full operating system. In many cases, this is unnecessary. Anderson [61] pointed out that, in many cases, the process can optimize the use of system resources better than the generic algorithms used by the operating system. For example, consider a process that accesses SSD secondary storage, which operates much like memory. An operating system that optimizes reading and writing for a disk drive head adds unnecessary overhead to those operations. Anderson proposed a kernel with two functions. The first is to use hardware protections to prevent processes from overwriting one another or accessing the memory of another process. The second is to control access to physical resources that must be shared among the executing processes. All other functions normally in the kernel are in user space.

EXAMPLE: The V++ Cache Kernel [401] implemented this idea. The Cache Kernel tracks operating system objects that are in use, such as address spaces, and handles process coordination such as scheduling. It runs in supervisor mode. The application kernel manages process resources. For example, the application kernel handles page faults by loading a new page mapping descriptor into the Cache Kernel. It runs in user mode. The Exokernel [639] goes a step further, separating resource protection and resource management. A small kernel, Aegis, provides interfaces to the hardware resources and multiplexes them among the processes. A "library OS," ExOS, provides an interface to Aegis that enables the process to use the resources as appropriate. It also provides isolation through the protection of resources.

The goal of a library OS is to move as much of the operating system as is feasible to the user level, thus minimizing the overhead of context switches and providing processes with maximum flexibility. For example, ExOS implements virtual memory abstractions. Thus, the process can take into account any particular memory referencing patterns to use its own virtual memory management algorithm, and other processes may use different virtual memory management algorithms.

> **Definition 18–5.** A *library operating system* is a library or set of libraries that provide operating system functionality at the user level.

One issue is the level of abstraction that the library OS provides. Those that the Exokernel and Cache Kernel provide are low level, in that the process needs to understand details of how the library OS interacts with the supervisor-mode kernel. Higher level abstractions limit the changes necessary for existing programs and applications.

EXAMPLE: Drawbridge [1536] is a library OS architecture developed for Windows 7. It supports standard Windows applications such as Microsoft Excel and the web server IIS, and provides access to Windows features such as DirectX. It uses higher-level abstractions than the Cache Kernel and the Exokernel.

Drawbridge consists of a library OS and a security monitor. The security monitor provides an application binary interface (ABI) to the underlying operating system, thereby virtualizing the system resources. Processes use the library OS to access the ABI, and all interactions with the operating system go through that interface. The library OS provides application services such as frameworks and rendering engines. The ABI provides calls to manage virtual memory, processes and threads, and I/O streams, as well as calls for cryptographically strong random sequences of bits, wall clock time, and other information. One of the goals of Drawbridge was to keep the ABI compact and easy to work with, a design decision that led to a logical organization of the calls.

Drawbridge handles kernel dependencies using a Windows NT emulator at the lowest layer of the library OS. This allows all server dependencies and Windows subsystems to be moved out of the operating system and into the user layer (either in the library OS or another user-level library). Human-computer interaction uses emulated device drivers that tunnels input and output between the desktop and the security monitor.

Drawbridge provides process isolation. When malware that deleted all registry keys was run, under Drawbridge only the malware process was affected, but without Drawbridge, all processes were affected. Similarly, under Drawbridge, a keystroke logger captured the keystrokes of the application with the keystroke logger, but without Drawbridge, it captured all keystrokes for all applications. Another test involved five attack vectors that caused Internet Explorer to escape its normal protected mode that restricted its actions (for example, preventing programs run under Explorer from writing to disk). Drawbridge mitigated all the attacks.

18.2.1.3   Sandboxes

A playground sandbox provides a safe environment for children to stay in. If the children leave the sandbox, they will leave a contained environment in which they can be watched and, if needed, prevented from hurting themselves or others. The computer sandbox is similar. It provides a safe environment for programs to execute in. If the programs "leave" the sandbox, they may do things that they are not supposed to do. Both types of sandboxes restrict the actions of their occupants.

Definition 18–6. A *sandbox* is an environment in which the actions of a process are restricted according to a security policy.

Systems may enforce restrictions in two ways. First, the sandbox can limit the execution environment as needed. This is usually done by adding extra security-checking mechanisms to the libraries or kernel. The program itself is not modified. For example, the VMM kernel discussed earlier is a sandbox because it constrains the accesses of the (unmodified) operating systems that run on it. The Java virtual machine, in which downloaded applets are executed, is a sandbox because its security manager limits access of downloaded programs to system resources as dictated by a security policy [1185].

EXAMPLE: The operational kernel of the Sidewinder firewall [1877] uses type enforcement to confine processes (see the example on page 529 in Section 16.3.1). This is an example of a sandbox built into a kernel, and it has the property that the sandbox is defined by the vendor. It is not intended to be altered at the site. Such a design is typical for a turnkey system, which is the intended use for a Sidewinder firewall.

DTE, the type enforcement mechanism for DTEL (see page 122 in Section 4.5.1), is an example in which kernel modifications enable system administrators to configure their own sandboxes. The kernel enforces the constraints.

The second enforcement method is to modify the program (or process) to be executed. Dynamic debuggers [15, 866, 1259, 1811, 1812, 2054] and some profilers [217] use this technique by adding breakpoints to the code and, when the trap occurs, analyzing the state of the running process. A variant, known as *software fault isolation* [1709, 1956, 2097], adds instructions that perform memory access checks or other checks as the program runs, so any attempt to violate the security policy causes an error.

EXAMPLE: Janus [786] implements a user-level sandbox. It is an execution environment in which system calls are trapped and checked. Users execute it to restrict the objects and modes of access of an untrusted program. Janus consists of a *framework*, which does the runtime checking, and *modules*, which determine which accesses are to be allowed.

Janus first reads a configuration file. This file instructs it to load certain modules. Along with the module identification is a list of constraints. The following example configuration file defines the environment variable **IFS** for the child and restricts the child's access to the file system. The child cannot access any files except those that are named below (this meets the principle of fail-safe

defaults discussed in Section 14.2.2). The child can read or write to any file in the
/usr file system except for those in the */usr/lib* and */usr/local/lib* directories (which
are read only) and in */usr/bin* (read and execute). The child can read any file in the
/lib directory and can read and execute any file in the */sbin* and */bin* directories. In
the following configuration file, the first word in each instruction line is the name
of the module and the other words are the arguments passed to the modules ("#"
begins a comment):

```
# basic module
basic

# define subprocess environment variables
putenv IFS="\t\n " PATH=/sbin:/bin:/usr/bin TZ=PST8PDT

# deny access to everything except files under /usr
path deny read,write *
path allow read,write /usr/*
# allow subprocess to read files in library directories
# needed for dynamic loading
path allow read /lib/* /usr/lib/* /usr/local/lib/*
# needed so child can execute programs
path allow read,exec /sbin/* /bin/* /usr/bin/*
```

Each module constrains system calls. The framework uses the modules to build a
linked list for each monitored system call. The list defines allowed and disallowed
actions. Once this list has been constructed, the Janus framework invokes the
program in such a way that all monitored system calls are trapped.

When the program executes a monitored system call, the program traps
and the Janus framework is invoked. It has access to the arguments supplied to
the system call. It validates that the system call, with these specific parameters,
is allowed. If the system call is not allowed, the framework sets the child's
environment so that the system call appears to have failed. If the system call is
allowed, the framework returns control to the child, which in turn passes control
to the kernel. On return, control goes to the framework, which updates any
internal state and returns the results to the child.

An example use would be in reading MIME mail. One could have set the
mail reading program to pass control to a Postscript display engine. Some such
engines have a mechanism for executing system-level commands embedded in
the Postscript file. Hence, an attacker could put a file deletion command in the
Postscript file. The recipient would run the display engine to read the file, and some
of her files would be deleted [2160]. However, the user (or system administrator)
can set up the Janus configuration file to disallow execution of any subprograms.
Then the embedded command will be detected (on the system call to execute it)
and rejected.

Some sandboxing mechanisms use both program and kernel modifications. These redefine some aspect of the system calls, which requires both kernel modifications and program modifications.

EXAMPLE: Capsicum [1983] is a framework developed to sandbox a single application. Kernel modifications enforce the sandbox limits set by the application.

In UNIX-like systems such as Linux and FreeBSD, file descriptors control read and write access, but given a file descriptor the application can obtain and modify metadata such as file permissions and times of last access and modification. Capsicum extends the notion of UNIX file descriptors by providing fine-grained rights for accessing and manipulating the underlying file. The extended file descriptor is called a *capability*, and the process can create capabilities that allow a subprocess to read a file but not access the file permissions, for example.

The process issues the *cap_enter* system call to activate the sandbox; the process is now in *capability mode*. The process remains in this mode until the process terminates. Any subprocesses that it creates will also be in capability mode and will inherit those capabilities that the parent process allows it to.

The system call *cap_new* creates capabilities from file descriptors or existing capabilities. It takes a mask of rights that are to be set. If a capability is given, the mask must be a subset of the rights in that capability. For example, the mask F_READ | F_SEEK allows a file to be read with the *read* system call.

The global namespaces for the system are not available in capability mode. So any system call that depends upon access to the namespace, for example *open*, is unavailable. The other system calls may be constrained. For example, the system call that creates memory objects can create anonymous ones but not named ones (as the names would be in the global namespace). Opening a file requires a special form of the *open* system call, in which the containing directory is given as a file descriptor. So for example if the file descriptor is that of the directory "/lib," the system call could open the file "libc.so.7" (for which "lib" is an ancestor directory) but not "/etc/passwd" or "../etc/passwd" (as "/lib" is not an ancestor directory for those files). Subprocesses of a sandboxed process cannot elevate privileges. This means they cannot be setuid or setgid. However, a setuid or setgid program may enter capability mode by issuing the *cap_enter* system call. All these constraints are applied at the point in the kernel where the relevant service is provided, and not at the system call interface.

At the user level, the *libcapsicum* library provides an interface to start sandboxed processes and to explicitly delegate rights to the sandbox. When it starts a sandboxed process, all nondelegated file descriptors are closed and the address space is flushed. A UNIX domain socket is returned to the parent process; this allows communication between the parent and the sandboxed child process. In addition, there is a runtime linker designed to support capability mode.

Applications can either work directly with capabilities or use the *libcapsicum* interface. As an example, and a way to test performance, the program *tcpdump* was sandboxed. This program takes a user-supplied pattern and passes it to a filter that reads network traffic looking for packets that match the pattern.

These are then saved. Having it work directly with capabilities is straightforward, as it acquires the resources it needs (such as access to the underlying network to get the packets) when it starts, and uses those resources throughout its execution. Unnecessary privileges, such as unconstrained access to the user's keyboard, are not acquired, and hence the modified *tcpdump* cannot read user input—which it should not read in the first place. These modifications took eight lines of code.

One complication was the use of the DNS resolver. As *tcpdump* provides the ability to change IP addresses into host names, it needs access to the DNS. But the standard DNS resolver needs access to files in the file system, which requires access to the global namespace and is therefore blocked. The solution was to use a simple DNS resolver that communicates with a local daemon, and that daemon does the resolution and sends the result back to the simple resolver.

More complex programs, such as the Google Chrome web browser, have also been sandboxed using Capsicum. Sandboxing is essential as each tab uses a renderer process to display the web page, and the renderer includes the ability to execute JavaScript applets. The design of Chrome for Linux systems and Mac OS X systems compartmentalized many functions, so the task was less complex than might be assumed. The implementation of shared memory had to be changed to the POSIX shared memory code and about 100 lines of code were needed to limit access to file descriptors given to sandboxed processes.

Like a virtual machine monitor, a sandbox forms part of the trusted computing base. If the sandbox fails, it provides less protection than it is believed to provide. Hence, ensuring that the sandbox correctly implements a desired security policy is critical to the security of the system.

18.2.2   Program Modification

The second class of techniques to confine applications relies on transforming the source or binary code of the application to ensure that the confinement constraints are satisfied. These transformations may be carried out by a code rewriter, which is usually a preprocessor; the compiler, which transforms the program as it compiles; a binary code rewriter, which is a postprocessor that transforms the machine instructions in the executable; or a loader that transforms the linkages between the program and the libraries and operating system calls to validate interactions. All transformations are controlled by a policy that states which interactions are to be allowed and which are forbidden.

18.2.2.1   Rewriting

Software fault isolation considers programs with both trusted and untrusted modules. The untrusted modules are placed in special virtual segments, and the code is modified so that control flow remains in that segment whenever the module is invoked. Additionally, all memory accesses are to data in that segment; the module cannot refer to any data not in the module. The rewriting may occur before or after compilation.

EXAMPLE: Wahbe et al. [1956] propose two ways to implement software fault isolation for untrusted modules. Each module is placed in its own segment, and each such segment has a unique pattern of bits (the *segment identifier*) in the upper part of the virtual addresses in the segment. An instruction that accesses (transfers control to or stores in) an address that cannot be verified to be in the module's segment is an *unsafe instruction*. The first technique, called *segment matching*, is to statically analyze the program and identify all unsafe instructions. Then they are wrapped to check the actual addresses when the program executes. If the check shows that the address is not in the segment, a trap occurs. Checking is straightforward as only the segment identifier in the address need be checked. An alternate technique simply sets the upper bits of any target virtual address to the segment identifier. An illegal address resulting from this is handled in the usual way.

System calls in untrusted modules pose a problem, as the module can use that to interfere with the operation of trusted modules, for example by closing a file that a trusted module relies on. To prevent this, trusted *arbitration code* is placed into its own segment. This code accepts RPC requests from other modules and translates them into system calls, returning the results via the RPC. The arbitration module filters these requests. Then the untrusted modules are rewritten so any system calls are translated into RPC calls to the arbitration code.

Taking software fault isolation a step further, one can place the security-sensitive parts of the application into a separate trusted process. The application is then rewritten so the untrusted part invokes the trusted part through IPC. To run the application, both the untrusted part and the trusted part are executed. The trusted process handles all security-sensitive operations and mediates access to security-sensitive data.

EXAMPLE: An implementation of separation of trusted modules and untrusted modules into different processes is built upon the Nizza architecture [1757]. This architecture provides a trusted computing environment. The trusted process, AppCore, is executed on this architecture and the untrusted process on a virtual system running the appropriate operating system.

Creating the trusted AppCore is a three-step process. First, the application is analyzed to identify the security-sensitive components. This can be automated to some extent, but is typically done manually. Next, these components are placed in a stand-alone AppCore process. In this step, these components may be rewritten to ensure they satisfy the requisite security policy, and whenever possible the interfaces between the AppCore and the untrusted process are reused. Finally, the rest of the application is transformed to invoke the AppCore to execute security-sensitive components. Experiments showed the AppCores were small compared to the original programs, and that this approach had a low impact on performance.

18.2.2.2   Compiling

A security policy can specify confinement for a compiler to implement. The goal of the resulting compiled code is to provide the isolation defined by the security policy. As an example, type-safe programming languages provide this type of confinement because the typing places restrictions on the actions that can be taken with objects. The compiler checks the program to verify that the use of types is consistent; if it is not, then the process will not be properly confined. In addition to this static checking, compilers can determine when runtime checking is necessary, and add code to do that. Type-safe high-level and assembly languages have been developed.

EXAMPLE: The programming language Java is a type-safe language. This means that a Java program with no type errors will act in a known, understood way. For example, in Java, if an array access is out of bounds, the behavior is well-defined: an exception (ArrayIndexOutOfBoundsException) is thrown. By way of contrast, the C programming language is not type-safe, because the behavior of such a reference is undefined and, in fact, the program may crash, or it may continue to run with incorrect values in memory.

CCured is a system that imposes type safety on C programs [1434]. It adds semantics to constructs in C that can produce undefined results. For example, three types of pointer attributes are defined: safe, sequence, and dynamic. Each pointer has a set of invariants to be maintained. If a safe pointer points to an object of type t, then it can only contain 0 (the **NULL** pointer) or the address of an object of type t. Thus, when dereferencing this type of pointer, the system need only check that it is not 0. A sequence pointer is either an integer or a pointer into a memory area containing objects of type t. This type of pointer is used as a pointer to elements in data structures such as arrays. Thus, the checks here are that the pointer is indeed a pointer, and that it points to an object of type t in that memory area when cast to a safe pointer or dereferenced. A dynamic pointer does not have information about the type of data it references. It can be used to point to untyped areas of memory, or memory of arbitrary type (which must be tagged with the type of values in that area).

Given an existing C program, a type inference algorithm constructs a CCured program that honors the type rules. This algorithm first gathers constraints that control the pointers in the program. If the pointer is used in pointer arithmetic, it cannot be a safe pointer. If used in a cast, the pointer being cast must be a safe pointer, and the one being cast to a sequence pointer. If the pointer points to another pointer and is a dynamic pointer, the pointer it points to must be dynamic also. Finally, if two pointers have the dynamic attribute, their types must be equivalent. These constraints are then simplified and the attributes assigned accordingly. The algorithm maximizes the number of safe and sequential pointers because tags need not be maintained when those pointers are involved.

The results of running CCured over the SPECINT95 benchmarks resulted in detecting several bugs in those benchmarks. Performance on those benchmarks and the Olden benchmark was impacted, leading to execution times increasing by 30% to 150% in most cases.

An alternate approach is to use a certifying compiler that includes a proof that a program satisfies specified security properties. Then the proof can be validated before execution.

EXAMPLE: Touchstone [1433] is a compiler and certifier for a type-safe subset of C. In this language, the bounds of all array references are checked. To facilitate this, arrays are represented as pairs of base address and array length.

The compiler translates the program into assembly language. Loop invariants that describe the types of registers used in the loops annotate the code. Type specifications declare the types of arguments (preconditions) and return values (postconditions) for each function. This goes to the VCGen, which generates verification conditions. VCGen works on a per-function basis and uses symbolic execution. First, it initializes variables corresponding to the machine registers. Then, it builds a predicate based on the assembly language instructions emitted by the compiler. Both branches of a conditional branch are evaluated, and the appropriate condition is included in the evaluation. When VCGen encounters a return instruction, it puts out a predicate that includes a check on the instantiation of the preconditions, the predicate built up from the assembly language, and the postcondition. This predicate can be proved if and only if the program satisfies the postcondition, and the registers that were preserved on entry to the function are not changed by the function.

A theorem prover for first-order logic verified the proof. The theorem prover produces proofs that can be checked independently, and it proves the predicates automatically. The prover has a set of inference rules such as it being safe to read an element of an array if the index of the element being accessed is within the bounds of the array. These inference rules and the rules of first-order predicate logic suffice to have the theorem prover validate the proof.

18.2.2.3   Loading

This approach loads libraries that will apply constraints to keep the process appropriately confined. It is similar to the sandboxing discussed in Section 18.2.1.3, except that the framework is embedded in the libraries and is not a separate user-level process. When the process calls one of the constrained libraries, the library applies its policy rules to determine whether it should carry out the request or take some other action.

EXAMPLE: To prevent Android apps from exfiltrating sensitive data or misusing resources, Aurasium [2038] transforms (repackages) the app by adding code to monitor all interactions with the phone's resources to enforce security and privacy policies. These policies can be considerably more granular than the default permissions set upon installation. When the policies are violated, the user is notified and asked whether the app should proceed.

Aurasium has two parts. The first part is the tool that inserts the code to enforce various policies when the app calls upon resources in the underlying operating system such as SMS messaging. The second part is a modified version of the Android standard C libraries called the *Bionic libc*. These libraries receive the system call requests from the app, and determine whether the system call should be blocked based on the policy. If not, the call proceeds. The importance of this library is that all higher-level frameworks invoke functions that in turn use the Android standard C libraries—and the Bionic libc stands in for those libraries with the same functionality, plus the policy checking feature.

The developers of Aurasium noted that Android apps are typically signed, so modifying them will cause the signature to not match the app, and thus be rejected. Their approach is to validate the original signature before transforming the app. Then, after the transformation, Aurasium simply signs the modified app with its own certificate.

When applied to apps from a third-party app store and to apps known to be malicious, Aurasium was able to repackage well over 99% of those apps. The performance impact on these was negligible.

18.3 Covert Channels

Covert channels use shared resources as paths of communication. This requires sharing of space or sharing of time.

> **Definition 18–7.** A *covert storage channel* uses an attribute of the shared resource. A *covert timing channel* uses a temporal or ordering relationship among accesses to a shared resource.

EXAMPLE: The covert channel in the example on page 581 is a covert storage channel. The shared resource is the directory and the names of the files in that directory. The processes communicate by altering characteristics (file names and file existence) of the shared resource.

EXAMPLE: A study of the security of the KVM/370 system [1675] found that two virtual machines could establish a covert channel based on the CPU quantum that each virtual machine received. If the sending virtual machine wished to send a 0 bit, it would relinquish the CPU immediately; to send a 1 bit, it would use its full quantum. By determining how quickly it got the CPU, the second virtual machine could deduce whether the first was sending a 1 or a 0 bit. The shared resource is the CPU. The processes communicate by using a real-time clock to measure the intervals between accesses to the shared resource. Hence, this is a covert timing channel.

A covert timing channel is usually defined in terms of a real-time clock or a timer, but temporal relationships sometimes use neither. An ordering of events implies a time-based relationship that involves neither a real-time clock nor a timer.

EXAMPLE: Consider a variant of a channel identified in KVM/370 [784, 2025]. Two virtual machines share cylinders 100 through 200 on a disk. The disk uses a SCAN algorithm [1748] to schedule disk accesses. One virtual machine has security class *High*, and the other has class *Low*. A process on the *High* machine is written to send information to a process on the *Low* machine.

The process on the *Low* machine issues a read request for data on cylinder 150. When that request completes, it relinquishes the CPU. The process on the *High* machine runs, issues a seek to cylinder 140, and relinquishes the CPU. The process on the *Low* machine runs and issues seek requests to cylinders 139 and 161. Because the disk arm is moving over the cylinders in descending order, the seek issued to cylinder 139 is satisfied first, followed by the seek issued to cylinder 161. This ordering represents a 1 bit.

To send a 0 bit, the process on the *High* machine issues a read request for data on cylinder 160 instead of cylinder 140. Then the process on the *Low* machine's requests will be satisfied first on cylinder 161 and then on cylinder 139.

Is this a covert timing channel or a covert storage channel? Because it does not involve a real-time clock or timer, the usual definition implies that it is a covert storage channel.

Modify the example slightly to postulate a timer. The process on the *Low* machine uses this timer to determine how long it takes for its requests to complete. If the timer shows that the time required to satisfy the request for a seek to cylinder 139 is less than the time required to satisfy the request for a seek to cylinder 161, then a 1 bit is being sent. If the timings indicate the opposite, a 0 bit is being sent. This modification clearly uses a covert timing channel.

The difference between the modified example and the original example is the presence of a timer. The timer changes nothing about the way the channel works. For this reason, we include relative ordering of events as a covert timing channel.

A second property distinguishes between a covert channel that only the sender and receiver have access to and a covert channel that others have access to as well.

Definition 18–8. A *noiseless covert channel* is a covert channel that uses a resource available to the sender and receiver only. A *noisy covert channel* is a covert channel that uses a resource available to subjects other than the sender and receiver, as well as to the sender and receiver.

The difference between these two types of channels lies in the need to filter out extraneous information. Any information that the receiver obtains from a noiseless channel comes from the sender. However, in a noisy channel, the sender's information is mixed with meaningless information, or noise, from other entities using the resource. A noisy covert channel requires a protocol to minimize this interference.

The key properties of covert channels are *existence* and *bandwidth*. Existence tells us that there is a channel along which information can be transmitted.

Bandwidth tells us how rapidly information can be sent. Covert channel analysis establishes both properties. Then the channels can be eliminated or their bandwidths can be reduced.

18.3.1   Detection of Covert Channels

Covert channels require sharing. The manner in which the resource is shared controls which subjects can send and receive information using that shared resource. Detection methods begin with this observation.

18.3.1.1   Noninterference

Models such as the Bell-LaPadula Model represent information transfer using read and write operations and develop controls to restrict their use. Viewing "information transfer" more broadly, one can consider any operation that a second process can detect as being a write command. This immediately leads to the use of an interference model to detect these covert channels. If a subject can interfere with another subject in some way, there is a covert channel, and the nature of the interference identifies the channel.

EXAMPLE: The SAT system has a multilevel security policy analyzed in terms of noninterference [846]. The formal model of the SAT was analyzed to locate covert channels [845]. The first analysis, using noninterference, introduced the $\pi(i, l)$ function, which removes all instructions issued by subjects dominated by level l from the instruction stream i. $A(i, \sigma)$ is the state resulting from the execution of the instruction stream i on the state σ. $\sigma.v(s)$ describes the subject s's view of the state σ. Then, by Definition 9–4, the system is noninterference-secure if and only if, for all instruction sequences i, subjects s with security level $l(s)$, and states σ,

$$A(\pi(i, l(s)), \sigma).v(s) = A(i, \sigma).v(s)$$

This leads to a version of the unwinding theorem (Theorem 9.1):

Theorem 18.1. Let Σ be the set of states of the system. A specification is noninterference-secure if, for each subject s at security level $l(s)$, there exists an equivalence relation $\equiv: S \times S$ such that:

(a) For $\sigma_1, \sigma_2 \in S$, when $\sigma_1 \equiv \sigma_2$, $\sigma_1.v(s) = \sigma_2.v(s)$.
(b) For $\sigma_1, \sigma_2 \in S$ and any instruction i, when $\sigma_1 \equiv \sigma_2$, $A(i, \sigma_1) \equiv A(i, \sigma_2)$.
(c) For $\sigma \in S$ and instruction i, if $\pi(i, l(s))$ is empty, $A(\pi(i, l(s)), \sigma).v(s) = \sigma.v(s)$.

Intuitively, this theorem states that the system is noninterference-secure if equivalent states have the same view for each subject, the view remains the same when any instruction is executed, and instructions from higher-level subjects do not affect the state from the viewpoint of lower-level subjects.

The designers looked at several parts of the SAT specification. The relevant parts were for the object creation instruction and the readable object set.

Let s be a subject with security level $l(s)$, and let o be an object with security level $l(o)$ and type $\tau(o)$. Let σ be the current state. The set of existing objects is listed in a global object table $T(\sigma)$. Then the object creation specification *object_create* is as follows.

Specification 18.1.

$$[\sigma' = object\_create(s, o, l(o), \tau(o), \sigma) \wedge \sigma' \neq \sigma] \Leftrightarrow [o \notin T(\sigma) \wedge l(s) \leq l(o)]$$

The object is created if it does not exist and if the subject's clearance is sufficient to permit the creation of an object at the desired level.

The readable object set contains the set of existing objects that the subject could read in at the current, or at least at a future, state. We ignore discretionary controls for this predicate. Let s be a subject and o an object. Let l and T be as before, and let $can_read(s, o, \sigma)$ be true if, in state σ, o is of a type to which s can apply the read operation (ignoring permissions). Then:

Specification 18.2.

$$o \in readable(s, \sigma) \Leftrightarrow [o \in T(\sigma) \vee \neg(l(o) \leq l(s)) \vee \neg(can\_read(s, o, \sigma))]$$

An object is not in the set if it does not exist, if the subject's security level does not dominate the object's security level, or if the subject is of the wrong type to read the object (or vice versa).

Because the SAT system model was tranquil, adding an object to the readable set requires a new object to be created. Let s' be the subject that creates it. Then,

Specification 18.3.

$$[o \notin readable(s, \sigma) \wedge o \in readable(s, \sigma')] \Leftrightarrow$$
$$[\sigma' = object\_create(s', o, l(o), \tau(o), \sigma) \wedge o \notin T(\sigma) \wedge l(s') \leq l(o) \leq l(s)$$
$$\wedge can\_read(s, o, \sigma')]$$

For an object to be added to a subject's readable set, it initially cannot exist; it must first be created, and then its levels and discretionary access controls must be set appropriately.

Consider two states σ_1 and σ_2. These states differ only in that an object o exists in state σ_2 and not in σ_1 and that in state σ_2, $l(s)$ does not dominate $l(o)$. By Specification 18.2, $o \notin readable(s, \sigma_1)$ (because o does not exist) and $o \notin readable(s, \sigma_2)$ (because $\neg(l(o) \leq l(s))$). Thus, $\sigma_1 \equiv \sigma_2$. Now, s issues a command to create o with $l(o) = l(s)$ and of a type that it can read (that is, $can\_read(s, o, \sigma_1')$ is true, where σ_1' is the state after $object\_create(s, o, \sigma_1)$). By Specification 18.1, σ_1' differs from σ_1 by the addition of o to the table $T(\sigma_1)$. This new entry would satisfy $can\_read(s, o, \sigma_1')$ and $l(s') \leq l(o) \leq l(s)$, where s' is the subject that created the object.

Next, because o exists in σ_1, $\sigma_2' = object\_create(s', o, l(o), \tau(o), \sigma_2) = \sigma_2$. So, $\sigma_1 \equiv \sigma_2$ is true, but $A(object\_create(s', o, l(o), \tau(o), \sigma_1), \sigma_1) \equiv A(object\_create (s', o, l(o), \tau(o), \sigma_2), \sigma_2)$ is false. This means that condition 2 in Theorem 18.1 is false. Thus, Theorem 18.1 does not apply.

Exploiting this covert channel is straightforward. To send a 1, the subject at a high level creates an object at a high level. The recipient (a second subject) tries to create the same object but at a low level. The creation fails, but no indication of the failure is given. The second subject then gives a different subject type permission to read and write the object. It writes a 1 to the object and reads the object. The read returns nothing. To send a 0, the subject at the high level creates nothing, but the subject at the low level follows the same steps. In this case, the read returns a 1.

Because noninterference techniques reason in terms of security levels and not in terms of time, these techniques are most useful for analyzing covert storage channels.

18.3.1.2   The Shared Resource Matrix Methodology

Kemmerer introduced a methodology for identifying shared channels and determining in what ways they are shared [1024, 1025, 1027]. First, the analyst identifies all shared resources and the attributes of those resources that are visible to subjects. These attributes make up the rows of the matrix. Next, the analyst determines the operations that either reference (read) or modify (alter) the attributes. These operations make up the columns of the matrix. The contents of each element of the matrix indicate whether the operation references, modifies, or both references and modifies the attribute.

EXAMPLE: Consider a system that implements a multilevel security model. Files have four attributes: file existence, file owner, file label, and file size. Two subjects, one *High* and one *Low*, are active. The file manipulation operations are *read_file*, *write_file*, *delete_file*, and *create_file*. Reading succeeds if the file exists and the subject's label is greater than or equal to the file's label. Writing and deletion succeed if the file exists and the subject's label is less than or equal to the file's label. Creation succeeds if no file with the given name exists. The file is given the creating process as its owner and the label of the creating process as its label.

The shared resource matrix is as follows:

	read_file	write_file	delete_file	create_file
file existence	R	R	R, M	R, M
file owner			R	M
file label	R	R	R	M
file size	R	M	M	M

Because all four operations check for the existence of the file, they reference the attribute. The "R" in each matrix location reflects this. The *create-file* and *delete-file* operations also modify that attribute. This is reflected by the "M." Read and write do not check ownership, but delete and create do; create modifies the owner, and delete references it. The file label is set by *create-file* and referenced by the other operations, and all but *read-file* modify the file size. The *read-file* operation checks the size of the the file to determine if the end of the file will be (or has been) encountered.

The next step is to determine whether any of these shared resources provide covert channels. The following properties must hold for a covert storage channel to exist:

1. Both the sending and receiving processes must have access to the same attribute of a shared object.
2. The sending process must be able to modify that attribute of the shared object.
3. The receiving process must be able to reference that attribute of the shared object.
4. A mechanism for initiating both processes, and properly sequencing their respective accesses to the shared resource, must exist.

Hence, we need to consider only those attributes with both "R" and "M" in their rows.

EXAMPLE: The *High* process is not allowed to communicate directly with the *Low* process. For this example, the sending process is the *High* one and the receiving process is the *Low* one. Consider the *create-file* operation, which both references and modifies the attribute file existence. Both the *High* and *Low* processes have access to the file existence attribute. The *High* process can modify the file existence attribute using *create-file* or *delete-file*. The *Low* process can use *create-file* to reference this attribute regardless of the file label because if the file exists the creation will fail. All that remains is to devise a mechanism for sequencing the accesses to the attribute of the shared resource, the file.

Let two files be named *ready* and *done* and a third be named *1bit*. Both processes begin. The *Low* process creates a file named *ready* at the *High* level. The *High* process references the file existence attribute of this file and sees it exists. If the *High* process is to send a 1, it creates the file *1bit* at the *High* level. The lack of this file will indicate a 0 bit. The process then deletes the *ready* file and creates the file *done* at the *High* level.

The *Low* process periodically tries to create the *done* file at level *High*. When it fails, the file exists. The process then tries to create the file named *1bit* at the *High* level. On success, it records a 0. On failure, it records a 1. The process then deletes the file named *done* and creates *ready* at the *High* level. This continues until the message is sent. This is a covert storage channel.

The requirements for covert timing channels are similar to those for covert storage channels:

1. Both the sending and receiving processes must have access to the same attribute of a shared object.
2. Both the sending and receiving processes must have access to a time reference, such as a real-time clock, a timer, or the ordering of events.
3. The sending process must be able to control the timing of the detection of a change in the attribute by the receiving process.
4. A mechanism for initiating both processes, and properly sequencing their respective accesses to the shared resource, must exist.

As with covert storage channels, we need to consider only those attributes with both "R" and "M" in their rows.

EXAMPLE: The variant of the KVM/370 channel (on page 595) is an example of a timing channel. Both the sender and receiver have access to the same attribute— the ordering of requests by the disk-arm scheduler. Both have access to a time reference—the ordering of the requests. The *High* process can control the ordering of the requests of the *Low* process by the cylinder number of the request that the *High* process issues, so it can control the (relative) timing of the detection of a change in the attribute (ordering) by the *Low* process. Whether this channel can be exploited therefore depends on the initiating and sequencing mechanisms required by requirement 4.

Kemmerer demonstrates the use of the shared resource matrix (SRM) methodology at various stages of the software life cycle ranging from English requirements and formal specifications to implementation code. Its flexibility is one of its strengths.

The SRM methodology was used to analyze the Secure Ada Target [844, 845]. The participants constructed the matrix manually from a flow analysis of the model. From the transitive closure of the elements of the matrix, two potential covert channels were found, one using the assigned level attribute of an object and the other using the assigned type attribute.

The SRM methodology is comprehensive but incomplete. In particular, it does not address the problem of determining what the shared resources are and what the primitives used to access them are. In some ways, this is appropriate, because the techniques used differ at the different steps of the software life cycle. The generality of the SRM method makes it suitable for use throughout the life cycle. However, the absence of detail makes its application sensitive to the analysis of the particular stage of development: specification, design, or implementation. The next approach looks at these issues at the implementation, or source code, level.

18.3.1.3   Information Flow Analysis

The methods of Denning and Denning and of Reitman and Andrews discussed in Sections 17.3.3 and 17.3.4 can uncover covert channels. When an exception occurring depends on the value of a variable, a covert channel exists because information leaks about the value in that variable. Synchronization and inter-process communication primitives also cause problems because one process can control when it sends a message or blocks to receive a message, something the second process can typically detect. This differs from shared variables, which are legitimate channels of information flow. The covert channel occurs because of timing considerations or shared resources (such as a file system).

Tsai, Gligor, and Chandersekaran [1897] have developed a method for identifying covert storage channels in source code. The method asserts that covert (storage) channels arise when processes can view or alter kernel variables. It focuses on identifying variables that processes can refer to directly or that processes can view or alter indirectly (through system calls).

The first step is to identify the kernel functions and processes for analysis. The processes involved are those that function at the highest level of privilege and perform actions on behalf of ordinary users. Processes executing on behalf of administrators are ignored because administrators have sufficient privilege to leak information directly; they do not need to use covert channels. System calls available only to the administrator are ignored for the same reason.

The second step identifies the kernel variables that user processes can read and/or alter. The process must be able to control *how* the variable is altered and be able to detect *that* the variable has been altered. For example, if a system call assigns the fixed value 7 to a particular variable whenever that system call is made, the process cannot control how that variable is altered. Similarly, error conditions affect visibility. If the variable *count* being zero causes an error, the state of *count* can be determined from the setting of the error indicator: if it is set on exit, *count* is 0; otherwise, it is nonzero. The specific criteria are as follows:

1. The value of a variable is obtained from a system call.
2. A calling process can detect at least two different states of that variable.

EXAMPLE: In Figure 18–1, the variable x is visible because it is returned directly to the calling process. The variable y is not directly visible because its value is never returned. However, its state (zero or nonzero) is visible through the value of the variable z.

The detection of such variables requires that the data flow through the kernel be analyzed to ensure that all dependencies (both data and functional) are detected. If the variable is a record or structure, the analysis process must consider changes in its attributes. If the variable is an array of records, changes both in the

```
                                          y := func(abc, def);
                                          if y = 0 then
    x := func(abc, def);                         z := 1;
    if x = 0 then                         else
            x := x + 10;                         z := 0;
    return x;                             return z;
```

Figure 18–1 Visibility of variables. The code fragments represent the body of system calls. The return value is the value returned by the system call. At the left, *x* is visible directly. The value of *y* at the right is not directly visible, but information about its state can be deduced from the returned value.

attributes of each element and in the array as a whole affect the analysis. Finally, the analysis must consider pointers to the variables in question.

The third step is to analyze these shared variables, looking for covert channels. The analysis here is similar to the analysis in the SRM method. The results are given in terms of the primitives that alter or view the shared variables. Primitives associated with variables that can *only* be altered or *only* be viewed are discarded. Complicating this process is the observation that many variables may be associated with a single covert channel, or one variable with many covert channels.

The resulting primitives are then compared with the model of nondiscretionary access control under the assumption that the recipient's security clearance does not dominate the sender's.

An analysis of the Secure Xenix kernel using this method found two kernel variables involved in covert channels. Four classes of generic covert channels were identified, including an *unexploitable* class that could be exploited only when the system failed (one such channel caused a reboot) and a *noiseless* channel that could not be eliminated without discarding the semantics of regular Xenix. The analysts also used the SRM method to analyze the top-level specification of Secure Xenix and noted that it failed to detect several covert channels. (This was expected, because the top-level specifications did not specify the data structures in which the covert channels were found.)

Tsai, Gligor, and Chandersekaran conclude that the shared variables could have been detected by informal code analysis but claim it unlikely that informal analysis would make all the associations of those variables with system calls. Hence, informal analysis would have missed several covert channels that their methodology found.

18.3.1.4   Covert Flow Trees

Porras and Kemmerer have devised an approach to representing security violations that springs from the application of fault trees [1028]. They model the flow of information through shared resources with a tree. The paths of flow are identified in this structure. The analyst determines whether each flow is legitimate or covert.

A covert flow tree is a tree-structured representation of the sequence of operations that move information from one process to another. It consists of five types of nodes:

1. *Goal symbols* specify states that must exist for the information to flow. There are several such states:

    a. A *modification goal* is reached when an attribute is modified.

    b. A *recognition goal* is reached when a modification of an attribute is detected.

    c. A *direct recognition goal* is reached when a subject can detect the modification of an attribute by referencing it directly or calling a function that returns it.

    d. An *inferred recognition goal* is reached when a subject can detect the modification of an attribute without referencing it directly and without calling a function that references the attribute directly. For example, the subject may call a function that performs one of two computations depending on the value of the attribute in question.

    e. An *inferred-via goal* is reached when information is passed from one attribute to other attributes using a specified primitive operation (such as a system call).

    f. A *recognize-new-state goal* is reached when an attribute that was modified when information was passed using it is specified by an inferred-via goal. The value need not be determined, but the fact that the attribute has been modified must be determined.

2. An *operation symbol* is a symbol that represents a primitive operation. The operation symbols may vary among systems if they have different primitive operations.

3. A *failure symbol* indicates that information cannot be sent along the path on which it lies. It means that the goal to which it is attached cannot be met.

4. An *and symbol* is a goal that is reached when both of the following hold for all children:

    a. If the child is a goal, then the goal is reached.

    b. The child is an operation.

5. An *or symbol* is a goal that is reached when either of the following holds for any children:

    a. If the child is a goal, then the goal is reached.

    b. The child is an operation.

Constructing the tree is a three-step process. To make the steps concrete, we present a simple set of operations and then ask if they can create a covert channel.

EXAMPLE: Consider a file system in which each file has three attributes. The boolean attribute *locked* is true when the file is locked, and false otherwise. The second attribute, *inuse*, is a set that contains the process ID of each process that has the file open. The function *read_access*(*p,f*) is true if process *p* has read rights over file *f*, and *empty*(*s*) is true if set *s* has no members. The function *random* returns one of its arguments chosen at random. The following operations are defined:

```
(* lock the file if it is not locked and not opened *)
(* otherwise indicate it is locked by returning false *)
procedure Lockfile(f: file): boolean;
begin
        if not f.locked and empty(f.inuse) then
                f.locked := true;
end;

(* unlock the file *)
procedure Unlockfile(f: file);
begin
        if f.locked then
                f.locked := false;
end;

(* say whether the file is locked *)
function Filelocked(f: file): boolean;
begin
        Filelocked := f.locked;
end;

(* open the file if it isn't locked and the *)
(* process has the right to read the file *)
procedure Openfile(f: file);
begin
        if not f.locked and read_access(process_id, f)
        then
                (* add the process ID to the inuse set *)
                f.inuse = f.inuse + process_id;
end;

(* if the process can read the file, say if the *)
(* file is open, otherwise return a value at random *)
function Fileopened(f: file): boolean;
begin
        if not read_access(process_id, f) then
                Fileopened := random(true, false);
```

```
              else
                    Fileopened := not isempty(f.inuse);
       end
```

Assuming that processes are not allowed to communicate with one another, the reader is invited to try to find a covert storage channel.

The first step in constructing a covert flow tree is to determine what attributes (if any) the primitive operations reference, modify, and return.

EXAMPLE: The functions in the preceding example affect file attributes in different ways, as follows:

	Lockfile	Unlockfile	Filelocked	Openfile	Fileopened
reference	*locked, inuse*	*locked*	*locked*	*locked, inuse*	*inuse*
modify	*locked*	∅	∅	*inuse*	∅
return	∅	∅	*locked*	∅	*inuse*

The symbol ∅ means that no attribute is affected in the specified manner.

The second step begins with the goal of locating a covert storage channel that uses some attribute. The analyst constructs the covert flow tree. The type of goal controls the construction, as follows:

1. The *topmost goal* requires that the attribute be modified and that the modification be recognized. Hence, it has one child (an *and* symbol), which in turn has two children (a modification goal symbol and a recognition goal symbol).

2. A *modification goal* requires some primitive operation to modify the attribute. Hence, it has one *or* child, which has one child operation symbol per operation for all operations that modify the attribute.

3. A *recognition goal* requires that a subject either directly recognize or infer a change in an attribute. It has an *or* symbol as its child. The *or* symbol has two children, one a direct recognition goal symbol and the other an inferred recognition goal symbol.

4. A *direct recognition goal* requires that an operation access the attribute. Like the modification goal, it has one *or* child, and that child in turn has one child operation symbol for each operation that returns the attribute. If no operation returns the attribute, a failure symbol is attached.

5. An *inferred recognition goal* requires that the modification be inferred on the basis of one or more other attributes. Hence, it has one child, an *or* symbol, which has one child inferred-via symbol for each operation that references an attribute and that modifies some attribute (possibly the same one that was referenced).

6. An *inferred-via goal* requires that the value of the attribute be inferred via some operation and a recognition of the new state of the attribute resulting from that operation. Hence, it has one child (an *and* symbol), which has two children (an operation symbol representing the primitive operation used to draw the inference and a recognize-new-state goal symbol).

7. A *recognize-new-state goal* requires that the value of the attribute be inferred via some operation and a recognition of the new state of the attribute resulting from that operation. The latter requires a recognition goal for the attribute. So, the child node of the recognize-new-state goal symbol is an *or* symbol, and for each attribute enabling the inference of the modification of the attribute in question, the *or* symbol has a recognition goal symbol child.

Tree construction ends when all paths through the tree terminate in either an operation symbol or a failure symbol. Because the construction is recursive, the analyst may encounter a loop in the tree construction. Should this happen, a parameter called repeat defines the number of times that the path may be traversed. This places an upper bound on the size of the tree.

EXAMPLE: We build the covert flow tree for the attribute *locked* in our previous two examples. The goal state is "covert storage channel via attribute *locked.*" The *and* node beneath it has two children, "modification of attribute *locked*" and "recognition of attribute *locked.*" At this point, the tree looks like Figure 18–2.

From the table in the preceding example, the operations *Lockfile* and *Unlockfile* modify the attribute *locked.* That branch of the tree is shown in Figure 18–3.

The recognition branch expands into direct recognition and inferred recognition branches. The direct recognition branch has an *and* with one child, *Filelocked*, because *Filelocked* returns the value of the *locked* attribute. The inferred

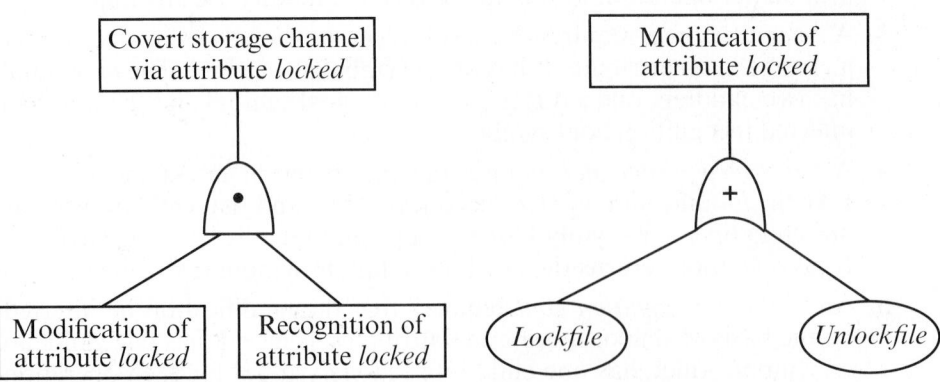

Figure 18–2 First stage of building tree.

Figure 18–3 Second stage of building tree.

recognition branch has an *or* child with one child, an inferred-via node that infers *locked* from *inuse*. This branch comes from comparing the "reference" row of the table in the preceding example with the "modify" row. If an operation references the *locked* attribute and modifies another attribute, inference is possible (assuming that the modification can be detected). Figure 18–4 shows the recognition branch at this point.

Inferring that the attribute *locked* has changed from the attribute *inuse* requires the operation *Openfile*. After that operation, the recognize-new-state goal represents the change in the attribute *inuse*, as shown in Figure 18–5.

This in turn requires the recognition of modification of the attribute *inuse* (hence, a recognition state). The operation *Fileopened* recognizes this change directly; nothing recognizes it indirectly. The result is shown in Figure 18–6.

Figure 18–7 shows the full covert flow tree.

The analyst now constructs two lists. The first list contains sequences of operations that modify the attribute, and the second list contains sequences of operations that recognize modifications in the attribute. A sequence from the first list followed by a sequence from the second list is a channel along which information can flow. The analyst examines these channels to determine which are covert.

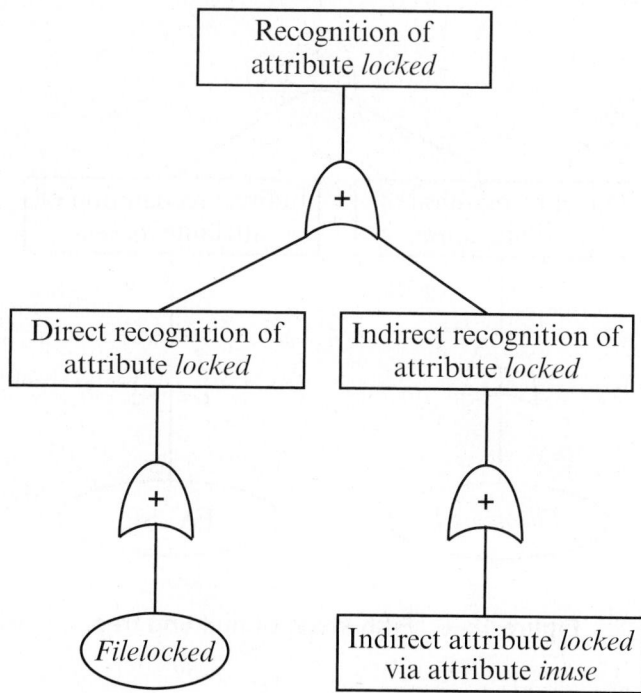

Figure 18–4   Third stage of building tree.

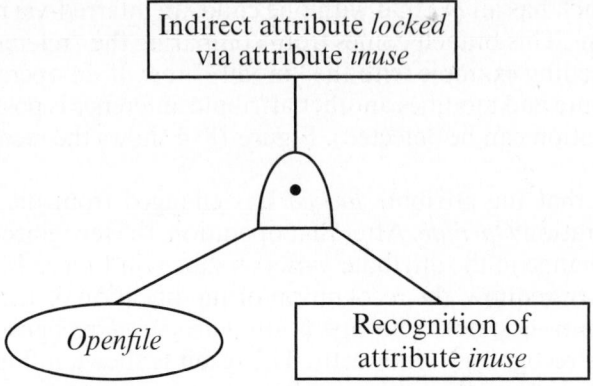

Figure 18–5   Fourth stage of building tree.

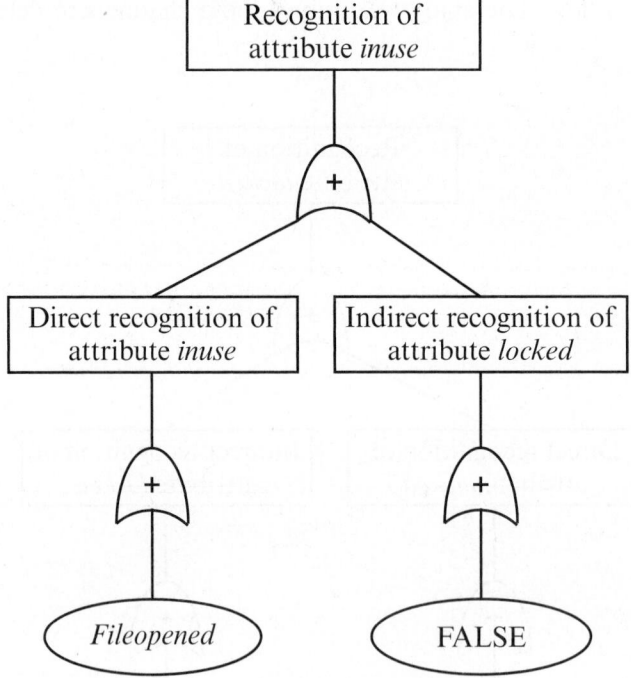

Figure 18–6   Fifth stage of building tree.

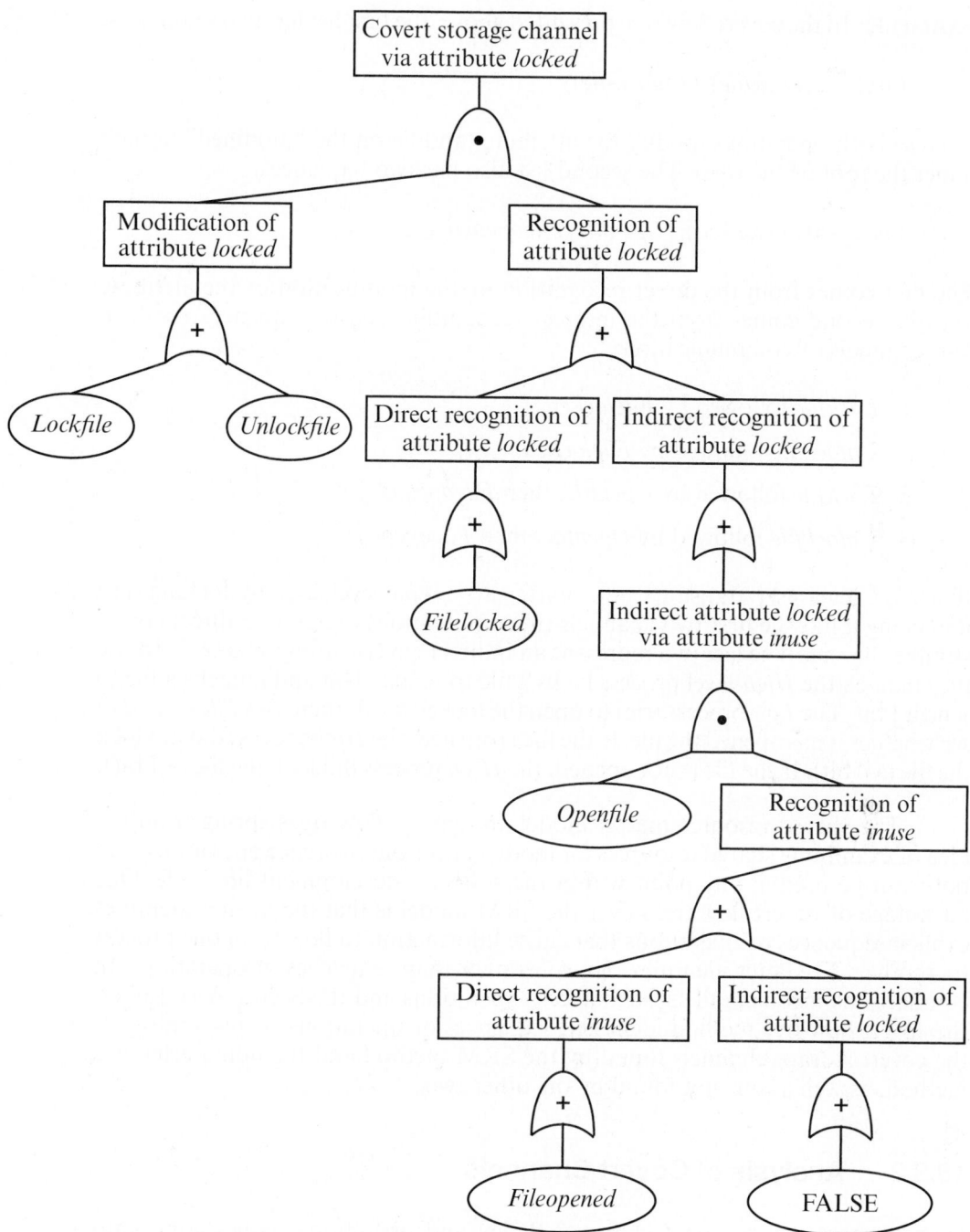

Figure 18–7 The covert flow tree for the operations.

EXAMPLE: In the covert flow tree presented above, the first list has two sequences:

List1 = ((*Lockfile*), (*Unlockfile*))

because both operations modify the attribute (and lie on the "modified" branch under the root of the tree). The second list also has two sequences:

List2 = ((*Filelocked*), (*Openfile, Fileopened*))

The first comes from the direct recognition of the modification of the attribute and the second comes from the indirect recognition. These sequences result in four channels of communication:

1. *Lockfile* followed by *Filelocked*
2. *Unlockfile* followed by *Filelocked*
3. *Lockfile* followed by *Openfile*, then *Fileopened*
4. *Unlockfile* followed by *Openfile*, then *Fileopened*

If a *High*-level user transmits information to a *Low*-level user by locking and unlocking a file, the first two channels (in combination) represent a direct covert storage channel. The last two represent an indirect covert storage channel. To use the channel, the *High*-level process locks a file to send a 0 bit and unlocks a file to send a 1 bit. The *Low* process tries to open the locked file. It then uses *Fileopened* to see whether it has opened the file. If the file is opened, the *High* process did not lock the file (a 0 bit). If the file is not opened, the *High* process did lock the file (a 1 bit).

The shared resource matrix model and covert flow trees spring from the idea of examining shared resources for modification and reference operations, and both can be used at any point within the software development life cycle. One advantage of covert flow trees over the SRM model is that the former identifies explicit sequences of operations that cause information to flow from one process to another. The latter identifies *channels* rather than sequences of operations. In comparisons involving file system access operations and the Secure Ada Target, the covert flow tree method identified sequences of operations corresponding to the covert storage channels found by the SRM method and the noninterference method, as well as one not found by the other two.

18.3.2   Analysis of Covert Channels

How dangerous is a covert channel? Policy and operational issues come into play, and we do not consider those issues here. For our purposes, the security policy in force deems covert channels a serious problem. However, the *amount* of information that can be transmitted over a covert channel affects how serious a problem that channel presents. If the rate were one bit per hour, the channel would be harmless in most circumstances. If the rate were 1,000,000 bits per second, the channel would be dangerous. Following Millen [1337], we examine the problem of measuring this bandwidth.

18.3.2.1   Covert Channel Capacity and Noninterference

We begin by asking when the bandwidth is 0. Suppose Alice wants to send Bob information over a covert channel. Alice feeds her input into a machine that passes the output to Bob. We define the following random variables:

- W represents the inputs to the machine.
- A represents the inputs from Alice.
- V represents the inputs to the machine from users other than Alice.
- B represents all possible outputs to Bob.

Define $I(A ; B)$ as the amount of information transmitted over the covert channel. We are interested in the greatest amount of information that can be transmitted.

Definition 18–9. The *covert channel capacity* is $max_A I(A ; B)$.

This capacity is measured in bits. The rate is then established by dividing the capacity by the number of trials (or the amount of time) required to send the information.

We first establish that noninterference is sufficient to make the capacity of a covert channel 0.

Theorem 18.2. [1337] If A and V are independent and A is noninterfering with B, then $I(A ; B) = 0$.

Proof It suffices to show that the conditions of the theorem mean that A and B are independent—that is, to prove that $p(A = a, B = b) = p(A = a)p(B = b)$. Recall that

$$p(A = a, B = b) = \sum_V p(A = a, B = b, V = v)$$

By Definition 9–4, A being noninterfering with B means that deleting that part of the input making up a will not change the output b. Thus, we need to consider only those values of B that can result from values of V. Hence,

$$p(A = a, B = b) = \sum_V p(A = a, V = v)p(B = b \mid V = v)$$

By independence of A and V, this becomes

$$p(A = a, B = b) = \sum_V p(A = a)p(V = v)p(B = b \mid V = v)$$

Standard manipulations yield

$$p(A = a, B = b) = p(A = a)(\sum_V p(B = b \mid V = v)p(V = v))$$

$$= p(A = a)p(B = b)$$

establishing independence and hence the desired result.

However, noninterference is not necessary [1337]. To see this, consider a system with one bit of state; three inputs I_A, I_B, and I_C; and one output O_X. Each input flips the state, and the value of the state (0 or 1) is output. Let the system initially be in state 0, and let w be the sequence of inputs corresponding to the output $x(w)$. Then the value $x(w)$ depends on the length of the input; $x(w) = length(w) \bmod 2$. Clearly, I_A is not noninterfering with O_X because if the inputs from I_A are deleted, the length of the input sequence is affected and so the value $x(w)$ may also be affected. We consider two cases. In the following discussion, let W represent the random variable corresponding to the length of the input sequences, let A represent the random variable corresponding to the length of the components of the input subsequence contributed by input I_A, let V represent the random variable corresponding to the length of the components of the input sequence not contributed by I_A, and let X represent the random variable corresponding to the output state. Let A and V be independent and consider two distributions of V. Without loss of generality, we restrict A and V to representing single bits.

1. If $V = 0$, because $W = (A + V) \bmod 2$, then $W = A$. So A and W are not independent, and neither are A and X. Hence, if $V = 0$, $I(A \, ; X) \neq 0$.
2. Let inputs I_B and I_C produce inputs such that $p(V = 0) = p(V = 1) = 0.5$. Then

   $$p(X = x) = p(V = x, A = 0) + p(V = 1 - x, A = 1)$$

   Because A and V are independent,

   $$p(X = x) = p(V = x)p(A = 0) + p(V = 1 - x)p(A = 1)$$

   This yields $p(X = x) = 0.5$. Moreover,

   $$p(X = x \mid A = a) = p(X = (a + x) \bmod 2) = 0.5$$

   Hence, A and X are independent, yielding I(A; X) = 0.

This means that even though A and X are not noninterfering, the channel capacity may be 0. In other words, the covert channel capacity will be 0 if either the input is noninterfering with the output or the input sequence is produced from independent sources and all possible values from at least one source are equiprobable. In the latter case, the distribution in effect "hides" the interference.

18.3.2.2 Measuring Covert Channel Capacity

When an attacker uses a covert channel, he modulates the output by providing specific inputs. Suppose that, when no modulation occurs, the uncertainty in the output is eight bits. When modulation occurs, the uncertainty is reduced to five bits. Then the covert channel capacity is three bits, because the input "fixes" those bits. We formalize this idea as follows [1337].

The capacity of the covert channel with inputs A and V, and output X, is the measure of the *certainty* in X given A. In terms of entropy, this means that we maximize

$$I(A;X) = H(X) - H(X \mid A)$$

with respect to A.

EXAMPLE: Return to the example in the preceding section. We assume that A and V are independent. Let $p = p(A = 0)$ and $q = p(V = 0)$. Then

$$p(A = 0, V = 0) = pq \qquad p(A = 1, V = 0) = (1 - p)q$$
$$p(A = 0, V = 1) = p(1 - q) \quad p(A = 1, V = 1) = (1 - p)(1 - q)$$

and $p(X = 0) = pq + (1 - p)(1 - q)$ and $p(X = 1) = (1 - p)q + p(1 - q)$. Also,

$$p(X = 0 \mid A = 0) = q \qquad p(X = 1 \mid A = 0) = 1 - q$$
$$p(X = 0 \mid A = 1) = 1 - q \quad p(X = 1 \mid A = 1) = q$$

This means that

$$
\begin{aligned}
H(X) &= -p(X = 0) \lg p(X = 0) - p(X = 1) \lg p(X = 1) \\
&= -[pq + (1 - p)(1 - q)] \lg [pq + (1 - p)(1 - q)] \\
&\quad -[(1 - p)q + p(1 - q)] \lg [(1 - p)q + p(1 - q)]
\end{aligned}
$$

and

$$
\begin{aligned}
H(X|A) &= \sum_A p(A = a)[\sum_X p(X = x \mid A = a) \lg p(X = x \mid A = a)] \\
&= -p(A = 0)[p(X = 0 \mid A = 0) \lg p(X = 0 \mid A = 0) \\
&\quad +p(X = 1 \mid A = 0) \lg p(X = 1 \mid A = 0)] \\
&\quad -p(A = 1)[p(X = 0 \mid A = 1) \lg p(X = 0 \mid A = 1) \\
&\quad +p(X = 1 \mid A = 1) \lg p(X = 1 \mid A = 1)] \\
&= -p[q \lg q + (1 - q) \lg (1 - q)] - (1 - p)[(1 - q) \lg (1 - q) + q \lg q] \\
&= -q \lg q - (1 - q) \lg (1 - q).
\end{aligned}
$$

So

$$I(A ; X) = -[pq + (1 - p)(1 - q)] \lg [pq + (1 - p)(1 - q)]$$
$$-[(1 - p)q + p(1 - q)] \lg [(1 - p)q + p(1 - q)]$$
$$+q \lg q + (1 - q) \lg (1 - q).$$

This is a maximum when $p = 0.5$. At that value,

$$I(A ; X) = 1 + q \lg q + (1 - q) \lg (1 - q) = 1 - H(V)$$

which agrees with the intuition from the earlier example. In particular, if $q = 0$ (so V is a constant), the capacity of the covert channel is $I(A ; X) = 1$ bit, and if $q = p = 0.5$, the capacity of the covert channel is $I(A ; X) = 0$ bits.

We now examine a model for computing the capacity for a storage channel and a timing channel.

18.3.2.3   Analyzing a Noisy Covert Channel's Capacity

Costich and Moskowitz [462] examined the covert channel created by a multilevel secure database that used replication to ensure data availability. The database used the two-phase commit protocol to ensure atomicity of transactions. One *coordinator* process managed global execution; the other processes were *participants*.

1. The coordinator sends a message to each participant requesting whether to commit or abort the transaction. Each participant replies as it deems appropriate. If a participant replies to abort, it stops its process.
2. The coordinator gathers the replies from the participants. If all replies are to commit, the coordinator sends commit messages back to the participants. If any reply is to abort, the coordinator sends abort messages to the participants. Each participant that has sent a commit waits for the reply from the coordinator, and then acts accordingly.

In the database under discussion, if either the coordinator does not receive a reply from a participant or a participant does not receive a reply from the coordinator, the protocol times out and the parties act as though the transaction has been aborted.

Suppose the replicated database consists of two types of components—one at a *Low* security level and another at a *High* security level. If a *Low* component begins the two-phase commit, both *Low* and *High* components must cooperate in the two-phase commit protocol. A *High* component can transmit information to a *Low* component by selectively aborting transactions (either by sending abort messages or simply by not sending anything, causing a timeout). This is a covert channel.

EXAMPLE: If transactions always succeeded except when a *High* component is sending information, this channel would not be noisy. The capacity of the channel would be one bit (abort/commit) per trial.

This channel is noisy because transactions may abort for reasons other than the sending of information. The analysis must take this into account.

EXAMPLE: Let X be the random variable corresponding to what the *High* user wants to send. Without loss of generality, we treat an aborted transaction as the *High* user sending a 1 and a committed transaction as the *High* user sending a 0. Let A be the random variable corresponding to what the *Low* user receives. (Note that for a noiseless channel, $X = A$.)

Let $p = p(X = 0)$ be the probability that the *High* user sends a 0. We also assume that the n users other than the sender and receiver act independently of one another, and that the probability of a transaction being aborted at any of these users is q. Thus

$$p(A = 0 \mid X = 0) = (1 - q)^n \quad p(A = 1 \mid X = 0) = 1 - (1 - q)^n$$
$$p(A = 0 \mid X = 1) = 0 \quad\quad\quad p(A = 1 \mid X = 1) = 1$$

This yields $p(A = 0) = p(1 - q)^n$ and $p(A = 1) = 1 - p(1 - q)^n$. From this, we have

$$p(X = 0 \mid A = 0) = 1 \quad\quad\quad\quad p(X = 1 \mid A = 0) = 0$$
$$p(X = 0 \mid A = 1) = \frac{p[1 - (1 - q)^n]}{1 - p(1 - q)^n} \quad p(X = 1 \mid A = 1) = \frac{1 - p}{1 - p(1 - q)^n}$$

This means that

$$H(X) = -p(X = 0)\lg p(X = 0) - p(X = 1)\lg p(X = 1)$$
$$-p\lg p - (1 - p)\lg(1 - p)$$

and

$$H(X \mid A) = -\sum_A p(A = a)[\sum_X p(X = x \mid A = a)\lg p(X = x \mid A = a)]$$
$$= -p(A = 0)[p(X = 0 \mid A = 0)\lg p(X = 0 \mid A = 0)$$
$$+p(X = 1 \mid A = 0)\lg p(X = 1 \mid A = 0)]$$
$$-p(A = 1)[p(X = 0 \mid A = 1)\lg p(X = 0 \mid A = 1)$$
$$+p(X = 1 \mid A = 1)\lg p(X = 1 \mid A = 1)]$$
$$= -p(1 - q)^n[0 + 0]$$
$$-p[1 - (1 - q)^n]\lg\{p[1 - (1 - q)^n]/[1 - p(1 - q)^n]\}$$
$$-(1 - p)\lg\{(1 - p)/[1 - p(1 - q)^n]\}$$
$$= -p[1 - (1 - q)^n]\lg p - p[1 - (1 - q)^n]\lg[1 - (1 - q)^n]$$
$$+[1 - p(1 - q)^n]\lg[1 - p(1 - q^)n] - (1 - p)\lg(1 - p)$$

So,

$$I(A \; ; X) = -p(1 - q)^n \lg p + p[1 - (1 - q)^n] \lg [1 - (1 - q)^n]$$
$$-[1 - p(1 - q)^n] \lg [1 - p(1 - q)^n]$$

We maximize this with respect to p to obtain the covert channel capacity. For notational convenience, take $m = (1 - q)^n$ and $M = (1 - m)^{(1-m)}$. Then $I(A \; ; X)$ is a maximum when $p = \frac{M}{Mm+1}$. So the channel capacity is

$$I(A \; ; X) = \frac{Mm \lg p + M(1 - m) \lg(1 - m) + \lg(Mm + 1)}{Mm + 1}$$

18.3.3   Mitigation of Covert Channels

Covert channels convey information by varying the use of shared resources. An obvious way to eliminate all covert channels is to require processes to state what resources they need before execution and provide these resources in such a manner that only the process can access them. This includes runtime, and when the stated runtime is reached, the process is terminated and the resources are released. The resources remain allocated for the full runtime even if the process terminates earlier. Otherwise, a second process could infer information from the timing of the release of the resources (including access to the CPU). This strategy effectively implements Lampson's idea of total isolation, but it is usually unworkable in practice.

   An alternative approach is to obscure the amount of resources that a process uses. A receiving process cannot determine what amount of resource usage is attributable to the sender and what amount is attributable to the obfuscation. This can be done in two ways.

   First, the resources devoted to each process can be made uniform. This is a variant of isolation, because each process gets the same amount of resources and cannot tell whether a second process is accessing the resource by measuring the timing or amount of resources available. In essence, the system eliminates meaningful irregularities in resource allocation and use.

EXAMPLE: The covert channel involving the CPU usage in KVM (see the second example on page 594) can be mitigated by assigning each virtual machine a time slice of fixed magnitude and not allowing any virtual machine to surrender the CPU until the end of the slice. No virtual machine can shorten its time slice by relinquishing the CPU early, thereby sending a "0" or a "1." This closes the timing channel.

   Second, a system can inject randomness into the allocation and use of resources. The goal is to make the covert channel a noisy one and to have the noise dominate the channel. This does not close the covert channel (because it still exists) but renders it useless.

EXAMPLE: Return to the noisy covert channel in the multilevel secure database discussed in Section 18.3.2.3. If the probability of a transaction being aborted by a participant that is neither the sender nor the receiver approaches 1, then the channel capacity approaches 0. Hence, increasing the probability of such an abort decreases the calculated bandwidth of the channel. One suggestion [462] is to resolve conflicts by aborting; this increases the probability of aborts from participants that are neither senders nor receivers. A second idea is to cause participants to abort transactions randomly.

Both these techniques affect efficiency. Assigning fixed allocations and constraining use waste resources. Fixing the time slices on the KVM system means that the CPU will be unused (or will execute an idle process) when another virtual machine could run a nonidle process. Increasing the probability of aborts in the multilevel secure database system will abort some transactions that would normally commit, increasing the expected number of tries to update the database. Whether the closing of the covert channel or the limiting of the bandwidth compensates adequately for the loss in efficiency is a policy decision.

EXAMPLE: Hu [931] describes an interesting approach to limiting covert timing channels on the VAX virtualizing security kernel. "Fuzzy time" reduces the accuracy of system clocks by using the programmable system clock to generate random clock ticks. The random interrupts can take any desired distribution. For example, virtual machines receive timer interrupts with a uniform distribution and a mean of 20 milliseconds, rather than every 10 milliseconds (as the native timer would create). The system clock is updated only after each timer interrupt, and the kernel rounds the time to the nearest tenth of a second before supplying it to the virtual machine (so it cannot be any more accurate than that of the interrupts). I/O operations have delays added randomly. The kernel distinguishes between event time (when the I/O event occurs) and notification time (when the virtual machine is told that the I/O operation has occurred). The random delay between these two times prevents the virtual machine from determining exactly when an event occurred. The random length of the interval can be distributed as desired. In the security kernel, the interval is between 1 and 19 milliseconds. The "fuzz" added to the timings adds noise to the covert timing channel, thereby making it more difficult to exploit. Trostle [1893] improved on this technique by modifying the scheduler to run processes in increasing order of security level and by observing that countermeasures are needed only when a transition from a dominating virtual machine to a dominated virtual machine occurs. He also suggested adding random intervals between quanta at these transitions.

A device known as a *pump* is the basis of several techniques for defeating covert channels.

EXAMPLE: The pump [999] is a (hardware or software) tool for controlling a communication path between a *High* process and a *Low* process. It consists of a buffer for messages to and from the *High* process, a buffer for messages to and from the *Low* process, and a communications buffer of length n that is connected to both of the other buffers (see Figure 18–8). We assume that messages are numbered and that the communications buffer preserves messages if the pump crashes. Under these assumptions, the processes can recover (so that either the messages in the pump are delivered or the sender detects that they are lost and resends the messages; see Exercise 10).

A covert timing channel occurs when the *High* process can control the rate at which the pump passes messages to it. The *Low* process fills the communications buffer by sending messages to the pump until it fails to receive an acknowledgment. At that point, the *High* and *Low* processes begin their trials. At the beginning of each trial, if the *High* process wants to send a 1, it allows the pump to send it one of the queued messages. If the *High* process wants to send a 0, it does not accept any messages from the pump. If the *Low* process receives an acknowledgment, it means that a message has moved from the *Low* buffer to the communications buffer. This can happen only if a space in the communications buffer opens. This occurs when the *High* process reads a message. Hence, if the *Low* process gets an acknowledgment, the *High* process is signaling a 1. By a similar argument, if the *Low* process does not get an acknowledgment, the *High* process is signaling a 0. Following the trial, if the *Low* process has received an acknowledgment, it must send another message to the pump to enter the state required for the next trial.

In what follows, we assume that the *Low* process and the pump can process messages more quickly than the *High* process. Let L_i be the random variable

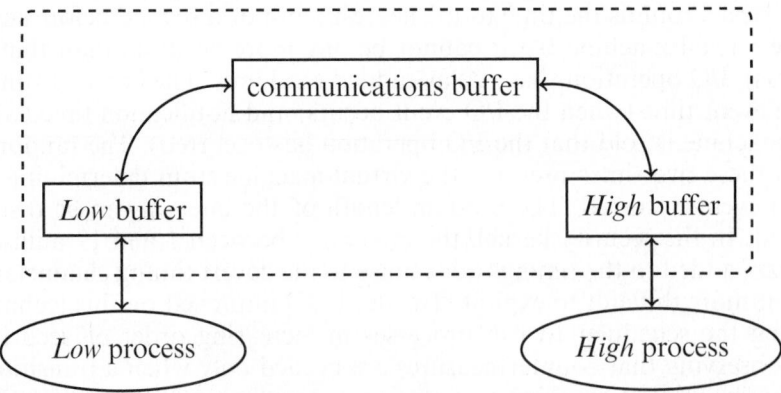

Figure 18–8 **The pump. Messages going between the High and Low processes enter the pump (represented by the dashed rectangle). The pump controls the rate at which the messages flow between the two processes. The pump acknowledges each message as it is moved from the process buffer to the communications buffer.**

corresponding to the time from the *Low* process sending a message to the pump to the *Low* process receiving an acknowledgment. Let H_i be the random variable corresponding to the average time required for the *High* process to acknowledge each of the last n messages. Three cases arise.

1. $E(L_i) > H_i$. This means that the *High* process can process messages in less time than it takes for the *Low* process to get the acknowledgment. Because this contradicts our assumption above, the pump must be artificially delaying acknowledgments. This means that the *Low* process will wait for an acknowledgment regardless of whether the communications buffer is full or not. Although this closes the covert timing channel, it is not optimal because the processes may wait even when they do not need to.

2. $E(L_i) < H_i$. This means that the *Low* process is sending messages into the pump faster than the *High* process can remove them. Although it maximizes performance, it opens the covert channel.

3. $E(L_i) = H_i$. This means that the pump and the processes handle messages at the same rate. It balances security and performance by decreasing the bandwidth of the covert channel (with respect to time) and increases performance. The covert channel is open, however, and performance is not optimal.

Kang and Moskowitz [999] showed that adding noise to the channel in such a way as to approximate the third case reduced the covert channel capacity to at most $1/nr$, where r is the time between the *Low* process sending a message to the pump and its receiving an acknowledgment when the communications buffer is not full. They concluded that the pump substantially reduces the capacity of covert channels between *High* and *Low* processes when compared with direct connection of those processes.

18.4 Summary

The confinement problem is the problem of preventing a process from illicitly leaking information. Its solutions lie in some form of separation or isolation. Virtual machines provide a basis for these mechanisms, as do less restrictive sandbox environments. Virtual machines and sandboxes limit the transfer of information by controlling expected paths used to send (or receive) data.

However, shared resources provide unexpected paths for transmission of information. Detecting and analyzing these covert channels require deduction of the common resources, which processes can manipulate (alter) the resources, which processes can access (read) the resources, and how much information per trial the channel can transmit. Several methods, among them a matrix methodology and tree analysis methodology, provide systematic ways to analyze systems for such channels.

Information flow and noninterference techniques focus on how information moves about the system. Information flow considers exceptions resulting from flows that are disallowed. The exception itself leads to a covert channel. Noninterference techniques work similarly and also provide a basis for measuring channel capacity. Statistical techniques are useful also.

Covert channels are difficult to eliminate. Countermeasures focus on making the channel less useful by decreasing its capacity, usually through the addition of randomness to obscure the regularity that sending and receiving requires.

18.5   Research Issues

Research into the confinement problem and its solutions includes research into malicious logic as well as covert channels.

Policy determines what information is to be confined. Policy representation is critical to a correct implementation of these requirements. So is a mechanism for translating these representations into effective, reliable security mechanisms. This is a fruitful area for research not only because of the technical issues, such as power of expression and constraint representation, but also because of the human interface issues.

Balancing security and functionality raises issues of controlling the channels through which systems communicate, as well as shared channels. A sandbox isolates some aspects of processes while providing access to system resources. Preventing other information from leaking requires development of precise mechanisms and is also an area of active research, particularly in mobile code. Sandboxes often reduce the performance and efficiency of processes. Minimizing this impact makes such security constraints more acceptable.

Covert channel research focuses on detection, measurement, and mitigation. Techniques for detecting covert channels require effort by a human analyst. Simplifying and reducing the effort required would aid the discovery of these channels. Techniques for discovering these channels at all levels of the software life cycle are varied. Current techniques for detecting the exploiting of covert channels are typically statistical.

The balance between minimizing the bandwidths of covert channels (or closing them entirely) and providing acceptable performance is delicate. Techniques for optimizing both simultaneously are primitive and rarely yield mechanisms that provide optimality. This is another active research area.

18.6   Further Reading

Confinement mechanisms are used to limit the actions of downloaded or untrusted programs [468, 555, 953, 1238, 1517, 1886, 2050]. McLean [1300] raises questions about the effectiveness of sandboxes, pointing out the complexity of hardening them against escape. The risks that Java applet and application containers pose depends in part upon their implementation and the environment in which the program is to execute [523, 897]. In addition to Xen, many hypervisors, such as VMware [587, 1454] and Virtual Box [1476, 1980], have been developed. Rosenblum and Garfinkel [1609] provide an overview of the different types of virtual machines, and Pearce, Zeadally, and Hunt [1503] discuss security issues specific to virtual machines. Agarwal, Jain, and Porter [20] compare virtual machines and containers. Techniques that detect that programs are being run in a virtual machine have been developed [673, 716], as have various countermeasures [350, 1841].

A number of sandboxing mechanisms have different emphases on desired attributes such as performance, complexity, and special environments, and all aim to isolate processes for protection [697, 907, 962, 1055, 1173]. Garfinkel [748] and Watson [1979] discuss some issues with intercepting system calls for sandboxing. Madhavapeddy and Scott [1232] present a detailed overview of library operating systems.

Millen [1335] provides a retrospective of covert channel research, including an amusing view of the disk-arm covert channel. Gold, Linde, and Cudney [783] review the successes and failures of KVM/370. Karger and Wray [1009] discuss covert storage channels in disk accesses. Hu [930] and Völp, Hamann, and Härtig [1944] discuss countermeasures against covert channels arising from process scheduling. Biswas, Ghosal, and Nagarja [236] present a survey of timing channels. Covert channels that use the L2 cache [2039], interrupts [1247], network traffic [333, 1719, 1996, 2077], shared hardware-based random number generators [646], and the cloud [1168] have also been studied, both in their detection and the detection of their exploitation.

Several studies describe the relationship between noise and the capacity of covert channels [1255, 1383, 1384, 1386, 1974, 2025, 2104]. Gray [816] suggests alternating between secure and nonsecure modes to limit bandwidth. Tsai and Gligor [1896] examine a Markov model for bandwidth computation in covert storage channels. Browne [305] examines state transitions to place upper bounds on covert channels. Meadows [1305] discusses covert channels in integrity lock architectures, in which a trusted component mediates access to databases. Venkatraman and Newman-Wolfe [1928] examine the capacity of a covert channel on a network. The "light pink book" [2164] looks at covert channels in the context of government security requirements.

Carrara and Adams [352] examine covert channels the exploitation of which has a low probability of being detected. Gianvecchio, Wang, Wijesekera, and Jajodia [765] and Kothari and Wright [1097] discuss approaches to evading detection of the use of a covert timing channel. Archibald and Ghosal [70] compare statistical techniques for identifying the use of covert channels.

Variations of the pump extend its concept to other arenas, including the network [800, 801, 1000–1002] and a nozzle for limiting the effectiveness of denial of service attacks [1838].

18.7   Exercises

1. Implement the transmission protocol in the example that follows Definition 18–2. Measure how much information is sent over a 10-minute period.

2. Two UNIX processes wish to communicate but cannot use standard IPC mechanisms. However, both can run *ps*(1) as a subprocess.

   a. Devise a protocol whereby the two processes can communicate using their environment lists.

   b. Implement the protocol. Measure the (actual) rate of transmission.

3. Consider the rule of transitive confinement. Suppose a process needs to execute a subprocess in such a way that the child can access exactly two files, one only for reading and one only for writing.

   a. Could capabilities be used to implement this? If so, how?

   b. Could access control lists implement this? If so, how?

4. A company wishes to market a secure version of the Swiss Cheese Operating System (SCOS), known as much for its advanced user and database management features as for its security vulnerabilities. The company plans to build a virtual machine to run SCOS and run that virtual machine on a second system, the Somewhat Secure Operating System (SSOS). The marketing literature claims that the VM running SCOS provides total isolation, thereby eliminating any potential security problems.

   a. Does this arrangement provide total isolation? If your answer is "no," discuss what features the VM would need to include to provide total isolation or show why this arrangement cannot provide total isolation.

   b. The literature states that "the VM mediates all accesses to real system resources, providing an impenetrable barrier to any attacker trying to break out of the SCOS and attack other copies of SCOS running on the SSOS." Do you agree or disagree with this statement? Why? (If you would need more information in order to make a decision, state what information you would need and why.)

5. In the Janus system, when the framework disallows a system call, the error code **EINTR** (interrupted system call) is returned.

   a. When some programs have read or write system calls terminated with this error, they retry the calls. What problems might this create?

   b. Why did the developers of Janus not devise a new error code (say, **EJAN**) to indicate an unauthorized system call?

6. A developer produces a program and VCGen generates the verification conditions from it. A user downloads the program, knowing it will be validated after

downloading. If the validation succeeds, the user will execute the downloaded program. However, an adversary wants to trick the user into executing a malicious program. So she intercepts and alters the downloading program without altering the predicates.

   a. Will the theorem prover validate the altered program?

   b. How could this attack be detected and thwarted?

7. The following system call adds read permission for a process (*for_pid*) if the caller (*call_pid*) owns the file, and does nothing otherwise. (The operating system supplies *call_pid*; the caller supplies the two latter parameters.)

```
function addread(call_pid, for_pid: process_id;
                             fid: file_id): integer;
begin
        if (call_pid = filelist[fid].owner) then
                addright(filelist[fid].
                access_control_list, for_pid, "r");
        addread := (call_pid = filelist[fid].owner);
end.
```

   a. Is the variable *addread* directly or indirectly visible, or not visible?

   b. Is the variable *filelist[fid].owner* directly or indirectly visible, or not visible?

   c. Is the variable *filelist[fid].access_control_list* directly or indirectly visible, or not visible?

8. In the covert flow tree technique, it is possible for some part of the tree to enter a loop in which recognition of attribute *a* depends on recognition of attribute *b*, which in turn is possible when attribute *a* is recognized.

   a. Give a specific example of such a loop.

   b. Should such a loop occur, the covert flow tree path is labeled with a repeat parameter that dictates the maximum number of times that branch may be traversed. Discuss the advantages and drawbacks of this solution.

9. Section 18.3.2.3 derives a formula for $I(A;X)$. Prove that this formula is a maximum with respect to p when $p = \dfrac{M}{Mm+1}$, with M and m as defined in that section.

10. Prove that if the pump crashes, either every message in the pump has been delivered or the sender detects that a message has been lost and resends it.

Part VI

Assurance

Contributed by Elisabeth Sullivan and Michelle Ruppel[1]

S ecurity policies are assumed to be internally consistent and to reflect the requirements of the organization to which they apply. Similarly, security mechanisms are assumed to work correctly and to perform the functions for which they are intended. These critical aspects of trustworthiness are commonly glossed over because they are difficult to quantify or analyze. However, they speak directly to the assumptions on which all security policies and mechanisms rest. Part VI explores the concepts and methodologies of assurance and describes the options available for receiving an evaluation of the level of trust that the assurance can provide in the system.

Chapter 19, "Introduction to Assurance," explores and motivates the concept of security assurance, provides fundamental definitions, and presents an overview of current assurance techniques.

Chapter 20, "Building Systems with Assurance," identifies what must be done differently to create a system that is built specifically for security by addressing life cycle issues of assurance.

Chapter 21, "Formal Methods," provides a look at the formal techniques used today to ensure the correctness of programs and designs. These techniques include specification, proof-based verification, model checking, and protocol verification.

---

[1]These chapters were written by Elisabeth C. Sullivan and Michelle Ruppel. Ms. Sullivan and Ms. Ruppel have granted permission for this material to be used in *Computer Security: Art and Science*. Any use of this material outside the scope of this text must have the permission of Ms. Sullivan and Ms. Ruppel.

Chapter 22, "Evaluating Systems," investigates the formal evaluation and certification techniques that are available today. The specific evaluation techniques and assignment of trust used in these methodologies are highlighted.

Chapter 19
Introduction to Assurance

> BOTTOM: Not a whit: I have a device to make all
> well. Write me a prologue; and let the prologue
> seem to say, we will do no harm with our swords,
> and that Pyramus is not killed indeed; and,
> for the more better assurance, tell them that I,
> Pyramus, am not Pyramus, but Bottom the
> weaver: this will put them out of fear.
> — *A Midsummer Night's Dream*, III, i, 17–23.

This chapter introduces the concepts of security assurance and trusted systems. Assurance for secure and trusted systems must be an integral part of the development process. The following chapters elaborate on the concepts and ideas introduced here.

19.1   Assurance and Trust

In previous chapters we have used the terms *trusted system* and *secure system* without defining them precisely. When looked on as an absolute, creating a secure system is an ultimate, albeit unachievable, goal. As soon as we have figured out how to address one type of attack on a system, other types of attacks occur. In reality, we cannot yet build systems that are guaranteed to be secure or to remain secure over time. However, vendors frequently use the term "secure" in product names and product literature to refer to products and systems that have "some" security included in their design and implementation. The amount of security provided can vary from a few mechanisms to specific, well-defined security requirements and well-implemented security mechanisms to meet those requirements. However, providing security requirements and functionality may not be sufficient to engender trust in the system.

Intuitively, *trust* is a belief or desire that a computer entity will do what it should to protect resources and be safe from attack. However, in the realm of computer security, trust has a very specific meaning. We will define trust in terms of a related concept.

> **Definition 19–1.** An entity is *trustworthy* if there is sufficient credible evidence leading one to believe that the system will meet a set of given requirements. *Trust* is a measure of trustworthiness, relying on the evidence provided.

These definitions emphasize that calling something "trusted" or "trustworthy" does not make it so. Trust and trustworthiness in computer systems must be backed by concrete evidence that the system meets its requirements, and any literature using these terms needs to be read with this qualification in mind. To determine trustworthiness, we focus on methodologies and metrics that allow us to measure the degree of confidence that we can place in the entity under consideration. The term *assurance* captures this notion. Assurance is the basis for trust. Essentially, trust depends upon assurance.

> **Definition 19–2.** *Security assurance*, or simply *assurance*, is confidence that an entity meets its security requirements, based on specific evidence provided by the application of assurance techniques.

Examples of assurance techniques include the use of a development methodology, formal methods for design analysis, and testing. Evidence specific to a particular technique may be simplistic or may be complex and fine-grained. For example, evidence that measures a development methodology may be a brief description of the methodology to be followed. Alternatively, development processes may be measured against standards under a technique such as the System Security Engineering Capability Maturity Model (SSE-CMM; see Section 22.9).

Assurance techniques can be categorized as informal, semiformal, or formal. Informal methods use natural languages for specifications and justifications of claims. They impose a minimum of rigor on the processes used. Semiformal methods also use natural languages for specifications and justifications but apply a specific overall method that imposes some rigor on the process. Often these methods mimic formal methods. Formal methods use mathematics and other machine-parsable languages with tools and rigorous techniques such as formal mathematical proofs.

Security assurance is acquired by applying a variety of assurance techniques that provide justification and evidence that the mechanism, as implemented and operated, meets the security requirements described in the security policy for the mechanism (or collection of mechanisms). Figure 19–1 illustrates this process.

A related term, *information assurance*, refers to the ability to access information and preserve the quality and security of that information [595]. It differs from security assurance, because the focus is on the threats to information and the mechanisms used to protect information and not on the correctness, consistency, or completeness of the requirements and implementation of those mechanisms.

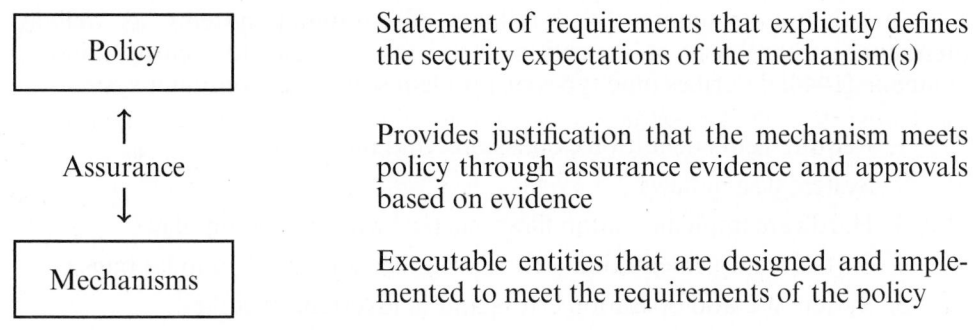

Policy	Statement of requirements that explicitly defines the security expectations of the mechanism(s)
↑ **Assurance** ↓	Provides justification that the mechanism meets policy through assurance evidence and approvals based on evidence
Mechanisms	Executable entities that are designed and implemented to meet the requirements of the policy

Figure 19–1   Assurance, policy, and mechanisms.

However, we use the word "assurance" to mean "security assurance" unless explicitly stated otherwise.

We are now in a position to define a trusted system.

> **Definition 19–3.** A *trusted system* is a system that has been shown to meet well-defined requirements under an evaluation by a credible body of experts who are certified to assign trust ratings or assurance levels to evaluated products and systems.

Specific methodologies aggregate evidence of assurance, and results are interpreted to assign levels of trustworthiness. The Trusted Computer System Evaluation Criteria [2239] and the Information Technology Security Evaluation Criteria [2177] are two standards that have been replaced by the Common Criteria (CC) [2129–2131]. These methodologies provide increasing "levels of trust," each level having more stringent assurance requirements than the previous one. When experts evaluate and review the evidence of assurance, they provide a check that the evidence amassed by the vendor is credible to disinterested parties and that the evidence supports the claims of the security requirements. Certification by these experts signifies that they accept the evidence.

19.1.1   The Need for Assurance

Applying assurance techniques is time-consuming and expensive. Operating systems, critical applications, and computer systems are often marketed as "secure," whereas in reality they have serious flaws that undermine their security features, or they are used in environments other than those for which their security features were developed. The marketing creates a false sense of well-being, which in turn encourages the users, system administrators, and organizations to act as though their systems were protected. So they fail to develop the defenses needed to protect critical information.

Accidental or unintentional failures of computer systems, as well as intentional compromises of security mechanisms, can lead to security failures. Neumann [1444] describes nine types of problem sources in computer systems.

1. Requirements definitions, omissions, and mistakes
2. System design flaws
3. Hardware implementation flaws, such as wiring and chip flaws
4. Software implementation errors, program bugs, and compiler bugs
5. System use and operation errors and inadvertent mistakes
6. Willful system misuse
7. Hardware, communication, or other equipment malfunction
8. Environmental problems, natural causes, and acts of God
9. Evolution, maintenance, faulty upgrades, and decommissions

Assurance addresses each of these problem sources (except for natural causes and acts of God). Design assurance techniques applied to requirements address items 1, 2, and 6. A specification of requirements must be rigorously analyzed, reviewed, and verified to address completeness, consistency, and correctness. If the security requirements are faulty, the definition of security for that system is faulty, so the system cannot be "secure." Proper identification of threats and appropriate selection of countermeasures reduce the ability to misuse the system. Design assurance techniques can detect security design flaws, allowing their correction prior to costly development and deployment of flawed systems.

Implementation assurance deals with hardware and software implementation errors (items 3, 4, and 7), errors in maintenance and upgrades (item 9), willful misuse (item 6), and environmentally induced problems (item 8). Thorough security testing as well as detailed and significant vulnerabilities assessment find flaws that can be corrected prior to deployment of the system.

Operational assurance can address system use and operational errors (item 5) as well as some willful misuse issues (item 6).

Neumann's list is not exclusive to security problems. It also addresses risks to safety, reliability, and privacy.

EXAMPLE: [1444] The space shuttle Challenger exploded on January 28, 1986, killing everyone on board. An essential failure was a decision to take shortcuts to meet an accelerated launch schedule. Among other steps, several sensors were removed from the booster rockets. The sensors might have enabled analysts to detect that the cold weather was affecting the booster rockets adversely and to delay the launch. Better assurance techniques might have detected the possible effects of removing the sensors, as well as other problems in the design of the booster rockets.

EXAMPLE: [1444] Three patients died from a radiation overdose attributed to a Therac 25 computer-based electron accelerator radiation therapy system. The flaws in the system resulted from two flaws in the design of the system's software and the removal of a hardware safety interlock. Assurance techniques would have detected the flaws in the software's design, and ongoing assurance techniques would have detected the removal of the interlock.

EXAMPLE: [1444] Although the most significant root cause of the Three Mile Island nuclear failure was a hardware problem (nonstandard instruments were used to measure core temperature), design and software problems contributed significantly. When the temperature rose very high, the system printed a string of question marks rather than the measured temperature. In addition, the intended, rather than the actual, valve settings were displayed. Assurance techniques would have detected these software flaws.

Sometimes safety and security measures can backfire. Assurance techniques highlight the consequences of these errors.

EXAMPLE: [1444] The Bell V22 Osprey is a high-technology helicopter. After a fifth Osprey had crashed, an analysis traced the cause to a failure to correct for malfunctioning components. The Osprey implemented a majority-voting algorithm, and the cross-wiring of two roll-rate sensors allowed two faulty components to outvote the third, correctly functioning, component. Although assurance techniques might not have prevented the incorrect voting, they would have emphasized the results that could have occurred if faulty components overrode the correctly functioning components.

Other failures have had less serious consequences. When bugs were found in the trigonometric functions of the Intel 486 chip, Intel's public reputation was damaged, and replacing the chips cost Intel time and money. As a result, Intel began using high-assurance methods to verify the correctness of requirements in their chip design [1545].

19.1.2   The Role of Requirements in Assurance

Although security policies define security for a particular system, the policies themselves are created to meet needs. These needs are the requirements.

Definition 19–4. A *requirement* is a statement of goals that must be satisfied.

A statement of goals can vary from generic, high-level goals to concrete, detailed design considerations. The term *security objectives* refers to the high-level security issues and business goals, and the term *security requirements* refers to the specific and concrete issues.

A brief review of definitions will prove helpful. Definition 4–1 states that a *security policy* is a statement that partitions the states of the system into a set of authorized or secure states and a set of unauthorized, or nonsecure, states. Equivalently, we can consider a security policy to be a set of specific statements that, when enforced, result in a secure system. The individual statements are the security requirements for the entity and describe what behavior must take place (or not take place) in order to define the authorized states of the system. Typically, requirements do not contain implementation details, which are the realm of the implementing *mechanism* (see Definition 4–7). On the other hand, a *security model* describes a family of policies, systems, or entities (see Definition 4–8) and is more abstract than a policy, which is specific to a particular entity or set of entities.

EXAMPLE: Suppose a high-level security goal for an entity is to ensure the confidentiality of certain data that the entity must process. A set of individual security requirements that specify an access control mechanism to restrict access to the information would address this objective. Individual requirements might describe the access control policy, the rules it implements, the security attributes associated with the data, and other specific issues. Another group of requirements that could address this objective might require encryption of the information when it is in transit from one part of the entity to another.

Selecting the right security requirements for a computer entity requires an understanding of the intended use of that entity as well as of the environment in which it must function. One can then examine policy models to determine if any are appropriate. Part III, "Policy," describes several types of policies and models that have been used in the past. These models have been subjected to significant analysis and peer review, and most have had corrections during their life spans. This process of acceptance is like the acceptance of mathematical proofs over the centuries. Typically, mathematicians study a mathematical proof to find its flaws and weaknesses. Some proofs have survived this test of time, and others have not.

19.1.3 Assurance throughout the Life Cycle

The goal of assurance is to show that an implemented and operational system meets its security requirements throughout its life cycle. Because of the difference in the levels of abstraction between high-level security requirements and low-level implementation details, the demonstration is usually done in stages. Different assurance techniques apply to different stages of system development. For this reason, it is convenient to classify assurance into policy assurance, design assurance, implementation assurance, and operational or administrative assurance.

> **Definition 19–5.** *Policy assurance* is the evidence establishing that the set of security requirements in the policy is complete, consistent, and technically sound.

Policy assurance is based on a rigorous evaluation of the requirements. Completeness and consistency are demonstrated by identifying security threats and objectives and by showing that the requirements are sufficient to counter the threats or meet the requirements. If a security policy model is used, the justifications in the model can support the technical soundness of the requirements.

Once the proper requirements have been defined, justified, and approved for the system, the design and development process can begin with confidence. The developers create the system design to implement the security requirements and provide assurance evidence that the design meets the security requirements. The next step is to show that the system implements the design correctly. The design and development approach is illustrated in Figure 19–2. As that figure shows, following every design and implementation refinement step is an assurance justification step that shows that the requirements continue to be met at successive levels of development of the trusted system.

This process is usually iterative, because assurance steps identify flaws that must be corrected. When this happens, the affected steps must be rechecked.

EXAMPLE: If assurance step 4 indicates a flaw in the implementation, the implementation will have to be adjusted and the affected parts of step 4 redone. If this flaw in the implementation in turn indicates a flaw in the design, the design must be adjusted, causing steps 1, 2, 3, and 4 to be revisited. On rare occasions, a flaw in the implementation or design may point to a flaw in the requirements.

Assurance must continue throughout the life of the system. Because maintenance and patching usually affect the system design and implementation, the assurance requirements are similar to those described above.

Definition 19–6. *Design assurance* is the evidence establishing that a design is sufficient to meet the requirements of the security policy.

Design assurance includes the use of good security engineering practices to create an appropriate security design to implement the security requirements. It also includes an assessment of how well the system design meets the security requirements.

Design assessment techniques use a policy or model of the security requirements for the system as well as a description or specification of the system design.

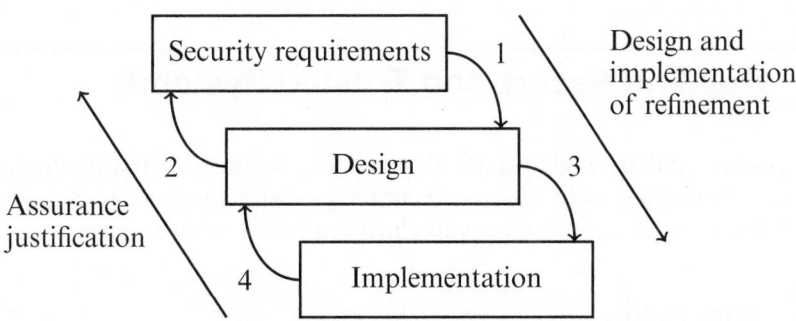

Figure 19–2 Development of a trusted system. There may be multiple levels of design and implementation. Note that the refinement steps alternate with the assurance steps.

Claims are made about the correctness of the design with respect to security requirements. The design assurance techniques provide a justification or proof of such claims.

> **Definition 19–7.** *Implementation assurance* is the evidence establishing that the implementation is consistent with the security requirements of the security policy.

In practice, implementation assurance shows that the implementation is consistent with the design, which design assurance showed was consistent with the security requirements found in the security policy. Implementation assurance includes the use of good security engineering practices to implement the design correctly, both during development and through the maintenance and repair cycles. It also includes an assessment of how well the system as implemented meets its security requirements through testing and proof of correctness techniques, as well as vulnerability assessment.

Design assurance and implementation assurance verify that the security policy requirements are properly designed and built into the system. However, computer systems and applications must be delivered, installed, and operated as assumed during design and implementation. Typically, the vendor provides procedures and processes in the form of supporting automated tools and documentation. The customer is responsible for ensuring their correct use.

> **Definition 19–8.** *Operational* or *administrative assurance* is the evidence establishing that the system sustains the security policy requirements during installation, configuration, and day-to-day operation.

One fundamental operational assurance technique is a thorough review of product or system documentation and procedures, to ensure that the system cannot accidentally be placed into a nonsecure state. This emphasizes the importance of proper and complete documentation for computer applications, systems, and other entities.

19.2   Building Secure and Trusted Systems

Building secure and trusted systems depends on standard software engineering techniques augmented with specific technologies and methodologies. Hence, a review of the life cycles of systems will clarify much of what follows.

19.2.1   Life Cycle

The concept of a *life cycle* addresses security-relevant decisions that often are made outside the engineering disciplines in business situations. There is more to building a product or system than just the engineering steps. Security goals may impact both the life cycle and the engineering process used. Such processes establish both discipline and control and provide confidence in the consistency and quality of the resulting system. Assurance requires a life cycle model and engineering process in every situation, although the size and complexity of the project, the project team, and the organization guide selection of the appropriate model and process. In a small operation, where individuals play multiple roles, an informal structure of the life cycle process may work best. In a larger company with complex roles, distributed development environments, and interactions among several projects and project team members, a more rigorous and formal process might be more appropriate.

A life cycle starts when a system is considered for development and use. The life cycle ends when the system is no longer used. A life cycle includes a set of processes that define how to perform activities, as well as methods for managing activities. Examples of such activities are writing of marketing literature, sales training, and design and development of code. Management activities include planning, configuration management, and selection and use of standards. Both types of activities follow the system from its initial conception through the decision to create the system, the steps required to develop, sell, and deploy the system, the maintenance of the system, and the decommissioning and retirement of the system.

A typical life cycle process is defined in stages. Some stages depend on previous stages, whereas others do not. Each stage describes activities of all the involved disciplines and controls interdisciplinary interactions. As work progresses, the project ideally transitions from one stage to the next. In practice, there is often some iteration of the stages—for example, when a more advanced stage uncovers flaws or omissions in the work of the previous stage.

Consider a very general life cycle "metamodel" to illustrate these concepts. This model captures the fundamental areas of system life for any type of project, although the focus is on software engineering projects. An actual, functioning life cycle process may be more detailed, but this metamodel addresses the needs of any business application. It incorporates the four stages of conception, manufacture, deployment, and fielded product life. Engineering processes tend to focus on manufacture and, to a lesser degree, on fielded product life, although engineering function responsibilities may exceed this typical view.

19.2.1.1   Conception

The conception stage starts with an idea. Ideas come from anywhere—for example, from customers, engineers, other disciplines, user groups, or others. The organization decision makers may decide to

- fund the idea and make it a project;
- reject the idea; or
- ask for further information or for a demonstration that the idea has merit.

How decisions are made varies. A decision may be rather spontaneous in a very small and self-contained organization, where communication is ubiquitous and informal. A larger company may have formalized processes for initiation of new projects requiring many layers of approval.

> **Definition 19–9.** A *proof of concept* is a demonstration that an idea has merit.

The decision makers may ask for a proof of concept if they are unsure, or not convinced, that the idea is worth pursuing. Developing proofs of concept typically involves small projects. A request for a proof of concept may result in a rapid prototype, an analysis, or another type of proof. It need not involve the engineering staff, and it need not use steps in the engineering process.

The output of the conception stage must provide sufficient information for all disciplines to begin their tasks in the next stage. This information may be an overview of the project; high-level requirements that the project should meet; or schedule, budget, staffing, or planning information. The planning information could be a detailed project plan or more general high-level plans for each of the disciplines involved in the project. The exact nature of the information depends on the size and complexity of the project.

Security feasibility and high-level requirement analysis should begin during this stage of the life cycle. Before time and resources are invested in development or in proof of concept activities, the following questions should be considered:

- What does "secure" mean for this concept?
- Is it possible for this concept to meet this meaning of security?
- Is the organization willing to support the additional resources required to make this concept meet this meaning of security?

Identification of threats and assumptions comprises another important set of security issues. It is especially important to determine the expected usage of the product and the threats that are visible at the conception stage. This allows those threats to be addressed in rapid prototypes and proofs of concept. It also helps develop realistic and meaningful requirements at later stages. It provides the basis for a detailed threat analysis that may be required in the manufacturing phase to refine requirements.

Development of assurance considerations is important at this stage. A decision to incorporate assurance, and to evaluate mechanisms and other evidence of assurance, will influence every subsequent step of development. Assurance decisions will affect schedules and time to market.

19.2.1.2   Manufacture

Once a project has been accepted, funded, approved, and staffed, the manufacturing stage begins. Each required discipline has a set of substages or steps determined in part by the size of, complexity of, and market for the system. For most disciplines, the manufacturing stage is the longest.

Manufacturing begins with the development of more detailed plans for each of the involved disciplines, which could include marketing plans, sales training plans, development plans, and test plans. These documents describe the specific tasks for this stage of the life cycle within each discipline. The actual work required by each discipline depends on the nature of the system. For example, a system designed for internal use would not have sales requirements, and marketing requirements might target internal groups who may use the completed entity. Alternatively, a product designed for commercial use could require massive marketing campaigns and significant effort on the part of the sales force.

The software development or engineering process lies in this stage. It includes procedures, tools, and techniques used to develop and maintain the system. Technical work may include design techniques, development standards and guidelines, and testing tools and methods. Management aspects may include planning, scheduling, review processes, documentation guidelines, metrics, and configuration management such as source code control mechanisms and documentation version controls.

The output of this stage from each discipline should be the materials necessary to determine whether to proceed. These materials are the masters that are then used to distribute and deploy the product. Marketing groups could complete marketing collateral such as white papers and data sheets. Sales groups could develop documented leads and sales channels, as well as training materials for the sales force. Engineering groups would develop a tested, debugged system that is ready for use. Documentation groups would complete manuals and guides. Service groups would be trained on the product and may need to add staffing to handle telephone calls, installation support, bug tracking, and the like. The focus of this book is on the engineering steps of this stage.

19.2.1.3   Deployment

Once the system has passed the acceptance criteria in the manufacturing stage, it is ready for deployment. This stage is the process of getting the system out to the customer. It is divided into two substages.

The first substage is the domain of production, distribution, and shipping. The role of the other disciplines (such as engineering and marketing) is to deliver masters to the production staff. That staff creates and packages the materials that are actually shipped. If there is no assurance that masters have been appropriately protected from modification, and that copies are replicas of the masters, then the painstaking assurance steps taken during manufacture may be for naught.

The distribution organization ships systems to customers and to other sales organizations. In the case of an internal system, this step may be small. Users of the system may require specific types of documentation. Security and assurance issues in this part of deployment are focused on the integrity of the delivery, that is knowing that what was received is actually what was shipped.

The second substage of deployment is proper installation and configuration of the system in its production setting. Accurate installation and administrative guidance that includes security considerations and descriptions of security measures are necessary. The developers must ensure that the system will work appropriately in this environment. The developers are also responsible for appropriate assurance measures for functionality, tools, and documentation. Service personnel must know appropriate security procedures as well as all other aspects of the system.

19.2.1.4   Fielded Product Life

The primary tasks of fielded product life are patching or fixing of bugs, maintenance, and customer service. In some organizations, routine maintenance and emergency patching may be the responsibility of engineering. Alternatively, maintenance and patching may the responsibility of an organization entirely separate from the product development organization. Wherever this responsibility lies, an engineering process must track maintenance and patches, and a deployment process must distribute patches and new releases. Modifications and enhancements must meet the same level of assurance rigor as the original development.

Commercial systems often have separate customer service and support organizations and engineering organizations. The support organization tasks could include answering questions, recording bugs, and solving routine customer problems. The engineering organization handles maintenance and patching.

Product retirement, or the decision to take a product out of service, is a critical part of this stage of the life cycle. Vendors need to consider migration plans for customers, routine maintenance for retired products still in use, and other issues.

The importance of the configuration of the fielded product and its role in the security of the network system cannot be overlooked. There are many large, expensive breaches lately that have been the result of improper security architectures, improper remote connections, or unpatched systems. In addition to the Target and Equifax breaches mentioned below, since 2000 there have also been breaches at Yahoo!, Home Depot, Inc., Anthem, Inc., and the U.S. Office of Management and Budgeting (OMB) that have affected large numbers of individuals.

EXAMPLE: [1011, 1745] The Target Corporation breach of 2013 is an example of a system network that was architected with improper security controls. This breach started by compromising a third-party vendor with access to the Target network. Once in the Target network, the attackers were able to compromise internal servers and install malware on the point-of-sale (POS) systems in order to steal tens of millions of debit and credit cards.

EXAMPLE: [799] The Equifax breach of 2017 is an example of improperly maintained and configured systems with possible insufficient data security policies and practices. Based on current information, an important system patch was not installed, causing the breach of private personal financial information for hundreds of millions of individuals.

19.2.2   The Waterfall Life Cycle Model

We have discussed life cycles in terms of stages. The waterfall model captures this.

> **Definition 19–10.** [1616] The *waterfall life cycle model* is the model of building in stages, whereby one stage is completed before the next stage begins.

This model is not the only technique for building secure and trusted systems, but it is perhaps the most common. It consists of five stages, pictured in Figure 19–3. The solid arrows show the flow from each stage to the next.

19.2.2.1   Requirements Definition and Analysis

In this phase, the high-level requirements are expanded. Development of the overall architecture of the system may lead to more detailed requirements. It is likely that there will be some iteration between the requirements definition step and the architecture step before either can be completed.

Requirements may be functional requirements or nonfunctional requirements. Functional requirements describe interactions between the system and its environment. Nonfunctional requirements are constraints or restrictions on the system that limit design or implementation choices. Requirements describe what and not how. They should be implementation-independent.

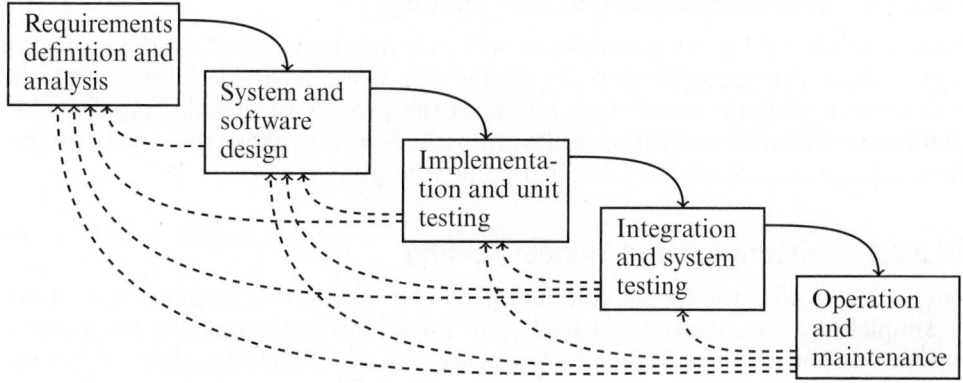

Figure 19–3 Development of a trusted system. There may be multiple levels of design and implementation. Note that the refinement steps alternate with the assurance steps.

Often, two sets of requirements are defined. A requirements definition of what the customer can expect the system to do is generally presented in natural language. A technical description of system characteristics, sometimes called a requirements specification, may be presented in a more precise form. The analysis of the requirements may include a feasibility study and may examine whether or not the requirements are correct, consistent, complete, realistic, verifiable, and traceable.

System design includes the development of the overall system architecture by partitioning requirements into hardware and/or software systems. The nature of the overall architecture may place additional constraints or requirements on the system, thus creating the need for iteration between this step and the previous one. An architecture document may or may not be required. In projects that are revisions or new releases of previous products, the basic architecture may be already defined. The architecture and the requirements must be reconciled to be consistent—that is, the architecture must be able to support the requirements.

19.2.2.2 System and Software Design

Software design further partitions the requirements into specific executable programs. Typically, at this stage, external functional specifications and internal design specifications are written. The external functional specifications describe the inputs, outputs, and constraints on functions that are external to the entity being specified, whereas the internal design specifications describe algorithms to be used, data structures, and required internal routines.

This stage is sometimes broken into the two phases *system design*, in which the system as a whole is designed, and *program design*, in which the programs of the system are individually designed.

19.2.2.3 Implementation and Unit Testing[1]

Implementation is the development of software programs based on the software design from the previous step. Typically, the work is divided into a set of programs or program units. *Unit testing* is the process of establishing that the unit as implemented meets its specifications. It is in this phase that many of the supporting processes described earlier come into play.

19.2.2.4 Integration and System Testing

Integration is the process of combining all the unit-tested program units into a complete system. Automated tools and guidelines governing the integration process may be in place. *System testing* is the process of ensuring that the system as a whole meets the requirements. System testing is an iterative step because invariably bugs and errors are found that have to be corrected. Typically, the errors

---

[1]Some authors break this phase into two parts: implementation testing and unit testing. In practice, the developer of a program is usually responsible for the unit testing of that program. Because the two are often done concurrently, it seems appropriate to treat them as a single phase.

are sent back to the development team to be corrected. This requires iteration with the previous step. The corrected code is reintegrated into the system, and system testing is repeated.

19.2.2.5   Operation and Maintenance

Once the system is finished,[2] it is moved into production. This is called *fielding the system*. Maintenance involves correction of errors that have been reported from the field and that have not been corrected at earlier stages. This stage also involves routine maintenance and the release of new versions of the system. Finally, retirement of the system also falls under this phase.

19.2.2.6   Discussion

In reality, there is usually some iteration between the processes at each stage of the waterfall because a later process may uncover deficiencies in a previous stage, causing it to be revisited. For example, implementation errors in the fielded system may not become clear until the operation and maintenance stage. Correction of such a deficiency will "trickle down" through the waterfall of phases. For example, if an error discovered in system testing is found to impact the software design, that change would feed into the system and software design phase, through implementation and unit testing to integration and system testing. An error found in the field may affect any stage from requirements to integration and system testing. Figure 19–3 shows the waterfall model, depicted by the solid arrows, and the potential error paths, represented by the dotted arrows. In practice, the stages may be performed in parallel during the development of certain features and/or parts of the system. For example for an appliance, the hardware may be in development while the operating system and other software is still in design.

Use of good system engineering practices provides discipline and process control during development and maintenance. Security analysis and development of assurance evidence on a regular basis, and as an integral part of the development and maintenance activities, increase confidence that the resulting system meets its security requirements. Use of a life cycle model and reliable supporting tools cannot ensure freedom from flaws or compliance with requirements. However, an appropriate process may help limit the number of flaws, especially those that can lead to security violations. Hence, building security into a product increases its trustworthiness. This demonstrates that the methods used to build a system are critical to the security of that system.

19.2.3   Agile Software Development

Software development is still a relatively young field. After the past few decades of building software, the industry has realized that software development is a creative process. Software development is always changing and is never really

---

[2]That is, the system meets the criteria established to define when it has been completed.

completed. To adjust to the unique nature of software development, Agile software development was developed. Agile software development is a term first coined in the Manifesto for Agile Software Development [143].

Agile software development is centered around Agile teams and focuses on working together. There are really no Agile methods or processes, but there are several Agile methodologies that fall under Agile software development. Instead, an Agile team learns how to efficiently work together in their environment to develop quality software. In addition, Agile engages the customer to be involved in the software development as a member of an Agile team. Customers are involved in the requirements and scoping of the software development projects. This allows the developers to learn firsthand how the product will be used and what features are the most important.

Agile software development accepts and adapts to changing requirements, allowing for continuous improvement of features. It involves quickly creating working software and demonstrating to the customer prior to continuing with development.

19.2.3.1   Manifesto for Agile Software Development

Agile software development was born at The Lodge at Snowbird ski resort by 17 engineers with years of software development experience. They wrote:

> We are uncovering better ways of developing software by doing it. Through this work we have come to value:
>
> - *Individuals and Interactions* more than processes and tools
> - *Working Software* more than comprehensive documentation
> - *Customer Collaboration* more than contract negotiation
> - *Responding to Change* more than following a plan
>
> That is, while there is value in the items on the right we value the items on the left more.[3]

The 17 engineers also documented the principles behind the Agile Manifesto.

19.2.3.2   Agile Methodologies or Implementations?

As mentioned above, Agile software development is not a methodology or set of processes. It is an overarching term used to describe any one of a number of Agile methodologies. These methodologies include Scrum, Kanban, eXtreme Programming (XP), Crystal, Feature-Driven Development (FDD), Dynamic Systems Development Method (DSDM), and Pragmatic Programming.

The following subsections provide an overview of the Scrum, Kanban, and extreme programming methodologies.

---

[3] Manifesto for Agile Software Development [143].

19.2.3.2.1 Scrum

Scrum is a simple, adaptive framework used to iteratively manage projects, allowing for fast development and continuous improvement. First, the project is split into small parts that can be completed within a short timeframe (called a *sprint*). This is called a *product backlog* and is created by the product owner, who is responsible for representing the customer and product stakeholders. The Scrum team agrees on a small subset from the top of the product backlog and decides how to design and implement that subset. The team's goal is to complete that subset within the sprint. To accomplish this, the team gathers each day in a daily Scrum "stand up" meeting to evaluate progress and adjust as needed to deliver a workable solution within every sprint. When the sprint is over, the work completed should be ready to ship, demonstrate, or place back in the product backlog if not complete. At the end of the sprint, the team meets to consider any lessons learned. The project continues with the team choosing another subset from the product backlog and starting again [1121, 1700].

19.2.3.2.2 Kanban

The Kanban methodology originated at Toyota manufacturing. Its goal is to deliver a valuable product to the customer in an expected timeframe. Kanban ensures that feedback is provided throughout the software development process to evaluate effort and product at each stage of development. Kanban manages projects by identifying lanes of work: work to be done, work in progress, work completed, and work deployed. Each lane, except for the work deployed lane, has a limit on the number of items within that lane, based on the staff available to perform the work. Teams can take items off of the work to be done lane and work on it until completion. When implemented correctly, a team is completing work on the top item in a lane when another work item is coming into the lane. [1121].

19.2.3.2.3 Extreme Programming

Extreme programming is a development methodology based on rapid prototyping and best practices such as separate testing of components, frequent reviewing, frequent integration of components, and simple design. A project is driven by business decisions, not by project stakeholders, and requirements are open until the project is complete. The design evolves as needed to remove complexity and add flexibility. Programmers work in teams or pairs. Component testing procedures and mechanisms are developed before the components are developed. The components are integrated and tested several times a day. One objective of this model is to put a minimal system into production as quickly as possible and then enhance it as appropriate.

19.2.3.2.4 Discussion

Use of Agile software development for security has several benefits and several drawbacks. The nature of an evolving design leaves the product vulnerable to the problems of an add-on product (see Section 20.1.2.2). Leaving requirements open does not ensure that security requirements will be properly implemented into the system. If assurance is needed, using Agile will require that the software development include checkpoints for security of the features and system overall at appropriate points of the development process. If threats are analyzed and appropriate security requirements developed before the system is designed, a secure or trusted system could result. However, evidence of trustworthiness would need to be adduced after the system was developed and implemented.

19.2.4   Other Models of Software Development

A few words on other life cycle models will illuminate the differences between those models and the waterfall model with respect to assurance [1787].

19.2.4.1   Exploratory Programming

In exploratory programming approaches, a working system is developed quickly and then modified until it performs adequately. This approach is commonly used in artificial intelligence (AI) system development, in which users cannot formulate a detailed requirements specification and in which adequacy rather than correctness is the aim of the system designers. The key to using this approach successfully is to use techniques that allow for rapid system iterations. Using a very high-level programming language may facilitate rapid changes.

In this technique, there are no requirements or design specifications. Hence, assurance becomes difficult. A system subjected to continual modification suffers the same vulnerabilities that plague any add-on system. The focus on adequacy rather than correctness leaves the implementation potentially vulnerable to attack. Therefore, this model is not particularly useful for building secure and trusted systems because such systems need precise requirements and detailed verification that they meet those requirements as implemented.

19.2.4.2   Prototyping

Prototyping is similar to exploratory programming. The first phase of development involves rapid development of a working system. However, in this case, the objective of the rapid development is specifically to establish the system requirements. Then the software is reimplemented to create a production-quality system. The reimplementation can be done using another model that is more conducive to development of secure and trusted systems.

19.2.4.3   Formal Transformation

In the formal transformation model, developers create a formal specification of the software system. They transform this specification into a program using correctness-preserving transformations. The act of formal specification, if tied to well-formed security requirements, is beneficial to security and to design in general. The use of correctness-preserving transformations and automated methods can assist in developing a correct implementation. However, a system developed by such a method should be subjected to the same rigorous implementation testing and vulnerabilities analysis that are applied to any other methodology.

19.2.4.4   System Assembly from Reusable Components

This technique assumes that systems are made up mostly of components that already exist. The system development process becomes one of assembly rather than creation. Developing trusted systems out of trusted components is complex because of the need to reconcile the security models and requirements of each component, and developing trusted systems out of untrusted components is even more complex. However, this is a common approach to building secure and trusted systems.

19.3   Summary

Assurance is the foundation for determining the trustworthiness of a computer system. Assurance techniques test the appropriateness of requirements and the effectiveness of specification, design, implementation, and maintenance. These techniques cannot guarantee system security or safety, but they can significantly increase the likelihood of finding security flaws during requirements definition, design, and implementation. Errors found early can be corrected early. A well-defined life cycle process provides rigorous, well-defined steps with checks and balances that contribute significantly to the quality of the software developed and also increases the credibility of the measures of assurance that are used.

19.4   Research Issues

Probably the most important area in assurance research is getting people to understand the importance and the value of assurance and trust. Assurance techniques are expensive and time-consuming, but they result in more reliable products. Moreover, assurance techniques support the identification of more clearly defined problems for products to solve and functions for them to perform. Most current systems are fragile—particularly systems used as infrastructure. Applying increasingly rigorous assurance techniques would strengthen these systems, not only in terms of security but also in terms of reliability and robustness. However, the level of assurance used with systems and products is driven by regulation and consumer demand as well as by the ability to hire people who know these techniques. Therefore, the problem of getting assurance techniques to be more widely used is in large part a problem of persuading consumers, developers, vendors, and regulators of their importance.

Part of the problem is cost; most assurance techniques are expensive. If assurance techniques were more effective, more efficient, less costly, and easier to use, would they be used more often? How can their cost be lowered? How can the use of these techniques, and the techniques themselves, be automated? In particular, formal methods require organizations not just to invest money but also to find qualified people who can use those methods effectively. Automating the less formal testing of software and systems, and providing better tools for evaluation methodologies such as those discussed in Chapter 22, "Evaluating Systems," would help.

This leads to the issue of selecting appropriate assurance techniques. Some assurance technologies are appropriate in specific environments or for meeting specific goals. How does one determine which of the many techniques to use? Given specific environments and goals, how do the techniques compare?

One important area for research and standardization is the strength of security functionality. The effectiveness of a cryptographic algorithm has several measures (none of them perfect): the size of the key, the arrangement of elements in a substitution table, the size of the possible message space, and the strength of the cipher when used as a pseudorandom number generator. Other types of security functionality have more obscure, or more meaningless, measures. Of course, not all such functions lend themselves to computational measures, but there may be other methods that can be applied.

Another important area is the investigation of new approaches to assurance. Assurance is generally measured by the performance of the resulting product or system rather than the process by which it was developed. Several models and methodologies, notably the SSE-CMM (see Section 22.9), deal with the process of development rather than its result. In practice, which approach produces systems with some level of assurance and with lowest cost? Would combining the two approaches improve the level of assurance, or would it make the development process more cumbersome with no added benefit?

19.5   Further Reading

Any serious student of assurance should read James Anderson's seminal paper [50]. This paper defines many key concepts on which assurance is based.

Recent work on automobile [394, 1096, 2026] and medical device security [321, 855, 856] has shown the necessity of applying assurance techniques. These techniques have been applied for a variety of specialized systems, including outer space [1156, 1452, 1577], systems that control trains [1263], and aviation [192, 672].

Metrics have been used to measure assurance with respect to specific properties, such as failure tolerance [530, 1939], abnormal system behavior [645], and test coverage [40,2098]. The Visual Network Rating Methodology (VNRM) [1492] helps users organize and document assurance arguments.

Berzins and Luqi [187] discuss applications of formal methods to software engineering. Brooks's description of the development of OS/360 [300] focuses on the human practices and problems as well as the technical ones. It is a classic in the field of software engineering.

19.6   Exercises

1. Definition 19–2 defines assurance in terms of "confidence." A vendor advertises that its system was connected to the Internet for three months, and no one was able to break into it. It claims that this means that the system cannot be broken into from any network.

   a. Do you share the vendor's confidence? Why or why not?

   b. If a commercial evaluation service had monitored the testing of this system and confirmed that, despite numerous attempts, no attacker had succeeded in breaking into it, would your confidence in the vendor's claim be increased, decreased, or left unchanged? Justify your answer.

2. A computer security expert contends that most break-ins to computer systems today are attributable to flawed programming or incorrect configuration of systems and products. If this claim is true, do you think design assurance is as important as implementation and operational assurance? Why or why not?

3. Suppose you are the developer of a computer product that can process critical data and will likely run in a hostile environment. You have an outstanding design and development team, and you are very confident in the quality of their work.

   a. Explain why you would add assurance steps to your development environment.

   b. What additional information (if any) would you need in order to decide whether or not the product should be formally evaluated?

4. Requirements are often difficult to derive, especially when the environment in which the system will function, and the specific tasks it will perform, are unknown. Explain the problems that this causes during development of assurance.

5. Why is the waterfall model of software engineering the most commonly used method for development of trusted systems?

6. The goal of a researcher is to develop new ideas and then test them to see if they are feasible. Software developed to test a new idea is usually similar to

software developed for proof of concept (see Definition 19–9). A commercial firm trying to market software that uses a new idea decides to use the software that the researchers developed.

  a. What are the problems with this decision from an assurance point of view?

  b. What should the company do to improve the software (and save its reputation)?

7. A company develops a new security product using the extreme programming software development methodology. Programmers code, then test, then add more code, then test, and continue this iteration. Every day, they test the code base as a whole. The programmers work in pairs when writing code to ensure that at least two people review the code. The company does not adduce any additional evidence of assurance. How would you explain to the management of this company why their software is in fact not "high-assurance" software?

Chapter 20
Building Systems with Assurance

LORD BARDOLPH: When we mean to build,
We first survey the plot, then draw the model;
And when we see the figure of the house,
Then must we rate the cost of the erection;
Which if we find outweighs ability,
What do we then but draw anew the model
In fewer offices, or at last desist
To build at all?
— *King Henry IV, Part II*, I, iii, 41–48.

Designing and implementing systems with assurance requires that every step of the process involve an appropriate level of assurance. This chapter discusses how to provide the levels of assurance during the steps of building a system. It emphasizes the documentation and methods required to obtain evidence to support claims of assurance and provides the context for detailed discussions of methodologies such as formal program verification and testing.

20.1 Assurance in Requirements Definition and Analysis

Understanding the role of assurance in the development of requirements means understanding what requirements must provide. The set of requirements must be complete and correct in the context of security policy models. Defining requirements is an iterative process that normally begins with threat definition and culminates with the detailed level requirements that are used in the design, implementation, and maintenance of the system.

20.1.1   Threats and Security Objectives

In building a secure or trusted system, it is a mistake to assume that threats to the system are obvious or well-defined. This section briefly discusses identification of the security threats to the system and development of high-level security requirements, or security objectives, to mitigate the threats. This approach parallels that of the Common Criteria (see Section 22.8).

> **Definition 20–1.** A *threat* is a potential occurrence that can have an undesirable effect on the system assets or resources. It is a danger that can lead to undesirable consequences.

Threats are different from vulnerabilities.

> **Definition 20–2.** A *vulnerability* is a weakness that makes it possible for a threat to occur.

At the highest layer of abstraction, security threats are breaches of confidentiality, disruptions of integrity, or denials of service. It is important to refine these threats in relation to the specific system and the environment in which it must operate. Threats may come from either outside or inside some boundary that defines the system. Threats can come from authorized users or from unauthorized users who masquerade as valid users or find ways to bypass security mechanisms. Threats can also come from human errors or from acts of God.

EXAMPLE: An attacker from the Internet penetrating a computer system is an example of an outside threat. A penetration could result in a breach of confidentiality, a breach of integrity, or a denial of service. A successful penetration could result in theft of secrets, compromising of secret information, or the setting up of a denial of service attack.

EXAMPLE: Another example of an outsider threat involves an organizational LAN having restricted access to certain machines. A valid user of the LAN could be an outsider to a specific host and could theoretically mount an outsider attack on that host.

If the system is not connected to external networks, outside attackers may not be a threat. Elimination or mitigation of the threat of penetration does not, however, eliminate the threat of disclosure of secrets, breaches of integrity, or denials of service. Typically, inside users are trusted to use the system correctly, but there are many ways in which this trust can go wrong. One way is through intentional misuse of authorizations, whether for fun, profit, or revenge. An example of intentional misuse of authorizations is abuse of privileges to commit fraud within the system, including exfiltrating personally identifiable information. Another way trust can go wrong is the so-called fat-finger error, whereby an authorized user makes a mistake or inadvertently corrupts or misuses the system. Other means of misusing systems include finding ways to defeat or bypass authorization and access controls or other security mechanisms to reach information that would ordinarily be denied the perpetrator.

Every identified threat must be addressed by some countermeasure that mitigates it. Security objectives are high-level requirements that can serve this purpose. For example, threats regarding unauthorized use of the system can be mitigated by an objective that requires user identification and authentication before a user is given access to any system resources. Objectives are requirements at the highest level, and they provide clues about the kinds of mechanisms that are needed to implement them. In addition, objectives reveal information that can help in the subsequent development of a detailed requirement specification. Objectives suggest models and other existing policies. Sometimes security objectives are not sufficient to address all threats, which leads to assumptions about the operating environment, such as physical protection mechanisms.

Mapping the security threats into the set of objectives and assumptions partially addresses the completeness of the system security requirements. Note that every threat must be addressed. Threats may be mitigated by a combination of assumptions or objectives. Often a single objective or assumption can address multiple threats.

20.1.2 Architectural Considerations

An early architectural decision is to determine the primary focus of control of security enforcement mechanisms. Computer security centers on access to information, but the primary focus of control of security protection and enforcement mechanisms may be on user identity or on operations. In operating systems, for example, the focus of control is on the data. Access decisions are based on predefined permissions to data for processes acting on behalf of users. User-based mechanisms include mandatory access control mechanisms, discretionary access control mechanisms, and privileges assigned to users. In applications, the focus of control may be on operations that a user is allowed to perform. A user may be restricted to certain operations. These operations control access to the data needed to perform their functions. Role-based access control mechanisms focus on operations.

Another architectural decision is whether to centralize some security functions or to distribute them among systems or system components. There are trade-offs between a centralized security enforcement mechanism and a distributed mechanism. In distributed systems, a function may be spread across components or centralized in a single component. In a single-host system, a function may be distributed across modules or consolidated into a single module. An example in a distributed system is the collection of security audit information. The system could forward all auditing information to a central audit repository, or each component could do its own auditing. As another example, an operating system can use centralized or distributed mandatory access control checks. The mechanism may be centralized and called by other routines or may be distributed and duplicated within the operating system where needed.

Generally, it is easier to analyze and develop sound assurance evidence for centralized mechanisms. A mechanism that is in one place need only be analyzed once, and the remainder of the assurance steps simply argue that the routine is called appropriately. However, a centralized mechanism may be a bottleneck and may impact performance.

20.1.2.1   Security Mechanisms and Layered Architecture

Computer architectures are layered, and security enforcement mechanisms may reside at any architectural layer. Systems designed and built using layers describe the functionality of each layer precisely.

EXAMPLE: Consider an architecture with four layers.

1. The uppermost layer is the *application layer*. Application programs are those special-purpose programs that are used to perform specific tasks on behalf of a user, varying from personal applications to business applications to web applications.

2. The next layer is the *services* or *middleware layer*. It provides support services for applications. These services, however, are not part of the operating system. Examples of tools at this layer include database management systems and object reference brokers.

3. The next layer is the *operating system layer*. Software at this layer manages memory, file systems, I/O, and peripheral devices and may be responsible for scheduling and process control. The operating system kernel, which is at this layer, is the part of the operating system that is restricted to specially authorized users and is at the heart of the control of the physical resources of the underlying processor.

4. The lowest layer is the *hardware layer*. This layer includes firmware, which is code that has been built into the hardware itself and cannot be altered or removed without making a physical change in the processor.

When an application receives a request, it passes the request to the layer underneath the application. That layer processes the request and passes it to the next layer. This continues until the request reaches the layer that can fulfill the request. Successive layers simply follow the instructions they are given by the preceding layers. When the request is satisfied, the pertinent information is passed back up the layers to the user at the application layer.

An early architectural decision is selecting the correct layer for a mechanism. Designers must select the layer at which the mechanism will be the most efficient and the most effective. Security mechanisms for controlling user actions may be most effective at the application level, but security mechanisms for erasing data in freed disk blocks may be most effective at the operating system level.

Once a layer has been chosen for a security mechanism, one must consider how to protect the layers below that layer. For example, a secure operating system requires security mechanisms in the hardware layer as well as in the operating system itself. A secure application requires security mechanisms inside the application as well as at the services, operating system, and hardware layers.

The security mechanisms at the hardware layer may be a combination of physical security mechanisms that isolate the hardware in rooms requiring special access and administrative procedures that restrict access to them. Some computer manufacturers suggest that security mechanisms be built into the firmware and hardware [82, 2243] as well as into the software.

It may not be possible to place a mechanism in the desired layer unless what is being developed includes all the pertinent architectural layers. For example, when developing an application, the builder may not be able to make changes in the operating system layer. Doing so would mean defining requirements for the operating system and acquiring an operating system that meets those requirements. If no such operating system exists, the mechanism must be placed at a less optimal layer, or the builders must consider a special-purpose operating system.

EXAMPLE: Consider an application program that uses a database management system to manage information. The user requests access to a particular data item from the application. The application forwards this request to the database management system. That system processes the request and sends appropriate requests to the operating system. The database management system may use operating system commands or may issue system calls directly to continue the request. The operating system kernel issues commands to the firmware and hardware to physically retrieve the data and pass it back to the operating system. Then the operating system passes the retrieved data to the database management system, which returns the data to the application.

The security enforcement mechanisms of the application and the database management system can only control accesses to the underlying operating system that use the internal mechanisms of the application and the database management system. Application and database mechanisms cannot control a system user from accessing the operating system directly, bypassing the controls of the application or the database mechanism entirely. If a user can access application or database information by accessing the operating system directly, then the system is vulnerable. Regardless of the security mechanisms within the database management system, the operating system must also enforce security. For this reason, all evaluated and rated database management systems require the underlying operating system to provide specific security features and to be a rated and evaluated operating system.

20.1.2.2   Building Security In or Adding Security Later

Like performance, security is an integral part of a computer system. It should be integrated into the system from the beginning, rather than added on later.

Imagine trying to create a high-performance product out of one that has poor performance. If the poor performance is attributable to specific functions, those functions must be redesigned. However, the fundamental structure, design, and style of the system are probably at the heart of the performance problem. Fixing the underlying structure and system design is a much harder problem. It might be better to start over, redesigning the system to address performance as a primary goal. Creating a high-security system from one that previously did not address security is similar to creating a high-performance system. Products claiming security that are created from previous versions without security cannot achieve high trust because they lack the fundamental and structural concepts required for high assurance.

A basic concept in the design and development of secure computer systems is the concept of a reference monitor and its implementation—the reference validation mechanism.

> **Definition 20–3.** [50] A *reference monitor* is an access control concept of an abstract machine that mediates all accesses to objects by subjects.

> **Definition 20–4.** [50] A *reference validation mechanism* (RVM) is an implementation of the reference monitor concept. An RVM must be tamper-proof, must always be invoked, can never be bypassed, and must be small enough to be subject to analysis and testing, the completeness of which can be assured.

Any secure or trusted system must obviously meet the first three requirements. The "analysis and testing" of the reference monitor provides evidence of assurance. The fourth requirement engenders trust by providing assurance that the operational system meets its requirements.

> **Definition 20–5.** [50] A *security kernel* is a combination of hardware and software that implements a reference monitor.

Security kernels were early examples of reference validation mechanisms. The idea of a security kernel was later generalized by the definition of a trusted computing base, which applies the reference validation mechanism rules to additional security enforcement mechanisms.

> **Definition 20–6.** [2239] A *trusted computing base* (TCB) consists of all protection mechanisms within a computer system—including hardware, firmware, and software—that are responsible for enforcing a security policy.

A TCB consists of one or more components that together enforce the security policy of a system. The ability of a TCB to enforce a security policy depends solely on the mechanisms within the TCB and on the correct input of parameters (such as a user's clearance) related to the security policy.

If a system is designed and implemented so as to be "small enough to be subject to analysis and testing, the completeness of which can be assured," it will be more amenable to assurance than a system that is not so designed and implemented. Design analysis is possible using a variety of formal and informal methods. More thorough testing is possible because what must be tested is clear from the structured, analyzed design. More and deeper assurance leads to a higher level of trust in the resulting system. However, trade-offs may occur between features and simplicity. Inclusion of many features often leads to complexity, which limits the ability to analyze the system, which in turn lowers the potential level of assurance.

Systems in which security mechanisms are added to a previous product are not as amenable to extensive analysis as those that are specifically built for security. Often the functions are spread throughout the system in such a way that a thorough design analysis must analyze the entire system. Rigorous analysis of large and complex designs is difficult. So, it may not be feasible to determine how well the design implements the requirements. Assurance may be limited to test results. Testing of conformance to a flawed design is similar to designing a system to meet inappropriate requirements. The gap in abstraction between security requirements and implementation code may prohibit complete requirements testing. Hence, systems with security mechanisms added after development has been completed are inherently less trustworthy.

Building a system with security as a significant goal may provide the best opportunity to create a truly secure system. In the future, this may be the norm. However, many products today, including many high-assurance products, are developed by rearchitecting existing products and reusing parts as much as possible while addressing fundamental structure as well as adding new security features.

EXAMPLE: Multics [1477] was one of the early general-purpose operating systems that was built for secure applications. It borrowed much from the other operating systems of the day. Although it is no longer in use, many security experts consider Multics to be the best example of an operating system built for security.

EXAMPLE: Gemsos [1677] is a high-assurance, formally verified operating system that has a minimal UNIX-like kernel and limited functionality. Seaview [649] was a high-assurance database management system that was intended to run on the Gemsos operating system. Seaview was designed for security but was implemented by rearchitecting an existing database product.

EXAMPLE: Information flow control mechanisms, called *guards*, are often high-assurance devices. The RECON guard [53] controls the flow of information from a highly classified reconnaissance database to an unclassified network. The Restricted Access Processor [1547] controlled the flow of information between two differently classified networks. Firewalls are a form of guards, although they are usually single-purpose applications built on security-hardened versions of existing operating systems rather than systems developed specifically for high assurance.

EXAMPLE: In the late 1980s and early 1990s, AT&T undertook two projects to provide secure versions of UNIX System V that supported mandatory access controls. The first project was market-driven, in response to specific requests from customers. The underlying goals of this project were quick time to market and minimal impact on the user interface and on the look and feel of the resulting UNIX system, called SV/MLS [286, 687]. The chosen approach was to add security functionality to AT&T UNIX System V Release 3.2. The second project was focused on restructuring and recreating a UNIX system to provide a medium-to-high level of trust. This version, called SVR4.1ES, involved significant rearchitecting of the UNIX system with security built in [1618]. The technical differences between these two products illustrate the superiority of building security in over adding it on.

The SVR4.1ES project involved extensive restructuring of the UNIX kernel to meet high-modularity requirements and to incorporate an implementation of the principle of least privilege that was integral to the UNIX kernel. SV/MLS used the existing UNIX kernel modular structure and did not provide an implementation of least privilege. The basic architecture of SVR4.1ES was new, and the architecture of SV/MLS was essentially unchanged from its parent product.

In UNIX systems, the inode structure contains attribute information about each file or object, such as access permission information and file owner. The inode also has a pointer to the file or object itself. There is insufficient space in the inode to house security labels of any significant size. SV/MLS chose not to disturb the existing inode structure. The designers created a separate table to hold mandatory access control labels and used a free location in the inode structure to point to the table. When an object is created, a code defining both the mandatory access control label and the discretionary security attributes is stored in the table. Security attributes for subjects are stored internally in the same code structure. An access control check becomes a comparison of the codes for the subject and object, effectively doing a mandatory access control check and a discretionary access control check in one operation.

Even if the implementation of this table is correct and the comparison of the codes properly reflects the mandatory and discretionary access control requirements, there are potential weaknesses in this design. The coupling between the table and the file is inherently weaker than the coupling between the inode and the file. Two accesses are required to reach the coded mandatory and discretionary access control attributes of the object (first to the inode, then to the table), potentially weakening the tie between the actual object and its security attributes. Updating of discretionary access control security attributes is done to the inode version of the discretionary access control requirements. An additional step to update the table entry occurs whenever the permissions or owner is changed. This introduces the potential for inconsistency between the inode attributes and the coded interpretation. During a table update, the mandatory access control information for that object may be exposed. Finally, if the table is corrupted, the mandatory and discretionary access permissions for the entire file system may be impacted. Although the SV/MLS implementations addressed these issues satisfactorily, the potential for these vulnerabilities still existed.

The SVR4.1ES implementation simply redefined the inode structure. These new inodes, called vnodes, contained the mandatory access control label as well as the discretionary access control attributes in the vnode. Access to the vnode provided access to the mandatory and discretionary attributes. SVR4.1ES reused the UNIX discretionary access control mechanisms and augmented them with access control lists. Checks of mandatory and discretionary access were independent checks. SVR4.1ES was not constrained by minimal impact requirements, resulting in a stronger set of access control mechanisms. Because of the structural change, SVR4.1ES was able to reuse other parts of the system with little impact.

20.1.3   Policy Definition and Requirements Specification

Recall from Section 19.1.2 that we can consider a security policy to be a set of specific statements or security requirements.

> **Definition 20–7.** A *specification* is a description of characteristics of a computer system or program. A *security specification* specifies desired security properties.

Good specifications are as important as the properties of the systems or programs that they describe. Specifications can be written at many different levels of abstraction. For example, some specifications may describe the security requirements, whereas other specifications may describe an architectural view of the system. More detailed specifications may describe individual components. Even more detailed specifications may describe individual functions. As this example implies, there may be multiple levels of specifications at different layers of abstraction.

Specifications must be clear, unambiguous, and complete. This is difficult when using informal methods that rely on natural language because natural languages do not have precise syntax or semantics.

EXAMPLE: A specification or an operating system gave "meet C2 security" as a requirement. The specification provided no details of the C2 requirements [2239], which included 34 requirements in 11 different categories. Other requirements in the same specification were extremely detailed, such as those for adding a new file system, adding several new devices, and making very detailed changes in the memory control subsystem. The unevenness of the specification made it difficult to use. The developers chartered to "meet C2 security" neither understood what it meant nor knew how to find the detailed requirements.

Precision in stating requirements can be difficult to achieve.

EXAMPLE: The requirement that "users of the system must be identified and authenticated" is ambiguous. It does not specify the type of identification required. Is a driver's license presented to the system operator sufficient? It does not unambiguously specify the entities to be authenticated. Is the user, the representation of the identity, or the system to be authenticated? It also does not specify who is to perform the authentication. Is the system, some other system, or some other entity (such as a guard at the door) to perform the authentication? It is not necessary to name specific identification or authentication mechanisms to answer these questions and clear up the ambiguities.

A second iteration might change this requirement to "users of the system must be identified to the system and must have that identification authenticated by the system." This is more precise. The "system" both identifies and authenticates the representation of the user's identity (not the system or the user). However, it still does not address the conditions under which the user must be identified to the system. Is the user to be identified at entry to the site, at login, at a particular time of day, or before certain operations are to be performed?

A third iteration produces the requirement that "users of the system must be identified to the system and must have that identification authenticated by the system before the system performs any functions on behalf of that identity." This form addresses the concerns from the previous two versions.

There are several different methods of defining policies or requirement specifications. One technique is to extract applicable requirements from existing security standards, such as the Common Criteria. These specifications tend to be semiformal because of the structure of the requirements and the mappings among them. Another method is to create a new policy by combining the results of a threat analysis with components of existing policies.

A third technique is to map the system to an existing model. If the model is appropriate for the goals of the system, creating a mapping between the model and the system may be simpler and cheaper than constructing a requirements specification by other methods. If the mapping is accurate, the proofs of the original model establish the correctness of the resulting policy.

The expression of the specification can be formal or informal in nature. Section 21.2 contains an example of a formal specification of the Bell-LaPadula Model in the specification language SPECIAL.

EXAMPLE: System X is a product that enhances standard UNIX security mechanisms with mandatory access controls and auditing. The confidentiality components are based on the Bell-LaPadula (BLP) Model discussed in Section 5.2.

The designers use a mapping technique to develop the System X confidentiality policy.

1. The designers map the elements and state variables of BLP to entities in System X. They also justify the existence and functions of any entities in System X that have no counterparts in BLP:

   • System X processes are subjects in the set S of the BLP model.

   • Inode objects (disk files, directories, and other file system constructs), interprocess communication objects, mail messages, processes as destinations for messages, and other passive entities in System X are the objects in the set O of the BLP model.

- Each system function of System X is given a right from the set P of the BLP model. Functions that create entities (such as *creat*, which creates a file) have the access type <u>w</u>; functions that read and write entities (such as the system calls *read* and *write*) have the types <u>r</u> and <u>w</u>, respectively. Execution and search accesses are mapped to the access type <u>r</u>.

- The access set b in the BLP model defines the types of access allowed for each object. For example, subjects can use the rights <u>r</u>, <u>w</u>, and <u>a</u> to access inode objects.

- The access control matrix a for the current state in the BLP model is the current state of both mandatory and discretionary controls in System X.

- The functions f_s, f_o, and f_c in the BLP model map into three functions in System X. The function $f(s)$ is the maximum security level of the subject s, the function *current-level(s)* is the current security level of the subject, and $f(o)$ is the security level of an object.

- The hierarchy H in the BLP model maps differently for different types of objects. For example, inode objects are hierarchical trees represented by the file system hierarchy, whereas other object types map to discrete points in the hierarchy.

2. Next, the designers define BLP properties in the language of System X and demonstrate that each property is consistent with BLP.

- The mandatory access control property of BLP is translated as a user having read access over an object if and only if the user's clearance dominates the object's classification, and as a user having write access over an object if and only if the object's classification dominates the user's clearance.

- The discretionary access control property of BLP is translated as giving a user access to an object if and only if the owner of the object has explicitly granted that user access to the object.

- Label inheritance and user level changes are properties specific to System X. The security level of a newly created object is inherited from the creating subject. The security level of the initial process at user login, and the security level of the initial process after a user level change, are bounded by the security level range defined for that user and by the security level range defined for the terminal. The security level of a newly spawned process is inherited from the parent, except for the first process after a user level change. When a user's level is raised, the child process does not inherit write access to the objects opened by the parent. When a user's level is lowered, all processes and all accesses associated with the higher privilege are terminated.

- Reclassification is also a property of System X. Specially trusted users are allowed to downgrade objects they own within the constraints of the user's authorizations.

- The System X property of owner/group transfer allows the ownership or group membership of the process to be transferred to another user or group.

- Finally, the status property is a property of System X. It restricts the visibility of status information available to users when they use the standard System X set of commands.

3. In this step, the designers define System X rules by mapping System X system calls, commands, and functions to BLP rules. The simple security condition, the *-property, and the discretionary security property are all interpreted for each type of access. From these interpretations, the designers can extract specific requirements for specific accesses to particular types of objects.

4. Finally, the designers demonstrate that the System X rules preserve the security properties. They either show that the rules enforce the properties directly or map the rules directly to a BLP rule or a sequence of BLP rules. System X has nine rules about current access, five rules about functions and security levels, eight access permission rules, and eight more rules about subjects and objects. The designers must show that each rule is consistent with the actions of System X.

The results of these steps provide a high degree of assurance that System X correctly enforces the rules of the Bell-LaPadula Model.

20.1.4   Justifying Requirements

Once the policy has been defined and specified, it must be shown to be complete and consistent. This section examines part of a security policy developed in accordance with the ITSEC [2177] guidelines. It also provides a partial informal demonstration that the resulting security policy meets the threats defined for the system.

The ITSEC (see Section 22.3) is a harmonization of security evaluation criteria of several European countries. ITSEC introduced the concept of a security target (ST) that defines the security threats to the system and the functional requirements of the system under evaluation. An ITSEC suitability analysis justifies that the security functional requirements are sufficient to meet the threats to the system.

The suitability analysis maps threats to requirements and assumptions in tabular form. For each threat, a prose description describes how the references address the threat.

EXAMPLE: Consider a system called Y that is under evaluation. A subset of the threats, requirements, and assumptions relevant to our security target are as follows:

- *Threat T1*: A person not authorized to use the system gains access to the system and its facilities by impersonating an authorized user.
- *Requirement IA1*: A user is permitted to begin a user session only if the user presents a valid unique identifier to the system and if the claimed identity of the user is authenticated by the system by authenticating the supplied password.
- *Requirement IA2*: Before the first user/system interaction in a session, successful identification and authentication of the user take place.
- *Assumption A1*: The product must be configured such that only the approved group of users has physical access to the system.
- *Assumption A2*: Only authorized users may physically remove from the system the media on which authentication data is stored.
- *Assumption A3*: Users must not disclose their passwords to other individuals.
- *Assumption A4*: Passwords generated by the administrator shall be distributed in a secure manner.

The security analysis mapping is as follows:

Threat   **Security Target Reference**
T1   IA1, IA2, A1, A2, A3, A4

The justification for this mapping requires an examination of the effects of the security target references.

- The referenced requirements and assumptions guard against unauthorized access. Assumption A1 restricts physical access to the system to those authorized to use it. Requirement IA1 requires all users to supply a valid identity and confirming password. Requirement IA2 ensures that requirement IA1 cannot be bypassed.
- The referenced assumptions prevent unauthorized users from gaining access by using a valid user's identity and password. Assumption A3 ensures that users keep their passwords secret. Assumption A4 prevents unauthorized users from intercepting new passwords when those passwords are distributed to users. Finally, assumption A2 prevents

unauthorized access to authentication information stored on removable media.

The justification provides an informal basis for asserting that, if the assumptions hold and the requirements are met, the threat is adequately handled.

20.2   Assurance during System and Software Design

Design assurance is often neglected. Design flaws are usually uncovered when tests produce numerous flaws that cannot be fixed easily. Had the design been analyzed, the security flaws could have been corrected at that level, and then the implementation flaws would have been easier to fix. Hence, identifying and correcting security flaws at the design level not only enhances the trustworthiness of the system but also supports both implementation and operational assurance.

Design assurance is the process of establishing that the design of the system is sufficient to enforce the security requirements for the system. Design assurance techniques employ a specification of the requirements, a specification of the system design, and processes for examining how well the design (as specified) meets the requirements (as specified). This is also important when creating a design that utilizes externally hosted systems. The assurance requirements of the internal and external system must be consistent and well-defined. The assurance and security techniques of the internal and external systems must be compatible, and the interfaces of the externally hosted systems and internal systems must be well-defined.

20.2.1   Design Techniques That Support Assurance

Modularity and layering are techniques of system design and implementation that can simplify the system, thus making it more amenable to security analysis. If a complex system has well-defined independent modules, it may be amenable to a security analysis. Similarly, layering simplifies the design. Layering supports a better understanding of the system and therefore leads to more assurance. Layering can also support data hiding. For example, global variables span all layers and modules and therefore may allow sensitive information to be available to functions for which that information is not needed. This type of unnecessary interaction between layers or between modules should be eliminated. This reduces the risk that errors in one layer or module will contaminate another.

The reference validation mechanism suggests that functions not related to security be removed from modules supporting security functionality. This makes those modules smaller and thus easier to analyze. These design concepts must be carefully described in design documentation and in the implementations derived from them.

Large systems can be broken down into layers, making it easier to develop specifications at different levels of abstraction. The following terminology describes the different levels of a system.

Definition 20–8. A *subsystem* or *component* is a special-purpose division of a larger entity.

The subsystems or components of an operating system may include the memory management system or file systems, whereas a subsystem or component of a web store may be the collection of credit-card processing activities. A component consists of data structures and subcomponents or modules. A system that does not have subsystems in the traditional sense may be subdivided by other means, such as layers or servers. A solution utilizing externally hosted systems may identify each externally hosted system as a subsystem or component.

It may be easier to describe a large component if it is broken into smaller parts, each having a specific functionality or purpose.

Definition 20–9. A *subcomponent* is a part of a component.

For example, in an operating system, an I/O component may be broken down into I/O management and I/O drivers. It may be useful to break a subcomponent into even lower subsystems, such as a component for each I/O driver. The lowest level of decomposition is made up of modules.

Definition 20–10. A *module* is a set of related functions and pertinent data structures.

A set of modules may be a subcomponent or component. The functions that may make up a module include commands, system calls, library routines, and other supporting routines. Functions have inputs, outputs, exception conditions, error conditions, and effects on data or other functions. Function descriptions may include internal logic and algorithms or just address interfaces.

EXAMPLE: A system may be decomposed into components and subcomponents in many ways. The I/O system of Windows 10 and Windows Server 2016 may be viewed as a three-layer component decomposition: I/O System component, Drivers component, and HAL component. The I/O System component comprises the first layer with the following subcomponents: the Windows Management Instrumentation (WMI) Routines, the Plug and Play (PnP) Manager, the Power Manager, and the I/O Manager. The Drivers component includes the kernel mode device drivers. There are three basic types of kernel-mode device drivers: file system drivers, plug and play drivers, and non–plug and play drivers. The hardware abstraction layer (HAL) component has no subcomponents [2062]. The subcomponents of the I/O System and Drivers components define the second layer of the decomposition (see Figure 20–1).

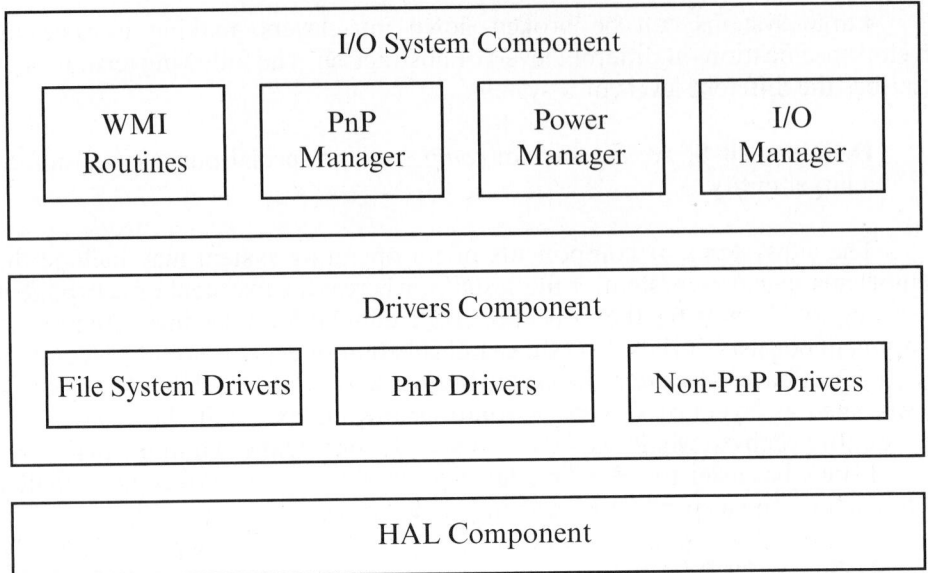

Figure 20–1   Decomposition of the Windows 10 and Windows Server 2016 I/O System.

The subcomponent I/O file system drivers can be broken down into a third layer, consisting of the compact disk file system (CDFS), the NT file system (NTFS), the fast file allocation table file system (FAT), and the encrypting file system (EFS). Below this layer sits the module and function layers.

Because the HAL has no subcomponents, it has no second or third layer. The other subcomponents do have third layers, but for reasons of space we will not discuss them.

The I/O System utilizes data stored in the Registry (a database storing system configuration information including hardware devices and driver initialization settings), INF files (driver installation files), and CAT files (stores digital signatures for drivers).

Another design consideration is the principles of secure design (see Chapter 14). For example, consider the principle of least privilege (see Section 14.2.1). The modular structure of a design can support the use of this principle. Each level of the design should address privilege. At the time of implementation, it may be tempting to give more privilege than is required, because it is simpler, because the privilege may be needed again shortly, or for other reasons. This temptation should be resisted. Implementers should understand how to write programs and configure systems so that the assignment of privilege is tightly controlled and privileges are revoked when no longer needed.

20.2.2   Design Document Contents

Most life cycle models require design documentation, although the documentation requirements are not always sufficient for developing design assurance. A more rigorous specification may be necessary to establish that the system design is sufficient to enforce the security requirements. Design specifications can be informal, semiformal, or formal in style. Specifications that are more formal can be subjected to more rigorous security analysis and justification, providing a higher level of assurance. A significant benefit of writing specifications is the ability to correct a design as one defines it in writing. Creating formal design specifications is time intensive, but the added assurance can be valuable in the long term. The more precise the descriptions, the more likely one can find and correct flaws.

For security analysis, documentation must specify three types of information.

1. *Security functions.* High-level descriptions of the functions that enforce security on the system, such as identification and authentication, access controls, and auditing, provide an overview of the protection approach of the system.

2. *External interfaces.* The interfaces visible to the users are the mechanisms through which users access system resources and information. The system security enforcement functions control these actions, and security enforcement depends on the constraints and effects that determine their behavior.

3. *Internal design.* High-level design descriptions of the system address the architecture of the entity being described in terms of the next layer of decomposition. For example, system high-level designs describe the system architecture in terms of its major subsystems. The low-level or detail design is a description of the internal function of a module. The low-level description identifies and describes all the interfaces and data structures of the module.

The next three subsections expand on each of these types of information.

20.2.2.1   Security Functions Summary Specification

This is the highest level of specification of security enforcement and is significant to the development of all subsequent specifications and to the security analysis on which they depend.

> **Definition 20–11.** A *security functions summary specification* identifies the high-level security functions that are defined for the system.

These functions are the protection mechanisms defined to meet the security functional requirements in a requirement specification. The content of the security functions summary specification should include the following information:

1. *Description of individual security functions.* This description should be complete enough to show the intent of the function. The activities of each function relate to one or more security requirements and may specify behavior that is not explicitly a part of the security requirements.
2. *Overview of the set of security functions.* This overview should describe how the security functions work together to satisfy security requirements.
3. *Mapping to requirements.* This section should specify a mapping between the security functions and the security requirements. It is often presented as a table.

20.2.2.2   External Functional Specification

A description of the expected behavior of each external interface should include parameters, syntax, effects, security constraints, and security error conditions. Each of the security functions mentioned above may have several user-visible interfaces, which are of particular importance for a specification of a secure or trusted product or system.

> **Definition 20–12.** An *external functional specification*, also called a *functional specification*, is a high-level description of external interfaces to a system, component, subcomponent, or module.

The interface descriptions provide details about parameters, effects, exceptions, and error conditions. An external functional specification can be written for an entire system, a component, a subcomponent, or even a module. The technical content of this specification should include the following information:

1. *Component overview.* This overview identifies the component, its parent component, and how the component fits into the design structure of the parent component. It also identifies the substructures (such as modules) to be specified in this document as well as in related documents.
2. *Data descriptions.* These descriptions identify and define data types and data structures that are necessary to support the external interface descriptions specific to this component. They provide references to definitions of data types and structures that are defined outside the scope of this component but that are used in this component. Finally, they identify security issues or protection requirements relevant to data structures.

3. *Interface descriptions.* External interfaces are methods available for use by external entities (human users, applications, devices, etc.) to interact with the system, component, subcomponent, or module. External interfaces include commands, system calls, library calls, functions, protocols, and application program interfaces. They may be visible to the user or may be application program interfaces to the particular component being specified. Interfaces visible to the user should be explicitly identified as visible to the user. An interface description should follow a standard syntax and should identify input and output parameters, exception conditions, effects, and error messages. The exception conditions and effects are especially important.

EXAMPLE: The following external functional specification describes a routine for an error handling subsystem. This routine adds a new event to an existing log file. The specification has a fixed C-like format. Each required piece of information is carefully identified.

Interface Name

```
error_t add_logevent (
    handle_t handle;
    data_t event;
);
```

Input Parameters

handle   a valid handle returned from a previous call to open_log
event   the buffer of event data with event records in *logevent* format

Exceptions

Caller does not have permission to add to EVENT file.
There is inadequate memory to add to an EVENT file.

Effects

Event is added to EVENT log.

Output Parameters

```
status   status_ok             /* routine completed
                                  successfully */
         no_memory             /* routine failed due to
                                  insufficient memory */
         permission_denied     /* routine failed, caller does not
                                  have permission */
```

Note

add_logevent is a user-visible interface.

EXAMPLE: The following external functional specification describes a web user interface used for changing a user password.

Interface Name

`User Manager / Change Password`

Input Parameters

Old password   Current user's old password
New password   Current user's new password
Confirm new password Confirmation of current user's new password

OK button is used to submit the change password request
CANCEL button is used to cancel the change password request and return to the previous screen / window

Exceptions

Caller does not have permission to change their password.
The new supplied password does not meet password complexity requirements.
The new supplied password does not match the confirm password.

Effects

Event is added to EVENT log.
If the correct old password is supplied, the new password and confirm password are identical, and the new password meets complexity requirements, the user's password is changed.

Output Parameters

Event is added to EVENT log.
A dialog box appears indicating that the password is changed, the password did not meet the complexity requirements, or the new password and confirm password did not match.

Note

`User Manager / Change Password` is a user-visible interface.

20.2.2.3   Internal Design Description

> **Definition 20–13.** An *internal design description* describes the internal structures and functions of the components of the system.

The description of the internal structures and functions of the system consists of a set of one or more documents. The complexity of the system and its decomposition into components and subcomponents determine the decomposition of the high-level design documentation.

High-level design documents focus on subsystems or components and address their structures, functions, and the ways in which they are used. The architecture of the system, in terms of its major subsystems, is the most abstract layer of the high-level design. The high-level design documents of each major subsystem provide specific information about the subsystem design in terms of the subcomponents, regardless of the layer of the design decomposition.

The high-level design documents for each layer, from the system architecture through all intermediate layers, provide the same fundamental information and should follow the same structure. The technical content of a high-level design document includes the following information:

1. *Overview of the parent component.* Only the highest level of the design or system architecture lacks a parent component. If there is a parent component, the high-level design identifies its high-level purpose and function. The description identifies all subsystems of the parent component, describes their purpose and function, and includes how they interact with each other to transfer data and control. A description of the security relevance of the parent component, including a mapping of the security requirements met by the parent component, completes this overview.

2. *Detailed description of the component.* This document expands on the purpose and functionality of the component. It includes a description of the features and functions that the component provides. The component structure is described in terms of the subcomponents, providing an overview of how the subcomponents support the component in accomplishing its purpose and functionality. Any underlying hardware, firmware, and software that the component or its subcomponents need are also identified. The document describes the data model for the component in terms of the variables and data structures that are global to it and describes the data flow model in terms of how subcomponents of the component interact and communicate to transfer information and control. The document describes the interactions of the component with other components. The document identifies all interfaces to the component and explicitly notes which are externally visible. A more complete description includes a description of the interfaces in terms of effects, exceptions, and error messages, as appropriate.

3. *Security relevance of the component.* This section identifies the relevance of the component and its subcomponents to the system security in terms of the security issues that the component and its subcomponents should address. It is recommended that this security description include a mapping of the security requirements (or part of the security requirements) met by the component. It includes specific information on the protection needs of global variables, data structures, and other information under the control of the component. Other issues include correctness of particular routines and management of security attributes. The mechanisms supporting security in the underlying hardware, firmware, and software mechanisms must also be identified and described.

EXAMPLE: This example documents the high-level design of the audit mechanism from the preceding section.

Overview of the Parent Component   The audit component is responsible for recording an accurate representation of all security-relevant events that occur in the target of evaluation (the system) and ensuring that the integrity and confidentiality of the records are maintained. The audit component is broken into three different subcomponents.

- *Audit view*. This subcomponent provides authorized users with a mechanism for viewing audit records.
- *Audit logging*. This subcomponent records the auditable events, as requested by the system, in the format defined by the requirements. For example, the audit record includes the date and time of the event, the user identifier of the process causing the event, and the success or failure of the event.
- *Audit management*. This subcomponent handles the administrative interface used to define what is audited.

The audit management subcomponent manages the information that the audit logging subcomponent uses to decide whether to generate an audit record for a given event. Each subcomponent is responsible for maintaining the integrity and confidentiality of the audit records.

The audit component satisfies the security requirements related to logging of security-relevant events. All security-relevant events must be audited, and all audit records must include the date and time of the event, the user identifier of the process causing the event, and the success or failure of the event.[1]

Detailed Description of the Component   The audit logging subcomponent records the auditable events, as requested by the system, in a secure fashion. When the audit logging subcomponent receives a request to write an audit record, it determines whether the audit system has been configured to audit records with those characteristics. For example, if the audit system is configured to record login failures and not to record login successes, then a request to record a login success will not generate an audit record.

The audit logging subcomponent formats the audit record and includes all attributes of the security-relevant event. It generates the audit record in the predefined format, which includes the date and time of the event, the user and group identifiers of the process causing the event, the record number, the function or application identifier, the system name, and the success or failure of the event.

---

[1] The exact security requirements would be listed here.

In addition, the audit logging subcomponent handles exception conditions, such as an error writing to the log (for example, when the disk containing the log is full). The audit logging subcomponent uses one global structure:

```
struct audit_config      /* defines configuration of
                            which events */
                         /* are to be audited */
```

The audit logging subcomponent has two external interfaces:

```
add_logevent()  /* ask to log multiple events of a given
                   type */
logevent()      /* ask to log event */
```

Security Relevance of the Component   The audit logging subcomponent is supplied security-relevant events and records those events that match the configurable audit selection criteria. Security-relevant events include attempts to violate the security policy and successful completion of security-relevant actions.

Low-level design documents focus on the internal design of modules, describing relevant data structures, interfaces, and logic flow. These documents include detailed descriptions of interface functions such as application program interface routines, system calls, library calls, and commands. This specification focuses on how a function is to be implemented and may include specific algorithms and pseudocode.

A low-level design description of a module should contain sufficient information for a developer to write the implementation code for the module. The design description includes the following information:

1. *Overview of the module being specified.* This overview describes the purpose of the module and its interrelations with other modules—especially dependencies on other modules. The description of the module structure is in terms of interfaces and internal routines as well as global data structures and variables of the module and provides details of the logic and data flow throughout the module.

2. *Security relevance of the module.* This section identifies how the module is relevant to system security in terms of the security issues that the module and its interfaces should address. It provides specific information on the protection needs of global variables, data structures, or other information under the control of the module.

3. *Individual module interfaces.* This section identifies all interfaces to the module, explicitly naming those that are externally visible. It describes the purpose and method of use of each routine, function, command, system

call, protocol, and other interface, in terms of effects, exceptions, and error messages. The documentation must provide details of the flow of control and of the algorithms used.

EXAMPLE: This example documents the low-level design of the audit mechanism from the preceding section.

Overview of the Module Being Specified   The audit logging subcomponent is responsible for monitoring and recording security-relevant events. This subcomponent depends on the I/O system and process system components. The audit management subcomponent depends on the audit logging subcomponent for accurate implementation of the audit parameters configured by the audit management subcomponent. All system components depend on the audit logging component to produce their audit records.

The audit logging subcomponent uses the following variables:

```
structure logevent_t    structure defining the audit record
structure audit_ptr     points to current position in audit file
file_ptr audit_fd       file descriptor to current audit file
```

The audit logging subcomponent uses the following global structure, which the audit management subcomponent initializes and updates:

```
structure audit_config   /* defines configuration of
                            which events are to be audited */
```

The audit logging subcomponent has two external interfaces:

```
add_logevent()  /* ask to log multiple events of a given
                   type */
logevent()      /* ask to log event */
```

Security Relevance of the Component   The audit logging subcomponent is supplied security-relevant events and records those events that match the configurable audit selection criteria. Security-relevant events include attempts to violate security policy and successful completion of security-relevant actions. The audit logging subcomponent must ensure that no audit records are lost and that the audit records are protected from tampering.

Individual Module Interfaces   The *logevent*() function is the only non-privileged external interface to the audit logging subcomponent. This function determines if the system has been configured to audit the reported event. If so, the function creates the audit record for the event and writes it to the audit log. The function must ensure that no audit records are lost. Pseudocode for *logevent*() is as follows:

```
verify function parameters
call check_selection_parameters to determine if the
          system has been configured to audit the event
if check_selection_parameters is true then
        call create_logevent
        call write_logevent
        return success or error number
else
        return success
```

Refer to the functional specification for *logevent*() in Section 20.2.2.2 for details on using this function.

The *add_logevent*() function is a privileged external interface to the audit logging subcomponent that allows multiple events to be written to the audit log. This function is available only to privileged users and requires that the audit records be provided in the correct format.

Pseudocode for *add_logevent*() is as follows:

```
verify the caller has privilege/permission to use this
          function
if the caller does not have permission
        return permission_denied
verify function parameters
call write_logevent for each event record
return success or error number from write_logevent
```

20.2.2.4 Internal Design Specification

The internal design specification is slightly more complex than either the security functions summary specification or the external functional specification. Previous sections discussed content. They did not show how to relegate various designs to specific documents, thus making a set of documents that is a useful, readable, and complete set. Developers may use an internal design specification document, which covers parts of both the low-level and high-level design documents. The internal design specification is most useful when specifying the lowest layer of decomposition of a system and the modules that make up that layer. However, the internal design specification is not always used to describe the higher levels of design, making them incomplete for security analysis or for developers who are new to the system.

The following two examples present an outline of an internal design specification and an approach for dividing the internal design documentation for the I/O system, following the component decomposition described in the example in Section 20.2.1.

EXAMPLE: This example presents an outline of an internal design specification of a low-level component that consists of modules. The internal design specification contains elements of the high-level design of the component and the low-level design of each module in the component.

1. *Introduction.* The introduction defines the purpose and scope, identifies the target audience, and presents definitions new to this document.

2. *Component overview.* This overview identifies and describes the modules, data structures, and other data mechanisms in the component. It describes how data is transmitted through the modules and data structures in the component. Depending on the type of product, this section might describe interfaces, protocols, installation, signals and interrupts, and diagnostic processing. This section also describes the security relevance of the component in terms of what security functionality it provides.

3. *Detailed module designs.* A separate section describes each module and all of its interfaces.

   3.1 *Module #1.* This section describes the module's interrelations with other modules, its local data structures and variables, its control and data flows through the module, and the relevance of the module to security.

   3.1.1 *Interface designs.* A separate section describes each interface.

   3.1.1.1 *Interface 1a.* This describes security relevance and external visibility and provides a detailed description including purpose and method of use in terms of input/output parameters, effects, exceptions, error messages, and results. It describes logic flow, data flow, and algorithms as appropriate.

EXAMPLE: The example in Section 20.2.1 identified the decomposition of the Windows I/O system. High-level design documents for each component and subcomponent of the decomposition would be excessive. A high-level design document describing the I/O system as a whole, including all the necessary descriptions of the three components (I/O System, Drivers, and HAL), is more useful. This document addresses the I/O system high-level design and the high-level design of the I/O System, Drivers, and HAL components. The next level of decomposition could be documented with a high-level design document for each of the subcomponents of the Drivers component. An internal design specification for the HAL component (which has no subcomponents) and I/O System subcomponents would be documented. Internal design specifications for each of the modules of the Drivers subcomponents complete the documentation of the I/O system.

20.2.3   Building Documentation and Specification

Considerations other than the kind of specification required to support design assurance affect the development of documentation. Time, cost, and efficiency issues may impact how a development organization creates a complete set of documents. For example, a time constraint may compel an organization to write informal rather than formal specifications. Other shortcuts can result in effective documentation if done carefully.

20.2.3.1   Modification Specifications

When a system or product is built from previous versions or components, the specification set may consist of specifications of previous versions or parent products, together with modification specifications that describe the required changes. Time and cost constraints may compel developers to write specifications that are restricted to changes in the existing parts. These *modification specifications* describe the changes in existing modules, functions, or components; the addition of new modules, functions, or components; and possibly the methods for deleting discarded modules, functions, or components.

The use of modification specifications is most effective in developing new (or maintenance) releases of existing products, where security requirements and specifications are well defined for the older releases. Creating modification specifications gives the developer the advantage of understanding the specifications, design, and implementation of the system on which the new release is built. However, it can create problems for security analysis. The security analysis must rest on the specification of the resulting product, not just the changes. If there are full specifications of the previous versions of the parts, it may be possible to do an informal analysis based on the two sets of specifications. Modifications of modifications make the analysis even more complex.

Problems arise when the modification specifications are the only specifications of the system. Because there are no specifications for the parts not being modified, security analysis must be based on incomplete specifications.

20.2.3.2   Security Specifications

When external and internal design specifications are adequate in every way except for security issues, a supplemental specification may be created to describe the missing functionality. One approach is to develop a document that starts with the security functions summary specification. It is expanded to address the security issues of components, subcomponents, modules, and functions. Depending on the size and organization of the existing documentation, the information can be organized in the same way as the existing documentation. It can also be organized by security function.

EXAMPLE: Section 20.1.3 described the security policy for System X. Recall that System X is a UNIX operating system enhanced to include mandatory access control, auditing, and other functionality in order to meet certain evaluation requirements. The underlying UNIX implementation is completely specified. The specification includes complete functional specification and internal design specification documentation. However, because security had not been a significant consideration in the UNIX system on which System X was based, the functional specification and internal design specification documentation did not cover security issues sufficiently well, nor did it include information about the new functionality.

The System X security team addresses the missing parts of the documentation with a set of documents to supplement the existing functional specification and internal design specification documentation. A security architecture document provides an overview of the base product architecture, including the operating system, firmware, and hardware. It addresses some security shortcomings of the existing design documentation. The remainder of the security architecture document provides a complete overview of each security function. Some functions are entirely new to the product (such as mandatory access control, labeling, and audit). Others are a part of the existing product and require modification for the new product (such as discretionary access control and identification and authentication). Still others are a part of the base product but are unchanged in the new version (such as object reuse). Four documents, one for each of the four security functional areas, support the security architecture document. These other documents describe the external interfaces and internal design of each of the functions in the functional area. In some cases, the supporting documentation references base product documentation; in others, the security architecture documents replace the base product documentation.

20.2.3.3   Formal Specifications

Any of the four specification types discussed above (requirements specifications, security functions summary specifications, functional specifications, and design specifications) can be informal, semiformal, or formal. Informal methods use natural language for specifications. Semiformal methods also use natural language for specifications but apply a specific overall method that imposes some rigor on the process. Formal methods use mathematics and machine-parsable languages. Formal specifications are written in formal languages based on well-defined syntax and sound semantics. The languages themselves are usually supported by parsers and other tools that help the author check the resulting specification for consistency and proper form. The semantics of the language may help catch some oversights in the specification, but in general the author determines the completeness and correctness of the specification. Some high-level formal languages are appropriate for requirements specifications or functional specifications. Other languages are more like programming languages and can easily describe algorithms and logic flow. Chapter 21, "Formal Methods," describes a variety of formal languages and discusses their use.

20.2.4 Justifying That Design Meets Requirements

The nature of the specification limits the techniques that can validate the specified design. Informal specifications and semiformal specifications cannot be analyzed using formal methods because of the imprecision of the specification language. However, it is possible to do some informal security analysis. An informal specification can justify the correct implementation of requirements or justify consistency between two levels of specification. The most common informal techniques are requirements tracing, informal correspondence, and informal arguments. An excellent technique for verifying any of the informal techniques is called *review*. Other methods, producing higher assurance, are formal in nature, such as formal specifications and precise mathematical proofs of correctness. Chapter 21, "Formal Methods," discusses these methods.

20.2.4.1 Requirements Tracing and Informal Correspondence

Two techniques help prevent requirements and functionality from being discarded, forgotten, or ignored at lower levels of design. They also highlight functionality that may creep into the design but does not meet specific requirements.

> **Definition 20–14.** *Requirements tracing* is the process of identifying specific security requirements that are met by parts of a specification.

> **Definition 20–15.** *Informal correspondence* (also called *representation correspondence*) is the process of showing that a specification is consistent with an adjacent level of specification.

Together, these two methods can provide confidence that the specifications constitute a complete and consistent implementation of the security requirements defined for the system.

A typical set of design documentation for a system contains security requirements, external functional specifications, and internal design specifications, presented by one of the methods described in Section 20.2.2. The final level of decomposition of this design is the implementation code. Figure 20–2 shows the requirements tracing steps and the informal correspondence steps in such a design decomposition.

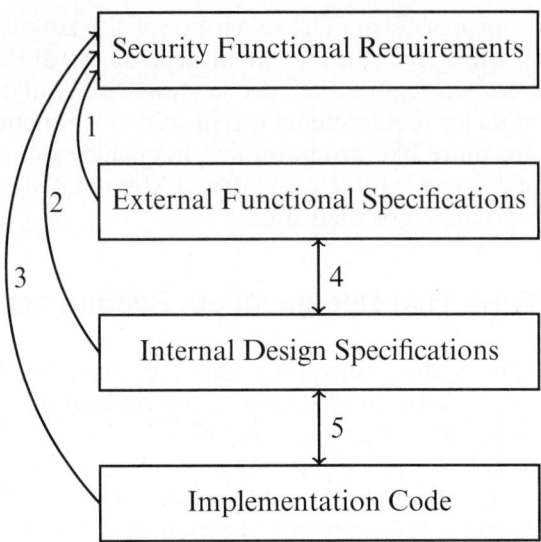

Figure 20–2   Requirements mapping and informal correspondence. Arrows 1, 2, and 3 indicate requirements tracing for each of the three levels of specification. Arrows 4 and 5 represent informal correspondence between adjacent levels of specification.

Identifying how a very high-level and abstract requirement applies to a very specific and concrete function in an external functional specification is not always straightforward. The difference in level of abstraction may obscure the relationship. Having an intermediate level between the very abstract and the very concrete often makes the process simpler. A security functions summary specification provides such an intermediate step between the requirements and the external functional specification. High-level design documentation can bridge the gap between functional specifications and low-level design specifications.

Requirements tracing and informal correspondence are most appropriate when all levels of specification or representation of the system have identified requirements and all adjacent pairs of specifications have been shown to be consistent. In addition to the security functions summary specification, the external functional specification, and the high- and low-level design specifications, the implementation (source) code is the final and lowest level. The adjacent pairs of specifications are as follows:

- Security functions summary specification and functional specification
- Functional specification and high-level design specification
- High-level design specification and low-level design specification
- Low-level design specification and implementation code

If requirements have been traced to the nth level of specification, developing an informal correspondence between level n and level $n + 1$ provides a straight path to the identities of specific requirements in the descriptions of specification level $n + 1$.

EXAMPLE: Consider a family of specifications across several levels.

R2 is a security requirement from the requirement specification. It requires users of the system to be identified to the system and to have that identification authenticated by the system prior to use of any system functions.

I&A (identification and authentication) is a high-level security-enforcing function from a security functions summary specification.

- Using a *login_ID*, users identify themselves to the system before they can use any of the system resources.
- Users authenticate their identities to the system by providing a password. The password must be accepted as authentic by the system before any system resources can be used.
- The password must meet specific password size and character constraints.
- The life of a password shall not exceed 12 months.

The interfaces *login* and *change_password* are described in a functional specification.

The *login* function allows a user to enter his or her identity and, when prompted to do so, enter authentication information; it returns a message indicating success or failure. If *login* fails, the user cannot use any resources of the system except to start the *login* process again.

The *change_password* function allows the user to change his or her password by entering the old password and then entering the new password when prompted. A failure message results if the new password does not meet the size and character constraints, and the user is prompted to try again. If the proposed password meets the constraints, the user is prompted to enter it a second time.

Writing of the external functional specifications for these functions is left as an exercise for the reader (see Exercise 5).

The requirements mapping between the requirements specification and the security functions summary specification is represented by a table followed by an explanation. In this example, R2 is the only requirement mapping to I&A.

Security requirements	Function 1	I&A	...	Function *m*
R1			...	...
R2		X		
...				
R*n*				

The informal correspondence between the functional specification and the security functions summary specification relevant to these two functions is as follows:

- *login* maps to the first two list items in the description of I&A.
- *change_password* maps to the second and third list items in the description of I&A.

The informal correspondence shows that the requirement R2 maps to *login*, but not to *change_password*.

The requirements trace and the informal correspondence information may be included in the design specifications described above by adding sections from the security functions summary specifications, functional specifications, high-level design documentation, and low-level design documentation. These sections describe the informal correspondence to the next-higher level of specification and identify the security requirements met by the lowest-level entities of the specification. Requirements tracing and correspondence mapping can also be written in a separate document, with high-level overviews or references to the relevant parts of the specifications themselves.

20.2.4.2   Informal Arguments

Requirements tracing identifies the components, modules, and functions that meet requirements, but this technique does not fully address how well the requirements are met. This requires analysis beyond simple mappings. A technique called *informal arguments* uses an approach similar to mathematical proofs.

Common Criteria protection profiles and security targets (see Section 22.8.1) provide examples of informal arguments. Protection profiles define threats to the system and security objectives for the system. The rationale section of the protection profile presents an argument justifying that the objectives are adequate to prevent the threats. A security target identifies the mechanisms used to implement the security requirements and justifies that the mechanisms are sufficient to meet the objectives. This technique helps the writer analyze the completeness and correctness of security objectives (in protection profiles) and of security mechanisms (in security targets).

EXAMPLE: Consider the modification specifications of System W, a new version of an existing product. The previous version had adequate requirement specifications, security functions summary specifications, external functional specifications, and design specifications.

System W included numerous bug fixes and added several new features to the product. Some were large and pervasive. The developers created both external functional specification documents and internal design specification documents for all modifications of the system. Each document carefully defined the scope to be modifications only and, where applicable, referred to the documentation of the previous version. The modification specifications provided by the development staff were almost adequate to understand the issues. The security analysts asked developers many questions. The developers reviewed the author's work. The resulting combined security specification and analysis document addressed the impacts of the changes on the security of the previous, evaluated system. The analysis documentation contained a system overview document, a security analysis document, and a test coverage analysis (omitted here). The security analysis of the modifications contained individual documents for each of approximately 15 different functional areas. Some described new functionality, and others presented modifications of existing subsystems. Each subsystem document described the results of the analysis in terms of problems and recommendations for the code, documentation, and testing of the component.

The documentation was semiformal in nature. It was written in a natural language supported with code excerpts where practical.

Design overview. The design overview gave a high-level description of the component as well as the security issues relevant to the component. This section described the impact of the component on security by enumerating new object types and decomposing the component into subcomponents or modules. The rest of the section described the subcomponents or modules.

Requirements section. This section identified the security functionality in the module and traced it to the applicable security functional requirements. An explanation was provided for each security functional requirement not applicable to this module.

Interface analysis. This section described each new or impacted interface and mapped requirements to them. It also identified and documented security problems and analyzed documentation and test coverage to uncover additional problems and to make recommendations.

20.2.4.3   Formal Methods: Proof Techniques

Producing a formal specification is expensive. Thus, the specifiers usually intend to process the specification using an automated tool such as a proof-based technology or a model checker. Requirements tracing for a formal specification will check that the specification satisfies the requirements. Creating informal justifications before applying formal methods provides intuition about the proofs. Chapter 21, "Formal Methods," discusses formal proof technologies and model checking.

Formal proof mechanisms are general-purpose techniques. They are usually based on logic such as the predicate calculus. They are generally highly interactive and are sometimes called *proof checkers* to indicate that the user constructs the proof and the tool merely verifies the steps in the proof. Proof technologies are designed to allow one to show that a specification satisfies certain properties (such as security properties). An automated theorem prover processes the properties and the specification. There may be many intermediate steps, such as proving of supporting lemmata and splitting of cases. Some proof technologies use a separate tool to generate formulas that can be given to the prover. The formula generator takes the specification of the system and a specification of properties as input. The generator develops formulas claiming that the specification parts meet the properties.

Model checking, on the other hand, checks that a model satisfies a specification. A model checker is an automated tool with a specific security model and processes a specification to determine if the specification meets the constraints of the model. This type of checking is designed for systems such as operating systems that do not terminate. Model checkers are usually based on temporal logic. Chapter 21, "Formal Methods," discusses them in detail.

20.2.4.4   Review

A mechanism for gaining consensus on the appropriateness of assurance evidence is especially important when the assurance technique used for the evidence is informal in nature. A formal review process can meet this need. Every meaningful review process has three critical parts: review guidelines, conflict resolution methods, and completion procedures.

The reviewers receive (or determine) guidelines on how to review the entity. These guidelines vary from general directions to specific instructions. For example, a review guideline might instruct a reviewer to focus on the correctness of a particular section of a document. It might request that the reviewer ensure that relevant requirements are described for each interface in an external functional specification.

Reviewers will have different strengths, opinions, and expertise. The review process must have a method for resolving any conflicts among the reviewers and authors.

Finally, the review must terminate, ensuring the completion of the entity being reviewed. This may include techniques for tracking and organizing feedback, ensuring the correct implementation of feedback, final approval procedures, and the like.

EXAMPLE: The following formal review process may be used by large software development organizations with assurance goals. The review participants have four critical roles: moderator, reviewer, scribe, and author. In some cases, an observer may be included in the review meeting. The observer's role is to observe silently and to not participate in the review process in any way. Managers may not be moderators, scribes, or observers and may be selected as reviewers only if their technical expertise is needed and cannot be provided otherwise. The absence of managers often eases the process and allows reviewers to speak more openly.

This review process is designed for individual documents such as specifications or other engineering documents. However, it can be used for other items such as code walkthroughs.

Setting Up the Review   When the author is ready to have the entity reviewed, he informs the appropriate person to select a review moderator to manage the review process.

The first responsibility of the moderator is to decide if she agrees that the entity is ready for review. If not, then the moderator and the author's manager will discuss additional requirements with the author. Otherwise, the manager, author, and moderator determine if the size of the entity warrants dividing the review into chapters or sections. Whether or not the division is done, the entity in its entirety must be reviewed eventually. This may require more than one review meeting. If the entity to be reviewed is large and is to be subdivided, then at least two reviewers should review each pertinent part of the entity, as well as the entity in its entirety.

The moderator selects the review team, defines the review guidelines (ground rules), schedules the review meeting, and distributes the review materials to the reviewers. The moderator also arranges for appropriate facilities and materials for the review. Ground rules include the minimum amount of time a reviewer should spend on the entity review and may include special assignments to focus on specific areas.

When feasible, the moderator should indicate what the reviewers should look for with respect to security. A document template or a list of issues may be helpful in this regard. Such materials should be circulated with the item to be reviewed.

The Technical Review   Reviewers study the entity with respect to the ground rules and guidelines provided, answering any specific questions and commenting on any issues they uncover. If a reviewer feels that the entity is not ready for review because it does not meet a predefined ground rule, is incomplete, has major errors, or is unreadable, the reviewer can request that the moderator send the entity back to the author for changes. The moderator decides whether to continue or stop the technical review. If the review is stopped, the moderator and the manager discuss additional requirements with the author. This step can save time and effort in the end.

Reviewers provide general, specific, and grammatical comments. General comments apply to the entity as a whole and include comments on structure, organization, style, major omissions, and duplications. Specific comments apply to a particular section of the entity and address technical content. Grammatical comments include comments on clarity, style, spelling, and grammar, and include other issues such as missing reference markings. When the entity being reviewed is a document, the reviewers tie specific and grammatical comments to the documents by providing line, page, and section numbers. The reviewers record all comments in writing and give them to the scribe at the end of the review meeting.

The Review Meeting   First, the moderator determines whether or not each reviewer has had sufficient time to review the entity. If not, she reschedules the review meeting. Otherwise, the meeting begins with grammatical comments being presented to the scribe.

These comments are not discussed unless they present clarity issues that need amplification.

The moderator does not participate as a reviewer, but acts as an independent master of ceremonies. If the moderator has been a reviewer as well,[2] another reviewer should represent the moderator's comments.

Typically, the moderator first asks for general comments. After all general comments have been made, the moderator starts at the beginning of the entity and goes through it sequentially, collecting comments from the reviewers. The reviewers must make concise, clear comments about the content of the document and not reiterate grammatical comments that have already been submitted. A good moderator will instruct reviewers to keep comments constructive and positive, not demeaning or personal. The reviewers may ask the author for clarification on parts of the entity being reviewed. Similarly, the author may ask for clarification of a reviewer's comment.

The goal of the review meeting is to collect all comments on the entity. It is not to resolve conflicting opinions between reviewers or between a reviewer and the author. These conflicts are handled outside the review meeting.

Once a comment is understood, the scribe writes down the comment, including the name of the person who made the comment. The reviewer may need to assist the scribe in correct phrasing. All meeting attendees should see what the scribe records, and the person making the comment can attest to its correctness.

Conflict and Comment Resolution   After the review meeting, the scribe creates a Master Comment List. This list is circulated to the reviewers. Each reviewer marks each comment with a code of "Agree" or "Challenge" and the reviewer's identity. When all reviewers have completed this process, the scribe moves comments that all reviewers marked "Agree" or all marked "Challenge" to an Official Comment List. The remaining comments are recirculated. Reviewers must resolve their differences. This allows reviewers with conflicting views to discuss their differences. As disputes are resolved, the scribe adds them to the Official Comment List. If the reviewers cannot resolve a dispute, the review moderator must resolve the conflict or call a meeting to do so.

When all conflicts have been resolved, the moderator and the reviewers decide whether to accept the entity as it stands, reject the entity for major revision, or accept the entity with changes as indicated on the Official Comment List. If the entity is accepted, the review is complete. Otherwise, the moderator and the manager meet with the author to discuss additional requirements.

The scribe gives the completed Official Comment List to both the moderator and the author. The author changes the entity to reflect the comments as he sees fit. When all changes have been made, the author reviews the changes with the reviewers. He explains how he handled each comment to the reviewer who made the comment. When all comments have been resolved to the satisfaction

---

[2]This is not recommended.

of the author and the reviewers, the conflict and comment resolution phase is complete and the review goes to completion.

Completion of the Review   After the moderator is satisfied with all changes, the review is completed. All reviewers and the moderator sign off on the review, and the completed entity is put under configuration management.

Notes   Due to the fast pace of releases and bug fixes, a simplified, informal review process is commonly used by developers. The review process for many development organizations does not include a moderator or scribe. In addition, reviews are frequently performed via electronic communications with only one reviewer.

20.3   Assurance in Implementation and Integration

The most well-known technique for showing that an implementation meets its security requirements is testing. Section 20.3.3.1 discusses security testing methodologies, but other techniques also increase assurance in implementation and integration.

20.3.1   Implementation Considerations That Support Assurance

A system should be modular, with well-defined modules having a minimal number of well-defined interfaces. Whenever possible, functionality not relevant to security should be removed from modules that enforce security functionality.

The choice of the programming language for the implementation can affect the assurance of the implementation. Some languages strongly support security by providing built-in features that help to avoid commonly exploited flaws. Programs written in these languages are often more reliable. For example, the C programming language can produce programs with limited reliability, because C does not constrain pointers adequately and has only rudimentary error-handling mechanisms. Implementations of C usually allow a program to write past the bounds of the program's memory and buffers. The extra data goes into the next contiguous piece of memory, overwriting what was already there. The C language does not provide checks to prevent this overwriting, leaving the responsibility for preventing this type of buffer overflow to the C programmer.

Languages that provide features supporting security will detect many implementation errors. Languages having features such as strong typing, built-in buffer overflow protections (such as array bounds handling), data hiding, modularity, domains and domain access protections, garbage collection, and error handling support the development of more secure, trustworthy, and reliable programs. For example, the programming language Java was designed to support the development of secure code as a primary goal. Other languages provide some support for security. Perl, a general-purpose programming language, provides a "taint mode," which monitors input and warns when a program uses the information inappropriately.

Sometimes it is not feasible to use a high-level language because of efficiency constraints or the need to exploit system features that the high-level language cannot access. In such cases, coding standards can compensate for some of the security enforcement limitations. Although not as reliable as built-in features, coding standards help programmers avoid many errors. Another technique is to restrict the use of lower-level languages to specific situations in which high-level languages are inadequate.

20.3.2   Assurance through Implementation Management

Teams of programmers often develop systems designed in modules. Each programmer develops modules independently of the others. Well-defined module interfaces are critical, especially when the work of the different programmers is integrated into a single system. This is especially important when the programmers working on the system are part of a large team or many small distributed teams. Supporting tools and processes are important for small and large systems, whether developed by one programmer or a large team of programmers.

> **Definition 20–16.** *Configuration management* is the control of changes made in the system's hardware, software, firmware, documentation, testing, test fixtures, and test documentation throughout the development and operational life of the system.

Configuration management tools and processes provide discipline and control of the refinement and modification of configuration items such as the source code and other information such as documentation. The configuration management system is made up of several tools or manual processes and should perform several functions.

1. *Version control and tracking*. Most development organizations use a source code control system that stores code modules and subsequent versions of them. Other configuration items, such as documents or document sections, require similar version control and tracking, whether using the same or a different tool. These tools allow an individual to make a copy of a particular version of a configuration item under control of the system and to return a new version later.

2. *Change authorization*. Version control and tracking tools do not always control who can make a change in a document. Typically, these tools allow anyone to have a copy of a version and to place the new version in the database. Hence, there must be a mechanism that allows only

authorized individuals to "check in" versions. Consider the case in which two programmers each need to make changes in a module. They both request a copy of the module, make their changes, and return the changed module to the database. Without any change in authorization controls, both versions will be kept, but the version from the first programmer will not include the changes made by the second programmer, and vice versa. Hence, some changes will be lost. Some tools require that a specific individual or gatekeeper check versions in. Other version control and tracking tools restrict check-in to the first person to check out the configuration item. Others can check out review copies but cannot check them back in. When the authorized first user checks in the new version, others can then check that item out and merge their changes. Some version control and tracking tools provide change collision features allowing the second user to check in the item to decide how to resolve the conflicts between the two sets of changes.

3. *Integration procedures.* Integration procedures define the steps that must be taken to select the appropriate versions of configuration items to generate the system. This ensures that the system generation tools process properly authorized versions.

4. *Tools for product generation.* Product generation creates the current system from the properly authorized versions provided by the integration procedures. It may include various steps of compiling source code and linking binaries to create the full executable system.

The development of code standards is another implementation management tool that supports assurance. Coding standards support improved software development practices. Coding standards may require or recommend naming conventions, style considerations, and commenting guidelines. Although useful, these standards provide limited support for development of good code that produces secure and trusted systems. No programming language solves all the security problems, and coding standards may address some issues not covered by the language itself. Other coding guidelines address constraints on the use of the language that help prevent common security flaws. Still other guidelines may be specific to handling of permissions or processing of secret or sensitive information, or may address specification of error handling or security exceptions.

20.3.3   Justifying That the Implementation Meets the Design

Code reviews, requirements tracing, informal correspondence, security testing, and formal proof techniques can be used to enhance assurance about the implementation. Code walkthroughs, or code reviews, take place at system implementation. Section 20.2.4.4 describes the review process. That description applies to code reviews. The review guidelines, however, will be specific to software development techniques rather than to documentation.

Requirements tracing and informal correspondence apply to the code. Comments in the code typically show the results of a requirement trace and a correspondence between the code and the lowest level of design documentation.

20.3.3.1   Security Testing

There are two types of testing techniques.

> **Definition 20–17.** *Functional testing*, sometimes called *black box testing*, is testing of an entity to determine how well it meets its specification.

> **Definition 20–18.** *Structural testing*, sometimes called *white box testing*, is testing based on an analysis of the code in order to develop test cases.

Testing occurs at different times during the engineering process.

> **Definition 20–19.** *Unit testing* consists of testing by the developer on a code module before integration. Unit testing is usually structural.

> **Definition 20–20.** *System testing* is functional testing performed by the integration team on the integrated modules of the system. It may include structural testing in some cases.

> **Definition 20–21.** *Third-party testing*, sometimes called *independent testing*, is functional testing performed by a group outside the development organization, often an outside company.

> **Definition 20–22.** *Security testing* is testing that addresses the product security.

Security testing consists of three components.

1. *Security functional testing* is functional testing specific to the security issues described in the relevant specification.
2. *Security structural testing* is structural testing specific to security implementation found in the relevant code.
3. *Security requirements testing* is security functional testing specific to the security requirements found in the requirements specification. It may overlap significantly with security functional testing.

In general, security functional testing and security requirements testing are parts of unit testing and system testing. Third-party testing may include security functional testing or just security requirements testing. Security structural testing can be part of a unit test or a system test.

Security functional testing differs from ordinary functional testing in its focus, coverage, and depth. Normal testing focuses on the most commonly used functions. Security testing focuses on functions that invoke security mechanisms, particularly on the least used aspects of such mechanisms. The least used parts often contain the exploitable flaws. Security functional testing focuses on pathological cases, boundary value issues, and the like.

Test coverage describes how completely the entity has been tested against its functional specification. Security testing requires broader coverage than normal testing. It covers system security functions more consistently than ordinary testing. A completed test coverage analysis provides a rigorous argument that all external interfaces have been completely tested. An interim test coverage analysis indicates additional test requirements.

Finally, security testing against high-level and low-level specifications shows how well the testing covers the specifications of the subsystem, module, and routine. A completed test depth analysis provides a rigorous argument that testing at all levels is sufficient. An interim test depth analysis indicates additional test requirements that must be met.

During a unit test, the programmer should perform extensive security and requirements tests. A unit test should focus on the least used aspects, pathological cases, or boundary value issues. Most structural testing occurs during unit testing.

Most development organizations perform system testing on their systems. For the most part, security system testing takes place at the external interface level. In this context, an interface is a point at which processing crosses the security perimeter. Users access the system services through external interfaces. Therefore, violations of policy occur through external interfaces. Occasionally, noninterface tests are required. Typically, there are two parallel efforts, one by the programming team and the other by the test team. Figure 20–3 illustrates this.

Security test suites are very large. Automated test suites are essential, as are configuration management and documentation. The testers must also develop and document test plans, test specifications, test procedures, and test results.

Writing test plans, specifications, and procedures gives the author the ability to examine and correct approaches as the writing proceeds. This provides assurance about the test methodology. This documentation increases the assurance of the testing because it enables analysis of the test suite for completeness and correctness.

The reports of the results of security testing are the tangible evidence of the test effort. These reports identify which tests the entity has passed. Ideally, it will pass all tests. In practice, the entity will fail some tests, so unusual results must be examined. In particular, automated test suites can introduce some problems; the entity may fail a test when the test is part of an automated test suite but pass the test when it is run independently of the test suite. Also, the tester may demonstrate the desired result by means other than execution of the particular test.

20.3.3.2 Security Testing Using PGWG

PGWG, the PAT (Process Action Team) Guidance Working Group, presents a systematic approach to system and requirements test development using successive decomposition of the system and requirements tracing. This methodology

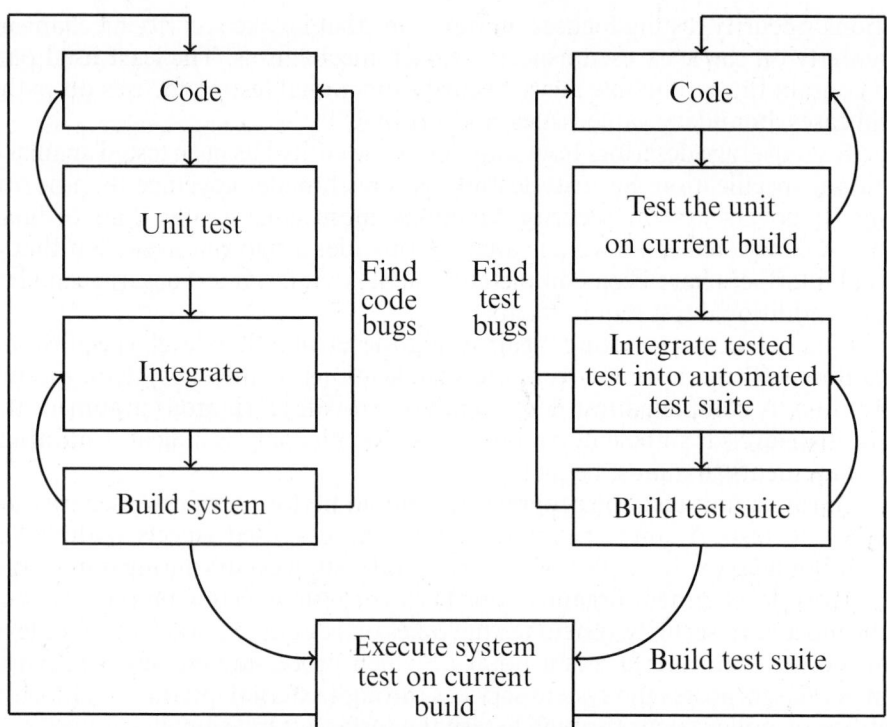

Figure 20–3 Relationship between code development and testing. At the left are the development tasks, and at the right are the testing tasks. Reverse arrows indicate iterative steps.

works well in a system defined into successively smaller components, such as systems, components, modules, and functions, as described in previous sections of this chapter. Requirements are mapped to successively lower levels of design using *test matrices*. At the lowest level of decomposition, usually the individual function and interface level, *test assertions* claim that the interfaces meet the specifics of each requirement for those interfaces. These test assertions are used to develop test cases, which may be individual tests or families of tests. This strategy is accompanied by a documentation approach that fits nicely with traditional test planning and documentation.

20.3.3.2.1 Test Matrices

The PGWG methodology defines two levels of test matrices (high and low). Rows reflect the decomposition of the entity to be tested. If design decomposition is previously defined in the design documentation, identifying row headers is a simple task. The rows of the high-level matrix are the entity subsystems or major components. The columns in the high-level matrix reflect security areas to be considered. Selection of security areas should be a simple task, because security requirements should already be well-defined. The security areas focus on functional requirements (as opposed to assurance requirements or documentation requirements). Examples of security functional areas may be discretionary access controls, nondiscretionary access controls, audit, integrity controls, cryptography, trusted communications, and the like. The cells of the high-level test matrix provide pointers to relevant documentation and to lower-level test matrices.

In a large and complex system with a multiple-layer design decomposition, it may be useful to create intermediate levels of test matrices to address components or even modules of components in individual matrices. If intermediate levels are used, there is one lower-level matrix for each row of the higher-level matrix until the lowest level is reached. At the intermediate levels, it may be useful to refine the security areas that define the columns. For example, discretionary access could be decomposed into protection-bit-based access controls and access-control-list-based controls. The cells of intermediate levels have contents similar to those of a high-level matrix.

At the lowest level, matrix rows are the interfaces to the subsystem or component. The columns could be represented as security areas, subdivisions of security areas, or even individual requirements. The size and complexity of the system are the determining factors. The cells of the lowest level are the heart of the decomposition methodology. They contain test assertions (or pointers to test assertion sets). Each assertion applies to a single interface and a single requirement, and all assertions relative to each cell in the low-level test matrix must be identified. Once the assertions have been developed, it is a simple matter to fill in the cells in the higher-level matrices.

When the low-level matrices are completed, any empty cells must be justified to ensure that coverage is complete. The cells should refer to a rationale that justifies why a particular requirement class does not apply to a particular interface.

EXAMPLE: Consider security testing of a typical security-enhanced UNIX product. The subsystems include file management, memory management, process management, process control, I/O interfaces, I/O devices, and IPC management. The security functional requirement areas of this UNIX system are discretionary access controls (DAC), privileges, identification and authentication (I&A), object reuse protection, security audit, and system architecture constraints. The mechanisms implementing the DAC requirements include the abbreviated access controls of UNIX systems (see Section 16.1.1) as well as full access control lists. The privilege implementation uses a "privilege vector" to allow normal users to access certain functions that are usually restricted to the root user. I&A mechanisms include login, password, password constraints, and system entry constraints. Object reuse mechanisms are the standard purge-on-reallocation and revocation-of-access-rights-on-deallocation mechanisms found in UNIX systems. Security audit mechanisms expand beyond the standard UNIX logging capabilities. System architecture mechanisms include isolation and private execution domain issues.

In this system, testing is done using an interpretation of the PGWG methodology. The high-level matrix used is as follows.

	Security Requirement Area					
Component	**DAC**	**Priv**	**I&A**	**OR**	**Audit**	**Arch**
Process management					x	
Process control	x	x		x	x	x
File management	x	x		x	x	x
Audit subsystem		x	x	x	x	x
I/O subsystem interfaces	x	x	x	x	x	
I/O device drivers		x		x	x	x
IPC management	x	x		x	x	x
Memory management	x	x		x	x	x

An "x" in a cell indicates that there are requirements in that security area that apply to that component. If a cell is empty, then the security area does not apply to the particular subsystem. Forward references are provided for the low-level matrices, which contain justifications of the empty cells in all matrices.

One low-level matrix is developed for each row of the system's high-level matrix. The rows are the system calls of the pertinent subsystem, and the columns are expanded to address subdivisions of the security areas.

System Call	**DAC u/g/o**	**DAC ACL**	**Priv**	**I&A**	**OR**	**Security Audit**	**Logging**	**Isolation**	**Protection Domains**
brk					x			x	x
madvise								x	x
mmap	x	x			x	x	x	x	x
mprotect	x	x				x		x	x
msync								x	x
munmap			x		x	x		x	x
plock	x	x	x		x	x		x	x
vm-ctl	x	x	x		x	x	x	x	x

(The column labeled "DAC u/g/o" refers to DAC using the UNIX style of permissions; see Section 16.1.1.) An "x" in a cell means that high-level test specification (HLTS) documents contain the relevant assertions for the (interface, security requirement area) pair.

20.3.3.2.2 Test Assertions

Test assertions are created by reviewing design documentation and identifying conditions that are security-relevant, testable, and analyzable. If the documentation contains requirements tracing, creating test assertions is greatly simplified and developing assertions provides an excellent review of the existing requirement trace. Assertions are at a very fine level of granularity, and each assertion should generate one or more individual tests that illustrate that the assertion is met. In rare cases, an assertion will not be testable. It should then be verified by other means, such as analysis.

PGWG presents three methods for stating assertions. The first technique is to develop brief statements describing behavior that the tester must verify, such as "Verify that the calling process needs DAC write access permission to the parent directory of the file being created. Verify that if access is denied, the return error code is 2." The second technique is very similar to the first, but the form of the statement is different, making claims that the tester must prove or disprove with tests. For example, an assertion might be "The calling process needs DAC write access permission to the parent directory of the file being created, and if access is denied, it returns error code 2." The third method states assertions as claims that are embedded within a structured specification format.

20.3.3.2.3 Test Specifications

Define one or more test cases to verify the truth of each assertion for each interface. The test cases are specified by test specifications. PGWG suggests the use of high-level test specifications (HLTS) to describe and specify the test cases for each interface, and low-level test specifications (LLTS), which provide specific information about each test case, such as setup conditions, cleanup conditions, and other environmental conditions.

EXAMPLE: We present a high-level test specification for the interface *stime*(). The HLTS should include an overview of the interface being specified and relevant documentation references as well as the assertion and test case specifications shown below.

Assertion Number	Requirement Area and Number	Assertion	Relevant Test Cases
1	PRIV AC_1	Verify that only the root can use the system call *stime*() successfully	Stime_1, 2
2	PRIV AC_3	Verify that an audit record is generated for every failed call to *stime*()	Stime_1, 2
3	PRIV AC_3	Verify that an audit record is generated for every successful call to *stime*()	Stime_1, 2

Test case specifications describe specific tests required to meet the assertions.

Test Case Name and Number	Is UserID = *root*?	Expected Results
Stime_1	Yes	Call to *stime*() should succeed. An audit record should be generated noting the successful attempt and the new clock time.
Stime_2	No	Call to *stime*() should fail. An audit record should be generated noting the failed attempt.

EXAMPLE: We now show a low-level test specification (LLTS) for stime_1. These specifications are written for each individual test. The LLTS should identify the test name, test descriptions, any assumptions about the hardware or the environment that are necessary to run the test, the test case setup, algorithms, and procedures. The LLTS can be put into the test case code as comments and extracted for documentation if necessary.

Test case name: K_MIS_stime_1

Test case description: Call *stime* as a non*root* user to change the system time. The *stime* call should fail, verifying that only *root* can use the *stime* system call successfully.

Expected result: The *stime* call should fail with a return value of −1, the system clock should be unchanged, and the error number should be set to **EPERM** (indicating that permission for the access is denied). The audit record should be as specified below.

Test specific setup:

1. Log in as the non*root* user (*secusr1*).

2. Get the current system time.

Algorithm:

1. Do the setup as above.

2. Call *stime* to change the system time to 10 minutes ahead of the current time.

3. If the return value from the *stime* call is −1, the error number is **EPERM**, and the current system time is not the new time passed to *stime* as a parameter, declare that the *stime* call passed the test; otherwise, declare that it failed.

Cleanup: Restore the system time (if it has changed) by reducing the current time by 10 minutes.

Audit record field values for failure (success):

Authid	secusr1
RUID	secusr1
EUID	secusr1
RGID	scgrp1
EGID	secgrp1
Class	tune
Reason	Privilege failure (success)
Event	SETTHETIME_1
Message	Privilege failure (none)

20.3.3.3   Formal Methods: Proving That Programs Are Correct

Just as there are formal methods for specification and for proving that a design specification is consistent with its security requirements, there are techniques for proving properties about programs. Used during the coding process, these techniques help avoid bugs. They work best on small parts of a program that performs a well-defined task. This technique can be used for some programs that enforce security functionality. Chapter 21, "Formal Methods," covers these techniques.

20.4   Assurance during Operation and Maintenance

While a system is in operation, bugs will occur, requiring maintenance on the system. A *hot fix* addresses bugs immediately and is sent out as quickly as possible. Hot fixes correct bugs that can immediately affect the security or operation of the system. A *regular fix* addresses less serious bugs or provides long-term solutions to bugs already addressed with hot fixes. Regular fixes are usually collected until some condition is met. Then the vendor issues a maintenance release containing those fixes. If the system involved is not sold to others but instead is used internally, the problems that hot fixes address are usually not addressed by regular fixes also.

As part of the maintenance of a system, well-defined procedures track reported flaws. The information about each flaw should include a description of the flaw, remedial actions taken or planned, the flaw's priority severity, and the progress in fixing the code, documentation, a pointer to the configuration management system entries related to the flaw corrections, and other aspects of the flaw.

The action taken for a maintenance release or bug fix should follow the same security procedures used during the original development. Any new design should follow the modularity considerations, design principle considerations, documentation, and justifications for the first release. Furthermore, the vendor must apply to the bug fix or maintenance release all security considerations and assurance measures that were used in the implementation, integration, and security testing of the original product. The vendor must update the assurance evidence appropriately. For fixes, the vendor must rerun the pertinent parts of the security test suite. For maintenance releases, the vendor must rerun the security tests for the system.

20.5   Summary

Security assurance is an integral part of the life cycle of product or system development. Assurance measures are taken at every step of the process, from requirements development through design and development to testing and release, and must be supported during product or system operation. Consistency between distributed development teams in terms of assurance techniques and implementation of security features accessing large components is critical to security assurance of the product or system.

The process begins with analyses of the goals of the system and the threats against which the system must be protected. These analyses guide the development of the architecture of the system and its security policy and mechanisms. As part of this process, the requirements for each of these elements are stated and justified.

System and software design must also include assurance. There are specific design goals that lead to the desired level of assurance. Documentation of decisions, designs, and the process through which these decisions and designs were developed provides information on which beliefs of assurance can be based. The design documents and software specification documents include both external and internal interfaces and functions and justify that the design meets the requirements. Formal (or informal) methods of implementation and testing provide assurance at the implementation level.

20.6   Research Issues

Research issues abound. One important issue is creating systems and products from commercial off-the-shelf (COTS) components and providing as high a level of assurance as possible that the resulting system meets its requirements. The problem lies in the difficulty of assessing composition and assessing the COTS components, few of which are constructed using high-assurance techniques. This is frequently addressed by reviewing the code provided for COTS components and performing functional and integration testing on the COTS components. When a COTS component is updated, developers normally review the changes made to the component and re-execute the functional and integration tests. As discussed in this chapter, these techniques alone do not provide a high level of assurance.

Adding appropriate assurance measures at appropriate times in the software engineering life cycle is another critical issue. The process by which the system or product is developed affects the degree of assurance. For example, use of a methodology such as the SSE-CMM (see Section 22.9) imparts a certain level of assurance.

Requirements analysis is often overlooked in the security arena, and yet it forms the basis for the definition of security by guiding the development of a security policy. Expressing requirements unambiguously but in a way that is easily understood and analyzing requirements for feasibility in a particular environment and for consistency are difficult problems.

Testing of systems and products for security is another area of active research. Property-based testing abstracts security as a set of properties and then tests conformance to those properties. Other types of testing, notably software fault injection, assess the assurance of existing systems and products.

20.7 Further Reading

Yen and Paul [2052] present a short survey of six areas in which high assurance is critical. Assurance is also critical in safety-related software [274, 728, 856, 1147, 1224, 1237, 1455, 1937, 2060].

An early methodology for assertion-based testing and requirements correspondence in security is discussed by Bullough, Loomis, and Weiss [312].

Several papers consider the problem of providing assurance when components are assembled for a system [341, 860, 1187]. Programming languages provide a foundation for assurance, and the design and iteration of assurance into both languages and supporting subsystems such as libraries is critical [796].

Technologies that aid the processes described in this chapter include requirements analysis and checking [862, 1223, 1283, 1756, 2078], architectural description languages [1898], and documentation [214, 1375]. Several authors have described methodologies and experiences [749, 1059, 1286, 1933, 2009].

Arbo, Johnson, and Sharp [69] present a network interface that allows System V/MLS to be used in a network MLS environment. Kang, Moore, and Moskowitz analyze the design of the NRL pump for assurance [998]. Smith [1769] discusses the cost-benefit impacts of using formal methods for software assurance.

Property-based testing [678, 679, 771, 1077] tests process conformance to a stated security policy. Software fault injection [77, 463, 464, 764, 1940, 1941] tests how systems react to failures of components. Both methods can be adapted to testing for other, nonsecurity problems as well.

20.8   Exercises

1. Distinguish between a policy requirement and a mechanism. Identify at least three specific security requirements for a system you know and describe at least two different mechanisms for implementing each one.

2. Justify that the four security properties in System X (see the example that begins on page 658) are consistent with the Bell-LaPadula properties. Use the System X statements in this chapter. Identify any information you may need to complete the justification that you do not find in this material.

3. In System Y (see the example on page 661), assumption A3 restricts the access to authentication data to administrators. Should this assumption have been used in the justification of threat T1? Why or why not? If yes, create the appropriate statements to add to the justification given above.

4. Pick a life cycle development model not discussed in Chapter 19 and describe how useful it is for development of secure and trusted products.

5. This exercise deals with the external specifications discussed in Section 20.2.4.1.

   a. Write the external functional specification for the *login* function in the example that begins on page 679.

   b. Write the external functional specification for the *change_password* function in the example that begins on page 679.

   c. Write the low-level test matrix, test assertions, and test case specifications for the *login* function for the external functional specification written in part (a).

   d. Write the low-level test matrix, test assertions, and test case specifications for the *change_password* function for the external functional specification written in part (b).

6. Discuss the benefits and disadvantages of building secure and trusted products or systems with assurance using an Agile software development methodology.

7. Write an informal review process for a small development organization.

Chapter 21
Formal Methods

> PETRUCHIO: And, for an entrance to my entertainment,
> I do present you with a man of mine
> [*Presenting Hortensio.*]
> Cunning in music and the mathematics,
> To instruct her fully in those sciences,
> Whereof I know she is not ignorant:
> Accept of him, or else you do me wrong:
> His name is Licio, born in Mantua.
> — *The Taming of the Shrew*, II, i, 54–60.

Previous chapters have addressed the topic of assurance in general and have described how assurance can be acquired throughout the life cycle of a product or system. To this point, the methods and techniques that have been discussed have been informal in nature and dependent on documentation and written requirements statements for design assurance and on testing for implementation assurance. Chapter 20, "Building Systems with Assurance," introduced the concepts of formal specification languages for specifying requirements and systems as well as mathematically based automated formal methods for proving properties of specifications and programs. This chapter discusses these topics more fully, examining past and present formal specification and proof technologies.

21.1 Formal Verification Techniques

As in the techniques discussed in previous chapters, formal verification techniques rely on descriptions of the properties or requirements of interest, descriptions of systems to be analyzed, and verification techniques for showing that the system descriptions are sufficient to meet the requirements. The difference between the formal methods and those described in Chapter 20 is the degree of formality of the approach.

Part III, "Policy," presented a variety of formal and informal security policy models. The formal models are presented in the language of mathematics. This chapter introduces other formal languages, called *specification languages*, that are useful for representing policies, models, and system descriptions. These languages have well-defined syntax and semantics and are based on a mathematical logic system. This chapter also addresses formal verification techniques that process the formal specifications, determining how well each specification meets the requirements stated in the policy/model or requirements specification. All verification techniques rely on the underlying structure of some mathematical logic system and the proof theory of that logic. Appendix E, "Symbolic Logic," provides a very brief overview of several logical systems that are used in formal proof technologies and presents fundamental definitions and theories. The reader who is inexperienced in logical systems should review that chapter before proceeding.

Although all formal verification techniques implement similar concepts and approaches, current trends have divided these techniques into inductive verification techniques and model checking techniques. The differences between these two types of techniques are based on the intended use, degree of automation, general logical approach, and underlying logic system. Huth and Ryan [937] provide an excellent set of criteria for classifying verification technologies.

- *Proof-based versus model-based techniques.* Proof-based techniques define a set of formulas called *premises* that embody the system description and another formula called the *conclusion* that represents what is to be proved (the properties). These techniques rely on finding a set of intermediate formulas that allow the verifier to reach the desired conclusion beginning from the premises. Model-based techniques rely on establishing that the premises and the conclusion exhibit the same truth table values.

- *Degree of automation.* Approaches vary from fully automated to fully manual, with every possibility in between.

- *Full verification versus property verification.* The system specification may describe an entire system or parts of it, and the property specification may be as small as a single property or may contain many properties.

- *Intended domain of application.* This may be hardware or software, sequential or concurrent, reactive[1] or terminating, or other types of systems.

- *Predevelopment versus postdevelopment.* A verification technique may be intended to be used as a design aid or for verification of the system after the design is complete.

Inductive verification techniques are typically more general in nature. Some of the techniques we discuss below were designed to be general-purpose software

---

[1]Huth and Ryan [937] define a reactive system as one that is not meant to terminate. Examples include operating systems, embedded systems, and computer hardware.

development methodologies, addressing all stages of the life cycle. Other inductive verification systems simply provide mechanisms for proof of theorems. All are based on generation of formulas that show that a specification of a system meets the requirements of a set of properties. These techniques often have separate steps to create formulas that claim that the specification meets the properties. These formulas are submitted to a theorem prover that uses a higher-order logic such as predicate calculus. The theorem prover attempts to show that the premises and conclusion are provably equivalent by finding a series of proof steps starting with the premises of the formula and eventually reaching the conclusion of the formula. The user of an inductive verification technique generally guides a theorem prover in finding a proof by supplying lemmata and previous results that can be used to prove more complex theorems. Some inductive verification techniques are used in the development cycle to find flaws during the design process. Others are used to verify the properties of computer programs.

Model checking techniques also establish how well a specification of a system meets a set of properties. The systems modeled are state transition systems, and a formula may be true in some states and false in others. Formulas may change truth values as the system evolves from one state to another. The properties to be verified by a model checker are formulas in a temporal logic. In temporal logic, truth or falsehood of a formula is dynamic and is not statically true or false as in propositional and predicate logic. Section E.3, "Temporal Logic Systems," presents an example of a temporal logic system.

Typically, a model checker addresses a single model that is built into a tool or given to the tool as a specification of external properties. The tool is usually automatic, with little or no interaction with the users' point of view. Formula generation and proof are a single step from the user view. The model checker attempts to show that the model of the system and the desired properties are semantically equivalent, which can be described by saying that the model and properties exhibit the same truth table. The user initiates the model checker and waits for the results. The model checking approach is often used after development is complete but before a product is released to the general market. Model checking was designed for concurrent systems and systems that react to the environment and that are not expected to terminate.

EXAMPLE: The Hierarchical Development Methodology (HDM) of SRI International will be used in many examples in this chapter. HDM began as a general-purpose proof-based formal verification methodology addressing design through implementation. It was an automated and general-purpose (rather than property-oriented) methodology. It supported formal descriptions of a system at various levels of abstraction, using specification languages, implementation languages, and verification techniques to demonstrate that successive levels of abstraction were consistent.

HDM also provided one of the earliest so-called model checkers with its Multilevel Security (MLS) tool, although the theorem prover uses a proof-based technique. The input to the MLS tool was a formal specification in the language SPECIAL, a nonprocedural design specification language that was very effective for writing external functional specifications. This tool is a fully auto-mated, property-oriented verification system. The MLS tool embodies the SRI model, which is an interpretation of the Bell-LaPadula Model. MLS processed SPECIAL specifications to determine potential violations of the model within the specification. This was accomplished by the MLS verification condition generator, which created formulas that asserted that the specifications correctly implemented the embedded SRI model. The Boyer-Moore theorem prover processed these formulas. The output of the MLS program was a list of formulas that passed and those that failed.

The final section of this chapter addresses the analysis of cryptographic protocols, which lends itself nicely to the use of formal methods. The protocols themselves are relatively small and contained but may present complex and exploitable flaws. Protocol verification has been a hugely popular topic in the computer security research community over the past decade. Protocol verification has been accomplished using inductive proof methodologies as well as model checkers, and there are several special-purpose protocol verification methodolo-gies in wide use. Many are based on the knowledge and belief logics of Burrows, Abadi, and Needham [325], and others describe the interactions of a set of state machines to attempt to prove that a protocol is secure.

21.2   Formal Specification

Recall that a *specification* is a description of characteristics of a computer system or program. A *security specification* specifies desired security properties. (See Definition 20–7.) To this we add the definition of a formal specification.

> **Definition 21–1.** A *formal specification* is a specification written in a formal language with a restricted syntax and well-defined semantics based on well-established mathematical concepts.

Formal specifications use a language with precise semantics. This avoids ambiguity and may allow for proofs of properties about the specification. These languages support precise descriptions of the behavior of system functions and generally eliminate implementation details.

EXAMPLE: One good example of the use of formal mathematical specifications can be seen in the Bell-LaPadula security policy model (see Section 5.2.3). The elements and rules of this security policy model are precisely defined in mathe-matical language. Using this well-defined specification, theorems were generated showing the consistency of the model rules with its axioms. Precise mathematical proofs of the theorems complete this model. Other formal specification languages resemble programming languages and are usually supported by automated tools that verify correct syntax and semantics of a specification in the language.

Generally, the specification languages are supported by automated tools for verifying the correct use of the language syntax and semantics. Inductive verification, protocol verifiers, and model checkers use formal specification languages as input to the tools of the technique, making a formal specification a part of any formal verification technology. Formal specification is also important as a stand-alone technique. The specification may or may not be needed for some proof process. The process of writing formal specifications helps us to understand the design better and to see potential flaws, even without claims and proofs.

SPECIAL is a first-order logic-based language developed at SRI International as a stand-alone specification language. SPECIAL provides an excellent example of a nonprocedural and strongly typed specification language that is well suited for writing functional specifications, as described in Chapter 20. The strengths of SPECIAL are the richness of its expressive capability and its ability to describe inputs, constraints, errors, and outputs without implementation details. SPECIAL has a rich set of built-in operators, including set operations such as UNION and DIFF; logical operators such as AND, OR, and => (implies); universal and existential quantifiers (FORALL, EXISTS); IF/THEN/ELSE constructs; arithmetic operators; and many others. SPECIAL also has a mechanism for distinguishing an old value of a variable from a new value.

A specification in SPECIAL represents a module, and the specifier defines the scope of the module. Several modules can be used to describe a system. Two good reasons to make smaller modules are convenience and ease of manipulation, but another reason is to take advantage of the ability to hide information between modules.

A SPECIAL module specification has several sections for describing types, parameters, assertions, and functions. SPECIAL types are identified syntactically using keywords in capital letters. Two examples are the DESIGNATOR type, which allows the use of a type whose specifics are to be defined at a lower level of abstraction, and the BOOLEAN type, which includes the values TRUE and FALSE. SPECIAL also supports discrete sets, sets defined in terms of other types, and structured types. Parameters define constants and entities whose ability to change is outside the scope of the specification. Definitions are a shortcut for complex expressions that need to be used repeatedly. Global assertions can be made about the other elements of the module and can be used in proving theorems about the specification.

The heart of the SPECIAL specification is the functions, which define state variables and state transitions. Any function can be defined as private to the scope of the module in which that function is defined or as visible and addressable outside the specific module description. The visible functions define the external interface to the module. A visible function may have an exceptions clause that lists the conditions to be tested and passed for the effects of the function to take place. VFUNs describe variable data. Primitive VFUNs describe the system state variables, whereas derived VFUNs provide values determined by expressions involving primitive VFUNs, which have an initial value. VFUNs are viewed as functions that return a value to the caller and thus contribute to the definition of the system state. OFUNs and OVFUNs describe state transitions. They have exception sections as well as an effects section that describes changes in VFUN values. Like OFUNs, OVFUNs describe state transitions, but, like VFUNs, they also return a value and thus are state transition functions and contribute to the state of the system. Any function specification can contain "local" assertions that are specific to the function.

EXAMPLE: The specification below represents parts of the SPECIAL specification of the Bell-LaPadula Model. The *give-access* rule is a generalization of the *give-read* rule described in Section 5.2.4.2.

```
MODULE Bell_LaPadula_Model give-access
TYPES
Subject_ID:     DESIGNATOR;
Object_ID:      DESIGNATOR;
Access_Mode:    {OBSERVE_ONLY, ALTER_ONLY, OBSERVE_AND_ALTER};
Access: STRUCT_OF(    Subject_ID    subject;
                      Object_ID     object;
                      Access_Mode   mode);
FUNCTIONS
VFUN active (Object_ID object) -> BOOLEAN active:
HIDDEN;
INITIALLY
        TRUE;
VFUN access_matrix () -> Accesses accesses:
HIDDEN;
INITIALLY
        FORALL Access a: a INSET accesses => active(a.object);
OFUN give-access(Subject_ID giver; Access access);
ASSERTIONS
        active(access.object) = TRUE;
EFFECTS
        access_matrix() = access_matrix() UNION (access);
END_MODULE
```

This example defines four types. The Subject_ID and Object_ID are to be described at a lower level of abstraction, and so are of type DESIGNATOR. Variables of type Access_Mode may take only the values OBSERVE_ONLY, ALTER_ONLY, and OBSERVE_AND_ALTER. The type Access is a structure with three fields—namely, a Subject_ID, an Object_ID, and an Access_Mode. The first VFUN defines the state variable active for an object to be TRUE. The second VFUN defines the state variable access_matrix to be the set of triplets of (subject, object, right). The OFUN defines the transition occurring when a new element is added to the matrix. It requires that the state variable active for the object be **TRUE** (in the ASSERTIONS). Then the value of the variable `access_matrix` after the transition is the value of that variable before the transition, with the additional access right added to the `access_matrix` variable. An interpretation of this specification is that the triples in `access_matrix` define the current set of access rights in the system and the `active` state variable for an `object` is **TRUE** if the object is in `access_matrix`—that is, if the `object` exists.

21.3 Early Formal Verification Techniques

Some early work in formal methods attempted to mechanize and formalize the entire development process. This approach met with only limited success but provided invaluable lessons that led to further research that produced more useful results. Other early work led to modern-day model checkers, and still other early work analyzed communications protocols. This work demonstrated the importance of the individual components by themselves and not just as parts of an overall method. More recent research has focused on more specific entities (for example, one part of the overall picture, such as proofs, and one type of system, such as cryptographic protocols).

In the 1970s and 1980s, several formal verification systems were developed. The most well-known of these systems are described in Cheheyl et al. [395], from which much of the material in this section is drawn. We will discuss two verification systems to illustrate the basic concepts of verification. The Enhanced Hierarchical Development Methodology focuses on proofs of design, whereas the Gypsy Verification Environment focuses on proofs of implementation.

21.3.1 The Hierarchical Development Methodology

The Enhanced Hierarchical Development Methodology (EHDM) was strongly based on its predecessor, the Hierarchical Development Methodology (HDM) [1449]. HDM was a general-purpose design and implementation methodology. Its goal was to mechanize and formalize the entire development process, providing reliable, verifiable, and maintainable software. The HDM package addressed design specification and verification as well as implementation specification and verification, using the concept of successive refinement of specifications.

The system design specification was created as a hierarchy that consisted of a series of abstract machines at increasing levels of detail. The hierarchy began with requirements. These requirements were expanded into a model that was proven to be internally consistent. Next, layers of abstract machines represented the system at increasingly lower levels of detail, as shown in Figure 21–1.

The *hierarchy specification* was written in the Hierarchy Specification Language (HSL). It identified the abstract machines of the hierarchy. The abstract machines were made up of sets of module specifications written in SPECIAL, as

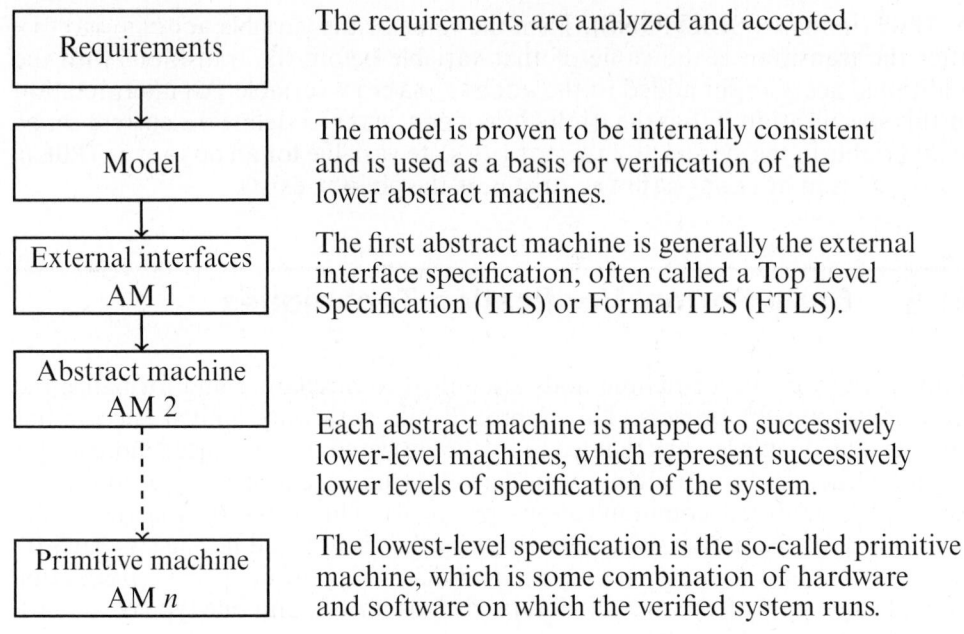

The requirements are analyzed and accepted.

The model is proven to be internally consistent and is used as a basis for verification of the lower abstract machines.

The first abstract machine is generally the external interface specification, often called a Top Level Specification (TLS) or Formal TLS (FTLS).

Each abstract machine is mapped to successively lower-level machines, which represent successively lower levels of specification of the system.

The lowest-level specification is the so-called primitive machine, which is some combination of hardware and software on which the verified system runs.

Figure 21–1   Levels of abstract machines in HDM.

shown in the example that begins on page 704. Each abstract machine specification had one or more module specifications, each of which defined a group of related functions. Modules could be reused in one or more abstract machines.

Mapping specifications defined the functions of one abstract machine in terms of the next higher machine. HDM module and mapping specifications were written in SPECIAL. Module and mapping specifications each had some unique constructs and a large set of common constructs. Several tools supported module and mapping specifications, including syntax checkers and consistency checkers.

A *hierarchy consistency checker* ensured consistency among the hierarchy specifications, the associated module specifications for each machine, and the mapping specifications between the abstract machines.

The basis for HDM implementation specification was the design hierarchy. The specification was accomplished by looking at each pair of consecutive abstract machines and the mapping between them. For each function in the higher-level abstract machine, programs were written to show how the function was implemented in terms of calls to the lower-level abstract machine. These programs were to be written in a high-order language that had a compiler. To verify these programs, a translator mapped the program into a Common Internal Form (CIF) that the HDM tools understood. Such a translator existed for a restricted version of Modula. Using the mappings, the two levels of specifications were translated into an intermediate language. This language, together with the

CIF, generated verification conditions to be sent to the Boyer-Moore theorem prover. Assuming that the lower-level machine worked as specified, the higher-level machine was verified to work correctly. Given the correspondence of the CIF to the real programs, correctness of the CIF implied correctness of the real implementation. See Figure 21–2.

21.3.1.1 Verification in HDM

The implementation specification and verification parts of HDM were never used outside the research environment, nor was the originally planned design verification in HDM. The approach centered on the proof that the top-level specification correctly implemented a set of predefined properties within a model. The original intent was to be able to provide design verification for a wide variety of models and properties, but the difficulty in formally stating properties other than those found in U.S. Department of Defense (DOD) policy limited the utility of this approach. HDM was used as a design verification package for the Multilevel Security (MLS) tool [655]. This tool implemented a version of the Bell-LaPadula Model known as the SRI model and processed SPECIAL specifications for consistency with the model properties.

The SRI model differed from an implementation of the Bell-LaPadula Model in several aspects [1862]. The SRI model was specifically constructed to function within the MLS tool. As a result, some entities differed from their Bell-LaPadula counterparts. Some entities had no counterparts. For example, the SRI model addressed visible function references and results (from VFUNs or OVFUNs), whereas the Bell-LaPadula Model did not have these elements. On the other hand, the Bell-LaPadula Model addressed discretionary access control and had a concept of current access triples as well as an access permission matrix.

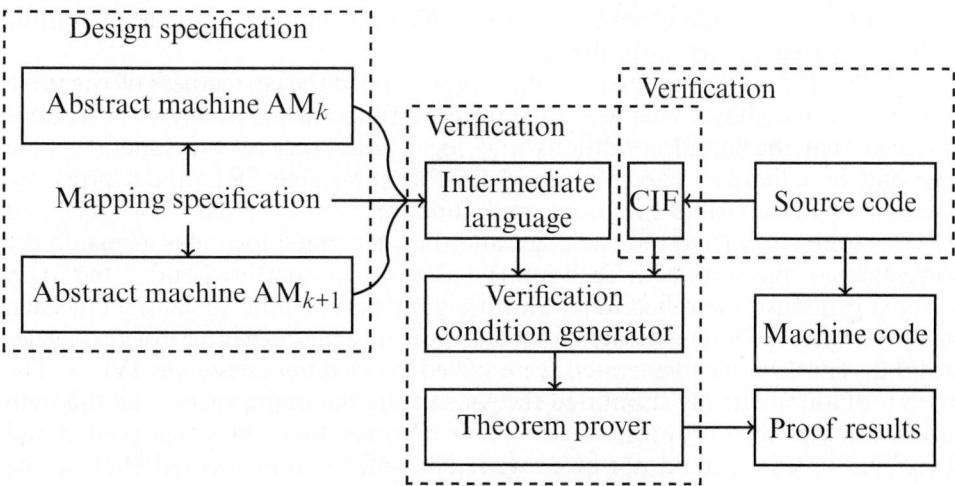

Figure 21–2 Implementation verification in HDM.

These entities did not appear in the SRI model. Both models had mandatory access control properties, and both called the mandatory rules the simple security condition and the *-property, but the rules differed slightly between the two models. Subjects were implicitly defined in the SRI model (as the invokers of functions). They were explicitly defined in the Bell-LaPadula Model. In the Bell-LaPadula Model, the *-property was expressed in terms of allowable access, but in the SRI model, that property addressed downward flow of information. Thus, they were not the same [1862].

The SRI model embedded in the MLS tool has three properties:

1. The information being returned by a specific function invocation could depend only on information at a security level lower than or equal to that of the subject.

2. The information flowing into a state variable (VFUN) could depend only on other state variables that had security levels lower than that of the first state variable.

3. If the value of a state variable was modified, the modification could be done only by a function invocation whose level is the same as or lower than the level of the state variable.

The underlying model of the MLS tool was a reasonable interpretation of the multilevel policy of the U.S. Department of Defense. It was used successfully for several years to analyze the mandatory access control properties of systems and products.

The MLS tool processed a SPECIAL specification that described the externally visible interfaces to the SPECIAL model, as shown in Figure 21–1. When the MLS tool was used, one abstract machine was represented, and there were no mappings, but there might have been multiple modules in the specification. The SPECIAL module checker had to verify each module, and the hierarchy consistency tool had to verify the set of modules.

The MLS tool generated formulas that claimed the correctness of the three properties listed above. This was done for each function separately. All formulas assumed that the initial conditions and local assertions of the function were true and hypothesized the correctness of the applicable SRI model property. Exceptions from visible functions and function returns from OVFUNs and VFUNs were considered return values and thus generated formulas asserting the correctness of property 1 for each return value. For properties 2 and 3, the MLS formula generator identified new value assignments for state variables. For each such reference, the tool generated formulas asserting the correctness of properties 2 and 3. The formulas generated were called *verification conditions* (VCs). The MLS tool automatically submitted the VCs to the theorem prover. The theorem prover attempted to prove the theorems. It reported those VCs that passed and those that failed or could not be proved. This information was fed back to the MLS tool.

21.3.1.2   The Boyer-Moore Theorem Prover

The Boyer-Moore theorem prover [283] was a fully automated program. It did not have an interface for commands or directions to the theorem prover to take user-defined actions. The user had to provide any theorems, axioms, lemmata, and assertions that were needed to assist in the proof process. These were expressed in a LISP-like notation. For example, when proving VCs from the MLS tool, the theorem prover needed fundamental axioms about the elements of the VCs, such as rules of transitivity, reflexivity, and antisymmetry of the partial ordering relationship between security levels (see Section 5.2). The MLS tool provided these axioms to the theorem prover.

This approach made it easier for the user to prove simple theorems but potentially more difficult to prove more complex theorems. The user needed to understand the underlying theory used by the theorem prover in order to structure input in such a way that the theorem prover could find a proof. The Boyer-Moore theorem prover maintained a file of previously proven theorems and axioms that it could use in future proofs. In spite of the limitations, this theorem prover was capable of complex mathematical proofs.

The theory behind the Boyer-Moore theorem prover used an extended propositional calculus. This was enhanced to support the needs of computer programs. The heuristics of the theorem prover were organized to find a proof in the most efficient manner. The prover then performed a series of steps on a formula in search of a proof. The fundamental steps were as follows:

- *Simplify* the formula by applying axioms, lemmata, and function definitions. Other simplifications included rerepresenting the formula by converting it to a conjunction of *if*-free clauses.
- *Reformulate* the formula by trading terms for equivalent terms that are easier for the theorem prover to process. For example, if a theorem involved the term $x - 1$ $(x \neq 0)$, the theorem prover would replace x by $y + 1$. The formula now contained the terms y and $y + 1$ rather than $x - 1$ and x.
- *Substitute equalities* by replacing equality expressions with appropriate substitutions, eliminating the equality clauses. For example, if (EQUAL s t) appeared in the formula, the theorem prover replaced t with s elsewhere in the formula and eliminated the equality.
- *Generalize* the formula by introducing variables for terms whose roles have been completed.
- *Eliminate* irrelevant terms from the formula.
- *Induct* to prove theorems when necessary.

The first step was always simplification, which could have resulted in a conclusion of the proof process by reducing the formula to "TRUE" or "FALSE." If a conclusion was not reached, the theorem prover attempted the next step.

If this did not result in a conclusion, processing returned to the simplification step. Processing iterated between simplification and reformulation until a conclusion was reached, or simplification or reformulation did not produce additional changes to the formula. The prover then attempted equality substitution, and if a conclusion was not reached, it returned to the simplification step and the process was repeated. In this way, the theorem prover iterated between simplification, reformulation, and equality substitution until a conclusion was reached or actions were exhausted. The prover might have split off subgoals at any step, and these were addressed separately. After carrying out each step in the sequence, the prover returned to the simplification step and proceeded to the next step if nothing could be done on any previous steps. Thus induction was only carried out if a proof could not be reached via the other steps.

21.3.2 Enhanced HDM

HDM had some limitations that were addressed in a new, enhanced version of the system called *Enhanced HDM*, or EHDM. The fundamental framework of HDM was preserved but was enhanced to work more smoothly and with less complexity for the user. Like HDM, EHDM used modules as the building blocks of specifications. It supported multiple abstract machines and mappings between them and had an MLS tool for design verification. Like HDM, EHDM supported implementation verification. The difficulties with HDM focused on three areas: the language SPECIAL, some of the tools, and limitations of the theorem prover.

SPECIAL, which had been designed as a stand-alone specification language before HDM was developed, was not defined in terms that the Boyer-Moore theorem prover could readily use. This was attributable in part to the richness of the language and in part to the lack of specific constructs needed by the theorem prover. The missing constructs made formula generation and proof difficult. As a result, the toolset lacked a general-purpose verification condition generator to create verification conditions from SPECIAL that the Boyer-Moore theorem prover could use. Finally, the theorem prover itself was not interactive, requiring the user to understand the underlying theory used by the theorem prover in order to structure input in such a way that the theorem prover could find a proof.

To remedy these problems, new language constructs were needed. Eventually SPECIAL was eliminated as the specification language for EHDM, and a new language was developed. The new language bore many similarities to SPECIAL but was much more powerful. It had the rich, expressive capabilities of SPECIAL but had more logical constructs, allowing for more reusable specifications and proofs. The new language used the concepts of AXIOM, THEOREM, and LEMMA, which helped make it more conducive to the use of a theorem prover.

The HDM theorem prover was not interactive. The user had to understand the underlying theory used by the theorem prover in order to structure input so that the theorem prover could find a proof. The EHDM theorem prover was based on the Boyer-Moore theorem prover but was interactive. The MLS tool that worked with EHDM was one of the formal verification tools approved by the

National Computer Security Center (NCSC) for use in high-assurance evaluations of computer products (see Section 22.2.3).

21.3.3 The Gypsy Verification Environment

This discussion of the Gypsy Verification Environment (GVE) and its language Gypsy is based on the work of Cheheyl et al. [395]. GVE focused on implementation proofs rather than design proofs, and the verification system attempted to prove a correspondence between specifications and their implementation. It was also possible to use the GVE to prove properties of Gypsy specifications. The GVE was based on structured programming, formal proof, and formal specification methods. It supported a set of tools that included a Gypsy language parser, a verification condition generator, and a theorem prover.

21.3.3.1 The Gypsy Language

Gypsy was a program description language and combined specification language constructs with a programming language. Using Gypsy, specifications could be added to program code at appropriate places in an implementation program. Alternatively, Gypsy could be used as an abstract specification language, using abstract types and their operations.

Gypsy was based on the programming language Pascal [966], with some notable changes. The primary goal of the language was verifiability, including both formal proof and runtime validation. This fundamental requirement led to the following limitations on the Pascal language base. Gypsy routines could not be nested, but instead could be grouped together in a named "scope." There were no global variables in Gypsy. Only constants, types, procedures, and functions were visible between routines. This helped to eliminate side effects from functions. Only constant parameters were allowed, and these parameters could be passed only by reference. Furthermore, Gypsy did not allow routine names to be passed as parameters. The data types in Gypsy were different from those in Pascal. Pointers were replaced by dynamic structures consisting of sets, sequences, mappings, and buffers, allowing for a variable number of components and three basic operations (addition, deletion, and moving a component to a different structure). Finally, statements were slightly different from Pascal statements, to support optimal placement of assertions.

A second goal of the Gypsy language was to support incremental development. A Gypsy program was made up of small, independently verifiable units including functions, procedures, lemmata, types, and constants. The units were defined so that they could be removed and replaced easily. They also supported verification. The proof of a unit depended only on the external specifications of those other units it referenced.

Gypsy provided facilities for detection, isolation, and recovery from hardware and software faults. It supported concurrency by allowing the security properties of concurrent routines to be specified and verified.

Gypsy also included an extensive set of specification constructs. Gypsy external specifications defined the effects of a routine, function, or procedure on its parameters at specified points in its execution. Gypsy provided keywords and specification statements for this purpose:

- *Entry*: conditions that were assumed to be true when the routine was activated
- *Exit*: conditions that must have been true if the routine exited
- *Block*: conditions that must have held if the routine were blocked waiting on access to shared memory

Gypsy internal specifications addressed the internal behavior of a routine. These specifications could not be accessed outside the routine. The keywords and specification statements were as follows:

- *Assert*: conditions that had to be satisfied at a specific point of execution
- *Keep*: conditions that had to remain true throughout the execution of the routine

Gypsy supported the execution of *lemmata* as separate units. These lemmata defined a relation among a number of functions and global constraints. Lemmata could be used to state algebraic properties of abstract data types.

Gypsy provided a *hold* specification, which defined a constraint on the value set of the concrete representation of an abstract data type.

At the expressive level, specification statements were made up of boolean expressions that had to be true as specified by the keywords (listed above). For example, an expression with the *entry* keyword had to be true at the time the routine was activated. The boolean expressions were made up of constants, variables, and function references allowed in the program code. Gypsy also supported existential quantifiers using the keyword *some*, and universal quantifiers using the keyword *all*. Like SPECIAL, there was a mechanism to distinguish the old value of a variable from the new, so that the exit specification could describe the computed value of a variable parameter in terms of its prior value. Each expression in a specification statement also could contain a *validation directive*, which determined if the condition were to be proved during verification, validated at runtime, or both.

The GVE was not intended as a design verification package but rather as an environment for proving properties of implementation programs. However, MITRE developed a tool of the same nature as the HDM MLS tool that performs security flow analysis on specifications written in a limited subset of Gypsy.

21.3.3.2   The Bledsoe Theorem Prover

The Bledsoe theorem prover was an interactive natural deduction system that used an extended first-order logic. This logic allowed subgoaling, matching, and rewriting. In order to prove a Gypsy program unit by inductive assertion, every loop had to be broken by at least one assert specification. Thus, there was a finite number of paths through the program that covered all possible execution sequences. Each verification condition was a theorem corresponding to a single path. The condition stated that the specification at the beginning of the path implied the specification at the end of the path. An analyst could guide the theorem prover, or the theorem prover could be instructed to choose the next step.

21.4   Current Verification Systems

Many formal verification systems are being developed and used. We present a sampling of three: the inductive proof system called the Prototype Verification System, the model checker called the Symbolic Model Verifier, and the cryptographic protocol verifier called the NRL Protocol Analyzer. These three examples demonstrate the key concepts underlying each type of verification system.

21.4.1   The Prototype Verification System

The Prototype Verification System (PVS) [1485] builds on the successes and failures of other systems developed at SRI International. HDM and EHDM focused on providing a means of proving programs correct and supporting a full life cycle of program development. PVS was built as a "lightweight prototype" to explore the next-generation verification system based on EHDM. PVS provides mechanically checked specifications and readable proofs but does not attempt to be a full development methodology. There is no concept of successive layers of abstraction or mappings between levels as in HDM and EHDM.

    PVS is a system for writing specifications and constructing proofs. It focuses on creating good specifications and proving appropriate properties for critical systems. PVS consists of a specification language that is tightly integrated with a powerful theorem prover. The theorem prover is highly interactive, allowing the user to guide the proof, and is often referred to as a "proof checker." The use of powerful inference tools allows the enrichment of the language. Conversely, several of the features of the language, including data types, predicate subtypes, and dependent types, contribute to the effectiveness of the inference mechanisms used in the proof checker. PVS also includes tools such as a syntax checker, a type checker, and parsers.

21.4.1.1   The PVS Specification Language

The PVS language is a strongly typed language based on first-order logic. It is used to construct compact specifications. This language is especially designed to describe computer systems but, like SPECIAL, is generally nonprocedural, focusing on what is to occur and how it is to be accomplished. This highly expressive language supports modularity by allowing the specifier to describe *theories*, which are somewhat similar in concept to the modules in SPECIAL. The typing of the PVS language is rich and includes the notion of a *predicate subtype* as well as type constructors for function, tuple, record, and abstract data types.

Each theory contains a series of statements called *declarations*. The declarations identify types, constants, variables, axioms, and formulas used by the theory. Theories are reusable, and many have been incorporated into the PVS package. These predefined theories have been named *preludes*. A PVS library provides a wealth of such preludes. They include fundamental definitions and theorems of set theory, functions, relations, and ordering, as well as the properties of the integers and the real numbers. External PVS libraries provide finite sets, bit vectors, coalgebras, real analysis, graphs, quaternions, lambda calculus, and linear and branching time temporal logics.

EXAMPLE: The following example of a PVS specification language is an abbreviated version of an example taken from the PVS tutorial [481]. It is a theory that is built into the PVS library. This example shows how the PVS language declarations are formed and illustrates some of the types and subtypes the language provides. The theory is called *rats* and begins to build a theory of rational numbers.

```
rats THEORY
BEGIN
     rat: TYPE
     zero: rat

     nonzero : TYPE {x | x ≠ zero}
     / : [rat, nonzero -> rat]
     * : [rat, rat -> rat]
     x, y : VAR

     left_cancellation : AXIOM zero ≠ x IMPLIES
         x * (y/x) = y
     zero_times : AXIOM zero * x = zero
END rats
```

The type *rat* is not interpreted (just as DESIGNATOR in SPECIAL marks the type as primitive). This specification describes the types *rat* and *nonzero* and identifies a constant *zero* of type *rat* as well as a "division" function "/" and a multiplication function "*"—each of which takes two arguments and returns a value of type *rat*. The type *nonzero* is called a *predicate subtype* of type *rat*, because membership in type *nonzero* consists of members of type *rat* that satisfy the given predicate (namely, all members not equal to zero). The "/" function addresses division by zero by taking a parameter of type *rat* and one of type *nonzero*. The multiplicative function "*" takes two arguments of type *rat*.

When the PVS type checker checks the types for an occurrence of the "/" operator in left cancellation, the type checker generates a type correctness condition (TCC) and adds it to the specification. For the example above, the added declaration is

```
Left_cancellation _TCC1: OBLIGATION
        (FORALL (x: rat): zero ≠ x IMPLIES x ≠ zero)
```

TCCs are called obligations because they must be proved in order to show that the theory is type correct. Such proofs may be deferred until a later time, but they are required to complete the proof of the theory.

21.4.1.2 The PVS Proof Checker

The PVS proof checker uses a life cycle concept with four phases:

1. *Exploratory phase*: The specification is debugged. The developer tests the specification proofs and revises key high-level proof ideas.
2. *Development phase*: The developer constructs a proof in larger steps and works on the efficiency of the proof.
3. *Presentation phase*: The proof is honed, polished, and checked.
4. *Generalization phase*: The developer analyzes the proof and the lessons learned for future proofs.

The PVS proof checker is highly interactive, supporting a goal-directed proof search. The prover starts from the conclusion and progressively applies inference steps to generate subgoals. The prover repeats this process until the subgoals are trivially provable.

One goal is to support efficient development of readable proofs in all stages of the proof development life cycle. The PVS prover has a small set of powerful primitive inference rules and a mechanism for composing rules into proof strategies. It can also rerun proofs and check that secondary proof obligations (such as type correctness conditions) have been met. Among the PVS proof checker primitive inference rules are the following:

- *Propositional rules*, such as a cut rule for introducing case splits, a rule for lifting *if*-conditionals to the top level of the formula, and a rule for deleting formulas from a goal (weakening rule)
- *Quantifier rules*, such as a rule for instantiating existentially quantified variables with terms
- *Equality rules*, such as replacing one side of an equality premise by another

Other rules introduce lemmata, axioms, type constraints, and decision procedures to limit the number of cases.

Proof strategies are frequently used patterns of proofs that have been composed into single steps. Examples of proof strategies are propositional simplifications, use of decision procedures, and rewriting with a definition or lemma.

21.4.1.3   Experience with PVS

PVS has been used in a variety of applications in many areas, not just computer security. NASA centers have analyzed requirements for several spacecraft projects and for avionics control. PVS has been used to verify microarchitectures as well as complex circuits, algorithms, and protocols in hardware devices. PVS has been used successfully to analyze both fault-tolerant algorithms and distributed algorithms. The model checker integrated into the PVS theorem prover enables PVS to analyze finite-state systems. Finally, PVS has also been used in real-time and hybrid systems, for compiler correctness, and in other applications.

21.4.2   The Symbolic Model Verifier

The Symbolic Model Verifier (SMV) [317] is based on Control Tree Logic (CTL) [425]. Control Tree Logic (see Section E.3) adds eight temporal connectives to those of the predicate calculus. Two letters represent each connective. The first is an "A" or an "E." Intuitively, one can think of "A" as inevitability, or meaning "along all paths." "E" is called possibility and means "along at least one path." The second symbol is "X," "F," "G," or "U." An "X" refers to the next state, an "F" means some future state, "G" means all future states (globally), and "U" means "until." Therefore, "AX" means "along all possible next paths," and "EX" means "there is at least one next path."

CTL can represent a model specifying a system as a directed graph whose nodes represent the states. The propositional atoms of the system that hold in that state can be indicated within the graph of the node, and the possible state transitions are represented by arrows connecting the appropriate nodes.

EXAMPLE: Suppose that M is a model that specifies a system with three states s_0, s_1, and s_2 and three propositional atoms p_1, p_2, and p_3. Suppose further that the possible state transitions are $s_0 \rightarrow s_1$, $s_0 \rightarrow s_2$, $s_1 \rightarrow s_0$, $s_1 \rightarrow s_2$, and $s_2 \rightarrow s_2$. Finally, suppose that p_1 is true in state s_1, p_1 and p_3 are true in s_0, and p_2 and p_3 are true in s_2. The graph in Figure 21–3 completely represents this model.

We can unwind this graph, creating an infinite tree of all computational paths beginning in a given state. This provides a graphical representation that clarifies the new temporal connectives such as "AX" and "EX." See Figure 21–4.

21.4.2.1   The SMV Language

An SMV program specifies the system and includes a description of the properties to be verified. The property specifications are written as CTL formulas. The

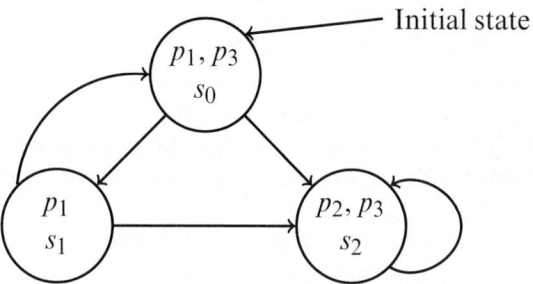

Figure 21–3   Graphical representation of the model *M*.

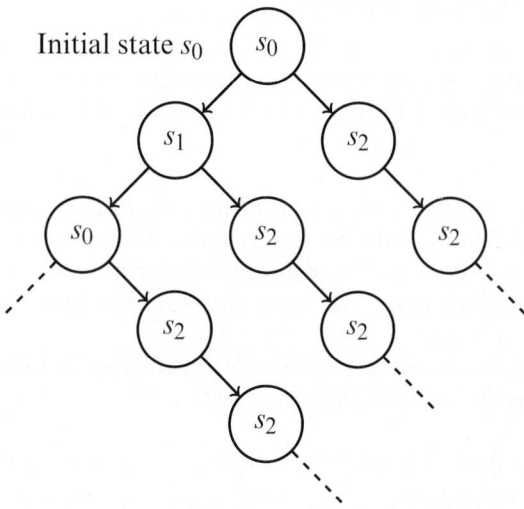

Figure 21–4   Unwinding the graph of *M*.

SMV tool processes the program and returns either a "true,'" indicating that the specifications hold for all initial states, or a trail of actions to help in debugging.

The SMV program may consist of several modules. The module called *main* takes no parameters and identifies the modules of the program. This module forms the root of the model hierarchy. It is the starting point for building the finite-state model for a given description. Individual module specifications contain declarations describing a set of variables. A module may be parameterized and may contain instances of other modules. Alternatively, a module can be reused as necessary.

The SMV program may have many types of declarations. The VAR declaration defines a variable and identifies its type. The language supports boolean, scalar, and fixed array types, as well as static structured data types. The ASSIGN declaration assigns initial and next values to variables. Next values are described in terms of current values of other variables, as in SPECIAL and Gypsy. The DEFINE declaration assigns values to variables in terms of other variables, constants, logical and arithmetic operators, and case and set operators. The INVAR declaration describes an invariant on the state transition system. The SPEC declaration introduces a CTL specification of the properties to be proved about the module.

The SMV language includes other features. One of the more interesting is a set of fairness constraints that can be used to rule out infinite executions. It describes deterministic and nondeterministic transitions as well as specifying synchronous or interleaving composition.

21.4.2.2   The SMV Proof Theory

The SMV model checking tool uses the proof logic of CTL. The proof technique is to establish semantic equivalence of the premises (from the specification of the system) and the conclusion, represented by the properties following the SPEC declaration in the CTL program.

EXAMPLE: Suppose that two concurrent processes share a resource but must not have access to it at the same time. To ensure correctness, we must define a critical section of each process's code and a protocol to determine which process can enter its critical section at which time. We verify our solution by confirming that some expected properties are met.

The model M is defined as follows. Let p_1 and p_2 be two processes. Define each of the following states for each process p_i:

- A noncritical state n_i corresponding to the process not attempting entry
- A state t_i in which the process is trying to enter the critical section
- A critical state c_i corresponding to the process being in its critical section

A process moves from its noncritical state to trying to enter its critical state to being in its critical state to back to its noncritical state, and so on. The set of possible system states is (n_1, n_2), (n_1, t_2), (n_1, c_2), (t_1, n_2), (t_1, t_2), (t_1, c_2), (c_1, n_2), (c_1, t_2), and (c_1, c_2). However, the state (c_1, c_2) is not included in the model because it is the condition that the model is to show is not possible. We also model the (t_1, t_2) state twice in our model, as shown in Figure 21–5. Both occurrences record that both processes are in their trying states, but s_3 describes p_1's turn and s_8 describes p_2's turn.

Suppose that the properties we want to show about the model are as follows:

- *Safety*: Only one process at a time can be in the critical section.
- *Liveness*: A process trying to enter its critical section will eventually do so.
- *Nonblocking*: A process can always request to enter its critical section.

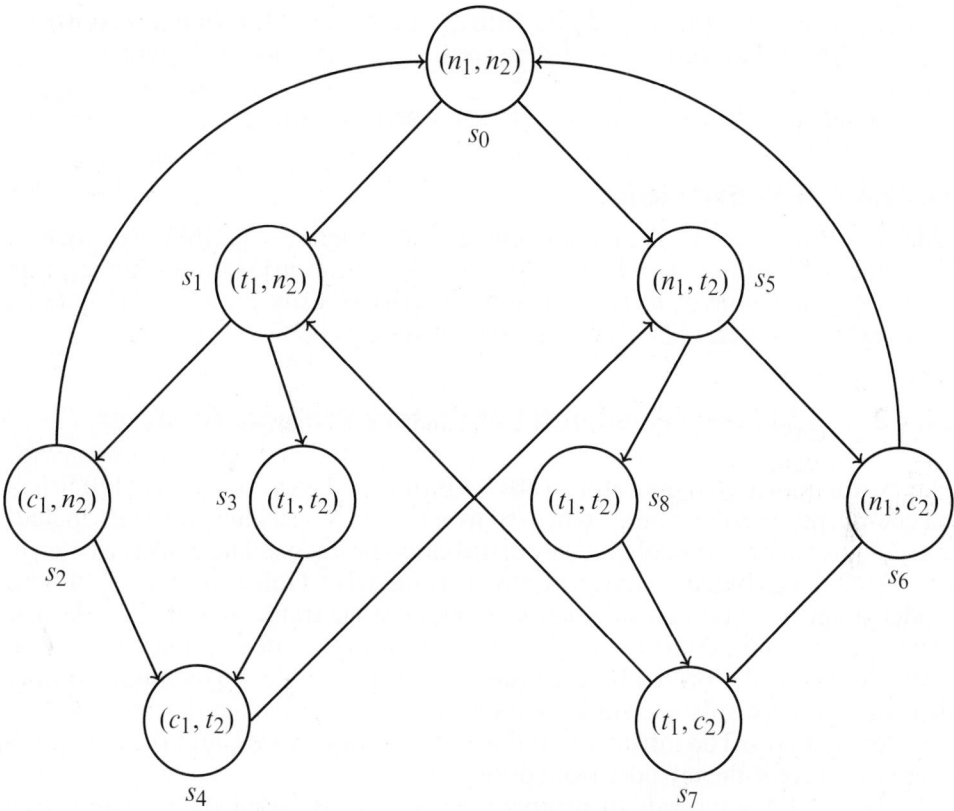

Figure 21–5 Graph of mutual exclusion model.

The model for this system is represented by the graph in Figure 21–5. Consider each of these desired properties separately:

- *Safety*: In terms of the model, this property requires that, for all paths, c_1 and c_2 cannot be true simultaneously. The CTL formula is $AG\neg(c_1 \wedge c_2)$. Because the state (c_1, c_2) is not defined in our model, this formula trivially holds.

- *Nonblocking*: In terms of the model, this property requires that, for every computational path, every state n_i has a successor state t_i. The CTL formula for this is $AG(n_i \rightarrow EXt_i)$. Inspection of Figure 21–5 shows that this is true.

- *Liveness*: In terms of the model, this property requires that, for all paths, if t_i is true, then there is some future state (on the same path) in which c_i is true. More simply, if the first process attains its trying state, then it will always eventually reach its critical state. The CTL formula is $AG(t_i \rightarrow AFc_i)$. This proof can also be verified by inspection of Figure 21–5.

Thus we have verified that all three properties hold.

21.4.2.3   SMV Experience

SMV has been used to verify sequential circuit designs [316]. SMV was used to verify the IEEE Futurebus+ Logical Protocol Specification [344]. Researchers also used SMV and some of its predecessors to verify security protocols [426], finite state real-time systems [345], and concurrent systems [425].

21.4.3   The Naval Research Laboratory Protocol Analyzer

The Naval Research Laboratory (NRL) Protocol Analyzer (NPA) [1307] is a special-purpose verification system used to verify cryptographic protocols, including authentication protocols and key distribution protocols. The NPA is written in Prolog [429]. It is based on the term-rewriting model of Dolev and Yao [580]. This model assumes that an intruder can read all message traffic, modify and destroy any messages, and perform any operation (encryption or decryption) that can be read, altered, or performed by a legitimate user. The model further assumes that there are certain words, such as keys or encrypted messages, that the intruder does not already know. The intruder's goal is to learn these words, and the defender's goal is to prevent the intruder from doing so.

The NPA approach to protocol verification is based on an interaction among a set of state machines. The user specifies nonsecure states and attempts to prove that they are unreachable. The proof uses an exhaustive backward search from the unreachable state. The NPA can also use proof techniques for reasoning about state machine models and for finding flaws and identifying potential attacks as well.

21.4.3.1   NPA Languages

The NPA Temporal Requirements Language (NPATRL) is the fundamental language of the NPA. It expresses generic requirements of key distribution or key agreement protocols.

The work in protocol verification includes the development of protocol specification languages and tools for generating formulas and searching for proofs. Each method has its own language. The large number of protocol verification systems led to the development of CAPSL, the Common Authentication Protocol Specification Language. CAPSL is a high-level language for cryptographic authentication and key distribution protocols. This allows a protocol to be specified once, after which, theoretically, translators can be provided to convert the specification automatically into another language supported by a protocol verification system.

A CAPSL specification has three parts. The *protocol specification* describes the protocol. A *types specification* describes the encryption operations. An *environment specification* provides scenario-specific details that can help in finding a proof for a protocol. The NRL Protocol Analyzer has a CAPSL interface [285].

21.4.3.2   NPA Experience

The NPA has been widely used to verify protocols. Among the protocols tested with this tool are the Internet Key Exchange protocol [1309] and the Needham-Schroeder public key protocol [1312].

21.5   Functional Programming Languages

Functional programming is a declarative style of developing computer programs using mathematical expressions that are evaluated, instead of using statements that can change the state. Functional programs utilize expressions that are only dependent upon the inputs provided ensuring that the outputs and effects of the function are not dependent upon global variables or local states. Functions in functional programming are treated like any other value, so they can be modified and used as input or output parameters. Functional programming languages are well-defined and well-typed lending to analysis that is comparatively simple compared to nonfunctional programming languages [2166].

The increased use of functional programming languages has given a more promising future to the ability to formally verify a program. Because state changes are dependent solely on the inputs to the function construct and syntaxes are well-defined, mathematically proving a program developed using functional programming is simpler and more straightforward.

There are three well known functional programming languages: OCaml, Haskell, and Rust. A brief description of each is provided below.

OCaml is a functional programming language. OCaml programs are verified by the compiler prior to execution resulting in a reduction in programming errors. As such OCaml programs lend to easier formal verification. OCaml is used in environments where speed and error-free functionality is critical [2197].

Haskell is a purely functional programming language that offers built-in memory management and is strongly typed (e.g., no core dumps). Programs written in Haskell tend to be shorter, lending to a program that is easier to verify [2166].

Rust is a new system programming language that combines the speed of the C programming language with functional programming language characteristics, providing thread safety and preventing segmentation faults [2212]. The Rust programming language has recently undergone a formal proof for the Rust ownership discipline to demonstrate that unsafe implementations are safely encapsulated [983].

21.6   Formally Verified Products

As mentioned earlier, most of the formally verified products are security kernels. There have been recent advances in scalability of formal verification methods. Due to the increased computing power and cheaper computer systems, the ability to formally verify a product is becoming more feasible.

EXAMPLE: The seL4 microkernel is an open source operating system kernel that was designed using high assurance techniques; it has undergone formal verification by SSRG@NICTA (now known as Trustworthy Systems@Data61). It has been formally verified against its own specification, including the ability to enforce security properties [1065].

More commonly, annotations are used. In this method, hypotheses about the program are embedded in the program, and when one is encountered, the hypothesis is checked. If the hypothesis fails, the program or system takes some action such as warning the user or aborting execution.

EXAMPLE: The Security-Oriented Analysis of Application Programs (SOAAP) analysis tool [829, 830] is based on a number of annotations related to compartmentalization of execution. They describe what parts of a program should be in a sandbox, and how those parts can communicate among themselves. Consider a function to decipher a file and put the cleartext into a second file:

```
__soaap_var_read("decrypt")
int retval;

__soaap_sandbox_persistent("decipher")
void decipher(fdes in, fdes out)
{
        char key[128] __soaap_private;
        if (getkey("Key:", key) < 0)
                retval = -1;
        while((n = read(buf, 1023, in)) > 0)
                decrypt(buf, key);
                if (write(buf, n, out) != n)
                        retval = -1;
        retval = 0;
}
```

In the above, `__soaap_sandbox_persistent("decrypt")` specifies that the function `decrypt` is to be run in a sandbox. The value of `key`, the key to decrypt the file, is marked as `__soaap_private` so any leaks of it via library functions (here, `decrypt`) will be detected. Because `decipher` is in a sandbox, it cannot communicate with the rest of the program to return success or failure. The variable `retval` is to be 0 on success and −1 if an error occurs. Hence, it is annotated with `__soaap_var_read("decrypt")` to indicate that the function decipher may change the value of that variable even though it is outside the sandbox.

Annotated programs are first compiled into an intermediate representation, and the representations for all files making up the program are linked. SOAAP then performs both static and dynamic control and dataflow analysis to identify violations, and also to warn if the overhead added by the additional checks causes performance requirements not to be met.

SOAAP was developed as part of a project to develop a high assurance capability-based system designed for software compartmentalization [1984, 2022].

21.7 Summary

Formal verification begins with a specification stated in an appropriate language. The language has a precise syntax and well-defined semantics based on mathematical principles. The system design and the properties to be verified are described in formal specifications. The specification of the design is proved to meet the specification of the properties. The proof may use general, inductive techniques or be tied to a specific model, in which case model checking techniques are appropriate.

The Hierarchical Development Methodology (HDM) was an early formal verification technique. It treated the specification as a hierarchy of abstract machines. The requirements and model were first proven consistent internally and with one another. The model was mapped into the top-level abstract machine, which in turn was mapped into the next lower abstract machine, and so forth. Each layer was expressed in terms of the lower layer, and each mapping between machines was verified to be correct. A later version, called Enhanced HDM (EHDM), used a different specification language and an interactive theorem prover to verify the system.

A second early verification environment focused not on verifying design but on proving properties of implementations. It combined a specification language with a programming language. The specifications were embedded in the programs. It supported incremental development as well as handling of hardware and software faults.

The Prototype Verification System (PVS) evolved from EHDM. Its goals are to provide a system for proving theorems about specifications. It does not attempt to support the full life cycle of program development. Specifications written in PVS use a specification language coupled with an interactive theorem prover. PVS has been used successfully to analyze requirements for spacecraft and to verify protocols in hardware devices.

The Symbolic Model Verifier (SMV) is a model checking tool. It represents a model of the system in a specification language. The properties to be verified are written in CTL, a temporal logic. An automated program tests the model against properties to verify that the properties hold. Circuit designs, security protocols, and real-time systems have been verified using this methodology. Protocols, especially cryptographic protocols, are notoriously difficult to get right. The NRL Protocol Analyzer is a system used to verify protocols. It is a state-based analysis engine that determines whether the protocol can enter states labeled as nonsecure. It can also identify potential attacks.

21.8   Research Issues

One area of research is how to define, and how to select, security properties in a way that is amenable to formal analysis and applies to realistic situations with precision. Security properties are often defined at an abstract level, and the mapping of the properties to that level removes much of the detail that affects security at the implementation level. Furthermore, many security-relevant properties are difficult to analyze in the context of formal methods. The issue of noninterference, for example, falls outside most formal analysis methods that operate on implemented systems. A good counterpoint is the analysis of cryptographic protocols. Formal methods work well with cryptographic protocols because the protocols can be expressed mathematically and the implementing software is small, but the current methods do not scale well to large systems.

This suggests restructuring of systems to make formal verification of security-critical components easier. Developing architectures that lend themselves to formal verification is a deep area. The concept of reference monitors comes into play, but in most instances systems are simply too large to structure as single reference monitors. How can systems be architected to achieve a compact or simple enough form so that formal methods can be used to verify the key components?

Expressions of security properties, designs, and implementations can simplify the use of formal methods. Different environments and different uses lead to different verification methodologies. Currently, there are many languages that can express policies at various levels of abstraction and others that can tie code to specifications. Can one create languages that support the implementation of verified designs without introducing flaws that create vulnerabilities?

In the realm of security and safety, ongoing work includes verification of cryptographic protocols and verification of code on active networks. The latter is particularly critical because active networks change the software that controls traffic while the network is in use. Protocols supporting these changes, and the code being introduced, must meet security requirements that are suitable for the network, but the verification of the code must be done at the time the code arrives, and so must be quick. How to speed up the verification of code is an important issue. The ideas of proof-carrying code (see Section 23.9.5.1) may work well in this environment. This is an important area of research.

21.9   Further Reading

McLean [1301] provides a terse but enlightening review of 20 years of formal methods. Snow [1775, 1776] discusses the future of assurance, including the role of formal methods. Wing [2010] discusses the relationship of formal methods and security. Bowen and Hinchley [277–279] discuss guidelines for and misperceptions of formal methods.

Many other specification languages are available. Among these are ACL2 [1014], Estelle [1905], HOL [802], LOTOS [257], SDL [1905], Z [567], and Isabelle [1997]. Comparisons of these languages are instructive [72, 92].

Similarly, several model checkers are in use. In addition to SMV, the model checker Spin [123, 918] is based on a temporal logic system and FDR2 [1605] is based on a process algebra. SyMP [172] and Forte [1315] combine model checking and theorem proving.

Many papers discuss formal methods and tools for protocol analysis. Kemmerer [1026] laid the basis for this work. The Interrogator [1336, 1340, 1341] is another Prolog-based protocol analysis system. Kemmerer, Meadows, and Millen [1030] contrast three protocol analysis systems. Abadi and Needham [4] present 11 principles for creating cryptographic protocols.

Formal methods have benefited in the past decade or so by the emergence of advancements in Satisfiability Modulo Theories (SMT). SMT checks whether the first-order formula expressions have a model or solution [130, 521]. A sample SMT solver is Z3, an SMT theorem prover from Microsoft Research [520].

The use of formal methods in the certification of aircraft systems is a current area of development and research. Muñoz [1400] discusses the use of formal methods in air traffic management for unmanned aircrafts. Cofer and Miller [432] discuss case studies for different formal methods of software development projects in the avionics industry.

21.10   Exercises

1. Add a SPECIAL specification to the example beginning on page 704 that describes *get-access* (see Section 5.2.4.1).

2. Section 21.3.1.1 presents three properties of the SRI model as embedded in the MLS tool. Compare and contrast these properties with the simple security property and the *-property of the Bell-LaPadula Model.

3. Why does the Boyer-Moore theorem prover perform induction only when the other five steps fail to simplify the formula? Why does it not try induction first?

4. Contrast the goals of the Gypsy Verification Environment with those of HDM. In particular, when is using HDM appropriate, and when is using Gypsy appropriate? Can HDM and Gypsy be used interchangeably?

5. Add rules to the *rats* example for PVS in Section 21.4.1.1 for exponentiation (^) and remainder (%). Remember that 0 and the remainder of anything when divided by 0 are both undefined.

6. Compare the life cycle concept that the PVS proof checker uses with the waterfall model of software engineering (see Section 19.2.1). Can the life cycle concept be expressed as a form of the waterfall model?

7. Consider the example in Section 21.4.2.2. The proof of the nonblocking condition states that "for every computational path, every state n_i has a successor state t_i." But the path $s_0 s_1 s_2$ is a cycle in which n_2 never changes to t_2. Reconcile this observation with the statement in the proof that "Inspection of Figure 21–5 shows that this is true."

Chapter 22
Evaluating Systems

> LEONATO: O! she tore the letter into a thousand
> halfpence; railed at herself, that she should be
> so immodest to write to one that she knew would
> flout her; 'I measure him,' says she, 'by my own
> spirit; for I should flout him, if he writ to me;
> yea, though I love him, I should.'
> — *Much Ado About Nothing*, II, iii, 156–161.

Evaluation is a process in which the evidence for assurance is gathered and analyzed against criteria for functionality and assurance. It can result in a measure of trust that indicates how well a system meets particular criteria. The criteria used depend on the goals of the evaluation and the evaluation technology used. The Trusted Computer System Evaluation Criteria (TCSEC) was the first widely used formal evaluation methodology, and subsequent methodologies built and improved on it over time. The Common Criteria for Information Security Evaluation (Common Criteria or CC) is an internationally developed standard for certification of security features within products. CC was developed in the mid-1990s and is still in use today by many countries. The Federal Information Processing Standard (FIPS) Publication 140-2 (FIPS PUB 140-2) is a standard cosponsored by the U.S. and Canadian governments to accredit cryptographic modules. This chapter explores several past and present evaluation methodologies, emphasizing the differences among them and the lessons learned from each methodology.

22.1 Goals of Formal Evaluation

Perfect security is an ultimate, but unachievable, goal for computer systems. As the complexity of computer systems increases, it becomes increasingly difficult to address the reference validation mechanism concept of a system being simple enough to analyze. A trusted system is one that has been shown to meet specific security requirements under specific conditions. The trust is based on assurance evidence. Although a trusted system cannot guarantee perfect security, it does provide a basis for confidence in the system within the scope of the evaluation.

Formal security evaluation techniques were created to facilitate the development of trusted systems. Typically, an evaluation methodology provides the following features:

- A set of requirements defining the security functionality for the system or product.
- A set of assurance requirements that delineate the steps for establishing that the system or product meets its functional requirements. These requirements usually specify required evidence of assurance.
- A methodology for determining that the product or system meets the functional requirements based on analysis of the assurance evidence.
- A measure of the evaluation result (called a *level of trust*) that indicates how trustworthy the product or system is with respect to the security functional requirements defined for it.

Definition 22–1. A *formal evaluation methodology* is a technique used to provide measurements of trust based on specific security requirements and evidence of assurance.

Several evaluation standards have affected formal evaluation methodologies. Among the major standards have been the Trusted Computer System Evaluation Criteria (TCSEC) [2239] and the Information Technology Security Evaluation Criteria (ITSEC) [2177]. The Common Criteria (CC) [2129–2131, 2133] has supplanted these standards as a standard evaluation methodology. This chapter discusses components of each standard.

Even when a system is not formally evaluated, the security functional requirements and assurance requirements provide an excellent overview of the considerations that improve assurance. These considerations are invaluable to any development process.

22.1.1 Deciding to Evaluate

A decision to evaluate a system formally must take into consideration the many trade-offs between security and cost, such as time to market and the number of features. Vendors typically seek validation or certification for a product due to government acquisition requirements. In the U.S., the Committee on National Security Systems (CNSS) established a policy for acquisition of information assurance (IA) and IA-enabled products, called NSTISSP #11. NSTISSP #11 mandates that COTS products used on national security systems within the Executive branch be evaluated or validated against CC or FIPS 140-2 [2196].

Groups seeking formal evaluation usually have to pay the evaluator's charge as well as staffing costs for skilled experts to develop security documentation and assurance evidence. Interaction with the evaluator for training, clarification, or corrections takes development staff time and could affect development and delivery schedules. Unfortunately, security evaluation cannot prove that a system is invulnerable to attack. Most systems today must operate in hostile environments, and the systems must provide their own protections from attacks and inadvertent errors.

Security and trust are no longer the exclusive realm of the government and military, nor are they of concern only to financial institutions and online businesses. Computers are at the heart of the economy, medical processes and equipment, power infrastructures, and communications infrastructures. Systems having no security are unacceptable in most environments today. Systems providing some security are a step in the right direction, but a trusted system that reliably addresses specifically defined security issues engenders stronger confidence. Evaluation provides an independent assessment by experts and a measure of assurance, which can be used to compare products.

The independent assessment by experts of the effectiveness of security mechanisms and the correctness of their implementation and operation is invaluable in finding vulnerabilities and flaws in a product or system. An evaluated product has been scrutinized by security experts who did not design or implement the product and can bring a fresh eye to the analysis. Hence, the evaluated product is less likely to contain major flaws than a product that has not been evaluated. The analysis of such a system begins with an assessment of requirements. The requirements must be consistent, complete, technically sound, and sufficient to counter the threats to the system. Assessing how well the security features meet the requirements is another part of the evaluation. Evaluation programs require specific types of administrative, user, installation, and other system documentation, which provide the administrators and maintainers the information needed to configure and administer the system properly, so that the security mechanisms will work as intended.

The level of risk in the environment affects the level of trust required in the system. The measure of trust associated with an evaluated product helps find the optimum combination of trust in the product and in the environment to meet the security needs.

22.1.2 Historical Perspective of Evaluation Methodologies

Government and military establishments were the early drivers of computer security research. They also drove the creation of a security evaluation process. Before evaluation methodologies were available for commercial products, government and military establishments developed their own secure software and used internal methodologies to make decisions about their security. With the rapid expansion of technology, government and military establishments wanted to use commercial products for their systems rather than developing them. This drove the development of methodologies to address the security and trustworthiness of commercial products.

Evaluation methodologies provide functional requirements, assurance requirements, and levels of trust in different formats. Some list requirements and use them to build trust categories. Others list the requirements only within the description of a trust category. To help the reader compare the development of the methodologies, we present each methodology in a standard manner. We first present overview information about the methodology. Descriptions of functional requirements (when they exist), assurance requirements, and levels of trust follow. If the methodology was widely used to evaluate systems, we describe the evaluation process. The final discussion for each methodology addresses its strengths, its weaknesses, and the contributions it makes to the evaluation technology. Unfortunately, the methodologies use slightly different terminologies. In the discussion of each methodology, we will describe the terminology specific to that technique and relate it to the specific terminologies of previous methodologies.

22.2   TCSEC: 1983–1999

The Trusted Computer System Evaluation Criteria (TCSEC), also known as the Orange Book, was developed by the U.S. government and was the first major computer security evaluation methodology. It presents a set of criteria for evaluating the security of commercial computer products. The TCSEC defined criteria for six different *evaluation classes* identified by their rating scale of C1, C2, B1, B2, B3, and A1. Each evaluation class contains both functional and assurance requirements, which are cumulative and increasing throughout the evaluation classes. Classes were subdivided into three different "divisions" of lesser importance to our discussion than individual evaluation classes. A fourth division, D, was provided for products that attempted evaluation but failed to meet all the requirements of any of the six classes. The vendor could select the level of trust to pursue by selecting an evaluation class but otherwise had no say in either the functional or assurance requirements to be met.

The reference monitor concept (see Section 20.1.2.2) and the Bell-LaPadula security policy model (see Section 5.2) heavily influenced the TCSEC criteria and approach. Recall that a trusted computing base (TCB) is a generalization of the reference validation mechanism (RVM). The TCB is not required to meet the RVM requirements (always invoked, tamperproof, and small enough to analyze) for all classes. In the TCSEC, the TCB need not be a full RVM until class B3.

The TCSEC emphasizes confidentiality, with a bias toward the protection of government classified information. Although there is no specific reference to data integrity in the TCSEC, it is indirectly addressed by the *-property of the embedded Bell-LaPadula Model.[1] However, this is not a complete data integrity solution, because it does not address the integrity of data outside the mandatory access control policy. System availability is not addressed.

During the first few years that the TCSEC was available, the National Computer Security Center published a large collection of documents that expanded on requirement areas from the TCSEC. These "Rainbow Series" documents[2] discussed the requirements in specific contexts such as networks, databases, and audit systems, and some are still applicable today.

The TCSEC provides seven levels of trust measurement called *ratings*, which are represented by the six evaluation classes C1, C2, B1, B2, B3, and A1, plus an additional class, D. An evaluated product is a *rated product*. Under the TCSEC, some requirements that this text considers to be functional in nature appear under headings that use the word *assurance*. These requirements are identified in the text below.

22.2.1   TCSEC Requirements

The TCSEC is organized by evaluation class and uses an outline structure to identify named requirement areas. It defines both functional and assurance requirements within the context of the evaluation classes. The actual requirements are embedded in a prose description of each named area. The divisions and subdivisions of the document are of lesser importance than the actual requirement areas found within them.

22.2.1.1   TCSEC Functional Requirements

Discretionary access control (DAC) requirements identify an access control mechanism that allows for controlled sharing of named objects by named individuals and/or groups. Requirements address propagation of access rights, granularity of control, and access control lists.

Object reuse requirements address the threat of an attacker gathering information from reusable objects such as main memory or disk memory. The requirements address the revocation of access rights from a previous owner when the reusable object is released and the inability of a new user to read the previous contents of that reusable object.

Mandatory access control (MAC) requirements, not required until class B1, embody the simple security condition and the *-property from the Bell-LaPadula Model. These requirements include a description of the hierarchy of labels. Labels attached to subjects reflect the authorizations they have and are derived

---

[1] Recall that the *-property addresses writing of data, which provides some controls on the unauthorized modification of information (see Section 5.2.1).

[2] Each document had a different colored cover.

from approvals such as security clearances. Labels attached to objects reflect the protection requirements for objects. For example, a file labeled "secret" must be protected at that level by restricting access to subjects who have authorizations reflecting a secret (or higher) clearance.

Label requirements, also not required until class B1, enable enforcement of mandatory access controls. Both subjects and objects have labels. Other requirements address accurate representation of classifications and clearances, exporting of labeled information, and labeling of human-readable output and devices.

Identification and authentication (I&A) requirements specify that a user identify herself to the system and that the system authenticate that identity before allowing the user to use the system. These requirements also address the granularity of the authentication data (per group, per user, and so on), protecting authentication data, and associating identity with auditable actions.

Trusted path requirements, not required until class B2, provide a communications path that is guaranteed to be between the user and the TCB. For example, in Windows the CTRL-ALT-DELETE can be configured to be required for login. The CTRL-ALT-DELETE key sequence cannot be intercepted, so spoofed login screens are not possible.

Audit requirements address the existence of an audit mechanism as well as protection of the audit data. They define what audit records must contain and what events the audit mechanism must record. As other requirements increase, the set of required auditable events increases, causing the auditing requirements to expand as one moves to higher classes.

The TCSEC presents other requirements that it identifies as system architecture requirements. They are in fact functional requirements, and they include a tamperproof reference validation mechanism, process isolation, the principle of least privilege, and well-defined user interfaces.

TCSEC operational assurance requirements that are functional in nature include the following. Trusted facility management requires the separation of operator and administrator roles and are required starting at class B2. Trusted recovery procedure requirements ensure a secure recovery after a failure (or other discontinuity). These requirements are unique to class A1. Finally, a system integrity requirement mandates hardware diagnostics to validate the on-site hardware and firmware elements of the TCB.

22.2.1.2   TCSEC Assurance Requirements

Configuration management requirements for the TCSEC begin at class B2 and increase for higher classes. They require identification of configuration items, consistent mappings among all documentation and code, and tools for generating the TCB.

The *trusted distribution requirement* addresses the integrity of the mapping between masters and on-site versions as well as acceptance procedures for the customer. This requirement is unique to class A1.

TCSEC system architecture requirements mandate modularity, minimization of complexity, and other techniques for keeping the TCB as small and simple as possible. These requirements begin at class C1 and increase until class B3, where the TCB must be a full reference validation mechanism.

Design specification and verification requirements address a large number of individual requirements, which vary dramatically among the evaluation classes. Classes C1 and C2 have no requirements in this area. Class B1 requires an informal security policy model that is shown to be consistent with its axioms. Class B2 requires that the model be formal and be proven consistent with its axioms and that the system have a descriptive top level specification (DTLS). Class B3 requires that the DTLS be shown to be consistent with the security policy model. Finally, class A1 requires a formal top level specification (FTLS) and that approved formal methods be used to show that the FTLS is consistent with the security policy model. Class A1 also requires a mapping between the FTLS and the source code.

Testing requirements address conformance with claims, resistance to penetration, and correction of flaws followed by retesting. A requirement to search for covert channels includes the use of formal methods at higher evaluation classes.

Product documentation requirements are divided into a Security Features User's Guide (SFUG) and an administrator guide called a Trusted Facility Manual (TFM). The SFUG requirements include a description of the protection mechanisms, how they interact, and how to use them. The TFM addresses requirements for running the product securely, including generation, startup, and other procedures. All classes require this documentation, and as the level of the class increases, the functional and assurance requirements increase.

Internal documentation includes design and test documentation. The design documentation requirements and the design specification and verification requirements overlap somewhat. Design documentation requirements include a statement of the philosophy of protection and a description of interfaces. Test documentation requirements specify test plans, procedures, tests, and test results. As with the user and administrator documentation, requirements for test and design documentation increase as the functional and assurance requirements increase as the classes increase.

22.2.2   The TCSEC Evaluation Classes

Class C1, called *discretionary protection*, has minimal functional requirements only for identification and authentication and for discretionary access controls. The assurance requirements are also minimal, covering testing and documentation only. This class was used only briefly, and no products were evaluated under this class after 1986.

Class C2, called *controlled access protection*, requires object reuse and auditing in addition to the class C1 functional requirements and contains somewhat more stringent security testing requirements. This was the most commonly used class for commercial products. Most operating system developers incorporated class C2 requirements into their primary product by the end of the lifetime of the TCSEC.

Class B1, called *labeled security protection*, requires mandatory access controls, but these controls can be restricted to a specified set of objects. Labeling supports the MAC implementation. Security testing requirements are more stringent. An informal model of the security policy, shown to be consistent with its axioms, completes class B1. Many operating system vendors offered a class B1 product in addition to their primary products. Unfortunately, the B1 products did not always receive the updates in technology that the main line received, and they often fell behind technically.

Class B2, called *structured protection*, is acceptable for some government applications. At class B2, mandatory access control is required for all objects. Labeling is expanded, and a trusted path for login is introduced. Class B2 requires the use of the principle of least privilege, which requires all users operate with the least set of privileges necessary to perform the specific task. Assurance requirements include covert channel analysis, configuration management, more stringent documentation, and a formal model of the security policy that has been proven to be consistent with its axioms.

Class B3, called *security domains*, implements the full reference validation mechanism and increases the trusted path requirements. It also constrains how the code is developed in terms of modularity, simplicity, and use of techniques such as layering and data hiding. It has significant assurance requirements that include all the requirements of class B2 plus more stringent testing, more requirements on the DTLS, an administrator's guide, and design documentation.

Class A1, called *verified protection*, has the same functional requirements as class B3. The difference is in the assurance. Class A1 requires significant use of formal methods in covert channel analysis, design specification, and verification. It also requires trusted distribution and increases both test and design documentation requirements. A correspondence between the code and the FTLS is required.

22.2.3   The TCSEC Evaluation Process

Government-sponsored evaluators staffed and managed TCSEC evaluations at no fee to the vendor. Some products began the TCSEC evaluations during the product design and implementation phases. The evaluation had three phases: application, preliminary technical review (PTR), and evaluation. If the government did not need a particular product, the application might be denied. The PTR was essentially a readiness review, including comprehensive discussions of the evaluation process, schedules, the development process, product technical content, requirement discussions, and the like. The PTR determined when an evaluation team would be provided, as well as the fundamental schedule for the evaluation.

The evaluation phase was divided into design analysis, test analysis, and a final review. In each part, the results obtained by the evaluation team were presented to a technical review board (TRB), which approved that part of the evaluation before the evaluation moved to the next step. The TRB consisted of senior evaluators who were not on the evaluation team being reviewed.

The design analysis consisted of a rigorous review of the system design based on the documentation provided. Because TCSEC evaluators did not read the source code, they imposed stringent requirements on the completeness and correctness of the documentation. Evaluators developed the initial product assessment report (IPAR) for this phase. Test analysis included a thorough test coverage assessment as well as an execution of the vendor-supplied tests. The evaluation team produced a final evaluation report (FER) after approval of the initial product assessment report and the test review. Once the TRB had approved the final evaluation report, and the evaluators and vendor had closed all items, the rating was awarded.

The Ratings Maintenance Program (RAMP) maintained assurance for new versions of an evaluated product. The vendor took the responsibility for updating the assurance evidence to support product changes and enhancements. A TRB reviewed the vendor's report and, when the report had been approved, the evaluation rating was assigned to the new version of the product. RAMP did not accept all enhancements. For example, structural changes and the addition of some new functions could require a new evaluation. The RAMP program required that the vendor have a trained Vendor Security Analyst on staff to perform the RAMP process.

22.2.4   Impacts

The TCSEC created a new approach to identifying how secure a product is. The approach was based on the analysis of design, implementation, documentation, and procedures. The TCSEC was the first evaluation technology, and it set several precedents for future methodologies. The concepts of evaluation classes, assurance requirements, and assurance-based evaluations are fundamental to evaluation today. The TCSEC set high technical standards for evaluation. The technical depth of the TCSEC evaluation came from the strength of the foundation of requirements and classes, from the rigor of the evaluation process, and from the checks and balances provided by reviews from within the evaluation team and the TRBs from outside the evaluation team.

However, the TCSEC was far from perfect. Its scope was limited. The evaluation process was difficult and often lacked needed resources. The TCSEC bound assurance and functionality together in the evaluation classes, which troubled some users. Finally, the TCSEC evaluations were recognized only in the United States, and evaluations from other countries were not valid in the United States.

22.2.4.1   Scope Limitations

The TCSEC was written for operating systems and does not translate well to other types of products or to systems. Also, the TCSEC focused on the security needs of the U.S. government and military establishments, who funded its development. All evaluation classes except C1 and C2 require mandatory access control, which most commercial environments do not use. Furthermore, the TCSEC did not address integrity, availability, or other requirements critical to business applications.

The National Computer Security Center (NCSC) tried to address the scope problems by providing criteria for other types of products. After an attempt to define a criteria document for networks, the NCSC chose to develop the Trusted Network Interpretation (TNI) of the TCSEC [2242], released in 1987. The TNI offered two approaches: evaluation of networks and evaluation of network components. The TNI network approach addressed centralized networks with a single accreditation authority, policy, and Network TCB (NTCB). In the first part of the TNI, the TCSEC criteria were interpreted for networks, and one could evaluate a network at the same levels offered by the TCSEC. The second part of the TNI offered evaluation of network components. A network component may be designed to provide a subset of the security functions of the network as a whole. The TNI could provide an evaluation based on the specific functionality that the component offered.

In 1992, a Trusted Database Management System Interpretation (TDI) [2240] of the TCSEC was released. In the early 1990s, IBM and Amdahl pushed for a Trusted Virtual Machine Monitor Interpretation [2207] of the TCSEC, but this project was eventually dropped. The interpretations had to address issues that were outside the scope of the TCSEC, and each had limitations that restricted their utility. Not many evaluations resulted from the TNI or the TDI.

22.2.4.2   Process Limitations

The TCSEC evaluation methodology had two fundamental problems. The first was "criteria creep," or the gradual expansion of the requirements that defined the TCSEC evaluation classes. Evaluators found that they needed to interpret the criteria to apply them to specific products. Rather than publish frequent revisions of the TCSEC to address these requirement interpretations, the NCSC chose to develop a process for approval of interpretations and to publish them as an informal addendum to the TCSEC. The interpretations were sometimes clearer and more specific than the original requirement. Over time, the list became quite large and expanded the scope of the individual criteria in the TCSEC and its interpretations. The requirements of the classes became the union of the requirements in the TCSEC and the set of applicable interpretations. Thus, a class C2 operating system may have been required to meet stronger requirements than a system evaluated a few years before. This put an additional burden on the newer products under evaluation and meant that the minimum-security enforcement of all C2 operating systems was not the same. Although there were many problems with these differences, it caused the security community to learn more about security and create better security products.

The second problem with the evaluation process was that evaluations took too much time. Three factors contributed to this problem. Many vendors misunderstood the depth of the evaluation and the required interactions with the evaluation teams. The practices of the evaluation management caused misunderstandings and scheduling problems. Finally, the motivation to complete a free evaluation was often lacking. Typically, both vendors and evaluators caused delays in the schedule. Vendors often had to do additional unanticipated work. Evaluators were assigned to multiple evaluations, and the schedule of one evaluation could cause delays for another vendor. Many evaluations took so long to complete that the product was obsolete before the rating was awarded. Toward the end of the life of the TCSEC, commercial labs approved by the government were allowed to do TCSEC evaluations for a fee. Vendors had to be prepared for evaluation, and there was significantly less interaction between evaluators and vendors. This change addressed much of the timeliness problem, with labs completing evaluations in roughly a year.

A related problem was that RAMP cycles were as difficult as full evaluations and suffered from similar delays. Consequently, RAMP was not used very much.

22.2.4.3   Contributions

The TCSEC provided a process for security evaluation of commercial products. Its existence heightened the awareness of the commercial sector to the needs for computer security. This awareness would have arisen later if not for the influence of the TCSEC.

In the 1990s, new varieties of products emerged, including virus checkers, firewalls, virtual private networks, IPsec implementations, and cryptographic modules. The TCSEC remained centered on operating systems, and its interpretations were insufficient to evaluate all types of networks or the new varieties of products. The commercial sector was dissatisfied with the functional requirements of the evaluation classes. These inadequacies of the TCSEC stimulated a wave of new approaches to evaluation that significantly affected evaluation technology. Commercial organizations wrote their own criteria. Other commercial organizations offered a pass-fail "certification" based on testing. The Computer Security Act of 1987 gave the responsibility to the NSA for security of computer systems processing classified and national security-relevant information. NIST received a charter for systems processing sensitive and unclassified information. In 1991, NIST and the NSA began working on new evaluation criteria called the Federal Criteria (FC). All these activities sprang from the impact of the TCSEC.

22.3   International Efforts and the ITSEC: 1991–2001

By 1990, several Western countries had developed their own security evaluation criteria. Canada released the first version of the Canadian Trusted Computer Product Evaluation Criteria (CTCPEC) [107, 2124] in 1989. The CTCPEC relied heavily on the TCSEC in the beginning but also incorporated some new ideas through successive releases. The CTCPEC espouses separation of assurance and functionality. It offers a catalogue of functional requirements in several categories. It introduces the concept of functionality "profiles" based on sets of well-defined requirements from the catalogue. It also addresses new functional requirement areas such as integrity and availability and new assurance areas such as the developer environment.

Some Western European countries—notably, France, Germany, the United Kingdom, and the Netherlands—also had security evaluation criteria by this time. The lack of reciprocity of evaluation among European nations created a move to harmonize the criteria of these countries, resulting in the Information Technology Security Evaluation Criteria (ITSEC), the European standard published in 1991. The European Union officially endorsed the ITSEC as a Recommendation by the Council of the European Union in 1995. The ITSEC was widely used over a 10-year period until the Common Criteria (see Section 22.8) became available. The ITSEC took a different approach to evaluation than that of the TCSEC, and consequently it successfully addressed some of the shortcomings of the TCSEC. However, it created a new set of shortcomings of its own.

The ITSEC provided six levels of trust, called *evaluation levels*, E1, E2, E3, E4, E5, and E6. A seventh level, E0, was used for products that did not meet other levels. A product or system successfully evaluated under the ITSEC was called a *certified product* or *certified system*, and a certified product or system was said to have a *certification*. ITSEC did not provide functional criteria. It required the vendor to define the security functional criteria in a *security target* (ST). This effectively split functionality and assurance into distinct categories. Having vendor-defined or externally defined functional requirements permitted evaluation of any type of product or system. There was no equivalent to the concept of a TCB in the ITSEC. However, a new term was introduced by the ITSEC.

> **Definition 22–2.** A *target of evaluation* (TOE) is a product or system, and its associated administrator and user documentation, that is the subject of an evaluation.

We use the acronym "TOE" and "product" or "system" interchangeably in this text, avoiding the use of "TOE" where appropriate.

The United Kingdom IT Security Evaluation and Certification Scheme Certification Body defined exemplary sets of functional requirements that were consistent with the functional requirements for TCSEC classes C1 through B3, as well as other fixed *functionality classes*. An evaluated product using these predefined sets of functional requirements received certification that had two components: one for the functional class (for example, FC2 was the U.K. functional requirement specification that mimicked TCSEC class C2) and one for the assurance class. Therefore, an operating system evaluated under the ITSEC could end up with a certification for "FC2-E3," indicating that it met the assurance requirements stated in the E3 assurance class and the functional requirements stated in the FC2 functionality class.

22.3.1   ITSEC Assurance Requirements

The ITSEC assurance requirements were similar to those in the TCSEC, although there were substantial differences in terminology. As in the TCSEC, assurance requirements were defined within the constraints of the evaluation levels. ITSEC assurance was viewed in terms of correctness and effectiveness. The six effectiveness requirements applied equally to all levels of ITSEC evaluation. The first two effectiveness requirements were as follows:

1. *Suitability of requirements.* This requirement addressed consistency and coverage of the security target by showing how the security requirements and environmental assumptions found in the security target were sufficient to counter the threats defined in the security target.
2. *Binding of requirements.* This analysis investigated the security requirements and the mechanisms that implemented them. This ensured that the requirements and mechanisms were mutually supportive and provided an integrated and effective security system. The assessment took both the requirements and the implementing mechanisms into account.

These requirements applied to the security target and provided an analysis of the security target that contained the security requirements. There was no correspondence between the ITSEC and the TCSEC in this area because the corresponding analysis was done in defining the TCSEC evaluation classes.

This section discusses the remaining four effectiveness requirements along with the correctness requirements. The correctness requirements are subdivided, and, as with the TCSEC, the subdivisions are not as significant as the individual requirement areas. This section will identify the differences between the requirements of the ITSEC and those of the TCSEC.

22.3.1.1   Requirements in the ITSEC Not Found in the TCSEC

The ITSEC required an assessment of the security measures used for the developer environment during the development and maintenance of the product or system. The TCSEC had no such requirement.

Starting at level E2, the ITSEC required that a correspondence be defined between all levels of representation of the TOE (such as mappings of specifications to requirements, mappings between successive levels of specification, and mappings between the lowest specification and the code). The TCSEC required only a mapping from the top-level specification to the code, and only for higher evaluation classes. The ITSEC had requirements on compilers and languages that the TCSEC did not have. Finally, the ITSEC required the submission of source code at several levels and of object code at the highest level. The TCSEC evaluations were done without examining code.

The ITSEC requirements for delivery and generation procedures, and for approved distribution procedures, addressed many aspects of those procedures, whereas the TCSEC addressed only the use of masters in the distribution process. Furthermore, the distribution requirements began at the lowest level of the ITSEC, whereas the TCSEC required them only at the highest level. Secure start and operation requirements in the ITSEC addressed more aspects than did the TCSEC requirements, which addressed only recovery after a discontinuity.

The effectiveness requirements of the ITSEC required several forms of vulnerability assessment that the TCSEC did not require. The design vulnerability analysis, which assessed vulnerabilities at the design level, had no equivalent in the TCSEC. The TCSEC had no equivalent to the ITSEC's ease of use analysis, which determined how the system could be misused based on a study of the system documentation. The ITSEC known vulnerabilities analysis was similar to the TCSEC design vulnerability analysis but addressed the implemented system. The strength of mechanisms effectiveness requirement applied to each security mechanism whose strength could be measured. For example, it applied to cryptographic algorithms (the measure was based on key size) and passwords (the measure was based on the size of the password space). The TCSEC has no corresponding requirement.

22.3.2   The ITSEC Evaluation Levels

The ITSEC levels were listed from lowest to highest. Each level included the requirements of the preceding level. If a product or system did not meet the requirements for any level, it was rated as level E0 (which corresponded to the TCSEC level D).

Level E1 required a security target against which to evaluate the product or system. It also required an informal description of the product or system architecture. The product or system had to be tested to demonstrate that it satisfied its security target.

Level E2 also required an informal description of the detailed design of the product or system TOE, as well as configuration control and a distribution control process. Evidence of testing had to be supplied.

Level E3 had more stringent requirements on the detail design and also required a correspondence between the source code and the security requirements.

Level E4 also required a formal model of the security policy, a more rigorous, structured approach to architectural and detailed design, and a design level vulnerability analysis.

Level E5 also required a correspondence between the detailed design and the source code, and a source code level vulnerability analysis.

Level E6 also required extensive use of formal methods. For example, the architecture design had to be stated formally and shown to be consistent with the formal model of the security policy. Another requirement was the partial mapping of the executable code to the source code.

22.3.3   The ITSEC Evaluation Process

Each participating country had its own methodology for doing evaluations under the ITSEC. All were similar and followed well-defined guidelines. This discussion uses the U.K. methodology.

Certified, licensed evaluation facilities (CLEFs) performed evaluations for a fee. The U.K. government certified the CLEFs. Evaluations typically started much later in the development cycle than did TCSEC evaluations. CLEFs often had an evaluation division and a consulting division. Vendors sought guidance and support from the consulting division to prepare for the evaluation, and consequently the products and systems were better prepared before evaluation began. Because fees were involved, all parties were motivated to finish the evaluation quickly. The evaluation process was much more structured and did not have the lengthy (but technically sound) checks and balances that were provided by TCSEC technical review boards.

The process began with an evaluation of the security target, based on the suitability and binding of assurance requirements. When the security target was approved, the evaluators evaluated the product against the security target. The documentation required for the ITSEC followed a slightly more rigid structure than that for the TCSEC, making it easier in some ways for vendors to provide useful evidence to the evaluators. ITSEC evaluators read the code for clarification when documentation proved inadequate.

The U.K. scheme for the ITSEC had a very straightforward and simplistic certificate maintenance scheme. It required a plan and evidence to support correct implementation of the plan. Like the evaluation process, it did not have technical reviews such as those of the technical review boards of the TCSEC.

22.3.4   Impacts

The ITSEC evaluation allowed flexibility in requirement definition and in mixtures of assurance and functionality. Commercial labs performed the ITSEC evaluations, which effectively reduced the length of the evaluation process. Additionally, the ITSEC methodology lent itself to any kind of products or systems. ITSEC provided guidance on what documentation was required. Reciprocity of evaluation existed within the European states. The four effectiveness requirements were a very useful addition to assurance requirements.

In spite of the somewhat stronger assurance requirements in some areas, the ITSEC evaluations were often viewed as technically inferior to the TCSEC evaluations for two reasons. The first was a fundamental potential weakness in the development of functional requirements. The second dealt with the evaluation process itself, which was somewhat lacking in technical rigor.

Another limit of the ITSEC was the lack of reciprocity of evaluation with Canada and the United States.

22.3.4.1   Vendor-Provided Security Targets

Unfortunately, vendors did not always have qualified security experts to develop appropriate security targets. This raised the concern that ITSEC evaluations did not determine if a claim made sense; it merely verified that the product met the claim. In fact, security target evaluation was often the work of one or two individuals. No official review provided checks and balances. No board of experts (such as the TCSEC's technical review board) assessed the quality of the evaluators' work. The use of predefined functionality classes eased this limitation somewhat.

22.3.4.2   Process Limitations

Some considered using the same company for both evaluation preparation support and evaluation itself to be a conflict of interest. Different personnel provided the consulting and evaluation services, but their biases could be the same. Separation of these duties among different organizations may produce stronger results because this approach offers more diversity of opinion.

ITSEC product and system evaluations could have had one- or two-person teams. Usually, one or two people made all the decisions, and there was insufficient review of the decisions. One- or two-person teams cannot generate the rich set of opinions and internal review that a team of five or six security experts can provide.

Efficiency of process and ease of use are not substitutes for rigor or depth. There was no body of experts to approve evaluator design analysis or to test coverage analysis. The small evaluation team made the decision to move to the next phase of the evaluation. There was no equivalent to a final review by experts. A government body provided the final approval for the evaluation, but that body usually took the recommendation of the evaluation team.

22.4   Commercial International Security Requirements: 1991

The Commercial International Security Requirements (CISR) [486] was a joint effort of individuals from American Express and Electronic Data Systems (EDS). They used the TCSEC, Germany's IT-Security Criteria [2183], and the newly released ITSEC. Their approach was to develop a "C2+" security evaluation class that stressed the areas of importance to business. As before, the following discussion focuses on the differences between the requirements of the CISR and the TCSEC.

22.4.1   CISR Requirements

The CISR had its roots in the TCSEC evaluation class C2. Because one level of trust was involved, the functional and assurance requirements were stated directly and not embedded in the description of several levels of trust. The CISR functional and assurance requirements included only those requirement areas required by the TCSEC evaluation class C2. This effectively eliminated design specification and verification, labeling, mandatory access control, trusted path, trusted facilities management, and trusted recovery. Assurance requirements were identical to the TCSEC C2 requirements with one small addition. The administrator guide had to contain a threat analysis that identified the protection measures addressing each threat. CISR functional requirements for object reuse and system integrity were identical to the TCSEC class C2 requirements. The other C2 functional requirement areas were enhanced.

1. CISR discretionary access control requirements included the B3 TCSEC requirements of access control lists and limiting of access by specific modes. Several new access modes were added.

2. CISR I&A requirements included password management constraints, as identified in the Password Management Guide of the Rainbow Series [2202]. The CSIR offered one-time passwords as an alternative to fixed, stored passwords and required one-way encryption to protect stored passwords.

3. CISR made minor modifications to address the auditing of new discretionary access control attributes, added a few auditable events, and included small issues from TCSEC evaluation classes B1 and B3. The CISR added B1, B2, and B3 requirements to the system architecture requirements from the TCSEC.

The CISR added several new categories of requirements that were not found in the TCSEC. Session controls included login attempt thresholds, limits on multiple concurrent sessions, and keyboard locking. System entry constraints could be set to limit a user's access to the system based on time, location, and mode of access. CISR provided a set of workstation security requirements that included the use of encryption, virus deterrents, and restrictions on use of peripheral devices and operating commands. CISR network security requirements included the use of a centralized administrative interface as well as alternative user authentication methods such as tokens, challenge response techniques, and public key cryptography.

22.4.2   Impacts

Although the CISR never became a generally available evaluation methodology, it did contribute to the rapid growth of evaluation technology in the early 1990s.

Perhaps the most significant contribution of this work was the awareness it brought to the U.S. federal government regarding the security evaluation needs of the commercial sector. The CISR influenced the Federal Criteria, which included many of the new requirements stated by the CISR.

22.5   Other Commercial Efforts: Early 1990s

In the late 1980s and early 1990s, private commercial companies in the United States and the United Kingdom began evaluating other types of products. These evaluations were oriented toward testing and did not include requirement analysis, design analysis, or other classical evaluation techniques. This approach offered no level of trust but rather used a "pass-or-fail" process. A product or system that passed the process was called *certified*, and a certified product received periodic recertification as part of the initial agreement. These companies evaluated products such as antivirus software, network firewalls, Internet filter software, cryptographic products, biometric products, and IPsec products with this technique. In the absence of U.S. government criteria, some of these evaluations were an effective stopgap measure for security evaluations of products that could not be addressed using the TCSEC. They are still available today, but they must compete with the lowest level of trust Common Criteria evaluations that provide similar services at similar costs but provide a government-validated assurance rating.

22.6   The Federal Criteria: 1992

The National Institute of Standards and Technology (NIST) and the National Security Agency (NSA) together developed the Federal Criteria (FC) [2155] in 1992 to replace the TCSEC with a new evaluation approach. The FC attempted to address the shortcomings of the TCSEC and of the ITSEC and to address the concerns of the CISR authors. It was heavily influenced by the TCSEC technically but followed the lead of the ITSEC in its separation of assurance and functional requirements. The FC used a catalogue of functional requirements, which had been done in the CTCPEC. A new direction in the FC is evaluation of products with respect to protection profiles, with each profile identifying requirements and other information particular to a family of products or systems.

> **Definition 22–3.** A *protection profile* (PP) is an abstract specification of the security aspects of an IT product. A protection profile is product-independent, describing a range of products that could meet this same need.

It contains both functional and assurance requirements that are bound together in a profile with a rationale describing the anticipated threats and intended method of use.

NIST and NSA planned to create a set of FIPS for each protection profile. The Minimum Security Functionality Requirements for Multi-User Operating Systems (MISR) was an example of such a profile. Before the FC approach could come to fruition, the Canadian Security Establishment (CSE) and the ITSEC community approached the U.S. government to encourage it to use the FC as a basis for a new set of international criteria.

22.6.1   FC Requirements

The FC included a catalogue of all functional requirements of the TCSEC. New functional requirements adopted from the CISR included the system entry constraints based on time, mode of entry, and location, and other functional issues. Possibly for the first time, there appeared an availability policy based on requirements for resource allocation and fault tolerance. Security management requirements were identified, enhanced, and added to a new section of the functional requirements. Assurance requirements met both TCSEC and ITSEC requirements. The FC included a new assurance requirement for a life cycle process.

22.6.2   Impacts

The most significant contribution of the FC was the concept of an evaluated protection profile. This approach also appears in the 1993 CTCPEC. The functional requirements sections of protection profiles are similar to the ITSEC functionality classes, but the protection profile requirements were selected from the FC functional requirements catalogue. The FC methodology supported evaluation of protection profiles. In contrast, the ITSEC functionality classes were not included in the ITSEC evaluation methodology.

The FC protection profile included the information needed for identification and cross-referencing as well as a brief description of the nature of the problem that the profile addressed. The rationale portion included identification of threats, the environment, and assumptions and provided the justification for the profile. The subsequent sections of the protection profile contained the functional and assurance requirements as stated in the FC. The FC also introduced the concept of a product-dependent security target that implemented the requirements of an approved protection profile.

A second significant contribution was the development of a profile registry that made FC-approved protection profiles available for general use.

22.7   FIPS 140: 1994–Present

During the time of the TCSEC, the U.S. government had no mechanism for evaluating cryptographic modules. Evaluation of such modules was needed in order to ensure their quality and security enforcement. Evaluation of cryptographic modules outside the United States under the ITSEC or within the United States under the commercial pass-or-fail techniques did not meet these needs. In 1994, NIST and the Canadian Security Establishment (CSE) jointly established FIPS 140-1 as an evaluation standard for cryptographic modules for both countries. This standard was updated in 2001 to FIPS 140-2 [2217] to address changes in technology and process since 1994. The program is now sponsored jointly by NIST and CSE under the Cryptographic Module Validation Program (CMVP). Since May 25, 2002, the CMVP only accepts validations against FIPS 140-2. Certification laboratories are accredited in Canada, the United States, Australia, Germany, Spain, Japan, and Taiwan to perform the evaluations, which are validated jointly under the CMVP, sponsored by CSE and NIST. This scheme for evaluating cryptographic products has been highly successful and is actively used today [2141].

A cryptographic module is a set of hardware, firmware, or software, or some combination thereof, that implements cryptographic logic or processes. If the cryptographic logic is implemented in software, then the processor that executes the software is also a part of the cryptographic module. The evaluation of software cryptographic modules automatically includes the operating system.

The Cryptographic Algorithm Validation Program (CAVP) provides for the evaluation of approved cryptographic algorithms against specific algorithm specifications. This list of approved cryptographic algorithms is dynamic. The CAVP tests the following types of cryptographic algorithms: block ciphers, block cipher modes, digital signatures (including elliptic curves), key derivation functions, key management, message authentication, random number generation, secure hashing, and component testing. CMVP requires validation testing for claimed approved cryptographic algorithms to be performed by the CAVP. It is also possible for vendors to obtain validations for approved algorithms using CAVP without CMVP [2141].

22.7.1   FIPS 140 Requirements

FIPS 140-1 and FIPS 140-2 provide the security requirements for a cryptographic module implemented within federal computer systems. Each standard defines four increasing, qualitative levels of security (called security levels) intended to cover a wide range of potential environments. The requirements for FIPS 140-1 cover basic design and documentation, module interfaces, roles and services, physical security, software security, operating system security, key management, cryptographic algorithms, electromagnetic interference/electromagnetic compatibility, and self-testing. The requirements for FIPS 140-2 include areas related to the secure design and implementation of cryptographic modules: specification; ports and interfaces; roles, services, and authentication; a finite state model; physical security; the operational environment; cryptographic key management; electromagnetic interference/electromagnetic compatibility; self-testing; design assurance; and mitigation of other attacks.

22.7.2 FIPS 140-2 Security Levels

In this section we present an overview of the security levels of FIPS 140-2. Changes from those of FIPS 140-1 reflect changes in standards (particularly the move from the TCSEC to the Common Criteria), changes in technology, and comments from users of FIPS 140-1.

Security Level 1 provides the lowest level of security. It specifies that the encryption algorithm be a FIPS-approved algorithm but does not require physical security mechanisms in the module beyond the use of production-grade equipment. Security Level 1 allows the software and firmware components of a cryptographic module to be executed on a general-purpose computing system using an unevaluated operating system. An example of a Level 1 cryptographic module is a personal computer board that does encryption.

Security Level 2 dictates greater physical security than Security Level 1 by requiring tamper-evident coatings or seals, or pick-resistant locks. Level 2 provides for role-based authentication, in which a module must authenticate that an operator is authorized to assume a specific role and perform a corresponding set of services. Level 2 also allows software cryptography in multiuser timeshared systems when used in conjunction with an operating system evaluated at EAL2 or better under the Common Criteria (see Section 22.8) using one of a set of specifically identified Common Criteria protection profiles.

Security Level 3 requires enhanced physical security generally available in many existing commercial security products. Level 3 attempts to prevent potential intruders from gaining access to critical security parameters held within the module. It provides for identity-based authentication as well as stronger requirements for entering and outputting critical security parameters. Security Level 3 requirements on the underlying operating system include an EAL3 evaluation under specific Common Criteria protection profiles (see Section 22.8.1), a trusted path, and an informal security policy model. An equivalent evaluated trusted operating system may be used.

Security Level 4 provides the highest level of security. Level 4 physical security provides an envelope of protection around the cryptographic module with the intent of detecting and responding to all unauthorized attempts at physical access. Level 4 also protects a cryptographic module against a security compromise resulting from environmental conditions or fluctuations outside the module's normal operating ranges of voltage and temperature. Level 4 allows the software and firmware components of a cryptographic module to be executed on a general-purpose computing system using an operating system that meets the functional requirements specified for Security Level 3 and that is evaluated at the CC evaluation assurance level EAL4 (or higher). An equivalent evaluated trusted operating system may be used.

22.7.3   Additional FIPS 140-2 Documentation

To promote consistency and repeatability, validation testing of cryptographic modules is performed using the Derived Test Requirements for FIPS PUB 140-2, Security Requirements for Cryptographic Modules (DTR). The DTR contains all vendor and certification laboratory requirements for validating a cryptographic module. The FIPS 140-2 certified laboratories use the DTR as the basis for their validation activities.

An Implementation Guidance for FIPS PUB 140-2, Security Requirements for Cryptographic Modules (IG) provides programmatic guidance of the CMVP. It contains clarification and guidance for the DTR. It includes testing guidance and guidance related to the implementation of Approved and non-Approved functions. The content of the IG is based on responses provided by NIST and CSE to questions received from the FIPS 140-2 certification laboratories. The IG includes guidance on how a validated software or firmware module can be ported to a similar environment and still maintain its validation.

22.7.4   Impact

The CMVP has improved the quality and security of cryptographic modules. By 2002, 164 cryptographic modules and 332 cryptographic algorithms had been tested. Of the 164 modules, approximately half had security flaws and more than 95% had documentation errors. Of the 332 algorithms, approximately 25% had security flaws and more than 65% had documentation errors. Vendors were able to correct these problems before their modules and algorithms were deployed and used. By 2018, more than 1,100 cryptographic modules and more than 7,000 cryptographic algorithms had been validated.

In 2006, the first edition of ISO/IEC 19790 *Information Technology — Security Techniques — Security Requirements for Cryptographic Modules* [2170] was published by the Joint Technical Committee ISO/IEC JTC 1, Information technology, Subcommittee SC 27, IT Security techniques. This requirements standard was derived from FIPS 140-2. A second edition of ISO/IEC 19790 was published in 2012 [2171]. In 2008, a companion to this standard, ISO/IEC 24759 *Information Technology — Security Techniques — Test Requirements for Cryptographic Modules* [2173] was published by the same committee. A second edition of ISO/IEC 24759 [2174] was published in 2014, and a third in 2017 [2175]. The CMVP does not validate cryptographic modules against these standards.

22.7.5   Future

In 2005, NIST announced plans to develop FIPS 140-3, Security Requirements for Cryptographic Modules. NIST solicited comments from the public for suggested modifications and enhancements to FIPS 140-2. Between 2007 and 2012, NIST released drafts of the revised standard for public review. The most recent draft of FIPS 140-3 was released on August 30, 2012 and the public comment period ended on October 1, 2012. FIPS 140-3 is currently in the internal review process. It will probably be released in the latter half of 2018.

22.8   The Common Criteria: 1998–Present

The Common Criteria (CC) approach to security evaluation draws from the strengths of TCSEC, ITSEC, CTCPEC, and FC, as well as from commercial efforts. The original participants in the Common Criteria Project included Canada, NIST and the NSA from the United States, the United Kingdom, France, Germany, and the Netherlands. Although all participants had the common goal of developing a technically strong, easy to use, mutually reciprocal evaluation technology, each of the participants represented previous methodologies. The United Kingdom, France, Germany, and the Netherlands represented the ITSEC community. NIST and the NSA represented the work done for the Federal Criteria Project, and the NSA also represented the TCSEC and the interests of the U.S. military establishment for very high assurance systems. Canada represented the CTCPEC.

Common Criteria version 1.0 was published in 1994. In 1998, the first signers of the Arrangement on the Recognition of the Common Criteria Certifications in the Field of Information Technology Security were the United States, the United Kingdom, France, Germany, and Canada. This arrangement is called the Common Criteria Recognition Arrangement (CCRA), and also the Mutual Recognition Arrangement (MRA), in the literature. This version of the CCRA required nations to develop an appropriate evaluation scheme in order to join. In 1999, Australia and New Zealand signed the MRA. Also in 1999, the CC became Standard 15408 of the International Standards Organization (ISO).

The CCRA was expanded to allow nations to join as either authorizing nations (also known as certificate-producing nations) or consuming nations (also known as certificate-consuming). Authorizing nations have developed evaluation schemes to accredit laboratories to perform CC evaluations that conform to the CC. The consuming nations do not yet have an evaluation scheme developed, but agree to recognize the evaluations performed by the authorizing nations. As of May 2002, Australia, New Zealand, Finland, Greece, Israel, Italy, the Netherlands, Spain, Sweden, and Norway had signed the CCRA. As of November 2017, Austria, Czech Republic, Denmark, Ethiopia, Finland, Greece, Hungary, Israel, India, Japan, Malaysia, Pakistan, Qatar, Republic of Korea, Russia, Singapore,

Turkey, and South Korea have signed the CCRA, bringing the total number of nations in the CCRA to 28. As of November 2017, Australia, Canada, France, Germany, India, Italy, Japan, Malaysia, the Netherlands, New Zealand, Norway, Republic of Korea, Spain, Sweden, Turkey, United Kingdom, and the United States were the 17 authorizing nations.

The CC became the de facto security evaluation standard in the United States in 1998. The TCSEC was retired in 2000, when the last TCSEC evaluation was completed. European countries that used the ITSEC similarly retired it, although remnants of the old evaluation programs still exist.

The Common Criteria evaluation methodology has three parts: the CC documents, the CC Evaluation Methodology (CEM), and a country-specific evaluation methodology called an *Evaluation Scheme* or *National Scheme*. The CC provides an overview of the methodology and identifies functional requirements, assurance requirements, and Evaluation Assurance Levels (EALs). The CEM provides detailed guidelines for the evaluation of products and systems at EAL1–EAL4 as well as some commonly used assurance requirements not included in any EAL. This document is useful to developers and invaluable to evaluators. The first four EALs address low and medium levels of trust, whereas the higher three levels are specific to what are called high-assurance products and systems. Individual country Evaluation Schemes provide the infrastructure necessary to implement CC evaluation. Each country implements the methodology in its own way. The CC documents and the CEM set the fundamental criteria, EALs, and evaluation strategy, but countries may have different methods of selecting evaluators, awarding certifications, structuring interactions between evaluators and vendors, and the like. In the United States, for example, the Evaluation Scheme is the Common Criteria Evaluation and Validation Scheme (CCEVS), which is implemented within NIST. Under this scheme, NIST accredits commercial evaluation laboratories, which then perform product and system or protection profile evaluations. The sponsoring agencies of NIST then validate the evaluation and award the appropriate EALs.

The CC uses the following terms.

Definition 22–4. A *TOE Security Policy* (TSP) is a set of rules that regulate how assets are managed, protected, and distributed within a product or system.

Definition 22–5. The *TOE Security Functions* (TSF) is a set consisting of all hardware, software, and firmware of the product or system that must be relied on for the correct enforcement of the TSP.

Notice that the TSF is a generalization of the TCSEC concept of a trusted computing base (TCB).

There have been many versions of the CC and its companion CC Evaluation Methodology (CEM). Significant changes were made to the CC in September 2006 with the release of CC v3.1 and CEM v3.1. In April 2017, CC Version 3.1

Revision 5 and CEM Version 3.1 Revision 5 were released. In May 2017, CC and CEM addenda describing additional criteria were released.

Due to the amount of content and current relevancy in the field, the following discussion is based on Version 3.1 Revision 5 of the Common Criteria. Previous versions of the CC are still available on the international CC web portal [2132].

22.8.1 Overview of the Methodology

The CC supports two kinds of evaluations: evaluations of protection profiles and evaluations of products or systems against security targets (STs). Product evaluations are awarded at one of seven predefined EALs or at another, user-defined, EAL. All CC evaluations that meet the conditions of the CCRA are reciprocal to the signers of the CCRA. Initially member nations recognized evaluations of products or systems up to EAL4. Then, member nations recognized evaluations of products or systems up to EAL2 and possibly up to EAL4 based on approved protection profiles (PPs). On October 1, 2009, CCEVS began only accepting products into evaluation that claimed compliance to an NIAP-approved PP.

In 2014, the members of the CCRA decided to encourage the development of PPs by collaborating with member government agencies, product vendors, and CC licensed laboratories. PPs developed by this process are called collaborative Protection Profiles (cPP). The intent is that the member nations will utilize the cPPs as a procurement tool. Under the current CCRA dated July 2, 2014, all signatories to the CCRA recognize the results of the evaluation of a product or system claiming compliance to a cPP and results of the evaluations claiming EAL1 or EAL2 with a flaw remediation claim [2118]. Each group of organizations working together to develop a cPP forms a Technical Community. Currently, there are six technical communities: USB Portable Storage Devices, Full Disk Encryption, Network Fundamentals and Firewalls, Application Software, Dedicated Security Component, and Biometrics Security.

The concept of a protection profile evolved from the Federal Criteria, the CTCPEC profiles, and the ITSEC functionality classes. The form, structure, and terminology of a CC protection profile differs from that of an FC protection profile, although the concepts are similar.

> **Definition 22–6.** A *CC protection profile* (PP) is an implementation-independent set of security requirements for a category of products or systems that meet specific consumer needs.

The PP provides a thorough description of a family of products in terms of threats, environmental issues and assumptions, security objectives, and CC requirements. The requirements include both functional requirements, chosen from the CC functional requirements by the PP author, and assurance requirements, which include one of the seven EALs and may include additional assurance requirements as well. The final section of the PP provides the assurance evidence in the form of a rationale that the PP is complete, consistent, and technically sound. PPs do not have to be evaluated and validated. Currently, many NIAP-approved PPs have not undergone evaluation. PPs that are evaluated must undergo evaluation in accordance with the methodology outlined in the CC assurance class APE: Protection Profile Evaluation.

A PP consists of six sections.

1. *Introduction.* This section contains

   a. the *PP Reference*, which is precise information used to identify, catalogue, register, and cross reference the PP; and

   b. the *TOE Overview*, which is a narrative summary of the TOE that should identify and describe the type of the product or system and its features and be acceptable as a stand-alone abstract for use in catalogues and registries.

2. *Conformance Claims.* This section defines whether or not the PP claims conformance to any other PPs and/or packages. It also contains a conformance rationale that justifies how it meets the PP it claims to comply with and a conformance statement that indicates how STs and/or other PPs must claim conformance to that PP. *Strict conformance* requires evidence that all PP requirements are met and that the ST/PP claiming conformance is an instantiation of the PP while allowing the ST/PP claiming conformance to be broader than itself. *Demonstrable conformance* requires evidence that the ST/PP claiming conformance solve the generic security problem described in the PP, providing a solution equivalent to or more restrictive than that described in the PP. *Exact conformance* requires that the ST claiming conformance use the exact same security requirements, no more and no less. Exact conformance is a type of strict conformance.

3. *Security Problem Definition.* This section presents

   a. *assumptions* about the intended usage and the environment of use;

   b. *threats* to the assets requiring protection, in terms of threat agents, types of attacks, and assets that are the targets of the attacks; and

   c. *organizational security policies* (OSPs) by which the product or system must abide.

4. *Security Objectives.* This section defines the security objectives and provides rationale for those security objectives. There are two types of security objectives:

   a. the *security objectives for the TOE* must be traced back to aspects of identified threats and/or organizational security policies; and

   b. the *security objectives for the operational environment* must be traced back to threats not completely countered by the product or system and/or organizational policies or assumptions not completely met by the product or system.

This section also defines a security objectives rationale, which demonstrates that the security objectives counter the threats, enforce the OSPs, and uphold the assumptions.

5. *Extended Components Definition*. The section defines components needed in a PP that are not defined in CC Part 2 or CC Part 3. The new definitions must be modeled after existing CC Part 2 components.

6. *Security Requirements*. This section covers functional and assurance requirements.

   a. The *security functional requirements* (SFRs) are usually drawn from CC Part 2. If no CC requirements are appropriate, the PP author may supply other requirements explicitly without reference to the CC.
      PPs are allowed to include *optional* SFRs that contribute to the PP's security problem, but can be included in the ST at the discretion of the ST author. PPs are also allowed to include selection-based requirements, which are mandatory requirements that depend upon the selections made by the ST author in the rest of the PP.

   b. The *security assurance requirements* are usually drawn from CC Part 3 and may be based on an EAL. The PP author may augment an EAL by adding extra security assurance requirements from the CC or may supply other requirements explicitly without reference to the CC. This includes security requirements for the environment, as applicable.

   c. The *security requirements rationale* demonstrates that the requirements are traceable to and meet the security objectives. This section also includes justification for any security requirement dependencies that are not satisfied.

A PP-Module is a uniquely referenced construct that defines a set of elements (i.e., security problem definition, security objectives, and security requirements) that address an optional set of security features added to a base product type. A PP-Module must refer to at least one Base-PP that provides the mandatory requirements and base TOE type. The PP-Module complements the security problem definition, security objectives, and security requirements of the Base-BB by introducing new elements or providing a more detailed set of elements. A PP-Module cannot be evaluated stand-alone; it must be evaluated as part of a PP-Configuration. CC Part 1 describes the required sections of a PP-Module.

A PP-Configuration is also uniquely referenced. It is a composite of one or more PP-Modules with their associated Base-PPs. A PP-Configuration cannot have any additional content not found in the selected PP-Modules or Base-PPs. Evaluation rules for PP-Configurations are based on the evaluation rules for standard PPs. CC Part 1 describes the required sections of a PP-Configuration.

The second form of evaluation offered by the CC is the evaluation of a product or system against a security target (ST). This type of evaluation has two parts. The first is the evaluation of the ST in accordance with assurance class ASE: Security Target Evaluation (see Section 22.8.4). The product or system itself is then evaluated against the ST.

Under the CC, the functional requirements for a specific product or system are defined in an ST, just as was done under the ITSEC. The concept of a security target evolved from the ITSEC, and the idea of evaluating a security target against an evaluated protection profile evolved from the FC.

> **Definition 22–7.** A *security target* (ST) is an implementation-dependent set of security requirements and specifications to be used as the basis for evaluation of an identified product or system.

There are two approaches to developing an ST. The first approach is to develop an ST based on a PP. The second approach is to develop an ST directly from the CC. If an evaluated PP is used, the ST process is generally simpler because much of the security problem definition, security objectives, and security objectives rationale in the ST can be taken directly from the PP. The ST addresses the same fundamental issues as the PP, with some notable differences. A significant difference is that the ST addresses the issues for the specific product or system, not for a family of potential products or systems.

An ST consists of seven sections.

1. *ST Introduction.* This section has four parts.

   a. The *ST Reference* gives precise information that is used to control and identify the ST.

   b. The *TOE Reference* gives precise information that is used to control and identify the product or system to which the ST refers.

   c. The *TOE Overview* is a brief description of the TOE that should be acceptable as a stand-alone abstract for use in evaluated product lists. The TOE overview also states the type of the TOE, such as router, operating system, or firewall. Any non-TOE hardware, software, and/or firmware required by the TOE is identified in the TOE Overview.

   d. The *TOE Description* provides a more detailed description of the TOE as an aid to understanding its security requirements. It addresses the product or system type and the scope and boundaries of the TOE (both physically and logically).

2. *Conformance Claims.* This section has four parts.

   a. The *CC conformance claim* is a statement of conformance to the CC. An ST is *part 2 conformant* if it uses only functional requirements found in part 2 of the CC. If it uses extended requirements defined by the vendor, it is called *part 2 extended. Part 3 conformant* and *part 3 extended* are similarly defined.

b. The *PP claim* lists the PPs to which the ST is conformant if it is compliant with all parts of the PP.

c. The *package claim* identifies the packages (e.g., EALs) to which the ST claims conformance. A PP is conformant to a package if the security functional requirements or security assurance requirements of the ST are identical to all of those in the package. A PP is augmentation of a package if the security functional requirements or security assurance requirements of the ST include all of those in the package plus at least one additional requirement.

d. The *conformance rationale* demonstrates that the TOE type is consistent with claimed PP, that the SPD in the ST is consistent with the SPD in the claimed PP, that the security objectives in the ST are consistent with the security objectives in the claimed PP, and that the security requirements in the ST are consistent with the security requirements in the claimed PP.

3. *Security Problem Definition*. This section includes

   a. *assumptions* about the intended usage and about the environment of use;

   b. *threats* to the assets requiring protection, in terms of threat agents, types of attacks, and assets that are the targets of attacks; and

   c. *organizational* security policies by which the product or system must abide.

4. *Security Objectives*. There are two types of security objectives:

   a. The *security objectives for the TOE* must be traced back to aspects of identified threats and/or organizational security policies.

   b. The *security objectives for the operational environment* must be traced back to threats not completely countered by the product or system and/or organizational policies or assumptions not completely met by the product or system.

   This section also defines a security objectives rationale, which demonstrates that the security objectives counter the threats, enforce the OSPs, and uphold the assumptions.

5. *Extended Components Definition*. The section defines components needed in a ST that are not defined in CC Part 2 or CC Part 3. The new definitions must be modeled after existing CC Part 2 components.

6. *Security Requirements*. This section covers functional and assurance requirements.

   a. The *security functional requirements* are usually drawn from the CC Part 2. If no CC requirements are appropriate, the ST author may supply other requirements explicitly without reference to the CC.

   b. The *security assurance requirements* are usually drawn from CC Part 3 and may be based on an EAL. The ST author may augment an EAL by adding extra security assurance requirements from the CC or may supply other requirements explicitly without reference to the CC. This includes security requirements for the environment, as applicable.

   c. The *security requirements rationale* demonstrates that the requirements for the product or system and the requirements for the environment are traceable to the objectives and meet them.

   d. The section includes justification for any security requirement dependencies that are not satisfied.

7. *TOE Summary Specification.* This specification defines the instantiation of the security requirements for the product or system and includes

   a. a high-level description of how the TOE meets each of the claimed security functional requirements; and

   b. a high-level description of how the TOE protects itself from interference, logical tampering, and bypass.

As shown in the previous list, in addition to the PP issues, the ST includes a TOE summary specification. A PP claims section identifies claims made to PPs that the ST implements. An ST that claims to implement a PP must state those claims and justify them in the rationale.

The CC also has a scheme for assurance maintenance. The goal of such activities is to build confidence that assurance already established for a product or system will be maintained and that the product or system will continue to meet the security requirements through changes in the product or system or its environment.

22.8.2   CC Requirements

The heart of the CC is the requirements themselves. The CC defines both functional and assurance requirements and then builds EALs out of the assurance requirements. The requirements are organized into a somewhat elaborate naming and numbering scheme. However, this scheme is much easier to use than the textual descriptions of multiple requirements in a single section, as is done in other methodologies. Functional and assurance requirements are divided into classes based on common purpose. Classes are broken into smaller groups called families. Families contain components, which contain definitions of detailed requirements as well as dependent requirements and a definition of hierarchy of requirements.

22.8.3   CC Security Functional Requirements

There are 11 classes of security functional requirements, each having one or more families. Two of the security functional requirement classes are auditing and security management. The related requirements are unique in the sense that many requirements in other classes generate auditing and/or management requirements.

A management section of each family overview provides specific information about management issues relevant to the subdivisions and requirements of the family. Similarly, the audit section of the family overview identifies relevant auditable events associated with the requirements of the family. Requirements may be hierarchical in nature. Requirement A is hierarchical to requirement B if the functional elements of requirement A offers more security (or is more restrictive) than requirement B. Finally, nonhierarchical dependencies, which may cross classes, are also identified with each requirement. These four structural approaches (identification of management requirements, audit requirements, hierarchical relationships, and nonhierarchical dependencies) help define a consistent and complete specification using the CC.

Consider the security functional requirements of the CC by class and family. The class is indicated by the title, and the families are identified in the descriptive text. All other requirements are derived from previously discussed methodologies.

- Class FAU: *Security Audit*. This class contains six families of requirements that address audit automatic response, audit data generation, audit analysis, audit review, audit event selection, and audit event storage.

- Class FCO: *Communication*. This class contains two families that address nonrepudiation of origin and nonrepudiation of receipt. The CC is the first methodology to contain this requirement.

- Class FCS: *Cryptographic Support*. This class contains two families that address cryptographic key management and cryptographic operation. Encryption algorithms and other implementation issues can be addressed using FIPS 140-2.

- Class FDP: *User Data Protection*. This class has 13 families. It includes two different types of security policies: access control policies and information flow policies. The difference between these two types of policies is essentially that an access control policy makes decisions based on discrete sets of information, such as access control lists or access permissions, whereas an information flow control policy addresses the flow of information from one repository to another. A discretionary access control policy is an access control policy and a mandatory access control policy is an information flow control policy. These families are also represented in other methodologies, but they are generalized in the CC, for flexibility.

  The residual information protection family addresses the issues called "object reuse" in previous criteria. Other families address data authentication, rollback, stored data integrity, inter-TSF user data confidentiality transfer protection, inter-TSF user data integrity transfer protection, exporting to outside the TSF control, and importing from outside the TSF control.

- Class FIA: *Identification and Authentication*. This class has six families that include authentication failures, user attribute definition, specification of secrets, user authentication, user identification, and user/subject binding.

- Class FMT: *Security Management*. This class contains seven families that include management of security attributes, management of TSF data, management roles, management of functions in TSF, security attribute expiration, specification of management functions, and revocation.
- Class FPR: *Privacy*. The CC is the first evaluation methodology to support this class. It has four families that address anonymity, pseudonymity, unlinkability, and unobservability.
- Class FPT: *Protection of Security Functions*. This class has 14 families. These families address TSF physical protection, fail secure, trusted recovery, availability of exported TSF data, confidentiality of exported TSF data, integrity of exported TSF data, internal TOE TSF data transfer, replay detection, state synchrony protocol, timestamps, inter-TSF TSF data consistency, testing of external entities, internal TOE TSF data replication consistency, and TSF self-tests.
- Class FRU: *Resource Utilization*. The three families in this class deal with fault tolerance, resource allocation, and priority of service (first used in the CC).
- Class FTA: *TOE Access*. This class has six families. They include limitations on multiple concurrent sessions, session locking and termination, TOE access history, TOE session establishment, TOE access banners, and limitations on the scope of selectable attributes (system entry constraints).
- Class FTP: *Trusted Path*. This class has two families. The inter-TSF trusted channel family (which is first defined in the CC) and the trusted path family.

EXAMPLE: As indicated above, Class FAU contains six families. The management section for each family identifies potential management functions of class FMT that should be considered relative to the components of that family. The audit section for each family description identifies auditable events that must be addressed if the component FAU_GEN is selected in the PP or ST.

Component FAU_SAA addresses security audit analysis. Within FAU_SAA there are four components, two of which are described here. FAU_SAA.1, potential violation analysis, is a component that is hierarchical to no other components. This means that there is no lesser requirement in this family on this topic. FAU_SAA.1 depends on requirement FAU_GEN.1, a requirement from another FAU family. This means that if FAU_SAA.1 is selected, FAU_GEN.1 must also be selected. Within FAU_SAA.1 there are two functional requirements. The next component is FAU_SAA.2, profile-based anomaly detection. It is hierarchical to FAU_SAA.1, meaning that the requirements of FAU_SAA.2 are more stringent than those of FAU_SAA.1 and subsume the requirements of

FAU_SAA.1. FAU_SAA.2 is also dependent on FIA_UID.1, a requirement for a family in another class. FAU_SAA.2 contains two individual requirements.

22.8.4   Assurance Requirements

There are nine security assurance classes. One assurance class relates to protection profiles, one to security targets, and one to the maintenance of assurance. The other six directly address assurance for the product or system.

- Class APE: *Protection Profile Evaluation*. This class has six families, one for each section of the PP.
- Class ACE: *Protection Profile Configuration Evaluation*. This class has eight families used to evaluate a PP-Configuration. The first six families are similar to the APE families. The other two families are PP-Module consistency and PP-Configuration consistency.
- Class ASE: *Security Target Evaluation*. This class contains seven families, one for each of the seven sections of the ST. They are similar to the APE families and include a family for TOE summary specification.
- Class ADV: *Development*. This class contains six families: security architecture, functional specification, implementation representation, TSF internals, TOE design, and security policy modeling.
- Class AGD: *Guidance Documentation*. The two families in this class are operational user guidance and preparative procedures.
- Class ALC: *Life Cycle*. There are seven families in this class. There are two configuration management (CM) classes: CM capabilities and CM scope. The other five families are delivery, development security, flaw remediation, tools and techniques, and life cycle definition.
- Class ATE: *Tests*. There are four families in this class: test coverage, test depth, functional tests, and independent testing.
- Class AVA: *Vulnerabilities Assessment*. There is only one family in this class: vulnerability analysis, which can include aspects of covert channel analysis and strength of function analysis.
- Class ACO: *Composition*. There are five families in this class: composition rationale, development evidence, reliance of dependent component, composed TOE testing, and composition vulnerability analysis.

22.8.5   Evaluation Assurance Levels

The CC has seven levels of assurance.

- EAL1: *Functionally Tested*. This level is based on an analysis of security functions using functional and interface specifications and an examination of the guidance documentation provided. It is supported by a search of the public domain for vulnerabilities and independent functional and vulnerability testing. EAL1 requires unique TOE identification. EAL1 is applicable to systems in which some confidence in correct operation is required but security threats are not serious.

- EAL2: *Structurally Tested*. In addition to the analysis performed at EAL1, EAL2 analyses a basic description of the TOE architecture. The analysis is supported by a public domain search for vulnerabilities, independent functional and vulnerability testing, as in EAL1, as well as by evidence of developer testing based on the functional specification and independent confirmation of developer test results, and a vulnerability analysis indicating resistance to attackers with a basic attack potential. EAL2 requires unique TOE identification, the use of a CM system, and secure delivery procedures. EAL2 is applicable to systems for which a low to moderate level of independent assurance is required but the complete developmental record may not be available, such as legacy systems.

- EAL3: *Methodically Tested and Checked*. At this level, the analysis of security functions is the almost same as at EAL2, except it requires an architectural description of the TOE design. The analysis is supported as in EAL2, with the addition of high-level design as a basis for developer testing and the use of development environment controls and configuration management.

- EAL4: *Methodically Designed, Tested, and Reviewed*. This level adds low-level design, a complete interface description, a basic modular design of the TOE, and a subset of the implementation to the inputs for the security function analysis. Other assurance measures at EAL4 require additional configuration management including automation and evidence of secure delivery procedures. The analysis is supported as in EAL3, with the addition of implementation representation and a vulnerability analysis indicating resistance to attackers with an enhanced-basic attack potential. This is the highest EAL that is likely to be feasible for retrofitting of an existing product line. It is applicable to systems for which a moderate to high level of independently assured security is required.

- EAL5: *Semiformally Designed and Tested*. This level adds a modular TSF design and the full implementation to the inputs for the security function analysis for EAL4. A semiformal functional specification and a semiformal modular high-level design are required. A methodical vulnerability search must address penetration attackers with moderate attack potential. Configuration management must be comprehensive. This level is the highest EAL at which rigorous commercial development practices supported by a moderate amount of specialist computer security engineering will suffice. This EAL is applicable to systems for which a high level of independently assured security is needed.

- EAL6: *Semiformally Verified Design and Tested.* This level requires a structured presentation of the implementation in addition to the inputs for the security function analysis for EAL5. A formal model of the security policies and a semiformal functional specification and TOE design must be included. The TSF design must be simple and support layering as well as modularity. Other assurance measures at EAL6 require additional configuration controls and development environment security measures. The methodical vulnerability search at EAL6 addresses penetration attackers with high attack potential. A structured development process must be used. EAL6 is applicable for systems in high-risk situations where the assets being protected are valuable enough to justify the high cost of development and certification.

- EAL7: *Formally Verified Design and Tested.* The final level requires a formal presentation of the functional specification and a high-level design, and formal and semiformal demonstrations must be used in the correspondence, as appropriate. The product or system design must be simple. The analysis requires that the implementation representation be used as a basis for testing. Independent confirmation of the developer test results must be complete. EAL 7 is applicable in extremely high-risk situations and requires substantial security engineering.

Figure 22–1 gives a rough matching of the levels of trust of various methodologies. Although the correspondences are not exact, they are reasonably close. The table indicates that the CC offers a level that is lower than any previously offered level.

22.8.6 Evaluation Process

The CC evaluation process in the United States is controlled by the CC Evaluation Methodology (CEM) and NIST. Evaluations are performed by NIST-accredited commercial laboratories that do evaluations for a fee. In addition to using partner organizations, many of the evaluation laboratories also offer support for vendors

TCSEC	ITSEC	CC	Other
D	E0	*no equivalent*	
no equivalent	*no equivalent*	EAL1	Private testing lab
C1	E1	EAL2	OS for FIPS 140-2 L2
C2	E2	EAL3	OS for FIPS 140-2 L3
B1	E3	EAL4	OS for FIPS 140-2 L4
B2	E4	EAL5	
B3	E5	EAL6	
A1	E6	EAL7	

Figure 22–1 Comparison of levels of trust in various methodologies.

in getting ready for evaluations. Staff that assist vendors in getting ready for an evaluation are not allowed to work as evaluators on the evaluation. The size of an evaluation team is normally dependent upon the assurance level, size of the TSF, or PP. It is usually a team of two to six individuals but this may vary from laboratory to laboratory.

Typically, a vendor selects an accredited laboratory to evaluate a product or system. The laboratory performs the evaluation on a fee basis. Once negotiations and a baseline schedule have been developed, the laboratory must coordinate with the validating body. Under the U.S. scheme (CCEVS), the evaluation laboratory must develop a work plan and must submit the evaluation for eligibility.

Evaluation of a product or system is slightly more complex than evaluating a PP because there are more steps involved and more evaluation evidence deliverables. Some schemes require a completed ST that passes all CEM work units prior to accepting the evaluation project. Other schemes only require a ST that is mostly complete. CCEVS will only accept evaluations against an NIST-approved PP. Other schemes will accept evaluations that claim an EAL level. Each scheme has different evaluation acceptance criteria. The vendor and the evaluation laboratory must coordinate schedules for deliverables of evaluation evidence. The evaluation proceeds as outlined in the CEM. When the laboratory finishes the evaluation, it presents its findings to the validating agency, which decides whether or not to validate the evaluation and award the EAL rating.

22.8.7   Other International Organizations

Over the years, a few additional entities have been created as a result of the CC. Two of these are described in this section.

22.8.7.1   SOG-IS International Cooperation Agreement

The Senior Officials Group Information Systems Security (SOG-IS) agreement is a mutual recognition agreement between participating government organizations and agencies from countries in the European Union (EU) or European Free Trade Association (EFTA). The development of the agreement was a result of EU decisions in the fields of security of information systems and common information technology security evaluation criteria. The agreement was originally signed in 1997. In 1999, the agreement was updated to incorporate CC.

The current SOG-IS agreement was modified in January 2010. The 2010 version of the agreement included the concept of *authorizing* (or certificate producing) participants and *consuming* participants. This update also limited levels of recognition above EAL4 to approved technical areas. There are two levels of certificate producers within SOG-IS: the recognition of CC certificates claiming EAL1–EAL4 and the recognition of CC certificates at higher levels for defined technical areas if the SOG-IS management committee has approved the scheme for that level. As of 2017, there are eight authorizing participants: France,

Germany, Italy, Netherlands, Norway, Spain, Sweden, and UK. In addition there are six consuming participants: Austria, Croatia, Estonia, Finland, Luxembourg, and Poland.

SOG-IS participants collaborate to standardize CC PPs and CC certificate policies between the CC schemes within Europe to present a common position within the CCRA and to develop PPs when the EU Commission issues an IT security-related directive that should be incorporated in EU national laws. Authorizing nations still perform EAL3 and EAL4 evaluations of products, including operating systems and network devices. There are currently two technical areas covered by the SOG-IS agreement: smartcards and similar devices, and hardware devices with security boxes. The SOG-IS participants have developed 16 smartcard and similar device PPs, including PPs for passports and secure signature creation devices. Ten PPs have been developed by the SOG-IS participants for hardware devices with security boxes.

22.8.7.2   Common Criteria Users Forum

The Common Criteria Users Forum is comprised of international individual members from the following sectors: academia, consultants, end users, governments, CC laboratories, schemes, solution providers, standards organizations, and vendors. The CCUF provides a communication mechanism between individuals in the CC community. It strives to promote worldwide mutual recognition of CC evaluations, focused technical communities to develop cPPs, viable policies and processes for evaluation maintenance on future product versions, and viable policies and processes for evaluation of systems comprised of evaluated products. It also encourages the development of methods/techniques for minimizing the time and resources required to successfully complete an evaluation.

The CCUF is governed by the CCUF Management board, which is comprised of seven elected members. The CCUF hosts a portal used for collaboration and communication between CCUF members as well as Technical Communities.

22.8.8   Impacts

The CC addresses many issues with which other evaluation criteria and methodologies have struggled. However, the CC is not perfect. At first glance, one might think that the protection profiles and security targets of the CC suffer the same weaknesses as those that plagued the security targets of the ITSEC. In some sense, this is true. A PP or ST may not be as strong as TCSEC classes because fewer security experts have reviewed it and it has yet faced the test of time. Some of the CC requirements were derived from requirements of the previous methodologies. Such requirements may inherently have more credibility. Mature requirements and the CC process of identifying dependencies, audit requirements, and management requirements can contribute to the completeness, consistency, and technical correctness of a resulting PP or ST. The clarity of presentation of the requirements also helps, but ultimately the correctness of an ST lies in the hands of the vendor and the evaluation team.

The CC is much more complete than the functional requirements of most preceding technologies. However, it is not immune to "criteria creep." A CC project board manages interpretations to support consistent evaluation results. Interpretations can be submitted by any national scheme for international review. The final interpretations agreed on become required on all subsequent evaluations under the CC and form the basis for future CC updates. Although this is a well-managed process, it does not address the fact that a newer evaluation may have more stringent requirements levied on it than an older evaluation of the same type.

Having a team member who is not motivated by financial issues to complete the evaluation quickly lends support to the depth of the evaluation and in some respects addresses the functions of a technical review board by providing impartial review. The evaluation process itself is very well-monitored by the validating body; it is less subjective than some of the preceding methodologies because every step is well-defined and carefully applied.

22.8.9   Future of the Common Criteria

The CC documentation and methodology continue to evolve. As of 2017, there have been eight official versions of the CC/CEM. CCRA members can submit change proposals for consideration. New Technical Communities are continuing to be formed and cPPs are continuing to be developed by these new TCs.

The Common Criteria Management Board (CCMB) is an international body responsible for maintaining the Common Criteria and ensuring the CCRA is operated as defined by its rules. Each signatory of the CCRA has a representative on the CCMB. This group has the responsibility of accepting or rejecting change proposals of the CC submitted by national schemes or the general public. The charter of the CCMB is to facilitate consistent evaluation results under the CCRA.

The CCMB discusses change proposals forwarded by CCRA participants and makes one of the following determinations: Agreed, Concurred, Disagreed. Agreed indicates that the change proposal is worthy of international adoption by the CC. Concurred indicates that the change proposal is acceptable and does not violate mutual recognition, but is not worthy of international adoption. Disagreed means either the change proposal violates mutual recognition rules or is not complete enough to be acceptable. If a change proposal is assigned the designation of Disagreed, it is assumed that use of the change proposal will be halted as soon as possible.

The CCMB also supports the process required to obtain ISO/IEC standardization for the CC/CEM by responding appropriately to requests from ISO/IEC. When appropriate the CCMB is responsible for integrating the new material developed from the work projects into the CC/CEM. Technical consistency of CC/CEM-related work projects assigned to other groups are reviewed by the CCMB, and issues are reported to the Common Criteria Development

Board (CCDB). The CCDB is responsible for managing the technical facets of the CCRA, CC/CEM maintenance and continuous development, and development of cPPs created by Technical Communities. The CCDB also provides technical recommendations and guidance to the CCMB.

22.9   SSE-CMM: 1997–Present

The System Security Engineering Capability Maturity Model (SSE-CMM) [136, 889, 890, 2172, 2236] is a process-oriented methodology for developing secure systems based on the Software Engineering Capability Maturity Model (SE-CMM). SSE-CMM was developed by a team of security experts from the U.S. government and industries to advance security engineering as a defined, mature, and measurable discipline. It helps engineering organizations define practices and processes and focus on improvement efforts. The SSE-CMM became ISO Standard 21827 in 2002 [2172]. The ISO/IEC standard was updated in 2008 [2172].

Taking a very abstract view, there is a similarity between evaluation of processes using a capability model and evaluation of security functionality using an assurance model. Capability models define requirements for processes, whereas methodologies such as the CC and its predecessors define requirements for security functionality. Capability models assess how mature a development/engineering process is, whereas the CC type methodology evaluates how much assurance is provided for the functionality. SSE-CMM provides maturity levels, whereas the other methodologies provide levels of trust. In each case, there are specific requirements for the process or functionality and different levels of maturity or trust that can be applied to each.

The SSE-CMM can be used to assess the capabilities of security engineering processes and provide guidance in designing and improving them, thereby improving an organization's security engineering capability. It provides an evaluation technique for an organization's security engineering. Applying the SSE-CMM can support assurance evidence and increase confidence in the trustworthiness of a product or system.

22.9.1   The SSE-CMM Model

The SSE-CMM is organized into processes and maturity levels. Generally speaking, the processes define what needs to be accomplished by the security engineering process and the maturity levels categorize how well the process accomplishes its goals.

> **Definition 22–8.** A *process capability* is the range of expected results that can be achieved by following the process. It indicates potential and is a predictor of future project outcomes.

Definition 22–9. *Process performance* is a measure of the actual results achieved.

Definition 22–10. *Process maturity* is the extent to which a process is explicitly defined, managed, measured, controlled, and effective.

The SSE-CMM contains 11 systems security engineering process areas:

- Administer Security Controls
- Assess Impact
- Assess Security Risk
- Assess Threat
- Assess Vulnerability
- Build Assurance Argument
- Coordinate Security
- Monitor System Security Posture
- Provide Security Input
- Specify Security Needs
- Verify and Validate Security

The definition of each process area contains a goal for the process area and a set of base practices that support the process area. The SSE-CMM defines 61 base practices within the 11 process areas.

EXAMPLE: The definition of the Assess Threat process area contains the goal that threats to the security of the system be identified and characterized. The base processes are:

- Identify Natural Threats
- Identify Human-Made Threats
- Identify Threat Units of Measure
- Assess Threat Agent Capability
- Assess Threat Likelihood
- Monitor Threats and Their Characteristics

Eleven additional process areas related to project and organizational practices adapted from the SE-CMM are:

- Ensure Quality
- Manage Configuration
- Manage Project Risk
- Monitor and Control Technical Effort

- Plan Technical Effort
- Define Organization's Systems Engineering Process
- Improve Organization's Systems Engineering Process
- Manage Product Line Evolution
- Manage Systems Engineering Support Environment
- Provide Ongoing Skills and Knowledge
- Coordinate with Suppliers

The five Capability Maturity Levels that represent increasing process maturity are as follows:

1. *Performed Informally.* Base processes are performed.
2. *Planned and Tracked.* Project-level definition, planning, and performance verification issues are addressed.
3. *Well-Defined.* The focus is on defining and refining a standard practice and coordinating it across the organization.
4. *Quantitatively Controlled.* This level focuses on establishing measurable quality goals and objectively managing their performance.
5. *Continuously Improving.* At this level, organizational capability and process effectiveness are improved.

22.9.2   Using the SSE-CMM

Application of the SSE-CMM is a straightforward analysis of existing processes to determine which base processes have been met and the maturity levels they have achieved. The same process can help an organization determine which security engineering processes they may need but do not currently have in practice.

This is accomplished using the well-defined base processes and Capability Maturity Levels that were overviewed in the preceding section. One starts with a process area, identifying the area goals and base processes that SSE-CMM defines for the process area. If all the processes within a process area are present, then the next step of the analysis involves determining how mature the base processes are by assessing them against the Capability Maturity Levels. Such an analysis is not simple and may involve interactions with engineers who actually use the process. The result of the analysis culminates in identification of the current level of maturity for each base process in the process area.

The analysis continues as described above for each process area. Processes within an area may have varying levels of maturity, and the level of maturity for the process area would be the lowest level represented by the set of levels for the base process. A useful way of looking at the result of a complete SSE-CMM analysis is to use a Rating Profile, which is a tabular representation of process areas versus maturity levels. An example of such a profile is provided in Figure 22–2.

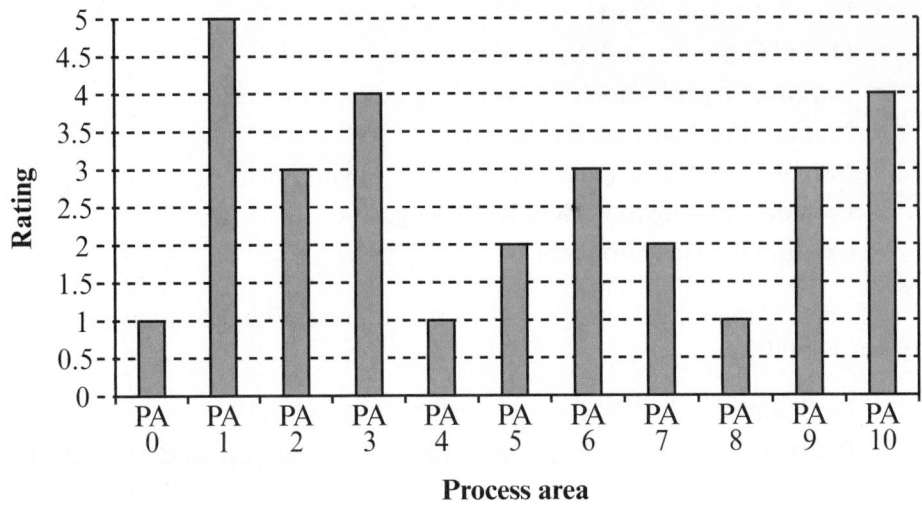

Figure 22–2 Example of a rating profile for the 11 process areas of the SSE-CMM (from [670]).

In a similar fashion, process area rating profiles can be used to show the ratings provided for individual base processes within a process area.

22.10   Summary

Since the early 1980s, the international computer security community has been developing criteria and methodologies for the security evaluation of IT products and systems. The first public and widely used technique was provided by the Trusted Computer System Evaluation Criteria (TCSEC), which was driven by the U.S. Department of Defense. Although the TCSEC was widely used for nearly two decades, criticisms of it inspired research and development of other approaches that addressed many areas of concern, including limitations of scope, problems with the evaluation process, binding of assurance and functionality, lack of recognition of evaluations in one country by the authorities of another, and inflexibility in selection of requirements, to name the most significant ones. New methodologies were developed to address these issues. Most notable of these were the Information Technology Security Evaluation Criteria (ITSEC) in Europe, the Canadian Trusted Computer Product Evaluation Criteria (CTCPEC), and the Federal Criteria (FC) in the United States. These foundational methodologies have culminated in the Common Criteria, which has obtained worldwide support for over a decade.

Other evaluation techniques include FIPS 140-2 (a special-purpose evaluation of cryptographic modules, jointly managed by NIST and the Canadian CSE) and the process-oriented System Security Engineering Capability Maturity Model (SSE-CMM).

22.11 Research Issues

The Common Criteria (CC) methodology is the focus of much current research. Aside from the issues discussed in Section 22.8.8, mechanisms for spreading the use of the CC and other evaluation criteria are receiving much attention. Evaluations are expensive and time-consuming. Reducing both cost and time without diminishing the quality of the evaluation is a critical area of research.

Another interesting research topic is reuse of evaluations in new environments or for systems composed of evaluated parts. Consumers of products and systems need to determine how effective those products and systems are in their current environments. Formal evaluation is suitable when one can determine precise security requirements and the environment in which the product or system is to be used and can provide appropriate evidence that the requirements are met in the defined environment. Today's evaluation techniques and approaches do not readily support reuse of evidence, for reasons of intellectual property ownership and proprietary information. Without detailed assurance evidence from the product or system developer, evaluation options for consumers may be limited. Current approaches that are alternatives to evaluation include various types of testing, such as penetration testing (see Section 24.2). Penetration testing is an excellent technique for identification of vulnerabilities but lacks the "total picture" view of formal evaluation. More complete and effective functional and structural testing is another alternative for finding problems. How can one make the testing as effective as possible, and what is the highest possible level of effectiveness?

22.12 Further Reading

The evaluation process of the TCSEC has been widely discussed and critiqued [80, 167, 408, 970, 1445, 1541, 1714], and changes have been proposed for specific environments such as real-time embedded systems [39]. Several products and systems aimed at levels of the TCSEC have also been analyzed [286, 561, 641, 1618, 1868, 2012]. Pfleeger [1521] compares the TCSEC with then-current European evaluation methodologies.

The results of ITSEC evaluations have also been presented [334, 929]. Straw [1835] compares the ITSEC with the Federal Criteria, and Borrett [270] discusses the differences between evaluation under the TCSEC and under the U.K. ITSEC.

The basis for CC requirements arises in several papers, including one that describes the functional criteria for distributed systems [482]. Other papers discuss various aspects of CC ratings and protection profiles [256, 938], including the use of SSE-CMM processes to develop those profiles [81, 2008]. Some evaluations have also been discussed [9, 871].

Hefner [889, 890] and Menk [1320] discuss the origins and evaluation partnerships under the SSE-CMM. Some papers [1043, 1044] discuss the relationships between product-oriented evaluation and process-oriented evaluation. In particular, Ferraiolo [670] discusses the contribution of process capability to assurance and the definition of metrics to support process-based assurance arguments. Ferraiolo's tutorial [669] provides a good introduction to SSE-CMM.

Some systems have demanded their own specialized certification processes [685], as have some environments [385, 628].

Lipner [1191] gives a short, interesting historical retrospective on evaluation, and Snow [1775, 1776] briefly discusses the future.

The most current information on evaluation standards and processes can be found on the World Wide Web. For example, the CMVP website [2142] gives information about NIST's cryptographic module validation program and the CAVP website gives information about NIST and CSE's cryptographic algorithm validation program [2141]. The international Common Criteria website [2127] contains copies of the Common Criteria documents. It also offers historical information, information about current projects, registries of evaluated and unevaluated protection profiles, evaluated product and system listings (most of which include the security target for the product or system), and information on testing laboratories and recognition agreements among the participating countries. National schemes have their own websites that usually provide scheme announcements, a list of evaluation facilities licensed by the scheme, scheme-approved PPs, a list of products certified by the scheme, the scheme's accreditation process, and a list of products and PPs currently undergoing evaluation in that scheme. Examples of scheme websites include that of the United States scheme (known as CCEVS) [2193], the Canadian scheme (known as CSE) [2139], the Germany scheme (known as BSI) [2122], and the Swedish scheme (known as CSEC) [2144].

22.13   Exercises

1. The issue of binding assurance requirements to functional requirements versus treating them as mutually exclusive sets has been debated over the years. Which approach do you think is preferable, and why?

2. What are the values of doing formal evaluation? What do you see as the drawbacks of evaluation?

3. Recall that "criteria creep" is the process of refining evaluation requirements as the industry gains experience with them, making the evaluation criteria something of a moving target. (See Section 22.2.4.2.) This issue is not confined to the TCSEC, but rather is a problem universal to all evaluation technologies. Discuss the benefits and drawbacks of the CC methodology for handling criteria creep.

4. What are the conceptual differences between a reference validation mechanism, a trusted computing base, and the TOE Security Functions?

5. Choose a Common Criteria protection profile and a security target of a product that implements that profile (see the CCEVS website [2193]). Identify the differences between the PP and the ST that implements the PP.

6. Identify the specific requirements in the Common Criteria that describe a reference validation mechanism. *Hint*: Look in both security functional classes and security assurance classes.

7. Use the Common Criteria to write security functional requirements for identifying the security functional and assurance requirements that define a security policy that implements the Bell-LaPadula Model.

8. Map the assurance requirements of the TCSEC (as defined in this chapter) to the assurance requirements of the ITSEC and the CC. Map the ITSEC assurance requirements to the CC assurance requirements. Justify your mappings.

9. Map the security functional requirements of the CC to the functional requirements of the TCSEC (as described in this chapter). Justify your mappings.

10. Describe a family of security functional requirements that is not covered in the Common Criteria. Using the CC style and format, develop several requirements.

11. Use the Common Criteria Part 2 to write security functional requirements for a security feature that requires passwords to be 15 or more characters in length and include at least one uppercase character, at least one lowercase character, at least one number, and at least one special character.

12. Use the Common Criteria Part 2 to write security functional requirements for a security feature that requires the following security-related events to be audited: startup and shutdown of the audit functions, all login and logout attempts, all password resets, cryptographic key management, all attempts to update the TOE, all attempts to change time, and all user management activities.

13. Select a certified Security Target (see the Common Criteria Certified Products website [2128]) and complete the ASE evaluator work units in the CEM.

Part VII
Special Topics

Part VII explores five topics that play important roles in computer security. They underlie the security of modern systems and networks.

Chapter 23, "Malware," discusses programs set up by attackers to perform actions that violate the site's security policy. The programs act with the privileges of an authorized user but execute without that user's knowledge.

Chapter 24, "Vulnerability Analysis," describes penetration testing. Although important as a standard a posteriori testing technique, penetration testing models the way attackers analyze a system when determining how best to attack it. The insight gained from this mode of thinking is invaluable to defenders. This chapter also discusses models of vulnerabilities to gain insight into why they occur.

Chapter 25, "Auditing," considers auditing and logging. These operations are important in the analysis of attacks. However, they introduce complexities, particularly in the areas of knowing what to log and how to correlate logs kept on different systems.

Chapter 26, "Intrusion Detection," examines the different ways to detect and respond to various types of intrusions. Intrusion detection automates analysis of logs and systems to detect attacks and, in some cases, counter them.

Chapter 27, "Attack Analysis," presents techniques to determine how an attack works and what it did, to varying degrees of certainty based on the information recorded in logs and the visible results of the attack.

Chapter 23
Malware

TITUS ANDRONICUS: Ah! wherefore dost thou urge the name of hands?
To bid Aeneas tell the tale twice o'er,
How Troy was burnt and he made miserable?
— *The Tragedy of Titus Andronicus*, III, ii, 26–28.

Trojan horses, computer viruses, and spyware are effective tools with which to attack computer systems. They assume an authorized user's identity. Thus, access control methods based upon identity or role are ineffective. This chapter presents several types of malicious logic, and discusses defenses.

23.1 Introduction

Odysseus, of Trojan War fame, found the most effective way to breach a hitherto-impregnable fortress was to have people inside bring him in without knowing they were doing so [919, 1936]. The same approach works for computer systems.

Definition 23–1. *Malicious logic*, more commonly called *malware*, is a set of instructions that cause a site's security policy to be violated.

EXAMPLE: The following UNIX script is named *ls* and is placed in a directory:

```
#! /bin/sh
# make a privileged, hidden copy of the shell (command
# interpreter)
cp /bin/sh /tmp/.xxsh
chmod o+s,w+x /tmp/.xxsh

# do what the victim thinks is *all* you're doing
ls $*
```

```
# delete this file
rm ./ls
```

It creates a copy of the UNIX shell that is setuid to the user executing this program (see Section 15.3). The correct *ls* command is executed, and then this program is deleted. On most systems, it is against policy to trick someone into creating a shell that is setuid to themselves. If someone is tricked into executing this script, a violation of the (implicit) security policy occurs. This script is an example of malicious logic.

This chapter presents several different types of malware. It is important to understand that a single piece of malware may embody several different types, as several examples in what follows will show.

23.2   Trojan Horses

Suppose the user *root* executed the script in Section 23.1 unintentionally (for example, by typing "ls" in the directory containing this file). This would be a violation of the security policy. However, if *root* deliberately typed

```
cp /bin/sh /tmp/.xxsh
chmod o+s,w+x /tmp/.xxsh
```

the security policy would not be violated. This illustrates a crucial component of the problems with malware. The system cannot determine whether the instructions being executed by a process are known to the user or are a set of instructions that the user does not intend to execute. The next definition makes this distinction explicit.

> **Definition 23–2.** A *Trojan horse* is a program with an overt (documented or known) purpose and a covert (undocumented or unexpected) purpose.

EXAMPLE: In the preceding example, the overt purpose is to list the files in a directory. The covert purpose is to create a shell that is setuid to the user executing the script. Hence, this program is a Trojan horse.

Dan Edwards was the first to use this term [50]. Trojan horses are often used in conjunction with other tools to attack systems.

EXAMPLE: Geinimi [1836] is a Trojan horse designed for Android cell phones. It was placed in several Android apps on Android markets and forums. When an unsuspecting victim downloaded and ran the app, Geinimi installed itself. It then connected to a remote command and control server, announced its presence, and waited for commands. Among the commands it could execute were a command to delete some or all SMS messages, send them to a remote server named in the command, dump the contact list and list of installed apps, and other functions. It also used several techniques to hide itself, making discovery difficult.

23.2.1   Rootkits

A rootkit is a pernicious Trojan horse. It hides itself on a system so it can carry out its actions without detection. The earliest rootkits first installed backdoors and other traps at various places in the system. The rootkit then changes various system programs that reported on the status of the system and its components. For example, a program that listed the contents of a directory would be altered to not report the presence of certain files; a network status program would be altered so it would not show network connections from specific hosts.

EXAMPLE: The Linux Rootkit IV [307] required superuser access to install. It replaced several programs that might reveal the presence of rootkit-related files (*ls*, *find*, *du*), processes (*ps*, *top*, *pidof*), and other changes (*killall* to not terminate any rootkit-related processes and *crontab* to not reveal any entries causing rootkit-related processes to run). Several programs (*chfn*, *chsh*, *passwd*) gave a user a privileged shell if that user entered a particular password. Similarly, the *login* program allowed the attacker to log in using any name if a particular password were entered, and doing so suppressed the logging information normally saved when one logs in.

It also altered several programs to allow the attackers to return as privileged users, and to gather information. Changing various network status programs (*netstat*, *tcpd*, *syslogd*) prevented adding entries in log files, or displaying network information, that would reveal the presence of the attackers. Some network servers (*inetd*, *rshd*) would allow attackers to connect with root privileges when they entered a particular password.

The installation of the rootkit created several programs useful to attackers. One would install the Trojan horse version of the programs above, but restore the timestamps of the original program and add meaningless data to restore the checksum information.[1] Programs to erase log entries were also added, as was a network sniffer; this enabled the attacker to gather user names and passwords sent over the network. Of course, the network status program *ifconfig*, which would reveal the presence of such a sniffer by reporting the network was accepting all network traffic, was altered to hide this behavior.

Similar rootkits were developed for other systems such as FreeBSD, SunOS, Irix, and Solaris [1466].

---

[1]This is a CRC checksum, which is not a cryptographic hash function and so could be matched easily.

The obvious approach to counter rootkits, used very successfully, was to run nonstandard programs that obtained the same information as the system programs. For example, a program might access the directory directly and read its contents, which would be a list of files and other ancillary information. Other techniques included looking for specific strings in the Trojaned executables, and using cryptographically strong checksums to determine when changes had occurred (see page 125 for a brief example). The reason is that these programs bypassed the system programs, using system calls and information from the kernel to obtain the required information.

Later rootkits were more sophisticated. They altered parts of the kernel, typically by changing modules loaded into it, so that *any* program accessing the kernel (for example, through system calls or other means) to retrieve information would get information that had been filtered by the rootkit.

EXAMPLE: Three Linux rootkits use slightly different methods of hiding themselves.

The Knark rootkit [1109, 1158, 1350] modifies entries in the system call table to invoke new versions in a kernel-loadable module, *sysmod.o*. These routines hijack the system calls that examine the file system and network connections, spawn new processes, and supply new versions that conceal the presence of the rootkit. Knark also uses several exploits enabling an attacker to obtain root privileges easily.

One detection method compares the system call table stored in the kernel with a copy of that table stored on disk at boot time. Instead of modifying entries in the system call table, the SucKIT rootkit [1158, 1588] changes a variable in the kernel that contains the address of the system call table. The new value points to a new system call table with modified entries. This defeats the earlier-mentioned defense.

The adore-ng rootkit [314, 1109, 1820] works differently. On Linux systems, as on UNIX systems, operating system entities such as processes and devices can be accessed through the file system interface; indeed, this uniformity is part of what makes these systems so elegant. Linux implements many actions, such as gathering information about processes and network connections, through the file system. The adore-ng rootkit takes advantage of this by compromising the virtual file system (VFS) layer, which translates system call requests into file system actions. If a process trying to read a file has a UID and a GID with the rootkit's values, adore-ng will show all files; otherwise, it will hide files with the given UID and GID. By manipulating the file system /proc, which has entries corresponding to the active processes, it can manipulate what process monitoring programs report. It also hides processes and any log messages they generate.

A rootkit was once used for digital rights management—with unintended results.

EXAMPLE: In 2005, Sony BMG, a major music vendor, released a music CD with anti-piracy software called XCP from the First 4 Internet Ltd. company [360,

849, 1626, 1627]. To play the music on a Windows computer system, users had to use a proprietary music playing program. When the user installed this software from the disk, the XCP software was installed. This software tried to prevent users from bypassing the proprietary music player by altering certain functions of the Windows operating system. After the alteration, if the user tried to access the music on the CD in any way other than with the proprietary program, the access would be blocked. Otherwise, the normal operating system CD access methods would be invoked. In addition to altering the CD access functions of the CD, the XCP software concealed itself by altering the kernel not to list any files, including folders, with a name beginning with "sys" and placing its software into a folder with such a name.

XCP also contacted Sony during system startup. It obtained new advertising material for the proprietary program to display when music was played. Further, the web-based uninstaller that Sony released had several vulnerabilities; Sony quickly replaced it with a downloadable uninstaller without those problems.

Shortly after the rootkit was made public, attackers took advantage of one of its actions. A variant of one Trojan horse created a file called "sysdrv.exe" in the Windows system directory [1161]. A system running the rootkit would hide this file even though it had no association with the rootkit.

This illustrates the problem of using a malicious technology for purposes the perpetrator believes are benign. Not only did the Sony rootkit fail to achieve its objectives, it created new vulnerabilities in systems, and resulted in lawsuits and a flood of bad publicity, as well as a recall of CDs with the rootkit on them [721, 1396, 1688].

23.2.2 Propagating Trojan Horses

Some Trojan horses can make copies of themselves. One of the earliest Trojan horses was a version of the game *animal*. When this game was played, it created an extra copy of itself. These copies spread, taking up much room. The program was modified to delete one copy of the earlier version and create two copies of the modified program. Because it spread even more rapidly than the earlier version, the modified version of *animal* soon completely supplanted the earlier version. After a preset date, each copy of the later version deleted itself after it was played [556].

> **Definition 23–3.** A *propagating Trojan horse* (also called a *replicating Trojan horse*) is a Trojan horse that creates a copy of itself.

Karger and Schell [1008], and later Thompson [1875], examined detection of Trojan horses. They constructed a Trojan horse that propagated itself slowly and in a manner that was difficult to detect. The central idea is that the Trojan horse modifies the compiler to insert itself into specific programs, including future versions of the compiler itself.

EXAMPLE: Thompson [1875] created a version of the *login* program that was a Trojan horse. When a user logged in, the Trojan horse would accept a fixed password as well as the user's normal password. However, anyone reading the source code for the *login* program would instantly detect this Trojan horse. To obscure it, Thompson had the compiler check the program being compiled. If that program was *login*, the compiler added the code to use the fixed password. Now, no code needed to be added to the *login* program. Thus, an analyst inspecting the *login* program source code would see nothing amiss. If the analyst compiled the *login* program from that source, she would believe the executable to be uncorrupted.

The extra code is visible in the compiler source. To eliminate this problem, Thompson modified the compiler. This second version checked to see if the compiler (actually, the C preprocessor) was being recompiled. If so, the code to modify the compiler so as to include both this Trojan horse and the *login* Trojan horse code would be inserted. He compiled the second version of the compiler and installed the executable. He then replaced the corrupted source with the original version of the compiler. As with the *login* program, inspection of the source code would reveal nothing amiss, but compiling and installing the compiler would insert the two Trojan horses.

Thompson took special pains to ensure that the second version of the compiler was never released. It remained on the system for a considerable time before someone overwrote the executable with a new version from a different system [1592]. Thompson's point was that "no amount of source-level verification or scrutiny will protect you from using untrusted code,"[2] a point to be reiterated later.

23.3   Computer Viruses

A replicating Trojan horse propagates itself only as specific programs (in the preceding example, the compiler and the *login* program). When the Trojan horse can propagate freely and insert a copy of itself into another file, it becomes a computer virus.

> **Definition 23–4.** A *computer virus* is a program that inserts (a possibly transformed version of) itself into one or more files and then performs some (possibly null) action.

The first phase, in which the virus inserts itself into a file, is called the *insertion phase*. The second phase, in which it performs some action, is called

---

[2]See [1875, p. 763].

the *execution phase*. The following pseudocode fragment shows how a simple computer virus works:

```
beginvirus:
    if spread-condition then begin
        for some set of target files do begin
            if target is not infected then begin
                determine where to place virus instructions
                copy instructions from beginvirus to
                    endvirus into target
                alter target to execute added instructions
            end;
        end;
    end;
    perform some action(s)
    goto beginning of infected program
endvirus:
```

As this code indicates, the insertion phase must be present but need not always be executed. As a simple example, one of the earliest viruses [903] would check for an uninfected boot file (the *spread-condition* mentioned in the pseudocode) and, if one was found, would infect that file (the *set of target files*). Then it would increment a counter and test to see if the counter was at 4. If so, it would erase the disk. These operations were the *action(s)*.

Authorities differ on whether or not a computer virus is a type of Trojan horse. Most equate the purpose of the infected program with the overt action and consider the insertion and execution phases to be the covert action. To them, a computer virus is a Trojan horse [586,951]. However, others argue that a computer virus has no covert purpose. Its overt purpose is to infect and execute. To these authorities, it is not a Trojan horse [435, 1405]. In some sense this disagreement is semantic. In any case, defenses against a Trojan horse inhibit computer viruses.

According to Ferbrache [665], programmers wrote the first computer viruses on Apple II computers. A virus developed for research purposes in 1980 wrote itself to the disk boot sectors when the catalogue command was executed. Another one infected many copies of the game "Congo," which stopped working. Friends of its author had released it before it was fully debugged. The author rewrote it to replace existing copies of itself with the fully debugged version. Released into the wild, it rapidly supplanted the buggy copies.

In 1983, Fred Cohen was a graduate student at the University of Southern California. During a seminar on computer security, he described a type of Trojan horse that the teacher, Len Adleman, christened a "computer virus" [436]. To demonstrate the effectiveness of the proposed attack, Cohen designed a computer virus to acquire privileges on a VAX-11/750 computer running the UNIX operating system. He obtained all system rights within half an hour on the average, the longest time being an hour and the shortest being less than five minutes. Because the virus did not degrade response time noticeably, most users never knew the system was under attack.

In 1984, an experiment involving a UNIVAC 1108 computer showed that viruses could spread throughout that system, too. Unlike the UNIX system, the UNIVAC partially implemented the Bell-LaPadula Model, using mandatory protection mechanisms.[3] Cohen's experiments indicated that the security mechanisms of systems that did not inhibit writing using mandatory access controls did little if anything to inhibit computer virus propagation [435, 436].

The Brain (or Pakistani) virus, written for IBM PCs, is thought to have been created in early 1986 [665] but was first reported in the United States in October 1987. It alters the boot sectors of floppy disks, possibly corrupting files in the process. It also spreads to any uninfected floppy disks inserted into the system. Since then, numerous variations of this virus have been reported [904].

In 1987, computer viruses infected Macintosh, Amiga, and other computers. The MacMag Peace virus would print a "universal message of peace" on March 2, 1988, and then delete itself [683]. This computer virus infected copies of the Aldus FreeHand program, which were recalled by their manufacturer [665].

In 1987, Tom Duff experimented on UNIX systems with a small virus that copied itself into executable files. The virus was not particularly virulent, but when Duff placed 48 infected programs on the most heavily used machine in the computing center, the virus spread to 46 different systems and infected 466 files, including at least one system program on each computer system, within eight days. Duff did not violate the security mechanisms in any way when he seeded the original 48 programs [593]. He wrote another virus in a Bourne shell script. It could attach itself to any UNIX program. This demonstrated that computer viruses are not intrinsically machine-dependent and can spread to systems of varying architectures.

In 1989, Dr. Harold Joseph Highland developed a virus for Lotus 1-2-3 [904]. This virus, stored as a set of commands for that spreadsheet, was loaded automatically when a file was opened. Because the virus was intended as a demonstration only, it changed the value in a specific row and column and then spread to other files. This demonstrated that macros for office-type programs on personal computers could contain viruses.

Computer viruses infect computers in different ways, and use various techniques to conceal themselves.

23.3.1   Infection Vectors

Computer viruses can infect systems in three ways: through a boot sector, executables, or data.

---

[3]Specifically, it implemented the simple security condition but not the *-property [951].

The *boot sector* is the part of a disk used to bootstrap the system or mount a disk. When the system boots, any virus in that sector is executed. (The actual boot code is moved to another place, typically another sector.)

Definition 23–5. A *boot sector infector* is a virus that inserts itself into the boot sector of a disk.

EXAMPLE: The Brain virus for the IBM PC is a boot sector infector. When the system boots from an infected disk, the virus is in the boot sector and is loaded. It moves the disk interrupt vector (location 13H or, in decimal, 19) to an alternative interrupt vector (location 6DH or, in decimal, 109) and sets the disk interrupt vector location to invoke the Brain virus now in memory. It then loads the original boot sector and continues the boot.

Whenever the user reads a floppy, the interrupt at location 13H is invoked. The Brain virus checks for the signature 1234H. If the signature is present, control is transferred to the interrupt vector at location 6DH so that a normal read can proceed. Otherwise, the virus infects the disk.

To do this, it first allocates to itself three contiguous clusters (of two contiguous sectors each). The virus then copies the original boot sector to the first of the six contiguous sectors and puts copies of itself into the boot sector and the remaining five sectors.

If there are no unused clusters, the virus will not infect the disk. If it finds only one unused cluster, it will simply overwrite the next two. This accounts for the sometimes destructive nature of the Brain virus.

Definition 23–6. An *executable infector* is a virus that infects executable programs.

Figure 23–1 illustrates how infection can occur. The virus can prepend itself to the executable (as shown in the figure) or append itself.

EXAMPLE: The Jerusalem virus (also called the Israeli virus) is triggered when an infected program is executed. The virus first puts the value 0E0H into register ax and invokes the DOS service interrupt (21H). If on return the high eight bits of register ax contain 03H, the virus is already resident on the system and the executing version quits, invoking the original program. Otherwise, the virus sets itself up to respond to traps to the DOS service interrupt vector.

The Jerusalem virus then checks the date. If the year is 1987, it does nothing. Otherwise, if it is not a Friday and not the 13th (of any month), it sets itself up to respond to clock interrupts (but it will not infect on clock calls). It then loads and executes the file originally executed. When that file finishes, the virus puts itself in memory. It then responds to calls to the DOS service interrupt.

If it is a Friday and the 13th (of any month), and the year is not 1987, the virus sets a flag in memory to be destructive. This flag means that the virus will delete files instead of infecting them.

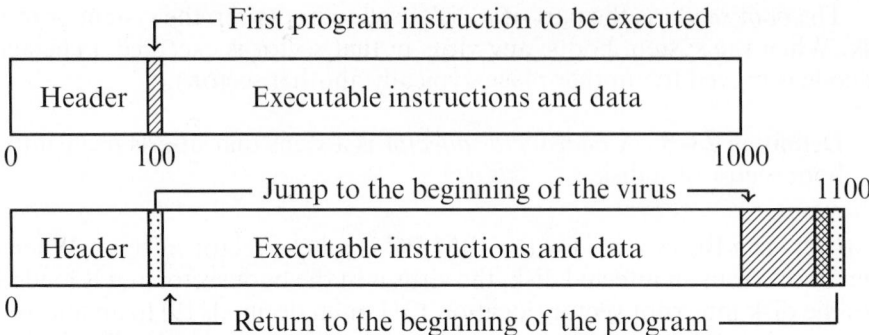

Figure 23–1   How an executable infector works. It inserts itself into the program so that the virus code will be executed before the application code. In this example, the virus is 100 words long and appends itself to the executable code. The first instruction is changed to a branch to the computer virus, and the computer virus arranges to execute the replaced instruction.

Once in memory, the virus checks all calls to the DOS service interrupt, looking for those asking that files be executed (function 4B00H). When this happens, the virus checks the name of the file. If it is *COMMAND.COM*, the virus does nothing. If the memory flag is set to be destructive, the file is deleted. Otherwise, the virus checks the last five bytes of the file. If they are the string "MsDos", the file is infected.[4] If they are not, the virus checks the last character of the file name. If it is "M", the virus assumes that a *.COM* file is being executed and infects it; if it is "E", the virus assumes that a *.EXE* file is being executed and infects it. The file's attributes, especially the date and time of modification, are left unchanged.

Some computer viruses can infect both boot sectors and executables.

Definition 23–7. A *multipartite* virus is one that can infect both boot sectors and applications.

These typically have two parts, one for each type. When it infects an executable, it acts as an executable infector; when it infects a boot sector, it works as a boot sector infector.

---

[4]According to Compulit, as cited in Highland [904, p. 47], "[t]he author of the virus apparently forgot to set the signature during .EXE file infection. This will cause multiple infections of .EXE files." Analysts at the Hebrew University of Jerusalem found that the size of a *.COM* file increased only one time, but the size of an *.EXE* file increased every time the file was executed.

In addition to infecting boot sectors and executable files, some computer viruses infect data. This data is then interpreted as a set of instructions, and the computer virus causes the interpreter to spread the virus.

Definition 23–8. A *macro* virus is a virus composed of a sequence of instructions that is interpreted, rather than executed directly.

Conceptually, macro viruses are no different from ordinary computer viruses. Like Duff's *sh* computer virus, they can execute on any system that can interpret the instructions. For example, a spreadsheet virus executes when the spreadsheet interprets these instructions. If the macro language allows the macro to access files or other systems, the virus can access them, too.

EXAMPLE: The Melissa virus infected Microsoft Word 97 and 98 documents on Windows and Macintosh systems. It is invoked when the program opens an infected file. It installs itself as the *open* macro and copies itself into the Normal template (so any Word documents that the Word program opens are infected). It then invokes a mail program and sends copies of itself to people in the user's address book associated with the program.

A macro virus can infect either executables or data files (the latter leads to the name *data virus*). If it infects executable files, it must arrange to be interpreted at some point. Duff's experiments did this by wrapping the executables with shell scripts. The resulting executables invoked the Bourne shell, which interpreted the virus code before invoking the usual executable.

Macro viruses are not bound by machine architecture. They use specific programs, and so, for example, a macro virus targeted at a Microsoft Word program will work on any system running Microsoft Word. The effects may differ. For example, most Macintosh users do not use the particular mail program that Melissa invoked, so although Macintosh Word files could be infected, and the infection could spread, the virus did not mail itself to other users. On a Windows system, where most users did use that mail program, the infection was spread by mail.

23.3.2 Concealment

One of the goals of computer viruses is to remain undiscovered until executed, and possibly even after that. As detection methods became more sophisticated, so did the methods of concealment. We begin with techniques used by the earliest computer viruses, and describe the defenses that virus writers have evolved.

Definition 23–9. A *terminate and stay resident* (*TSR*) virus is one that stays active (resident) in memory after the application, bootstrapping, or macro interpretation has terminated.

TSR viruses can be boot sector infectors or executable infectors. Both the Brain and Jerusalem viruses are TSR viruses.

Viruses that are not TSR execute only when the host application is executed, the disk containing the infected boot sector is mounted, or the macro is interpreted. An example is the Encroacher virus, which appends itself to the ends of executables.

TSR viruses can be detected by examining the files they infect, and noting that the contents have changed (because of the infection). The next step in computer virus evolution was to hide the changes.

Definition 23–10. *Stealth* viruses are viruses that conceal the infection of files.

To present the appearance of a noninfected file, the virus intercepts calls to the operating system that access files. If the call is to obtain file attributes, the original attributes of the file are returned. If the call is to read the file, the file is disinfected as its data is returned. But if the call is to execute the file, the infected file is executed. Some viruses use all these techniques; others, only some.

EXAMPLE: The Stealth virus (also called the IDF virus or the 4096 virus) is an executable infector. It modifies the DOS service interrupt handler (rather than the interrupt vector; this way, checking the values in the interrupt vector will not reveal the presence of the virus). If the request is for the length of the file, the length of the uninfected file is returned. If the request is to open the file, the file is temporarily disinfected; it is reinfected on closing. The Stealth virus also changes the time of last modification of the file in the file allocation table to indicate that the file is infected.

A second type of concealment obscures the virus rather than the fact of infection. These transformation techniques aim to prevent the file from containing known sequences of code that identify computer viruses, called *signatures* (see Section 23.9.1). To conceal these sequences, some viruses encipher most of the virus code, leaving only a small decryption routine and a random cryptographic key in the clear. Thus, the encryption is used only to obscure the virus, not conceal it. Figure 23–2 summarizes this technique.

Definition 23–11. An *encrypted* virus is a virus that encrypts all of the virus except the cryptographic key and a decryption key.

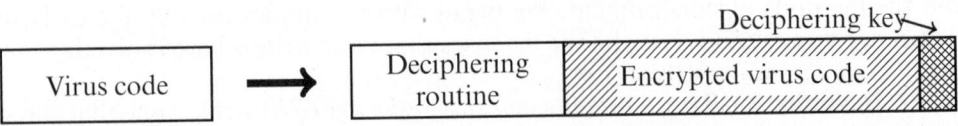

Figure 23–2 An encrypted virus. The ordinary virus code is at the left. The encrypted virus, plus encapsulating decryption information, is at the right.

EXAMPLE: Ferbrache [665, p. 75] cites the following as the decryption code in the 1260 virus. It uses two keys, stored in $k1$ and $k2$. The virus code itself begins at the location *sov* and ends at the location *eov*. The pseudocode is as follows:

```
(* initialize the registers with the keys *)
rA := k1;
rB := k2;
(* initialize rC with the message *)
rC := sov;
(* the encipherment loop *)
while (rC != eov) do begin
        (* encipher the byte of the message *)
        (* ^rC means the value at the address stored
            in rC *)
        (^rC) := (^rC) xor rA xor rB;
        (* advance all the counters *)
        rC := rC + 1;
        rA := rA + 1;
end
```

The dual keys and the shifting of the first key prevent a simple *xor*'ing from uncovering the deciphered virus.

The encrypted part of the virus now varies depending on the key chosen, so detecting known sequences of instructions will not detect the virus. However, the decryption algorithm can be detected. So the next step was to hide decryption signatures by allowing a virus to use different sequences of instructions to carry out a task. Polymorphic viruses were designed to do this.

Definition 23–12. A *polymorphic* virus is a virus that changes the form of its decryption routine each time it inserts itself into another program.

The deciphering code is the segment of the virus that is changed to something different but equivalent. In some sense, they are successors to the encrypting viruses and are often used in conjunction with them.

Consider polymorphism at the instruction level. All of the instructions

```
add 0 to operand
or (word of all 1's) with operand
no operation
subtract 0 from operand
```

have exactly the same effect, but they are represented as different bit patterns on most architectures. A polymorphic virus would insert these instructions into the deciphering segment of code.

EXAMPLE: A polymorphic version of the 1260 computer virus might look like the following. (The lines marked "random line" do not affect the decryption of the computer virus and are changed whenever the virus replicates.)

```
(* initialize the registers with the keys *)
rA := k1;
rA := rA + 0;                    (* random line *)
rB := k2;
rD := k1 + k2;                   (* random line *)
(* initialize rC with the message *)
rC := sov;
rC := rC + 1;                    (* random line *)
(* the encipherment loop *)
while (rC != eov) do begin
        rC := rC - 1;            (* random line *)
        (* encipher the byte of the message *)
        (* ^rC means the value at the address stored in rC *)
        (^rC) := (^rC) xor rA xor rB;
        (* advance all the counters *)
        rC := rC + 2;            (* counter incremented ... *)
        (* to handle random line X *)
        rD := rD - 0;            (* random line *)
        rA := rA + 1;
end
(* the next block does nothing *)
while (rC != sov) do begin
        rD := rD - 1;
        rC = rC - 1;
end
```

Examination shows that these instructions have the same effect as the four instructions listed above.

The production of polymorphic viruses at the instruction level has been automated. At least two tool kits, the Mutation Engine (MtE) and the Trident Polymorphic Engine (TPE), were available in 1992 [2053]; since then, many such tools have been created [1850].

One characteristic of polymorphic viruses is that the computer virus they decrypt is the same regardless of the deciphering key used. Thus, while each occurrence of a polymorphic virus is different when not executing, once it executes the same computer virus is loaded into memory. This makes them susceptible to detection.

Virus writers realized that polymorphism can exist at many levels, including that of the internal structure of the computer virus—for example, the order in which instructions are executed. This led to the next step.

Definition 23–13. A *metamorphic* virus is a virus that changes its internal structure but performs the same actions each time it is executed.

Metamorphic viruses are different even when loaded into memory; in this, they differ from polymorphic viruses. For example, once the virus is decrypted, it may have two completely different implementations, or two different algorithms that produce the same result. For example, the computer virus might change the registers used (W95/Regswap). It might vary the order of functions (W32/Ghost) or instructions, in the latter case with branches ensuring they are executed in the proper order (W95/Zperm).

EXAMPLE: The Zmist (W95/Zmist) [675] computer virus is a complex metamorphic virus that includes elements of polymorphism and other evasion techniques. One of the most sophisticated of its time, it introduced the code integration technique, in which the virus rearranges executable code in the file being infected, distributes parts of it through the rearranged instructions and data, and then updates references in the file so that the infected executable will perform its expected function.

When Zmist executes, it hides the original process if possible and allocates memory to create room for the virus engine, Mistfall, to create a new instance of the virus with some instructions changed, instructions added that do nothing, and other transformations.

When Zmist finds a file to infect, it loads the file into memory. It then takes one of three actions, chosen randomly:

1. With probability 0.1, insert jump instructions between each set of non-jump instructions. In this case the file is not infected, merely altered.

2. With probability 0.1, infect the file with an unencrypted copy of Zmist.

3. With probability 0.8, infect the file with a polymorphic, encrypted copy of Zmist. This requires that the file being infected have a section with initialized data that is writeable. If so, when the infected file is executed, the virus expands this section and uses it to store the virus code as it is decrypted, and then executes that code. Otherwise, the file is infected with an unencrypted copy of the virus.

When the third action is taken, the decryptor is scattered throughout the executable file, with jumps ensuring that the flow of control is correct. The decryptor code takes care to preserve the registers, so once done the original values can be restored. It also rewrites addresses and instructions as needed to ensure the program works as it did before.

In 2007, the Crimea virus that targeted Linux used many of the same evasion techniques as did Zmist [674].

23.3.3   Summary

The number and variety of computer viruses has evolved rapidly. The later viruses are far more complex than the early ones—indeed, the development of virus writing toolkits has placed these into the hands of both expert and nonexpert attackers. Undoubtedly the future will bring even more computer viruses.

23.4   Computer Worms

A computer virus infects other programs. A variant of the virus is a program that spreads from computer to computer, spawning copies of itself on each one.

> **Definition 23–14.** A *computer worm* is a program that copies itself from one computer to another.

Research into computer worms began in the mid-1970s. Shoch and Hupp [1741] developed distributed programs to render computer animations, broadcast messages, and perform other computations. These programs probed workstations. If the workstation was idle, the worm copied a segment onto the system. The segment was given data to process and communicated with the worm's controller. When any activity other than the segment's began on the workstation, the segment shut down.

EXAMPLE: On November 2, 1988, a program targeting Berkeley and Sun UNIX-based computers entered the Internet; within hours, it had rendered several thousand computers unusable [619, 621, 1600, 1706, 1707, 1796, 1797, 1830]. Among other techniques, this program used a virus-like attack to spread: it inserted some instructions into a running process on the target machine and arranged for those instructions to be executed. To recover, these machines had to be disconnected from the network and rebooted, and several critical programs had to be changed and recompiled to prevent reinfection. Worse, the only way to determine if the program had suffered other malicious side effects (such as deletion of files) was to disassemble it. Fortunately, the only purpose of this worm[5] turned out to be

---

[5]We use the conventional terminology of calling this program a "computer worm" because its dominant method of propagation was from computer system to computer system. Others, notably Eichin and Rochlis [619], have labeled it a "computer virus."

self-propagation. Infected sites were extremely lucky that the worm did not infect a system program with a virus designed to delete files and did not attempt to damage attacked systems.

The Father Christmas worm, which appeared shortly after the Internet worm, was interesting because it was a form of macro worm.

EXAMPLE: On December 22, 1988, an electronic "Christmas card" was passed around several IBM-based networks. This card was an electronic letter instructing the recipient to save the message and run it as a program. The program drew a Christmas tree (complete with blinking lights) and printed "Merry Christmas!" It then checked the recipient's list of previously received mail and the recipient's address book to create a new list of email addresses. It then sent copies of itself to all these addresses. The worm quickly overwhelmed the IBM networks and forced the networks and systems to be shut down [817].

This worm had the characteristics of a macro worm. It was written in a high-level job control language, which the IBM systems interpreted, just as the Microsoft Word program interpreted the Visual Basic instructions forming the Melissa virus.

Computer worms generally exhibit three phases. The first, *target selection*, occurs when the worm determines what systems to attempt to spread to. Then the *propagation* begins, with the worm attempting to infect the set of chosen targets. After this, the worm enters the *execution* phase once it is resident on the target. The last phase may be empty, in which case the worm is simply spreading. These phases are similar to the phases of a computer virus, with the target selection and propagation phases corresponding to the infection phase of the virus.

EXAMPLE: The Internet worm is a good example of this structure (see above). The target selection phase of the Internet worm began with the worm examining lists of trusted hosts and hosts trusted by users whose passwords the worm had cracked. During the propagation phase, the worm attempted to exploit four vulnerabilities: one involving an SMTP server in debugging mode, one using a buffer overflow attack on an information server, one involving using guessed passwords to connect to the target host, and one exploiting trust relationships. Once resident on a system, the worm then took actions to hide its presence, prevent reinfection, and then attempt to guess passwords on the local system, to be used in target selection and propagation. It is worth noting that several of these steps were programmed incorrectly, resulting in the rapid spread of the worm, as noted above.

Since then, numerous computer worms have caused many problems. In 2001, Code Red I and its variants exploited a vulnerability in Microsoft's IIS web servers [1376]. If the system was infected between the first and 19th of the month, the worm generated a random list of target IP addresses and tried to propagate to them. From the 20th to the 28th, the worm was set up to send 400MB of meaningless data to the U.S. White House IP address; estimates are that 359,000 systems were ready to do this when the worm was discovered [174]. Code Red II, which has no relationship with Code Red I other than the name, used the same infection vector, but then created a backdoor, and after 24 hours rebooted the system. Its target selection involved randomly generated IP addresses but then masked them to bias infection towards the network containing the system [1376]. The danger here was from the backdoor, which allows an attacker to use the system in nefarious ways.

In 2010, the Stuxnet worm had spread to systems in industrial sites in Iran [653, 1116, 1137]. It targeted Siemens centrifuges used in a process to enrich uranium, first compromising the Windows-based software and then the programmable logic (PLC) in the centrifuges. The centrifuges could also be spun at nonstandard speeds, tearing themselves apart. That the worm spread to industrial control (SCADA) was unusual; equally unusual was the sophistication of the worm's spread and actions. It used state-of-the-art exploits, evasion techniques, and both Windows and (the first identified) PLC rootkits. Symantec estimates that between 8,000 and 9,000 new infections occurred per day [737].

Stuxnet propagated in two ways. First, it would be put onto a system from an infected USB stick via a Trojan horse. Then, it looked on the local network for Windows-based systems to infect. It would then infect no more than three additional systems. Once on such a system, it determined whether that system is part of a specific Siemens industrial control system. If not, the worm did nothing. If it was, the worm then tried to download a later version of itself. It then exploited vulnerabilities of the system's PLC, and took control of the attached centrifuges. It also corrupted the information sent to the controllers, so they would not detect that anything was wrong until the centrifuges went out of control.

Earlier research had shown that physical systems such as power generators are vulnerable to attacks from connected computers. For example, the U.S. Idaho National Laboratories sent a series of commands turning a generator off and on in such a way that the generator tore itself apart [55]. The implication of Stuxnet is that such attacks can be launched over the Internet, and that systems thought to be isolated are in fact connected to the Internet. Stuxnet focused only on Siemens systems. A worm with a less selective payload could cause widespread damage [444].

Stuxnet infected a number of sites in Iran, India, Indonesia, and other countries. Its authorship is unknown, but there has been considerable speculation that its complexity and sophistication mean it was developed by one or more nation-states [299]. Since then, analysts have discovered other equally sophisticated worms. For example, the Flame worm [1761] spreads using techniques similar to Stuxnet, but the attackers must enable the propagation mechanism. It then gathers information such as audio from the microphone, keystrokes, screenshots, and network traffic. Attackers can then retrieve this information. Perhaps even more sophisticated, stealthy worms are active but have yet to be discovered.

23.5   Bots and Botnets

Sometimes attackers coordinate actions among malware on different systems. The malware can preset specific actions to occur with specific triggers. The attackers also can have the malware take actions based on particular messages that the attacker sends.

> **Definition 23–15.**   A *bot* is malware that carries out some action in coordination with other bots. The attacker, called a *botmaster*, controls the bots from one or more systems called *command and control (C&C) servers* or *motherships*. They communicate over paths called *C&C channels*. A collection of bots is a *botnet*.

The distinguishing characteristic of a bot is its using a C&C channel. The bots can be updated or triggered through this channel.

Each bot in a botnet has four stages in its life cycle [364]:

1. The bot first infects a system. This can be done in any number of ways, for example as a computer worm or Trojan horse resident in a program that an unsuspecting user installs and executes. It can also exploit vulnerabilities to enter the system.
2. The bot then checks for a network connection, and looks for either a C&C server or another node that it can communicate with.
3. The bot is then given commands to execute by the C&C server or other node. This may also involve downloading additional components to the bot to add to its capabilities.
4. The bot executes the commands. If appropriate, it sends the results to another site.

Steps 3 and 4 repeat as often as needed.

Botnets can be organized in three basic ways [454]. The botnet may be centralized, in which case each bot communicates directly with the C&C server. However, the C&C server would then become a bottleneck for large botnets. Thus, many botnets use a hierarchical control scheme in which the C&C server communicates with a set of bots that are in turn C&C servers for other bots. This allows control over a large botnet. Indeed, during a study of the Torpig botnet, the researchers observed over 180,000 bots using approximately 1,250,000 unique IP addresses [1834]. The Mirai Internet-of-Things botnet footprint was estimated to be 493,000 instances [1090].

EXAMPLE: One of the earliest bots, GTBot, used an IRC channel as the C&C channel. The bot would be placed on a Windows system running the mIRC client. This was coupled with some scripts to monitor the IRC channel looking for specific keywords, a program to hide the presence of the bot, and in some cases programs to propagate to other Windows systems and install servers on the infected systems. An example of this bot, Backdoor.IRC.Aladinz, installs itself in an invisible directory, then takes additional steps to hide itself, and finally connects to a particular IRC channel and notifies the attacker that it is resident. The bot had tools to launch a large number of attacks, such as flooding the victim with UDP packets, launching a Smurf attack that also floods the victim, gathering and sending information about the system to the attacker, and rebooting the host [346].

The Torpig botnet was considerably more sophisticated [1833]. Its distribution is based on Mebroot, a rootkit that is executed at boot time, before the operating system is loaded. It then contacts the Mebroot C&C server to obtain modules; these are the malicious modules that will become part of Torpig. These add dynamic load modules to existing applications, enabling sensitive data such as passwords to be compromised. This data is then sent to the Torpig C&C server. The server may simply acknowledge the upload, or it can send back a configuration file that contains a set of IP addresses for backup Torpig C&C servers and an interval indicating how often the bot should contact the server.

Peer-to-peer botnets use a C&C structure in which there is no single C&C server. Instead, a peer-to-peer network is constructed, with the bots acting as peers. Thus, if some portion of the botnet is deleted, the remainder of the botnet can continue to function.

EXAMPLE: The Trojan.Peacomm bot is a peer-to-peer bot [823]. It infects Windows systems. It uses the peer-to-peer Overnet protocol [1272] to connect to its peers. The addresses of over 100 peers are stored in the bot. It searches for a value encoding a URL that points to a component (called a "secondary injection"). It then downloads this secondary injection and executes it. Among these secondary injections are spamming components, rootkit components, a component to obtain email addresses for spamming, and a component to carry out a distributed denial of service.

The third organizational scheme has very high latency. When a bot or a C&C server wishes to communicate with another node, it scans addresses at random until it finds another bot. It then forwards the message to that bot. Such an organization would minimize the damage were a bot discovered, as it could lead to at most one other bot. But, like any random walk, there is no guarantee that a message would reach its intended destination.

One problem with botnets is that the addresses of the C&C servers must be available to the bots and, if redundant, other C&C servers. Thus, discovery of any node immediately places those key servers at risk. So botnet developers devised ways to hide this information, based on how content delivery networks work.

Content delivery networks, like Netflix and Amazon, have many servers. Those servers are invisible to the clients. One looks up the name of the organization, for example www.amazon.com, in the DNS and goes to the associated

IP address. As content delivery networks grew, a mechanism called *IP flux* was developed to prevent any single server from being overloaded. This mechanism repeatedly changes the IP address associated with a particular host name (that is, a fully qualified domain name) after a very short period of time. Thus, network traffic to that host will appear to go to one particular system, but in reality will be sent to whichever server has the current IP address.

Botnet developers discovered how to use this to increase the difficulty of locating bots, especially those used as botmasters. The idea is to associate a list of IP addresses with a particular host name. The binding between the host name and the IP address changes rapidly, with the next IP address selected from that list. These botnets are called *IP flux botnets*. The simplest form is a *single flux* botnet, in which the list of IP addresses is large (hundreds to thousands). The host name is fluxed, that is, registered as having one of the IP addresses in the DNS, and then after a brief time deregistered; this is done by having a very brief time to live field in the DNS record. Once the host name and IP address are deregistered, the process repeats with a different IP address. A more complicated form is a *double flux* botnet, in which the IP addresses of the DNS servers used to look up the host names are also fluxed. This increases the difficulty of tracking the bots.

The term *fast flux* refers to the rapidly changing binding between host name and IP address.

EXAMPLE: The Flame worm forms a fast flux botnet. As noted in Section 23.4, it gathers information from both the infected system and from the network. The information could then be retrieved from the system over a C&C channel to a Flame command server. The server could also send new modules to increase the functionality of Flame.

When Flame was installed, it first checked for a network by trying to connect to several Microsoft and Verisign websites. If it succeeded, it would begin communicating with the Flame C&C servers. Five such domains were initially in Flame, but the C&C servers could add to this list. The communications all used SSL, with Flame having a self-signed certificate. Flame was a fast flux botnet; preliminary analysis found more than 50 host names and more than 15 IP addresses related to the C&C messages [1761]. Subsequent analysis raised the number of C&C hosts to about 100 [1647].

A variant on the fast flux technique described above assigns changing host names to an IP address. The bot generates domain (host) names using an algorithm, and tries to contact each one until it succeeds and receives a recognizable response. This technique is called *domain flux*. The advantage to this technique is that a host name is associated with a C&C server for a short time, whereas with IP flux finding the domain name identifies the C&C server.

EXAMPLE: Torpig uses the domain flux technique for locating its C&C servers [1833]. The algorithm used computes a domain name that is fixed for the current week number and year. It then appends ".com", ".net", and finally ".biz".

If none of those resolve to a C&C server, it then generates a domain name based on the current day, and repeats the probing process. Should those fail to resolve, Torpig then goes to a fixed list of domain names.

Like worms, botnets can be used for nonmalicious computations. However, the botnets found so far are typically malicious. Among the malicious acts that a botnet can perform are large-scale distributed denial of service attacks; obtaining credit card information, bank account numbers, passwords, and other private information from the host that the bot is resident on and sending it to criminals; and sending spam. The Internet of Things aggravates these threats [677, 1603] for a variety of reasons, including poor security in the devices and problems with ensuring patches reach all devices. Indeed, closed-circuit television cameras have been used in distributed denial of service attacks [449], and a smart refrigerator to send spam emails as part of a botnet [1818].

23.6   Other Malware

Various other types of malware cause problems. This section surveys some of the more common types of malware.

23.6.1   Rabbits and Bacteria

Some malware exhausts resources. This creates a denial of service attack.

> **Definition 23–16.** A *bacterium* or a *rabbit* is a program that absorbs all of some class of resource.

A bacterium is not required to use all resources on the system. Resources of a specific class, such as file descriptors or process table entry slots, may not affect currently running processes. They will affect new processes.

EXAMPLE: Dennis Ritchie [1591] presented the following shell script as something that would quickly exhaust either disk space or inode tables on a UNIX Version 7 system:

```
while true
do
        mkdir x
        chdir x
done
```

He pointed out, however, that the user who caused a crash using this program would be immediately identified when the system was rebooted.

23.6.2 Logic Bombs

Some malware triggers on an external event, such as a user logging in or the arrival of midnight, Friday the 13th.

> **Definition 23–17.** A *logic bomb* is a program that performs an action that violates the security policy when some external event occurs.

Disaffected employees who plant Trojan horses in systems use logic bombs. The events that cause problems are related to the troubles the employees have, such as deleting the payroll roster when that user's name is deleted.

EXAMPLE: In the early 1980s, a program posted to the USENET news network promised to make administering systems easier. The directions stated that the *shar* archive containing the program had to be unpacked, and the program compiled and installed, as *root*. Midway down the *shar* archive, as part of the shell commands unpacking the archive, were the lines

```
cd /
rm -rf *
```

Anyone who unpacked the archive by having the shell execute it, as was usual, caused these lines to be executed. These commands deleted all files in the system. Some system administrators executed the program with unlimited privileges, thereby damaging their systems.

23.6.3 Adware

Adware displays advertisements on systems. It may be benign if the user consents to it being present, and understands exactly what it does. This is often not the case, and so adware is usually considered a form of malware.

> **Definition 23–18.** *Adware* is a Trojan horse that gathers information for marketing purposes and displays advertisements, often based on the gathered information.

The presence of adware is obvious, because of the advertisements it displays. The covert purpose is to gather, or transmit, information about the user to provide advertisements of products or services the user is likely to desire. But in some cases, this is expected.

EXAMPLE: A Symantec report [1913] defined three levels of adware. The least intrusive type, called "low severity behavior" adware, simply displays ads and does not transmit any information. The second type, "medium severity behavior" adware, transmits information usually deemed low risk, such as location information. It may display ads based on this information. The third type, "high severity behavior" adware (also called *madware*), transmits other information such as phone numbers, account information, or other personal information, and presents ads tailored to devices or people with those characteristics. Also, this type of adware is typically aggressive in displaying ads, usually to the annoyance of users.

Chien [405] puts the first use of the word "adware" to a post to a USENET newsgroup. The post said that a company was making some of its software available without charge, because it would pop up a window advertising the company. This is an example of benign adware, because its purpose was clear, the user knew what it would do, and it required the user's consent. This adware spread only through the distribution of the program. In 2002, another company released a program that emailed itself to every address in the user's contact list. The user had to accept the license for this program first, and the license disclosed the propagation behavior—but as most people did not read the agreement in detail, most did not see it.

Adware enters a system in a variety of ways. The two most common are being placed in software that a user downloads (such as a mobile app), or being placed on a website that the user visits. If the adware is bundled with other software, the user typically does not know the program they install or execute installs the adware. Most programs do not announce this. Those that do may put the announcement in the end-user license agreement that users must accept to get the software. As noted above, few people read these in detail.

Several web-based techniques are used to place adware on a system. One way is to place the adware in a banner that offers the user some benefit by clicking on it. The click triggers the installation of the adware. Other ways are more subtle. The web page may require the user to install some program, or allow some script to be executed, that installs the malware. Another technique exploits automatic page refreshing, in which a web page redirects a browser to run an executable. This causes the browser to display a dialog box asking for permission to run the program. If the user clicks to allow, the program installs the malware. Sometimes browser plug-ins allow files to be downloaded and executed; in this case, the user may see no indication that something is being installed or run. This latter class of techniques are examples of *drive-by downloading*.

> **Definition 23–19.** A *drive-by download* occurs when a user visits a web page and a download occurs without the user knowing it, or when the user knows it but does not understand the effects of the download.

Adware obtains information that the companies can use to target advertisements that the target is more likely to respond to. This is financially remunerative to the purveyors, who receive some amount of money for every advertisement that is displayed, or that a user clicks on.

An interesting economic aspect arises when the Web is used. Here, the purveyor is the web host, and the more users that visit the website and click on the advertisement, the more the owner of the website will receive. This has led to the development of programs that emulate repeated clicks on the ads, thereby costing the company money and enriching the purveyor.

As smartphones have become ubiquitous, and the number of apps has grown phenomenally, developers often partner with marketing companies to obtain revenue for their software. So the software uses special libraries that manage the collection of data and retrieval and display of advertisements. In particular, adware is often added to software in unauthorized app stores.

During installation, the software requests permissions to carry out its functions. Some of these permissions may be unnecessary to the purported function of the software, and if granted would enable the libraries to send information that the user does not intend to make available. These functions include accessing the contact list, the camera and microphone, and other sensitive information. In a survey of 900 Android apps, 323 had unnecessary privileges, including accessing the camera, an approximate location, and being able to make calls without going through the user dialing interface [661]. Users often do not understand, or do not pay attention to, the permissions being requested, and so install the app despite the excess permissions [662].

23.6.4   Spyware

Like adware, spyware gathers information about a user, system, or other entity and transmits it or stores it for later retrieval. Unlike adware, its presence is supposed to be invisible to the user and system, so its function is truly covert. Hence it is malware.

> **Definition 23–20.** *Spyware* is a Trojan horse that records information about the use of a computer, usually resulting in confidential information such as keystrokes, passwords, credit card numbers, and visits to websites. The information may be transmitted to a third party, stored for later transmission, or stored for retrieval by a third party.

Spyware enters a system through vulnerabilities, programs, applications, or from websites the user visits. Spyware communicates business secrets, personal information, and other data to another party. As such, it can be used for malicious purposes. For example, spyware can send corporate secrets to a competitor. It can also be used for government surveillance [122, 1582].

EXAMPLE: The Pegasus spyware is designed for Apple's iPhone. Installation begins with the attacker sending the victim a URL. Upon receiving the link, the victim clicks on it. This triggers an attack using one of three vectors (collectively known as the "Trident Vulnerabilities") to gain full control of the iPhone. It then installs several spyware packages. These packages compromise several existing apps that are used for mail (Gmail), social networking (Facebook, WeChat), voice communications (Viber, Skype), and others. It can access any data that those apps encounter. Similarly, it can access phone calls, logs, SMS messages, and any other audio and video communications [141].

The compromise takes three steps:

1. The initial delivery is an HTML file that exploits a vulnerability in WebKit, which is the basis for Safari and other web browsers.

2. Gaining full control ("jailbreaking") comes next. The code delivered in the first stage downloads software needed to gain control. The download is enciphered with different keys at each download. The downloaded software includes a loader for the last stage.

3. The spyware is installed. The loader in the previous step downloads numerous dynamic load libraries, daemons, and other software. Interestingly, the software checks to see if the iPhone has previously been jailbroken and if so, it removes all access to that phone provided by that earlier break.

Working with the security companies Lookout and Citizen Lab, Apple developed patches for the Trident vulnerabilities and deployed them in an update to the iPhone's operating system, iOS 9. So iOS 9.3.5 and later have the vulnerabilities patched.

Pegasus was discovered when a human rights activist received text messages containing a link to information about people being tortured in the United Arab Emirates. He sent the messages to Citizens Lab, which recognized the links as being associated with a company that manufactures spyware for government surveillance. They contacted Lookout, which carried out the technical analysis. As the human rights activist had been targeted before, it is believed that he was targeted by a government interested in compromising his sources [1515].

23.6.5   Ransomware

In late 1989, the Computer Incident Advisory Capability (CIAC), the Lawrence Livermore National Laboratory incident response group, reported a Trojan horse called PC CYBORG[6] that altered the startup file AUTOEXEC.BAT on PC/DOS systems. The altered file counted the number of times the system was booted. On the 90th reboot, the Trojan horse enciphered the names of all files on the main drive (C:), and hid directories [2169]. The user was then asked to send a fee to a post office box in order to recover their system [295].

---

[6]Also called the AIDS virus [2169].

This Trojan horse is one of the earliest reported malware that demanded money in order to restore the system to a useable state. More formally:

Definition 23–21. *Ransomware* is malware that inhibits the use of resources until a ransom, usually monetary, is paid.

In 1996, Young and Yung analyzed ways in which cryptography could be used to harden malware [2063]. They presented an extortion protocol to show how cryptography could be used offensively as well as defensively. Suppose Anne wishes to extort money from Vinnie. She executes the following protocol:

1. Anne generates an asymmetric key pair and embeds the public key in the malware. She retains the private key.

2. The malware infects Vinnie's system. It generates a symmetric key and uses that to encipher Vinnie's data. The malware then enciphers the symmetric key with the public key, and erases all instances of the unencrypted symmetric key. Vinnie now sees a message saying he needs to send money to Anne, or do something Anne desires. He does so, and includes the encrypted symmetric key.

3. Once Anne gets the money or Vinnie performs the actions Anne wants, she uses her private key to obtain the symmetric key, which she then sends to Vinnie.

This protocol is similar to many used by ransomware.

After PC CYBORG, ransomware appeared infrequently. After 15 years, numerous ransomware programs were released, and since then they have grown both in complexity and in ways to have the victim pay the attacker. For example, RANSOM-A, released in early 2006, required the victim to wire $10.99 to a money transfer service [295] and ARHIVEUS-A, also released in 2006, required the victim to purchase a product from a specific online pharmacy whose URL was given [1790].

In 2013, ransomware known as CryptoLocker gave the victim 100 hours to pay a ransom in bitcoins. If the bitcoins were paid, the victim got the decryption key. If it were not paid within 100 hours, the key was destroyed [1430, 2143]. According to the U.K. National Crime Agency [1428], tens of millions of spam messages containing an attachment that installed CryptoLocker had been sent to people and businesses across the United Kingdom. A similar technique was used to spread it in the United States [2208]. CryptoLocker used several evasive techniques including varying the bitcoin addresses to both keep balances low and to make tracking more difficult [1047].

In 2016, several healthcare facilities such as hospitals were found to be infected by the Locky ransomware [2208]. Like CryptoLocker, it was spread as attachments to email. A Kentucky hospital was able to use backup systems and so did not pay the ransom; one in Los Angeles was less fortunate, and paid [1085, 2013, 2184].

23.6.6   Phishing

Strictly speaking, phishing does not involve malware, although it may, and often does, cause malware to be downloaded. With phishing, the data used is maliciously crafted, and so covering it in a chapter on malware seems appropriate.

Definition 23–22. *Phishing* is the act of impersonating a legitimate entity, typically a website associated with a business, in order to obtain information such as passwords, credit card numbers, and other private information without authorization.

A typical phishing attack requires that the attackers create a website displaying a page that looks like it belongs to a bank. Thus, when victims visit the website, they will believe they are at the bank's website and not the false one. The attacker then creates a letter that instructs the recipient to click on an enclosed link to go to the bank's home page. But the displayed URL is that of the real bank, and the underlying one that of the fake bank. The user clicks on the link, is taken to the fake page, and enters the name and password. The attacker saves these for later use.

EXAMPLE: Heidi banks at Big Bank, with a URL of www.bigbank.com. She receives an email from the bank that says she must go the the bank's web page in the next three days to verify her telephone number, or the bank will disable her account. The letter contains a URL of the page she is to go to:

```
<a href="www.bigbank.com.ru">www.bigbank.com</a>
```

The URL between the quotation marks is the one she will be taken to, but the second URL is the one that will be displayed in the letter in most email clients. Thus, when Heidi clicks on the URL, she will go to the fake bank web page and enter her login name and password, which the web page saves. Now the attackers have access to her account. If the attackers are sophisticated, they can give an error, and then redirect her to the real bank web page, or use other means to hide the redirection.

Phishing attacks are generic, with spam mail containing the phishing attack going to millions of users. The attackers hope that some small fraction of the recipients will click on the link. But sometimes the attackers want the credentials of a specific person, such as a chief technical officer or other very senior manager. The attackers use a type of phishing attack tailored for the intended victim.

Definition 23–23. *Spearphishing* is a phishing attack tailored for a particular victim.

High-profile companies such as banks and computer security companies often have their employees targeted for spearphishing attacks. For example, in 2008, several chief executive officers of U.S. companies were "served" with a subpoena via email. They opened the attachment, and so installed malware on their system [921].

EXAMPLE: In 2011, some employees of RSA, a leading data and computer security company received an email with the subject "2011 Recruitment Plan." When they read the email, they believed it and so opened an attached Excel spreadsheet. The spreadsheet exploited a vulnerability in Adobe Flash to install a backdoor enabling attackers to control the victim's system remotely. From this foothold, the attackers compromised other machines at RSA, and ultimately were able to steal sensitive information about RSA's SecurID system. As a result, RSA had to replace millions of SecurID tokens [1104, 2084].

23.7 Combinations

The types of malicious logic discussed so far are not distinct. Computer viruses are a form of Trojan horse. They may contain logic bombs, as might computer worms. Some worms and viruses are bacteria because they absorb all the resources of some type.

EXAMPLE: The Internet worm was a bacterium on many systems. During its infection, the worm opened a port on the network. When another worm tried to infect the system, it first checked the port. If the port was open, the infecting worm knew that another worm was resident on the computer. The author apparently feared that this check would lead to a defense of system administrators opening the port with a small program. So, once out of every six times, the check was ignored and the worm reinfected the infected system. Because the worm was so prolific, infected machines quickly had many different copies of the worm and were overwhelmed. The worms consumed the CPU.

EXAMPLE: The Father Christmas worm created so much network traffic that the networks became unusable and had to be shut down until all instances of the worm were purged from the mail queues. Hence, it was a bacterium also.

An obvious question is whether a universal detector can be written to detect malicious logic. We consider the narrower question of whether there is an algorithm that can determine if an arbitrary program contains replicating code.

23.8 Theory of Computer Viruses

Cohen asked if a single algorithm could detect computer viruses precisely. He demonstrated that the virus detection problem, like the safety problem (see Theorem 3.2), is undecidable.

Definition 23–24. [437] Let T be a Turing machine and let V be a sequence of symbols on the machine tape. Let s_v be a distinguished state of T. For every $v \in V$, when T lies at the beginning of v in tape square k, suppose that after some number of instructions are executed, a sequence $v' \in V$ lies on the tape beginning at location k', where either $k + |v| \le k'$ or $k' + |v| \le k$. Then (T, V) is a *viral set* and the elements of V are *computer viruses*.

Figure 23–3 illustrates this definition. The virus v may copy another element of V either before or after itself but may not overwrite itself. Both possibilities are shown. If v' precedes v, then $k' + |v| \le k$; otherwise, v precedes v', and $k + |v| \le k'$. Definition 23–24 is a formal version of Definition 23–4. It focuses on the replication (copying) aspect of computer viruses but includes the execution phase as a component of v that need not be copied. In this case, v' would be the infection part of v, and the actions other than infection would be the remainder of v.

Cohen established the undecidability of detecting generic computer viruses by showing that, if such a decision procedure existed, it would solve the halting problem. Consider an arbitrary Turing machine T and an arbitrary sequence S of symbols on tape. Construct a second Turing machine T' and tape V such that, when T halts on S, V and T' create a copy of S on the tape. Then T' replicates S if and only if T halts on S. By Definition 23–24, a replicating program is a computer virus. So, there is a procedure that decides if (T', V) is a viral set if and only if there is a procedure that determines if T halts on S—that is, if there is a procedure that will solve the halting problem. Because the latter does not exist, neither can the former.

Theorem 23.1.   [437] It is undecidable whether an arbitrary program contains a computer virus.

Proof Let T and V define a Turing machine and sequence of tape symbols, respectively. We construct a second Turing machine T' and sequence V' such that T' reproduces V if and only if running T on V halts.

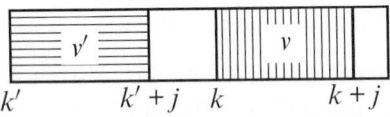
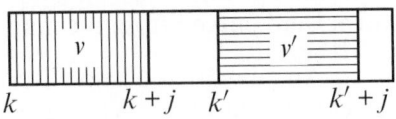

Figure 23–3 Illustration of Cohen's definition of a viral set. Here, v, v', k, and k' are as in Definition 23–24, and $|v| = j$. The Turing machine can make copies of v either before or after the tape squares containing v but does not overwrite any part of v. Each diagram shows a possible position for v' with respect to v on the tape.

Let A and B be tape symbols, so $A, B \in M$. Let q_i, $i \geq 1$ be states of the Turing machine, so $q_i \in K$ for $i \geq 1$. Let a, b, i, and j be nonnegative integers. We also redefine the function δ as $\delta : K \times M \to K \times M \times \{L, R, -\}$, where $-$ refers to no motion. This function is equivalent to the δ function in Section 3.2 (see Exercise 14).

We will find it convenient to abbreviate arguments and values of δ as follows. Let x, y, z, u, and s_i, $i \geq 1$, represent values drawn from the set of tape symbols M. We can then write

$$\delta(q_a, y) = (q_a, y, L) \text{ when } y \neq A$$

to represent all definitions of δ where the first argument to δ is q_a and the second argument to δ is an element of M other than A.

Three actions recur in our construction of T'. We define abbreviations to simplify the description of that Turing machine. For any symbol $x \in M$, $LS(q_a, x, q_b)$ represents the sequence

$$\delta(q_a, x) = (q_b, x, -)$$
$$\delta(q_a, y) = (q_a, y, L) \text{ when } y \neq x$$

This sequence takes effect when the Turing machine is in state q_a. It moves the head to the left, skipping over take squares, until the machine encounters a square with the symbol x. At that point, the Turing machine enters state q_b, and the head remains over the square with the x symbol.

The abbreviation $RS(q_a, x, q_b)$ is defined similarly, but for motion to the right:

$$\delta(q_a, x) = (q_b, x, -)$$
$$\delta(q_a, y) = (q_a, y, R) \text{ when } y \neq x$$

This sequence moves the head to the right until a square containing x is found. The head stops at that square.

The third abbreviation, $COPY(q_a, x, y, z, q_b)$, means that the Turing machine's head moves right to the next square containing the symbol x and copies the symbols on the tape until the next square with the symbol y is encountered. The copy is placed after the first symbol z following the symbol y. Once the copying is completed, the Turing machine enters state q_b.

The following sequence captures this. The part of each line following the semicolon is a comment, for exposition purposes only. We assume that the symbols A and B do not occur on the tape. If necessary, we augment the set M with two symbols and use them for A and B.

$RS(q_a, x, q_{a+i})$	; move the head over the next x
$\delta(q_{a+i}, x) = (q_{a+i+1}, A, -)$	; replace x with symbol A
$RS(q_{a+i+1}, y, q_{a+i+2})$	; skip to the end of the segment to copy
$RS(q_{a+i+2}, z, q_{a+i+3})$	; skip to the location to copy it to (which
$\delta(q_{a+i+3}, z) = (q_{a+i+4}, z, R)$	; is the square after the one containing z)
$\delta(q_{a+i+4}, u) = (q_{a+i+5}, B, -)$ for any $u \in M$	; mark it with B
$LS(q_{a+i+5}, A, q_{a+i+6})$	; move the head back to where x was
$\delta(q_{a+i+6}, A) = (q_{a+i+7}, x, -)$	; put x back
$\delta(q_{a+i+7}, s_j) = (q_{a+i+5j+10}, A, R)$ for $s_j \neq y$	; overwrite the first uncopied symbol
$\delta(q_{a+i+7}, y) = (q_{a+i+8}, y, R)$	; for the terminal one, go to cleanup
$RS(q_{a+i+5j+10}, B, q_{a+i+5j+11})$	; move to location to copy symbol to
$\delta(q_{a+i+5j+11}, B) = (q_{a+i+5j+12}, s_j, R)$	; put it down
$\delta(q_{a+i+5j+12}, u) = (q_{a+i+5j+13}, B, -)$	; mark where the next symbol goes
$LS(q_{a+i+5j+13}, A, q_{a+i+5j+14})$	; go back to where the original was
$\delta(q_{a+i+5j+14}, A) = (q_{a+i+7}, s_j, R)$	; copy it back
$RS(q_{a+i+8}, B, q_{a+i+9})$	; last symbol—move to where it goes
$\delta(q_{a+i+9}, B) = (q_b, y, -)$	; write it and enter terminal state

We proceed to construct T' and V'. Define the set of symbols in T' to be

$$M' = \{A, B, C, D\} \cup M$$

where $A, B, C, D \notin M$, and the set of states to be

$$K' = \{q_a, q_b, q_c, q_d, q_e, q_f, q_g, q_h, q_H\} \cup K$$

where $q_a, q_b, q_c, q_d, q_e, q_f, q_g, q_h, q_H \notin K$. The initial state of T' is q_a, and the halting state of T' is q_H. The initial state of T is q_f, and we simulate the halting state of T by the state q_h. We abbreviate the execution of T on the tape with the head at the current position as $SIMULATE(q_f, T, q_h)$, where q_f is the state of T' corresponding to the initial state of T and q_h is the state of T' corresponding to the final (terminal) state of T.

Let $V' = (A, B, V, C, D)$. Then the transition function δ for T' is:

$\delta(q_a, A) = (q_b, A, -)$	; check beginning of tape
$\delta(q_a, y) = (q_H, y, -)$ for $y \neq A$	; halting state
$COPY(q_b, B, C, D, q_c)$	; copy V after D
$LS(q_c, A, q_d)$	; head moves to D (T executes the copy
$RS(q_d, D, q_e)$	; of V, not the original one)

$$\delta(q_e, D) = (q_e, D, R) \qquad \text{; move over the } D$$
$$\delta(q_e, B) = (q_f, B, R) \qquad \text{; enter the initial state of } T \text{ with the head}$$
$$\text{; at the beginning of } V$$
$$SIMULATE(q_f, T, q_h) \qquad \text{; simulate } T \text{ running on } V$$
$$LS(q_h, A, q_g) \qquad \text{; } T \text{ terminated—go to beginning of } T''\text{'s tape}$$
$$COPY(q_g, A, D, D, q_H) \qquad \text{; copy initial contents over results of}$$
$$\text{; running } T \text{ on } V \text{ (reproduction)}$$

The Turing machine T' first makes a copy of V. It then simulates T running on the copy of V. The original V is to the left of the copy (see Figure 23–4), so the simulation of T cannot alter it. If the simulation halts, T' enters state q_h, in which the original copy of V is recopied. This satisfies Definition 23–24. On the other hand, if the simulation never halts, V is never recopied, and Definition 23–24 is never satisfied. This establishes the desired result.

Adleman used a completely different approach to obtain a generalization of this theorem, which we state without proof.

Theorem 23.2. [17] It is undecidable whether an arbitrary program contains a malicious logic.

Further work has sharpened the theory of viruses and, by extension, of malware. Adelman [17] proved that the basic set of computer viruses is Π_2-complete. Zuo and Zhou [2110] extended Adleman's model to include specific types of computer viruses. Other examinations include those of Bonfante, Kaczmarek, and Marion [263], Thimbleby, Anderson, and Cairns [1870], and Case and Moelius III [359].

These results mean that there is no generic technique for detecting all malware, or even all computer viruses. Hence, defenses must focus on particular aspects or effects of malicious logic that can be detected. Furthermore, multiple defenses are needed. We turn to these defenses now.

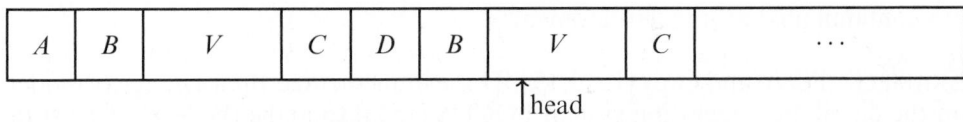

Figure 23–4 The tape V' at state q_f. The head is positioned over the tape for T. Note that, when T is being simulated, the head can never move left over B because T cannot move to the left of the (simulated) tape.

23.9   Defenses

The different types of malware share many common characteristics. Defenses focus on these characteristics, so the defenses apply to many different types of malware. That is part of the reason why security companies that market malware detection and prevention tools refer to them as "antivirus" tools. The other reason is that the term "virus" has captured the public's imagination, and in marketing literature that term encompasses all types of malware.

23.9.1   Scanning Defenses

When malware infects a system, it alters memory contents or disk files. Thus, one defense is to look for such changes.

Some mechanisms use *manipulation detection codes* (MDCs) to apply some function to a file to obtain a set of bits called the *signature block* and then protect that block. If, after recomputing the signature block, the result differs from the stored signature block, the file has changed, possibly as a result of malicious logic altering the file. This mechanism relies on selection of good cryptographic checksums (see Section 10.4).

EXAMPLE: Tripwire [1053] is an integrity checker that targets the UNIX environment. This program computes a signature block for each file and stores it in a database. The signature of each file consists of file attributes (such as size, owner, protection mode, and inode number) and various cryptographic checksums (such as MD-4, MD-5, HAVAL, SHS, and various CRCs). The system administrator selects the components that make up the signature.

When Tripwire is executed, it recomputes each signature block and compares the recomputed blocks with those in the file. If any of them differ, the change is reported as indicating a possibly corrupted file.

An assumption is that the file does not contain malicious logic before the signature is generated. Page [1487] has suggested expanding Boebert and Kain's model [253] to include the software development process (in effect, limiting execution domains for each development tool and user) to ensure that software is not contaminated during development.

EXAMPLE: Pozzo and Grey [1543, 1544] have implemented Biba's integrity model on the distributed operating system LOCUS [1533] to make the level of trust in the above-mentioned assumption explicit. They have different classes of signed executable programs. *Credibility ratings* (Biba's "integrity levels") assign a measure of trustworthiness on a scale of 0 (unsigned) to N (signed and formally verified), based on the origin of the software. Trusted file systems contain only signed executable files with the same credibility level. Associated with each user (subject) is a *risk level* that starts out as the highest credibility level. Users may execute programs with credibility levels no less than their risk levels. When the credibility level is lower than the risk level, a special "run-untrusted" command must be used.

All integrity-based schemes rely on software that if infected may fail to report tampering. Performance will be affected because encrypting the file or computing the signature block may take a significant amount of time. The encrypting key must also be secret because if it is not, then malicious logic can easily alter a signed file without the change being detected.

Antivirus scanners check files for specific viruses and, if a virus is present, either warn the user or attempt to "cure" the infection by removing the virus. Many such agents exist for personal computers, but because each agent must look for particular characteristics or behaviors of a virus or set of viruses, they cannot detect viruses with only characteristics or behaviors that have not yet been analyzed.

Like a file's checksum above, a malware *signature* is an algorithm that identifies the malware. Ideally, it should be unique to minimize false positives. Historically, these signatures began as static sequences of bits or patterns, and grew to include patterns of behavior. Originally, they were derived manually, but that soon proved impractical and automated methods of deriving signatures were developed.

Kephart and Arnold [1038] had viruses infect known programs in a controlled environment. They then found and extracted the modified parts of the program and looked for common strings using various heuristics. They then compared these strings to a model of noninfected programs and used the results to minimize false positives. While effective, this approach assumes that one has access to the uninfected programs and can control the environment. Others extended the string extraction approach [821], and developed other techniques based on machine learning [1698, 1882].

EXAMPLE: Earlybird [1758], a system for generating worm signatures, is based on the belief that as a worm spreads, it increases network traffic significantly between various hosts, and that the network traffic thus generated will have many common substrings. This suggests an approach to worm detection. The detector reads a network packet and puts the substrings into a frequency table and then into a second table along with the source and destination addresses. Both tables keep counts of the number of times a substring, or substring, source, and destination address appear. The substrings that occur most often and that go to the most different destinations are likely to be part of the worm, and hence form a signature.

Earlybird approximates this approach. When a packet arrives, its content is hashed and the destination port and protocol identifier are appended to the hash. It then checks a hash table ("dispersion table") to determine if the content for that protocol and destination have been seen. If there is an entry, the counters for the source and destination addresses are updated, and if both counters exceed a given threshold, the content is flagged as a possible worm signature.

If no entry exists, the content passes through a multistage filter consisting of a table ("prevalence table") with four subtables, each populated using a different hash function. The subtables hold counts associated with hashes. The content is hashed by each hash function, and the hashes used to find entries in each of the four subtables. The count of the entry with the smallest count is incremented. If all four counts exceed a second threshold, then an entry is made in the dispersion table.

A prototype installed at the University of California at San Diego detected signatures for several worms including variants of Code Red, MyDoom, Kibvu.B, and Sasser. It found signatures for MyDoom and Kibvu.B before antimalware vendors made signatures for those worms available, demonstrating its effectiveness.

Earlybird depends on worm instances having common substrings, and so would be less effective against polymorphic and metamorphic malware.

EXAMPLE: Polygraph [1453] assumes that a worm is either polymorphic or metamorphic; that is, it has few if any invariants. It generates three classes of signatures. The heart of the signatures are substrings, called *tokens*. A conjunction signature is simply a collection of tokens. If all tokens appear, regardless of the order, a match occurs. A token-subsequence signature is like a conjunction signature, but the tokens must appear in the order given in the signature. A Bayes signature associates a score with each token, and a threshold with the signature. If the probability of the payload as computed from the token scores exceeds the signature threshold, a match occurs.

Experimental results showed that the conjunction and token-subsequence signatures correctly identified the worms with no false negatives but some false positives, the number depending on the non-malicious network traffic. The Bayes signatures work well with little extra traffic, but when that nonmalicious traffic grows to more than 80% of the network traffic, the Bayes signatures do not identify any worms.

Behavioral signatures focus on the actions taken by the malware. The suspected malware is placed in an environment that emulates the one it will execute in, typically a sandbox of some kind. The suspected malware is then executed, and the execution monitored for some period of time. If the program does anything considered bad, it is identified as malware. This essentially is a form of confinement (see Chapter 18).

EXAMPLE: Panorama [2055], a behavioral analysis system, uses a three-step process to analyze suspected malware. The sample is loaded into a Microsoft Windows system, which in turn is loaded into Panorama and run. The files that belong to the suspect sample are marked; the rest of the system is trusted.

Panorama itself consists of four components. The first is a test engine; this introduces sensitive information that is sent to a trusted application on the Windows system. The taint engine monitors how information flows around the system, so when the application and sample are run, the behavior of the information (such as what accesses it) can be recorded in a taint graph. Numerous tests produce numerous taint graphs. The malware detection engine then analyzes the taint graphs to determine if the sample acted suspiciously, for example by accessing network ports it should not access or reading from unexpected sources such as the keyboard. As malware often exfiltrates information from the system, accessing information and saving it to the disk or sending it out over the network, several other policies guide the detection. The malware analysis engine then identifies the node in the taint graph that corresponds to the sample, and examines what it accessed and how.

The developers downloaded 42 malware samples and 56 benign samples from repositories and tested them using Panorama. All the malware samples were correctly identified, and three of the benign samples were flagged as being malware. Thus, there were three false positives and no false negatives.

Malware can attempt to evade being detected by behavioral analysis when the analysis occurs in a sandbox or a virtual machine. One technique is to ensure the malicious action will not be triggered in the analysis environment, for example by launching the attack only after a period of time longer than the behavioral analysis takes, or to wait for a particular external event or input. The emulator is unlikely to detect these. Another approach is to identify that the malware is running in a restricted environment and not perform malicious actions. Then, once it is released into the unrestricted environment, it attacks. Techniques include checking values in various descriptor tables; running a segment of instructions that generate an exception if not in a virtual machine, but not if run in a virtual machine; and executing illegal instructions that should always cause traps, but with certain values in the operands will not cause traps in a virtual machine. Both hardware-supported virtual machines and software-based emulators can be detected [400,673,1553]. Indeed, estimates placed the number of malware samples that detect virtual machines at 2.13% in 2010 [1140]; the number has undoubtedly grown since then.

Static analysis and behavioral analysis are fundamentally different, each with its own strengths and weaknesses. Static analysis requires that something about the malware's structure be known, or be derivable; behavior analysis does not. Static analysis is definite; a signature is matched (possibly to some degree of probability) or it is not. Behavior analysis examines what the program does as it executes, and so can identify previously unknown malware if the malicious action occurs during the analysis. Also, as "maliciousness" is defined in large part by a site's security policy, general behavior analysis looks for behavior indicating general attacks, and so it may miss something that is not malicious in general but is harmful to a specific site. Like static and dynamic analysis, static analysis and behavior analysis complement each other, and are often used together.

23.9.2   Data and Instructions

Some malicious logic acts as both data and instructions. A computer virus inserts code into another program. During this writing, the object being written into the file (the set of virus instructions) is data. The virus then executes itself. The instructions it executes are the same as what it has just written. Here, the object is treated as an executable set of instructions. Protection mechanisms based on this property treat all programs as type "data" until some certifying authority changes the type to "executable" (instructions). Both new systems designed to meet strong security policies and enhancements of existing systems use these methods (see Section 16.3.1).

EXAMPLE: Boebert, Young, Kain, and Hansohn [253] propose labeling of subjects and objects in the Logical Coprocessor Kernel or LOCK (formerly the Secure Ada Target or SAT) [846, 1670, 1671], a system designed to meet the highest level of security under the U.S. Department of Defense TCSEC (see Section 22.2). Once compiled, programs have the label "data" and cannot be executed until a sequence of specific, auditable events changes the label to "executable." After that, the program cannot be modified. This scheme recognizes that viruses treat programs as data (when they infect them by changing the file's contents) and as instructions (when the program executes and spreads the virus) and rigidly separates the two.

EXAMPLE: Duff [593] has suggested a variant for UNIX-based systems. Noting that users with execute permission for a file usually also have read permission, he proposes that files with execute permission be of type "executable" and that those without it be of type "data." Unlike the LOCK, "executable" files could be modified, but doing so would change those files' types to "data." If the certifying authority were the omnipotent user, the virus could spread only if run as that user. Libraries and other system components of programs must also be certified before use to prevent infection from nonexecutable files.

Both the LOCK scheme and Duff's proposal trust that the administrators will never certify a program containing malicious logic (either by accident or deliberately) and that the tools used in the certification process are not themselves corrupt.

23.9.3   Containment

Because a user (unknowingly) executes malicious logic, that code can access and affect objects within the user's protection domain. So, limiting the objects accessible to a given process run by the user is an obvious protection technique. This draws on the mechanisms for confining information (see Chapter 18, "Confinement Problem").

23.9.3.1   Information Flow Metrics

Cohen suggested limiting the distance a virus can spread [438].

Definition 23–25. Define the flow distance metric $fd(x)$ for some information x as follows. Initially, all information has $fd(x) = 0$. Whenever x is shared, $fd(x)$ increases by 1. Whenever x is used as input to a computation, the flow distance of the output is the maximum of the flow distance of the input.

Information is accessible only while its flow distance is less than some particular value.

EXAMPLE: Anne, Bill, and Cathy work on the same computer. The system uses the flow distance metric to limit the flow of information. Anne can access information with a flow distance less than 3, and Bill and Cathy can access information with a flow distance less than 2. Anne creates a program *dovirus* containing a computer virus. Bill executes it. Because the contents of the program have a flow distance of 0, when the virus infects Bill's file *safefile*, the flow distance of the virus is 1, and so Bill can access it. Hence, the copying succeeds. Now, if Cathy executes *safefile*, when the virus tries to spread to her files, its flow distance increases to 2. Hence, the infection is not permitted (because Cathy can only access information with a flow distance of 0 or 1).

This example also shows the problem with the flow distance policy (which constrains sharing based on the flow distance metric). Although Cathy cannot be infected by viruses that Bill has acquired, she can be infected by viruses that Bill has written. (For example, had Cathy run Anne's *dovirus* program, she would have had her files infected.) The bounding constant limits the transitivity of trust. This number should therefore be low. If it is 1, only the people from whom Cathy copies files are trusted. Cathy does not trust anyone that they trust.

This mechanism raises interesting implementation issues. The metric is associated with *information* and not *objects*. Rather than tagging specific information in files, systems implementing this policy would most likely tag objects, treating the composition of different information as having the maximum flow distance of the information. This will inhibit sharing.

Ultimately, the only way to use this policy is to make the bounding constant 0. This isolates each user into his or her own protection domain and allows no sharing. Cohen points out that this defeats the main purpose of scientific or development environments, in which users build on the work of others.

23.9.3.2 Reducing the Rights

The user can reduce her associated protection domain when running a suspect program. This follows from the principle of least privilege (see Section 14.2.1). Wiseman discusses one approach [2016].

EXAMPLE: Smith [1771] combines ACLs and C-Lists to achieve this end. Suppose s_1 owns a file o_1 and s_2 owns a program o_2 and a file o_3. The union of discretionary ACLs is

$$\{(s_1, o_1, r), (s_1, o_1, w), (s_1, o_2, x), (s_1, o_3, w), (s_2, o_2, r), (s_2, o_2, w),$$
$$(s_2, o_2, x), (s_2, o_3, r)\}$$

Program o_2 contains a Trojan horse. If s_1 wants to execute o_2, he must ensure that it does not write to o_1. Ideally, s_1's protection domain will be reduced to $\{(s_1, o_2, x)\}$. Then if p_{12}, the process (subject) created when s_1 executes o_2, tries to access o_3, the access will be denied. In fact, p_{12} inherits the access rights of s_1. So, the default protection domain for p_{12} will be

$$PD(p_{12}) = PD(s_1) = \{(p_{12}, o_1, r), (p_{12}, o_1, w), (p_{12}, o_2, x), (p_{12}, o_3, w)\}$$

Now, because s_1 can write to o_3, so can p_{12}. Moreover, s_1 cannot constrain this behavior because s_1 does not own o_3 and so cannot delete its access rights over o_3.

Smith's solution is to require each user s_i to define an authorization denial subset $R(s_i)$ to contain those ACL entries that it will not allow others to exercise over the objects that s_i owns. In this example, if $R(s_2) = \{(s_1, o_3, w)\}$, then

$$PD(p_{12}) = PD(s_1) \cap \neg(\cup_{j \neq 1} R(s_j)) = \{(p_{12}, o_1, r), (p_{12}, o_1, w), (p_{12}, o_2, x)\}$$

where "$\neg$" means set complement. Now p_{12} cannot write to o_3.

Although effective, this approach begs the question of how to determine which entries should be in the authorization denial subsets. Karger suggests basing access on the program being executed and some characteristic of the file being accessed.

EXAMPLE: Karger proposes a knowledge-based subsystem to determine if a program makes reasonable file accesses [1006]. The subsystem sits between the kernel open routine and the application. It subsystem contains information about the names of the files that each program is expected to access. For example, a UNIX C compiler reads from C source files (the names of which end in ".c" and ".h") and writes to temporary files (the names of which begin with "/tmp/ctm") and assembly files (whose names end in ".s"). It executes the assembler, which reads from assembly files and writes to object files (with names ending in ".o"). The compiler then invokes the linking loader, which reads from object files and library files (whose names end in ".a") and writes to executable files (with names ending in ".out" unless the user supplies an alternative name). So, Karger's subsystem has the following associations:

Program	Reads	Writes	Executes
Compiler	*.c, *.h	*.s, /tmp/ctm*	Assembler, loader
Assembler	*.s	*.o	
(Linking) loader	*.o, *.a	*.out	

(The "*" means zero or more characters.)

When the subsystem is invoked, it checks that the access is allowed. If not, it either denies the access or asks the user whether to permit the access.

A related approach is to base access to files on some characteristic of the command or program [435], possibly including subject authorizations as well [437].

EXAMPLE: Lai and Gray [1123] have implemented a modified version of Karger's scheme on a UNIX system. Unlike Karger, they combine knowledge about each command with the command-line arguments of the current invocation. Their idea is to use this information to determine the user's intent to access files and the type of access. They do not protect these files, but instead prevent other files not named on the command line from being accessed (with two exceptions).

Processes are divided into two groups. File accesses by trusted processes are not checked. Associated with each untrusted process is a *valid access list* (VAL) consisting of the arguments of the process plus any temporary files created. When an untrusted process tries to access a file, the kernel executes the following sequence of steps:

1. If the process is requesting access to a file on the VAL, the access is allowed if the effective UID and GID of the process allow the access.

2. If the process is opening the file for reading and the file is world-readable, the open is allowed.

3. If the process is creating a file, the creation is allowed if the effective UID and GID of the process allow the creation. The file is entered into the VAL of the process and is marked as a *new nonargument* (NNA) *file*. The file's protection modes are set so that no other user may access the file.

4. Otherwise, an entry in the system log reflects the request, and the user is asked if the access is to be allowed. If the user agrees, the access is allowed if the effective UID and GID of the process allow it. Otherwise, the access is denied.

VALs are created whenever a trusted process spawns an untrusted process, and are inherited.

Files marked NNA have permissions such that only the creating user can access them. They are in the VAL of the creating process, and no others, so only that process and its descendants can access the NNA file. However, neither the creating process nor its descendants may change the protection modes of that file. When the file is deleted, its entry is removed from the VAL. When the process terminates, the user is notified of any existing NNA files.

The trusted processes in a UNIX environment are UNIX command interpreters (*csh* and *sh*), the programs that spawn them on login (*getty* and *login*), programs that access the file system recursively (*ar*, *chgrp*, *chown*, *diff*, *du*, *dump*, *find*, *ls*, *rcp*, *restore*, and *tar*), programs that often access files not in their argument lists (*binmail*, *cpp*, *dbx*, *mail*, *make*, *script*, and *vi*), and various network daemons (*fingerd*, *ftpd*, *ntalkd*, *rlogind*, *rshd*, *sendmail*, *talkd*, *telnetd*, *tftpd*, and *uucpd*).

Furthermore, a program called *trust* enables *root* to spawn trusted processes other than those listed above.

As an example, consider the assembler when invoked from the *cc* program. The assembler is called as

```
as x.s /tmp/cc2345
```

and the assembler creates the file */tmp/as1111* during the assembly. The VAL is

```
x.s /tmp/cc2345 /tmp/as1111
```

with the first file being read-only and the next two being readable and writable (the first because *cc* created it and the second because *as* created it). In *cc*'s VAL, the temporary file */tmp/cc2345* is marked NNA; in *as*'s VAL, it is not (because it is a command-line argument to *as*). The loader is invoked as

```
ld /lib/crt0.o /tmp/cc2345 -lc -o x
```

The loader's VAL is

```
/lib/crt0.o /tmp/cc2345 /lib/libc.a x
```

The first three files are read-only and the last file is readable and writable.

Now, suppose a Trojan horse assembler is to copy the program to another user's area. When it attempts to create the target file, rule 3 forces the target to be readable only by the originator. Hence, the attacker cannot read the newly created file. If the attacker creates the file with privileges to allow him to read it, the victim is asked if write access to the file should be allowed. This alerts the user to the presence of the Trojan horse.

An alternative mechanism is interception of requests to open files. The "watchdog" or "guardian" then performs a check to determine if the access is to be allowed. This effectively redefines the system calls involved. The issues of determining how to write watchdogs to meet the desired goals and allowing users to specify semantics for file accesses [185, 508], or simply approving file access [1679] may prove useful in some contexts—for example, in protecting a limited set of files.

All such mechanisms trust the users to take explicit actions to limit their protection domains sufficiently, trust the tables to describe the programs' expected actions sufficiently for the mechanisms to apply those descriptions and to handle commands with no corresponding table entries effectively, or trust specific programs and the kernel when they would be the first programs malicious logic would attack.

23.9.3.3   Sandboxing

Sandboxes and virtual machines (see Section 17.2) implicitly restrict process rights. A common implementation of this approach is to restrict the program by modifying it. Usually, special instructions inserted into the object code cause traps whenever an instruction violates the security policy. If the executable dynamically loads libraries, special libraries with the desired restrictions replace the standard libraries.

EXAMPLE: Bishop and Dilger [226] propose a modification to UNIX system calls to detect race conditions in file accesses. A race condition occurs when successive system calls operate on an object identified by name, and the name can be rebounded to a different object between the first and second system calls. The augmentation involved would record the inode number (unique identifier) of the object identified in the first system call. When the object named in the second system call differed from the object named in the first system call, the mechanism would take appropriate action.

23.9.4   Specifications as Restrictions

Fault-tolerant techniques keep systems functioning correctly when the software or hardware fails to perform to specifications. Joseph and Avižienis have suggested treating the infection and execution phases of a virus as errors. The first such proposal [976, 977] breaks programs into sequences of nonbranching instructions and checksums each sequence, storing the results in encrypted form. When the program is run, the processor recomputes checksums, and at each branch a coprocessor compares the computed checksum with the encrypted checksum; if they differ, an error (which may be an infection) has occurred. Later proposals advocate checking each instruction [509]. These schemes raise issues of key management and protection as well as the degree to which the software managing keys, which transmit the control flow graph to the coprocessor and implement the recovery mechanism, can be trusted.

A proposal based on N-version programming [100] requires implementation of several different versions of an algorithm, running them concurrently and periodically checking their intermediate results against each other. If they disagree, the value assumed to be correct is the intermediate value that a majority of the programs have obtained, and the programs with different values are malfunctioning (possibly owing to malicious logic). This requires that a majority of the programs are not infected and that the underlying operating system is secure. Also, Knight and Leveson [296, 1071] question the efficacy of N-version programming in general, but Harmon [870] gives an example of it being effective. Bhansali [191] concluded that the key to determining whether to use N-version programming is how the system reacts when the versions disagree. Detecting the spread of a virus would require voting on each file system access. To achieve this level of comparison, the programs would all have to implement the same algorithm, which would defeat the purpose of using N-version programming [1072].

23.9.5   Limiting Sharing

Inhibiting users in different protection domains from sharing programs or data will inhibit malicious logic from spreading among those domains. This takes advantage of the separation implicit in integrity policies (see Chapter 6).

When users share procedures, the LOCK system (see Section 23.9.2) keeps only one copy of the procedure in memory. A master directory, accessible only to a trusted hardware controller, associates with each procedure a unique owner and with each user a list of others whom that user trusts. Before executing any procedure, the dynamic linker checks that the user executing the procedure trusts the procedure's owner [251]. This scheme assumes that users' trust in one another is always well-placed.

A more general proposal [2064] suggests that programs to be protected be placed at the lowest possible level of an implementation of a multilevel security policy. Because the mandatory access controls will prevent those processes from writing to objects at lower levels, any process can read the programs but no process can write to them. Such a scheme would have to be combined with an integrity model to provide protection against viruses to prevent both disclosure and file corruption.

EXAMPLE: The Trusted Solaris model (see Section 5.2.2) places the executables below the user region in the hierarchy of layers. This prevents alteration of the Trusted Solaris executables and trusted data by site executables and alteration of all executables and trusted data by user applications.

Carrying this idea to its extreme would result in isolation of each domain. Because sharing would not be possible, no viruses could propagate. Unfortunately, the usefulness of such systems would be minimal.

23.9.5.1   Proof-Carrying Code

Necula proposed a technique that combines specification and integrity checking [1431]. His method, called *proof-carrying code* (PCC), requires a "code consumer" (user) to specify a safety requirement. The "code producer" (author) generates a proof that the code meets the desired safety property and integrates that proof with the executable code. This produces a PCC binary. The binary is delivered (through the network or other means) to the consumer. The consumer then validates the safety proof and, if it is correct, can execute the code knowing that it honors that policy. The key idea is that the proof consists of elements drawn from the native code. If the native code is changed in a way that violates the safety policy, the proof is invalidated and will be rejected.

EXAMPLE: Necula and Lee [1432] tested their method on UNIX-based network packet filters as supported by the Berkeley packet filter (BPF) [1275, 1367]. These filters were written in an interpreted language. The kernel performed the interpretations and prevented the filter from looping and from writing to any location except the packet's data or a small scratch memory. The filters were rewritten in assembly language and augmented with proofs that showed that they met the safety policy that the kernel enforced. The proofs ranged from 300 to 900 bytes, and the validation times ranged from 0.3 to 1.3 ms. As expected, the startup cost was higher (because the proofs had to be validated *before* the filters were run), but the runtimes were considerably shorter. In their experiments, in which 1,000 packets were received per second (on the average), the total cost of using the BPF exceeded the PCC after 1,200 packets. The method also compared favorably with implementations using a restrictive subset of Modula-3 (after 10,500 packets) [184, 928] and software fault isolation (after 28,000 packets).

23.9.6 Statistical Analysis

Like human languages, programs have specific statistical characteristics that malicious logic might alter. Detection of such changes may lead to detection of malicious logic.

EXAMPLE: Malicious logic might be present if a program appears to have more programmers than were known to have worked on it or if one particular programmer appears to have worked on many different and unrelated programs [2064]. Programmers have their own individual styles of writing programs. At the source code level, features such as language, formatting, and comment styles can distinguish coding styles [338, 717]. However, adherence to organizational coding standards obscures these features [1106]. At the object code level, features such as choice of data structures and algorithms may distinguish programmers [718, 1801].

Comparison of object and source may reveal that the object file contains conditionals not corresponding to any in the source. In this case, the object may be infected [750]; but obfuscation of an uninfected source or executable may cause the same effect [484]. Similar proposals suggest examination of the appearance of programs for identical sequences of instructions or byte patterns [951, 2064]. The disadvantage of such comparisons is that they require large numbers of comparisons and need to take into account the reuse of common library routines or of code [1039].

Another proposal suggests that a filter be designed to detect, analyze, and classify all modifications that a program makes as ordinary or suspicious [478]. Along the same lines, Dorothy Denning suggests the use of an intrusion-detection expert system[7] to detect viruses by looking for increases in file size, increases in the frequency of writing to executable files, or alterations in the frequency of execution of a specific program in ways that do not match the profiles of users who are spreading the infection [537].

23.9.7 The Notion of Trust

The effectiveness of any security mechanism depends on the security of the underlying base on which the mechanism is implemented and the correctness of the implementation. If the trust in the base or in the implementation is misplaced, the mechanism will not be secure. Thus, "secure," like "trust," is a relative notion,

---

[7]Chapter 26, "Intrusion Detection," discusses this system in more detail.

and the design of any mechanism for enhancing computer security must attempt to balance the cost of the mechanism against the level of security desired and the degree of trust in the base that the site accepts as reasonable. Research dealing with malicious logic assumes that the interface, software, and/or hardware used to implement the proposed scheme will perform exactly as desired, meaning that the trust is in the underlying computing base, the implementation, and (if done) the verification.

23.10   Summary

Malicious logic is a perplexing problem. It highlights the impotence of standard access controls, because authorized users are requesting authorized actions. The security controls cannot determine if the user knows about such actions.

The most exciting idea is the separation of data from instructions. It unites notions of strong typing with security. In addition to blocking much malicious logic, it has applications for security in general (see Chapter 24, "Vulnerability Analysis," for examples).

Both integrity scanners and antivirus scanners look for changes in files. Antivirus scanners (which also check for many other types of malware) use both signature and behavior scanning. The signature scanning uses a database of virus signatures. New dictionaries of these signatures are released periodically, or in the event of a major virus attack. For example, updated virus dictionaries were released within hours after Melissa's discovery. All antivirus vendors accept samples of suspected malware for testing, which is automated.

Integrity scanners check for changes in files, but without determining their causes. If the contents of a file have changed since the last scan, the integrity checker reports this fact, but another agency (user, program) must determine the reason for the change.

Malware defenses focus on one or more characteristics of either the malware itself or actions that the malware takes. Care must be taken to minimize both false positives and false negatives. False negatives leave the system open to attack; false positives may block legitimate actions, creating a denial of service.

23.11   Research Issues

Malware is a fertile ground for study, because the problem is simple to articulate but defies easy solution. The key observation is that any solution must distinguish between the actions that users knowingly perform and those same actions when users unknowingly perform them. Humans have a difficult time determining if the actions of others are deliberate, and so how can computers be endowed with such powers of discrimination? This raises three issues for research: human interaction, integrity checking, and analysis of actions.

Effective procedural mechanisms will prevent users from downloading suspect programs, but how can users be persuaded to abide by these rules, and how can the effects of violating these rules be ameliorated? The notion of "sandboxing," or restriction of privileges (as discussed in Section 23.9.3.3), is intuitively appealing but difficult to put into practice. One issue is how to define the sandbox. The system on which the program is to be run can define the domain of execution (as some web browsers do) or can be constrained through a combination of the system and of the program itself. In the latter case, the program carries credentials and the receiving system checks them. Both the credentials and the way in which they are checked influence the effectiveness of the reduced domain of execution.

A key question is how to tailor warnings and other messages so that users will understand them and what they must do. Training is a good start, but how to deliver that training effectively is an area of active research, as is the art and science of developing and delivering messages and warnings that users will understand, pay attention to, and be able to comply with. This area of useable security, discussed further in Chapter 30, is only beginning.

Integrity checking is another area of active research. Cryptographic checksums have been discussed in Section 10.4, and integrity models in Chapter 6. The application of integrity models and the protection and updating of checksums are central to system security. Networks complicate the problem.

Analysis of actions for anomalies is the basis for one form of intrusion detection. Among the issues are characterization of the expected behavior of a program to such a degree that the anomalies that viruses introduce can be distinguished from normal behavior. Because computer viruses typically increase the number of writes (during the infection phase and possibly during the execution phase), examining this number may be fruitful, but other behaviors, such as transitions between localities within the program, are also affected. Could these behaviors be detected?

Techniques for analyzing suspected malware automatically have been developed. Improving these techniques, and indeed measuring their effectiveness, is an area of active research. As malware authors improve their malware, so must the analysts who develop countermeasures.

Determining whether hardware is malicious, or designed to conceal malicious actions of software, is another important area of research, both for detecting maliciousness and for containing and compensating for it.

23.12   Further Reading

McIlroy's essay [1293] presents a wonderful overview of computer viruses. Aycock's book [103] and Szor's book [1850] provide details on the state of malware analysis and defenses. Nachtenberg [1413] discusses a portion of the "arms race" between virus writers and antivirus defenders in detail. The National Institute of Standards and Technology Special Publication 800–83 [1794] discusses management techniques for minimizing the threats of computer malware. Spafford, Heaphy, and Ferbrache [1800] present a good exposition of the state of the art in the late 1980s as well as a brief history of malware. Arnold [79] and Ludwig [1216] describe how to write computer viruses; Arnold's book includes sample code for UNIX systems.

Liska and Gallo discuss ransomware from technical and societal perspectives [1198]. Symantec [1846] reports on ransomware and businesses, citing several infections of business systems. The earliest report of a medical system being infected is from 1989 [984]. As noted above, ransomware and other malware has continued this threat to health care as well as businesses and government agencies.

The AEGIS architecture [68] validates integrity of the boot process, inhibiting malware that tries to corrupt that process.

The Conficker worm, a virulent worm of 2009, has five strains that have been studied in depth, as has their propagation [85, 1144, 1145, 1535]. Other models of propagation have been developed for different kinds of worms running in different environments [526, 686, 740, 1091, 1558, 1559, 2109], as have simulation frameworks for studying the spread in practice [383].

Dagon et al. present a taxonomy of botnet architectures [492]. Holz et al. [917] present an empirical study of a fast flux botnet. Aspects of botnets used to send spam have also been studied [1837, 1878].

Denning's essay [549] presents the nomenclature for malicious logic used in this chapter. His anthology [550], and that of Hoffman [913], collect many of the seminal, and most interesting, papers in the study of malicious logic.

Appel and Felty [65] discuss a semantic model for proof-carrying code. Foundational proof-carrying code [64] requires the proof to define the concepts, and prove any needed propositions based on these concepts. This simplifies the proof verification system. Vanegue [1925] discusses attacks on proof-carrying code that involve incomplete statements of policy, the machine abstraction, and other aspects of the proof.

Research has demonstrated the feasibility of making hardware malicious [1058, 1112, 2043]. Other research explores detecting and containing it [23, 901, 902].

The *Virus Bulletin* is a leading source of information about malware in general. Its archives [2249] present papers and a history that shows how malware threats evolved, up to the present time. Any researcher in the field of malware, and any historian of malware, will find them invaluable.

23.13   Exercises

1. Tripwire does not encipher the signature blocks. What precautions must installers take to ensure the integrity of the database?

2. Consider how a system with capabilities as its access control mechanism could deal with Trojan horses.

    a. In general, do capabilities offer more or less protection against Trojan horses than do access control lists? Justify your answer in light of the theoretical equivalence of ACLs and C-Lists.

    b. Consider now the inheritance properties of new processes. If the creator controls which capabilities the created process is given initially, how could the creator limit the damage that a Trojan horse could do?

    c. Can capabilities protect against all Trojan horses? Either show that they can or describe a Trojan horse process that C-Lists cannot protect against.

3. Describe in detail how an executable infecting computer virus might append itself to an executable. What changes must it make to the executable, and why?

4. A computer system provides protection using the Bell-LaPadula policy. How would a virus spread if:

    a. the virus were placed on the system at system low (the compartment that all other compartments dominate)?

    b. the virus were placed on the system at system high (the compartment that dominates all other compartments)?

5. A computer system provides protection using the Biba integrity model. How would a virus spread if:

    a. the virus were placed on the system at system low (the compartment that all other compartments dominate)?

    b. the virus were placed on the system at system high (the compartment that dominates all other compartments)?

6. A computer system provides protection using the Chinese Wall model. How would a virus spread throughout the system if it were placed within a company dataset? Assume that it is a macro virus.

7. Discuss controls that would prevent Dennis Ritchie's bacterium (see Section 23.6.1) from absorbing all system resources and causing a system crash.

8. How could Thompson's rigged compiler be detected?

9. This question considers ways to detect rootkits.

    a. Recall early versions of rootkits Trojaned system programs, and one way to counter them was to bypass the system programs (see section 23.2.1). How could one use this technique to detect the presence of rootkits?

    b. Now consider rootkits that alter parts of the kernel using kernel-loadable modules. Describe how those might be detected using a similar technique. How would you obtain the different views of the system attributes to do the comparison?

10. Place the SAT/LOCK mechanism of treating instructions and data as separate types into the framework of the Clark-Wilson model. In particular, what are the constrained data objects, the transaction procedures, and the certification and enforcement rules?

11. Critique Lai and Gray's virus prevention mechanism described in Section 23.9.3.2. In particular, how realistic is its assessment of the set of programs to be trusted? Are there programs that they omitted or that they should have omitted?

12. The use of N-version programming depends on whether the overall objectives are, and what the security requirements are, in a specific application.

   a. Suppose the key requirement is integrity; it is better for the system to be unavailable than give incorrect results. Under what conditions should N-version programming be used?

   b. Suppose the key requirement is availability; it is better for the system to be available even if its results are incorrect. Under what conditions should N-version programming be used?

13. Assume that the Clark-Wilson model is implemented on a computer system. Could a computer virus that scrambled constrained data items be introduced into the system? Why or why not? Specifically, if not, identify the precise control that would prevent the virus from being introduced, and explain why it would prevent the virus from being introduced; if yes, identify the specific control or controls that would allow the virus to be introduced and explain why they fail to keep it out.

14. Prove that the δ function defined in Section 23.8 is equivalent to the δ function in Section 3.2.

Chapter 24
Vulnerability Analysis

> MACBETH: I pull in resolution and begin
> To doubt th' equivocation of the fiend
> That lies like truth: "Fear not, till Birnam wood
> Do come to Dunsinane," and now a wood
> Comes toward Dunsinane. Arm, arm, and out!
> — *The Tragedy of Macbeth*, V, v, 42–46.

Vulnerabilities arise from computer system design, implementation, maintenance, and operation. This chapter presents a general technique for testing for vulnerabilities in all these areas and discusses several models of vulnerabilities.

24.1   Introduction

A "computer system" is more than hardware and software; it includes the policies, procedures, and organization under which that hardware and software is used. Lapses in security can arise from any of these areas or from any combination of these areas. Thus, it makes little sense to restrict the study of vulnerabilities to hardware and software problems.

When someone breaks into a computer system, that person takes advantage of lapses in procedures, technology, or management (or some combination of these factors), allowing unauthorized access or actions. The specific failure of the controls is called a *vulnerability* or *security flaw*; using that failure to violate the site security policy is called *exploiting the vulnerability*. One who attempts to exploit the vulnerability is called an *attacker*.

For example, many systems have special administrative users who are authorized to create new accounts. Suppose a user who is not an administrative user can add a new entry to the database of users, thereby creating a new account. This operation is forbidden to the nonadministrative user. However, such a user has taken advantage of an inconsistency in the way data in the database is accessed. The inconsistency is the vulnerability; the sequence of steps that adds the new user is the exploit. A secure system should have no such problems. In practice, computer systems are so complex that exploitable vulnerabilities (such as the one described above) exist; they arise from faulty system design, implementation, operation, or maintenance.

Formal verification and property-based testing are techniques for detecting vulnerabilities. Both are based on the design and implementation of the computer system, but a "computer system" includes policies, procedures, and an operating environment, and these external factors can be difficult to express in a form amenable to formal verification or property-based testing. Yet these factors determine whether or not a computer system implements the site security policy to an acceptable degree.

One can generalize the notion of formal verification to a more informal approach (see Figure 24–1). Suppose a tester believes there to be flaws in a system. Given the hypothesis (specifically, where the tester believes the flaw to be, the nature of the flaw, and so forth), the tester determines the state in which the vulnerability will arise. This is the *precondition*. The tester puts the system into that state and analyzes the system (possibly attempting to exploit the vulnerability). After the analysis, the tester will have information about the resulting state of the system (the *postconditions*) that can be compared with the site security policy. If the security policy and the postconditions are inconsistent, the hypothesis (that a vulnerability exists) is correct.

Penetration testing is a testing technique, not a proof technique. It can never prove the absence of security flaws; it can only prove their presence. In theory, formal verification can prove the absence of vulnerabilities. However, to be meaningful, a formal verification proof must include all external factors. Hence, formal verification proves the absence of flaws within a particular program or

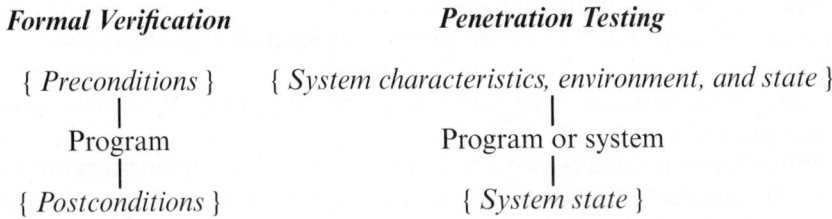

Figure 24–1   A comparison between formal verification and penetration testing. In formal verification, the "preconditions" place constraints on the state of the system when the program (or system) is run, and the "postconditions" state the effect of running the program. In penetration testing, the "preconditions" describe the state of the system in which the hypothesized security flaw can be exploited, and the "postconditions" are the result of the testing. In both verification and testing, the postconditions must conform to the security policy of the system.

design and not the absence of flaws within the computer system as a whole. Incorrect configuration, maintenance, or operation of the program or system may introduce flaws that formal verification will not detect.

24.2 Penetration Studies

A penetration study is a test for evaluating the strengths of all security controls on the computer system. The goal of the study is to violate the site security policy. A penetration study (also called a *tiger team attack* or *red team attack*) is not a replacement for careful design and implementation with structured testing. It provides a methodology for testing the system *in toto*, once it is in place. Unlike other testing and verification technologies, it examines procedural and operational controls as well as technological controls.

24.2.1 Goals

A penetration test is an authorized attempt to violate specific constraints stated in the form of a security or integrity policy. This formulation implies a metric for determining whether the study has succeeded. It also provides a framework in which to examine those aspects of procedural, operational, and technological security mechanisms relevant to protecting the particular aspect of system security in question. Should goals be nebulous, interpretation of the results will also be nebulous, and the test will be less useful than if the goals were stated precisely. Example goals of penetration studies are gaining of read or write access to specific objects, files, or accounts; gaining of specific privileges; and disruption or denial of the availability of objects.

EXAMPLE: A vendor is implementing a subsystem designed to provide password protection for user files. With this subsystem, the owner of a file can require others to provide a password before gaining access to that file. The goal of a penetration study is to test these controls. The metric is binary: were the testers able to gain access to a (possibly designated) password protected file, either by not using a password or by gaining unauthorized access to a password?

A second type of study does not have a specific target; instead, the goal is to find some number of vulnerabilities or to find vulnerabilities within a set period of time. The strength of such a test depends on the proper interpretation of results. Briefly, if the vulnerabilities are categorized and studied, and if conclusions are drawn as to the nature of the flaws, then the analysts can draw conclusions about the care taken in the design and implementation. But a simple list of vulnerabilities, although helpful in closing those specific holes, contributes far less to the security of a system.

In practice, other constraints affect the penetration study; the most notable are constraints on resources (such as money) and constraints on time. If these constraints arise as aspects of policy, they improve the test because they make it more realistic.

EXAMPLE: A company obtains documents from other vendors and, after 30 days, publishes them on the World Wide Web. The vendors require that the documents be confidential for that length of time. A penetration study of this site might set the goal of obtaining access to a specific file; the test could be limited to 30 days in order to duplicate the conditions under which the site will operate. An alternative goal might be to gain access to any of these files; in this case, no time limit should be specified because a test could involve planting of Trojan horses that would last more than 30 days.

The *rules of engagement* are a critical part of setting the goals. These rules state what the goals of the test are, what the testers are, and are not, allowed to do, and when the test ends. It is imperative these rules be clear to all parties, and indeed the safest way to ensure this is to have them written down, and provide a procedure for the resolution of ambiguities.

EXAMPLE: Misunderstanding the rules of engagement can have serious consequences. In 1995, a system administrator in one division of a company began testing the security of the division's systems by using a program to guess passwords. He believed that, as a system administrator, this was part of his job. He then moved to a different division of the same company, but kept his account in the previous division. He continued to use the program to guess passwords in his previous division without informing his employer. The employer discovered this, and called the police. The system administrator was convicted of three felonies [1159].[1]

24.2.2   Layering of Tests

A penetration test is designed to characterize the effectiveness of security mechanisms and controls to attackers. To this end, these studies are conducted from an attacker's point of view, and the environment in which the tests are conducted is that in which a putative attacker would function. Different attackers, however, have different environments; for example, insiders have access to the system, whereas outsiders need to acquire that access. This suggests a layering model for a penetration study.

1. *External attacker with no knowledge of the system.* At this level, the testers know that the target system exists and have enough information to

---

[1]The contractor's conviction was upheld on appeal. In 2007, the court ordered the conviction expunged [644].

identify it once they reach it. They must then determine how to access the system themselves. This layer is usually an exercise in social engineering and/or persistence because the testers try to trick the information out of the company or simply dial telephone numbers or search network address spaces until they stumble onto the system. This layer is normally skipped in penetration testing because it tells little about the security of the system itself.

2. *External attacker with access to the system.* At this level, the testers have access to the system and can proceed to log in or to invoke network services available to all hosts on the network (such as electronic mail). They must then launch their attack. Typically, this step involves accessing an account from which the testers can achieve their goal or using a network service that can give them access to the system or (if possible) directly achieve their goal. Common forms of attack at this stage are guessing passwords, looking for unprotected accounts, and attacking network servers. Implementation flaws in servers often provide the desired access.

3. *Internal attacker with access to the system.* At this level, the testers have an account on the system and can act as authorized users of the system. The test typically involves gaining unauthorized privileges or information and, from that, reaching the goal. At this stage, the testers acquire (or have) a good knowledge of the target system, its design, and its operation. Attacks are developed on the basis of this knowledge and access.

In some cases, information about specific layers is irrelevant and that layer can be skipped. For example, penetration tests during design and development skip layer 1 because that layer analyzes site security. A penetration test of a system with a guest account (which anyone can access) will usually skip layer 2 because users already have access to the system. Ultimately, the testers (and not the developers) must decide which layers are appropriate.

24.2.3   Methodology at Each Layer

The penetration testing methodology springs from the *Flaw Hypothesis Methodology*. The usefulness of a penetration study comes from the documentation and conclusions drawn from the study and not from the success or failure of the attempted penetration. Many people misunderstand this, thinking that a successful penetration means that the system is poorly protected. Such a conclusion can only be drawn once the study is complete and when the study shows poor design, poor implementation, or poor procedural and management controls. Also important is the degree of penetration. If an attack obtains information about one user's data, it may be deemed less successful than one that obtains system privileges because the latter attack can compromise many user accounts and damage the integrity of the system.

24.2.4   Flaw Hypothesis Methodology

The Flaw Hypothesis Methodology was developed at the System Development Corporation and provides a framework for penetration studies [1183, 1993, 1994]. It consists of four steps.

1. *Information gathering*. In this step, the testers become familiar with the system's functioning. They examine the system's design, its implementation, its operating procedures, and its use. The testers become as familiar with the system as possible.

2. *Flaw hypothesis*. Drawing on the knowledge gained in the first step, and on knowledge of vulnerabilities in other systems, the testers hypothesize flaws of the system under study.

3. *Flaw testing*. The testers test their hypothesized flaws. If a flaw does not exist (or cannot be exploited), the testers go back to step 2. If the flaw is exploited, they proceed to the next step.

4. *Flaw generalization*. Once a flaw has been successfully exploited, the testers attempt to generalize the vulnerability and find others similar to it. They feed their new understanding (or new hypothesis) back into step 2 and iterate until the test is concluded.

A fifth step is often added [1993, 1994]:

5. *Flaw elimination*. The testers suggest ways to eliminate the flaw or to use procedural controls to ameliorate it.

The following sections examine each aspect of this methodology and show how it is used in practice.

24.2.4.1   Information Gathering and Flaw Hypothesis

In the steps of the Flaw Hypothesis Methodology, the design of the system is scrutinized, with particular attention to discrepancies in the components. The testers devise a model of the system, or of its components, and then explore each aspect of the designs for internal consistency, incorrect assumptions, and potential flaws. They then consider the interfaces between the components and the ways in which the components work together. At this stage, some of the testers must be very knowledgeable about the system (or acquire expertise quickly) to ensure that the model or models of the system represent the implementation adequately. If the testers have access to design documents and manuals, they can often find parts of the specification that are imprecise or incomplete. These parts will be very good places to begin, especially if different designers worked on parts of the system that used the unclear specification. (Occasionally, a single designer may interpret an unclear specification differently during the design of two separate components.) If a privileged user (such as *root* on UNIX systems or *administrator* on Windows systems) is present, the way the system manages that user may reveal flaws.

The testers also examine the policies and procedures used to maintain the system. Although the design may not reveal any weak points, badly run or incorrectly installed systems will have vulnerabilities as a result of these errors. In particular, any departure from design assumptions, requirements, or models will usually indicate a vulnerability, as will sloppy administrative procedures and unnecessary use of privileges. Sharing of accounts, for example, often enables an attacker to plant Trojan horses, as does sharing of libraries, programs, and data.

Implementation problems also lead to security flaws. Models of vulnerabilities offer many clues to where the flaws may lie. One strategy is for the testers to look in the manuals describing the programs and the system, especially any manuals describing their underlying implementation, assumptions, and security-related properties [214]. Wherever the manuals suggest a limit or restriction, the testers try to violate it; wherever the manuals describe a sequence of steps to perform an action involving privileged data or programs, the testers omit some steps. More often than not, this strategy will reveal security flaws.

Critical to this step is the identification of the structures and mechanisms that control the system. These structures and mechanisms are the programs (including the operating system) that will enable an attacker to take control of (parts of) the system, such as the security-related controllers. The environment in which these programs have been designed and implemented, as well as the tools (compilers, debuggers, and so on) used to build them, may introduce errors, and knowledge of that environment helps the testers hypothesize security flaws.

Throughout all this, the testers draw on their past experience with the system, with penetrating systems in general, and on flaws that have been found in other systems. Later sections of this chapter present several models and frameworks of vulnerabilities and analyze them with respect to their ability to model system vulnerabilities. The classification of flaws often leads to the discovery of new flaws, and this analysis is part of the flaw hypothesis stage.

24.2.4.2   Flaw Testing

Once the testers have hypothesized a set of flaws, they determine the order in which to test the flaws. The priority is a function of the goals of the test. For example, if the testing is to uncover major design or implementation flaws, hypothetical flaws that involve design problems or flaws in system-critical code will be given a very high priority. If the testing is to uncover the vulnerability of the system to outsider attack, flaws related to external access protocols and programs will be given a very high priority and flaws affecting only internal use will be given a low priority. Assigning priorities is a matter of informed judgment, which emphasizes the need for testers to be familiar with the environment and the system.

Once the priorities have been determined, the testers study the hypothetical flaws. If a flaw can be demonstrated from the analysis, so much the better; this commonly occurs when a flaw arises from faulty specifications, designs, or operations. If the flaw cannot be demonstrated in this way, the tester must understand exactly why the flaw might arise and how to test for it in the least intrusive manner. The goal is to demonstrate that the flaw exists and can cause system compromise, but to minimize the impact of that demonstration.

Ideally, when a system must be tested, it should be backed up and all users should be removed from it. This precautionary measure saves grief should the testing go awry. This is not always possible, especially if the penetration test is being conducted without notice to the system users and operators, to test both the system and the procedures that protect it. The tester verifies that the system is configured as needed for the test and takes notes (or helps an observer take notes) of the requirements for detecting the flaw. The tester then verifies the existence of the flaw. In many cases, this can be done without exploiting the flaw; in some cases, it cannot. The latter cases are often political, in which the system developers or managers refuse to believe that the flaw exists until it is demonstrated. The test should be as simple as possible but must demonstrate that the exploitation succeeded; for example, a test might copy a protected file to a second protected file or change the date of modification of a system file by one second (unless the precise time of modification is critical). The tester's goal is to demonstrate what a hostile exploiter of the flaw could do, not to be that hostile exploiter. The notes of the test must be complete enough to enable another tester to duplicate the test or the exploitation on request; thus, precise notes are essential.

24.2.4.3   Flaw Generalization

As testers successfully penetrate the system (either through analysis or through analysis followed by testing), classes of flaws begin to emerge. The testers must confer enough to make each other aware of the nature of the flaws, and often two different flaws can be combined for a devastating attack. As an example, one flaw may enable a tester to gain access to an unprivileged account on a Windows 10 system, and a second flaw may enable an ordinary user to gain administrator privileges. Separately, the impact of these flaws depends on the site policy and security concerns. Together, they allow anyone who can connect to the system to become supervisor.

As a second example, some privileged programs on the UNIX system read input into a buffer on the user stack and fail to check the length. By supplying an appropriate input, the attacker can overwrite the return address and make it invoke code in a way that compromises the system. Similarly, many programs place a copy of command-line arguments onto the stack. Generalizing the former flaw suggests that programs that do the latter are equally vulnerable to compromise in a similar fashion (but the string is supplied as a command-line argument rather than as input).

24.2.4.4   Flaw Elimination

The flaw elimination step is often omitted because correction of flaws is not part of the penetration. However, the flaws uncovered by the test must be corrected.

Proper correction of a flaw requires an understanding of the context of the flaw as well as of the details of both the flaw and its exploitation. This implies that the environment in which the system functions is relevant to correction of the flaw. For example, if a design flaw is uncovered during development as part of the testing cycle, the developers can correct the design problem and reimplement those portions of the system that are affected by the flaw. In this case, knowledge of how to exploit that flaw is not critical. If, however, a design flaw is uncovered at a production site, that site (and the vendor) may not be able to correct the flaw quickly enough to prevent attackers from exploiting it. In this case, understanding how the flaw can be exploited becomes critical because all the site can do is to try to block those paths of exploitation or to detect any attacker who tries to exploit the flaw. This justifies the extensive analysis during the flaw hypothesis and generalization phase. Understanding the origins of the flaw, its context, and its affect on the system leads to proper corrective measures based on the system and the environment in which it functions.

24.2.5   Versions

The Flaw Hypothesis Methodology lacks details on how to carry out its steps. This is both a strength and a weakness—a strength because it gives the tester the freedom to use any strategy to perform the tests, a weakness because the lack of structure provides little guidance. Since its introduction, various methods have been developed to guide the application of the Flaw Hypothesis Methodology.

24.2.5.1   ISSAF

The Information Systems Security Assessment Framework (ISSAF) [1570], developed by the Open Information Systems Security Group, is a methodology designed to evaluate the security of systems (including networks and applications). The methodology defines three main steps:

- The planning and preparation step sets up the test. It includes the legal and contractual bases for the test, including establishing the goals and what is and is not allowed as part of the test. This corresponds to preparing to apply the Flaw Hypothesis Methodology.
- The assessment phase consists of nine steps. The first two steps, Information Gathering and Network Mapping, make up step 1 of the Flaw Hypothesis Methodology. The third step, Vulnerability Identification, corresponds to step 2 of the Flaw Hypothesis Methodology. The remaining steps (Penetration, Gaining Access and Privilege Escalation, Enumerating Further, Compromise Remote Users/Sites, Maintaining Access, and Cover the Tracks) make up step 3 of the Flaw Hypothesis Methodology. The ISSAF offers general suggestions on how to do each of these steps.
- The final phase consists of reporting and cleaning up. In it, testers write the reports and, if necessary, purge the target system of all attack tools and other artifacts that they used. The report-writing corresponds to the

documentation in the Flaw Hypothesis Methodology. It is performed *after* the testing, though, and not during it.

This methodology has no step corresponding to step 4, the generalization step. The Enumerating Further step lists specific information gathering techniques, and then says to try the earlier steps with the newly gathered data as a starting point. Similarly, the Compromise Remote Users/Sites step suggests compromising users and systems, and then, using the newly gained access, trying the earlier steps again. This "cycle" (really, a feedback loop) enables one to exploit known vulnerabilities that require additional privileges, access, or changes to the environment. It does not synthesize two known vulnerabilities into a different new (third) one.

The strength of ISSAF is its clear and very intuitive structure, which guides the tester through the complicated assessment steps. Its problem is its lack of emphasis on generalizing new vulnerabilities from commonalities or properties of existing ones.

24.2.5.2   OSSTMM

The Open Source Security Testing Methodology Manual (OSSTMM) [898] is a widely used standard for security testers. It describes a testing methodology with a scope comprised of three classes:

- *COMSEC* is the communications security class.
- *PHYSSEC* is the physical security class.
- *SPECSEC* is the spectrum security class.

Classes are the means of interacting with assets. An asset is what is valuable to the owner. The scope requires that all the threats must be considered possible, even if not probable.

The three main classes are in turn split into five channels:

- The *human class* comprises all the human elements of communications.
- The *physical class* comprises the tangible elements of security where interaction requires physical effort or an energy transmitter to manipulate.
- The *wireless communication class* comprises all the electronic communications, signals and emanations that take place over the known electromagnetic spectrum.
- The *data networks class* comprises all the electronic systems and data networks where interactions take place over established cables and wired network lines.
- The *telecommunication class* comprises all the telecommunication networks, digital or analog, where the interaction takes place over established telephone or telephone-like network lines.

OSSTMM describes 17 modules to analyze each of the channels. The modules are divided into four phases. Each methodology phase covers a different audit depth, each phase being equally important:

- The *induction phase* provides legal information and the resulting technical restrictions.
- The *interaction phase* defines the scope of the test and the interrelations between its components.
- The *inquest phase* has the testers uncover specific information about the system. This may require some testing, for example to determine the actual control settings rather than the way those controls should be set.
- The *intervention phase* tests the specific targets, trying to compromise them. It follows the inquest phase so that the penetration testing does not disrupt the gathering of the specific information in that phase.

In terms of the Flaw Hypothesis Methodology, the induction and first part of the interaction phases correspond to pretesting preparation, because they set up the goals of the test and ensure the requirements for the test are met. The rest of the interaction phase and the inquest phase together correspond to steps 1 and 2 of the Flaw Hypothesis Methodology, because during those steps, the testers gather and organize information about the target and its environment, and then use that information to think of vulnerabilities and design plans to test for them. The actual tests are conducted in the last phase of the methodology, which corresponds to step 3 of the Flaw Hypothesis Methodology. The OSSTMM supplies specific modules for tests.

As with the ISSAF, there is no explicit generalization step. The standard, however, notes that many of the steps of each phase feed back into one another, and at the end, the alert and log review (part of the intervention phase) feeds back into the testing [898, §6.3]. The implication is that the testers learn from later parts of this methodology, and then cycle back to use their new knowledge. This is a part of generalization.

The strength of the OSSTMM is its organization of resources and environmental considerations into classes, channels, modules, and phases. This provides a methodical approach to analyzing the system. Its weakness is the same as that for the ISSAF: it provides no guidance on how to generalize new vulnerabilities from commonalities or properties of existing ones, and indeed omits discussion of that step.

24.2.5.3 GISTA

The NIST Technical Guide to Information Security Testing and Assessment (GISTA) [1673] introduces a four-phase process for penetration testing:

- In the planning phase, the testers and the management agree on the rules for the test, and set the goals for success.

- In the discovery phase, the testers search the system. The first part of this phase gathers information, especially identifying and examining potential targets. The second part examines the information gathered, and based on vulnerability databases and the testers' experiences and knowledge of vulnerabilities, hypothesizes vulnerabilities to test.

- In the attack phase, the testers verify whether the hypothesized vulnerabilities can be exploited. In some cases, the additional privileges will suggest additional possible exploits; in other cases, the testers will merely learn something about the system. They will then add this information to the pool of knowledge, and go back to the discovery phase to see if they can think of new vulnerabilities.

- The reporting phase occurs in parallel with the other phases, and results in a report to the management describing what was found and how to mitigate these problems.

This is the closer to the Flaw Hypothesis Methodology than either ISSAF or OSSTMM. Step 4, again, is hinted at more directly than in other methods in the link between the attack and discovery phases. However, this method is quite general, and does not provide the same discipline of system resource guidance as do the ISSAF and OSSTMM methodologies.

24.2.5.4   PTES

The Penetration Testing Execution Standard [1031, 2204] defines a seven-phase testing plan:

1. During the pre-engagement interactions, the testers and clients agree on the scope of the test, its goals, and the terms of the engagement. Legal and contractual issues are resolved here.

2. Intelligence gathering follows. To identify potential targets, the testers scour sources provided by the client as well as public information such as DNS records, social media, web pages, company reports, and probes. For example, a port scan during this phase gives an indication of what services the client provides, which provides insights into the systems as well as the software.

3. Threat modeling uses information gathered in the previous phases to analyze the threats. In this phase, the data gathered may require more investigation of potential threats, including nontechnical ones. The testers identify potential vulnerabilities, or combinations of vulnerabilities, that an attacker could exploit to realize the threat.

4. In the vulnerability analysis phase, the testers determine which of the potential vulnerabilities actually exist. They use a variety of techniques, including automated tools to scan the network gathering data (such as network port numbers and login banners) that will confirm the presence of specific vulnerabilities.

5. The exploitation phase tests whether the vulnerabilities identified in the previous step can be exploited. Depending on the agreed-upon rules for the test, the testers may use social engineering means as well as technical means to achieve their goal. Note that the testers may discover preventative mechanisms that block the exploits of some vulnerabilities found in the previous step.

6. The post-exploitation phase occurs next. It expands upon the exploits, leading to an understanding of the effects of a successful exploitation. The attackers focus on the most damaging attacks, including planting backdoors and access to backups. They must also try to conceal their efforts, unless the terms of the test say not to.

7. The reporting phase is where the testers document their actions and what they found. In addition to successful attacks, hypothesized but failed attacks are documented, as are attacks and vulnerabilities that have not been tried. The first goal of the report is to provide the clients with a foundation for decisions about the allocation or resources to harden their systems. The second is to provide a starting point for future penetration tests, to minimize the time needed to review the attacks tried here and to suggest possibly fruitful starting points for new attacks. The report will contain recommendations and suggestions for improving security.

The pre-engagement and intelligence gathering phases correspond to step 1 of the Flaw Hypothesis Methodology as both are information gathering steps. The next steps, threat modeling and vulnerability analysis, result in hypotheses about possible flaws and vulnerabilities, so this is step 2 of the Flaw Hypothesis Methodology. The exploitation and post-exploitation steps combine to be step 3 of the Flaw Hypothesis Methodology. The reporting phase is implicit in the Flaw Hypothesis Methodology, being a critical part of each step. The technical guide [2204] provides information to help the testers use the methodology.

Although the post-exploitation step sounds like flaw generalization, it synthesizes possible results of attacks. That is, if the attacker compromises one system, the attacker looks through that system to determine whether the compromise can provide information that helps her attain the test goal. It does not generalize vulnerabilities, which is the goal of step 4 of the Flaw Hypothesis Methodology.

24.2.6   Example: Penetration of the Michigan Terminal System

As an exercise, a graduate computer science class at the University of Michigan launched a penetration test against the Michigan Terminal System, a general-purpose operating system that ran on the University of Michigan's IBM 360 and 370 computer systems [885]. Their goal was to acquire access to the terminal control structures. The students had the approval and support of the computer center staff. They began by assuming that the attackers had access to an authorized account (step 3 on page 830).

The first step was to learn the details of the system's control flow and supervisor. When an individual user ran a program, memory was split into segments. Segments 0 to 4 contained the supervisor, system programs, and system state and were protected by hardware mechanisms. Segment 5 was a system work area, recording process-specific information such as privilege level, accounting information, and so forth. The process should not have been able to alter any of this information. Segments numbered 6 and higher contained user process information, and the process could alter them.

Segment 5 was protected by a virtual memory protection system. The virtual system had two states. In "system" mode, the process could access or alter its segment 5 and could issue calls to the supervisor. In "user" mode, segment 5 was not present in the address space of the process and so could not be modified. The process would run in user mode whenever user-supplied code would be executed. If the user code needed a system service, it would issue a system call; that code could in turn issue a supervisor call, in which case the supervisor would perform the needed function. The system code had to check parameters to ensure that the system (or supervisor) would access authorized locations only. Complicating this check was the way in which parameters were passed. A list of addresses (one per parameter) was constructed in user segments, and the address of this list was given to the system call in a register; hence, checking of parameters required following of two levels of indirection. All such addresses, of course, had to be in user segments numbered 6 (or higher).

The testing now entered the flaw hypothesis stage. The observation that many security problems arise at interfaces suggested focusing on the switch from user to system mode because system mode required supervisor privileges. The study focused on parameter checking, and it was discovered that an element of the parameter list could point to a location within the parameter list (see Figure 24–2). In other words, one could cause the system or supervisor procedure to alter a parameter's address after the validity of the old address had been verified.

In order to exploit this flaw, the testers had to find a system routine that used this calling convention, took two parameters, altered at least one, and could

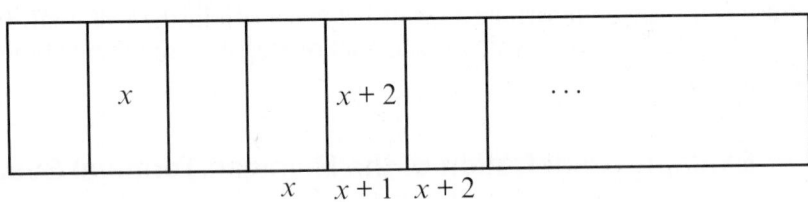

Figure 24–2 An example of the parameter passing conventions. Here, *x* is the address of the parameter list, and locations *x*, *x*+1, and *x*+2 contain addresses of the actual parameters. Note that location *x* + 1 contains the address *x* + 2, meaning that the last address in the parameter list is itself the location of a parameter (as well as containing the address of another parameter).

be made to change the parameter to any of a specific set of values (which lay in the system segment). Several such routines were found; the one that was exploited was the line input routine, which returned the line number and length of the line as well as the line itself. The testers set up the parameter list so that the address for storing the line number was the location of the address of the line length. When called, the system routine validated the parameter list (all addresses were indeed in user segments), and it then read the input line. The line number was stored in the parameter list itself and was set to be an address within the system segment. The line length corresponded to the desired value of that location in the system segment. Thus, the testers were able to alter data in segment 5. However, they could not alter anything in the supervisor segments because those segments were protected by hardware.

During the flaw generalization stage, the testers realized the full implications of this flaw. The privilege level in segment 5 controlled the ability of the process to issue supervisor calls (as opposed to system calls). One of these calls turned off the hardware protection for segments 0 to 4. This enabled the process to alter any data or instructions in those segments and thus effectively control the computer completely.

During the test, the testers found numerous flaws that allowed them to acquire sufficient privileges to meet their goal. The penetration study was a success because it demonstrated how an attacker could obtain control of the terminal control structures.

24.2.7   Example: Compromise of a Burroughs System

The penetration study of a Burroughs B6700 system [2007] is particularly interesting because of the architecture of that system. Again as a class project, a graduate computer systems class at the University of Canterbury attempted to penetrate a Burroughs B6700 computer system running the 3.0 P.R.#1 release. The goal was to obtain the status of a privileged user and thus be able to alter privileged programs. The group explored four aspects of the system, in all cases beginning with an authorized account on the system (step 3 on page 830); we will discuss only the part that focused on file security.

The Burroughs B6700 system security is based on strict file typing. There are four relevant entities: ordinary users, privileged users, privileged programs, and operating system tasks. Ordinary users are tightly restricted; the other three classes can access file data without restriction but are still constrained from compromising integrity. Furthermore, the Burroughs system provides no assemblers; its compilers all take high-level languages as input and produce executable code. The B6700 distinguishes between data files and executable files by the type of the file. Only compilers can produce executable files. Moreover, if any user tries to write into a file or into a file's attributes, that file's type is immediately set to data, even if the file was previously an executable.

The group hypothesized that the system would not be able to detect a file that was altered offline. To test this hypothesis, the members of the group wrote and compiled a program to change the type of any file. It could not be run successfully yet because it would have to alter the file's attributes. Because it was not a recognized compiler, the file so altered would immediately become a data file. They then copied the machine code version of this program to tape. The tape utility created a header record indicating the file type. A second tape was mounted, and the contents of the first tape were copied to the second. During the transfer, the copying program altered the file type of the machine code to be a compiler. They then copied the file from the second tape to disk, and the file was installed as a compiler. The testers wrote a second subroutine, compiled it using the regular compiler, altered the machine code to give privileges to any user calling it, and used the bogus compiler to change the type of the altered file to executable. They then wrote a program to call that routine. It succeeded, and the user became privileged. This gave the user complete control of the system, achieving the goal.

A procedural corrective measure was to prevent unprivileged users from loading executables off tape. The testers noted the impracticality of this measure in many environments, such as academic and development sites.

24.2.8   Example: Penetration of a Corporate Computer System

This study [2011] is instructive because it began at step 1 of the list on page 830 and looked only at gathering nontechnical information needed to breach the computer system. It shows the importance of proper operations and organizational proce- dures in securing a system. Although the specific example is an amalgamation of techniques used in several real penetrations, the techniques are very effective and have repeatedly succeeded. Specifics are disguised to protect the corporations so penetrated.

The goal of the study was to determine whether corporate security mea- sures were effective in keeping external attackers from accessing the system. The corporation had a variety of policies and procedures (both technical and nontechnical) that were believed to protect the system.

The testers began by gathering information about the site. They searched the Internet and obtained information on the corporation, including the names of some employees and officials. They obtained the telephone number of a local branch of the company and from that branch got a copy of the annual report. From the report and the other data, the testers were able to construct much of the company's organization, as well as a list of some of the projects on which individuals were working.

The testers determined that a corporate telephone directory would provide them with needed information about the corporate structure. One impersonated a new employee, and through judicious telephone calls found out that two numbers were required to have something delivered off-site: the number of the employee requesting the shipment and a Cost Center number. A tester promptly called the secretary of the executive about whom the testers knew the most; by impersonating another employee, the caller obtained the executive's employee number. A second tester impersonated an auditor and obtained that executive's

Cost Center number. The testers used these numbers to have a corporate directory sent to a "subcontractor."

At this point, the testers decided to contact newly hired personnel and try to obtain their passwords. They impersonated the secretary of a very senior executive of the company, called the appropriate office, and claimed that the senior executive was very upset that he had not been given the names of the employees hired that week. The information was promptly provided.

The testers then began calling the newly hired people. They claimed to be with the corporate computing center and provided a "Computer Security Awareness Briefing" over the telephone. In the process of this briefing, the testers learned the types of computer systems used, the employees' numbers, their logins, and their passwords. A call to the computing center provided modem numbers; the modems bypassed a critical security system. At this point, the testers had compromised the system sufficiently that the penetration study was deemed successful.

24.2.9   Example: Penetrating a UNIX System

In this example, the first goal is to gain access to the system. Our target is a system connected to the Internet.

We begin by scanning the network ports on the target system. Figure 24–3 shows some of these ports, together with a list of protocols that servers listening on those ports may use. Note that protocols are running on ports 79, 111, 512, 513, 514, and 540; these ports are typically used on UNIX systems. Let us make this assumption.

Many UNIX systems use *sendmail* as their SMTP server. This large program has had many security problems [420, 2121, 2167, 2190, 2219–2225]. By connecting to the port, we determine that the target is using *sendmail* Version 3.1. Drawing on previous experience and widely known information [216],

```
ftp        21/tcp   File Transfer
telnet     23/tcp   Telnet
smtp       25/tcp   Simple Mail Transfer
finger     79/tcp   Finger
sunrpc     111/tcp  SUN Remote Procedure Call
exec       512/tcp  remote process execution (rexecd)
login      513/tcp  remote login (rlogind)
shell      514/tcp  rlogin style exec (rshd)
printer    515/tcp  spooler (lpd)
uucp       540/tcp  uucpd
nfs        2049/tcp networked file system
xterm      6000/tcp x-windows server
```

Figure 24–3   The output of the UNIX port scan. These are the ports that provide network services.

```
220 zzz.com sendmail 3.1/zzz.3.9, Dallas, Texas, ready
  at Wed, 2 Apr 97 22:07:31 CST
helo xxx
250 zzz.com Hello xxx.org, pleased to meet you
wiz
250 Enter, O mighty wizard!
shell
#
```

Figure 24–4   A successful accessing of a UNIX system.

we hypothesize that the SMTP agent will recognize the command shell and give us a *root*-owned shell on the system. To do this, we need to execute the *wiz* command first. We are successful, as Figure 24–4 shows. On this particular system, we have obtained root privileges.

The key to this attack is an understanding of how most UNIX systems are configured and a knowledge of known vulnerabilities. Most UNIX systems use some variant of *sendmail* as their SMTP agent, and that program prints version information when a connection is made. The information enabled the testers to determine what set of attacks would be likely to be fruitful. Given the wide variation in *sendmail*s (owing to differences in vendors' patches), the flaw had to be tested for. The test succeeded.

Now assume we are at step 3 of the list on page 830. We have an unprivileged account on the system. We determine that this system has a dynamically loaded kernel; the program used to add modules to the kernel is *loadmodule*. Because such a program must be privileged (or else it could not update the kernel tables), an unprivileged user can execute a privileged process. As indicated before, this suggests that the program does some sort of validation or authorization check. Our vulnerabilities models (see Section 24.4) indicate that this is a source of many problems. Let us examine this program more closely.

The program *loadmodule* validates the module as being a dynamically loadable module and then invokes the dynamic loader *ld.so* to perform the actual load. It also needs to determine the architecture of the system, and it uses the program arch to obtain this information. A logical question is how it executes these programs. The simplest way is to use the library function *system*. This function does not reset any part of the environment. Hence, if the system call is used, the environment in which we execute *loadmodule* is passed to the subprocesses, and these subprocesses are run as *root*. In this case, we can set our environment to look for programs in our local directory first, and then in system directories (by setting the **PATH** variable to have "." as the first directory).

We accept this as a working hypothesis, and we set out to verify that this flaw exists. We write a small program that prints its effective UID, name it *ld.so*, and move it to the current working directory. We then reset our **PATH** variable as indicated above and run *loadmodule*. Unfortunately, our program does not execute; nothing is printed.

Why not? Once we understand this, we may be able to figure out a way to bypass this check, and our understanding of the system will increase. We scan the executable looking for ASCII strings, to see exactly how their dynamic loader invokes those subprograms. We see that the invocations are "/bin/arch" and "/bin/ld.so". So our attempt to change the search path (**PATH** environment variable) was irrelevant; the system never looked at that variable because full path names were given.

Rereading the manual page for the library function system, we notice that it invokes the command interpreter *sh*. Looking at *sh*'s manual page, we learn that the **IFS** environment variable has as its value characters used to separate words in commands that *sh* executes. Given that *loadmodule* invokes "/bin/arch", if the character "/" were in the value of the environment variable **IFS**, *sh* would treat this command as "bin arch". Then we could use the idea that just failed, but call the program *bin* rather than *ld.so*.

We could verify this idea without a test, but it would require disassemby of the *loadmodule* executable unless we had source code (we would look for anything that reset the environment within *loadmodule*). Assuming that we do not have source code, we change the value of **IFS** to include "/", reset **PATH** and **IFS** as described above, change the name of our small program from *ld.so* to *bin*, and run *loadmodule*. The process prints that its effective UID is 0 (*root*). Our test has succeeded. (Chapter 31, "Program Security," discusses corrective measures for problems of this type. The vendor fixed the problem [2232].)

Incidentally, this example leads to a simple flaw generalization. The problem of subprocesses inheriting environment variables and their values suggests that the privileged program did not adequately sanitize the (untrusted) environment in which that program executes before invoking subprograms that are to be trusted. Hence, *any* privileged program may have this flaw. One could even hypothesize that a standard library routine or system call is invoked. So, a general class of flaws would involve failure to sanitize the environment, and the indicator of such a flaw might be one or more specific function calls. At this point, the testers would look in the programmers' manuals to see if such routines existed; if so, they would analyze programs to see which privileged programs called them. This could lead to a large number of other vulnerabilities.

This penetration test demonstrates how failure can lead to success. When a test fails, the testers may have not understood the system completely and so need to study why the test failed. In this example, the failure led to a reexamination of the relevant library function, which led to a review of one of the system command interpreters. During this review, one of the testers noticed an obscure but documented control over the way the command interpreter interpreted commands. This led to a successful test. Patience is often said to be a virtue, and this is certainly true in penetration testing.

24.2.10   Example: Penetrating a Windows System

As in the preceding example, we begin at step 2 of the list on page 830, and all we know is that the system is connected to the Internet. We begin as before, by

```
qotd            17/tcp   Quote of the Day
ftp             21/tcp   File Transfer [Control]
loc-srv         135/tcp  Location Service
netbios-ssn     139/tcp  NETBIOS Session Service [JBP]
```

Figure 24–5 The output of the Windows port scan. These are the ports that provide network service.

probing network ports, and from the results (see Figure 24–5)—especially the service running on port 139—we conclude that the system is a Windows server.

We first probe for easy-to-guess passwords. We discover that the system administrator has chosen the password "Admin", and we obtain access to the system. At this point, we have administrator privilege on the local system. We would like to obtain rights to other systems in the domain.

We examine the local system and discover that the domain administrator has installed a service that is running with the privileges of a domain administrator. We then obtain a program that will dump the local security authority database, and load it onto the system. After executing it, we obtain the service account password. Using this password, we acquire domain administrator privileges and can now access any system in the domain.

This penetration test uncovered a serious administrative problem. For some reason, a sensitive account had a password that was easy to guess. This indicates a procedural problem within the company. Perhaps the system administrators were too busy, or forgot, to choose a good password. Two generalizations are appropriate. First, other systems should be checked for weak passwords. Second, the company's security policies should be reviewed, as should its education of its system administrators and its mechanisms for publicizing the policies.

24.2.11   Debate

Considerable debate has arisen about the validity of penetration studies for testing system security. At one end of the spectrum are some vendors who report that "after one year of our system being on the Internet, no one has successfully penetrated the system," implying (and in some cases stating) that this shows that their product is quite secure. At the other end is the claim that penetration testing has no validity, and only rigorous design, implementation, and validation comprise an adequate test of security.

The resolution lies somewhere between two these extremes. Penetration testing is no substitute for good, thorough specification, rigorous design, careful and correct implementation, and meticulous testing. It is, however, a very valuable component of the final stage, "testing"; it is simply a form of a posteriori testing. Ideally, it should be unnecessary; but human beings are fallible and make mistakes, and computer systems are so complex that no single individual, or group, understands all aspects of the hardware's construction, the software's design and implementation, and the computer system's interactions with users and the environment. Hence, errors will be introduced. Properly done, penetration tests examine the design and implementation of security mechanisms from the point of view of an attacker. The knowledge and understanding gleaned from such a viewpoint is invaluable.

24.2.12   Conclusion

Penetration testing is a very informal, nonrigorous technique for checking the security of a system. Two problems with the Flaw Hypothesis Methodology described in Section 24.2.4 are its dependence on the caliber of the testers and its lack of systematic examination of the system. High-caliber testers will examine the design systematically, but all too often the testing degenerates into a more scattered analysis.

In an attempt to make the process more systematic, and less dependent on the knowledge of the individuals conducting the test, various elaborations of the Flaw Hypothesis Methodology have been developed. These guide testers through various stages of that methodology, but are not checklists; the testers must still apply their knowledge and intuition. So testers also look at flaws that exist on other systems and decide which ones could translate into the tested system's model. Classification schemes can help in this regard; they group similar vulnerabilities together and enable the analyst to extract common features. Hence, such schemes are important in the flaw hypothesis step and are worth exploring.

24.3   Vulnerability Classification

Vulnerability classification frameworks describe security flaws from various perspectives. Some frameworks describe vulnerabilities by classifying the techniques used to exploit them. Others characterize vulnerabilities in terms of the software and hardware components and interfaces that make up the vulnerability. Still others classify vulnerabilities by their nature, in hopes of discovering techniques for finding previously unknown vulnerabilities.

The goal of vulnerability analysis is to develop methodologies that provide the following abilities:

1. The ability to specify, design, and implement a computer system without vulnerabilities.
2. The ability to analyze a computer system to detect vulnerabilities (which feeds into the Flaw Hypothesis Methodology step of penetration testing).

3. The ability to address any vulnerabilities introduced during the operation of the computer system (possibly leading to a redesign or reimplementation of the flawed components).

4. The ability to detect attempted exploitations of vulnerabilities.

Ideally, one can generalize information about security flaws. From these generalizations, one then looks for underlying principles that lead toward the desired goals. Because the abstraction's purpose is tied to the classifiers' understanding of the goal, and of how best to reach that goal, both these factors influence the classification system developed. Hence, the vulnerability frameworks covering design often differ from those covering the detection of exploitation of vulnerabilities. Before we present several different frameworks, however, a discussion of two security flaws will provide a basis for understanding several of the problems of these frameworks.

24.3.1   Two Security Flaws

This section presents two widely known security vulnerabilities in some versions of the UNIX operating system. We will use these vulnerabilities as examples when comparing and contrasting the various frameworks.

The program *xterm* is a program that emulates a terminal under the X11 window system. For reasons not relevant to this discussion, it must run as the omnipotent user *root* on some UNIX systems. It enables the user to log all input and output to a log file. If the file does not exist, *xterm* creates it and assigns ownership to the user; if the file already exists, *xterm* checks that the user can write to it before opening the file. Because any *root* process can write to any file in the system, the extra check is necessary to prevent a user from directing *xterm* to append log output to (say) the system password file and gaining privileges by altering that file [2255].

Suppose the user wishes to log to an existing file. The following code fragment opens the file for writing:

```
if (access("/usr/tom/X", W_OK) == 0){
        if ((fd = open("/usr/tom/X", O_WRONLY|O_APPEND))
                        < 0){
                /* handle error: cannot open file */
        }
}
```

The semantics of the UNIX operating system cause the name of the file to be loosely bound to the data object it represents, and the binding is asserted each time the name is used. If the data object corresponding to */usr/tom/X* changes after the *access* but before the *open*, the *open* will not open the file checked by *access*. So if, during that interval, an attacker deletes the file and links a system file (such as the password file) to the name of the deleted file, *xterm* appends logging output to the password file. At this point, the user can create a root account without a password and gain root privileges. Figure 24–6 shows this graphically.

The Internet worm of 1988 [619, 842, 1600, 1796, 1797] publicized our second flaw. It continues to recur—for example, in implementations of various network servers [487, 1456, 2014, 2120, 2218, 2234]; indeed, the CVE database has over 8,000 entries of buffer overflow vulnerabilities since 1999, with 32 reports in the first two months of 2017. The *finger* protocol [2106] obtains information about the users of a remote system. The client program, called *finger*, contacts a server, called *fingerd*, on the remote system and sends a name of at most 512 characters. The server reads the name and returns the relevant information, but the server does not check the length of the name that finger sends. The storage space for the name is allocated on the stack, directly above the return address for the I/O routine. The attacker writes a small program (in machine code) to obtain a command interpreter and pads it to 512 bytes. She then sets the next 24 bytes to return to the input buffer instead of to the rightful caller (the main routine, in this case). The entire 536-byte buffer is sent to the daemon. The first 512 bytes go into the input storage array, and the excess 24 bytes overwrite the

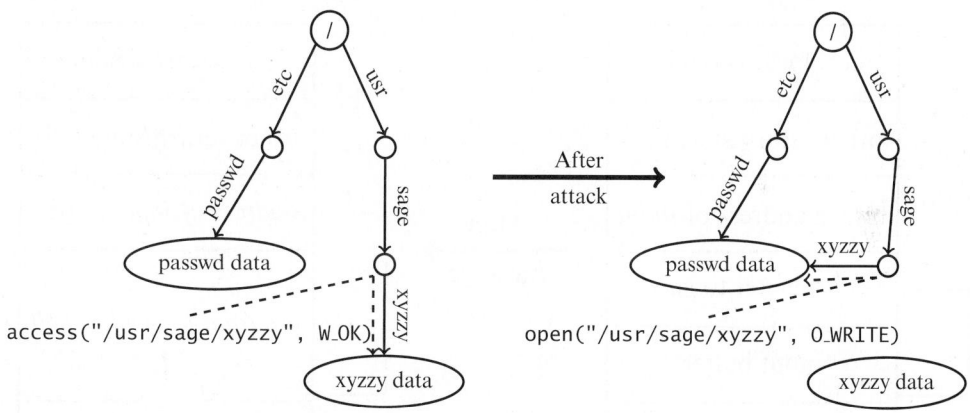

Figure 24–6 (a) The state of the system at the time of the access system call. The labeled arrows indicate the name of the target. Both */usr/sage/xyzzy* and */etc/passwd* name distinct objects containing their own data. The *access* system call checks that the data in */usr/sage/xyzzy* can be overwritten; this is shown by the dashed arrow in (a). However, before the process makes its *open* system call, */usr/sage/xyzzy* is deleted and a direct alias (hard link) for */etc/passwd* is created and named */usr/sage/xyzzy*; the data associated with the previous */usr/sage/xyzzy* is no longer accessible by that name. Then the *open* accesses the data associated with */etc/passwd* when it opens */usr/sage/xyzzy* because */usr/sage/xyzzy* and */etc/passwd* now refer to the same file. This is shown in (b), with the dashed arrow indicating which data is actually read.

stack locations in which the caller's return address and status word are stored. The input routine returns to the code to spawn the command interpreter. The attacker now has access to the system. Figure 24–7 shows the changes in the user stack.

Variants of buffer overflows do not require the attacker to upload executable code. An *arc attack*, also called a *return-to-libc attack*, replaces the return address with the address of a function in memory; arguments to that function can also be pushed onto the stack, so the invoked function can use those arguments [554]. For example, the C library function *system* passes its argument to the command interpreter to be executed as if it were typed directly to the interpreter. Thus, if a privileged program has this vulnerability and function, an attacker can have that program execute an arbitrary command.

A more subtle exploitation of buffer overflows is called *return oriented programming* (ROP) [1717]. This attack pushes a sequence of return addresses onto the stack. The return addresses correspond to small code fragments, called *gadgets*, that execute operations in the sequence desired by the attacker. Each gadget ends in a return instruction that pops the next return address off the stack, causing the flow of control to go to the next gadget. This effectively creates a program within the program.

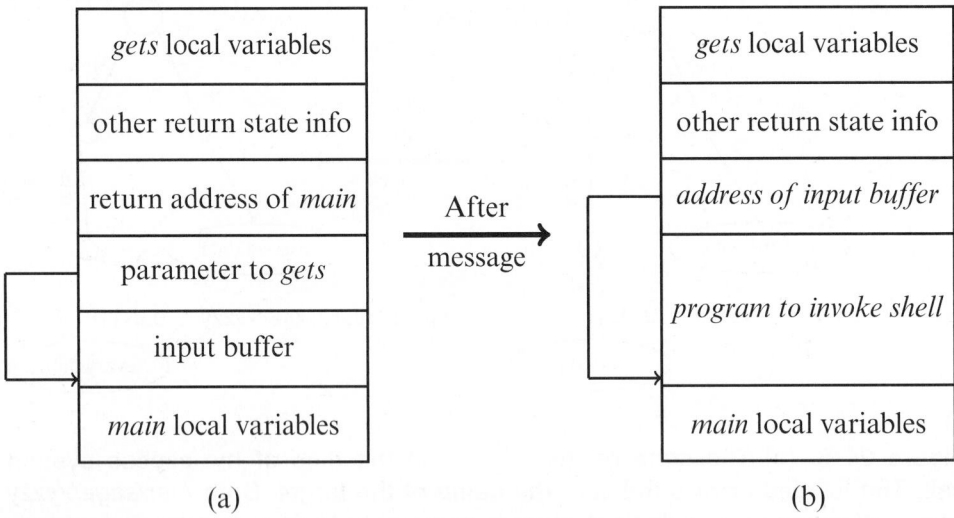

gets local variables	*gets* local variables
other return state info	other return state info
return address of *main*	*address of input buffer*
parameter to *gets*	*program to invoke shell*
input buffer	
main local variables	*main* local variables
(a)	(b)

After message →

Figure 24–7   **(a) The stack frame of *fingerd* when input is to be read. The arrow indicates the location to which the parameter to *gets* refers (it is past the address of the input buffer). (b) The same stack after the bogus input is stored. The input string overwrites the input buffer and parameter to *gets*, allowing a return to the contents of the input buffer. The arrow shows that the return address of main was overwritten with the address of the input buffer. When *gets* returns, it will pop its return address (now the address of the input buffer) and resume execution at that address.**

24.4   Frameworks

The goals of a framework dictate the framework's structure. For example, if the framework is to guide the development of an attack detection tool, the focus of the framework will be on the steps needed to exploit vulnerabilities. If the framework is intended to aid the software development process, it will emphasize programming and design errors that cause vulnerabilities. Each of the following classification schemes was designed with a specific goal in mind.

Each of the following frameworks classifies a vulnerability as an *n*-tuple, the elements of the *n*-tuple being the specific classes into which the vulnerability falls. Some have a single set of categories; others are multidimensional ($n > 1$) because they are examining multiple characteristics of the vulnerabilities.

24.4.1   The RISOS Study

The RISOS (Research Into Secure Operating Systems) study [5] was prepared to aid computer and system managers and information processing specialists in understanding security issues in operating systems and to help them determine the level of effort required to enhance their system security. The investigators classified flaws into seven general classes.

1. Incomplete parameter validation
2. Inconsistent parameter validation
3. Implicit sharing of privileged/confidential data
4. Asynchronous validation/inadequate serialization
5. Inadequate identification/authentication/authorization
6. Violable prohibition/limit
7. Exploitable logic error

The investigators discussed techniques for avoiding, or ameliorating, the flaws in each class. They also attempted to develop methodologies and software for detecting incomplete parameter validation flaws. The survey examined several operating systems (MULTICS, BBN's TENEX, DEC's TOPS-10, Honeywell's GECOS, IBM's OS/MVT, SDS's SDS-940, and UNIVAC's EXEC-8) but noted that the flaw classes applied to other systems as well.

24.4.1.1   The Flaw Classes

Incomplete parameter validation occurs when a parameter is not checked before use. The buffer overflows discussed earlier are the classic example of this type of flaw. Another example is a flaw in one computer's software emulator for integer division [2191]. The caller provided two addresses as parameters, one for the quotient and one for the remainder. The quotient address was checked to ensure that it lay within the user's protection domain, but the remainder address was not similarly checked. By passing the address of the user identification number for the remainder, the programmer was able to acquire system privileges. Parameters need to be checked for type (and possibly format), ranges of values, access rights, and presence (or absence).

Inconsistent parameter validation is a design flaw in which each individual routine using data checks that the data is in the proper format for that routine, but the routines require different formats. Basically, the inconsistency across interfaces causes this flaw. An example occurs in a database in which each record is one line, with colons separating the fields. If one program accepts colons and newlines as part of data but other programs read the colons so accepted as field separators and the newlines so accepted as record separators, the inconsistency can cause bogus records to be entered into the database.

When an operating system fails to isolate processes and users properly, an *implicit sharing of privileged/confidential data* flaw occurs. The ability to recover a file's password in TENEX is an example of this type of flaw [1856]. TENEX allowed the user to determine when paging occurred. Furthermore, when a file access required a password, the password was checked character by character, and the checking stopped at the first incorrect character. So, an attacker would position a guess for the password so that a page boundary lay between the first and second characters. He would then try to access the file. If paging occurred, the first character of the password was correct; if not, it was incorrect. Continuing in this fashion, the attacker could quickly recover the password needed to access the file. Kocher's timing attack against RSA, in which small variations in the speed of encipherment enable an attacker to deduce the private key (see Section 9.6), is another example of this type of flaw [1084].

Race conditions and time-of-check to time-of-use flaws such as that shown in Figure 24–6 are members of the *asynchronous validation/inadequate serialization* class of flaws.

Inadequate identification/authorization/authentication flaws arise when a system allows a user to be erroneously identified, when one user can assume another's privilege, or when a user can trick the system (or another user) into executing a program without authorization. Trojan horses are examples of this type of flaw, as are accounts without passwords, because any user can access them freely. The UNIVAC 1100 provides an example related to file naming [5]. On that system, access to the system file $SYS\$*DLOC\$$ meant that the process was privileged. The system checked this by seeing if the process could access any file with the first three characters of the qualifier name "SYS" and the first three characters of the file name "DLO." So, any process that could access the file $SYSA*DLOC\$$, which was an ordinary (nonsystem) file, was also privileged and could access any file without the file access key.

Violable prohibition/limit flaws arise when system designers fail to handle bounds conditions properly. For example, early versions of TENEX kept the operating system in low memory and gave the user process access to all memory cells with addresses above a fixed value (marking the last memory location of the operating system). The limit of memory addressing was the address of the highest memory location; but when a user addressed a location beyond the end of memory, it was reduced modulo the memory size and so accessed a word in the operating system's area. Because the address was a large number, however, it was treated as being in user space—and hence could be altered [1856].

Exploitable logic error flaws encompass problems not falling into any of the other classes; examples include incorrect error handling, unexpected side effects of instructions, and incorrect allocation of resources. One such flaw that occurred in early versions of TENEX requires an understanding of how the TENEX monitor implemented a return to the user's program. Basically, the monitor would execute a *skip return* to the address following the one stored in the user's program counter; the system would simply add 1 to the user's return word and return. On the PDP-10, the index field was a bit in the return word. If the return word was set to −1, the addition would overflow into the index field and change its semantics to refer to the contents of register 1, so the return would be to the location stored in that register. The attacker would load a bootstrap program into other registers, manipulate the contents of register 1 through a series of system calls so that it contained the address of the first bootstrap instruction, and then cause the monitor to execute a *skip return*. The bootstrap program would execute, loading the attacker's program and executing it with system privileges [1134].

24.4.1.2   Legacy

The RISOS project created a seminal study of vulnerabilities. It provided valuable insights into the nature of flaws, among them that security is a function of site requirements and threats, that there are a small number of fundamental flaws that recur in different contexts, and that operating system security is not a critical factor in the design of operating systems. It spurred research efforts into detection and repair of vulnerabilities in existing systems; the Protection Analysis study was the most influential of these efforts.

24.4.2   Protection Analysis Model

The Protection Analysis (PA) study [210] attempted to break the operating system protection problem into smaller, more manageable pieces. The investigators hoped that this would reduce the expertise required of individuals working on operating systems. The study aimed at developing techniques that would have an impact within 10 years. It developed a general strategy, called *pattern-directed protection evaluation*, and applied it to several operating systems. In one case, the investigators found previously unknown security vulnerabilities. From this approach grew a classification scheme for vulnerabilities. Neumann's presentation [1443] of this study organizes the 10 classes of flaws in order to show the connections among the major classes and subclasses of flaws (the italicized names in parentheses are the names used in the original study).

1. Improper protection domain initialization and enforcement

   a. Improper choice of initial protection domain (*domain*)

   b. Improper isolation of implementation detail (*exposed representations*)

   c. Improper change (*consistency of data over time*)

   d. Improper naming (*naming*)

   e. Improper deallocation or deletion (*residuals*)

2. Improper validation (*validation of operands, queue management dependencies*)

3. Improper synchronization

   a. Improper indivisibility (*interrupted atomic operations*)

   b. Improper sequencing (*serialization*)

4. Improper choice of operand or operation (*critical operator selection errors*)

24.4.2.1   The Flaw Classes

The investigators identified 10 classes of errors and noted that a simple hierarchy could be built; however, the subclasses overlapped. We follow Neumann's reorganization, which eliminates the overlap and is conceptually simpler than the original.

The first class is *improper protection domain initialization and enforcement*; it includes security flaws arising from initialization of the system or programs and enforcement of the security requirements. For example, when a system boots, the protection modes of the file containing the identifiers of all users logged in can be altered by any user. Under most security policies, the initial assignment of protections is incorrect, and hence a vulnerability exists. The subclass in which this particular flaw lies is *improper choice of initial protection domain*, which includes any flaw related to an initial incorrect assignment of privileges or of security and integrity classes, especially when that flaw allows untrusted users to manipulate security-critical data.

Improper protection flaws often arise when an abstraction is mapped into an implementation. The covert timing channel in the IBM KVM/370 system (see the example that begins on page 595) is an example of an *improper isolation of implementation detail*. This subclass also includes flaws that allow users to bypass the operating system and write directly to absolute I/O locations or to alter data structures in ways that are inconsistent with their functions (for example, altering the rights of a process by writing directly to memory).

Another example of an improper protection flaw can arise when a privileged program needs to open a file after checking that some particular condition holds. The goal of the adversary is to have the privileged program open another file for which the condition does not hold. The attack is an attempt to switch the binding of the name between the check and the open. Figure 24–6 shows an example for the UNIX system [224]. This is an instance of the subclass called *improper change*. Another instance of this subclass is when some object, such as a parameter, a file, or the binding of a process to a network port, changes unexpectedly.

If two different objects have the same name, a user may access or execute the wrong object. The classic example is the venerable Trojan horse (see Section 23.2): an attacker crafts a program that will copy data to a hidden location for later viewing and then invoke an editor, and gives it the same name as the widely used system editor. Now, a user invoking the editor may get the correct program or may get the bogus editor. Other examples of *improper naming* arise in networking. The best example occurs when two hosts have the same IP address. Messages intended for one of the hosts may be routed to the other, without any indication to the sender.

Failing to clear memory before it is reallocated, or to clear the disk blocks used in a file before they are assigned to a new file, causes *improper deallocation or deletion* errors. One example occurs when a program dumps core in a publicly readable file and the core dump contains sensitive information such as passwords.

The second major class of flaws is improper validation. These flaws arise from inadequate checking, such as *fingerd*'s lack of bounds checking (with the results shown in Figure 24–7). A second example occurs in some versions of Secure NIS. By default, that protocol maps the *root* user into an untrusted user *nobody* on the theory that the server should not trust any claim to *root* privileges from remote systems unless the credentials asserting those privileges are cryptographic. If the Secure NIS server is misconfigured so that *root* has no private key, however, the remote client can claim to be *root* and supply credentials of the *nobody* user. The flawed system will determine that it cannot validate *root*'s credentials and will promptly check for *nobody*'s private key (because *root* is remapped when needed). Because the credentials will be validated, the remote client will be given *root* privileges [2209].

Improper synchronization arises when processes fail to coordinate their activities. These flaws can occur when operations that should be uninterruptable are interrupted (the oxymoron "interrupting atomic operations" is often used to describe this phenomenon), or the flaws can arise when two processes are not synchronized properly. The flaw in the UNIX *mkdir* command in Version 7 is an example of the first case [1856]. That command created directories by executing a privileged operation to create the directory and then giving it to the requester by changing the ownership of the directory. This should be done as a single operation, but in Version 7 UNIX systems two distinct system calls were needed:

```
mknod("xxx", directory)
chown("xxx", user, group)
```

If an attacker changed the binding of the name "xxx" to refer to the password file between these calls, the attacker would own that file and so could create and delete accounts with impunity. Thus, such a flaw is an example of *improper indivisibility*. The second subtype, *improper sequencing*, arises in at least one one-time password scheme. If the target system is running multiple copies of the server and two users attempt to access the same account, both may be granted access even though the password should be valid for at most one use. Essentially, accesses to the file need to be paired as a read followed by a write; but if multiple copies of the server run, nothing enforces this ordering of access types. This system suffers from improper sequencing.

The last category, *improper choice of operand or operation*, includes calling of inappropriate or erroneous functions. Examples include cryptographic key generation software calling pseudorandom number generation functions that produce predictable sequences of numbers or sequences of numbers with insufficient randomness. The Kerberos authentication system [579], as well as numerous other security-related programs, have suffered from this problem.

24.4.2.2   Analysis Procedure

One of the goals of the PA project was to study the automated detection of instances of the aforementioned flaws in operating systems. The pattern-directed protection evaluation approach sprang from the observations that similar protection errors appear in different systems, and in different functional areas of the same system, and that the success of automated searching depends on the specificity with which the targets of the search are described. These observations, and the desire to develop widely applicable search techniques that nonexperts could use, led to the following procedure:

1. Collect descriptions of protection problems. The project gathered more than 100 security problems from six systems (EXEC-8, GECOS, MULTICS, OS/360, TENEX, and UNIX), not counting minor variations.

2. Convert these problems to a more formalized notation (called *raw error patterns*). This notation expressed a flaw as a set of conditions, possibly including relations among them. The set's membership was minimal, in that if any of the conditions was removed, the raw pattern no longer represented a security flaw. Complicating this process was a lack of a common vocabulary for describing the features of the system and of the flaw; furthermore, because the flaw depended on the security policy, a single error could produce multiple patterns.

3. Eliminate irrelevant features and abstract system-specific components into system-independent components. The goal of this step was to generalize the raw pattern so that it was independent of the specific system on which it arose. As an example, files, memory locations, and other data areas can be abstracted into a "memory cell" and the generalized raw patterns can refer to that cell.

4. Determine which features in the operating system code are relevant to the flaw, and abstract the relevant contexts of those features. These features are expressed independently of the system and are used to construct a pattern from which a search procedure can be derived.

5. Compare the combination of the relevant features in the operating system and their contexts with generic error patterns. This simply executes the search procedure derived in step 4.

EXAMPLE: One MULTICS flaw [210, 211] enabled a user to terminate any process. In early versions of MULTICS, *STOP_PROCESS* was a privileged procedure that halted other processes. A user invoked this procedure with the process ID of the process to be terminated. The gate (user entry point) checked that the user's ID was authorized to stop the process and, if so, called the traffic controller module to halt the process. The flaw was that the process ID could be changed after validation but before being passed to the traffic controller module.

The raw error pattern was as follows:

1. A user process invokes the procedure *STOP_PROCESS* with a user-supplied parameter.

2. The *STOP_PROCESS* interface validates the user-supplied parameter.

3. The traffic controller module uses the user-supplied parameter to identify the process to be terminated.

4. The user may modify the validated parameter between steps 2 and 3.

The generalized pattern for this class of flaws was

```
B:M(x) and for some operation L occurring before M,
        [for operation L which does not modify Value(x),
               Value(x) before L NOT = Value(x) before M]
```

and

```
        Value(x) after L NOT = Value(x) before M
```

This pattern indicated that the memory cell of interest was x and that some operation L occurred. If L did not affect the value of x, then the value of x changed before M; if L did affect the value of x, then the value of x changed after L but before M. In other words, the value of x changed unexpectedly. A similar generalized pattern could be created for a corresponding operating system policy.

From this generalized pattern, we see that this condition arose because two operations (L and M) accessed the variable x. L could read or alter x, but

M simply read x. L occurred before M, and M was critical to B. Furthermore, for this specific example, x was bound to a parameter and so B could be called by user procedures with one parameter. These statements made up the system-independent description of the flaw; the following features were the relevant ones:

1. Procedure callable by user procedures

2. Parameter

3. Code that reads or writes a variable x

4. Code that reads a variable x

5. The temporal relation "before"

6. A critical function

The search procedure was to find a routine in which all those features were present.

1. Ignore everything but user-callable procedures (feature 1).

2. Ignore all user-callable procedures without parameters (feature 2).

3. For each parameter, identify all statements involving reading from or writing to that parameter (features 3 and 4).

4. Identify all statements containing operators that control the flow of execution (feature 5).

5. Ignore all noncritical reads and writes meeting the conditions above (feature 6).

This process was applied to a set of 47 critical procedures (feature 6) in the MULTICS system. A list of reads from, and writes to, parameters was automatically generated, and the list was manually searched for reads, writes, and reads and writes followed by a write; when such a write was found, it was checked for criticality. Of the 47 procedures examined, errors were found in seven of them.

24.4.2.3   Legacy

The Protection Analysis project was the first project to explore automatic detection of security flaws in programs and systems. Its methods were not widely used, in part because of the inability to automate part of the procedure, in part because of its complexity, and in part because the procedure for reducing flaws to system-independent patterns was not complete. However, the efficacy of the idea was demonstrated, and the classification scheme of flaws greatly influenced the study of vulnerabilities. The PA project was a milestone in computer security research and was the last published vulnerability study for some time, because efforts were turned toward development of methods that were free of these errors.

24.4.3   The NRL Taxonomy

In 1992, Landwehr, Bull, McDermott, and Choi [1134] developed a taxonomy to help designers and operators of systems enforce security. They tried to answer three questions: how did the flaw enter the system, when did it enter the system, and where in the system is it manifest? They built three different classification systems, one to answer each of the three questions, and classified more than 50 vulnerabilities in these schemes.

24.4.3.1   The Flaw Classes

The first classification scheme classified vulnerabilities by genesis. The class of *inadvertent* flaws was broken down using the RISOS categories (except that the incomplete and inconsistent validation classes were merged), and the class of *intentional* flaws was broken into *malicious* and *nonmalicious* flaws. Figure 24–8 summarizes these classes. The investigators felt that because most security flaws were inadvertent, better design and coding reviews could eliminate many of them; but if the flaws were intentional, measures such as hiring more trustworthy designers and programmers and doing more security-related testing would be more appropriate.

The second scheme classified vulnerabilities by time of introduction; Figure 24–9 summarizes the subclasses. The investigators wanted to know if security errors were more likely to be introduced at any particular point in the software life cycle in order to determine if focusing efforts on security at any specific point would be helpful. They defined the *development* phase to be all activities up to the release of the initial version of the software, the *maintenance* phase to be all activities leading to changes in the software performed under configuration control, and the *operation* phase to be all activities involving patching of the

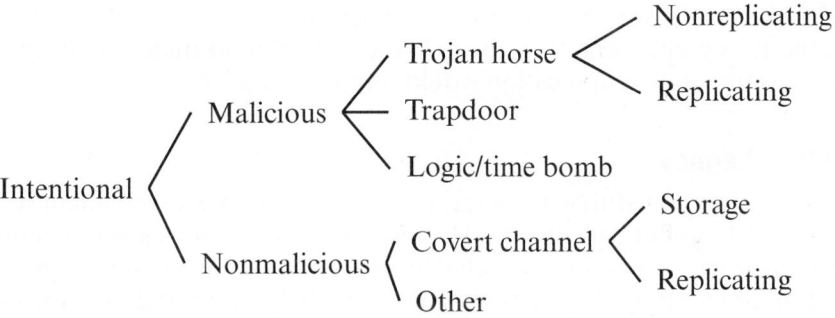

Figure 24–8 NRL taxonomy: flaws by genesis. This diagram shows only the intentional portion of the taxonomy; the inadvertent portion is similar to the RISOS taxonomy except that the first two RISOS classes are merged.

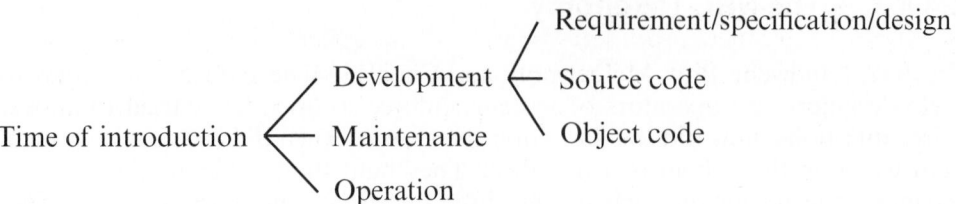

Figure 24–9   NRL taxonomy: flaws by time of introduction.

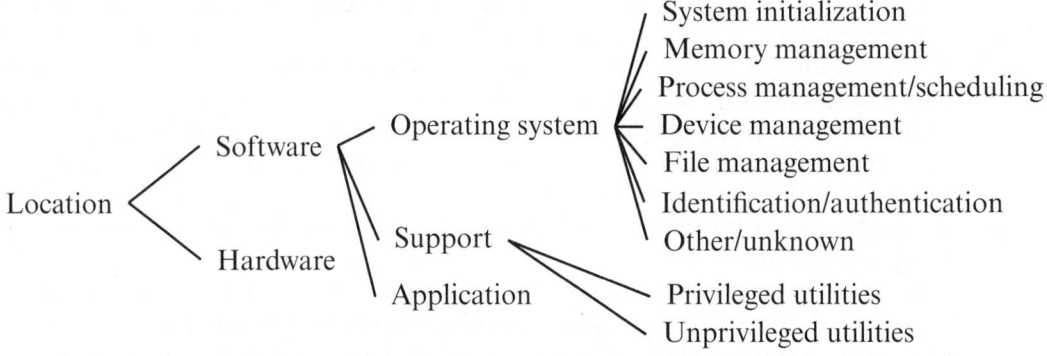

Figure 24–10   NRL taxonomy: flaws by location.

software and not under configuration control (for example, installing a vendor patch).

The third scheme classified by location of the flaw; Figure 24–10 summarizes the classes. The intent is to capture where the flaw manifests itself and to determine if any one location is more likely to be flawed than any other. If so, focusing resources on that location would improve security.

24.4.3.2   Legacy

The investigators noted that their sample size (50 flaws) was too small to draw any statistically sound conclusions. However, by plotting the classes against one another on scatter plots, they concluded that with a large enough sample size, an analyst could study the relationships between location and genesis, genesis and time of introduction, and location and time of introduction. The knowledge gained from such a study would help developers concentrate on the most likely places, times, and causes of security flaws.

Landwehr's taxonomy differs from the others in that it focuses on social processes as well as technical details of flaws. In order to classify a security flaw correctly on the time of introduction and genesis axes, either the precise history of the particular flaw must be known or the classifier must make assumptions. This ambiguity is unsettling, because this information is not always available. However, when available, this information is quite useful, and the study was the first to approach the problem of reducing vulnerabilities by studying the environments in which they were introduced.

24.4.4   Aslam's Model

Aslam [87] developed a classification scheme for security flaws that categorized faults and grouped similar faults together. It differed from both the PA and RISOS studies in that it drew on software fault studies to develop its categories, and it focused specifically on implementation flaws in the UNIX system. Moreover, the categories and classes in both PA and RISOS had considerable overlap; Aslam presented a decision procedure for classifying faults unambiguously. This made it useful for organizing vulnerability data in a database, one of the goals of his study.

24.4.4.1   The Flaw Classes

Aslam distinguished between *coding faults*, which were introduced during software development, and *emergent faults*, which resulted from incorrect initialization, use, or application. For example, a program that fails to check the length of an input string before storing it in an array has a coding fault, but allowing a message transfer agent to forward mail to an arbitrary file on the system is an emergent fault. The mail agent is performing exactly according to specification, but the results produce a dangerous security hole.

The class of coding faults is subdivided into *synchronization errors* and *condition validation errors*. Synchronization errors arise when a timing window between two operations allows a fault to be exploited or when operations are improperly serialized. For example, the *xterm* flaw discussed previously is a classic synchronization error. Condition validation errors arise when bounds are not checked, access rights are ignored, input is not validated, or authentication and identification fails. The *fingerd* flaw is an example of this.

Emergent faults are either *configuration errors* or *environment faults*. The former arise from installing a program in the wrong place, with the wrong initialization or configuration information, or with the wrong permissions. For example, if the *tftp* daemon is installed so that any file in the system can be accessed, the installer has caused a configuration error. Environment faults are those faults introduced by the environment as opposed to those from the code or from the configuration. On older UNIX systems, for example, any shell whose name began with "-" was interactive, so an attacker could link a setuid to *root* shell script to the name "-gotcha" and execute it, thereby getting a setuid to root shell [212].

Aslam's decision procedure [87] consisted of a set of questions for each class of flaws, the questions being ordered so that each flaw had exactly one classification.

24.4.4.2   Legacy

The contribution of Aslam's taxonomy was to tie security flaws to software faults and to introduce a precise classification scheme. In this scheme, each vulnerability belonged to exactly one class of security flaws. Furthermore, the decision procedure was well-defined and unambiguous, leading to a simple mechanism for representing similar flaws in a database.

24.4.5   Comparison and Analysis

Consider the flaws described in Section 24.3.1. Both depend on the interaction of two processes: the trusted process (*xterm* or *fingerd*) and a second process (the attacker). For the *xterm* flaw, the attacker deletes the existing log file and inserts a link to the password file; for the *fingerd* flaw, the attacker writes a name the length of which exceeds the buffer size. Furthermore, the processes use operating system services to communicate. So, three processes are involved: the flawed process, the attacker process, and the operating system service routines. The view of the flaw when considered from the perspective of any of these processes may differ from the view when considered from the perspective of the other two. For example, from the point of view of the flawed process, the flaw may be an incomplete validation of a parameter because the process does not adequately check the parameter it passes to the operating system by means of a system call. From the point of view of the operating system, however, the flaw may be a violable prohibition/limit, because the parameter may refer to an address outside the space of the process. Which classification is appropriate?

Levels of abstraction muddy this issue even more. At the lowest level, the flaw may be, say, an inconsistent parameter validation because successive system calls do not check that the argument refers to the same object. At a higher level, this may be characterized as a race condition or an asynchronous validation/inadequate serialization problem. At an even higher level, it may be seen as an exploitable logic error because a resource (object) can be deleted while in use.

The levels of abstraction are defined differently for every system, and this contributes to the ambiguity. In the following discussion, the "higher" the level, the more abstract it is, without implying precisely where in the abstraction hierarchy either level occurs. Only the relationship, not the distance, of the levels is important in this context.

We now expand on these questions using our two sample flaws.

24.4.5.1   The *xterm* Log File Flaw

We begin with the PA taxonomy. From the point of view of the *xterm* process, the flaw is clearly an improper change flaw because the problem is that between the time of check (*access*) and the time of use (*open*), the referent of the name changes. However, with respect to the attacker process, the flaw is an improper deallocation or deletion flaw because something (in this case, the binding between the name and the referent) is being deleted improperly. And from the operating system's point of view, the flaw is an improper indivisibility flaw because the opening of the file should atomically check that the access is allowed.

Reconsider the problem at a higher level of abstraction from the point of view of the operating system. At this level, a directory object is seen simply as an object; deletion and creation of files in the directory are semantically equivalent to writing in the directory, and obtaining file status and opening a file require that the directory be read. In this case, the flaw may be seen as a violation of the Bernstein conditions [177] (requiring no reading during writing, and a single writer), which means that the flaw is one of improper sequencing.

At the abstraction level corresponding to design, the attacking process should not be able to write into the directory in the first place, leading to a characterization of the flaw as one of improper choice of initial protection domain. This is not a valid characterization at the implementation level because both the attacking process and the *xterm* are being executed by the same user and the semantics of the implementation of the UNIX operating system require that both processes be able to access the same objects in the same way.

At the implementation level, with respect to the *xterm* process and the RISOS taxonomy, the *xterm* flaw is clearly an asynchronous validation/inadequate serialization flaw because the file access is checked and then opened nonatomically. From the point of view of the attacker, the ability to delete the file makes the flaw an exploitable logic error as well as a violable prohibition/limit flaw because the attacker is manipulating a binding in the system's domain. And from the operating system's point of view, the flaw is an inconsistent parameter validation flaw because the access check and open use the same parameters, but the objects they refer to are different, and this is not checked.

Interestingly, moving up in the hierarchy of abstractions, the flaw may once again be characterized as a violation of the Bernstein conditions, or the nonatomicity of an operation that should be atomic; in either case, it is an asynchronous validation/inadequate serialization flaw. So the process view prevails.

At the design level, a write being allowed where it should not be is an inadequate identification/authentication/authorization flaw because the resource (the containing directory) is not adequately protected. Again, owing to the nature of the protection model of the UNIX operating system, this would not be a valid characterization at the implementation level.

Hence, this single flaw has several different characterizations. At the implementation level, depending on the classifier's point of view, the *xterm* flaw can be classified in three different ways. Trying to abstract the underlying principles under one taxonomy places the flaw in a fourth class, and under the other taxonomy, one view (the *xterm* process view) prevails. Moving up to the design level, a completely different classification is needed. Clearly, the ambiguity in the PA and RISOS classifications makes it difficult to classify flaws with precision.

The classification under the NRL taxonomy depends on whether this flaw was intentional or not; the history is unclear. If it was intentional, at the lowest level, it is an inadvertent flaw of serialization/aliasing; if it was unintentional (because on earlier systems *xterm* need not be privileged), it is a nonmalicious: other flaw. In either case, at higher levels of abstraction, the classification would parallel that of the RISOS scheme. Given the history, the time of introduction is clearly during development, and the location is in the class support: privileged utilities. So, this taxonomy classifies this particular flaw unambiguously on two axes. However, the third classification is ambiguous even when points of view and levels of abstraction are ignored.

The selection criteria for fault classification in Aslam's taxonomy places the flaw in the object installed with incorrect permissions class from the point of view of the attacking program (because the attacking program can delete the file), in the access rights validation error class from the point of view of the *xterm* program (because *xterm* does not properly validate the file at the time of access), and in the improper or inadequate serialization error class from the point of view of the operating system (because the deletion and creation should not be interspersed between the access and open). As an aside, in the absence of the explicit decision procedure, the flaw could also have been placed in a fourth class, race conditions. So, although this taxonomy classifies flaws into specific classes, the class into which a flaw is placed is a function of the decision procedure as well as the nature of the flaw itself. The fact that this ambiguity of classification is not a unique characteristic of one flaw is apparent when we study the second flaw—the *fingerd* flaw.

24.4.5.2   The *fingerd* Buffer Overflow Flaw

With respect to the *fingerd* process and the PA taxonomy, the buffer overflow flaw is clearly an improper validation flaw because the problem is failure to check parameters, leading to addressing of memory not in its memory space by referencing through an out-of-bounds pointer value. However, with respect to the attacker process (the *finger* program), the flaw is one of improper choice of operand or operation because an operand (the data written onto the connection) is improper (specifically, too long, and arguably not what *fingerd* is to be given). And from the operating system's point of view, the flaw is an improper isolation of implementation detail flaw because the user is allowed to write directly into what should be in the space of the process (the return address) and to execute what should be treated as data only.

Moving still higher in the layers of abstraction, the storage space of the return address is a variable or an object. From the operating system's point of view, this makes the flaw an improper change flaw because a parameter— specifically, the return address—changes unexpectedly. From the *fingerd* point of view, however, the more abstract issue is the execution of data (the input); this is improper validation—specifically, failure to validate the type of the instructions being executed. So, again, the flaw is an improper validation flaw.

At the highest level, the system is changing a security-related value in memory and is executing data that should not be executable. Hence, this is again an improper choice of initial protection domain flaw. But this is not a valid characterization at the implementation level because the architectural design of the system requires the return address to be stored on the stack, just as the input buffer is allocated on the stack, and, because the hardware supporting most versions of the UNIX operating system cannot protect specific words in memory (instead, protection is provided for all words on a page or segment), the system requires that the process be able to write to, and read from, its stack.

With respect to the *fingerd* process using the RISOS taxonomy, the buffer overflow flaw is clearly an incomplete parameter validation flaw because the problem is failure to check parameters, allowing the buffer to overflow. However, with respect to the *fingerd* process, the flaw is a violable prohibition/limit flaw because the limit on input data to be sent can be ignored (violated). And from the operating system's point of view, the flaw is an inadequate identification/authentication/authorization flaw because the user is allowed to write directly to what should be in the space of the process (the return address) and to execute what should be treated as data only.

Moving still higher, the storage space of the return address is a variable or an object. From the operating system's point of view, this makes the flaw one of asynchronous validation/inadequate serialization because a parameter—specifically, the return address—changes unexpectedly. From the *fingerd* point of view, however, the more abstract issue is the execution of data (the input); this is improper validation—specifically, failure to validate the type of the instructions being executed. So the flaw is an inadequate identification/authentication/authorization flaw.

At the highest level, this is again an inadequate identification/authentication/authorization flaw because the system is changing a security-related value in memory and is executing data that should not be executable. Again, owing to the nature of the protection model of the UNIX operating system, this would not be a valid characterization at the implementation level.

The NRL taxonomy suffers from similar problems in its classification by genesis, which—for inadvertent flaws, as this is—uses the RISOS taxonomy. In this case, the time of introduction is clearly during development, and the location is in the support: privileged utilities class. So, this taxonomy classifies this particular flaw unambiguously on two axes. Note that knowledge of the history of the program is needed to perform the classification. A rogue programmer could easily have inserted this vulnerability into a patch distributed to system administrators, in which case the genesis classification would be as a malicious flaw, falling in the trapdoor category, and the time of introduction would be in the operating class.

Finally, under Aslam's taxonomy, the flaw is a boundary condition error from the point of view of the attacking program (because the limit on input data can be ignored) and from the point of view of the *fingerd* program (because the process writes beyond a valid address boundary) and an environment fault from the point of view of the operating system (because the error occurs when the program is executed on a particular machine—specifically, a stack-based machine). As an aside, in the absence of the explicit decision procedure, the flaw could also have been placed in the class of access rights validation errors because the code executed in the input buffer should be data only and because the return address is outside the protection domain of the process and yet is altered by it. So, again, this taxonomy satisfies the decision procedure criterion, but not the uniqueness criterion.

The RISOS classifications are somewhat more consistent among the levels of abstraction because the improper authorization classification runs through the layers of abstraction. However, point of view plays a role here because that classification applies to the operating system's point of view at two levels and to the process view between them. This, again, limits the usefulness of the classification scheme. Because Landwehr's work is based on RISOS, it has similar problems.

24.4.5.3   Summary

Flaw classification is not consistent among different levels of abstraction. Ideally, a flaw should be classified the same at all levels (possibly with more refinement at lower levels). This problem is ameliorated somewhat by the overlap of the flaw classifications because as one refines the flaws, the flaws may shift classes. However, the classes themselves should be distinct; they are not, leading to this problem.

The point of view is also a problem. The point of view should not affect the class into which a flaw falls, but, as the examples show, it clearly does. So, can we use this as a tool for classification—that is, identify flaws on the basis of the three classes into which they fall? The problem is that the classes are not partitions; they overlap, and so it is often not clear which class should be used for a component of the triple.

In short, the *xterm* and *fingerd* examples demonstrate weaknesses of the PA, RISOS, NRL, and Aslam classifications: either the classifications of some flaws are not well defined or they are arbitrary and vary with the levels of abstraction and points of view from which the flaws are considered.

24.5   Standards

Although not frameworks in the above sense, several descriptive databases have been used to examine vulnerabilities. Here, we examine the two most widely used ones.

24.5.1   Common Vulnerabilities and Exposures (CVE)

Originally called "Common Vulnerabilities Enumeration" (CVE), the CVE grew out of a need to standardize terminology for vulnerabilities [2134]. Vendors often identified, and described, the same vulnerability differently. Thus, one could not tell whether two vulnerabilities were the same without analysis. In addition, databases of attacks viewed vulnerabilities as parts of attacks; databases of software faults considered vulnerabilities as faults; and other databases described vulnerabilities through their own perspective. Correlating the vulnerabilities in the databases required considerable analysis.

CVE's goal was to change this state of affairs. Started at MITRE Corp. [1243], it assigned a label to each vulnerability. Then vendors and databases could simply cite the number to make clear which vulnerability was being discussed. CVE was designed to enable interoperability among the many tools and databases that identified vulnerabilities, and thus needed to be independent of their perspectives. MITRE also developed governance procedures, including a CVE Board to provide input on the nature of specific vulnerabilities, to determine whether two or more vulnerabilities overlap, and the CVE program's management and direction [116]. CVE Numbering Authorities are organizations authorized to assign CVE numbers for a distinct scope, usually for their products. Initially, CVE numbers had exactly four digits to simplify automated parsing. With the explosion of vulnerability reports, MITRE and the CVE Board decided to allow CVE numbers to have four or more digits; the change took effect in January 2014.

A CVE entry consists of several fields. It gives an identifier consisting of the year the CVE number is requested and a CVE number, a brief description, and then references public reports from groups that have reported this vulnerability.

EXAMPLE: The entry for the *xterm* race condition in Section 24.3.1 contains the following information [2135]:

CVE-ID: CVE-1999-0965
Description: Race condition in xterm allows users to modify arbitrary files via the logging option
References:

- CERT:CA-93.17
- XF:xterm

Date Entry Created: 20000104

The entry was created on January 4, 2000. The Computer Emergency Response Team (CERT) created an advisory (CA-93.17) for this vulnerability, and the X-Force, a corporate vulnerability reporting group, reported this as "xterm."

A buffer overflow in a function in the GNU C library has the following entry [2136]:

CVE-ID: CVE-2016-3706
Description: Stack-based buffer overflow in the getaddrinfo function in sysdeps/posix/getaddrinfo.c in the GNU C Library (aka glibc or libc6) allows remote attackers to cause a denial of service (crash) via vectors involving hostent conversion. NOTE: this vulnerability exists because of an incomplete fix for CVE-2013-4458.

References:

CONFIRM:https://sourceware.org/bugzilla/show_bug.cgi?id=20010
CONFIRM:https://sourceware.org/git/gitweb.cgi?p=glibc.git;
        h=4ab2ab03d4351914ee53248dc5aef4a8c88ff8b9
CONFIRM:http://www-01.ibm.com/support/docview.wss?uid
        =swg21995039
SUSE:openSUSE-SU-2016:1527
URL:http://lists.opensuse.org/opensuse-updates/2016-
        06/msg00030.html
SUSE:openSUSE-SU-2016:1779
URL:http://lists.opensuse.org/opensuse-updates/2016-
        07/msg00039.html
BID:88440
URL:http://www.securityfocus.com/bid/88440

Date Entry Created: 20160330

This more recent vulnerability shows several more public announcements of the vulnerability.[2] SUSE is a version of Linux, and the BID entry refers to the Bugtraq Identification database. The entry was created on March 30, 2016.

The CVE database was started in 1999, and currently has over 82,000 entries. It is used by over 150 organizations, including major security vendors such as McAfee, Inc., Tripwire, Inc., Trend Micro, Inc., and Symantec, computer and software vendors such as Apple, Inc., Juniper Networks, Inc., IBM, and Red Hat, Inc., and other groups such as the CERT/CC and the U.S. National Institute for Standards and Technology [487].

24.5.2   Common Weaknesses and Exposures (CWE)

As work to expand the CVE database continued, the developers realized that another database was needed to list the weaknesses that underlie these vulnerabilities. Such a database would provide useful information to analysts describing vulnerabilities in programs, and especially to describe the coverage of automated code analyzers. This database would enumerate the weaknesses, idiosyncrasies, flaws, and faults (WIFF), and so initially was the Common WIFF Enumeration, or CWE; the acronym subsequently evolved to Common Weaknesses and Exposures. The developers worked with NIST, the vulnerabilities research community, and vendors to develop the list. The initial proposed CWE contained 28 weaknesses [1256].

The CWE is a list of common software weaknesses [2137]. It encompasses most of the software weaknesses underlying the vulnerabilities in the CVE list. An entry in the CWE list contains an identifier, description, applicable

---

[2]The second, third, fifth, and seventh lines in the References of the GNU C library example are shown as two lines for readability.

environment, common consequences, how likely the weakness is to be exploited, examples, possible mitigations, a list of relationships to other CWE entries, and other information. The web interface to the database allows a variety of views of each entry, so the user can focus on the parts of the entry deemed most critical.

Although organized as a list, the CWE elements can be viewed as a graph because some weaknesses are refinements of others. It is not, however, a tree because some nodes with no children have multiple parents.

EXAMPLE: The "Development Concepts" (CWE-699) view has a number of child entries. One, the "Violation of Secure Design Principles" (CWE-657), is the parent to "Execution with Unnecessary Privileges," which has no children. However, it is a child of numerous other entries such as "Privilege/Sandbox Issues" (CWE-265) and "Improper Privilege Management" (CWE-269). The former is a child of "Permissions, Privileges, and Access Controls" (CWE-264), which is in turn a child of "Security Features" (CWE-254); that entry in turn is a child of "Source Code" (CWE-18), itself a child of "Code" (CWE-17), and that entry has no parent.

There are seven types of entries. In these, a "weakness" is defined as a "mistake in software that could contribute to the introduction of vulnerabilities within that software" [2145].

- A *category* entry is an entry that identifies a set of entries having a characteristic in common with the current entry.
- A *chain* entry is a sequence of distinct weaknesses that can be linked together within software; for example, one weakness can create the conditions necessary to cause another weakness to become exploitable.
- A *compound element composite* entry is an entry that consists of multiple weaknesses that all must be present to enable an exploit.
- A *view* entry provides a view of the CWE database for a particular weakness or set of weaknesses.
- A *weakness variant* entry presents a weakness that is described in terms of a particular technology or language.
- A *weakness base* entry is an entry that describes weakness more abstractly than a weakness variant entry, but in sufficient detail to lead to specific methods of detection and remediation.
- A *weakness class* entry is an entry that describes a weakness in a way that is independent of any specific language or technology.

EXAMPLE: An example of a view entry is CWE-631, Resource-specific Weaknesses. It refers to those CWE entries that occur when the software handles resources of different types. Its children are CWE-632 (Weaknesses that Affect Files or Directories), CWE-633 (Weaknesses that Affect memory), and CWE-634

(Weaknesses that Affect System Processes). These in turn are parents of other weaknesses.

An example of a chain entry is CWE-680, Integer Overflow to Buffer Overflow. It begins with integer overflow (CWE-190), which leads to a failure to restrict some operation to within the bounds of a buffer (CWE-119). Other composite entries may have chains of more than two entries.

An example of a composite entry is CWE-61, UNIX Symbolic Link (Symlink) Following. It requires five weaknesses to be present before it can be exploited, including a particular setting of permissions (CWE-275), the symbolic name not being mapped to the right object (CWE-3856), and concurrent execution using a shared resource and lacking proper synchronization (CWE-362).

One important element of the CWE entries is the abstraction level of the weakness because this tries to avoid the abstraction problem described in Section 24.4.5. The CWE defines three levels of abstraction [2153]:

- *Class* describes a weakness at an abstract level, but independently of any particular programming language or environment.
- *Base* describes a weakness at an abstract level but with enough detail for the reader to develop specific methods of detection, prevention, and mediation for a technology.
- *Variant* describes a weakness at a low level, usually tied to a specific programming language, system, or technology.

These levels are not formally defined, but they provide a useful demarcation of vulnerabilities related to design, implementation, or both design and implementation. The importance of this field is it can be used to determine which weaknesses are most relevant to the current step in the software development life cycle.

The CWE list enables developers to anticipate problems and guard against them. By providing a set of entries describing weaknesses, developers can determine which tools are best suited for their use. Like CVE, CWE provides a common language for describing weaknesses.

24.6   Gupta and Gligor's Theory of Penetration Analysis

Gupta and Gligor [836] developed a formal analysis technique arising from failure to perform adequate checks. This is not a vulnerabilities model, because it presupposes classification—that is, the vulnerabilities that their technique detects are asserted to be vulnerabilities arising from failure to perform adequate checks. As a scheme for classifying flaws, this obviously is not adequate. As a method for detecting previously undetected flaws of the designated class, it is very elegant.

We present this model here because it is an excellent example of the use of a classification scheme.

Gupta and Gligor make two hypotheses.

Hypothesis of Penetration Patterns. *"[S]ystem flaws that cause a large class of penetration patterns can be identified in system (i.e., TCB) source code as incorrect/absent condition checks or integrated flows that violate the intentions of the system designers."*[3]

If true, this hypothesis implies that an appropriate set of design and implementation principles would prevent vulnerabilities. This leads to the next hypothesis:

Hypothesis of Penetration-Resistant Systems. *"[A] system (i.e., TCB) is largely resistant to penetration if it adheres to a specific set of design properties."*[4]

Gupta and Gligor select and formalize several properties, and from those properties derive checks to determine if the system correctly obeys them.

- System isolation or tamperproofness, which states that users must not be able to tamper with the system. This encompasses parameter checking at the system boundary, separation of user and system addresses, and allowing entry to the system only at well-defined gates at which parameters and privileges can be validated.
- System noncircumventability, which states that the system must check all references to objects.
- Consistency of global objects belonging to the system, with respect to both timing and storage.
- Elimination of undesirable system and user dependencies, which usually refers to prevention of denial-of-service attacks.

For modeling purposes, Gupta and Gligor focus on the consistency principle and set as their policy that accesses to system entities and functions are allowed only if the conditions for access are validated atomically.

24.6.1 The Flow-Based Model of Penetration Analysis

Gupta and Gligor's model focuses on the flow of control during the validation of parameters. Consider the system function *rmdir* [837]. It takes a single parameter. When invoked, it allocates space for a copy of the parameter on the stack and copies that parameter into the allocated storage. Thus, control flows through three

---

[3]See [836], p. 67.
[4]See [836], p. 67.

steps: the allocation of storage, the binding of the parameter with the formal argument, and the copying of the formal argument (parameter) to the storage. The failure to check the length of the parameter is the flaw.

The model represents the system as a sequence of states and state transitions. The *abstract cell set* $C = \{c_1, \ldots, c_n\}$ is the set of system entities that holds information. The *system function set* $F = \{f_1, \ldots, f_x\}$ is the set of all system functions that the user may invoke; those involving time delays (such as *sleep* and *pause*) are also in the set $Z \subseteq F$. The *system condition set* $R = \{r_1, \ldots, r_m\}$ is the set of all parameter checks. The information flow set is the set of all possible information flows between pairs of abstract cells and is represented as $IF = C \times C$, where each (c_i, c_j) means that information flows from c_i to c_j. Similarly, the call relationship between system functions is denoted by $SF = F \times F$, where each (f_i, f_j) means that f_i calls f_j or f_i returns to f_j. The latter two sets capture the flow of information and control throughout the system.

System-critical functions are functions that the analysts deem critical with respect to penetration; examples include functions that cause time delays (because this may allow a window during which checked parameters are changed) and functions that can cause the system to crash. These functions are represented by the set $K = \{k_1, \ldots, k_s\}$. System entry points are the gates through which user processes invoke system functions; they are represented by the set $E = e_1, \ldots, e_t$.

EXAMPLE: Consider the *rmdir* function. Figure 24–11 shows the flow of control and information. *fname* points to a global entity and therefore is a member of C. *rmdir* is a system function and thus is in F; it is also an entry point and thus is in E. The parameter *fname* cannot be an illegal address, and the string it points to

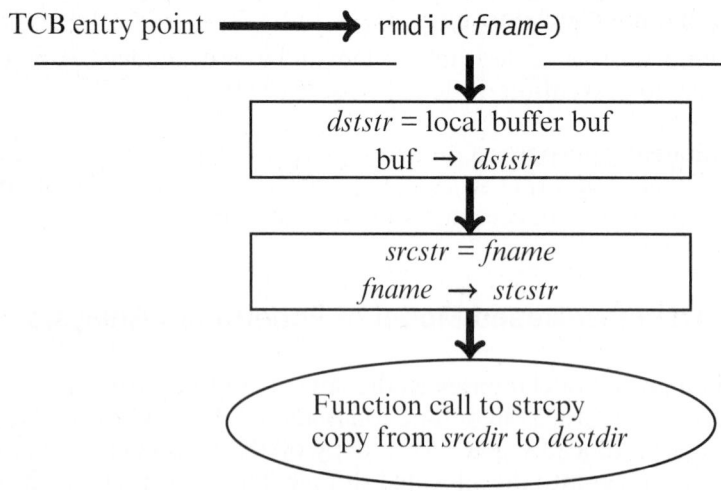

Figure 24–11 The integrated flow path for the *rmdir* system function in one version of the UNIX operating system. From [837], Figure 11(a), p. 178.

must be smaller than the space allocated to *buf*. This means that the predicates *islegal(fname)* and *length(fname)* < *spacefor(buf)* are in R. We deem *strcpy* to be a system-critical function because it does not check destination bounds or source addresses, so *strcpy* is in K. Because information flows from *fname* to *buf*, the tuple $(fname, buf) \in IF$, and because the *rmdir* function calls *strcpy*, $(rmdir, strcpy) \in SF$.

The alter set $AC = \{(c_1, R_1), \dots, (c_n, R_n)\}$, where $R_i \subseteq R$, is the set of abstract cells that can be altered and the conditions that must be validated first. The predicate $Element(c_i, R_i)$ means that the conditions in R_i must be checked before c_i is viewed or altered. The view set $VC = \{(c_1, R'_1), \dots, (c_n, R'_n)\}$, where $R'_i \subseteq R$, is the set of abstract cells that can be viewed and the conditions that must be validated first. The critical function set $KF = \{(k_1, R''_1), \dots, (k_s, R''_s)\}$ and the entry point set $EF = \{(e_1, R'''_1), \dots, (e_t, R'''_t)\}$ are defined analogously.

EXAMPLE: Before *strcpy* views *fname*, it must validate the address as legal, and before *strcpy* alters *buf*, it must validate the size of *fname* as being small enough. Thus, $(strcpy, islegal(fname) \wedge length(fname) < spacefor(buf)) \in KF$.

The model defines three functions for capturing the history of transitions. Each triple in the *altered cells set* $ACS = \{(c_1, e_1, pathcond_1), \dots, \}$ means that c_i has been altered by invoking entry point e_i, and $pathcond_i \subseteq IF \cup SF \cup R$ is the sequence (ordered set) of information flows, function flows, and conditions along the path. The *viewed cells set* $VCS = \{(c_1, e_1, pathcond'_1), \dots, \}$ and the *critical functions invoked set* $KFS = \{(k_1, e_1, pathcond''_1), \dots, \}$ are defined analogously. The triplet (ACS, VCS, KFS) makes up the state of the system.

A *state* is said to be *penetration-resistant* if it meets the following three requirements:

1. For all states $(c, e, p) \in ACS$:
   (a) The conditions associated with the entry point $e \in EF$ are a subset of the conditions checked in p.
   (b) The conditions associated with the cell $c \in AC$ are a subset of the conditions checked in p.
   (c) There is a subsequence of p that contains the last element of p, contains the conditions in part (b), and does not contain any elements $(f, g) \in SF$ with $f \in Z$ or $g \in Z$.

2. Requirement 1, but for $(c, e, p) \in VCS$ rather than ACS

3. Requirement 1, but for $(k, e, p) \in KFS$ rather than $(c, e, p) \in ACS$

These requirements define a state invariant SI. Intuitively, SI says that if the system function checks all conditions on the global variables and parameters to be altered (requirement 1) or viewed (requirement 2), and all conditions on the system-critical functions (requirement 3), then the system cannot be penetrated using a technique that exploits a failure to check the conditions. Part (a) of each requirement requires checking of conditions on entry. Part (b) requires checking of conditions on the memory locations or system-critical functions. Part (c) requires checking of changes in previously checked parameters as a result of a time delay caused by a function.

State transition rules control the updating of information as the system changes. If τ is a state transition function and $S = (ACS, VCS, KFS)$ is the current state, then $\tau(S) = S' = (ACS', VCS', KFS')$. In this model, τ is *alter_cell*, *view_cell*, or *invoke_crit_func*.

The function *alter_cell*(c, e, p) checks that $c \in C$, $e \in E$, and $p \in IF \cup SF \cup R$ and that requirement 1 holds. If so, $ACS' = ACS \cup \{(c, e, p)\}$, $VCS' = VCS$, and $KFS' = KFS$. If not, the function has attempted to move the system into a state that is not penetration-resistant.

The function *view_cell*(c, e, p) checks that $c \in C$, $e \in E$, and $p \in IF \cup SF \cup R$, and that requirement 2 holds. If so, $ACS' = ACS$, $VCS' = VCS \cup \{(c, e, p)\}$, and $KFS' = KFS$. If not, the function has attempted to move the system into a state that is not penetration-resistant.

Finally, the function *invoke_crit_func*(k, e, p) checks that $k \in K$, $e \in E$, and $p \in IF \cup SF \cup R$ and that requirement 3 holds. If so, $ACS' = ACS$, $VCS' = VCS$, and $KFS' = KFS \cup \{(f, e, p)\}$. If not, the function has attempted to move the system into a state that is not penetration-resistant.

> **Theorem 24.1.** Let the system be in a state V that satisfies the state invariant SI. Then, if a state transition function is applied to V, the resulting state V' will also satisfy SI.

EXAMPLE: Consider the *rmdir* function, and assume that the system is in a penetration-resistant state. The call to *strcpy* is a state transition in which a system-critical function is invoked, so the tuple is (*strcpy*, *rmdir*, p), where p is the sequence of conditions, information flows, and function invocations so far. The *invoke_crit_func* function tells us that requirement 3 must hold. Because there is no condition associated with the entry point *rmdir*, 3(a) holds. However, requirement 3(b) does not hold: the conditions for *strcpy*, {*islegal*(*fname*) $\land$ *length*(*fname*) < *spacefor*(*buf*)} $\not\subset p$ because they have not been checked within the TCB. After the *rmdir* system call, the system is no longer in a penetration-resistant state. The specific attack on this system call is to give it an argument sufficiently long to overflow *buf* and alter the stack, much as the *fingerd* bug in Section 24.3.1 did.

24.6.2   The Automated Penetration Analysis Tool

Gupta and Gligor designed and implemented an automated penetration analysis (APA) tool that performed this testing. The *primitive flow generator* reduces

C statements to Prolog facts recording data and control flow information, condition statements, and sequencing information. Two other modules, the *information flow integrator* and the *function flow integrator*, integrate execution paths derived from the primitive flow statements to show pertinent flows of information, flows of control among functions, and how the conditions affect the execution paths. The *condition set consistency prover* analyzes conditions along an execution path and reports inconsistencies. Finally, the *flaw detection module* applies the Hypothesis of Penetration Patterns by determining whether the conditions for each entry point conform to penetration-resistant specifications.

24.6.3   Discussion

The Gupta-Gligor theory presents a formalization of one of the classes of vulnerabilities—specifically, inconsistent and incomplete parameter validation (possibly combined with improper change). The formalization builds preconditions for executing system functions; the APA tool verifies that these preconditions hold (or determines that they do not).

Whether or not this technique can be generalized to other classes of flaws is an open question. In particular, the technique is extremely sensitive to the level of detail at which the system is analyzed and to the quality of the specifications describing the policy. This work is best seen as a foundation on which future automation of penetration analysis may build and a reinforcement of the idea that automated tools can aid an analyst in uncovering system vulnerabilities.

Could the theory be generalized to classify vulnerabilities? The model assumes an existing classification scheme (specifically, improper or inadequate checks) and describes a technique and a tool for detecting vulnerabilities of this class. Were the purpose of the model to classify vulnerabilities (rather than to detect them), basing classification on the nature of the tools that detect them is tautological and a single vulnerability could fall into several classes depending on how the tool was crafted. Hence, such an (inverted) application of the Gupta-Gligor approach would suffer from the same flaws that plague the other classification schemes. However, the purpose of the model is to detect, not to classify, vulnerabilities of one specific type.

24.7   Summary

As the Internet has grown, so has connectivity, enabling attackers to break into an increasing number of systems. Often very inexperienced attackers appear to have used extremely sophisticated techniques to break into systems, but on investigation it can be seen that they have used attack tools. Indeed, attack tools are becoming very widespread, and most systems cannot resist a determined attack.

In the past, attention was focused on building secure systems. Because of the large number of nonsecure systems in use today, it is unrealistic to expect that new, secure systems will be deployed widely enough to protect the companies and individuals connected to the Internet. Instead, existing systems will be made more secure, and as vulnerabilities are found they will be eliminated or monitored. The vulnerability models discussed in this chapter guide us in improving the software engineering cycle and in reducing the risk of introducing new vulnerabilities, and penetration analyses enable us to test admittedly nonsecure systems to determine whether or not they are sufficiently secure for the uses to which they are put.

24.8   Research Issues

Research in the area of vulnerability analysis focuses on discovery of previously unknown vulnerabilities and quantification of the security of systems according to some metric. All agree that the security of existing systems is poor—but how poor is another matter.

Adaptive security springs from fault-tolerant methods. When a system is under attack, security mechanisms limit the actions of suspect processes. When a system is not under attack, less stringent controls are applied. Under what conditions should one begin adapting in order to minimize the impact of the attack while still maximizing openness? Do the attack-detecting sensors themselves introduce vulnerabilities? Minimizing false alarms (and thus unnecessary impact on system performance) is a difficult problem.

The best test of a model is how well it describes real-world phenomena. Ideally, a vulnerability model can describe all the security holes in a system and can provide guidance on how to verify or refute the existence of those holes. Most vulnerability models are based on formal methods. Those methods are adapted to systems in which security policies cannot be rigorously defined. One research issue is how to retain enough formalism to prove that a model works and yet eliminate any formalism that is not relevant to the existing system.

Vulnerability databases add to this question. They provide much of the historical basis for the first step in the Flaw Hypothesis Methodology. The databases support research on characterization of vulnerabilities. The data collected about the vulnerabilities varies depending on the purpose of the database. Sharing data raises problems of trust and interpretation. Two workshops on sharing information from vulnerability databases concluded that a central database is impractical and emphasized the need to share data. One interesting aspect of such sharing is the provision of a common numbering scheme. Each database uses its own scheme but also includes the number from the common enumeration scheme. Researchers at MITRE have pioneered a numbering scheme called Common Vulnerabilities and Exposures (CVE), which provides each vulnerability with a unique number. Vendors and vulnerability databases can use these numbers to correlate vulnerabilities. What constitutes a "vulnerability" for the purposes of this scheme is vague. Currently, an editorial board determines whether a proposed vulnerability is one vulnerability, many vulnerabilities, a repeat of a vulnerability that has already been numbered, or not a vulnerability.

Finally, the precise definitions of "attack" and "vulnerability" are under study. Although the current definitions have much in common, the various nuances of each paper and study color its precise meaning. Rigorous definitions of these two terms would lead to a clearer understanding of how and why systems fail.

24.9   Further Reading

Geer and Harthorne [755] assert that penetration testing is an art. Thompson [1874] gives an overview of testing applications. McLaughlin et al. discuss penetration testing in the smart grid [1295]. Dimkov et al. present methodologies for using social engineering in penetration testing [569].

Studies of vulnerabilities analyses and countermeasures have become common. For example, many buffer overflow analyses and countermeasures have been developed [32, 193, 228, 237, 406, 467, 469, 470, 880, 1099, 1717, 1952, 2086]. Race conditions too have been studied thoroughly, especially in the context of time-of-check to time-of-use flaws [226, 269, 336, 337, 525, 1162, 1894, 1988, 2068]. Similar analyses exist for other types of vulnerabilities.

Some analyses focus on vulnerabilities in specific domains such as electronic voting systems [121, 1088], automobiles [394, 1096], medical devices [551, 856] and hardware [581, 712, 1056]. These studies, and others, indicate that security is usually an afterthought in systems developed for nontechnical applications.

Numerous techniques have been used to find vulnerabilities such as static and dynamic analysis [981, 1201, 1630, 1931, 1977, 2034, 2040]. Some work combines static and dynamic analysis [21, 1531]. Other methods include fault injection [764, 1426], examining execution traces [678, 1720]. Perl et al. [1513] look specifically at finding vulnerabilities in code repositories. Kupsch and Miller compare manual and automated vulnerability assessment [1115].

Other taxonomies focus on the use of vulnerabilities. Lindqvist and Jonsson [1186] present a classification of intrusions partially based on the vulnerabilities exploited, inducing a classification of vulnerabilities. Krsul [1105] used Aslam's scheme as a basis for classifying vulnerabilities based on programmer assumptions. Tsipenyuk, Chess, and McGraw [1901] present a taxonomy intended for programmers. McPhee [1303] discusses how IBM's OS/VS2 Release 2 handles vulnerabilities related to system integrity. Gray [814] gives a historical perspective of vulnerability analysis. Igure and Williams [941] present a valuable review of taxonomies and classification schemes of both vulnerability and attack models. Several efforts have examined how and when to disclose vulnerabilities [373, 924, 2161, 2250].

Numerous other lists of common weaknesses can be mapped into the CWE list. These other lists identify the weaknesses deemed most common in the particular environment for which they were created. For example, the OWASP Top 10 [1483] list focuses on web-based weaknesses, whereas the SANS Top 25 Programming Errors [414] focuses on software design.

24.10   Exercises

1. Classify the following vulnerabilities using the RISOS model. Assume that the classification is for the implementation level. Justify your answer.

   a. The presence of the "wiz" command in the *sendmail* program (see Section 24.2.9).

   b. The failure to handle the **IFS** shell variable by *loadmodule* (see Section 24.2.9).

   c. The failure to select an *Administrator* password that was difficult to guess (see Section 24.2.10).

   d. The failure of the Burroughs system to detect offline changes to files (see Section 24.2.7).

2. Classify the vulnerabilities in Exercise 1 using the PA model. Assume that the classification is for the implementation level. Justify your answer.

3. The C shell does not treat the **IFS** variable as a special variable. (That is, the C shell separates arguments to commands by white spaces; this behavior is built in and cannot be changed.) How might this affect the *loadmodule* exploitation?

4. A common error on UNIX systems occurs during the configuration of *bind*, a directory name server. The time-to-expire field is set at 0.5 because the administrator believes that this field's unit is minutes (and wishes to set the time to 30 seconds). However, *bind* expects the field to be in seconds and reads the value as 0—meaning that no data is ever expired.

   a. Classify this vulnerability using the RISOS model, and justify your answer.

   b. Classify this vulnerability using the PA model, and justify your answer.

   c. Classify this vulnerability using Aslam's model, and justify your answer.

5. Can the UNIX Bourne shell variable **HOME**, which identifies the home directory of a user to programs that read startup files from the user's home directory, be used to compromise a system? If so, how?

6. An attacker breaks into a web server running on a Windows 10–based system. Because of the ease with which he broke in, he concludes that Windows 10 is an operating system with very poor security features. Is his conclusion reasonable? Why or why not?

7. Generalize the vulnerability described in Section 24.2.7 in order to suggest other ways in which the system could be penetrated.

8. Generalize the example in Section 24.2.8 in order to describe other weaknesses that the security of the computer system might have.

9. Why might an analyst care how similar two vulnerabilities are?

10. One expert noted that the PA model and the RISOS model are isomorphic. Show that the PA vulnerability classifications correspond to the RISOS vulnerability classes and vice versa.

11. The NRL classification scheme has three axes: genesis, time of introduction, and location. Name two other axes that would be of interest to an analyst. Justify your answer.

12. In the NRL classification scheme for the "time of introduction" axis, must the development phase precede the maintenance and operation phases, and must the maintenance phase precede the operation phase? Justify your answer.

13. In the NRL classification scheme for the "genesis" axis, how might one determine whether a vulnerability is "malicious" or "nonmalicious"?

14. In the NRL classification scheme for the "genesis" axis, can the classes "Trojan horse" and "covert channel" overlap? Justify your answer. If your answer is yes, describe a Trojan horse that is also a covert channel or vice versa.

15. Aslam's classification scheme classifies each vulnerability into a single category based on a decision tree that requires "yes" or "no" answers to questions about the vulnerability. A researcher has suggested replacing the tree with a vector, the components of which correspond to questions about the vulnerability. A "1" in the vector corresponds to a "yes" answer to the question; a "0" corresponds to a "no" answer. Compare and contrast the two approaches.

16. For the *fingerd* security hole to be exploited, certain conditions must hold. Based on the discussion in Section 24.3.1, enumerate these conditions.

17. For the *xterm* security hole to be exploited, certain conditions must hold. Based on the discussion in Section 24.3.1, enumerate these conditions.

18. Use Gupta and Gligor's technique to analyze a UNIX kernel for security flaws in the *open* system call. Check for problems with the first argument, which is a character string.

19. Generalize Gupta and Gligor's technique to extend to integer values. You should check for overflow (both negative and positive).

   a. Describe how to check for problems with the second argument. You will need to determine the maximum meaningful value for that argument.

   b. Describe how to check for problems with the third argument, which is a UNIX protection mode. Its maximum meaningful value is (octal) 7777, and its minimum meaningful value is 0.

20. Perform a penetration test on a system *after you obtain authorization to do so*. Apply the Flaw Hypothesis Methodology to obtain a meaningful assessment of the system's security.

Chapter 25
Auditing

LADY MACBETH: Your servants ever
Have theirs, themselves and what is theirs, in compt,
To make their audit at your highness' pleasure,
Still to return your own.
— *The Tragedy of Macbeth*, I, vi, 27–30.

Auditing is a technique for determining security violations. This chapter presents the notions of logging (recording of system events and actions) and auditing (analysis of these records). Auditing plays a major role in detecting security violations and in postmortem analysis to determine precisely what happened and how. This makes an effective auditing subsystem a key security component of any system.

25.1   Definition

The development of techniques for auditing computer systems sprang from the need to trace access to sensitive or important information stored on computer systems as well as access to the computer systems themselves. Anderson [52] first proposed the use of audit trails to monitor threats. The use of existing audit records suggested the development of simple tools that would check for unauthorized access to systems and files. The premise—that the logging mechanism was in place and active and logged the relevant events—required that the logs be augmented with additional information, but Anderson did not propose modification of the basic structure of the system's logging design, the implication being that redesign of the security monitoring mechanism was beyond the scope of the study.

> **Definition 25–1.** *Logging* is the recording of events or statistics to provide information about system use and performance.

The log need not be on the computer. For example, images from a camera may play a role in the analysis of system state. For our purposes, we simply note these records may be treated as log records.

> **Definition 25–2.** *Auditing* is the analysis of records to present information about the system in a clear and understandable manner.

With respect to computer security, logs provide a mechanism for analyzing the system security state, either to determine if a requested action will put the system in a nonsecure state or to determine the sequence of events leading to the system being in a nonsecure (compromised) state. If the log records all events that cause state transitions, as well as the previous and new values of the objects that are changed, the system state can be reconstructed at any time. Even if only a subset of this information is recorded, one might be able to eliminate some possible causes of a security problem; what remains provides a valuable starting point for further analysis.

Gligor [773] suggests other uses for the auditing mechanism. It allows systems analysts to review patterns of usage in order to evaluate the effectiveness of protection mechanisms. These patterns can be used to establish expected patterns of resource usage, which are critical for some intrusion detection systems. (See Chapter 26, "Intrusion Detection.") Auditing mechanisms must record any use of privileges. A security control that would restrict an ordinary user may not restrict the empowered user. Finally, audit mechanisms might deter attacks because of the record and the analysis, thereby providing some level of assurance that any violation of security policies will be detected.

Two distinct but related problems arise: which information to log and which information to audit. The decision of which events and actions should be audited requires a knowledge of the security policy of the system, what attempts to violate that policy involve, and how such attempts can be detected. The question of how such attempts can be detected raises the question of what should be logged [1504, 1506, 1507]: what commands must an attacker use to (attempt to) violate the security policy, what system calls must be made, who must issue the commands or system calls and in what order, what objects must be altered, and so forth. Logging of all events implicitly provides all this information; the problem is how to discern which parts of the information are relevant, which is the problem of determining what to audit.

25.2   Anatomy of an Auditing System

An auditing system consists of three components: the logger, the analyzer, and the notifier. These components collect data, analyze it, and report the results.

25.2.1   Logger

Logging mechanisms record information. The type and quantity of information are dictated by system or program configuration parameters. The mechanisms may record information in binary or human-readable form or transmit it directly to an analysis mechanism (see Section 25.2.2). A log-viewing tool is usually provided if the logs are recorded in binary form, so a user can examine the raw data or manipulate it using text-processing tools.

EXAMPLE: RACF [2256] is a security enhancement package for many IBM systems such as z/OS and OS/390. Among other events, it logs failed access attempts and the use of privileges to change security levels, and it can be set to log RACF interactions. The command *LISTUSER* lists information about RACF users as follows:

```
USER=EW125004    NAME=S.J.TURNER    OWNER=SECADM
  CREATED=88.004
  DEFAULT-GROUP=HUMRES    PASSDATE=88.004
  PASS-INTERVAL=30
  ATTRIBUTES=ADSP
  REVOKE DATE=NONE    RESUME-DATE=NONE
  LAST-ACCESS=88.020/14:15:10
  CLASS AUTHORIZATIONS=NONE
  NO-INSTALLATION-DATA
  NO-MODEL-NAME
  LOGON ALLOWED    (DAYS)  (TIME)
  -------------------------------
  ANYDAY                    ANYTIME
    GROUP=HUMRES AUTH=JOIN CONNECT-OWNER=SECADM
      CONNECT-DATE=88.004
      CONNECTS= 15  UACC=READ LAST-CONNECT=88.018/16:45:06
      CONNECT ATTRIBUTES=NONE
      REVOKE DATE=NONE RESUME DATE=NONE
    GROUP=PERSNL AUTH=JOIN CONNECT-OWNER=SECADM
      CONNECT-DATE:88.004
      CONNECTS= 25 UACC=READ LAST-CONNECT=88.020/14:15:10
      CONNECT ATTRIBUTES=NONE
      REVOKE DATE=NONE RESUME DATE=NONE
    SECURITY-LEVEL=NONE SPECIFIED
    CATEGORY AUTHORIZATION
       NONE SPECIFIED
```

RACF can also log its interactions with users, so that if a user attempts to modify it in any way, a log entry will be made.

EXAMPLE: Microsoft's Windows 10 records events using the Windows Event Log Service, and stores them in log files [273]. The *system event* log contains records of events that Windows and other system-level routines generate, for example a device driver failing to load. The *application event* log contains records that applications have produced; the developers determine what events to log, and whether the event should be recorded in the application event log or a program-specific event log. The *security event* log contains records corresponding to security-critical events such as logging in and out, system resource overuses, and accesses to system files as defined by the audit policy. The *setup event* log records events occurring during application installations, and the *forwarded event* log records entries forwarded from other systems.

The Windows 10 logger defines a record as a header followed by a description and possibly an additional data field. The header contains an event identifier, user identity information (a user identifier and, if appropriate, an impersonation identifier), the date and time, the source that caused the record to be generated, the specific policy setting that triggered the record, and the computer involved. All records are kept in binary form. A tool called the *event viewer* translates the records into readable form.

An example security event log record might look like the following (but would be displayed in a graphic format):

```
================================
Log Name: Security
Source:   Microsoft        Logged:         03/20/2017
          Windows security                 12:02:59 PM
Event ID: 4634             Task Category:  Logoff
Level:    Information      Keywords:       Audit Success
User:     N/A              Computer:       McLaren
OpCode:   Info


General:
An account was logged off.
Subject:
        Security ID:       MCLAREN\matt
        Account Name:      matt
        Account Domain:    MCLAREN
        Logon ID:          0xACBA30

Details:
+ System
- EventData
    TargetUserSID          S-1-5-22-2039872233-608055118-
                             4446661516-2001
    TargetUserName         matt
```

```
TargetDomainName     MCLAREN
TargetLogonId        0xacba30
```

The system logs logins (logon) and logoffs in the security log. This event arose from the user "matt" logging out of the system named "McLaren."

25.2.2   Analyzer

An analyzer takes a log as input and analyzes it. The results of the analysis may lead to changes in the data being recorded, to detection of some event or problem, or both.

EXAMPLE: Suppose a system administrator wants to be notified whenever there is an attempt to login to a nonexistent account using *ssh*. The following *swatchdog* patterns [864, 865, 2192] match the lines generated by these remote connections:

```
/sshd\[[0-9]*\]:/&/Invalid user/
```

This line matches all log file entries containing the string "sshd" followed by a string of digits in square brackets and a colon, and the words "Invalid user."

EXAMPLE: An intrusion detection system (see Chapter 26) detects attacks by analyzing log records for unexpected activity or for activity that is known to be an attempt to compromise the system. The analysis mechanism of the intrusion detection system is an example of an audit analysis mechanism.

25.2.3   Notifier

The analyzer passes the results of the analysis to the notifier. The notifier informs the analyst, and other entities, of the results of the audit. The entities may take some action in response to these results.

EXAMPLE: The *swatchdog* mentioned above provides a notification facility. The following item matches the lines generated by the remote connections, as above, and sends the lines to *root* and the administrator's personal account, *heidi*. The subject line contains the IP address or host name of the system from which the attempted connection originated (the tenth field of the line).

```
watchfor   /sshd\[[0-9]*\]:/&/Invalid user/
     echo red
     mail addresses=root:heidi,subject="Bad ssh
          login from $_[10]"
```

This line matches all log file entries containing the string "sshd" followed by a string of digits in square brackets and a colon, and the words "Invalid user."

It then prints the line, in red, on the standard output, and sends the requisite letter to the accounts *root* and *heidi*.

EXAMPLE: Consider the login system described on page 431, in which three consecutive failed login attempts disable the user's account. The logging mechanism records each attempt. The audit mechanism checks the number of consecutive failed login attempts. When this number reaches 3, the audit mechanism invokes the notifier, which reports the problem to the system administrator and disables the account.

25.3   Designing an Auditing System

A single, well-unified logging process is an essential component of computer security mechanisms [267]. The design of the logging subsystem is an integral part of the overall system design. The auditing mechanism, which builds on the data from the logging subsystem, analyzes information related to the security state of the system and determines if specific actions have occurred or if certain states have been entered.

The goals of the auditing process determine what information is logged [124, 1504, 1506, 1507]. In general, the auditors desire to detect violations of policy. Let A_i be the set of possible actions on a system. The security policy provides a set of constraints p_i that the design must meet in order for the system to be secure. This implies that the functions that could cause those constraints to fail must be audited.

EXAMPLE: Consider the design hierarchy suggested by PSOS [656, 1447, 1448]. At each level, the design of the abstract machine is verified not to violate the predicates p_i. The predicates control specific actions at that level. By auditing those actions, one can determine if an attempt to breach security has occurred. Enough information must be logged to allow auditing at these points.

Represent constraints as "*action* $\Rightarrow$ *condition*." Implication requires that the action be true (which means that the *action* occurred, in this context) before any valid conclusion about the *condition* can be deduced. Although this notation is unusual, it allows us simply to list constraints against which records can be audited. Furthermore, the goal of the auditing is to determine if the policy has been violated (causing a breach of security), so the result (success or failure) of the operation should match the satisfaction of the constraint. That is, if the constraint is true, the result is irrelevant, but if the constraint is false and the operation is successful, a security violation has occurred.

EXAMPLE: Recall that the simplest form of the Bell-LaPadula Model linearly orders the security levels L_i. A subject S has the level $L(S)$, and the object O has the level $L(O)$. Under this policy, a system state is illegal if S reads O when $L(S) < L(O)$ or if S writes to O when $L(S) > L(O)$. The corresponding constraints are

1. S reads $O \Rightarrow L(S) \geq L(O)$
2. S writes $O \Rightarrow L(S) \leq L(O)$

Auditing for security violations merely requires auditing for writes from a subject to a lower-level object or reads from a higher-level object and checking for violations of these constraints. Logs must contain security levels of the subjects and objects involved, the action (to determine which constraint applies), and the result (success or failure). From these logs, testing for the violation of the constraints above is trivial.

Surprisingly, the *names* of the subject and object need not be recorded. However, in practice, the site security policy would require the security analyst to identify both the object of the violation and the user who attempted the violation. With this modification of the policy, the names of the subject and object would also be recorded.

Removing the assumption of tranquility (see Section 5.3) adds very little complication from an auditing perspective. Without tranquility, a subject can change the security level or the categories of any subject or object it controls to a level no greater than its own (this allows declassification). The command to do this and the old and new security levels and categories must be recorded.

To summarize, in this limited case, auditing of Bell-LaPadula-based systems requires logging of the following items:

- For reads and writes, the subject's security level, the object's security level, and the result of the action
- For systems without tranquility, the subject or object, its old and new security levels, the security level of the subject changing the security level, and the result

EXAMPLE: The Chinese Wall policy model partitions the set of all subjects and objects into "conflict of interest" classes (called COIs) and partitions each COI into "company datasets" (called CDs). Let the COI of subject S be $COI(S)$ and let the company dataset of subject S be $CD(S)$; for object O, define $COI(O)$ and $CD(O)$ similarly. O may contain sanitized information, which can be read by anyone, or unsanitized information, which can be read only by a subject in another COI class or by one that is in the COI class of the object and has already accessed another object in $CD(O)$. The predicate $san(O)$ is true if O contains only sanitized information and is false if it contains unsanitized information.

Let $CD_H(S)$ be the set of all CDs accessed by the subject S so far. Intuitively, if S has read some object in a dataset, it can read other objects in the same dataset, but it cannot read objects in other datasets in the same COI class as that of the original object. Then S can read O if and only if $COI(O) \neq COI(S)$ or

$CD(O) \in CD_H(S)$. Intuitively, if S can read O, then S can write to O unless S can read an object in a different CD and that object contains unsanitized information. This means S can write to O if and only if S can read O and $\neg\exists O'(CD(O) \neq CD(O') \wedge S$ can read $O' \wedge \neg san(O'))$. The constraints follow immediately:

1. S reads $O \Rightarrow COI(O) \neq COI(S) \vee CD(O) \in CD_H(S)$

2. S writes $O \Rightarrow (S \; canread \; O) \wedge \neg\exists O'(COI(O) \neq COI(O') \wedge S \; canread \; O' \wedge \neg san(O'))$

where $S \; canread \; O$ is true if the consequent of constraint 1 holds.

To validate that these constraints hold for each transaction, the auditor must be able to determine for each transaction the elements of each COI and CD as well as the set of CDs that a particular subject has accessed. Any sanitization is also relevant. For each transaction, logging of the subject and object identifiers, the action, a time, and the result (success or failure) will enable the auditor to determine whether or not the two constraints are satisfied.

25.3.1   Implementation Considerations

The example models above showed that analyzing the specific rules and axioms of a model reveal specific requirements for logging enough information to detect security violations. Interestingly enough, one need not assume that the system begins in a secure (or valid) state because all the models assert that the rules above are necessary but not sufficient for secure operation and auditing tests necessity. That is, if the auditing of the logs above shows a security violation, the system is not secure; but if it shows no violation, the system may still not be secure because if the initial state of the system is nonsecure, the result will (most likely) be a nonsecure state. Hence, if one desires to use auditing to detect that the system is not secure rather than detect actions that violate security, one needs also to capture the initial state of the system. In all cases, this means recording at start time the information that would be logged on changes in the state.

The examples above discussed logging requirements quite generically. The discussion of the Bell-LaPadula Model asserted that specific types of data should be recorded during a "write." In an implementation, instantiating "write" may embody other system-specific operations ("append," "create directory," and so on). Moreover, the notion of a "write" may be quite subtle—for example, it may include alteration of protection modes, setting the system clock, and so forth. How this affects other entities is less clear, but typically it involves the use of covert channels (see Section 18.3) to write (send) information. These channels also must be modeled.

Naming also affects the implementation of logging criteria. Typically, objects have multiple names by which they can be accessed. However, if the criteria involve the entity, the system must log all constrained actions with that entity regardless of the name used. For example, each UNIX file has at least two representations: first, the usual one (accessed through the file system), and second, the low-level one (composed of disk blocks and an inode and accessed through the raw disk device). Logging all accesses to a particular file requires that the system log accesses through both representations. Systems generally do not provide logging and auditing at the disk block level (owing to performance considerations). However, this means that UNIX systems generally cannot log all accesses to a given file.

25.3.2 Syntactic Issues

One critical issue is *how* to log: what data should be placed in the log file, and how it should be expressed, to allow an audit to draw conclusions that can be justified through reference to the log [1504, 1506–1508]. This enables the analyst to display the reasoning behind the conclusions of the audit. The problem is that many systems log data ambiguously or do not present enough context to determine to what the elements of the log entry refer.

EXAMPLE: A UNIX system logs the names of files that a user retrieves using *ftp*. The log contains the file name *letc/passwd*. If the associated user is the anonymous user (indicating an anonymous login), then the file *actually* retrieved is the password file in the anonymous *ftp* subtree, not the system's password file. This is an example of the naming issue discussed in the preceding section.

This example demonstrates that a single log entry may not contain all the information about a particular action. The context of the entry conveys information. An analysis engine benefits from analyzing the context at the time the entries were made as well as the entries themselves.

Flack and Atallah [684] suggest using a grammar-based approach to specifying log content. The grammar, expressed using a notation such as BNF, forces the designer to specify the syntax and semantic content of the log. Because the grammar of the log is completely specified, writing tools to extract information from the log requires development of a parser using the stated grammar. The analyzer can then process log entries using this grammar.

EXAMPLE: Suppose the following grammar describes log entries in a typical UNIX system's log for failed attempts to change user privileges:

```
entry : date host prog [ bad ] user [ "from" host ] "to"
        user "on" tty
date  : daytime
host  : string
prog  : string ":"
bad   : "FAILED"
user  : string
tty   : "/dev/" string
```

Here, "string" and "daytime" are terminals and the quoted strings are literals. An analyst would check that this log entry format contained all the information needed for analysis. Then all programs that created these login entries would use a format derived from this grammar. This would provide consistency for the entries and would allow a single tool to extract the desired information from the log file.

Flack and Atallah point out that most current log entries are not specified using grammars. They examined the description and entries of the Basic Security Module (BSM) (see Section 25.5.2) and found some ambiguities. For example, one BSM entry has two optional text fields followed by two mandatory text fields. The documentation does not specify how to interpret a sequence of three text fields in this context, so it is unclear which of the two optional text fields is present. They developed a BSM grammar that treats the optional fields as either both present or both absent, so three text fields generate a parse error. Any ambiguous log entries will thereby generate the exception. The analyst can then examine the log entry and best determine how to handle the situation.

25.3.3   Log Sanitization

A site may consider a set of information confidential. Logs may contain some of this information. If the site wishes to make logs available, it must delete the confidential information.

> **Definition 25–3.** Let U be a set of users. The policy P defines a set of information $C(U)$ that members of U are not allowed to see. Then the log L is *sanitized* with respect to P and U when all instances of information in $C(U)$ are deleted from L.

Confidentiality policies may impact logs in two distinct ways. First, P may forbid the information to leave the site. For example, the log may contain file names that give indications of proprietary projects or enable an industrial spy to determine the IP addresses of machines containing sensitive information. In this case, the unsanitized logs are available to the site administrators. Second, P may forbid the information to leave the system. In this case, the goal is to prevent the system administration from spying on the users. For example, if the Crashing Machine Company (CMC) rents time on Denise's Distributed System, CMC may not want the administrators of the system to determine what they are doing. Privacy considerations also affect the policy. Laws may allow the system administration to monitor users only when they have reason to believe that users are attacking the system or engaging in illegal activities. When they do look at the logs, the site must protect the privacy of other users so that the investigators cannot determine what activities the unsuspected users are engaged in.

The distinction controls the organization of the logging. Figure 25–1 shows where the sanitizers are applied. The top part of the figure shows a sanitizer that removes information from an existing log file before the analysts examine

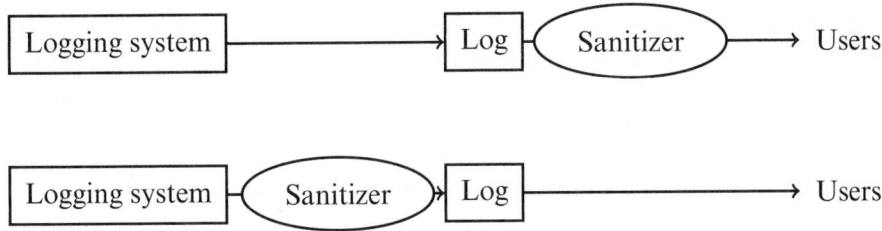

Figure 25–1   The different types of sanitization. The top image shows logs being sanitized for external viewing. The bottom image shows logs being sanitized for privacy of users. In this case, the sanitizer may save information in a separate log that enables the reconstruction of the omitted information. Cryptographic techniques enforce separation of privilege, so multiple administrators must agree to view the unsanitized logs.

it. This protects company confidentiality because the external viewers are denied information that the company wishes to keep confidential. It does not protect users' privacy because the site administration has access to the unsanitized log. The bottom part of the figure shows a configuration in which users' privacy is protected, because the data is sanitized before it is written to the log. The system administrators cannot determine the true value of the sanitized data because it is never written to the log file. If they must be able to recover the data at some future point (to satisfy a court order, for example), the sanitizer can use cryptography to protect the data by encrypting it or by using a cryptographic scheme allowing a *re-identifier* to reassemble the unsanitized data.

This suggests two different types of sanitization.

> **Definition 25–4.** An *anonymizing sanitizer* deletes information in such a way that it cannot be reconstructed by either the recipient or the originator of the data in the log. A *pseudonymizing sanitizer* deletes information in such a way that the originator of the log can reconstruct the deleted information.

These issues affect the design of the log. The sanitizer must preserve information and relationships relevant to the analysis of the data in the log. Otherwise, the analyzers may miss information that would enable them to detect attacks.

EXAMPLE: The Humongous Corporation wishes to conceal the IP addresses of a set of hosts containing proprietary data. The actual IP addresses are 10.163.5.10 through 10.163.5.14. The corporation wants to make its logs available to a consultant for analysis. It must replace the IP addresses.

The log shows connections to port 25 (the electronic mail port) of the IP addresses in question. The order of the probing is as follows:

10.163.5.10, 10.163.5.11, 10.163.5.12, 10.163.5.13, 10.163.5.14

If the corporation replaces the IP addresses at random, the log entries will reflect email being sent to a set of random hosts. If the corporation preserves the sequential order of the IP addresses, the log entries will reflect a port scanning probe. This often precedes an attack of some sort.

While critical, concealing identifiers may not be enough.

Definition 25–5. A *quasi-identifier* is a set of elements in data of entities that, considered together, are associated with either a specific entity or a very small set of entities [494].

EXAMPLE: In Massachusetts, USA, the commission responsible for purchasing insurance for state employees released records containing information about medical visits, diagnoses, procedures, medications, and other medical information, along with the ZIP code,[1] gender, and birth date of around 135,000 patients. No names or addresses were in the records. Sweeney obtained the voter list for the state, and looked up the governor's registration. The voter list contained the name, address, party affiliation, birth date, and gender for each voter. According to the list for the city in which the governor lived, six people had the same birth date as one of the medical records; only three were the same gender as the governor, and only one had the governor's ZIP code. Thus, the elements (ZIP code, gender, and birth date) in this dataset form a quasi-identifier. From them, Sweeney identified the records in the medical data belonging to the governor [1845].

Biskup and Flegel [235] point out that one need not sanitize data that is not collected. Therefore, if a log is to be sanitized to provide anonymity, the simplest technique is simply not to collect the data. However, pseudonymity requires that the data be collected. Two techniques provide the hiding ability.

Suppose the policy allows site administrative personnel to view the data but others to see only the sanitized log. The first step is to determine a set of pseudonyms that preserve the relationships that are relevant to the analysis. The sanitizer replaces the data with the pseudonyms and maintains a table mapping pseudonyms to actual values (similar to a pseudonymous remailer; see Definition 15–5). Because all site administrators have access to this table, any of them could reconstruct the actual log.

The second technique is appropriate when the policy requires that some set of individuals, *not* including the system administrators, be able to see the unsanitized data (for example, law enforcement officers or intrusion analysts at a remote site) [235]. The unsanitized data cannot be stored in the clear on the system because the system security officers could then obtain the unsanitized data. One approach is to use a random enciphering key to encipher each sensitive datum and treat the decryption key as the representation of the datum. Then a secret

---

[1] A postal code composed of five digits used by the U.S. Post Office. It is based on geographical location of the address.

sharing scheme such as Shamir's (see Section 16.3.2) allows the shadows of the decryption key to be split among as many people (or entities) as desired. Using a (t, n)-threshold scheme allows any t of n recipients to reconstruct the decryption key and reverse the pseudonymity.

The key to sanitization is not simply hiding data; as noted above, it also requires hiding the relationships between the hidden data and the data that is not hidden [225].

EXAMPLE: In 2006, Netflix created a contest to improve their movie recommendation system, which predicts what movies customers would like based on their previous selections and other ancillary information. They provided each entering team with a set of anonymized training data, and offered a large cash prize to the team or teams that were able to predict better than the Netflix algorithm which movies the customers would select based on that data. The training data consisted of more than 100,000,000 ratings; the test set, not released, consisted of 3,000,000 ratings [151]. The names of the Netflix customers were anonymized, and the rest of the data was subject to perturbation [1422].

Narayanan and Shmatikov asked how much an adversary needs to know about someone to deanonymize that person's records [1422]. They analyzed the Netflix training dataset, and compared it to external information—that stored in the public Internet Movie Database (IMDB) [2181]. They assumed there was a strong correlation between the users, their movie ratings, and movie titles. Other factors, such as time, also helped them reconstruct relationships. Because of restrictions on their gathering data from IMDB, they worked with a sample of 50 IMDB users. Because Netflix did not release the deanonymized data, the researchers took action to minimize false positives. They concluded that they could identify IMDB posting names for 2 anonymized customers.

This example shows the fallacy of making a closed world assumption, in which the only data available to the adversary who wants to deanonymize the data is the data in the anonymized dataset [475]. In practice, external information may well be available, as was true for both examples above. Given the rapid spread of information in many of today's societies, making the closed world assumption should be done very carefully and deliberately.

25.3.4 Application and System Logging

Application logs consist of entries made by applications. These entries typically use high-level abstractions, such as

```
su: bishop to root on /dev/ttyp0
smtp: delivery failed; could not connect to
      abcxy.net:25
```

They describe the problems (or results) encountered at the application layer. These logs usually do not include detailed information about the system calls that are made, the results that are returned, or the sequence of events leading up to the log entry.

System logs consist of entries of kernel events. These entries do not include high-level information. They report system calls and events. The first part of a system log corresponding to the *su* line above on a FreeBSD system is as follows:

```
3876 ktrace    RET   ktrace 0
3876 ktrace    CALL  execve(0x7fffffffea62,0x7fffffffe7e8,
                            0x7fffffffe800)
3876 ktrace    NAMI  "/usr/bin/su"
3876 ktrace    NAMI  "/usr/libexec/ld-elf.so.1"
3876 su        RET   execve 0
3876 su        CALL  mmap(0,0x8000,0x3<PROT_READ|PROT_
                            WRITE>,0x1002<MAP_PRIVATE|
                            MAP_ANON>,0xffffffff,0)
3876 su        RET   mmap 34366169088/0x80062200
3876 su        CALL  issetugid
3876 su        RET   issetugid 0
3876 su        CALL  getuid
3876 su        RET   getuid 0
3876 su        CALL  getegid
```

The system log consists of 6,929 lines detailing the system calls (the "CALL" lines), their return values ("RET"), file name lookups ("NAMI"), file I/O (including the data read or written), and any other actions requiring the kernel.

The difference in the two logs is their focus. If the audit is to focus on application events, such as failures to provide correct passwords (the *su* entry) or failures to deliver letters (the SMTP entry), an application log provides a simple way of recording the events for analysis. If system events such as file accesses or memory mapping affect the outcome of the auditing, then system logging is appropriate. In some cases, audits using both logs can uncover the system events leading up to an application event.

The advantage of system logs is the completeness of the information recorded. Rather than indicating that a configuration file could not be accessed, the system level log will identify the particular file, the type of access, and the reason for the failure. This leads to large log files that may require special handling. If a log overflows, the system can turn off logging, begin overwriting the least recent log entries, or shut down the system. Many systems allow the auditor to specify the types of information, or the specific system events, to be logged. By a judicious choice of which events to log, the danger of logs overflowing can be minimized.

The advantage of application logs is the level of abstraction. The applications provide the auditor with data that has undergone some interpretation before being entered. For example, rather than identifying a particular file as inaccessible, an application log should indicate the reason for accessing the file:

```
appx: cannot open config file appx.cf for reading:
      no such file
```

The correlation problem relates system and application logs. Given a system log composed of events from one execution of an application, and the corresponding application log, how can one determine which system log entries correspond to entries in the application log, and vice versa? This issue identifies the need to understand what an application level failure means at a system level and what application failures are caused by system level problems. The point is that the application logs are abstractions of system level events interpreted by the application in view of the previous application level events. By understanding the events at both the system and application levels, the auditor can learn about the causes of failures and determine if they are the results of attempts to breach system security.

25.4   A Posteriori Design

The design of an effective auditing subsystem is straightforward when one is aware of all possible policy violations and can detect them. Unfortunately, this is rarely the case. Most security breaches arise on existing systems that were not designed with security considerations in mind. In this case, auditing may have two different goals. The first goal is to detect *any* violations of a stated policy; the second is to detect actions that are known to be part of an attempt to breach security.

The difference is subtle but important. The first goal focuses on the policy and, as with the a priori design of an auditing subsystem, records (attempted) actions that violate the policy. The set of such actions may not be known in advance. The second goal focuses on specific actions that the managers of the system have determined indicate behavior that poses a threat to system security. Thus, one approaches the first goal by examining the desired policy, whereas one approaches the second goal by examining the actions (attacks) that pose the threat.

25.4.1   Auditing to Detect Violations of a Known Policy

Implementation of this type of auditing is similar to the auditing subsystem design discussed in Section 25.3. The idea is to determine whether or not a state violates the policy. Unlike mechanisms designed into the system, the auditing mechanisms must be integrated into the existing system. Analysts must analyze the system to determine what actions and settings are consistent with the policy. They then design mechanisms for checking that the actions and settings are in fact consistent with the policy. There are two ways to proceed: state-based auditing and transition-based auditing.

25.4.1.1   State-Based Auditing

The designer can opt for a state-based approach, in which states of the system are analyzed to determine if a policy violation exists.

> **Definition 25–6.** A *state-based logging mechanism* records information about a system's state. A *state-based auditing mechanism* determines whether or not a state of the system is unauthorized.

Typically, a state-based auditing mechanism is built on a state-based logging system. There is a tacit assumption that a state-based logging mechanism can take a snapshot of the system. More generally, the state-based logging mechanism must obtain a consistent state. Algorithms such as Chandy-Lamport [380] can supply a consistent state for distributed resources, but obtaining a state for nondistributed resources requires the resources to be quiescent while the state is obtained. On most systems in which multiple resources supply components of the state, this is infeasible.

Consider a set of resources on a system. Each resource supplies a component (called an *attribute*) of the state. Hence, state-based auditing mechanisms analyze attributes of the state. Let the state s_i be a vector $(c_{i0}, \ldots, c_{in})$, where $c_{ij} \in C$ is an attribute of the state. If the system is quiescent, then the audit analyzes $(c_{i0}, \ldots, c_{in})$. We call this *consistent static analysis*. However, if the system is not quiescent, then the audit analyzes $(c_{i0}, c_{j1}, \ldots, c_{kn})$. Here, the "state" is a vector of attributes of different states and does not correspond to any particular state. Although the intent is to examine a single state, the audit actually examines attributes from multiple states. This type of analysis is called *inconsistent static analysis*.

EXAMPLE: File system auditing tools such as *tripwire* (see the example beginning on page 125 in Section 4.5.2) are usually discussed under the rubric of "static analysis tools." This implies that they analyze a single state of the system. In fact, unless they are run on quiescent file systems, these tools take slices of different states because the attributes are read while the system transitions as other programs access the resource. The effect of this incremental construction of a union of slices of the states during the tool's run can affect the correctness of the report. If a test that the scanner performs near the end of the tool's run depends on some assumptions derived from a check made near the beginning of its run, the state may change and the test may appear to succeed, when in reality it reveals no (or misleading) information. With consistent static analysis, because the state does not change during the run of the tool, the tool may rely on the assumptions, but with inconsistent static analysis, such reliance leads to a classic "time of check to time of use" flaw. The same observation holds for any inconsistent static tool that relies on assumptions deduced from an earlier part of its current incarnation.

25.4.1.2 Transition-Based Auditing

The designer can opt for a transition-based approach, in which actions that could violate the policy are checked to determine if they do indeed cause violations.

> **Definition 25–7.** A *transition-based logging mechanism* records information about an action on a system. A *transition-based auditing mechanism* examines the current state of the system and the proposed transition (command) to determine if the result will place the system in an unauthorized state.

An important observation is that transition-based logging may not be sufficient to enable a transition-based auditing mechanism to determine if the system will enter an unauthorized state. Specifically, if the system begins in a state that violates policy, a transition-based auditing mechanism will not detect the security problem if the transition alone was analyzed and determined not to move the system from a secure state to a nonsecure state. For this reason, transition-based logging is used only when specific transitions always require an examination (as in the example of changes of privilege) or when some state analysis is also performed.

EXAMPLE: The program *tcp_wrappers* intercepts TCP connections to UNIX-based systems and determines whether or not the connections are to be allowed. The connections that are to be denied are identified in the file *hosts.deny*. The logging mechanism determines where the connection comes from. The auditing mechanism compares that point of origin (the IP address, the destination port, and possibly the user name) with the data in the *hosts.deny* file. If the point of origin matches the data in the *hosts.deny* file, the connection is blocked. This is transition-based auditing because the mechanism analyzes a command (the putative connection) to determine if it will put the system in an unauthorized state (by allowing a connection in the *hosts.deny* file). The current state of the system is not examined.

EXAMPLE: Some instant messaging systems allows a user to sign on from at most one computer at a time. The mechanism that detects when a user tries to sign on from two computers simultaneously is a mixture of state-based and transition-based auditing. It examines the transition (the sign-on) and the current state (whether or not that user signed on already). If the transition would put the system in an unauthorized state (the user signed on twice), the audit mechanism reports the problem. The system responds by blocking the second sign-on.

25.4.2 Auditing to Detect Known Violations of a Policy

In many cases, the security policy is not stated explicitly. However, certain behaviors are considered to be "nonsecure." For example, an attack that floods a network to the point that it is not usable, or accessing of a computer by an unauthorized person, would violate the implicit security policy. Under these conditions, analysts can determine specific sequences of commands, or properties of states, that indicate a security violation and look for that violation.

EXAMPLE: Daniels and Spafford [498] present an analysis of the Land attack [2182], which causes a denial of service by causing the target of the attack to hang or to respond very slowly. This attack is built on an exchange that begins a TCP connection (see Figure 7–1).

When a TCP connection begins, the source sends a SYN packet to the destination. This packet contains a sequence number s. The destination receives the packet and returns a SYN/ACK packet containing the acknowledgment number $s + 1$ and a second sequence number t. The source receives this packet and replies with the acknowledgment number $t + 1$. Figure 7–1 illustrates this exchange, called a *three-way handshake*.

The Land attack arises from an ambiguity in the TCP specification [1537]. When the source and destination differ, or the TCP port numbers of the source and destination differ, the two sequence numbers s and t are from different processes. But what happens if the source and destination addresses and ports are the same? The TCP specification is ambiguous.

Consider what happens in the three-way handshake in this case. The target host receives a SYN packet with sequence number s. It responds with a SYN/ACK packet containing sequence number t and acknowledgment number $s + 1$. At this point, the internal state of the connection in that host is that the next acknowledgment number will be $t + 1$. Because the source and destination addresses and ports are the same, the packet returns to the host. The host checks the packet and finds that the acknowledgment number ($s + 1$) is incorrect. At this point, the TCP specification suggests two different ways to handle the situation.

According to one part of the specification,[2] the connection should send a reset (RST). If this is done, it terminates the connection and the attack fails.

According to a different part of the specification,[3] the host should reply with an empty packet with the current sequence number and the expected acknowledgment number. Hence, the host sends a packet with sequence number $t+1$ and acknowledgment number $s+1$. Naturally, it receives that packet. It checks that the acknowledgment number is correct, and—again—it is not. Repeating the sequence causes the same packet to be generated, resulting in an infinite loop. If the host has disabled interrupts during this part, the system hangs. Otherwise, it runs very slowly, servicing interrupts but doing little else. The denial of service attack is now successful.

Detecting this attack requires that the initial Land packet be detected. The characteristic of this packet is that the source and destination addresses and port numbers are the same. So, the logging requirement is to record that information.

---

[2]See p. 36 of the TCP specification [1537].
[3]See p. 69 of the TCP specification [1537].

The audit requirement is to report any packets for which the following condition holds:

```
(source address = destination address) and
    (source port number = destination port number)
```

25.5   Auditing Mechanisms

Different systems approach logging in different ways. Most systems log all events by default and allow the system administrator to disable the logging of specific events. This leads to bloated logs.

In this section, we present examples of information that systems record and give some details of the auditing mechanisms.

25.5.1   Secure Systems

Systems designed with security in mind have auditing mechanisms integrated with the system design and implementation. Typically, these systems provide a language or interface that allows system managers to configure the system to report specific events or to monitor accesses by a particular subject or to a particular object. This is controlled at the audit subsystem so that irrelevant actions or accesses are not recorded.

EXAMPLE: The VAX VMM system is designed to meet the requirements of the A1 classification of the TCSEC [2239]. This classification requires that impending security violations be detected, actions be taken to protect the system, auditing based on user or object be allowed, and extensive administrative support be provided. Because the VAX VMM was intended to be a production system, the audit mechanism could have only minimal impact on system performance and had to be highly reliable [1710].

The system is designed as a layered kernel, and so the logging mechanisms are not unified. Logging occurs at each place in the hierarchy where events of interest occur. Each layer also audits accesses to the objects it controls. In essence, the auditing mechanisms are distributed throughout the layers.

After each layer has audited its information, the logs and results of the audit are passed to the audit subsystem for future use. The audit subsystem manages the system log and has a single entry point (called *AUD$audit*). The parameters are event identification, status (the result), auxiliary data (which depends on the event), and the caller's name. The audit subsystem records the event if the event affects a subject or object listed in an audit table and if the severity of the event (derived from the status code) exceeds that associated with the entity in the audit table. The audit subsystem then adds the date and time, the subject's name and type, and other data to the log entry, dumps the entry into a buffer, and signals the audit logging process, which writes the log event to the log.

Two types of events are always logged. The first results from the caller's setting a special flag and is under the programmers' control. The second is an attempt to violate policy and is required by the criteria used to certify systems. Protection violations and login failures are recorded when the event occurs repeatedly. Use of covert channels is also flagged.

When the log reaches 75% of its capacity, the kernel notifies the audit process to archive the log contents. This resets the log. This follows the philosophy that the kernel never runs without auditing. Should archiving be impossible (as a result of full disks, for example), the system stops.

Audit reduction is based on time (before or after a particular date and time), security or integrity level (at or above a given level), and severity.

EXAMPLE: The Compartmented Mode Workstation [483] auditing subsystem interface [1525] illustrates how the auditing mechanisms interact with users, processes, and the kernel. The auditing subsystem maintains a table of auditable events for the system. Each entry indicates whether or not logging is turned on and what type of logging to use. At the user level, the command *chaud* allows the system manager to turn auditing on or off, to indicate what events and objects are to be audited, and to find out which events and objects are being logged. If the auditor changes the entities being audited, the log is not interrupted.

At the process level, the system call *audit_on* turns on logging for an event and identifies the log file in which to place records. The call *audit_off* turns off logging for that event. The *audit_write* system call takes a pointer to a log entry, validates the putative ID number, and writes it out if logging is turned on for that event. This allows processes to write their own log entries. Finally, the calls *audit_suspend* and *audit_resume* allow the process to turn off system logging for that process. Any calls to *audit_write* are honored.

Some processes, such as the window manager, perform their own auditing. The problem is that low-level auditing, at the system call level, does not map easily into more abstract, high-level events. By disabling low-level auditing and writing its own records, the window manager can maintain a high level of abstraction for its logged events.

Once the process makes a system call, the interface checks that the process is to be audited and that the *audit_suspend* is not in effect. The first three system call arguments are recorded, but if any of them is a pointer, the pointer is not resolved.

At the kernel level, the *audit_write* routine determines what to do with the record. If there is room in the log, it writes the record out. If not, it can halt the system, discard the record, or disable the events that will cause logging. This last technique is unusual, but its goal is to impact system functionality as little as possible while ensuring that auditing will record all events of interest.

The logged events are analyzed using a tool called *redux*. This tool converts records into a printable format and prints events that satisfy conditions based on users, objects, security levels, and events.

25.5.2   Nonsecure Systems

Auditing subsystems for systems not designed with security in mind are generally for purposes of accounting. Although these subsystems can be used to check for egregious security violations, they rarely record the level of detail or the types of events that enable security officers to determine if security has been violated. The level of detail needed is typically provided by an added subsystem.

EXAMPLE: The Basic Security Module (BSM) [2233] is an enhanced auditing system for Solaris, Trusted BSD, FreeBSD, MacOS X, and many other systems. Each log consists of files, and each file is composed of individual records. A record is made up of a sequence of tokens. The record size is not fixed; there is a begin token and an end token. Each record refers to an auditable event. These events are defined either at the system level ("kernel event"), such as a system call, or through library function calls from an application ("application event"), such as a failure to authenticate successfully to the login program. Finally, BSM groups records into audit event classes. These classes are based on the event triggering the generation of the record and can be created either before an audit log is created (in which case the event classes that are defined tell the system which events to generate records for) or after the log is created (in which case the classes that are defined control which records are given to the analysis tools). The latter is an example of log reduction, and the program *auditreduce* allows analysts to define the classes of events about which records are to be extracted.

BSM defines a token as an identification field followed by a series of information fields. These tokens encapsulate user identity (a real, effective, and original UID and effective group ID as well as process ID), group list, file system information (pathname and attributes), IPC usage (IPC token, IPC attributes), networking (IP port number, IP address), and process and system call information (return value, arguments) as well as more general information (text, data, opaque). This enables an analyst to tie tokens and records to events of interest and to extract enough information to determine what was done, who did it, and (if applicable) what the outcome was.

An example BSM log record might look like this:

```
header,35,AUE_EXIT,Wed Sep 18 11:35:28 1991,
      + 570000 msec,
process,bishop,root,root,daemon,1234,
return,Error 0,5
trailer,35
```

The information is stored in a binary format to minimize log size. A program called *praudit* formats and prints records when a human-readable form is needed.

The determination of what to log and what to audit is left to the system managers. This allows BSM to be used in multiple environments and under different policies. This is consistent with BSM being an add-on security module. It provides other security mechanisms as well.

25.6   Examples: Auditing File Systems

The difference between designing a logging and auditing mechanism for an existing file system protocol and designing a logging and auditing mechanism for a new file system protocol illuminates the differences between a priori and a posteriori audit design. This section compares and contrasts the design of an audit mechanism for NFSv2 and the design of a new file system intended to provide logging and auditing.

A bit of background first. Many sites allow computers and users to share file systems, so that one computer (called a *client host*) requests access to the file system of another computer (a *server host*). The server host responds by *exporting* a directory of its file system; the client host *imports* this information and arranges its own file system so that the imported directory (called the *server host's mount point*) appears as a directory in the client host's file system (this directory is called the *client host's mount point*).

25.6.1   Audit Analysis of the NFS Version 2 Protocol[4]

Consider a site connected to the Internet. It runs a local area network (LAN) with several UNIX systems sharing file systems using the Network File System version 2 (NFSv2) [1462] protocol. What should be logged?

We first review the NFSv2 protocol. When a client host wishes to mount a server's file system, its kernel contacts the server host's MOUNT server with the request. The MOUNT server first checks that the client is authorized to mount the requested file system and how the client will mount the requested system. If the client is authorized to mount the file system, the MOUNT server returns a *file handle* naming the mount point of the server's file system. The client kernel then creates an entry in its file system corresponding to the server's mount point. In addition, either the client host or the server host may restrict the type of accesses to the networked file system. If the server host sets the restrictions, the programs on the server host that implement NFSv2 will enforce the restrictions. If the client host sets the restrictions, the client kernel will enforce the restrictions and the server programs will be unaware that any restrictions have been set.

When a client process wishes to access a file, it attempts to open the file as though the file were on a local file system. When the client kernel reaches the client host's mount point in the path, the client kernel sends the file handle of

---

[4]This analysis was done with Jeremy Frank and Christopher Wee.

the server host's mount point (which it obtained during the mount) to resolve the next component (name) of the path to the server host's NFSv2 server using a LOOKUP request. If the resolution succeeds, this server returns the requested file handle. The client kernel then requests attributes of the component (a GETATTR request), and the NFSv2 server supplies them. If the file is a directory, the client kernel iterates (passing the directory's file handle and the next component of the path in a LOOKUP request and using the obtained file handle to get the attributes in a GETATTR request) until it obtains a file handle corresponding to the desired file object. The kernel returns control to the calling process, which can then manipulate the file by name or descriptor; the kernel translates these manipulations into NFSv2 requests, which are sent to the server host's NFSv2 server.

Because NFSv2 is a stateless protocol, the NFSv2 servers do not keep track of which files are in use. The file handle is a capability. Furthermore, many versions of NFSv2 require the kernel to present the requests,[5] although some accept requests from any user. In all cases, the server programs can identify the user making the request by examining the contents of the underlying messages.

The site policy drives the logging and auditing requirements because we are capturing events relevant to violations of that policy. In our example, the site wishes to regulate sharing of file systems among all systems on its LAN (with individual restrictions enforced through the NFSv2 mechanism). All imported file systems are supposed to be as secure as the local file systems. Therefore, the policy is as follows:

P1. NFSv2 servers will respond only to authorized clients.
The site authorizes only local hosts to act as clients. Under this policy, the site administrators could allow hosts not on the LAN to become clients, and so the policy could be less restrictive than the statement above suggests.

P2. The UNIX access controls regulate access to the server's exported file system.
Once a client has imported a server host's file system, the client host's processes may access that file system as if it were local. In particular, accessing a file requires search permission on all the ancestor directories (both local and imported).
An important ramification is the effect of the UNIX policy on file type. Only the local superuser can create device (block and character special) files locally, so users should not be able to create device files on any imported file system (or change an existing file's attributes to make it a device file). However, this policy does not restrict a client host from importing a file system that has device files.

---

[5]Validation is from the originating port number; the NFSv2 implementations assume that only the superuser (operator) can send requests from ports with numbers less than 1024.

P3. No client host can access a nonexported file system.
This means that exporting a file system allows clients to access files at or below the server host's mount point. Exporting a file system does not mean that a client host can access any file on the server host; the client can access only exported files.

These policies produce several constraints.

C1. File access granted ⇒ client is authorized to import file system, user can search all parent directories and can access file as requested, and file is descendant of server host's file system mount point.

C2. Device file created or file type changed to device ⇒ user has UID of 0.

C3. Possession of a file handle ⇒ file handle issued to that user.
Because the MOUNT and NFSv2 server processes issue file handles when a user successfully accesses a file, possession of a file handle implies that the user could access the file. If another user acquires the file handle without accessing either server, that user might access files without authorization.

C4. Operation succeeds ⇒ a similar operation local to the client would succeed.
This follows from the second policy rule. Because an ordinary user cannot mount a file system locally, the MOUNT operation should fail if the requesting user is not a superuser.

These constraints follow immediately from the three policy rules.

A transition from a secure to a nonsecure state can occur only when an NFSv2-related command is issued. Figure 25–2 lists the NFSv2 commands that a client may issue. One set takes no arguments and performs no actions; these commands do not affect the security state of the system. A second set takes file handles as arguments (as well as other arguments) and returns data (including status information). The third set also takes file handles as arguments and returns file handles as results.

Those operations that take file handles as arguments require that the auditor validate the constraint. When a server issues a file handle, the file handle, the user to whom it is issued, and the client to which it is sent must be recorded.

L1. When a file handle is issued, the server must record the file handle, the user (UID and GID) to whom it is issued, and the client host making the request.

The semantics of the UNIX file system say that access using a path name requires that the user be able to search each directory. However, once a file has been opened, access to the file requires the file descriptor and is not affected by the search permissions of parent directories. From the operation arguments, file handles seem to refer to open objects. For example, SYMLINK creates a symbolic link, which is effectively a write to a directory object; the argument to SYMLINK

Request	Arguments	Action
No arguments		
NULL	None	No action
WRITECACHE	None	*Unused*
Returns nonfile handle		
GETATTR	*fh*	Get attributes of the file
SETATTR	*fh, attrib*	Set attributes of the file
READ	*fh, off, ct*	Get *ct* bytes at position *off* from file
WRITE	*fh, off, ct*, data	Write *ct* bytes of data at position *off* to file
REMOVE	*dh, fn*	Delete named file in directory
RENAME	*dh1, dh2, fn1, fn2*	Rename file
LINK	*fh, dh, fn*	Create link named *fn* for file in directory
SYMLINK	*dh, fn1, fn2, attrib*	Create slink named *fn1* for *fn2* in directory
READLINK	*fh*	Get file name that symbolic link refers to
RMDIR	*dh, fn*	Delete named directory in directory
READDIR	*dh, off, ct*	Read *ct* bytes at position *off* from directory
STATFS	*dh*	Get file system information
Returns file handle		
ROOT	none	Get root file handle (*obsolete*)
CREATE	*dh, fn, attrib*	Create file *fn* in directory with attributes
MKDIR	*dh, fn, attrib*	Create directory *fn* in directory with attributes
LOOKUP	*dh, fn*	Get file handle of named file in directory

Figure 25–2   NFSv2 operations. In the Arguments and Action columns, *fh* is "file handle," *fn* is "file name," *dh* is "directory handle" (effectively, a file handle), *attrib* is "file attributes," *off* is "offset" (which need not be a byte count; it is positioning information), *ct* is "count," "link" is "direct alias," and "slink" is "indirect alias."

is the directory's handle. Hence, file handles resemble descriptors more than path names, so the auditor need not verify access permission whenever a user supplies a file handle. The only issue is whether the server issued the file handle to the user performing the operation.

L2. When a file handle is supplied as an argument, the server must record the file handle and the user (UID and GID).

A file handle allows its possessor to access the file to which the handle refers. Any operation that generates a file handle must record the user and relevant permissions for the object in question. For example, on a LOOKUP, recording the search permissions of the containing directory enables the auditor to determine if the user should have had access to the named file. On a CREATE, recording the write permissions of the containing directory indicates whether the user could legitimately write to the containing directory.

> L3. When a file handle is issued, the server must record the relevant attributes of any containing object.

Finally, whether the operation succeeds or fails, the system must record the operation's status so that the auditor can verify the result.

> L4. Record the results of each operation.

Because each operation performs a different function, we consider the audit criteria of each operation separately. We illustrate the process for mount and lookup and leave the rest as an exercise for the reader.

Constraints C1 and C4 define the audit criteria for MOUNT.

> A1. Check that the MOUNT server denies all requests by unauthorized client hosts or users to import a file system that the server host exports.

("Unauthorized users" refers specifically to those users who could not perform the operation locally.) This means that the MOUNT server must record L3 and L4.

Constraints C1 and C3 give the audit criteria for LOOKUP.

> A2. Check that the file handle comes from a client host and a user to which it was issued.
>
> A3. Check that the directory has the file system mount point as an ancestor and that the user has search permission on the directory.

The check for the client being authorized to import the file system (in C1) is implicit in A3 because if the client host is not authorized to import the file system, the client host will not obtain the file handle for the server host's mount point. Performing this audit requires logging of L2, L3 (the relevant attributes being owner, group, type, and permission), and L4. Audit criterion A3 requires recording of the name of the file being looked up; from this and the file handle, the auditor can reconstruct the ancestors of the file.

> L5. Record the name of the file argument in the LOOKUP operation.

Given the logs and the auditing checks, an analyst can easily determine if the policy has been violated. This is a transition-based mechanism because checks are performed during the actions and not during an evaluation of the current state of the system.

The most recent version of NFS, version 4.2, is stateful [883]. It also allows commands to be batched and sent to the server using COMPOUND. File locking is supported on the server. Further, many more file attributes are available and the protocol provides the ability to set them atomically. The security features have been made more compatible with Microsoft Windows access control lists. Thus, validation of the constraints are slightly different, and the validation more complex.

EXAMPLE: NFSv4 servers export a pseudo-file system that contains directories leading to exported file systems, so the clients can traverse the file system freely without seeing anything that is not to be exported. The root of this pseudo-file system is the root file handle. The server operates on the file identified as the *current file handle* (CFH). Many operations do not require that the client pass the file handle explicitly; instead, the CFH is used.

Suppose a client wishes to read a file on the NFSv4 file server [1500]. There is no MOUNT operation, but the PUTROOTFH operation sets the CFH to that of the root of the pseudo-file system. Thus:

A1. Check that the server denies all requests by unauthorized client hosts or users to execute the PUTROOTFH operation.

The server then looks up the requested root of the exported file system.

A2. Check that the directory being looked up is in the pseudo-file system and that the user has search permission on the directory.

Of course, this should always be true; but an error in implementation may enable the client to evade the restrictions of the pseudo-file system.

The server next receives a request to set the CFH to that of the requested root, and a request to open the file and read from it. The server can then verify the user is authorized to open the file.

A3. Check that the file being looked up is in the pseudo-file system and that the user has search permission on the directory containing it and read permission for the file.

The logging requirements are those of NFSv2, with one difference. NFSv4 has both persistent and volatile file handles. When a volatile file handle expires, that must be logged to indicate its validity has expired. Then an attempt to reuse the expired file handle will be logged and the reason for its rejection clear. If an expired file handle is not rejected, the logs will also show that.

25.6.2   The Logging and Auditing File System (LAFS)

LAFS [1986] takes a different approach. LAFS is a file system that records user level actions taken on files. A policy language allows an auditor to automate checks for violations of policy.

The LAFS file system is implemented as an extension of an existing file system, NFSv2, in the prototype. A user creates a directory using the *lmkdir* command and then attaches it to LAFS with the *lattach* command. For example, if the file policy contains a policy for LAFS, the commands

```
lmkdir /usr/home/xyzzy/project policy
lattach /usr/home/xyzzy/project /lafs/xyzzy/project
```

attach the directory and its contents to LAFS. All references to the files through LAFS will be logged.

LAFS consists of three main components, along with a name server and a file manager. The *configuration assistant*, which interacts with the name server and protection mechanisms of the underlying file system, sets up the required protection modes. This part is invoked when a file hierarchy is placed under LAFS (using *lattach*) and by the LAFS name server. The *audit logger* logs accesses to the file. The LAFS file manager invokes it whenever a process accesses the file. This allows LAFS to log accesses by LAFS-unaware applications. It in turn invokes the file manager of the underlying file system. At no point does the LAFS file manager perform access checking; that is left to the underlying file system. The *policy checker* validates policies and checks that logs conform to the policy.

A goal of LAFS is to avoid modifying applications to enable the logging. This allows users to use existing applications rather than having to develop new ones. The interface is therefore a set of three "virtual" files associated with each file in the LAFS hierarchy. The file *src.c* is a regular file. The file *src.c%log* contains a log of all accesses to *src.c*. The file *src.c%policy* contains a description of the access control policy for the file *src.c*. Accessing the virtual file *src.c%audit* triggers an audit in which the accesses of *src.c* are compared with the policy for the file. Any accesses not conforming to the policy are listed. The virtual files do not appear in file listings; the LAFS interface recognizes the extensions and provides the required access.

The policy language is simple yet powerful. It consists of a sequence of lines in the *%policy* files of the form

```
action:date&time:file:user:application:operation:
       status
```

For example, the following line says that users may not play the game *wumpus* from 9 a.m. to 5 p.m. The status field is omitted, because the policy checker is to report any attempts to play *wumpus* whether they succeed or not.

```
prohibit:0900-1700:*:*:wumpus:exec
```

The following lines describe a policy for controlling accesses to source code files in a project under development:

```
allow:*:Makefile:*:make:read
allow:*:Makefile:Owner:makedepend:write
```

```
allow:*:*.o,*.out:Owner,Group:gcc,ld:write
allow:-010929:*.c,*.h:Owner:emacs,vi,ed:write
allow:010930-:RCS/:librarian:rcs,co,ci:write
```

The first line allows the *make* program to read the Makefile on behalf of any user on the system. The second line allows the owner of the Makefile (indicated by the distinguished user "Owner") to change the Makefile by running the command *makedepend* (which adds dependencies among source code). The owner, or anyone in the group, of an object file can re-create the object file. Line 4 allows the owner of the source code to modify the source files using the *emacs* editor, the *vi* editor, or the *ed* editor, provided that the modification occurs before September 29, 2001. The last line allows the user "librarian" to write into the directory RCS using the *rcs*, *co*, and *ci* commands on any date from September 30, 2001, on. The purpose of this line is to allow the librarian to commit source code changes. The preceding line requires that all such changes be made before September 30, so (presumably) the project code is to be frozen on September 30, 2001.

As users access files, LAFS logs the accesses in a human-readable format, and when the user accesses the appropriate *%audit* file, the audit reports all violations of the relevant policy.

25.6.3   Comparison

The NFSv2 auditing mechanism and the LAFS have important similarities. In both cases, a security policy controls access, and the goal of both mechanisms is to detect and report attempted violations of the policy. Both have auditing mechanisms built into the file system.

The differences are also crucial. LAFS is "stacked" on top of NFSv2, so if a file is not bound to LAFS, no accesses to it are logged or audited. With the modifications of NFSv2, an attacker could avoid being audited only by not using NFSv2. (This is a typical problem with security mechanisms layered on top of existing protocols or other mechanisms.) The auditing mechanisms in NFSv2 are at a lower layer than those in LAFS (because of the stacking). However, LAFS allows users to specify policies for sets of files and to perform audits. The analysis of NFSv2 above is not as flexible. There, a site sets the policy for NFSv2. Users cannot define their own policies. Thus, the NFSv2 auditing mechanism will examine all file accesses, whereas LAFS may not. This affects not only auditing but also performance because if only a few files need to be audited, much of the effort by the NFSv2 mechanisms is unnecessary. Finally, modifying NFSv2 for auditing requires changes in several privileged daemons, whereas adding LAFS requires no modifications to existing system daemons and a kernel.

Which scheme to use depends on several factors, such as the ability to modify the NFSv2 daemons. The NFSv2 auditing modifications and LAFS can work together, the NFSv2 modifications being for the low-level system checking and LAFS for user-level auditing.

25.6.4   Audit Browsing

In addition to running audit mechanisms to analyze log files, auditors sometimes look through the log files themselves. The audit mechanisms may miss information or irregularities in the log that a knowledgeable auditor can detect. Furthermore, the audit mechanisms may be unsophisticated. By examining the logs directly, the auditors may uncover evidence of previously unknown patterns of misuse and attack. Finally, few systems provide a fully integrated suite of logs. Most have several different log files, each for a different set of applications or kernel events. The logs are usually ordered by timestamp and do not show relations other than the time of day and the program (process) creating the entry. For example, a log typically does not indicate two different programs making a sequence of accesses to a particular file.

The goal of an audit browsing tool is to present log information in a form that is easy for the analyst to understand and use. Specifically, the tool must indicate associations between log entries that are of interest to the analyst. Hoagland, Wee, and Levitt [908] identify six basic browsing techniques.

1. *Text display* shows the logs in a textual format. The format may be fixed, or it may be defined by the analyst through post-processing. The auditor may search for events based on name, time, or some other attribute; however, the attribute must be recorded in the log file. This method does not indicate relationships among events, entries, and entities.

2. *Hypertext display* shows the logs as a set of hypertext documents with associated log entries linked by hypertext constructs. This allows the auditor to follow relationships between entries and entities by following the links. The browser can include additional information about entities as well. The disadvantage is that the view of the log information is local because the browser does not highlight global relationships in a manner that is clear and easy to understand.

3. *Relational database browsing* requires that the logs be stored in a relational database. The auditor then issues queries to the database, and the database performs the correlations and associations before it replies to the query. The advantage of this method is that the database performs the correlations and can do so after the logs have been preprocessed. That is, the auditor need not know in advance what associations are of interest. The disadvantage is that the representation of the output to the query is usually textual. Furthermore, some preprocessing is required because the elements of the logs must be separated to provide the information for the database. The expected queries imply how this is to be done. This may limit the associations between entities and events that the database can exhibit.

4. *Replay* presents the events of interest in temporal order. It highlights temporal relationships. For example, if three logs are replayed on a single screen, the temporal order of the events in the log will be intermingled

and the order of occurrence across the logs will clearly indicate the order of the events in a way that the analyst can see.

5. *Graphing* provides a visual representation of the contents of logs. Typically, nodes represent entities such as processes and files, and edges represent associations. The associations indicate relationships between various entities. For example, processes may have incoming edges from their parents and outgoing edges to their children. The process hierarchy then becomes clear. One problem with this technique is the size of the drawing. If the area in which the graph is drawn is too small, the information may be unreadable. Reducing the logs to eliminate some information ameliorates this problem. The graph may also represent high-level entities (such as groups of processes or file systems) and their relationships, and the auditor can expand the high-level entities in order to examine relationships within the components of those entities.

6. *Slicing* obtains a minimum set of log events and objects that affect a given object. This comes from the traditional notion of slicing [1991], a program debugging technique that extracts a minimum set of statements that affect a given variable. Its advantage is that it focuses attention on the sequence of events, and related objects, that affect some entity. Its disadvantage, like that of hypertext browsing, is the locality of the technique.

Audit browsing tools emphasize associations that are of interest to the auditor. Hence, their configurations depend on the goals of the audit.

EXAMPLE: The Visual Audit Browser tool kit [908] was designed for general-purpose audit browsing. It consists of four tools. Each tool takes BSM logs as input. The *frame visualizer* generates a graphical representation of the logs. The *movie maker* generates a sequence of graphs corresponding to the logs. Each successive audit event generates a new graph with a new node and edge(s) corresponding to the audit event. The *hypertext generator* produces one page for each user in the log, one page for each file modified in the log, a page summarizing the audit records, and an index page. The pages are in HTML, so any web browser can view them. The *focused audit browser* combines slicing and graphing. The auditor enters the name of a node, and the browser displays that node, the node's incoming and outgoing edges, and the nodes at the ends of those edges.

Suppose a file is changed. The auditor uses the focused audit browser, with the file as the initial focus. The edges show which processes have altered the file and how. The auditor determines which process(es) may have caused the unexpected change, focuses on one of the suspect processes, and iterates until it is determined how the attacker gained access to the system (through a login, through a network daemon, and so on). At this point, the auditor needs to determine whether a masquerade is occurring. From the processes seen earlier, the auditor knows the audit UID of the attacker. She uses the hypertext generator to access the page with all audit records involving that audit UID and examines all entries on that page for irregular activity. She can also use the frame visualizer to graph the sequence of process creations. Once the auditor has found the entry point, she can probably uncover the vulnerability and then work forward to construct the actions that the attacker took. Finally, the movie maker can generate a small movie showing the actions that the attacker took. This will be a compelling visual record for law enforcement authorities and may aid the auditor during presentations to nontechnical people.

EXAMPLE: MieLog [1852] computes counts of single words and word pairs in logs. It allows the auditor to define a threshold count. Words and word pairs with counts higher than the threshold are colored to make them stand out. The display of MieLog consists of four fields. The *tag appearance frequency area* has a colored tile indicating the frequency of appearance (red meaning rare). The *time information area* contains a bar graph indicating the number of log entries in that period of time. Clicking on the bar brings up the log entries for that time period. The *outline of message area* shows the outline of the log messages, colored to match the frequency in the tag appearance frequency area. The fourth field, the *message in text area*, displays the log entry under study and its surrounding areas. The words and word pairs are colored to reflect their frequencies.

As an example, an administrator examining a log file notices an unusual gap in the time information area. There are no log messages recorded during the period of time in the gap. The system administrator focuses on the log entries just before and just after the gap, to determine why the logging turned off and then turned back on. The color of the words in those log entries will aid the auditor in looking for unusual log entries, words, or phrases indicating an attack.

Developing a visual interface to logs is as much an art as a science. The science lies in determining what to display; the art lies in the graphics used to express the desired relationships and entities. The human should be able to grasp the relevant parts of the log quickly and to pursue lines of inquiry quickly and easily.

25.7 Summary

Logging is the collection of information; auditing is its analysis. Auditing consists of analysis, which is the study of information gleaned from the log entries and ancillary information, and notification, which is the reporting of the results of the study (and possibly the taking of appropriate actions).

Designing an audit system requires that the goals of the audit be well formed. Typically, the security policy defines these goals. The audit mechanism reports attempts to violate the constraints imposed by the security policy, such as a subject's attempt to write to a lower-level object. Several considerations affect the auditing. For example, names in the logs must be resolvable to an object. The logs must be well structured to allow unambiguous and consistent parsing. They may need to be sanitized before or after analysis. Application logs reflect actions of the application; system logs reflect events within the operating system.

Auditing mechanisms should be designed into the system. These mechanisms may also be added after the system is completed. In this case, the mechanism may report violations of a defined security policy or may report actions that are considered to be security threats (whether a security policy is defined precisely or not).

Some logs need to be anonymized before they are used. In that case, the relationships between the suppressed data and the nonsuppressed data are as important as the method used for anonymization.

A mechanism enabling auditors to browse the logs aids in the analysis. Such a browser helps auditors locate problems that they have not thought of and may speed the analysis of problems that other audit mechanisms have reported.

25.8 Research Issues

The sanitization of logs is an important research topic. The key issue is the preservation of relationships needed to perform a useful audit and the protection of sensitive data. The former requires a careful analysis of the goals of the audit and the security policy involved. In real situations, the policy is often not explicit. The audit system itself looks for known violations of the policy. The analysts are also attempting to discover previously unknown methods of attack. If the audit detects violations of a known policy, then the analysts need to determine the sequence of events leading up to the breach. In either case, the analyst may not know what information he is looking for until he has done considerable analysis, at which point the required data may have been sanitized and the original data may be unavailable. But if information about the relationship of sanitized data is left in the log, someone may be able to deduce confidential information. Whether or not this dilemma can be resolved and, if not, how to sanitize the logs to best meet the needs of the analysts and the people being protected are open questions.

Determining what to record is also an area of active research. Given a system with a precise specification, the events to be logged are simply those that enable the audit to determine whether those specifications were violated. But few systems have precise specifications. For these systems, analyzing the nature of events that violate the security policy is complex, and indeed the security policy itself may be incomplete or inconsistent. How to decide what to record without making the logs unmanageable, and how to deal with incomplete logs, affects the completeness of the audit.

Correlation of logs is another open problem. The first type of correlation is development of a general method that maps a set of system log entries to the corresponding application log entries. Conversely, an analyst may want to map a single application log entry to a set of system log entries to determine what happens at the lower (system) level. A second type of correlation involves ordering of logs from systems spread over a network. If the clocks are synchronized, the log entries may be placed in temporal order. If not, Lamport's clock algorithm [1129] provides a partial ordering of the entries, provided that the sends and receives between systems are logged. However, Lamport's scheme assumes either that the systems communicate directly with one another or that the logs of all intermediate systems record sends and receives and be available to the analyst. How to correlate the events when this information is not available, or when the logs do not record sends and receives, is an open problem.

Data provenance is a type of logging that records details of who accesses the data and how, especially if the data is altered or transformed in any way. It is critical for validating the integrity of data in workflows, and the relationships between provenance, workflow, and forensics are areas of active research. Maintaining provenance logs securely, and validating the information in the provenance logs, are under study.

Audit browsing techniques are in their infancy. Like other user interface mechanisms, audit browsing mechanisms take advantage of human psychology and cognitive abilities. How best to use these mechanisms to enable people to study logs and draw conclusions, or to determine where to focus the analysis, is an open question, and another one is how to create or determine associations of entities on the fly as the interest of the human analyst shifts from one set of data to another.

25.9   Further Reading

The analysis of log files, and auditing techniques, relating to detecting attacks is discussed in Chapter 26, "Intrusion Detection." Many analyses of log files require that times be correlated. Lamport's clock algorithm is based on events that correlate among multiple systems. If only timestamps are available, then Ristenpart [1590] showed that temporal relationships can only be determined from them if they are created using synchronized clocks.

Logs and auditing are critical components of systems designed for security, and papers discuss the auditing mechanism and the rationale behind it, usually pointing to the relevant requirements. Sibert [1746] discusses auditing in the SunOS MLS system. Banning and her colleagues [124] discuss auditing of distributed systems. Shieh and Gligor [1733] discuss auditing of covert channels. Retroactive auditing can be used to identify that problems have occurred by examining security patches [398, 1973].

What is logged, and how those logs are analyzed, depends upon the domain of use of the system. Rao [1566] discusses auditing in an avionics system. Auditing systems for healthcare environments must take regulations such as the U. S. Health Insurance Portability and Accountability Act into consideration [248, 594]. Electronic voting systems have unusual audit requirements, in that the information logged cannot enable a voter to be correlated with his or her ballot [63, 139,

232, 973, 1509, 1951]. Introspection of virtual systems enables system logs to be analyzed by an observer outside the virtual system [113, 597, 906].

One technique to aid analysis is visualization. It has been used to enhance audits of spreadsheets [375, 1638]. Other visualization techniques are designed to aid analysts in using logs to detect intruders. Researchers have explored using a visual interface for logs used to detect intruders [1089, 1853]. Analysts also use other visualization tools to explore the logs for events of interest [450, 935].

Information sharing is critical to both science in general and security in particular. Differential privacy [601, 602, 1304] captures the risk to one's privacy that being in a dataset poses. That quasi-identifiers can arise from unexpected combinations of data elements was shown in studies of the 1990 and 2000 censuses of the United States [792, 1844]. Prefix-preserving IP address anonymization [654, 1562] hides the actual addresses without disguising the relationship of addresses being on the same network or subnet. Sweeney proposed anonymizing data by grouping entities into sets with a lower bound on size [1845], and others built upon her work to handle cases in which the partitioning does not provide the requisite anonymity [1165, 1228]. The trade-off between privacy and utility has been studied for network traces [320, 465, 1490]. Other studies discuss approaches to deanonymizing sanitized data [466, 739, 1423].

To counter the threat of the attacker finding and altering logs or log entries, researchers have proposed cryptographic methods to secure the logs themselves [12, 480, 1227, 1689]. These have been implemented in file systems [1519]. Secure logging as a service, analogous to infrastructure as a service, has also been explored [1046, 2079]. The S4 service [1839] uses journaling techniques to secure logs even if the system has been compromised. A number of papers discuss security in provenance logs [753, 878, 2037].

25.10 Exercises

1. Extend the example of deriving required logging information to the full Bell-LaPadula Model with both security levels and compartments.

2. In the example of deriving required logging information for the Chinese Wall model, it is stated that the time must be logged. Why? Can something else be logged to achieve the same purpose?

3. The Windows system logger allows the system administrator to define events to be entered into the security log. In the example, the system administrator configured the logger to record process execution and termination. What other events might the system administrator wish to record?

4. Suppose a notifier sends email to the system administrator when a successful compromise of that system is detected. What are the drawbacks of this approach? How would you notify the appropriate user?

5. Describe a set of constraints for the Clark-Wilson model that lead to a description of the conditions that an audit mechanism should detect. Give these conditions.

6. Why is adherence to the principle of complete mediation (see Section 14.2.4) a necessity for logging of file accesses?

7. A network monitor records the following information while recording a network connection:

   a. System prompts that name neither the user nor the system

   b. System control files such as the password file

   c. A file containing a list of dictionary words

   d. A user's startup file

   e. A system banner

   f. A source code file

   g. A web page downloaded from a remote site

   Which type of information should the monitor check to see if it must sanitize the data to conceal the names of the users and the names and addresses of the computers involved?

8. Fisch, White, and Pooch [680] define four levels of log sanitization.

   a. Simple sanitization, in which all information except the commands issued by an intruder are deleted

   b. Information-tracking sanitization, in which sensitive information is entered into a symbol table as it is encountered, a unique identifier is assigned, and whenever that information is encountered it is replaced with the associated identifier

   c. Format sanitization, in which compressed or encoded data is transformed into its original form, the original form is sanitized using information-tracking sanitization, and the resulting data is returned to its transformed format

   d. Comprehensive sanitization, in which all data is analyzed and sanitized as in information-tracking and format sanitization

   Discuss the level of anonymity of each level of sanitization. Which level could be automated, and to what degree would human oversight be required?

9. Prove or disprove that state-based logging and transition-based logging are equivalent if and only if the state of the system at the first transition is recorded.

10. Suppose a remote host begins the TCP three-way handshake with the local host but never sends the final ACK. This is called a *half-open connection*. The local host waits for some short time and then purges the information from its network tables. If a remote host makes so many half-open connections that

the local host cannot accept connections from other hosts, the remote host has launched a *syn flood attack* (see Section 7.4 for more details). Derive logging and auditing requirements to detect such an attack.

11. What are the logging and auditing requirements for the NFSv2 operations MKDIR and WRITE?

12. In the LAFS file system, what does the following policy line say?

    ```
    prohibit:0800-1700:*:root:solitaire:exec:ok
    ```

    What is the effect of specifying the status field?

13. Write a program that will slice a log file with respect to a given object. Your program should take an object identifier (such as a process or file name) and a log file as input. Your program should print the minimum set of statements that affect the object, either directly or indirectly.

Chapter 26
Intrusion Detection

> HIPPOLYTA: How chance Moonshine is gone before
> Thisbe comes back and finds her lover?
> THESUS: She will find him by starlight. Here
> she comes; and her passion ends the play.
> — *A Midsummer Night's Dream*, V, i, 320–323.

System managers must protect computer systems from attack. The mechanisms and techniques discussed throughout this book help protect systems, data, and resources. However, nothing is perfect. Even the best protected systems must be monitored to detect successful (and unsuccessful) attempts to breach security. This chapter discusses automated systems for detecting intrusions.

26.1   Principles

Computer systems that are not under attack exhibit several characteristics.

1. The actions of users and processes generally conform to a statistically predictable pattern. A user who does only word processing when using the computer is unlikely to perform a system maintenance function.

2. The actions of users and processes do not include sequences of commands to subvert the security policy of the system. In theory, any such sequence is excluded; in practice, only sequences known to subvert the system can be detected.

3. The actions of processes conform to a set of specifications describing actions that the processes are allowed to do (or not allowed to do).

Denning [537] hypothesized that systems under attack fail to meet at least one of these characteristics.

EXAMPLE: If the goal is to put in a backdoor, the intruder may modify a system configuration file or program. If the attacker enters the system as a nonprivileged user, he or she must acquire system privileges to change the files. The nonprivileged user may not be a user who normally acquires system privileges (characteristic 1). The techniques used to acquire those privileges may involve sequences of commands designed to violate the security policy of the system (characteristic 2). If they do not, the alterations in the system files may introduce elements that cause processes to act in ways that violate specifications (characteristic 3).

If the attacker modifies a user file, processes executing on behalf of that user can now behave in abnormal ways, such as allowing network connections from sites not able to connect earlier, or by executing commands that the user did not execute before (characteristic 1). The commands may subvert the security policy, thereby gaining system privileges for the user—and the attacker (characteristic 2).

EXAMPLE: Cliff Stoll noticed an anomaly in one of the systems he was administering: a 79¢ discrepancy in the output of an accounting log [1829]. On investigation, he realized that an intruder was breaking in to search for classified information. This caused the discrepancy. As a result, authorities broke up an espionage ring [1831].

26.2   Basic Intrusion Detection

The characteristics listed above guide the detection of intrusions. Once the province of the technologically sophisticated, attacks against systems have been automated. So a sophisticated attack need not be the work of a sophisticated attacker. These attack tools do not change the nature of intrusion detection fundamentally. They do eliminate many errors arising from incorrect installation and perform routine steps to clean up detritus of the attack, but they cannot eliminate all traces.

EXAMPLE: Consider an attack involving the Linux Rootkit IV described in Section 23.2.1. If the configuration files controlling *netstat*, *ps*, *ls*, and *du* are set up correctly, these programs will not report any network connections, files, or processes associated with *rootkit*. The files and processes will still be present, and other programs that perform the same functions as *netstat*, *ps*, *ls*, and *du* will report the presence of *rootkit*-related files. For example, *du* prints the number of blocks used by a set of files, and *df* reports the number of free blocks on a file system. Their sum should be approximately the size of the file system (less some space for disk management blocks). The number of files in directories should agree with *ls*'s count. Other programs, such as a locally written directory listing program, can check this. The load average should be consistent with the running processes. Programs other than *ps*, such as local process listers, can list processes.

The point is that *rootkit* does not conceal the files, connections, and processes by altering kernel or file structures. It alters the programs that interpret the data in those structures. So, if *rootkit* fails to alter any program that retrieves the data, that program will reveal the correct data. This inconsistency indicates an anomaly, which—by characteristic 1—indicates an attack.

EXAMPLE: When the network sniffer in the Linux Rootkit IV (*rootkit*) accesses the network device, it puts that device into promiscuous mode.[1] On some systems, this creates a log entry. Such an entry indicates a known attack, and—by characteristic 2—an intrusion.

Denning [537] suggests automation of the intrusion detection process. Her specific hypothesis is that exploiting vulnerabilities requires an abnormal use of normal commands or instructions, so security violations can be detected by looking for abnormalities. Her model is very general and includes abnormalities such as deviation from usual actions (anomaly detection), execution of actions that lead to break-ins (misuse detection), and actions inconsistent with the specifications of privileged programs (specification-based detection).

Systems that do this are called *intrusion detection systems* (IDS). Their goals are fourfold:[2]

1. Detect a wide variety of intrusions. Intrusions from within the site, as well as those from outside the site, are of interest. Furthermore, both known and previously unknown attacks should be detected. This suggests a mechanism for learning or adapting to new types of attacks or to changes in normal user activity.

2. Detect intrusions in a timely fashion. "Timely" here need not be in real time. Often, it suffices to discover an intrusion within a short period of time. Real-time intrusion detection raises issues of responsiveness. If every command and action must be analyzed before it can be executed, only a very simple analysis can be done before the computer (or network) being monitored becomes unusable. On the other hand, in all but a few rare cases, determining that an intrusion took place a year ago is probably useless.

3. Present the analysis in a simple, easy-to-understand format. Ideally, this should be a light that glows green for no detected intrusions and that changes to red when an attack is detected. Unfortunately, intrusions are rarely this clear-cut, so intrusion detection mechanisms must present more complex data to a site security officer. The security officer determines what action (if any) to take. Because intrusion detection

---

[1] Unless the network device is in promiscuous mode, the network sniffer can record only packets intended for the host on which the sniffer resides.

[2] Intrusion detection systems may simply log traffic for later analysis. In this case, they are logging engines rather than intrusion detection mechanisms (see Section 25.2.1).

mechanisms may monitor many systems (not just one), the user interface is of critical importance. This leads to the next requirement.

4. Be accurate. A *false positive* occurs when an intrusion detection system reports an attack, but no attack is underway. False positives reduce confidence in the correctness of the results as well as increase the amount of work involved. However, *false negatives* (occurring when an intrusion detection system fails to report an ongoing attack) are worse, because the purpose of an intrusion detection system is to report attacks. The goal of an intrusion detection system is to minimize both types of errors.

Formalizing this type of analysis provides a statistical and analytical basis for monitoring a system for intrusions. Three types of analyses—anomaly detection, misuse (or signature) detection, and specification detection—look for violations of the three characteristics in Section 26.1. Before discussing these types of analyses, let us consider models of an intrusion detection system.

26.3   Models

Intrusion detection systems determine if actions constitute intrusions on the basis of one or more models of intrusion. A model classifies a sequence of states or actions, or a characterization of states or actions, as "good" (no intrusions) or "bad" (possible intrusions). Anomaly models use a statistical characterization, and actions or states that are statistically unusual are classified as "bad." Misuse models compare actions or states with sequences known to indicate intrusions, or sequences believed to indicate intrusions, and classify those sequences as "bad." Specification-based models classify states that violate the specifications as "bad." The models may be *adaptive* models that alter their behavior on the basis of system states and actions, or they may be *static* models that are initialized from collected data and do not change as the system runs.

In this section we examine representative models of each class. In practice, models are often combined, and intrusion detection systems use a mixture of two or three different types of models.

26.3.1   Anomaly Modeling

Anomaly detection uses the assumption that unexpected behavior is evidence of an intrusion. Implicit is the belief that some set of metrics can characterize the expected behavior of a user or a process. Each metric relates a subject and an object.

Definition 26–1. *Anomaly detection* analyzes a set of characteristics of the system and compares their behavior with a set of expected values. It reports when the computed statistics do not match the expected measurements.

Central to anomaly detection is the idea of being able to detect "outliers" or values that do not match, or fall within, a set of "reasonable values." These outliers are the anomalies, but characterizing a value as abnormal implies that there is a method for characterizing "normal" values. Several methods have been developed to do this.

26.3.1.1 Threshold Metrics

Denning proposed using a threshold metric. A minimum of m and a maximum of n events are expected to occur (for some event and some values m and n). If, over a specific period of time, fewer than m or more than n events occur, the behavior is deemed anomalous.

EXAMPLE: Microsoft Windows systems allow the administrator to lock a user out after some number n of failed login attempts. This is an intrusion detection system using the threshold metric with the lower limit 0 and the upper limit n. The attempted logins are deemed anomalous after n failed attempts to log in.

Determining the threshold complicates use of this model. The threshold must take into account differing levels of sophistication and characteristics of the users. For example, if n were set to 3 in the example above for a system in France, and the primary users of that system were in the United States, the difference in the keyboards would result in a large number of false alarms. But if the system were located in the United States, setting n to 3 would be more reasonable. One approach is to combine this approach with the other two models to adapt the thresholds to observed or predicted behavior.

26.3.1.2 Statistical Methods

The simplest statistical method, also proposed by Denning, uses statistical moments. The analyzer knows the mean and standard deviation (first two moments) and possibly other measures of correlation (higher moments). If values fall outside the expected interval for that moment, the behavior that the values represent is deemed anomalous. Because the profile, or description of the system, may evolve over time, anomaly-based intrusion detection systems take these changes into account by aging (or weighting) data or altering the statistical rule base on which they make decisions.

EXAMPLE: The Intrusion Detection Expert System (IDES) [965, 1219] was developed at SRI International based on Denning's original model. It uses anomaly detection, among other techniques. It represents subjects, which can include a user, a login session, applications, routers, and so on, as an ordered sequence of statistics $<q_{0,j}, \ldots, q_{n,j}>$, where $q_{i,j}$ is the ith statistic on day j. The metrics are counts or time intervals, as discussed in a preceding example. The profile for each subject is updated every day on the basis of observed behavior.

IDES weights its statistics to favor recent behavior over past behavior. Let $A_{k,l}$ be the summation of counts making up the metric for the kth statistic on day l. Then the statistic $q_{k,l+1} = A_{k,l+1} - A_{k,l} + 2^{-rt}q_{k,l}$, where t is the number of log entries or the total time elapsed since time 0, and r is a half-life determined through experience. This is an exponential decay of previous values and is quite sensitive to changes in behavior over a short period of time.

EXAMPLE: Haystack [1764] used a similar representation of events, but considered behavior anomalous based on values larger than or smaller than certain limits. It used a single variable. Let A_n be a count or time interval, and let T_L and T_U be bounds such that 90% of values for A_i, $i = 0, \ldots, n$, lie between T_L and T_U. Then, when A_{n+1} is computed, it is deemed anomalous if it does not fall between T_L and T_U. In this model, rapid changes in the values of A_n are not considered relevant. But a value is anomalous if it lies outside the bounds of an interval containing 90% of the previous values.

This mechanism is also adaptive. As the values of the variable change, so do the thresholds. This leads to a system that can adapt to changes in user behavior over a long period of time.

The statistical moments model provides more flexibility than the threshold model. Administrators can tune it to discriminate better than the threshold model. But with flexibility comes complexity. In particular, an explicit assumption is that the behavior of processes, and users, can be statistically modeled. If this behavior matches a statistical distribution (such as a Gaussian or normal distribution), determining the parameters requires experimental data that can be obtained from the system. But if not, the analysts must use other techniques, such as clustering, to determine the model and the values that indicate abnormal behavior.

26.3.1.3   Markov Models

Denning's third model is a Markov model. Examine a system at some particular point in time. Events preceding that time have put the system into a particular state. When the next event occurs, the system transitions into a new state. Over time, a set of probabilities of transition can be developed. When an event occurs that causes a transition that has a low probability, the event is deemed anomalous. This model suggests that a notion of "state," or past history, can be used to detect anomalies. The anomalies are now no longer based on statistics of the occurrence of individual events, but on sequences of events. This approach heralded misuse detection and was used to develop effective anomaly detection mechanisms.

Teng, Chen, and Lu used this approach in Digital Equipment Corporation's TIM research system [1866]. Their scheme used an artificial intelligence technique called time-based inductive learning. The system is given a type of event to be predicted. It develops a set of temporally related conditions that predict the time that the event will occur with respect to the set.

EXAMPLE: Consider the sequence of events *abcdedeabcabc*. The goal is to predict these events. The following rules are examples that TIM might derive:

$$R_1 : ab \rightarrow c \ (1) \quad R_2 : c \rightarrow d \ (0.5) \quad R_3 : c \rightarrow e \ (0.5)$$
$$R_4 : d \ \rightarrow e \ (1) \quad R_5 : e \rightarrow a \ (0.5) \quad R_6 : e \rightarrow d \ (0.5)$$

The left side of each rule is the antecedent, and the right side is the event being predicted. The number in parentheses is the probability that the antecedent event(s) is (are) followed by the event on the right side of the rule. Rules R_1 and R_4 are good indicators of expected behavior. The other rules are not particularly good, and will either be dropped (should the probability decrease over time) or become better (should the probability increase over time).

Anomalies are detected when a sequence of events matches the left side of a rule but the succeeding event differs from the expected right side. Using the rules above, if the sequence *abd* occurs, an alert will be triggered because *c* should always come after *ab*. But the sequence *acf* will not cause an alert, because multiple events may follow *c*. This sequence could cause a new rule to be added, namely, $R_7 : c \rightarrow f \ (\frac{1}{3})$—and the probabilities for rules R_2 and R_3 would change to $\frac{1}{3}$.

EXAMPLE: Hofmeyr, Somayaji, and Forrest [703,915] defined "normal behavior" in terms of sequences of system calls of various lengths, called *traces*. They built a database of these traces by observing process behavior during normal runs of the program. For example, if the trace length were 4 and the process had the trace

```
open read write open mmap write fchmod close
```

then the database would contain the following traces:

open	read	write	open
read	write	open	mmap
write	open	mmap	write
open	mmap	write	fchmod
mmap	write	fchmod	close

If the sequence of system calls of this program on a later run were

```
open read read open mmap write fchmod close
```

that trace would differ from the traces in the database in five positions (the second call after the first *open* is not *write*, the call following the first *read* is not *write*, the call following the second *read* is not *write*, the second call is not *open*, and the third call is not *mmap*). The maximum number of pairwise mismatches for this sequence is 18, so the mismatch rate is about 26%.

Using this technique to monitor the UNIX *sendmail* program and the line printer daemon showed that this technique could distinguish between these two programs and other programs. They also showed promise for detecting anomalous behavior. Comparisons of other statistical methods suggested that more sophisticated statistical analysis could enhance the accuracy of intrusion detection systems using system call sequences.

The effectiveness of Markov-based models depends on the adequacy of the data used to establish the model. This data (called *training data*) is obtained experimentally, usually from populations that are believed to be normal (not anomalous). For example, TIM could obtain data by monitoring a corporate system to establish the relevant events and their sequence. Hofmeyr, Forrest, and Somayaji obtained traces of system calls from processes running in a normal environment. If this training data accurately reflects the environment in which the intrusion detection system is to run, the model will work well, but if the training data does not correspond to the environment, the Markov model will produce false alarms and miss abnormal behaviors. In particular, unless the training data covers all possible normal uses of the system in the environment, the intrusion detection mechanism will issue false reports of abnormalities.

26.3.1.4   Machine Learning

The anomaly detection methods discussed so far make assumptions about the statistics of the underlying data. For example, IDES builds its anomaly detection scheme on the assumption that values of events have a Gaussian distribution. If the distribution is Gaussian, the model works well. If it is not, the model will not match the events, and either too many anomalous events will occur (a high *false positive rate*) or anomalous events will be missed (a high *false negative rate*). The former will overwhelm the security officers with data and possibly cause them to miss truly anomalous behavior. The latter will simply not report events that should be reported.

Experience indicates, however, that the distribution is typically not Gaussian. So various machine learning methods can be used to classify data as anomalous. These methods, discussed in the next few sections, fall into two broad categories.

Supervised learning methods begin with data that has already been classified. First, the data is split into two sets. The first set is the "training set" and the system uses that to learn what is anomalous and what is not. Once the training is complete, the second set of classified data is used to test the training. As the data has already been classified, the results reported by the system can be compared to these classifications. Ideally, the two results should match.

Unsupervised learning methods, on the other hand, have no training data. The system is given the data to be classified and, based on characteristics of the data, determines what is anomalous and what is not. This method assumes that anomalous data is a small part of the data; otherwise, the system will assume that the anomalous data is normal, leading to a large number of false positives.

Several measures are commonly used to evaluate intrusion detection methods. Define *TP* and *TN* as the number of true positives and true negatives, respectively. Similarly, define *FP* and *FN* as the number of false positives and false negatives, respectively.

Definition 26–2. [2029]

1. The *accuracy* (sometimes called the *classification rate*) is defined as $\frac{TP+TN}{TP+TN+FP+FN} \times 100\%$, or the percentage of events classified correctly.
2. The *detection rate*, also called the *true positive rate*, is $\frac{TP}{TP+FN} \times 100\%$, or the percentage of reported attack events that are real attack events.
3. The *false alarm rate*, also called the *false positive rate*, is $\frac{FP}{FP+TN} \times 100\%$, or the percentage of nonattack events reported as attack events.

These are sometimes expressed as fractions rather than percentages.

Evaluating intrusion detection methods requires a common set of data, and gathering or generating data for testing is a perennial problem [11, 1636, 1738, 1786, 1871]. The DARPA off-line intrusion detection evaluations [1194, 1195] were the first large-scale evaluation of intrusion detection systems. The researchers developed a synthetic dataset, IDEVAL, based on network traffic of a U.S. Air Force base, with attacks injected into the dataset that was used in the testing. McHugh's critique of the tests [1291] noted that generating synthetic data to match a particular context means that the data may not be valid for evaluating systems used in other contexts. A variant of the IDEVAL dataset, the KDD-CUPS-99 (or KDD-99) dataset, is widely used to compare anomaly detection methods and systems.

EXAMPLE: The network traffic at an academic institution is most likely quite different than that of the KDD-CUPS-99 dataset, and so an intrusion detection system that performs well on the KDD-CUP-99 data may perform poorly on an academic research network. Indeed, a comparison of the KDD-CUP-99 dataset with traffic collected from the main server for the computer science department at the Florida Institute of Technology (FIT) [1236] showed some anomalies in the FIT traffic not in the KDD-CUPS-99 traffic, such as the TCP ACK field being nonzero when the ACK flag was not set. Higher-level protocols also showed differences; the KDD-CUPS-99 HTTP requests were all regular, used the keyword GET, and were HTTP version 1.0, whereas in the FIT data some of the commands were not GET, inconsistencies in the requests abounded, and the protocol was either version 1.0 or 1.1. They concluded that using the KDD-CUPS-99 data to evaluate anomaly detection techniques for their network would result in an overestimation of how well some of those techniques performed.

26.3.1.5   Clustering

Clustering is a statistical technique that does not assume any *a priori* distribution of events. It requires some set of data to be available, usually obtained by monitoring the system for some period of time. The data is then grouped into subsets, or *clusters*, based on some property (called a *feature*). Instead of analyzing individual data points, the clusters are analyzed. This greatly reduces the amount of data analyzed, at the cost of some preprocessing time (to cluster the data). This approach is sensitive to the features and the statistical definitions of clustering.

EXAMPLE: Suppose an intrusion detection system bases anomaly detection on the number of reads and writes that a process does. Figure 26–1 shows a sample of the relevant data for a system. Rather than deal with six data points, we cluster them. (In practice, the data sample would be many thousands of values.)

Our first clustering scheme is to group the data into four clusters. The first cluster contains all entries whose CPU times fall into the first 25th percentile of the data; the second, the entries whose CPU times fall into the second 25th percentile of the data; and so forth. Using this grouping, we have four clusters, with only one value in the last quartile. This could be selected as an anomalous cluster.

Our second clustering reduces the number of clusters to two, divided into those events with CPU times above the 50th percentile, and those with the CPU times below it. Here, the two clusters contain three values each, so no conclusions about anomalies can be drawn.

As this example shows, determining how to cluster the data can be tricky. Even more difficult is determining which features are meaningful. For example, the CPU time used may show anomalies but may not indicate violations of the security policy, but the number of I/O requests may indicate a violation if the data falls into a particular cluster. To overcome this problem, systems using clustering require *training data* in which the anomalous data indicating intrusions is marked. The feature selection program will use this data to derive features and build clusters that will reflect the anomalous data (to some degree of accuracy).

Process	User	CPU Time	CPU Time (cluster 1)	CPU Time (cluster 2)
p1	matt	359	4	2
p2	holly	10	1	1
p3	heidi	263	3	2
p4	steven	68	1	1
p5	david	133	2	1
p6	mike	195	3	2

Figure 26–1   Clustering. The relevant measure, CPU time, is clustered in two ways. The first uses intervals of 25th percentiles, and the second uses the 50th percentile.

EXAMPLE: Frank demonstrated how feature selection can aid detection of potential problems [713]. He recounts an experiment in which network traffic was classified by features. Normally, network traffic is characterized by its source and destination port numbers, but on many systems the port numbers and services can be remapped, so (for example) the telnet port could be 3925 rather than the traditional 23. This remapping is internal to the system, and is undetectable unless the contents of the traffic are read and analyzed. Frank used 15,947 network connections obtained by monitoring a local area network to test the classification program. He also gathered port numbers to train the classification program (the assumption being that there was not enough illicit port mapping to corrupt the results).

Frank collected the following characteristics about each connection:

- Index in the set of connections
- Length of time of the connection
- Number of packets from the source to the destination, and vice versa
- Number of data bytes from the source to the destination, and vice versa
- Expert system warning, an indication of how likely the NSM (see Section 26.5.1) thought it was that the event was an attack

Initially, each characteristic was considered as a possible feature. Frank then used three types of algorithms to determine the best feature set to use for classifying connections as suspicious. The first was a backward sequential search algorithm, which began with the full set of features, computed error rates, and eliminated one of the features to reduce the error rate. This continued for some number of steps. For Frank's test data, the error rate was roughly 0.011%. The best set of features used all six recorded characteristics (the index was omitted).

The second algorithm was a beam search algorithm. In this algorithm, a metric ordered the possible clusters from best to worst, took the best, and extended the search from that state. As new potential clusters were generated, they were added to the list. This algorithm achieved the same error rate as the backward sequential search algorithm, and produced a best features set of the same size.

The third algorithm selected sequential data beginning at randomly chosen places in the set of network connections. This generated a random feature set, and then both backward and forward analyses were performed. This was the slowest algorithm and had the same error rate and best features set as those of the other two algorithms.

All three of these algorithms found that if the time in seconds, number of packets from the destination, and number of data bytes from the source were the only three features used, the classification error was less than 0.02%. Adding the other features reduced the error even further.

Frank then considered the set of features that would best classify connections as being of a particular type, such as SMTP (electronic mail) connections. He found that for all three algorithms, the best features set had five features (the index and number of data bytes from the destination were unnecessary), with an error rate of 0.007%. If the number of packets from the source and the expert system warning were omitted, the error rate crept to 0.009%. He obtained similar results for remote login connections (four features, with an error rate of 0.001%). When he analyzed remote command sessions, all algorithms found that the best features set was of size four, but the randomly generated sequential search method chose a different set of features (it omitted the number of destination packets and included the time), and halved the error rate obtained by the other two algorithms.

26.3.1.6   Neural Nets

A neural net is a structure that has an input layer, an output layer, and one or more layers between them (the "hidden layers"). Each node in a layer is connected to all the nodes in the preceding and following layer, and has an internal function that transforms the inputs coming into the node into outputs leaving the node. Each of the connections has an associated weight.

The goal of the neural net is to classify values as anomalous or expected. It is first given training data that is used as input to the neural net, and the net produces outputs. These actual outputs are compared to the ideal outputs. The weights of the connections are adjusted according to a function that takes into account the discrepancies between the ideal and actual outputs. The data is then run through the neural net again, the weights adjusted again, and this process repeats until the neural net output matches the ideal output. This approach is called "backpropagation" because the outputs are used to adjust the internal weights. When the training is finished, the weights are set, and testing and analysis begins.

Other types of neural networks have been used for intrusion detection. The simplest is the *perceptron*, which has one intermediate neuron. Feedforward networks have multiple internal neurons distributed among one or more hidden layers (see Figure 26–2); the backpropagation network is an example of this. Other types include multilayer perceptrons and autoassociative networks.

EXAMPLE: Mukkamala, Janoski, and Sung [1395] used three types of neural nets to analyze the KDD-CUP-99 dataset. As they used all 41 features of that dataset, all the neural nets had 41 inputs and 1 output node. The first neural net had three hidden layers of 20 neurons each; the second, two hidden layers of 40 neurons each; and the third, two hidden layers of 25 and 20 neurons. They split the dataset into two parts. The training part had 7,312 elements and the testing part had 6,980 elements. The second neural net had the highest accuracy, 99.50%, the first, 99.05%, and the third, 99%.

26.3.1.7   Self-Organizing Maps

Self-organizing maps are unsupervised learning methods. They map nonlinear statistical relationships between data points into geometrical relationships between points in a two-dimensional map.

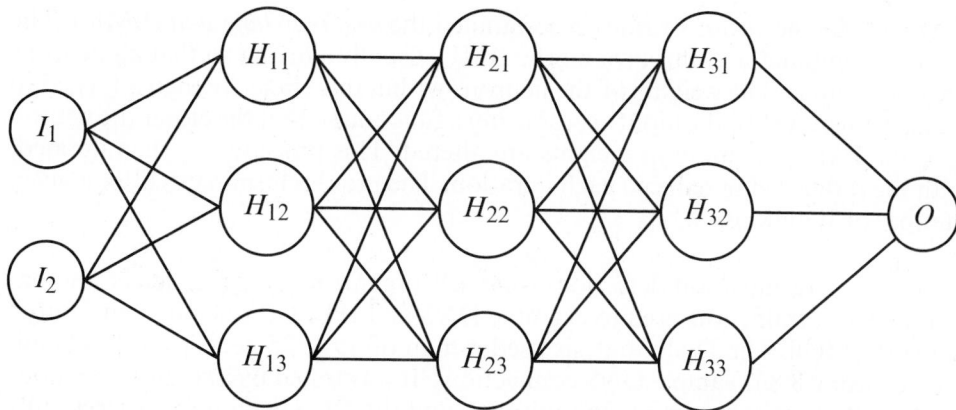

Figure 26–2 A neural net with input nodes I_1 and I_2, output node O, and three hidden layers of three neurons each. Note the neurons in a layer are not connected to one another. Each connection between neurons also has a weight assigned to it.

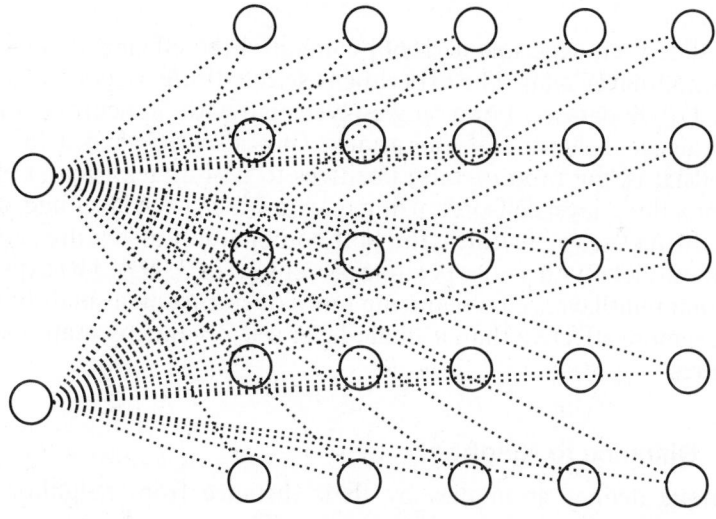

Figure 26–3 A self-organizing map with two inputs. The inputs are connected to each neuron in the lattice, and none of the lattice neurons are connected to one another.

The self-organizing map consists of a set of neurons arranged in a lattice, with each input neuron connected to every neuron in the lattice (see Figure 26–3). Say the classification is to use n features $(v_1, \ldots, v_n)$. Each lattice neuron is given a vector of weights $(w_1, \ldots, w_n)$, one per feature. A vector from the training set is then compared to the weights in each neuron, and the neuron whose weights are most like the vector's values is designated the *best matching unit* (BMU). The method computes a radius around the BMU, usually starting so that all neurons are in this circle. The weights of the neurons within this circle are then adjusted to make them more like the input vector using a function so that the closer the neuron is to the BMU, the more its weights are altered. This procedure is then iterated, with the radius being reduced each iteration. The process terminates after a given number of iterations.

EXAMPLE: An intrusion detection using self-organizing maps to detect anomalous network traffic was used to examine DNS and HTTP traffic on a university's network [1560]. The DNS analysis used a map of 19×25 neurons and was initialized using 8,857 sample DNS connections. It was tested by a set of anomalous DNS traffic with a known exploit injected, and the DNS exploit was successfully identified as anomalous. The HTTP analysis used 7,194 connections to train a map of 16×27 neurons. Then the self-organizing map was given anomalous HTTP traffic that included an HTTP tunnel through which *telnet* was run. The commands setting up the tunnel were identified as anomalous.

Some experiments involved multiple layers of self-organizing maps.

EXAMPLE: One such experiment [1666] compared the efficacy of a single-layer map with a multilayer map. The experiment selected three sets of features from the KDD-CUP-99 dataset. For a single-layer map with 36 neurons, the best set of features detected 99.91% of the attacks, but also reported a false positive percentage (that is, the ratio of false positives to non-attack events) of 77.53%. However, for a three-layer self-organizing map in which each layer had 48 neurons and used a distinct set of features, the best combination of feature sets detected 93.46% of the attacks with a false positive percentage of 3.99%. The experimenters concluded that multilayer self-organizing maps operating on a small subset of the features were more effective than a single-layer self-organizing map operating on all the features.

26.3.1.8   Distance to Neighbor

This technique defines anomalies by their distance from neighbor elements. Different measures are used for this purpose. The most common one is based on the distance to the kth nearest neighbor [1563]. Essentially, the system uses a clustering algorithm to partition the data into disjoint subsets. It then computes upper and lower bounds for the distances of the elements in the partition, and from that determines which partitions are likely to contain outliers. These partitions are then examined.

EXAMPLE: Liao and Vermuri [1175] used this approach to analyze the IDEVAL dataset. They examined system call data from processes; this data was labeled so that the system calls for each process could be identified. This enabled them to use a text-based analysis method. Each system call is considered a word, and the system calls issued by a process make up a document. This allowed them to create a matrix with rows corresponding to words and columns to documents. They calculated the elements of the matrix using the term frequency–inverse document frequency weighting. This takes into account the word frequency over all documents, and compensates for the documents being of different lengths. This matrix is constructed using the training data.

When a new document is to be tested, a similarity function is used to compute the distance (similarity) to the documents. The k closest are selected, and the average of the distances is computed. This is compared to a threshold; if the threshold is exceeded, the document is considered normal.

The values of k tested varied between 5 and 25. The value $k = 10$, with a threshold value of 0.72, detected all attacks, and had a false positive rate of 0.44%. The experiment was repeated but this time using frequency weighting; there, the value $k = 15$ with a threshold value of 0.99 detected all attacks, and had the lowest false positive rate of 0.87%. They concluded that this classification method could detect attacks with an acceptably low false positive rate.

Sometimes the distances can be used to define a new feature, which is then used for classification. In the triangle area nearest neighbor [1895], the data is clustered, and the center of each cluster obtained. Some function of the areas of the triangles formed by the center of each pair of clusters and one point from the dataset forms a new feature of the data point. The data is then classified using the k nearest neighbor algorithm.

EXAMPLE: This method was used on the KDD-CUP-99 data [1895]. That dataset contains four types of attacks, so k was set to 5. The experimenters calculated the five clusters, and then formed the triangles with each data point and two cluster centers. The new feature was defined to be the sum of the areas of these 10 triangles.

The KDD-CUP-99 data was split into two sets. The testing and training set consisted of 10% of the data; the remaining 90% was used to validate the results. With $k = 17$, the method gave an accuracy of 99.01%, a detection rate of 99.27%, and a false alarm rate of 2.99%. A k nearest neighbor algorithm worked best when $k = 21$, giving an accuracy of 93.87%, a detection rate of 93.39%, and a false alarm rate of 28.69%.

26.3.1.9   SVM

Consider a set of data with n features. Represent each data point as a point in n-dimensional space, one dimension per feature. The support vector machine (SVM) is a supervised learning model that derives a hyperplane dividing the space into two parts. The similarity of two points is determined using a function called a *kernel function*; a common one is the Gaussian radial base function (RBF) $e^{-\gamma||x-y||^2}$, where x and y are two points, γ a constant parameter, and

$||x - y||^2 = \sum_1^n (x_i - y_i)^2$. New data is mapped into the n-dimensional space, and thus falls into one class or the other. This method works well when the data can be divided into two distinct classes with a clear separation between them.

EXAMPLE: Mukkamala, Janoski, and Sung [1395] used an SVM to analyze the same data as they analyzed using neural nets (see Section 26.3.1.6). They used the Gaussian RBF to determine similarity. The SVM was trained on 7,312 data points, and then tested on 6,980 points. It achieved an accuracy of 99.50%, and the SVM training time was much quicker than the neural nets (18 seconds as opposed to 18 minutes).

26.3.1.10   Other Methods

Other methods for applying machine learning to detecting anomalies abound. Several use biology, and more specifically immunology, as a model [558, 700–702, 704, 1855]. Others anomaly detection methods include Bayesian networks [169, 1108] and information theoretic approaches [828, 1464]. A common practice is to combine two or more methods.

Critical to understanding the machine learning methods is to know that they classify data. When applied to anomaly detection, these classifications identify anomalous data. But "anomalous" does not necessarily mean "bad" (that is, data indicating an attack). So the data used to initialize or train the machine learning system must contain enough "normal" (that is, nonattack) data for the system to identify the values of the relevant features, and in some cases the features that indicate nonanomalous data; otherwise, the bad data will appear normal, and the normal data will appear anomalous.

26.3.2   Misuse Modeling

In some contexts, the term "misuse" refers to an attack by an insider or authorized user. In the context of intrusion detection systems, it means "rule-based detection."

> **Definition 26–3.** *Misuse detection* determines whether a sequence of instructions being executed is known to violate the site security policy being executed. If so, it reports a potential intrusion.

Modeling of misuse requires a knowledge of system vulnerabilities or potential vulnerabilities that attackers attempt to exploit. The intrusion detection system incorporates this knowledge into a rule set. When data is passed to the intrusion detection system, it applies the rule set to the data to determine if any sequences of data match any of the rules. If so, it reports that a possible intrusion is underway.

Misuse-based intrusion detection systems often use expert systems to analyze the data and apply the rule set. These systems cannot detect attacks that are unknown to the developers of the rule set. Previously unknown attacks, or even variations of known attacks, can be difficult to detect. Later intrusion detection systems used adaptive methods involving neural networks and Petri nets to improve their detection abilities.

EXAMPLE: Kumar and Spafford [1113] have adapted colored Petri nets to detect both attack signatures and the actions following previously unknown attacks in their system Intrusion Detection In Our Time (IDIOT). They define an event as a change in the system state. The observation that an "event can represent a single action by a user or system, or it can represent a series of actions resulting in a single, observable record"[3] is key. They have developed a model of attacks on the UNIX operating system based on temporal ordering of events. Their model classified attacks in five ways:

1. *Existence*: The attack creates a file or some other entity at some time.

2. *Sequence*: The attack causes several events to occur sequentially.

3. *Partial order*: The attack causes two or more sequences of events, and the events form a partial order under the temporal relation.

4. *Duration*: Something exists for an interval of time.

5. *Interval*: Two events occur exactly n units of time apart.

In these attacks, the sequence of events may be interlaced with other events. Regular expressions and attribute- and context-free grammars cannot easily capture this. Hence, Kumar and Spafford use colored Petri nets. Each signature corresponds to an automaton called a Colored Petri Automaton (CPA). The nodes represent tokens; the edges represent transitions. The final state of each signature is the compromised state. Each automaton may have multiple start states (see Figure 26–4). At the beginning, a token is placed in each node corresponding to a start state. As events transition the states, the tokens move from one node along the appropriate edge to the next node.

Associated with each transition is a set of expressions protected by (possibly empty) guards. The expressions dictate assignments to variables when the transition is taken, and the guards determine whether or not conditions hold for the transitions to be taken. In a guard or expression, the function *this* instantiates itself to the attributes of the last event. In Figure 26–4, the guard for transition t_4 requires that the UID of the process executing the *mknod* be 0 but that *root* not be running it (this[euid] == 0 && this[ruid] != 0). If it is, the variable *FILE1* is bound to the true name of the object being created, and the transition is made. Similarly, the guard for transition t_1 (the *unlink*) requires that the UID of the process not be 0 and that *FILE1* be instantiated and be the same as the name of the object being unlinked (FILE1 == true_name(this[obj])). If both hold,

---

[3] See [1113], p. 15.

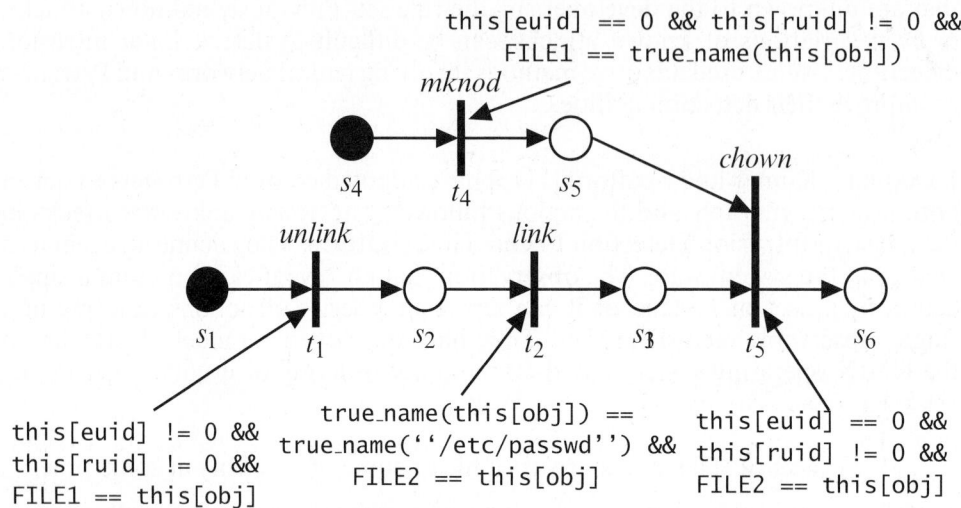

Figure 26–4 The *mkdir* attack on page 853 described using a Colored Petri Automaton. The circles represent states, and the thick bars represent the commands causing transitions.

the token is moved to s_2, which represents transitioning of the system into a new state. When transition t_5 occurs, it merges the two branches into one. *FILE2* obtains its value from the s_1-s_2-s_3 branch, but the restrictions on the user IDs come from the s_4-s_5 branch. If those conditions are met, the transition t_5 occurs, the tokens merge at node s_6, and the system enters the corresponding (compromised) state.

   This model has two important features. The first is the ability to add new signatures dynamically. The partially matched signatures need not be cleared and rematched; existing representations of the CPAs maintain their states. Furthermore, the patterns can be prioritized by ordering the CPAs. Even more, sequences that are known to be likely to occur (perhaps because they were recently published) can be prioritized by appropriately ordering the initial branches of the CPAs.

   IDIOT monitors audit logs looking for a sequence of events that correspond to an attack. An alternative point of view is to ignore the actual states and focus on the commands that change them. Researchers at the University of California at Santa Barbara have built several systems that analyze the results of commands to breach a security policy.

EXAMPLE: STAT [942] views a computer as being in a particular state, and commands move it from one state to another. The effect of the command is to cause a state transition. Ilgun, Kemmerer, and Porras use this to model attacks. Ilgun developed the first STAT prototype, called USTAT.

Although the notion of "state" encompasses all data stored on the computer, down to the level of caches and registers, the architects of STAT noted that they needed to track only those portions of the state that affected security. For example, suppose that a process is running as the superuser (UID 0) without authorization. The system has been compromised. But rather than detect the compromised state, STAT looks at the manner in which the user obtained the special privileges. This focuses on transitions. All compromises may be described in this way—that is, a process goes from a limited state to a state in which some other right is acquired. The key to STAT is to find how this can happen.

Associated with each state is a set of assertions. Consider an attack on a UNIX system in which an attacker renames a setuid to *root* shell script so its name begins with "-." The user executes it. Because some shells have a bug that makes any invocation of the shell beginning with "-" interactive, the attacker gets superuser privileges.

```
ln target -s
-s
```

The state transition diagram is

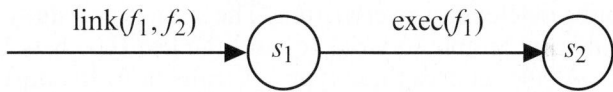

The state diagram is now augmented to capture the result of the attack by placing postconditions under the state. Let USER be the user's effective UID. The transition of the process into a state where it has superuser privileges means that the effective UID is no longer that of the user:

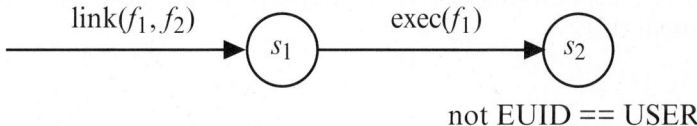

Finally, the state diagram needs to establish conditions under which the state s_1 can be entered. In order to enter that state, the new file name must start with "-" and cannot be owned by *USER* (otherwise, the user could not acquire additional privileges). Furthermore, it must be a script, it must be setuid, and *USER* must be able to execute the file. This leads to

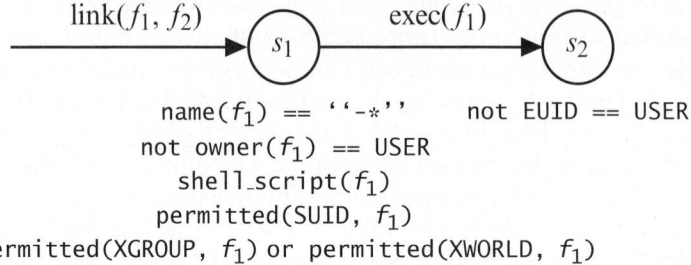

$$\text{name}(f_1) \; == \; ``\text{-*''} \qquad \text{not EUID} \; == \; \text{USER}$$
$$\text{not owner}(f_1) \; == \; \text{USER}$$
$$\text{shell\_script}(f_1)$$
$$\text{permitted(SUID, } f_1)$$
$$\text{permitted(XGROUP, } f_1) \text{ or permitted(XWORLD, } f_1)$$

USTAT uses records generated by BSM to obtain system information. A preprocessor extracts events of interest and maps them into USTAT's internal representation. It also removes events in which the attempted system calls failed (because such events do not change the system state).

It then uses an inference engine to determine when a state transition compromising a system occurs. The system has a fact base of seven types of transitions. The first type lists files that no unprivileged user should be able to access (read or write). The second type lists files that no unprivileged user should be able to write to. The third and fourth types list executable programs that are authorized to read from files in the first list and write to files in the second list, respectively. The fifth type lists files that are common places for Trojan horses and should not be deleted nor overwritten. The sixth type lists system directories that users should not be able to write to, and the last type lists UNIX files with multiple names. A rule set uses these types of transitions to constrain the actions that should be reported.

The inference engine constructs a series of state table entries corresponding to the transitions. Consider the attack described above, and suppose that the rule base consists of the one state transition rule above. Initially, the table appears as

	s_1	s_2
1		

because there is one state transition rule with two states. After the first command (the *ln*), all five preconditions of state s_1 are satisfied, so the system creates a new row to represent this:

	s_1	s_2
1		
2	X	

The first row will be used if another file is created with the same properties as those in the state transition diagram. The second row asserts that a process has already done so. The attacker now executes the file *-x* and, because the EUID of the process is no longer that of the user, the system enters state s_2. The matrix is not augmented, but the violation is noted. The row remains present until something negates the preconditions on s_1 (such as the file not being a shell script or not being setuid).

The load that USTAT places on a system does not increase as the system load increases, because USTAT reopens log files repeatedly to read new records. Nevertheless, its approach is interesting because, unlike other intrusion detection mechanisms, it focuses on the changes of state rather than on the existing state.

One important feature for intrusion detection systems is an interface into which new users and/or maintainers can add new rules or data. The widely used Bro intrusion detection system does exactly this.

EXAMPLE: Bro [1501] is a network-based intrusion detection system that provides a mechanism for users to configure its analysis. Its architecture consists of two components, an *event engine* and a *policy script interpreter*. The event engine reads packets from the network (using various lower-level libraries) and processes them into a stream of events that is fed to the policy script interpreter. The event engine does not consider any events "good" or "bad"; that is left to the policy script interpreter. That performs the analysis, and notifies the analyst when events of interest occur. Policy scripts control the analysis.

The key to this architecture is the separation of policy from mechanism. The event engine uses a variety of protocol analyzers to map the network flows into events. For example, one protocol analyzer detects a new TCP connection, another HTTP requests, and so forth. Once an event is found, it is passed up to the policy layer, where the policy script interpreter executes the appropriate script.

Bro comes with numerous policy scripts, and the site administrator can write others. As an example, the following script [1784] detects SSH servers on the network:

```
# holds a list of SSH servers
global ssh_hosts: set[addr];

event connection_established(c: connection)
{
        local responder = c$id$resp_h;   # address of
                                         # responder (server)
        local service = c$id$resp_p;     # port on server

        if ( service != 22/tcp )          # SSH port is 22
                return;

        # if you get here, it's SSH
        if ( responder in ssh_hosts )     # see if we saw
                                         # this already
                return;

        # we didn't -- add it to the list and say so
```

```
        add ssh_hosts[responder];
        print "New SSH host found", responder;
}
```

This script assumes that every connection to a server on port 22 is a connection to an SSH server. The first two lines set variables to the address and port number being accessed. If the port number is not 22, the client is not accessing an SSH server. Otherwise, the server (responder) is a putative SSH host. The script then checks whether this server has been seen before; if not, it adds the address to the list of SSH servers seen, and prints a message announcing the discovery.

The Bro scripting language offers many features. As in the above, the scripts can preserve state over multiple invocations, and can access domain-specific information such as IP addresses and port numbers. They can also execute external programs.

26.3.3   Specification Modeling

Anomaly detection has been called the art of looking for unusual states. Similarly, misuse detection is the art of looking for states known to be bad. Specification detection takes the opposite approach; it looks for states known not to be good, and when the system enters such a state, it reports a possible intrusion.

> **Definition 26–4.** *Specification-based detection* determines whether or not a sequence of instructions violates a specification of how a program, or system, should execute. If so, it reports a potential intrusion.

For security purposes, only those programs that in some way change the protection state of the system need to be specified and checked. For example, because the policy editor in Windows changes security-related settings, it needs to have an associated specification.

Specification-based detection relies on traces, or sequences, of events [1079].

> **Definition 26–5.** A *system trace* is a sequence of events $t_0, t_1, \ldots, t_i, t_{i+1}, \ldots$ during the execution of a system of processes. Event t_i occurs at time $C(t_i)$, and this imposes a total ordering on the events.

Contrast this with the notion of trace in Chapter 9, "Noninterference and Policy Composition." This definition uses events as elements of the sequence, whereas the definition in Chapter 9 uses inputs and outputs as elements of the sequence.

> **Definition 26–6.** A *subtrace* of a trace $T = t_0, t_1, \ldots, t_i, t_{i+1}, \ldots, t_n$ is a sequence of events $t'_0, \ldots, t'_k$, where $t'_0, \ldots, t'_k$ is a subsequence of $t_0, t_1, \ldots, t_i, t_{i+1}, \ldots, t_n$.

For example, if U is the system trace for the system, and V is a system trace for one process in that system, then V will be a subtrace of U.

Definition 26–7. A trace $T = t_0, \ldots, t_{m+n}$ is the *merge of two traces* U and V if and only if there are two subtraces $u_1, \ldots, u_m$ and $v_0, \ldots, v_n$ of T such that $U = u_1, \ldots, u_m$ and $V = v_0, \ldots, v_n$.

When a distributed process executes, its trace is the merged trace of its components. The merge of traces U and V is written $T = U \oplus V$.

Definition 26–8. A *filter p* is a function that maps a trace T to a subtrace T' such that, for all events t_i in T', $p(t_i)$ is true.

The filter allows the monitoring to weed out events that are of no interest.

Definition 26–9. An *execution trace of a subject s* is the sequence of operations performed by the processes making up the subject.

For example, if the subject s is composed of processes p, q, and r, with traces T_p, T_q, and T_r, respectively, then the trace of s is $T_s = T_p \oplus T_q \oplus T_r$.

A trace policy takes a set of selection expressions and applies them to the system trace of interest.

EXAMPLE: If the filtering function can filter on process, program, host, or user, one can represent each subject as a quadruple *<proc, prog, host, user>*. Thus, the filter

```
< ANY, emacs, ANY, bishop >
```

applied to a system trace will produce a list of subjects with program *emacs* and user *bishop*. The filter

```
< ANY, ANY, progress, ANY >
```

produces a list of subjects on the host *progress*.

EXAMPLE: Ko, Ruschitzka, and Levitt [1079] developed a specification-based intrusion detection system for the UNIX environment. They specified 15 security-related programs. The specifications constrained object access, sequencing of operations, synchronization, and race conditions. The researchers applied this to monitoring of the program *rdist*.

The UNIX program *rdist* (for remote distribution) updates programs on remote systems. It first creates a temporary file */tmp/rdistxxxxx*. It then copies the contents of the new file into the temporary file, changes the protection mask as required, and copies the temporary file over the file to be replaced. The problem is that *rdist* modifies protection modes by acting on the file name, so if an attacker can replace the file by a symbolic link, he can force *rdist* to modify the protection modes of any file in the system. For example, he can turn on the setuid bit for the program */bin/sh*, which would give him superuser privileges instantly.

A specification in the PE-grammar language describes the accepted behavior of *rdist*. The SPEC line defines the set of subjects (events) to which the rule should be applied (namely, any process on the host *progress* created from the program *rdist*, regardless of which user executes it):

```
SPEC rdist <?, rdist, *, client>
```

The next lines set up the environment:

```
ENV User U = getuser();
ENV int PID = getpid();
ENV int FILECD[int];
ENV int PATHCD[str];
ENV str HOME = "/export/home/U.name"
```

The top line names the user. The next line identifies the process, and the next two lines obtain the inode of the relevant directories. The last line sets **HOME** to be the user's home directory.

The rest of the specification sets up the validation:

```
SE: <rdist>
<rdist> -> <valid_op> <rdist> |.
<valid_op> -> open_r_worldread
|     open_r_not_worldread
      {     if !Created(F)
            then violation(); fi; }
|     creat_dir
      {     if !(Inside(P, "/tmp") or Inside(P. HOME))
            then violation(); fi; }
|     creat_file
      {     if !(Inside(P, "/tmp") or Inside(P. HOME))
            then violation(); fi;
            FILECD[F.nodeid] = 1;
            PATHCD[P] = F.nodeid'; }
...
```

The first line here specifies the top-level rule, and the next line says that the operations of interest are in the rule *valid_op*. The third line on says when the operations of interest are valid. For example, the operation **open_r_worldread**, meaning open an object that is world readable for reading, is always valid. The operation **open_r_not_worldread**, meaning open for reading an object that is not world readable, is not valid unless *rdist* created the file; if it did not, a violation exception is raised. Similarly, if the operation **creat_dir**, meaning create a directory, occurs, it is not valid if that directory is created as a subdirectory of the user's home directory or the */tmp* directory, and a violation exception occurs. The same is true for the create file (**creat_file**) operation, and on success of that operation, the appropriate variables are set for later use.

The checks for validity of other file system operations, namely **open_rw**, **symlink**, **chown**, **chmod**, **rename**, are left as an exercise to the reader.

The distributed program execution monitor (DPEM) has a set of agents for generating traces from audit logs, and a director for collecting the traces, comparing them with the specifications, and analyzing the results. In the experiments, specifications for all network daemons (including copies of *rdist* and *sendmail* known to have vulnerabilities) were developed, and several attacks were launched. On average, detecting an attack from *rdist* took 0.06 seconds. Similarly, a race condition involving two editing sessions of a password file took 0.05 seconds to detect.

Specification-based intrusion detection is in its infancy. Among its appealing qualities are the formalization (at a relatively low level) of what should happen. This means that intrusions using unknown attacks will be detected. Balanced against this desirable feature is the extra effort needed to locate and analyze the programs that may cause security problems. The subtlety of this last point is brought home when one realizes that any program is a potential security threat when executed by a privileged user.

26.3.4 Summary

Reflecting on the differences between the three basic types of intrusion detection will clarify the nature of each type.

Some observations on misuse detection will provide a basis for what follows. Definition 26–3 characterizes misuse detection as detection of violations of a policy. The policy may be known (explicit) or implicit. In the former case, one uses the techniques described in Section 25.4.1 to develop the rules for the misuse detection system. In the latter case, one must describe the policy in terms of actions or states that are known to violate the policy, which calls on the techniques described in Section 25.4.2 to develop the relevant rules. This distinction, although subtle, is crucial. In the first case, the rules database is sufficient to detect all violations of policy because the policy itself was used to populate the rule set. In the second case, the rule set contains descriptions of states and/or actions that are known to violate the policy, *but not all such states or actions*. This kind of misuse detection system will not detect all violations of system policy.

Now consider the difference between misuse detection and anomaly detection. The former detects violations of a policy. The latter detects violations of expectation, which may (or may not) violate the policy. For example, TIM uses rules that it derives from logs to construct its Markov model. If the training data contain attacks, the Markov model will accept those attacks as normal. Hence, it is an anomaly detection mechanism. By way of contrast, IDIOT does not construct models from data on the fly. It contains a rule base of sequences that describe known attacks. Hence, it is a misuse detection mechanism.

The distinction between specification-based detection and misuse detection is also worth consideration. The former detects violations of per-program specifications, and makes an implicit assumption that if all programs adhere to their specifications, the site policy cannot be violated. The latter makes no such assumption, focusing instead on the overall site policy. Suppose an attacker could attack a system in such a way that no program violated its specifications but the combined effect of the execution of the programs during the attack did violate the site policy. Misuse intrusion detection might detect the attack (depending on the completeness of the rule set). Anomaly intrusion detection might also detect the attack (depending on the characterization of expected behavior). However, specification-based intrusion detection would not detect this attack. In essence, if the specification of a program is its "security policy," specification-based detection is a local (per-program) form of misuse detection.

26.4   Architecture

An intrusion detection system is also an automated auditing mechanism. Like auditing systems, it consists of three parts (see Section 25.2). The agent corresponds to the logger. It acquires information from a target (such as a computer system). The director corresponds to the analyzer. It analyzes the data from the agents as required (usually to determine if an attack is in progress or has occurred). The director then passes this information to the notifier, which determines whether, and how, to notify the requisite entity. The notifier may communicate with the agents to adjust the logging if appropriate. Figure 26–5 illustrates this.

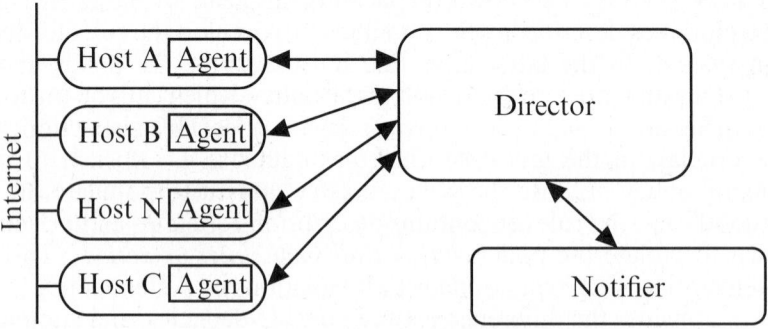

Figure 26–5 Architecture of an intrusion detection system. Hosts A, B, and C are general-purpose computers, and the agents monitor activity on them. Host N is designed for network monitoring, and its agent reports data gleaned from the Internet to the director.

26.4.1   Agent

An agent obtains information from a data source (or set of data sources). The source may be a log file, another process, or a network. The information, once acquired, may be sent directly to the director. Usually, however, it is preprocessed into a specific format to save the director from having to do this. Also, the agent may discard information that it deems irrelevant.

EXAMPLE: If the agent is to transmit the time and location of a failed login attempt, it will scan the appropriate log file, discard any records of successful logins, and send the remainder to the director.

The director may determine that it needs more information from a particular information source. In that case, the director can instruct the agent to collect additional data, or to process the data it collects differently. The director can use this to cut down on the amount of processing it must do, but can increase the level of information it receives when an attack is suspected.

EXAMPLE: When the director determines that an attack on some other system is underway, it might direct all agents to report all login attempts involving the suspect accounts, whether successful or not.

An agent can obtain information from a single host, from a set of hosts (in which case it may also function as a director; see Section 26.4.2), or from a network. Let us consider the types of information that are available from each, and how they might be gathered.

26.4.1.1   Host-Based Information Gathering

Host-based agents usually use system and application logs to obtain records of events, and analyze them to determine what to pass to the director. The events to look for, and to analyze, are determined by the goals of the intrusion detection mechanism. The logs may be security-related logs (such as BSM and the Windows logs discussed in Chapter 25, "Auditing") or other logs such as accounting logs. Crosbie and Spafford [479] point out that the logs may even be virtual logs if the agent is put directly in the kernel. The agent then simply copies records that the kernel puts into the logs. This eliminates the need to convert from one log format to an internal representation. It also means that the agents are not portable among heterogeneous computers. There is also a drawback involving the granularity of information obtained, which we will discuss in Section 26.4.1.3.

A variant of host-based information gathering occurs when the agent generates its own information. Policy checkers do this. They analyze the state of the system, or of some objects in the system, and treat the results as a log (to reduce and forward). However, these agents are usually somewhat complex, and a fundamental rule of secure design is to keep software simple, usually by restricting its function to one task. This arrangement violates that rule. So, the policy checker usually logs its output, and the agent simply analyzes that log just as it would analyze any other log.

26.4.1.2   Network-Based Information Gathering

Network-based agents use a variety of devices and software to monitor network traffic. This technique provides information of a different flavor than host-based monitoring provides. It can detect network-oriented attacks, such as a denial of service attack introduced by flooding a network. It can monitor traffic for a large number of hosts. It can also examine the contents of the traffic itself (called content monitoring).

Network-based agents may use network sniffing to read the network traffic. In this case, a system provides the agent with access to all network traffic passing that host. If the medium is point-to-point (such as a token ring network), the agents must be distributed to obtain a complete view of the network messages. If the medium is a broadcast medium (such as Ethernet), typically only one computer needs to have the monitoring agent. Arranging the monitoring agents so as to minimize the number required to provide complete network coverage is a difficult problem. In general, the policy will focus on intruders entering the network rather than on insiders. In this case, if the network has a limited number of points of access, the agents need to monitor only the traffic through those points. If the computers controlling those entry points do extensive logging on the network traffic that they receive, the network-based information gathering is in effect reduced to host-based information gathering.

Monitoring of network traffic raises several significant issues. The critical issue is that the analysis software must ensure that the view of the network traffic is *exactly* the same as at all hosts for which the traffic is intended. Furthermore, if the traffic is end-to-end enciphered, monitoring the contents from the network is not possible.

26.4.1.3   Combining Sources

The goal of an agent is to provide the director with information so that the director can report possible violations of the security policy (intrusions). An aggregate of information is needed. However, the information can be viewed at several levels.

EXAMPLE: Consider a FreeBSD UNIX system with two sources of information. The first is the application level log. Whenever a user changes privileges by executing the program *su*, a log entry is written into that log. The second is the system call log that the (nonstandard, instrumented) kernel generates.

The application level log presents a very high-level view of actions:

```
Apr  2 14:24:05 nob su: bishop to root on /dev/pts/3
```

The system call level log generates a very different view of this action. The log contains 1,941 entries for the single command. A few such entries from the middle of the process give the flavor of the entire log. The entries that follow correspond to obtaining the user's effective UID, opening the password file, and obtaining the password of the user with that effective UID:

```
79878 su      CALL   geteuid
79878 su      RET    geteuid 0
79878 su      CALL   open(0x800fc539a,0x100000
                              <O_CLOEXEC>,<unused>0)
79878 su      NAMI   "/etc/spwd.db"
79878 su      RET    open 3
79878 su      CALL   fstat(0x3,0x7fffffffdf00)
79878 su      RET    fstat 0
79878 su      CALL   read(0x3,0x80164d000,0x104)
79878 su      RET    read 260/0x104
79878 su      CALL   pread(0x3,0x801656000,0x1000,0x6000)
79878 su      RET    pread 4096/0x1000
79878 su      CALL   pread(0x3,0x80165c000,0x1000,0x4000)
79878 su      RET    pread 4096/0x1000
79878 su      CALL   close(0x3)
79878 su      RET    close 0
```

If one views the issue at the application level, the single-line log entry is sufficient, but from a system level view, it is not, because it obscures the many system calls actually made. Similarly, from an application level view, the system level view is inadequate, because the sequence of system calls does not make clear what their combined function is (specifically, to log in a user).

The difference between application and system views (which is, essentially, a problem of layers of abstraction) affects what the agent can report to the director and what the director can conclude from analyzing the information. The agent, or the director, must either obtain information at the level of abstraction at which it looks for security problems or be able to map the information into an appropriate level.

26.4.2   Director

The director itself *reduces* the incoming log entries to eliminate unnecessary and redundant records. It then uses an analysis engine to determine if an attack (or the precursor to an attack) is underway. The analysis engine may use any of, or a mixture of, several techniques to perform its analysis.

Because the functioning of the director is critical to the effectiveness of the intrusion detection system, it is usually run on a separate system. This allows the system to be dedicated to the director's activity. It has the side effect of keeping the specific rules and profiles unavailable to ordinary users. Then attackers lack the knowledge needed to evade the intrusion detection system by conforming to known profiles or using only techniques that the rules do not include.

The director must correlate information from multiple logs.

EXAMPLE: A particular user logs in during the day to perform system maintenance functions. Occasionally she logs in during the late evening to write reports. One day, she apparently logs in during the late evening and begins altering the kernel (a system maintenance procedure). Agents provide information from both the log of login times and the log of commands executed. Neither set of data by itself will give an indication of a security problem. However, if the director correlates the two sets of data, the anomaly will be apparent.

Many types of directors alter the set of rules that they use to make decisions. These *adaptive directors* alter the profiles, add (or delete) rules, and otherwise adapt to changes in the systems being monitored.

EXAMPLE: A *science DMZ* [499, 500, 1505] is a high-speed network used for big data science. Because of the throughput that is required, security mechanisms must be simple and not interfere with the flow of legitimate data. The architecture of this type of network uses routers to provide security. When a connection begins, the beginning of the connection is copied to a system and analyzed. If the connection is malicious, the system reconfigures the router to discard packets coming from the source of the connection. This way, legitimate connections pass through the router onto the science DMZ with no interference, but illegitimate connections are blocked.

Directors rarely use only one analysis technique, because different techniques highlight different aspects of intrusions. The results of each are combined, analyzed and reduced, and then used.

26.4.3   Notifier

The notifier accepts information from the director and takes the appropriate action. In some cases, this is simply a notification to the system security officer that an attack is believed to be underway. In other cases, the notifier may take some action to respond to the attack.

Many intrusion detection systems use graphical interfaces. A well-designed graphics display allows the intrusion detection system to convey information in an easy-to-grasp image or set of images. It must allow users to determine what attacks are underway (ideally, with some notion of how likely it is that this is not a false alarm). This requires that the GUI be designed with a lack of clutter and unnecessary information.

EXAMPLE: The Graphical Intrusion Detection System (GrIDS) [1816], intended for monitoring very large networks, uses a graph-oriented user interface to show the progress of attacks across multiple systems. The hosts are represented as nodes, and as an attack from one system to another is identified, the nodes are

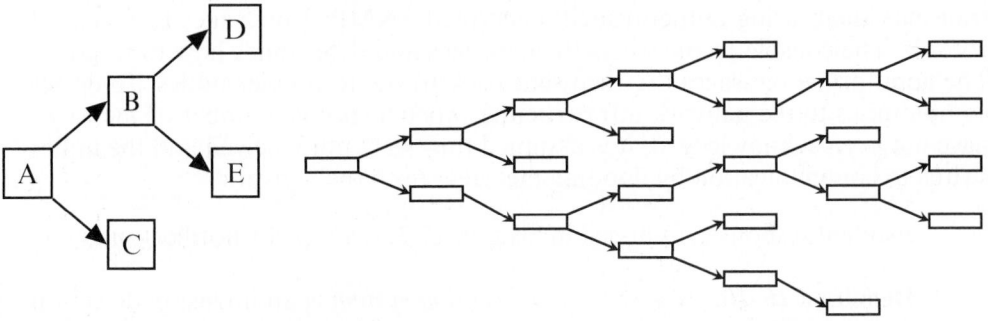

Figure 26–6 An example of GrIDS output showing the spread of a worm. The left image shows the graph shortly after the spread has begun. The right image shows the graph after further spread.

connected with edges labeled to show the progress of the attack. Figure 26–6 is an example of one of the user displays of GrIDS. It shows the progress of a worm attack as it progresses through a network.

The notifier may contact the appropriate person or make entries into the appropriate log files.

EXAMPLE: Credit card companies often allow customers to set up alerts notifying them when their card is used. This capability helps detect fraudulent purchases using the card. If a cardholder has set up SMS notification when the card is used for a purchase over $500, then the credit card company will text the cardholder a message informing her when a purchase with the card exceeds that amount. The cardholder can then challenge the charge if she believes it to be fraudulent, for example if she is in San Francisco at the time the purchase was made in Dubai.

When the intrusion detection system is a distributed one, or a set of cooperating intrusion detection systems, they must communicate among themselves and change firewall and router rules as appropriate to block attacks.

EXAMPLE: The Intrusion Detection Message Exchange Format (IDMEF) [527] describes messages that different intrusion detection systems can exchange, using a protocol such as the Intrusion Detection Exchange Protocol (IDXP) [657]. These have been used in an intrusion detection system for computational grids [1697]. This system consists of host- and network-based intrusion detection systems that feed information to a higher level grid intrusion detection system (GIDS), which analyzes the data and reports any intrusions it, or one of the lower level intrusion detection systems, detects. The lower level intrusion detection systems send IDMEF messages using the IDXP. An intrusion detection system for MANETS [1066] converts IDMEF-format messages to an internal form and transmits them using authenticated, encrypted SNMPv3 messages to a central console. The console reconstructs the messages and determines how to respond. The appropriate messages are then sent back to the responder nodes. To detect compromises to the network infrastructure, when a specific number of messages have not been acknowledged, it is assumed they were not received and the nodes switch to communication by flooding messages onto the network.

Incident response, discussed in Section 27.3, is a type of notification.

Definition 26–10. An *intrusion prevention system* is an intrusion detection system with a notifier that responds to attacks by taking action to block or mitigate that attack and future similar attacks.

In addition to any human-intelligible notifications, the intrusion detection system communicates with other entities to counteract the attack. Responses include disconnecting from the network, filtering packets from attacking hosts, increasing the level of logging, and instructing agents to forward information from additional sources.

26.5   Organization of Intrusion Detection Systems

An intrusion detection system can be organized in several ways. This section explores three such paradigms using research intrusion detection systems. The first system examined network traffic only. The second explored how to combine network and host sources. The third system distributed the director among multiple systems to enhance security and reliability.

26.5.1   Monitoring Network Traffic for Intrusions: NSM

The Network Security Monitor (NSM) [887] develops a profile of expected usage of a network and compares current usage with that profile. It also allows the definition of a set of signatures to look for specific sequences of network traffic that indicate attacks. It runs on a local area network and assumes a broadcast medium. The monitor measures network utilization and other characteristics and can be instructed to look at activity based on a user, a group of users, or a service. It reports anomalous behavior.

The NSM monitors the source, destination, and service of network traffic. It assigns a unique *connection* ID to each connection. The source, destination, and service are used as axes for a matrix. Each element of the matrix contains the number of packets sent over that connection for a specified period of time, and the sum of the data of those packets. The NSM also generates expected connection data from the network. The data in the array is "masked" by the expected connection data, and any data not within the expected range is reported as an anomaly.

The developers of the NSM quickly found that too much data was being generated during the network analysis. To reduce the overhead, they constructed a hierarchy of elements of the matrix and generated expected connection data for those elements. If any group in the hierarchy showed anomalous data, the system security officer could ask the NSM to break it down into the underlying elements. The groups were constructed by folding axes of the matrix. For example, one group would be the set of traffic between two hosts for each service. It would have the elements $\{(A, B, \mathrm{SMTP}), (A, B, \mathrm{FTP}), \ldots\}$, where A and B are host names. The next group would collapse the service names and simply group all traffic into source-destination pairs. At the highest level, traffic would be grouped into its source. The NSM would analyze the data at the source level. If it flagged an anomaly, the system security officer could have the NSM examine each component of the underlying group and determine which specific source-destination pair had the anomaly. From there, it could be broken into the specific service or services involved.

The NSM's use of a matrix allowed a simple signature-based scheme to look for known patterns of misuse. For example, repeated telnet connections that lasted only as long as the normal setup time would indicate a failed login attempt. A specific rule could look in the matrix for this occurrence (although, as the designers point out, these patterns can be hidden as one moves up the hierarchy).

The implementation of the NSM also allowed the analyst to write specific rules against which to compare network traffic. The rules initially used were to check for excessive logins, a single host communicating with 15 or more hosts, or any attempt to communicate with a nonexistent host.

The NSM provided a graphical user display to enable the system security officer to see at a glance the state of the network. Furthermore, the display manager was independent of the NSM matrix analyzer, so the latter could devote full time to the analysis of the data. The prototype system, deployed at the University of California at Davis, detected many attacks. As with all intrusion detection systems, it also reported false positives, such as alumni logging into accounts that had laid dormant for some time. But its capabilities revealed the need for and feasibility of monitoring the network as well as individual hosts.

The NSM is important for two reasons. First, it served as the basis for a large number of intrusion detection systems. Indeed, 11 years after its creation, it was still in use at many sites (although with an augmented set of signatures). Second, it proved that performing intrusion detection on networks was practical. As network traffic becomes enciphered, the ability to analyze the contents of the packets diminishes, but NSM did not look at the contents of the traffic. It performed traffic analysis. Hence, its methodology will continue to be effective even after widespread deployment of network encryption.

26.5.2   Combining Host and Network Monitoring: DIDS

The Distributed Intrusion Detection System (DIDS) [1773, 1774] combined the abilities of the NSM with intrusion detection monitoring of individual hosts.

It sprang from the observation that neither network-based monitoring nor host-based monitoring was sufficient. An intruder attempting to log into a system through an account without a password would not be detected as malicious by a network monitor. Subsequent actions, however, might make a host-based monitor report that an intruder is present. Similarly, if an attacker tries to telnet to a system a few times, using a different login name each time, the host-based intrusion detection mechanism would not report a problem, but the network-based monitor could detect repeated failed login attempts.

DIDS used a centralized analysis engine (the *DIDS director*) and required that agents be placed on the systems being monitored as well as in a place to monitor the network traffic. The agents scanned logs for events of interest and reported them to the DIDS director. The DIDS director invoked an expert system that performed the analysis of the data. The expert system was a rule-based system that could make inferences about individual hosts and about the entire system (hosts and networks). It would then pass results to the user interface, which displayed them in a simple, easy-to-grasp manner for the system security officer.

One problem is the changing of identity as an intruder moves from host to host. An intruder might gain access to the first system as user *alice*, and then to the second system as user *bob*. The host-based mechanisms cannot know that *alice* and *bob* are the same user, so they cannot correlate the actions of those two user names. But the DIDS director would note that *alice* connected to the remote host and that *bob* logged in through that connection. The expert system would infer that they were the same user. To enable this type of correlation, each user was identified by a *network identification number* (NID). In the example above, because *alice* and *bob* are the same user, both would share a common NID.

The host agents and network agent provide insight into the problems distributed intrusion detection faces. The host logs are analyzed to extract entries of interest. In some cases, simple reduction is performed to determine if the records should be forwarded; for example, the host agents monitor the system for attacks using signatures. Summaries of these results go to the director. Other events are forwarded directly. To capture this, the DIDS model has host agents report *events*, which are the information contained in the log entries, and an *action* and *domain* (see Figure 26–7). Subjects (such as active processes) perform actions; domains characterize passive entities. Note that a process can be either a subject (as when it changes the protection mode of a file) or an object (as when it is terminated). An object is assigned to the highest-priority domain to which it belongs. For example, a file may be tagged as important. If the file contains authentication data and also is tagged, it will be reported as a tagged object. A hand-built table dictates which events are sent to the DIDS director based on the actions and domains associated with the events. Events associated with the NID are those with *session_start* actions, and execute actions with network domains. These actions are forwarded so that the DIDS director can update its system view accordingly.

The network agent is a simplified version of the NSM. It provides the information described above.

Type of Action		Type of Domain	
session_start	create	tagged	sys_info
session_end	delete	authentication	user_info
read	move	audit	utility
write	change_rights	network	owned
execute	change_user_id	system	not_owned
terminate			

Figure 26–7 DIDS actions and domains. The domains are listed in order of priority, from top to bottom.

The expert system, a component of the DIDS director, derives high-level intrusion information from the low-level data sent to it. The rule base comes from a hierarchical model of intrusion detection. That model supplies six layers in the reduction procedure.

1. At this lowest layer, the log records are all visible. They come from the host and the network agent, and from any other sources the DIDS director has.
2. Here, the events abstract relevant information from the log entries.
3. This layer defines a subject that captures all events associated with a single user. The NID is assigned to this subject. This layer defines the boundary between machine-dependent information and the abstraction of a user (subject) and associated events.
4. This layer adds contextual information. Specifically, temporal data such as wall clock time, and spacial data such as proximity to other events, are taken into account. If the user tries to log in at a time when that user has never tried to log in before, or if a series of failed logins follows commands to see who is using a system, the context makes the events suspicious.
5. This layer deals with network threats, which are combinations of events in context. A threat is *abuse* if the protection state of the system is changed (for example, making a protected file world-writable). A threat is *misuse* if it violates policy but does not change the state of the system (for example, copying a world-readable homework file, which is a clear violation of policy at most universities). A threat is a *suspicious act* if it does not violate policy but is of interest (for example, a *finger* probe may be a prelude to an attack).
6. This layer assigns a score, from 1 to 100, representing the security state of the network. This score is derived from the threats to the system developed in layer 5. This is a user convenience, because it enables the

system security officer to notice problems quickly. Because the raw data (and intermediate data) used to derive the figure is present, the specifics can be provided quickly.

Within the expert system, each rule has an associated *rule value*. This value is used to calculate the score. The system security officer gives feedback to the expert system, and if false alarms occur, the expert system lowers the value associated with the rules leading to the false alarm.

GrIDS, mentioned in Section 26.4.3, extended DIDS to wide area networks. In addition to monitoring hosts and network traffic, the GrIDS directors could obtain data from network infrastructure systems (such as DNS servers). Figure 26–6 shows that GrIDS deployed a hierarchy of directors, each one reducing data from its children (agents or other directors) and passing the information to its parent. GrIDS directors can be in different organizations. This leads to the ability to analyze incidents occurring over a wide area, and to coordinate responses.

26.5.3   Autonomous Agents: AAFID

In 1995, Crosbie and Spafford examined intrusion detection systems in light of fault tolerance [479]. They noted that an intrusion detection system that obtains information by monitoring systems and networks is a single point of failure. If the director fails, the IDS will not function. Their suggestion was to partition the intrusion detection system into multiple components that function independently of one another, yet communicate to correlate information.

> **Definition 26–11.** An *autonomous agent* is a process that can act independently of the system of which it is a part.

Crosbie and Spafford suggested developing autonomous agents each of which performed one particular monitoring function. Each agent would have its own internal model, and when the agent detected a deviation from expected behavior, a match with a particular rule, or a violation of a specification, it would notify other agents. The agents would jointly determine whether the set of notifications were sufficient to constitute a reportable intrusion.

The beauty of this organization lies in the cooperation of the agents. No longer is there a single point of failure. If one agent were compromised, the others can continue to function. Furthermore, if an attacker shoud compromise one agent, she has learned nothing about the other agents in the system or monitoring the network. Moreover, the director itself is distributed among the agents, so it cannot be attacked in the same way that an intrusion detection system with a director on a single host can be. Other advantages include the specialization of each agent. The agent can be crafted to monitor one resource, making the agent small and simple (and meeting the principle of economy of mechanism; see Section 14.2.3). The agents could also migrate through the local network and process data on multiple systems. Finally, this approach appears to be scalable to larger networks because of the distributed nature of the director.

The drawbacks of autonomous agents lie in the overhead of the communications needed. As the functionality of each agent is reduced, more agents are needed to monitor the system, with an attendant increase in communications overhead. Furthermore, the communications must be secured, as must the distributed computations.

EXAMPLE: The Autonomous Agents for Intrusion Detection (AAFID) system [56, 958] implements these ideas. Each host has a set of agents and a *transceiver*, which controls the execution of the agents, collates the information, and forwards it to a monitor (director). If the transceiver's host does not have a monitor, the transceiver simply transmits the information to a monitor on another host.

In theory, each agent obtains its own data. This approach causes unnecessary duplication of work and leads to agents that are highly system-dependent. To avoid this problem, AAFID uses *filters* to provide access to monitored resources in a system-independent way. An agent subscribes to a filter by specifying which records it needs. The filter collects the data, transforms it into a system-independent form, and sends each agent the requested records. Multiple agents may subscribe to a single filter.

Transceivers collect data from the local agents, process it, and forward it to other agents or to monitors as appropriate. A transceiver also tracks the agents on its host, and can initiate them or terminate them. For example, if a system begins to accept TCP connections, the transceiver can initiate the SMTP monitoring agent. When TCP networking is shut down, the transceiver can then terminate that agent.

Monitors are the distributed components of the AAFID director. They accept information from transceivers and can communicate with the transceivers and other monitors. They perform high-level correlations for one or more hosts. Multiple monitors may receive data from, and transmit commands to, a single transceiver. In such cases, the AAFID system must ensure that the transceiver receives consistent information and commands.

Finally, the *user interface* plays one of the roles of a notifier. This interface interacts with the monitors. It may be graphical (for human interaction) or textual (for command scripts).

The implemented AAFID prototype runs on Linux and Solaris systems. It focused on testing the ideas and architecture outlined above. It was implemented in Perl [415] for ease of programming, portability, and modification. Because the prototype was a proof of concept and not a production system, the loss of performance was considered acceptable. The prototype validated the architecture and demonstrated that autonomous agents were a practical method for intrusion detection systems.

26.6   Summary

Intrusion detection is a form of auditing that looks for break-ins and attacks. Automated methods aid in this process, although it can be done manually. There are three basic models of intrusion detection.

Anomaly detection looks for unexpected behavior. A baseline of expected actions or characteristics of processes, users, or groups of users is developed. Whenever something deviates from that baseline, it is reported as a possible intrusion. In some cases, the profiles are changed over time. In this way, the expected behavior of users is updated as their actual behavior changes over time.

Misuse detection looks for sequences of events known to indicate attacks. A rule set (or database) of attacks provides the requisite information. Ideally, an expert system will use the rule set to detect previously unknown attacks (but efforts of this type have been singularly unsuccessful). Both state-based and transition-based techniques capture the sequence of events in attacks.

Specification-based detection looks for actions outside the specifications of key programs. Each program has a set of rules specifying what actions it is allowed to take. If the program tries to take any other action, the intrusion detection mechanism reports a probable intrusion. This method requires that specifications for programs be written.

Intrusion detection systems are auditing engines, so models of auditing systems can describe their architecture. The director, or analysis engine, may be centralized or distributed, and may be hierarchical or fragmented. Each organization has advantages and disadvantages, but for wide area networks, a distributed director provides the greatest flexibility and power. Information may be gathered from hosts, from the network, from both, or from other directors.

26.7   Research Issues

Models of intrusion detection are being studied. In particular, techniques for developing profiles of expected behavior that allow deviations to be quickly determined would improve the state of anomaly detection, such as mechanisms that learn program or user behavior or mechanisms allowing for rapid adaptation of profiles. The acme of misuse detection would be to develop methods of detecting previously unseen attacks. Research on attack taxonomies and attack languages provides a better understanding of how attacks work. Vulnerabilities analysis is another approach that is compatible with research on attacks.

The architecture of a wide area intrusion detection system is critical to successful deployment. Technical problems abound. Should the director be distributed or centralized? Should intrusion detection systems be organized hierarchically? How can existing security tools be integrated into an intrusion detection system? Cooperation among intrusion detection systems would allow different organizations to work together to detect, ameliorate, and possibly trace attacks. Several techniques for enabling communication among such systems are under study.

Related to communication is the data processing required to analyze large amounts of data from distributed agents and directors. Intrusion detection agents can gather large amounts of data, and when this data is combined with output from other agents, storing, sending, and processing the data becomes difficult. The layering methodology of GrIDS lessens the amount of raw data that the higher-level directors need, but at lower levels the problem persists. Unless the hierarchy involves few directors, the problem can exist even when the abstractions are used. Data mining and other techniques for processing large amounts of data are proving useful for this problem.

If end-to-end encryption becomes pervasive, intrusion detection techniques that rely on analysis of unencrypted network traffic will become less useful, and intrusion detection mechanisms will move to the endpoints. Similarly, if link level encryption becomes widely used, intrusion detection will take place at the intermediate hosts. How this will impact the organization, efficiency, and effectiveness of intrusion detection systems is not fully understood.

The most technically exacting area of research is testing of intrusion detection systems. Determining the rate of false negatives is difficult unless the data has been thoroughly analyzed before the test by people other than the designers (and, even then, the analysts may miss attacks). Furthermore, comparison of intrusion detection systems requires an understanding of the policies that each intrusion detection system assumes, as well as development of a basis for comparison. These areas will grow in importance as the need to determine efficiency with respect to various metrics increases.

Privacy issues pervade intrusion detection. In particular, how does one ensure that the data being analyzed does not reveal information about nonattackers? The data can be sanitized, but sanitization risks elimination of data that the intrusion detection system needs in order to detect intrusions. Moreover, if different organizations decide to cooperate, how can each organization sanitize the data that it wishes to keep private? Although the heart of these questions is nontechnical, their resolution is central to maintaining people's trust in the system and the security mechanisms. The technologies used to protect individuals and organizations raise sublime technical questions.

26.8   Further Reading

Several authors describe intrusion detection in detail. Bace [106] provides a wonderful overview with much historical information. Kemmerer and Vigna [1029] provide a history of the field. Collins [443], Bejtlich [146], and Sanders and Smith [1650] give a practitioner's overview. Others [636, 1548, 1672] present both managerial and technical information, and discuss tools such as Snort [366, 471, 676, 1601]. Intrusion detection systems and techniques have been developed for a variety of environments such as cyber-physical systems [1362], critical infrastructure [1182], wireless networks [329, 1361], and MANETs [1414]. Chandola, Banerjee, and Kumar [377] provide an excellent survey of anomaly detection methods.

Work on the Bro intrusion detection system includes augmenting it to perform host-based intrusion detection [588] and developing protocol parsers to aid in the creation of policies [1491]. Both Bro [1176] and Snort [2045] have been used to monitor SCADA systems.

Many methods of evaluating intrusion detection systems have been proposed [347, 827, 1270]. Sommer and Paxson [1785] challenge the widespread acceptance of machine learning techniques being suitable for finding attacks in real network data, and offer guidelines for applying machine learning effectively in that domain.

Honeydocuments, sometimes called *decoy documents*, appear to be an effective tool for detecting intruders targeting particular information [1828]. Stoll used one to catch a spy [1829]. Honeydocuments must be developed, deployed, and monitored with care to fool attackers [168, 275, 276, 1948].

Specification-based anomaly detection has been used with the ad hoc on-demand distance vector routing protocol [1900]. It also served as the basis for pecification-based anomaly intrusion detection, which augments that with statistics that can be used to detect anomalies [1711].

Evaluating intrusion detection systems is an area of active research. Axelsson [102] discusses the relationship between false positives and false negatives. Several papers describe techniques for testing [599, 730, 847, 1334, 1406, 1551] intrusion detection systems. Tavallaee et al. [1861] describe two problems with the KDD-CUP-99 dataset and suggest ways to ameliorate them. Ptacek and Newsham [1550] take advantage of packet fragmentation to evade intrusion detection systems; mimicry attacks [1107, 1954] use exploits that craft a set of allowed interactions with the system to carry out malicious actions; as the interactions are allowed, the intrusion detection system does not detect the attack.

Sobirey, Fischer-Hübner, and Rannenberg raise the issue of privacy in an intrusion detection context [1778]. Others have analyzed this problem and suggested approaches [235, 1218]. Lakkaraju and Slagell [1126] examine how anonymization affects the results of an intrusion detection mechanism.

26.9   Exercises

1. You have been hired as the security officer for Compute Computers, Inc. Your boss asks you to determine the number of erroneous login attempts that should be allowed before a user's account is locked. She is concerned that too many employees are being locked out of their accounts unnecessarily, but is equally concerned that attackers may be able to guess passwords. How would you determine an appropriate value for the threshhold?

2. Why should the administrator (or the superuser) account never be locked regardless of how many incorrect login attempts are made? What should be done instead to alert the staff to the attempted intrusion, and how could the chances of such an attack succeeding be minimized?

3. Consider the trace-based approach to anomaly-based intrusion detection. An intrusion detection analyst reports that a particular pattern of system usage results in processes with "low entropy," meaning that there is little uncertainty about how the system processes behave. How well would a cluster-based analysis mechanism for anomaly-based intrusion detection work with this system? Justify your answer.

4. Use a Colored Petri Automaton (see Section 26.3.2) to describe the *xterm* attack discussed in Section 24.3.1.

5. One view of intrusion detection systems is that they should be of value to an analyst trying to disprove that an intrusion has taken place. Insurance companies and lawyers, for example, would find such evidence invaluable in assessing liability. Consider the following scenario. A system has both classified and unclassified documents in it. Someone is accused of using a word processing program to save an unclassified copy of a classified document. Discuss if, and how, each of the three forms of intrusion detection mechanisms could be used to disprove this accusation.

6. GrIDS uses a hierarchy of directors to analyze data. Each director performs some checks, then creates a higher-level abstraction of the data to pass to the next director in the hierarchy. AAFID distributes the directors over multiple agents. Discuss how the distributed director architecture of AAFID could be combined with the hierarchical structure of the directors of GrIDS. What advantages would there be in distributing the hierarchical directors? What disadvantages would there be?

7. As encryption conceals the contents of network messages, the ability of intrusion detection systems to read those packets decreases. Some have speculated that *all* intrusion detection will become host-based once all network packets have been encrypted. Do you agree? Justify your answer. In particular, if you agree, explain why no information of value can be gleaned from the network; if you disagree, describe the information of interest.

Chapter 27
Attacks and Responses

ROMEO: Courage, man; the hurt cannot be much.
MERCUTIO: No, 'tis not so deep as a well, nor so wide
as a church-door; but 'tis enough,'twill serve—ask
for me to-morrow, and you shall find me a grave man.
— *The Tragedy of Romeo and Juliet*, III, i, 98–101.

Preparing for attacks, handling them, and recovering from them requires both preparation and an understanding of how attacks work. Attack models are an attempt to frame the general ideas underlying attacks into a form that provides a basis for developing attacks or countering them. Understanding what happened in an attack, including its possible goals, requires that the attack be analyzed. Often, the model guides the analysis. This chapter examines models of attacks and how attacks are analyzed.

27.1 Attacks

Security policies define what is, and is not, allowed.

> **Definition 27–1.** An *attack* is a sequence of actions that create a violation of a security policy.

When attackers launch an attack, they have a particular goal in mind. The goal may be ill-formed, as in one of exploration; it may be very general, as in simply disrupting the proper operation of the system; or it may be very specific, as in acquiring a copy of a particular file.

> **Definition 27–2.** A *goal* is that which the attacker hopes to achieve.

For example, the students' goal in attacking the University of Michigan's system (see Section 24.2.6) was to acquire access to the terminal control structures.

The goal of the attack on the Burroughs machine (see Section 24.2.7) was to obtain privileged status. These are both technical goals, relating specifically to the use of a computer. Other goals may be more general: cracking a safe, or embarrassing a public figure or political party.

An attacker launches an attack against an entity or entities. The attack may affect other entities, but that is incidental to the purpose of the attack.

> **Definition 27–3.** A *target* of an attack is the entity that the attacker wishes to affect.

The targets of the two attacks mentioned above were the computer system. Acquiring control of a computer may be simply a step towards achieving a larger goal, for example obtaining a copy of a confidential document or changing information on the system, causing the company to take actions (or not to take actions) that it otherwise would (or would not) take.

> **Definition 27–4.** A *multistage attack* is an attack that requires several steps to achieve its goal.

Most attacks are multistage. Describing them requires considering the details of system configuration and operation, and the environment in which it is held. This suggests some sort of graphical representation, the nodes representing steps in the attack and the edges providing relationships among them.

27.2   Representing Attacks

The notion of layers of abstraction is important in representing attacks. Attacks can be viewed at many layers. As one goes down from the highest layer, the attack steps become more detailed. What appears to be one step becomes several. Each step is designed to achieve a *subgoal* that must be satisfied in order to achieve the larger goal.

EXAMPLE: Consider the penetration of the corporate computer system described in Section 24.2.8. The system managers wanted to determine the effectiveness of the corporation's defenses against unauthorized people accessing their computers. In order to accomplish this, the testers played the role of attackers whose goal was to gain access to the corporate computer system.

Their approach was to try to get people to reveal their account information and change their passwords to something the attackers knew. They targeted newly hired employees who had not had the "Computer Security Awareness Briefing." So, one subgoal was to find those people.

To obtain this list, the attackers needed to know who had it. This required them to learn about the company's organization. To achieve this subgoal, they chose a method that required them to get the company's annual report and a telephone directory. The former was simple, as the report was public; the latter required the attackers to find out how to acquire that directory.

Acquiring the directory required two numbers, so obtaining those numbers became another subgoal. Both were obtained by impersonating employees, one an auditor. So successful impersonation of these employees were additional subgoals.

Had the corporation controls prevented the attackers from meeting a subgoal, they would have tried to find other ways to achieve the corresponding goal. This shows the benefit of viewing an attack as a set of subgoals all directed to achieving a particular goal.

The above example shows that an attack, and its goals, can be framed as a sequence of subgoals that must be satisfied in order to achieve the attack's goal. In essence, a series of very specific attacks can be combined to achieve a higher-level goal. The question is how best to represent these steps.

27.2.1 Attack Trees

An obvious way to represent a sequence of hierarchical steps is as a tree.

EXAMPLE: Longley and Rigby [1207] developed a program to examine cryptographic key management schemes for security flaws. Their goal was to develop a package that would allow attackers to ask (for example) what data is needed to determine the encryption key. Their system has only two functions, $E_k(m)$ (encrypt message m with key k) and $D_k(c)$ (decrypt ciphertext c with key k).

The package sets up an attack tree (called a "search tree" in the paper). Each node represents a subgoal, and the root of the tree represents the information that the attacker requires. Nodes are of two types: "required" and "available." A "required" node represents information that is necessary for the parent, and is said to be *satisfied* when that information becomes available. An "available" node represents information that is known. Thus, a node may be of type "available" if it represents information known initially or if all its "required" children have been satisfied. When all the children of the root node become "available" nodes, then the package has found an attack.

As each level of the tree is constructed, the system looks for leaf nodes that are "required" using a breadth-first search, and then constructs one additional layer. See Exercise 1.

As an example, assume that Sage knows $E_k(m)$, $E_{k'}(k)$, and k'. She wants to determine m. Thus, the node representing m is a "required" node, and the nodes representing $E_k(m)$, $E_{k'}(k)$, and k' are marked "available."

The next step is the construction of the tree. The goal is to determine m. One way to determine this is to use k to decrypt $E_k(m)$. Figure 27–1a shows this tree. The system determines that one node, representing the subgoal of finding k, is "required"; all other subgoals are "available." To find k, then, one approach is to determine whether it is encrypted, and if so try decrypt it. Figure 27–1b shows this tree.

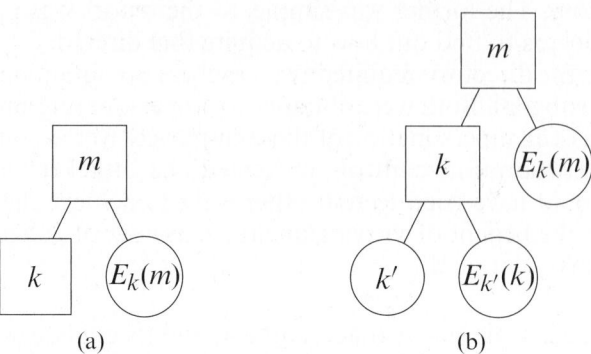

Figure 27–1   Search trees. The square nodes are "required"; the circular ones are "available."

At this point, all k's child nodes are "available," so the subgoal of determining k can be satisfied. Thus, the k node becomes "available." Now, all children of m are "available," so the node k becomes "available," satisfying the goal. Thus, Sage can determine the required message m.

Schneier [1685] generalized the idea of using trees to describe ways to attack systems. He defined two types of nodes. An "and" node requires all its children to be satisfied before it is satisfied. An "or" node requires one of its children to be satisfied before it is satisfied. Each node may have a *weight* indicating a relevant characteristic of the node, such as a measure of the difficulty in satisfying the node. In this case, the weights of the interior nodes depend upon the weights of the child nodes. The weights of the leaf nodes must be assigned based on the analyst's assessment of the characteristic.

To build an attack tree, represent the goal as the root node of the tree. Then determine what steps are necessary to satisfy the goal. These become the children of the root. For each child, repeat this process, until the leaves are at an appropriate layer of abstraction.

EXAMPLE: Schneier presents an attack tree for reading a message encrypted using PGP [741, 1213]. Here, we show how the first few levels of a modified version are generated.

Sage wants to read a message that Skyler is sending to Caroline. Knowing this, Skyler encrypts the message using PGP. Sage has five ways she can read the plaintext message:

1. Read the message before Skyler encrypts it; or

2. Read the message after Caroline decrypts it; or

3. Break the encryption used to encrypt the message; or

4. Determine the symmetric key used to encrypt the message; or

5. Obtain Caroline's private key.

Here, we focus on 2. Once Caroline has decrypted the message, she may forward it to someone she trusts. So, monitoring her outgoing mail may provide Sage with the plaintext message. Similarly, Caroline may reply to the message, and the reply may contain parts of the original message or enable Sage to deduce the original message. The problem here is the reply will almost certainly be enciphered. If so, Sage can try to spoof a "Reply-To" field, causing Caroline to use Sage's public key rather than Skyler's. Sage can also read the message directly by compromising Caroline's computer. Thus, the next layer of the tree under the root node is:

1. Monitor Caroline's outgoing mail; or

2. Add a "Reply-To" field to the header (or change the address in the existing "Reply-To" field); or

3. Compromise Caroline's computer and read the decrypted message.

The last is really two steps:

1. Compromise Caroline's computer; and

2. Read the decrypted message.

Focusing on the former, Sage can compromise Caroline's computer in a number of ways:

1. Copy decrypted message from memory; or

2. Copy decrypted message from secondary storage; or

3. Copy decrypted message from backup; or

4. Monitor network to observe Caroline sending the plaintext message; or

5. Use a Van Eck device [1922] to monitor the display of the message on Caroline's monitor as it is displayed.

We end here, although each of these leaf nodes can be expanded further.

Schneier also suggests a text-based representation of attack trees, with indentation indicating the level of the node. "(AND)" after an interior node indicates it is an "and" node, "(OR)" an "or" node. So, the trees in Figure 27–1 would be written as follows:

1. m (AND)

    1.1. k

    1.2. $E_k(m)$

and

1. m (AND)
    1.1. k (AND)
        1.1.1 k'
        1.1.2 $E_{k'}(m)$
    1.2. $E_k(m)$

The tree for the previous example is:

1. Read a message that Skyler is sending to Caroline. (OR)
    1.1. Read the message before Skyler encrypts it.
    1.2. Read the message after Caroline decrypts it. (OR)
        1.2.1. Monitor Caroline's outgoing mail.
        1.2.2. Add a "Reply-To" field to the header (or change the address in the existing "Reply-To" field).
        1.2.3. Compromise Caroline's computer and read the decrypted message. (AND)
            1.2.3.1. Compromise Caroline's computer. (OR)
                1.2.3.1.1. Copy decrypted message from memory.
                1.2.3.1.2. Copy decrypted message from secondary storage.
                1.2.3.1.3. Copy decrypted message from backup.
                1.2.3.1.4. Monitor network to observe Caroline sending the cleartext message.
                1.2.3.1.5. Use a Van Eck device to monitor the display of the message on Caroline's monitor as it is displayed.
            1.2.3.2. Read the decrypted message.
    1.3. Break the encryption used to encrypt the message.
    1.4. Determine the symmetric key used to encrypt the message.
    1.5. Obtain Caroline's private key.

The key to developing an attack tree is creativity, that is, being able to think of the ways to attack a system. The PGP attack tree is an excellent example, because most people focus on the cryptography (branch 1.3) or on the key management infrastructure (branch 1.5). However, in practice, compromising the system on which the cryptography is executed will often prove simpler and equally effective.

27.2.2   The Requires/Provides Model

Attack trees provide a mechanism for organizing the steps needed to achieve a particular goal. Templeton and Levitt [1865] generalize this approach by describing attacks in terms of their building blocks.

> **Definition 27–5.** A *capability* is a semantic object that encapsulates a number of semantically typed attributes.[1]

Intuitively, a capability represents information or a situation to advance the attack. For example, Sage must be physically proximate to Caroline's computer in order to use a Van Eck device to read the message. Thus, a capability would represent "close enough" in this context. If one capability exists, it may imply that another exists. For example, the capability of knowing someone's password means that that a capability to read their files on that system also exists. This is called *inherent implication*.

Capabilities differ from leaves in attack trees because they are representations of the results of the step. Sage can copy the decrypted message from memory (see leaf 1.2.3.1.1) in several ways, and indeed the "leaf" node in the attack tree would be the root of a subtree detailing these methods. In practice, though, the exact method may not be known until the system is examined, and the set of methods may change over time. The capability, however, represents the situation of reading the memory, encapsulating the result of *any* method to do so. So multiple events—here, the different ways to gain access and read memory—provide the same, or equivalent, capabilities.

> **Definition 27–6.** A *concept* is a set of required capabilities and a mapping from that set of required capabilities to another set of capabilities that are provided.

Concepts are descriptions of subgoals of an attack. To realize the subgoal, the attacker must have the required capabilities. The attacker then receives the additional, provided capabilities with the values given by the concept. This leads to several features.

First, it captures variants of attacks. As the concepts focus on the capabilities and not the method by which those capabilities are required, the focus of detection is on the *effect* of the attack and not the manner of the attack. Similarly, from the attacker's point of view, the focus is on the capabilities to be obtained, and any method that obtains them reaches the desired concept. Similarly, this moves away from the notion of having to know all unique methods of attacks. Only the effects need be known, as those are the capabilities fed into the concepts. Finally, it allows the composition of attacks based solely on the effects and not the methods of attack. Thus, it captures multistage attacks naturally.

---

[1] Contrast this with the "capability" used for access control (see Section 16.2).

EXAMPLE: The remote shell (*rsh*) program allowed remote execution of commands with authentication based on the IP address, user name, and password of the requester. It also allowed *trusted hosts* to execute commands remotely; no user name or password was required.

Consider an *rsh* connection spoofing attack, in which host *attacker* wishes to spoof host *trusted* so it can execute a command remotely on host *victim* (see Figure 27–2). The goal of *attacker* is to execute a command remotely on *victim*. This is done using a TCP connection, which immediately poses a problem.

Recall the three-way handshake that occurs when opening the connection. The host *victim* responds by sending a SYN/ACK packet back, with a sequence number t associated with the SYN. When it gets a responding ACK packet, it checks that the sequence number is $t+1$. But as *attacker* is spoofing *trusted*, *victim* replies to *trusted* and not *attacker*. So *attacker* must block *trusted* from receiving the SYN/ACK packet, and be able to send the ACK packet with the right sequence number.

To do this, *attacker* first launches a denial of service attack against *trusted*. It then probes *victim* to determine what sequence number t will be in the SYN/ACK packet. Once it determines this, it begins the TCP three-way handshake by sending a SYN packet to *victim*, which promptly sends *trusted* a reply with sequence number t. But *trusted* never sees this because of the denial of service attack. So *attacker* sends a spoofed ACK packet to *victim* bearing the sequence number $t+1$. The payload of this TCP packet is the command to be executed, usually a command to insert a vulnerability that *attacker* can later exploit. Note *attacker* cannot get any output from *victim*, because *victim* would send the output to the host *trusted*.

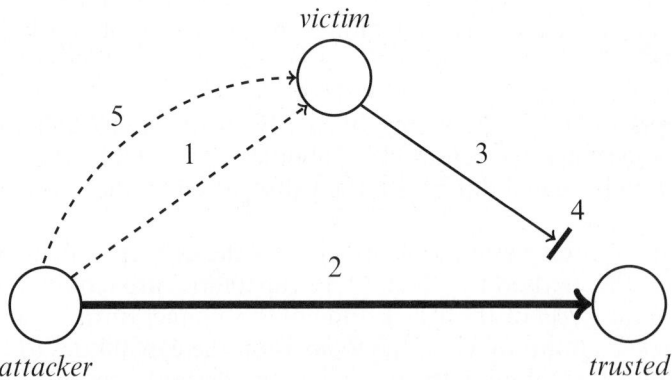

Figure 27–2 The *rsh* attack. Step 1: *attacker* launches a denial of service attack against *trusted*, a host trusted by the *victim*. Step 2: *attacker* sends a spoofed packet purportedly from *trusted* to *victim*. Step 3: *victim* replies to *trusted*, but the packet never arrives (step 4) due to the denial of service attack. Step 5: *attacker* sends another forged packet, purportedly from *trusted*, to *victim*, which executes the command in the packet because it ostensibly came from *trusted*.

In this context, one capability would be blocking of a connection between *trusted* and *victim*. The capability itself would have a source and destination address, and a time interval indicating when the communication is blocked. The concept would be to spoof the *rsh* host.

Templeton and Levitt designed a domain-specific language called JIGSAW. The basis of the language are two constructs, *capabilities* and *concepts*. Capabilities are simply sets of typed attributes and their values. Concepts are two sets of capabilities. Those required to satisfy the concept are listed in a **requires** block, followed by a **with** block that lists the required relationships among the attributes. When those required relationships hold, the capabilities provided by the concept are in a **provides** block. An optional **action** field describes an action to take place when the concept is is active; typical actions are to report a potential or actual problem. The keyword **extern** when applied to a capability means it is defined elsewhere, much as a variable in a program may be labeled **extern** if it is defined in another file.

EXAMPLE: Templeton and Levitt [1865] present a JIGSAW representation of *rsh* connection spoofing. They first define the form of a capability in this context:

```
capability nosend is
   true_src, src, dst:  type Host;
   using:            type Service;
end.
```

Here, `true_src` is the real source of whatever the capability allows the attacker to do (so it is usually the attacking host), `src` is the ostensible source (for example, the host the attacker is spoofing; for nonspoofing capabilities, it may well be the same as `true_src`), and `dst` is the target or destination. Finally, `using` is the requisite service, if any. They then build the concept:

```
concept rsh_connection_spoofing is
   requires
      TP:       type Trusted_Partner;
      SA:       type Active_Service;
      PPS:      type Prevent_Packet_Send;
      FPS:      type Forged_Packet_Send;
      extern SNP: type SeqNumProbe;
   with            #- These instantiate the capabilities
      TP.service is RSH,       #- Service is RSH
      PPS.host is TP.trusted,  #- Blocked host is
                               #-      trusted host
```

```
        FPS.dst.host is TP.trustor,#- Spoofed packets go to host
                                  #-       trusting TP
        FPS.src is [PPS.host,PPS.port], #- Apparent source
                                  #-     of forged
                                  #-     packets is blocked
        SNP.dst is [SA.host,SA.port],  #- Probed host must be
                                  #-     running
        SA.port is TCP/RSH,        #-     RSH on usual port
        SA.service is RSH,

        SNP.dst is FPS.dest,       #- Forged packets go to
                                  #-     probed
        active(FPS) during active(PPS) #-   host while DOS of
                                  #-     trusted
                                  #-     host is active
    end;

    provides
        PSC: type push_channel;
        REX: type remote_execution;
    with
        PSC.src <- FPS.true_src,        #- Capability to move
                                  #-     code from

        PSC.dst <- FPS.dst,            #-     attacker to rsh
                                  #-     server (target)
        PSC.true_src <- FPS.true_src
        PSC.using <- rsh;

        REX.src <- FPS.true_src,        #- Capability to execute
                                  #-     code on
        REX.dst <- FPS.dst,            #-     to rsh server
        REX.true_src <- FPS.true_src
        REX.using <- rsh;
    end;

    action
        true -> report ("rsh connection spoofing: " +
                        TP.hostname)
    end;
end.
```

This concept uses a capability called SeqNumProbe that is defined elsewhere.

The **requires** block requires a trusted host *TP*, a service *SA* (in this case, the *rsh* server), and three capabilities, *PPS*, which enables the "src" host to block the "dst" host from sending packets, *FPS*, which enables the "src" host to send a forged packet to the "dst" host, and *SNP* which enables the "src" host to determine the next sequence number of the "dst" host. Note the full "src" and "dst" of the capabilities also includes the appropriate port number, here the one for the *rsh* service. For the **requires** conditions to be met, a number of relationships, in the **with** part of the block, must hold. These conditions are that the trusted host must be running the *rsh* service, the attacker must have the capability to both block the trusted host from sending packets and be able to send packets spoofed to appear to come from the trusted host to the victim (here, the "victim" is expressed as "the host that trusts the trusted host"). Finally, the host whose sequence number can be probed is the victim, and when the attack on the victim (*FPS*) is being carried out, the attack on the trusted host (*PPS*) is also being carried out.

Given all these conditions, the attacker acquires two new capabilities as shown in the **provides** block. The first, *PSC*, is the ability to send code or commands to the victim and the second, *REX*, is the ability to execute that code or those commands on the victim.

Finally, when this concept is realized (that is, all the conditions in the **requires** block hold), the events in the **action** block occur: a message is printed out alerting the observer that an *rsh* spoofing attack is under way.

27.2.3   Attack Graphs

Attack trees are actually a subset of the more general *attack graph*. These describe an attack in terms of a general graph. Meadows used such a graph to model stages of an attack on cryptographic protocols [1308]. Moskowitz and Kang used graphs to represent circuits in their study of how a lack of security can spread throughout composed systems [1385]. More generally, Dacier and Deswarte proposed a graph-based extension to the typed access control matrix model and describe its use for detecting attacks [488, 489]. Misuse intrusion detection systems have also used graphical representations to represent attacks, as discussed in Section 26.3.2. The difference between these models and the attack tree is that the earlier models focus on the detailed representation of attacks rather than on the goals that motivated the attack. In other words, the earlier work views the attack as the end; Schneier's attack tree and the requires/provides model treat the attack as a means to a given end, the goal.

Phillips and Swiler [1524] use a graphical method to identify attacks on network resources, and further to prune the set to those that have a high probability of success. They consider paths based on the configuration of systems, and focus on both probabilistic risk assessment and on the instantiation of their model to assess the attack paths. The graph represents attack states and transitions. This is very close to the attack trees; the primary difference is their focus on network topology, vulnerabilities, and configurations. The attack trees discussed above are much more general. Further, Phillips and Swiler generate their attack graphs based on configuration information. The corresponding requires/provides model would use capabilities to eliminate potential attack paths, and thus can be used for classes of systems and networks. So it is more general in that sense also.

EXAMPLE: McDermott [1284] shows how to use attack graphs to guide penetration testing.

The nodes $P = \{p_1, \ldots, p_n\}$ of the net are states of entities relevant to the security of the system under attack, and the edges $T = \{t_1, \ldots, t_n\}$ are the transitions between states. The tokens move from node to node to indicate the attack's progress; when a token is present on a node, the attacker has obtained the appropriate control of that entity. The edges are directed in the sense that, if node P_i precedes p_j, then the attacker must gain control of the entity represented by p_i before being able to control the entity represented by p_j.

McDermott's approach is to hypothesize individual flaws as two nodes connected by a transition. The nodes are then examined for relationships that allow them to be linked.

Consider the *rsh* connection spoofing attack discussed previously. The first steps in the attack are as shown in Figure 27–3. These steps can be combined as shown in Figure 27–4. This is in fact a method of carrying out the flaw hypothesis step in that methodology.

Figure 27–4a shows the attack graph representation of the attack. The dotted circle in node p_0 in Figure 27–4a indicates the starting point of the

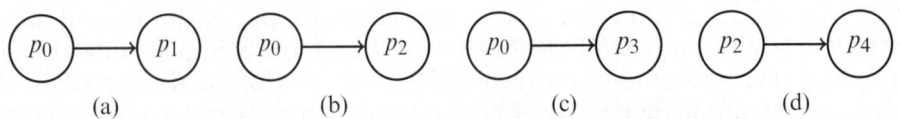

Figure 27–3 Four steps in an attack. **(a) represents the initial scan of the target. (b) represents identifying an unused address. (c) represents establishing that the target trusts another host. (d) is the forging of a SYN packet.**

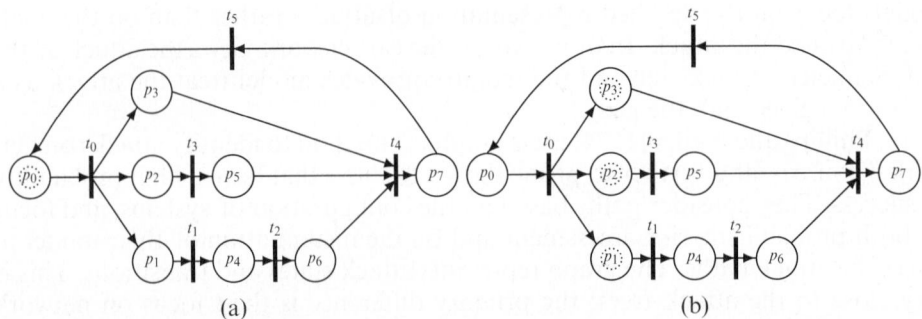

Figure 27–4 An attack graph representing the *rsh* spoofing attack using a Petri net. The small dashed circles represent the tokens. Graph (a) is before the attack; graph (b) is after the first stages.**

attack. Transition t_0 is the initial scan of the system. Note that it splits into three transitions, as successful completion leads to three states of interest. To proceed, all three states must be found: identifying an unused address on the target network (p_1), a trusted host (p_2), and the target (p_3) that trusts the trusted host. As each is found, the token in p_0 advances into each of p_1, p_2, and p_3. The graph of Figure 27–4b shows this state.

Transition t_1 corresponds to the creation of a forged SYN packet, with address that of the trusted host. Transition t_2 is the attacker launching a SYN flood against the trusted host. The token in p_1 can move to p_4 via t_1 and then to p_6, representing the (saturated) state of the network connections of the trusted host. Similarly, transition t_3 represents the attacker figuring out how to predict the TCP sequence numbers of the target host, and p_5 represents that ability. Transition t_4 represents the actual attack using the entities above, producing a system state in which the target has established a spoofed TCP session with the trusted host—but actually, with the attacker's host.

Transition t_5 represents the attacker modifying the trusted host list on the target, enabling the attacker to acquire *root* privileges on the host and thus continue the attack on other hosts.

27.3   Intrusion Response

Once an attack is detected, how can the system be protected? The field of intrusion response deals with this problem. Its goal is to handle the (attempted) attack in such a way that damage is minimized (as determined by the security policy). Some intrusion detection mechanisms may be augmented to thwart intrusions. Others require human intervention to respond to the attack and attempt to repair any damage.

27.3.1   Incident Prevention

Ideally, intrusion attempts will be detected and stopped before they succeed. This typically involves closely monitoring the system, usually with an intrusion detection mechanism, and taking action to defeat the attack.

In the context of response, prevention requires that the attack be identified *before* it completes. Defenders typically use real-time intrusion detection systems and other techniques for monitoring the logs and systems to identify attacks. The defenders then take measures to prevent the attack from completing. This may be done manually or automatically.

EXAMPLE: *Jailing* of attackers is an approach that allows the attackers to think that their attacks have succeeded, but places them in a confined area in which their observed behavior can be controlled and, if necessary, manipulated. Cheswick [402] used this approach to examine an attack. His system recorded a break-in attempt using the SMTP server. After several attempts to break in had failed, Cheswick created a highly restrictive account and monitored the intruder's actions, including which machines were attacked. (None of the attempts succeeded; Cheswick notified the administrators of those systems.) The jail had a file system that closely resembled a real UNIX file system (but without some programs that would reveal system information, and the deception), and access times to certain critical files were also masked. The attacker returned numerous times. Cheswick finally shut down the jail at the request of his management.

Amoroso [45] points out that multilevel secure systems are excellent places to implement jails, because they provide much greater degrees of confinement than do ordinary systems. The attacker is placed into a security compartment isolated from other compartments. The built-in security mechanisms are designed to limit the access of the subjects in the compartment, thereby confining the attacker.

More sophisticated host-based approaches may be integrated with intrusion detection mechanisms. Signature-based methods enable one to monitor transitions for potential attacks. Anomaly-based methods enable one to monitor relevant system characteristics to identify anomalies and to react when anomalies are detected in real time.

EXAMPLE: Somayaji and Forrest [1783] extended intrusion detection using system calls (see the example that begins on page 923) to respond to suspected intrusions. They first modified the intrusion detection system to record anomalous system calls in the *locality frame buffer*. When the number of anomalous system calls (the *locality frame count* or LFC) exceeded a user-defined threshold, the system delayed the evaluation of system calls by $d \times 2^{LFC}$, where d was a tunable parameter. If the maximum LFC exceeded an *abort_execve* parameter, any attempt to spawn a child process failed.

This scheme was implemented in the kernel of a Linux system. The first test examined an *ssh* daemon, and found that attempts to use a global password installed as a backdoor in the daemon were detected. In one set of experiments, the attacker's connection was slowed down significantly. In a second set, the *abort_execve* parameter was set to 1. This prevented the attacker from obtaining a login shell. The second set used *sendmail*, the standard Linux SMTP daemon. In those experiments, the delays that were produced quickly grew to more than two hours, discouraging all but the most patient attacker.

The performance impact of the mechanism was minimal if delays were turned off. When delays were turned on and programs were being used legitimately, the performance of system calls was substantially degraded. However, this did not appear to affect the user's view of system performance significantly. Because system calls are a small part of the runtimes of most programs, this result is not surprising.

Diversity is an attempt to increase the difficulty of successful attacks. In a monoculture, where all systems are the same, an attack that works against one will work against all. But if systems are of different types, then attacks that work against one type of system are likely to fail against another. Thus, varying system types, or even configurations within systems of the same types, limits the extent to which an attack against a particular system can be used. But this diversity may increase the number of attacks that would compromise the overall system.

One such mechanism, *moving target defense*, focuses on changing the system as it runs to thwart attacks. They are based on the asymmetry of the attacker and defender.

> **Definition 27–7.** [1239] An *attack surface* is the set of entry points and data that attackers can use to compromise a system.

The attacker need only find one such avenue to compromise the system. Traditionally, defenses simply hardened the system to reduce the attack surface. But that surface was not empty, so there were still ways for the attacker to gain entry. This is the asymmetry: elements of the attack surface either stay the same, or are diminished, or are eliminated. But the attacker is free to change tactics, and thus has considerably more flexibility than the defender. This asymmetry is called the *defender's dilemma*.

Moving target defenses reduce this asymmetry. They change the attack surface while the system is running, so that attacks that work at one time may not work at another time. Thus, elements of the attack surface now can change. One example, used in network defense, is IP address hopping.

EXAMPLE: The defenses of IP address and port hopping [89] are designed to confuse attackers as they probe a system, and to hide services. Essentially, when a client needs to contact a server, a component maps the destination address and port numbers to different addresses and port numbers. The packet goes to the network on which the server is located, and a mechanism there maps the destination address and port number to the actual address and port number of the server. The mapped address and port number are selected from a set of possible addresses and port numbers pseudorandomly.

If the client and server are on different networks, the changed IP address must be on the same network as the server. Further the components that do the mapping and reverse mapping must be synchronized, so the reverse mapping matches the original IP address and port number. The mapping changes frequently (for example, every minute) so that an attacker monitoring the connections cannot determine the actual IP address and port number from the packets, and further can only piggyback on the connection to attack the server and service between changes to the map.

As an example of how the mapping is done, one implementation of port hopping [1139, 1146] divides time into a series of discrete intervals of length τ at times $t_0, t_1, \ldots, t_i, \ldots$. Let f be a pseudorandom number generator, and s a seed for it. Then, at time k, the port $p_k = f(k, s)$ is used. Further, the ports overlap at the interval boundaries, so (for example) p_k is valid from $t_k - L\tau$ to $t_{k+1} + L\tau$, where L is the amount of overlap in the interval. Another implementation uses an encryption algorithm [1045]. As each packet is received, the low-order eight bits of the IP address (identifying the host) and the bits of the port number are put into a three-byte array that is left-rotated by four bits, and then encrypted using a key shared by both the mapping component and the reverse mapping component. The high-order byte becomes the low-order eight bits of the IP address, and the rest of the bytes become the port number. The reverse mapping component simply reassembles the array, decrypts it, and restores the correct IP address and port number.

Network-based moving target defense mechanisms [818] must not introduce any impediments to authorized clients connecting to the target while they prevent unauthorized clients from doing so. The defense must rely on randomness to prevent unauthorized clients from predicting the changes to the attack surface. If they could do so, they would simply act in anticipation of the next change. Finally, the defender must be able to distinguish between clients that are trustworthy, in the sense that they are to be allowed to connect, and clients that are not.

EXAMPLE: In the example above, the changed IP address acts as a valid IP address. It introduces only the cost of the mapping and reverse mapping, which is negligible compared to the network transit times. A similar observation applies to the port number mappings. Both use pseudorandomness (the key and encryption algorithm for the IP address and the seed act as a pseudorandom number generator). Both hopping schemes determine whether a client is to be allowed to connect by the mapping and reverse mapping mechanisms. If the client uses the correct IP address and port number, then the packets will arrive at the correct server and service, which means the packet's destination address was reverse mapped correctly, and hence mapped correctly. Otherwise, the reverse mapping will change the destination address and port number to invalid ones, and the packet will be dropped. So, these two examples have all the characteristics for a network-based moving target defense.

Moving target defenses at the host level defend against attackers who have access to the host. The access may be as an authorized user with an account or as a remote client connecting to a server. Now, the attack surface is within the host, and that must be changed as the system runs.

EXAMPLE: *Address space layout randomization* (ASLR) is a host-level moving target defense. Consider how the binary of a program is structured. It has several segments, the number depending on the particular type of system and compiler. When loaded into memory for execution, the segments are arranged in a particular order, so the position of the variables and functions in virtual memory are fixed. Thus, an attack tool that (for example) overflows a buffer causing a branch to a function within the program (a *return-to-libc* or an *arc* attack) will work on every invocation of the program. ASLR perturbs the placement of segments, variables, and functions in virtual memory so that attacks that depend on knowing the location of variables and functions will fail.

The key question is how the perturbation is done. The simplest version simply randomizes the placement of the segments in virtual memory [1863]. Other forms randomize the order of functions and variables within their segments or the location of those functions and variables, or add a random amount of space between variables and between functions [194].

The effectiveness of ASLR depends in large part upon the entropy (amount of randomness) introduced into the address space. For example, on 32-bit Linux systems, the uncertainty in the base address of a library loaded into memory is around 16 bits, which can be searched by brute force quickly. But in a 64-bit system, the uncertainty can be as large as 40 bits of uncertainty, which increases the time needed sufficiently so that such an attack is likely to be detected. Interestingly, compile-time randomization is more effective than runtime randomization, and re-randomizing the address space during runtime increases the number of attempts by at most a factor of 2 [1718] (see Exercise 11).

27.3.2   Intrusion Handling

When an intrusion occurs, the security policy of the site has been violated. Handling the intrusion means restoring the system to comply with the site security policy and taking any actions against the attacker that the policy specifies. Intrusion handling consists of several phases [419, 1460].

1. *Preparation* for an attack. This step occurs before any attacks are detected. It establishes procedures and mechanisms for detecting and responding to attacks.
2. *Identification* of an attack. This triggers the remaining phases.
3. *Containment* (confinement) of the attack. This step limits the effects of the attack as much as possible.
4. *Eradication* of the attack. This step stops the attack and blocks further similar attacks.
5. *Recovery* from the attack. This step restores the system to a secure state (with respect to the site security policy).
6. *Follow-up* to the attack. This step involves taking action against the attacker, identifying problems in the handling of the incident, and recording lessons learned.

In the following discussions, we focus on the containment, eradication, and follow-up phases.

27.3.2.1   Containment Phase

Containing or confining an attack means limiting the access of the attacker to system resources. The protection domain of the attacker is reduced as much as possible. There are two approaches: passively monitoring the attack, and constraining access to prevent further damage to the system. In this context, "damage" refers to any action that causes the system to deviate from a "secure" state as defined by the site security policy.

Passive monitoring simply records the attacker's actions for later use. The monitors do not interfere with the attack in any way. This technique is marginally useful. It will reveal information about the attack and, possibly, the goals of the attacker. However, not only is the intruded system vulnerable throughout, the attacker could attack other systems.

EXAMPLE: It may be helpful to know the type of operating system from which the intruder is entering. A passive monitor can examine settings of the TCP and IP headers of incoming connections to generate a signature. For example, some systems change the window size field more often, and in different ways, than others. This signature can be compared with known signatures of operating systems, and the analyst may be able to draw some conclusions about the type of the remote system from which the packets have been generated [95, 820, 1226, 1765].

The other approach, in which steps are taken to constrain the actions of the attacker, is considerably more difficult. The goal is to minimize the protection domain of the attacker while preventing the attacker from achieving her goal. But the system defenders may not know what the goal of the attacker is, and thus may misdirect the confinement so that the data or resources that the attacker seeks lie within the minimal protection domain of the attacker.

EXAMPLE: Stoll [1831] detected an attacker in a computer system at the Lawrence Berkeley Laboratory. After a period of monitoring, Stoll concluded that the attacker was looking for documents related to nuclear weaponry. He arranged for a trace over network and telephone lines, but the tracing ended at the attacker's point of entry into the United States. The foreign authorities reported that they would need a longer connection to trace the attacker to his point of origin in Europe. Stoll created a very large file containing some of the keywords for which the attacker had been searching. When the attacker next entered, he found the file and began to download it. The time required for the upload was more than ample for the trace to be completed, and the attacker was identified and subsequently arrested.

The document that Stoll wrote is an example of a *honeypot* (or, more specifically, a *honeyfile* or *honeydocument*) deception technology. The file was carefully designed to entice the attacker to download it, but in fact contained false and meaningless information. This technique can be extended to systems and networks. Honeypots, sometimes called *decoy servers*, are servers that offer many targets for attackers. The targets are designed to entice attackers to take actions that indicate their goals. Honeypots are also instrumented and closely monitored. When a system detects an attack, it takes actions to shift the attacker onto a honeypot system. The defenders can then analyze the attack without disrupting legitimate work or systems. Two good examples are the Deception Tool Kit and the tools produced by the Honeynet Project.

EXAMPLE: Cohen's Deception Tool Kit (DTK) [439] creates a false network interface that allows the user of the tool kit to present any desired configuration to incoming connections. When an attacker probes the putative network, the DTK returns a wide range of vulnerabilities. The attacker may then choose some subset of the presented network addresses to attack. The defender can configure illusionary systems and servers, and monitor the attacks, so while the attacker is probing nonexistent systems the defender can analyze the attacks to determine the goals and abilities of the attacker.

EXAMPLE: The Honeynet Project [1804] was created to learn about the "black hat" (attacker) community. The organizers were interested in the motives, techniques, and tools of the attackers. The honeypot work was split into phases. The first phase was to identify common threats against specific operating systems and configurations. These Gen-I honeynets were crude but remarkably effective. The next phase was to develop a Gen-II honeypot network that could collect data more efficiently while being easier to deploy and harder to detect. Honeynets are used in research, to gather attack signatures, and to enable defenders to analyze attacks and counter them without endangering production systems [418, 1522, 1572, 1573, 1805, 1980].

27.3.2.2   Eradication Phase

Eradicating an attack means stopping the attack. The usual approach is to deny access to the system completely (such as by terminating the network connection) or to terminate the processes involved in the attack. An important aspect of eradication is to ensure that the attack does not immediately resume. This requires that attacks be blocked.

A common method for implementing blocking is to place wrappers around suspected targets. The wrappers implement various forms of access control. Wrappers can control access locally on systems or control network access.

EXAMPLE: Wrappers that control local access to resources are usually embedded in the kernel to make them difficult to bypass. In an experiment that used wrappers to improve the security of commercial off-the-shelf programs, Fraser, Badger, and Feldman [720] used loadable kernel modules to place wrappers in the kernels of UNIX systems. When the wrappers were invoked, they waited for some specified event (such as a system call, possibly with particular privilege settings or arguments). When the event occurred, the wrapper would take control of the process and perform a specified action. The action could be to log the call, to deny access (by returning a failure code to the caller), or to generate and process auxiliary data such as system call counts. The wrappers were specified using an extension of the C programming language. The performance impact of using the wrappers was measured at less than 7%.

The researchers noted that the functionality of the wrappers was varied, ranging from access control and auditing to intrusion detection and response. Others [1078] focused on the latter, designing wrappers that would detect intrusions. Their mechanism accepted notifications from multiple wrappers. In one experiment, when two wrappers determined that a process appeared to be launching an attack, they notified a wrapper that was monitoring program execution, which terminated the process.

EXAMPLE: Wrappers can also control access from the network. Bina, McCool, Jones, and Winslett [209] describe an application in which a web server accepts requests for database records and returns the desired records if so authorized. Access to the records is determined by the role of the requester. To determine this, the web server obtains information from the client (including a public key for authentication) and passes the data to a script that assigns the appropriate role to the request. The role and request are given to the database engine, which returns an appropriate response. The script is a wrapper around the database. It mediates access to the database.

Firewalls (see Section 17.6.2) sit between an organization's internal network and some other external network (such as the Internet). The firewall controls access from the external network to the internal network and vice versa. The advantage of firewalls is that they can filter network traffic *before* it reaches the target host. They can also redirect network connections as appropriate, or throttle traffic to limit the amount of traffic that flows into (or out of) the internal network.

EXAMPLE: Consider the example of a firewall that filters Java applets (see p. 572). An interesting approach, similar to rewriting the HTML tag, is to use a proxy situated on the firewall. Spout [407], one such proxy, forwards HTML requests from a client to the web server. When the server responds, the requested page goes to the proxy. If the HTML includes a Java applet, the proxy replaces the applet name with that of a template applet, and maintains the association between the requested applet name and the template applet name. It then forwards the HTML file to the client. When the client issues a request for the applet, Spout gets the request, and forwards to the web server a request for the real applet. When the applet arrives at the proxy, it routes the applet to a Java application server and forwards the bytecode of the template applet to the client. The Java application server executes the applet. The template applet links the input from the client browser to the real applet, and the output from the real applet to the client's browser.

An organization may have several firewalls on its perimeter, or several organizations may wish to coordinate their responses. The Intruder Detection and Isolation Protocol (IDIP) [1680] provides a protocol for coordinated responses to attacks.

The IDIP protocol runs on a set of computer systems. A *boundary controller* is a system that can block connections from entering a perimeter. Typically, boundary controllers are firewalls or routers. A boundary controller and another system are *neighbors* if they are directly connected. If they send messages to one another, the messages go directly to their destination without traversing any other system. If two systems are not boundary controllers and can send messages to each other without the messages passing through a boundary controller, they are said to be in the same *IDIP domain*. This means that the boundary controllers form a perimeter for an IDIP domain.

When a connection passes through a member of an IDIP domain, the system monitors the connection for intrusion attempts. If one occurs, the system reports the attempt to its neighbors. The neighbors propagate information about the attack and proceed to trace the connection or datagrams to the appropriate boundary controllers. The boundary controllers can then coordinate their responses, usually by blocking the attack and notifying other boundary controllers to block the relevant communications.

EXAMPLE: Kahn [987] discusses the use of IDIP to handle network flooding attacks, in which one or more sources spew large numbers of packets to a target. This effectively prevents legitimate traffic from being processed, either because the target is overwhelmed with processing the flooding packets or because the legitimate traffic cannot reach the destination (target).

Consider Figure 27–5. Suppose host f launches a flooding attack against host A along the path f, Z, Y, X, W, a, A. The flood effectively stops all traffic along that path. Host a detects the flood and begins blocking traffic for host A. It also notifies its neighbor W, a boundary controller. W detects traffic targeting A, suppresses it, and notifies its neighbor X. X detects the traffic targeting A, suppresses it, and notifies its neighbors Y and C. W then notices the traffic for A has stopped, and it eliminates its suppression. At this point, A, a, W, and b can again communicate freely, because the traffic formerly saturating the links has been eliminated by X. C detects no traffic for A and so does nothing. Y does detect the traffic, and suppresses it. X detects that the traffic going through it for A has stopped, and X eliminates its suppression. Y then communicates with Z, and Z detects and suppresses the traffic. Y also communicates with D, which detects no relevant traffic. This process continues until all traffic from f to A is suppressed.

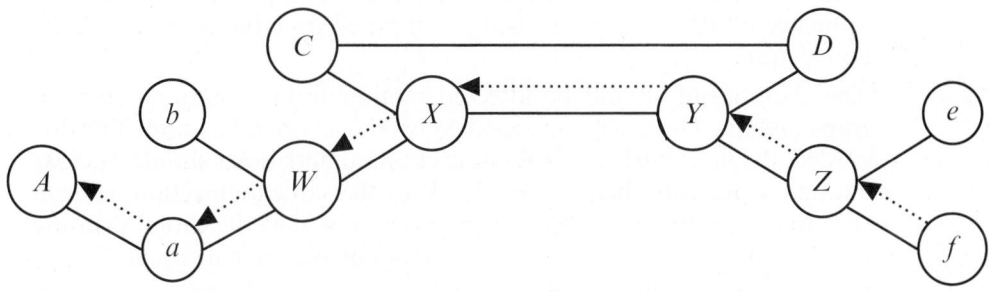

Figure 27–5 Example of IDIP. *C*, *D*, *W*, *X*, *Y*, and *Z* are boundary controllers. Host *a* runs the IDIP protocol but is not a boundary controller. The flooding attack follows the dashed arrows from *f* to A.

The IDIP protocol is flexible, because if multiple sources attempt to flood a host, the boundary controllers will block the traffic along each path that the sources use. Of course, if any path has no IDIP controllers, the traffic can flow freely along that path. Kahn and Zurko suggest that IDIP, or a similar protocol, should be widely deployed throughout the Internet to handle flooding attacks. They argue that economic and other incentives will encourage Internet Service Providers and other network providers to cooperate in suppressing distributed flooding attacks.

27.3.2.3   Follow-Up Phase

In the follow-up phase, the systems take some action against the attacker. The most common follow-up is to pursue some form of legal action, either criminal or civil. The requirements of the law vary among communities, and indeed vary within communities over time. So, for our purposes, we confine ourselves to the technical issue of tracing the attack through a network. Two techniques for tracing are thumbprinting and IP header marking.

Thumbprinting takes advantage of connections passing through several hosts. An attacker may go from one host, through many intermediate hosts, until he reaches his target. If one monitors the connections at any two hosts that the connections pass through, the contents of the connections will be the same (excluding data added at the lower layers). By comparing contents of connections passing through hosts, one can construct the chain of hosts making up the connections.

Staniford-Chen and Heberlein [1817] list five characteristics of a good thumbprint.

1. The thumbprint should take as little space as possible, to minimize storage requirements at each site.
2. If two connections have different contents, the probability that their thumbprints are the same should be low. Notice that two connections with *identical* contents will have the same thumbprint. This is a consequence of the thumbprint being computed over the contents of the connection.
3. The thumbprint should be affected minimally by common errors in transmission. Thus, if traffic between two hosts often has some bits discarded, the thumbprints of the connections at both hosts should be close enough to identify them as belonging to the same connection. (Recall that thumbprints are computed passively, and that the thumbprinting program may not have access to the error correction features of TCP.)
4. Thumbprints should be additive so that two thumbprints over successive intervals can be combined into a single thumbprint for the total interval.
5. Finally, thumbprints should cost little to compute and compare.

There are several possible sources of error (see Exercise 8).

EXAMPLE: Staniford-Chen and Heberlein [1817] experimented with thumbprints made up of linear combinations of character frequencies in telnet and rlogin connections. The thumbprints were computed over a set of connections drawn from normal network traffic. First, a control experiment checked that thumbprints were unlikely to match randomly paired connections. Out of 4,000 pairings, only one match was identified. On inspection, the two connections had identical contents over the period of thumbprinting (a prompt and a logout command). Next, they computed thumbprints from connections passing through multiple hosts (one thumbprint per host for each connection) on a local area network. These thumbprints were injected into a collection of thumbprints made at the same time. Comparison identified these thumbprints as belonging to the same connections. Experiments on long haul networks (across the United States and the Atlantic Ocean) also showed that the comparison procedure was able to find the connections correctly.

An alternative approach is to ignore the contents of the packets and examine the headers. *IP header marking* does just this. A router places extra information into the IP header of each packet to indicate the path that the packet has taken. This information may be examined in order to to trace the packet's route back through the Internet [1669].

The keys to IP header marking are selection of the packets to mark, and marking of the packets. Packet selection may be *deterministic* or *probabilistic*. Packet marking may be *internal* or *expansive*.

Deterministic packet selection means that packets are selected on the basis of a nonrandom algorithm. For example, every second packet may have the router's IP address inserted as the marking. It is unreliable because an attacker can enter false data into the header area and prevent the marking (see Exercise 3). In general, it is also expensive. Probabilistic packet selection reduces this somewhat by selecting a subset of the packets based on a given probability.

Internal packet marking places the router's marking in the packet header without expanding it. For example, Dean, Franklin, and Stubblefield [524] have identified several bits in an IPv4 header that could be used for marking. Expansive packet marking means that the packet header is expanded to include extra space for the marking.

EXAMPLE: Doeppner, Klein, and Koyfman [578] suggest a probabilistic, expansive packet marking scheme. They propose adding space ("slots") for s markings. The probability that a packet will be marked is p. The following algorithm describes how the router handles an incoming packet:

```
/* generate random number between 0, 1 */
x = random(0, 1);
/* stamp the packet appropriately */
if x < s * p then
        slot[x/p] = /* router's stamp */;
```

Note that the slot into which the router's marking is placed depends on the random number generated.

The markings can enable one to trace certain attacks back to their sources. As an example, consider the SYN flood attack [498], in which an attacker generates a large number of TCP SYN packets (see Section 7.4). The target receives them and sends the SYN/ACK packet in the second step of the three-way handshake (see Section 25.4.2). The attacker never sends the third packet, so the connection is pending until it times out. At that point, the target grabs the next incoming SYN packet and repeats the cycle. Because the attacker is flooding the target with SYN packets, the probability of any other host's SYN packet initiating the three-way handshake is very low. The attack therefore denies service to all other hosts.

Consider the network in Figure 27–6. Host E experiences a SYN flood. The administrators identify 3,150 packets that could be a result of the attack. Figure 27–7 shows the number of packets that have been marked as taking each route. Counting, there are 1,200 packets with A's mark, 750 with B's mark, 700 with C's mark, and 2,450 with D's mark. Assuming that the probability of marking is the same on each router, the number of packets that D received is more than three times as great as the number that B received. Thus, B is probably the source of the flooding.

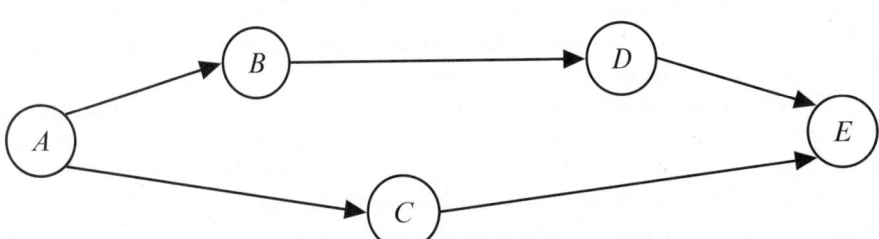

Figure 27–6 Example network. Routers A, B, C, and D mark packets. The destination host E is experiencing a SYN flood. The administrators at host E use the markings to identify the flooder.

Number	Route	Number	Route
600	(A, B, D)	150	(B, D)
200	(A, D)	300	(C)
400	(A, C)	1500	(D)

Figure 27–7 The number of packets marked with a route from Figure 27–6. Some routes are incomplete as not every router marks every packet it routes.

EXAMPLE: Dean, Franklin, and Stubblefield [524] employ an algebraic technique to encode suffixes of the paths taken by packets. Evaluating an nth-degree polynomial requires $n + 1$ data points. Consider the packets being sent from host A to host B along path P. The first router in path P labels the jth packet with the integer x_j. Let the routers' IP addresses on path P be $a_0, \ldots, a_n$. Then, when the jth packet arrives at B, its marking will be the value of the polynomial $f(x) = a_0 x^n + \ldots + a_n$ at x_j. When $n + 1$ packets along that path arrive, the coefficients of the polynomial can be determined. The routers can use Horner's rule [1076] to evaluate the polynomial, so they need not know the path P. Router a_i needs to know $a_0 x_j^i + \ldots + a_{i-1}$. It then computes $(a_0 x_j^i + \ldots + a_{i-1})x_j + a_i$.

This approach has several problems. First, recording the entire path requires that a router know it is the first router on path P so that it can assign x_j and begin computing the polynomial. This is infeasible given the current structure of the Internet. One approach is to select a number from a weighted random distribution of integers to determine if the router is the first on P. If so, it assigns x_j; if not, the router evaluates the polynomial as described above. Furthermore, if x_j is assigned, the router assigns similar values to the next k packets (k being a tunable parameter). This increases the number of packets needed to reconstruct the full path. Moreover, an attacker can place arbitrary information into the marking, so if the router does not select the packet for marking, the erroneous information is passed along. Ultimately, the destination will not be able to distinguish the erroneous information from legitimate packet markings.

An alternative approach modifies the scheme so that at most l routers mark the packet. The first router sets this parameter; each marking router decrements it by 1. This scheme records subsequences of P, rather than suffixes of P or the entire path. This keeps the degree of the polynomials small (of degree $l - 1$ at most).

Dean, Franklin, and Stubblefield used this last scheme to mark packets. The bits of the values of the polynomials were distributed over 11 bits in the IP header. In their simulations, they analyzed 20,000 packets and recovered paths of length 25 more than 98% of the time, demonstrating the efficacy of their scheme.

Counterattacking, or attacking the attacker, takes several forms.

Legal mechanisms, such as filing criminal complaints, require protecting a "chain of evidence" so that legal authorities can establish that the attack was real (in other words, that the attacked site did not invent evidence) and that the evidence can be used in court. The precise requirements of the law change over time and jurisdictions, so this first form of counterattacking lies outside the scope of this discussion.

Related to this is the ability to attribute the attack to a set of entities [227, 229, 936]. This helps determine the set of legal remedies available, if any. The degree of accuracy of the attribution will also affect those remedies, as will the intentions of the attackers. If the attackers do not want to be identified, then accurate attribution will be a deterrent.

A technical counterattack has the goal of damaging the attacker seriously enough to stop the current attack and discourage future attacks. This approach has several important consequences that must be considered.

1. The counterattack may harm an innocent party. The attacker may be impersonating another site. In this case, the counterattack could damage a completely innocent party, putting the counterattackers in the same position as the original attackers. Alternately, the attackers may have broken into the site from which the attack was launched. Attacking that host does not solve the problem. It merely eliminates one base from which future attacks might be launched.

2. The counterattack may have unintended consequences. For example, if the counterattack consists of flooding a specific target, the flood could block portions of the network that other parties need to transit, which would damage them.

3. The counterattack is antithetical to the shared use of a network. Networks exist to share data and resources and provide communication paths. By attacking, regardless of the reason, the attackers make networks less usable because they absorb resources and make threats more immediate. Hence, sites must protect themselves by limiting the sharing and communication on the network beyond what is needed for their safe operation.

4. The counterattack may be legally actionable. If an attacker can be prosecuted or sued, it seems reasonable to assume that one who responds to the attack by counterattacking can also be prosecuted or sued, especially if other innocent parties are damaged by the counterattack.

Under exceptional circumstances, counterattacking may be appropriate. In general, it should be avoided, and legal avenues of prosecution (either civil or criminal) should be pursued. Improving defenses will also hinder attacks. The efforts used to develop and launch counterattacks could be spent far more effectively in that way.

EXAMPLE: Recall the example of the two versions of the *animal* game (see page 779). In that case, the new version of *animal* targeted a specific, older version written by the same authors, and it was unlikely that any organization depended on the existence of that game. Consider moving this example into the world of distributed systems and networks. Imagine a computer worm that enters systems through a widely used network server. The worm spreads rapidly, and despite attempts to eradicate it, systems continue to be reinfected. One company designs a "counterworm." Whenever a break-in comes from a remote site, the "counterworm" detects the break-in, deletes the connection, and uses the same infection technique as that of the original worm to enter the attacking host. On that host, it deletes all worm processes (except its own). It then waits until that system is attacked, and the cycle repeats.

This response raises several questions. First, how can the "counterworm" be set to ensure that it deletes only those processes belonging to the original worm? Second, what if the invaded machine is gathering data for research or countermeasures? Third, how can the originators of the "counterworm" ensure that it does no damage to any system it is sent to? Fourth, can they be held legally liable for any problems that a site encounters if that site is sent the "counterworm"? The answers to these questions are complex, and illustrate clearly why one needs informed, full consent of a remote site before sending an automated response.

27.3.2.4   Incident Response Groups

When a security incident occurs, it rarely affects one system, and the response must be coordinated with other affected sites. Even if only one system is affected, the system administrators may not know how to handle the situation.

> **Definition 27–8.** A *computer security incident response team* (CSIRT) is a team established to assist and coordinate responses to a security incident among a defined constituency.

A constituency may be a company, an organization, a sector (such as academic institutions), or even broader.

EXAMPLE: As several groups dealt with the Internet Worm (see Section 24.3.1), members of the groups communicated with people they knew at other affected sites. In some cases, establishing the connection required a third party trusted by all groups; in other cases, the groups were not aware of other groups analyzing the worm, resulting in a duplication of work. This raised the concern of how to enhance communication and coordinate responses, leading to the formation of the Computer Emergency Response Team (CERT/CC) located at Carnegie Mellon University. It had several purposes, among them the coordination of responses to incidents and preserving information about incidents that were reported to better understand whether they were separate incidents or different facets of a larger attack. CERT/CC worked with vendors and others to ensure vulnerabilities reported in products were fixed, and issued vulnerability advisories to report to the community.

Many CSIRTs have been formed, such as national CSIRTs that have the country as their constituency, vendor CSIRTs that deal with vulnerabilities in the vendor's products or services, and internal CSIRTs that deal with incidents involving their organization. The mission of a CSIRT depends in large part upon its constituency. A critical part of all missions is to keep the constituency informed about the services the CSIRT will provide and how members of the constituency can communicate with the CSIRT. A CSIRT would not have much value if the procedures used to report an incident were not known to those who are expected to do the reporting.

CSIRT missions generally have at least three aspects [306].

1. *Publication.* As above, the CSIRT should publish its policies and procedures to inform its constituency of what it can do, how it will communicate information to the constituency, and how the constituency can inform it of incidents and requests.

2. *Collaboration.* Given the scope of many attacks over the Internet, the CSIRT will almost certainly collaborate with other CSIRTs in gathering information about such attacks, disseminating information about attacks, and responding to them.

3. *Secure communication.* A key component of any CSIRT is its credibility. Thus, the constituency needs to be sure that its members are communicating with the CSIRT and not some rogue group masquerading as the CSIRT. Similarly, when dealing with an incident, the CSIRT must be certain it is dealing with the affected members of its constituency, and other CSIRTs, and not the attackers impersonating members of the constituency or other CSIRTs.

Underlying a CSIRT's functioning are policies and procedures, plans, and management [419].

The policy of a CSIRT defines what it will, and will not, do. For example, will the CSIRT handle news media requests for information about an ongoing incident? Can the CSIRT order systems isolated from the network during an attack? At what point might the CSIRT conclude the incident has been responded to appropriately, and either end its involvement or transfer the response to another group, such as law enforcement? With what other CSIRTs will it collaborate, and what information will it share? Many of these questions illustrate aspects of the policy driven by the needs and constraints of the organization that the CSIRT is a part of. For example, the information that a medical CSIRT can share is much more limited than that of a public agency, because medical records are protected by different, more restrictive laws.

A CSIRT also needs a plan to respond to incidents. How will an incident report be handled? What actions might the CSIRT take to contain an attack, and how does it enable members of its constituency to continue to do their jobs during the attack—or does it? How does the CSIRT interact with management? How will it report the status of the attack and its own efforts to its constituency? How will it interact with other CSIRTs and interested parties? Do laws or regulations require the CSIRT, or the reporters, to take specific actions such as notifying law enforcement or regulatory bodies and if so, when and how? Again, the plans for handling incidents are driven by the needs and constraints of the organization.

The management component deals with the organization and staffing of the CSIRT. It can be centralized or distributed, and internal to the organization or contracted to an outside group. Cost, availability needs, and other factors will guide this. A key factor is morale—the members of the CSIRT will be on call (whether all the time or part time is up to the organization), and this combined with the importance of their work to the organization will undoubtedly cause stress. To keep the CSIRT functioning well, the organization must have a plan to deal with this.

The CSIRT must take care to avoid a simply technical approach [27]. Often a strategic analysis coupled with the technical analysis will reveal organizational issues that contribute to an incident, or hinder appropriate responses. Understanding the impacts of the attack on the organization's mission is critical, and involves nontechnical aspects of the organization such as human resources, economics, and the law.

Finally, the CSIRT should disseminate information that will prevent or limit attacks. This information includes reports of vulnerabilities so system administrators can patch them, reports of attacks so users and administrators know what to look for, and contact information for the CSIRT. The more involved the constituency is in protecting the systems and the data on it, the more effective a CSIRT can be.

27.4   Digital Forensics

As part of incident response, determining what happened and what failed requires an analysis of the detritus of the attack.

> **Definition 27–9.** *Digital forensics* is the science of identifying and analyzing entities, states, and state transitions of events that have occurred or are occurring.

The distinction between this and the legal notion of forensics is important. Digital forensics, also called *computer forensics*, may in fact be a component of a legal forensic analysis, in which case the computer analysts must acquire the information and perform the analysis in such a way that they meet the appropriate legal requirements. More commonly, digital forensics is used to figure out what caused an anomaly or to understand the nature of an attack, including how the attackers entered the system, what they did there, and how the defenses failed, without following legal strictures. This complicates matters should the analysis uncover information requiring legal intervention.

27.4.1   Principles

Locard's Exchange Principle states that "every contact leaves a trace" [922, p. 45]. This principle is widely applied in the investigation of physical crime scenes. The principles of digital forensics create an environment in which Locard's Exchange Principle also holds. They are based on the notion that the entire system must be considered, because attacks on one component may affect other components. In particular, multistage attacks often leverage access to one system to gain access to other systems. Further, while the analyst may expect an attack to have a certain effect, often the attack has other, or additional, effects that are unexpected—another reason to consider the system as a whole rather than only looking at the attacked components. Finally, an attack occurs when the system is active, and hence data about the attack gathered while the system is running can be critical to the analysis. Post-intrusion analysis is helpful, but the analyst often must deduce what happened rather than observe it in comprehensive logs. Such deductions may be incorrect due to erroneous assumptions, or the analyst may not know which of several possible transitions occurred.

Five principles build upon these bases [1506]:

1. Consider the entire system.
2. Assumptions should not control what is logged.
3. Consider the effects of actions as well as the actions.
4. Context assists in understanding meaning.
5. Information must be processed and presented in an understandable way.

We consider these separately.

27.4.1.1   Consider the Entire System

The analyst must have access to at least the information that the intruder had both before and during the attack. This is necessary to be able to deduce what the intruder did. This includes changes to the memory, kernel, file systems, and files. On most systems, such information is rarely recorded continuously, so the analyst will have incomplete information for her analysis. Logging and auditing tools typically record information about connections, the state of services, and which programs are executed. But they do not identify the directories searched to find the libraries loaded when the programs are executed, which would reveal both how an attacker is exploring the file system, and whether the standard library or a modified version of the library was loaded. Nor do they reveal the contents of memory or the functions called during program execution, all of which would provide valuable information about the attack. In addition, many applications do not log security-relevant information, leaving the analyst to reconstruct actions taken by the application from incomplete, system-level logs.

27.4.1.2   Assumptions Should Not Control What Is Logged

Forensic analysts work from logs of information captured before, during, and after the attack. Thus, what is logged affects the analysis. So if assumptions inhibit information from being logged, the analysts may have incomplete information, leading to an incomplete or incorrect analysis of the attack. Instead, as much information as needed to reconstruct the system state at any point in time should be recorded.

Virtual machine introspection provides an avenue for examining a running system. It also can be used to record the state of the system. Introspection systems usually focus on nondeterministic events, such as user input or hardware interrupts, because deterministic events can be reconstructed.

EXAMPLE: Oliveira et al. [522] developed an architecture to enable replay of events with minimal overhead and no modification to the running systems. Their system consists of three components: a checkpoint mechanism, a logging mechanism, and a replay mechanism, ExecRecorder. These reside in the virtual machine monitor Bochs, and so are invisible to the operating system being monitored. The checkpoint component takes a snapshot of the state of the system. In addition, Bochs supports a disk mode enabling recovery of the state of the disk at any point in time. The logging component records nondeterministic events in sufficient detail to allow them to be reproduced exactly in the way they occurred, down to the instruction, number of bytes moved, and where they are moved (register or memory). The contents are recorded when necessary, but for I/O from the disk, this is not needed as the state of the disk at that moment can be reproduced. The replay component allows the state of the system to be restored and system activity continued from that point, reproducing what happened. During this time, all interrupts and other nondeterministic events are disabled or blocked so as not to affect the execution.

27.4.1.3   Consider the Effects of Actions as Well as the Actions

One of the goals of forensic analysis is to establish what happened to the system as well as what the attacker did. Logging will record actions, and in some cases the effects of actions, but rarely the causes that allow those actions to occur. Consider a remote attacker who is able to gain sufficient access to execute commands on another system. The logs will show which server she connected to, perhaps the commands she issued to that server, and that she executed an unauthorized command remotely. But the logs will not show the vulnerability in the server that allowed this. Other attackers can use the same vulnerability in different ways to gain access. Thus, while one effect of the commands is to allow remote execution of a program, a second effect might be a way to escalate privileges so that program runs as *root* or *admin*. The forensic analysts must consider these possibilities.

27.4.1.4   Context Assists in Understanding Meaning

Complicating the application of the previous principle, the same actions may create two different effects depending on the context in which they occur. The simplest example is typing a command to the Linux shell. If the full path name of the command is not used, then the actual program executed depends on the user's search path, which is part of the context. Keystroke logging suffers from the same defect; the same set of keystrokes may cause wildly different actions depending on what program they are given to as input.

Another example is a file system monitoring tool that logs accesses to files by file names. The problem is that a file name may refer to one file at one point in time, and then a different file in another point in time because the first was deleted and a new file, with the same name, was created. The omitted context here is the information in the file allocation table, which would enable the tool to distinguish between the files.

27.4.1.5   Information Must Be Processed and Presented in an Understandable Way

This principle simply requires that those who need to understand the forensic analysis can do so. Two aspects must be considered.

The first audience is the analysts themselves. The interfaces to tools that do the analysis and reconstruction should be designed with usability in mind, and—perhaps most importantly—indicate where gaps in the analysis exist. The forensic analysts should be able to use the tools so they can find needed information, and generate intelligible output. The results should be clear to a technical audience.

The second audience is nontechnical. They should be provided the information needed to understand what happened, how it happened, and what the effects of the attack were. Thus, they must be shown the results of the analysis, and the root causes of the successful attack, or the reasons the unsuccessful attack failed. In some cases, they will require access to evidence collected in accordance with legal or regulatory requirements, or information gathered to a particular level of assurance that it is correct. This may be difficult if the analysts had to reconstruct actions and intermediate results, because they may have to justify the reasons for their reconstruction—and those reasons may be highly technical.

We now consider the practice of forensics in light of the above principles.

27.4.2   Practice

The practice of digital forensics depends in large part upon the intended use of the forensic information. If the information is to be gathered for use in a court of law, then legal evidentiary procedures must be followed in order to ensure the data can be used in court. As courts and laws vary among jurisdictions, we forego that discussion and instead focus on the gathering of information to determine what happened.

Reconstructing the state of the system (including system inputs and outputs such as network traffic) and sequence of actions of interest typically requires four steps:

1. Capture and preserve the current state of the system and network data.
2. Extract information about that state and about prior states.
3. Analyze the data gathered to determine the sequence of actions, which objects they affected, and how.
4. Prepare and report the results of the analysis to the intended audience.

The first two steps may be reversed if the system on which the forensics is being performed is active, perhaps because the cost of shutting it down is unacceptable. The active nature of the system typically precludes obtaining the exact, correct state of the system because gathering that data takes time, and the system state changes while (and sometimes even as a result of) gathering that data [353].

The results of the forensic analysis can be used to determine which system defenses need to be hardened, changed, or added. If the analysis would have benefitted from more data, the systems can be tuned to save that data. It can also be used in legal proceedings, in reports to management, in media statements, and other ways. Because the requirements for how the investigation is to be conducted and the evidence preserved depends on the goals of the forensic investigation, plans for these possible uses should be prepared and approved with the relevant parties in advance. As in incident handling, contingencies may arise that force the plans to be altered, but being prepared will enable the analysts, and others involved, to cope with these changes readily. These show the importance of the principle of processing information in a way useful to the goals of the analysis.

When performing forensic analysis, the principle of considering the complete system means that a complete image of all components should be made at the time of compromise. In most cases this is infeasible because the compromise is discovered after it occurs or the system is active, so any snapshot of it will include changes over the time of the snapshot. So the analyst must acquire as complete an image of the system as possible. For example, an image of the disks affected by the attack can be made. Data from backups and other sources may also be useful. Similarly, any network traffic stored will prove valuable; if none is available, the logs from intrusion detection systems and other network monitoring tools may suffice. As soon as the data is acquired, a cryptographic hash of it needs to be computed and saved not on the media, so that an independent observer can verify the data was not changed after acquisition.

Persistent data remains when the system or data storage is powered off; data stored on a hard drive is an example.

EXAMPLE: One evening a junior system administrator notices something odd about a UNIX system—one of the disks is full, but on inspection, the total space used by the files on the system is much less than the size of the disk. He sends out a message saying the system is having hardware problems, and shuts the system down. He then removes the disk, attaches it to another system, mounts it read-only (as there are no physical write blockers available), and uses the *dc3dd*(1) command to create an image of it on some other media (like a second, wiped disk). This command also creates a cryptographic checksum of the image, which can be used to show the image was not altered since its creation. The analyst then uses a separate program to compute the checksum from the image, and verifies that it matches the one *dc3dd* generated.

Volatile data is not permanent; it disappears at at some point in time, for example when the system is powered off. Data stored in memory is a good example. Capturing the contents of memory of a running system is much more difficult that capturing the contents of a disk because, as noted above, any capture using software alters the contents of memory. Further, capturing the contents of kernel memory requires using the kernel, which alters the contents of the kernel memory.

EXAMPLE: Carrier and Grand [354] use specialized hardware to capture the contents of memory. They add a custom PCI card to the bus before any incident occurs. When the computer boots, the card configures itself and then disables its controller so it is invisible to any programs scanning the PCI bus. When a switch is thrown, the card reenables the controller, suspends the CPU, and then dumps the contents of memory to a nonvolatile storage medium. Once that is done, it has the CPU resume and again disables the PCI controller. Some architectures restrict access to physical RAM for protection reasons, which also blocks access for forensic analysis.

Another approach is to embed memory-reading software in a trusted location. Then attackers cannot alter the software. The software freezes the operating system and all associated processes, captures the contents of memory and transmits it or saves it, and then unfreezes the operating system.

EXAMPLE: The System Management Mode on Intel IA-32 platforms [2178] provide such a trusted, protected area of memory. Software drivers for a standard network PCI card reside in the SMM. To obtain a snapshot of memory, the SMM obtains the contents of the CPU registers, and the PCI card reads memory. This is transmitted to a waiting server. The use of the SMM suspends the operating system, and hence the memory remains in a consistent state [1964].

An alternate approach is to put acquisition software between the operating system and the hardware. Virtual machine introspection provides this capability. When memory is to be captured, the virtual machine monitor stops the virtual machine and captures the contents of its memory [597, 882, 906]. Rather than a full-fledged virtual machine, specialized software that has complete control of the hardware can capture memory, but the software must execute in an area of memory that the system does not use for anything else [374, 1676].

Finally, memory retains its contents for a very short time after power is lost—and cooling the memory increases the time significantly [850]. This remanence effect has enabled forensics on Android phones [932].

The next step is to extract information from the data. For system data, the file systems and other data are analyzed to determine the events and a timeline. To do this, the analysts first obtain a list of files from the image, and also check for deleted files and data stored in the free space. Then the analysts determine which files are critical, based on the effects of the attack, and look not only at those files but also any earlier versions that have been deleted or are in the free space to see what changes were made. Similarly, for network packet captures, the analysts look for data that involves interaction with the computers under investigation or that are themselves attacked. Data and logs from intrusion detection systems can help in this.

EXAMPLE: To continue the Linux example from above, the analysts begin extracting information from the disk. First, they obtain a list of all files on the disk from the disk image. They then check for deleted files, and find several corresponding to undeleted files. They then examine the free space on the disk, and find a large number of files stored there.

The analysis phase begins. The specific questions to be answered depends upon the nature of the attack, the resources involved (both as potential targets and compromised resources), and also in part on what is found.

EXAMPLE: The analysts begin by examining the files stored in the free space. They are copies of recently released movies. As they are hidden, this focuses on the effects of the (as yet unknown) actions. Given that the system was being used to store recently released movies without authorization, an obvious question is how the attackers got access to the system, when they obtained that access, and how they hid the movies.

The analysts first extract the log files of the network servers and user actions—for this system, the logins, logouts, and changes of privilege. They begin with the logins, and find a user name with control characters in it. There is no corresponding entry in the list of users who logged out; indeed, there is no user with that name. They then execute the login program, and give it a user name that is 1,000 characters long. The login program crashes. This suggests a buffer overflow.

The next question is how the attackers gained access to the system. They examine the logs of the servers, and see nothing suspicious. They then look at the configuration files controlling the servers being run, and there is nothing suspicious. But as the attackers did not have physical access to the system, the analysts look through other log files—and in one, they see an entry made by a program that starts the *telnet* service. That service should never run. So they scan the list of file names looking for the file, and find it in a system administrator's directory.

They then go to the network logs. The organization's intrusion detection systems capture packets and store them for 30 days, then delete the packet bodies and store the headers for 5 more months. They look through these logs for *telnet* packets. They find several, including one the contents of which match the user name with control characters that they found earlier. Without the context of the strange login, this would probably be interpreted as a failed attack. But given the context and the match, the context means that these packets are how the attackers first entered the system. The analysts copy these packets to a separate file, and create a textual representation of these packets in another file. Both files are then checksummed and saved on read-only media.

The last question is how the attackers put the movies into the free space. The obvious answer is that they simply deleted them. However, this contradicts previously gathered evidence—that the total space used by the files on the system was much less than the size of the disk. Were the movie files stored as ordinary files in the file system, the discrepancy would not exist. Further, had the attackers simply stored the files in the free space by writing directly to the raw disk, the files would not be counted in the total space used by the files on the system. Thus, the disk blocks used by the files were marked used, but the file was not present in the file hierarchy. This means the attacker created the file, opened it, and then deleted the file while it was opened. This removes the file name from the hierarchy, so a program that determines the amount of used disk space by traversing the hierarchy will not count it, but a program that looks directly at the disk maps will. This explains the discrepancy.

Finally, the analysts must deliver a report on the findings. They must take into account the principle of presenting information in an understandable way. So the contents of the delivered report depends on the audience. If the audience were nontechnical, the report could simply state the movies were put into unused space on the disk, and provide information about the number of movies found, their titles, and so forth. If the audience were technical, then the report should also describe how the movies were stored and how they were found. Perhaps the most comprehensive approach is to prepare a detailed technical report for reference, and then other types of reports based on the technical report as needed.

EXAMPLE: The analysts need to present a report to the organization's legal team. Because the lawyers may take legal action based on the results, the analysts must ensure the data and analysis are gathered in such a way that they will stand up in court. Everything from the imaging on must have the chain of possession and access documented, so the courts can determine whether the evidence is trustworthy. The report must reflect this, and explain what happened in terms that nontechnical readers can understand. It must also justify the analysis done, to ensure that the methods used meet the criteria of acceptability in court. As part of this, the report must also demonstrate that the analysts followed accepted industry best practices or standard methodologies. Finally, it needs to state the qualifications and experience of those doing the analysis.

If the lawyers are not involved, then the chain of evidence is less important. The analysts need to track who has access to ensure only authorized people can perform authorized actions on the image, but they need not document it as rigorously as they would need to were it to be introduced in a court of law.

27.4.3   Anti-Forensics

The term "anti-forensics" has many definitions [447], all of which have the idea of interfering with a forensic analysis. We focus on the following:

Definition 27–10. [872] *Anti-forensics* is the attempt to compromise the availability or usefulness of evidence to the forensics process.

Several goals flow from this [743].

The first is to interfere with the forensic tools gathering information, for example by hiding the data or obscuring the type or sequence of events. Disk wiping is a very simple anti-forensic mechanism. It prevents the collection of any data from that disk. So it hides events that occurred, although it may indicate that events that left traces on the disk and that the attacker wants to hide did occur. Similarly, forensic tools may not scan all parts of the system, so anti-forensic tools can hide data there. Rather than wiping the disk, the attacker may wish the forensic tools to construct an incorrect timeline of file accesses. To do this, the anti-forensic mechanism changes the times of last access in the file metadata. Then any forensic tool that uses the metadata to construct a timeline will be using incorrect data, and hence give incorrect results.

EXAMPLE: *Timestomp* is a Metasploit [1031] plug-in that enables the user to change file access times. A second plug-in, *event_manager*, enables the user to modify log files to delete entries corresponding to events the user wishes to delete.

Forensics is often used to determine the authenticity of a digital image. Consequently, some anti-forensic techniques are designed to hinder this validation.

EXAMPLE: The JPEG image format compresses the digital representation of the picture into multiple bands of transform coefficients. This compression technique introduces a unique signature into the transform coefficients. The coefficients in a band generally follow a smooth distribution. Altering the image introduces perturbations in the coefficients, called "transform coefficient quantization artifacts." Forensic analysis methods look for such irregularities to determine whether the image has been altered. Anti-forensic tools attempt to remove these artifacts to smooth the transform coefficients' distribution by adding dithering to make the modified distribution approximate the original one, hiding the alterations to the image [1813].

A second goal is to exploit weaknesses in forensic analysis tools.

EXAMPLE: One Windows forensic analysis tool determines whether a file is an executable by checking file extensions for ".exe", and if found then checks whether the first two bytes of the file are "MZ". If so, the file is an executable. Thus, this tool will not detect executable files if the user changes the file extension [743]. This technique has also been used to evade spam filters, which look for and block attached files with certain extensions.

The free space on a disk is also a good place to hide information [512]. The danger of doing this is the operating system allocating the blocks to a file, thereby overwriting the contents of the hidden data. If the disk space allocation algorithm is known, though, it is possible to minimize this threat. Also, if a file size is not a multiple of the block length, then data can be stored in the empty space between the end of the file and the end of the block (called "the slack space").

Other goals are detecting active forensic tools and attacking the user of the forensic tools, either indirectly, for example by increasing the time needed to analyze the event, or directly, for example by crashing the analyst's system. Perhaps the most insidious goal is simply to cast doubt on the results of the forensic analysis, which would diminish its credibility in (for example) a court of law.

Anti-forensic tools sometimes leave traces [757]. For example, the JPEG anti-forensic tools introduce a slight distortion, and thus can itself be detected [1918]. Some anti-forensic techniques, such as encryption, are easily detected. But others, such as storing data in free disk space, will not be detected unless the analyst knows what to look for and where to look.

27.5   Summary

The goal of modeling attacks is to understand the attackers, and the systems they are attacking. Attack graphs, and attack trees in particular, represent the way in which attacks proceed. Beginning from a knowledge of some aspects of the system, including the human, social, and procedural aspects, the attacks achieve intermediate goals, and combine the results of those goals to incrementally approach, and achieve, the ultimate goal of the attack. The requires/provides model formalizes what is necessary to achieve the goals (preconditions) and what achieving the goals provide (postconditions).

When an intrusion occurs, some response is appropriate. If the intrusion attempt is detected before the attack is successful, the system can take action to prevent the attack from succeeding, including modifying itself to negate the value of the results of any information gleaned from reconnaissance or previous attacks. Otherwise, the intrusion must be handled. Among the steps involved are confinement of the attack to limit its effectiveness, eradication to eliminate the attacking processes or connections, and follow-up to take action against the attacker as well as learn from the attack.

As part of the response, or after the attack, the detritus of the attack must be analyzed to determine the effects of the attack and how it was carried out, and to glean information to enable analysts to determine the goals of the attack. This is the realm of digital or computer forensics. The principles that underlie the practice require considering the entire system, the effects of actions as well as the actions themselves, understanding the context to properly interpret the data, and presenting the results in a way that the audience can understand. The practice requires preserving the information on the system and extracting information from that data, then analyzing the data to determine the steps of the attack, what it accessed, and how, and reporting the results. How these steps are carried out depends in part on the use to which the results will be put. For example, preserving evidence for use in a court of law requires special steps to meet legal requirements. Thus, planning for forensic analysis is critical.

27.6   Research Issues

There is a semantic gap between understanding the technical goals of an attack, as discussed in this chapter, and how those goals fit into the overall goals of an attacker. For example, if an attacker wishes to shut down a factory, the technical attack on the factory's computerized equipment may be tied to financial manipulations designed to inhibit its ability to obtain the resources and people necessary to recover. Representing attacks in terms that span this gap would enable analysts to interpret data from attacks in light of the overall goals of the attacker. This interpretation is particularly helpful in predicting future attacks, allowing defenders to focus their resources to develop and support plans to handle those attacks, as well as harden their defenses.

Moving target defenses have existed for many years, although not under that name. As system complexity increases, the complexity of the moving target defense also increases. Further, the danger of such a defense corrupting legitimate activities may require additional precautions, ideally within the defense or system itself, but possibly within an application or library, adding to their complexity. Complicating this is the use of multiple moving target defenses simultaneously, and ensuring they do not conflict. Adversaries aware of the defenses may alter their behavior in the hope that the adaptation will decrease, or even nullify, the effectiveness of the moving target defense.

The interest in counterattacking, and its legal and technical consequences, has increased in importance as attacks targeting specific people or entities becomes more prominent. Several nations have formed military groups focusing on cyberwarfare, specifically both attacking and defending. Although the virtual world is different than the physical world, warfare in cyberspace is expected to share much of the strategies and tactics of warfare in the physical world, including counterattacking. But the problems are the same, and the consequences may be much more severe, than responding to attacks launched by nonstate actors.

Techniques to gather volatile data, especially on running systems, has two problems. The first occurs when the volatile data is gathered while the system is active. The data changes while it is being gathered, so the image of the storage represents the state of a number of parts of the storage in several states, rather than an image of the storage at a particular state. The obvious answer is to freeze the system (or just the storage) while the volatile data is gathered. This introduces the second problem, that the system's responsiveness drops drastically (or the system is nonresponsive) while the data is gathered. Determining how to gather the image at a particular state with minimal impact on the system will improve the ability of forensic analysis to capture the state of a system.

In order to pursue culprits, it is necessary to have evidence that will satisfy a court or a jury that a tort (or crime) has been committed and that the accused is guilty. The legal rules for collecting and handling evidence must be followed if the evidence is to be admissible in court. An area of active research is the development of intrusion detection systems, methodologies, and procedures that will supply evidence of this caliber.

27.7   Further Reading

Attack trees and attack graphs have been used and studied extensively. Mauw and Oostdijk [1266] provide a formal model of attack trees. They have been used to assess security of systems and networks [41, 940, 1392]. Studies have examined ways to automate their generation and analysis [945, 1016, 1482, 1732]. Some work has combined attack steps and corresponding defense steps [1094, 1615, 1667].

Papers describing security incident handling and response [27, 306, 419], and examples of incidents [402, 1736, 1829, 1831] often describe both successful and unsuccessful attacks. Some books and papers [32, 653, 826, 886, 1582, 2251] describe attacks in detail. Parker [1496] outlines several techniques that unsuccessful criminals have used.

Honeynets and honeypots have their counterpart in honeydocuments and honeyfiles [168, 1828, 1948, 2073]. Rowe [1611, 1612] discusses modeling and designing good deception. Almeshekah and Spafford [36] discuss planning deception and how to integrate it into defenses. Most deception presents a consistent image ("fiction") of a nonexistent system or server. Bishop and Neagoe [1429] introduced inconsistency in deception as a tactic in computer defenses; Rowe and Goh evaluated it [1612]. Game theory is a useful tool for analyzing deception as a defense [357]. Honeypots provide an opportunity for forensics when no production systems will be disrupted [1522, 1572, 1573].

Carvalho and Ford present an overview of the philosophy and goals of moving target defenses [358]. Atighetchi and his colleagues expand on this [90]. Zhu, Hu, and Liu suggest using machine learning to guide moving target defenses [2102]. One model for evaluating IP address hopping analyzes the cost for users, and that the defense is most effective if the number of vulnerable systems is small compared to the address space [356]. The greater address space size of IPv6 makes IP address hopping particularly attractive for IPv6 addresses [598]. It has been used to protect Smart Grids [824] and VPN servers [900]. Operating system hopping [1876] and instruction set randomization [129] have also been proposed, as has permuting the locations of code and variables at load time [1051].

An "anti-worm" counters a malicious worm by changing it into a worm that disinfects the original. Simulations show it would be effective [361]. Other work takes a more strategic view [2072]. Characteristics of an attack provide information about whether the attacker was launched by a nation-state [230]. Information warfare, in which two nation-states come into conflict in cyberspace, is now an important concern, involving psychology, organization, economics, politics, civil liberties, and law as much as technology [411, 412, 539, 819, 1137, 1484, 2206].

A critical part of testing forensic tools is determining how effective anti-forensic measures are against the tools. Moses [1382] proposes a framework to do this. Others [515] consider how aware investigators are of anti-forensic methods. Machine learning appears to be a promising approach to coping with anti-forensics [1233]. Böhme and Kirchner [255] discuss the theory of anti-forensics in images. Rekhis and Boudriga [1579] discuss a formal model for doing digital forensics in the presence of anti-forensic tools.

27.8   Exercises

1. In the example on page 961, why is the tree constructed using a breadth-first search rather than a depth-first search?

2. In the IP address and port number hopping example on page 974, the mapping mechanisms use a pseudorandom sequence rather than a random sequence. Why?

3. This exercise examines deterministic packet selection (see Section 27.3.2.3). Assume that the packet header contains spaces for routers to enter their IP addresses.

    a. Suppose the header contains space for 30 router addresses. Initially, these spaces contain all zero bits. As the packet passes through a router, the router inserts its IP address into the first available location in this space. If there is no room left (because the packet has passed through 30 routers), the router does not insert its address. Describe how an attacker could conceal the route that the packet takes as it travels to its destination.

    b. Now suppose the header uses variable-sized space for a list of router addresses. Initially, no router addresses are attached. As the packet passes through a router, the router adds its IP address to this list. Would this prevent the attack in your answer to part (a)? Why or why not? What other problems would this variable-length router address field cause?

4. Consider the "counterworm" in the example that begins on page 984.

    a. Pretend you are a technical expert called as a witness in a lawsuit between the sender of the "counterworm" and the target. What arguments could you make for and against the sending of the worm?

    b. How might the arguments for a company providing "worms" to fix security problems in their software differ from those for providing a "counterworm"? How would they be the same?

5. The last example in Section 27.3.1 states that "compile-time randomization is more effective than runtime randomization." Give an intuitive explanation of why this is so.

6. Systems can log both successful and unsuccessful attempts to access files. This is often not enabled. Why?

7. Every time a process is started on a Microsoft Windows system, a corresponding event is entered into the security log. Although the name of the file being executed is logged, no parameters (such as command-line arguments) are logged. In earlier versions of the system, the full command, including parameters, was logged by default.

   a. Why would one want to enable the logging of both the name of the executed file and parameters?

   b. Why would one want to enable the logging of the name of the executed file and *not* want to log parameters?

8. This exercise asks you to consider sources of errors in thumbprints (see Section 27.3.2.3). Recall that a thumbprint is computed from the contents of a connection over some interval of time. Consider clocks on two different computers. Initially, they are synchronized. After some period of time has passed, the clocks will show different times. This is called *clock skew*.

   a. Why might clock skew introduce differences in the thumbprints of a connection?

   b. Why might propagation delays introduce differences in the thumbprints of a connection?

   c. Staniford-Chen and Heberlein computed thumbprints based on contents only, rather than on contents plus information gleaned from the packet header. Suppose they computed the thumbprint over the contents plus the packet header. What errors might this introduce? Could they have chosen some fields of the TCP and IP headers that would not have introduced errors? If so, state which ones, and why.

9. Consider how enciphering of connections would affect thumbprinting.

   a. If the connection contents were enciphered using an end-to-end encipherment protocol, would thumbprinting work? Why or why not?

   b. If the connection contents were enciphered using a link encipherment protocol, would thumbprinting work? Why or why not?

10. The benefit of diversity, discussed on page 972, is to prevent an attack that is successful against one system to be successful against other systems. Consider a set of systems $s_1, \ldots, s_n$ each running a different operating system. What advantages do these diverse attack surfaces present to an attacker, compared to a monoculture?

11. An attack can succeed on a system using ASLR if the attacker can guess n bits of randomness in the placement of each of the segments. The attacker launches a brute force attack in which she probes the address space repeatedly until she finds the right address.

    a. How many possibilities for the placement of each of the segments are there?

    b. Assume the ASLR is done at compile time, so the address space is fixed once loaded into memory. What is the expected number of probes required for the attack to succeed?

    c. Assume the ASLR is done at runtime, and the address space is re-randomized after each probe. What is the probability that a brute force attack will succeed after exactly t probes?

12. Systems can log both successful and unsuccessful file accesses. But this is often not enabled. Why not?

13. A Microsoft Windows security log contains an entry (called an *event*) every time a process is created or started. The name of the executable file is logged, but by default the parameters to the command are not logged. So, for example, the command "`edit.exe file1`" would cause the system to log the name "edit.exe" but not "file1". In some earlier versions of Windows, the default was to log the name of the executable file and all the parameters. What were the advantages and disadvantages to the change of default behavior?

Part VIII

Practicum

The practice of computer security draws on the principles and mechanisms discussed in Parts I through VII. Part VIII explores the application of these ideas and tools in four different settings. Each chapter considers a particular situation and discusses solutions that include various levels of security. Beginning with policy considerations, each chapter develops a security architecture and deploys appropriate mechanisms to provide the desired level of security.

Chapter 28, "Network Security," considers a corporation that must provide public access to some information but limit access to other information even within the company. It derives parts of a network configuration and security mechanisms that support the policy.

Chapter 29, "System Security," examines two systems in the corporation's network. One is an infrastructure machine in the DMZ (demilitarized zone) and the other is a developer workstation. This chapter discusses an appropriate policy for each, and from parts of that policy derives system configurations and mechanisms that support the security policy.

Chapter 30, "User Security," shows how components of a site policy and a user's personal policy lead to the user configuring her environment to provide protection for her programs and data.

Chapter 31, "Program Security," begins with the requirements for a program. Policy considerations flow from these requirements and from the environment in which the program is to be used, and from these policy considerations are developed the security mechanisms that the program must implement. This chapter concludes with a discussion of common errors that cause vulnerabilities in privileged programs.

Chapter 28
Network Security

> JOHN OF GAUNT: This fortress built by Nature for herself
> Against infection and the hand of war,
> This happy breed of men, this little world,
> This precious stone set in the silver sea,
> Which serves it in the office of a wall,
> Or as a moat defensive to a house
> Against the envy of less happier lands.
> — *The Tragedy of King Richard the Second*, II, i, 43–49.

The goals of an organization, and its security policy, dictate the functionality required of the site. The distribution of functionality throughout the site's network is critical to improving the security of the site. The functionality of each part of the network controls the nature and configuration of each host on the network. This chapter applies some of the principles and concepts of computer security to the network of the organization.

28.1   Introduction

The Dribble Corporation builds and sells dribbles, an electronic item popularly seen as the successor to the Pet Rock. The Drib (the popular name for the corporation) has decided to develop a network infrastructure that would enable it to connect to the Internet, to provide a web and electronic mail presence that consumers, suppliers, and other partners could access, and to protect its proprietary information. Because of its need to add meaningless but entertaining information gleaned from various Internet websites, the Drib developers must have access to the Internet, but external users cannot be allowed to access the development sites. Finally, because dribbles look like their main competitor, gibbles (from the Gibble Gabble Gobble Git Company), the Drib has many lawyers working to defend its patents on dribbles, and its corporate officers are preparing to fight a hostile takeover from GGGGC. Hence, the corporate officers and lawyers also need access to developer data, but the developers are not to have access to the corporation's private or legal information.

The goals of the Drib's security policy are to be as follows:

- Data related to company plans is to be kept secret. In particular, sensitive corporate data, such as data involved in developing potential products, is to be available only to those who need to know.

- When a customer provides data (such as a credit card number) to the Drib as part of a purchase, the data, and all information about the customer, are to be available only to those who fill the order. Company analysts may obtain statistics about a number of orders for planning purposes.

- Releasing sensitive data requires the consent of the company's officials and lawyers.

Our goal is to design a network infrastructure that will meet these requirements. We begin by analyzing the goals of the policy so that we can make them precise.

28.2   Policy Development

The Drib requires a policy that minimizes the threat of data being leaked to unauthorized entities. However, it is unclear what "unauthorized" should mean. The Drib's internal structure suggests one answer.

The Drib has three main internal organizations. The first is the Customer Service Group (CSG), which handles all dealings with customers. This group maintains all customer data and serves as the interface between the other groups and the clients of the Drib. The second group is the Development Group (DG), which develops, modifies, and maintains products. Members of the DG rely on the CSG for descriptions of customer complaints, suggestions, and ideas; at no time do they talk directly with customers. This prevents them from accidentally revealing confidential information or from learning confidential information such as credit card numbers. The Corporate Group (CG) handles the Drib's debentures, lawsuits, patents, and other corporate-level work.

The policy is to describe the way information is to flow among these groups.

When one looks at the actual functions of the three groups, how they restrict information, and how they share information, a pattern emerges. Specifications of current products, as well as marketing and sales literature, are publicly available. However, other information about current products, such as problems (especially those that are the subjects of lawsuits), patent applications, and budgets, is not public. The CG and DG groups share this information for planning, budgeting, and development purposes, but beyond this sharing, each group keeps its own private information. The CG keeps corporate information private so that it can be protected by attorney privilege and so that it can comply with government stock regulations. The DG plans and prototypes future products. The DG waits until it is convinced that production is feasible before it proposes a new product to the CG. The CSG keeps track of customer credit card information and specific clients' ordering information for its own purposes, and it does not share this information (except in the aggregate) with either the CG or the DG. This forms the basis for the policy.

28.2.1 Data Classes

We classify information into five classes that reflect the divisions outlined above. The classification reflects the principle of least privilege[1] by separating the data in such a way that the ability to view one class of data does not imply the ability to view another class of data. Also, the policy and all its rules are not secret, reflecting the principle of open design.[2] Note that "open design" does *not* mean that this information is available to the public. It simply means that anyone within the Drib who is affected by the policy, or who wants to know what the policy is and why it was designed that way, can find out.

- *Public data* (*PD*) is available to anyone. It includes product specifications, price information, marketing literature, and any other data that will help the Drib sell dribbles without compromising its secrets.
- *Development data for existing products* (*DDEP*) is available only internally. Because of pending lawsuits, it must be available to the company lawyers and officers as well as to the developers. It is kept secret from all others.
- *Development data for future products* (*DDFP*) is available to the developers only. The specifications may change, as may various aspects of development, but the Drib never announces information about products under development, and does not intend to change this style of operation.
- *Corporate data* (*CpD*) includes legal information that is privileged and information about corporate actions that is not to become known publicly (such as actions that may affect stock values). The corporate officials and lawyers need access to this information; no one else does.
- *Customer data* (*CuD*) is data that customers supply, such as credit card information. The Drib protects this data as strongly as it protects its own data.

---

[1] See Section 14.2.1, "Principle of Least Privilege."
[2] See Section 14.2.5, "Principle of Open Design."

Data may change from the DDFP class to the DDEP class as products become implemented; from the DDEP class to the PD class when deemed advantageous to publicize some development details; and from the CpD class to the PD class as privileged information becomes publicly known through mergers, lawsuit filings, or the ordinary course of business. There is no provision for revealing CuD directly; this protects the privacy of the Drib's customers.

28.2.2   User Classes

Four classes of people may access data. The user classes are based on the same principles as the classes of data: separation of privilege[3] and least privilege. Some users may be placed in multiple classes. If so, an underlying assumption of the model is that they will not bypass the restrictions by copying data from one class to another without using the mechanisms provided for that purpose.

- *Outsiders* (members of the public) get access to some of the Drib's data such as prices, product descriptions, and public corporate information. The public can also order merchandise, download new drivers for their dribbles, and send electronic mail to the company.

- *Developers* get access to both classes of development data. They cannot alter development data for existing products because that data describes how to manufacture the product. It also provides a historical record for use in developing new products. Developers can modify development data for future products, however.

- *Corporation executives* (corporation counsel, members of the board of directors, and other executives) get access to corporate data. They can see development data for both existing and future products but may not alter it. They may read customer data (for legal purposes or analysis). Under specific conditions (described below), they may make sensitive data public.

- *Employees* get access to customer data only.

Figure 28–1 summarizes the access that each class of users has to each class of data. This table is an access control matrix[4] and defines the access control policy. It reflects a mandatory access control policy;[5] the discretionary component is fixed at "allow always." This matrix combines elements of confidentiality[6] and integrity.[7] Left as an implementation detail is the security officer who puts people

---

[3] See Section 14.2.6, "Principle of Separation of Privilege."
[4] See Chapter 2, "Access Control Matrix."
[5] See Section 4.4, "Types of Access Control."
[6] See Chapter 5, "Confidentiality Policies."
[7] See Chapter 6, "Integrity Policies."

	Outsiders	Developers	Corporation Executives	Employees
Public data	read	read	read	read
Development data for existing products		read	read	
Development data for future products		read, write	read	
Corporate data			read, write	
Customer data	write		read	read, write

Figure 28–1 The classes of users, data, and the allowed accesses.

and data into the appropriate classes (see Lipner's integrity matrix model[8] and Exercise 1).

Specific classes of people can move data from one class to another, as indicated above. The specific transformation rules are as follows:

- The developers must propose that a proposed future product be realized. Corporation executives must determine if the proposed action is wise, from both legal and economic standpoints. Hence, both developers and corporation executives must agree to reclassify data from the DDFP class to the DDEP class.

- The employees may identify certain development data as important for answering technical questions from outsiders, or for market literature. In these cases, the employees notify the corporation executives, who then decide whether or not to make the information public. Both employees and corporation executives must agree to reclassify data from the DDEP class to the PD class.

- Corporation executives may reveal corporate data in filings or when revealing that the data will not harm the company. Thus, they can reclassify data from CpD to PD. However, at least two members must agree to do the reclassification.

The principle of separation of privilege dictates that moving data from one class to another requires approval of more than one user. In the first two cases, the users must come from separate classes because the data involved may reveal internal information that would be of use to a competitor. (Two users in different classes may be the same user in two different roles.[9] Hence, the requirement for two different users.) The third case involves corporate business, usually in legal matters (such as lawsuits or stock filings). In this case, the Drib lawyers (all of whom are in

---

[8]See Section 6.3, "Lipner's Integrity Matrix Model."
[9]See Section 15.4, "Groups and Roles."

the "corporate executive" user class) have the expertise to determine what must be revealed, and because the consequences may involve criminal charges, the lawyers and corporate executives must make the decisions. Because the Drib is a well-run company, they will obtain the appropriate information and recommendations from people in the other user classes as required. However, the requirement that the two members be in the corporate executive class is an acknowledgment of the responsibility of the corporate executives.

28.2.3   Availability

The Drib is a worldwide, multinational corporation and does business on all seven continents (although its Antarctic operation is quite small). Orders come from all over the world. Thus, the corporate officers want employees and the public to be able to contact the Drib at any time. In practice, this means that the Drib's systems must be available 99% of the time, the remaining 1% being used for planned maintenance and unexpected downtimes.

28.2.4   Consistency Check

The policy described above should meet the goals of the Drib. Otherwise, it is not an appropriate policy. We will now review the goals of the policy and discuss consistency.

The first goal is to keep sensitive information confidential, on a "need to know" basis. Public data is, by definition, not confidential, and is available to all. Developers clearly need access to both current and future development data, but not to customer data or corporate information (because they do not decide which products to market). They can alter development data as they investigate possibilities and test ideas. Corporate executives need access to corporate data to plan business actions. Some of these actions may be based on development data for existing products; for example, should the Drib invest in a company developing faster CPUs for the Drib's products? Hence, corporate executives also need access to development data for existing products. They can alter corporate data, but not development data. So, the first goal of the policy is met.

The second goal requires that only employees who handle purchases can access customer data, and only they and the customers themselves can alter the customer data. The policy above provides this restriction.

The third goal is met by the rules for changing security classes. Moving data from the DDFP class to the DDEP class requires consent of both a developer and a corporate executive. Moving data from the DDEP class to the PD class requires the consent of an employee and a corporate executive. Finally, moving data from the corporate class to the public class requires consent of a corporate executive. In all cases, a corporate executive can prevent the release of company information. Furthermore, because no other class of users can write public class data, only the corporate executives can release the information.

Thus, the policy is valid, because it meets the security requirements of the Drib.[10]

We next verify the consistency of the policy, to show that it is not self-contradictory. We construct the transitive closure of all paths along which information can flow among the classes. From this closure, it is clear that the only way information can flow into the public class is when a corporate executive moves it there. Hence, the key point of trust is in the corporate executive class. Without an executive acting, information simply cannot become public. Furthermore, by the rules for moving data out of the DDEP and DDFP classes, some other entity beyond the corporate executives must consent to the release of the information. This satisfies the principle of separation of privilege as well as the corporate goals. Because there is no contradiction among the rules in the policy, the policy is self-consistent.

We have now (informally) both validated and verified the policy. Validation and verification are basic aspects of information assurance[11] and provide a basis for asserting that the policy is correct.

We have now defined the confidentiality, integrity, and availability aspects of the Drib's basic security policy. We will now expand this into a simple network architecture.

28.3 Network Organization

The policy discussed above suggests that the network be partitioned into several parts, with firewalls[12] between parts to prevent information from leaking. Each type of data resides in one of the parts (we combine both types of development data into one type, DD). The resulting partition is shown in Figure 28–2. It is an instantiation of the configuration in Figure 17–4(b), with one part available to the public and a second part available only internally.

Definition 28–1. The *DMZ*[13] is a portion of a network that separates a purely internal network from an external network.

When information moves from the Internet to the internal network, confidentiality is not at issue. However, integrity is. Firewalls separate the Internet, the DMZ, and the internal network. They must not accept messages that will cause servers to work incorrectly or to crash. When information moves from the internal network to the Internet, confidentiality and integrity are both at issue. The firewalls must ensure that no confidential information goes to the Internet and

---

[10]See Section 19.1.2, "The Role of Requirements in Assurance."
[11]See Chapter 19, "Introduction to Assurance."
[12]See Section 17.6.2, "Firewalls."
[13]"DMZ" stands for "demilitarized zone."

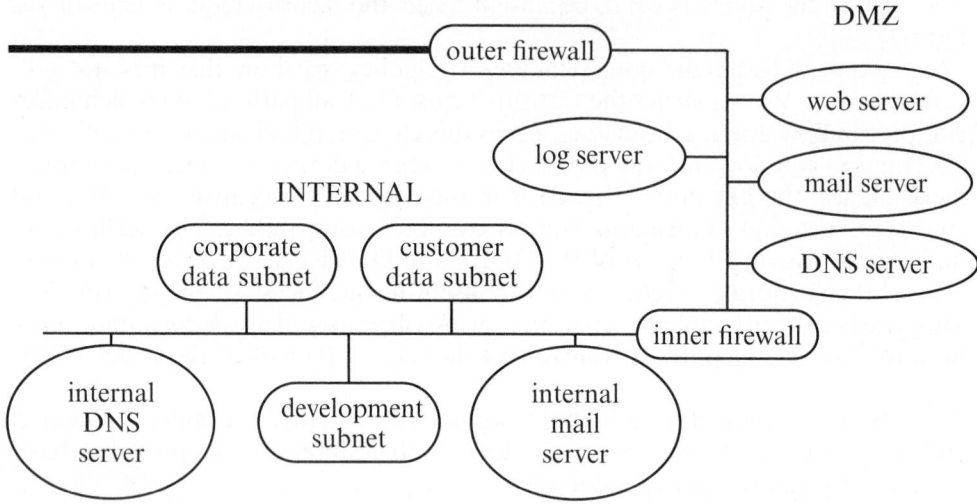

Figure 28–2 The network designed for the Dribble Corporation. The "outer firewall" sits between the Internet and the company network. The subnet labeled "DMZ" provides limited public access to various servers. The "inner firewall" sits between the DMZ and the subnets that are not to be accessed by the public. These subnets share common mail and DNS servers that, like the other hosts, are not publicly accessible.

that the information that reaches the Internet is correct.[14] The latter issue requires simply that information not be altered in transit from the internal network to the Internet. For simplicity, we make the assumption that the systems as deployed will not change any information in transit (except delivery information, such as packet headers). If such changes are made, then the system has been compromised by an attacker. This would require the attacker to gain access to the system. This is equivalent to the problem of disallowing certain types of information (namely, attack mechanisms) from entering the internal or DMZ subnets from the Internet—in other words, ensuring the integrity of this information.[15]

The arrangement and configuration of the firewalls provide the supporting access control mechanisms used to implement the policy. A different point of view is to see the firewall as an audit mechanism.[16] It analyzes the packets that enter or leave. Firewalls can then base actions on this analysis, leading to traffic shaping (in which percentages of bandwidth are reserved for specific types of traffic), intrusion response,[17] and other controls.

---

[14]See Chapter 17, "Information Flow."
[15]See Chapter 24, "Vulnerability Analysis."
[16]See Chapter 25, "Auditing."
[17]See Section 27.3, "Intrusion Response."

With these definitions in mind, the reason for this structure of the network falls into place.

28.3.1 Analysis of the Network Infrastructure

The benefits of this design flow from the security policy and the principle of least privilege. The security policy distinguishes "public" entities from those internal to the corporation, but recognizes that some corporate resources must be available to the public. The network layout described above provides this functionality. The public entities may enter the corporate perimeter (bounded by the "outer firewall") but are confined to the DMZ area (bounded inside by the "inner firewall").[18] The next few paragraphs give an overview of the technical details of this arrangement. We then expand on the configurations of the infrastructure systems.

The key decision is to limit the flow of information from the internal network to the DMZ. The public cannot communicate directly with any system in the internal network, nor can any system in the internal network communicate directly with other systems on the Internet (beyond the "outer firewall"). The systems in the DMZ serve as mediators, with the firewalls providing the guards. This setup is derived from the notion of the "pump" (see page 617 in Section 18.3.3). The firewalls and the DMZ systems make up the pump, because they control all access to and from the Internet and filter all traffic in both directions.

The first step is to conceal the addresses of the internal network. In general, the internal network addresses can be any IP addresses (the families of addresses specifically allocated to private networks are $10.x.y.z$, $172.a.x.y$ (where $16 \leq a \leq 31$), and $192.168.x.y$[19] [1580]), and the inner firewall can use a protocol such as the Network Address Translation protocol [1806] to map these internal host addresses to the firewall's Internet address. A more common method is to assign each host an address but not allow those addresses to leave the corporate network. This is particularly simple, because all services are implemented as proxies in the outer firewall. However, electronic mail presents a special problem.

The DMZ mail server must know an address in order for the internal mail server to pass mail back and forth. This need not be the actual address of the internal mail server. It could be a distinguished address that the inner firewall will recognize as representing the internal mail server. Similarly, the internal mail server must know an address for the DMZ mail server. These addresses can be fixed (in which case the DMZ DNS server is unnecessary). For flexibility, we will assume that the Drib has decided to use a DNS server on both the internal and DMZ subnets. As a backup, each system in the DMZ has the network addresses of both firewalls stored locally, so if the DNS system is unavailable, the other servers can function.

---

[18]See Section 17.6.2, "Firewalls."
[19]In classless IP terminology, 10.0.0.0/8, 172.16.0.0/12, and 192.168.0.0/16.

The web server lies in the DMZ for the same reasons that a mail server lies in the DMZ. External connections to the web server go into the DMZ and no farther. If any information is to be transmitted from the web server to the internal network (for example, the customer data subnet), the transmission is made separately, and not as part of a web transaction.

This network organization reflects several of Saltzer and Schroeder's design principles [1644]. The containment of internal addresses reflects the principle of least privilege[20] as well as the Drib's solution to the confinement problem.[21] The inner firewall mediates every access involving the DMZ and the internal networks, meeting the principle of complete mediation.[22] Going out of the inner network to the Internet requires that several criteria be met, to implement the principle of separation of privilege.[23] The firewalls are distinct computers, as are the DMZ servers, leading to a duplication rather than a sharing of network services. If the mail server stops working, for example, the WWW server is not affected. The principle of least common mechanism[24] suggests this design. The shared DNS server in the DMZ violates this principle, because multiple systems are affected if it is corrupted or unavailable. The reason for the local, fixed addresses of the two firewalls is to handle the case of unavailability, mitigating this threat. Finally, the applications of confinement, access control,[25] and information flow control[26] have been discussed earlier.

We now examine each component in more detail.

28.3.1.1 Outer Firewall Configuration

The goals of the outer firewall are to restrict public access to the Drib's corporate network and to restrict the Drib's access to the Internet. This arises from the duality of information flow.[27] In the Bell-LaPadula Model,[28] for example, one cannot read information from a higher level (here, by restricting public access to the Drib's network), but one cannot write information to a lower level, either (here, by restricting the Drib's employees' access to the Internet). Certain sanitized exchanges, however, are allowed. To implement the required access control, the firewall uses an access control list,[29] which binds source addresses and ports and destination addresses and ports to access rights.

The public needs to be able to access the web server and mail server, and no other services; under some conditions, employees working remotely may need

---

[20] See Section 14.2.1, "Principle of Least Privilege."
[21] See Section 18.1, "The Confinement Problem."
[22] See Section 14.2.4, "Principle of Complete Mediation."
[23] See Section 14.2.6, "Principle of Separation of Privilege."
[24] See Section 14.2.7, "Principle of Least Common Mechanism."
[25] See Chapter 16, "Access Control Mechanisms."
[26] See Chapter 17, "Information Flow."
[27] See Chapter 17, "Information Flow."
[28] See Section 5.2, "The Bell-LaPadula Model."
[29] See Section 16.1, "Access Control Lists."

to access an encrypted virtual private network (VPN) used to communicate with the internal network. The firewall therefore presents an interface that allows connections to the WWW services (HTTP and HTTPS), to electronic mail (SMTP), and to the inner firewall using the VPN. Sites on the Internet see the addresses of these servers as the same—that of the firewall. No other services are provided to sites on the Internet.

The firewall is a proxy-based firewall. When an electronic mail connection is initiated, the SMTP proxy on the firewall collects the mail. It then analyzes it for computer viruses and other forms of malicious logic. If none is found, it forwards the mail to the DMZ mail server. When a web connection (or datagram) arrives, the firewall scans the message for any suspicious components (such as extraordinarily long lines or other evidence of attacks) and, if none is found, forwards it to the DMZ web server. These two DMZ servers have different addresses, neither of which is the address of the firewall. When a VPN session is initiated, the outer firewall is configured to route it directly to the inner firewall.

Attackers trying to penetrate the firewall have four methods of entry. The first is to enter through the web server ports. The unsecured (HTTP) port proxy checks for invalid or illegal HTTP requests and rejects them. The second is to enter through the SMTP port. The mail proxy will detect and reject such attempts. The third is through the VPN port. The firewall immediately forwards those messages to the inner firewall, which will validate the communication. The fourth is to attempt to bypass the low-level firewall checks by exploiting vulnerabilities in the firewall itself.

The discussion of vulnerabilities in Chapter 24, "Vulnerability Analysis," implies that there is no way to ensure that the firewall software and hardware cannot be breached. Designing the firewall mechanisms to be as simple as possible, in accordance with the principle of economy of mechanism,[30] using assurance techniques such as those described in Part VI minimizes, but does not eliminate, this possibility. So we apply the principle of separation of privilege[31] in the form of a technique called "defense in depth." In order to attack a system in the DMZ by bypassing the firewall checks, the attacker must know something about the internal addresses of the DMZ. If, for example, the attacker knows that the internal address of the DMZ mail server is 10.34.231.19, the attacker may be able to use that information to piggyback packets to that host.[32] But if the attacker has no idea of the internal DMZ mail server's address, even if the attacker is able to bypass the firewall checks, he or she will not know where to have the packets sent.

---

[30]See Section 14.2.3, "Principle of Economy of Mechanism."

[31]See Section 14.2.6, "Principle of Separation of Privilege."

[32]The description here is vague out of necessity. Whether or not such a method exists, and how to exploit it, are properties of individual hosts, software, and vendors. The curious reader is invited to use the Flaw Hypothesis Methodology (see Section 24.2.4) to analyze his or her organization's firewall after obtaining written permission from the responsible officials.

28.3.1.2   Inner Firewall Configuration

The internal network is where the Drib's most sensitive data resides. It may contain data, such as proprietary information, that the Drib does not want outsiders to see. For this reason, the inner firewall will block all traffic except for that specifically authorized to enter (the principle of fail-safe defaults[33]). All such information will come from the DMZ, and never directly from the Internet.

EXAMPLE: The Drib uses the Network File System (NFS) protocol to share files among its systems. The NFS protocol (see Section 25.6.1) sends the contents of files around a network. Were any of these packets containing sensitive information to leak to the Internet, the Drib would be compromised. The outer firewall is configured to disallow NFS packets from leaking to the Internet. However, the principle of least privilege says that, unless hosts in the DMZ require access to the internal NFS information, the packets should not even reach the DMZ. Furthermore, the principle of separation of privilege says that multiple mechanisms should prevent NFS packets from leaking to the Internet. If one mechanism fails, the others will still prevent the leak. Hence, the inner firewall should also disallow NFS packets from going to the DMZ.

Like the outer firewall, the inner firewall allows a limited set of traffic through (using the same type of access control mechanism as does the outer firewall). It allows SMTP connections using proxies, but all electronic mail is sent to the DMZ mail server for disposition. It allows limited transfer of information to the DNS server in the DMZ. It also allows system administrators to access the systems in the DMZ from a trusted administrative server. All other traffic, including web access, is blocked.

The administrator's connection uses the Secure Shell (SSH) protocol and differs from the other protocols in that a direct connection through the SSH port is allowed (that is, no SSH proxies). This allows the address of the administrative server to leave the internal network. However, the firewall filter ensures that the SSH connection can go only to one of the DMZ servers. This use of cryptography provides message secrecy and integrity as well as strong (cryptographic) authentication of the endpoints.[34] Because the requisite public keys are embedded into the system when SSH is configured, the issue of an infrastructure for public key distribution[35] is finessed.

The access allowed to system administrators violates the principle of least privilege,[36] because the connection allows the administrators full control over the DMZ systems. Several precautions ameliorate this violation. First, if the connection to the systems in the DMZ does not originate from a special system in the internal network (dubbed the "administrative server"), the firewall will

---

[33]See Section 14.2.2, "Principle of Fail-Safe Defaults."
[34]See Chapter 10, "Basic Cryptography," and Chapter 12, "Cipher Techniques."
[35]See Section 11.4, "Cryptographic Key Infrastructures."
[36]See Section 14.2.1, "Principle of Least Privilege."

disallow the connection. Second, the Drib trusts its system administrators, so only trusted users will be allowed unrestricted access to the DMZ servers. Third, the administrators can use the SSH protocol only to connect to the DMZ servers, and all administrative traffic is protected using SSH. This means that an attacker would not only have to spoof the internal network host addresses, but also find the correct set of cryptographic keys. Although not perfect, these precautions reduce the risk of compromise.

28.3.2   In the DMZ

Four servers reside in the DMZ. They are the mail, WWW, DNS, and log servers. We will discuss these servers separately.

28.3.2.1   DMZ Mail Server

The mail server in the DMZ performs address and content checking on all electronic mail messages. The goal is to hide internal information from the outside while being transparent to the inside. When the mail server receives a letter from the Internet, it performs the following steps:

1. The mail proxy reassembles the message into a set of headers, a letter, and any attachments. The attachments are assembled into their native form (not the form used to transmit them through electronic mail). This allows the mail server to work on the original mail, as opposed to a packetized form of the letter. It simplifies the checking.

2. The mail proxy scans the letter and attachments, looking for any "bad" content. "Bad" content here is defined as a computer virus or known malicious logic. The attachments are then restored to the form used to transmit them through electronic mail. The headers, the letter, and the attachments are rescanned for any violation of the SMTP specification [1068]. This is the basic content checking. Any binary data (which might indicate a buffer overflow or other attack) is weeded out, as are excessively long lines.[37] Although address lines are limited in length to 1,000 characters, the mail proxy will split them as needed to keep lines less than 80 characters long. The scanning also detects and eliminates known malicious logic (computer viruses and worms, logic bombs, and so forth). The analysis of content for malicious logic uses standard techniques.[38]

3. The mail proxy scans the recipient address lines. The addresses that directed the mail to the Drib are rewritten to direct the mail to the internal mail server. The DMZ mail server then forwards the mail to the

---

[37] See Chapter 24, "Vulnerability Analysis."
[38] See Section 23.9.1, "Scanning Defenses."

internal mail server. This step forwards the mail to the Drib's internal network, on which it will be delivered. Identification is by host name and not user name,[39] because the mail server determines the identity of the correct host to forward the mail to on the basis of host name, not user name.

The procedure for sending mail out of the Drib is similar. All outgoing mail comes from the internal mail server. Steps 1 and 2 are the same (although the content checking in step 2 may be enhanced to detect keywords such as "proprietary"). But the sanitization for step 3 is different.

3′. The mail proxy scans the header lines. All lines that mention internal hosts are rewritten to identify the host as "drib.org," the name of the outside firewall. All header lines must be checked. In addition to the source address lines, any "Received" lines are to be removed, and any destinations that name the Drib must also be changed. Following this sanitization, the letter is forwarded to the firewall for delivery. This step forwards the mail to the Internet after hiding all details of the Drib's networks. This idea comes from the principle of least privilege,[40] because those who do not need to know about the internals of the Drib's network do not get that information.

The primary goals of the mail server are to handle mail and to perform all needed checks and sanitization. This way, the firewalls only need to perform rudimentary checks (such as checks on line length and character type) and leave the detailed checking to the mail servers.

The DMZ mail server also runs an SSH server. This server is configured to accept connections only from the trusted administrative host in the internal network. This allows the system administrators to configure and maintain the DMZ mail host remotely (a great convenience) without unnecessarily exposing that host to compromise.

28.3.2.2   DMZ WWW Server

The web server accepts and services requests from the Internet. It does not contact any servers or information sources within the internal network. This means that if the web server is compromised, the compromise cannot affect internal hosts. Although the web server runs CGI scripts, the scripts have been checked for potential attacks and hardened to prevent their success.[41] The server itself contains no confidential data.

The web server also identifies itself as "www.drib.org" and uses the IP address of the outside firewall. This hides part of the DMZ configuration in

---

[39]See Section 15.6.1, "Host Identity."

[40]See Section 14.2.1, "Principle of Least Privilege."

[41]See Chapter 24, "Vulnerability Analysis," and Chapter 31, "Program Security."

accordance with the principle of least privilege[42] (because people outside the network need not know the address), and forces external entities to send web traffic to the firewall.

A system in the internal network known as the "WWW-clone" is used to update the DMZ web server. People authorized to update the Drib's web page can access this system. Periodically (or on request), an administrator will copy the contents of the WWW-clone to the DMZ web server (see Section 29.3.1). This follows from the principle of separation of privilege,[43] because any unauthorized changes in the web server are mitigated by the updates. Like the mail server, the WWW server also runs an SSH server for maintenance and updating. The server provides the cryptographic support necessary to ensure confidentiality and data and origin integrity.[44]

The Drib accepts orders for its merchandise through the web. The data entered by the consumer is saved to a file. After the user confirms an order, the web server invokes a simple program that checks the format and contents of the file and creates an enciphered version of the file using the public key of a system on the internal customer subnet. This file resides in a spooling area that is *not* accessible to the web server (see Exercise 2). The program deletes the original file. This way, even if the attacker can obtain the file, the attacker cannot determine the order information or credit card numbers associated with customers. Indeed, because the customer names are in the enciphered files, the attacker cannot even determine the names. Formally, not keeping valuable information online and in the clear follows from the principle of least privilege,[45] because the users of that machine are not authorized to read the data, and from the principle of separation of privilege,[46] because the cryptographic key is needed to read the data. Using public key cryptography means that only a public key need be on the DMZ web server. This prevents an attacker from deciphering the data on that system should it be compromised, which is an application of the principle of fail-safe defaults.[47]

The internal trusted administrative server periodically connects to the web server using the SSH protocol, uploads the enciphered order files, and transmits them to the appropriate system on the internal customer subnet. The SSH server on the web server is configured to reject connections from any host other than the trusted internal administrative server, so an attacker cannot connect from outside (assuming the attacker is able to penetrate the outer firewall). The principle of denying unknown connections, rather than allowing them and then authenticating them, follows the principle of fail-safe defaults.[48]

---

[42] See Section 14.2.1, "Principle of Least Privilege."
[43] See Section 14.2.6, "Principle of Separation of Privilege."
[44] See Chapter 10, "Basic Cryptography," and Chapter 12, "Cipher Techniques."
[45] See Section 14.2.1, "Principle of Least Privilege."
[46] See Section 14.2.6, "Principle of Separation of Privilege."
[47] See Section 14.2.2, "Principle of Fail-Safe Defaults."
[48] See Section 14.2.2, "Principle of Fail-Safe Defaults."

28.3.2.3   DMZ DNS Server

The DMZ DNS host contains directory name service information about those hosts that the DMZ servers must know. It contains entries for the following:

* DMZ mail, web, and log hosts
* Internal trusted administrative host
* Outer firewall
* Inner firewall

Note that the DNS server does not know the addresses of the internal mail server. The inner firewall will forward mail to that server. The DMZ mail server need only know the addresses of the two firewalls (for mail transfers), and the trusted administrative server. If the mail server knows the address of the DNS server, it can obtain these three addresses. This gives the internal network the flexibility to rearrange its host addressing. The DMZ DNS server must be updated only if the address of the internal trusted administrative host is changed.

The limited information in the DNS server reflects the principle of least privilege,[49] because those entries are sufficient for the systems in the DMZ.

28.3.2.4   DMZ Log Server

The log server performs an administrative function. All DMZ machines have logging turned on. In the event of a compromise (or an attempted compromise), these logs will be invaluable in assessing the method of attack, the damage (or potential damage), and the best response. However, attackers can delete logs, so if the logs were on the attacked machines, they might be tampered with or erased.

The Drib has located a fourth server in the DMZ. All other servers log messages by writing them to a local file and then to the log server. The log server also writes them to a file and then to write-once media, which is a precaution in case some attacker is able to overwrite log files on both the target server and the log server. It is also an application of the principle of separation of privilege.[50]

The log system is placed in the DMZ to confine its activity.[51] It never initiates transfer to the inner network. Only the trusted administrative host does that, and then only if the administrators choose not to read logs by reading the media on which the logs reside.

Like the other servers, the log server accepts connections from the internal trusted administrative host. Administrators can view the logs directly, or they can replace the write-once media with another instance of the media and read the extracted media directly. The use of write-once media is an example of applying the principle of least privilege[52] and fail-safe defaults,[53] because the media cannot

---

[49]See Section 14.2.1, "Principle of Least Privilege."
[50]See Section 14.2.6, "Principle of Separation of Privilege."
[51]See Chapter 18, "Confinement Problem."
[52]See Section 14.2.1, "Principle of Least Privilege."
[53]See Section 14.2.2, "Principle of Fail-Safe Defaults."

be altered; it can only be destroyed, and then only if the attacker has physical access to the system.

28.3.2.5   Summary

Each server has the minimum knowledge of the network necessary to perform its task. This follows the principle of least privilege. Compromise of the servers on these systems will restrict the transfer of information, but will not lead to compromise of the systems on the internal network.

Ideally, the operating systems of the server computers should be very small kernels that provide only the system support services necessary to run the appropriate servers. In practice, the operating systems are trusted operating systems (developed using assurance techniques,[54]) or—more commonly—commercial operating systems in which all unnecessary features and services have been disabled. This minimizes the operations that a server can perform on behalf of a remote process. Hence, even if the server is compromised, the attacker cannot use it to compromise other hosts such as the inner firewall.

The use of proxies on the firewalls prevents direct connections across the firewalls. Moreover, the data passing through the firewalls can be checked and, based on the content, filtered or blocked. The only exception is the SSH connection from the internal network to the DMZ. The inner firewall checks the origination of the connection, to ensure that it comes from the internal administrative host, and the destination, to ensure that it goes to one of the servers.

28.3.3   In the Internal Network

The internal network may be organized in several ways. Each of the subnets may have its own firewall and its own server, and may filter traffic just as the inner firewall does. The subnets may share servers. If the primary goal is to guard the Drib's internal data from being stolen by an outside attacker, what goes on behind the inner firewall is irrelevant.

The Drib's policy imposes the opposite requirement. The subnets must guard against unauthorized access to information as dictated by the policy. For these purposes, "read" corresponds to fetching or retrieving a file, and "write" corresponds to putting or depositing a file. For the moment, we ignore electronic mail, updating of web pages on the DMZ, and the internal administrative host.

The constraints on information flow[55] dictate the arrangement of the network. The firewalls impose the confinement[56] required at the interfaces.

The data and users are distributed among the three subnets of the internal network in the obvious way. The firewall on the developer network allows read access from the corporate network but blocks write access to all other subnets.

---

[54]See Part VI, "Assurance."
[55]See Chapter 17, "Information Flow."
[56]See Chapter 18, "Confinement Problem."

The firewall on the corporate network does not allow read or write access from the other networks. The firewall for the customer subnet allows read access from the corporate network. It also allows write access for information placed by the public onto the DMZ web server. However, the write access is constrained to be mediated only by the DMZ web server and the inner firewall, so the public does not have unrestricted access. These firewalls may be proxy firewalls or filtering firewalls.

The internal mail server must be free to communicate with hosts behind each of the subnet firewalls. Either the subnet may have its own mail server, or the internal mail server can deliver mail directly to each host on the subnets. The former has the advantage of flexibility, because the internal DNS server need only know the addresses of the subnet firewalls and (possibly) the mail servers. Thus, other host addresses can be changed freely within each subnet. The latter requires the internal DNS to have the addresses of all hosts on the internal network, but is simpler to configure and maintain. Either arrangement will satisfy the Drib's policy.

In addition to the mail server, an internal web server provides a staging area for the Drib's web pages. All internal firewalls allow both read and write access to this server. (The server itself controls the specific access that individuals have to each web page.) The DMZ web server's pages are synchronized with the web pages on this server by using the trusted internal administrative host. This provides a test bed for changes in the pages, so corporate and other internal personnel can review and approve changes before they are made visible to the public. Furthermore, if the DMZ web server is ever compromised, the web pages can be restored very quickly.

Finally, the trusted internal administrative server has strict access rules: only system administrators authorized to administer the DMZ systems have access to it. All connections to the DMZ through the inner firewall must use this server, except for the mail server and (possibly) the DNS server. The server itself uses SSH to access systems in the DMZ, and the DMZ servers recognize it as the only host authorized to access their SSH daemons. This prevents a user on the internal network from sending SSH commands from a local workstation to DMZ servers.

With respect to the internal network, the DMZ servers know only about the inner firewall's address and the trusted administrative host's address, by the principle of least privilege.[57] The DMZ servers never communicate directly with the internal servers. They instead send information to the firewall, which routes the messages appropriately. DMZ servers accept only incoming SSH connections from the trusted administrative host. These connections use public key authentication to establish identity,[58] so an attacker cannot forge addresses.

This arrangement is layered with checks. A single action affecting a host on the DMZ requires that several tests be passed (implementing the principle of

---

[57] See Section 14.2.1, "Principle of Least Privilege."
[58] See Section 10.3, "Public Key Cryptography," and Section 15.6.1, "Host Identity."

separation of mechanism). Only a few administrators can alter or update systems on the DMZ. In general, the only data in the DMZ that nonadministrators can alter is the data in the web pages. However, the alterations occur on a copy on the internal network. An administrator must invoke special functions to move the updated pages to the web server on the DMZ.

The only data that is written from the DMZ to the internal network comes from customer orders, but the data so received has been checked for potential errors (or deliberately corrupt data), is enciphered, and is transferred to an internal machine in such a way that it cannot be executed. This applies the analysis techniques for analyzing existing systems[59] and developing systems with some level of assurance.[60] This again limits the ability of an attacker to use this data to attack systems on the internal network.

28.3.3.1   The Wireless Network

The Drib maintains two sets of wireless networks. The first set is a single wireless network. It is for guests who need access to the Internet and are not authorized to access any Drib resources or data. The access points for this wireless network bypass the firewalls for the subnets, connecting directly to the inner firewall and through that to the outer firewall. A virtual private network provides the connection, so all traffic to the outer firewall is encrypted. At that firewall, the traffic is decrypted and routed to its destination. Similarly, responses to any queries are returned to the user via the same virtual private network.

The second set of wireless network is for Drib employees. It consists of three subnets, one for each subnet on the internal network. Each of these is connected to an access point that uses a virtual private network to connect to the appropriate firewall. The firewalls check all communication to and from the wireless access points to ensure that it is not malicious. It also enforces the controls described above.

The Drib handles mobile computing in a number of ways. Personal devices, such as cell phones, tablets, and personal laptops are allowed to connect to the guest wireless network but not the others. Laptops owned by the Drib may connect to the other wireless networks. The reason for this arrangement lies in the control of the mobile systems. The Drib laptops have all software installed and maintained by the Drib administrators. Some laptops are designated as "internal" and are not to be removed from the physical premises. Others are designated "external" and may be taken off the premises, but these are configured so that any network connection will be tunneled directly to the outer firewall, and then the inner firewall, over an encrypted VPN. This arrangement enables employees to take laptops on trips, but imposes the same controls on Internet access as are imposed on users of the Drib's internal network. So, for example, an employee cannot use a web browser to visit a website as the internal firewall blocks such

---

[59]See Chapter 24, "Vulnerability Analysis."
[60]See Part VI, "Assurance."

connections. In addition, the disks of all external laptops are encrypted, and the user must supply both a password and an appropriate fingerprint scan to log into the system. This minimizes the risk to the Drib should the laptop be stolen.

The VPN server resides on the inner firewall. The external laptops each have a different public key pair known to the server. These are generated randomly and changed whenever the laptop is given to an employee. Thus, the server can tell whether an attempt to connect using the VPN is from an authorized laptop. Note there is a risk of an employee copying the key pair to a personal laptop and using that system. To mitigate this risk, the Drib has procedures for checking laptops when they are returned. The logs in the laptop are extracted and the actions compared to those logged by the other Drib systems. Discrepancies indicate a potential problem and lead to further investigation.

28.3.3.2   The Cloud

> **Definition 28–2.** A *cloud* is "a model for enabling ubiquitous, convenient, on-demand network access to a shared pool of configurable computing resources (e.g., networks, servers, storage, applications, and services) that can be rapidly provisioned and released with minimal management effort or service provider interaction" [1316, p. 2].

A cloud has several properties that have caused the Drib to consider using it. The client (here, the Drib) can obtain computing resources such as time and storage without manual intervention by the provider of the cloud. Further, as the client's needs expand, the cloud can provide the needed resources; similarly, as those needs contract, the cloud can reallocate resources that are no longer needed. Thus, the Drib pays for the resources it needs, and resources that are no longer necessary are not paid for. Network accessibility allows the Drib to use the cloud remotely.

Using these properties, the cloud can provide several services: software as a service, platform as a service, and infrastructure as a service [1316].

A *software as a service* cloud provides the applications that a client needs, and the client supplies the data. The client does not control how the data is managed, how the application is run, or any other aspect of the execution. But the Drib uses its own software to develop widgets, so the Drib immediately rejected the idea of using such a cloud.

A *platform as a service* cloud is similar, except that the client develops the software using cloud resources such as libraries, programming languages and systems, tools, and other services of the cloud provider. This type of cloud platform has exactly the same drawbacks for the Drib as does the cloud providing software as a service: the Drib's software executes on the cloud provider, and hence is visible to them. Again, the Drib rejected the idea of using this type of cloud.

A cloud providing *infrastructure as a service* enables the client to run its own software on the cloud rather than on the client's local systems. The cloud provider manages the execution of the software. The client provides the software and the input, and the provider returns the output. This means the cloud provider has access to the software in order to run it. Fortunately, the Drib's computations are well within the resources the Drib has locally, so the Drib need not use the cloud to execute its software—and as the software is proprietary, the Drib decided to keep the computations local.

But this type of cloud provides other services, including storage. Of course, the Drib cannot store raw data on such a cloud because the provider can see it, contrary to the Drib's need to protect the data as noted above. The cloud may offer an encrypted storage service, in which the cloud provider enciphers the data as it enters the cloud, and when the client requests the data, the provider deciphers the data as it goes back to the client. While this protects data in the cloud from many attackers, the provider has the keys to the encryption, and—more directly—can see the data before it is encrypted or after it is encrypted. The obvious solution, then, is for the data to be encrypted on the Drib systems and that sent to the cloud. The Drib can then retrieve the data and decrypt it locally, so neither the cloud provider nor anyone who gains access to the data stored in the cloud will see the Drib's raw data. So the Drib should choose a provider whose client does the encryption and decryption on the Drib's system, or the Drib should encrypt the data itself before uploading it to the cloud.

The Drib considered this possibility for two purposes. The first was to minimize the need for local storage. But as secondary storage is inexpensive and the Drib did not have or need massive amounts of data, a cost analysis showed the Drib's management that the cost of sufficient local storage was affordable and, indeed, reasonable. Should this change, the Drib management agreed that they would revisit the issue. The second was for doing backups of its data. As the data would be stored off-site, any data at the Drib's site that was damaged or erased could then be retrieved. The issue for the Drib was the reliance on a second party; if the cloud provider suffered failures, or for some reason cut the Drib's access to the cloud, the backups would be unavailable. The Drib management felt that this was an unacceptable risk. So backups are performed daily, and stored on storage media, a copy of which is physically transported to a remote site (in the Drib's case, a bank vault located in a nearby city). Thus, the Drib can make immediate use of the copy of the backup on-site, and if needed retrieve a copy of the backups from the off-site media.

28.3.4 General Comment on Assurance

All of the defenses discussed above depend on software that has been written defensively. This is particularly true of software on the firewalls. Although the amount of software running on the firewalls is minimized, and the software is written to perform only necessary functions and has been extensively audited and tested, the Drib defensive mechanisms all trust that the software is correct and cannot be compromised. If this trust is misplaced, the defensive mechanisms can be breached. This is another reason why the configuration of servers and firewalls is based extensively on the principle of separation of mechanism. If one mechanism fails, another may prevent the attacker from exploiting that failure.

A similar remark applies to hardware. Suppose the network interface card connected to the Internet never cleared its buffer. An attacker could craft a packet that contained data of the form of a legal packet addressed to an interior system. The containing packet would be validated as allowed to go to the interior network and then would be passed to the interior network. The next packet would be short enough to overwrite the contents of the buffer from the beginning up to the data in the form of the valid packet. If the card then flushed the contents of its buffer to the inside network, the legal but unvalidated packet would be sent on too. The separation of mechanism inherent in a proxy firewall hinders attacks based on failures in single network cards, but other types of malfunctions may allow other attacks.

Assurance at all levels is important. Here, the informal policy model of the Drib (see Section 28.2) guides the design of the network architecture as well as the analysis of the software and hardware configurations. Infrastructure, software, and hardware all provide the basis for claims that the network actually enforces the policy model correctly.

28.4   Availability

The availability component of the Drib's policy requires that the systems must be available to the public and to Drib personnel. This means that access over the Internet must be unimpeded. We consider this in the context of flooding attacks, in which attackers attempt to overwhelm system resources.

The SYN flood[61] is a common type of flooding attack. There are two aspects of SYN flooding. The first is the consumption of bandwidth. If the flooding is more than the capacity of the physical network medium, or of intermediate nodes, legitimate handshakes may be unable to reach the target. The second is the use of resources—specifically, memory space—on the target. If the flooding absorbs all the memory allocated for half-open connections, then the target will discard the SYN packets from legitimate handshake attempts.

The Drib focused on the second aspect, because the first involves infrastructure elements not under the control of the Drib. Their countermeasures combined using intermediate hosts such as routers to divert or eliminate traffic, as described in Section 7.4.2, and host-based defenses as described in Section 7.4.3. In this way, any flooding that the intermediate hosts passes on to the end hosts will affect those hosts as little as possible.

---

[61] See Section 7.4, "Availability and Network Flooding."

28.5   Anticipating Attacks

In spite of the measures outlined above, the Drib security officers realize that their network and systems might be compromised through unanticipated means. They have taken steps to prepare for, and handle, such attacks. The extensive logging described above is one step. The DMZ log server contains an intrusion detection mechanism that scans through the logs looking for evidence of known attacks and of anomalous behavior. The reasons, and settings, are bound in the Drib's philosophy of defense.

The Drib security officers are aware of the multitude of attacks that can be launched against networks and systems. They expect these attacks to come from the Internet against the outer firewall. If the attacks are stopped by the firewall, they are logged and ignored. For example, should someone attempt a known buffer overflow attack against the SMTP mail proxy, the proxy will reject the attack, log the attempt, and continue to function. The security officers will not pursue the attacker, and are interested in the attack only as a statistic they can use when higher management asks them to justify their budget, or when they are training new system administrators in security procedures and techniques.

However, should the SMTP proxy be attacked successfully, the Drib's security officers will be very interested. At that point, the SMTP mail proxy will cease to function as a mail proxy. Instead, it will start nonstandard programs (such as a command interpreter or some other program that gives the attacker access to, or information about, the system). At this point, the anomaly detection component of the intrusion detection mechanism will detect the unusual behavior and report a potential problem. The Drib's security staff monitors the intrusion detection system around the clock, so they can act quickly on such reports.

The Drib's security officers are very interested in attempted attacks within the DMZ. Unlike the Internet, where attack tools are commonplace, use of the DMZ is restricted only to those who have access to the internal administrative trusted host or who are using a small set of services. If a known attack occurs on this network, someone who has obtained access to the network has launched it. This means that some trusted administrator should not have been trusted (entry through the administrative trusted host), that one of the servers on the firewall has been compromised (entry through the outer firewall), or that the software on the DMZ systems either is corrupted (already in the DMZ) or does not restrict actions sufficiently tightly (entry through the DMZ web or mail server). Hence, network traffic is monitored using both anomaly and misuse detection methods, and all attempted compromises are reported.

The philosophy of ignoring attacks that fail seems dangerous, because when an attacker succeeds in compromising the system, the attacker probably has tried—and failed—numerous times before. Although this is true, the Drib's answer is, "So what? We do not have the personnel to handle the false alarms and the failed attacks. Instead, we focus on what we are most concerned about: successful attacks, and failed attacks in areas where attacks ought not to be launched. A failed attack within the DMZ tells us that someone or something is acting in a forbidden way and that some compromise has occurred. But a failed attack from the Internet tells us that someone may have found a new attack script and used us as the target. We put our efforts where we can obtain useful results."

Finally, the Drib security officers analyzed many commercial intrusion detection systems to find one that met their needs. All reported many false positives. Some even failed to detect attacks launched by the security officers. The Drib therefore purchased an intrusion detection system that allowed them to add signatures of known attacks and to tune parameters to control reporting of events. After considerable experimentation, they found a group of settings that seemed to work well. To verify this, every month the Drib security officers select two one-hour periods at random and analyze the logs for attacks, probes, and other nefarious events. The results of the analysis are compared with the reported events. If they match, the current set of settings is accepted; if not, the settings are retuned.

28.6   Summary

This chapter demonstrated how to develop a network infrastructure from security requirements. The security goals led directly to the development of a security policy, which in turn suggested the form of the network. One firewall limits the types of traffic to public servers; the other firewall blocks all external traffic from reaching the innermost portions of the corporate network. The servers available to the public are dedicated systems that provide only one service. The firewalls are application level firewalls, so they can check the contents of any connection. Finally, meeting the availability policy requirements led to a discussion of defenses against attackers using SYN floods to prevent legitimate connections from accessing the publicly available servers.

28.7   Research Issues

Distributed denial of service (DDoS) attacks are insidious and difficult to handle. Research into handling them, as well as tracing them, focuses on both the end system and the infrastructure. One difficult problem is to distinguish between an attack and a large number of attempted connections over a short period of time; the effect is the same, but the response may need to be different.

The dissonance between policy and implementation means that systems often do not enforce the stated policy. Policies include procedural issues, some of which cannot be enforced by technical means. However, the host and infrastructure systems should be configured to implement those parts of the policy that can be enforced by technical means. An automated method of deriving settings for a system from a given policy would reduce the inconsistencies and provide a higher degree of assurance that the site enforces those aspects of the policy correctly. Conversely, many sites do not have a clear policy for controlling access to their networks. Application of reverse engineering techniques to deduce the actual policy that the configurations of the systems support, and expression of that policy in a clearly understood manner, also constitute a deep research problem that involves not just technical analysis but also human factors. The elements of policy languages are critical to both of these problems.

The structure of the network architecture resembles that of a medieval fortress: a single gateway to the outside world, an outer keep (the DMZ) in which people from outside the fortress may enter for limited purposes, and an inner keep, in which the inhabitants of the fortress dwell. This structure ignores the historical problem of the frailty of medieval fortresses, and can be attacked in the same way—through an insider. The problem of defending systems from unauthorized access is simpler than defending them from unauthorized acts by authorized users. This "insider problem" suggests a different approach. The skin of the human body is designed to protect people from certain bacteria, but if the skin is breached (through a cut, or through breathing in bacteria or viruses), the body responds with antibodies. Perhaps this could be extended to a network architecture other than the one shown here. How to do this is a research question, and how to do it effectively involves not only technical considerations but also human factors.

28.8 Further Reading

Architecting networks for security requires an understanding of the environment in which the network will function and what its function is to be. Convery [452] discusses network security architectures in general. Others discuss architectures for specific types of networks such as ad hoc networks among vehicles [640, 1571], networks with programmable infrastructure [33, 1127, 1999], and the smart grid [1050, 1967, 2165, 2194]. Science DMZs are networks designed to transfer massive amounts of data; as stateful firewalls that analyze the contents of packets would impose an unacceptable performance delay, these networks instead use routers to control access [499, 1371, 2111]. Such networks relating to medical science have more stringent constraints and so use firewalls, but does not put them in the path of the traffic [1505].

Virtual private networks (VPNs) build virtual infrastructures on existing infrastructures. They are ideal for corporations with geographically distributed offices, or when telecommuting is used. Several books discuss their creation and management [642, 1073, 1772, 2071]. Caronni, Kumar, Schuba, and Scott present a layering approach to VPNs that hides the existing infrastructure [349].

Web commerce and security uses principles and practices that are common to other systems in which security is desired. Several authors [746, 1417, 1909] have described the issues and approaches specifically in terms of the web and electronic commerce.

28.9   Exercises

1. Suppose a new class of users, the *system security officers* (SSOs), were to be added to the access control matrix discussed in Section 28.2. Augment the matrix with the *change* right. This right allows the user to alter the classes of other users in that category. For example, if user Amy had change rights over the class "developers," she could change the class of user Tom, who is currently in the "developers" class, to any of the other four classes.

   a. Let Alice be a member of the SSO class, and let her have change rights over the "developers" and "employees" classes. Let Bob be a member of the SSO class, with change rights over "outsiders" and "employees." Redraw the matrix for this situation and write rules describing the allowed transformations of the matrix.

   b. Describe any problems that might occur if Alice and Bob were not careful about the changes of classes they made. Could information leak in undesired ways? If so, give an example. If not, show why not.

   c. Should members of the SSO class be allowed to apply the change right to members of that class? Justify your answer. In particular, state what damage could occur if this were allowed, and if it were not allowed.

2. Consider the scheme used to allow customers to submit their credit card and order information. Section 28.3.2.2 states that the enciphered version of the data is stored in a spooling area that the web server cannot access.

   a. Why is the file kept inaccessible to the web server?

   b. Because the file is inaccessible to the web server, and no other services are available to an attacker from the Internet, the encipherment may seem unnecessary. Discuss this issue, but assume that the attacker is on the internal network.

3. The organization of the network provides a DMZ to which the public has controlled access. This follows the principle of least privilege, as noted in Section 28.3.2.2. For each of Saltzer and Schroeder's other design principles [1644] (see Chapter 14), explain how the principle is relevant to the creation of the DMZ. Justify your answer.

4. A security analyst wishes to deploy intrusion detection monitors to determine if any attackers penetrate the Drib's network.

   a. Where should the intrusion detection monitors be placed in the network's topology, and why?

b. If the analyst wished to monitor insider attacks (that is, attacks by people with access to the Drib's internal network), how would your answer to part (a) change (if at all)? Justify your changes (or lack of changes).

5. The Drib has hired the computer security firm of Dewey, Cheatham, and Howe to audit their networks. The analyst from DC&H arrives and produces a floppy disk. She states that the disk is to be loaded onto a system on the internal network. She will then run the program. It will scan the Drib's networks and send the information to DC&H's headquarters in Upper Bottom. There, DC&H analysts will determine whether the Drib's security is acceptable, and will recommend changes.

   a. The analyst informs the Drib that the program works by sending the data to DC&H's headquarters over the Internet using a proprietary protocol. She requests that the firewalls be opened to allow communications to remote hosts with destination port 80. The audit department manager, who was told to hire DC&H by the Drib's CEO, is nervous. Should his security expert recommend that the communication be allowed, or not? Why?

   b. The analyst is asked exactly what the program does. She assures the Drib that it does nothing harmful. Given that she is so vague, the Drib security officers want to find out more information. Suggest four or five questions that they should ask to obtain the information they seek.

   c. The analyst admits that her answers are based on what the DC&H auditors have told her. When asked for the source code of the program on the floppy, she states that it is proprietary and cannot be released. What could the Drib's officers do to assure themselves that the program is not harmful?

   d. Based on the actions of the analyst, and assuming that finances are not a consideration, would you hire DC&H to analyze your network security? Why or why not?

6. This exercise asks you to compare an SMTP server such as *sendmail* with an SMTP proxy for an application level firewall. Your answers should assume that the questions refer to the Drib's network.

   a. The SMTP server must be able to parse electronic mail addresses. It may have to change the destination address (so the mail can be delivered correctly) and/or the source address (so the recipient can reply). Would an SMTP proxy on the outer firewall need to rewrite addresses of mail moving from the Internet to the DMZ? From the DMZ's mail server to the Internet? If not, explain why not. If so, explain which addresses would need to be rewritten, and how.

   b. The SMTP server must be able to deliver mail locally. Does the SMTP proxy server need to deliver mail locally (that is, on the outer firewall)? Why or why not?

   c. Considering your answers to the previous two parts, how does the complexity of the SMTP proxy compare with the complexity of the SMTP server? From the point of view of security, is this important? Justify your answer.

7. Suppose the Drib wished to allow employes to telecommute. In order to protect the network, they require all remote connections (other than those for the web and mail servers) to use SSH.

   a. Discuss the required changes in the network infrastructure. In particular, should the outer firewall provide an SSH proxy or a packet filter to incoming SSH connections? Why?

   b. The destination of an SSH connection from the Internet might be the address of any host on the internal network. Such addresses, however, are not broadcast to the Internet and in fact may be addresses that routers on the Internet should not pass (such as 10.*x.x.x*). Devise a method or protocol that will continue to conceal the addresses of the hosts on the internal network but still allow SSH connections from the Internet to arrive at the proper destinations. What supporting infrastructure must the Drib add to its network?

   c. The inner firewall will pass SSH connections, provided that one endpoint is the trusted administration server on the internal network. With the above-mentioned change, the destination of the incoming SSH connection may be any host on the internal network. For this question, assume that the addresses of the hosts on the internal network are kept within the internal network—in other words, that the method or protocol in part (b) is implemented. What are the security implications of allowing SSH connections to *any* internal host through the inner firewall? Should such connections be restricted (for example, by requiring users to register the hosts from which they will be connecting)?

   d. An alternative to allowing the SSH connections through the firewall is to provide a specific host (the "SSH host") on the internal network that is also connected to the Internet. Telecommuters could use SSH to log into this system, and from it reach systems on the internal network. (The difference between this method and allowing connections through the firewall is that the user must log into the intermediate host, and from there move to the internal system. The firewall approach makes the intermediate system transparent.) Identify the *minimum* number of services that this system should run in order to fulfill its function. Why must these services be run? As part of your answer, identify any other systems (such as DNS servers, mail servers, and so on) that this SSH host would have to trust.

   e. From the point of view of Saltzer and Schroeder's design principles [1644] (see Chapter 14), is the solution suggested in part (d) better than, worse than, or the same as the solutions involving access through the firewall? Justify your answer.

8. The Drib routers use the approach described in the first example of Section 7.4.2.

    a. Why does the router not save time by opening a connection to the destination host before the pending connection completes its three-way handshake?

    b. The router is protecting a target from being flooded. Is the router itself vulnerable to a flooding attack? If not, why not, and why won't the same property make the target immune? If the router is vulnerable, does the attack on the router differ from the attack on the target? How?

Chapter 29
System Security

> IMOGEN: To your protection I commend me, gods.
> From fairies and the tempters of the night
> Guard me, beseech ye.
> — *Cymbeline*, II, ii, 8–10.

System configuration and administration relies on many principles of security and assurance. This chapter considers how the administration of security affects the system. It begins with a policy for the DMZ web server system and for a development system in the internal network. It explores the configuration and maintenance of several system components in light of the policy and in light of principles of computer security. This illuminates how the practice of computer security is guided by the fundamental principles discussed throughout this book.

29.1   Introduction

Among the many functions of system administration is the security of the system and the data it contains. For our purposes, we consider the security policy of the WWW server within the DMZ and a user system in the development subnet. This will contrast the manner in which an administrator secures a system that many users use for development of software with the methods used to secure a system that is likely to be attacked and that is not intended for the use of nonadministrative users.

Section 28.3.2.2 discusses the WWW server's function in relation to the rest of the Drib's network infrastructure. Briefly, the WWW server system provides access to untrusted users through a WWW server, and access to trusted users through SSH. Untrusted users can come from any system on the Internet. Trusted users are those users who have access to the trusted administrative host on the internal network. For the purposes of our policy, we assume that any user in that system has been correctly authenticated to that system and is "trusted" as we use the term.

The development system is a standard UNIX or UNIX-like system. A set of developers are allowed to use the system.

29.2   Policy

Policy is at the heart of every decision involving security. The DMZ WWW server has a policy very different from that of the development system. This section discusses portions of the policies in order to provide a foundation for the remainder of this chapter. We then compare and contrast the policy elements.

29.2.1   The WWW Server System in the DMZ

Section 28.3.2.2, "DMZ WWW Server," discusses the basic security policy of the WWW server. Some of the consequences of the policy are as follows:

1. All incoming web connections come through the outer firewall, and all replies are sent through the outer firewall.
2. All users log in from an internal trusted server running SSH. Web pages are never updated locally. New web pages are downloaded through the SSH tunnel.
3. Log messages are transmitted to the DMZ log server only.
4. The WWW server may query the DMZ DNS system for IP addresses.
5. Other than those expressly mentioned here, no network services are provided.
6. The WWW server runs various scripts. One of these scripts will write enciphered information (transaction data) to a spooling area. The enciphered file will be retrieved from the trusted internal administrative host using the SSH tunnel.
7. The WWW server must implement its services correctly, and must restrict access to those services as much as possible.
8. The public key of the principal who will decipher and process the transaction data must reside on the DMZ WWW server.

From these implications, several constraints emerge. The WWW server consequences (WCs) of interest are as follows:

WC1. Policy consequence 1 requires that no unrequested network connections except those from the outer firewall over the HTTP and HTTPS ports, and those from the internal trusted administrative server over SSH, should be accepted. Replies to DNS queries should be accepted provided that they can be verified to come from the DMZ DNS server. If other network clients are to be run, only replies to messages originating from the DMZ WWW server should be accepted.

WC2. Policy consequence 2 states that user access to the system is to be limited to those users on the internal trusted administrative server. Furthermore, the number of users who need access to the WWW server should be as small as possible, with only those privileges needed to perform their tasks. All actions must be attributable to an individual, as opposed to a role, user.

WC3. Policy consequences 4 and 5 suggest that the WWW server should be configured to provide minimal access to the system. This prevents an attacker who compromises the WWW server from accessing other parts of the system. This requirement leads to one unexpected, interesting consideration. If an attacker gains access to the system through the WWW server, she can delete all uncollected transaction files. This denial of service attack would blemish the Drib's reputation. Some other mechanism should capture the transaction files and copy them to an area that the WWW server cannot reach. Then, if an attacker compromises the WWW server, that attacker cannot reach the transaction files.

WC4. Policy consequences 5, 6, and 8 imply that all software must have a very high assurance of functioning correctly (as specified by its documentation). In practice, this means that the software must be either developed or checked very carefully. It also requires that extensive logging occur, to verify that the software is functioning correctly even when under attack. In essence, we view attacks as situations in which software functions correctly (and the attack fails) or incorrectly (and the attack succeeds).

WC5. Policy consequence 7 states that the WWW server must contain as few programs, and as little software, configuration information, and other data, as possible. If the system is compromised, this will minimize the effects of the attack.

29.2.2 The Development System

The development system lies in the internal network, on the development subnet (called the "devnet"). It must provide an environment in which developers can produce code for dribbles. Because users will be active on the system, its policy is considerably different than that of the WWW server system.

The devnet has both infrastructure and user systems. The infrastructure systems are the devnet firewall (which separates it from other internal subnets), a DNS server, a logging host (which provides a central repository for logs), one or more file servers, and one or more systems containing user information common to the workstations (the UINFO servers). There is also an isolated system used to build a "base system configuration" (system files, configuration files, company-approved software, and so on) and to create the bootable media. The policy that follows does not apply to these systems. They are under much tighter controls. The components of the security policy relevant to our discussion are as follows:

1. Only authorized users are allowed to use the devnet systems. They may work on any devnet workstation. All actions and system accesses must be tied to an individual user, rather than to a role account.

2. Workstation system administrators must be able to access the workstations at all times, unless the particular workstation has crashed. The set of devnet workstation administrators differs from the set of devnet central server administrators.

3. Within the devnet itself, users are trusted not to attack devnet systems. Users not on the devnet are not trusted. They are not allowed to access devnet resources except as permitted by the network security policy (for internal Drib users). Furthermore, devnet users are not allowed to access systems not on the devnet except as permitted by the network policy.

4. All network communications, except electronic mail, are to be confidential and are to be checked to ensure that the messages are not altered in transit.

5. The base standard configuration for each devnet system cannot be changed on that system. There is to be a local area in each system in which developers may install programs that are nonstandard. Before doing this, they must obtain approval from the security officers and system administrators. Should the software prove useful, it may be integrated into the standard configuration.

6. Backups shall enable system administrators to restore any devnet system with the loss of at most one day's changes in user and local files.

7. Security officers shall perform both periodic and ongoing audits of devnet systems. Compromised systems shall be removed from the devnet until they have been restored to an uncompromised state.

These components have several consequences, two of which affect the infrastructure and configuration of workstations. Policy component 3 leads to the use of a firewall at the boundary of the devnet and the other subnets to enforce the network security policy. This allows the network security administrators to enforce changes in the network policy without having to alter each system on the devnet. Any changes need only be made at the firewall. Also, the systems on the devnet need not be so tightly configured as must the firewalls. The firewalls enforce the policy that hosts outside the devnet see; the hosts inside the devnet enforce the policy specific to the developers and their hosts (the policy outlined above).

Policy component 3 also bars direct access between the Internet and devnet systems. This decision was based on a risk analysis. The security officers and management of the Drib realized that the Drib would benefit from allowing access to remote websites. However, the dangers of opening up an avenue of attack from Internet hosts to internal hosts, and allowing unsuspecting Drib employees to download untrusted, and possibly malicious, code, outweighed the perceived benefits.

Some developers need access to the Internet to determine what equipment to obtain as they plan new mechanisms and devices to enhance the value of the Drib's products. These developers are given separate workstations connected to a commercial Internet Service Provider (ISP) outside the Drib's perimeter. These "ISP workstations" are physically separated from the internal network, and the ISP workstation cannot easily be connected with the devnet workstation. These procedural mechanisms enforce the desired separation.

Other consequences of the policy apply to the devnet workstations. The development system consequences (DCs) of interest are as follows:

DC1. Policy components 1 and 4 imply the need for authenticated, enciphered, integrity-checked communications. These policy components also imply a consistent naming scheme across systems, so that a user name refers to the same user on all devnet systems.

DC2. Policy component 2 requires that each workstation have one or more local privileged accounts to administer the system locally. Policy components 1 and 2 imply that multiple local administrative accounts may be used to limit access to particular administrative functions. This division of power into roles allows the administrators to designate special system accounts, such as *mail*, as being limited in their power. Policy requirement 2 also requires that the workstation be able to run without any network connections.

DC3. Policy component 1 also requires that there be a notion of a "login" or "audit" user (see Section 29.4). This identity must be recorded in logs, to tie individuals to actions. Furthermore, users should not be able to log directly into role accounts such as *root*, because this would eliminate the ability to tie an individual to an action. Instead, they must log in to an individual account and change to the role account, or add a new role to their individual account.

DC4. If a developer wants to install a program from the outside onto his devnet workstation, he must first obtain approval from the security officers. Once approved, he installs it in an area separate from the base system configuration (see policy component 5). Adding a program to the base system configuration requires that it be added to the isolated system first. This requires testing and analysis of the program to ensure (to an appropriate level of integrity) that the software is not malicious and will not accidentally damage the system on which it runs.

DC5. Policy component 5 requires that each workstation protect the base system configuration, as installed, from being altered. One approach is to mount the disks containing that configuration as read-only disks. A far simpler and more effective approach is to use read-only media. This meets policy requirements and ensures that all devnet workstations are up to date. A writable hard drive provides space for local files such as spool and temporary files.

DC6. Policy component 1 requires that an employee's files be available to her continuously. This requires that the files be stored on systems other than the workstations, in case a workstation goes down. As a corollary, the file controls should enforce the same sets of permissions regardless of the workstations from which they are accessed.

DC7. Policy component 6 requires regular backups. As explained in Section 29.3.2, the development workstations store only transient files on writable media. Hence, they need not be backed up. Restoration involves rebooting and remounting of file systems from the file servers, which are regularly backed up.

DC8. Policy component 7 requires several security precautions. The primary one is a logging system to which all systems send log messages. Furthermore, security officers need access to both devnet systems and the devnet network. They conduct periodic (and irregular) sweeps of the network, looking for unauthorized servers. They also conduct periodic (and irregular) sweeps of each system looking for dangerous settings in user accounts and the local areas.

Two points about this policy, and its implications, are apparent. First, the system security policy relies on the outer and inner firewalls to prevent Internet users from reaching the system. If one firewall fails, the other will still block such accesses.[1] Also, the firewall at the perimeter of the developer's subnet enforces the access restrictions among the users of the other two subnets and the systems on the developer's subnet.[2] So the system policy assumes that those who can connect to the system are authorized to access developer systems.

The security policy also requires procedural enforcement mechanisms.

EXAMPLE: Consider a system administrator for the development network who has both an ISP workstation and a devnet workstation on her desk. She could download a program to her ISP workstation, copy it onto a floppy disk, and move the floppy disk to the devnet workstation. This clearly would violate policy, but there is no reasonable technical means of preventing it. (See Exercise 1.)

Here, the Drib must rely on procedural mechanisms to enforce the policy. In this case, the procedures should specify both the prohibition and the

---

[1] See Section 14.2.6, "Principle of Separation of Privilege."
[2] See Section 14.2.4, "Principle of Complete Mediation."

consequences of violating it. This puts all employees on notice that the prohibition will be enforced, and encourages them to use the allowed methods to obtain approval.

29.2.3   Comparison

The differences between the policies of the DMZ WWW system and the devnet developer system arise from their different roles. The DMZ WWW server is not a general-use system. It exists only to serve web pages and accept orders over the web. The devnet developer system is a general-use computer. It must allow compilation, editing, and other functions that programmers and software engineers need to design, implement, and test software.

The DMZ WWW server system's security policy focuses on the single purpose of the server: to run the web server. Two sets of users can access the server: the system administrators, who maintain the security and the web pages; and the users from the Internet, who must go through the outer firewall and can access only the web server. The developer system's security policy focuses on more complex purposes. These purposes include software creation, testing, and maintenance. The developer system requires more supporting software than does the DMZ WWW server system. The user population is different and provides an environment more amenable for attackers than does the DMZ WWW server system, because the users may not be as security-conscious as the security officers comprising the user population of the DMZ WWW server system.

That the system administrators of the DMZ WWW server system are trained in security (hence, the term "security officers") should be expected. The developer systems are more numerous and require more administrative effort to maintain. More system administrators are required. The administrators will also have different skills and abilities; some may be very senior and experienced, whereas others will be junior and inexperienced. Hence, the system administrators for the developer systems may not be trained in security. So the system security officers may not be administrators. This leads to situations in which system administrators and security officers disagree on what actions are appropriate. The policy must have some mechanism for resolving these disputes. The mechanism typically involves a person, or a group of people, performing a cost-benefit analysis of each option and selecting the option that provides the greatest benefit at the least cost. This type of analysis was briefly discussed in Section 1.6.1.

29.2.4   Conclusion

We now examine several areas of system administration in light of these security requirements. Our goal is to install and manage as secure a system as possible. Our approach is to compare and contrast these two systems. What follows is organized into areas, and each system is examined with respect to the mechanisms used to enforce the policy. We then compare the two systems.

29.3   Networks

Both the DMZ WWW server system and the devnet user system are connected to the network. Although the firewalls provide some measure of protection, the principle of separation of privilege says that access should be limited even when the firewalls fail.[3] So we consider how the administrators should set network configurations and services to protect the systems in the case that the firewalls fail.

29.3.1   The WWW Server System in the DMZ

Item WC1 limits network access to the WWW server.[4] External users can reach the system only by using web services and connecting through the outer firewall. Internal users can reach the system by using SSH from the trusted administrative system, through the inner firewall. A security mechanism must block any other types of connections, or any connections from sources other than the outer firewall or the trusted administrative server.[5] Moreover, item WC4 requires that *all* attempts to connect be monitored[6] to validate that the security mechanism functions according to this policy (or to detect failures).[7]

Consider the WWW server first. Although requests can come from any IP address on the Internet, all such requests go to the outer firewall's web proxy. That firewall forwards well-formed requests to the DMZ WWW server. Hence, the WWW server's access control mechanism can discard any requests from sites other than the outer firewall. Whether to accept requests from the inner firewall depends on several policy factors. The current policy for the Drib is not to allow the WWW server to accept these requests.[8] However, the policymakers have realized that some situations may require internal users to access the WWW server directly (these situations typically will involve debugging or checking for errors). Should this be necessary, the security officers will reconfigure the inner firewall to run a web proxy identical to the one on the outer firewall. Thus, the DMZ WWW server is configured to accept requests from the inner firewall as well as the outer firewall. The server will not accept requests from other DMZ systems, because they are not to be used for accessing the web server.

EXAMPLE: The Apache web server can control access to specific parts of the web pages based on IP address. The configuration file controls which addresses are allowed access and which ones are denied access. By default, all accesses are allowed.

---

[3] See Section 14.2.6, "Principle of Separation of Privilege."
[4] See Section 14.2.1, "Principle of Least Privilege."
[5] See Section 17.6, "Example Information Flow Controls."
[6] See Chapter 25, "Auditing."
[7] See Chapter 26, "Intrusion Detection."
[8] See Section 14.2.2, "Principle of Fail-Safe Defaults."

The system administrator sets the configuration file to load the module *mod_authz_host*, and sets the host authorizations to allow connections from the inner and outer firewall:

```
<RequireAll>
     Require ip outer_firewall
     Require ip inner_filewall
<RequireAll>
```

where *inner_firewall* and *outer_firewall* are the addresses of those hosts. If either condition holds, that is the connecting IP address matches the address in either line, the connection is allowed. If not, it is denied.

Item WC1 requires the DMZ WWW server to allow administrative access from the trusted administrative WWW host. This allows system administrators to update web pages, reconfigure and modify software, and perform other administrative tasks. The WWW server runs an SSH server. This server provides enciphered, authenticated access to the web server system using cryptographic mechanisms to provide those security services. Of interest here is that the server requires both the host and the user to be authenticated.[9] This allows the system administrators to restrict access to users connecting from the trusted administrative WWW host only.

EXAMPLE: The simplest way to control access to the SSH server is to use the "hosts.allow" file. This file controls access to network services on a per-host, per-server basis. The relevant lines in this file are:

```
sshd : trusted_admin_WWW_host : allow
sshd : ALL : deny
```

where *trusted_admin_WWW_host* is the name of the trusted administrative WWW host.

The lines in this file are matched in order, and on a match the respective access is used. As the request is for the SSH server, *sshd*, the first field matches that service. If the incoming connection is from the administrative host, the name matches the name of the host in the first line, and the access is allowed. Otherwise, the host name matches the wild card "ALL" in the second line, and the access is denied.

If the DMZ WWW server has an internal firewall, that can also be used. For example, the following lines block all attempts to connect to the SSH server except those from the trusted administrative WWW host:

```
ipfw add 100 allow tcp from ip_trusted_WWW_host to me 22 in
ipfw add 101 deny tcp from any to me 22 in
```

---

[9]See Section 14.2.6, "Principle of Separation of Privilege."

where *ip_trusted_WWW_host* is the IP address of the trusted administrative WWW host.

Each packet is matched to these firewall rules. The first line allows incoming packets from the trusted administrative WWW host to the SSH server, which listens at port 22. If the host is another, the first line does not match and the second line is checked. If the packet is destined for the SSH server, it is discarded. Other lines in the file control which outgoing packets are allowed.

Section 29.4.1 discusses users, and authentication of both hosts and users, on the WWW server system.

To maximize availability, the WWW server system wraps each server with a small script. If the server terminates, the script starts a new instance of the server.

EXAMPLE: The web server and the SSH server are started at boot time. Both are wrapped so that, should either fail, a new copy will be run. For example, the web server *webd* is run from the following shell script:

```
#! /bin/sh
echo $$ > /mnt/users/servers/webdwrapper.pid
while true
do
        /usr/local/bin/webd
        sleep 30
done
```

Now, if the web server terminates, the script will automatically start a new web server process after a wait of 30 seconds.

By virtue of item WC3, the WWW server system should run a minimum of network servers. Because access is to be given only to web requests and administrative logins, no network servers other than the web server and the SSH server are needed.[10]

The web server runs several network clients, however. Because the web server system must request IP addresses and host names, it must make requests of, and receive replies from, a DMZ DNS server. At any time, multiple requests may be outstanding. By virtue of item WC1, this satisfies the policy. However, several types of attacks on DNS clients involve "piggybacking" of multiple host name and address associations onto a reply to a request for a single such association.[11] The WWW server system's DNS client will use only the requested data. It will discard any additional data as well as any logs that such data has been received.[12] Furthermore, if the client receives a response that provides information that was not requested, or if two responses provide different answers to the same query,

---

[10]See Section 14.2.2, "Principle of Fail-Safe Defaults."
[11]See Section 15.6.1.2, "Security Issues with the Domain Name Service."
[12]See Section 14.2.1, "Principle of Least Privilege."

both are logged and discarded, and the client acts as though the DNS request has timed out.

The WWW server system also runs a logging client to send log messages to the log server. Programs use an internal message delivery system to send messages to the logging client, which then delivers them to the appropriate hosts and files. The delivery addresses lie in a configuration file. Each log message is timestamped and has the name of the process and (WWW server) system attached.

The system is configured to log any attempts to connect to network ports on which no servers are listening. The three reasons for doing this follow from item WC4. First, it serves as a check that the outer firewall is intercepting all probes from the Internet to the Drib's WWW server. Second, it detects probes from the internal network to the DMZ WWW server. Because the inner firewall has one port that is filtered rather than proxied (the SSH port), such probing is possible if the filter does not check the destination port number. This should never happen, of course, unless the inner firewall is misconfigured or compromised. Thus, in order for an attack on the firewall to be undetectable, two failures must occur (the firewall fails to block, and the DMZ WWW server fails to log).[13] Third, probes to other ports from within the DMZ indicate unauthorized activities on the DMZ systems, meaning that one of them has been compromised. This requires immediate investigation.

29.3.2 The Development System

Item DC1 requires that the development system accept user connections only when they are authenticated and encrypted. Like the DMZ WWW server, the development systems run SSH servers to provide such access. Both hosts and users use public key authentication.[14]

Unlike the DMZ WWW server system, the development system runs several other servers. It runs a line printer spooler to send print requests to a print server. It runs a logging server to accept log messages and dispose of them properly. It also runs servers to support access to both the file server and the user information database system. These servers are necessary in order for the developers to be productive on that system.

The development system does not have FTP or web services. Instead, special FTP and web server systems mount directories from the central file servers. The workstations run an SMTP server as a convenience to users,[15] but all mail is forwarded to a central mail server and is never delivered locally. (This allows workstation SMTP servers to be very simple programs.[16]) Users can access mail on any workstation, because the mail spooling directory resides on the central file

---

[13]See Section 14.2.6, "Principle of Separation of Privilege."
[14]See Section 10.3, "Public Key Cryptography."
[15]See Section 14.2.8, "Principle of Least Astonishment."
[16]See Section 14.2.3, "Principle of Economy of Mechanism."

server. Similarly, users can make files available for FTP and web access by placing them into user-specific directories on the central file server. The corresponding servers mount these directories for remote access. They cannot access other parts of the file systems on the file servers.

Placing the mail, FTP, and web services on systems other than the development workstations has two advantages that satisfy item DC2. First, it minimizes the set of network servers that each workstation has to run. Second, it minimizes the number of systems that provide the services.[17] This enables the firewall to be configured to allow traffic for these services through to a small set of systems, and the security administrators can configure those systems to handle access control appropriately.

The development system uses access control wrappers to support access controls. The firewall provides this control for systems not on the devnet, but the workstation's access control wrappers provide this control for other devnet workstations, as well as duplicating the firewall's control rules. If the firewall's access controls fail (for example, as a result of a configuration error), the workstation will still honor the network security policy.[18] Furthermore, the development system logs all attempts to access servers. These logs provide both evidence of intrusions and verification of the correct functioning of the security mechanisms, as required by item DC8.

EXAMPLE: *TCP wrappers* [1927] is a program that provides host-based wrappers to intercept requests (connections or datagrams) to some set of servers. The wrapper determines the origin of the request from the packet. It then looks in the configuration file. If the wrapper is configured to allow the connection, it then spawns the appropriate server and passes the open port to the server. Otherwise, the request is ignored. In either case, the wrapper logs the request and its origin.

On some systems, this functionality is folded into the program. The SSH server configuration in the example on page 1043 shows this. The configuration file is "hosts.allow," and the code in the TCP wrappers program that controls access is in a library available to all network servers and used by the SSH server.

Item DC8 requires checking of the security of the development workstations. To ensure that they remain at the desired level of security, the system security officers occasionally scan each system. Their scanner probes each port and records those that are open. The results are compared with the list of ports that are expected to be open. Any discrepancies are reported to the security officers. Moreover, the scanners record the address of each system on the network. Any unauthorized system is reported immediately, as are any unexpected changes in addresses. The security officers make these scans periodically. To prevent an attacker from determining the schedule, the security officers launch additional scans at irregular intervals as well.[19]

---

[17]See Section 14.2.3, "Principle of Economy of Mechanism."
[18]See Section 14.2.6, "Principle of Separation of Privilege."
[19]See Chapter 25, "Auditing."

Finally, the security officers occasionally attack devnet systems to determine how well they withstand attacks.[20] These operations are sustained and take some time, but the information gleaned from them has proven invaluable. When flaws are discovered, the security officers determine whether they are attributable to the initial configuration or to user changes in the system. In the former case, the security officers develop a patch or modification of the standard configuration. In the latter case, they assess the situation in more detail, and act on the basis of that analysis.

29.3.3   Comparison

The difference between approaches to network services and accesses springs from the use of, and the locations of, the systems.

The DMZ WWW server system is dedicated to two specific tasks—serving web pages and accepting commercial transactions. Only those functions and processes required to support this specific task are allowed. Any other programs, such as those required for general use, are simply not present in the system. It need not provide access to a line printer, or handle remote file systems from central servers. Everything is present in the system itself. No extraneous services are provided or used.[21]

The development system performs many tasks, all designed to achieve the goal of providing an environment in which the developers can be productive.[22] It has general-purpose tools ranging from compilers and text editors to electronic mail reading programs. It shares user files with other workstations using a central file server, and user information with a central user information system. Users can run processes freely.

The environment plays a role in configuration. Both systems use a "defense in depth" strategy of providing access controls that duplicate some of the firewall controls.[23] The DMZ WWW server system does not depend on the firewall to filter or block web client requests. Even if the inner firewall allowed messages to flow through it with no control, the DMZ WWW server system would function as required by policy. However, access to the development systems depends on the devnet firewall's filtering abilities. If a user from another internal subnet tries to access a development system, the devnet firewall will determine whether or not access to the devnet is allowed. If it is, then the developer system determines whether or not to accept the connection. This allows the Drib network administrators to control access among the three subnets and the DMZ independently of the system administrators within the subnets (who do not control the firewalls). It also allows the developer workstations to support developers on other subnets if the Drib policy allows it.

---

[20] See Section 24.2, "Penetration Studies."
[21] See Section 14.2.7, "Principle of Least Common Mechanism."
[22] See Section 14.2.8, "Principle of Least Astonishment."
[23] See Section 14.2.6, "Principle of Separation of Privilege."

29.4   Users

Our first step is to determine the accounts needed to run the systems. The user accounts, as distinguished from the system administration accounts (system administrators), require enough privileges to use the computer to perform their jobs, but as few others as possible.[24] Creating, configuring, and maintaining their accounts are crucial to the successful use of the computer. For brevity, we refer to a user account as a "user" and a system administration account as a "sysadmin" in this section.

29.4.1   The WWW Server System in the DMZ

Items WC2 and WC3 suggest that the number of user accounts on the system be minimal. The WWW server requires at most two users and a sysadmin. The first user is a user with enough privileges to read (and serve) web pages and to write to the web server transaction area. The second user is a user who can move files from the web server transaction area to the commerce transaction spooling area. The reason the web server has minimal privileges lies in the assumption that the WWW server, which interacts with other systems on the Internet, may be compromised. A compromised web server running with sysadmin privileges could allow the attacker to control the system, but if the web server had only enough privileges to read web pages, then compromising it would be less likely to compromise the WWW system. The commerce server and the web server should be different users in order to prevent an attacker from compromising the web server and then deleting files from the commerce server's area. Access control mechanisms[25] can inhibit this, but defense should not depend on one control only.[26] If the web server and commerce server are different users, and the web server is compromised, the attacker must then compromise either the sysadmin or the commerce server user.

EXAMPLE: Let the web server account's name be *webbie*, and let the commerce server's account be *ecommie*. The web server's scripts would create the transaction file, with an ACL allowing *ecommie* to read and delete the file. The commerce server then could simply copy the contents of the file into a file in the spooling area, set the ACL to allow the administrator to read and delete the file, and delete the original file. Note that with the given ACL, *webbie* can no longer read the file. This protects transactions against attack if the web server is attacked.

---

[24] See Section 14.2.1, "Principle of Least Privilege."
[25] See Chapter 16, "Access Control Mechanisms."
[26] See Section 14.2.6, "Principle of Separation of Privilege."

Some systems (such as many UNIX systems) use a simplified mechanism that does not allow individual users to be placed in an access control list.[27] However, group mechanisms achieve the same end.

EXAMPLE: The web server's transaction directory is group-owned by the group *trans*. That group contains two members, *webbie* and *ecommie*. The scripts write a transaction file group-owned by *trans* and group-readable. The commerce server can read the file and, because the directory is group-writable,[28] delete the file.

There is a tension between the desire to minimize the number of accounts (item WC2) and the desire to minimize the privileges of these accounts (item WC3). Most computer systems allow the assignment of privilege to accounts independently of name. This means that there can be multiple sysadmin accounts. Each person designated as a system administrator could have a separate sysadmin account or could use a single, role account.[29] The reason for having separate sysadmin accounts is to tie each action to a *particular* user. Whether or not this can be done depends to some extent on the implementation of the WWW server system.

EXAMPLE: Most UNIX systems represent accounts by UIDs. The particular UID determines the level of privilege, with 0 being the sysadmin. Having separate system administration accounts would require the account names to be different, but the account UIDs to be the same (0). Hence, the only benefit is to be able to track who logged in as a system administrator. All logged actions would show up as having been executed by the user with UID 0.

Some UNIX systems support an audit, or a login, UID.[30] This UID is assigned at login and is not changed throughout the lifetime of the process. Furthermore, all children of the process inherit that audit UID. Assigning each system administrator a unique user account (each with a unique UID) associates that UID with every action that account takes. This includes acquiring administrator privileges.

EXAMPLE: FreeBSD 10.3 supports an audit UID. When the WWW server system is set up, each system administrator is assigned a separate, unprivileged account. After the system administrator logs in as the ordinary user, she switches to the sysadmin role. Each action will have three associated UIDs: the real, effective, and audit UIDs. Any action that the sysadmin takes will be tied to the individual account of the particular system administrator who takes it.

---

[27] See Section 16.1.1, "Abbreviations of Access Control Lists."

[28] Some UNIX variants allow the group owner of a file to delete it only if the directory *and the file itself* are group-writable. In this case, the transaction file must be group-writable as well.

[29] See Section 15.3, "Users," and Section 15.4, "Groups and Roles."

[30] See Section 15.3, "Users."

Because item WC4 requires strict user accountability, the WWW server system is set up to disallow direct logins from system administrators. Each user must log in to the system from the trusted administrative server. As stated in Section 29.3.1, this requires the use of SSH, so the user must be an authorized user of the WWW server system.[31] The set of allowed users is enumerated in the SSH configuration file in the WWW server system. Once logged in, the user may switch to a role account. To do so, the user supplies a password. The program checks that the user has self-authenticated correctly, and then that the user is authorized to access the requested role account. If so, the user is switched into this role.

Direct login to a sysadmin account is allowed in one situation only. The WWW server system allows logins to role accounts (such as *root*) from the system console. Although the system cannot identify the individual logging into the role, the console itself is in a locked room to which only a few highly trusted individuals have access. At least three people are in that room at all times, including one security officer. The officer can identify by sight the set of people authorized to enter the room.[32] If someone walks up to the console and logs into a role account, the security officer will log that individual's use of the console.[33] Thus, should the SSH server become unexpectedly unavailable, a system administrator could fix it.

29.4.2   The Development System

Unlike the DMZ WWW server system, the development system requires at least one user account per developer (items DC1, DC3, and DC6). It also requires administrative accounts, as well as groups corresponding to projects (items DC2 and DC3). Furthermore, an account on different development systems must refer to the same individual, role, or project (item DC1). Otherwise, inconsistent use of identifiers may allow access rights that exceed the level authorized by the security policy.

EXAMPLE: The *r*-protocols [1005] define a set of protocols that implement a trusted host relationship. The host *stokes* names host *navier* in the file */etc/hosts.equiv*. Then, if the user Abby has an account *abby* on *navier*, and there is an account *abby* on *stokes*, Abby can log in to *abby* on *stokes* without supplying a password. The system administrator configures the *hosts.equiv* file.

Suppose a site[34] had two different users named Abraham and Abigail, both of whom use the nickname "Abby." Abraham's account on *navier* is *abby*, and Abigail's account on *stokes* is *abby*. If *navier* trusts *stokes* as described above, then Abraham can log in to Abigail's account on *stokes*. This violates the security policy requirement of being able to tie actions to individual users (item DC3).

---

[31] See Section 14.2.6, "Principle of Separation of Privilege."
[32] See Section 14.2.6, "Principle of Separation of Privilege."
[33] See Section 14.2.4, "Principle of Complete Mediation."
[34] Not the Drib. SSH provides the same functionality as the *r*-protocols, but with added security. So the Drib does not use the *r*-protocols.

Shared files increase the risk of accidental or deliberate damage.[35] The Network File System (NFS) protocol for sharing files bases access on the UID of the user requesting access. If *abby* has UID 8924 on *navier*, and *sioban* has UID 8924 on *stokes*, both have access to files owned by the user with UID 8924 on the NFS file server. This violates the security policy requirement of users being able to control access to their files from any development system (item DC6).

To meet the requirement for consistency of naming, the Drib developers have decided to use a central repository to define users and accounts, the UINFO system. They use the LDAP protocol [875, 1713, 2082, 2200] to allow distribution of user information. All systems on the developer subnet, except the firewall, use the LDAP server to obtain information about users and accounts. Any new account must be instantiated on the databases of this server. No user accounts are created on the developer workstations themselves, and all system accounts have entries in the server databases.

The developers benefit from this arrangement. Because their files are kept on NFS file servers, a developer can access them at any devnet workstation, as required by item DC6. If one workstation cannot function, the developer can walk to another workstation and continue development. The system and network administrators can then repair the malfunctioning workstation with minimal loss of developer time.

To satisfy item DC2, each developer workstation has a local *root* account and one local account for each system administrator.[36] This account gives administrators access should the workstation be unable to contact the LDAP server. Because there are both primary and secondary LDAP servers, and backups for each, the only reason that this situation might arise would be either a network problem or a workstation problem. Using the local *root* account, the administrator could access the workstation, diagnose the problem, and (if possible) correct the problem at the client.

As allowed by item DC2, the Drib administrators have set up several accounts to perform system functions. Examples are the *mail* account, which allows the user to manipulate mail queues and configuration files, and the *daemon* user, under which most network daemons run. These accounts do not have *root* privileges. This is an application of the principle of least privilege,[37] because few functions require the powers of the *root* account.

EXAMPLE: Backups require access to the raw disk device. Rather than require *root* to do the backups, the Drib administrators have created the *operator* user. This user is in the group devices. All files corresponding to raw disk devices are in that group and are group-readable. The *operator* user can therefore dump the contents of the disk using a backup program.

---

[35]See Section 14.2.1, "Principle of Least Privilege."
[36]See Section 14.2.7, "Principle of Least Common Mechanism."
[37]See Section 14.2.1, "Principle of Least Privilege."

To enforce the individual accountability of item DC3, the *operator* account does not allow password authentication. To access the account, the user must log in to her normal account, and then change to the *operator* account. The version of the UNIX operating system that is used here has a login UID, so when the user changes to the *operator* account, the new process inherits the login UID. This is logged (along with the real and effective UIDs), so each action taken as operator can be tied to a particular user's UID.

The LDAP mechanism uses TLS connections to transmit user information, and so satisfies requirement DC1.

29.4.3 Comparison

The difference between selecting users for the DMZ WWW server system and selecting users for the development system reflects the differences between the security policies of the two systems. The root lies in the intended use of each system.

The DMZ WWW server system is in an area that is accessible to untrusted users (specifically, from the Internet). Although access is controlled, the controls may have vulnerabilities. Limiting the number of users on the system, and ensuring that untrusted users access servers running with minimal privileges, increase the difficulty of an attacker obtaining unauthorized access to the system.[38] Except for the superuser, users can perform only restricted actions. Finally, the user information is kept on the system, so attackers cannot inject false information (such as information on other users) into the system's accesses to a user information database.[39]

The development system allows general user access, so it has many more accounts. Furthermore, the development system shares its user population with other systems on the same subnet, so it accesses a centralized database containing the information. This keeps the user and file information consistent across platforms. The features of the LDAP system allow each devnet system administrator to control authorization to use that particular system. System accounts other than that of the superuser allow the system administrators to control administrative actions to a fairly high degree of granularity. The trade-off is that these administrative accounts can access files on the file server, whereas the superuser can access only public files.

Finally, the difference in means of access reflects the differences in the environments and uses of the two systems. The DMZ WWW server system allows access only through a small set of tightly controlled access points: the web server (from the outer firewall), the SSH server (from the inner firewall), and a login server bound to the physical console of the system. This reflects the classes of

---

[38]See Section 14.2.1, "Principle of Least Privilege."
[39]See Section 14.2.7, "Principle of Least Common Mechanism."

users who are authorized to use the system, as well as the ways in which they are authorized to use it.[40] External users can access only the web server, internal users only the SSH server. However, the devnet system is in the internal network. Hence, users can come from a wide variety of systems and can access any server. The only controls on access are that the accesses must come from within the devnet, unless *explicitly* stated otherwise, and that the users must have accounts on the devnet centralized database system.

29.5   Authentication

Authentication binds the identity of the user to processes. Incorrect or compromised authentication leads to security problems. In this section, we consider the authentication techniques used in the two systems.

29.5.1   The WWW Server System in the DMZ

As required by WC1 and WC2, the SSH server uses cryptographic authentication to ensure that the source of the connection is the trusted administrative host. If the connection is from any other host, the SSH server is configured to reject the connection. Furthermore, SSH uses a cryptographic method of authentication rather than relying on IP addresses.[41]

When a user connects to the SSH server, that server attempts to perform cryptographic authentication. If that attempt fails, that server requests a password from the user. Were this likely to remain unchanged, the administrator would configure the authentication routines directly in the SSH daemon. However, the Drib is experimenting with one smart card system and plans to try two more. Because such a system would require changes in the authentication methods, the system administrator has elected to use PAM to avoid having to modify the source to the SSH server, recompile, and reinstall.[42]

The UNIX system used for the web server system allows the use of a SHA-256-based password hashing mechanism. The advantage of this scheme over the standard UNIX scheme is that the passwords may be of arbitrary length. The password changing program on the web server system is set to require passwords to have a mixture of letters, numbers, and punctuation (including white space) characters. When a password is changed, the password changing program runs the proposed password through a series of checks to determine if it is too easy to guess.[43] If not, the change is allowed.

---

[40]See Section 14.2.1, "Principle of Least Privilege."
[41]See Section 10.3, "Public Key Cryptography."
[42]See Section 13.9, "Multifactor Authentication."
[43]See Section 13.3.3, "User Selection of Passwords."

The system administrator has disabled password aging. Password aging is suitable when reusable passwords may be tried repeatedly until guessed, or if the hashed passwords can be obtained and cracked.[44] Here, all user connections come from the trusted administrative host, so only users who are authorized to use that system can get to the WWW server system's SSH server. These users are trusted. The purpose of password aging is to limit the danger of passwords being guessed. Because the only users who could guess passwords are trusted not to do so, password aging is unnecessary.

29.5.2   Development Network System

The development system supports several users. It is in a physically secure area, accessible only to Drib employees. However, employees other than developers (such as custodians and managers) have access to the restricted area, so authentication controls are required.[45]

Item DC1 means that each user must self-authenticate at login. Although the Drib is moving toward a smart card system, each user currently has a reusable password. Each proposed password is checked to ensure that it is not easy to guess.[46] The criteria include a mixture of case, character type, length, and testing against various word lists and transformations of those lists. Like the WWW server system, the development system uses a password hashing scheme based on SHA-256.

Although the Drib does not expect to upgrade the methods of authentication on the development system, that system uses PAM to provide a uniform, consistent interface for authentication. The system maintainers found that providing consistency and simplicity, as the interface to PAM does, eases the burden of administration.

To allow developers to access the system from anywhere within the Drib's offices, the development system runs an SSH server. This is configured to accept connections from any system within the internal network. It validates host identities using public key encryption and validates users using public key authentication, smart card authentication, and (if needed) password authentication.[47] However, to meet item DC3, *root* access is blocked. A system administrator must log in as an ordinary user and then change to *root*. To enforce this, the server's configuration file disallows *root* logins, and the system is set to disallow *root* logins on all terminals (network terminals and console). Other role accounts simply have a password hash that cannot be produced when any password is entered. Thus, users cannot log in to them. To gain access, administrators must use a special

---

[44]See Section 13.5, "Password Aging."

[45]See Section 14.2.6, "Principle of Separation of Privilege."

[46]See Section 13.4.3, "Password Strength."

[47]See Section 15.6.1, "Host Identity."

program on the workstation that validates their identities, and then checks their authorization to access the desired role account.[48]

EXAMPLE: The programs *lsu* [219] and *sudo* [1214, 1438] both implement role-based access control for a variety of UNIX systems. These programs require that the user enter his or her password and then, if the password is validated, determine whether or not the user is authorized to assume the requested role.

29.5.3   Comparison

Both the DMZ WWW server system and the devnet system use strong authentication measures to ensure that users and hosts are correctly authenticated. The SSH server requires cryptographic authentication of not only the user but also the host from which the user is connecting, and the server responds only to known hosts. Host and user identities are established using the RSA public key cryptosystem. The certificates are initialized by trusted system administrators, so systems that are set up by unauthorized personnel will not be able to connect over SSH to any Drib system.

29.6   Processes

A system runs a collection of processes to perform specific tasks. Each process is a potential vulnerability. This section examines the processes run on both systems.

29.6.1   The WWW Server System in the DMZ

As required by WC5, the WWW server system runs a minimum set of processes[49] because its function is only to serve web pages and batch transactions for off-line processing. The required services are as follows:

- Web server
- Commerce server
- SSH server
- Login server, if there is a physical terminal or console
- Any essential operating system services (such as paging daemons)

---

[48]See Section 15.4, "Groups and Roles."
[49]See Section 14.2.1, "Principle of Least Privilege."

Items WC2 and WC3 require each server to run with a minimum of privileges. The SSH and login servers need enough privileges to change to the user logging in. The web and commerce servers run with minimal privileges, because they only need to access public data. Neither the login nor the commerce server accepts network connections.[50] The former is tied to specific, hardwired terminals (such as a console); the latter simply responds to interprocess communication from the web server.

EXAMPLE: A typical UNIX-like system will have the following daemons running:

- *init*, the login server
- *sshd*, the SSH server
- *webd*, the web server
- *commerced*, the commerce server
- Various servers for the operating system

For example, a Solaris system running with minimal services will include a scheduling process, a paging process, a file system flushing process, and a process for recording logins and logouts. Enabling of accounting creates one more process, but the information gleaned may provide guidance for optimizing the performance of the system.

Consider the level of privilege that the servers need.[51] The SSH server must run with sysadmin privileges to support the remote access and tunneling facilities. The login server (if present) must run with this level of privilege also. The web server requires enough privileges to read web pages and invoke subordinate scripts. The web pages can be world-readable, so the web server simply needs minimal privileges. The scripts manipulate web pages or generate transaction data, and with appropriate settings of file permissions can write into the web server's area. The commerce server needs enough privileges to copy transaction files from the web server area to the transaction spooling area. However, it should not have enough privileges to alter web pages. Other required servers run with appropriate privileges.

EXAMPLE: A program may require extra privileges when it begins. Most UNIX-like systems require that only *root* programs be able to access network ports with numbers of 1023 or lower. These systems do not enforce the principle of complete mediation, because access is checked only when the port is opened. This allows two approaches to minimizing of privileges.

The web server can run with *root* privileges. As soon as it opens the network port, it discards those privileges. So it runs as the user *webbie*. This requires special code in the web server to drop the privileges. If the web server does not do this,

---

[50]See Section 14.2.2, "Principle of Fail-Safe Defaults."
[51]See Section 14.2.1, "Principle of Least Privilege."

a second approach is to write a wrapper program that runs as *root*, opens the port, spawns the web server (as the user *webbie*), and passes the file descriptor corresponding to the port to that process. The wrapper then terminates.

File access is an important issue. File system access control lists[52] provide one defense. We can adapt another defense from capabilities.[53] Recall that in a pure capability system, the capability names the object; if the subject does not possess the capability, it cannot even identify an object. An access control–based system does not work this way. However, if we can change the meaning of a file system name, then we can confine all references to a particular part of the file system. The web server, for example, needs to reference only programs and files within the hierarchy of web pages (and scripts). The commerce server needs access only to the transaction spooling area and the area where the web server's scripts place transactions.

EXAMPLE: Most UNIX-like systems provide a system call *chroot* that changes the process's notion of the root of the file hierarchy. For example, suppose a process wishes to open the file */usr/web/pages/index.html*. The appropriate system call would be

```
if ((fd = open("/usr/web/pages/index.html", O_RDONLY)) < 0)
    perror("open /usr/web/pages/index.html for reading failed");
```

But the system call *chroot*("/usr/web") changes the process's notion of root to */usr/web* rather than */*. After this, the system call that would open the same file as above is

```
if ((fd = open("/pages/index.html", O_RDONLY)) < 0)
    perror("open /pages/index.html for reading failed");
```

because the kernel maps the first */* in */pages/index.html* to the directory */usr/web*. Every full path name that the process refers to uses */usr/web* as its beginning. The process could not directly refer to the file */usr/trans/1*.

Depending on the nature of the hierarchy, the process may be able to refer indirectly to the file */usr/trans/1*. Some variants of these system allow the superuser to make links to a directory. Consider the hierarchy shown in Figure 29–1. The directory *xdir* is a child of *trans*, so the entry *..* in *xdir* refers to *trans*. The superuser has created a hard link in *web* that refers to *xdir*. Now suppose a process executes the call *chroot*("/usr/web"). The process can no longer access */usr/trans/1* by that

---

[52] See Section 16.1, "Access Control Lists."
[53] See Section 16.2, "Capabilities."

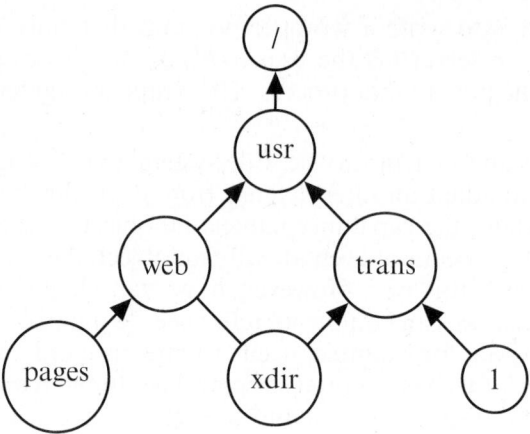

Figure 29–1   A UNIX file system. The directed edges indicate the parents of each directory. A hard link to *xdir* lies in *web*.

name, but it can access it as *xdir/../1* because the change in root does not affect the interpretation of the path name. This shows that, in addition to the *chroot*, the file hierarchy in which the process is rooted must not have any hard links extending to directories not in that file hierarchy.

Finally comes interprocess communication. Processes should be able to communicate only through known, well-defined communication channels.[54] The issue here is how the web server communicates with the commerce server to tell it that transaction files are present, and the names of those files.

The simplest method of communication is to use the directory that both the web server and commerce server share. The commerce server periodically checks for files with names consisting of *trans* followed by a set of digits. When a transaction begins, the scripts create a temporary transaction file. It builds the transaction data and enciphers it using the appropriate public key. It then renames the temporary file with a name consisting of *trans* followed by the integer representation of the date and time, followed by one or more digits. (See Exercise 5.) When the commerce server checks the directory, it moves any files with that type of name to the spooling area.

If the web server and commerce server run with the same real or effective UID, or either runs with superuser privileges,[55] then they can communicate using the signaling (asynchronous interrupt) mechanism. If an attacker acquires access through the web server, and can signal the commerce server, then the attacker can damage the Drib with a denial of service attack. Hence, the web server and the commerce server should run as distinct users, with different privileges.

---

[54]See Chapter 18, "Confinement Problem."
[55]See Section 15.3, "Users."

29.6.2   The Development System

Unlike the DMZ WWW server system, the development workstation serves developers who will compile, test, debug, and manage software. They will also write reports and analyses, communicate with other developers on different systems in the devnet, and send and receive electronic mail over the Internet. The system must support all these functions.

Consider servers and clients first. The devnet workstations may run servers to provide administrative information (such as who is currently logged into the system). These servers require administrative users. As discussed in Section 29.4.2, item DC2 requires these users to be local. Item DC1 requires that users be named (and numbered) consistently. The LDAP protocol provides user information to clients, ensuring this consistency. Hence, the devnet workstation runs LDAP clients. Similarly, the workstation runs NFS clients to satisfy item DC6. Servers run with the fewest privileges necessary to perform their tasks. In many cases, servers begin with *root* privileges to open privileged ports. They then drop privileges to a more restricted user.[56]

EXAMPLE: Consider a mail server on the devnet mail server system. It must listen for connections on port 25. That port (and all ports with numbers less than 1024) can be opened only by *root* processes, but the mail server itself need not run as *root* to perform other functions. It can forward mail to the central mail server as an ordinary user. Thus, two alternatives arise.

Some mail servers allow the system administrator to specify an execution UID. The mail server begins execution as *root* (either by being setuid to *root* or, more commonly, by being started at boot time), opens port 25, and then switches to the execution UID. The disadvantage of this approach is that the saved UID is *root*. If an attacker can trick the server into executing a system call to set the UID to *root*, the mail server can do so. This means that the mail server must be carefully programmed, as discussed in Chapter 31, "Program Security."

The second approach is to use a wrapper. The wrapper runs as *root*. It opens port 25, redirects standard input and output to that port, drops privileges, and then spawns the mail server. For this to work, the mail server must be able to read messages from the standard input and write messages to the standard output.

The abilities of the mail server dictate which approach to use.

Server processes on the development machine run with as few privileges as necessary, as required by item DC2. Whenever possible, they run with the *nobody* UID and the *nogroup* GID to ensure that the clients can obtain only information that the developers deem public (that is, available to others within the confines of the Drib's internal network).[57] When access to privileged ports is required, one of two methods is used. In the first, the *inetd* daemon (which runs with *root* privileges) listens for messages at the port. When a message is received, *inetd*

---

[56]See Section 14.2.1, "Principle of Least Privilege."
[57]See Section 14.2.1, "Principle of Least Privilege."

spawns the server with the limited privileges. In the second method, the server starts with *root* privileges, opens the ports and other files accessible only to *root*, and drops to a lesser privilege level. This minimizes the actions that the process takes when it has unlimited privilege.[58] It also allows the operating system to enforce normal file system access checks.[59] As with the WWW server system, the servers run in a subtree of the file system whenever possible.

To satisfy item DC3, the development system has a logging mechanism that can record any operating system call, its parameters, and the result.[60] Logged information is recorded locally and sent to a central logging server. The security officers monitor the logs from that server using an intrusion detection system.[61] If an attack is suspected, the central logging server can instruct the kernel to begin (or cease) recording data to augment the current set of data. Initially, the system logs process initiation and termination, along with the audit UID and effective UID of the user executing the command.

In addition to requiring the use of file servers, item DC6 requires that the workstations have sufficient disk space available for local users' work. To meet this goal, every night, or when disk space reaches 95% of capacity, a program scans the file system and deletes auxiliary files such as editor backup files and files in temporary directories that are not in current use (defined as not having been accessed within the last three days).

As required by item DC1, the devnet workstations allow remote access using SSH. This allows devnet users to test software using multiple workstations, which is useful when the software involves network connections or concurrency. It also allows system administrators to log in remotely to perform maintenance activities.

29.6.3   Comparison

The DMZ WWW server system uses a minimalist approach: only those processes necessary for the web server, remote administration, and the operating system are present. All other processes are eliminated. This requires that any new software be compiled on other systems and that all development be done elsewhere. Only those programs essential to the serving of web pages, to remote administration, and to the operating system are available. The number of processes active at any time on this system is small.[62] By way of contrast, the devnet system must provide an environment in which developers can be productive. This requires that more programs be available, and that more processes be active, than on the DMZ WWW server system. Compilers, scripting languages, web servers, and other tools help the developers carry out their tasks.

---

[58]See Section 14.2.1, "Principle of Least Privilege."
[59]See Section 14.2.4, "Principle of Complete Mediation."
[60]See Section 25.3, "Designing an Auditing System," and Section 25.4, "A Posteriori Design."
[61]See Chapter 26, "Intrusion Detection."
[62]See Section 14.2.1, "Principle of Least Privilege."

Both systems run servers with the minimum level of privilege needed. This includes not only minimizing user privileges but also restricting the environment in which the process runs.[63] The difference between the systems is that the "minimum environment" for the DMZ WWW server system is different from the minimum environment for the web servers on the devnet systems. In the latter, users wish to share data, so users must be able to place data into areas in which the devnet system's web server can make it available to other users on the development network. The DMZ WWW server system has no such requirement.[64] The *root* user installs all new web pages. So the web server needs to serve data only from a part of the file system to which the *root* user can write. No other user needs access, except for the commerce user—and that user has tightly restricted access.

Both systems have processes that log information, but the types of the logging processes differ. The devnet system has a log server that accepts messages from other programs, timestamps and formats them, and writes them to locations specified in a control file. This conforms to the way most UNIX-like systems handle logging and allows devnet systems to use off-the-shelf software. The DMZ WWW server system has no such daemon. Each program writes log entries to a local log and to a remote daemon on the log server.[65] This minimizes the number of servers on the DMZ WWW server system.

29.7 Files

The setting of protection modes, and the contents of files, affect the protection domains of users and so are critical to a system satisfying a security policy. Again, consider each system separately.

29.7.1 The WWW Server System in the DMZ

The WWW server system's goal is to serve the web pages. The system programs and configuration files will not change; only the web pages, log files, and spooling area for the electronic commerce transactions will change. To preserve their integrity, as required by item WC4, all system programs and files are on read-only media such as a CD-ROM or DVD-R. When the system boots, it boots from the read-only media. That media is mounted as a file system, so even if attackers can break into the web server, they cannot alter system or configuration files.[66] A hard drive provides space for temporary and spooled files, for the home directories of authorized users, and for portions of the web pages.

---

[63] See Section 14.2.1, "Principle of Least Privilege."
[64] See Section 14.2.7, "Principle of Least Common Mechanism."
[65] See Section 14.2.6, "Principle of Separation of Privilege."
[66] See Section 14.2.1, "Principle of Least Privilege."

Because the web pages change often, it is not feasible to have them on read-only media. However, the scripts change very infrequently, and are to be protected from any attacker who might gain access to the system, as required by item WC4. Hence, the web page root directory, and the subdirectory containing the scripts, are on the read-only media. In the web page root directory is a subdirectory called *pages* that serves as a mount point for a file system on the hard drive. That file system contains the web pages. In other words, an attacker can alter web pages, but cannot alter the scripts or the internal public key, which is also kept in a directory under the web page root directory on the read-only media. (See Exercise 10.)

When the system boots, one of its startup actions is to mount two directories from the hard drive onto mount points on the read-only media. The hard drive file system containing the web pages is mounted onto the mount point in the web page root directory. A separate area, containing user home directories for the system administrators, a temporary file area, and spooling directories for transactions, is also mounted on the root file system.

As dictated by item WC3, the web server runs confined to the web page root directory and its subdirectories.[67] An attacker who compromises the web server cannot alter the scripts, nor add new ones, but can only damage the web pages on the server.

The commerce server has access to the web page directory and the spooling area. When the scripts have processed a request for an electronic transaction, they name the transaction file appropriately (see Section 29.6.1). The commerce server copies the data to the spooling area and deletes the original data. Because the web server is confined to the web page partition, an attacker who seizes control of the web server will be unable to control the commerce server. Moreover, because the scripts (and the containing directory) cannot be altered, an attacker could not alter the programs to send raw data to the attacker. Because the scipts encipher all data using a public key system before writing the data to disk, the attacker cannot read the raw data there.[68] The corresponding private key is on the internal network, not the DMZ system, so the attacker cannot decipher the data without breaking the public key system.[69]

The system administrator partition provides a home directory area when an administrator logs in. It is small and intended for emergency use only.

EXAMPLE: Suppose the WWW server system is a UNIX-like system and the web server runs as the user *webbie*. This user has access to all world-readable files, but to no others. Moreover, the web server changes its notion of the root directory to the root of the web page directory—on this system */mnt/www*. The scripts are owned by *root* and are located in a separate directory, */mnt/www/scripts*, on the read-only media. The public key used by the scripts to encipher the data is in the directory */mnt/www/keys*. All three of these directories are owned by *root* and are not writable by anyone else. The scripts place all transaction data into the directory

---

[67]See Section 18.2, "Isolation."
[68]See Section 14.2.7, "Principle of Least Common Mechanism."
[69]See Section 10.3, "Public Key Cryptography."

/mnt/www/pages/trans. Because the executing process runs as the user *webbie*, this directory is writable by a group containing the users *webbie* and *ecommie*.

The commerce server, running as the user *ecommie*, periodically checks the directory */mnt/www/pages/trans* for transaction files. When a transaction is completed, the scripts name it appropriately. The commerce server then copies the contents of the named file into the transaction directory spool */home/com/transact* area. Both the commerce server and the web server log to the log server.

Finally, WC5 also specifies that the number of programs on the system be minimal.[70] Fortunately, the system itself requires few programs. No compilers or software development tools are available. Because all executables are statically linked, the dynamic loader is not present (see Exercise 3). The only programs that are available allow the users to log in and out; run commands (command interpreters); monitor the system; copy, create, edit, or delete files; and stop and start servers. Programs such as mail readers, news readers, batching systems (the *at* and *cron* commands), and web browsers are not present. This minimizes what an attacker can compromise.

WC4 suggests that the integrity of the system should be checked. Periodically, or whenever there is a question about the integrity of the system, the web server is stopped, transaction files are transferred, the system is rebooted from the read-only media, the hard drive is reformatted, and the contents of the user and web page areas are reloaded from the internal WWW server system clone mirroring the DMZ system (see Section 28.3.2.2). This restores the web pages and user directories to a known, safe state. If an attacker has left any backdoors or other processes to gather information, the reformatting of the hard drive eliminates them.

29.7.2   The Development System

The development system's goal is to provide the resources that developers need to develop new software for the Drib's products and (if necessary) infrastructure and systems. This requires a variety of software. A site can take two approaches.

The first approach is to allow each developer to configure his or her own workstation. The Drib rejected this approach because it would create too many different systems for the system administrators to manage. Furthermore, tools available on one workstation might not be available on another, violating the interchangeability required by item DC6. Meeting item DC5 would also be infeasible because read-only media would have to be created for each workstation separately—an effort that was deemed unacceptable.[71]

The second approach is to develop a standard configuration that provides developers and system administrators with needed software tools and configuration settings. To create such a configuration, the Drib policy managers gathered

---

[70]See Section 14.2.1, "Principle of Least Privilege."
[71]See Section 14.2.8, "Principle of Least Astonishment."

developers, system administrators, security officers, and all other users of the development workstations. The group developed a configuration that met the Drib's policies and that was acceptable to as many people as possible, and ensured that all members of the group were willing and able to use systems with that configuration.[72] The system administrators then installed and configured a base system on an isolated workstation system and created a bootable media that, once written, cannot be overwritten. This was copied and given to all developers. The developers use this to boot their workstations, ensuring that the resulting configuration is the standard one. All updates and upgrades are made to that isolated workstation system and tested, and a new bootable media is created. The bootable media is copied and distributed to the developers. This eliminates the problem of inconsistent patching or upgrading of workstations.[73] It also ensures that files are available on all workstations (through mounting of the central file server's file systems) and that the naming scheme is consistent (through use of the same user database system), satisfying items DC1 and DC5. Finally, the local system configurations of all workstations are identical, so all have the same administrative accounts.

Some members of the group pointed out the need for local writable storage. In the event that no file servers are available, the local administrators may need to create files (for example, to save output from a program for analysis). Furthermore, spool files require space, and many programs use temporary storage. Hence, each workstation has a hard drive with several file systems. When the computer boots from the media, the root file system is located on the media itself. All system programs and configuration files lie on this media, as indicated above. During the boot, the workstation mounts the file systems on the hard drive at mount points in the file system loaded from the media. This provides the workstation with appropriate writable storage, satisfying item DC5.

This approach also prevents developers from adding new system programs to the workstations. Programs can of course be added to the writable file systems, but adding a program to the configuration requires that it be added to the isolated system and that new bootable media.[74] This satisfies part of item DC4. Procedural mechanisms (ranging from warnings to firings) enforce the requirement that programs be inspected before they are added to the writable file system. The organization of the various file systems allows the writable media to be wiped during the boot procedure, eliminating any and all programs added to the workstation. This is part of the recommended boot procedure, but it can be skipped if spool files are queued.

Wiping the writable disks deletes some local log files. However, the logging server also forwards log messages to an infrastructure system that records messages from all workstations. Security analysts examine these logs using various analysis tools, including host-based and network-based intrusion detection tools,

---

[72]See Section 14.2.5, "Principle of Open Design."
[73]See Section 14.2.7, "Principle of Least Common Mechanism."
[74]See Section 14.2.6, "Principle of Separation of Privilege."

to detect misuse and attacks. To validate that the analysis tools are working as expected and are configured correctly, every day the analysts select 30 minutes' worth of log entries and examine them to determine if the analysis tools correctly analyzed those entries. The analysis either validates the security mechanisms and procedures as effective, or reports (or finds) problems. This serves two purposes: validation of the current configuration and software (item DC4)[75] and detection of security incidents (item DC8).[76]

The use of read-only media eliminates the need for integrity checking of the development system binaries and configuration files. Scans of the writable media locate files that match patterns of intrusions. When such files are found, the security officer merely reboots the system, wiping the writable hard drive. This cleans up the workstation. An extensive check of the file servers follows.

29.7.3   Comparison

Both the WWW server system and the development system rely on physical protection of media to prevent unauthorized alteration of system programs and configuration files. Both boot from read-only media and use the file system on that media as the main file system. Because some files on both systems must change (for example, transaction files on the WWW server system and spooled files on the development system), both have file systems on writable media that are mounted on the main file system.[77]

When the WWW server system must be reloaded (because the integrity of the system may have been violated), the spooled transaction files are removed from the system, the system is booted, and the writable medium is reformatted. Then the web pages and user directories are reloaded from a clone kept in a state known to be safe. The development system does not require this, because any nontransient files are kept on a centralized file server that is itself regularly checked. The only local files are temporary files that the users can re-instantiate when they log back in, so the system is simply rebooted and the media reformatted. Because the main file system is on storage that cannot be altered, its integrity is ensured.

The differences between the approaches used in developing the two read-only media spring from the question of attack from within the company. The developers are all trusted not to attack the workstation, because at any time a developer may have to use any workstation. However, the developers may be used as "vectors of attack" if they should (accidentally or deliberately) make errors in programming or bring in software from untrusted sources.[78] This led to the consensus-based development of the workstation media. The developers had great influence, because they would be using the workstations. Security was a consideration, but it was weighted against productivity and morale. The outer,

---

[75]See Section 20.3.3, "Justifying That the Implementation Meets the Design."
[76]See Chapter 26, "Intrusion Detection."
[77]See Section 14.2.1, "Principle of Least Privilege."
[78]See Section 23.9, "Defenses."

inner, and devnet firewalls were to provide the bulwark of the security for the development network systems.[79]

The set of users trusted to work on the DMZ WWW server system was much smaller. Thus, the DMZ WWW server system was designed to withstand attack from both the Internet and the internal network. For example, the web server originally was intended to handle transactions; the security people vetoed this as allowing too many potential attacks, and instead suggested the staging approach, in which the DMZ WWW server system acts as a proxy for the transaction processing systems on the customer data subnet (see Figure 28–2). The construction of that media began with the security officers devising the most secure, minimal WWW server system they could construct and then adding those features necessary for the Drib's special needs.[80] They monitor activities on the web server, and several vulnerability tracking lists and news services, to ensure that they are up to date on all potential problems.

The DMZ WWW server system is self-contained in that all files are local. None are served remotely.[81] If an attacker alters files, a reboot and a reload restore the files to their original state. No other system depends on those files. However, the development workstation relies on file servers. This removes user file integrity from the purview of the development workstation's security. Integrity of the configuration becomes critical, to ensure that the right servers are used, but the read-only ensures that the configuration file data is correct. However, the security of the development systems depends more on the security of the infrastructure of the development network than the security of the DMZ WWW server system depends on the security of the infrastructure of the DMZ network.

29.8   Retrospective

This section briefly reviews the basics of the security of the systems.

29.8.1   The WWW Server System in the DMZ

The web server on the DMZ WWW server system runs a minimal set of services. It keeps everything possible on unalterable media.[82] Except for the web server process, the system accepts only enciphered, authenticated connections from a known, trusted host by known, trusted users.[83]

---

[79]This approach violates the principle of fail-safe defaults, but it was deemed necessary to allow the developers to be as productive and effective as possible. This illustrates a tension between the principle of fail-safe defaults and the principle of least astonishment (see Exercise 11).

[80]See Section 14.2.2, "Principle of Fail-Safe Defaults."

[81]See Section 14.2.7, "Principle of Least Common Mechanism."

[82]See Section 14.2.1, "Principle of Least Privilege."

[83]See Section 14.2.4, "Principle of Complete Mediation."

The web server process must accept connections from any host on the Internet. However, all such connections go through an outer firewall that can (if desired) be configured to reject requests.[84] This means that denial of service attacks could be handled at the outer firewall and not by the DMZ WWW server system.

The web server and commerce server run with minimal privileges. Neither may communicate with the other except through a shared directory used to transfer transaction requests from the public web server area to a private spooling area from which they can be retrieved through the enciphered link.[85] The transaction files themselves are enciphered using a public key algorithm, so an attacker who compromises the web server cannot alter the transaction files, but can only delete them. To minimize this risk, the commerce server moves the transaction files as quickly as possible to an area that is inaccessible to the web server.

Access to the administrative account requires that the user access a trusted host (the internal trusted administrative host) and then authenticate to the DMZ WWW server system using a public key protocol. Automated processes will authenticate on the basis of the host from which they are run, which is the internal trusted administrative host. The SSH server ignores connections from other hosts, and host identity is determined using public key authentication, not IP addresses.

Other servers and programs are simply deleted from the system, so they cannot be run even by accident.[86] This simplifies system maintenance. It also deprives any attackers of available tools should they penetrate the DMZ WWW server system.

29.8.2   The Development System

The development system also runs a minimal set of programs and services.[87] The notion of "minimal" is different for the development system than for the DMZ WWW server system, because the systems must serve many functions. Users compile and debug programs. They test programs, and they integrate different programs into a single software system. They may use ancillary hardware (such as embedded systems) to support the development. The development systems must support this functionality.

Given this, security plays a prominent but not dominant role. Hidden behind three firewalls, each development workstation has sufficient security mechanisms to hinder attackers, and to allow quick recovery if an attack does occur,[88] but these systems rely more on the infrastructure than does the DMZ WWW server system.

---

[84]See Section 14.2.6, "Principle of Separation of Privilege."
[85]See Section 18.2, "Isolation."
[86]See Section 14.2.2, "Principle of Fail-Safe Defaults."
[87]See Section 14.2.1, "Principle of Least Privilege."
[88]See Section 27.3.2, "Intrusion Handling."

The development system allows a large number of users access from any development network system and (possibly) from systems in other subnets of the internal network. User information resides in a centralized repository to maintain consistency across all development systems. Reusable passwords are supported. However, passwords are tested for strength before they are accepted, and the security officers periodically try to guess passwords. Other password schemes are also supported.

Backups occur daily. Because each workstation has a local writable area, users may keep files in that area rather than place them on the file servers. These areas are backed up. The dumps are typically small, because most users work on directories mounted from the file servers. The main reason for these backups is to preserve the log files should an investigation require them.

29.9   Summary

This chapter refined parts of a security policy to derive requirements for mechanisms on systems to implement the policy. The mechanisms rely in part on infrastructure systems and the environment in which those systems function. The server in the DMZ is based on assumptions under which a small set of users is trusted, and everyone else is distrusted. This leads to a system that provides minimal services. System files are kept on protected media so that they cannot be physically altered. Other files, such as those containing transactions, are protected using cryptographic mechanisms so that alterations will be detected, and sanity checks are performed on their contents both before encryption and after delivery and decryption. By way of contrast, the development workstations are general-purpose workstations designed to support a development environment. They support many more functions, and more open access, than the DMZ server. Furthermore, their user population is trusted to a greater degree than that of the DMZ WWW server system. This leads to differences in infrastructure support and workstation configuration.

29.10   Research Issues

The role of a security policy in system development raises several research issues. The first is realism and consistency of policy. A security policy must be consistent with the requirements of the organization. The second issue is the difficulty of ensuring that a policy is internally consistent. Aggravating this issue is the manner of expression of the policy. If the policy can be expressed mathematically, one can apply mathematical techniques to determine its internal consistency. In practice, few policies can be so expressed, and those that can are usually abstractions of the policy in use (that is, they are policy models). Analyzing the actual policies in use at a site requires techniques and methodologies that have not yet been developed.

A third issue is to express the policy in a way users and other people can understand, which is usually in opposition to mathematical expression. Creating the policy in both forms requires establishing consistency between the mathematical version and the natural language version. Methods to do this are highly informal, and more rigorous methods are needed.

Part of the problem is how to map policy components to security mechanisms. Although such mapping appears clear in many cases, the influences of the environment, the users, and the organization affect the selection of mechanisms. For example, the nature of the authentication mechanism determines whether an access control list is sufficient to restrict access as required by the policy, because if users are improperly identified through a weak authentication mechanism, unauthorized users may gain access to data. One research issue is the development of automated (or semiautomated) techniques for guiding the selection of mechanisms for enforcing policies.

The inverse of this problem is also an interesting research topic. Given a system, one would like to derive a high-level exposition of the policy it enforces. Given a set of systems, one would like to demonstrate that the policy they collectively enforce is consistent. Security mechanisms work at a low level. Translating those implementation-specific mechanisms to higher-level expositions, whether formal or informal, is an area that is ripe for study.

Developing methodologies for maintaining large collections of systems consistently seems straightforward. It is not. The difficulty arises from the administration of the distribution system and from the need to ensure that any failures in the process will be detected and reported. This problem is related to the problem of updating distributed databases, and some protocols from that field ameliorate the problem. But human factors, such as keeping the distribution versions up to date, often create problems, as does the desire for control over one's own system. Much work remains to be done in the area of distributing upgrades and patches to systems in a trusted manner, and in the area of determining whether installing a patch or an upgrade will interfere with the system's ability to meet the security policy of the local site.

29.11   Further Reading

Many books discuss system administration and security for UNIX and UNIX-like systems [747, 1095, 1438, 1795], Windows systems [273, 1628, 1760, 1781], and Macintosh systems [1060, 1610].

As sites grow in complexity and number of systems, automated system administration tools are becoming more important. Several authors [145, 175, 318, 319, 909, 1003, 2076] discuss systems for administering sites.

29.12   Exercises

1. A system administrator on a development network workstation wants to execute a program stored on a DVD. What steps could the Drib take to configure the workstation to prevent the system administrator from mounting the DVD and executing the program?

2. Suppose a user has physical access to computer hardware (specifically, the box containing the CPU and a hard drive). The user does not have an account on the computer. How can the user force the computer to shut down? To reboot?

3. Some systems support dynamic loading, in which system library routines are not loaded until they have been referenced. A library can be updated independently of any programs that use the library. If the program loads the library routines dynamically, the updated routines will be used. If the program does not load the library routines dynamically, the program will use the versions of the routines that were in the library at link time. This exercise examines this property from the viewpoint of security.

   a. From the point of view of assurance, what problems might dynamic loading introduce? (*Hint*: Think about the assumptions the programmer made when writing the code that calls the library functions.)

   b. Does dynamic loading violate any of Saltzer and Schroeder's principles of secure design?[89] Justify your answer.

   c. If an attacker wanted to implant a Trojan horse into as many processes as possible, how would dynamic loading lower the amount of work that the attacker would need to do?

4. Suppose there is no system dedicated to the bootable media discussed in Section 29.7.2. How would you go about constructing such a bootable media? Discuss procedures, and justify them. What is the problem with updating a running system and writing only the changes onto the write-once media?

5. The web server system on the DMZ renames temporary files used to record transactions. The name has the form *trans* followed by the integer representation of the date and time, followed by one or more digits. Why are the extra digits necessary?

6. Consider a developer who has both an ISP workstation and a devnet workstation on his desk, and who wants to move a program from the ISP workstation to the devnet workstation.

   a. Assume that the user is not allowed to mount media such as a DVD. Thus, he would not be able to access the data on the disk as though it were a file system. Would he be able to access the data in some other

---

[89] See Chapter 14.

way? (*Hint*: Must data on all media be accessed as though it were a file system, or can it be read in some other way?)

b. Assume that the *root* user is asked to mount the DVD for the user, so he can access data on it. What precautions should *root* take before making the data available to the user?

c. Suppose the ISP workstation were removed. How could the Drib prevent the developer from bringing a DVD into his office?

d. Suppose the DVD reader were removed from the development network workstation. Would this solve the problem? Why or why not? Discuss the advantages and disadvantages of this approach.

7. The second line of the web server starting script puts the process ID number of the web server wrapper into a file. Why? (*Hint*: Think of how to terminate the process automatically.)

8. This exercise reconsiders the use of NIS or some other name service to distribute user information such as password hashes.

a. In general, why might an administration want to use encryption techniques to protect the transmission of NIS records over a network?

b. Why is secrecy of the NIS records not important to the system administrators?

c. Assume the devnet firewall (and the inner and outer firewalls) did not prevent outside users from monitoring the development network. How important would secrecy of the NIS records be then? Why?

d. The NIS client accepts the first response to its query that it receives from *any* NIS server. Why is physical control of the development network critical to the decision not to use cryptography to protect the NIS network traffic?

9. The system administrators on the development network believe that any password can be guessed in 180 days of continuous trial and error. They set the lifetime of each password at a maximum of 90 days. After 90 days, a password must be changed. Why did they use 90 days rather than 180 days?

10. Section 29.7.1 discusses using executable scripts on the DMZ web server system. It points out that web pages change too frequently to be placed on write-once media, but that the scripts are changed infrequently enough to allow them to be placed on the media.

a. In light of the fact that the scripts do not contain data, why is their alteration a concern?

b. The scripts can generate web pages from data stored on the server. Discuss the integrity issues arising from storing of the data that those scripts use on writable media but storing of the scripts themselves on read-only media. In particular, how trustworthy are the pages resulting from the script's use of stored data? (*Hint*: See Section 6.2.)

    c. Assume that the scripts are to be changed frequently. Devise a method that allows such changes and also keeps the interface to those scripts on read-only media. Where would you store the actual scripts, and what are the benefits and drawbacks of such a scheme?

11. Brian Reid has noted that "[p]rogrammer convenience is the antithesis of security" [1576]. Discuss how the Drib's trade-off between security and convenience exemplifies the conflict between users (programmers) and security. In particular, when should the principle of least astonishment (see Section 14.2.8) override other principles of secure design?

12. Computer viruses and worms are often transmitted as attachments to electronic mail. The Drib's development network infrastructure directs all electronic mail to a mail server. Consider an alteration of the development network infrastructure whereby workstations download user mail rather than mounting the file system containing the mailboxes.

    a. The Drib has purchased a tool that scans mail as it is being received. The tool looks for known computer worms and viruses in the contents of attachments, and deletes them. Should this antivirus software be installed on the mail server, on the desktop, or on both? Justify your answer.

    b. What other actions should the Drib take to limit incoming computer worms and viruses in attachments? Specifically, what *attributes* should cause the Drib to flag attachments as suspicious, even when the antivirus software reports that the attachment does not contain any known virus?

    c. What procedural mechanisms (such as warnings) should be in place to hinder the execution of computer worms and viruses that are not caught by the antivirus filters? Specifically, what should users be advised to do when asked to execute a set of instructions to (for example) print a pretty picture?

Chapter 30
User Security

COMINIUS: Away! the tribunes do attend you: arm yourself
To answer mildly; for they are prepar'd
With accusations, as I hear, more strong
Than are upon you yet.
— *Coriolanus*, III, ii, 138–141.

Although computer systems provide security mechanisms and policies that can protect users to a great degree, users must also take security precautions for a variety of reasons. First, although system controls limit the access of unauthorized users to the system, such controls often are flawed and may not prevent all such access. Second, someone with access to the system may want to attack an authorized user—for example, by reading confidential or private data or by altering files. The success of such attacks may depend on the victim's failure to take certain precautions. Finally, users may notice problems with their accounts, causing them to suspect compromises. The system administrator can then investigate thoroughly.

This chapter considers a user of a workstation on the development network at the Drib. The user's primary job is to develop products or support for the Drib. It is not to secure her system. We explore the precautions, settings, and procedures that such a user can use to limit the effect of attacks on her account.

30.1 Policy

Most users have informal policies in mind when they decide on security measures to protect their accounts, data, and programs. Few analyze the policies or even write them down. However, as with the development of a network infrastructure, and of the configuration and operation of a system, users' security policies are central to the actions and settings that protect them.

The components of users' policies that we focus on are as follows:

U1. Only users have access to their accounts.

U2. No other user can read or change a file without the owner's permission.

U3. Users shall protect the integrity, confidentiality, and availability of their files.

U4. Users shall be aware of all commands that they enter, or that are entered on their behalf.

30.2   Access

Component U1 requires that users protect access to their accounts. Consider the ways in which users gain access to their accounts. These points of entry are ideal places for attackers to attempt to masquerade as users. Hence, they form the first locus of users' defenses.

30.2.1   Passwords

Section 13.3, "Password Selection," discussed the theory behind good password selection. Ideally, passwords should be chosen randomly.[1] In practice, such passwords are difficult to remember. So, either passwords are not assigned randomly, or they require that some information be written down. And if a user chooses a password that is easy to guess, it may cause a violation of policy component U1.

Writing down passwords is popularly considered to be dangerous. In reality, the degree of danger depends on the environment in which the system is accessed and on the manner in which the password is recorded.

EXAMPLE: Consider the isolated system that the development network administrators use to create the CD-ROM from which other workstations boot (see Section 29.7.2). This system is kept in a locked room, and only the authorized users of the system have keys. The system is not connected to networks or telephone lines and can be accessed only from within that room. The password for the role account used to construct the CD-ROM is written on a whiteboard in the room. Given that all users of the isolated system are authorized to know that password, and that anyone else entering the room is under observation, this arrangement meets policy component U1. (But see Exercise 1.)

Users with accounts on many systems will choose the same password for each system, choose passwords that follow a pattern, or write passwords down.[2]

---

[1] See Section 13.3.1, "Random Selection of Passwords."
[2] See Section 13.3.3, "User Selection of Passwords."

On the development network, the first of these is a result of centralizing the user database. Even there, users (especially system administrators) may have multiple accounts, including some on infrastructure systems that do not use the centralized user database. These users must take precautions to protect their passwords.

EXAMPLE: The development network has 10 infrastructure systems (mail, file, web, and other servers). Anne and Paul are the lead system administrators for the infrastructure systems. They must have privileged access to all those systems. To make the *root* and *Administrator* passwords as difficult as possible to guess, those passwords are chosen randomly. But Paul and Anne cannot remember 10 random passwords. Instead, each has decided on a transformation algorithm.[3] Anne's is "Change the third letter's case, and delete the last character." Paul's is "Add 2 mod 10 to the first digit, and delete the first letter." The following table summarizes the actual passwords and what Paul and Anne have written on small pieces of paper that they carry with them.

Actual password	Anne's version	Paul's version
IbhEpZqYre<7RCPI	IbHEpZqYre<7RCPI$	QIbhEpZqYre<5RCPI
t/?rctp*e(V(R9v-	t/?rCtp*e(V(R9v-p	Rt/?rctp*e(V(R7v-
(tY8t#`M!8J,8?gc	(tY8T#`M!8J,8?gc%	(mtY8t#`M!6J,8?gc
Ym=.P.sIwW*u2F!j	Ym=.p.sIwW*u2F!j(	sYm=.P.sIwW*u0F!j
P8%KJ'TiGx@9P+j.	P8%Kj'TiGx@9P+j.r	aP6%KJ'TiGx@9P+j.
IOKFsnNS=m:1Xuqe	IOkFsnNS=m:1Xuqe,	TIOKFsnNS=m:9Xuqe
kaE6el#:?[ODeSDJ	kae6el#:?[ODeSDJ;	nkaE4el#:?[ODeSDJ
I.Jc&G/+zXXd4(Au	I.JC&G/+zXXd4(Au*	fI.Jc&G/+zXXd2(Au
@pa/63yb*:vaR2UD	@pa/63Yb*:vaR2UD=	@Vpa/43yb*:vaR2UD
8dpq:L9;'5wW<RY7	8dpQ:L9;'5wW<RY7+	g6dpq:L9;'5wW<RY7

If someone obtains either Anne's or Paul's list, the thief will not be able to determine the correct password before Anne or Paul notices that the list is missing and takes appropriate action.

The users of development network workstations can choose their own passwords, but a proactive password checking program checks the proposed password before accepting it.[4] The proactive password checker rejects proposed passwords that are deemed too easy to guess.[5] Most users choose verses of poetry or sayings, and use them to generate their passwords.

---

[3]See Section 13.3.1, "Random Selection of Passwords."
[4]See Section 13.3.3, "User Selection of Passwords."
[5]An example set of criteria begins on page 421.

EXAMPLE: The third verse of the nonsense poem *Jabberwocky* [355] is

> He took his vorpal sword in hand:
> Long time the manxome foe he sought—
> So rested he by the Tumtum tree,
> And stood awhile in thought.

Marilyn, a developer at the Drib, chose her password by taking the first letter of the second and fourth words from each line, the last letter of the third and fifth words on each line, putting various nonalphanumerics between them, and her age (22) after. Her password is "ttrs-vmbi&seee+deet22".

30.2.2   The Login Procedure

The Drib uses two-factor login. Every Drib system is equipped with a fingerprint scanner. To log in, the user must supply her login name and authentication information. First, the user obtains a prompt at which she can enter the information. She is then prompted to use the fingerprint scanner to supply biometric data. The data is encrypted using a session key shared with the biometric validation server; this key is different each time the fingerprint scanner is used. If the fingerprint is validated, the user obtains access; otherwise, access is denied. The fingerprint is requested at all login attempts, so the user is not told whether the login name, password, or biometric is incorrect when access is denied.

This approach has another advantage. In order to communicate with the Drib servers, the client must have the private key associated with the public key for the client. The public key is resident on the Drib servers. Thus, only someone with access to the Drib's authorized clients can access the Drib's network. This is intended to limit access to those whom the Drib authorizes when the client (for example, a laptop) is off-site.

If only passwords are used, there is a potential attack that arises from the lack of mutual authentication on most systems. An attacker may place a program at the access point that emulates the login prompt sequence. Then, if the user has a reusable password, the name and password are captured. Crude versions of this Trojan horse[6] save the name and password to a file and then terminate by spawning a legitimate login session. The user will be re-prompted for the information. Most users simply assume that they have mistyped some part of the password (which, after all, is usually not printed) and proceed to repeat the login procedure. A more sophisticated version saves the name and password to a file and then spawns the login process and feeds it the name and password. The program terminates, giving control of the access point to the login process.

---

[6]See Section 23.2, "Trojan Horses."

EXAMPLE: Students at many university sites in the 1970s tried this attack in public terminal rooms. They had varying degrees of success. An early version of one operating system had a feature that defeated the crude versions of this attack. If a user mistyped his name or password, the login program would re-prompt him for this information. However, the prompt for the user name would change from "Login:" to "Name:." If a user saw the prompt "Login:" twice in a row, he had reason to believe that a spoof was underway.

EXAMPLE: Secure Xenix [775] had an alternative approach that is common to systems that desire high assurance authentication of users. When a user wished to log in, he struck a particular combination of keys that created a trusted path to the kernel. No application program could disable this feature; no application program could read or alter the information given to the kernel over that path. The kernel then performed the identification and authentication processing and granted or denied the user access.

Windows systems have a similar feature. The control-alt-delete key sequence is trapped by the operating system. Typing this sequence to begin logging in ensures the user is connected to the authentication system of Windows and not a rogue program impersonating the login procedure.[7] Once logged in, that key sequence invokes the Windows task manager.

A second potential attack arises from an attacker reading the password as it is entered. At a later date, the attacker can reuse the password. This differs from the first attack in that it succeeds even when the user and system mutually authenticate each other. The problem is that the password is no longer confidential.

EXAMPLE: "Shoulder surfing" is a technique in which an attacker watches the target enter the password. Variations on this attack include reading of the characters from kernel variables, which requires that the attacker have access to those structures (usually as a result of a system configuration error[8]), and passive wiretapping of an unenciphered connection.

The latter opportunity for reading the password is important. Many protocols, such as *ftp* and *telnet*, do not encipher messages. If a user name and password are sent over such a connection, they are visible at every intermediate node and network. Other protocols, such as SSH and TLS, provide enciphered tunnels through which other protocols can be sent.[9] This provides the user with confidentiality even when the protocols themselves do not. In some environments, this is unnecessary. For example, the Drib firewalls block any traffic to the Internet, and hosts and networks within the Drib are trusted not to capture network traffic. In other environments, *especially when messages are sent over untrusted links*, enciphering of all messages is prudent.

---

[7]A system administrator can disable this.
[8]See Section 29.2.2, "The Development System."
[9]See the examples in Section 12.5, "Example Protocols."

The second potential attack is thwarted by use of the biometric. The first may be; it depends on whether the Trojan horse can read the biometric data and encrypt it using the session key supplied by the biometric validator. If so, then it can replay the login.

As part of the login procedure, many systems print useful information. If the date, time, and location of the last successful login are shown, the user can verify that no one has used her account since she last did. If the access point is shown, the user can determine if some program is intercepting and rerouting her communications.

EXAMPLE: Suppose a user logs in from the console. After the login, the system prints a message indicating that she last successfully logged in on the previous Tuesday and was currently using a network terminal. The time of login happens to be correct, but the terminal is not, and the user should contact the system administrator. One possible explanation is that a Trojan horse is capturing all commands, saving them in a file, and then passing the commands back to the normal system login process over a network connection.

Policy component U1 suggests that the user should be alert when logging in. If something suspicious occurs, or the link to the system is not physically or cryptographically protected, an unauthorized user may acquire access to the system.

30.2.2.1   Trusted Hosts

The notion of "trusted hosts" comes from the belief that if two hosts are under the same administrative control, each can rely on the other to authenticate a user. It allows certain mechanisms, such as backups, to be automated without placing passwords or cryptographic keys on the system.

EXAMPLE: The Drib uses a remote backup scheme run from a backup system. It logs into each system as the user *backup* and executes a backup program. The backup program sends the data to be backed up over the network connection. If logging in required a password, then an administrator password would have to be present on the backup system. The Drib development network administrators considered this to be an unacceptable risk. Instead, they made all systems trust the backup host. Then the backup user could simply log in without a password.

The trusted host mechanism requires accurate identification of the connecting host. The primary identification token of a host is its IP address,[10] but the authentication mechanism can be either the IP address itself [1005] or a challenge-response exchange[11] based on cryptography [2059]. The Drib uses the latter. This prevents IP spoofing.

---

[10]See Section 15.6.1, "Host Identity."
[11]See Section 13.6, "Challenge-Response."

The development network workstations use the cryptographically based trusted host mechanism. The implementation provides enciphered and integrity-checked connections. Because all development network workstations use the same user information database, a developer need only log in to one using a password. She can then access any workstation on that subnet.

Hence, the development network provides an infrastructure that supports this aspect of policy component U1.

30.2.3   Leaving the System

The Drib has many physical and procedural controls that limit access to its facility, but some people not authorized to use the systems have access to the rooms in which those systems reside. For example, custodians clean the rooms. If lights or air conditioning units need to be repaired, maintenance workers need entry. Hence, physical security is not sufficient to control access to the systems.

Users must authenticate themselves to begin a session. However, once authenticated, the user must also control access to the session. A common problem is that users will leave their sessions unattended—for example, by walking away from their monitors to go to the bathroom. If a custodian came into the room, she would see that the monitor was logged in and could enter commands, thereby obtaining access to the system even though she was not authorized to do so.

When a user of a system leaves a session unattended, he must restrict physical access to the endpoint of the session.[12] When that endpoint is a monitor or terminal, a screen locking program provides an appropriate defense against this threat.

EXAMPLE: The X window system provides a program called *xlock*. When run, *xlock* blocks access to the monitor until the user's password is entered. Only the user or the system administrator can terminate the program without the password by sending an appropriate termination signal to it from another session.

Screen locking programs may have security holes. The most common is a "master password" that unlocks the terminal if the user forgets the password used to lock it.[13]

EXAMPLE: In one version of the UNIX operating system, the *lock* program prompted the user for a password and then locked access to the terminal until the password was entered. If the user forgot the password, the master password "Hasta la vista!" would unlock the terminal. (See Exercise 2.)

---

[12] See Section 14.2.1, "Principle of Least Privilege."

[13] Section 1.4, "Assumptions and Trust," discusses the role of beliefs underlying security mechanisms such as a screen locking program. Section 19.1.3, "Assurance throughout the Life Cycle," discusses the role of assurance in developing software.

30.3   Files and Devices

Users keep information and programs in files. This makes file protection a security mechanism that users can manipulate to refine the protection afforded their data. Similarly, users manipulate the system through devices of various types. Their protection is to some degree under the user's control. This section explores both.

30.3.1   Files

Users must protect confidentiality and integrity of the files to satisfy policy component U2. To this end, they use the protection capabilities of the system to constrain access. Complicating the situation is the interpretation of permissions on the containing directories.

EXAMPLE: Peter is using a UNIX-based system. He wants to allow Deborah to read the file design but prevent other users from doing so. He can use the abbreviated ACL mechanism of standard UNIX systems[14] to do this in three ways.

If Deborah and Peter are the only members of a group, Peter can make the file owned by that group and readable by that group but not readable by others.

If Deborah is the only member of a group and the UNIX system semantics allow the owner of a file to give the file to a group of which the owner is not a member, Peter can give group ownership of the file to Deborah's group and then set the group ownership privileges as described above.

An alternative approach is to set permissions on the containing directory. Peter can set the permissions of the directory to allow search access only for himself and for the group of which Deborah is the only member by turning on read and execute permissions for the group owner of the directory. Then the protections of the file can allow anyone to read the file. Because only Peter and Deborah can search the directory (the execute permission), only they can reach the file.

This example illustrates the cumbersome nature of abbreviated ACLs (see Exercise 3; Exercise 4 explores an approach to the situation in which Peter and Deborah are the only members in common to two groups). Ordinary ACLs make the task considerably simpler.

EXAMPLE: The Windows 10 access control lists[15] allow Peter to give Deborah access directly. Peter creates an ACL for design with two entries:

```
(Peter, full control)  (Deborah, read)
```

The semantics of Windows 10 disallow access to any user or group omitted from the ACL. Hence, only Peter and Deborah can access the file.

---

[14]See Section 16.1.1, "Abbreviations of Access Control Lists."

[15]See Section 16.1.4, "Example: NTFS and Access Control Lists."

Users can control several aspects of file protection. The remainder of this section explores some of these aspects.

30.3.1.1 File Permissions on Creation

Many systems allow users to specify a template of permissions to be given to a file when it is created. The owner can then modify this set as required.

EXAMPLE: When Roger creates a directory on Windows 10, it inherits the ACL of its parent directory.

UNIX-like systems take an alternative approach. A user can identify specific permissions to be *denied* on creation.

The variable *umask* contains a set of permissions to be disabled. It uses the nine-bit format of the standard UNIX protection mask, in which the first set of three bits corresponds to the owner, the second set corresponds to the group, and the third set corresponds to others (everyone except the owner and members of the group). The first bit in each triplet controls read access, the second bit controls write access, and the third bit controls execute access. So, if a user sets her *umask* to 022, then, when she creates a file, group and other write permissions are turned off, *regardless* of the permissions she requested. If she wants the group members to have write access, she can use a command or system call such as *chmod* to enable that access. (See Exercise 5.)

30.3.1.2 Group Access

Group access provides a selected set of users with the same access rights.[16] The problem is that the membership of the group is not under the control of the owner of the file. This has an advantage and a disadvantage.

The advantage arises when the group is used as a role.[17] Then, as users are allowed to assume the role, their access to the file is altered. Because the owner of the file is concerned only with controlling access of those role users, reconfiguration of the access to the role reconfigures user access to the file, which is what the user wants.

EXAMPLE: Tom is working on a project to develop the next generation of widgets, called Widget-NG. All members of the Widget-NG design team are in the group *widgetngd*. The files that contain the design are group-owned by *widgetngd*, and the members of that group can read from and write to the file.

Even when the membership of the group changes, the function of the group does not. Hence, the new users are given access to the Widget-NG information. The group ownership mechanism provides that access.

---

[16]See Section 15.4, "Groups and Roles."
[17]See Section 15.4, "Groups and Roles."

The disadvantage arises when a group is used as a shorthand for a set of specific users. If the membership of the group changes, unauthorized users may obtain access to the file, or authorized users may be denied access to the file.

EXAMPLE: Maria wants her friends Anne and Joan to have access to the file *movies*. She has the system administrator create a group called *maj*, which contains those three users, and makes the file group-owned, readable, and writable by the group *maj*.

The system administrator is later asked to create a group containing Maria, Anne, Joan, and Lorraine. He notices that the group *maj* contains three of those four users, and he simply adds Lorraine to the group. Now Lorraine can read and alter the file *movies*, even though Maria never intended for her to do so.

In general, users should limit access as much as possible when creating new files. So ACLs and C-Lists should include as few entries as possible, and permissions for each entry should be as restrictive as possible. Constructs such as the *umask* should be set to deny permissions to as many users as possible (in the specific case of UNIX systems, *umask* should deny all permissions to all but the owner, unless there are specific reasons to set it differently).

30.3.1.3 File Deletion

A user deletes a file. Either the file data or the file name is discarded. The effects of these differ widely.

Computer systems store files on disk. The *file attribute table* contains information about the file. The *file mapping table* contains information that allows the operating system to locate the disk blocks that compose the file. Systems represent a file being in a directory in a variety of ways. All involve an entry in the directory for that file, but the entry may contain attribute information (such as permissions and file type) or may merely point to an entry in the file attribute table.

> **Definition 30–1.** A *direct alias* is a directory entry that points to (names) the file. An *indirect alias* is a directory entry that points to a special file containing the name of the target file. The operating system interprets the indirect alias by substituting the contents of the special file for the name of the indirect alias file.

All direct aliases that name the same file are equal. Each direct alias is an alternative name for the same file.[18]

The representation of containment in a directory affects security. If each direct alias can have different permissions, the owner of a file must change the access modes of each alias in order to control access. To avoid this, most systems

---

[18]See Section 15.2, "Files and Objects."

associate the file attribute information with the actual data, and directory entries consist of a pointer to the file attribute table.

When a user deletes a file, the directory entry is removed. The system tracks the number of directory entries for each file, and when that number becomes 0, the data blocks and table entries for that file are released. This means that deleting a file does *not* ensure that the file is unavailable; it merely deletes the directory entry.

EXAMPLE: Anna uses a UNIX-based system. She has a program *runasanna* that is setuid to herself.[19] She wishes to delete it so that no one can use it. However, if she executes the command

```
rm runasanna
```

she will delete the directory entry for that file. If no one else has a direct alias (or, in UNIX terminology, a *hard link*) to the file, it will be removed from the system.

Sandra, however, has made a direct alias to the file. Anna has deleted the file, but there is still a directory entry (Sandra's direct alias) corresponding to the file, so the file has not been deleted. Sandra can still execute the program. Because it is still setuid to Anna, the program runs with Anna's, not Sandra's, permissions.

On UNIX systems, Anna can delete the file from Sandra's directory only if Sandra has given Anna write permission to the directory. To prevent anyone from using the program, Anna must change the permissions of the program to disable it. She can then delete her direct alias. The first line turns off *all* access permissions to the file, including the setuid permission.

```
chmod 000 runasanna
rm runasanna
```

Sandra will retain her alias, and the program will still reside on disk, but it will be useless.

The second issue affecting file deletion is persistence. When a file is deleted, its disk blocks are returned to the pool of unused disk blocks, and they may be reused. However, the data on them remains, and if an attacker can read those blocks, he may read information that was intended to be confidential. When sensitive files are deleted, the contents should be erased before deletion.[20]

EXAMPLE: Many Windows and Macintosh system utilities programs have mechanisms for "wiping" files before they are deleted. These mechanisms overwrite the contents of the file with a bit pattern. The patterns used, and the number of times the contents of the file are overwritten, are configurable. Some versions of the *rm* (file deletion) command on UNIX systems have a similar option.

---

[19]See Section 15.3, "Users."
[20]See, for example, Section 22.2.1.1, "TCSEC Functional Requirements" and Section 22.8.3, "CC Security Functional Requirements."

The third issue lies in the difference between direct and indirect aliases. When a command that affects a file is executed, it may have different effects depending on whether the file is a direct alias or an indirect alias. This may mislead a user into believing that certain information has been protected or deleted when in fact the protection or deletion applied only to the indirect alias and not to the file itself.

EXAMPLE: Suppose Angie executes a command to add read permission to a file for Lucy. If the file is a direct alias, Lucy will be able to read the contents of the file, but if it is an indirect alias, does Lucy have permission to read the file or the indirect alias file? The answer depends entirely on the semantics of the system. The semantics may not be consistent. For example, on Fedora Linux release 25, the *chmod* command changes the permissions of the file named by the indirect alias, whereas the *rm* command deletes the indirect alias file itself.

30.3.2   Devices

Users communicate with the system through devices. The devices may be virtual, such as network ports, or physical, such as terminals. Policy components U1 and U4 require that these devices be protected so that the user can control what commands are sent to the system in her name and so that others are prevented from seeing her interactions.

30.3.2.1   Writable Devices

Devices that allow any user to write to them can pose serious security problems. Unless necessary for the correct functioning of the system, devices should restrict write access as much as possible.[21] Two examples will demonstrate why.

EXAMPLE: Many systems have tape drives set so that anyone can write to them. When a process begins writing, the ACL of the device changes so that only that process (or the user executing the process) can write to the device. However, between the mounting of the media and the execution of the process is an interval during which another user's process can access the tape drive and read, or overwrite, the tape. For this reason, users should always write-protect mounted media unless they are to be altered.[22] If possible, processes should be attached to such devices, or the devices should be locked to prevent anyone except the user from accessing them, before the media are mounted.

EXAMPLE: If any user can write to another user's terminal, an attacker can erase the terminal screen by writing an appropriate control sequence to it. On some early UNIX systems, such a denial of service attack could terminate sessions because

---

[21] See Section 14.2.1, "Principle of Least Privilege."
[22] See Section 14.2.2, "Principle of Fail-Safe Defaults."

the attacker could set the communications speed of the terminal line to 0. The terminal session would immediately terminate [212].

The development network users have a default configuration that denies write privileges to everyone except the user of a terminal.

30.3.2.2   Smart Terminals

A *smart terminal* provides built-in mechanisms for performing special functions. Most importantly, a smart terminal can perform a *block send*. Using this mode, a process can instruct a terminal to send a set of characters that are printed on the screen. The instructions are simply a sequence of characters that the process sends to the terminal. This can be used to implant a Trojan horse.[23]

EXAMPLE: Robert wants to trick Craig into executing the command

```
chmod 666 .profile
```

so that Robert can add commands to Craig's startup file. Robert carefully crafts a letter that contains the following:

```
Dear Craig,
Please be careful. Someone may ask you to execute
chmod 666 .profile
You shouldn't do it!
Your friend,
Robert
<BLOCK SEND (-3,18), (-3,18)>
<BLOCK SEND (-4,0), (-4,18)><CLEAR>
```

The sequence

```
<BLOCK SEND (a,b), (c,d)>
```

sends all characters from screen position (a,b) to position (c,d) to the system, as though the user had typed them. On Craig's terminal, a newline is stored as an invisible character at the end of each line. The sequence

```
<CLEAR>
```

clears the terminal screen. When Craig reads this letter, the command

```
!chmod 666 .profile
```

will be sent to the system as though the user had typed it. In this particular mail reading program, the "!" causes the mail program to send the rest of the line to a command interpreter. That interpreter promptly executes the forbidden command and clears the screen to hide the visible traces of the command.

---

[23]See Section 23.2, "Trojan Horses."

The difference between a smart terminal and a writable terminal is subtle. Only the user of the terminal need have write access to the smart terminal, whereas the earlier attacks required the attacker as well as the user of the terminal to be able to write to the terminal. An attacker must therefore trick the user into reading data in order to spring the smart terminal attack. This requires malicious logic (or, in this context, malicious data).[24]

30.3.2.3   Monitors and Characters

A more subtle form of this attack involves the use of Unicode characters that resemble, but are not, Latin characters [513]. This attack, called an *international domain name homograph attack*, is particularly effective in phishing attacks.[25]

EXAMPLE: As in the example in Section 23.6.6, Heidi banks at Big Bank, with a URL of www.bigbank.com. She receives an email from the bank that says she must go the the bank's web page in the next three days to verify her telephone number, or the bank will disable her account. The letter contains a URL of the page she is to go to:

```
<a href="https://www.bigbank.com">https://www.bigbank.com</a>
```

She carefully checks the underlying URL, and sees the above. Believing it is safe, she clicks on the link. And as in the earlier example, she goes to the attackers' website—because the "a" in the actual URL is a Cyrillic letter, not the Latin letter that the bank uses.

30.3.2.4   Monitors and Window Systems

Window systems provide a graphical user interface to a system. Typically, a process called the *window manager* controls what is displayed on the monitor and accepts input from input devices. Other processes, called *clients*, register with the window manager. They can then receive input from the window manager and send output to the window manager. The window manager draws the output on the monitor screen if appropriate. The window manager is also responsible for routing input to the correct client.

The obvious question is how the window manager determines which clients it may talk to. If an attacker is able to register a client with the window manager, the attacker can intercept input and send bogus output to the monitor.

EXAMPLE: In some versions of the X window system [747], it was possible for an attacker to overlay an invisible window the size of the monitor screen. The attacker could then record all mouse motions and keystrokes from that monitor

---

[24]See Chapter 23, "Malware."
[25]See Section 23.6.6, "Phishing."

and then transmit them to the appropriate window on the screen. The effect was to record everything, including passwords and cryptographic keys. Effectively, this was a keylogger.

Window systems can use any of the access control mechanisms described in Chapter 16 to control access to the window manager. The granularity of the access control mechanism varies among different window systems.

EXAMPLE: The X window system controls access on the basis of host name or possession of a token [1394]. If access is granted to the window manager, the client may control the display. The window manager cannot control which parts of the display, or which clients, the new client communicates with. The X window system offers two modes of control. Neither provides any confidentiality.

The first mode, called the *xhost* method, determines the name of the host from which the client is trying to connect.[26] The window manager then checks a list of hosts from which processes are authorized to connect. If the process comes from one of those hosts, access is granted. Otherwise, access is denied.

The second mode, called the *xauth* method, requires that a process be able to supply a fixed random number (called a *magic cookie*).[27] When the X window manager starts, it creates (or is given) a magic cookie. This cookie is stored in the file .*Xauthority* in the user's home directory. Any client that attempts to connect to the window manager for that user's display must supply that magic cookie. If the process is local and is run by the user, it can obtain the magic cookie directly from the .*Xauthority* file. If the process is to be run on a remote host, the user must ensure that the process has the magic cookie before it connects to the window manager (this is usually done by copying the .*Xauthority* file to the remote system).

30.4   Processes

Processes manipulate objects, including files. Policy component U3 requires the user to be aware of how processes manipulate files. This section examines several aspects of this requirement.

30.4.1   Copying and Moving Files

Copying a file duplicates its contents. The semantics of the copy command determine if the file attributes are also copied. If the attributes are not copied, the user may need to take steps to preserve the integrity and confidentiality of the file.

---

[26]See Section 15.6.1, "Host Identity."
[27]See Section 15.6.2, "State and Cookies."

EXAMPLE: Suppose Mona Anne wants to copy the file *xyzzy* on a UNIX system. She gives the following command:

```
cp xyzzy plugh
```

If the file *plugh* does not exist, this command creates it and copies the contents of *xyzzy* into it. The permissions will be the same as for *xyzzy*, except that the setuid and setgid attributes will be discarded if she does not own *xyzzy* (see Section 30.4.5).

If the file *plugh* exists, the command copies the contents of *xyzzy* into it. It does not alter the permissions of *plugh*. This is a security problem, because if *xyzzy* is not readable by everyone but *plugh* is, the contents of *xyzzy* will no longer be confidential because anyone reading *plugh* will learn them.

Similarly, sometimes the semantics of moving files involve copying a file and deleting the original copy. In this case, the file attributes of the move command follow those of the copy command. Otherwise, the move command may preserve the attributes of the original command.

EXAMPLE: Now Mona Anne decides to move the file *plugh* to another directory. She gives the command

```
mv plugh /usr/monaanne/advent
```

If the directory resides in the same file system, the direct alias is deleted from the current directory and placed in the directory */usr/monaanne/advent*. Otherwise, the *mv* command executes:

```
cp plugh /usr/monaanne/advent/plugh
rm plugh
```

In the first case, the permissions of *plugh* are preserved. In the second, those permissions may be changed, as noted above.

The semantics of the commands, and how well the user knows those semantics and can take steps to handle potential security problems, affect their ability to satisfy policy component U3.

30.4.2   Accidentally Overwriting Files

Part of policy component U3 is to protect users from themselves.[28] Sometimes people make mistakes when they enter commands. These mistakes can have unpleasant consequences.

---

[28] See Section 14.2.2, "Principle of Fail-Safe Defaults."

EXAMPLE: Scout wants to delete all the files in her directory whose names end in the characters ".o". She uses the pattern "*.o" to match these file names. The "*" is a wildcard that matches 0 or more characters, so the pattern is read as "all file names that end in .o". Unfortunately, she mistypes the command, putting a space between the "*" and the ".o" accidentally:

```
rm * .o
```

This command says to delete all files in the current directory, and the file ".o". Scout will discover this when the command prints the error message

```
.o: No such file or directory
```

after all the files have been deleted.

Many programs that delete or overwrite files have an interactive mode. Before any file is deleted or overwritten, the program requests confirmation that the user intends for this to happen.[29] Policy component U3 strongly suggests that these modes be used. In fact, the development workstations have these modes set in user startup files. The users can disable the modes, but generally do not.

30.4.3 Encryption, Cryptographic Keys, and Passwords

The basis for encryption is trust. Cryptographic considerations aside, if the encryption and decryption are done on a multiuser system, the cryptographic keys are potentially visible to anyone who can read memory and, possibly, swap space. Anyone who can alter the programs used to encipher and decipher the files, or any of the supporting tools (such as the operating system), can also obtain the cryptographic keys or the cleartext data itself. For this reason, unless users trust the privileged users,[30] and trust that other users cannot acquire the privileges needed to read memory, swap space, or alter the relevant programs, the sensitive data should never be on the system in cleartext.[31]

EXAMPLE: PGP protects a user's private key by enciphering it with a passphrase. Mary Ann receives a letter that the sender has enciphered for confidentiality using PGP. She enters her passphrase to allow the PGP deciphering program to obtain her private key. It uses her key to decipher the data encryption key, and then the message. Unknown to Mary Ann, Eve has broken into her system and has implanted a keystroke recording module. When Eve retrieves the log of the session, she will have the passphrase, from which she can obtain Mary Ann's private key, and thus her identity (as far as Mary Ann's PGP recipients are concerned).

---

[29] See Section 14.2.8, "Principle of Least Astonishment."
[30] Here, "privileged users" means those who can read memory, swap space, or alter system programs.
[31] See Section 14.2.1, "Principle of Least Privilege."

The saving of passwords on a multiuser system suffers from the same problem. In addition, some programs that allow users to put passwords into a file do not rely on enciphering the passwords; they simply require the user to set file permissions so that only the owner can read the file.

EXAMPLE: An implementation of the *ftp* client under some versions of the UNIX system allows users to keep account names, host names, and passwords in a file called *.netrc*. Kathy uses the remote host *gleep* to store files, so she often connects using *ftp*. Her *.netrc* file looks like this:

```
machine gleep
login kathy
password oi4ety98
```

The security risks of keeping her information in this file were brought home when one day *ftp* ignored the file. On investigation, Kathy determined that the *.netrc* file was readable by all users on the system. By looking at her previously typed commands, Kathy realized that she had mistyped one of them. The unfortunate effect of that command was to make the *.netrc* file readable.

The circumstances under which a password should reside in a system are few.[32] Unless unavoidable, no password should reside unenciphered in a system, either on disk or in memory. The Drib has modified its *ftp* programs to ignore *.netrc* files. This discourages their use. Furthermore, system administrators have embedded a check for such files in their audit tools that check the systems.

30.4.4   Startup Settings

Many programs, such as text editors and command interpreters, use startup information. These variables and files contain commands that are executed when the program begins but before any input is accepted from the user. The set of startup files, and the order in which they are accessed, affect the execution of the program.

EXAMPLE: When a user logs in to a FreeBSD 11.0 system, her login shell *sh* initializes itself by accessing startup information in the following order:

1. The contents of the startup file */etc/profile*

2. The contents of the startup file *.profile* in the user's home directory

3. The contents of the startup file named in the environment variable **ENV**

If any of these files do not exist, the step is skipped.

---

[32]See Section 14.2.2, "Principle of Fail-Safe Defaults."

The security threat lies in the program's trust of the startup information. For example, if the environment variable **ENV** were to name a file that an untrusted user could alter, then that user could insert commands to delete files or give the attacker privileges to perform actions that violate policy. This Trojan horse can be difficult to detect, especially because it can erase itself after execution but before the shell allows interaction.

30.4.5   Limiting Privileges

Users should know which of their programs grant additional privileges to others. They should also understand the implications of granting such privileges.

EXAMPLE: Part of Toni's job as a secretary to the manager of the Drib Development Group is to read mail sent to her boss, Fran. Because Fran knew about the dangers of sharing passwords, she copied the UNIX command interpreter into a file that she owned, and turned on the setuid permission.[33] This allowed Toni to read Fran's mail.

Toni quickly discovered that the command interpreter allowed her to do anything as Fran. She suggested to Fran that perhaps some other approach could be found.[34] After some discussion, the two decided to forward to Toni a copy of every letter that Fran received. This enabled Toni to process Fran's mail without having access to her account.

The two had considered an alternative approach—to make a copy of the mail reading program setuid to Fran. Unfortunately, the mail program had an escape mechanism that allowed the user to pass commands to a command interpreter—and that had the same effect as giving Toni the shell.

30.4.6   Malicious Logic

Section 29.2.2 discusses mechanisms for preventing users from bringing malicious software from outside the development network. However, insiders can write malicious programs in order to gain additional privileges or to sabotage others' work. Also, if an attacker breaks in, he may not acquire the desired privileges and may leave traps for authorized users to spring. Hence, users need to take precautions.

> **Definition 30–2.** A *search path* is a sequence of directories that a system uses to locate an object (program, library, or file).

Because programs rely on search paths, users must take care to set theirs appropriately.

---

[33]See Section 15.3, "Users."
[34]See Section 14.2.2, "Principle of Fail-Safe Defaults."

EXAMPLE: Johannes's coworker wants to see Johannes's confidential designs. The coworker has created a small program called *ls* that will copy the designs to a public area, from which the coworker can retrieve them. She has placed copies of *ls* in various publicly writable directories, including */tmp*. Johannes changed to that directory to clean up files he had left there. Johannes's program search path was

```
.  /bin /usr/bin /usr/local/bin
```

where "." means the current directory. Johannes executed the *ls* program. The command interpreter first looked in the current directory for an executable named *ls*, found it, and executed it. The coworker got the desired files.

Some systems have many types of search paths. In addition to searching for executables, a common search path contains directories that are used to search for libraries when the system supports dynamic loading. In this case, an attacker can create a new library that the unsuspecting victim will load, much as Johannes executed the wrong program in the example above.[35]

Part of policy component U4 requires that the users have only trusted directories in their search paths. Here, "trusted" means that only trusted users can alter the contents of the directory. The default startup files for all the development workstation users have search paths set in this way.[36]

30.5   Electronic Communications

Electronic communications deserves discussion to emphasize the importance of users understanding basic security precautions. Electronic mail may pass through firewalls (as the Drib policy allows; see Section 28.3). Although it can be checked for malicious content, such checking cannot detect all forms of such content.[37] Finally, users may unintentionally send out more material than they realize. Hence, users must understand the threats and follow the procedures that are appropriate to the site policy.

30.5.1   Automated Electronic Mail Processing

Some users automate the processing of electronic mail. When mail arrives, a program determines how to handle it. The mail may be stored for the user, or

---

[35]See Section 24.2.9, "Example: Penetrating a UNIX System."
[36]See Section 14.2.2, "Principle of Fail-Safe Defaults."
[37]See Section 23.8, "Theory of Computer Viruses."

it may be interpreted as a sequence of commands causing execution of either programs already on the system or part of the content of the message, or both. The danger is that the execution may have unintended side effects.

EXAMPLE: The NIMDA worm [1230] used several methods to propagate itself. One method involved the use of email. The worm would mail itself to a user on the target system, encapsulated as an attachment to a letter. When the user opened the letter, the default configuration of the mail programs involved would pass the attachment to another program to be displayed. The other program would execute the code comprising the worm, thereby infecting the system.

The WannaCry ransomware, which was also a worm, worked similarly [427, 1912]. When U.K. National Health Service personnel opened an email attachment, the WannaCry program was started. It spread among systems by exploiting a vulnerability in the implementation of SMB on various types of Windows systems. It is believed to have spread to other institutions through a combination of phishing and exploiting the SMB vulnerability.

Electronic mail may come from untrusted sources. Hence, in general, the contents of email messages are not trustworthy. Mail programs should be configured not to execute attachments, or indeed any component of the letter.[38] The trust in the result of such execution is the same as the trust the reader puts in the data contained in the mail message.

30.5.2   Failure to Check Certificates

Electronic signatures can be misleading. In particular, a certificate may validate a signature, but the certificate itself may be compromised, invalid, or expired. Mail reading programs must notify the user of these problems, as well as provide a mechanism for allowing the user to validate certificates.

EXAMPLE: Someone pretending to be a Microsoft employee obtained two certificates that could be used to sign programs under the name of Microsoft Corporation [2247].[39] The issuer (*not* Microsoft Corporation) immediately revoked both certificates and placed them on the Certificate Revocation List,[40] but sites that had not received the revocation notice would accept the certificates as valid and could execute malicious logic that the attackers had signed. Although the mechanism involved used web pages, the generalization to electronic mail is obvious.

The Drib has enhanced all mail reading programs that use certificates to validate the certificates as far as possible. The programs then display the certificates that could not be validated, to allow users to determine how to proceed. It does so in a form designed to minimize the threat of "click-through," where

---

[38] See Section 23.9.2, "Data and Instructions."
[39] See Section 15.5, "Naming and Certificates."
[40] See Section 11.5.2, "Key Revocation."

users simply click acceptance without reading the warning or error messages because there are too many of them.

30.5.3   Sending Unexpected Content

Attachments to electronic mail may contain data of which the sender is not aware. When these files are sent, the recipient may see more than the sender intended.

EXAMPLE: A sales director once sent her sales team a chart showing the effects of a proposed reorganization. Unfortunately, she did not realize that the spreadsheet in which she had created the chart also contained confidential information such as names and addresses, salaries, and personal comments about each employee. The information disrupted the efficiency of the sales force [96].

Some programs perform "rapid saves," in which data is appended to the file and pointers are updated. When the program rereads the file, the document appears as it was last saved, and the extraneous data is ignored. However, if the file is sent to a different system, or if other programs are used to access the file, the "deleted" contents will be accessible.

The users of the development workstations are periodically warned about this risk. Furthermore, all programs with "rapid saves" have them disabled by default.[41]

30.6   Summary

This chapter covered only a few aspects of how users can protect the data and programs with which they work. The security policy of the site and the desires of the user combine to provide a personalized, if unwritten, security policy.

Well-chosen reusable passwords, or (even better) one-time passwords, inhibit unauthorized access. Other authentication mechanisms allow users to control access to some degree on the basis of the host of origin and cryptographic keys (although in some cases the system administrator can override these access controls). Users can prevent interference with their sessions by using enciphered, integrity-checked sessions and by physically securing the monitors or terminals they use to interact with the system (as well as the system of origin, if they are working remotely).

Basic file permission mechanisms help protect the confidentiality and integrity of data and programs. The user can check programs for an "interactive" mode that will require verification of any request to delete or overwrite files. Other aspects of file handling, such as erasing files before deleting them, and verifying that deletion of a file does not delete only an alias and leave the file accessible, also affect file security.

---

[41]See Section 14.2.8, "Principle of Least Astonishment."

Equally important are the controls on devices. The sophistication of most modern equipment allows devices to be programmed from the computer to which they are connected. Hence, devices should be configured to refuse unexpected or untrusted connections. Ideally, access control mechanisms will provide sufficient granularity to allow access based on users or processes.

Processes act on the user's behalf, and can perform any action that the user requests. Malicious logic, or corrupt input, can cause the process to act in ways that the user does not want. Users can minimize this risk by setting up their environments carefully and by not executing untrusted programs or giving untrusted data to trusted programs.

30.7   Research Issues

There is a tension between allowing security features to be highly configurable and expecting users to configure them correctly (as defined by adherence to a security policy). Users view security as an infrastructure measure, designed to support work, and not as an end goal in itself. Because their primary goal is not security, many users find security mechanisms cumbersome and difficult to use. Designing mechanisms that can be readily understood, and that can be configured with a minimum of effort by untrained users, is a critical area of research that has received little attention. Striking the right balance between configurability and usability is a topic that combines security, psychology, and user interfaces.

30.8   Further Reading

Discussions of user level mechanisms in various systems abound. Books on the security of various systems (such as Gibson [767], Garfinkel, Spafford, and Schwartz [747], Kalsi [994], and Soyinka [1795]) focus on the system administration aspects of security but also describe user level mechanisms. Books on how to use the systems (such as Pogue [1527]) cover the material more effectively for ordinary users.

Zurko and Simon discuss the notion of user-centered security as fundamental to secure systems [2112]. This theme has gained acceptance with the recognition of the importance of the user in security. West [1998] gives a good overview of the problem. Security and usability are often seen to conflict. Thus, users choose the action that provides the most direct, immediate benefit. Herley [895] argues that this leads to the rejection of security advice because users feel that understanding and following the advice is a greater burden than dealing with an attack that, to them, appears unlikely. Another study [650] examines how gaps in perception motivate users' security decisions. A second factor is that many security indicators and warnings are simply ineffective. One study [616] examined passive alerts (which do not interrupt the user's task) and active warnings (which force the user to interrupt their task to deal with the warning) in web browsers, and found that most participants heeded active warnings about a spearphishing attack, whereas most ignored passive alerts. Designing warnings that meet users' mental models to better communicate risk in personal firewalls increased the probability that users would act on the warnings [1555]. Acquisti and his colleagues provide an insightful survey and synthesis of many results [13]. Other studies have examined the mental models that guide home computer users in their security interactions [1552, 1975, 1976] and the effect of social influences in those interactions [501, 502, 617].

30.9   Exercises

1. Consider the isolated system described in the first example in Section 30.2.1. If custodians and other people not authorized to use the isolated system were allowed into the room without observation, would that violate policy component U1? Justify your answer.

2. Reconsider the lock program discussed in Section 30.2.3.

   a. The program requires a user to choose a password (rather than using her login password) to lock the screen. Does this violate the principle of least astonishment (see Section 14.2.8)? Justify your answer.

   b. If a user forgets her password, how might she terminate the program without using the master password? (*Hint*: Although she cannot use that terminal, she can use another terminal to access the system.)

   c. How might a user determine the master password? Discuss steps that the implementer could take to prevent such a discovery. In particular, could a per-system master password be implemented (rather than a single master password for the program)? How?

3. The example of Peter and Deborah on the UNIX system in Section 30.3.1 assumes that Deborah is the only member, or that Deborah and Peter are the only members, of a group. If this is not so, can Peter give only himself and Deborah access to the file by using the abbreviated ACL? Explain either how he can or why he cannot.

4. Suppose that Deborah, Peter, and Kathy are the only members of the group *proj* and that Deborah, Peter, and Elizabeth are the only members of the group *exeter*. Show how Peter can restrict access to the file design to himself and Deborah using *only* abbreviated ACLs. (*Hint*: Consider both *design* and its containing directory.)

5. The UNIX *umask* disables access by default. The Windows scheme enables it. Discuss the implications of enabling access by default and of disabling access by default with respect to security. In particular, which of Saltzer and Schroeder's design principles (see Chapter 14, "Design Principles") is violated by either enabling or disabling access by default?

6. Many UNIX security experts say that the umask should be set to 077 (that is, to allow access only to the owner). Why? What problems might this cause?

7. The problem in the example in Section 23.6.6 is that there is no visual difference between the Cyrillic character "a" and the Latin character "a." Thus, Heidi cannot tell that the displayed URL is not the same as the actual URL.

   a. What actions can Heidi take to ensure that the attack fails?
   b. How could the web browser be modified to ensure Heidi knows the two URLs differ?
   c. How could the web browser be modified to detect this attempted attack?

8. For file deletion programs, the goal of an interactive mode is to enable the user to change his or her mind and not delete certain files. Many systems do not provide such a mode on their file deletion programs. Instead, they move deleted files to a holding area. The user can then use another command to actually remove the files from the system. If the system runs out of file system space, it will then automatically delete enough files in the holding area to create the necessary room. Compare and contrast these two approaches. What are the advantages of the interactive mode over the other method, and what are the disadvantages?

Chapter 31
Program Security

<blockquote>
CLOWN: What is he that builds stronger than either
the mason, the shipwright, or the carpenter?
OTHER CLOWN: The gallows-maker; for that frame outlives
a thousand tenants.
— *Hamlet*, V, i, 42–45.
</blockquote>

The software on systems implements many mechanisms that support security. Some of these mechanisms reside in the operating system, whereas others reside in application and system programs. This chapter discusses the design and implementation of a program to grant users increased privileges. It also presents common programming errors that create security problems, and offers suggestions for avoiding those problems. Finally, testing and distribution are discussed.

This chapter shows the development of the program from requirements to implementation, testing, and distribution.

31.1   Problem

The purpose of this chapter is to provide a glimpse of techniques that provide better than ordinary assurance that a program's design and implementation satisfy its requirements. This chapter is not a manual on applying high-assurance techniques. In terms of the techniques discussed in Part VI, "Assurance," this chapter describes low-assurance techniques.

However, given the current state of programming and software development, these low-assurance techniques enable programmers to produce significantly better, more robust, and more usable code than they could produce without these techniques. So, using a methodology similar to the one outlined in this chapter will reduce vulnerabilities and improve both the quality and the security of code.

A specific problem will illustrate the methods in this chapter. On the Drib's development network infrastructure systems, numerous system administrators must assume certain roles, such as *bin* (the installers of software), *mail* (the manager of electronic mail), and *root* (the system administrator). Each of these roles is implemented as a separate account, called a *role account*. Unfortunately, this raises the problem of password management. To avoid this problem, as well as to control when access is allowed, the Drib will implement a program that verifies a user's identity, determines if the requested change of account is allowed, and, if so, places the user in the desired role.

31.2   Requirements and Policy

The problem of sharing a password arises when a system implements administrative roles as separate user accounts.

EXAMPLE: Linux systems implement the administrator role as the account *root* (and several other accounts that have more limited functionality).[1] All individuals who share access to the account know the account's password. If the password is changed, all must be notified. All these individuals must remember to notify the other individuals should they change the password.

An alternative to using passwords is to constrain access on the basis of identity and other attributes. With this scheme, a user would execute a special program that would check the user's identity and any ancillary conditions. If all these conditions were satisfied, the user would be given access to the role account.

31.2.1   Requirements

The first requirement comes directly from the description of the alternative scheme above. The system administrators choose to constrain access through known paths (locations) and at times of day when the user is expected to access the role account.

> **Requirement 31.1.** Access to a role account is based on user, location, and time of request.

Users often tailor their environments to fit their needs. This is also true of role accounts. For example, a role account may use special programs kept in a subdirectory of the role account's home directory. This new directory must be on the role account's search path, and would typically be set in the startup file

---

[1]See Section 14.2.1, "Principle of Least Privilege," for an explanation of how the existence of the *root* account violates the principle of least privilege.

executed when the user logged in. A question is whether the user's environment should be discarded and replaced by the role account's environment, or whether the two environments should be merged. The requirement chosen for this program is as follows.

> **Requirement 31.2.** The settings of the role account's environment shall replace the corresponding settings of the user's environment, but the remainder of the user's environment shall be preserved.

The set of role accounts chosen for access using this scheme is critical. If unrestricted access is given (essentially, a full command interpreter), then any user in the role that maintains the access control information can change that information and acquire unrestricted access to the system. Presumably, if the access control information is kept accessible only to *root*, then the users who can alter the information—all of whom have access to *root*—are trusted. Thus:

> **Requirement 31.3.** Only *root* can alter the access control information for access to a role account.

In most cases, a user assuming a particular role will perform specific actions while in that role. For example, someone who enters the role of *oper* may perform backups but may not use other commands. This restricts the danger of commands interacting with the system to produce undesirable effects (such as security violations) and follows from the principle of least privilege.[2] This form of access is called "restricted access."

> **Requirement 31.4.** The mechanism shall allow both restricted access and unrestricted access to a role account. For unrestricted access, the user shall have access to a standard command interpreter. For restricted access, the user shall be able to execute only a specified set of commands.

Requirement 31.4 implicitly requires that access to the role account be granted to authorized users meeting the conditions in Requirement 31.1. Finally, the role account itself must be protected from unauthorized changes.

> **Requirement 31.5.** Access to the files, directories, and objects owned by any account administered by use of this mechanism shall be restricted to those authorized to use the role account, to users trusted to install system programs, and to *root*.

We next check that these requirements are complete with respect to the threats of concern.

---

[2] See Section 14.2.1, "Principle of Least Privilege."

31.2.2   **Threats**

The threats against this mechanism fall into distinct classes. We enumerate the classes and discuss the requirements that handle each threat.

31.2.2.1   **Group 1: Unauthorized Users Accessing Role Accounts**

There are four threats that involve attackers trying to acquire access to role accounts using this mechanism.

Threat 31.1. An unauthorized user may obtain access to a role account as though she were an authorized user.

Threat 31.2. An authorized user may use a nonsecure channel to obtain access to a role account, thereby revealing her authentication information to unauthorized individuals.

Threat 31.3. An unauthorized user may alter the access control information to grant access to the role account.

Threat 31.4. An authorized user may execute a Trojan horse (or other form of malicious logic),[3] giving an unauthorized user access to the role account.

Requirements 31.1 and 31.5 handle Threat 31.1 by restricting the set of users who can access a role account and protecting the access control data. Requirement 31.1 also handles Threat 31.2 by restricting the locations from which the user can request access. For example, if the set of locations contains only those on trusted or confidential networks, a passive wiretapper cannot discover the authorized user's password or hijack a session begun by an authorized user. Similarly, if an authorized user connects from an untrusted system, Requirement 31.1 allows the system administrator to configure the mechanism so that the user's request is rejected.

The access control information that Requirement 31.1 specifies can be changed. Requirement 31.3 acknowledges this but restricts changes to trusted users (defined as those with access to the root account). This answers Threat 31.3.

Threat 31.4 is more complex. This threat arises from an untrusted user, without authorization, planting a Trojan horse at some location at which an authorized user might execute it. If the attacker can write into a directory in the role account's search path, this attack is feasible. Requirement 31.2 states that the role account's search path may be selected from two other search paths: the default search path for the role account, and the user's search path altered to include those components of the role account's search path that are not present. This leads to Requirement 31.5 which states that, regardless of how the search path is

---

[3]See Chapter 23, "Malware."

derived, the final search path may contain only directories (and may access only programs) that trusted users or the role account itself can manipulate. In this case, the attacker cannot place a Trojan horse where someone using the role account may execute it.

Finally, if a user is authorized to use the role account but is a novice and may change the search path, Requirement 31.4 allows the administrators to restrict the set of commands that the user may execute in that role.

31.2.2.2   Group 2: Authorized Users Accessing Role Accounts

Because access is allowed here, the threats relate to an authorized user changing access permissions or executing unauthorized commands.

Threat 31.5. An authorized user may obtain access to a role account and perform unauthorized commands.

Threat 31.6. An authorized user may execute a command that performs functions that the user is not authorized to perform.

Threat 31.7. An authorized user may change the restrictions on the user's ability to obtain access to the account.

The difference between Threats 31.5 and 31.6 is subtle but important. In the former, the user deliberately executes commands that violate the site security policy. In the latter, the user executes authorized commands that perform covert, unauthorized actions as well as overt, authorized actions—the classic Trojan horse. Threat 31.6 differs from Threat 31.4 because the action may not give access to authorized users; it may simply damage or destroy the system.

Requirement 31.4 handles Threat 31.5. If the user accessing the role account should execute only a specific set of commands, then the access controls must be configured to restrict the user's access to executing only those commands.

Requirements 31.2 and 31.5 handle Threat 31.6 by preventing the introduction of a Trojan horse, as discussed in the preceding section.

Requirement 31.3 answers Threat 31.7. Because all users who have access to *root* are trusted by definition, the only way for an authorized user to change the restrictions on obtaining access to the role account is to implant a backdoor (which is equivalent to a Trojan horse) or to modify the access control information. But the requirement holds that only trusted users can do that, so the authorized user cannot change the information unless he is trusted—in which case, by definition, the threat is handled.

31.2.2.3   Summary

Because the requirements handle the threats, and because all requirements are used, the set of requirements is both necessary and sufficient. We now proceed with the design.

31.3   Design

To create this program, we build modules that fit together to supply security services that satisfy the requirements. First, we create a general framework to guide the development of each interface. Then we examine each requirement separately, and design a component for each requirement.

31.3.1   Framework

The framework begins with the user interface and then breaks down the internals of the program into modules that implement the various requirements.

31.3.1.1   User Interface

The user can run the program in two ways. The first is to request unrestricted access to the account. The second is to request that a specific program be run from the role account. Any interface must be able to handle both.

The simplest interface is a command line. Other interfaces, such as graphical user interfaces, are possible and may make the program easier to use. However, these GUIs will be built in such a way that they construct and execute a command-line version of the program.

The interface chosen is

        role *role_account* [*command*]

where *role_account* is the name of the role account and *command* is the (optional) command to execute under that account. If the user wants unrestricted access to the role account, he omits *command*. Otherwise, the user is given restricted access and *command* is executed with the privileges of the role account.

The user need not specify the time of day using the interface, because the program can obtain such information from the system. It can also obtain the location from which the user requests access, although the method used presents potential problems (see Section 31.4.3.1). The individual modules handle the remainder of the issues.

31.3.1.2   High-Level Design

The basic algorithm is as follows.

1. Obtain the role account, command, user, location, and time of day. If the command is omitted, the user is requesting unrestricted access to the role account.

2. Check that the user is allowed to access the role account

   a. at the specified location;
   b. at the specified time; and
   c. for the specified command (or without restriction).

   If the user is not, log the attempt and quit.
3. Obtain the user and group information for the role account. Change the privileges of the process to those of the role account.
4. If the user has requested that a specific command be run, overlay the child process with a command interpreter that spawns the named command.
5. If the user has requested unrestricted access, overlay the child process with a command interpreter.

This algorithm points out an important ambiguity in the requirements. Requirements 31.1 and 31.4 do not indicate whether the ability of the user to execute a command in the given role account requires that the user work from a particular location or access the account at a particular time. This design uses the interpretation that a user's ability to run a command in a role account is conditioned on location and time.

The alternative interpretation, that access only is controlled by location and time, and that commands are restricted by role and user, is equally valid. But sometimes the ability to run commands may require that users work at particular times. For example, an operator may create the daily backups at 1 a.m. The operator is not to do backups at other times because of the load on the system. The interpretation of the design allows this. The alternative interpretation requires the backup program, or some other mechanism, to enforce this restriction. Furthermore, the design interpretation includes the alternative interpretation, because any control expressed in the alternative interpretation can be expressed in the design interpretation.

Requirement 31.4 can now be clarified. The addition is in boldface.

Requirement 31.6. The mechanism shall allow both restricted access and unrestricted access to a role account. For unrestricted access, the user shall have access to a standard command interpreter. For restricted access, the user shall be able to execute only a specified set of commands. **The level of access (restricted or unrestricted) shall depend on the user, the role, the time, and the location.**

Thus, the design phase feeds back into the requirements phase, here clarifying the meaning of the requirements. It is left as an exercise for the reader to verify that the new form of this requirement counters the appropriate threats (see Exercise 2).

31.3.2   Access to Roles and Commands

The user attempting access, the location (host or terminal), the time of day, and the type of access (restricted or unrestricted) control access to the role account. The access checking module returns a value indicating success (meaning that access is allowed) or failure (meaning that access is not allowed). By the principle of fail-safe defaults, an error causes a denial of access.

We consider two aspects of the design of this module. The interface controls how information is passed to the module from its caller, and how the module returns success or failure. The internal structure of the module includes how it handles errors. This leads to a discussion of how the access control data is stored. We consider these issues separately to emphasize that the interface provides an entry point into the module, and that the entry point will remain fixed even if the internal design of the module is completely changed. The internal design and structures are hidden from the caller.

31.3.2.1   Interface

Following the practice of hiding information among modules,[4] we minimize the amount of information to be passed to the access checking module. The module requires the user requesting access, the role to which access is requested, the location, the time, and the command (if any). The return value must indicate success or failure. The question is how this information is to be obtained.

The command (or request for unrestricted access) must come from the caller, because the caller provides the interface for the processing of that command. The command is supplied externally, so the principles of layering require it to pass through the program to the module.

The caller could also pass the other information to the module. This would allow the module to provide an access control result without obtaining the information directly. The advantage is that a different program could use this module to determine whether or not access *had been* or *would be* granted at some past or future point in time, or from some other location. The disadvantage is a lack of portability, because the interface is tied to a particular representation of the data. Also, if the caller of the module is untrusted but the module is trusted, the module might make trusted decisions based on untrusted data, violating a principle of integrity.[5] So we choose to have the module determine all of the data.

This suggests the following interface:

```
boolean accessok(role rname, command cmd);
```

where *rname* is the name of the requested role and *cmd* is the command to be executed (or is empty if unrestricted access is desired). The routine returns **true** if access is to be granted, and **false** otherwise.

----

[4]This is one aspect of the principle of least common mechanism (see Section 14.2.7).
[5]This follows from Biba's low-water-mark policy (see Section 6.2.1).

31.3.2.2   Internals

This module has three parts. The first part gathers the data on which access is to be based. The second part retrieves the access control information. The third part determines whether the data and the access control information require access to be granted.

The module queries the operating system to determine the needed data. The real user identification data is obtained through a system call, as is the current time of day. The location consists of two components: the entry point (terminal or network connection) and the remote host from which the user is accessing the local system. The latter component may indicate that the entry point is directly connected to the system, rather than using a remote host.

Part I: Obtain user ID, time of day, entry point, and remote host.

Next, the module must access the access control information. The access control information resides in a file. The file contains a sequence of records of the following form:

```
role account
user names
locations from which the role account can be accessed
times when the role account can be accessed
command and arguments
```

If the "command and arguments" line is omitted, the user is granted unrestricted access. Multiple command lines may be listed in a single record.

Part II: Obtain a handle (or descriptor) to the access control information. The programmer will use this handle to read the access control records from the access control information.

Finally, the program iterates through the access control information. If the role in the current record does not match the requested role, it is ignored. Otherwise, the user name, location, time, and command are compared with the appropriate fields of the record. If they all match, the module releases the handle and returns success.[6] If any of them does not match, the module continues on to the next record. If the module reaches the end of the access control information, the handle is released and the module returns failure. Note that records never deny access, but only grant it. The default action is to deny. Granting access requires an explicit record.[7]

If any record is invalid (for example, if there is a syntax error in one of the fields or if the user field contains a nonexistent user name), the module logs the error and ignores the record. This again follows the principle of fail-safe defaults, in which the system falls into a secure state when there is an error.

---

[6] If the time interval during which access is allowed expires after the access control check but before the access is granted, Requirement 31.1 is met (as it refers to the time of request). This eliminates a possible race condition.

[7] See Section 14.2.2, "Principle of Fail-Safe Defaults."

Part III: Iterate through the records until one matches the data or there are no more records. In the first case, return success; in the second case, return failure.

31.3.2.3   Storage of the Access Control Data

The system administrators of the local system control access to privileged accounts. To keep maintenance of this information simple, the administrators store the access control information in a file. Then they need only edit the file to change a user's ability to access the privileged account. The file consists of a set of records, each containing the components listed above. This raises the issue of expression. How should each part of the record be written?

For example, must each entry point be listed, or are wildcards acceptable? Strictly speaking, the principle of fail-safe defaults[8] says that we should list explicitly those locations from which access may be obtained. In practice, this is too cumbersome. Suppose a particular user was trusted to assume a role from any system on the Internet. Requiring the administrators to list all hosts would be time-consuming as well as infeasible. Worse, if the user were not allowed to access the role account from one system, the administrators would need to check the list to see which system was missing. This would violate the principle of least astonishment.[9] Given the dynamic nature of the Internet, this requirement would be absurd. Instead, we allow the following special host names, both of which are illegal [1365]:

> ***any*** (a wildcard matching any system)
> ***local*** (matches the local host name)

In BNF form, the language used to express location is

> *location* ::= '(' *location* ')' | 'not' *location* | *location* 'or' *location* | *basic*
> *basic* ::= '*any*' | '*local*' | '.' *domain* | *host*

where *domain* and *host* are domain names and host names, respectively. The strings in single quotation marks are literals. The parentheses are grouping operators, the "not" complements the associated locations, and the "or" allows either location.

EXAMPLE: A user is allowed to assume a role only when logged into the local system, the system "control.fixit.com", and the domain "watchu.edu". The appropriate entry would be

```
*local* | control.fixit.com | .watchu.edu
```

---

[8]See Section 14.2.2.
[9]See Section 14.2.8.

A similar question arises for times. Ignoring how times are expressed, how do we indicate when users may access the role account? Considerations similar to those above lead us to the following language, in which the keyword

any

allows access at any time. In BNF form, the language used to express time is

> *time* ::= '(' *time* ')' | 'not' *time* | *time* 'or' *time* | *time time* | *time* '–' *time* | *basic*
> *basic* ::= *day_of_year day_of_week time_of_day* | '*any*'
> *day_of_year* ::= *month* [*day*] [',' *year*] | *nmonth* '/' [*day* '/'] *year* | *empty*
> *day_of_week* ::= 'Sunday' | ... | 'Saturday' | 'Weekend' | 'Weekday' | *empty*
> *time_of_day* ::= *hour* [':' *min*] [':' *sec*] ['AM' | 'PM'] | *special* | *empty*
> *special* ::= 'noon' | 'midnight' | 'morning' | 'afternoon' | 'evening'
> *empty* ::= ''

where *month* is a string naming the month, *nmonth* is an integer naming the month, *day* is an integer naming the day of the month, and *year* is an integer specifying the year. Similarly, *hour*, *min*, and *sec* are integers specifying the hour, minute, and second. If *basic* is empty, it is treated as not allowing access.[10]

EXAMPLE: A user is allowed to assume a role between the hours of 9 o'clock in the morning and 5 o'clock in the evening on Monday through Thursday. An appropriate entry would be

> Monday-Thursday 9a.m.-5p.m.

This is different than saying

> Monday 9a.m.-Thursday 5p.m.

because the latter allows access on Monday at 10 p.m., whereas the former does not.

Finally, the users field of the record has a similar structure:

any

In BNF form, the language used to express the set of users who may access a role is

> *userlist* ::= '(' *userlist* ')' | 'not' *userlist* | *userlist* ',' *userlist* | *user*

where *user* is the name of a user on the system.

---

[10]By the principle of fail-safe defaults (see Section 14.2.2).

These "little languages" are straightforward and simple (but incomplete; see Exercise 5). Various implementation details, such as allowing abbreviations for day and month names, can be added, as can an option to change the American expression of days of the year to an international one. These points must be considered in light of where the program is to be used. Whatever changes are made, the administrators must be able to configure times and places quickly and easily, and in a manner that a reader of the access control file can understand quickly.[11]

The listing of commands requires some thought about how to represent arguments. If no arguments are listed, is the command to be run without arguments, or should it allow any set of arguments? Conversely, if arguments are listed, should the command be run only with those arguments? Our approach is to force the administrator to indicate how arguments are to be treated.

Each command line contains a command followed by zero or more arguments. If the first word after the command is an asterisk (" * "), then the command may be run with any arguments. Otherwise, the command must be run with the exact arguments provided.

EXAMPLE: Charles is allowed to run the install command when he accesses the *bin* role. He may supply any arguments. The line in the access control file is

```
/bin/install *
```

He may also copy the file log from the current working directory to the directory */var/install*. The line for this is

```
/bin/cp log /var/install/log
```

Finally, he may run the *id* command to ensure that he is working as *bin*. He may not supply other arguments to the command, however. This would be expressed by

```
/usr/bin/id
```

The user must type the command as given in the access control file. The full path names are present to prevent the user from accidentally executing the command *id* with *bin* privileges when *id* is a command in the local directory, rather than the system *id* command.[12]

---

[11]See Section 14.2.8, "Principle of Least Astonishment."
[12]See Chapter 23, "Malware."

31.4   Refinement and Implementation

This section focuses on the access control module of the program. We refine the high-level design presented in the preceding section until we produce a routine in a programming language.

31.4.1   First-Level Refinement

Rather than use any particular programming language, we first implement the module in pseudocode. This requires two decisions. First, the implementation language will be block-structured, like C or Java, rather than functional, like Scheme or ML. Second, the environment in which the program will function will be a UNIX-like system such as FreeBSD or Linux.

The basic structure of the security module is

```
boolean accessok(role rname, command cmd);
    status ← false
    user ← obtain user ID
    timeday ← obtain time of day
    entry ← obtain entry point (terminal line, remote host)
    open access control file
    repeat
       currecord ← obtain next record from file; EOF if none
       if currecord ≠ EOF then
            status ← match(currecord, rname, cmd, user,
                           timeday, entry)
    until currecord = EOF or status = true
    close access control file
    return status
```

We now verify that this sketch matches the design. Clearly, the interface is unchanged. The variable *status* will contain the status of the access control file check, becoming true when a match is found. Initially, it is set to false (deny access) because of the principle of fail-safe defaults. If *status* were not set, and the access control file were empty, *status* would never be set and the returned value would be undefined.

The next three lines obtain the user ID, the current time of day, and the system entry point. The following line opens the access control file.

The routine then iterates through the records of that file. The iteration has two requirements—that if any record allows access, the routine is to return true, and that if no record grants access, the routine is to return false. From the structure of the file, one cannot create a record to deny access. By default, access is denied. Entries explicitly grant access. So, iterating over the records of the file either produces a record that grants access (in which case the match routine returns true, terminating the loop and causing *accessok* to return with a value of true) or produces no such record. In that case, *status* is false, and *currecord* is set to EOF when the records in the access control file are exhausted. The loop then terminates, and the routine returns the value of *status*, which is false. Hence, this pseudocode matches the design and, transitively, the requirements.

31.4.2   Second-Level Refinement

Now we will focus on mapping the pseudocode above to a particular language and system. The C programming language is widely available and provides a convenient interface to UNIX-like systems. Given that our target system is a UNIX-like system, C is a reasonable choice. As for the operating system, there are many variants of the UNIX operating system. However, they all have fundamental similarities. The Linux operating system will provide the interfaces discussed below, and they work on a wide variety of UNIX systems.

On these systems, roles are represented as normal user accounts. The *root* account is really a role account,[13] for example. Each user account has two distinct representations of identity:[14] an internal user type *uid_t*,[15] and a string (name). When a user specifies a role, either representation may be used. For our purposes, we will assume that the caller of the *accessok* routine provides the *uid_t* representation of the role identity. Two reasons make this representation preferable. First, the target systems are unable to address privilege in terms of names, because, within the kernel, process identity is always represented by a *uid_t*. So the routines will need to do the conversion anyway. The second reason is more complex. Roles in the access control file can be represented by numbers or names. The routine for reading the access control file records will convert the roles to *uid_t*s to ensure consistency of representation. This also allows the input routine to check the records for consistency with the system environment. Specifically, if the role name refers to a nonexistent account, the routine can ignore the record. So any comparisons would require the role from the interface to be converted to a *uid_t*.

This leads to a design decision: represent all user and role IDs as integers internally. Fortunately, none of the design decisions discussed so far depend on the representation of identity, so we need not review or change our design.

Next, consider the command. On the target system, a command consists of a program name followed by a sequence of words, which are the command-line arguments to the command. The command representation is an array of strings, in

---

[13] See Section 15.4, "Groups and Roles."

[14] See Section 15.3, "Users."

[15] On Linux systems, and on most UNIX-like systems, this is an integer.

which the first string is the program name and the other strings are the command-line arguments.

Putting this all together, the resulting interface is

```
int accessok(uid_t rname, char *cmd[])
```

Next comes obtaining the user ID. Processes in the target system have several identities, but the key ones are the *real UID* (which identifies the user running the process) and the *effective UID* (which identifies the privileges with which the process runs).[16] The effective UID of this program must have *root* privileges (see Exercise 4) regardless of who runs the process. Hence, it is useless for this purpose. Only the real UID identifies the user running the program. So, to obtain the user ID of the user running the program, we use

```
userid = getuid();
```

The time of day is obtained from the system and expressed in internal format. The internal representation can be given in seconds since a specific date and time (the *epoch*)[17] or in microseconds since that time. It is unlikely that times will need to be specified in microseconds in the access control file. For both simplicity of code and simplicity of the access control data,[18] the internal format of seconds will be used. So, to obtain the current time, we use

```
timeday = time(NULL);
```

Finally, we need to obtain the location. There is no simple method for obtaining this information, so we defer it until later by encapsulating it in a function. This also localizes any changes should we move this program to a different system (for example, the methods used on a Linux system may differ from those used on a FreeBSD system).

```
entry = getlocation();
```

Opening the access control file for reading is straightforward:

```
if ((fp = fopen(acfile, "r")) == NULL){
    logerror(errno, acfile);
    return(0);
}
```

---

[16]See Section 15.3, "Users."

[17]On Linux and most other UNIX-like systems, the epoch is midnight on January 1, 1970 (UTC).

[18]See Section 14.2.3, "Principle of Economy of Mechanism," and Section 14.2.8, "Principle of Least Astonishment."

Notice first the error checking, and the logging of information on an error. The variable `errno` is set to a code indicating the nature of the error. The variable `acfile` points to the access control file name. The processing of the access control records follows:

```
do {
    acrec = getnextacrec(fp);
    if (acrec != NULL)
        status = match(acrec, rname, cmd, user, timeday,
                entry);
} while (acrec == NULL || status == 1);
```

Here, we read in the record—assuming that any records remain—and check the record to see if it allows permission. This looping continues until either some record indicates that permission is to be given or all records are checked. The exact internal record format is not yet specified; hence, the use of functions. The routine concludes by closing the access control file and returning status:

```
(void) fclose(fp);
return(status);
```

31.4.3   Functions

Three functions remain: the function for obtaining location, the function for getting an access control record, and the function for checking the access control record against the information of the current process. Each raises security issues.

31.4.3.1   Obtaining Location

UNIX and Linux systems write the user's account name, the name of the terminal on which the login takes place, the time of login, and the name of the remote host (if any) to the *utmp* file. Any process may read this file. As each new process runs, it may have an associated terminal. To determine the *utmp* record associated with the process, a routine may obtain the associated terminal name, open the *utmp* file, and scan through the record to find the one with the corresponding terminal name. That record contains the name of the host from which the user is working.

This approach, although clumsy, works on most UNIX and Linux systems. It suffers from two problems related to security.

1. If any process can alter the *utmp* file, its contents cannot be trusted. Several security holes have occurred because any process could alter the *utmp* file [2254].

2. A process may have no associated terminal. Such a detached process must be mapped into the corresponding *utmp* record through other means.

However, if the *utmp* record contains only the information described above, this is not possible because the user may be logged into multiple terminals. The issue does not arise if the process has an associated terminal, because only one user at a time may be logged into a terminal.

In the first case, we make a design decision that if the data in the *utmp* file cannot be trusted because any process can alter that file, we return a meaningless location. Then, unless the location specifier of the record allows access from any location, the record will not match the current process information and will not grant access. A similar approach works if the process does not have an associated terminal.

The outline of this routine is

```
hostname getlocation()
    status ← false
    myterm ← name of terminal
    obtain access control list for utmp
    if any user other than root can alter it then
        return "*nowhere*"
    open utmp
    repeat
        term ← obtain next entry from utmp; otherwise EOF
        if term ≠ EOF and myterm = term then
                status ← true
    until term = EOF or status = true
    if host field of utmp entry = empty
        host = "localhost"
    else
        host = host field of utmp entry
    close utmp
    return host
```

We omit the implementation due to space limitations.

31.4.3.2   The Access Control Record

The format of the records in the access control file affects both the reading of the file and the comparison with the process information, so we design it here.

Our approach is to consider the match routine first. Four items must be checked: the user name, the location, the time, and the command. Consider these items separately.

The user name is represented as an integer. Thus, the internal format of the user field of the access control record must contain either integers or names that the match routine can convert to integers. If a match occurs before all user names have been checked, then the program needs to convert no more names to integers. So, we adopt the strategy of representing the user field as a string read directly from the file. The match routine will parse the line and will use lazy evaluation to check whether or not the user ID is listed.

A similar strategy can be applied to the location and the set of commands in the record.

The time is somewhat different, because in the previous two cases, the process user ID and the location had to match one of the record entries exactly. However, the time does not have to do so. Time in the access control record is (almost always) a range. For example, the entry "May 30" means any time on the date of May 30. The day begins at midnight and ends at midnight, 24 hours later. So, the range would be from May 30 at midnight to May 31 at midnight, or in internal time (for example) between 1527638400 and 1527724800. In those rare cases in which a user may assume a role only at a precise second, the range can be treated as having the same beginning and ending points. Given this view of time as ranges, checking that the current time falls into an acceptable range suggests having the match routine parse the times and checking whether or not the internal system time falls in each range as it is constructed.

This means that the routine for reading the record may simply load the record as a sequence of strings and let the match routine do the interpretation. This yields the following structure:

```
record
    role rname
    string userlist
    string location
    string timeofday
    string commands[]
    integer numcommands
end record;
```

The *commands* field is an array of strings, each command and argument being one string, and *numcommands* containing the number of commands.

Given this information, the function used to read the access control records, and the function used to match them with the current process information, are not hard to write, but error handling does deserve some mention.

31.4.3.3   Error Handling in the Reading and Matching Routines

Assume that there is a syntax error in the access control file. Perhaps a record specifies a time incorrectly (for example, "Thurxday"), or a record divider is garbled. How should the routines handle this?

The first observation is that they cannot ignore the error. To do so violates basic principles of security (specifically, the principle of least astonishment[19]). It also defeats the purpose of the program, because access will be denied to users

---

[19]See Section 14.2.8, "Principle of Least Astonishment."

who need it.[20] So, the program must produce an indication of error. If it is printed, then the user will see it and should notify the system administrator maintaining the access control file. Should the user forget, the administrator will not know of the error. Hence, the error must be logged. Whether or not the user should be told why the error has occurred is another question. One school of thought holds that the more information users have, the more helpful they will be. Another school holds that information should be denied unless the user needs to know it, and in the case of an error in the access control file, the user only needs to know that access will be denied.

Hence, the routines must log information about errors. The logged information must enable the system administrator to locate the error in the file. The error message should include the access control file name and line or record number. This suggests that both routines need access to that information. Hence, the record counts, line numbers, and file name must be shared. For reasons of modularity, this implies that these two routines should be in a submodule of the access checking routine. If they are placed in their own module, no other parts of the routine can access the line or record numbers (and none need to, given the design described here). If the module is placed under the access control routine, no external functions can read records from the access control file or check data against that file's contents.

31.4.4   Summary

This section has examined the development of a program for performing a security-critical function. Beginning with a requirements analysis, the design and parts of the implementation demonstrate the need for repeated analysis to ensure that the design meets the requirements and that design decisions are documented. From the point at which the derivation stopped, the implementation is simple.

We will now discuss some common security-related programming problems. Then we will discuss testing, installation, and maintenance.

31.5   Common Security-Related Programming Problems

Unfortunately, programmers are not perfect. They make mistakes. These errors can have disastrous consequences in programs that change the protection domains. Attackers who exploit these errors may acquire extra privileges (e.g., access to a system account such as *root* or *Administrator*). They may disrupt the normal functioning of the system by deleting or altering services over which they

---

[20]Note that a record with a syntax error will never grant access (see Exercise 6).

should have no control. They may simply be able to read files to which they should have no access.[21] So the problem of avoiding these errors, or security holes, is a necessary issue to ensure that the programs and system function as required.

We present both management rules (installation, configuration, and maintenance) and programming rules together. Although there is some benefit in separating them, doing so creates an artificial distinction by implying that they can be considered separately. In fact, the limits on installation, configuration, and maintenance affect the implementation, just as the limits of implementation affect the installation, configuration, and maintenance procedures.

Researchers have developed several models for analyzing systems for these security holes.[22] These models provide a framework for characterizing the problems. The goal of the characterization guides the selection of the model. Because we are interested in technical modeling and not in the reason or time of introduction, many of the categories of the NRL model[23] are inappropriate for our needs. We also wish to analyze the multiple components of vulnerabilities rather than force each vulnerability into a particular point of view, as Aslam's model[24] does. So either the PA model[25] or the RISOS model[26] is appropriate. We have chosen the PA model for our analysis.

We examine each of the categories and subcategories separately. We consider first the general rules that we can draw from the vulnerability class, and then we focus on applying those rules to the program under discussion.

31.5.1   Improper Choice of Initial Protection Domain

Flaws involving improper choice of initial protection domain arise from incorrect setting of permissions or privileges. There are three objects for which permissions need to be set properly: the file containing the program, the access control file, and the memory space of the process. We will consider them separately.

31.5.1.1   Process Privileges

The principle of least privilege[27] dictates that no process have more privileges than it needs to complete its task, but the process must have enough privileges to complete its task successfully.

Ideally, one set of privileges should meet both criteria. In practice, different portions of the process will need different sets of privileges. For example, a process may need special privileges to access a resource (such as a log file) at the beginning

---

[21] See Chapter 24, "Vulnerability Analysis."
[22] See Section 24.4, "Frameworks."
[23] See Section 24.4.3, "The NRL Taxonomy."
[24] See Section 24.4.4, "Aslam's Model."
[25] See Section 24.4.2, "Protection Analysis Model."
[26] See Section 24.4.1, "The RISOS Study."
[27] See Section 14.2.1, "Principle of Least Privilege."

and end of its task, but may not need those privileges at other times. The process structure and initial protection domain should reflect this.

Implementation Rule 31.1. Structure the process so that all sections requiring extra privileges are modules. The modules should be as small as possible and should perform only those tasks that require those privileges.

The basis for this rule lies in the reference monitor.[28] The reference monitor is verifiable, complete (it is always invoked to access the resource it protects), and tamperproof (it cannot be compromised). Here, the modules are kept small and simple (verifiable), access to the privileged resource requires the process to invoke these modules (complete), and the use of separate modules with well-defined interfaces minimizes the chances of other parts of the program corrupting the module (tamperproof).

Management Rule 31.1. Check that the process privileges are set properly.

Insufficient privileges could cause a denial of service. Excessive privileges could enable an attacker to exploit vulnerabilities in the program. To avoid these problems, the privileges of the process, and the times at which the process has these privileges, must be chosen and managed carefully.

One of the requirements of this program is availability (Requirements 31.1 and 31.4). On Linux and UNIX systems, the program must change the effective identity of the user from the user's account to the role account. This requires special (setuid) privileges of either the role account or the superuser.[29] The principle of least privilege[30] says that the former is better than the latter, but if one of the role accounts is *root*, then having multiple copies of the program with limited privileges is irrelevant, because the program with privileges to access the *root* role account is the logical target of attack. After all, if one can compromise a less privileged account through this program, the same attack will probably work against the *root* account. Because the Drib plans to control access to *root* in some cases, the program requires setuid to *root* privileges.

If the program does not have root privileges initially, the UNIX protection model does not allow the process to acquire them; the permissions on the program file corresponding to the program must be changed. The process must log enough information for the system administrator to identify the problem,[31] and should notify users of the problem so that the users can notify the system administrator. An alternative is to develop a server that will periodically check the permissions on the program file and reset them if needed, or a server that the program can notify should it have insufficient privileges. The designers felt that the benefits of

---

[28]See Section 20.1.2.2, "Building Security In or Adding Security Later." Programs implemented following this rule are *not* reference monitors.
[29]See Section 15.3, "Users."
[30]See Section 14.2.1, "Principle of Least Privilege."
[31]See Section 25.3, "Designing an Auditing System."

these servers were not sufficient to warrant their development. In particular, they were concerned that the system administrators investigate any unexpected change in file permissions, and an automated server that changed the permissions back would provide insufficient incentive for an analysis of the problem.

As a result, the developers required that the program acquire *root* permission at start-up. The access control module is executed. Within that module, the privileges are reset to the user's once the log file and access control file have been opened.[32] Superuser privileges are needed only once more—to change the privileges to those of the role account should access be granted. This routine, also in a separate module, supplies the granularity required to provide the needed functionality while minimizing the time spent executing with *root* privileges.

31.5.1.2   Access Control File Permissions

Biba's models[33] emphasize that the integrity of the process relies on both the integrity of the program and the integrity of the access control file. The former requires that the program be properly protected so that only authorized personnel can alter it. The system managers must determine who the "authorized personnel" are. Among the considerations here are the principle of separation of duty[34] and the principle of least privilege.[35]

Verifying the integrity of the access control file is critical, because that file controls the access to role accounts. Some external mechanism, such as a file integrity checking tool, can provide some degree of assurance that the file has not changed. However, these checks are usually periodic, and the file might change after the check. So the program itself should check the integrity of the file when the program is run.

> **Management Rule 31.2.** The program that is executed to create the process, and all associated control files, must be protected from unauthorized use and modification. Any such modification must be detected.

In many cases, the process will rely on the settings of other files or on some other external resources. Whenever possible, the program should check these dependencies to ensure that they are valid. The dependencies must be documented so that installers and maintainers will understand what else must be maintained in order to ensure that the program works correctly.

> **Implementation Rule 31.2.** Ensure that any assumptions in the program are validated. If this is not possible, document them for the installers and maintainers, so they know the assumptions that attackers will try to invalidate.

---

[32]Section 14.2.3, "Principle of Complete Mediation," provides detail on why this works.
[33]See Section 6.2, "The Biba Model."
[34]See Section 6.1, "Goals."
[35]See Section 14.2.1, "Principle of Least Privilege."

The permissions of the program, and its containing directory, are to be set so only *root* can alter or move the program. According to Requirement 31.2, only *root* can alter the access control file. Hence, the file must be owned by *root*, and only *root* can write to it. The program should check the ownership and permissions of this file, and the containing directories, to validate that only *root* can alter it.

EXAMPLE: The naive way to check that only *root* can write to the file is to check that the owner is *root* and that the file permissions allow only the owner to write to it. But consider the group permissions. If *root* is the only member of the group, then the group permissions may allow members of the group to write to the file. The problem is that checking group membership is more complicated than looking up the members of the group. A user may belong to a group without being listed as a member, because the GID of the user is assigned from the password file, and group membership lists are contained in a different file.[36] Either the password file and the group membership list must both be checked, or the program should simply report an error if anyone other than the user can write to the file. For simplicity,[37] the designers chose the second approach.

31.5.1.3   Memory Protection

As the program runs, it depends on the values of variables and other objects in memory. This includes the executable instructions themselves. Thus, protecting memory against unauthorized or unexpected alteration is critical.

Consider sharing memory. If two subjects can alter the contents of memory, then one could change data on which the second relies. Unless such sharing is required (for example, by concurrent processes), it poses a security problem because the modifying process can alter variables that control the action of the other process. Thus, each process should have a protected, unshared memory space.

If the memory is represented by an object that processes can alter, it should be protected so that only trusted processes can access it. Access here includes not only modification but also reading, because passwords reside in memory after they are types. Multiple abstractions are discussed in more detail in the next section.

> **Implementation Rule 31.3.** Ensure that the program does not share objects in memory with any other program, and that other programs cannot access the memory of a privileged process.

---

[36]Specifically, if the group field of the password file entry for *matt* is 30, and the group file lists the members of group 30 as *root*, the user *matt* is still in group 30, but a query to the group file (the standard way to determine group membership) will show that only *root* is a member.

[37]See Section 14.2.3, "Principle of Economy of Mechanism."

Interaction with other processes cannot be eliminated. If the running process obtains input or data from other processes, then that interface provides a point through which other processes can reach the memory. The most common version of this attack is the buffer overflow.

Buffer overflows involve either altering of data or injecting of instructions that can be executed later. There are a wide variety of techniques for this [32, 706].[38] Several remedies exist. For example, if buffers reside in sections of memory that are not executable, injecting instructions will not work. Similarly, if some data is to remain unaltered, the data can be stored in read-only memory.

Management Rule 31.3. Configure memory to enforce the principle of least privilege. If a section of memory is not to contain executable instructions, turn execute permission off for that section of memory. If the contents of a section of memory are not to be altered, make that section read-only.

These rules appear in three ways in our program. First, the implementers use the language constructs to flag unchanging data as constant (in the C programming language, this is the keyword *const*). This will cause compile-time errors if the variables are assigned to, or runtime errors if instructions try to alter those constants.

The other two ways involve program loading. The system's loader places data in three areas: the *data* (initialized data) segment, the *stack* (used for function calls and variables local to the functions), and the *heap* (used for dynamically allocated storage). A common attack is to trick a program into executing instructions injected into three areas. The vector of injection can be a buffer overflow,[39] for example. The characteristic under discussion does not stop such alteration, but it should prevent the data from being executed by making the segments or pages of all three areas nonexecutable. This suffices for the data and stack segments and follows Management Rule 31.3.

If the program uses dynamic loading to load functions at runtime, the functions that are loaded may change over the lifetime of the program. This means that the assumptions the programmers make may no longer be valid.[40] One solution to this problem is to compile the program in such a way that it does not use dynamic loading. This also also prevents the program from trying to load a module at runtime that may be missing. This could occur if a second process deleted the appropriate library. So disabling of dynamic loading also follows Implementation Rule 31.3.[41]

Finally, some UNIX-like systems (including the one on which this program is being developed) allow execution permission to be turned off for the stack. The boot file sets the kernel flag to enforce this.

---

[38] However, alternative techniques involving corrupting data, causing the flow of control to change improperly, do work. See Section 31.5.6, "Improper Validation."

[39] Buffer overflows can also alter data. See Section 31.5.3.1, "Memory," for an example.

[40] See Section 31.5.3.2, "Changes in File Contents."

[41] Other considerations contributed. See Section 31.5.4, "Improper Naming."

31.5.1.4   Trust in the System

This analysis overlooks several system components. For example, the program relies on the system authentication mechanisms to authenticate the user, and on the user information database to map users and roles into their corresponding UIDs (and, therefore, privileges). It also relies on the inability of ordinary users to alter the system clock. If any of this supporting infrastructure can be compromised, the program will not work correctly. The best that can be done is to identify these points of trust in the installation and operation documentation so that the system administrators are aware of the dependencies of the program on the system.

> **Management Rule 31.4.** Identify all system components on which the program depends. Check for errors whenever possible, and identify those components for which error checking will not work.

For this program, the implementers should identify the system databases and information on which the program depends, and should prepare a list of these dependencies. They should discuss these dependencies with system managers to determine if the program can check for errors. When this is not possible, or when the program cannot identify all errors, they should describe the possible consequences of the errors. This document should be distributed with the program so that system administrators can check their systems before installing the program.

31.5.2   Improper Isolation of Implementation Detail

The problem of improper isolation of implementation detail arises when an abstraction is improperly mapped into an implementation detail. Consider how abstractions are mapped into implementations. Typically, some function (such as a database query) occurs, or the abstraction corresponds to an object in the system. What happens if the function produces an error or fails in some other way, or if the object can be manipulated without reference to the abstraction?

The first rule is to catch errors and failures of the mappings. This requires an analysis of the functions and a knowledge of their implementation. The action to take on failure also requires thought. In general, if the cause cannot be determined, the program should fail by returning the relevant parts of the system to the states they were in when the program began.[42]

> **Implementation Rule 31.4.** The error status of every function must be checked. Do not try to recover unless the cause of the error, and its effects, do not affect any security considerations. The program should restore the state of the system to the state before the process began, and then terminate.

---

[42]See Section 14.2.2, "Principle of Fail-Safe Defaults."

The abstractions in this program are the notion of a user and a role, the access control information, and the creation of a process with the rights of the role. We will examine these abstractions separately.

31.5.2.1   Resource Exhaustion and User Identifiers

The notion of a user and a role is an abstraction because the program can work with role names and the operating system uses integers (UIDs). The question is how those user and role names are mapped to UIDs. Typically, this is done with a user information database that contains the requisite mapping, but the program must detect any failures of the query and respond appropriately.

EXAMPLE: A mail server allowed users to forward mail by creating a forwarding file [2225]. The forwarding file could specify files to which the mail should be appended. In this case, the mail server would deliver the letter with the privileges of the owner of the forwarding file (represented on the system as an integer UID). In some cases, the mail server would queue the message for later delivery. When it did so, it would write the name (not the UID) of the user into a control file. The system queried a database, supplying the UID, and obtaining the corresponding name. If the query failed, the mail server used a default name specified by the system administrator.

Attackers discovered how to make the queries fail. As a result, the user was set to a default user, usually a system-level user (such as *daemon*). This enabled the attackers to have the mail server append mail to any file to which the default user could write. They used this to implant Trojan horses into system programs. These Trojan horses gave them extra privileges, compromising the system.

The designers and implementers decided to have the program fail if, for any reason, the query failed. This application of the principle of fail-safe defaults[43] ensured that in case of error, the users would not get access to the role account.

31.5.2.2   Validating the Access Control Entries

The access control information implements the access control policy (an abstraction). The expression of the access control information is therefore the result of mapping an abstraction to an implementation. The question is whether or not the given access control information correctly implements the policy. Answering this question requires someone to examine the implementation expression of the policy.

The programmers developed a second program that used the same routines as the role-assuming program to analyze the access control entries. This program prints the access control information in an easily readable format. It allows the system managers to check that the access control information is correct. A specific procedure requires that this information be checked periodically, and always after the file or the program is altered.

---

[43] See Section 14.2.2, "Principle of Fail-Safe Defaults."

31.5.2.3   Restricting the Protection Domain of the Role Process

Creating a role process is the third abstraction. There are two approaches. Under UNIX-like systems, the program can spawn a second, *child*, process. It can also simply start up a second program in such a way that the parent process is replaced by the new process. This technique, called *overlaying*, is intrinsically simpler than creating a child process and exiting. It allows the process to replace its own protection domain with the (possibly) more limited one corresponding to the role. The programmers elected to use this method. The new process inherits the protection domain of the original one. Before the overlaying, the original process must reset its protection domain to that of the role. The programmers do so by closing all files that the original process opened, and changing its privileges to those of the role.

EXAMPLE: The effective UIDs and GIDs[44] control privileges. Hence, the programmers reset the effective GID first, and then the effective UID (if resetting were done in the opposite order, the change to GIDs would fail because such changes require *root* privileges). However, if the UNIX-like system supports saved UIDs, an authorized user may be able to acquire *root* privileges even if the role account is not *root*. The problem is that resetting the effective UID sets the saved UID to the previous UID—namely, *root*. A process may then reacquire the rights of its saved UID. To avoid this problem, the programmers used the *setuid* system call to reset *all* of the real, effective, and saved UIDs to the UID of the role. Thus, all traces of the *root* UID are eliminated and the user cannot reacquire those privileges.

Similarly, UNIX-like systems check access permissions only when the file is opened. If a *root* process opens a privileged file and then the process drops *root* privileges, it can still read from (or write to) the file.

The components of the protection domain that the process must reset before the overlay are the open files (except for standard input, output, and error), which must be closed, the signal handlers, which must be reset to their default values, and any user-specific information, which must be cleared.

31.5.3   Improper Change

This category describes data and instructions that change over time. The danger is that the changed values may be inconsistent with the previous values. The previous values dictate the flow of control of the process. The changed values cause the program to take incorrect or nonsecure actions on that path of control.

The data and instructions can reside in shared memory, in nonshared memory, or on disk. The last includes file attribute information such as ownership and access control list.

---

[44]See Section 15.3, "Users."

31.5.3.1   Memory

First comes the data in shared memory. Any process that can access shared memory can manipulate data in that memory. Unless all processes that can access the shared memory implement a concurrent protocol for managing changes, one process can change data on which a second process relies. As stated above, this could cause the second process to violate the security policy.

EXAMPLE: Two processes share memory. One process reads authentication data and writes it into the shared memory space. The second process performs the authentication, and writes a boolean *true* back into the shared memory space if the authentication succeeds, and *false* if it fails. Unless the two processes use concurrent constructs to synchronize their reading and writing, the first process may read the result before the second process has completed the computation for the current data. This could allow access when it should be denied, or vice versa.

> **Implementation Rule 31.5.** If a process interacts with other processes, the interactions should be synchronized. In particular, all possible sequences of interactions must be known and, for all such interactions, the process must enforce the required security policy.

A variant of this situation is the asynchronous exception handler. If the handler alters variables and then returns to the previous point in the program, the changes in the variables could cause problems similar to the problem of concurrent processes. For this reason, if the exception handler alters any variables on which other portions of the code depend, the programmer must understand the possible effects of such changes. This is just like the earlier situation in which a concurrent process changes another's variables in a shared memory space.

> **Implementation Rule 31.6.** Asynchronous exception handlers should not alter any variables except those that are local to the exception handling module. An exception handler should block all other exceptions when begun, and should not release the block until the handler completes execution, unless the handler has been designed to handle exceptions within itself (or calls an uninvoked exception handler).

A second approach applies whether the memory is shared or not. A user feeds bogus information to the program, and the program accepts it. The bogus data overflows its buffer, changing other data, or inserting instructions that can be executed later.

EXAMPLE: The buffer overflow attack on *fingerd* described in Section 24.4.5.2 illustrates this approach. The return address is pushed onto the stack when the input routine is called. That address is not expected to change between its being pushed onto the stack and its being popped from the stack, but the buffer overflow changes it. When the input function returns, the address popped from the stack is that of the input buffer. Execution resumes at that point, and the input instructions are used.

This suggests one way to detect such transformations (the *stack guard approach*) [469]. Immediately after the return address is pushed onto the stack, push a random number onto the stack (the *canary*). Assume that the input overflows the buffer on the stack and alters the return address on the stack. If the canary is n bits long and has been chosen randomly, the probability of the attacker not changing that cookie is 2^{-n}. When the input procedure returns, the canary is popped and compared with the value that was pushed onto the stack. If the two differ, there has been an overflow.[45]

In terms of trust, the return address (a trusted datum) can be affected by untrusted data (from the input). This lowers the trustworthiness of the return address to that of input data. One need not supply instructions to breach security.

EXAMPLE: One (possibly apocryphal) version of a UNIX login program allocated two adjacent arrays. The first held the user's cleartext password and was 80 characters long, and the second held the password hash[46] and was 13 characters long. The program's logic loaded the password hash into the second array as soon as the user's name was determined. It then read the user's cleartext password and stored it in the first array. If the contents of the first array hashed to the contents of the second array, the user was authenticated. An attacker simply selected a random password (for example, "password") and generated a valid hash for it (here, "12CsGd8FRcMSM"). The attacker then identified herself as *root*. When asked for a password, the attacker entered "password", typed 72 spaces, and then typed "12CsGd8FRcMSM". The system hashed "password", got "12CsGd8FRcMSM", and logged the user in as *root*.

A technique in which canaries protect data, not only the return address, would work, but raises many implementation problems (see Exercise 7).

Implementation Rule 31.7. Whenever possible, data that the process trusts and data that it receives from untrusted sources (such as input) should be kept in separate areas of memory. If data from a trusted source is overwritten with data from an untrusted source, a memory error will occur.

In more formal terms, the principle of least common mechanism[47] indicates that memory should not be shared in this way.

---

[45]If the goal is to alter data on the stack other than the return address, the canary will not be altered. This technique will not detect the change. (See Exercise 7.)

[46]See Section 13.2, "Passwords."

[47]See Section 14.2.7, "Principle of Least Common Mechanism."

These rules apply to our program in several ways. First, the program does not interact with any other program except through exception handling.[48] So Implementation Rule 31.5 does not apply. Exception handling consists of calling a procedure that disables further exception handling, logs the exception, and immediately terminates the program.

Illicit alteration of data in memory is the second potential problem. If the user-supplied data is read into memory that overlaps with other program data, it could erase or alter that data. To satisfy Implementation Rule 31.7, the programmers did not reuse variables into which users could input data. They also ensured that each access to a buffer did not overlap with other buffers.

The problem of buffer overflow is solved by checking all array and pointer references within the code. Any reference that is out of bounds causes the program to fail after logging an error message to help the programmers track down the error.

31.5.3.2   Changes in File Contents

File contents may change improperly. In most cases, this means that the file permissions are set incorrectly or that multiple processes are accessing the file, which is similar to the problem of concurrent processes accessing shared memory. Management Rule 31.2 and Implementation Rule 31.5 cover these two cases.

A nonobvious corollary is to be careful of dynamic loading. Dynamic load libraries are not part of this program's executable. They are loaded, as needed, when the program runs. Suppose one of the libraries is changed, and the change causes a side effect. The program may cease to function or, even worse, work incorrectly.

If the dynamic load modules cannot be altered, then this concern is minimal, but if they can be upgraded or otherwise altered, it is important. Because one of the reasons for using dynamic load libraries is to allow upgrades without having to recompile programs that depend on the library, security-related programs using dynamic load libraries are at risk.

> **Implementation Rule 31.8.** Do not use components that may change between the time the program is created and the time it is run.

This is another reason that the developers decided not to use dynamic loading.

31.5.3.3   Race Conditions in File Accesses

A race condition in this context is the *time-of-check-to-time-of-use* problem. As with memory accesses, the file being used is changed after validation but before

---

[48] If the access control information or the authentication information came from servers, then there would be interaction with other programs (the servers). The method of communication would need to be considered, as discussed above.

access.[49] To thwart it, either the file must be protected so that no untrusted user can alter it, or the process must validate the file and use it indivisibly. The former requires appropriate settings of permission, so Management Rule 31.2 applies. Section 31.5.7, "Improper Indivisibility," discusses the latter.

This program validates that the owner and access control permissions for the access control file are correct (the check). It then opens the file (the use). If an attacker can change the file after the validation but before the opening, so that the file checked is not the file opened, then the attacker can have the program obtain access control information from a file other than the legitimate access control file. Presumably, the attacker would supply a set of access control entries allowing unauthorized accesses.

EXAMPLE: The UNIX operating system allows programs to refer to files in two ways: by name and by file descriptor.[50] Once a file descriptor is bound to a file, the referent of the descriptor does not change. Each access through the file descriptor always refers to the bound file (until the descriptor is closed). However, the kernel reprocesses the file name at each reference, so two references to the same file name may refer to two *different* files. An attacker who is able to alter the file system in such a way that this occurs is exploiting a race condition. So any checks made to the file corresponding to the first use of the name may not apply to the file corresponding to the second use of the name. This can result in a process making unwarranted assumptions about the trustworthiness of the file and the data it contains.

In the *xterm* example[51] the program can be fixed by opening the file and then using the file descriptor (handle) to obtain the owner and access permissions.[52] Those permissions belong to the opened file, because they were obtained using the file descriptor. The validation is now ensured to be that of the access control file.

The program does exactly this. It opens the access control file and uses the file descriptor, which references the file attribute information directly to obtain the owner, group, and access control permissions. Those permissions are checked. If they are correct, the program uses the file descriptor to read the file. Otherwise, the file is closed and the program reports a failure.

31.5.4   Improper Naming

Improper naming refers to an ambiguity in identifying an object. Most commonly, two different objects have the same name. The programmer intends the name to refer to one of the objects, but an attacker manipulates the environment and the

---

[49]Section 24.3.1, "Two Security Flaws," discusses this problem in detail.
[50]See Section 15.2, "Files and Objects."
[51]See Section 24.3.1, "Two Security Flaws."
[52]The system call used would be *fstat*.

process so that the name refers to a different object. Avoiding this flaw requires that every object be unambiguously identified. This is both a management concern and an implementation concern.

Objects must be uniquely identifiable or completely interchangeable. Managing these objects means identifying those that are interchangeable and those that are not. The former objects need a controller (or set of controllers) that, when given a name, selects one of the objects. The latter objects need unique names. The managers of the objects must supply those names.

> **Management Rule 31.5.** Unique objects require unique names. Interchangeable objects may share a name.

A name is interpreted within a context. At the implementation level, the process must force its own context into the interpretation, to ensure that the object referred to is the intended object. The context includes information about the character sets, process and file hierarchies, network domains, and any accessible variables such as the search path.

EXAMPLE: Stage 3 in Section 24.2.9 discussed an attack in which a privileged program called *loadmodule* executed a second program named *ld.so*. The attack exploited *loadmodule*'s failure to specify the context in which *ld.so* was named. *Loadmodule* used the context of the user invoking the program. Normally, this caused the correct *ld.so* to be invoked. In the example, the attacker changed the context so that another version of *ld.so* was executed. This version had a Trojan horse that would grant privileged access. When the attacker executed *loadmodule*, the Trojan horse was triggered and maximum privileges were acquired.

> **Implementation Rule 31.9.** The process must ensure that the context in which an object is named identifies the correct object.

This program uses names for external objects in four places: the name of the access control file, the names of the users and roles, the names of the hosts, and the name of the command interpreter (the *shell*) that the program uses to execute commands in the role account.

The two file names (access control file and command interpreter) must identify specific files. Absolute path names specify the location of the object with respect to a distinguished directory called / or the "root directory." However, a privileged process can redefine / to be any directory.[53] This program does not do so. Furthermore, if the root directory is anything other than the root directory of the system, a trusted process has executed it. No untrusted user could have done so. Thus, as long as absolute path names are specified, the files are unambiguously named.

---

[53]Specifically, the system call *chroot* resets / to mean the named directory. All absolute path names are interpreted with respect to that directory. Only the superuser, *root*, may execute this system call.

The name provided may be interpreted in light of other aspects of the environment. For example, differences in the encoding of characters can transform file names. Whether characters are made up of 16 bits, 8 bits, or 7 bits can change the interpretation, and therefore the referent, of a file name. Other environment variables can change the interpretation of the path name. This program simply creates a new, known, safe environment for execution of the commands.[54]

This has two advantages over sanitization of the existing context. First, it avoids having the program analyze the environment in detail. The meaning of each aspect of the environment need not be analyzed and examined. The environment is simply replaced. Second, it allows the system to evolve without compromising the security of the program. For example, if a new environment variable is assigned a meaning that affects how programs are executed, the variable will not affect how this program executes its commands because that variable will not appear in the command's environment. So this program closes all file descriptors, resets signal handlers, and passes a new set of environment variables for the command.

These actions satisfy Implementation Rule 31.9.

The developers assumed that the system was properly maintained, so that the names of the users and roles would map into the correct UIDs. (Section 31.5.2.1 discusses this.) This applies to Management Rule 31.5.

The host names are the final set of names. These may be specified by names or IP addresses. If the former, they must be fully qualified domain names to avoid ambiguity. To see this, suppose an access control entry allows user *matt* to access the role *wheel* when logging in from the system *amelia*. Does this mean the system named *amelia* in the local domain, or any system named *amelia* from any domain? Either interpretation is valid. The former is more reasonable,[55] and applying this interpretation resolves the ambiguity. (The program implicitly maps names to fully qualified domain names using the former interpretation. Thus, *amelia* in the access control entry would match a host named *amelia* in the local domain, and not a host named *amelia* in another domain.) This implements Implementation Rule 31.9.[56]

As a side note, if the local network is mismanaged or compromised, the name *amelia* may refer to a system other than the one intended. For example, the real host *amelia* may crash or go offline. An attacker can then reset the address of his host to correspond to *amelia*. This program will not detect the impersonation.

31.5.5   Improper Deallocation or Deletion

Failing to delete sensitive information raises the possibility of another process seeing that data at a later time. In particular, cryptographic keywords, passwords,

---

[54]The principle of fail-safe defaults (see Section 14.2.2) supports this approach.

[55]According to the principle of least privilege (see Section 14.2.1).

[56]As discussed in Section 15.6.1, "Host Identity," host names can be spoofed. For reasons discussed in the preceding chapters, the Drib management and security officers are not concerned with this threat on the Drib's internal network.

and other authentication information should be discarded once they have been used. Similarly, once a process has finished with a resource, that resource should be deallocated. This allows other processes to use that resource, inhibiting denial of service attacks.

A consequence of not deleting sensitive information is that dumps of memory, which may occur if the program receives an exception or crashes for some other reason, contain the sensitive data. If the process fails to release sensitive resources before spawning unprivileged subprocesses, those unprivileged subprocesses may have access to the resource.

> **Implementation Rule 31.10.** When the process finishes using a sensitive object (one that contains confidential information or one that should not be altered), the object should be erased, then deallocated or deleted. Any resources not needed should also be released.

Our program uses three pieces of sensitive information. The first is the cleartext password, which authenticates the user. The password is hashed, and the hash is compared with the stored hash. Once the hash of the entered password has been computed, the process must delete the cleartext password. So it overwrites the array holding the password with random bytes.

The second piece of sensitive information is the access control information. Suppose an attacker wanted to gain access to a role account. The access control entries would tell the attacker which users could access that account using this program. To prevent the attacker from gaining this information, the developers decided to keep the contents of the access control file confidential. The program accesses this file using a file descriptor. File descriptors remain open when a new program overlays a process. Hence, the program closes the file descriptor corresponding to the access control file once the request has been validated (or has failed to be validated).

The third piece of sensitive information is the log file. The program alters this file. If an unprivileged program such as one run by this program were to inherit the file descriptor, it could flood the log. Were the log to fill up, the program could no longer log failures. So the program also closes the log file before spawning the role's command.

31.5.6   Improper Validation

The problem of improper validation arises when data is not checked for consistency and correctness. Ideally, a process would validate the data against the more abstract policies to ensure correctness. In practice, the process can check correctness only by looking for error codes (indicating failure of functions and procedures) or by looking for patently incorrect values (such as negative numbers when positive ones are required).

As the program is designed, the developers should determine what conditions must hold at each interface and each block of code. They should then validate that these conditions hold.

What follows is a set of validations that are commonly overlooked. Each program requires its own analysis, and other types of validation may be critical to the correct, secure functioning of the program, so this list is by no means complete.

31.5.6.1   Bounds Checking

Errors of validation often occur when data is supposed to lie within bounds. For example, a buffer may contain entries numbered from 0 to 99. If the index used to access the buffer elements takes on a value less than 0 or greater than 99, it is an invalid operand because it accesses a nonexistent entry. The variable used to access the element may not be an integer (for example, it may be a set element or pointer), but in any case it must reference an existing element.

> **Implementation Rule 31.11.** Ensure that all array references access existing elements of the array. If a function that manipulates arrays cannot ensure that only valid elements are referenced, do not use that function. Find one that does, write a new version, or create a wrapper.

In this example program, all loops involving arrays compare the value of the variable referencing the array against the indexes (or addresses) of both the first and last elements of the array. The loop terminates if the variable's value is outside those two values. This covers all loops within the program, but it does not cover the loops in the library functions.

For loops in the library functions, bounds checking requires an analysis of the functions used to manipulate arrays. The most common type of array for which library functions are used is the character string, which is a sequence of characters (bytes) terminating with a 0 byte. Because the length of the string is not encoded as part of the string, functions cannot determine the size of the array containing the string. They simply operate on all bytes until a 0 byte is found.

EXAMPLE: The program sometimes must copy character strings (defined in C as arrays of character data terminating with a byte containing 0). The canonical function for copying strings does no bounds checking. This function, strcpy(x, y), copies the string from the array y to the array x, even if the string is too long for x. A different function, strncpy(x, y, n), copies at most n characters from array y to array x. However, unlike *strcpy*, *strncpy* may not copy the terminating 0 byte.[57] The program must take two actions when *strncpy* is called. First, it must insert a 0 byte at the end of the x array. This ensures that the contents of x meet the definition of a string in C. Second, the process must check that both x and y are arrays of characters, and that n is a positive integer.

The programmers use only those functions that bound the sizes of arrays. In particular, the function *fgets* is used to read input, because it allows the

---

[57] If the string in y is longer than n characters, *strncpy* will not add a 0 byte to the characters copied into x.

programmer to specify the maximum number of characters to be read. (This solves the problem that plagued *fingerd*.[58])

31.5.6.2   Type Checking

Failure to check types is another common validation problem. If a function parameter is an integer, but the actual argument passed is a floating point number, the function will interpret the bit pattern of the floating point number as an integer and will produce an incorrect result.

> **Implementation Rule 31.12.** Check the types of functions and parameters.

A good compiler and well-written code will handle this particular problem. All functions should be declared before they are used. Most programming languages allow the programmer to specify the number and types of arguments, as well as the type of the return value (if any). The compiler can then check the types of the declarations against the types of the actual arguments and return values.

> **Implementation Rule 31.13.** When compiling programs, ensure that the compiler reports inconsistencies in types. Investigate all such warnings and either fix the problem or document the warning and why it is spurious.

31.5.6.3   Error Checking

A third common problem involving improper validation is failure to check return values of functions. For example, suppose a program needs to determine ownership of a file. It calls a system function that returns a record containing information from the file attribute table. The program obtains the owner of the file from the appropriate field of the record. If the function fails, the information in the record is meaningless. So, if the function's return status is not checked, the program may act erroneously.

> **Implementation Rule 31.14.** Check all function and procedure executions for errors.

This program makes extensive use of system and library functions, as well as its own internal functions (such as the access control module). Every function returns a value, and the value is checked for an error before the results of the function are used. For example, the function that obtains the ownership and access permissions of the access control file would return meaningless information should the function fail. So the function's return value is checked first for an error; if no error has occurred, then the file attribute information is used.

---

[58] See Section 24.4.5.2, "The *fingerd* Buffer Overflow."

As another example, the program opens a log file. If the open fails, and the program tries to write to the (invalid) file descriptor obtained from the function that failed, the program will terminate as a result of an exception. Hence, the program checks the result of opening the log file.

31.5.6.4   Checking for Valid, Not Invalid, Data

Validation should apply the principle of fail-safe defaults.[59] This principle requires that valid values be known, and that all other values be rejected. Unfortunately, programmers often check for invalid data and assume that the rest is valid.

EXAMPLE: A *metacharacter* is a character that is interpreted as something other than itself. For example, to the UNIX shells, the character "?" is a metacharacter that represents all single character files. A vendor upgraded its version of the command interpreter for its UNIX system. The new command interpreter (shell) treated the character " ` " (back quote) as a delimiter for a command (and hence a metacharacter). The old shell treated the back quote as an ordinary character. Included in the distribution was a program for executing commands on remote systems. The set of allowed commands was restricted. This program carefully checked that the command was allowed, and that it contained no metacharacters, before sending it to a shell on the remote system. Unfortunately, the program checked a list of metacharacters to be rejected, rather than checking a list of characters that were allowed in the commands. As a result, one could embed a disallowed command within a valid command request, because the list of metacharacters was not updated to include the back quote.

Implementation Rule 31.15. Check that a variable's values are valid.

This program checks that the command to be executed matches one of the authorized commands. It does not have a set of commands that are to be denied. The program will detect an invalid command as one that is not listed in the set of authorized commands for that user accessing that role at the time and place allowed.

As discussed in Section 31.3.2.3, it is possible to allow all users *except some specific users* access to a role by an appropriate access control entry (using the keyword *not*). The developers debated whether having this ability was appropriate because its use could lead to violations of the principle of fail-safe defaults. On one key system, however, the only authorized users were system administrators and one or two trainees. The administrators wanted the ability to shut the trainees out of certain roles. So the developers added the keyword and recommended against its use except in that single specific situation.

---

[59]See Section 14.2.2, "Principle of Fail-Safe Defaults."

Implementation Rule 31.16. If a trade-off between security and other factors results in a mechanism or procedure that can weaken security, document the reasons for the decision, the possible effects, and the situations in which the compromise method should be used. This informs others of the trade-off and the attendant risks.

31.5.6.5   Checking Input

All data from untrusted sources must be checked. Users are untrusted sources. The checking done depends on the way the data is received: into an input buffer (bounds checking) or read in as an integer (checking the magnitude and sign of the input).

Implementation Rule 31.17. Check all user input for both form and content. In particular, check integers for values that are too big or too small, and check character data for length and valid characters.

The program determines what to do on the basis of at least two pieces of data that the user provides: the role name and the command (which, if omitted, means unrestricted access).[60] Users must also authenticate themselves appropriately. The program must first validate that the supplied password is correct. It then checks the access control information to determine whether the user is allowed access to the role at that time and from that location.

The length of the input password must be no longer than the buffer in which it is placed. Similarly, the lines of the access control file must not overflow the buffer allocated for it. The contents of the lines of the access control file must make up a valid access control entry. This is most easily done by constraining the format of the contents of the file, as discussed in the next section.

An excellent example of the need to constrain user input comes from formatted print statements in C.

EXAMPLE: The *printf* function's first parameter is a character string that indicates how *printf* is to format output data. The following parameters contain the data. For example,

```
printf("%d %d\n", i, j);
```

prints the values of *i* and *j*. Some versions of this library function allow the user to store the number of characters printed at any point in the string. For example, if *i* contains 2, *j* contains 21, and *m* and *n* are integer variables,

```
printf("%d %d%n %d\n%n", i, j, &m, i, &n);
```

prints

```
2 21 2
```

---

[60]See Section 14.2.6, "Principle of Separation of Privilege."

and stores 4 in *m* and 7 in *n*, because four characters are printed before the first "%n" and seven before the second "%n" (the sequence "\n" is interpreted as a single character, the newline). Now, suppose the user is asked for a file name. This input is stored in the array *str*. The program then prints the file name with

```
printf(str);
```

If the user enters the file name "log%n", the function will overwrite some memory location with the integer 3. The exact location depends on the contents of the program stack, and with some experimentation it is possible to cause the program to change the return address stored on the stack. This leads to the buffer overflow attack described earlier.

31.5.6.6   Designing for Validation

Sometimes data cannot be validated completely. For example, in the C programming language, a programmer can test for a NULL pointer (meaning that the pointer does not hold the address of any object), but if the pointer is not NULL, checking the validity of the pointer may be very difficult (or impossible). Using a language with strong type checking is another example.

The consequence of the need for validation requires that data structures and functions be designed and implemented in such a way that they can be validated. For example, because C pointers cannot be properly validated, programmers should not pass pointers or use them in situations in which they must be validated. Methods of data hiding, type checking, and object-oriented programming often provide mechanisms for doing this.

Implementation Rule 31.18. Create data structures and functions in such a way that they can be validated.

An example will show the level of detail necessary for validation. The entries in the access control file are designed to allow the program to detect obvious errors. Each access control entry consists of a block of information in the following format:

```
role name
    user comma-separated list of users
    location comma-separated list of locations
    time comma-separated list of times
    command program and arguments
    . . .
    command program and arguments
endrole
```

This defines each component of the entry. (The lines need not be in any particular order.) The syntax is well-defined, and the access control module in the program checks for syntax errors. The module also performs other checks, such as searching for invalid user names in the **user** field and requiring that the full path names of all commands be specified. Finally, note that the module computes the number of commands for the module's internal record. This eliminates a possible source of error—namely, that the user may miscount the number of commands.

In case of any error, the process logs the error, if possible, and terminates. It does not allow the user to access the role.

31.5.7   Improper Indivisibility

Improper indivisibility[61] arises when an operation is considered as one unit (indivisible) in the abstract but is implemented as two units (divisible). The race conditions discussed in Section 31.5.3.3 provide one example. The checking of the access control file attributes and the opening of that file are to be executed as one operation. Unfortunately, they may be implemented as two separate operations, and an attacker who can alter the file after the first but before the second operation can obtain access illicitly. Another example arises in exception handling. Often, program statements and system calls are considered as single units or operations when the implementation uses many operations. An exception divides those operations into two sets: the set before the exception, and the set after the exception. If the system calls or statements rely on data not changing during their execution, exception handlers must not alter the data.

Section 31.5.3 discusses handling of these situations when the operations cannot be made indivisible. Approaches to making them indivisible include disabling interrupts and having the kernel perform operations. The latter assumes that the operation is indivisible when performed by the kernel, which may be an incorrect assumption.

> **Implementation Rule 31.19.** If two operations must be performed sequentially without an intervening operation, use a mechanism to ensure that the two cannot be divided.

In UNIX systems, the problem of divisibility arises with root processes such as the program under consideration. UNIX-like systems do not enforce the principle of complete mediation.[62] For *root*, access permissions are not checked. Recall the *xterm* example in Section 24.3.1. A user needed to log information from the execution of *xterm*, and specified a log file. Before appending to that file, *xterm* needed to ensure that the real UID could write to the log file. This required an extra system call. As a result, operations that should have been indivisible (the access check followed by the opening of the file) were actually divisible. One way to make these operations indivisible on UNIX-like systems is to drop privileges to those of the real UID, then open the file. The access checking is done in the kernel as part of the open.

---

[61] This is often called "atomicity."
[62] See Section 14.2.4, "Principle of Complete Mediation."

Improper indivisibility arises in our program when the access control module validates and then opens the access control file. This should be a single operation, but because of the semantics of UNIX-like systems, it must be performed as two distinct operations. It is not possible to ensure the indivisibility of the two operations. However, it is possible to ensure that the target of the operations does not change, as discussed in Section 31.5.3, and this suffices for our purposes.

31.5.7.1   Improper Sequencing

Improper sequencing means that operations are performed in an incorrect order. For example, a process may create a lock file and then write to a log file. A second process may also write to the log file, and then check to see if the lock file exists. The first program uses the correct sequence of calls; the second does not (because that sequence allows multiple writers to access the log file simultaneously).

> **Implementation Rule 31.20.** Describe the legal sequences of operations on a resource or object. Check that all possible sequences of the program(s) involved match one (or more) legal sequences.

In our program, the sequence of operations in the design shown in Section 31.3.1.2 follows a proper order. The user is first authenticated. Then the program uses the access control information to determine if the requested access is valid. If it is, the appropriate command is executed using a new, safe environment.

A second sequence of operations occurs when privileges to the role are dropped. First, group privileges are changed to those of the role. Then all user identification numbers are changed to those of the role. A common error is to switch the user identification numbers first, followed by the change in group privileges. Because changing group privileges requires *root* privileges, the change will fail. Hence, the programmers used the stated ordering.

31.5.8   Improper Choice of Operand or Operation

Preventing errors of choosing the wrong operand or operation requires that the algorithms be thought through carefully (to ensure that they are appropriate). At the implementation level, this requires that operands be of an appropriate type and value, and that operations be selected to perform the desired functions. The difference between this type of error and improper validation lies in the program. Improper implementation refers to a validation failure. The operands may be appropriate, but no checking is done. In this category, even though the operands may have been checked, they may still be inappropriate.

EXAMPLE: The UNIX program *su* allows a user to substitute another user's identity, obtaining the second user's privileges. According to an apocryphal story, one version of this program granted the user *root* privileges if the user information database did not exist (see Exercise 10 in Chapter 14). If the program could not open the user information database file, it assumed that the database did not exist. This was an inappropriate choice of operation because one could block access to the file even when the database existed.

Assurance techniques[63] help detect these problems. The programmer documents the purpose of each function and then checks (or, preferably, others check) that the algorithms in the function work properly and that the code correctly implements the algorithms.

Management Rule 31.6. Use software engineering and assurance techniques (such as documentation, design reviews, and code reviews) to ensure that operations and operands are appropriate.

Within our program, many operands and operations control the granting (and denying) of access, the changing to the role, and the execution of the command. We first focus on the access part of the program, and afterwards we consider two other issues.

First, a user is granted access only when an access control entry matches all characteristics of the current session. The relevant characteristics are the role name, the user's UID, the role's name (or UID), the location, the time, and the command. We begin by checking that if the characteristics match, the access control module returns *true* (allowing access). We also check that the caller grants access when the module returns true and denies access when the module returns *false*.

Next, we consider the user's UID. That object is of type *uid_t*. If the interface to the system database returns an object of a different type, conversion becomes an issue. Specifically, many interfaces treat the UID as an integer. The difference between the types *int* and *uid_t* may cause problems. On the systems involved, *uid_t* is an unsigned integer. Since we are comparing signed and unsigned integers, C simply converts the signed integers to unsigned integers, and the comparison succeeds. Hence, the choice of operation (comparison here) is proper.

Checking location requires the program to derive the user's location, as discussed above, and pass it to the validator. The validator takes a string and determines whether it matches the pattern in the location field of the access control entry. If the string matches, the module should continue; otherwise, it should terminate and return false.

Unlike the location, a variable of type *time_t* contains the current time. The time checking portion of the module processes the string representing the allowed times and determines if the current time falls in the range of allowed times. Checking time is different than checking location because legal times are ranges, except in one specific situation: when an allowed time is specified to the exact second. A specification of an exact time is useless, because the program may not obtain the time at the exact second required. This would lead to a denial of service, violating Requirement 31.4. Also, allowing exact times leads to ambiguity.

---

[63]See Chapter 20, "Building Systems with Assurance."

EXAMPLE: The system administrator specifies that user *matt* is allowed access to the role *mail* at 9 a.m. on Tuesdays. Should this be interpreted as *exactly* 9 a.m. (that is, 9:00:00 a.m.) or as *sometime during* the 9 a.m. hour (that is, from 9:00:00 to 9:59:59 a.m.)? The latter interprets the specification as a range rather than an exact time, so the access control module uses that interpretation.

The use of signal handlers provides a second situation in which an improper choice of operation could occur. A signal indicates either an error in the program or a request from the user to terminate, so a signal should cause the program to terminate. If the program continues to run, and then grants the user access to the role account, either the program has continued in the face of an error or it has overridden the user's attempt to terminate the program.

31.5.9   Summary

This type of top-down analysis differs from the more usual approach of taking a checklist of common vulnerabilities and using it to examine code. There is a place for each of these approaches. The top-down approach presented here is a design approach, and should be applied at each level of design and implementation. It emphasizes documentation, analysis, and understanding of the program, its interfaces, and the environment in which it executes. A security analysis document should describe the analysis and the reasons for each security-related decision. This document will help other analysts examine the program and, more importantly, will provide future developers and maintainers of the program with insight into potential problems they may encounter in porting the program to a different environment, adding new features, or changing existing features.

Once the appropriate phase of the program has been completed, the developers should use a checklist to validate that the design or implementation has no common errors. Given the complexity of security design and implementation, such checklists provide valuable confirmation that the developers have taken common security problems into account.

Appendix H lists the implementation and management rules in a convenient form.

31.6   Testing, Maintenance, and Operation

Testing provides an informal validation of the design and implementation of the program. The goal of testing is to show that the program meets the stated requirements. When design and implementation are driven by the requirements, as in the method used to create the program under discussion, testing is likely to uncover only minor problems, but if the developers do not have well-articulated requirements, or if the requirements are changed during development, testing may uncover major problems, requiring changes up to a complete redesign and reimplementation of a program. The worst mistake managers and developers can make is to take a program that does not meet the security requirements and add features to it to meet those requirements. The problem is that the basic design does not meet the security requirements. Adding security features will not ameliorate this fundamental flaw.

Once the program has been written and tested, it must be installed. The installation procedure must ensure that when a user starts the process, the environment in which the process is created matches the assumptions embodied in the design. This constrains the configuration of the program parameters as well as the manner in which the system is configured to protect the program. Finally, the installers must enable trusted users to modify and upgrade the program and the configuration files and parameters.

31.6.1   Testing

The results of testing a program are most useful if the tests are conducted in the environment in which the program will be used (the production environment). So, the first step in testing a program is to construct an environment that matches the production environment. This requires the testers to know the intended production environment. If there are a range of environments, the testers must test the programs in all of them. Often there is overlap between the environments, so this task is not so daunting as it might appear.

The production environment should correspond to the environment for which the program was developed. A symptom of discrepancies between the two environments is repeated failures resulting from erroneous assumptions. This indicates that the developers have implicitly embedded information from the development environment that is inconsistent with the testing environment. This discrepancy must be reconciled.

The testing process begins with the requirements. Are they appropriate? Do they solve the problem? This analysis may be moot (if the task is to write a program meeting the given requirements), but if the task is phrased in terms of a problem to be solved, the problem drives the requirements. Because the requirements drive the design of the program, the requirements must be validated before designing begins.

As many of the software life cycle models indicate, this step may be revisited many times during the development of the program. Requirements may prove to be impossible to meet, or may produce problems that cannot be solved without changing the requirements. If the requirements are changed, they must be reanalyzed and verified to solve the problem.

Then comes the design. Section 31.4 discusses the stepwise refinement of the program. The decomposition of the program into modules allows us to test the program as it is being implemented. Then, once it has been completed, the testing of the entire program should demonstrate that the program meets its requirements in the given environment.

The general philosophy of testing is to execute all possible paths of control and compare the results with the expected results. In practice, the paths of control are too numerous to test exhaustively. Instead, the paths are analyzed and ordered. Test data is generated for each path, and the testers compare the results obtained from the actual data with the expected results. This continues until as many paths as possible have been tested.

For security testing, the testers must test not only the most commonly used paths but also the *least commonly used* paths.[64] The latter often create security problems that attackers can exploit. Because they are relatively unused, traditional testing places them at a lower priority than that of other paths. Hence, they are not as well scrutinized, and vulnerabilities are missed.

The ordering of the paths relies on the requirements. Those paths that perform multiple security checks are more critical than those that perform single (or no) security checks because they introduce interfaces that affect security requirements. The other paths affect security, of course, but there are no interfaces.

First, we examine a module that calls no other module. Then we examine the program as a composition of modules. We conclude by testing the installation, configuration, and use instructions.

31.6.1.1   Testing the Module

The module may invoke one or more functions. The functions return results to the caller, either directly (through return values or parameter lists) or indirectly (by manipulation of the environment). The goal of this testing is to ensure that the module exhibits correct behavior regardless of what the functions returns.

The first step is to define "correct behavior." During the design of the program, the refinement process led to the specification of the module and the module's interface. This specification defines "correct behavior," and testing will require us to check that the specification holds.

We begin by listing all interfaces to the module. We will then use this list to execute four different types of tests. The types of test are as follows:

1. *Normal data tests.* These tests provide unexceptional data. The data should be chosen to exercise as many paths of control through the module as possible.

2. *Boundary data tests.* These tests provide data that tests any limits to the interfaces. For example, if the module expects a string of up to 256 characters to be passed in, these tests invoke the module and pass in arrays of 255, 256, and 257 characters. Longer strings should also be used in an effort to overflow internal buffers. The testers can examine the source code to determine what to try. Limits here do not apply simply to arrays or strings. In the program under discussion, the lowest allowed UID is 0, for *root*. A good test would be to try a UID of -1 to see what happens. The module should report an error.

---

[64]See Section 20.3.3.1, "Security Testing."

EXAMPLE: One UNIX system had UIDs of 16 bits. The system used a file server that would not allow a client's *root* user to access any files. Instead, it remapped root's UID to the public UID of −2. Because that UID was not assigned to any user, the remapped root could access only those files that were available to all users. The limit problem arose because one user, named Mike, had the UID 65534. Because 65534 = −2 in two's complement 16-bit arithmetic, the remote root user could access all of Mike's files—even those that were not publicly available.

3. *Exception tests.* These tests determine how the program handles inter-rupts and traps. For example, many systems allow the user to send a signal that causes the program to trap to a signal handler, or to take a default action such as dumping the contents of memory to a core file. These tests determine if the module leaves the system in a nonsecure state—for example, by leaving sensitive information in the memory dump. They also analyze what the process does if ordinary actions (such as writing to a file) fail.

EXAMPLE: An FTP server ran on a system that kept its authentication informa-tion confidential. An attacker found that she could cause the system to crash by sending an unexpected sequence of commands, causing multiple signals to be generated before the first signal could be handled. The crash resulted in a core dump. Because the server would be restarted automatically, the attacker simply connected again and downloaded the core dump. From that dump, she extracted the authentication information and used a dictionary attack[65] to obtain the passwords of several users.

4. *Random data tests.* These tests supply inputs generated at random and observe how the module reacts. They should not corrupt the state of the system. If the module fails, it should restore the system to a safe state.[66]

EXAMPLE: In a study of UNIX utilities [1345], approximately 30% crashed when given random inputs. In one case, an unprivileged program caused the system to crash. In 1995, a retest showed some improvement, but still "significant rates of failure" [1346, p. 1]. Other tested systems fared little better [705, 1344].

Throughout the testing, the testers should keep track of the paths taken. This allows them to determine how complete the testing is. Because these tests are highly informal, the assurance they provide is not as convincing as the techniques discussed in Chapter 20. However, it is more than random tests, or no tests, would provide.

---

[65] See Section 13.4, "Attacking Passwords."
[66] See Section 14.2.2, "Principle of Fail-Safe Defaults."

31.6.2   Testing Composed Modules

Now consider a module that calls other modules. Each of the invoked modules has a specification describing its actions. So, in addition to the tests discussed in the preceding section, one other type of test should be performed.

> 5. *Error handling tests*. These tests assume that the called modules violate their specifications in some way. The goal of these tests is to determine how robust the caller is. If it fails gracefully, and restores the system to a safe state, then the module passes the test. Otherwise, it fails and must be rewritten.

EXAMPLE: Assume that a security-related program, running with *root* privileges, logs all network connections to a UNIX system. It also sends mail to the network administrator with the name of the connecting host on the subject line. To do this, it executes a command such as

```
mail -s hostname netadmin
```

where *hostname* is the name of the connecting host. This module obtains *hostname* from a different module that is passed the connecting host's IP address and uses the Domain Name Service to find the corresponding host name. A serious problem arose because the DNS did not verify that *hostname* was composed of legal characters. The effects were discovered when one attacker changed the name of his host to

```
hi nobody; rm -rf *; true
```

causing the security-related program to delete critical files. Had the calling module expected failure, and checked for it, the error would have been caught before any damage was done.

31.6.3   Testing the Program

Once the testers have assembled the program and its documentation, the final phase of testing begins. The testers have someone follow the installation and configuration instructions. This person should not be a member of the testing team, because the testing team has been working with the program and is familiar with it. The goal of this test is to determine if the installation and configuration instructions are correct and easy to understand. The principle of least astonishment[67] requires that the tool be as easy to install and use as possible. Because most installers and users will not have experience with the program, the

---

[67]See Section 14.2.8, "Principle of Least Astonishment."

testers need to evaluate how they will understand the documentation and whether or not they can install the program correctly by following the instructions. An incorrectly installed security tool does not provide security; it may well detract from it. Worse, it gives people a false sense of security.

31.7   Distribution

Once the program has been completed, it must be distributed. Distribution involves placing the program in a repository where it cannot be altered except by authorized people, and from which it can be retrieved and sent to the intended recipients. This requires a policy for distribution. Specific factors to be considered are as follows.

1. *Who can use the program?* If the program is licensed to a specific organization, or to a specific host, then each copy of the program that is distributed must be tied to that organization or host so it cannot be redistributed or pirated. This is an originator controlled policy.[68] One approach is to provide the licensee with a secret key and encipher the software with the same key. This prevents redistribution without the licensee's consent, unless the attacker breaks the cryptosystem or steals the licensee's key.[69]

2. *How can the integrity of the master copy be protected?* If an attacker can alter the master copy, from which distribution copies are made, then the attacker can compromise all who use the program.

EXAMPLE: The program *tcp_wrappers* provides host-level access control for network servers. It is one of the most widely used programs in the UNIX community. In 1996, attackers broke into the site from which that program could be obtained [2238]. They altered the program to allow all connections to succeed. More than 50 groups obtained the program before the break-in was detected.

Part of the problem is credibility. If an attacker can pose as the vendor, then all who obtain the program from the attacker will be vulnerable to attack. This tactic undermines trust in the program and can be surprisingly hard to counter. It is analogous to generating a cryptographic checksum for a program infected with a computer virus.[70] When an uninfected program is obtained, the integrity checker complains because the checksum is wrong. In our example, when the real vendor

---

[68] See Section 8.3, "Originator Controlled Access Control."
[69] See Section 14.2.5, "Principle of Open Design."
[70] See Section 23.9.1, "Scanning Defenses."

contacts the duped customer, the customer usually reacts with disbelief, or is unwilling to concede that his system has been compromised.

3. *How can the availability of the program be ensured?* If the program is sent through a physical medium, such as a read-only DVD, availability is equivalent to the availability of mail or messenger services between the vendor and the buyer. If the program is distributed through electronic means, however, the distributor must take precautions to ensure that the distribution site is available. Denial of service attacks such as SYN flooding may hamper the availability.

Like a program, the distribution is controlled by a policy. All considerations that affect a security policy affect the distribution policy as well.

31.8   Summary

This chapter discussed informal techniques for writing programs that enforce security policies. The process began with a requirements analysis and continued with a threat analysis to show that the requirements countered the threats. The design process came next, and it fed back into the requirements to clarify an ambiguity. Once the high-level design was accepted, we used a stepwise refinement process to break the design down into modules and a caller. The categories of flaws in the program analysis vulnerability helped find potential implementation problems. Finally, issues of testing and distribution ensured that the program did what was required.

31.9   Research Issues

The first research issue has to do with analysis of code. How can one analyze programs to discover security flaws? This differs from the sort of analysis that is performed in the development of high-assurance systems, because the program and system are already in place. The goal is to determine what, and where, the problems are. Some researchers are developing analysis tools for specific problems such as buffer overflows and race conditions. Others are using flow analysis tools to study the program for a wide variety of vulnerabilities.

Related to this issue is the development of languages that are safer with respect to security. For example, some languages automatically create an exception if a reference is made beyond the bounds of an array. How much overhead does this add? Can the language use special-purpose hardware to minimize the impact of checking the references? What else should a language constrain, and how should it do so?

31.10   Further Reading

Robust programming—the art of writing programs that work correctly and handle errors gracefully—is a topic of great interest, often in the guise of "secure programming." Kernighan and Plauger's book [1039] describes the principles and ideas underlying good programming style. Kernighan and Pike [1040] also discuss style and other elements of good programming. Stavely's book [1819] combines formalisms with informal steps. Maguire's book [1234] is much more informal, and is a collection of tips on how to write robust programs. Martin [1257] focuses on robust practices for agile programming, while McConnell [1277] discusses robust programming in the general context of software construction.

Howard and LeBlanc [926] discuss secure coding, emphasizing the Windows and .NET environment. Howard, LeBlanc, and Viega's book [927] describes 24 serious but common software flaws and how programmers can avoid them.

Much focus is on the C and C++ programming languages, because of their wide use, lack of type-safe features, and ability to manipulate memory directly. Seacord [1704] and Viega and Messier [1935] discuss ways to make programs in these languages more robust and secure. Sutter and Alexandrescu [1843] present a set of coding standards for C++. Similarly, developing robust, secure web applications is critical, and several books [119, 1241, 1393, 1734] discuss how to do so.

Graff and van Wyk [804] provide a general overview of principles and practice, and much sound advice. Viega and McGraw's book [1932] is also general, with many examples focusing on UNIX and Linux systems. Its design principles give good advice. McGraw [1287] expands on these in a later book. Garfinkel, Schwartz, and Spafford [747] has a wonderful chapter on trust, which is must reading for anyone interested in security-related programming. Wheeler [2000] also provides valuable information and insight.

31.11   Exercises

1. Consider the two interpretations of a time field that specifies "1 a.m." One interpretation says that this means exactly 1:00 a.m. and no other time. The other says that this means any time during the 1 a.m. hour.

   a. How would you express the time of "exactly 1 a.m." in the second interpretation?

   b. How would you express "any time during the 1 a.m. hour" in the first interpretation?

   c. Which is more powerful? If they are equally powerful, which do you think is least astonishing? Why?

2. Verify that the modified version of Requirement 31.4 shown as Requirement 31.6 on page 1105 counters the appropriate threats.

3. Assume the alternative interpretation of Requirement 31.4 given in Section 31.3.1.2, so that access only is controlled by location and time, and that commands are restricted by role and user. This means that if a user is authorized to run a command, she can run it from any location he is authorized to use. How would you change the way information is stored in the access control file described in Section 31.3.2.2?

4. Currently, the program described in this chapter is to have setuid-to-*root* privileges. Someone observed that it could be equally well-implemented as a server, in which case the program would authenticate the user, connect to the server, send the command and role, and then let the server execute the command.

   a. What are the advantages of using the server approach rather than the single program approach?

   b. If the server responds only to clients on the local machine, using interprocess communication mechanisms on the local system, which approach would you use? Why?

   c. If the server were listening for commands from the network, would that change your answer to the previous question? Why or why not?

   d. If the client sent the password to the server, and the server authenticated, would your answers to any of the three previous parts change? Why or why not?

5. The little languages presented in Section 31.3.2.3 have ambiguous semantics. For example, in the location language, does "not host1 or host2" mean "neither at host1 nor at host2" or "at host2 or not at host1"?

   a. Rewrite the BNF of the location language to make the semantics reflect the second meaning (i.e., the precedence of "not" is lower than that of "or"). Are the semantics unambiguous now? Why or why not?

   b. Rewrite the BNF of the time language to make the semantics reflect the second meaning (i.e., the precedence of "not" is higher than that of "or"). Are the semantics unambiguous now? Why or why not?

6. Suppose an access control record is malformed (for example, it has a syntax error). Show that the access control module would deny access.

7. The canary for StackGuard simply detects overflow that might change the return address. This exercise asks you to extend the notion of a canary to detection of buffer overflow.

   a. Assume that the canary is placed directly after the array, and that after every array, access is checked to see if it has changed. Would this detect a buffer overflow? If so, why do you think this is not suitable for use in practice? If not, describe an attack that could change a number beyond the buffer without affecting the canary.

b. Now suppose that the canary was placed directly after the buffer but— like the canary for StackGuard—was only checked just before a function return. How effective do you think this method would be?

Part IX

Appendices

This part presents background and additional material that may prove helpful with some of the chapters of this book.

Appendix A, "Lattices," reviews the mathematical properties of lattices.

Appendix B, "The Extended Euclidean Algorithm," presents a very useful number-theoretic algorithm used in various cryptosystems.

Appendix C, "Entropy and Uncertainty," presents an overview of probability and entropy.

Appendix D, "Virtual Machines," reviews the notion of a virtual machine.

Appendix E, "Symbolic Logic," discusses different types of logic, including propositional logic and temporal logic.

Appendix F, "The Encryption Standards," discusses the Data Encryption Standard and its successor, the Advanced Encryption Standard.

Appendix G, "Example Academic Security Policy," presents real acceptable use and electronic communications policies.

Appendix H, "Programming Rules," lists rules for programming implementation and management.

Appendix A
Lattices

A lattice is built on the notion of a group. First, we review some basic terms. Then we discuss lattices.

A.1 Basics

For a set S, a relation R is any subset of $S \times S$. For convenience, if $(a, b) \in R$, we write aRb.

EXAMPLE: Let $S = \{1, 2, 3\}$. Then the relation *less than or equal to* is defined on S by the set $R = \{(1, 1), (1, 2), (1, 3), (2, 2), (2, 3), (3, 3)\}$. We write $1R2$ and $2R3$ for convenience, because $(1, 2) \in R$ and $(2, 3) \in R$, but $3R2$ does not hold, because $(3, 2) \notin R$. Of course, the symbol used for R is simply $\leq$.

The following definitions describe properties of relations.

Definition A–1. A relation R defined over a set S is *reflexive* if aRa for all $a \in S$.

Definition A–2. A relation R defined over a set S is *antisymmetric* if aRb and bRa imply $a = b$ for all $a, b \in S$.

Definition A–3. A relation R defined over a set S is *transitive* if aRb and bRc imply aRc for all $a, b, c \in S$.

EXAMPLE: Consider the set of complex numbers $\mathbb{C}$. For any $a \in \mathbb{C}$, define a_R as the real component and a_I as the imaginary component (that is, $a = a_R + a_I i$). Let $a \leq b$ if and only if $a_R \leq b_R$ and $a_I \leq b_I$. This relation is reflexive, antisymmetric, and transitive.

A *partial ordering* occurs when a relation orders some, but not all, elements of a set. Such a set and relation are often called a *poset*. If the relation imposes an ordering among all elements, it is a *total ordering*.

EXAMPLE: The relation "less than or equal to," as defined in the usual sense, imposes a total ordering on the set of integers, because, given any two integers, one will be less than or equal to the other. However, the relation in the preceding example imposes a partial ordering on the set $\mathbb{C}$. Specifically, the numbers $1 + 4i$ and $2 + 3i$ are not related under that relation (because $1 \leq 2$ but $4 \nleq 3$).

Under a partial ordering (and a total ordering), we define the upper bound of two elements to be any element that follows both in the relation.

> **Definition A–4.** For two elements $a, b \in S$, if there exists a $u \in S$ such that aRu and bRu, then u is an *upper bound* of a and b.

A pair of elements may have many upper bounds. Intuitively, the one "closest" to the two elements but greater than or equal to both is the least upper bound. The following definition formalizes "closest."

> **Definition A–5.** Let U be the set of upper bounds of a and b. Let $u \in U$ be an element such that there is no $t \in U$ for which tRu. Then u is the *least upper bound* of a and b (written $lub(a, b)$ or $a \otimes b$).

Lower bounds, and greatest lower bounds, are defined similarly.

> **Definition A–6.** For two elements $a, b \in S$, if there exists an $l \in S$ such that lRa and lRb, then l is a *lower bound* of a and b.

> **Definition A–7.** Let L be the set of lower bounds of a and b. Let $l \in L$ be an element such that there is no $m \in L$ for which lRm. Then l is the *greatest lower bound* of a and b (written $glb(a, b)$ or $a \oplus b$).

EXAMPLE: Consider the subset of the set of complex numbers for which the real and imaginary parts are integers from 0 to 10, inclusive, and the relation defined in the second example in this appendix. The set of upper bounds for $1 + 9i$ and $9 + 3i$ is $\{9 + 9i, 9 + 10i, 10 + 9i, 10 + 10i\}$. The least upper bound of $1 + 9i$ and $9 + 3i$ is $9 + 9i$. The set of lower bounds is $\{1 + 1i, 1 + 0i, 0 + 0i\}$. The greatest lower bound is $1 + 1i$.

A.2   Lattices

A *lattice* is a set of elements S and a relation R meeting the following criteria:

1. R is reflexive, antisymmetric, and transitive on the elements of S.
2. For every $s, t \in S$, there exists a greatest lower bound.
3. For every $s, t \in S$, there exists a least upper bound.

EXAMPLE: The set $\{0, 1, 2\}$ forms a lattice under the relation "less than or equal to" ($\leq$). By the laws of arithmetic, the relation is reflexive, antisymmetric, and transitive. The greatest lower bound of any two integers is the smaller, and the least upper bound is the larger.

EXAMPLE: Consider the subset $\mathbb{C}'$ of the set of complex numbers for which the real and imaginary parts are integers from 0 to 10, inclusive. For any $a \in \mathbb{C}'$, define a_R as the real component and a_I as the imaginary component (that is, $a = a_R + a_I i$). Let $a \leq b$ if and only if $a_R \leq b_R$ and $a_I \leq b_I$. This set and relation define a lattice, because the relation is reflexive, antisymmetric, and transitive (see the second example of this appendix) and any pair of elements a, b have a least upper bound and a greatest lower bound.

A.3   Exercises

1. Determine the least upper bound and greatest lower bound for the pair of complex integers a and b in the subset $\mathbb{C}'$ used in the examples.

2. Prove that the set of all subsets of a given set S (that is, the *power set* of S) forms a lattice under the relation "subset" ($\subseteq$).

3. Consider a set with elements that are totally ordered by a relation. Does the set form a lattice under that relation? If so, show that it does. If not, give a counterexample.

A.2 Exercises

Appendix B
The Extended Euclidean Algorithm

The Extended Euclidean Algorithm is a staple of number theory and is used to solve equations of the form $ax \bmod n = b$. This appendix reviews this algorithm and its applications. We begin with the classical algorithm, and then extend it to solve simple equations.

B.1 The Euclidean Algorithm

Euclid's algorithm determines the greatest common divisor of two integers. The algorithm is based on the observation that, if x divides both a and b, then x divides their difference $a - b$. The trick is to find the largest such x.

Assume (without loss of generality) that $a > b$. If x divides $a - b$, then it also divides $a - qb$, where q is an integer. Let $r = a - qb$. If $r \neq 0$, and x divides $a - qb$, then x divides r. We have now reduced the problem of finding the largest x such that x divides a and b to the problem of finding the largest x such that x divides b and r. (To see this, realize that if x divides b and r, then x divides $qb + r$, or a.) We iterate until r is 0. Then x is the greatest common divisor of a and b.

If we take q to be the integer portion of $\frac{a}{b}$, these operations can form a simple table, as follows.

EXAMPLE: Find the greatest common divisor of 15 and 12.
Take $a = 15$ and $b = 12$. Then:

a	b	q	r
15	12	1	3
12	3	4	0

The greatest common divisor of 15 and 12 is 3.

EXAMPLE: Find the greatest common divisor of 35,731 and 24,689.
Take $a = 35731$ and $b = 24689$. Then:

a	b	q	r
35731	24689	1	11042
24689	11042	2	2605
11042	2605	4	622
2605	622	4	117
622	117	5	37
117	37	3	6
37	6	6	1
6	1	6	0

The numbers 35,731 and 24,689 have 1 as the greatest (and only) common factor.

The algorithm (in pseudocode) is as follows:

```
function gcd(a : integer, b : integer) : integer;
var r : integer;
    rprev: integer;
begin
    rprev := r := 1;
    while r <> 0 do begin
        rprev := r;
        r := a mod b;
        write 'a = ', a, 'b =', b, 'q = ', a div b,
            'r = ', r, endline;
      a := b;
      b := r;
    end;
    gcd := rprev;
    write 'the gcd is ', gcd, endline;
end.
```

The "write" corresponds to the lines in the tables in the examples above.

B.2   The Extended Euclidean Algorithm

The Extended Euclidean Algorithm determines two integers x and y such that

$$xa + yb = 1$$

In order for these integers to exist and be unique, the greatest common divisor of a and b must be 1. The following algorithm (in pseudocode) returns x and y:

```
proc eeuclid(a : integer, b : integer,
        var x : integer, var y : integer) : integer;
var q, u: integer;
    xprev, yprev, uprev: integer;
    xtmp, ytmp, utmp: integer;
begin
    uprev := a; u := b;
    xprev := 0; x := 1; yprev := 1; y := 0;
    write 'u = ', uprev, ' x = ', xprev, ' y = ', yprev,
            endline;
    write 'u = ', u, ' x = ', x, ' y = ', y, endline;
    while u <> 0 do begin
        q := uprev div u;
        write 'q = ', q, endline;
        utmp := uprev - u * q; uprev := u; u := utmp;
        xtmp := xprev - x * q; xprev := x; x := xtmp;
        ytmp := yprev - y * q; yprev := y; y := ytmp;
        write 'u = ', u, ' x = ', x, ' y = ', y, endline;
    end;
    x := xprev; y := yprev;
    write 'the values are x = ', x, ' y = ', y, endline;
end.
```

The "write" corresponds to the lines in the tables in the examples below. The variable u contains $xa + yb$ at each step.

EXAMPLE: Find x and y such that $51x + 100y = 1$.

u	x	y	q
100	0	1	
51	1	0	$100/51 = 1$
49	-1	1	$51/49 = 1$
2	2	-1	$49/2 = 24$
1	-49	25	$2/1 = 2$
0	100	-51	

So, $51 \times (-49) + 100 \times 25 = 1$.

EXAMPLE: Find x and y such that $24689x + 35731y = 1$.

u	x	y	q
35731	0	1	
24689	1	0	35731/24689 = 1
11042	−1	1	24689/11042 = 2
2605	3	−2	11042/2605 = 4
622	−13	9	2605/622 = 4
117	55	−38	622/117 = 5
37	−288	199	117/37 = 3
6	919	−635	37/6 = 6
1	−5802	4009	
0	35731	−24689	

So $24689 \times (-5802) + 35731 \times 4009 = 1$.

B.3 Solving $ax \bmod n = 1$

Recall that if $ax \bmod n = 1$, then there exists an integer k such that $ax = 1 + kn$. Rewriting this, $ax - kn = 1$. Define $j = -k$, to yield $ax + jn = 1$. So, to find x and j, use the Extended Euclidean Algorithm. As before, a and n must be relatively prime.

EXAMPLE: Find x such that $51x \bmod 100 = 1$.
  Because $51 \times (-49) + 100 \times 25 = 1$ from the first example in Section B.2,

$$x = -49 \bmod 100 = 51$$

Checking,
$$51 \times 51 \bmod 100 = 2601 \bmod 100 = 1$$

EXAMPLE: Find x such that $24689x \bmod 35731 = 1$.
  From the last example in Section B.2, $24689 \times (-5802) + 35731 \times 4009 = 1$. Therefore,
$$x = -5802 \bmod 35731 = 29929$$

Checking,
$$24689 \times 29929 \bmod 35731 = 738917081 \bmod 35731 = 1$$

B.4   Solving *ax* mod *n* = *b*

From the fundamental laws of modular arithmetic,

$$xy \bmod n = (x \bmod n)(y \bmod n)$$

Thus, if x solves the equation $ax \bmod n = 1$, we can multiply both sides by b to get

$$b(ax \bmod n) = a(bx) \bmod n = b \times 1 = b$$

So, we first solve $ax \bmod n = 1$ for x and then compute $bx \bmod n$.

EXAMPLE: Find x such that $51x \bmod 100 = 10$.
    Solving $51y \bmod 100 = 1$, $y = -49 \bmod 100 = 51$. Then,

$$x = by \bmod n = 10 \times 51 \bmod 100 = 510 \bmod 100 = 10$$

EXAMPLE: Find x such that $24689x \bmod 35731 = 1753$.
    Solving $24689y \bmod 35731 = 1$, $y = -5802 \bmod 35731 = 29929$. Then,

$$x = by \bmod n = 1753 \times 29929 \bmod 35731 = 52465537 \bmod 35731 = 12429$$

B.5   Exercises

1. Find the greatest common divisor of 234 and 124.

2. Find r and s such that $8092r + 1111s = 1$.

3. Find a counterexample to the claim that if the greatest common divisor of a and b is not 1, there exists a unique r and a unique s such that $ra + sb = 1$.

4. Solve for x: $324x \bmod 121 = 1$.

5. Solve for x: $99997x \bmod 8888 = 1234$.

Appendix C
Entropy and Uncertainty

Entropy is an information-theoretic measure of the amount of uncertainty in a variable. Beginning with Shannon's seminal works [1725–1727], cryptographers and information theorists have used entropy to determine how well transformations on messages obscure their meaning. Entropy has applications in a wide variety of disciplines, including cryptography, compression, and coding theory. This chapter reviews the basics of entropy, which has its roots in probability theory.

C.1 Conditional and Joint Probability

Definition C–1. A *random variable* is a variable that represents the outcome of an event.

EXAMPLE: Let X be a variable representing some random event. X is a random variable. For example, X might be the result of rolling a six-sided die. Then X has a value selected from the set $\{1, 2, 3, 4, 5, 6\}$. Assuming the die is fair, the six possible outcomes are equiprobable. So,

$$p(X = 1) = p(X = 2) = p(X = 3) = p(X = 4) = p(X = 5) = p(X = 6) = \frac{1}{6}$$

Were the die loaded, so that 2 came up twice as often as the other faces, $p(X = 2) = 2/7$ and $p(X = i) = 1/7$ for $i = 1, 3, 4, 5, 6$.

A word about notation. We write $p(X = x_1)$ for the probability that the random variable X has value x_1. When the specific value does not matter (for example, when all values are equiprobable), we abbreviate this as $p(X)$.

Sometimes the results of two different events are of interest.

EXAMPLE: Let X be a random variable representing the roll of one die, and let Y be a random variable representing the flip of a coin. Assuming that both die and coin are fair, the probability of the die coming up 6 and the coin being heads is $\frac{1}{12}$.

Definition C–2. The *joint probability* of X and Y, written $p(X, Y)$, is the probability that the random variables X and Y will simultaneously assume particular values.

This example involves the probability $p(X = 6, Y = \text{heads})$. If the two random variables are independent (that is, if the value of one does not affect the value of the other), then

$$p(X, Y) = p(X)p(Y)$$

Now suppose that the two random variables are not independent.

EXAMPLE: Let X represent the roll of a red die, and let Y represent the sum of the values from rolling the red die and a blue die. Then,

$$
\begin{array}{lll}
p(Y = 2) = 1/36 & p(Y = 3) = 2/36 & p(Y = 4) = 3/36 \\
p(Y = 5) = 4/36 & p(Y = 6) = 5/36 & p(Y = 7) = 6/36 \\
p(Y = 8) = 5/36 & p(Y = 9) = 4/36 & p(Y = 10) = 3/36 \\
p(Y = 11) = 2/36 & p(Y = 12) = 1/36 &
\end{array}
$$

If both dice are fair, this formula yields

$$p(X = 1, Y = 11) = p(X = 1)p(Y = 11) = \left(\frac{1}{6}\right)\left(\frac{2}{36}\right) = \frac{1}{108}$$

But if $Y = 11$, then the only two possible throws of the red die are 5 and 6 (the corresponding numbers on the blue die are 6 and 5, respectively). The events $X = 1$ and $Y = 11$ cannot be simultaneously true. So, $p(X = 1, Y = 11) = 0$.

This example shows that if two events are not independent, then the formula for joint probability is more complicated. The next definition captures the notion of dependence.

Definition C–3. The *conditional probability* of X given Y (written $p(X|Y)$) is the probability that X takes on a particular value, given that Y has a particular value.

EXAMPLE: Returning to our previous example, $p(Y = 11|X = 1) = 0$, because when $X = 1$, Y cannot be 11. However, $p(Y = 7|X = 1) = 1/6$, because in one of the six ways to throw a 7, the number on the red die is 1.

We can now write the formula for joint probability in terms of conditional probability:

$$p(X, Y) = p(X|Y)p(Y) = p(X)p(Y|X)$$

EXAMPLE: Consider $p(X = 3, Y = 8)$. The two events are dependent. So,

$$p(X = 3, Y = 8) = p(X = 3 \mid Y = 8)p(Y = 8) = \left(\frac{1}{5}\right)\left(\frac{5}{36}\right) = \frac{1}{36}$$

This matches intuition, because by constraining the total throw and the value of the red die, there is only one value for the blue die that will produce the desired sum.

In fact, the formula for joint probability of two independent events is a special case of the formula above. When X and Y are independent random variables,

$$p(X \mid Y) = p(X)$$

C.2   Entropy and Uncertainty

Definition C–4. Let the random variable X take values from some set $\{x_1, ... x_n\}$. The value x_i occurs with probability $p(X = x_i)$, where $\sum_{i=1}^{n} p(X = x_i) = 1$. The *entropy*, or uncertainty, of x is

$$H(X) = -\sum_{i=1}^{n} p(X = x_i)\lg p(X = x_i)$$

where "$\lg x$" is the base 2 logarithm of x. (For purposes of this definition, we define $0 \lg 0$ to be 0.)

This definition measures the uncertainty of a message in bits.

EXAMPLE: Suppose the message m is either "yes" or "no," with either message being equally likely. Because there are two possibilities for the message, intuitively there is 1 bit of uncertainty. The message can be represented as either a 0 or a 1. From the previous discussion,

$$
\begin{aligned}
H(M) &= -\sum_{i=1}^{2} p(M = m_i)\lg p(M = m_i) \\
&= -p(M = \text{yes})\lg p(M = \text{yes}) - p(M = \text{no})\lg p(M = \text{no}) \\
&= -2^{-1}\lg 2^{-1} - 2^{-1}\lg 2^{-1} = 2^{-1} + 2^{-1} = 1
\end{aligned}
$$

as expected.

EXAMPLE: Suppose each message is equally likely—that is, $p(M = m_i) = 1/n$. Then

$$H(M) = -\sum_{i=1}^{n} p(M = m_i) \lg p(M = m_i)$$

$$= -\sum_{i=1}^{n} \frac{1}{n} \lg \frac{1}{n} = -n\left[\frac{1}{n} \lg \frac{1}{n}\right] = -\lg n^{-1} = \lg n$$

The uncertainty of m is the number of bits needed to represent n.

EXAMPLE: Suppose Ann, Paul, and Pamela are finalists in a game. Ann and Pamela are twice as likely to win as Paul is. Let W be the random variable representing the winner, and let w_1 = Ann, w_2 = Pamela, and w_3 = Paul. Then $p(W = w_1) = 2/5, p(W = w_2) = 2/5, p(W = w_3) = 1/5$, and

$$H(W) = \sum_{3i=1}^{3} p(W = w_i) \lg p(W = w_i)$$

$$= -p(W = w_1) \lg p(W = w_1) - p(W = w_2) \lg p(W = w_2)$$
$$-p(W = w_3) \lg p(W = w_3)$$

$$= -\frac{2}{5} \lg \frac{2}{5} - \frac{2}{5} \lg \frac{2}{5} - \frac{1}{5} \lg \frac{1}{5} = -\frac{4}{5} + \lg 5 \approx 1.52$$

Were all three players equally likely to win, the uncertainty would be $\lg 3 \approx 1.58$, again matching our intuition that the winner is less uncertain if two of the three are more likely to win. To take an extreme case, were Paul 100 times more likely to win than either Ann or Pamela, the uncertainty would be 0.14, considerably lower still.

EXAMPLE: Given a fair die, the uncertainty of the result of rolling it is $\lg 6 \approx 2.58$. When two fair dice are rolled, the uncertainty of the result is 3.27.

C.3   Joint and Conditional Entropy

Joint and conditional entropy are analogous to joint and conditional probability.

C.3.1   Joint Entropy

Definition C–5. Let the random variable X take values from some set $\{x_1, ...x_n\}$. The value x_i occurs with probability $p(X = x_i)$, where

$\sum_{i=1}^{n} p(X = x_i) = 1$. Let the random variable Y take values from some set $\{y_1, ...y_m\}$. The value y_j occurs with probability $p(Y = y_j)$, where $\sum_{j=1}^{n} p(Y = y_j) = 1$. The *joint entropy* of X and Y is

$$H(X, Y) = - \sum_{j=1}^{m} \sum_{i=1}^{n} p(X = x_i, Y = y_j) \lg p(X = x_i, Y = y_j)$$

EXAMPLE: Let X be a random variable representing the roll of one die, and let Y be a random variable representing the flip of a coin. (See the second example in Section C.1.) Assuming that both die and coin are fair, the entropy of X and Y taken jointly is

$$H(X, Y) = - \sum_{j=1}^{m} j = 1 \sum_{i=1}^{n} p(X = x_i, Y = y_j) \lg p(X = x_i, Y = y_j)$$

$$= -2 \left[6 \left[\frac{1}{12} \lg \frac{1}{12} \right] \right] = \lg 12 \approx 3.59$$

C.3.2   Conditional Entropy

Definition C–6.   Let the random variable X take values from some set $\{x_1, ...x_n\}$. The value x_i occurs with probability $p(X = x_i)$, where $\sum_{i=1}^{n} p(X = x_i) = 1$. Let the random variable Y take values from some set $\{y_1, ...y_m\}$. The value y_j occurs with probability $p(Y = y_j)$, where $\sum_{j=1}^{n} p(Y = y_j) = 1$. The *conditional entropy*, or *equivocation*, of X given $Y = y_j$ is

$$H(X | Y = y_j) = - \sum_{i=1}^{n} p(X = x_i | Y = y_j) \lg p(X = x_i | Y = y_j)$$

The conditional entropy of X given Y is

$$H(X | Y) = - \sum_{j=1}^{m} p(Y = y_j) \left[\sum_{i=1}^{n} p(X = x_i | Y = y_j) \lg p(X = x_i | Y = y_j) \right]$$

The latter is the weighted mean of the conditional entropies of X given $Y = y_j$ for the possible values of Y.

EXAMPLE: Let X represent the roll of a red die, and let Y represent the sum of the values from rolling the red die and a blue die. Then the conditional entropy of X given $Y = 2$ is

$$H(X|Y = 2) = -\sum_{i=1}^{n} p(X = x_i | Y = 2)\lg p(X = x_i | Y = 2) = 0$$

because $p(X = 1 | Y = 2) = 1$ and $p(X = i | Y = 2) = 0$ for $i = 2, ..., 6$. However, the conditional entropy of X given $Y = 7$ is

$$H(X|Y = 7) = -\sum_{i=1}^{n} p(X = x_i | Y = 7)\lg p(X = x_i | Y = 7) = \lg 6 \approx 2.58$$

Intuitively, these results make sense. If the total of the red and blue dice comes up 2, both must be 1, and so in the first case the conditional entropy is 0 because, given the value of Y, there is no uncertainty in the value of X. In the second case, the red die may take on any of its six possible values, so, assuming that it is fair, the uncertainty corresponds to each possible value of X being equally likely.

The conditional entropy of X given Y is

$$H(X|Y) = -\sum_{j=2}^{12} p(Y = y_j)\left[-\sum_{i=1}^{6} p(X = x_i | Y = y_j)\lg p(X = x_i | Y = y_j) \right]$$

$$= p(Y = 2)\left[-\sum_{i=1}^{6} p(X = x_i | Y = 2)\lg p(X = x_i | Y = 2) \right] + ... +$$

$$p(Y = 12)\left[-\sum_{i=1}^{6} p(X = x_i | Y = 12)\lg p(X = x_i | Y = 12) \right]$$

$$\approx 1.8955$$

C.3.3   Perfect Secrecy

Perfect secrecy arises when knowing the ciphertext does not decrease the uncertainty of the plaintext. More formally:

Definition C–7. Let M be a random variable that takes values from the set of messages $\{m_1, \ldots m_n\}$. The cipher $C = E(M)$ achieves *perfect secrecy* if $p(M|C) = p(M)$.

EXAMPLE: The one-time pad (see Section 10.2.2.2) meets this requirement. Let M be a random variable representing a message selected from a set of n four-letter messages. The probability of this variable is $p(M)$. An attacker intercepts $C = \text{AAVG}$. Given this, the probability of M is $p(M|C)$. However, the attacker has gleaned no more information than was initially available, because the key is four randomly chosen letters. Any message could produce the intercepted ciphertext. Hence, $p(M|C) = p(M)$, and the cipher achieves perfect secrecy.

C.4   Exercises

1. Let X represent the roll of a red die, and let Y represent the sum of the values from rolling the red die and a blue die. Prove that $p(X = 3| Y = 8) = 1/5$.

2. Prove that the maximum entropy for an unknown message chosen from the set of possible messages {"yes", "no"} occurs when the probability of each message is $1/2$.

3. Let X and Y be random variables that take values from finite sets. Prove that

$$H(X, Y) \leq H(X) + H(Y)$$

with equality holding when X and Y are independent.

4. Let X and Y be random variables that take values from finite sets. Prove that

$$H(X, Y) = H(X|Y) + H(Y)$$

5. Let M and C be random variables that take values from the set of possible plaintexts and the set of possible ciphertexts for some cryptosystem. Prove that the cryptosystem provides perfect secrecy if and only if $H(M|C) = H(M)$.

Appendix D
Virtual Machines

Virtual memory provides the illusion of physical memory. The abstraction allows a process to assume that its memory space both is contiguous and begins at location 0. This simplifies the process's view of memory and hides the underlying physical locations of the process's memory. The physical memory corresponding to the virtual memory need not be contiguous. Indeed, some of the locations in virtual memory may have no corresponding physical addresses until the process references them.

Like virtual memory, a *virtual machine* provides the illusion of a physical machine. The abstraction allows operating systems to assume that they are running directly on the hardware. This allows one to run the operating system, and allows the operating system to run processes, with no changes in either the operating system or the programs. A second, lower *virtual machine monitor* runs directly on the hardware and provides the illusion of hardware to the operating systems run above it. The physical machine may support many virtual machines, each running its own operating system.

This appendix reviews the structure of a virtual machine.

D.1 Virtual Machine Structure

A virtual machine runs on a virtual machine monitor. That monitor virtualizes the resources of the underlying system and presents to each virtual machine the illusion that it and it alone is using the hardware.

EXAMPLE: IBM's VM/370 and its successors provide each user with the illusion that she has complete access to the resources of a single IBM mainframe system. Many users will use the same physical machine, but each one is isolated from the others.

D.2 Virtual Machine Monitor

The virtual machine monitor keeps track of the state of each virtual machine just as an ordinary operating system keeps track of the states of its processes.

When a privileged instruction is executed, the hardware causes a trap to the virtual machine monitor. The monitor services the interrupt and restores the state of the caller.

EXAMPLE: Suppose the virtual machine monitor VMM is running the operating system OS. Process p running under OS makes a system call to read data from a disk. The system call causes a trap. VMM is invoked and detects that the trap occurred from within OS. It updates the state of OS to make it appear that the hardware on which OS is running (the virtual machine) invoked OS. OS then tries to read from the disk to service the interrupt. This causes another trap, and VMM is again invoked. It services the trap by carrying out the read and placing the results in the locations that OS indicates. It then returns control to OS, which updates the appropriate parts of process p (such as the return value of the system call). OS then performs a context switch to return control to p. This is a privileged instruction, so VMM is again invoked. It updates the virtual machine on which OS runs to make it appear that OS performed the context switch, and then performs the context switch itself. The process p now resumes execution.

A virtual machine monitor is sometimes called a *hypervisor*. A *type-1 hypervisor* runs directly on the hardware, just like a regular operating system; a *type-2 hypervisor* runs as a process or processes on a regular operating system. Figure D–1 illustrates the difference.

D.2.1   Privilege and Virtual Machines

The Digital Equipment Corporation VAX/VMM project examined the issues of privilege in virtual machines [1010]. Consider the requirements for a computer architecture to be virtualizable [1532].

> **Definition D–1.** A *sensitive instruction* is an instruction that discloses or alters the state of privilege of the processor. A *sensitive data structure* is a data structure that contains information about the state of privilege of the system.

EXAMPLE: The VAX architecture had four levels of privilege: user, supervisor, executive, and kernel. On the VAX architecture, the CHMK instruction was privileged because it changed the privilege level (to kernel mode), and the MOVPSL instruction copied the processor status longword (PSL) to a memory location. The former instruction was a sensitive instruction because it altered the state of privilege (moving it to kernel mode). The latter was also sensitive because it revealed information about the current level of privilege (the level of privilege was encoded in two bits in the PSL).

Page table entries were sensitive data structures because they contained information about the protection state of the processor (notably, they could contain a copy of the PSL for the process).

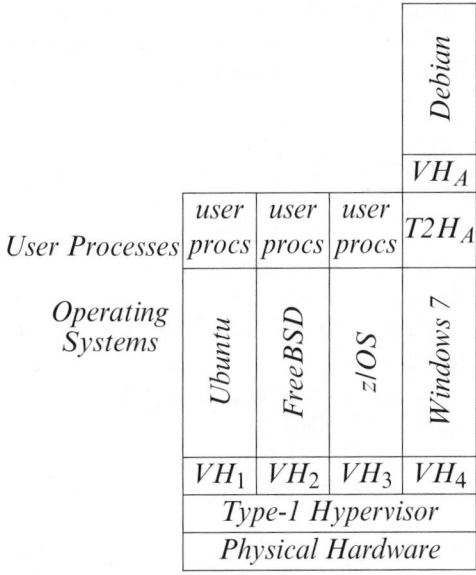

Figure D–1 A virtual machine environment. To the left is a type-1 hypervisor running four virtual machines VH_1, ..., VH_4 each with a different operating system. The Windows 7 operating system is itself running a type-2 hypervisor that runs a Debian Linux system. To the right is a set of type-2 hypervisors $T2H_1$, $T2H_2$, $T2H_3$ each running at least one virtual machine VH_5, ..., VH_8. $T2H_2$ is running two virtual machines, each with its own operating system. VH_5 is running Ubuntu Linux, which in turn is running another type-2 hypervisor that runs Windows 7.

A computer architecture is virtualizable if it meets the following requirements:

1. All sensitive instructions cause traps when executed by processes at lower levels of privilege.
2. All references to sensitive data structures cause traps when executed by processes at lower levels of privilege.

EXAMPLE: The CHMK instruction met requirement 1, because it caused a trap unless it was executed in kernel mode. The MOVPSL instruction met neither requirement, because it did not cause a trap regardless of the level of privilege of the process executing it. User level processes could alter page table entries, so references to those data structures also failed to meet the second requirement (but see Exercise 1).

If the hardware supports n levels of privilege, each virtual machine must appear to support n levels of privilege.

On some architectures only the virtual machine monitor runs at the highest level of privilege. This makes $n - 1$ levels of privilege available to each virtual machine. The virtual machine monitor virtualizes the levels of privilege. This technique is called *ring compression*.

EXAMPLE: Recall that the VAX system had four levels of privilege: user, supervisor, executive, and kernel. The VMM monitor had to emulate all of these levels for each virtual machine that it ran. However, it could not allow the operating system of any of those virtual machines to enter kernel mode, because then that operating system could access the physical resources directly, bypassing the virtual machine monitor. Yet to run the VAX standard operating system, VAX/VMS, the virtual machine had to appear to provide all four levels.

The solution was to virtualize the executive and kernel privilege levels. The executive and kernel levels of the virtual machine (called the *VM executive* and *VM kernel* levels, respectively) were mapped into the physical executive mode. The architects of VAX/VMM added three extensions to the VAX hardware to support this compression.

First, a virtual machine bit was added to the PSL. If this bit were set, the current process was running on a virtual machine. Second, a special register, the VMPSL register, recorded the PSL of the running virtual machine. Third, all sensitive instructions that could reveal the level of privilege either obtained their information from the VMPSL or caused a trap to the virtual machine monitor. In the latter case, the virtual machine monitor emulated the instruction.

Yet another approach is used in the Intel architectures [1908]. This defines a virtualization mode, so that each virtual machine can execute instructions at any privilege level, but certain instructions cause a transition to the nonvirtualized mode so the virtual machine monitor can take control.

EXAMPLE: The VT-i architecture, which adds virtualization support to Itanium processors, adds a bit to the processor status register and a new fault, the "virtualization fault." This bit, PSR.vm, is set when the system is running a guest operating system, and cleared when the virtual machine monitor is running. All four privilege levels (rings 0 to 3) are supported whether the bit is set or cleared, but when PSR.vm is set, privileged instructions cause a virtualization fault. When an interrupt occurs, the PSR.vm bit is automatically cleared so the virtual machine monitor can service it. A special instruction changes the bit with minimal overhead, avoiding a full context switch.

The processor abstraction layer provides an abstract interface to the hardware; this hides changes in the architecture of the hardware from the virtual machine monitors. Interfaces include procedures to create and destroy virtual machines as well as saving and restoring part of the state of a virtual machine.

The VT-x architecture, which adds virtualization support to IA-32 processors, also defines two modes of operation, called "VMX root operation" and "VMX nonroot operation." This is similar to the VT-i architecture, but is implemented differently. A control structure (the VMCS) contains parts of the state of the guest operating system and of the virtual machine monitor. Context switches between the virtual machine monitor and the guest system save and restore state from the VMCS. Like the VT-i, all four privilege levels are available in both modes, but in VMX nonroot operation, some instructions cause a transition to VMX root operation.

A third approach to privilege is to divide users into different classes and control access to the system by limiting the access of each class.

EXAMPLE: The IBM VM/370 uses this approach to associate various CP commands with users [528]. Each CP command is associated with one or more *user privilege classes*. For example, class G is the "general user" class. Members of that class can start a virtual machine. Class A is the "primary system operator" class. Members of that class can control system accounting, the availability of virtual machines, and other system resources. Members of class "Any" can gain access to, or surrender access to, a virtual machine.

D.2.2   Physical Resources and Virtual Machines

The virtual machine monitor manages the physical resources by distributing them among the virtual machines as appropriate. Each virtual machine therefore appears to have a reduced amount of resources. For example, if the control program is to allocate space on a single disk for 10 virtual machines, it will divide the disk into 10 minidisks. Each virtual machine will have access to a different portion of the physical disk. The size of each minidisk is less than the size of the actual disk (although the sizes of the 10 minidisks may differ). The virtual machine monitor handles the mapping from the minidisk address (presented to it by the virtual machine) and the physical disk.

EXAMPLE: When a virtual machine's operating system tries to write to a disk, the I/O instruction is privileged and causes a trap to the virtual machine monitor. The virtual machine monitor translates the addresses to be accessed (read from or written to), verifies that the I/O references disk space allocated to that virtual machine, and services the request. It returns control to the virtual machine when the request is satisfied (completed for synchronous I/O, begun for asynchronous I/O).

D.2.3   Paging and Virtual Machines

On an ordinary machine, paging occurs at the highest level of privilege. When a virtual machine attempts to page, it does so from the virtual machine's level of privilege. The attempt to read from, or write to, the disk causes a transfer to the virtual machine monitor. At that point, the request is handled as any other request for I/O. However, two problems unique to virtual machines arise.

First, because of the way some operating systems are designed, some pages may be accessible only to processes running at the highest level of privilege, but the virtual machine operating systems run at a lower level of privilege. The virtual machine must change the protection level of these pages to the appropriate level of privilege.

EXAMPLE: On the VAX/VMS system, only kernel level processes could read some pages. Hence, the virtual machine monitor on the VAX/VMM system had to ensure that executive level processes on a virtual machine could not read the pages for kernel level processes on that virtual machine. This was necessary because the kernel level processes on the virtual machine were actually running at the VM kernel level, which was in the physical executive level of privilege.

In theory, reducing the level of protection for these pages posed a security risk (because processes at the VM executive level could then access the pages). In practice, the VMS system allowed processes in executive mode to change to kernel mode freely. Hence, there was no loss of security. But if the process running at the VM executive level attempted to access one of these pages, the access would have been allowed. Were the VAX/VMS system running directly on the hardware and not under a virtual machine, the access would have been denied. Hence, there was a loss of reliability.

The second problem is performance. The virtual machine monitor paging its own data or instructions is transparent to the virtual machines. If the virtual machines attempt to page, the virtual machine monitor must handle the request as described above. If the virtual machine operating system pages heavily, this indirection may cause significant delays.

EXAMPLE: IBM's VM/370 provided support for several different operating systems. OS/MFT and OS/MVT were designed to access storage on disk. If the jobs being run under those systems depended on timings, the delays caused by the virtual machine might have affected the success of the jobs. With a system that supported virtual storage, such as MVS, either MVS or CP (the virtual machine monitor) might have caused paging. Again, if timings were important, the delays could have caused failure of a process that would not have failed were there no intermediate CP.

D.3   Exercises

1. The second example in Section D.2.1 states that "user level processes could alter page table entries, so references to those data structures also failed to meet the second requirement." How can an operating system prevent a user level process from altering its page table entries?

2. Suppose a virtual machine monitor (call it V_1) is running another virtual machine monitor (V_2), which in turn is running a version of the Linux operating system L. The user running the Linux system is editing a file with the E text editor. The user requests that the editor write the file to disk.

    a. Is the instruction RFT (Return From Trap) sensitive? Why or why not?

    b. Trace the flow of control among V_1, V_2, L, and E.

    c. How many RFT instructions will be executed? Justify your answer.

3. The Intel VT-i architecture deals with the problem of privileges by having a bit that indicates whether the hypervisor or the guest system is executing. What advantages does this have over the architectures that do virtualization by having the hypervisor run in the ring with highest privilege, and the virtual machine in the other rings? What are the disadvantages of the Intel approach?

Appendix E
Symbolic Logic

This appendix provides background on various types of logic. One can use symbols to represent data and functions to create formulas using the rules of logic. Then the rules of a logic system allow the analyst to reason about formulas made out of the symbols.

E.1   Propositional Logic

Propositional logic, also called the *propositional calculus*, is based on propositions, or atomic, declarative sentences that can be shown to be either true or false (but not both). Examples of such statements are "The sky is blue today," "Nine divided by 3 equals 3," and "All people like chocolate." Questions and statements such as "Let's go!" and "Here's hoping for the best" are not considered declarative because they cannot be argued to be true or false. Propositions are usually represented by lowercase letters—usually those in the middle of the alphabet such as p and q—or by letters with subscripts, such as $p_1, p_2, \ldots$, to make more than 26 symbols.

Propositions can be composed into compound sentences using connectives. These compound sentences are more complex propositions, or *formulas*. Formulas are generally represented by lowercase Greek letters, notably ϕ and ψ. The connectives of propositional logic are as follows:

- *Negation*, written as "¬", reverses the truth value of a proposition. If proposition p is true, then $\neg p$ is false, and if p is false, $\neg p$ is true.
- *Disjunction*, written as "∨", joins propositions. If one or both of p and q are true, then $p \vee q$ is true. If both p and q are false, then $p \vee q$ is false.
- *Conjunction*, written as "∧", also joins propositions. If both p and q are true, then $p \wedge q$ is true. If either p or q is false, then $p \wedge q$ is false.
- *Implication*, written as "→", suggests that one proposition is the logical consequence of another. Formally, $p \rightarrow q$ if and only if $(\neg p) \vee q$. In the implication $p \rightarrow q$, p is called the *premise* of the formula and q is the *conclusion* of the formula. Implication is also referred to as "if … then," but there are slight differences. In natural language, "if … then" assumes

a causal role in which the premise enables the conclusion. Implication in logic languages indicates a preservation of truth and not necessarily a causal relationship.

As in arithmetic, logic formulas consisting of symbols and connectives can be ambiguous. Arithmetic expressions and programming language expressions are evaluated according to specific rules, and when the rules are insufficient to distinguish ambiguities, distinctions are generally made using parentheses. For example, in arithmetic, $ab + c$ is not the same as $a(b + c)$. We know that multiplication and division have higher precedence than addition and subtraction, so the expression $ab + c$ is interpreted to mean "multiply a and b and add c" rather than "add b to c and multiply the result by a." Propositional logic has rules of precedence that behave in a similar fashion.

- Negation ($\neg$) has higher precedence than conjunction ($\wedge$) and disjunction ($\vee$).
- Conjunction ($\wedge$) and disjunction ($\vee$) have equal precedence.
- Implication ($\rightarrow$) has lower precedence than conjunction ($\wedge$) and disjunction ($\vee$).

Parentheses group operands and operators, and, as in arithmetic, operations within parentheses have the highest precedence. For example, $(\neg p) \wedge q$ can be written as $\neg p \wedge q$ to distinguish it from $\neg(p \wedge q)$, illustrating the first rule of precedence above. Similarly, $(p \wedge q) \rightarrow r$ can be written as $p \wedge q \rightarrow r$, but $p \wedge (q \rightarrow r)$ requires the parentheses.

E.1.1   Natural Deduction in Propositional Logic

Natural deduction is a means of reasoning about propositions, allowing us to draw conclusions. *Proof rules* let us infer formulas from other formulas. The rules can be applied to a set of *premises*, formulas that we know or assume to be true, to reach a conclusion, or the formula we wish to establish. A *contradiction* is a formula that is always false, regardless of p. For example, $p \wedge \neg p$ is a contradiction. All contradictions are equivalent and are denoted by a special symbol, $\bot$, called *bottom*. A *tautology* is a formula that is always true, regardless of p. For example, the expression $p \vee \neg p$ is a tautology. All tautologies are equivalent and are denoted by a special symbol, $\top$, called *top*.

E.1.2   Rules

We present 11 rules of natural deduction. For each of the logical connectives, there is an *introduction rule* and an *elimination rule*. The introduction rules allow us to deduce information about the conclusion from the premises. The elimination rules allow us to conclude information about the variables used in the premise from the conclusion.

EXAMPLE: An introduction rule for the connective "$*$" would allow us to draw conclusions about $p * q$ based on information about p and q. An elimination rule for "$*$" would allow us to draw conclusions about p (or q) based on what we know about $p * q$.

- *And introduction*: If we have concluded (the truth of) p and q, then we can also conclude (the truth of) $p \wedge q$. In other words, we can say that if p is true and q is true, then $p \wedge q$ is also true.
- *And elimination*: If we have concluded $p \wedge q$, then we can also conclude p and we can also conclude q. In other words, if $p \wedge q$ is true, then p is true and q is true.
- *Implication introduction*: Assume that p is true temporarily, and, based on this assumption, prove q. Thus, we can conclude $p \rightarrow q$. More generally, if we assume the premise and reach the conclusion, we can say that the premise implies the conclusion.
- *Implication elimination*, also called *modus ponens*: If we have concluded p and $p \rightarrow q$, we can also conclude q. More generally, if the premise is true and the implication is true, then the conclusion must be true.
- *Disjunction introduction*: If we can conclude p, then we can conclude $p \vee q$. Similarly, if we can conclude q, then we can conclude $p \vee q$. If either p or q is true, then $p \vee q$.
- *Disjunction elimination*: If we can conclude $p \vee q$ and want to use it to conclude X, we first assume p and conclude X. Then we assume q and conclude X. Given $p \vee q$ and these two proofs, we can infer X.
- *Negation introduction*: If we assume p and conclude bottom ($\perp$), we infer $\neg p$.
- *Negation elimination*: If we assume p and $\neg p$, we conclude bottom ($\perp$).
- *Bottom elimination*: If we assume $\perp$, a contradiction, then we can prove any proposition p.
- *Double negation introduction*: If we have concluded p, then we can also conclude the double negation of p, $\neg\neg p$. In other words, if p is true, then $\neg\neg p$ is also true.
- *Double negation elimination*: If we have concluded $\neg\neg p$, then we can also conclude p. In other words, if $\neg\neg p$ is true, then p is also true.

E.1.3   Derived Rules

Two commonly used rules that are derived from the rules above are *modus tollens* and *reductio ad absurdum*. *Modus tollens* eliminates an implication. If we have concluded $\neg q$ and $p \rightarrow q$, we can also conclude $\neg p$.

Suppose that $\neg q$ holds. Suppose we assume that a premise p holds and we can prove that $p \to q$ holds. By the implication elimination rule above, q holds. But it is impossible for both q and $\neg q$ to hold, so our assumption about p must be false, which means $\neg p$. In other words, if the conclusion is false and the implication is true, then the premise must be false. This is an example of a proof technique called *reductio ad absurdum* or *proof by contradiction*. A succinct description is: to prove p, assume $\neg p$ and reach bottom (or a contradiction).

E.1.4   Well-Formed Formulas

Any set of symbols using symbols for propositions, connectors, and parentheses is a *word* in the alphabet of a logical language. But not all words are meaningful. An important class of meaningful words is the set of *well-formed formulas* (WFFs). They are defined inductively.

- A propositional atom is a WFF.
- The negation of a WFF is a WFF.
- The conjunction of WFFs is a WFF.
- The disjunction of WFFs is a WFF.
- An implication between two WFFs is a WFF.

E.1.5   Truth Tables

The previous sections show how one may reach a conclusion based on a set of premises and applying the laws of natural deduction. Another way of approaching such a proof is by using *truth tables*. A truth table is a set of the possible values of a compound proposition based on the possible values (in this case, T for true or F for false) of the atomic propositions. Truth tables for conjunction, disjunction, implication, and negation are shown below.

p	q	$p \wedge q$	$p \vee q$	$p \to q$	$\neg p$
T	T	T	T	T	F
T	F	F	T	F	F
F	T	F	T	T	T
F	F	F	F	T	T

To reach a "proof" by using truth tables, create a truth table for a formula that states that the conjunction of the premises implies the conclusion. Of course, the more atomic propositions there are, the larger the truth table and the more complex this technique becomes. If the truth table of the conjunction of the premises is the same as the truth table of the conclusion, then we say that we have reached a proof.

Definition E–1. A *sequent* is a set of formulas (premises) $\phi_1, \phi_2, \ldots, \phi_n$ and a conclusion ψ. It is denoted by $\phi_1, \phi_2, \ldots, \phi_n \vdash \psi$.

Definition E–2. A sequent is *valid* if a proof for it can be found.

Definition E–3. Two formulas ϕ and ψ are *provably equivalent* if and only if $\phi \vdash \psi$ and $\psi \vdash \phi$ both are valid.

Definition E–4.   Two formulas that have the same truth table values are called *semantically equivalent*. If ψ evaluates to true whenever $\phi_1, \phi_2, \ldots, \phi_n$ evaluate to true, this is denoted by $\phi_1, \phi_2, \ldots, \phi_n \vDash \psi$.

These definitions lead to two critical theorems in propositional logic.

The first theorem says that if there is a proof of a conclusion given a set of premises, then the premises and conclusion are semantically equivalent. Formally:

Theorem E.1. *Soundness Theorem of Propositional Logic:* Let $\phi_1, \phi_2, \ldots, \phi_n$ and ψ be propositional logic formulas. If $\phi_1, \phi_2, \ldots, \phi_n \vdash \psi$, then $\phi_1, \phi_2, \ldots, \phi_n \vDash \psi$.

The second theorem says that if a set of premises and a conclusion are semantically equivalent, then there is a natural deduction proof for the sequent. Formally:

Theorem E.2. *Completeness Theorem of Propositional Logic:* Let $\phi_1, \phi_2, \ldots, \phi_n$ and ψ be propositional logic formulas. If $\phi_1, \phi_2, \ldots, \phi_n \vDash \psi$, then $\phi_1, \phi_2, \ldots, \phi_n \vdash \psi$.

E.1.6   Mathematical Induction

Mathematical induction is a proof technique that allows us to prove equations true when dealing with arbitrary values. Suppose we want to show that a property $M(n)$ holds for all natural numbers n. To use mathematical induction, we proceed as follows:

- Prove that $M(1)$ holds. This is called the *base case* or *basis*.
- Assert that $M(n)$ holds for $n = 1, \ldots, k$. This is called the *induction hypothesis*.
- Prove that if $M(k)$ holds, then $M(k+1)$ holds. This is called the *induction step*.

Then $M(n)$ is true for all natural numbers n.

EXAMPLE: We wish to prove that the formula for the sum of the first n natural numbers is

$$1 + \ldots + n = \frac{n(n + 1)}{2}$$

We use mathematical induction. Call this formula $M(n)$.

Basis. $M(1)$ is $1 = \frac{1(1+1)}{2}$, which is clearly true.

Induction Hypothesis. $M(n)$ is true for $n = 1, \ldots, k$.

Induction Step. Consider $1 + \ldots + k + (k + 1)$:

$$
\begin{aligned}
1 + \cdots + k + (k + 1) &= \frac{k(k + 1)}{2} + (k + 1) & \text{induction hypothesis} \\[2mm]
&= \frac{k^2}{2} + \frac{k}{2} + \frac{2k}{2} + \frac{2}{2} & \text{simplifying} \\[2mm]
&= \frac{k^2 + 3k + 2}{2} & \text{simplifying} \\[2mm]
&= \frac{(k + 1)(k + 2)}{2} & \text{factoring} \\[2mm]
&= \frac{(k + 1)[(k + 1) + 1]}{2} & \text{rewriting}
\end{aligned}
$$

But this is simply $M(k + 1)$. Hence, if $M(k)$ holds, then $M(k + 1)$ holds. This completes the proof.

E.2   Predicate Logic

Predicate logic, also called *predicate calculus* or *first order logic*, is based on the concept of predicates and may contain variables, quantifiers, constants, and functions in addition to the components of propositional calculus. Consider the sentence "Every directory contains some files." We would like to express this concept in terms of logic. To do this, we need to introduce the concepts of variables and predicates and a means of capturing the ideas of "every" and "some."

We define predicates that describe the properties represented by the sentence, using variables x and y to describe any file or directory. Let us assume the following:

- $F(x)$: x is a file.
- $D(y)$: y is a directory.
- $C(x, y)$: x is a file in directory y.

We next need to define the concepts of "every" and "some." We define the symbol ∃, the *existential quantifier*, to denote that something exists. Therefore, a statement containing the notation "∃x" is read "there exists x" or "there is some x." The concept of "all" is represented by the symbol ∀, called the *universal quantifier*. The phrase "∀x" is read "for all x." Both ∃ and ∀ can be combined with the negative connector, ¬, to mean "there does not exist" or "not all." The sentence "Every file belongs to some directory" becomes "∀$xF(x) \rightarrow (\exists y(D(y) \wedge C(x, y)))$." More precisely read, our sentence becomes "for every x, if x is a file, then there is some y such that y is a directory and directory y contains file x."

Variables and constants are the basic terms of predicate logic. More complex terms are constructed using function references on terms. The definition of a function is consistent with the usual definition from mathematics: a function provides a unique output for each input. If one views constants as "functions" without any variable references, then we see that the entire predicate vocabulary consists of function symbols and predicate symbols that range over the set of terms.

A variable is said to be *bound* if it is quantified with either ∀ or ∃. A variable that is not bound is said to be *unbound* or *free*. For example, in ∀$x\Phi(x, y)$, x is a bound variable and y is a free variable.

A formula in predicate calculus with predicates P and functions Φ is defined as follows:

- If P is a predicate taking n arguments ($n \geq 1$) and the arguments are terms $t_1, \ldots, t_n$, defined over the set Φ of functions, then $P(t_1, t_2, \ldots, t_n)$ is a formula.
- If ϕ is a formula, then ¬ϕ is also a formula.
- If ϕ and ψ are formulas, so are $\phi \wedge \psi$, $\phi \vee \psi$, and $\phi \rightarrow \psi$.
- If ϕ is a formula and x is a variable, then ∀$x\phi$ and ∃$x\phi$ are also formulas.

E.2.1   Natural Deduction in Predicate Logic

The natural deduction rules for predicate logic are similar to those in propositional logic. They add new rules for existential and universal quantifiers as well as the distinguished predicate *equals*, represented by the equality sign (=). The new rules are as follows:

- *Equality*: A term t is equal to itself.
- *Substitution*: Equals may be substituted for equals. If $t_1 = t_2$ and x is a free variable in $\phi(x)$, then $\phi(t_1) = \phi(t_2)$.
- *Universal quantifier elimination*: If you have ∀$x\phi(x)$, then you can replace the x in $\phi(x)$ by any term t that is free in $\phi(x)$.
- *Universal quantifier introduction*: If you can prove some formula $\phi(x)$ with x a free variable, you can derive ∀$x\phi(x)$.

E.3   Temporal Logic Systems

There are many temporal logic systems. *Linear time logic systems* view events as sequential. *Branching time logic systems* view events as concurrent "alternative universes." Temporal logic systems view time as either a *continuous* flow of events or a set of *discrete* events.

Section 21.4.2 discussed the use of Control Tree Logic (CTL) in the study and verification of hardware and communications protocols. This section describes the logic itself. CTL views time as branching and discrete.

E.3.1   Syntax of CTL

CTL builds on the concepts of propositional logic. Its building blocks are propositions; the connectors $\neg$, $\wedge$, $\vee$, and $\rightarrow$; the concepts of $\perp$ (bottom, never true) and $\top$ (top, always trivially true); the signs of aggregation ( ), [ ], and { }; and the notion of a well-formed formula.

CTL adds eight temporal connectives to this list. Each connective has two identifying symbols. The first symbol is either "A" or "E"; these symbols are somewhat similar in concept to the symbols $\forall$ and $\exists$ of predicate logic. "A" means "along all paths," whereas "E" means "along at least one path." The second symbol is "X," "F," "G," or "U." An "X" refers to "the next state," an "F" means "some next state," a "G" means "all future states," and a "U" means "until some future state."

The precedence rules for CTL are as follows:

- The unary operators $\neg$, AG, EG, AF, EF, AX, and EX have the highest precedence.
- The operators $\wedge$ and $\vee$ have the next-highest precedence.
- The operator $\rightarrow$ has the next-highest precedence.
- The operators AU and EU have the lowest precedence.

We define a well-formed CTL formula as follows:

- Top ($\top$) is a formula.
- Bottom ($\perp$) is a formula.
- All atomic descriptions are formulas.
- If ϕ and ψ are formulas, so are $\phi \wedge \psi$, $\phi \vee \psi$, $\neg\phi$, $\phi \rightarrow \psi$, AXϕ, EXϕ, A[ϕUψ], E[ϕUψ], AGϕ, EGϕ, AFϕ, and EFϕ.

E.3.2   Semantics of CTL

It is easiest to define the syntax of CTL in terms of a model of a system. The basic unit of a system model is a set of atoms defined for the system. The model consists of the states of the system, an operator that represents the changes of state, and a function that gives the atoms that hold for a state. More formally:

> **Definition E–5.** A *model* is formally defined within CTL as $M = (S, \Rightarrow, L)$, where S is a set of states, $\Rightarrow$ is the transition operator on the set S such that $\forall s \in S (\exists s' \in S[s \Rightarrow s'])$, L is a labeling function, and $L : S \to \mathcal{P}(\text{atoms})$.

Here, $\mathcal{P}(\text{atoms})$ is the power set (set of all subsets) of the defined atoms.

If M is a model and s is a state, the state satisfies a formula ϕ if the formula is true in that state. Again, formally:

> **Definition E–6.** *Satisfaction Relation.* Let $M = (S, \Rightarrow, L)$ be a model for CTL. Given any $s \in S$, if a CTL formula ϕ holds in state s, we denote this by $M, s \vDash \phi$, and say we that state s of model M satisfies formula ϕ.

For convenience, we write $M, s \nvDash \phi$ if state s of model M does not satisfy formula ϕ.

Let M be a model, let s and s_i for $i = 1, \ldots$ be states of M, let p be an atomic proposition of M, and let ϕ, ϕ_1, and ϕ_2 be CTL formulas. Then:

- $\forall s \in S\,[M, s \vDash \top]$.
  This says that tautologies hold in all states of the model M.
- $\forall s \in S\,[M, s \nvDash \bot]$.
  This says that contradictions do not hold in any state of the model M.
- $M, s \vDash p$ if and only if $p \in L(s)$. This says that p holds in state s of model M whenever p is in the set of atoms that hold in state s. Conversely, if p is not in that set, then p does not hold in state s.
- If $M, s \nvDash \phi$, then $M, s \vDash \neg\phi$.
  This establishes that if a state does not satisfy a formula, then the state satisfies the negation of that formula.
- $M, s \vDash \phi_1 \wedge \phi_2$ if and only if $M, s \vDash \phi_1$ and $M, s \vDash \phi_2$.
  This says that a state satisfies the disjunction of two formulas if and only if it satisfies both formulas.
- $M, s \vDash \phi_1 \vee \phi_2$ if and only if $M, s \vDash \phi_1$ or $M, s \vDash \phi_2$.
  This says that a state satisfies the conjunction of two formulas if and only if it satisfies either formula.
- $M, s \vDash \phi_1 \to \phi_2$ if and only if $M, s \nvDash \phi_1$ or $M, s \vDash \phi_2$.
  This says that a state satisfies the implication of two formulas if and only if it satisfies the second, or satisfies neither the first nor the second, formula.

Now consider the temporal connectives:

- $M, s \vDash AX\phi$ if and only if $\forall s_1$ such that $s \to s_1$, then $M, s_1 \vDash \phi$.
  This says that a state satisfies a formula in all possible next states if and only if every state that the original state implies also satisfies the formula.

- $M, s \vDash EX\phi$ if and only if $\exists s_1$ such that $s \rightarrow s_1$, then $M, s_1 \vDash \phi$.
  This says that a state satisfies a formula in some next state if and only if at least one state that the original state implies also satisfies the formula.
- $M, s \vDash AG\phi$ if and only if for all paths $s_1 \rightarrow s_2 \rightarrow s_3 \rightarrow \ldots$, where $s = s_1$ and $\forall s_i$ on the path, $[M, s_i \vDash \phi]$.
  This says that a state satisfies a formula in all future states if and only if every state on every path of transitions beginning at the original state satisfies the formula.
- $M, s \vDash EG\phi$ if and only if there exists a path $s_1 \rightarrow s_2 \rightarrow s_3 \rightarrow \ldots$, where $s = s_1$ and $\forall s_i$ on the path, $[M, s_i \vDash \phi]$.
  This says that there is a path with all states satisfying a formula if and only if every state on a path of transitions beginning at the original state satisfies the formula.
- $M, s \vDash AF\phi$ if and only if for all paths $s_1 \rightarrow s_2 \rightarrow s_3 \rightarrow \ldots$, where $s = s_1$ and $\exists s_i [M, s_i \vDash \phi]$.
  This says that on all paths there will be a state satisfying the formula if and only if every path of transitions beginning at the original state contains at least one state that satisfies the formula.
- $M, s \vDash EF\phi$ if and only if there exists a path $s_1 \rightarrow s_2 \rightarrow s_3 \rightarrow \ldots$, where $s = s_1$ and $\exists s_i$ on the path, $[M, s_i \vDash \phi]$.
  This says that there is a path with one state satisfying the formula if and only if a state on a path of transitions beginning at the original state satisfies the formula.
- $M, s \vDash A[\phi_1 U \phi_2]$ if and only if for all paths $s_1 \rightarrow s_2 \rightarrow s_3 \rightarrow \ldots$,
  $$\exists i \, [i \geq 0 \land s_i \vDash \phi_2 \land \forall j \, [0 \leq j < i \rightarrow s_j \vDash \phi_1]].$$
  This says that on all paths there will be a state satisfying the formula if and only if every path of transitions beginning at the original state has a state satisfying the second formula and all previous states in that path satisfy the first formula.
- $M, s \vDash E[\phi_1 U \phi_2]$ if and only if for some path $s_1 \rightarrow s_2 \rightarrow s_3 \rightarrow \ldots$,
  $$\exists i \, [i \geq 0 \land s_i \vDash \phi_2 \land \forall j \, [0 \leq j < i \rightarrow s_j \vDash \phi_1]].$$
  This says that there is a path on which there is a state satisfying the formula if and only if every path of transitions beginning at the original state has a state satisfying the second formula and all previous states in that path satisfy the first formula.

E.4   Exercises

1. Prove that $p \lor (q \land r) = (p \lor q) \land (p \lor r)$ using the following methods.

   a. A truth table
   b. Natural deduction (show the rules that you apply at each step of the proof)

2. Use the logical connectives of propositional logic to express the following sentences in propositional logic. Be sure to define all propositional atoms.

   a. If the sun shines, we can make hay.
   b. For dinner I can have a potato or rice but not both.
   c. If you do all the homework, read the text, and study the lecture notes, then you will be prepared for the midterm exam. Otherwise, you may not be prepared for the exam.

3. Use mathematical induction to prove that, for $n \geq 1$,

$$1^2 + 2^2 + \ldots n^2 = \frac{n(n+1)(n+2)}{6}$$

4. Use predicate logic to state the following sentences. Be sure to define all predicates, constants, and variables.

   a. Not all birds can fly.
   b. Every child is younger than its mother.
   c. Mary and Sue have the same paternal grandfather.

5. State which of the following strings are well-formed CTL formulas.

   a. FGr
   b. A¬Fp
   c. ¬($\neg p$) ∧ ($q \rightarrow r$)
   d. ¬EXq
   e. pU(AX⊥)
   f. AFq ∧ EXr

6. Express the meaning of the following CTL WFFs in ordinary English:

   a. A[True U ϕ]
   b. E[True U ϕ]

Appendix F
The Encryption Standards

The two ciphers described in Chapter 10 are built upon iterations of functions both to encrypt and to generate keys. This appendix describes them in detail.

F.1 Data Encryption Standard

The DES (see section 10.2.3) takes as input a 64-bit plaintext message, and iterates through 16 rounds to generate a 64-bit ciphertext. Each round requires a 48-bit key, called a *round key*. A schedule of 16 round keys is generated from the 64-bit DES key. Section F.1.2 describes the generation of the round keys.

The input to the DES is 64 bits. The bits are permuted, and the resulting bits split into two halves. One half is given to a function, along with the round key for that round, and the output is combined with the other half. This becomes the first half, and the old first half becomes the second half. This continues for 15 rounds. The last round is the same except the two halves are not exchanged; they are concatenated, the result permuted again, and the result is the output.

The function combines the right half of the current round with the round key, and then uses a substitution function to replace sets of bits. The result is then permuted to form the output of the function.

The permutations and substitutions are described by tables shown in this section. The notation for these tables bears explaining. For all tables except the S-boxes, each entry in the table is a bit position from the input. The bits are output in the order shown in the table. Thus, for the initial permutation IP (see Figure F–2(a)), the first bit of the output of the permutation is bit 58 of the input to the permutation, the second bit of the output is the bit 50 of the input, the third bit of the output is the 42nd bit of the input, and so forth. All blocks begin with bit number 1, as in the standard. The notation for the S-box tables will be explained later.

F.1.1 Main DES Algorithm

The DES algorithm consists of 16 iterations, called *rounds*. Figure F–1(a) shows the structure of the algorithm. The 64-bit input is permuted as indicated by the

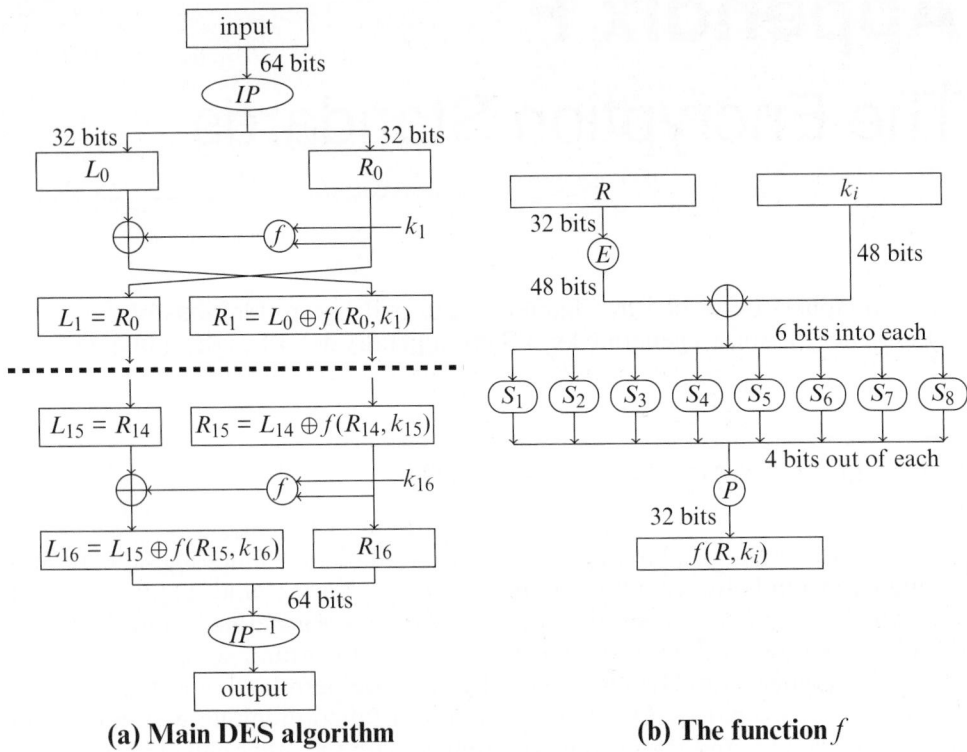

(a) Main DES algorithm   **(b) The function** f

Figure F–1   The DES algorithm.

permutation table IP (see Figure F–2(a)). The resulting 64 bits are split into two halves, L_0 and R_0.

The first round begins by transforming R_0 using a function f, which also takes as input the first round key k_1. The result of that function is exclusive or'ed with L_0, and the result becomes R_1. R_0 becomes L_1.

This process repeats for L_i and R_i for $i = 1, \ldots, 15$. The last round proceeds as do the earlier ones, except that the two haves are *not* exchanged. After the last round, L_{16} and R_{16} are concatenated to form a 64-bit quantity. This is then permuted according to the table IP^{-1}, the inverse of the initial permutation IP (see Figure F–2(b)). The resulting block is the output.

The function f lies at the heart of this algorithm. Figure F–1(b) shows the computation of f. For round i, the inputs to f are the right half R_i and the corresponding round key k_i. First, R_i is expanded from 32 to 48 bits by replicating some of its bits as indicated by the E table (see Figure F–3(a)). These 48 bits are exclusive or'ed with the round key k_i. The resulting 48 bits are split into 8 groups of 6 bits each, and group i is run through the ith S-box S_i. Each S-box replaces the 6-bit input with a 4-bit output. The 8 groups of 4 bits are concatenated into

58	50	42	34	26	18	10	2
60	52	44	36	28	20	12	4
62	54	46	38	30	22	14	6
64	56	48	40	32	24	16	8
57	49	41	33	25	17	9	1
59	51	43	35	27	19	11	3
61	53	45	37	29	21	13	5
63	55	47	39	31	23	15	7

(a) IP Table

40	8	48	16	56	24	64	32
39	7	47	15	55	23	63	31
38	6	46	14	54	22	62	30
37	5	45	13	53	21	61	29
36	4	44	12	52	20	60	28
35	3	43	11	51	19	59	27
34	2	42	10	50	18	58	26
33	1	41	9	49	17	57	25

(b) IP^{-1} Table

Figure F–2   Initial and final permutation tables.

32	1	2	3	4	5
4	5	6	7	8	9
8	9	10	11	12	13
12	13	14	15	16	17
16	17	18	19	20	21
20	21	22	23	24	25
24	25	26	27	28	29
28	29	30	31	32	1

(a) E Table

16	7	20	21
29	12	28	17
1	15	23	26
5	18	31	10
2	8	24	14
32	27	3	9
19	13	30	6
22	11	4	25

(b) P Table

Figure F–3   (a) Expansion table and (b) Permutation table.

32 bits, and those bits permuted as indicated by the P table (see Figure F–3(b)). The result is the output of f.

The way the S-boxes work is interesting. The eight S-boxes are shown in Figure F–4. All work the same way, so we consider S_1 as an example. The input is 6 bits. The first and last bits, taken as a pair, form an integer between 0 and 3 inclusive that is the row number in the table. The middle 4 bits form a number between 0 and 15 inclusive that is the column number in the table. Note that, unlike other tables, the first row of each S-box is numbered 0, as is the first column.

EXAMPLE: Consider S_1. If the input bits are 010011, then the row is 1 (01) and the column is 9 (1001), so the output bits corresponding to these input bits are 0110 (6). Similarly, if the input is 111000, then the row is 2 (10) and the column is 12 (1100), so the output bits are 0011 (3). For $S_2, ..., S_8$, the outputs corresponding to the input 010011 are 0000 (0), 1000 (8), 0111 (7), 0000 (0), 0001 (1), 0011 (3), and 0101 (5), respectively. The outputs corresponding to the input 111000 are 1001 (9), 0101 (5), 0101 (5), 0110 (6), 0001 (1), 0000 (0), and 1111 (15), respectively.

14	4	13	1	2	15	11	8	3	10	6	12	5	9	0	7
0	15	7	4	14	2	13	1	10	6	12	11	9	5	3	8
4	1	14	8	13	6	2	11	15	12	9	7	3	10	5	0
15	12	8	2	4	9	1	7	5	11	3	14	10	0	6	13

(a) S_1 Box

15	1	8	14	6	11	3	4	9	7	2	13	12	0	5	10
3	13	4	7	15	2	8	14	12	0	1	10	6	9	11	5
0	14	7	11	10	4	13	1	5	8	12	6	9	3	2	15
13	8	10	1	3	15	4	2	11	6	7	12	0	5	14	9

(b) S_2 Box

10	0	9	14	6	3	15	5	1	13	12	7	11	4	2	8
13	7	0	9	3	4	6	10	2	8	5	14	12	11	15	1
13	6	4	9	8	15	3	0	11	1	2	12	5	10	14	7
1	10	13	0	6	9	8	7	4	15	14	3	11	5	2	12

(c) S_3 Box

7	13	14	3	0	6	9	10	1	2	8	5	11	12	4	15
13	8	11	5	6	15	0	3	4	7	2	12	1	10	14	9
10	6	9	0	12	11	7	13	15	1	3	14	5	2	8	4
3	15	0	6	10	1	13	8	9	4	5	11	12	7	2	14

(d) S_4 Box

2	12	4	1	7	10	11	6	8	5	3	15	13	0	14	9
14	11	2	12	4	7	13	1	5	0	15	10	3	9	8	6
4	2	1	11	10	13	7	8	15	9	12	5	6	3	0	14
11	8	12	7	1	14	2	13	6	15	0	9	10	4	5	3

(e) S_5 Box

12	1	10	15	9	2	6	8	0	13	3	4	14	7	5	11
10	15	4	2	7	12	9	5	6	1	13	14	0	11	3	8
9	14	15	5	2	8	12	3	7	0	4	10	1	13	11	6
4	3	2	12	9	5	15	10	11	14	1	7	6	0	8	13

(f) S_6 Box

4	11	2	14	15	0	8	13	3	12	9	7	5	10	6	1
13	0	11	7	4	9	1	10	14	3	5	12	2	15	8	6
1	4	11	13	12	3	7	14	10	15	6	8	0	5	9	2
6	11	13	8	1	4	10	7	9	5	0	15	14	2	3	12

(g) S_7 Box

13	2	8	4	6	15	11	1	10	9	3	14	5	0	12	7
1	15	13	8	10	3	7	4	12	5	6	11	0	14	9	2
7	11	4	1	9	12	14	2	0	6	10	13	15	3	5	8
2	1	14	7	4	10	8	13	15	12	9	0	3	5	6	11

(h) S_8 Box

Figure F–4   S-boxes.

F.1.2 Round Key Generation

Figure F–5 shows the generation of the round keys. The initial 64-bit key is passed through permutation PC-1 (see Figure F–6(a)). This permutation discards 8 bits and scrambles the rest. These remaining 56 bits are then split into two 28-bit halves, called C_0 and D_0. Each half is *independently* rotated left[1] by the number of bits shown in the LSH table for that round (see Figure F–6(b); the shift is s_i bits for round i), producing C_1 and D_1. Then C_1 and D_1 are concatenated, and the resulting 56-bit quantity is permuted as indicated by the permutation table PC-2 (see Figure F–6(c)). Like PC-1, PC-2 eliminates 8 bits and scrambles the rest, resulting in a 48-bit output that is the round key k_1.

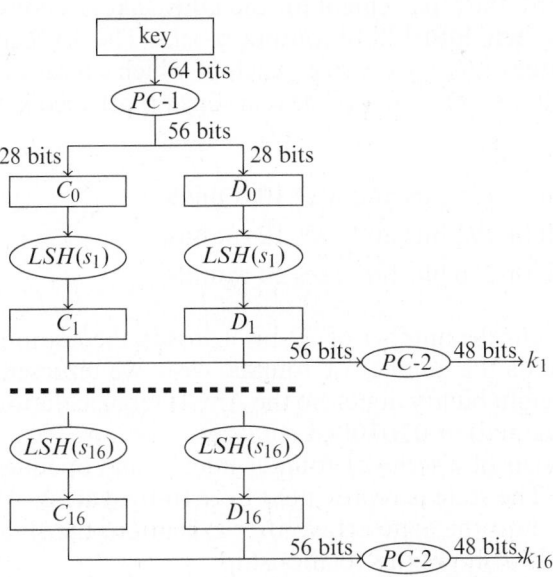

Figure F–5   Key schedule generation.

Then for each round, this process iterates: C_i and D_i are left rotated, and the combination permuted as indicated by PC-2. Each round produces the round key k_i. The process ends when 16 round keys are generated.

These 16 keys $k_1, \ldots, k_{16}$ form the key schedule. Key k_i is used as input to a function f in the main DES algorithm, as described below.

57	49	41	33	25	17	9
1	58	50	42	34	26	18
10	2	59	51	43	35	27
19	11	3	60	52	44	36
63	55	47	39	31	23	15
7	62	54	46	38	30	22
14	6	61	53	45	37	29
21	13	5	28	20	12	4

i	s_i	i	s_i
1	1	9	1
2	1	10	2
3	2	11	2
4	2	12	2
5	2	13	2
6	2	14	2
7	2	15	2
8	2	16	1

14	17	11	24	1	5
3	28	15	6	21	10
23	19	12	4	26	8
16	7	27	20	13	2
41	52	31	37	47	55
30	40	51	45	33	48
44	49	39	56	34	53
46	42	50	36	29	32

(a) PC-1 Table   **(b) LSH**   **(c) PC-2 Table**

Figure F–6   Key generation tables.

[1]The DES standard [2146] refers to this as a *left shift*.

F.2   Advanced Encryption Standard

The Advanced Encryption Standard, the replacement for the DES, takes as input blocks of 128 bits and transforms them into 128-bit output blocks. The AES, as defined in the standard, accepts three different key sizes, each of which causes the algorithm to perform a different number of rounds. The relationship between key size and rounds is:

- AES-128 has a key length of 128 bits and uses 10 rounds.
- AES-192 has a key length of 192 bits and uses 12 rounds.
- AES-256 has a key length of 256 bits and uses 14 rounds.

We use Nk and Nb to represent the number of 32-bit words in the key and block size, respectively. Nr represents the number of rounds. Also, we represent bytes as two hexadecimal digits or eight binary digits. So the ASCII representation of the character "Q" is 51 (hexadecimal) or 01010001 (binary).

Like the DES, the AES consists of a series of rounds. Each round operates on an internal *state* of the cipher. The state is represented by a 16-byte array. At the beginning, the input is copied into the state array; after execution, the state array becomes the output. Figure F–7 shows this relationship.

F.2.1   Background

Many of the internal transformations used by the AES rely on the manipulation of bytes. These manipulations all treat a byte as a polynomial in $GF(2^8)$, with each bit being a coefficient of the respective power of x. So, for example, the byte b5 in hexadecimal, which is 10110101 in binary, is treated as the polynomial $x^7 + x^5 + x^4 + x^2 + 1$. All arithmetic involving coefficients is done modulo 2.

The addition of two bytes is simply the exclusive or of the two bytes. This is equivalent to converting the two bytes into polynomial form, adding them in $GF(2^8)$, and converting the result back into binary form.

EXAMPLE: The sum of the bytes 5b and a4 is f3:

$$\begin{array}{r} 5b \\ \oplus\ a4 \\ \hline f3 \end{array} \quad \text{as, in binary,} \quad \begin{array}{r} 01011011 \\ \oplus\ 10101000 \\ \hline 11110011 \end{array}$$

	input bytes					state array					output bytes		
in_0	in_4	in_8	in_{12}		$s_{0,0}$	$s_{0,1}$	$s_{0,2}$	$s_{0,3}$		out_0	out_4	out_8	out_{12}
in_1	in_5	in_9	in_{13}	$\rightarrow$	$s_{1,0}$	$s_{1,1}$	$s_{1,2}$	$s_{1,3}$	$\rightarrow$	out_1	out_5	out_9	out_{13}
in_2	in_6	in_{10}	in_{14}		$s_{2,0}$	$s_{2,1}$	$s_{2,2}$	$s_{2,3}$		out_2	out_6	out_{10}	out_{14}
in_3	in_7	in_{11}	in_{15}		$s_{3,0}$	$s_{3,1}$	$s_{3,2}$	$s_{3,3}$		out_3	out_7	out_{11}	out_{15}

Figure F–7   Input, state, and output for the AES.

To multiply two bytes a and b (written $a \bullet b$), convert them to the corresponding polynomials and multiply them together modulo $x^8 + x^4 + x^3 + x + 1$. As we are working in $GF(2^8)$, addition of coefficients is done modulo 2.

EXAMPLE: To multiply the bytes 57 and 83, proceed as follows:

$$
\begin{aligned}
(x^6 + x^4 + x^2 + x + 1)(x^7 + x + 1) &= x^{13} + x^{11} + x^9 + x^8 + x^7 + \\
&\quad x^7 + x^5 + x^3 + x^2 + x + \\
&\quad x^6 + x^4 + x^2 + x + 1 \\
&= x^{13} + x^{11} + x^9 + x^8 + x^7 + x^7 + \\
&\quad x^6 + x^5 + x^4 + x^3 + x^2 + x^2 + \\
&\quad x + x + 1 \\
&= x^{13} + x^{11} + x^9 + x^8 + x^6 + x^5 + \\
&\quad x^4 + x^3 + 1
\end{aligned}
$$

Then reduce this product modulo $x^8 + x^4 + x^3 + x + 1$:

$$x^{13}+x^{11}+x^9+x^8+x^6+x^5+x^4+x^3+1 = (x^8+x^4+x^3+x+1)(x^5+x^3)+(x^7+x^6+1)$$

So, the product is 11000001 in binary, and therefore $57 \bullet 83 = $ c1.

F.2.2   AES Encryption

Each round of the AES is built up from four basic transformations: SubBytes, ShiftRows, MixColumns, and AddRoundKey.

F.2.2.1   SubBytes

This transformation takes a single byte as input, and replaces it with another byte. Figure F–8 defines this transformation. Thus, each byte of the state is changed with this transformation.

The substitution table is itself generated by composing two transformations. First, map the byte 00 to itself, and if the input byte is anything else, take the multiplicative inverse of the input byte in the field $GF(2^8)$. Then transform the resulting byte b to a new byte b' as follows. Let c_i be the ith bit of the byte 01100011. Then, for $i = 0, \ldots, 7$, generate b'_i as follows:

$$b'_i = b_i \oplus b_{(i+4) \bmod 8} \oplus b_{(i+5) \bmod 8} \oplus b_{(i+6) \bmod 8} \oplus b_{(i+7) \bmod 8} \oplus c_i$$

F.2.2.2   ShiftRows

This transformation shifts the rows of the state cyclically to the left, by the number of the row. Figure F–9 shows this transformation.

	0	1	2	3	4	5	6	7	8	9	a	b	c	d	e	f
0	63	7c	77	7b	f2	6b	6f	c5	30	01	67	2b	fe	d7	ab	76
1	ca	82	c9	7d	fa	59	47	f0	ad	d4	a2	af	9c	a4	72	c0
2	b7	fd	93	26	36	3f	f7	cc	34	a5	e5	f1	71	d8	31	15
3	04	c7	23	c3	18	96	05	9a	07	12	80	e2	eb	27	b2	75
4	09	83	2c	1a	1b	6e	5a	a0	52	3b	d6	b3	29	e3	2f	84
5	53	d1	00	ed	20	fc	b1	5b	6a	cb	be	39	4a	4c	58	cf
6	d0	ef	aa	fb	43	4d	33	85	45	f9	02	7f	50	3c	9f	a8
7	51	a3	40	8f	92	9d	38	f5	bc	b6	da	21	10	ff	f3	d2
8	cd	0c	13	ec	5f	97	44	17	c4	a7	7e	3d	64	5d	19	73
9	60	81	4f	dc	22	2a	90	88	46	ee	b8	14	de	5e	0b	db
a	e0	32	3a	0a	49	06	24	5c	c2	d3	ac	62	91	95	e4	79
b	e7	c8	37	6d	8d	d5	4e	a9	6c	56	f4	ea	65	7a	ae	08
c	ba	78	25	2e	1c	a6	b4	c6	e8	dd	74	1f	4b	bd	8b	8a
d	70	3e	b5	66	48	03	f6	0e	61	35	57	b9	86	c1	1d	9e
e	e1	f8	98	11	69	d9	8e	94	9b	1e	87	e9	ce	55	28	df
f	8c	a1	89	0d	bf	e6	42	68	41	99	2d	0f	b0	54	bb	16

Figure F–8 The SubBytes transformation. The first 4 bits of the byte identify the row, the last 4 bits the column. So, for example, the byte 7a would be transformed into the byte da.

state array before			
$s_{0,0}$	$s_{0,1}$	$s_{0,2}$	$s_{0,3}$
$s_{1,0}$	$s_{1,1}$	$s_{1,2}$	$s_{1,3}$
$s_{2,0}$	$s_{2,1}$	$s_{2,2}$	$s_{2,3}$
$s_{3,0}$	$s_{3,1}$	$s_{3,2}$	$s_{3,3}$

$\rightarrow$

state array after			
$s_{0,0}$	$s_{0,1}$	$s_{0,2}$	$s_{0,3}$
$s_{1,1}$	$s_{1,2}$	$s_{1,3}$	$s_{1,0}$
$s_{2,2}$	$s_{2,3}$	$s_{2,0}$	$s_{2,1}$
$s_{3,3}$	$s_{3,0}$	$s_{3,1}$	$s_{3,2}$

Figure F–9 The table on the left shows the state before ShiftRows is applied. The table on the right shows the state after ShiftRows is applied.

F.2.2.3   MixColumns

Let $s'_{0,c}$, $s'_{1,c}$, $s'_{2,c}$, and $s'_{3,c}$ be the bytes resulting from applying MixColumns to column c, where $c = 0, 1, 2, 3$. Then:

$$s'_{0,c} = (02 \bullet s_{0,c}) \oplus (03 \bullet s_{1,c}) \oplus s_{2,c} \oplus s_{3,c}$$

$$s'_{1,c} = s_{0,c} \oplus (02 \bullet s_{1,c}) \oplus (03 \bullet s_{2c}) \oplus s_{3,c}$$

$$s'_{2,c} = s_{0,c} \oplus s_{1,c} \oplus (02 \bullet s_{2,c}) \oplus (03 \bullet s_{3,c})$$

$$s'_{3,c} = (03 \bullet s_{0,c}) \oplus s_{1,c} \oplus s_{2,c} \oplus (02 \bullet s_{3,c})$$

F.2.2.4   AddRoundKey

This transformation adds a round key into the mix. Let w_i be the ith set of 32 bits (4 bytes) of the key schedule (see Section F.2.4). Let r be the current round, and $s'_{0,c}, s'_{1,c}, s'_{2,c}$ and $s'_{3,c}$ the bytes resulting from applying AddRoundKey to column c, where $c = 0, 1, 2, 3$. Then:

$$[s'_{0,c}, s'_{1,c}, s'_{2,c}, s'_{3,c}] = [s_{0,c}, s_{1,c}, s_{2,c}, s_{3,c}] \oplus [w_{r \times 4 + c}]$$

F.2.3   Encryption

First, the input bytes are copied into the state array (see Figure F–7).

The encryption begins with applying AddRoundKey to the state array, using round key 0. Then the transformations SubBytes, ShiftRows, MixColumns, and AddRoundKey (using the round key for the current round) are applied in succession, to form one round; in all, $Nr - 1$ rounds take place. The final round consists of an application of the SubBytes, ShiftRows, and AddRoundKey transformations.

At the end, the contents of the state array are the output bytes.

Figure F–10 shows this process.

```
encrypt(byte in[4*Nb], byte out[4*NB], word w[Nb*(Nr+1)])
begin
        byte state[4,Nb];

        state := in;
        AddRoundKey(state, w[0, Nb-1]);

        for round := 1 to Nr-1 do
        begin
                SubBytes(state);
                ShiftRows(state);
                MixColumns(state);
                AddRoundKey(state, w[round*Nb, (round+1)*Nb-1]);
        end

        SubBytes(state);
        ShiftRows(state);
        AddRoundKey(state, w[Nr*Nb, (Nr+1)*Nb-1]);

        out := state;
end
```

Figure F–10 Pseudocode for AES encryption (adapted from [2116, p. 15, Figure 5]).

F.2.3.1   AES Decryption

Like the encryption, the AES decryption is a series of rounds based on transformations similar to those used in the encryption. `InvShiftRows`, `InvSubBytes`, and `InvMixColumns` are the inverses of the corresponding encryption transformations, and are shown below.

F.2.3.2   InvSubBytes

This transformation takes a single byte as input, and replaces it with another byte. Figure F–11 defines this transformation. Thus, each byte of the state is changed with this transformation.

    The substitution table is simply the inverse of the `SubBytes` table used to encrypt.

F.2.3.3   InvShiftRows

This transformation shifts the rows of the state cyclically to the right, by the number of the row. Figure F–12 shows this transformation.

	0	1	2	3	4	5	6	7	8	9	a	b	c	d	e	f
0	52	09	6a	d5	30	36	a5	38	bf	40	a3	9e	81	f3	d7	fb
1	7c	e3	39	82	9b	2f	ff	87	34	8e	43	44	c4	de	e9	cb
2	54	7b	94	32	a6	c2	23	3d	ee	4c	95	0b	42	fa	c3	4e
3	08	2e	a1	66	28	d9	24	b2	76	5b	a2	49	6d	8b	d1	25
4	72	f8	f6	64	86	68	98	16	d4	a4	5c	cc	5d	65	b6	92
5	6c	70	48	50	fd	ed	b9	da	5e	15	46	57	a7	8d	9d	84
6	90	d8	ab	00	8c	bc	d3	0a	f7	e4	58	05	b8	b3	45	06
7	d0	2c	1e	8f	ca	3f	0f	02	c1	af	bd	03	01	13	8a	6b
8	3a	91	11	41	4f	67	dc	ea	97	f2	cf	ce	f0	b4	e6	73
9	96	ac	74	22	e7	ad	35	85	e2	f9	37	e8	1c	75	df	6e
a	47	f1	1a	71	1d	29	c5	89	6f	b7	62	0e	aa	18	be	1b
b	fc	56	3e	4b	c6	d2	79	20	9a	db	c0	fe	78	cd	5a	f4
c	1f	dd	a8	33	88	07	c7	31	b1	12	10	59	27	80	ec	5f
d	60	51	7f	a9	19	b5	4a	0d	2d	e5	7a	9f	93	c9	9c	ef
e	a0	e0	3b	4d	ae	2a	f5	b0	c8	eb	bb	3c	83	53	99	61
f	17	2b	04	7e	ba	77	d6	26	e1	69	14	63	55	21	0c	7d

Figure F–11 The InvSubBytes transformation. The first 4 bits of the byte identify the row, the last 4 bits the column. So, for example, the byte da would be transformed into the byte 7a.

state array before

$s_{0,0}$	$s_{0,1}$	$s_{0,2}$	$s_{0,3}$
$s_{1,0}$	$s_{1,1}$	$s_{1,2}$	$s_{1,3}$
$s_{2,0}$	$s_{2,1}$	$s_{2,2}$	$s_{2,3}$
$s_{3,0}$	$s_{3,1}$	$s_{3,2}$	$s_{3,3}$

$\rightarrow$

state array after

$s_{0,0}$	$s_{0,1}$	$s_{0,2}$	$s_{0,3}$
$s_{1,3}$	$s_{1,0}$	$s_{1,1}$	$s_{1,2}$
$s_{2,2}$	$s_{2,3}$	$s_{2,0}$	$s_{2,1}$
$s_{3,1}$	$s_{3,2}$	$s_{3,3}$	$s_{3,0}$

Figure F–12 The table on the left shows the state before InvShiftRows is applied. The table on the right shows the state after InvShiftRows is applied.

F.2.3.4 InvMixColumns

Let $s'_{0,c}$, $s'_{1,c}$, $s'_{2,c}$ and $s'_{3,c}$ be the bytes resulting from applying InvMixColumns to column c, where $c = 0, 1, 2, 3$. Then:

$$s'_{0,c} = (0e \bullet s_{0,c}) \oplus (0b \bullet s_{1,c}) \oplus (0d \bullet s_{2,c}) \oplus (09 \bullet s_{3,c})$$

$$s'_{1,c} = (09 \bullet s_{0,c}) \oplus (0e \bullet s_{1,c}) \oplus (0b \bullet s_{2,c}) \oplus (0d \bullet s_{3,c})$$

$$s'_{2,c} = (0d \bullet s_{0,c}) \oplus (09 \bullet s_{1,c}) \oplus (0e \bullet s_{2,c}) \oplus (0b \bullet s_{3,c})$$

$$s'_{3,c} = (0b \bullet s_{0,c}) \oplus (0d \bullet s_{1,c}) \oplus (09 \bullet s_{2,c}) \oplus (0e \bullet s_{3,c})$$

F.2.3.5 Decryption

First, the input bytes are copied into the state array (see Figure F–7). Next, the round keys are computed and the schedule reversed.

The decryption begins with applying AddRoundKey to the state array, using round key Nr. Then the transformations InvShiftRows, InvSubBytes, AddRoundKey (with the current round key from the reversed schedule), and MixColumns are applied in succession, to form one round; in all, $Nr - 1$ rounds take place. The final round consists of an application of the InvShiftRows, InvSubBytes, and AddRoundKey (using round key 0) transformations.

At the end, the contents of the state array are the output bytes.

Figure F–13 shows this process.

F.2.4 Round Key Generation

Like the DES, the AES takes a key k and generates 4-byte round keys $k_i = k_{i0}k_{i1}k_{i2}k_{i3}$. It is more convenient to consider these round keys as one array of 4-byte words. So let $[w_i]$ be the ith byte of this array. As there are Nr rounds, then $0 \leq i \leq Nb(Nr + 1)$.

```
encrypt(byte in[4*Nb], byte out[4*NB], word w[Nb*(Nr+1)])
begin
        byte state[4,Nb];

        state := in;
        AddRoundKey(state, w[Nr*Nb, (Nr+1)*Nb-1]);

        for round := Nr-1 downto 1 do
        begin
                InvShiftRows(state);
                InvSubBytes(state);
                AddRoundKey(state, w[round*Nb, (round+1)*Nb-1]);
                InvMixColumns(state);
        end

        SubBytes(state);
        ShiftRows(state);
        AddRoundKey(state, w[0, Nb-1]);

        out := state;
end
```

Figure F–13 Pseudocode for AES decryption (adapted from [2116, p. 21, Figure 12]).

The round key generation algorithm uses two transformations, SubWord and RotWord, and a round constant word array, Rcon.

F.2.4.1   SubWord

SubWord takes as input a 4-byte word. It applies the SubByte transformation to each byte individually, and returns the result. So the input [ae, 3f, 78, 21] produces the output [e4, 75, bc, fd].

F.2.4.2   RotWord

RotWord cyclically shifts the input 4-byte word right by one byte. So the input $[b_0, b_1, b_2, b_3]$ produces the output $[b_1, b_2, b_3, b_0]$.

F.2.4.3   Rcon

For the ith round, the round constant word array Rcon[i] has the value [x^{i-1}, 00, 00, 00], where x is 02, and x^i uses multiplication as described in Section F.2.1. Figure F–14 shows values for Rcon[1] through Rcon[10].

| 1 | 01000000 | 3 | 04000000 | 5 | 10000000 | 7 | 40000000 | 9 | 1b000000 |
| 2 | 02000000 | 4 | 08000000 | 6 | 20000000 | 8 | 80000000 | 10 | 36000000 |

Figure F–14 Values of Rcon[1] through Rcon[10] (adapted from [2116, Section A.2]).

```
roundkeys(byte key[4*Nk], word w[Nb*(Nr+1)], Nk)
begin
        word temp;

        for i:= 0 to Nk-1 do
                w[i] = word(key[4*i], key[4*i+1],
                            key[4*i+2], key[4*i+3]);

        for i := Nk to (Nr+1)*Nb-1 do
        begin
                temp := w[i-1];
                if (i mod Nk = 0)
                        temp = SubWord(RotWord(temp))
                                xor Rcon[i/Nk];
                else if (Nk > 6 and i mod Nk = 4)
                                temp = SubWord(temp);
                w[i] = w[i-Nk] xor temp;
        end
end
```

Figure F–15 Pseudocode for generating the round keys (adapted from [2116, p. 20, Figure 11]).

F.2.4.4 Round Key Schedule Generation

The round key schedule is generated as a sequence of words in the array w. In the algorithm presented in Figure F–15, word takes 4 bytes and combines them into a single word.

F.2.5 Equivalent Inverse Cipher Implementation

The order of transformations between AES encryption and AES decryption differ. Specifically, in encryption, the order of the transformations is SubBytes, ShiftRows, MixColumns, and AddRoundKeys, and in decryption the order of the transformations is InvShiftRows, InvSubBytes, AddRoundKeys, and InvMixColumns. But two properties allow a more efficient implementation of decryption.

```
for i = 0 to (Nr+1)*Nb-1 do
        dw[i] = w[i];

for round = 1 to Nr-1 do
        InvMixColumns(dw[round*Nb, (round+1)*Nb-1])
```

Figure F–16 Pseudocode to be added to the end of the roundkeys algorithm in Figure F–15 (adapted from Figure 15 [2116, p. 25]).

```
equivinvcipher(byte in[4*Nb], byte out[4*Nb], word
              dw[Nb*(Nr+1)])
begin
        byte state[4,Nb];

        state := in;
        AddRoundKey(state, dw[Nr*Nb, (Nr+1)*Nb-1]);

        for round = Nr-1 downto 1 do
        begin
                InvSubBytes(state);
                InvShiftRows(state);
                InvMixColumns(state);
                AddRoundKey(state, dw[round*Nb,
                                (round+1)*Nb-1]);
        end

        InvSubBytes(state);
        InvShiftRows(state);
        AddRoundKey(state, dw[0, Nb-1]);

        out := state;
end
```

Figure F–17 Pseudocode implementing the equivalent inverse cipher (AES decryption) (adapted from [2116, p. 25, Figure 15]).

The first two transformations in both sequences commute, so the order of SubBytes and ShiftRows is unimportant. The same is true for the order of InvShiftRows and InvSubBytes.

Also, the column mixing operations are linear in the column input, so

```
InvMixColumns(state xor roundkey) = InvMixColumns(state) xor
    InvMixColumns(roundkey)
```

This means the order of `InvMixColumns` and `AddRoundKey` can be reversed, providing the round key schedule is also modified by using `InvMixColumns`. This leads to the algorithm in Figures F–16 and F–17.

F.3 Exercises

1. Prove that the DES key consisting of all 0 bits and the DES key consisting of all 1 bits are both weak keys. What are the other two weak keys? (Note: Differences in the parity bits, which the PC-1 permutation drops, do not count; the keys must differ in the 56 bits that are used to generate the key schedule.)

2. Prove that the DES cipher satisfies the complementation property (see page 301).

3. Section F.2.5 states that the first two transformations in the rounds for both AES encryption and AES decryption commute.

   a. Prove that the `SubBytes` and `ShiftRows` transformations commute.

   b. Prove that the `InvShiftRows` and `InvSubBytes` transformations commute.

Appendix G

Example Academic Security Policy

The first policy statement presented here is the University of California at Davis's acceptable use policy for electronic communications. It is an informal statement, focusing on clear language and references to other resources. Next comes the University of California's Electronic Communications Policy.[1] The third statement gives the user advisories associated with this policy (and is the first attachment to the Electronic Communications Policy). This applies to all 10 University of California campuses. The User Advisories associated with this policy follow; again, these are written for the ordinary user, and have many references to the full policy. Last comes the University of California at Davis's implementing procedures for the Electronic Communications Policy.

The text of these policy statements is copyrighted by the Regents of the University of California, © 2000, 2005, 2006, 2013 and is used by permission. The text is taken directly from the University of California web pages and Policy and Procedure Manual. Section numbering has been changed to reflect the section numbering of this text, and all cross-references have been updated.[2] These changes do not affect the contents of the policy.

G.1 Acceptable Use Policy

This is from the University of California at Davis Policy and Procedure Manual, section 310-23, Exhibit A, issued on May 9, 2006 and reissued on September 6, 2013 [2115].

---

[1] The second attachment, "Implementation Guidelines," is omitted because the UC Davis procedures implementing the policy are presented.

[2] To convert the text's numbering to that of the original document, delete the leading "**G.**n." at the beginning of each section, and change the remaining digit to a Roman numeral. For example, section G.3.6 corresponds to Section VI of the User Advisories.

G.1.1   Introduction

The University encourages the use of electronic communications to share information and knowledge in support of the University's mission of education, research, community service, and patient care, and to conduct the University's business. To these ends, the University supports and provides electronic communications resources such as computers, networks, video and audio equipment, telecommunications devices, email, and the World Wide Web.

Incorporating the values affirmed by the UC Davis Principles of Community, this policy governs the use of electronic communications resources at UC Davis. All UC Davis users are responsible for reading and understanding this policy. Users must acknowledge, in writing, that they have read and understand this policy before they are allowed access to UC Davis electronic communications resources.

G.1.2   Rights and Responsibilities

Electronic communications provide access to resources on and off campus, as well as the ability to communicate with other users worldwide. Such open access is a privilege and requires that individual users act responsibly. Users must respect the rights of other users, respect the integrity of the systems and related physical resources, and observe all relevant laws, regulations, and contractual obligations. Since electronic information is volatile and easily reproduced, users must exercise care in acknowledging and respecting the work of others through strict adherence to software licensing agreements and copyright laws.

The University is the legal owner and operator of all electronic communications resources purchased or leased with University funds. Overall responsibility for administering the University's electronic communications resources is primarily that of the Vice Provost–Information & Educational Technology. The Vice Provost–Information & Educational Technology may delegate overall responsibility for certain resources.

Other organizations such as universities, companies, and governments that operate resources that are accessible via the UC Davis network may have their own policies governing the use of those resources. When accessing remote resources from UC Davis facilities, users are responsible for following the policy of UC Davis and/or the remote facility, whichever is more restrictive.

G.1.3   Privacy

The University recognizes that principles of academic freedom and shared governance, freedom of speech, and privacy hold important implications for the use of electronic communications resources. This policy reflects these principles within the context of the University's legal and other obligations. The University respects the privacy of electronic communications in the same way that it respects the privacy of paper correspondence and conversations, while seeking to ensure that University administrative records are accessible for the conduct of University business.

The University does not routinely inspect, monitor, or disclose electronic communications without the holder's consent. Nonetheless, the University may deny access to its electronic communications resources and may inspect, monitor, or disclose electronic communications under certain limited circumstances, subject to the requirements for authorization, notification, and recourse in the UC and UC Davis Electronic Communications Policies.

G.1.4   Enforcement of Laws and University Policies

Federal and state laws and University policies apply to electronic communications resources, including not only those that are specific to computers, but also those that apply generally to personal conduct.

Minor or accidental violations of this policy may be handled informally by the unit administering the accounts or network. This may be done through electronic mail or in-person discussion and education.

More serious violations (including repeated minor violations) may result in the temporary or permanent loss of access privileges or the modification of those privileges. Violators may be subject to disciplinary action up to and including dismissal or expulsion under applicable University policies and collective bargaining agreements. Violators may be referred to their sponsoring advisor, supervisor, manager, dean, vice chancellor, Student Judicial Affairs, or the Misuse of University Resources Coordinating Committee or other appropriate authority for further action.

G.1.5   Unacceptable Conduct

Unacceptable conduct includes, but is not limited to, the following attempted or completed actions:

A. Copyrights and licenses. Users shall respect copyrights and licensing agreements.

1. Copying. Software shall not be copied except as permitted by copyright law or a license agreement.

2. Number of simultaneous users. The number and distribution of copies shall be handled in such a way that the number of simultaneous users in a department does not exceed the number of copies purchased by that department, unless otherwise stipulated in the purchase contract.

3. Plagiarism. Copied material shall be properly attributed. Plagiarism of electronic communications information is subject to the same sanctions as in any other medium.

B. Integrity of electronic communications resources. Users shall not interfere with the normal operation of electronic communications resources.

1. Modification, damage, or removal. Users shall not modify, damage, or remove electronic communications resources that are owned by the University or other users without proper authorization.

2. Encroaching on others' access and use. Users shall not encroach on others' access and use of the University's electronic communications resources. This includes but is not limited to: the sending of chain-letters or excessive messages; printing excessive copies; running grossly inefficient programs when efficient alternatives are available; unauthorized modification of electronic communications resources; attempting to crash or tie up electronic communications resources.

3. Unauthorized or destructive programs. Users shall not intentionally develop or use programs such as, but not limited to, viruses, backdoors, and worms that disrupt other users, access private or restricted portions of the system, identify security vulnerabilities, decrypt secure data, or damage the software or hardware components of an electronic communications resource. Legitimate academic pursuits for research and instruction that are conducted under the supervision of academic personnel are authorized by the Vice Provost–Information and Educational Technology to the extent that the pursuits do not compromise the University's electronic communications resources.

4. Unauthorized equipment. Users shall not install or attach any equipment to a UCD electronic communications resource without the explicit approval of the system administrator for that electronic communications resource.

C. Unauthorized access. Users shall not seek or enable unauthorized access.

1. Authorization. Users shall not access electronic communications resources without proper authorization, or intentionally enable others to do so.

2. Password protection. A user who has been authorized to use a password-protected account shall not disclose the password or otherwise make the account available to others without authorization.

3. Misuse of EC records. Users may seek out, use, or disclose information contained in EC records only for University business.

D. Usage. Users shall comply with applicable law and University policy.

1. Hostile working environment. Users shall not use electronic communications resources in a manner that creates a hostile working

environment (including sexual or other forms of harassment), or that violates obscenity laws.

2. Unlawful activities. Users shall not use electronic communications resources for unlawful activities or activities that violate University policy, including fraudulent, libelous, slanderous, harassing, threatening, or other communications.

3. Mass messaging. Users shall avoid spamming, and other inappropriate mass messaging to newsgroups, bulletin boards, mailing lists, or individuals. Subscribers to an electronic mailing list will be viewed as having solicited any material delivered by the list so long as the material is consistent with the list's purpose.

4. Information belonging to others. Users shall not intentionally seek or provide information on, obtain copies of, or modify data files, programs, or passwords belonging to other users without the permission of those other users.

5. False identity. Users shall not use the identity of another user without the explicit approval of that user, or mask the identity of an account or machine.

6. Implying University endorsement. Users shall not imply University endorsement of products or services of a non-University entity from a University electronic communications resource without approval. Users shall not give the impression that the user is representing, giving opinions, or otherwise making statements on behalf of the University unless authorized to do so. To avoid this, the user may use a disclaimer such as "The opinions or statements expressed herein should not be taken as a position of or endorsement by the University of California."

7. Protection of restricted personal information. Employees are responsible for maintaining the security of individual's restricted personal information. Restricted personal information that is not necessary for an employees position responsibilities shall be removed from electronic communication devices. If the security of restricted personal information is compromised (e.g., loss of computer, theft, hacking), the employee must immediately inform their supervisor and the Security Coordinator at security@ucdavis.edu.

E. Political, religious, personal, and commercial use. The University is a not-for-profit, tax-exempt organization and, as such, is subject to federal, state, and local laws on the use of University property.

1. Political or religious use. In communications relating to religious or political activities or issues, the user's University title may be used only for identification. If such identification might reasonably be construed as implying the support, endorsement, or opposition of

the University with regard to any religious or political activity or issue, a disclaimer (see D.6[3] above) shall be used.

2. Personal use. University users may use electronic communications resources for incidental personal purposes provided that such use does not: (a) directly or indirectly interfere with the University's operation of electronic communications resources, (b) interfere with the user's employment or other obligations to the University, (c) burden the University with noticeable incremental costs, or (d) violate the law or University policy.

3. Commercial use. University electronic communications resources shall not be used for non-University commercial purposes, except as permitted under University policy or with the appropriate approval.

4. Advertisements. The University's electronic communications resources shall not be used to transmit commercial or personal advertisements, solicitations, or promotions, except as permitted under University policy or with the appropriate approval.

G.1.6   Further Information

UC Davis Policy & Procedure Manual Sections 310-23 and 310-24 (available on the Web at http://manuals. ucdavis.edu), and the University of California Electronic Communications Policy (available on the Web at http://www.ucop.edu /ucophome/policies/ec/), give further information and a list of relevant federal and state laws and University policies.

The Information & Educational Technology Services Website at http://iet .ucdavis.edu/ provides information on the use of the University's electronic communications resources.

G.2   University of California Electronic Communications Policy

This is the Electronic Communications Policy issued on November 17, 2000 and revised on August 18, 2005, for the University of California [2150]. The policy was issued by the University's Office of the President.

G.2.1   Introduction

The University of California encourages the use of electronic communications to share information and knowledge in support of the University's mission of education, research, and public service and to conduct the University's business.

---

[3]Section G.1.5.D.6 in this Appendix.

To this end, the University supports and provides interactive electronic communications services and facilities for telecommunications, mail, publishing, and broadcasting.

Recognizing the convergence of technologies based on voice, video, and data networks, as Presidential Policy [http://www.ucop.edu/ucophome /coordrev/policy/], the University of California Electronic Communications Policy establishes principles, rules, and procedures applying to all members of the University community to specifically address issues particular to the use of electronic communications. It clarifies the applicability of law to electronic communications and references other University guidelines to ensure consistent application of the Electronic Communications Policy on all University campuses (see Appendix B, References[4]).

G.2.2 General Provisions

A. Purpose
The purposes of this Policy are to:

- Establish policy on privacy, confidentiality, and security in electronic communications;
- Ensure that University electronic communications resources are used for purposes appropriate to the University's mission;
- Inform the University community about the applicability of laws and University policies to electronic communications;
- Ensure that electronic communications resources are used in compliance with those laws and University policies; and
- Prevent disruptions to and misuse of University electronic communications resources, services, and activities.

B. Scope
This Policy applies to:

- All electronic communications resources owned or managed by the University;
- All electronic communications resources provided by the University through contracts and other agreements with the University;
- All users and uses of University electronic communications resources; and
- All University electronic communications records in the possession of University employees or of other users of electronic communications resources provided by the University.

This Policy does not apply to electronic communications resources of the Department of Energy Laboratories managed by the University, or

---

[4]Section G.2.8 here

to users of such electronic communications resources who are employees and agents of those Laboratories. The Policy does apply to University users (as defined here) of the DOE Laboratories' electronic communications resources, to the extent that the provisions of the Policy are not superseded by those of DOE Laboratories managed by the University.

This Policy applies to the contents of electronic communications, and to the electronic attachments and transactional information associated with such communications.

This Policy applies only to electronic communications records in electronic form. The Policy does not apply to printed copies of electronic communications records or printed copies of transactional information. Electronic communications records in either printed or electronic form are subject to federal and state laws as well as University records management policies, including their provisions regarding retention and disclosure (see State of California Statutes, Federal Statutes and Regulations, and Business and Finance Bulletins in the Records Management and Privacy [RMP] series listed in Appendix B, References[5]).

C. Definitions

The following terms used in this Policy are defined in Appendix A, Definitions.[6] Knowledge of these definitions is important to an understanding of this Policy.

- Compelling Circumstances
- Electronic Communications
- Electronic Communications Resources
- Electronic Communications Records
- Electronic Communications Service Provider
- Electronic Communications Systems or Services
- Emergency Circumstances
- Faculty
- Holder of an Electronic Communications Record or Electronic Communications Holder
- Possession of Electronic Communications Record
- Public Record
- Substantiated Reason
- Time-Dependent, Critical Operational Circumstances
- Transactional Information
- University Administrative Record
- University Electronic Communications Record

---

[5]Section G.2.8 in this Appendix.
[6]Section G.2.7 in this Appendix.

- University Electronic Communications Systems or Services
- Use of Electronic Communications Services

D. Responsibilities

1. **Policy.** This Policy is issued by the President of the University of California. The Associate Vice President, Information Resources and Communications (IR&C) in the Office of the President is responsible for maintenance of this Policy.

2. **Implementation.** Each Chancellor, and for the Office of the President, the Senior Vice President, Business and Finance, shall designate a co-ordinator to administer the Policy. In consultation with faculty, students, and staff, the designated coordinator shall develop, maintain, and publish specific procedures and practices that implement this Policy. Campus procedures shall include information on accessibility of student information, authorized users, procedures for restricting or denying use of its electronic communications services, adjudication of complaints, network monitoring practices, and other matters as described in Attachment 2, Implementation Guidelines.[7] IR&C shall facilitate regular communication among campus coordinators to address consistency in campus implementing procedures.

3. **Informational Material.** Campuses shall provide users of University electronic communications resources with instructional material based on this Policy and on their own campus implementation guidelines.

E. Violations of Law and Policy

1. **Law.** Federal and state law prohibit the theft or abuse of computers and other electronic resources such as electronic communications resources, systems, and services. Abuses include (but are not limited to) unauthorized entry, use, transfer, tampering with the communications of others, and interference with the work of others and with the operation of electronic communications resources, systems, and services. The law classifies certain types of offenses as felonies (see Appendix B, References[8]).

2. **University Disciplinary Actions.** University policy prohibits the use of University property for illegal purposes and for purposes not in support of the mission of the University. In addition to legal sanctions, violators of this Policy may be subject to disciplinary action up to and including dismissal or expulsion, pursuant to University policies and collective bargaining agreements. Further information on permitted and prohibited uses is given in Section III, Allowable Use.[9]

---

[7] Not included in this Appendix.
[8] Section G.2.8 in this Appendix.
[9] Section G.2.3 in this Appendix.

G.2.3   Allowable Use

A. Introduction

The University encourages the use of electronic communications resources and makes them widely available to the University community. Nonetheless, the use of electronic communications resources is limited by restrictions that apply to all University property and by constraints necessary for the reliable operation of electronic communications systems and services. The University reserves the right to deny use of its electronic communications services when necessary to satisfy these restrictions and constraints.

In general, the University cannot and does not wish to be the arbiter of the contents of electronic communications. Neither can the University always protect users from receiving electronic messages they might find offensive.

B. Ownership

This Policy does not address the ownership of intellectual property stored on or transmitted through University electronic communications resources. Ownership of intellectual property is governed by law, the University of California Policy on Copyright Ownership (1992) and the 2003 Policy on Ownership of Course Materials, Academic Personnel Policy 020, Special Services to Individuals and Organizations (Regulation 4), and other University policies and contracts (see Appendix B, References[10]).

University policy issued by Vice President Bolton on October 31, 1969 and reiterated in Business and Finance Bulletin RMP-1, University Records Management Program (see Appendix B, References[11]) assigns the ownership of the administrative records of the University to The Regents of the University of California. This applies whether such records are in paper, digital, or other format. Electronic communications records pertaining to the administrative business of the University are considered public records (see Appendix A, Definitions[12]), whether or not the University owns the electronic communications resources, systems or services used to create, send, forward, reply to, transmit, store, hold, copy, download, display, view, read, print, or otherwise record them. Other records, although not owned by The Regents, nevertheless may be subject to disclosure as public records under the California Public Records Act if they pertain to the business of the University.

University electronic communications resources, systems and services are the property of The Regents of the University of California.

---

[10]Section G.2.8 in this Appendix.
[11]Section G.2.8 in this Appendix.
[12]Section G.2.7 in this Appendix.

These include all components of the electronic communications physical infrastructure and any electronic communications address, number, account, or other identifier associated with the University or any unit of the University or assigned by the University to individuals, units, or functions.

C. Allowable Users

1. **University Users.** University students, faculty, staff, and others affiliated with the University (including those in program, contract, or license relationships with the University) may, as authorized by the Chancellor, be eligible to use University electronic communications resources and services for purposes in accordance with Sections III.D, Allowable Use.[13]

2. **Public Users.** Persons and organizations that are not University Users may only access University electronic communications resources or services under programs sponsored by the University, as authorized by the Chancellor, or for the Office of the President, the Senior Vice President, Business and Finance, for purposes of such public access in accordance with Section III.D, Allowable Use.[14]

3. **Transient Users.** Users whose electronic communications merely transit University facilities as a result of network routing protocols are not considered "Users" for the purposes of this Policy.

D. Allowable Uses

Use of University electronic communications resources is allowable subject to the following conditions:

1. **Purpose.** Electronic communications resources may be provided by University units or sub-units in support of the teaching, research, and public service mission of the University, and of the administrative functions that support this mission.

2. **Non-Competition.** University electronic communications resources shall not be provided to individual consumers or organizations outside the University except by approval of the Chancellor. Such services shall support the mission of the University and not be in competition with commercial providers.

3. **Restrictions.** University electronic communications resources may not be used for:

   - unlawful activities;
   - commercial purposes not under the auspices of the University;
   - personal financial gain (except as permitted under applicable academic personnel policies);

---

[13] Section G.2.3 in this Appendix.
[14] Section G.2.3 in this Appendix.

- personal use inconsistent with Section III.D, Allowable Uses;[15] or

- uses that violate other University or campus policies or guidelines. The latter include, but are not limited to, policies and guidelines regarding intellectual property and sexual or other forms of harassment (see Appendix B, References[16]).

4. **Representation.** Use of the University's name and seal is regulated by the State of California Education Code 92000. Users of electronic communications resources must abide by this statute as well as by University and campus policies on the use of the University's name, seals, and trademarks (see Appendix B, References[17]). Users of electronic communications resources shall not give the impression that they are representing, giving opinions, or otherwise making statements on behalf of the University or any unit of the University unless appropriately authorized to do so.

5. **Endorsements.** Users of electronic communications resources must abide by University and campus policies regarding endorsements. References or pointers to any non-University entity contained in University electronic communications shall not imply University endorsement of the products or services of that entity.

6. **False Identity and Anonymity.** Users of University electronic communications resources shall not, either directly or by implication, employ a *false identity* (the name or electronic identification of another). However, when not prohibited by law or other University policy, a supervisor may direct an employee to use the supervisor's identity to transact University business for which the supervisor is responsible. In such cases, an employee's use of the supervisor's electronic identity does not constitute a false identity.

   A user of University electronic communications resources may use a *pseudonym* (an alternative name or electronic identification for oneself) for privacy or other reasons, so long as the pseudonym clearly does not constitute a false identity.

   A user of University electronic communications resources may remain *anonymous* (the sender's name or electronic identification are hidden) except when publishing web pages and transmitting broadcasts.

   Campus guidelines and procedures may further restrict the circumstances under which pseudonyms and anonymous electronic communications are permitted.

7. **Interference.** University electronic communications resources shall not be used for purposes that could reasonably be expected to cause

---

[15]Section G.2.3 in this Appendix.
[16]Section G.2.8 in this Appendix.
[17]Section G.2.8 in this Appendix.

excessive strain on any electronic communications resources, or to cause interference with others' use of electronic communications resources.

Users of electronic communications services shall not: (i) send or forward chain letters or their equivalents in other services; (ii) "spam," that is, exploit electronic communications systems for purposes beyond their intended scope to amplify the widespread distribution of unsolicited electronic messages; (iii) "letter-bomb," that is, send an extremely large message or send multiple electronic messages to one or more recipients and so interfere with the recipients' use of electronic communications systems and services; or (iv) intentionally engage in other practices such as "denial of service attacks" that impede the availability of electronic communications services.

8. **Personal Use.** University users of a University electronic communications facility or service may use that facility or service for incidental personal purposes provided that, in addition to the foregoing constraints and conditions, such use does not: (i) interfere with the University's operation of electronic communications resources; (ii) interfere with the user's employment or other obligations to the University, or (iii) burden the University with noticeable incremental costs. When noticeable incremental costs for personal use are incurred, users shall follow campus guidelines and procedures for reimbursement to the University.

The California Public Records Act requires the University to disclose specified public records. In response to requests for such disclosure, it may be necessary to examine electronic communications records that users consider to be personal to determine whether they are public records that are subject to disclosure (see the presumption in Appendix A, Definitions,[18] of a University Electronic Communications Record).

The University is not responsible for any loss or damage incurred by an individual as a result of personal use of University electronic communications resources.

9. **Accessibility.** All electronic communications intended to accomplish the academic and administrative tasks of the University shall be accessible to allowable users with disabilities in compliance with law and University policies. Alternate accommodations shall conform to law and University policies and guidelines.

10. **Intellectual Property.** The contents of all electronic communications shall conform to laws and University policies regarding protection of intellectual property, including laws and policies regarding copyright, patents, and trademarks. When the content and distribution of an electronic communication would exceed fair use as defined by

---

[18]Section G.2.7 in this Appendix.

the federal Copyright Act of 1976, users of University electronic communications resources shall secure appropriate permission to distribute protected material in any form, including text, photographic images, audio, video, graphic illustrations, and computer software.

E. Access Restriction

Eligibility to access or use University electronic communications services or electronic communications resources, when provided, is a privilege accorded at the discretion of the University. This privilege is subject to the normal conditions of use, including procedures for initiation and termination of service eligibility, established by the manager of the individual electronic communications resource.

In addition, use of University electronic communications resources may be restricted or rescinded by the University at its discretion when required by and consistent with law, when there is substantiated reason to believe that violations of law or University policies have taken place, when there are compelling circumstances, or under time-dependent, critical operational circumstances (see Appendix A, Definitions). Restriction of use is subject to established *campuswide* procedures or, in the absence of such procedures, to the approval of the appropriate Vice Chancellor(s) or, for the Office of the President, the Senior Vice President, Business and Finance. Electronic communications resource providers may, nonetheless, restrict use of University electronic communications systems and services on a temporary basis as needed in Emergency Circumstances and Compelling Circumstances (see Appendix A, Definitions[19]).

In compliance with the Digital Millennium Copyright Act, the University reserves the right to suspend or terminate use of University electronic communications systems and services by any user who repeatedly violates copyright law.

G.2.4   Privacy and Confidentiality

A. Introduction

The University recognizes that principles of academic freedom and shared governance, freedom of speech, and privacy hold important implications for the use of electronic communications. This Policy reflects these firmly-held principles within the context of the University's legal and other obligations. The University respects the privacy of electronic communications in the same way that it respects the privacy of paper correspondence and telephone conversations, while seeking to ensure that University administrative records are accessible for the conduct of the University's business.

---

[19]Section G.2.7 in this Appendix.

The University does not examine or disclose electronic communications records without the holder's consent. Nonetheless, subject to the requirements for authorization, notification, and other conditions specified in this Policy, the University may examine or disclose electronic communications under very limited circumstances as described in Section IV.B, Access Without Consent.[20]

University employees are prohibited from seeking out, using, or disclosing personal information in electronic communications without authorization (see Business and Finance Bulletin RMP-8, Legal Requirements on Privacy of and Access to Information). University policy requires that its employees take necessary precautions to protect the confidentiality of personal information encountered either in the performance of their duties or otherwise (see Business and Finance Bulletin IS-3, Electronic Information Security).

University contracts with outside vendors for electronic communications services shall explicitly reflect and be consistent with this Policy and other University policies related to privacy.

B. Access Without Consent

An electronic communications holder's consent shall be obtained by the University prior to any access for the purpose of examination or disclosure of the contents of University electronic communications records in the holder's possession, except as provided for below.

The University shall permit the examination or disclosure of electronic communications records without the consent of the holder of such records only: (i) when required by and consistent with law; (ii) when there is substantiated reason (as defined in Appendix A, Definitions[21]) to believe that violations of law or of University policies listed in Appendix C, Policies Relating to Access Without Consent,[22] have taken place; (iii) when there are compelling circumstances as defined in Appendix A, Definitions;[23] or (iv) under time-dependent, critical operational circumstances as defined in Appendix A, Definitions.[24]

When under the circumstances described above the contents of electronic communications records must be examined or disclosed without the holder's consent, the following shall apply:

1. **Authorization.** Except in emergency circumstances (as defined in Appendix A, Definitions[25]) in accordance with Section IV.B.2, Emergency Circumstances,[26] or except for subpoenas or search warrants

---

[20] Section G.2.4.B in this Appendix.
[21] Section G.2.7 in this Appendix.
[22] Section G.2.9 in this Appendix.
[23] Section G.2.7 in this Appendix.
[24] Section G.2.7 in this Appendix.
[25] Section G.2.7 in this Appendix.
[26] Section G.2.4.B.2 in this Appendix.

in accordance with Section IV.B.6, Search Warrants and Subpoenas,[27] such actions must be authorized in advance and in writing by the responsible campus Vice Chancellor or, for the Office of the President, the Senior Vice President, Business and Finance (see Section II.D, Responsibilities[28]).[29] This authority may not be further redelegated.

Authorization shall be limited to the least perusal of contents and the least action necessary to resolve the situation.

2. **Emergency Circumstances.** In emergency circumstances as defined in Appendix A, Definitions,[30] the least perusal of contents and the least action necessary to resolve the emergency may be taken immediately without authorization, but appropriate authorization must then be sought without delay following the procedures described in Section IV.B.1, Authorization,[31] above.

3. **Notification.** The responsible authority or designee shall at the earliest opportunity that is lawful and consistent with other University policy notify the affected individual of the action(s) taken and the reasons for the action(s) taken. Each campus will issue in a manner consistent with law an annual report summarizing instances of authorized or emergency nonconsensual access pursuant to the provisions of this Section IV.B, Access Without Consent,[32] without revealing personally identifiable data.

4. **Compliance with Law.** Actions taken under Sections IV.B.1, Authorization,[33] and IV.B.2, Emergency Circumstances,[34] shall be in full compliance with the law and other applicable University policies, including laws and policies listed in Appendix B, References.[35] Advice of legal counsel must always be sought prior to any action involving electronic communications records (a) stored on equipment not owned or housed by the University, or (b) whose content is protected under the federal Family Educational Rights and Privacy Act of 1974 (see Section IV.C.1.b, Student Information[36]).

---

[27] Section G.2.4.B.6 in this Appendix.

[28] Section G.2.2.D in this Appendix.

[29] On March 18, 2004 the Regents Committee on Audit approved changes to the Internal Audit Management Charter authorizing Internal Audit to have access to University information except where prohibited by law. [http://www.universityofcalifornia.edu/regents/regmeet/mar04.html]

[30] Section G.2.7 in this Appendix.

[31] Section G.2.4.B.1 in this Appendix.

[32] Section G.2.4.B in this Appendix.

[33] Section G.2.4.B.1 in this Appendix.

[34] Section G.2.4.B.2 in this Appendix.

[35] Section G.2.8 in this Appendix.

[36] Section G.2.4.C.1.b in this Appendix.

5. **Recourse.** Campus implementing procedures shall specify the process for review and appeal of actions taken under Sections IV.B.1, Authorization,[37] and IV.B.2, Emergency Circumstances[38] to provide a mechanism for recourse to individuals who believe that actions taken by employees or agents of the University were in violation of this Policy.

6. **Search Warrants and Subpoenas.** Search warrants and subpoenas are not subject to sections 1-2 and 4-5 above. Search warrants and subpoenas for electronic communications records shall be referred to University legal counsel at the Office of the General Counsel or designated officials at campus locations.

    Search Warrants. Duly signed search warrants shall be processed in accordance with federal and state laws, University policies, and instructions in the warrant.

    Subpoenas. Subpoenas shall be processed in accordance with applicable federal and state laws and University policies (see Business and Finance Bulletin RMP-10, Instructions for Responding to Subpoena). Campus officials shall provide advance notice to individuals whose records are the subject of a subpoena duces tecum in accordance with instructions and time requirements in RMP-10, section 6.2.3.C, "Responding to requests for personal records of a consumer."

C. Privacy Protection and Limits

1. Privacy Protections

a. **Personal Information.** Federal and California law provide privacy protections for some information that personally identifies an individual. Business and Finance Bulletin RMP-8, Legal Requirements on Privacy of and Access to Information, provides guidelines for the collection and use of personal information in conformance with the law. These guidelines apply to information collected and disseminated by electronic means just as they do to records stored on paper and other media.

b. **Student Information.** Users of electronic communications systems and services shall not disclose information about students in violation of the federal Family Educational Rights and Privacy Act of 1974 (FERPA), and the University policies that provide guidance in meeting FERPA requirements. See Business and Finance Bulletin RMP-8, Legal Requirements on Privacy of and Access to Information, and the University's Policy Applying to the Disclosure of Information from Student Records (Sections

---

[37] Section G.2.4.B.1 in this Appendix.
[38] Section G.2.4.B.2 in this Appendix.

130-134 of the Policies Applying to Campus Activities, Organizations, and Students).

c. **Electronically Gathered Data.** Any collection or distribution of personally identifiable information shall be consistent with federal and state law and University policy (see Business and Finance Bulletin RMP-8, Legal Requirements on Privacy of and Access to Information). Except when otherwise provided by law, users of University electronic communications systems and services shall be informed whenever personally identifiable information other than transactional information (see *Appendix A, Definitions[39]) will be collected and stored automatically by the system or service.

In addition, California law requires state agencies and the California State University to enable users to terminate an electronic communications transaction without leaving personal data (see Appendix B, References[40]). All electronic communications systems and services in which the University is a partner with a state agency or the California State University must conform to this requirement.

In no case shall electronic communications that contain personally identifiable information about individuals, including data collected by the use of "cookies" or otherwise automatically gathered, be sold or distributed to third parties without the explicit permission of the individual.

d. **Telephone Conversations.** In compliance with federal law, audio or video telephone conversations shall not be recorded or monitored without advising the participants unless a court has explicitly approved such monitoring or recording. Emergency services shall record 911-type emergency calls in accordance with federal and state laws and regulations.

Participants shall be informed when a call is being monitored or recorded for the purpose of evaluating customer service, assessing workload, or other business purpose permitted by law. University units that monitor or record telephone calls shall provide an alternative method of doing business with the University to clients who do not wish to be part of a monitored telephone call.

2. **Privacy Limits**

a. **Possession of Public Records.** University employees shall comply with University requests for copies of public records in their possession, regardless of whether such records reside on University electronic communications resources.

---

[39]Section G.2.7 in this Appendix.
[40]Section G.2.8 in this Appendix.

b. **System Monitoring.** University employees who operate and support electronic communications resources regularly monitor transmissions for the purpose of ensuring reliability and security of University electronic communications resources and services (see Section V.B, Security Practices[41]), and in that process might observe certain transactional information or the contents of electronic communications. Except as provided elsewhere in this Policy or by law, they are not permitted to seek out transactional information or contents when not germane to system operations and support, or to disclose or otherwise use what they have observed. In the process of such monitoring, any unavoidable examination of electronic communications (including transactional information) shall be limited to the least invasive degree of inspection required to perform such duties. This exception does not exempt systems personnel from the prohibition (see Section IV.A, Introduction[42]) against disclosure of personal or confidential information.

Except as provided above, systems personnel shall not intentionally search the contents of electronic communications or transactional information for violations of law or policy. However, if in the course of their duties systems personnel inadvertently discover or suspect improper governmental activity (including violations of law or University policy), reporting of such violations shall be consistent with the Policy on Reporting and Investigating Allegations of Suspected Improper Governmental Activities (the "Whistleblower Policy").

c. **Back-up Services.** Operators of University electronic communications resources shall provide information about back-up procedures to users of those services upon request.

G.2.5   Security

A. Introduction
The University makes reasonable efforts to provide secure and reliable electronic communications services. Operators of University electronic communications resources are expected to follow appropriate professional practices in providing for the security of electronic communications records, data, application programs, and systems following guidelines provided in Business and Finance Bulletin IS-3, Electronic Information Security.

---

[41] Section G.2.5.B in this Appendix.
[42] Section G.2.4.A in this Appendix.

IS-3 provides guidelines for managing the security of electronic information resources used to conduct activities in support of the University's mission. IS-3 guidelines apply to the security of University electronic information resources in the form of electronic communications, stored data, and electronic communications resources used to transmit and process such records and data.

B. Security Practices

Providers of electronic communications services ensure the integrity and reliability of systems under their control through the use of various techniques that include routine monitoring of electronic communications. Network traffic may be inspected to confirm malicious or unauthorized activity that may harm the campus network or devices connected to the network. Such activity shall be limited to the least perusal of contents required to resolve the situation. User consent is not required for these routine monitoring practices. Providers shall document and make available to their users general information about these monitoring practices. If providers determine that it is necessary to examine suspect electronic communications records beyond routine practices, the user's consent shall be sought. If circumstances prevent prior consent, notification procedures described in Section IV.B.3, Notification[43] shall be followed.

C. Integrity

No person shall attempt to breach any security mechanisms that protect electronic communications services or facilities or any records or messages associated with these services or facilities unless otherwise authorized by other provisions of this Policy.

D. Authentication

Electronic communications service providers (see Appendix A, Definitions[44]) shall maintain currency with authentication technologies supported by the University and implement them in accordance with Business and Finance Bulletin IS-3, Electronic Information Security, and commensurate with applicable security requirements.

E. Authorization

Service providers shall use authorization technologies commensurate with security requirements of the service, application, or system. See Business and Finance Bulletin IS-3, Electronic Information Security, for requirements regarding access management of the University's electronic information resources.

F. Encryption

Where deemed appropriate, electronic communications containing restricted data as defined in Business and Finance Bulletin IS-3, Electronic Information Security should be encrypted during transit across communications networks. Other communications may be encrypted

---

[43] Section G.2.4.B.3 in this Appendix.
[44] Section G.2.7 in this Appendix.

during transit. All encrypted communications shall be handled upon receipt in conformance with the storage requirements for electronic information resources, as defined in IS-3.

G. Recovery
Providers of campuswide or Universitywide electronic communications services shall implement recovery practices adequate to ensure rapid recovery from security intrusions and service interruptions.

H. Audit
Providers of electronic communications services shall use cost-effective audit technologies and practices to help identify security violators and speed up recovery from security incidents. The use of such audit technologies and practices shall not conflict with other provisions of this Policy, in particular Section IV, Privacy and Confidentiality.[45]

G.2.6   Retention and Disposition

A. Retention
Electronic communications records are subject to University records management policies as stated in the University of California Records Disposition Schedules Manual, which provides guidance for administering the retention and disposition of all records, regardless of the medium on which they are stored.

B. Disposition
The Record Proprietor, as defined in Business and Finance Bulletin RMP-1, University Records Management Program, is responsible for preserving those electronic communications records that have been identified as having lasting business purpose or historical value to the University.

C. Back-Up
The University does not maintain central or distributed electronic archives of all electronic communications records sent or received. Electronic communications records are normally backed up, if at all, only to assure system integrity and reliability, not to provide for future retrieval, although back-ups may at times serve the latter purpose incidentally. Operators of University electronic communications services are not required by this Policy to routinely retrieve electronic communications records from such back-up facilities for individuals.

G.2.7   Appendix A: Definitions

Compelling Circumstances: Circumstances in which failure to act might result in significant bodily harm, significant property loss or damage, loss of significant

---

[45]Section G.2.4 in this Appendix.

evidence of one or more violations of law or of University policies listed in Appendix C, Policies Relating to Access Without Consent,[46] or significant liability to the University or to members of the University community.

Electronic Communications: Any transfer of signals, writings, images, sounds, data or intelligence that is, created, sent, forwarded, replied to, transmitted, distributed, broadcast, stored, held, copied, downloaded, displayed, viewed, read, or printed by one or several electronic communications systems.[47] For purposes of this Policy, an electronic file that has not been transmitted is not an electronic communication.

Electronic Communications Records: The contents of electronic communications created, sent, forwarded, replied to, transmitted, distributed, broadcast, stored, held, copied, downloaded, displayed, viewed, read, or printed by one or several electronic communications systems or services. This definition of electronic communications records applies equally to attachments to such records and transactional information associated with such records.

Electronic Communications Resources: Telecommunications equipment, transmission devices, electronic video and audio equipment, encoding or decoding equipment, computers and computer time, data processing or storage systems, computer systems, servers, networks, input/output and connecting devices, and related computer records, programs, software, and documentation that supports electronic communications services.

Electronic Communications Service Provider: Any unit, organization, or staff with responsibility for managing the operation of and controlling individual user access to any part of the University's electronic communications systems and services.

Electronic Communications Systems or Services: Any messaging, collaboration, publishing, broadcast, or distribution system that depends on electronic communications resources to create, send, forward, reply to, transmit, distribute, broadcast, store, hold, copy, download, display, view, read, or print electronic records for purposes of communication across electronic communications network systems between or among individuals or groups, that is either explicitly denoted as a system for electronic communications or is implicitly used for such purposes.

Emergency Circumstances: Circumstances in which time is of the essence and there is a high probability that delaying action would almost certainly result in compelling circumstances.

Faculty: A member of the faculty as defined by Academic Personnel Policy 110-4 (14).

Holder of an Electronic Communications Record or Electronic Communications Holder: An electronic communications user who, at a given point in time, is in possession (see definition below) or receipt of a particular electronic communications

---

[46] Section G.2.9 in this Appendix.

[47] Definition is modeled on language contained in the Electronic Communications Privacy Act (see US Code Title 18 § 2510).

record, whether or not that electronic communications user is the original creator or a recipient of the content of the record.

Possession of Electronic Communications Record: An individual is in possession of an electronic communications record, whether the original record or a copy or modification of the original record, when that individual has effective control over the location of its storage or access to its content. Thus, an electronic communications record that resides on an electronic communications server awaiting download to an addressee is deemed, for purposes of this Policy, to be in the possession of that addressee. Systems administrators and other operators of University electronic communications services are excluded from this definition of possession with regard to electronic communications not specifically created by or addressed to them.

- Electronic communications users are not responsible for electronic communications records in their possession when they have no knowledge of the existence or contents of such records.

Public Record: A record as defined in Business and Finance Bulletin RMP-8, Legal Requirements on Privacy of and Access to Information, and/or the California Public Records Act. Public records include writings or other forms of recording that contain information relating to the conduct of the public's business in materials prepared, owned, used, or retained by the University regardless of physical form or characteristics [California Government Code Section 6252(e)]. Except for certain defined situations, such records are subject to disclosure under the California Public Records Act. For more information regarding the requirements of the Public Records Act, and the University's implementation of that Act, including exemptions from disclosure, see RMP-8.

Substantiated Reason: Reliable evidence indicating that violation of law or of University policies listed in Appendix C, Policies Relating to Access Without Consent,[48] probably has occurred, as distinguished from rumor, gossip, or other unreliable evidence.

Time-dependent, Critical Operational Circumstances: Circumstances in which failure to act could seriously hamper the ability of the University to function administratively or to meet its teaching obligations, but excluding circumstances pertaining to personal or professional activities, or to faculty research or matters of shared governance.

Transactional Information: Information, including electronically gathered information, needed either to complete or to identify an electronic communication. Examples include but are not limited to: electronic mail headers, summaries, addresses and addressees; records of telephone calls; and IP address logs.

---

[48] Section G.2.9 in this Appendix.

University Administrative Record: A Public Record (see definition above) that documents or contains information related to the organization, functions, policies, decisions, procedures, operations, or other business activities of the University.

University Electronic Communications Record: A Public Record in the form of an electronic communications record, whether or not any of the electronic communications resources utilized to create, send, forward, reply to, transmit, distribute, broadcast, store, hold, copy, download, display, view, read, or print the electronic communications record are owned by the University. This implies that the location of the record, or the location of its creation or use, does not change its nature (i) as a University electronic communications record for purposes of this or other University policy, and (ii) as having potential for disclosure under the California Public Records Act.

- Until determined otherwise or unless it is clear from the context, any electronic communications record residing on university-owned or controlled telecommunications, video, audio, and computing facilities will be deemed to be a University electronic communications record for purposes of this Policy. This would include personal electronic communications. Consistent with the principles of least perusal and least action necessary and of legal compliance, the University must make a good faith a priori effort to distinguish University electronic communications records from personal and other electronic communications in situations relevant to disclosures under the California Public Records Act and other laws, or for other applicable provisions of this Policy.

University Electronic Communications Systems or Services: Electronic communications systems or services owned or operated by the University or any of its subunits or provided through contracts with the University.

Use of Electronic Communications Services: To create, send, forward, reply to, transmit, distribute, broadcast, store, hold, copy, download, display, view, read, or print electronic communications with the aid of electronic communications services. An Electronic Communications User is an individual who makes use of electronic communications services.

- The act of receipt of electronic communications as contrasted with actual viewing of the record by the recipient is excluded from the definition of "use" to the extent that the recipient does not have advance knowledge of the contents of the electronic communications record.

G.2.8   Appendix B: References

The following list identifies significant sources used as background in the preparation of this Policy, whether or not they are directly referenced by this Policy. It does not include all applicable laws and University policies. Laws and policies change from time to time, so users of this Policy are encouraged to refer to the

Office of the President Universitywide Policy Manuals and Selected Guidelines website at http://www.ucop.edu/ucophome/coordrev/ucpolicies/policymanuals.html for up-dates.

University Policies and Guidelines

- *Business and Finance Bulletins:*
    A-56, Academic Support Unit Costing and Billing Guidelines
  BUS-29, Management and Control of University Equipment
  BUS-43, Materiel Management
  BUS-65, Guidelines for University Mail Services
  IS-3, Electronic Information Security
  RMP-1, University Records Management Program
  RMP-2, Records Retention and Disposition
  RMP-7, Privacy of and Access to Information Responsibilities
  RMP-8, Legal Requirements on Privacy of and Access to Information
  RMP-10, Instructions for Responding to Subpoena

- *Personnel Manuals and Agreements:*
    Academic Personnel Manual
  Personnel Policies for Staff Members and Appendix II for Senior Managers
  Collective Bargaining Contracts (Memoranda of Understanding)

- *Other Related Policies and Guidelines:*
    Campus Access Guidelines for Employee Organizations (Local Time, Place, and Manner Rules)
  Policies Applying to Campus Activities, Organizations, and Students
  Policy and Guidelines on the Reproduction of Copyrighted Materials for Teaching and Research
  Policy on Copyright Ownership (1992) and the 2003 Policy on Owner-ship of Course Materials
  Policy on Reporting and Investigating Allegations of Suspected Im-proper Governmental Activities (the "Whistleblower Policy")
  Policy on Sexual Harassment and Procedures for Responding to Reports of Sexual Harassment
  University of California Records Disposition Schedules Manual
  University Policy on Integrity in Research

State of California Statutes

State of California Information Practices Act of 1977 (Civil Code Section 1798 et seq.)
State of California Public Records Act (Government Code Section 6250 et seq.)

State of California Education Code, Section 67100 et seq.
State of California Education Code 92000
State of California Government Code, Section 11015.5
State of California Penal Code, Section 502 and 1523 et seq.

Federal Statutes and Regulations

Americans with Disabilities Act of 1990
Communications Decency Act of 1996
Copyright Act of 1976
Digital Millennium Copyright Act of 1998
Electronic Communications Privacy Act of 1986
Family Educational Rights and Privacy Act of 1974
Health Insurance Portability and Accountability Act of 1996
Privacy Act of 1974
Telecommunications Act of 1934
Telecommunications Act of 1996
Federal Communications Commission Rules and Regulations

G.2.9   Appendix C: Policies Relating to Access Without Consent

The Electronic Communications Policy cites circumstances under which access to electronic communications may occur without the prior consent of the holder (see Section IV.B, Access Without Consent).[49] Following are University policies that may trigger nonconsensual access following procedures defined in Section IV.B, Access Without Consent.[50]

1. University policies governing sexual or other forms of harassment, specifically: Policies Applying to Campus Activities, Organizations, and Students, Section 160; Section APM-035, Appendix A of Affirmative Action and Nondiscrimination in Employment; and Personnel Policies for UC Staff Members. Sexual harassment concerning students is covered by item 6 below.

2. Certain portions of policies governing access to University records, specifically RMP-1, Section IV.B; RMP-8, Sections on Disclosure of Information and Rules of Conduct.

3. The Academic Personnel Manual, APM-015, Section II, Part II, Professional Responsibilities, Ethical Principles, and Unacceptable Faculty Conduct, and the University Policy on Integrity in Research, APM 190, Appendix B.

---

[49]Section G.2.4.B in this Appendix.
[50]Section G.2.4.B in this Appendix.

4. Personnel Policies for Staff Members and Appendix II for Senior Managers

5. Collective bargaining agreements and memoranda of understanding.

6. Section 102 governing student conduct of the policy entitled Policies Applying to Campus Activities, Organizations, and Students.

7. Sections III, Allowable Use, and IV, Privacy and Confidentiality, of this Electronic Communications Policy.

Violations of other policies can normally be detected and investigated without requiring nonconsensual access to electronic communications. On occasion, attention to possible policy violations is brought about because of the receipt by others of electronic communications. However, it is acknowledged that electronic communications can be forged, the true identity of the sender can be masked, and the apparent sender might deny authorship of the electronic communication. In such circumstances and provided there is substantiated reason (as defined in Appendix A, Definitions[51]) that points to the identity of the sender, nonconsensual access to the purported sender's electronic communications may be authorized following the procedures defined in Section IV.B, Access Without Consent,[52] but only to the least extent necessary for verifying unambiguously the identity of the sender, and only for major violations of the following policies:

- Business and Finance Bulletin A-56, Section IV.H, governing sales of goods or services outside the University.
- Business and Finance Bulletin BUS-29, Section N, governing use of University materiel or property.
- Business and Finance Bulletin BUS-43, Part 3, Section X.A, governing use of University credit, purchasing power, or facilities.
- Policies Applying to Campus Activities, Organizations, and Students, Section 42.40, governing use of University properties for commercial purposes and personal financial gain.
- Business and Finance Bulletin BUS-65, Section VII, governing provision of University mailing lists to others.
- Policy and Guidelines on the Reproduction of Copyrighted Materials for Teaching and Research.
- Campus Access Guidelines for Employee Organizations.

Posting and Authority to Change

Because University policies are subject to change, this list may change from time to time. The authoritative list at any time will be posted under the listings of

---

[51] Section G.2.7 in this Appendix.
[52] Section G.2.4.B in this Appendix.

University policies posted on the Web. Authority to change this list rests with the President of the University acting, where policies affecting faculty are concerned, with the advice of the Academic Senate.

G.3   User Advisories

This is Attachment 1 of the University of California Electronic Communications Policy [2150]. It describes the parts of the policy that impact the users in a form that users can read.

G.3.1   Introduction

University policies often interpret the application of federal and state laws to the University community. The Electronic Communications Policy interprets the application of other University policies, as well as federal and state laws, to electronic communications. Users of electronic communications who are in doubt concerning the permissibility of an intended action should seek guidance from the Universitywide Electronic Communications Policy and, where they exist, local campus implementing guidelines and other computer policies that may interpret policy or address areas not explicitly covered by Universitywide policies.

G.3.2   User Responsibilities

A. **Compliance with Law**
   The Electronic Communications Policy refers to federal laws that prohibit:

   - Monitoring telephone conversations without informing participants or without a court order;
   - Using the Internet to make available intellectual property belonging to another in such a way as to cause the loss of $2500 or more;
   - Infringing copyright by electronic communications.

   The Electronic Communications Policy refers to California laws that govern the use of computer equipment, systems and services, and which apply to electronic communications as well. Section 502 of the California Penal Code prescribes criminal penalties for:

   - Using electronic means to defraud others;
   - Using data or documentation without permission;
   - Using electronic equipment without permission;
   - Tampering with data, software, or programs;
   - Disrupting or causing denial of services to authorized users;

- Accessing or providing access to others without permission;
- Introducing computer contaminants, such as viruses; and
- Using the Internet domain name of another.

In general, behaviors that are prohibited in the physical environment are also prohibited in the digital environment.

B. Allowable Uses

The Electronic Communications Policy identifies ten principles that govern the allowable use of University electronic communications resources. Users are advised to review local campus computing guidelines that specify how these are implemented and enforced at each University location (see Electronic Communications Policy, Section III.D, Allowable Use[53]).

In accordance with federal law, users should assume that material created by others, in electronic or other form, is protected by copyright unless such material includes an explicit statement that it is not protected, or unless such material is clearly in the public domain (see the Electronic Communications Policy, Section III.D.10, Intellectual Property[54]).

C. Courtesy

The University cannot protect users of University electronic communications resources from receiving communications they may not wish to receive. Members of the University community are strongly encouraged to use the same personal and professional courtesies and considerations in electronic communications as they would in other forms of communication (see Electronic Communications Policy, Section IV.A, Introduction[55]).

G.3.3   Privacy Expectations

Various laws and available security technologies affect the degree of privacy that users can expect. Generally, laws relating to more mature communications technologies are more fully developed than those governing newer technologies as a result of court interpretations that have led to consensus about their application. For example, laws that circumscribe the privacy of telephone communications are well established while those that apply to electronic mail are not. While some laws support higher expectations of privacy, other laws interfere with such expectations (see Electronic Communications Policy, Section IV.C, Privacy Protections and Limits[56]).

---

[53] Section G.2.3 in this Appendix.
[54] Section G.2.3.D.10 in this Appendix.
[55] Section G.2.4.A in this Appendix.
[56] Section G.2.4.C in this Appendix.

Users commonly associate different levels of privacy with various electronic communications technologies or with alternative uses of those technologies. For example:

- Users generally expect a high level of privacy with telephone conversations, and these expectations are generally protected by law;
- Users often expect a similarly high level of privacy with electronic mail, but (i) these expectations are not always supported by law, and (ii) recipients may compromise confidentiality by redirecting electronic mail messages;
- Users might expect a more moderate level of privacy with electronic communications intended for distribution to a limited audience, since privacy can be compromised by the limit of available security protections or by the behavior of members of the intended audience (a user, for example, might share a password without knowledge or consent of the originator of the communication); and
- Users should expect minimal or no privacy in broadcast communications, such as television or unprotected web pages, because they are accessible to a wide, unspecified audience.

G.3.4   Privacy Protections

Two categories of information that are protected from disclosure by law are information that personally identifies an individual and certain information pertaining to students. In addition, state and federal laws partially limit the use of automated electronic data gathering tools to collect and store personally identifiable information about individuals without their knowledge or consent (see Electronic Communications Policy, Section IV, Privacy and Confidentiality[57]). In spite of these legal protections users of electronic communications should exercise caution to protect their privacy.

A. Personal Information

Users of electronic communications systems and services should be aware of the difficulty of maintaining privacy and confidentiality on the web and should be particularly careful about posting personal information on the web. They should note that even web pages that have no pointers to or from other web pages might be found by search engines.

Users who do not want their electronic mail addresses made public are cautioned not to send electronic communications to mailing list systems, chat rooms, web pages, and newsgroups where they might be discovered or otherwise used for purposes over which the individual has no control.

---

[57] Section G.2.4 in this Appendix.

B. Student Privacy

Federal law protecting student privacy is incorporated into University policies. In accordance with the policies and procedures in the University's Policy Applying to the Disclosure of Information from Student Records (Sections 130-134 of the Policies Applying to Campus Activities, Organizations, and Students), campuses are responsible for designating the categories of personally identifiable information about a student that are public. Individual students may, consistent with the above policy, request the campus not to make public their electronic mail addresses and telephone numbers (see Electronic Communications Policy, Section II.D, Responsibilities[58] and Section IV.C, Privacy Protections and Limits[59]).

C. Electronic Data Gathering

Legislation protecting the privacy of electronic communications users is still evolving. There are currently few laws that would adequately protect users from electronic data gathering without their permission (see Electronic Communications Policy Section IV.C, Privacy Protections and Limits[60]).

G.3.5   Privacy Limits

A. Introduction

The privacy of electronic communications at the University is limited by: i) laws that protect the public's right to know about the public business; ii) policies that require employees to comply with management requests for University records in their possession; and iii) technical requirements for efficient operation of University electronic communications resources (see Electronic Communications Policy, Section IV, Privacy & Confidentiality[61]). Privacy and confidentiality might also be compromised by unintended redistribution or by the inadequacy of current technologies to protect against unauthorized access. Therefore, users should exercise extreme caution in using electronic communications to transmit confidential or sensitive matters. Guidance on storage, disposal, and preservation of records is addressed in the Appendices to RMP-2, "Records Retention and Disposition: Principles, Processes, and Guidelines."

B. Public Records

Users of University electronic communications services should be aware that the California Public Records Act and other similar laws make

---

[58] Section G.2.2.D in this Appendix.
[59] Section G.2.4.C in this Appendix.
[60] Section G.2.4.C in this Appendix.
[61] Section G.2.4 in this Appendix.

it impossible for the University to guarantee complete protection of an individual's personal electronic communications records resident on University facilities (see Electronic Communications Policy Section III.D.8, Personal Use[62]).

The University does not automatically comply with all requests for disclosure, but evaluates all such requests against the precise provisions of the California Public Records Act, other laws concerning disclosure and privacy, and other applicable law. Business and Finance Bulletin RMP-8 and personnel manuals and agreements provide guidelines for University implementation of the California Public Records Act.

Electronic communications records arising from personal use may be difficult to distinguish from public records, and such records may be subject to inspection or disclosure pursuant to the California Public Records Act (see the presumption in the Electronic Communications Policy, Appendix A, Definitions,[63] of a University Electronic Communications Record, regarding personal and other electronic communications records). Users should assess the implications of this presumption in their decision to use University electronic communications resources for personal purposes.

The California Public Records Act does not in general apply to records generated or held by students except in their capacity, if any, as employees or agents of the University. This exemption only applies to the Act and does not exclude students' electronic communications from other aspects of this Policy.

C. University Policies

In addition to University policies that require employees to comply with management requests for University records in their possession, other University policies affect the privacy of some forms of electronic communication.

In compliance with law, the University does not record or monitor audio or video telephone conversations except as described below, unless under court order. The law permits the University to monitor or record calls for the purpose of evaluating customer service, assessing workload, or other business purposes. In such cases the University advises the participants that the call is being monitored or recorded. Users who do not wish to be part of a monitored telephone call should be aware that University units are required to provide them with an alternative method of doing business with the University (see Electronic Communications Policy, Section IV.C, Privacy Protections and Limits[64]).

The use of University telephone equipment creates transaction records (which include the number called and the time and length of the call) that are reviewed by University units and sub-units as part

---

[62] Section G.2.3.D.8 in this Appendix.

[63] Section G.2.7 in this Appendix.

[64] Section G.2.4.C in this Appendix.

of routine accounting procedures. Employees who use University telephones for personal or other purposes should be aware that supervisors have access to records of all calls made from University telephones under their jurisdiction and that such records may be used for administrative purposes.

D. Unintended Distribution

Both the nature of electronic mail and the public character of the University's business make electronic mail less private than users might anticipate. For example, electronic mail intended for one person sometimes might be widely distributed because of the ease with which recipients can forward it to others. A reply to an electronic mail message posted on an electronic bulletin board or mailing list system intended only for the originator of the message might be distributed to all subscribers to the mailing list system. Users of workstations in public computer laboratories might forget to remove files after they finish their work. Even after a user deletes an electronic mail record, it might persist on back-up or local facilities and become subject to disclosure under the provisions of Section IV.B, Access Without Consent,[65] of this Policy. The University cannot routinely protect users against such eventualities.

Users of telephone, video teleconference, and other telecommunications services are advised that although electronic communications are subject to the non-consensual access provisions of the Electronic Communications Policy Section IV.B,[66] their privacy might be compromised by the presence of persons listening to speaker phones or participating in teleconference calls and video teleconferences without announcing their presence.

E. Electronic Data Gathering

Users of electronic communications systems or services should also be aware that by accessing electronic communications resources, users create transaction records that leave a trail of the electronic communications resources used and might give information about the users and their activities. Current state and federal laws governing such electronic data gathering may not fully protect the user from the gathering of such information without their knowledge or consent. Users are advised to read the privacy statement of any application that collects personally identifiable information to learn its disclosure and privacy policies.

G.3.6   Security Considerations

A. Security

Encryption technology enables the encoding of electronic communications so that for all practical purposes they cannot be read by anyone

---

[65]Section G.2.4.B in this Appendix.
[66]Section G.2.4.B in this Appendix.

who does not possess the commensurate technology needed to decrypt them. Users of electronic communications services should be aware that the University does not routinely encrypt electronic communications during transit across its facilities. If there is a concern about possible interception or disclosure of electronic communications, correspondents should implement appropriate encryption technology while ensuring conformance with BFB IS-3.

Since the University is not responsible for any loss or damage incurred by an individual as a result of personal use of University electronic communications resources, users should not rely on personal use of University electronic communications resources for communications that might be sensitive with regard to timing, financial effect, or privacy and confidentiality. (See the Electronic Communications Policy, Section III.D.8, Personal Use.[67])

B. Authentication

Unless authentication technologies are in use, there is no guarantee that an electronic communication received was in fact sent by the purported sender, since it is relatively straightforward, although a violation of the Electronic Communications Policy, for senders to falsify their identity. Electronic communications that are forwarded might also be modified. General purpose (in contrast to application specific) authentication technologies are not widely and systematically in use at the University as of the issuance of the Policy, but can be expected in future.

As with print documents, recipients of electronic communications should, in case of doubt, check directly with the purported sender to validate the authenticity of the sender or the content.

C. Back-Up

Electronic communications systems are backed up on a routine or occasional basis to protect system reliability and integrity, and to prevent potential loss of data. The back-up process entails the copying of electronic data onto storage media that might be retained for periods of time and in locations unknown to the originator or recipient of electronic communications. The practice and frequency of back-ups and the retention of back-up copies vary from system to system. Users are encouraged to request information on local back-up practices followed by the operators of University electronic communications resources, and such operators are required to provide such information to users upon request (see the Electronic Communications Policy, Section IV.C, Privacy Protections and Limits[68]).

Users of electronic communications resources should be aware that even if they have discarded copies of an electronic communication stored on devices they can control, back-up copies could exist on other devices. Back-up copies that are able to be retrieved might be subject to

---

[67] Section G.2.3.D.8 in this Appendix.
[68] Section G.2.4.C in this Appendix.

disclosure under the California Public Records Act or, in litigation, as the result of the discovery process.

D. Disposition

Electronic communications users should be aware that generally it is not possible to assure the longevity of electronic communications records for record-keeping purposes, in part because of the difficulty of guaranteeing that they can continue to be read in the face of changing formats and technologies, and in part because of the changing nature of electronic communications systems. Archiving is increasingly difficult as electronic communications encompass more digital forms, such as compound records composed of digital voice, music, image, and video in addition to text. In the absence of the use of authentication systems it is difficult to guarantee that electronic communications have not been intentionally or inadvertently altered (see the Electronic Communications Policy, Section IV.C, Privacy Protections and Limits[69] and Section V.D, Authentication[70]).

Those in possession of University records in the form of electronic communications are cautioned, therefore, to be prudent in their reliance on electronic means for purposes of maintaining a lasting record. Sound business practice suggests that consideration be given to the feasibility of transferring electronic communications records to a more lasting medium or format, such as acid-free paper or microfilm, for long-term accessibility as required.

G.4   Electronic Communications—Allowable Use

This is from the UC Davis Policies and Procedures Manual, Chapter 310, "Communications and Technology", Section 23, "Electronic Communications—Allowable Use," dated May 9, 2006 and reissued September 6, 2013 [2138]. It incorporates the "Acceptable Use Policy" in section G.1 as Exhibit A.

G.4.1   Purpose

This section provides UC Davis (UCD) implementing procedures for the allowable use of University Electronic Communications (EC). The UC and UCD EC policies apply to all EC resources owned by the University; provided by the University through contracts and other agreements; users and uses of University EC resources; and all University EC records in the possession of University employees or other users of University EC resources. See also Section 310-24, Electronic Communications—Privacy and Access to Records.

---

[69]Section G.2.4.C in this Appendix.
[70]Section G.2.5.D in this Appendix.

G.4.2   Definitions

The UC EC policy, Appendix A,[71] defines terms used in this policy. Some terms are further defined at UCD as follows:

A. Department head—the head of a teaching, research, administrative, or other organizational unit as designated by the Chancellor. For students, "department head" shall be the Director of Student Judicial Affairs.

B. Record (EC record)—EC records residing on University-owned or -controlled EC resources are University records for the purposes of this policy and subject to disclosure as required by the California Public Records Act.

C. Restricted personal information—unencrypted data in which the individual's first and last name appears in combination with the Social Security number, driver's license number, California identification card number, or credit card or account number together with the security code, access code, or password that would permit access to the account.

D. Security Coordinator—the Electronic Information Security Guidelines Coordinator, as designated by the Chancellor pursuant to UC Business and Finance Bulletin IS-3.

E. System administrator—department designee who has the physical or logical control over EC resources.

G.4.3   Policy

The use of electronic communications resources is limited by restrictions that apply to all University property and by constraints necessary for the reliable operation of electronic communications systems and services. The University reserves the right to deny use of its electronic communications services when necessary to satisfy these restrictions and constraints.

G.4.4   Allowable Users

A. University users may be granted access to University EC resources and services for purposes in accordance with allowable use. University users are defined as follows:

1. UCD students, staff, academic appointees, and emeriti. Department heads may grant access in support of teaching, research, public service, and patient care mission of the University, and the administrative functions that support that mission.

2. Other individuals who are affiliated with the University, including those in program, contract, or license relationships. Department

---

[71] Section G.2.7 in this Appendix.

heads may grant access for the term of the affiliation, when such access supports the mission of the University and is not in competition with commercial providers.

These individuals must be sponsored by a UCD department and must complete a Temporary Affiliate form (http://email.ucdavis.edu).

   a. Students, academic appointees, and staff at other UC campuses.

   b. University Extension students enrolled in courses requiring access.

   c. Retirees.

   d. Volunteers.

   e. Contractors, independent consultants, and certain agents of the University other than employees may be given access for the sole purpose of conducting their business on behalf of the University, unless agreed otherwise in writing.

B. Public users. Individuals and organizations that are not University users may only access University EC resources under programs sponsored by the University, as authorized by the Vice Provost–Information & Educational Technology or other administrator designated by the Chancellor for the purpose of public access in accordance with allowable use.

C. Separation from the University

  1. Access to records. If a separating individual is unable or unwilling to turn over the University records in his or her possession, the department may seek the records through the procedures for access without consent. (See Section 310-24.)

  2. Mail forwarding upon separation.

    a. Forwarding services for email may be provided indefinitely, subject to biennial renewal, for separated users unless they leave for disciplinary reasons.

    b. Separated employees whose mail is being forwarded must agree that any mail that pertains to the University's business will be returned to the department. The department head may require that all mail forwarded to a terminated user from the UCD address also be forwarded to a departmental account.

G.4.5   Allowable Uses

A. Acceptable Use Policy

All users must comply with the Acceptable Use Policy (Exhibit A[72]) and with applicable laws and University policies (see References, below).

---

[72]Section G.1 in this Appendix.

Users must acknowledge, in writing, that they have read and understand the Acceptable Use Policy before they are allowed access to UC Davis electronic communications resources.

B. Use for University Purposes

Access to EC resources is provided at the discretion of the department in consideration of educational requirements, job demands, departmental needs, and cost and efficiency factors. EC resources may be provided to UCD employees and others for the purpose of conducting the University's business and such other purposes that conform to the Acceptable Use Policy.

C. Incidental Personal Use

1. University users may use EC resources for incidental personal purposes provided that such use does not directly or indirectly interfere with the University's operation of EC resource; does not interfere with the user's employment or other obligations to the University; does not burden the University with noticeable incremental costs; and does not violate the law or University policy. Accordingly, regular or voluminous personal messages delivered via lengthy email lists are impermissible.

   a. University users are prohibited from, among other things, using EC resources in a manner that creates a hostile working environment (including sexual or other forms of harassment) in violation of the law, or violates obscenity laws.

   b. When noticeable incremental costs for personal use are incurred (e.g., telephone long distance charges), users shall reimburse the University.

2. Incidental personal use on behalf of an outside organization is permitted only under the circumstances listed below. Before such use, users shall verify with their supervisors that the proposed use complies with UC and UCD policy. A UCD EC resource shall not be published as the point of contact for non-University activities.

   a. Charities. UCD EC resources may be used only for charitable activities that have been approved by the Chancellor (e.g., the United Way campaign). Before such use, the user must obtain written authorization from the Chancellor or designee.

   b. Professional and public service organizations. UCD EC resources may be used on behalf of outside professional or public service organizations when the individual is participating as a representative of the University in the activities of an organization of which the University is a member, or when the individual is a member of an organization in support of the University's mission.

    c. Civic committees or task forces. UCD EC resources may be used on behalf of national, state, and local committees or task forces when associated with an approved University activity.

D. Policy Violations
Uses that violate this policy, other University policies, or any federal or state law or regulation may result in:

1. Service restriction;
2. Corrective action under applicable University policies and collective bargaining agreements; and/or
3. Civil lawsuit or criminal prosecution.

G.4.6   Restrictions on Use

A. Use of University EC resources is accorded at the discretion of the University and can be restricted or revoked without prior notice and without consent of the user.

1. A system administrator may temporarily restrict access to perform required maintenance. The system administrator shall give reasonable notice if possible.
2. A system administrator may temporarily restrict access to control an emergency or prevent damage or loss. The system administrator shall notify the department head and users as soon as possible.
3. A system administrator may restrict or rescind a user's access as described in UC Policy, III.E, Access Restriction.[73] The system administrator shall:

    a. Obtain approval from the department head prior to restricting the individual user's access.
    b. Notify the user of the reason for the restriction and the name of the person who authorized the restriction.
    c. Restore access when authorized to do so by the department head who authorized the restriction.

B. Recourse
The decision to restrict access may be appealed to the Vice Provost–Information and Educational Technology within 30 days of notification.

C. Copyright infringement
As permitted by the Digital Millennium Copyright Act (DMCA), the University may suspend access to EC systems by any user allegedly

---

[73]Section G.2.3.E in this Appendix.

violating copyright law upon receipt of a DMCA notification. (See Section 250-05.)

G.4.7   References and Related Policies

A. Office of the President: University of California Electronic Communications Policy (http://www.ucop.edu/ucophome/policies/ec/).

B. UCD Policy and Procedure Manual (http://manuals.ucdavis.edu /PPM/about.htm):

   1. Section 250-02, Use of Copyrighted Materials.

   2. Section 250-05, Digital Millennium Copyright Act.

   3. Section 270-20, Use of University Properties.

   4. Section 270-25, Commercial Activities.

   5. Section 310-10, Telecommunications Services.

   6. Section 310-24, Electronic Communications—Privacy and Access to Records.

   7. Section 310-65, Use of the University's Name and Seal.

   8. Section 310-70, World Wide Web (pending approval).

C. State of California, Education Code Section 92000 (http://www .leginfo.ca.gov/calaw.html).

D. Digital Millennium Copyright Act of 1998 (U.S. Code Title 17, Section 512) (http://uscode.house.gov/search/criteria.shtml).

E. UC Davis Principles of Community (http://occr.ucdavis.edu/poc/).

F. Business and Finance Bulletin IS-3, Electronic Information Security (http://www.ucop.edu/ucophome/policies/bfb/is3.pdf).

Appendix H
Programming Rules

This chapter lists the programming implementation and management rules in Chapter 31.

H.1   Implementation Rules

Implementation Rule 31.1. Structure the process so that all sections requiring extra privileges are modules. The modules should be as small as possible and should perform only those tasks that require those privileges.

Implementation Rule 31.2. Ensure that any assumptions in the program are validated. If this is not possible, document them for the installers and maintainers, so they know the assumptions that attackers will try to invalidate.

Implementation Rule 31.3. Ensure that the program does not share objects in memory with any other program, and that other programs cannot access the memory of a privileged process.

Implementation Rule 31.4. The error status of every function must be checked. Do not try to recover unless the cause of the error, and its effects, do not affect any security considerations. The program should restore the state of the system to the state before the process began, and then terminate.

Implementation Rule 31.5. If a process interacts with other processes, the interactions should be synchronized. In particular, all possible sequences of interactions must be known and, for all such interactions, the process must enforce the required security policy.

Implementation Rule 31.6. Asynchronous exception handlers should not alter any variables except those that are local to the exception handling module. An exception handler should block all other exceptions when begun, and should not release the block until the handler completes execution, unless the handler has been designed to handle exceptions within itself (or calls an uninvoked exception handler).

Implementation Rule 31.7. Whenever possible, data that the process trusts and data that it receives from untrusted sources (such as input) should be kept in separate areas of memory. If data from a trusted source is overwritten with data from an untrusted source, a memory error will occur.

Implementation Rule 31.8. Do not use components that may change between the time the program is created and the time it is run.

Implementation Rule 31.9. The process must ensure that the context in which an object is named identifies the correct object.

Implementation Rule 31.10. When the process finishes using a sensitive object (one that contains confidential information or one that should not be altered), the object should be erased, then deallocated or deleted. Any resources not needed should also be released.

Implementation Rule 31.11. Ensure that all array references access existing elements of the array. If a function that manipulates arrays cannot ensure that only valid elements are referenced, do not use that function. Find one that does, write a new version, or create a wrapper.

Implementation Rule 31.12. Check the types of functions and parameters.

Implementation Rule 31.13. When compiling programs, ensure that the compiler reports inconsistencies in types. Investigate all such warnings and either fix the problem or document the warning and why it is spurious.

Implementation Rule 31.14. Check all function and procedure executions for errors.

Implementation Rule 31.15. Check that a variable's values are valid.

Implementation Rule 31.16. If a trade-off between security and other factors results in a mechanism or procedure that can weaken security, document the reasons for the decision, the possible effects, and the situations in which the compromise method should be used. This informs others of the trade-off and the attendant risks.

Implementation Rule 31.17. Check all user input for both form and content. In particular, check integers for values that are too big or too small, and check character data for length and valid characters.

Implementation Rule 31.18. Create data structures and functions in such a way that they can be validated.

Implementation Rule 31.19. If two operations must be performed sequentially without an intervening operation, use a mechanism to ensure that the two cannot be divided.

Implementation Rule 31.20. Describe the legal sequences of operations on a resource or object. Check that all possible sequences of the program(s) involved match one (or more) legal sequences.

H.2   Management Rules

Management Rule 31.1. Check that the process privileges are set properly.

Management Rule 31.2. The program that is executed to create the process, and all associated control files, must be protected from unauthorized use and modification. Any such modification must be detected.

Management Rule 31.3. Configure memory to enforce the principle of least privilege. If a section of memory is not to contain executable instructions, turn execute permission off for that section of memory. If the contents of a section of memory are not to be altered, make that section read-only.

Management Rule 31.4. Identify all system components on which the program depends. Check for errors whenever possible, and identify those components for which error checking will not work.

Management Rule 31.5. Unique objects require unique names. Interchangeable objects may share a name.

Management Rule 31.6. Use software engineering and assurance techniques (such as documentation, design reviews, and code reviews) to ensure that operations and operands are appropriate.

References

1. I. Aad, J.-P. Hubaux, and E. W. Knightly. "Denial of Service Resilience in Ad Hoc Networks," *Proceedings of the Tenth Annual International Conference on Mobile Computing and Networking* pp. 202–215 (Sep. 2004).

2. M. Abadi. "Explicit Communication Revisited: Two New Attacks on Authentication Protocols," *IEEE Transactions on Software Engineering* **23**(3) pp. 185–196 (Mar. 1997).

3. M. Abadi and C. Fournet. "Access Control Based on Execution History," *Proceedings of the 2003 Symposium on Network and Distributed System Security* pp. 107–121 (Feb. 2003).

4. M. Abadi and R. Needham. "Prudent Engineering Practice for Cryptographic Protocols," *IEEE Transactions on Software Engineering* **22**(1) pp. 6–15 (Jan. 1996).

5. R. P. Abbott, J. S. Chin, J. E. Donnelley, W. L. Konigsford, S. Tokubo, and D. A. Webb. *Security Analysis and Enhancements of Computer Operating Systems*, NBSIR 76-1041, Institute for Computer Sciences and Technology, National Bureau of Standards, Washington, DC (Apr. 1976).

6. A. Abdul-Rahman and S. Hailes. "A Distributed Trust Model," *Proceedings of the 1997 Workshop on New Security Paradigms* pp. 48–60 (Sep. 1997).

7. J. Abel. "Do You Have to Keep the Government's Secrets? Retroactively Classified Documents, the First Amendment, and the Power to Make Secrets Out of the Public Record," *University of Pennsylvania Law Review* **163**(4) pp. 1037–1097 (Mar. 2015).

8. M. Abrams and D. Bailey. "Abstraction and Refinement of Layered Security Policy," in [10], pp. 126–136.

9. M. D. Abrams and P. J. Brusil. "Application of the Common Criteria to a System: A Real-World Example," *Computer Security Journal* **16**(2) pp. 11–21 (Mar. 2000).

10. M. D. Abrams, S. Jajodia, and H. J. Podell (*ed*). *Information Security: An Integrated Collection of Essays*, IEEE Computer Society Press, Los Alamitos, CA, USA (June 1995).

11. S. Abt and H. Baier. "Are We Missing Labels? A Study of the Availability of Ground-Truth in Network Security Research," *Proceedings of the Third International Workshop on Building Analysis Datasets and Gathering Experience Returns for Security* pp. 40–55 (Sep. 2014).

12. R. Accorsi. "BBox: A Distributed Secure Log Architecture," *Proceedings of the 2010 European Public Key Infrastructure Workshop: Public Key Infrastructures, Services and Applications* (*Lecture Notes in Computer Science* **6711**) pp. 109–124 (Sep. 2010).

13. A. Acquisti, I. Adjerid, R. Balebako, L. Brandimarte, L. F. Cranor, S. Komanduri, P. G. Leon, N. Sadeh, F. Schaub, M. Sleeper, Y. Wang, and S. Wilson. "Nudges for Privacy and Security: Understanding and Assisting Users' Choices Online," *ACM Computing Surveys* **50**(3) pp. 44:1–44:41 (Oct. 2017).

14. C. Adams and S. Lloyd. *Understanding the Public-Key Infrastructure: Concepts, Standards, and Deployment Considerations*, SAMS, Indianapolis, IN, USA (1999).

15. E. Adams and S. S. Muchnick. "Dbxtool: A Window-Based Symbolic Debugger for Sun Workstations," *Software: Practice and Experience* **16**(7) pp. 653–659 (July 1986).

16. B. Adida. "Helios: Web-Based Open-Audit Voting," *Proceedings of the 17th USENIX Security Symposium* pp. 335–348 (July 2008).

17. L. M. Adleman. "An Abstract Theory of Computer Viruses," *Advances in Cryptology — CRYPTO '88* (*Lecture Notes in Computer Science* **403**) pp. 354–374 (Aug. 1988).

18. Adobe Systems, Inc. *PostScript Language Reference*, Addison-Wesley, Reading, MA, USA (Mar. 1999).

19. D. Adrian, K. Bhargavan, Z. Durumeric, P. Gaudry, M. Green, J. A. Halderman, N. Heninger, D. Springall, E. Thomé, L. Valenta, B. VanderSloot, E. Wustrow, S. Zanella-Béguelin, and P. Zimmermann. "Imperfect Forward Secrecy: How Diffie-Hellman Fails in Practice," *Proceedings of the 22nd ACM SIGSAC Conference on Computer and Communications Security* pp. 5–17 (2015).

20. K. Agarwal, B. Jain, and D. E. Porter. "Containing the Hype," *Proceedings of the Sixth Asia-Pacific Workshop on Systems* pp. 8:1–8:9 (July 2015).

21. A. Aggarwal and P. Jalote. "Integrating Static and Dynamic Analysis for Detecting Vulnerabilities," *Proceedings of the 30th Annual International Computer Software and Applications Conference* (Sep. 2006).

22. G. B. Agnew. "Random Sources for Cryptographic Systems," *Advances in Cryptology — CRYPTO '87 (Lecture Notes in Computer Science 304)* pp. 77–81 (Apr. 1987).

23. D. Agrawal, S. Baktir, D. Karakoyunlu, P. Rohatgi, and B. Sunar. "Trojan Detection Using IC Fingerprinting," *Proceedings of the 2007 IEEE Symposium on Security and Privacy* pp. 296–310 (May 2007).

24. D. Agrawal, S. Calo, J. Giles, K.-W. Lee, and D. Verma. "Policy Management for Networked Systems and Applications," *Proceedings of the Ninth IFIP/IEEE International Symposium on Integrated Network Management* pp. 455–468 (May 2005).

25. D. Agrawal, S. Calo, K.-W. Lee, and J. Lobo. "Issues in Designing a Policy Language for Distributed Management of IT Infrastructures," *Proceedings of the Tenth IFIP/IEEE International Symposium on Integrated Network Management* pp. 30–39 (May 2007).

26. R. Agrawal, J. Kiernan, R. Srikant, and Y. Xu. "XPref: A Preference Language for P3P," *Computer Networks* **48**(5) pp. 809–827 (Aug. 2005).

27. A. Ahmad, J. Hadgkiss, and A. B. Ruighaver. "Incident Response Teams — Challenges in Supporting the Organisational Security Function," *Computers & Security* **31**(5) pp. 643–652 (July 2012).

28. G.-J. Ahn and R. Sandhu. "Role-Based Authorization Constraints Specification," *ACM Transactions on Information and System Security* **3**(4) pp. 207–226 (Nov. 2000).

29. R. Akella, H. Tang, and B. McMillin. "Analysis of Information Flow Security in Cyber–Physical Systems," *International Journal of Critical Infrastructure Protection* **3**(3-4) pp. 157–173 (Dec. 2010).

30. S. S. Al-Riyami and K. G. Paterson. "Certificateless Public Key Cryptography," *Advances in Cryptology — ASIACRYPT 2003 (Lecture Notes in Computer Science 2894)* pp. 452–473 (Nov. 2003).

31. E. Al-Shaer, H. Hamed, R. Boutaba, and M. Hasan. "Conflict Classification and Analysis of Distributed Firewall Policies," *IEEE Journal on Selected Areas in Communication* **23**(10) pp. 2069–2084 (Oct. 2005).

32. AlephOne. "Smashing the Stack for Fun and Profit," *Phrack* **7**(49) (Nov. 1996).

33. D. S. Alexander, W. A. Arbaugh, A. D. Keromytis, and J. M. Smith. "A Secure Active Network Environment Architecture: Realization in SwitchWare," *IEEE Network* **12**(3) pp. 37–45 (May 1998).

34. N. AlFardan, D. J. Bernstein, K. G. Paterson, B. Poettering, and J. C. Schuldt. "On the Security of RC4 in TLS," *Proceedings of the 22nd USENIX Security Symposium* pp. 305–320 (Aug. 2013).

35. P. G. Allen. "A Comparison of Non-Interference and Non-Deducibility Using CSP," *Proceedings of the Fourth Computer Security Foundations Workshop* pp. 43–54 (June 1991).

36. M. H. Almeshekah and E. H. Spafford. "Planning and Integrating Deception into Computer Security Defenses," *Proceedings of the 2014 Workshop on New Security Paradigms* pp. 127–138 (Sep. 2014).

37. F. T. Alotaiby and J. X. Chen. "A Model for Team-Based Access Control (TMAC 2004)," *Proceedings of the 2004 International Conference on Information Technology: Coding and Computing* pp. 450–454 (Apr. 2004).

38. M. Alsabah and I. Goldberg. "Performance and Security Improvements for Tor: A Survey," *ACM Computing Surveys* **49**(2) pp. 32:1–32:36 (Nov. 2016).

39. J. Alves-Foss, D. Frincke, and G. Saghi. "Applying the TCSEC Guidelines to a Real-Time Embedded System Environment," *Proceedings of the 19th National Information Systems Security Conference* pp. 89–97 (Oct. 1996).

40. P. E. Ammann and P. E. Black. "A Specification-Based Coverage Metric to Evaluate Test Sets," *Proceedings of the Fourth IEEE International Symposium on High-Assurance Systems Engineering* pp. 1–10 (Nov. 1999).

41. P. Ammann, J. Pamula, R. Ritchey, and J. Street. "A Host-Based Approach to Network Attack Chaining Analysis," *Proceedings of the 21st Annual Computer Security Applications Conference* pp. 72–83 (Dec. 2005).

42. P. Ammann and R. S. Sandhu. "The Extended Schematic Protection Model," *Journal of Computer Security* **1**(3-4) pp. 335–383 (1992).

43. P. Ammann and R. S. Sandhu. "Implementing Transaction Control Expressions by Checking for Absence of Access Rights," *Proceedings of the Eighth Annual Computer Security Applications Conference* pp. 131–140 (Nov. 1992).

44. P. Ammann, R. S. Sandhu, and R. Lipton. "The Expressive Power of Multi-Parent Creation in Monotonic Access Control Models," *Journal of Computer Security* **4**(2-3) pp. 149–165 (1996).

45. E. G. Amoroso. *Intrusion Detection: An Introduction to Internet Surveillance, Correlation, Trace Back, Traps, and Response*, Intrusion.Net Books, Sparta, NJ, USA (Feb. 1999).

46. E. Amoroso, T. Nguyen, J. Weiss, J. Watson, Lapiska, and T. Starr. "Toward an Approach to Measuring Software Trust," *Proceedings of the 1991 IEEE Symposium on Research in Security and Privacy* pp. 198–218 (May 1991).

47. P. Amthor, W. E. Kühnhauser, and A. Pölck. "Model-Based Safety Analysis of SELinux Security Policies," *Proceedings of the Fifth International Conference on Network and System Security* pp. 208–215 (Sep. 2011).

48. P. Amthor, W. E. Kühnhauser, and A. Pölck. "Heuristic Safety Analysis of Access Control Models," *Proceedings of the 18th ACM Symposium on Access Control Models and Technologies* pp. 137–148 (June 2013).

49. A. H. Anderson. "An Introduction to the Web Services Policy Language (WSPL)," *Proceedings of the Fifth IEEE International Workshop on Policies for Distributed Systems and Networks* pp. 189–192 (June 2004).

50. J. Anderson. *Computer Security Technology Planning Study*, Technical Report ESD-TR-73-51, ESD/AFSC, Hanscom AFB, Bedford, MA (Oct. 1972).

51. J. P. Anderson. "Information Security in a Multi-User Computer Environment," in *Information Security in a Multi-User Computer Environment*, edited by M. Rubinoff, Academic Press, New York, NY, USA pp. 1–36 (1972).

52. J. P. Anderson. *Computer Security Threat Monitoring and Surveillance*, Technical Report, James P. Anderson Co., Fort Washington, PA, USA (Apr. 1980).

53. J. P. Anderson. *On the Feasibility of Connecting RECON to an External Network*, Technical Report, James P. Anderson Co., Fort Washington, PA, USA (Mar. 1981).

54. R. Anderson. "Clinical System Security: Intermin Guidelines," *British Medical Journal* **312**(7023) pp. 109–111 (1996).

55. R. Anderson and S. Fuloria. "Security Economics and Critical National Infrastructure," Chapter 4 in *Security Economics and Critical National Infrastructure*, edited by T. Moore, D. J. Pym, and C. Ioannidis, Springer, New York, NY, USA pp. 55–66 (2010).

56. R. J. Anderson. "UEPS—A Second Generation Electronic Wallet," *Proceedings of the Second European Symposium on Research in Computer Security* (*Lecture Notes in Computer Science* **648**) pp. 409–418 (Nov. 1992).

57. R. J. Anderson. "A Security Policy Model for Clinical Information Systems," *Proceedings of the 1996 IEEE Symposium on Security and Privacy* pp. 30–43 (May 1996).

58. R. Anderson, C. Manifavas, and C. Sutherland. "NetCard—A Practical Electronic Cash System," *Proceedings of the International Workshop on Security Protocols* (*Lecture Notes in Computer Science* **1189**) pp. 49–57 (Apr. 1996).

59. R. Anderson and T. Moore. "Information Security Economics — and Beyond," *Advances in Cryptology — CRYPTO 2007* (*Lecture Notes in Computer Science* **4622**) pp. 68–91 (Aug. 2007).

60. R. Anderson and R. Needham. "Robustness Principles for Public Key Protocols," *Advances in Cryptology — CRYPTO '95* (*Lecture Notes in Computer Science* **963**) pp. 236–347 (Aug. 1995).

61. T. E. Anderson. *The Case for Application-Specific Operating Systems*, Technical Report UCB/CSD-93-738, Division of Computer Science, Electrical Engineering and Computer Science Department, University of California, Berkeley, Berkeley, CA, USA (1993).

62. G. R. Andrews and R. P. Reitman. "An Axiomatic Approach to Information Flow in Programs," *ACM Transactions on Programming Languages and Systems* **2**(1) pp. 56–76 (Jan. 1980).

63. T. Antonyan, S. Davtyan, S. Kentros, A. Kiayias, K. Michel, N. Nicolaou, A. Russell, and A. A. Shvartsman. "Automating Voting Terminal Event Log Analysis," *Proceedings of the 2009 Electronic Voting Technology Workshop/Workshop on Trustworthy Elections* pp. 1–15 (Aug. 2009).

64. A. A. Appel. "Foundational Proof-Carrying Code," *Proceedings of the 2003 Foundations of Intrusion Tolerant Systems* pp. 247–256 (Dec. 2003).

65. A. W. Appel and A. P. Felty. "A Semantic Model of Types and Machine Instructions for Proof-Carrying Code," *Proceedings of the 27th ACM SIGPLAN-SIGACT Symposium on Principles of Programming Languages* pp. 243–253 (Jan. 2000).

66. A. Apvrille and P. Makan. "XML Distributed Security Policy for Clusters," *Computers & Security* **23**(8) pp. 649–658 (Dec. 2004).

67. L. C. F. Araújo, L. H. R. Sucupira Jr., M. G. Lizárraga, L. L. Ling, and J. B. T. Yabu-Uti. "User Authentication Through Typing Biometrics Features," *IEEE Transactions on Signal Processing* **53**(2) pp. 851–855 (Feb. 2005).

68. W. A. Arbaugh, D. J. Farber, and J. M. Smith. "A Secure and Reliable Bootstrap Architecture," *Proceedings of the 1997 IEEE Symposium on Security and Privacy* pp. 65–71 (May 1997).

69. R. S. Arbo, E. M. Johnson, and R. L. Sharp. "Extending Mandatory Access Controls to a Networked MLS Environment," *Proceedings of the 12th National Computer Security Conference* pp. 286–295 (Oct. 1989).

70. R. Archibald and D. Ghosal. "A Comparative Analysis of Detection Metrics for Covert Timing Channels," *Computers & Security* **45**(5) pp. 284–292 (Sep. 2014).

71. C. A. Ardagna, R. Asal, E. Damiani, and Q. H. Vu. "From Security to Assurance in the Cloud: A Survey," *ACM Computing Surveys* **48**(1) pp. 2:1–2:50 (July 2015).

72. M. A. Ardis, J. A. Chaves, L. Jategaonkar, P. Mataga, C. Puchol, M. G. Staskauskas, and J. Von Olnhausen. "A Framework for Evaluating Specification Methods for Reactive Systems: Experience Report," *IEEE Transactions on Software Engineering* **22**(6) pp. 378–389 (June 1996).

73. R. Arends, R. Austein, M. Larson, D. Massey, and S. Rose. *DNS Security Introduction and Requirements*, RFC 4033 (Mar. 2005).

74. R. Arends, R. Austein, M. Larson, D. Massey, and S. Rose. *Protocol Modifications for the DNS Security Extensions*, RFC 4035 (Mar. 2005).

75. R. Arends, R. Austein, M. Larson, D. Massey, and S. Rose. *Resource Records for the DNS Security Extensions*, RFC 4034 (Mar. 2005).

76. S. Ariyapperuma and C. J. Mitchell. "Security Vulnerabilities in DNS and DNSSEC," *Proceedings of the 2007 International Conference on Availability, Reliability and Security* pp. 335–342 (Apr. 2007).

77. J. Arlat, Y. Crouzet, J. Karlsson, P. Folkesson, E. Fuchs, and G. Leber. "Comparison of Physical and Software-Implemented Fault Injection Techniques," *IEEE Transactions on Computers* **52**(9) pp. 1115–1133 (Sep. 2003).

78. ARM. *ARM11 MPCore Processor Revision r2p0 Technical Reference Manual*, Technical Report ARM DDI 0360F, ARM Ltd., San Jose, CA, USA (Oct. 2008).

79. N. D. Arnold. *UNIX Security: A Practical Tutorial*, McGraw-Hill, New York, NY, USA (1993).

80. J. J. Arnold Jr.. "Analysis Requirements for Low Assurance Evaluations," *Proceedings of the 18th National Computer Security Conference* pp. 356–365 (Oct. 1995).

81. A. Arsenault and R. Housley. "Protection Profiles for Certificate Issuing and Management Systems," *Proceedings of the 22nd National Information Systems Security Conference* pp. 189–199 (Oct. 1999).

82. W. Arthur and D. Challener. *A Practical Guide to TPM 2.0: Using the Trusted Platform Module in the New Age of Security*, Apress, Inc., New York, NY, USA (2015).

83. D. Artz and Y. Gil. "A Survey of Trust in Computer Science and the Semantic Web," *Journal of Web Semantics* **5**(2) pp. 58–71 (June 2007).

84. S. Arzt, S. Rasthofer, C. Fritz, E. Bodden, A. Bartel, J. Klein, Y. Le Traon, D. Octeau, and P. McDaniel. "FlowDroid: Precise Context, Flow, Field, Object-Sensitive and Lifecycle-Aware Taint Analysis for Android Apps," *Proceedings of the 35th ACM SIGPLAN Conference on Programming Language Design and Implementation* pp. 259–269 (June 2014).

85. H. Asghari, M. Ciere, and M. J. G. van Eeten. "Post-Mortem of a Zombie: Conficker Cleanup After Six Years," *Proceedings of the 24th USENIX Security Symposium* pp. 1–16 (Aug. 2015).

86. A. Askarov and A. Sabelfeld. "Gradual Release: Unifying Declassification, Encryption and Key Release Policies," *Proceedings of the 2007 IEEE Symposium on Security and Privacy* pp. 207–221 (May 2007).

87. T. Aslam. "A Taxonomy of Security Faults in the UNIX Operating System," Master's Thesis, Department of Computer Sciences, Purdue University, West Lafayette, IN, USA (Aug. 1995).

88. C. Asmuth and J. Bloom. "A Modular Approach to Key Safeguarding," *IEEE Transactions on Information Theory* **29**(2) pp. 208–210 (Mar. 1983).

89. M. Atighetchi, P. Pal, F. Webber, and C. Jones. "Adaptive Use of Network-Centric Mechanisms in Cyber-Defense," *Proceedings of the Second IEEE International Symposium on Network Computing and Applications* pp. 179–188 (Apr. 2003).

90. M. Atighetchi, P. Pal, F. Webber, R. Schantz, C. Jones, and J. Loyall. "Adaptive Cyberdefense for Survival and Intrusion Tolerance," *IEEE Internet Computing* **8**(6) pp. 25–33 (Nov. 2004).

91. D. Atkins and R. Austein. *Threat Analysis of the Domain Name System (DNS)*, RFC 3833 (Aug. 2004).

92. S. Atkinson and D. Scholefield. "Transformational vs Reactive Refinement in Real-Time Systems," *Information Processing Letters* **55**(4) pp. 201–210 (Aug. 1995).

93. V. Atluri, E. Bertino, and S. Jajodia. "Achieving Stricter Correctness Requirements in Multilevel Secure Databases," *Proceedings of the 1993 IEEE Symposium on Research in Security and Privacy* pp. 135–147 (May 1993).

94. V. Atluri, S. A. Chun, and P. Mazzoleni. "Chinese Wall Security for Decentralized Workflow Management Systems," *Journal of Computer Security* **12**(6) pp. 799–840 (2004).

95. P. Auffret. "SinFP, Unification of Active and Passive Operating System Fingerprinting," *Journal of Computer Virology* **6**(3) pp. 197–205 (Aug. 2010).

96. C. Augier. "Excel-lent Leaks," *Risks Digest* **21**(39) (May 2001).

97. T. Aura, M. Becker, M. Roe, and Zieliński. "Reconciling Multiple IPsec and Firewall Policies," *Proceedings of the 15th International Workshop on Security Protocols* (*Lecture Notes in Computer Science* **5964**) pp. 81–97 (Apr. 2007).

98. T. Aura, M. Bishop, and D. Sniegowski. "Analyzing Single-Server Network Inhibition," *Proceedings of the 13th Computer Security Foundations Workshop* pp. 108–117 (July 2000).

99. T. H. Austin and C. Flanagan. "Permissive Dynamic Information Flow Analysis," *Proceedings of the Fifth ACM SIGPLAN Workshop on Programming Languages and Analysis for Security* pp. 3:1–3:12 (2010).

100. A. Avižienis. "The *N*-Version Approach to Fault-Tolerant Software," *IEEE Transactions on Software Engineering* **SE-11**(12) pp. 1491–1501 (Dec. 1985).

101. A. Avižienis, J.-C. Laprie, B. Randell, and C. Landwehr. "Basic Concepts and Taxonomy of Dependable and Secure Computing," *IEEE Transactions on Dependable and Secure Computing* **1**(1) pp. 11–33 (Jan. 2004).

102. S. Axelsson. "The Base-Rate Fallacy and the Difficulty of Intrusion Detection," *ACM Transactions on Information and System Security* **3**(3) pp. 186–205 (Aug. 2000).

103. J. Aycock. *Computer Viruses and Malware* **22**, Springer Science+Business Media, LLC, New York, NY, USA (Dec. 2006).

104. A. Bacard. *The Computer Privacy Handbook: A Practical Guide to E-Mail Encryption, Data Protection, and PGP Privacy Software*, Peachpit Press, Berkeley, CA, USA (1995).

105. A. Bacard. *Anonymous Remailer FAQ* (July 1998).

106. R. Bace. *Intrusion Detection*, Macmillan Technical Publications, Indianapolis, IN, USA (2000).

107. E. M. Bačić. "The Canadian Trusted Computer Product Evaluation Criteria," *Proceedings of the Sixth Annual Computer Security Applications Conference* pp. 188–196 (Dec. 1990).

108. M. Backes and B. Pfitzmann. "Computational Probabilistic Noninterference," *International Journal of Information Security* **3**(1) pp. 42–60 (Oct. 2004).

109. A. Baddeley. "The Magic Number Seven: Still Magic After All These Years?" *Psychological Review* **101**(2) pp. 353–356 (Apr. 1994).

110. C. Badertscher, C. Matt, U. Maurer, P. Rogaway, and B. Tackmann. "Augmented Secure Channels and the Goal of the TLS 1.3 Record Layer," *Proceedings of the Ninth International Conference on Provable Security* pp. 85–104 (Nov. 2015).

111. L. Badger, D. F. Sterne, D. L. Sherman, and K. M. Walker. "A Domain and Type Enforcement UNIX Prototype," *Computing Systems* **9**(1) pp. 47–83 (Winter 1996).

112. J. Baek, R. Safavi-Naini, and W. Susilo. "Certificateless Public Key Encryption Without Pairing," *Proceedings of the Eighth International Information Security Conference* (*Lecture Notes in Computer Science* **3650**) pp. 134–148 (Sep. 2005).

113. S. Bahram, X. Jiang, Z. Wang, M. Grace, J. Li, D. Srinivasan, J. Rhee, and X. Dongyan. "DKSM: Subverting Virtual Machine Introspection for Fun and Profit," *Proceedings of the 29th IEEE Symposium on Reliable Distributed Systems* pp. 82–91 (Oct. 2010).

114. L. Bai, G. Kane, and P. Lyons. "Open Architecture for Contactless Smartcard-Based Portable Electronic Payment Systems," *Proceedings of the 2008 IEEE International Conference on Automation Science and Engineering* pp. 715–719 (Aug. 2008).

115. D. Bailey. "A Philosophy of Security Management," in [10], pp. 98–111.

116. D. W. Baker, S. M. Christey, W. H. Hill, and D. E. Mann. "The Development of a Common Enumeration of Vulnerabilities and Exposures," *Proceedings of the Second International Workshop on Recent Advances in Intrusion Detection* (Sep. 1999).

117. B. S. Bakloğlu. "The Gray Zone: Networks of Piracy, Control, and Resistance," *The Information Society* **32**(1) pp. 40–50 (2016).

118. D. Balenson and T. Markham. "ISAKMP Key Recovery Extensions," *Computers & Security* **19**(1) pp. 91–99 (Jan. 2000).

119. T. Ballad and W. Nallad. *Securing PHP Web Applications*, Addison-Wesley, Boston, MA, USA (2009).

120. L. Ballard, S. Kamara, and M. K. Reiter. "The Practical Subtleties of Biometric Key Generation," *Proceedings of the 17th USENIX Security Symposium* pp. 61–74 (July 2008).

121. D. Balzarotti, G. Banks, M. Cova, V. Felmetsger, R. A. Kemmerer, W. Robertson, F. Valeur, and G. Vigna. "An Experience in Testing the Security of Real-World Electronic Voting Systems," *IEEE Transactions on Software Engineering* **36**(4) pp. 453–473 (July 2010).

122. J. Bamford. "The Espionage Economy," *Foreign Policy* 216 pp. 70–72 (Jan. 2016).

123. K.-S. Bang, J.-Y. Choi, and C. Yoo. "Comments on 'The Spin Model Checker,'" *IEEE Transactions on Software Engineering* **27**(6) pp. 573–576 (June 2001).

124. D. Banning, G. Ellingwood, C. Franklin, C. Muckenhrin, and D. Price. "Auditing of Distributed Systems," *Proceedings of the 14th National Computer Security Conference* pp. 59–68 (Oct. 1991).

125. P. Barham, B. Dragovic, K. Fraser, S. Hand, T. Harris, A. Ho, R. Neugebauer, I. Pratt, and A. Warfield. "Xen and the Art of Virtualization," *Proceedings of the 19th ACM Symposium on Operating Systems Principles* pp. 164–177 (Dec. 2003).

126. E. Barker. *Recommendation for Key Management, Part 1: General (Revision 4)*, Special Publication 800-57 Part 1, Rev. 4, National Institute of Standards and Technology, Gaithersburg, MD, USA (Jan. 2016).

127. E. Barker and N. Mouha. *Recommendation for the Triple Data Encryption Algorithm (TDEA) Block Cipher*, Special Publication 800-67 Revision 2, National Institute of Standards and Technology, Gaithersburg, MD, USA (Nov. 2017).

128. T. H. Barr. *Invitation to Cryptology*, Prentice Hall, Inc, Upper Saddle River, NJ, USA (2002).

129. E. G. Barrantes, D. H. Ackley, S. Forrest, and D. Stefanović. "Randomized Instruction Set Emulation," *ACM Transactions on Information and System Security* **8**(1) pp. 3–40 (Feb. 2005).

130. C. Barrett, R. Sebastiani, S. Seshia, and C. Tinelli. "Satisfiability Modulo Theories," Chapter 26 in *Satisfiability Modulo Theories*, edited by A. Biere, M. Heule, H. Van Maaren, and T. Walsh (*Frontiers in Artificial Intelligence and Applications* **185**), IOS Press, Amsterdam, The Netherlands pp. 825–885 (Feb. 2009).

131. D. J. Barrett, R. E. Silverman, and R. G. Byrnes. *SSH, the Secure Shell: The Definitive Guide*, O'Reilly Media, Inc., Sebastopol, CA, USA (June 2009).

132. Y. Bartal, A. Mayer, K. Nissim, and A. Wool. "*Firmato*: A Novel Firewall Management Toolkit," *ACM Transactions on Computer Systems* **22**(4) pp. 381–420 (Nov. 2004).

133. A. Barth. *HTTP State Management Mechanism*, RFC 6265 (Apr. 2011).

134. G. Barthe, D. Naumann, and T. Rezk. "Deriving an Information Flow Checker and Certifying Compiler for Java," *Proceedings of the 2006 IEEE Symposium on Security and Privacy* pp. 229–242 (May 2006).

135. J. Bartlett. *Familiar Quotations*, Little, Brown and Co., Boston, MA, USA (1901).

136. R. Bate, A. Reichner, S. Garcia-Miller, J. Armitage, K. Cusick, R. Jones, D. Kuhn, I. Minnich, H. Pierson, and T. Powell. *A Systems Engineering Capability Maturity Model, Version 1.0*, Technical Report CMU/SEI-94-HB-004, Software Engineering Institute, Carnegie Mellon University, Pittsburgh, PA, USA (Dec. 1994).

137. B. L. A. Batista and M. P. Fernandez. "PonderFlow: A Policy Specification Language for Openflow Networks," *Proceedings of the 13th International Conference on Networks* pp. 204–209 (Feb. 2014).

138. M. Baum. *NIST Withdraws Outdated Data Encryption Standard*, National Institute of Standards and Technology, Gaithersburg, MD, USA (June 2005).

139. P. Baxter, A. Edmundson, K. Ortiz, A. M. Quevado, S. Rodriguez, C. Sturton, and D. Wagner. "Automated Analysis of Election Audit Logs," *Proceedings of the 2012 Electronic Voting Technology Workshop/Workshop on Trustworthy Elections* (Aug. 2012).

140. B. Bayh. "Unclassified Summary: Involvement of NSA in the Development of the Data Encryption Standard (United States Senate Select Committee on Intelligence)," *IEEE Communications Society Magazine* **16**(6) pp. 53–55 (Nov. 1978).

141. M. Bazaliy, S. Hardy, M. Flossman, K. Edwards, A. Blaich, and M. Murray. *Technical Analysis of Pegasus Spyware: An Investigation into Highly Sophisticated Espionage Software*, Technical Report 051-ESQ-475, Lookout, Washington, DC, USA (Aug. 2016).

142. C. Beame, B. Callaghan, M. Eisler, D. Noveck, D. Robinson, and R. Thurlow. *Network File System (NFS) Version 4 Protocol*, RFC 3530 (Apr. 2003).

143. K. Beck, M. Beedle, A. van Bennekum, A. Cockburn, W. Cunningham, M. Fowler, J. Grenning, J. Highsmith, A. Hunt, R. Jeffries, J. Kern, B. Marick, R. C. Martin, S. Mellor, K. Schwaber, J. Sutherland, and D. Thomas. *Manifesto for Agile Software Development* (2001).

144. M. Y. Becker and P. Sewell. "Cassandra: Flexible Trust Management, Applied to Electronic Health Records," *Proceedings of the 17th Computer Security Foundations Workshop* pp. 139–154 (June 2004).

145. K. M. Begnum. "Managing Large Networks of Virtual Machines," *Proceedings of the 20th Large Installation System Administration Conference* pp. 205–214 (Dec. 2006).

146. R. Bejtlich. *The Practice of Network Security Monitoring*, No Starch Press, Inc., San Francisco, CA, USA (2013).

147. H. Beker and F. Piper. *Cipher Systems: The Protection of Communications*, Northwood Books, London, UK (1982).

148. D. E. Bell. "Concerning 'Modeling' of Computer Security," *Proceedings of the 1988 IEEE Symposium on Security and Privacy* pp. 8–13 (Apr. 1988).

149. D. E. Bell and L. J. LaPadula. *Secure Computer Systems: Mathematical Foundations*, Technical Report MTR-2547, Vol. I, The MITRE Corporation, Bedford, MA, USA (Mar. 1973).

150. D. E. Bell and L. J. LaPadula. *Secure Computer System: Unified Exposition and Multics Interpretation*, Technical Report MTR-2997 Rev. 1, The MITRE Corporation, Bedford, MA, USA (Mar. 1976).

151. R. M. Bell, Y. Koren, and C. Volinsky. "All Together Now: A Perspective on the Netflix Prize," *Chance* **23**(1) pp. 24–29 (2010).

152. G. Bella, F. Massacci, and L. C. Paulson. "Verifying the SET Registration Protocols," *IEEE Journal on Selected Areas in Communication* **21**(1) pp. 77–87 (Jan. 2003).

153. G. Bella, F. Massacci, and L. C. Paulson. "Verifying the SET Purchase Protocols," *Journal of Automated Reasoning* **36**(1–2) pp. 5–37 (2006).

154. M. Bellare. "New Proofs for NMAC and HMAC: Security Without Collision-Resistance," *Journal of Cryptology* **28**(4) pp. 1–35 (Oct. 2015).

155. M. Bellare, R. Canetti, and H. Krawczyk. "Keying Hash Functions for Message Authentication," *Advances in Cryptology — CRYPTO '96* (*Lecture Notes in Computer Science* **1109**) pp. 1–15 (Aug. 1996).

156. M. Bellare and S. Micali. "Non-Interactive Oblivious Transfer and Applications," *Advances in Cryptology — CRYPTO '89* (*Lecture Notes in Computer Science* **435**) pp. 547–557 (Aug. 1989).

157. M. Bellare, D. Pointcheval, and P. Rogaway. "Authenticated Key Exchange Secure against Dictionary Attacks," *Advances in Cryptology — EUROCRYPT 2000* (*Lecture Notes in Computer Science* **1807**) pp. 139–155 (May 2000).

158. M. Bellare and R. L. Rivest. "Translucent Cryptography—An Alternative to Key Escrow, and Its Implementation via Fractional Oblivious Transfer," *Journal of Cryptology* **12**(2) pp. 117–139 (Mar. 1999).

159. M. Bellare and P. Rogaway. "Provably Secure Session Key Distribution: The Three Party Case," *Proceedings of the 27th Annual ACM Symposium on Theory of Computing* pp. 57–66 (May 1995).

160. M. Bellare, P. Rogaway, and D. Wagner. "The EAX Mode of Operation," *Proceedings of the 11th International Workshop on Fast Software Encryption* (*Lecture Notes in Computer Science* **3017**) pp. 389–407 (Feb. 2004).

161. S. Bellovin. "DRM, Complexity, and Correctness," *IEEE Security & Privacy* **5**(1) p. 80 (Jan. 2007).

162. S. M. Bellovin. "Security Problems in the TCP/IP Protocol Suite," *ACM SIGCOMM Computer Communications Review* **19**(2) pp. 32–48 (Apr. 1989).

163. S. M. Bellovin. "Using the Domain Name System for System Break-ins," *Proceedings of the Fifth USENIX UNIX Security Symposium* (June 1995).

164. S. M. Bellovin. "Probable Plaintext Cryptanalysis of the IP Security Protocols," *Proceedings of the 1997 Symposium on Network and Distributed System Security* pp. 52–59 (Feb. 1997).

165. S. M. Bellovin and M. Merritt. "Limitations of the Kerberos Authentication System," *Proceedings of the 1991 Winter USENIX Conference* pp. 253–267 (Winter 1991).

166. S. M. Bellovin and M. Merritt. "Encrypted Key Exchange: Password-Based Protocols Secure Against Dictionary Attacks," *Proceedings of the 1992 IEEE Symposium on Research in Security and Privacy* pp. 72–84 (May 1992).

167. F. Belvin, D. Bodeau, and S. Razvi. "Design Analysis in Evaluations Against the TCSEC C2 Criteria," *Proceedings of the 19th National Information Systems Security Conference* pp. 67–75 (Oct. 1996).

168. M. Ben Salem and S. J. Stolfo. "Decoy Document Deployment for Effective Masquerade Attack Detection," *Proceedings of the Eighth International Conference on the Detection of Intrusions and Malware, and Vulnerability Assessment* (*Lecture Notes in Computer Science* **6739**) pp. 35–54 (Aug. 2011).

169. S. Benferhat, T. Kenaza, and A. Mokhtari. "A Naive Bayes Approach for Detecting Coordinated Attacks," *Proceedings of the 32nd Annual IEEE International Computer Software and Applications Conference* pp. 704–709 (July 2008).

170. C. H. Bennett, F. Bessette, G. Brassard, L. Salvail, and J. Smolin. "Experimental Quantum Cryptography," *Journal of Cryptology* **5**(1) pp. 3–28 (1992).

171. J. Bennett. "Analysis of the Encryption Algorithm Used in the WordPerfect Processing Program," *Cryptologia* **11**(4) pp. 206–210 (Oct. 1987).

172. S. Berezin. "Model Checking and Theorem Proving: A Unified Framework," Ph.D. Dissertation, Carnegie Mellon University, Pittsburgh, PA, USA (Jan. 2002).

173. H. A. Bergen and W. J. Caelli. "File Security in WordPerfect 5.0," *Cryptologia* **15**(1) pp. 57–66 (Jan. 1991).

174. H. Berghel. "The Code Red Worm," *Communications of the ACM* **44**(12) pp. 15–19 (Dec. 2001).

175. J. Bergstra and M. Burgess (*ed*). *Handbook of Network and System Administration*, Elsevier, Amsterdam, The Netherlands (2007).

176. T. S. Bernard, T. Hsu, N. Perlroth, and R. Lieber. "Equifax Says Cyberattack May Have Affected 143 Million in the U.S.," *The New York Times* p. A1 (Sep. 7, 2017).

177. A. J. Bernstein. "Analysis of Programs for Parallel Processing," *IEEE Transactions on Electronic Computers* **15**(5) pp. 757–763 (Oct. 1966).

178. C. Bernstein and B. Woodward. *All the President's Men*, Simon & Schuster, New York, NY, USA (1974).

179. C. Bernstein and B. Woodward. *The Final Days*, Simon & Schuster, New York, NY, USA (1976).

180. D. J. Bernstein. "Curve25519: New Diffie-Hellman Speed Records," *Proceedings of the Ninth International Conference on Theory and Practice in Public-Key Cryptography* (*Lecture Notes in Computer Science* **3958**) pp. 207–228 (Apr. 2006).

181. D. J. Bernstein, T. Chou, C. Chuengsatiansup, Hülsing, T. Lange, R. Niederhagen, and C. van Vredendaal. "How to Manipulate Curve Standards: A White Paper for the Black Hat," *Proceedings of the Second International Conference on Research in Security Standardisation* (*Lecture Notes in Computer Science* **9497**) pp. 109–139 (Dec. 2015).

182. D. J. Bernstein, M. Hamburg, A. Krasnova, and T. Lange. "Elligator: Elliptic-Curve Points Indistinguishable from Uniform Random Strings," *Proceedings of the 20th ACM SIGSAC Conference on Computer and Communications Security* pp. 967–980 (Nov. 2013).

183. D. J. Bernstein and E. Schenk. *SYN Cookies* (Oct. 1996).

184. B. N. Bershad, S. Savage, P. Pardyak, E. G. Sirer, F. M. E., D. Becker, C. Chambers, and S. Eggers. "Extensibility, Safety and Performance in the SPIN Operating System," *Proceedings of the Fifteenth ACM Symposium on Operating Systems Principles* pp. 267–283 (Dec. 1995).

185. B. Bershad and C. Pinkerton. "Watchdogs: Extending the UNIX File System," *Proceedings of the 1988 Winter USENIX Conference* pp. 267–276 (Feb. 1988).

186. E. Bertino, P. A. Bonatti, and E. Ferrari. "TRBAC: A Temporal Role-Based Access Control Model," *ACM Transactions on Information and System Security* **4**(3) pp. 191–233 (Aug. 2001).

187. V. Berzins and L. Luqi. *Software Engineering with Abstractions*, Addison-Wesley Longman Publishing Co., Inc., Reading, MA, USA (1991).

188. T. Beth, H.-J. Knobloch, M. Otten, G. J. Simmons, and P. Wichmann. "Towards Acceptable Key Escrow Systems," *Proceedings of the Second ACM Conference on Computer and Communications Security* pp. 51–58 (Nov. 1994).

189. B. Beurdouche, K. Bhargavan, A. Delignat-Lavaud, C. Fournet, A. Kohlweiss, Markulf anf Pironti, P.-Y. Strub, and J. K. Zinzindohoue. "A Messy State of the Union: Taming the Composite State Machines of TLS," *Proceedings of the 2015 IEEE Symposium on Security and Privacy* pp. 535–552 (May 2015).

190. W. R. Bevier and W. D. Young. "A State-Based Approach to Noninterference," *Journal of Computer Security* **3**(1) pp. 55–70 (1994/1995).

191. P. V. Bhansali. "Software Dissimilarity Debate Revisited," *ACM SIGSOFT Software Engineering Notes* **30**(1) pp. 1–3 (Jan. 2005).

192. R. Bharadwaj and C. Heitmeyer. "Developing High Assurance Avionics Systems with the SCR Requirements Method," *Proceedings of the 19th Digital Avionics Systems Conference* pp. 1.D.1-1–8 (Oct. 2000).

193. S. Bhatkar, D. C. DuVarney, and R. Sekar. "Address Obfuscation: An Efficient Approach to Combat a Broad Range of Memory Error Exploits," *Proceedings of the 12th USENIX Security Symposium* pp. 105–120 (Aug. 2003).

194. S. Bhatkar, R. Sekar, and D. C. DuVarney. "Efficient Techniques for Comprehensive Protection from Memory Error Exploits," *Proceedings of the 15th USENIX Security Symposium* pp. 255–270 (July 2005).

195. R. Bhatti, E. Bertino, A. Ghafoor, and J. B. D. Joshi. "XML-Based Specification for Web Services Document Security," *IEEE Computer* **37**(4) pp. 41–49 (Apr. 2004).

196. K. J. Biba. *Integrity Considerations for Secure Computer Systems*, Technical Report MTR-3153, The MITRE Corporation, Bedford, MA, USA (June 1975).

197. R. Biddle, S. Chiasson, and P. C. van Oorschot. "Graphical Passwords: Learning from the First Twelve Years," *ACM Computing Surveys* **44**(4) pp. 19:1–19:41 (Aug. 2014).

198. N. Bielova, D. Devriese, F. Massacci, and F. Piessens. "Reactive Non-Interference for a Browser Model," *Proceedings of the Fifth International Conference on Network and System Security* pp. 97–104 (Sep. 2011).

199. E. Biham, R. Anderson, and L. Knudsen. "Serpent: A New Block Cipher Proposal," *Proceedings of the Fifth International Workshop on Fast Software Encryption* (*Lecture Notes in Computer Science* **1372**) pp. 222–238 (Mar. 1998).

200. E. Biham, A. Biryukov, and A. Shamir. "Cryptanalysis of Skipjack Reduced to 31 Rounds Using Impossible Differentials," *Journal of Cryptology* **18**(4) pp. 291–311 (Autumn 2005).

201. E. Biham, O. Dunkelman, and N. Keller. "Differential-Linear Cryptanalysis of Serpent," *Proceedings of the Tenth International Workshop on Fast Software Encryption* (*Lecture Notes in Computer Science* **2887**) pp. 9–21 (Feb. 2003).

202. E. Biham, O. Dunkelman, and N. Keller. "Related-Key Boomerang and Rectangle Attacks," *Advances in Cryptology — EUROCRYPT 2005* (*Lecture Notes in Computer Science* **3494**) pp. 507–525 (May 2005).

203. E. Biham, O. Dunkelman, and N. Keller. "A New Attack on 6-Round IDEA," *Proceedings of the 14th International Workshop on Fast Software Encryption* (*Lecture Notes in Computer Science* **4593**) pp. 211–224 (Mar. 2007).

204. E. Biham and A. Shamir. "Differential Cryptanalysis of DES-like Cryptosystems," *Journal of Cryptology* **4**(1) pp. 3–72 (1991).

205. E. Biham and A. Shamir. "Differential Cryptanalysis of Snefru, Khafre, Redoc-II, LOKI and Lucifer (Extended Abstract)," *Advances in Cryptology — CRYPTO '91* (*Lecture Notes in Computer Science* **576**) pp. 156–171 (Aug. 1991).

206. E. Biham and A. Shamir. "Differential Cryptanalysis of the Full 16-Round DES," *Advances in Cryptology — CRYPTO '92* (*Lecture Notes in Computer Science* **740**) pp. 487–496 (Aug. 1992).

207. E. Biham and A. Shamir. *Differential Cryptanalysis of the Data Encryption Standard*, Springer-Verlag, New York, NY, USA (1993).

208. L. Bilge, T. Strufe, D. Balzarotti, and E. Kirda. "All Your Contacts Are Belong to Us: Automated Identity Theft Attacks on Social Networks," *Proceedings of the 18th International World Wide Web Conference* pp. 551–560 (2009).

209. E. Bina, R. McCool, V. Jones, and M. Winslett. "Secure Access to Data Over the Internet," *Proceedings of the Third International Conference on Parallel and Distributed Information Systems* pp. 99–102 (Sep. 1994).

210. R. Bisbey II and D. Hollingsworth. *Protection Analysis: Final Report*, Technical Report ISI/SR-78-13, University of Southern California Information Sciences Institute, Marina Del Rey, CA (May 1978).

211. R. Bisbey II, G. Popek, and J. Carlstedt. *Protection Errors in Operating Systems: Inconsistency of a Single Value over Time*, Technical Report ISI/SR-75-4, University of Southern California Information Sciences Institute, Marina Del Rey, CA (Dec. 1975).

212. M. Bishop. "Reflections on UNIX Vulnerabilities," *Proceedings of the 25th Annual Computer Security Applications Conference* pp. 161–184 (Dec. 2009).

213. M. Bishop. "Hierarchical Take-Grant Protection Systems," *Proceedings of the Eighth ACM Symposium on Operating Systems Principles* pp. 109–122 (Dec. 1981).

214. M. Bishop. "Analyzing the Security of an Existing Computer System," *Proceedings of the 1986 ACM Fall Joint Computer Conference* pp. 1115–1119 (Nov. 1986).

215. M. Bishop. *The RIACS Intelligent Auditing and Checking System*, Technical Report 86.3, Research Institute for Advanced Computer Science, NASA Ames Research Center, Moffett Field, CA, USA (June 1986).

216. M. Bishop. *Sendmail Wizardry*, Research Memo 86.3, Research Institute for Advanced Computer Science, NASA Ames Research Center, Moffett Field, CA, USA (Jan. 1986).

217. M. Bishop. "Profiling Under UNIX by Patching," *Software: Practice and Experience* **17**(10) pp. 729–739 (Oct. 1987).

218. M. Bishop. "An Application of a Fast Data Encryption Standard Implementation," *Computing Systems* **1**(3) pp. 221–254 (Summer 1988).

219. M. Bishop. "Collaboration Using Roles," *Software: Practice and Experience* **20**(5) pp. 485–497 (May 1990).

220. M. Bishop. "A Security Analysis of the NTP Protocol Version 2," *Proceedings of the Sixth Annual Computer Security Applications Conference* pp. 20–29 (Dec. 1990).

221. M. Bishop. "Password Management," *Proceedings of Compcon Spring '91* pp. 167–169 (Feb. 1991).

222. M. Bishop. "A Proactive Password Checker," *Proceedings of the IFIP TC11 Seventh International Conference on Information Security: Creating Confidence in Information Processing* pp. 169–180 (May 1991).

223. M. Bishop. "Anatomy of a Proactive Password Changer," *Proceedings of the Third USENIX Security Symposium* pp. 171–184 (Sep. 1992).

224. M. Bishop and D. Bailey. *A Critical Analysis of Vulnerability Taxonomies*, Technical Report CSE-96-11, Dept. of Computer Science, University of California at Davis, Davis, CA, USA (Sep. 1996).

225. M. Bishop, J. Cummins, S. Peisert, A. Singh, B. Bhumiratana, D. Agarwal, D. Frincke, and M. Hogarth. "Relationships and Data Sanitization: A Study in Scarlet," *Proceedings of the 2010 Workshop on New Security Paradigms* pp. 151–164 (Sep. 2010).

226. M. Bishop and M. Dilger. "Checking for Race Conditions in File Accesses," *Computing Systems* **9**(2) pp. 131–152 (Mar. 1996).

227. M. Bishop, M. Doroud, C. Gates, and J. Hunker. "Effects of Attribution Policies: The Second Summer of the Sisterhood," *Proceedings of the 11th European Conference on Information Warfare and Security* pp. 63–69 (July 2012).

228. M. Bishop, S. Engle, D. Howard, and S. Whalen. "A Taxonomy of Buffer Overflow Characteristics," *IEEE Transactions on Dependable and Secure Computing* **9**(3) pp. 305–317 (May 2012).

229. M. Bishop, C. Gates, and J. Hunker. "The Sisterhood of the Traveling Packets," *Proceedings of the 2009 Workshop on New Security Paradigms* pp. 1–12 (Sep. 2009).

230. M. Bishop and E. Goldman. "The Strategy and Tactics of Information Warfare," *Contemporary Security Policy* **24**(1) pp. 113–139 (2003).

231. M. Bishop and D. V. Klein. "Improving System Security via Proactive Password Checking," *Computers & Security* **14**(3) pp. 233–249 (Apr. 1995).

232. M. Bishop, S. Peisert, C. Hoke, M. Graff, and D. Jefferson. "E-Voting and Forensics: Prying Open the Black Box," *Proceedings of the 2009 Electronic Voting Technology Workshop/Workshop on Trustworthy Elections* pp. 3:1–3:20 (Aug. 2009).

233. M. Bishop and L. Snyder. "The Transfer of Information and Authority in a Protection System," *Proceedings of the Seventh ACM Symposium on Operating Systems Principles* pp. 45–54 (Dec. 1979).

234. J. Biskup. "Some Variants of the Take-Grant Protection Model," *Information Processing Letters* **19**(3) pp. 151–156 (Oct. 1984).

235. J. Biskup and U. Flegel. "Transaction-Based Pseudonyms in Audit Data for Privacy Respecting Intrusion Detection," *Proceedings of the Third International Workshop on Recent Advances in Intrusion Detection* (*Lecture Notes in Computer Science* **1907**) pp. 28–48 (Oct. 2000).

236. A. K. Biswas, D. Ghosal, and S. Nagaraja. "A Survey of Timing Channels and Countermeasures," *ACM Computing Surveys* **50**(1) pp. 6:1–6:39 (Apr. 2017).

237. A. Bittau, A. Belay, A. Mashtizdeh, D. Mazières, and D. Boneh. "Hacking Blind," *Proceedings of the 2014 IEEE Symposium on Security and Privacy* pp. 227–242 (May 2014).

238. M. W. Blake, J. J. Lofe, and S. N. J.. "Using Fault Tree Methodologies in Availability Improvement Studies at Southern Company Services," *IEEE Transactions on Power Apparatus and Systems* **PAS-103**(3) pp. 656–661 (Mar. 1984).

239. G. R. Blakley. "Safeguarding Cryptographic Keys," *Proceedings of the AFIPS '79 International Workshop on Managing Requirements Knowledge* pp. 313–317 (June 1979).

240. G. R. Blakley. "One-Time Pads Are Key Safeguarding Schemes, Not Cryptosystems: Fast Key Safeguarding Schemes (Threshold Schemes) Exist," *Proceedings of the 1980 IEEE Symposium on Security and Privacy* pp. 108–113 (Apr. 1980).

241. J. Blasco, T. M. Chen, J. Tapiador, and P. Peris-Lopez. "A Survey of Wearable Biometric Recognition Systems," *ACM Computing Surveys* **49**(3) pp. 43:1–43:35 (Dec. 2016).

242. M. Blaze. "Protocol Failure in the Escrowed Encryption Standard," *Proceedings of the Second ACM Conference on Computer and Communications Security* pp. 59–67 (Nov. 1994).

243. M. Blaze. "Taking Surveillance Out of the Shadows," *IEEE Security & Privacy* **7**(5) pp. 75–77 (Sep. 2009).

244. M. Blaze, J. Feigenbaum, J. Ioannidis, and A. D. Keromytis. *The KeyNote Trust-Management System Version 2*, RFC 2704 (Sep. 1999).

245. M. Blaze, J. Feigenbaum, and A. D. Keromytis. "KeyNote: Trust Management for Public-Key Infrastructures," *Proceedings of the Ninth International Workshop on Services Computing* (*Lecture Notes in Computer Science* **1550**) pp. 59–63 (Apr. 1998).

246. M. Blaze, J. Feigenbaum, and J. Lacy. "Decentralized Trust Management," *Proceedings of the 1996 IEEE Symposium on Security and Privacy* pp. 164–173 (May 1996).

247. M. Blaze, J. Ioannidis, and A. D. Keromytis. "Trust Management for IPsec," *ACM Transactions on Information and System Security* **5**(2) pp. 95–118 (May 2002).

248. J. Blocki, N. Christin, A. Datta, and A. Sinha. "Audit Mechanisms for Privacy Protection in Healthcare Environments," *Proceedings of the Second USENIX Workshop on Health Security and Privacy* (Aug. 2011).

249. P. Bocij. *The Dark Side of the Internet: Protecting Yourself and Your Family from Online Criminals*, Praeger Publishers, Santa Barbara, CA, USA (2006).

250. W. E. Boebert. "On the Inability of an Unmodified Capability Machine to Enforce the *-Property," *Proceedings of the Seventh National Computer Security Conference* pp. 291–293 (Sep. 1984).

251. W. E. Boebert and C. Ferguson. "A Partial Solution to the Discretionary Trojan Horse Problem," *Proceedings of the Eighth National Computer Security Conference* pp. 245–253 (Sep. 1985).

252. W. E. Boebert and R. Y. Kain. "A Practical Alternative to Hierarchical Integrity Policies," *Proceedings of the Eighth National Computer Security Conference* pp. 18–27 (Sep. 1985).

253. W. E. Boebert, R. Y. Kain, W. D. Young, and S. A. Hansohn. "Secure Ada Target: Issues, System Design, and Verification," *Proceedings of the 1985 IEEE Symposium on Security and Privacy* pp. 176–183 (Apr. 1985).

254. C. Boettiger. "An Introduction to Docker for Reproducible Research," *ACM SIGOPS Operating Systems Review* **49**(1) pp. 71–79 (Jan. 2015).

255. R. Böhme and M. Kirchner. "Counter-Forensics: Attacking Image Forensics," in *Digital Image Forensics: There Is More to a Picture Than Meets the Eye*, edited by H. T. Sencar and N. Memon, Springer Science+Business Media, New York, NY, USA pp. 327–366 (2013).

256. D. Bolignano, D. Le Métayer, and C. Loiseaux. "Formal Methods in Context: Security and Java Card," *Proceedings of the First International Workshop on Java on Smart Cards: Programming and Security* (*Lecture Notes in Computer Science* **2041**) pp. 1–5 (Sep. 2000).

257. T. Bolognesi and E. Brinksma. "Introduction to the ISO Specification Language LOTOS," *Computer Networks and ISDN Systems* **14**(1) pp. 25–59 (1987).

258. J.-P. Boly, A. Bosselaers, R. Cramer, R. Michelsen, S. Mjølsnes, F. Muller, T. Pedersen, B. Pfitzmann, P. de Rooij, B. Schoenmakers, M. Schunter, L. Vallée, and M. Waidner. "The ESPRIT Project CAFE—High Security Digital Payment Systems," *Proceedings of the Third European Symposium on Research in Computer Security* (*Lecture Notes in Computer Science* **875**) pp. 217–230 (1994).

259. A. C. Bomberger, W. S. Frantz, A. C. Hardy, N. Hardy, C. R. Landau, and J. S. Shapiro. "The KeyKOS Nanokernel Architecture," *Proceedings of the USENIX Workshop on Micro-Kernels and Other Kernel Architectures* pp. 95–112 (Apr. 1992).

260. D. Boneh and M. Franklin. "Identity-Based Encryption from the Weil Pairing," *Advances in Cryptology — CRYPTO 2001* (*Lecture Notes in Computer Science* **2139**) pp. 213–229 (Aug. 2001).

261. D. Boneh and M. Franklin. "Identity-Based Encryption from the Weil Pairing," *SIAM Journal on Computing* **32**(3) pp. 586–615 (2003).

262. D. Boneh, C. Gentry, S. Halevi, and D. J. Wang, Frankand Wu. "Private Database Queries Using Somewhat Homomorphic Encryption," *Proceedings of the 11th International Conference on Applied Cryptography and Network Security* (*Lecture Notes in Computer Science* **7954**) pp. 102–118 (2013).

263. G. Bonfante, M. Kaczmarek, and J.-Y. Marion. "On Abstract Computer Virology from a Recursion Theoretic Perspective," *Journal of Computer Virology* **1**(3) pp. 45–54 (Mar. 2006).

264. J. Bonneau. "The Science of Guessing: Analyzing an Anonymized Corpus of 70 Million Passwords," *Proceedings of the 2012 IEEE Symposium on Security and Privacy* pp. 538–552 (May 2012).

265. J. Bonneau, C. Herley, P. C. van Oorschot, and F. Stajano. "The Quest to Replace Passwords: A Framework for Comparative Evaluation of Web Authentication Schemes," *Proceedings of the 2012 IEEE Symposium on Security and Privacy* pp. 553–567 (May 2012).

266. J. Bonneau, C. Herley, P. C. van Oorschot, and F. Stajano. "Passwords and the Evolution of Imperfect Authentication," *Communications of the ACM* **58**(7) pp. 78–87 (June 2015).

267. D. Bonyun. "The Role of a Well Defined Auditing Process in the Enforcement of Privacy Policy and Data Security," *Proceedings of the 1981 IEEE Symposium on Security and Privacy* pp. 19–25 (Apr. 1981).

268. D. A. Bonyun. "The Use of Architectural Principles in the Design of Certifiably Secure Systems," *Computers & Security* **2**(2) pp. 153–162 (June 1983).

269. N. Borisov, R. Johnson, N. Sastry, and D. Wagner. "Fixing Races for Fun and Profit: How to Abuse atime," *Proceedings of the 15th USENIX Security Symposium* pp. 303–314 (July 2005).

270. A. Borrett. "A Perspective of Evaluation in the UK Versus the US," *Proceedings of the 18th National Computer Security Conference* pp. 322–334 (Oct. 1995).

271. J. W. Bos, C. Costello, P. Longa, and M. Naehrig. "Selecting Elliptic Curves for Cryptography: An Efficiency and Security Analysis," *Journal of Cryptographic Engineering* **6**(4) pp. 259–286 (May 2016).

272. C. Bösch, P. Hartel, W. Jonker, and A. Peter. "A Survey of Provably Secure Searchable Encryption," *ACM Computing Surveys* **47**(2) pp. 18:1–18:51 (Aug. 2015).

273. E. Bott, C. Siechert, and C. Stinson. *Windows 10 Inside Out*, Microsoft Press, Redmond, WA, USA (Oct. 2016).

274. M. W. Bovee, D. L. Paul, and K. M. Nelson. "A Framework for Assessing the Use of Third-Party Software Quality Assurance Standards to Meet FDA Medical Device Software Process Control Guidelines," *IEEE Transactions on Engineering Management* **48**(4) pp. 465–478 (Nov. 2001).

275. B. M. Bowen, M. Ben Salem, A. D. Keromytis, and S. J. Stolfo. "Monitoring Technologies for Mitigating Insider Threats," in *Monitoring Technologies for Mitigating Insider Threats*, edited by C. W. Probst, J. Hunker, D. Gollmann, and M. Bishop (*Advances in Information Security* **49**), Springer Science+Business Media, LLC, New York, NY, USA pp. 197–217 (Jan. 2010).

276. B. M. Bowen, S. Hershkop, A. D. Keromytis, and S. J. Stolfo. "Baiting Inside Attackers Using Decoy Documents," *Proceedings of the Fifth International Conference on Security and Privacy in Communication Networks* (*Lecture Notes of the Institute for Computer Sciences, Social Informatics and Telecommunications Engineering* **19**) pp. 51–70 (Sep. 2009).

277. J. P. Bowen and M. G. Hinchey. "Seven More Myths of Formal Methods," *IEEE Software* **12**(4) pp. 34–41 (July 1995).

278. J. P. Bowen and M. G. Hinchey. "Ten Commandments of Formal Methods," *IEEE Computer* **28**(4) pp. 56–63 (Apr. 1995).

279. J. P. Bowen and M. G. Hinchey. "Ten Commandments of Formal Methods ... Ten Years Later," *IEEE Computer* **39**(1) pp. 40–48 (Jan. 2006).

280. J. Boyar. "Inferring Sequences Produced by a Linear Congruential Generator Mission Low Order Bits," *Journal of Cryptology* **1**(3) pp. 177–184 (Oct. 1989).

281. J. Boyar. "Inferring Sequences Produced by Pseudo-Random Number Generators," *Journal of the ACM* **36**(1) pp. 129–141 (Jan. 1989).

282. C. Boyd. "Hidden Assumptions in Cryptographic Protocols," *IEE Proceedings E – Computers and Digital Techniques* **137**(6) pp. 433–436 (Nov. 1990).

283. R. S. Boyer and J. S. Moore. "Proving Theorems About LISP Functions," *Journal of the ACM* **22**(1) pp. 129–144 (Jan. 1975).

284. J. L. Boyles, A. Smith, and M. Madden. *Privacy and Data Management on Mobile Devices*, Technical Report, The Pew Research Center's Internet & American Life Project, Washington, DC, USA (Sep. 2012).

285. S. Brackin, C. Meadows, and J. Millen. "CAPSL Interface for the NRL Protocol Analyzer," *Proceedings of the 1999 IEEE Symposium on Application-Specific Systems and Software Engineering and Technology* pp. 64–73 (Mar. 1999).

286. K. Brady. "Integrating B2 Security into a UNIX System," *Proceedings of the 14th National Computer Security Conference* pp. 338–346 (Oct. 1991).

287. J. Brainard, A. Juels, R. L. Rivest, M. Szydlo, and M. Yung. "Fourth-Factor Authentication: Somebody You Know," *Proceedings of the 13th ACM Conference on Computer and Communications Security* pp. 168–178 (Oct. 2006).

288. L. J. Brandeis. *Olmstead et al. v. United States*, 277 US 438 (June 1927).

289. S. Brands. "Electronic Cash on the Internet," *Proceedings of the 1995 Symposium on Network and Distributed System Security* pp. 84–84 (Feb. 1995).

290. G. Brassard, N. Lütkenhaus, T. Mor, and B. C. Sanders. "Security Aspects of Practical Quantum Cryptography," *Advances in Cryptology — EUROCRYPT 2000* (*Lecture Notes in Computer Science* **1807**) pp. 289–299 (May 2000).

291. D. M. Bressoud. *Factorization and Primality Testing*, Springer, New York, NY, USA (1989).

292. D. F. C. Brewer and M. J. Nash. "The Chinese Wall Security Policy," *Proceedings of the 1989 IEEE Symposium on Security and Privacy* pp. 206–214 (May 1989).

293. E. F. Brickell. "Breaking Iterated Knapsacks," *Advances in Cryptology — CRYPTO '84* (*Lecture Notes in Computer Science* **196**) pp. 342–358 (Aug. 1984).

294. E. F. Brickell and D. R. Stinson. "The Detection of Cheaters in Threshold Schemes," *Advances in Cryptology — CRYPTO '88* (*Lecture Notes in Computer Science* **403**) pp. 564–577 (Aug. 1988).

295. L. Bridges. "The Changing Face of Malware," *Network Security* **2008**(1) pp. 17–20 (Jan. 2008).

296. S. S. Brilliant, J. C. Knight, and N. G. Leveson. "The Consistent Comparison Problem in *N*-Version Software," *ACM SIGSOFT Software Engineering Notes* **12**(1) pp. 29–34 (Jan. 1987).

297. P. Brinch Hansen. *Operating System Principles*, Prentice Hall, Inc., Englewood Cliffs, NJ, USA (1973).

298. S. Brlek, S. Hamadou, and J. Mullins. "A Flaw in the Electronic Commerce Protocol SET," *Information Processing Letters* **97**(3) pp. 104–108 (Feb. 2006).

299. W. J. Broad, J. Markoff, and D. E. Sanger. "Israeli Test on Worm Called Crucial in Iran Nuclear Delay," *The New York Times* p. A1 (Jan. 16, 2011).

300. F. P. Brooks. *The Mythical Man-Month: Essays on Software Engineering Anniversary Edition*, Addison-Wesley, Reading, MA, USA (1996).

301. A. S. Brown, E. Bracken, S. Zoccoli, and K. Douglas. "Generating and Remembering Passwords," *Applied Cognitive Psychology* **18**(6) pp. 641–651 (June 2004).

302. L. Brown, M. Kwan, J. Pieprzyk, and J. Seberry. "Improving Resistance to Differential Cryptanalysis and the Redesign of LOKI," *Advances in Cryptology — ASIACRYPT '91* (*Lecture Notes in Computer Science* **739**) pp. 36–50 (Nov. 1991).

303. L. Brown and J. Pieprzyk. "Introducing the New LOKI97 Block Cipher," *unpublished* (1998).

304. L. Brown, J. Pieprzyk, and J. Seberry. "LOKI—A Cryptographic Primitive for Authentication and Secrecy Applications," *Advances in Cryptology—AUSCRYPT '90* (*Lecture Notes in Computer Science* **453**) (Jan. 1990).

305. R. Browne. "Mode Security: An Infrastructure for Covert Channel Suppression," *Proceedings of the 1994 IEEE Symposium on Research in Security and Privacy* pp. 39–55 (May 1994).

306. N. Brownlee and E. Guttman. *Expectations for Computer Security Inciudent Response*, RFC 2350 (June 1998).

307. D. Brumley. "Invisible Intruders: Rootkits in Practice," *;login:* **24**(9) pp. 69–71 (Sep. 1999).

308. K. Bryant and J. Campbell. "User Behaviours Associated with Password Security and Management," *Australasian Journal of Information Systems* **14**(1) (Nov. 2006).

309. T. A. Budd. "Safety in Grammatical Protection Systems," *International Journal of Computer and Information Sciences* **12**(6) pp. 413–431 (Dec. 1983).

310. S. Budiansky. *Battle of Wits: The Complete Story of Codebreaking in World War II*, Free Press, New York, NY, USA (2002).

311. J. A. Bull, L. Gong, and K. R. Sollins. "Towards Security in an Open Systems Federation," *Proceedings of the Second European Symposium on Research in Computer Security* (*Lecture Notes in Computer Science* **648**) pp. 3–20 (Nov. 1992).

312. G. Bullough, J. Loomis, and P. Weiss. "An Assertion Mapping Approach to Software Test Design," *Proceedings of the 13th National Computer Security Conference* pp. 266–276 (Oct. 1990).

313. J. Bunnell, J. Podd, R. Henderson, R. Napier, and J. Kennedy-Moffat. "Cognitive, Associative and Conventional Passwords: Recall and Guessing Rates," *Computers & Security* **16**(7) pp. 629–641 (1997).

314. A. Bunten. "UNIX and Linux Based Rootkits Techniques and Countermeasures," *Proceedings of the 16th Annual FIRST Conference on Computer Security Incident Handling* (June 2004).

315. J. Buolamwini and T. Gebru. "Gender Shades: Intersectional Accuracy Disparities in Commercial Gender Classification," *Proceedings of Machine Learning Research* pp. 77–91 (Feb. 2018).

316. J. R. Burch, E. M. Clarke, D. E. Long, K. L. McMillan, and D. L. Dill. "Symbolic Model Checking for Sequential Circuit Verification," *IEEE Transactions on Computer-Aided Design of Integrated Circuits and Systems* **13**(4) pp. 401–424 (Apr. 1994).

317. J. R. Burch, E. M. Clarke, and K. L. McMillan. "Symbolic Model Checking: 10^{20} States and Beyond," *Information and Computation* **98**(2) pp. 142–170 (June 1992).

318. M. Burgess. "Cfengine: A Site Configuration Engine," *Computing Systems* **8**(3) pp. 309–337 (Summer 1995).

319. M. Burgess. "On the Theory of System Administration," *Science of Computer Programming* **49**(1-3) pp. 1–46 (Dec. 2003).

320. M. Burkhart, D. Brauckhoff, and M. May. "On the Utility of Anonymized Flow Traces for Anomaly Detection," *Computing Research Repository* (Oct. 2008).

321. W. Burleson, S. S. Clark, B. Ransford, and K. Fu. "Design Challenges for Secure Implantable Medical Devices," *Proceedings of the 49th Annual Design Automation Conference* pp. 12–17 (June 2012).

322. M. Burmester, Y. Desmedt, and J. Seberry. "Equitable Key Escrow with Limited Time Span (Or, How to Enforce Time Expiration Cryptographically)," *Advances in Cryptology — ASIACRYPT '98* (*Lecture Notes in Computer Science* **1514**) pp. 380–391 (Oct. 1998).

323. W. E. Burr. "Selecting the Advanced Encryption Standard," *IEEE Security & Privacy* **1**(2) pp. 43–52 (Mar. 2003).

324. W. E. Burr, D. F. Dodson, E. M. Newton, R. A. Perlner, W. T. Polk, S. Gupta, and E. A. Nabbus. *Electronic Authentication Guideline*, NIST Special Publication 800-63-2, National Institute of Standards and Technology, Gaithersburg, MD, USA (Aug. 2013).

325. M. Burrows, M. Abadi, and R. Needham. "A Logic of Authentication," *ACM Transactions on Computer Systems* pp. 18–36 (Feb. 1990).

326. E. Bursztein, S. Bethard, C. Fabry, J. C. Mitchell, and D. Jurafsky. "How Good Are Humans at Solving CAPTCHAs? A Large Scale Evaluation," *Proceedings of the 2010 IEEE Symposium on Security and Privacy* pp. 399–413 (May 2010).

327. J. Burton. *The Pentagon Wars: Reformers Challenge the Old Guard*, Naval Institute Press, Annapolis, MD, USA (Sep. 1993).

328. C. Burwick, D. Coppersmith, E. D'Avignon, R. Gennaro, S. Halevi, C. Jutla, S. M. Matyas Jr., L. O'Connor, M. Peyravian, D. Safford, and N. Zunic. "MARS—A Candidate Cipher for AES," *unpublished* (June 1998).

329. I. Butan, S. D. Morgera, and R. Sankar. "A Survey of Intrusion Detection Systems in Wireless Sensor Networks," *IEEE Communications Surveys & Tutorials* **16**(1) pp. 266–282 (First Quarter 2014).

330. F. Butler, I. Cervesato, A. D. Jaggard, A. Scedrov, and C. Walstad. "Formal Analysis of Kerberos 5," *Theoretical Computer Science* **367**(1-2) pp. 57–87 (Nov. 2006).

331. J.-W. Byun, E. Bertino, and N. Li. "Purpose Based Access Control of Complex Data for Privacy Protection," *Proceedings of the 10th ACM Symposium on Access Control Models and Technologies* pp. 102–110 (2005).

332. J.-W. Byun and N. Li. "Purpose Based Access Control for Privacy Protection in Relational Database Systems," *The VLDB Journal* **17**(4) pp. 603–619 (July 2008).

333. S. Cabuk, C. E. Brodley, and C. Shields. "IP Covert Channel Detection," *ACM Transactions on Information and System Security* **12**(4) pp. 22:1–22:29 (Apr. 2009).

334. W. J. Caelli, A. W. Rhodes, and N. C. Russell. "An Evaluation of HP-UX (UNIX) for Database Protection Using the European ITSEC," *Computers & Security* **11**(5) pp. 463–479 (Sep. 1992).

335. N. Cai, J. Wang, and X. Yu. "SCADA System Security: Complexity, History, and New Developments," *Proceedings of the Sixth International Conference on Industrial Informatics* pp. 569–574 (July 2008).

336. X. Cai, Y. Gui, and R. Johnson. "Exploiting Unix File-System Races via Algorithmic Complexity Attacks," *Proceedings of the 2009 IEEE Symposium on Security and Privacy* pp. 27–41 (May 2009).

337. X. Cai, R. Lale, X. Zhang, and R. Johnson. "Fixing Races For Good: Portable and Reliable UNIX File-System Race Detection," *Proceedings of the Tenth ACM Symposium on Information, Computer and Communications Security* pp. 357–368 (2015).

338. A. Caliskan-Islam, R. Harang, A. Liu, A. Narayanan, C. Voss, F. Yamaguchi, and R. Greenstadt. "De-Anonymizing Programmers via Code Stylometry," *Proceedings of the 24th USENIX Security Symposium* pp. 255–270 (Aug. 2015).

339. J. Callas, Y. Desmedt, D. Nagy, A. Otsuka, J.-J. Quisquater, and M. Yung. "Real Electronic Cash Versus Academic Electronic Cash Versus Paper Cash (Panel Report)," *Proceedings of the 2008 International Conference on Financial Cryptography and Data Security* pp. 307–313 (Jan. 2008).

340. J. Callas, L. Donnerhacke, H. Finney, D. Shaw, and R. Thayer. *OpenPGP Message Format*, RFC 4880 (Nov. 2007).

341. B. A. Calloni, M. V. DelPrincipe, T. F. Marz, and K. Littlejohn. "INSERT: A COTS-Based Solution for Building High-Assurance Applications," *Proceedings of the 18th Digital Avionics Sstems Conference* pp. 2.D.6-1–8 (Oct. 1999).

342. J. Camenisch, A. Lysyanskaya, and M. Meyervich. "Endorsed E-Cash," *Proceedings of the 2007 IEEE Symposium on Security and Privacy* pp. 107–121 (May 2007).

343. J. P. Campbell Jr.. "Speaker Recognition: A Tutorial," *Proceedings of the IEEE* **85**(9) pp. 1437–1462 (Sep. 1997).

344. S. Campos, E. M. Clarke, and M. Minea. "Symbolic Techniques for Formally Verifying Industrial Systems," *Science of Computer Programming* **29**(1–2) pp. 79–98 (July 1997).

345. S. Campos, E. Clarke, W. Marrero, and M. Minea. "Verus: A Tool for Quantitative Analysis of Finite-State Real-Time Systems," *Proceedings of the ACM SIGPLAN 1995 Workshop on Languages, Compilers, & Tools for Real-Time Systems* pp. 70–78 (1995).

346. J. Canavan. *The Evolution of Malicious IRC Bots*, White Paper, Symantec, Inc., Cupertino, CA, USA (2005).

347. A. A. Cárdenas, J. S. Baras, and K. Seamon. "A Framework for the Evaluation of Intrusion Detection Systems," *Proceedings of the 2006 IEEE Symposium on Security and Privacy* pp. 63–77 (May 2006).

348. X. D. C. D. Carnavalet and M. Mannan. "A Large-Scale Evaluation of High-Impact Password Strength Meters," *ACM Transactions on Information and System Security* **18**(1) pp. 1:1–1:32 (June 2015).

349. G. Caronni, S. Kumar, C. Schuba, and G. Scott. "Virtual Enterprise Networks: The Next Generation of Secure Enterprise Networking," *Proceedings of the 16th Annual Computer Security Applications Conference* pp. 42–51 (Dec. 2000).

350. M. Carpenter, T. Liston, and E. Skoudis. "Hiding Virtualization from Attackers and Malware," *IEEE Security & Privacy* **5**(3) pp. 62–65 (May 2007).

351. B. Carrara and C. Adams. "You Are the Key: Generating Cryptographic Keys from Voice Biometrics," *Proceedings of the Eighth Annual International Conference on Privacy, Security, and Trust* pp. 213–222 (Aug. 2010).

352. B. Carrara and C. Adams. "Out-of-Band Covert Channels—A Survey," *ACM Computing Surveys* **49**(2) pp. 23:1–23:36 (Nov. 2016).

353. B. D. Carrier. "Risks of Live Digital Forensic Analysis," *Communications of the ACM* **49**(2) pp. 56–61 (Feb. 2006).

354. B. D. Carrier and J. Grand. "A Hardware-Based Memory Acquisition Procedure for Digital Investigations," *Digital Investigation* **1**(1) pp. 50–60 (Feb. 2004).

355. L. Carroll. *Through the Looking-Glass, and What Alice Found There, Macmillan and Co.*, London, 1882.

356. T. E. Carroll, M. Crouse, E. W. Fulp, and K. S. Berenhaut. "Analysis of Network Address Shuffling as a Moving Target Defense," *Proceedings of the 2014 IEEE International Conference on Communications* pp. 701–706 (June 2014).

357. T. E. Carroll and D. Grosu. "A Game Theoretic Investigation of Deception in Network Security," *Security and Communication Networks* **4**(10) pp. 1162–1172 (Oct. 2011).

358. M. Carvalho and R. Ford. "Moving-Target Defenses for Computer Networks," *IEEE Security & Privacy* **12**(2) pp. 73–76 (Mar. 2014).

359. J. Case and S. E. Moelius III. "Cautious Virus Detection in the Extreme," *Proceedings of the 2007 Workshop on Programming Languages and Analysis for Security* pp. 47–52 (June 2007).

360. S. Cass. "Antipiracy Software Opens Door to Electronic Intruders," *IEEE Spectrum* **43**(1) pp. 12–13 (Jan. 2006).

361. F. Castaneda, E. C. Sezer, and J. Xu. "WORM vs. WORM: Preliminary Study of an Active Counter-Attack Mechanism," *Proceedings of the 2004 ACM Workshop on Rapid Malcode* pp. 83–93 (Oct. 2004).

362. C. Castelfranchi and R. Falcone. "Trust Is Much More Than Subjective Probability: Mental Components and Sources of Trust," *Proceedings of the 33rd Annual Hawaii International Conference on System Sciences* (Jan. 2000).

363. C. Castelluccia, M. Dürmuth, and D. Perito. "Adaptive Password-Strength Meters from Markov Models," *Proceedings of the 2012 Symposium on Network and Distributed System Security* (Feb. 2012).

364. A. Castiglione, R. De Prisco, A. De Santis, U. Fiore, and F. Palmieri. "A Botnet-Based Command and Control Approach Relying on Swarm Intelligence," *Journal of Network and Computer Applications* **38** pp. 22–33 (Feb. 2014).

365. C. J. H. Castro, L. J. G. Villalba, J. C. H. Castro, and J. M. S. Cámara. "On MARS's S-Boxes Strength Against Linear Cryptanalysis," *Proceedngs of the International Conference on Computational Science and Its Applications, Part III* (*Lecture Notes in Computer Science* **2669**) pp. 79–83 (May 2003).

366. B. Caswell, J. Beale, and A. Baker. *Snort IDS and IPS Toolkit*, Syngress Press, Burlington, MA, USA (2007).

367. A. Cavoukian. "Privacy by Design: The Definitive Workshop," *Identity in the Information Society* **3**(2) pp. 247–251 (May 2010).

368. I. Cervesato, A. D. Jaggard, A. Scedrov, J.-K. Tsay, and C. Walstad. "Breaking and Fixing Public-Key Kerberos," *Revised Selected Papers from the 11th Asian Computing Science Conference on Secure Software and Related Issues* (*Lecture Notes in Computer Science* **4435**) pp. 167–181 (Dec. 2006).

369. I. Cervesato, A. D. Jaggard, A. Scedrov, and C. Walstad. "Specifying Kerberos 5 Cross-Realm Authentication," *Proceedings of the 2005 Workshop on Issues in the Theory of Security* pp. 12–26 (Jan. 2005).

370. D. W. Chadwick and G. Inman. "Attribute Aggregation in Federated Identity Management," *IEEE Computer* **42**(5) pp. 33–40 (May 2009).

371. A. Chakrabarti, A. Damodaran, and S. Sengupta. "Grid Computing Security: A Taxonomy," *IEEE Security & Privacy* **6**(1) pp. 44–51 (Jan. 2008).

372. L. S. Chalmers. "An Analysis of the Differences Between the Computer Security Practices in the Military and Private Sectors," *Proceedings of the 1984 IEEE Symposium on Security and Privacy* pp. 71–74 (Apr. 1984).

373. J. T. Chambers and J. W. Thompson. *Vulnerability Disclosure Framework*, Final Report and Recommendations by the Council, National Infrastructure Advisory Council (Jan. 2004).

374. E. Chan, S. Venkataraman, F. David, A. Chaugule, and R. Campbell. "Forenscope: A Framework for Live Forensics," *Proceedings of the 26th Annual Computer Security Applications Conference* pp. 307–316 (Dec. 2010).

375. H. C. Chan, C. Ying, and C. B. Peh. "Strategies and Visualization Tools for Enhancing User Auditing of Spreadsheet Models," *Information and Software Technology* **42**(15) pp. 1037–1043 (Dec. 2000).

376. R. Chandia, J. Gonzalez, T. Kilpatrick, M. Papa, and S. Shenoi. "Critical Infrastructure Protection," Chapter 9, "Security Strategies for SCADA Networks" in *Critical Infrastructure Protection*, edited by E. Goetz and S. Shenoi (*IFIP Advances in Information and Communication Technology* **253**), Springer, Boston, MA, USA pp. 117–131 (2008).

377. V. Chandola, A. Banerjee, and V. Kumar. "Anomaly Detection: A Survey," *ACM Computing Surveys* pp. 15:1–15:58 (July 2009).

378. D. Chandra and M. Franz. "Fine-Grained Information Flow Analysis and Enforcement in a Java Virtual Machine," *Proceedings of the 23rd Annual Computer Security Applications Conference* pp. 463–474 (Dec. 2007).

379. R. Chandramouli. "Implementation of Multiple Access Control Policies Within a CORBASEC Framework," *Proceedings of the 22nd National Information Systems Security Conference* pp. 112–130 (Oct. 1999).

380. K. M. Chandy and L. Lamport. "Distributed Snapshots: Determining Global States of Distributed Systems," *ACM Transactions on Computer Systems* **3**(1) pp. 63–75 (Feb. 1985).

381. D. Chang, S. Hines, P. West, G. Tyson, and D. Whalley. "Program Differentiation," *Proceedings of the 2010 Workshop on Interaction Between Compilers and Computer Architecture* pp. 9:1–9:8 (2010).

382. R. K. C. Chang. "Defending Against Flooding-Based Distributed Denial-of-Service Attacks: A Tutorial," *IEEE Communications Magazine* **40**(10) pp. 42–51 (Oct. 2002).

383. K. Channakeshava, D. Chafekar, K. Bisset, V. S. A. Kumar, and M. Marathe. "EpiNet: A Simulation Framework to Study the Spread of Malware in Wireless Networks," *Proceedings of the Second International Conference on Simulation Tools and Techniques* pp. 6:1–6:10 (Mar. 2009).

384. P. C. Chapin, C. Skalka, and X. S. Wang. "Authorization in Trust Management: Features and Foundations," *ACM Computing Surveys* **40**(3) pp. 9:1–9:48 (Aug. 2008).

385. E. C. Charles, D. A. Diodati, and W. J. Mozdzierz. "Trusted Systems: Applying the Theory in a Commercial Firm," *Proceedings of the 16th National Computer Security Conference* pp. 283–291 (Sep. 1993).

386. D. Chaum. "Security Without Identification: Transaction Systems to Make Big Brother Obsolete," *Communications of the ACM* **28**(10) pp. 1030–1044 (Oct. 1985).

387. D. Chaum. "The Dining Cryptographers Problem: Unconditional Sender and Recipient Untraceability," *Journal of Cryptology* **1**(1) pp. 65–75 (1988).

388. D. Chaum. "Online Cash Checks," *Advances in Cryptology — EUROCRYPT '89* (*Lecture Notes in Computer Science* **434**) pp. 288–293 (Apr. 1990).

389. D. Chaum. "Secret-Ballot Receipts: True Voter-Verifiable Elections," *IEEE Security & Privacy* **2**(1) pp. 38–47 (Jan. 2004).

390. D. Chaum, R. T. Carback, J. Clark, A. Essex, S. Popoveniuc, R. L. Rivest, P. Y. Ryan, E. Shen, A. T. Sherman, and P. L. Vora. "Scantegrity II: End-to-End Verifiability by Voters of Optical Scan Elections Through Confirmation Codes," *IEEE Transactions on Information Forensics and Security* **4**(4) pp. 611–627 (Dec. 2009).

391. D. Chaum, R. T. Carback, J. Clark, A. Essex, S. Popoveniuc, R. L. Rivest, P. Y. Ryan, E. Shen, A. T. Sherman, and P. L. Vora. "Corrections to 'Scantegrity II: End-to-End Verifiability by Voters of Optical Scan Elections Through Confirmation Codes," *IEEE Transactions on Information Forensics and Security* **5**(1) p. 194 (Mar. 2010).

392. D. Chaum, B. den Boer, E. van Heyst, S. Mjølsnes, and A. Steenbeek. "Efficient Offline Electronic Checks (Extended Astract)," *Advances in Cryptology — EUROCRYPT '89* (*Lecture Notes in Computer Science* **434**) pp. 294–301 (Apr. 1990).

393. D. L. Chaum. "Untraceable Electronic Mail, Return Addresses, and Digital Pseudonyms," *Communications of the ACM* **24**(2) pp. 84–90 (Feb. 1981).

394. S. Checkoway, D. McCoy, B. Kantor, D. Anderson, H. Shacham, S. Savage, K. Koscher, A. Czeskis, F. Roesner, and T. Kohno. "Comprehensive Experimental Analyses of Automotive Attack Surfaces," *Proceedings of the 20th USENIX Security Symposium* (Aug. 2011).

395. M. H. Cheheyl, M. Gasser, G. A. Huff, and J. K. Millen. "Verifying Security," *ACM Computing Surveys* **13**(3) pp. 279–339 (Sep. 1981).

396. B. Chen and V. Chandran. "Biometric Based Cryptographic Key Generation from Faces," *Proceedings of the Ninth Biennial Conference of the Australian Pattern Recognition Society on Digital Image Computing Techniques and Applications* pp. 394–401 (Dec. 2007).

397. F. Chen, A. X. Liu, J. Hwang, and T. Xie. "First Step Towards Automatic Correction of Firewall Policy Faults," *ACM Transactions on Autonomous and Adaptive Systems* **7**(2) pp. 27:1–27:24 (July 2012).

398. H. Chen, T. Kim, X. Wang, N. Zeldovich, and M. F. Kaashoek. "Identifying Information Disclosure in Web Applications with Retroactive Auditing," *Proceedings of the 11th USENIX Symposium on Operating Systems Design and Implementation* (Oct. 2014).

399. L.-C. Chen, T. A. Longstaff, and K. M. Carley. "Characterization of Defense Mechanisms Against Distributed Denial of Service Attacks," *Computers & Security* **23**(8) pp. 665–678 (Dec. 2004).

400. X. Chen, J. Andersen, Z. M. Mao, M. Bailey, and J. Nazario. "Towards an Understanding of Anti-Virtualization and Anti-Debugging Behavior in Modern Malware," *Proceedings of the 2008 IEEE International Conference on Dependable Systems and Networks* pp. 177–186 (June 2008).

401. D. R. Cheriton and K. J. Duda. "A Caching Model of Operating System Kernel Functionality," *Proceedings of the First USENIX Symposium on Operating Systems Design and Implementation* pp. 14:1–14:15 (Nov. 1994).

402. B. Cheswick. "An Evening with Berferd, in Which a Cracker Is Lured, Endured, and Studied," *Proceedings of the 1992 Winter USENIX Conference* pp. 163–174 (Jan. 1992).

403. W. R. Cheswick, S. M. Bellovin, and A. D. Rubin. *Firewalls and Internet Security: Repelling the Wily Hacker*, Addison-Wesley, Boston, MA, USA (Mar. 2003).

404. S. Chiasson and P. C. van Oorschot. "Quantifying the Security Advantage of Password Expiration Policies," *Designs, Codes and Cryptography* **77**(2) pp. 401–408 (Dec. 2015).

405. E. Chien. *Techniques of Adware and Spyware*, White Paper, Symantec, Inc., Cupertino, CA, USA (2005).

406. T.-C. Chiueh and F.-H. Hsu. "RAD: A Compile-Time Solution to Buffer Overflow Attacks," *Proceedings of the 21st International Conference on Distributed Computing Systems* (*ICDCS '01*) pp. 409–417 (Apr. 2001).

407. T.-c. Chiueh, H. Sankaran, and A. Neogi. "Spout: A Transparent Proxy for Safe Execution of Java Applets," *IEEE Journal on Selected Areas in Communication* **20**(7) pp. 1426–1433 (Sep. 2002).

408. S. Chokhani. "Trusted Products Evaluation," *Communications of the ACM* **35**(7) pp. 64–76 (July 1992).

409. L. Cholvy and F. Cuppens. "Analyzing Consistency of Security Policies," *Proceedings of the 1997 IEEE Symposium on Security and Privacy* pp. 103–112 (May 1997).

410. S. Chong and A. C. Myers. "End-to-End Enforcement of Erasure and Declassification," *Proceedings of the 21st Computer Security Foundations Workshop* pp. 98–111 (June 2008).

411. N. Choucri. *Cyberpolitics in International Relations*, MIT Press, Cambridge, MA, USA (2012).

412. N. Choucri and D. D. Clark. *Integrating Cyberspace and International Relations: The Co-Evolution Dilemma*, Research Paper 2012-29, Political Science Department, Massachusetts Institute of Technology, Cambridge, MA, USA (Nov. 2012).

413. S. Choudhury. *Public Key Infrastructure Implementation and Design*, John Wiley & Sons, Inc., New York, NY, USA (2002).

414. S. Christey. *2011 CWE/SANS Top 25 Most Dangerous Software Errors* (Sep. 13, 2011).

415. T. Christiansen, B. D. Foy, L. Wall, and J. Orwant. *Programming Perl*, O'Reilly Media, Sebastopol, CA, USA (Feb. 2012).

416. Y.-H. Chu, J. Feigenbaum, B. LaMacchia, P. Resnick, and M. Strauss. "REFEREE: Trust Management for Web Applications," *Computer Networks and ISDN Systems* **29**(8–13) pp. 953–964 (Sep. 1997).

417. R. Chugh, J. A. Meister, R. Jhala, and S. Lerner. "Staged Information Flow for Javascript," *Proceedings of the 30th ACM SIGPLAN Conference on Programming Language Design and Implementation* pp. 50–62 (June 2009).

418. A. Chuvakin. *An Overview of Unix Rootkits*, iAlert White Paper, iDefense Labs, Chantilly, VA, USA (Feb. 2003).

419. P. Cichonski, T. Millar, T. Grance, and K. Scarfone. *Computer Security Incident Handling Guide*, Special Publication 800-61 Revision 2, National Institute of Standards and Technology, Gaithersburg, MD, USA (Aug. 2012).

420. Cisco. *Sendmail Nested MIME Message Denial of Service Vulnerability* (June 2006).

421. A. J. Clark. "Key Recovery—Why, How, Who?" *Computers & Security* **16**(8) pp. 669–674 (1997).

422. D. D. Clark and S. Landau. "Untangling Attribution," *Harvard National Security Journal* **2**(2) pp. 323–352 (2011).

423. D. D. Clark and D. R. Wilson. "A Comparison of Commercial and Military Computer Security Policies," *Proceedings of the 1987 IEEE Symposium on Security and Privacy* pp. 184–194 (Apr. 1987).

424. D. Clarke, J.-E. Elien, C. Ellison, M. Fredette, A. Morcos, and R. L. Rivest. "Certificate Chain Discovery in SPKI/SDSI," *Journal of Computer Security* **9**(4) pp. 285–322 (2001).

425. E. M. Clarke, E. A. Emerson, and A. P. Sistla. "Automatic Verification of Finite-State Concurrent Systems Using Temporal Logic Specifications," *ACM Transactions on Programming Languages and Systems* **8**(2) pp. 244–263 (Apr. 1986).

426. E. M. Clarke, S. Jha, and W. Marrero. "Using State Space Exploration and a Natural Deduction Style Message Derivation Engine to Verify Security Protocols," *Proceedings of the IFIP TC2 / WG2.2, 2.3 International Conference on Programming Concepts and Methods* pp. 87–106 (June 1998).

427. R. Clarke and T. Youngstein. "Cyberattack on Britain's National Health Service — A Wake-up Call for Modern Medicine," *The New England Journal of Medicine* **377** pp. 409–411 (June 2017).

428. M. R. Clarkson and F. B. Schneider. "Hyperproperties," *Journal of Computer Security* **18**(6) pp. 1157–1210 (2010).

429. W. F. Clocksin and C. S. Mellish. *Programming in Prolog*, Springer-Verlag, Berlin, Germany (2003).

430. C. Cocks. "An Identity Based Encryption Scheme Based on Quadratic Residues," *Proceedings of the Eighth IMA International Conference on Cryptography and Coding* (*Lecture Notes in Computer Science* **2260**) pp. 360–363 (Dec. 2001).

431. T. Coe and P. T. P. Tang. "It Takes Six Ones to Reach a Flaw," *Proceedings of the 12th Symposium on Computer Arithmetic* pp. 140–146 (July 1995).

432. D. Cofer and S. P. Miller. *Formal Methods Case Studies for DO-333*, Technical Report NASA/CR-2014-218244, National Aeronautics and Space Administration Langley Research Center, Hampton, VA, USA (Apr. 2014).

433. E. Cohen and D. Jefferson. "Protection in the Hydra Operating System," *Proceedings of the Fifth ACM Symposium on Operating Systems Principles* pp. 141–160 (Nov. 1975).

434. E. Cohen, R. K. Thomas, W. Winsborough, and D. Shands. "Models for Coalition-Based Access Control (CBAC)," *Proceedings of the Seventh ACM Symposium on Access Control Models and Technologies* pp. 97–106 (June 2002).

435. F. Cohen. "Computer Viruses: Theory and Experiments," *Proceedings of the Seventh National Computer Security Conference* pp. 240–255 (Sep. 1984).

436. F. Cohen. "Computer Viruses: Theory and Experiments," *Computers & Security* **6**(1) pp. 22–35 (Feb. 1987).

437. F. Cohen. "Computational Aspects of Computer Viruses," *Computers & Security* **8**(4) pp. 325–344 (June 1989).

438. F. Cohen. "Models of Practical Defenses Against Computer Viruses," *Computers & Security* **8**(2) pp. 149–160 (Apr. 1989).

439. F. Cohen. "A Note on the Role of Deception in Information Protection," *Computers & Security* **17**(6) pp. 483–506 (Nov. 1998).

440. H. Cohen, G. Frey, R. Avanzi, C. Doche, T. Lange, K. Nguyen, and F. Vercauteren. *Handbook of Elliptic and Hyperelliptic Curve Cryptography*, Chapman and Hall/CRC, Boca Raton, FL, USA (2005).

441. K. Cohn-Gordon, C. Cremers, B. Dowling, L. Garratt, and D. Stebila. "A Formal Security Analysis of the Signal Messaging Protocol," *Proceedings of the 2017 IEEE European Symposium on Security and Privacy* pp. 451–466 (Apr. 2017).

442. E. Cole. *Online Danger: How to Protect Yourself and Your Loved Ones from the Evil Side of the Internet*, Morgan James Publishing, New York, NY, USA (2018).

443. M. S. Collins. *Network Security Through Data Analysis: Building Situational Awareness*, O'Reilly Media, Inc., Sebastopol, CA, USA (2014).

444. S. Collins and S. McCombie. "Stuxnet: The Emergence of a New Cyber Weapon and Its Implications," *Journal of Policing, Intelligence and Counter Terrorism* **7**(1) pp. 80–91 (Apr. 2012).

445. T. Combe, A. Martin, and R. Di Pietro. "To Docker or Not to Docker: A Security Perspective," *IEEE Cloud Computing* **3**(5) pp. 54–62 (Sep. 2016).

446. Comodo Group, Inc. *Comodo Fraud Incident March 23, 2011* (Mar. 2011).

447. K. Conlan, I. Baggili, and F. Breitinger. "Anti-Forensics: Furthering Digital Forensic Science Through a New Extended, Granular Taxonomy," *Digital Investigation* **18S** pp. S66–S75 (Aug. 2016).

448. J. R. Conrad, J. Alves-Foss, and S. S. Lee. "Analyzing Uncertainty in TG Protection Graphs with TG/MC," *Journal of Computer Security* **18**(5) pp. 667–699 (2010).

449. L. Constantin. "Attackers Hijack CCTV Cameras to Launch DDoS Attacks," *Computerworld* (Oct. 22, 2015).

450. G. Conti, K. Abdullah, J. Grizzard, J. Stasko, J. A. Copeland, M. Ahamad, H. L. Owen, and C. Lee. "Countering Security Information Overload Through Alert and Packet Visualization," *IEEE Computer Graphics and Applications* **26**(2) pp. 60–70 (Mar. 2006).

451. S. Contini and Y. L. Yin. "Forgery and Partial Key-Recovery Attacks on HMAC and NMAC Using Hash Collisions," *Advances in Cryptology — ASIACRYPT 2006* (*Lecture Notes in Computer Science* **4284**) pp. 37–53 (Dec. 2006).

452. S. Convery. *Network Security Architectures*, Cisco Press, Indianapolis, IN, USA (2004).

453. R. W. Conway, W. L. Maxwell, and H. L. Morgan. "On the Implementation of Security Measures in Information Systems," *Communications of the ACM* **15**(4) pp. 211–220 (Apr. 1972).

454. E. Cooke, F. Jahanian, and D. McPherson. "The Zombie Roundup: Understanding, Detecting, and Disrupting Botnets," *Proceedings of the Workshop on Steps to Reducing Unwanted Traffic on the Internet* pp. 39–44 (July 2005).

455. C. H. Coombs, R. M. Dawes, and A. Tversky. *Mathematical Psychology: An Elementary Introduction*, Prentice Hall, Inc, Englewood Cliffs, NJ, USA (1970).

456. D. A. Cooper. "A Model of Certificate Revocation," *Proceedings of the 15th Annual Computer Security Applications Conference* pp. 256–264 (Dec. 1999).

457. D. Cooper, S. Santesson, S. Farrell, S. Boeyen, R. Housley, and T. Polk. *Internet X.509 Public Key Infrastructure Certificate and Certificate Revocation List (CRL) Profile*, RFC 5280 (May 2008).

458. B. Copos. "Modeling Systems Using Side Channel Information," Ph.D. Dissertation, Department of Computer Science, University of California at Davis, Davis, CA, USA (2017).

459. D. Coppersmith. "The Data Encryption Standard (DES) and Its Strength Against Attacks," *IBM Journal of Research and Development* **38**(3) pp. 243–250 (May 1994).

460. D. Coppersmith, S. Halevi, and C. Jutla. "Cryptanalysis of Stream Ciphers with Linear Masking," *Advances in Cryptology — CRYPTO 2002* (*Lecture Notes in Computer Science* **2442**) pp. 117–128 (Aug. 2002).

461. F. J. Corbató and V. A. Vyssotsky. "Introduction and Overview of the Multics System," *Proceedings of the AFIPS '65 Fall Joint Computer Conference* pp. 185–196 (Nov. 1965).

462. O. L. Costich and I. S. Moskowita. "Analysis of a Storage Channel in the Two Phase Commit Protocol," *Proceedings of the Fourth Computer Security Foundations Workshop* pp. 201–208 (June 1991).

463. D. Cotroneo, A. Lanzaro, R. Natella, and R. Barbosa. "Experimental Analysis of Binary-Level Software Fault Injection in Complex Software," *Proceedings of the Ninth European Dependable Computing Conference* pp. 162–172 (May 2012).

464. D. Cotroneo and R. Natella. "Fault Injection for Software Certification," *IEEE Security & Privacy* **11**(4) pp. 38–45 (July 2013).

465. S. E. Coull, C. V. Wright, A. D. Keromytis, F. Monrose, and M. K. Reiter. "Taming the Devil: Techniques for Evaluating Anonymized Network Data," *Proceedings of the 2008 Symposium on Network and Distributed System Security* (Feb. 2008).

466. S. E. Coull, C. V. Wright, F. Monrose, M. P. Collins, and M. K. Reiter. "Playing Devil's Advocate: Inferring Sensitive Information from Anonymized Network Traces," *Proceedings of the 2007 Symposium on Network and Distributed System Security* (Feb. 2007).

467. C. Cowan, S. Beattie, J. Johansen, and P. Wagle. "PointGuard™: Protecting Pointers from Buffer Overflow Vulnerabilities," *Proceedings of the 12th USENIX Security Symposium* pp. 91–104 (Aug. 2003).

468. C. Cowan, S. Beattie, G. Kroah-Hartman, C. Pu, P. Wagle, and V. Gligor. "SubDomain: Parsimonious Server Security," *Proceedings of the 14th USENIX Systems Administration Conference* pp. 341–354 (Dec. 2000).

469. C. Cowan, C. Pu, D. Maier, J. Walpole, P. Bakke, S. Beattie, A. Grier, P. Wagle, Q. Zhang, and H. Hinton. "StackGuard: Automatic Adaptive Detection and Prevention of Buffer-Overflow Attacks," *Proceedings of the Seventh USENIX UNIX Security Symposium* pp. 63–77 (Jan. 1998).

470. C. Cowan, P. Wagle, C. Pu, S. Beattie, and J. Walpole. "Buffer Overflows: Attacks and Defenses for the Vulnerability of the Decade," *Proceedings of the Foundations of Intrusion Tolerant Systems (OASIS '03)* pp. 227-237 (Dec. 2003).

471. K. J. Cox and C. Gerg. *Managing Security with Snort and IDS Tools*, O'Reilly Media, Inc., Sebastopol, CA, USA (2004).

472. E. J. Coyne. "Role Engineering," *Proceedings of the First ACM Workshop on Role-Based Access Control* pp. I:15–I:16 (Dec. 1996).

473. M. Crabb. "Password Security in a Large Distributed Environment," *Proceedings of the Second UNIX Security Workshop* pp. 17–30 (Aug. 1990).

474. J. Crampton. "Specifying and Enforcing Constraints in Role-Based Access Control," *Proceedings of the Eighth ACM Symposium on Access Control Models and Technologies* pp. 43–50 (2003).

475. R. Crawford, M. Bishop, B. Bhumiratana, L. Clark, and K. Levitt. "Sanitization Models and Their Limitations," *Proceedings of the 2006 Workshop on New Security Paradigms* pp. 41–56 (Sep. 2006).

476. C. Cremers, M. Horvat, S. Scott, and T. van der Merwe. "Automated Analysis and Verification of TLS 1.3: 0-RTT, Resumption and Delayed Authentication," *Proceedings of the 2016 IEEE Symposium on Security and Privacy* pp. 470–485 (May 2016).

477. D. H. Crocker. *Standard for the Format of ARPA Internet Text Messages*, RFC 822 (Aug. 1982).

478. S. Crocker and M. Pozzo. "A Proposal for a Verification-Based Virus Filter," *Proceedings of the 1989 IEEE Symposium on Security and Privacy* pp. 319–324 (May 1989).

479. M. Crosbie and E. H. Spafford. "Defending a Computer System Using Autonomous Agents," *Proceedings of the 18th National Computer Security Conference* pp. 549–558 (Oct. 1995).

480. S. A. Crosby and D. S. Wallach. "Efficient Data Structures for Tamper-Evident Logging," *Proceedings of the 18th USENIX Security Symposium* (Aug. 2009).

481. J. Crow, S. Owre, J. Rushby, N. Shankar, and M. Srivas. *A Tutorial Introduction to PVS*, Technical Report, SRI International, Menlo Park, CA, USA (June 1995).

482. J. A. Cugini, R. W. Dobry, V. D. Gligor, and T. Mayfield. "Functional Security Criteria for Distributed Systems," *Proceedings of the 18th National Computer Security Conference* pp. 310–321 (Oct. 1995).

483. P. T. Cummings, D. A. Fullam, M. J. Goldstein, M. J. Gosselin, J. Picciotto, J. P. L. Woodward, and J. Wynn. "Compartmented Mode Workstation: Results Through Prototyping," *Proceedings of the 1987 IEEE Symposium on Security and Privacy* pp. 2–12 (Apr. 1987).

484. C. Curtsinger, B. Livshits, B. Zorn, and C. Seifert. "ZOZZLE: Fast and Precise In-Browser JavaScript Malware Detection," *Proceedings of the 20th USENIX Security Symposium* (Aug. 2011).

485. T. W. Cusick and M. C. Wood. "The Redoc-II Cryptosystem," *Advances in Cryptology – CRYPTO '90* (*Lecture Notes in Computer Science* **537**) pp. 546–563 (Aug. 1991).

486. K. Cutler and F. Jones. *Commercial International Security Requirements*, Final Draft, American Express and Electronic Data Systems (Sep. 1991).

487. CVE. *Linux Kernel Stack Based Buffer Overflow Vulnerability*, CVE Entry CVE-2017-17806, The MITRE Corporation, Bedford, MA, USA (Feb. 2017).

488. M. Dacier and Y. Deswarte. "Privilege Graph: An Extension to the Typed Access Matrix Model," *Proceedings of the Third European Symposium on Research in Computer Security* pp. 319–334 (Nov. 1994).

489. M. Dacier, Y. Deswarte, and M. Kaâniche. *Quantitative Assessment of Operational Security: Models and Tools*, Research Report 96493, Laboratory for Analysis and Architecture of Systems, Toulouse, France (May 1996).

490. J. Daemen and V. Rijmen. *The Design of Rijndael: AES — The Advanced Encryption Standard*, Springer-Verlag, Berlin, Germany (Mar. 2002).

491. J. Daemen and G. Van Assche. "Differential Propagation Analysis of Keccak," *Proceedings of the 19th International Workshop on Fast Software Encryption* (*Lecture Notes in Computer Science* **7549**) pp. 422–441 (Mar. 2012).

492. D. Dagon, G. Gu, C. P. Lee, and W. Lee. "A Taxonomy of Botnet Structures," *Proceedings of the 23rd Annual Computer Security Applications Conference* pp. 325–338 (Dec. 2007).

493. D. Dagon, N. Provos, C. P. Lee, and W. Lee. "Corrupted DNS Resolution Paths: The Rise of a Malicious Resolution Authority," *Proceedings of the 2008 Symposium on Network and Distributed System Security* (Feb. 2008).

494. T. Dalenius. "Finding a Needle in a Haystack or Identifying Anonymous Census Records," *Journal of Official Statistics* **2**(3) pp. 329–336 (Sep. 1986).

495. M. Dalton, H. Kannan, and C. Kozyrakis. "Raksha: A Flexible Information Flow Architecture for Software Security," *Proceedings of the 34th Annual International Symposium on Computer Architecture* pp. 482–493 (June 2007).

496. N. Damianou, N. Dulay, E. Lupu, and M. Sloman. "The Ponder Policy Specification Language," *Proceedings of the 2001 International Workshop on Policies for Distributed Systems and Networks* (*Lecture Notes in Computer Science* **1995**) pp. 18–38 (Jan. 2001).

497. G. Danezis, R. Dingledine, and N. Mathewson. "Mixminion: Design of a Type III Anonymous Remailer Protocol," *Proceedings of the 2003 IEEE Symposium on Security and Privacy* pp. 2–15 (May 2003).

498. T. E. Daniels and E. H. Spafford. "Identification of Host Audit Data to Detect Attacks on Low-Level IP Vulnerabilities," *Journal of Computer Security* **7**(1) pp. 3–35 (1999).

499. E. Dart, L. Rotman, B. Tierney, M. Hester, and J. Zurawski. "The Science DMZ: A Network Design Pattern for Data-Intensive Science," *Proceedings of the 2013 International Conference on High Performance Computing, Networking, Storage and Analysis* pp. 85:1–85:10 (Nov. 2013).

500. E. Dart, L. Rotman, B. Tierney, M. Hester, and J. Zurawski. "The Science DMZ: A Network Design Pattern for Data-Intensive Science," *Scientific Programming* **22**(2) pp. 173–185 (2014).

501. S. Das, T. H.-J. Kim, L. A. Dabbish, and J. I. Hong. "The Effect of Social Influence on Security Sensitivity," *Proceedings of the Tenth Symposium on Usable Privacy and Security* pp. 143–157 (July 2014).

502. S. Das, A. D. Kramer, L. A. Dabbish, and J. I. Hong. "Increasing Security Sensitivity with Social Proof: A Large-Scale Experimental Confirmation," *Proceedings of the 21st ACM SIGSAC Conference on Computer and Communications Security* pp. 739–749 (Nov. 2014).

503. J. G. Daughman. "High Confidence Visual Recognition of Persons by a Test of Statistical Independence," *IEEE Transactions on Pattern Analysis and Machine Intelligence* **15**(11) pp. 1148–1161 (Nov. 1993).

504. J. G. Daughman. "How Iris Recognition Works," *IEEE Transactions on Circuits and Systems for Video Technology* **14**(1) pp. 21–30 (Jan. 2004).

505. J. David. "Progress and Problems in Declassifying U. S. Government Records," *Journal of Government Information* **30**(4) pp. 443–450 (2004).

506. J. David. "What Should Nations Reveal About Their Spying from Space? An Examination of the US Experience," *Space Policy* **25**(2) pp. 117–127 (May 2009).

507. G. I. Davida, Y. Frankel, and B. J. Matt. "On Enabling Secure Applications Through Offline Biometric Identification," *Proceedings of the 1998 IEEE Symposium on Security and Privacy* pp. 148–157 (May 1998).

508. G. Davida and B. J. Matt. "UNIX Guardians: Delegating Security to the User," *Proceedings of the UNIX Security Workshop* pp. 14–23 (Aug. 1988).

509. Y. G. Davida, George I. amd Desmedt and B. J. Matt. "Defending Systems Against Viruses Through Cryptographic Authentication," *Proceedings of the 1989 IEEE Symposium on Security and Privacy* pp. 312–318 (May 1989).

510. D. Davies. "Defective Sign & Encrypt in S/MIME, PKCS#7, MOSS, PEM, PGP, and XML," *Proceedings of the 2001 USENIX Annual Technical Conference* (June 2001).

511. D. Davis, R. Ihaka, and P. Fenstermacher. "Cryptographic Randomness from Air Turbulence in Disk Drives," *Advances in Cryptology — CRYPTO '94* (*Lecture Notes in Computer Science* **839**) pp. 114–120 (Aug. 1994).

512. J. Davis, J. MacLean, and D. Dampier. "Methods of Information Hiding and Detection in File Systems," *Proceedings of the Fifth International Workshop on Systematic Approaches to Digital Forensic Engineering* pp. 66–69 (May 2010).

513. M. Davis and M. Suignard. *Unicode Security Considerations*, Technical Report 36, Unicode Consortium (Sep. 2014).

514. A. M. de Alvaré and E. E. Schultz. "A Framework for Password Selection," *Proceedings of the UNIX Security Workshop* pp. 8–9 (Aug. 1988).

515. R. de Beer, A. Stander, and J.-P. Van Belle. "Anti-Forensics: A Practitioner Perspective," *International Journal of Cyber-Security and Digital Forensics* **4**(2) pp. 390–403 (Jan. 2015).

516. C. De Cannière, F. Mendel, and C. Rechberger. "Collisions for 70-Step SHA-1: On the Full Cost of Collision Search," *Proceedings of the 14th International Workshop on Selected Areas in Cryptography* (*Lecture Notes in Computer Science* **4876**) pp. 56–73 (Aug. 2007).

517. W. De Groef, D. Devriese, N. Nikiforakis, and F. Piessens. "FlowFox: A Web Browser with Flexible and Precise Information Flow Control," *Proceedings of the 19th ACM SIGSAC Conference on Computer and Communications Security* pp. 748–759 (Oct. 2012).

518. A. De Luca, M. Denzel, and H. Hussmann. "Look Into My Eyes! Can You Guess My Password?" *Proceedings of the Fifth Symposium on Usable Privacy and Security* pp. 7:1–7:12 (July 2009).

519. A. De Luca, A. Hang, F. Brudy, C. Lindner, and H. Hussmann. "Touch Me Once and I Know It's You!: Implicit Authentication Based on Touch Screen Patterns," *Proceedings of the 2012 SIGCHI Conference on Human Factors in Computing Systems* pp. 987–996 (May 2012).

520. L. de Moura and N. Bjørner. "Z3: An Efficient SMT Solver," *Proceedings of the 14th Intenational Conference on Tools and Algorithms for the Construction and Analysis of Systems* (*Lecture Notes in Computer Science* **4963**) pp. 337-340 (Mar. 2008).

521. L. de Moura, B. Dutertre, and N. Shankar. "A Tutorial on Satisfiability Modulo Theories," *Proceedings of the 2007 International Conference on Computer Aided Verification* (*Lecture Notes in Computer Science* **4590**) pp. 20–36 (2007).

522. D. A. S. de Oliveira, J. R. Crandall, G. Wassermann, S. F. Wu, Z. Su, and F. T. Chong. "ExecRecorder: VM-Based Full-System Replay for Attack Analysis and System Recovery," *Proceedings of the First Workshop on Architectural and System Support for Improving Software Dependability* pp. 66–71 (Oct. 2006).

523. D. Dean, E. W. Felten, and D. S. Wallach. "Java Security: From HotJava to Netscape and Beyond," *Proceedings of the 1996 IEEE Symposium on Security and Privacy* pp. 190–200 (May 1996).

524. D. Dean, M. Franklin, and A. Stubblefield. "An Algebraic Approach to IP Traceback," *ACM Transactions on Information and System Security* **5**(2) pp. 119–127 (May 2002).

525. D. Dean and A. J. Hu. "Fixing Races for Fun and Profit: How to Use *access*(2)," *Proceedings of the 13th USENIX Security Symposium* (Aug. 2004).

526. W. H. Debany. "Modeling the Spread of Internet Worms via Persistently Unpatched Hosts," *IEEE Network* **22**(2) pp. 26–32 (Mar. 2008).

527. H. Debar, D. A. Curry, and B. S. Feinstein. *The Intrusion Detection Message Exchange Format (IDMEF)*, RFC 4765 (Mar. 2007).

528. H. M. Deitel. *An Introduction to Operating Systems*, Addison-Wesley Longman Publishing Co., Inc., Reading, MA, USA (1984).

529. M. Dell' Amico, P. Michiardi, and Y. Roudier. "Password Strength: An Empirical Analysis," *Proceedings of 2010 IEEE INFOCOM* pp. 1–9 (Mar. 2010).

530. T. A. DeLong, D. T. Smit, and B. W. Johnson. "Dependability Metrics to Assess Safety-Critical Systems," *IEEE Transactions on Reliability* **54**(3) pp. 498–505 (Sep. 2005).

531. R. A. DeMillo, D. P. Dobkin, A. K. Jones, and R. J. Lipton (*ed*). *Foundations of Secure Computation*, Academic Press, New York, NY, USA (1978).

532. H. Demirci. "Square-Like Attacks on Reduced Rounds of IDEA," *Proceedings of the Ninth International Workshop on Selected Areas in Cryptography* (*Lecture Notes in Computer Science* **2595**) pp. 147–159 (Aug. 2002).

533. D. Denning. *Cryptography and Data Security*, Addison-Wesley Publishing Company, Reading, MA, USA (1982).

534. D. E. Denning. "A Lattice Model of Secure Information Flow," *Communications of the ACM* **19**(5) pp. 236–243 (May 1976).

535. D. E. Denning. *On the Derivation of Lattice Structured Information Flow Policies*, CSD TR 180, Department of Computer Sciences, Purdue University, West Lafayette, IN, USA (Mar. 1976).

536. D. E. Denning. "Secure Personal Computing in an Insecure Network," *Communications of the ACM* **22**(8) pp. 476–482 (Aug. 1979).

537. D. E. Denning. "An Intrusion-Detection Model," *IEEE Transactions on Software Engineering* **SE-3**(2) pp. 222–232 (Feb. 1987).

538. D. E. Denning. "The US Key Escrow Encryption Technology," *Computer Communications* **17**(7) pp. 453–457 (July 1994).

539. D. E. Denning. *Information Warfare and Security*, Addison-Wesley, Reading, MA, USA (1999).

540. D. E. Denning, S. K. Akl, M. Heckman, T. F. Lunt, M. Morgenstern, P. G. Neumann, and R. R. Schell. "Views for Multilevel Database Security," *IEEE Transactions on Software Engineering* **SE-13**(2) pp. 129–140 (Feb. 1987).

541. D. E. Denning and D. K. Branstad. "A Taxonomy for Key Escrow Encryption Systems," *Communications of the ACM* **39**(3) pp. 34–40 (Mar. 1996).

542. D. E. Denning and P. J. Denning. "Certification of Programs for Secure Information Flow," *Communications of the ACM* **20**(7) pp. 504–513 (July 1977).

543. D. E. Denning, T. F. Lunt, R. R. Schell, W. R. Shockley, and M. Heckman. "The SeaView Security Model," *Proceedings of the 1988 IEEE Symposium on Security and Privacy* pp. 218–233 (Apr. 1988).

544. D. E. Denning and P. F. MacDoran. "Location-Based Authentication: Grounding Cyberspace for Better Security," *Computer Fraud & Security* **1996**(2) pp. 12–16 (Feb. 1996).

545. D. E. Denning and G. M. Sacco. "Timestamps in Key Distribution Protocols," *Communications of the ACM* **24**(8) pp. 533–536 (Aug. 1981).

546. D. E. Denning and M. Smid. "Key Escrowing Today," *IEEE Communications Magazine* **32**(9) pp. 58–68 (Sep. 1994).

547. P. J. Denning. "Third Generation Computer Systems," *ACM Computing Surveys* **3**(4) pp. 175–216 (Dec. 1971).

548. P. J. Denning. "Fault Tolerant Operating Systems," *ACM Computing Surveys* **8**(4) pp. 359–389 (Dec. 1976).

549. P. J. Denning. "The Science of Computing: Computer Viruses," *American Scientist* **76**(3) pp. 236–238 (May 1988).

550. P. J. Denning (*ed*). *Computers Under Attack: Intruders, Worms, and Viruses*, Addison-Wesley, Reading, MA, USA (1990).

551. T. Denning, K. Fu, and T. Kohno. "Absence Makes the Heart Grow Fonder: New Directions for Implantable Medical Device Security," *Proceedings of the Third USENIX Workshop on Hot Topics in Security* (July 2008).

552. J. B. Dennis and E. C. Van Horn. "Programming Semantics for Multiprogrammed Computations," *Communications of the ACM* **9**(3) pp. 143–155 (Mar. 1966).

553. A. W. Dent. "A Brief Introduction to Certificateless Encryption Schemes and Their Infrastructures," *Proceedings of the Sixth European Workshop on Public Key Infrastructures, Services and Applications* (*Lecture Notes in Computer Science* **6391**) pp. 1–16 (Sep. 2009).

554. S. Designer. "Getting Around Non-Executable Stack (and Fix)," *Bugtraq Mailing List* (Aug. 1997).

555. A. Dewald, T. Holz, and F. C. Freiling. "ADSandbox: Sandboxing JavaScript to Fight Malicious Websites," *Proceedings of the 2010 ACM Symposium on Applied Computing* pp. 1859–1864 (Mar. 2010).

556. A. K. Dewdney. "Computer Recreations: A Core War Bestiary of Viruses, Worms and Other Threats to Computer Memories," *Scientific American* **252**(3) pp. 14–23 (Oct. 1985).

557. P. A. DeWinstanley and E. L. Bjork. "Processing Strategies and the Generation Effect: Implications for Making a Better Reader," *Memory & Cognition* **32**(6) pp. 945–955 (Sep. 2004).

558. P. D'Haeseleer, S. Forrest, and P. Helman. "An Immunological Approach to Change Detection: Algorithms, Analysis and Implications," *Proceedings of the 1996 IEEE Symposium on Security and Privacy* pp. 110–119 (May 1996).

559. N. Dhanjani, B. Rios, and B. Hardin. *Hacking: The Next Generation*, O'Reilly Media, Inc., Sebastopol, CA, USA (2009).

560. M. Dhawan and V. Ganapathy. "Analyzing Information Flow in JavaScript-Based Browser Extensions," *Proceedings of the 25th Annual Computer Security Applications Conference* pp. 382–391 (Dec. 2009).

561. B. L. Di Vito, P. H. Palmquist, E. A. Anderson, and M. L. Johnston. "Specification and Verification of the ASOS Kernel," *Proceedings of the 1990 IEEE Symposium on Research in Security and Privacy* pp. 61–74 (May 1990).

562. U. Dieckmann, P. Plankensteiner, and T. Wagner. "SESAM: A Biometric Person Identification System Using Sensor Fusion," *Pattern Recognition Letters* **18**(9) pp. 827–833 (Sep. 1997).

563. T. Dierks and E. Rescorla. *The Transport Layer Security (TLS) Protocol Version 1.2*, RFC 5246 (Aug. 2008).

564. W. Diffie and M. Hellman. "New Directions in Cryptography," *IEEE Transactions on Information Theory* **IT-22**(6) pp. 644–654 (Nov. 1976).

565. W. Diffie and M. E. Hellman. "Exhaustive Cryptanalysis of the NBS Data Encryption Standard," *IEEE Computer* **10**(6) pp. 74–84 (June 1977).

566. E. W. Dijkstra. "The Structure of the 'THE'-Multiprogramming System," *Communications of the ACM* **11**(5) pp. 341–346 (May 1968).

567. A. Diller. *Z: An Introduction to Formal Methods*, John Wiley & Sons, Inc., New York, NY, USA (1994).

568. R. Dilmaghani, S. Geyik, K. Grueneberg, J. Lobo, S. Y. Shah, B. K. Szymanski, and P. Zerfos. "Policy-Aware Service Composition in Sensor Networks," *Proceedings of the Ninth International Workshop on Services Computing* pp. 186–193 (June 2012).

569. T. Dimkov, A. van Cleeff, W. Pieters, and P. Hartel. "Two Methodologies for Physical Penetration Testing Using Social Engineering," *Proceedings of the 26th Annual Computer Security Applications Conference* pp. 399–408 (Dec. 2010).

570. R. Dingledine, N. Mathewson, and P. Syverson. "Tor: The Second-Generation Onion Router," *Proceedings of the 13th USENIX Security Symposium* pp. 303–320 (Aug. 2004).

571. I. Dinur, O. Dunkelman, and A. Shamir. "Collision Attacks on Up to 5 Rounds of SHA-3 Using Generalized Internal Differentials," *Proceedings of the 20th International Workshop on Fast Software Encryption* (*Lecture Notes in Computer Science* **8424**) pp. 219–240 (Mar. 2013).

572. L. C. Dion. "A Complete Protection Model," *Proceedings of the 1981 IEEE Symposium on Security and Privacy* pp. 49–55 (Apr. 1981).

573. H. Dobbertin. "The Status of MD5 After a Recent Attack," *RSA Laboratories' CryptoBytes* **2**(2) pp. 1–6 (Summer 1996).

574. H. Dobbertin. "Cryptanalysis of MD4," *Journal of Cryptology* **11**(4) pp. 253–271 (Sep. 1998).

575. H. Dobbertin, A. Bosselaers, and B. Preneel. "RIPEMD-160: A Strengthened Version of RIPEMD," *Proceedings of the Fourth International Workshop on Fast Software Encryption* (*Lecture Notes in Computer Science* **1039**) pp. 71–82 (Feb. 1996).

576. H. Dobbertin, L. Knudsen, and M. Robshaw. "The Cryptanalysis of the AES—A Brief Survey," *Fourth International Conference on the Advanced Encryption Standard: Revised Selected and Invited Papers* (*Lecture Notes in Computer Science* **3373**) pp. 1–10 (May 2004).

577. Y. Dodis, R. Ostrovsky, L. Reyzin, and A. Smith. "Fuzzy Extractors: How to Generate Strong Keys from Biometrics and Other Noisy Data," *SIAM Journal on Computing* **38**(7) pp. 97–139 (2008).

578. T. W. Doeppner, P. N. Klein, and A. Koyfman. "Using Router Stamping to Identify the Source of IP Packets," *Proceedings of the Seventh ACM Conference on Computer and Communications Security* pp. 184–189 (Nov. 2000).

579. B. Dole, S. Lodin, and E. Spafford. "Misplaced Trust: Kerberos 4 Session Keys," *Proceedings of the 1997 Symposium on Network and Distributed System Security* pp. 60–70 (Feb. 1997).

580. D. Dolev and A. C. Yao. "On the Security of Public Key Protocols," *IEEE Transactions on Information Theory* **29**(2) pp. 198–208 (Mar. 1983).

581. C. Domas. "Breaking the x86 ISA," *Blackhat* (Aug. 2017).

582. F. J. Donner. *The Un-Americans*, Ballantine Books, New York, NY, USA (1961).

583. N. Doraswamy and D. Harkins. *IPSec: The New Security Standard for the Internet, Intranets, and Vitrtual Private Networks*, Prentice Hall, Inc, Upper Saddle River, NJ, USA (2003).

584. B. Dowling, M. Fischlin, F. Günther, and D. Stebila. "A Cryptographic Analysis of the TLS 1.3 Handshake Protocol Candidates," *Proceedings of the 22nd ACM SIGSAC Conference on Computer and Communications Security* pp. 1197–1210 (Oct. 2015).

585. I. Downnard. "Public-Key Cryptography Extensions into Kerberos," *IEEE Potentials* **21**(5) pp. 30–34 (Dec. 2002).

586. D. D. Downs, J. R. Rub, K. C. Kung, and C. S. Jordan. "Issues in Discretionary Access Control," *Proceedings of the 1985 IEEE Symposium on Security and Privacy* pp. 208–218 (Apr. 1985).

587. M. Dowty and J. Sugerman. "GPU Virtualization on VMware's Hosted I/O Architecture," *ACM SIGOPS Operating Systems Review* **43**(3) pp. 73–82 (July 2009).

588. H. Dreger, C. Kreibich, V. Paxson, and R. Sommer. "Enhancing the Accuracy of Network-Based Intrusion Detection with Host-Based Context," *Proceedings of the Second International Conference on Detection of Intrusions and Malware, and Vulnerability Assessment* (*Lecture Notes in Computer Science* **3548**) pp. 206–221 (July 2005).

589. R. Droms. *Dynamic Host Configuration Protocol*, RFC 2131 (Mar. 1997).

590. R. Droms, J. Bound, B. Volz, T. Lemon, C. E. Perkins, and M. Carney. *Dynamic Host Configuration Protocol for IPv6 (DHCPv6)*, RFC 3315 (July 2003).

591. R. Dua, A. R. Raja, and D. Kakadia. "Virtualization vs. Containerization to Support PaaS," *Proceedings of the 2014 IEEE International Conference on Cloud Engineering* pp. 610–614 (Mar. 2014).

592. B. Duc, E. S. Biglün, J. Bigün, G. Maître, and S. Fischer. "Fusion of Audio and Video Information for Multi Modal Person Authentication," *Pattern Recognition Letters* **18**(9) pp. 835–843 (Sep. 1997).

593. T. Duff. "Experiences with Viruses on UNIX Systems," *Computing Systems* **2**(2) pp. 155–171 (Spring 1989).

594. E. Duffy, S. Nyemba, C. A. Gunter, D. Liebovitz, and B. Malin. "Requirements and Design for an Extensible Toolkit for Analyzing EMR Audit Logs," *Proceedings of the 2013 USENIX Workshop on Health Information Technologies* (Aug. 2013).

595. C. W. Dukes. *Committee on National Security Systems (CNSS) Glossary*, Technical Report CNSSI No. 4009, Committee on National Security Systems, National Security Agency, Ft. George G. Meade, MD, USA (Apr. 2015).

596. O. Dunkelman, N. Keller, and A. Shamir. "Improved Single-Key Attacks on 8-Round AES-192 and AES-256," *Advances in Cryptology — ASIACRYPT 2010* (*Lecture Notes in Computer Science* **6477**) pp. 158–176 (Dec. 2010).

597. G. W. Dunlap, S. T. King, S. Cinar, M. A. Basrai, and P. M. Chen. "ReVirt: Enabling Intrusion Analysis Through Virtual-Machine Logging and Replay," *Proceedings of the Fifth Symposium on Operating Systems Design and Implementation* pp. 211–224 (Dec. 2002).

598. M. Dunlop, S. Groat, W. Urbanski, R. Marchany, and J. Tront. "MT6D: A Moving Target IPv6 Defense," *Proceedings of the 2011 Military Communications Conference* pp. 1321–1326 (Nov. 2011).

599. R. Durst, T. Champion, B. Witten, E. Miller, and L. Spagnuolo. "Testing and Evaluating Computer Intrusion Detection Systems," *Communications of the ACM* **42**(7) pp. 53–61 (July 1999).

600. Z. Durumeric, J. Kasten, D. Adrian, J. A. Halderman, M. Bailey, F. Li, N. Weaver, J. Amann, J. Beekman, M. Payer, and V. Paxson. "The Matter of Heartbleed," *Proceedings of the 2014 Conference on Internet Measurement* pp. 475–488 (Nov. 2014).

601. C. Dwork. "Differential Privacy," *Proceedings of the 33rd International Colloquium on Automata, Languages and Programming Part II* (*Lecture Notes in Computer Science* **4052**) pp. 1–12 (July 2006).

602. C. Dwork. "Differential Privacy in New Settings," *Proceedings of the 21st Annual ACM-SIAM Symposium on Discrete Algorithms* pp. 174–183 (Jan. 2010).

603. M. Dworkin. *Recommendation for Block Cipher Modes of Operation*, Special Publication 800-38A, National Institute of Standards and Technology, Gaithersburg, MD, USA (Dec. 2001).

604. M. Dworkin. *Recommendation for Block Cipher Modes of Operation: Galois/Counter Mode (GCM) and GMAC*, Special Publication 800-38D, National Institute of Standards and Technology, Gaithersburg, MD, USA (Nov. 2007).

605. K. P. Dyer, S. E. Coull, T. Ristenpart, and T. Shrimpton. "Protocol Misidentification Made Easy with Format-Transforming Encryption," *Proceedings of the 20th ACM SIGSAC Conference on Computer and Communications Security* pp. 61–72 (Oct. 2013).

606. D. E. Eastlake, 3rd. *Domain Name System Security Extensions*, RFC 2535 (Mar. 1999).

607. D. E. Eastlake, 3rd. *DSA Keys and SIGs in the Domain Name System (DNS)*, RFC 2536 (Mar. 1999).

608. D. E. Eastlake, 3rd. *RSA/MD5 Keys and SIGs in the Domain Name System (DNS)*, RFC 2537 (Mar. 1999).

609. D. E. Eastlake, 3rd. *Storage of Diffie-Hellman Keys in the Domain Name System (DNS)*, RFC 2538 (Mar. 1999).

610. D. E. Eastlake, 3rd and O. Gudmundsson. *Storing Certificates in the Domain Name System (DNS)*, RFC 2538 (Mar. 1999).

611. D. E. Eastlake, 3rd, J. I. Schiller, and S. Crocker. *Randomness Requirements for Security*, RFC 4086 (June 2005).

612. S. Eberz, K. B. Rasmussen, V. Lenders, and I. Martinovic. "Preventing Lunchtime Attacks: Fighting Insider Threats with Eye Movement Biometrics," *Proceedings of the 2015 Symposium on Distributed and Network System Security* (Feb. 2015).

613. S. T. Eckmann. "Eliminating Formal Flows in Automated Information Flow Analysis," *Proceedings of the 1994 IEEE Symposium on Research in Security and Privacy* pp. 30–38 (May 1994).

614. S. T. Eckmann, G. Vigna, and R. A. Kemmerer. "STATL: An Attack Language for State-Based Intrusion Detection," *Journal of Computer Security* **10**(1-2) pp. 71–103 (Jan. 2002).

615. W. M. Eddy. *TCP SYN Flooding Attacks and Common Mitigations*, RFC 4987 (Aug. 2007).

616. S. Egelman, L. F. Cranor, and J. Hong. "You've Been Warned: An Empirical Study of the Effectiveness of Web Browser Phishing Warnings," *Proceedings of the 2008 SIGCHI Conference on Human Factors in Computing Systems* pp. 1065–1074 (Apr. 2008).

617. S. Egelman, A. Sotirakopoulos, I. Muslukhov, K. Beznosov, and C. Herley. "Does My Password Go Up to Eleven? The Impact of Password Meters on Password Selection," *Proceedings of the 2013 SIGCHI Conference on Human Factors in Computing Systems* pp. 2379–2388 (Apr. 2013).

618. W. F. Ehrsam, S. M. Matyas, C. H. Meyer, and W. L. Tuchman. "A Cryptographic Key Management Scheme for Implementing the Data Encryption Standard," *IBM Systems Journal* **17**(2) pp. 106–125 (Apr. 1978).

619. M. W. Eichin and J. A. Rochlis. "With Microscope and Tweezers: An Analysis of the Internet Virus of November 1988," *Proceedings of the 1989 IEEE Symposium on Security and Privacy* pp. 326–343 (May 1989).

620. T. Eisenbarth, T. Kasper, A. Moradi, C. Paar, M. Salmasizadeh, and M. T. Manzuri Shalmani. "On the Power of Power Analysis in the Real World: A Complete Break of the KEELOQ Code Hopping Scheme," *Advances in Cryptology — CRYPTO 2008* (*Lecture Notes in Computer Science* **5157**) pp. 203–220 (Aug. 2008).

621. T. Eisenberg, D. Gries, J. Hartmanis, D. Holcomb, M. S. Lynn, and T. Santoro. "The Cornell Commission: On Morris and the Worm," *Communications of the ACM* **32**(6) pp. 706–709 (June 1989).

622. A. A. El Kalam, R. El Baida, and P. Balbiani. "Organization Based Access Control," *Proceedings of the Fourth IEEE International Workshop on Policies for Distributed Systems and Networks* pp. 120–131 (June 2003).

623. A. El-Sherbiny, M. Farah, I. Oueichek, and A. H. Al-Zoman. *Linguistic Guidelines for the Use of the Arabic Language in Internet Domains*, RFC 5564 (Feb. 2010).

624. A. J. Elbirt. "Accelerated AES Implementations Via Generalized Instruction Set Extensions," *Journal of Computer Security* **16**(3) pp. 265–288 (2008).

625. Electronic Frontier Foundation. *Cracking DES: Secrets of Encryption Research, Wiretap Politics & Chip Design*, O'Reilly Media, Sebastopol, CA, USA (May 1998).

626. D. Elenius, G. Denker, M.-O. Stehr, R. Senanayake, C. Talcott, and D. Wilkins. "CoRaL — Policy Language and Reasoning Techniques for Spectrum Policies," *Proceedings of the Eighth IEEE International Workshop on Policies for Distributed Systems and Networks* pp. 261–265 (June 2007).

627. T. ElGamal. "A Public Key Cryptosystem and Signature Scheme Based on Discrete Logarithms," *IEEE Transactions on Information Theory* **IT-31**(4) pp. 469–472 (July 1985).

628. J. Eller, M. Mastrorocco, and B. C. Stauffer. "The Department of Defense Information Technology Security Certification and Accreditation process (DITSCAP)," *Proceedings of the 19th National Information Systems Security Conference* pp. 46–53 (Oct. 1996).

629. J. H. Ellis. "The History of Non-Secret Encryption," *Cryptologia* **23**(3) pp. 267–273 (July 1999).

630. C. Ellison and S. Dohrmann. "Public-Key Support for Group Collaboration," *ACM Transactions on Information and System Security* **6**(4) pp. 547–565 (Nov. 2003).

631. C. M. Ellison. "Establishing Identity Without Certification Authorities," *Proceedings of the Sixth USENIX UNIX Security Symposium* (July 1996).

632. C. M. Ellison. "Naming and Certificates," *Proceedings of the Tenth Conference on Computers, Freedom and Privacy: Challenging the Assumptions* pp. 213–217 (Apr. 2000).

633. C. Ellison and B. Schneier. "Ten Risks of PKI: What You're Not Being Told About Public Key Infrastructure," *Computer Security Journal* **16**(1) pp. 1–7 (Winter 2000).

634. W. Enck, P. Gilbert, B.-G. Chun, L. P. Cox, J. Jung, P. McDaniel, and A. N. Sheth. "TaintDroid: An Information-Flow Tracking System for Realtime Privacy Monitoring on Smartphones," *Proceedings of the Ninth USENIX Symposium on Operating Systems Design and Implementation* pp. 393–408 (Oct. 2010).

635. W. Enck, P. Gilbert, S. Han, V. Tendulkar, B.-G. Chun, L. P. Cox, J. Jung, P. McDaniel, and A. N. Sheth. "TaintDroid: An Information-Flow Tracking System for Realtime Privacy Monitoring on Smartphones," *ACM Transactions on Computer Systems* **32**(2) pp. 5:1–5:29 (June 2014).

636. C. Endorf, E. Schultz, and J. Mellander. *Intrusion Detection and Prevention*, McGraw-Hill/Osborne, Emeryville, CA, USA (2004).

637. A. Ene, W. Horne, N. Milosavljevic, P. Rao, R. Schreiber, and R. E. Tarjan. "Fast Exact and Heuristic Methods for Role Minimization Problems," *Proceedings of the 13th ACM Symposium on Access Control Models and Technologies* pp. 1–10 (June 2008).

638. E. Engeler. *Introduction to the Theory of Computation*, Academic Press, New York, NY, USA (1973).

639. D. R. Engler, M. F. Kaashoek, and J. O'Toole Jr.. "Exokernel: An Operating System Architecture for Application-Level Resource Management," *Proceedings of the 15th ACM Symposium on Operating Systems Principles* pp. 251–266 (Dec. 1995).

640. R. G. Engoulou, M. Bellaïche, S. Pierre, and A. Quintero. "VANET Security Surveys," *Computer Communications* **44** pp. 1–13 (May 2014).

641. J. Epstein, J. McHugh, H. Orman, R. Pascale, A. Marmor-Squires, B. Danner, C. R. Martin, M. Branstad, G. Benson, and D. Rothnie. "A High Assurance Window System Prototype," *Journal of Computer Security* **2**(2-3) pp. 159–190 (Apr. 1993).

642. M. Erwin, C. Scott, and P. Wolfe. *Virtual Private Networks*, O'Reilly Media, Sebastopol, CA, USA (Dec. 1998).

643. K. R. Eschenfelder and A. C. Desai. "Software as Protest: The Unexpected Resiliency of U.S.-Based DeCSS Posting and Linking," *The Information Society* **20**(2) pp. 101–116 (Apr. 2004).

644. T. Espiner. "Intel 'Hacker' Sentence Expunged," *CNET* (Mar. 5, 2007).

645. S. Evans, S. F. Bush, and J. Hershey. "Information Assurance Through Kolmogorov Complexity," *Proceedings of the 2001 DARPA Information Survivability Conference and Exposition II* pp. 322–331 (June 2001).

646. D. Evtyushkin and D. Ponomarev. "Covert Channels Through Random Number Generator: Mechanisms, Capacity Estimation and Mitigations," *Proceedings of the 23rd ACM SIGSAC Conference on Computer and Communications Security* pp. 843–857 (Oct. 2016).

647. R. S. Fabry. "Capability-Based Addressing," *Communications of the ACM* **17**(7) pp. 403–412 (July 1974).

648. G. Faden. "RBAC in UNIX Administration," *Proceedings of the Fourth ACM Workshop on Role-Based Access Controls* pp. 95–101 (Oct. 1999).

649. G. Faden. "Multilevel Filesystems in Solaris Trusted Extensions," *Proceedings of the 12th ACM Symposium on Access Control Models and Technologies* pp. 121–126 (June 2007).

650. M. Fagan and M. M. Hasan Khan. "Why Do They Do What They Do? A Study of What Motivates Users to (Not) Follow Computer Security Advice," *Proceedings of the Twelfth Symposium on Usable Privacy and Security* pp. 59–75 (June 2016).

651. R. Fagin. "On an Authorization Mechanism," *ACM Transactions on Database Systems* **3**(3) pp. 310–319 (Sep. 1978).

652. R. C. Fairfield, R. L. Mortenson, and K. B. Coulthart. "An LSI Random Number Generator (RNG)," *Advances in Cryptology — CRYPTO '84* (*Lecture Notes in Computer Science* **196**) pp. 203–230 (Aug. 1984).

653. N. Falliere, L. O Murchu, and E. Chien. *W32.Stuxnet Dossier Version 1.4*, Technical Report, Symantec Corporation, Mountain View, CA, USA (Feb. 2011).

654. J. Fan, J. Xu, M. H. Ammar, and S. B. Moon. "Prefix-Preserving IP Address Anonymization: Measurement-Based Security Evaluation and a New Cryptography-Based Scheme," *Computer Networks* **46**(2) pp. 253–272 (Oct. 2004).

655. R. J. Feiertag, K. N. Levitt, and L. Robinson. "Proving Multilevel Security of a System Design," *Proceedings of the Sixth ACM Symposium on Operating Systems Principles* pp. 57–65 (Nov. 1977).

656. R. J. Feiertag and P. G. Neumann. "The Foundations of a Provably Secure Operating System (PSOS)," *Proceedings of the AFIPS '79 National Computer Conference* (*AFIPS Conference Proceedings* **48**) pp. 329–334 (June 1979).

657. B. S. Feinstein and G. A. Matthews. *The Intrusion Detection Exchange Protocol (IDXP)*, RFC 4767 (Mar. 2007).

658. H. Feistel. "Cryptography and Computer Privacy," *Scientific American* **228**(5) pp. 15–23 (May 1973).

659. M. Feldhofer, J. Wolkerstorfer, and V. Rijmen. "AES Implementation on a Grain of Sand," *IEE Proceedings on Information Security* **152**(1) pp. 13–20 (Oct. 2005).

660. D. C. Feldmeier and P. R. Kan. "UNIX Password Security—Ten Years Later," *Advances in Cryptology — CRYPTO '89* (*Lecture Notes in Computer Science* **435**) pp. 44–63 (Aug. 1989).

661. A. P. Felt, E. Chin, S. Hanna, D. Song, and D. Wagner. "Android Permissions Demystified," *Proceedings of the 18th ACM Conference on Computer and Communications Security* pp. 627–638 (Oct. 2011).

662. A. P. Felt, E. Ha, S. Egelman, A. Haney, E. Chin, and D. Wagner. "Android Permissions: User Attention, Comprehension, and Behavior," *Proceedings of the Eighth Symposium on Usable Privacy and Security* pp. 3:1–3:14 (July 2012).

663. W.-C. Feng, E. Kaiser, W.-C. Feng, and A. Luu. "The Design and Implementation of Network Puzzles," *Proceedings of the 24th Annual Joint Conference of the IEEE Computer and Communications Societies* pp. 2372–2382 (Mar. 2005).

664. J. S. Fenton. "Memoryless Subsystems," *The Computer Journal* **17**(2) pp. 143–147 (Jan. 1974).

665. D. Ferbrache. *A Pathology of Computer Viruses*, Springer-Verlag London, London, UK (1992).

666. N. Ferguson. "Authentication Weaknesses in GCM," *Comments on the Choice Between CWC or GCM*, Gaithersburg, MD, USA (June 2005).

667. N. Ferguson, B. Schneier, and T. Kohno. *Cryptography Engineering: Design Principles and Practical Applications*, John Wiley & Sons, New York, NY, USA (2010).

668. D. F. Ferraiolo and D. R. Kuhn. "Role-Based Access Controls," *Proceedings of the 15th National Computer Security Conference* pp. 554–563 (Oct. 1992).

669. K. Ferraiolo. "Tutorial: The Systems Secrity Engineering Capability Maturity Model," *Proceedings of the 21st National Information Systems Security Conference* pp. 719–729 (Oct. 1998).

670. K. Ferraiolo, L. Gallagher, and V. Thompson. "Building a Case for Assurance from Process," *Proceedings of the 21st National Information Systems Security Conference* pp. 719–729 (Oct. 1998).

671. A. Ferreira, R. Cruz-Correia, L. Antunes, P. Farinha, E. Oliveira-Palhares, D. W. Chadwick, and A. Costa-Pereira. "How to Break Access Control in a Controlled Manner," *Proceedings of the 19th IEEE International Symposium on Computer-Based Medical Systems* pp. 847–854 (June 2006).

672. T. Ferrell and U. Derrell. "Assuring Avionics — Updating the Approach for the 21st Century," *Proceedings of the SAFECOMP 2014 Workshops: Next Generation of System Assurance Approaches for Safety-Critical Systems* (*Lecture Notes in Computer Science* **8696**) pp. 375–383 (Sep. 2014).

673. P. Ferrie. *Attacks on Virtual Machine Emulators*, Symantee Advanced Research Threat Paper, Symantec Corporation, Mountain View, CA, USA (Dec. 2006).

674. P. Ferrie. "Crimea River," *Virus Bulletin* pp. 4–6 (Feb. 2008).

675. P. Ferrie and P. Szor. "Zmist Opportunities," *Virus Bulletin* pp. 6–7 (Mar. 2001).

676. J. Fichera and S. Bolt. *Network Intrusion Analysis: Methodologies, Tools, and Techniques for Incident Analysis and Response*, Syngress Press, Waltham, MA, USA (2013).

677. G. A. Fink, D. V. Zarzhitsky, T. E. Carroll, and E. D. Farquar. "Security and Privacy Grand Challenges for the Internet of Things," *Proceedings of the 2015 International Conference on Collaboration Technologies and Systems* (June 2015).

678. G. Fink and M. Bishop. "Property-Based Testing: A New Approach to Testing for Assurance," *ACM SIGSOFT Software Engineering Notes* **22**(4) pp. 74–80 (July 1997).

679. G. Fink and K. Levitt. "Property-Based Testing of Privileged Programs," *Proceedings of the Tenth Annual Computer Security Applications Conference* pp. 154–163 (Dec. 1994).

680. E. A. Fisch, G. B. White, and U. W. Pooch. "The Design of an Audit Trail Analysis Tool," *Proceedings of the Tenth Annual Computer Security Applications Conference* pp. 126–132 (Dec. 1994).

681. J. Fisch and L. J. Hoffman. "The Cascade Problem: Graph Theory Can Help," *Proceedings of the 14th National Computer Security Conference* pp. 88–100 (Oct. 1991).

682. A. Fischer and W. Kühnhauser. "Efficient Algorithmic Safety Analysis of HRU Security Models," *Proceedings of the 2010 International Conference on Security and Cryptography* pp. 49–58 (July 2010).

683. P. Fites, P. Jophnston, and M. Kratz. *The Computer Virus Crisis*, Van Nostrand Reinhold, New York, NY, USA (1989).

684. C. Flack and M. J. Atallah. "Better Logging Through Formality: Applying Formal Specification Techniques to Improve Audit Logs and Log Consumers," *Proceedings of the Third International Workshop on Recent Advances in Intrusion Detection* (*Lecture Notes in Computer Science* **1907**) pp. 1–16 (Oct. 2000).

685. E. Flahavin and R. Snouffer. "The Certification of the Interim Key Escrow System," *Proceedings of the 19th National Information Systems Security Conference* pp. 26–33 (Oct. 1996).

686. C. Fleizach, M. Liljenstam, P. Johansson, G. M. Voelker, and A. Mehes. "Can You Infect Me Now? Malware Propagation in Mobile Phone Networks," *Proceedings of the 2007 ACM Workshop on Recurring Malcode* pp. 61–68 (Nov. 2007).

687. C. W. Flink II and J. D. Weiss. "System V/MLS Labeling and Mandatory Policy Alternatives," *AT&T Technical Journal* pp. 53–64 (May 1988).

688. D. Florêncio and C. Herley. "A Large-Scale Study of Web Password Habits," *Proceedings of the 16th International World Wide Web Conference* pp. 657–666 (May 2007).

689. D. Florêncio and C. Herley. "Where Do Security Policies Come From?" *Proceedings of the Sixth Symposium on Usable Privacy and Security* pp. 10:1–10:14 (July 2010).

690. D. Florêncio, C. Herley, and P. C. van Oorschot. "An Administrator's Guide to Internet Password Research," *Proceedings of the Proceedings of the 28th Large Installation System Administration Conference* pp. 35–52 (Nov. 2014).

691. S. R. Fluhrer and D. A. McGrew. "Statistical Analysis of the Alleged RC4 Keystream Generator," *Proceedings of the Eighth International Workshop on Fast Software Encryption* (*Lecture Notes in Computer Science* **1978**) pp. 66–71 (Apr. 2001).

692. R. Focardi and M. Centenaro. "Information Flow Security of Multi-Threaded Distributed Programs," *Proceedings of the Third ACM SIGPLAN Workshop on Programming Languages and Analysis for Security* pp. 113–124 (June 2008).

693. R. Focardi and R. Gorrieri. "A Classification of Security Properties for Process Algebras," *Journal of Computer Security* **3**(1) pp. 5–33 (1994/1995).

694. S. N. Foley. "A Model for Secure Information Flow," *Proceedings of the 1989 IEEE Symposium on Security and Privacy* pp. 248–258 (May 1989).

695. S. N. Foley. "A Nonfunctional Approach to System Integrity," *IEEE Journal on Selected Areas in Communication* **21**(1) pp. 36–43 (Jan. 2003).

696. S. N. Foley and J. Jacob. "Specifying Security for CSCW Systems," *Proceedings of the Eighth Computer Security Foundations Workshop* pp. 136–149 (June 1995).

697. B. Ford and R. Cox. "Vx32: Lightweight User-Level Sandboxing on the x86," *Proceedings of the 2008 USENIX Annual Technical Conference* pp. 293–306 (June 2008).

698. D. Ford, F. Labelle, I. Popovici, M. Stokely, V.-A. Truong, L. Barroso, C. Grimes, and S. Quinlan. "Availability in Globally Distributed Storage Systems," *Proceedings of the Ninth USENIX Symposium on Operating Systems Design and Implementation* pp. 61–74 (Oct. 2010).

699. W. Ford and M. S. Baum. *Secure Electronic Commerce: Building the Infrastructure for Digital Signatures and Encryption*, Prentice Hall, Inc, Upper Saddle River, NJ, USA (Dec. 2000).

700. S. Forrest and C. Beauchemin. "Computer Immunology," *Immunological Reviews* **216**(1) pp. 176–197 (Apr. 2007).

701. S. Forrest, S. A. Hofmeyr, and A. Somayaji. "Computer Immunology," *Communications of the ACM* **40**(10) pp. 88–96 (Oct. 1997).

702. S. Forrest, S. A. Hofmeyr, and A. Somayaji. "The Evolution of System-Call Monitoring," *Proceedings of the 24th Annual Computer Security Applications Conference* pp. 418–430 (Dec. 2008).

703. S. Forrest, S. A. Hofmeyr, A. Somayaji, and T. A. Longstaff. "A Sense of Self for Unix Processes," *Proceedings of the 1996 IEEE Symposium on Security and Privacy* pp. 120–128 (May 1996).

704. S. Forrest, A. S. Perelson, L. Allen, and R. Cherukluri. "Self-Nonself Discrimination in a Computer," *Proceedings of the 1994 IEEE Symposium on Research in Security and Privacy* pp. 202–212 (May 1994).

705. J. E. Forrester and B. P. Miller. "An Empirical Study of the Robustness of Windows NT Applications Using Random Testing," *Proceedings of the Fourth USENIX Windows Systems Symposium* pp. 59–68 (Aug. 2000).

706. J. C. Foster, V. Osipov, N. Bhalla, and N. Heinen. *Buffer Overflow Attacks: Detect, Exploit, Prevent*, Syngress Publishing, Inc., Rockland, MA, USA (2005).

707. M. Foster. *The Secure CEO: How to Protect Your Computer Systems, Your Company, and Your Job*, Prime Concepts Group Publishing, Witchita, KS, USA (2007).

708. D. Fotakis and S. Gritzalis. "Efficient Heuristic Algorithms for Correcting the Cascade Vulnerability Problem for Interconnected Networks," *Computer Communications* **29**(11) pp. 2109–2122 (July 2006).

709. FreeBSD Foundation. *FreeBSD 9.0 Library Functions Manual: crypt(3) — Trapdoor Encryption* (Apr. 2011).

710. P.-A. Fouque, G. Leurent, and P. Q. Nguyen. "Full Key-Recovery Attacks on HMAC/NMAC-MD4 and NMAC-MD5," *Advances in Cryptology — CRYPTO 2007* (*Lecture Notes in Computer Science* **4622**) pp. 13–30 (Aug. 2007).

711. P.-A. Fouque, G. Martinet, F. Valette, and S. Zimmer. "On the Security of the CCM Encryption Mode and of a Slight Variant," *Proceedings of the Sixth International Conference on Applied Cryptography and Network Security* (*Lecture Notes in Computer Science* **5037**) pp. 411–428 (June 2008).

712. A. P. Fournaris, L. Pocero Fraile, and O. Koufopavlou. "Exploiting Hardware Vulnerabilities to Attack Embedded System Devices: A Survey of Potent Microarchitectural Attacks," *Electronics* **6**(3) pp. 52:1–52:15 (Sep. 2017).

713. J. Frank. "Artificial Intelligence and Intrusion Detection: Current and Future Directions," *Proceedings of the 17th National Computer Security Conference* pp. 22–33 (Oct. 1994).

714. M. Frank, D. Basin, and J. M. Buhmann. "A Class of Probabilistic Models for Role Engineering," *Proceedings of the 15th ACM Conference on Computer and Communications Security* pp. 299–310 (Oct. 2008).

715. S. Frankel and S. Krishnan. *IP Security (IPsec) and Internet Key Exchange (IKE) Document Roadmap*, RFC 6071 (Feb. 2011).

716. J. Franklin, M. Luk, J. M. McCune, A. Seshadri, A. Perrig, and L. van Doorn. "Remote Detection of Virtual Machine Monitors with Fuzzy Benchmarking," *ACM SIGOPS Operating Systems Review* **42**(3) pp. 83–92 (Apr. 2008).

717. G. Frantzeskou, S. MacDonell, E. Stamatatos, and S. Gritzalis. "Examining the Significance of High-Level Programming Features in Source Code Author Classification," *Journal of Systems and Software* **81**(3) pp. 447–460 (Mar. 2008).

718. G. Frantzeskou, E. Stamatatos, S. Gritzalis, and S. Katsikas. "Effective Identification of Source Code Authors Using Byte-Level Information," *Proceedings of the 28th International Conference on Software Engineering* pp. 893–896 (May 2006).

719. T. Fraser and L. Badger. "Ensuring Continuity During Dynamic Security Policy Reconfiguration in DTE," *Proceedings of the 1998 IEEE Symposium on Security and Privacy* pp. 15–26 (May 1998).

720. T. Fraser, L. Badger, and M. Feldman. "Hardening COTS Software with Generic Software Wrappers," *Proceedings of the 1999 IEEE Symposium on Security and Privacy* pp. 2–16 (May 1999).

721. C. Fredenburgh. "Judge Approves Settlement in SONY BMG Class Action," *Law 360* (May 2006).

722. A. Freedman. *How to Make BSD (SunOS) Kernels SYN-Attack Resistant* (Sep. 1996).

723. D. H. Freedman and C. C. Mann. *At Large: The Strange Case of the World's Biggest Internet Invasion*, Touchstone, New York, NY, USA (1998).

724. A. O. Freier, P. Karlton, and P. C. Kocher. *The Secure Sockers Layer (SSL) Protocol Version 3.0*, RFC 6101 (Aug. 2011).

725. M. Freire-Santos, J. Fierrez-Aguilar, and J. Ortega-Garcia. "Cryptographic Key Generation Using Handwritten Signature," *Proceedings of SPIE 6202: Biometric Technology for Human Identification III* pp. 62020N:1–7 (Apr. 2006).

726. Æ. Frisch. *Essential System Administration*, O'Reilly Media, Inc., Sebastopol, CA, USA (Aug. 2002).

727. A. M. Froomkin. "The Metaphor is the Key: Cryptography, the Clipper Chip, and the Constitution," *University of Pennsylvania Law Review* **143**(3) pp. 709–897 (1994–1995).

728. K. Fu and J. Blum. "Controlling for Cybersecurity Risks of Medical Device Software," *Communications of the ACM* **56**(10) pp. 35–37 (Oct. 2013).

729. S. V. K. Gaddam and M. Lal. "Efficient Cancellable Biometric Key Generation Scheme for Cryptography," *International Journal of Network Security* **11**(2) pp. 61–69 (Sep. 2010).

730. J. E. Gaffney Jr. and J. W. Ulvila. "Evaluation of Intrusion Detectors: A Decision Theory Approach," *Proceedings of the 2001 IEEE Symposium on Security and Privacy* pp. 50–61 (May 2001).

731. H. F. Gaines. *Cryptanalysis: A Study of Ciphers and Their Solution*, Dover Publications, New York, NY, USA (1956).

732. T. Gamage and B. McMillin. "Nondeducibility-Based Analysis of Cyber-Physical Systems," *Proceedings ot the Third Annual IFIP WG 11.10 International Conference on Critical Infrastructure Protection* (*IFIP Advances in Information and Communication Technology* **311**) pp. 169–183 (Mar. 2009).

733. D. Gambel. "Security Modeling for Public Safety Communication Specifications," *Proceedings of the 20th National Information Systems Security Conference* pp. 514–521 (Oct. 1997).

734. D. Gambetta (*ed*). *Trust: Making and Breaking Cooperative Relations*, Basil Blackwell Ltd., Oxford, UK (1988).

735. R. Ganesan. "The Yaksha Security System," *Communications of the ACM* **39**(3) pp. 55–60 (Mar. 1996).

736. R. Ganesan and C. Davies. "A New Attack on Random Pronounceable Password Generators," *Proceedings of the 17th National Computer Security Conference* pp. 184–187 (Oct. 1994).

737. L. Garber. "Worm Targets Industrial-Plant Operations," *IEEE Computer* **43**(11) pp. 15–16 (Nov. 2010).

738. A. V. Garcia and J.-P. Seifert. "On the Implementation of the Advanced Encryption Standard on a Public-Key Crypto-Coprocessor," *Proceedings of the 5th Smart Card Research and Advanced Application Conference* pp. 135–145 (Nov. 2002).

739. J. Gardner and L. Xiong. "An Integrated Framework for De-Identifying Unstructured Medical Data," *Data & Knowledge Engineering* **68**(12) pp. 1441–1451 (Dec. 2009).

740. M. Garetto, W. Ging, and D. Towsley. "Modeling Malware Spreading Dynamics," *Proceedings of the 22nd Annual Joint Conference of the IEEE Computer and Communications Societies* pp. 1869–1879 (Mar. 2003).

741. S. Garfinkel. *PGP: Pretty Good Privacy*, O'Reilly Media, Sebastopol, CA, USA (Dec. 1994).

742. S. Garfinkel. *Database Nation: The Death of Privacy in the 21st Century*, O'Reilly Media, Inc., Sebastopol, CA, USA (2000).

743. S. Garfinkel. "Anti-Forensics: Techniques, Detection and Countermeasures," *Proceedings of the Second International Conference on i-Warfare and Security* pp. 77–84 (Mar. 2007).

744. S. L. Garfinkel, D. Margrave, J. I. Schiller, E. Nordlander, and R. C. Miller. "How to Make Secure Email Easier to Use," *Proceedings of the 2005 SIGCHI Conference on Human Factors in Computing Systems* pp. 701–710 (Apr. 2005).

745. S. L. Garfinkel and R. C. Miller. "Johnny 2: A User Test of Key Continuity Management with S/MIME and Outlook Express," *Proceedings of the 2005 Symposium on Usable Privacy and Security* pp. 13–24 (July 2005).

746. S. Garfinkel and G. Spafford. *Web Security, Privacy & Commerce*, O'Reilly Media, Sebastopol, CA, USA (Nov. 2001).

747. S. Garfinkel, G. Spafford, and A. Schwartz. *Practical UNIX and Internet Security*, O'Reilly Media, Inc., Sebastopol, CA, USA (Feb. 2003).

748. T. Garfinkel. "Traps and Pitfalls: Practical Problems in System Call Interposition Based Security Tools," *Proceedings of the 2003 Symposium on Network and Distributed System Security* (Feb. 2003).

749. A. Gargantini, L. Liberati, A. Morzenti, and C. Zacchetti. "Specifying, Validating, and Testing a Traffic Management System in the TRIO Environment," *Proceedings of the 11th Annual Conference on Computer Assurance* pp. 65–76 (June 1996).

750. P. D. Garnett. "Selective Disassembly: A First Step Towards Developing a Virus Filter," *Proceedings of the Fourth Annual Computer Security Applications Conference* pp. 2–6 (Sep. 1988).

751. P. Garrett. *The Mathematics of Coding Theory*, Pearson Education, Englewood Cliffs, NJ, USA (2004).

752. M. Gasser. *A Random Word Generator for Pronounceable Passwords*, Technical Report ESD-TR-75-97, Electronic System Division, Hanscom Air Force Base, Bedford, MA, USA (Nov. 1975).

753. C. Gates and M. Bishop. "One of These Records Is Not Like the Others," *Proceedings of the Third USENIX Workshop on the Theory and Practice of Provenance* (June 2011).

754. X. Ge, F. Polack, and R. Laleau. "Secure Databases: An Analysis of Clark-Wilson Model in a Database Environment," *Proceedings of the 16th International Conference on Advanced Information Systems Engineering* (*Lecture Notes in Computer Science* **3084**) pp. 234–247 (June 2004).

755. D. Geer and J. Harthorne. "Penetration Testing: A Duet," *Proceedings of the 18th Annual Computer Security Applications Conference* (Dec. 2002).

756. E. F. Gehringer. "Changing Passwords: Security and Human Factors," *Proceedings of the 2002 International Symposium on Technology and Society* pp. 369–373 (June 2002).

757. M. Geiger. "Evaluating Commercial Counter-Forensic Tools," *Proceedings of the Fifth Digital Forensic Research Conference* pp. 1–12 (Aug. 2005).

758. E. Gelenbe and G. Loukas. "A Self-Aware Approach to Denial of Service Defence," *Computer Networks* **51**(5) pp. 1299–1314 (Apr. 2007).

759. S. Genaim and F. Spoto. "Information Flow Analysis for Java Bytecode," *Proceedings of the Sixth International Conference on Verification, Model Checking, and Abstract Interpretation* (*Lecture Notes in Computer Science* **3385**) pp. 346–362 (Jan. 2005).

760. D. Genkin, A. Shamir, and E. Tromer. "Acoustic Cryptanalysis," *Journal of Cryptology* **30**(2) pp. 392–443 (Apr. 2017).

761. C. Gentry. "A Fully Homomorphic Encryption Scheme," Ph.D. Dissertation, Stanford University, Stanford, CA, USA (Sep. 2009).

762. C. Gentry. "Computing Arbitrary Functions of Encrypted Data," *Communications of the ACM* **53**(3) pp. 97–105 (Mar. 2010).

763. A. K. Ghosh. *E-Commerce Security: Weak Links, Best Defenses*, John Wiley & Sons, Inc., New York, NY, USA (Jan. 1998).

764. A. K. Ghosh, T. O'Connor, and G. McGraw. "An Automated Approach for Identifying Potential Vulnerabilities in Software," *Proceedings of the 1998 IEEE Symposium on Security and Privacy* pp. 104–114 (May 1998).

765. S. Gianvecchio, H. Wang, D. Wijesekeran, and S. Jajodia. "Model-Based Covert Timing Channels: Automated Modeling and Evasion," *Proceedings of the 11th International Workshop on Recent Advances in Intrusion Detection* (*Lecture Notes in Computer Science* **5230**) pp. 211–230 (Sep. 2008).

766. C. Gibler, J. Crussell, J. Erickson, and H. Chen. "AndroidLeaks: Automatically Detecting Potential Privacy Leaks in Android Applications on a Large Scale," *Proceedings of the Fifth International Conference on Trust and Trustworthy Computing* (*Lecture Notes in Computer Science* **7344**) pp. 291–307 (June 2012).

767. D. Gibson. *Microsoft Windows Security Essentials*, Sybex, Indianapolis, IN, USA (2011).

768. K. L. Gibson and J. M. Smith. "The Emperor's New Masks: On Demographic Differences and Disguises," *Proceedings of the 2015 IEEE Conference on Computer Vision and Pattern Recognition Workshops* pp. 57–64 (June 2015).

769. D. K. Gifford. "Cryptographic Sealing for Information Secrecy and Authentication," *Communications of the ACM* **25**(4) pp. 274–286 (Apr. 1982).

770. H. Gilbert and G. Chassé. "A Statistical Attack of the FEAL-8 Cryptosystem," *Advances in Cryptology — CRYPTO '90* (*Lecture Notes in Computer Science* **537**) pp. 22–33 (Aug. 1990).

771. D. Gilliam, J. Kelly, J. Powell, and M. Bishop. "Development of a Software Security Assessment Instrument to Reduce Software Security Risk," *Proceedings of the Tenth IEEE International Workshop on Enabling Technologies: Infrastructure for Collaborative Enterprise* pp. 144–149 (June 2001).

772. V. D. Gligor. "A Note on Denial-of-Service in Operating Systems," *IEEE Transactions on Software Engineering* **SE-10**(3) pp. 320–324 (May 1984).

773. V. D. Gligor. *Guidelines for Trusted Facility Management and Audit*, Technical Report, University of Maryland (1985); cited in [2163].

774. V. D. Gligor. "Guaranteeing Access in Spite of Distributed Service-Flooding Attacks," *Proceedings of the 11th International Workshop on Security Protocols* (*Lecture Notes in Computer Science* **3364**) pp. 80–96 (Apr. 2003).

775. V. D. Gligor, C. S. Chandersekaran, R. S. Chapman, L. J. Dotterer, M. S. Hecht, W.-D. Jiang, A. Johri, G. L. Luckenbaugh, and N. Vasudevan. "Design and Implementation of Secure Xenix," *IEEE Transactions on Software Engineering* **13**(2) pp. 208–221 (Feb. 1987) (cited in [2166]).

776. V. D. Gligor and P. Donescu. "Integrity-Aware PCBC Encryption Schemes," *Proceedings of the Seventh International Workshop on Security Protocols* (*Lecture Notes in Computer Science* **1796**) pp. 153–168 (Apr. 1999).

777. V. D. Gligor and P. Donescu. "Fast Encryption and Authentication: XCBC Encryption and XECB Authentication Modes," *Proceedings of the Eighth International Workshop on Fast Software Encryption* (*Lecture Notes in Computer Science* **2355**) pp. 92–108 (Apr. 2001).

778. V. D. Gligor, S. I. Gavrila, and D. Ferraiolo. "On the Formal Definition of Separation-of-Duty Policies and Their Composition," *Proceedings of the 1998 IEEE Symposium on Security and Privacy* pp. 172–183 (May 1998).

779. V. Goel and N. Perlroth. "Yahoo Says 1 Billion User Accounts Were Hacked," *The New York Times* p. A1 (Dec. 15 2016).

780. J. A. Goguen and J. Meseguer. "Security Policies and Security Models," *Proceedings of the 1982 IEEE Symposium on Security and Privacy* pp. 11–20 (Apr. 1982).

781. J. Golbeck and J. Hendler. "Accuracy of Metrics for Inferring Trust and Reputation in Semantic Web-Based Social Networks," *Proceedings of the 14th International Conference on Engineering Knowledge in the Age of the Semantic Web* **3257** pp. 116–131 (Oct. 2004).

782. J. Golbeck (*ed*). *Computing with Social Trust*, Springer, London, UK (2009).

783. B. D. Gold, R. R. Linde, and P. F. Cudney. "KVM/370 in Retrospect," *Proceedings of the 1984 IEEE Symposium on Security and Privacy* pp. 13–23 (Apr. 1984).

784. B. Gold, R. Linde, R. Peeler, M. Schaefer, J. Scheid, and P. Ward. "A Security Retrofit of VM/370," *Proceedings of the AFIPS '79 International Workshop on Managing Requirements Knowledge* pp. 335–344 (June 1979).

785. I. Goldberg, D. Wagner, and E. Brewer. "Privacy-Enhancing Technologies for the Internet," *Proceedings of IEEE Compcon '97* pp. 103–109 (Feb. 1997).

786. I. Goldberg, D. Wagner, R. Thomas, and E. Brewer. "A Secure Environment for Untrusted Helper Applications (Confining the Wily Hacker)," *Proceedings of the Sixth USENIX UNIX Security Symposium* (July 1996).

787. O. Goldreich. *Foundations of Cryptography: Volume 1, Basic Tools*, Cambridge University Press, Cambridge, United Kingdom (2007).

788. O. Goldreich. *Foundations of Cryptography: Volume 2, Basic Applications*, Cambridge University Press, Cambridge, United Kingdom (2009).

789. D. M. Goldschlag, M. G. Reed, and P. F. Syverson. "Hiding Routing Information," *Proceedings of the First International Workshop on Information Hiding* (*Lecture Notes in Computer Science* **1174**) pp. 137–150 (May 1996).

790. Z. Gołębiewski, M. Kutyłowski, and F. Zagórski. "Stealing Secrets with SSL/TLS and SSH—Kleptographic Attacks," *Proceedings of the 5th International Conference on Cryptology and Network Security* (*Lecture Notes in Computer Science* **4301**) pp. 191–202 (Dec. 2006).

791. J. D. Golić, V. Bagini, and G. Morgari. "Linear Cryptanalysis of Bluetooth Stream Cipher," *Advances in Cryptology — EUROCRYPT 2002* (*Lecture Notes in Computer Science* **2332**) pp. 238–255 (Apr. 2002).

792. P. Golle. "Revisiting the Uniqueness of Simple Demographics in the US Population," *Proceedings of the Fifth ACM Workshop on Privacy in Electronic Society* pp. 77–80 (Oct. 2006).

793. P. Golle and A. Juels. "Dining Cryptographers Revisited," *Advances in Cryptology — EUROCRYPT 2004* (*Lecture Notes in Computer Science* **3027**) pp. 456–473 (May 2004).

794. L. Gong. "A Secure Identity-Based Capability System," *Proceedings of the 1989 IEEE Symposium on Security and Privacy* pp. 56–63 (May 1989).

795. L. Gong. "A Security Risk of Depending on Synchronized Clocks," *ACM SIGOPS Operating Systems Review* **26**(1) pp. 49–53 (Jan. 1992).

796. L. Gong and S. Dodda. "Security Assurance Efforts in Engineering Java 2 SE (JDK 1.2)," *Proceedings of the Fourth IEEE International Symposium on High-Assurance Systems Engineering* pp. 89–93 (Nov. 1999).

797. L. Gong and X. Qian. "The Complexity and Composability of Secure Interoperation," *Proceedings of the 1994 IEEE Symposium on Research in Security and Privacy* pp. 190–200 (May 1994).

798. L. Gong and X. Qian. "Computational Issues in Secure Interoperation," *IEEE Transactions on Software Engineering* **22**(1) pp. 43–52 (Jan. 1996).

799. D. Goodin. "Failure to Patch Two-Month-Old Bug Led to Massive Equifax Breach," *Ars Technica* (Sep. 2017).

800. S. K. Gorantia, S. Kadloor, T. P. Coleman, N. Kiyavash, I. S. Moskowitz, and M. H. Kang. "Directed Information and the NRL Network Pump," *Proceedings of the 2010 International Symposium on Information Theory and Its Applications* pp. 343–348 (Oct. 2010).

801. S. K. Gorantia, S. Kadloor, N. Kiyavash, T. P. Coleman, I. S. Moskowitz, and M. H. Kang. "Characterizing the Efficacy of the NRL Network Pump in Mitigating Covert Timing Channels," *IEEE Transactions on Information Forensics and Security* **7**(1) pp. 64–75 (Feb. 2012).

802. M. J. C. Gordon and T. F. Melham (*ed*). *Introduction to HOL: A Theorem Proving Environment for Higher Order Logic*, Cambridge University Press, New York, NY, USA (1993).

803. M. Gorski and S. Lucks. "New Related-Key Boomerang Attacks on AES," *Proceedings of the Ninth International Conference on Cryptology in India: Progress in Cryptology — INDOCRYPT 2008* (*Lecture Notes in Computer Science* **5365**) pp. 266–278 (Dec. 2008).

804. M. G. Graff and K. R. van Wyk. *Secure Coding: Principles and Practices*, O'Reilly and Associates, Sebastopol, CA, USA (2003).

805. G. S. Graham and P. J. Denning. "Protection: Principles and Practice," *AFIPS Conference Proceedings: 1971 Fall Joint Computer Conference* pp. 417–429 (Nov. 1972).

806. J. Graham-Cumming. "Some Laws of Non-Interference," *Proceedings of the Fifth Computer Security Foundations Workshop* pp. 22–33 (June 1992).

807. F. T. Grampp and R. H. Morris. "UNIX Operating System Security," *AT&T Bell Laboratories Technical Journal* **63**(8) pp. 1649–1672 (Oct. 1984).

808. G. Gran. *Understanding Digital Signatures: Establishing Trust Over the Internet and Other Networks*, McGraw-Hill, New York, NY, USA (1997).

809. T. Grandison and M. Sloman. "A Survey of Trust in Internet Applications," *IEEE Communications Surveys & Tutorials* **3**(4) pp. 2–16 (Fourth Quarter 2000).

810. T. Grandison and M. Sloman. "Trust Management Tools for Internet Applications," *Proceedings of the First International Conference on Trust Management* (*Lecture Notes in Computer Science* **2692**) pp. 91–107 (May 2003).

811. L. Grant. "DES Key Crunching for Safer Cypher Keys," *ACM SIGSAC Review* **5**(3) pp. 9–16 (Aug. 1987).

812. R. Graubart. "The Integrity-Lock Approach to Secure Database Management," *Proceedings of the 1984 IEEE Symposium on Security and Privacy* pp. 62–74 (Apr. 1984).

813. R. Graubart. "On the Need for a Third Form of Access Control," *Proceedings of the 12th National Computer Security Conference* pp. 296–304 (Oct. 1989).

814. A. Gray. "An Historical Perspective of Software Vulnerability Management," *Information Secuirty Technical Report* **8**(4) pp. 34–44 (Apr. 2003).

815. J. W. Gray III. "Toward a Mathematical Foundation for Information Flow Security," *Journal of Computer Security* **1**(3-4) pp. 255–294 (1992).

816. J. W. Gray III. "On Introducing Noise into the Bus-Contention Channel," *Proceedings of the 1993 IEEE Symposium on Research in Security and Privacy* pp. 90–98 (May 1993).

817. J. L. Green and P. L. Sisson. "The 'Father Christmas Worm,'" *Proceedings of the 12th National Computer Security Conference* pp. 359–368 (Oct. 1989).

818. M. Green, D. C. MacFarland, D. R. Smestad, and C. A. Shue. "Characterizing Network-Based Moving Target Defenses," *Proceedings of the Second ACM Workshop on Moving Target Defense* pp. 31–35 (Oct. 2015).

819. L. T. Greenberg, S. E. Goodman, and K. J. Soo Hoo. *Information Warfare and International Law*, National Defense University Press, Washington, DC, USA (1997).

820. L. G. Greenwald and T. J. Thomas. "Toward Undetected Operating System Fingerprinting," *Proceedings of the First USENIX Workshop on Offensive Technologies* (Aug. 2007).

821. K. Griffin, S. Schneider, X. Hu, and T.-c. Chiueh. "Automatic Generation of String Signatures for Malware Detection," *Proceedings of the 12th International Symposium on Recent Advances in Intrusion Detection* (*Lecture Notes in Computer Science* **5758**) pp. 101–120 (Sep. 2009).

822. P. P. Griffiths and B. W. Wade. "An Authorization Mechanism for a Relational Database System," *ACM Transactions on Database Systems* **1**(3) pp. 242–255 (Sep. 1976).

823. J. B. Grizzard, V. Sharma, C. Nunnery, B. B. Kang, and D. Dagon. "Peer-to-Peer Botnets: Overview and Case Study," *Proceedings of the First Workshop on Hot Topics in Understanding Botnets* pp. 1–8 (Apr. 2007).

824. S. Groat, M. Dunlop, W. Urbanski, R. Marchany, and J. Tront. "Using an IPv6 Moving Target Defense to Protect the Smart Grid," *Proceedings of the 2012 IEEE PES Innovative Smart Grid Technologies* (Jan. 2012).

825. E. Grosse and M. Upadhyay. "Authentication at Scale," *IEEE Security & Privacy* **11**(1) pp. 15–22 (Jan. 2013).

826. D. Gruss, C. Maurice, and S. Mangard. "Rowhammer.js: A Remote Software-Induced Fault Attack in Javascript," *Computing Research Repository* (arXiv:1507.06955v5 [cs.CR]) (Apr. 2016).

827. G. Gu, P. Fogla, D. Dagon, W. Lee, and B. Skorić. "Measuring Intrusion Detection Capability: An Information-Theoretic Approach," *Proceedings of the 13th ACM Conference on Computer and Communications Security* pp. 90–101 (Mar. 2006).

828. Y. Gu, A. McCallum, and D. Towsley. "Detecting Anomalies in Network Traffic Using Maximum Entropy Estimation," *Proceedings of the First ACM SIGCOMM Conference on Internet Measurement* pp. 345–350 (Oct. 2005).

829. K. Gudka, R. N. M. Waton, S. Hand, B. Laurie, and A. Madhavapeddy. "Exploring Compartmentalisation Hypotheses with SOAAP," *Proceedings of the 6th IEEE International Conference on Self-Adaptive and Self-Organizing Systems Workshops* pp. 23–30 (Sep. 2012).

830. K. Gudka, R. N. Watson, J. Anderson, D. Chisnall, B. Davis, B. Laurie, I. Marinos, P. G. Neumann, and A. Richardson. "Clean Application Compartmentalization with SOAAP," *Proceedings of the 22nd ACM SIGSAC Conference on Computer and Communications Security* pp. 1016–1031 (Oct. 2015).

831. M. Guennoun, N. Abbad, J. Talom, S. M. M. Rahman, and K. El-Khatib. "Continuous Authentication by Electrocardiogram Data," *Proceedings of the 2009 IEEE Toronto International Conference on Science and Technology for Humanity* pp. 40–42 (Sep. 2009).

832. S. Gueron. "Intel's New AES Instructions for Enhanced Performance and Security," *Proceedings of the 16th International Workshop on Fast Software Encryption: Revised Selected Papers* (*Lecture Notes in Computer Science* **5665**) pp. 51–66 (Feb. 2009).

833. S. Gueron. *Intel Advanced Encryption Standard (AES) New Instructions Set*, White Paper, Intel, Haifa, Israel (May 2010).

834. C. Gülcü and G. Tsudik. "Mixing Email with Babel," *Proceedings of the 1996 Symposium on Network and Distributed System Security* (Feb. 1996).

835. D. Gunetti and C. Picardi. "Keystroke Analysis of Free Text," *ACM Transactions on Information and System Security* **8**(3) pp. 312–347 (Aug. 2005).

836. S. Gupta and V. D. Gligor. "Towards a Theory of Penetration-Resistant Systems and Its Applications," *Proceedings of the Fourth Computer Security Foundations Workshop* pp. 62–78 (June 1991).

837. S. Gupta and V. D. Gligor. "Experience with a Penetration Analysis Method and Tool," *Proceedings of the 15th National Computer Security Conference* pp. 165–183 (Oct. 1992).

838. P. Gutmann. *Encrypt-then-MAC for Transport Layer Security (TLS) and Datagram Transport Layer Security (DTLS)*, RFC 7366 (Sep. 2014).

839. Z. Gutterman, B. Pinkas, and T. Reinman. "Analysis of the Linux Random Number Generator," *Proceedings of the 2006 IEEE Symposium on Security and Privacy* pp. 371–385 (May 2006).

840. J. Guttman. "Information Flow and Invariance," *Proceedings of the 1987 IEEE Symposium on Security and Privacy* pp. 67–73 (Apr. 1987).

841. J. D. Guttman and M. E. Nadel. "What Needs Securing?" *Proceedings of the First Computer Security Foundations Workshop* pp. 34–57 (June 1988).

842. K. Hafner and J. Markoff. *Cyberpunk: Outlaws and Hackers on the Computer Frontier*, Simon & Schuster, New York, NY, USA (1991).

843. S. Hai-Bo and H. Fan. "An Attribute-Based Access Control Model for Web Services," *Proceedings of the Seventh International Conference on Parallel and Distributed Computing, Applications and Technologies* pp. 74–79 (Dec. 2006).

844. J. T. Haigh, R. A. Kemmerer, J. McHugh, and W. D. Young. "An Experience Using Two Covert Channel Analysis Techniques on a Real System Design," *Proceedings of the 1986 IEEE Symposium on Security and Privacy* pp. 14–24 (Apr. 1986).

845. J. T. Haigh, R. A. Kemmerer, J. McHugh, and W. D. Young. "An Experience Using Two Covert Channel Analysis Techniques on a Real System Design," *IEEE Transactions on Software Engineering* **13**(2) pp. 157–168 (Feb. 1987).

846. J. T. Haigh and W. D. Young. "Extending the Non-Interference Version of MLS for SAT," *Proceedings of the 1986 IEEE Symposium on Security and Privacy* pp. 232–239 (Apr. 1986).

847. J. W. Haines, L. M. Rossey, R. P. Lippmann, and R. K. Cunningham. "Extending the DARPA Off-Line Intrusion Detection Evaluations," *Proceedings of the 2001 DARPA Information Survivability Conference and Exposition II* pp. 35–45 (June 2001).

848. V. Haldar, D. Chandra, and M. Franz. "Dynamic Taint Propagation for Java," *Proceedings of the 21st Annual Computer Security Applications Conference* pp. 311–320 (Dec. 2005).

849. J. A. Halderman and E. W. Felten. "Lessons from the Sony CD ROM Episode," *Proceedings of the 15th USENIX Security Symposium* pp. 77–92 (Aug. 2006).

850. J. A. Halderman, S. D. Schoen, N. Heninger, W. Clarkson, W. Paul, J. A. Calandrino, A. J. Feldman, Appelbaum, and E. W. Felten. "Lest We Remember: Cold Boot Attacks on Encryption Keys," *Communications of the ACM* **52**(5) pp. 91–98 (May 2009).

851. P. Hallam-Baker. "Comodo SSL Affiliate: The Recent RA Compromise," *Comodo Blog* (Mar. 2011).

852. N. Haller. "The S/Key One-Time Password System," *Proceedings of the 1994 Symposium on Network and Distributed System Security* pp. 151–157 (Feb. 1994).

853. N. Haller. *The S/Key One-Time Password System*, RFC 1760 (Feb. 1995).

854. S. E. Hallyn and A. G. Morgan. "Linux Capabilities: Making Them Work," *Proceedings of the Linux Symposium* pp. 163–172 (July 2008).

855. D. Halperin, T. S. Heydt-Benjamin, K. Fu, T. Kohno, and W. H. Maisel. "Security and Privacy for Implantable Medical Devices," *IEEE Pervasive Computing* **7**(1) pp. 30–39 (Jan. 2008).

856. D. Halperin, T. S. Heydt-Benjamin, B. Ransford, S. S. Clark, B. Defend, W. Morgan, K. Fu, T. Kohno, and W. H. Maisel. "Pacemakers and Implantable Cardiac Defibrillators: Software Radio Attacks and Zero-Power Defenses," *Proceedings of the 2008 IEEE Symposium on Security and Privacy* pp. 129–142 (May 2008).

857. H. Hamed, E. Al-Shaer, and W. Marrero. "Modeling and Verification of IPSec and VPN Security Policies," *Proceedings of the 13th IEEE International Conference on Network Protocols* pp. 259–278 (Nov. 2005).

858. A. Hamilton, J. Madison, and J. Jay. *The Federalist Papers*, edited by C. Rossiter, Signet Classics, New York, NY, USA (1982).

859. B. Hammond. *Digital Signatures*, McGraw-Hill Professional, New York, NY, USA (2002).

860. J. Han and Y. Zheng. "Security Characterisation and Integrity Assurance for Component-Based Software," *Proceedings of the 2000 International Conference on Software Methods and Tools* pp. 61–66 (Nov. 2000).

861. H. Handschuh and B. Preneel. "Key-Recovery Attacks on Universal Hash Function Based MAC Algorithms," *Advances in Cryptology — CRYPTO 2008 (Lecture Notes in Computer Science* **5157**) pp. 144–161 (Aug. 2008).

862. K. S. Hanks, J. C. Knight, and E. A. Strunk. "Erroneous Requirements: A Linguistic Basis for Their Occurrence and an Approach to Their Reduction," *Proceedings of the 26th Annual NASA Goddard Software Engineering Workshop* pp. 115–119 (Nov. 2001).

863. F. Hansen and V. Oleshchuk. "Spatial Role-Based Access Control Model for Wireless Networks," *Proceedings of the 58th IEEE Vehicular Technology Conference* pp. 2093–2097 (Oct. 2003).

864. S. E. Hansen and E. T. Atkins. "Centralized System Monitoring with Swatch," *Proceedings of the Third USENIX UNIX Security Symposium* pp. 105–117 (Sep. 1992).

865. S. E. Hansen and E. T. Atkins. "Automated System Monitoring and Notification with Swatch," *Proceedings of the USENIX Seventh System Administration Conference* pp. 145–152 (Nov. 1993).

866. D. R. Hanson. "A Machine-Independent Debugger – Revisited," *Software: Practice and Experience* **29**(10) pp. 849–862 (Aug. 1999).

867. S. Hardcastle-Kille. *X.500 and Domains*, RFC 1279 (Nov. 1991).

868. N. Hardy. "KeyKOS Architecture," *ACM SIGOPS Operating Systems Review* **19**(4) pp. 8–25 (Oct. 1985).

869. A. Harmon. "Hackers May 'Net' Good PR for Studio," *Los Angeles Times* p. D1 (Aug. 12, 1995).

870. T. Harmon and M. R. Lowry. "*N*-Version Programming in WCET Analysis: Revisiting a Discredited Idea," *Proceedings of the FSE/SDP Workshop on Future of Software Engineering Research* pp. 157–160 (Nov. 2010).

871. B. Harris and R. Hunt. "Firewall Certification," *Computers & Security* **18**(2) pp. 165–177 (Mar. 1999).

872. R. Harris. "Arriving at an Anti-Forensics Consensus: Examining How to Define and Control the Anti-Forensics Problem," *Digital Investigation* **3S** pp. 44–49 (Sep. 2006).

873. M. A. Harrison and W. L. Ruzzo. "Monotonic Protection Systems," in [531], pp. 337–363.

874. M. A. Harrison, W. L. Ruzzo, and J. D. Ullman. "Protection in Operating Systems," *Communications of the ACM* **19**(8) pp. 461–471 (Aug. 1976).

875. R. Harrison. *Lightweight Directory Access Protocol (LDAP): Authentication Methods and Security Mechanisms*, RFC 4513 (June 2006).

876. H. Härtig, O. Kowalski, and W. Kühnhauser. "The BirliX Security Architecture," *Journal of Computer Security* **2**(1) pp. 5–21 (1993).

877. H. R. Hartson and D. K. Hsiao. "Full Protection Specifications in the Semantic Model for Database Protection Languages," *Proceedings of the 1976 ACM Annual Conference* pp. 90–95 (Oct. 1976).

878. R. Hasan, R. Sion, and M. Winslett. "Introducing Secure Provenance: Problems and Challenges," *Proceedings of the 2007 ACM Workshop on Storage Security and Survivability* pp. 13–18 (Oct. 2007).

879. J. A. Haskett. "Pass-Algorithms: A User Validation Scheme Based on Knowledge of Secret Algorithms," *Communications of the ACM* **27**(8) pp. 777–781 (Aug. 1984).

880. E. Haugh and M. Bishop. "Testing C Programs for Buffer Overflow Vulnerabilities," *Proceedings of the 2003 Symposium on Network and Distributed System Security* pp. 123–130 (Feb. 2003).

881. P. Hawkes and L. O'Connor. "On Applying Linear Cryptanalysis to IDEA," *Advances in Cryptology — ASIACRYPT '96* (*Lecture Notes in Computer Science* **1163**) pp. 105–115 (Nov. 1996).

882. B. Hay and K. Nance. "Forensics Examination of Volatile System Data Using Virtual Introspection," *ACM SIGOPS Operating Systems Review* pp. 74–82 (Apr. 2008).

883. T. Haynes and D. Noveck. *Network File System (NFS) Version 4 Protocol*, RFC 7530 (Mar. 2015).

884. J. Heather, G. Lowe, and S. Schneider. "How to Prevent Type Flaw Attacks on Security Protocols," *Proceedings of the 13th Computer Security Foundations Workshop* pp. 255–268 (July 2000).

885. B. Hebbard, P. Grosso, T. Baldridge, C. Chan, D. Fishman, P. Goshgarian, T. Hilton, J. Hoshen, K. Hoult, G. Huntley, M. Stolarchuk, and L. Warner. "A Penetration Analysis of the Michigan Terminal System," *ACM SIGOPS Operating Systems Review* **14**(1) pp. 7–20 (Jan. 1980).

886. L. T. Heberlein and M. Bishop. "Attack Class: Address Spoofing," *Proceedings of the 19th National Information Systems Security Conference* pp. 371–377 (Oct. 1996).

887. L. T. Heberlein, G. V. Dias, K. N. Levitt, B. Mukherjee, J. Wood, and D. Wolber. "A Network Security Monitor," *Proceedings of the 1990 IEEE Symposium on Research in Security and Privacy* pp. 296–304 (May 1990).

888. D. Hedin, A. Birgisson, L. Bello, and A. Sabelfeld. "JSFlow: Tracking Information Flow in JavaScript and Its APIs," *Proceedings of the 29th ACM Annual Symposium on Applied Computing* pp. 1663–1671 (2014).

889. R. Hefner. "Lessons Learned with the Systems Security Engineering Capability Maturity Model," *Proceedings of the 19th International Conference on Software Engineering* pp. 566–567 (May 1997).

890. R. Hefner. "A Process Standard for System Security Engineering: Development Experiences and Pilot Results," *Proceedings of the Third IEEE International Software Engineering Standards Symposium and Forum* pp. 217–221 (June 1997).

891. J. S. Held and J. Bowers. *Securing E-Business Applications and Communications*, Auerbach Publications, New York, NY, USA (June 2001).

892. H. Hellman. *Great Feuds in Science: Ten of the Liveliest Disputes Ever*, John H. Wiley & Sons, New York, NY, USA (1998).

893. M. E. Hellman. "A Cryptanalytic Time-Memory Tradeoff," *IEEE Transactions on Information Theory* **26**(4) pp. 401–406 (July 1980).

894. J. Helsingius. *Johan Helsingius Closes His Internet Remailer* (Aug. 1996).

895. C. Herley. "So Long, and No Thanks for the Externalities: The Rational Rejection of Security Advice by Users," *Proceedings of the 2009 Workshop on New Security Paradigms* pp. 133–144 (Sep. 2009).

896. A. Herzberg and H. Leibowitz. "Can Johnny Finally Encrypt? Evaluating E2E-encryption in Popular IM Applications," *Proceedings of the Sixth Workshop on Socio-Technical Aspects in Security and Trust* pp. 17–28 (Dec. 2016).

897. A. Herzog and N. Shahmehri. "An Evaluation of Java Application Containers According to Security Requirements," *Proceedings of the 14th IEEE International Workshop on Enabling Technologies: Infrastructure for Collaborative Enterprise* pp. 178–183 (June 2005).

898. P. Herzon. *OSSTMM 3: Open Source Security Testing Methodology Manual*, Technical Report, Institute for Security and Open Methodologies, New York, NY, USA (Dec. 2010).

899. P. M. Hesse and D. P. Lemire. "Managing Interoperability in Non-Hierarchical Public Key Infrastructures," *Proceedings of the 2002 Symposium on Network and Distributed System Security* (Feb. 2002).

900. V. Heydari, S.-M. Yoo, and S.-i. Kim. "Secure VPN Using Mobile IPv6 Based Moving Target Defense," *Proceedings of the 2016 IEEE Global Communications Conference* (Dec. 2016).

901. M. Hicks, M. Finnicum, S. T. King, M. M. K. Martin, and J. M. Smith. "Overcoming an Untrusted Computing Base: Detecting and Removing Malicious Hardware Automatically," *Proceedings of the 2010 IEEE Symposium on Security and Privacy* pp. 159–172 (May 2010).

902. M. Hicks, C. Sturton, S. T. King, and J. M. Smith. "SPECS: A Lightweight Runtime Mechanism for Protecting Software from Security-Critical Processor Bugs," *ACM SIGARCH Computer Architecture News* pp. 517–529 (Mar. 2015).

903. H. J. Highland. "Random Bits & Bytes: Case History of a Virus Attack," *Computers & Security* **7**(1) pp. 3–5 (Feb. 1988).

904. H. J. Highland. *Computer Virus Handbook*, Elsevier Advanced Technology, Oxford, UK (1990).

905. H. J. Highland. "Random Bits & Bytes: Testing a Password System," *Computers & Security* **11**(2) pp. 110–120 (Apr. 1992).

906. J. Hizver and T.-C. Chiueh. "Real-Time Deep Virtual Machine Introspection and Its Applications," *Proceedings of the 10th ACM SIGPLAN/SIGOPS International Conference on Virtual Execution Environments* pp. 3–14 (Mar. 2014).

907. T.-H. Ho, D. Dean, X. Gu, and W. Enck. "PREC: Practical Root Exploit Containment for Android Devices," *Proceedings of the 4th ACM Conference on Data and Application Security and Privacy* pp. 187–198 (Mar. 2014).

908. J. A. Hoagland, C. Wee, and K. Levitt. *Audit Log-Analysis Using the Visual Audit Browser Toolkit*, Technical Report CSE-95-11, Dept. of Computer Science, University of California at Davis, Davis, CA, USA (Sep. 1995).

909. L. Hochstein. *Ansible: Up and Running*, O'Reilly Media, Sebastopol, CA, USA (2015).

910. L. J. Hoffman. "The Formulary Model for Flexible Privacy and Access Controls," *Proceedings of the AFIPS '72 Spring Joint Computer Conference* pp. 587–601 (May 1972).

911. L. J. Hoffman. *Modern Methods for Computer Security and Privacy*, Prentice Hall, Englewood Cliffs, NJ, USA (1977).

912. L. J. Hoffman and R. J. Davis. "Security Pipeline Interface (SPI)," *Proceedings of the Sixth Annual Computer Security Applications Conference* pp. 349–355 (Dec. 1990).

913. L. J. Hoffman (*ed*). *Rogue Programs: Viruses, Worms and Trojan Horses*, Van Nostrand Reinhold, New York, NY, USA (1990).

914. J. Hoffstein, J. Pipher, and J. H. Silverman. *An Introduction to Mathematical Cryptography*, Springer Science+Business Media, LLC, New York, NY, USA (2008).

915. S. A. Hofmeyr, S. Forrest, and A. Somayaji. "Intrusion Detection Using Sequences of System Calls," *Journal of Computer Security* **6**(3) pp. 151–180 (1998).

916. C. Holz and P. Baudisch. "Fiberio: A Touchscreen That Senses Fingerprints," *Proceedings of the 26th Annual Symposium on User Interface Software and Technology* pp. 41–50 (Oct. 2013).

917. T. Holz, C. Gorecki, K. Rieck, and F. C. Freiling. "Measuring and Detecting Fast-Flux Service Networks," *Proceedings of the 2008 Symposium on Network and Distributed System Security* (Feb. 2008).

918. G. J. Holzmann. "The Model Checker SPIN," *IEEE Transactions on Software Engineering* **23**(5) pp. 279–295 (May 1997).

919. Homer. *The Odyssey*, Penguin Classics, New York, NY, USA (Apr. 2003).

920. M. Honan. "How Apple and Amazon Security Flaws Led to My Epic Hacking," *Wired* (Aug. 2012).

921. J. Hong. "The State of Phishing Attacks," *Communications of the ACM* **55**(1) pp. 74–81 (Jan. 2012).

922. J. Horswell and C. Fowler. "The Practice of Crime Scene Investigation," Chapter Associative Evidence — The Locard Exchange Principle in *The Practice of Crime Scene Investigation*, edited by J. Horswell, CRC Press, Boca Raton, FL, USA pp. 45–55 (2004).

923. J. D. Horton, R. H. Cooper, W. F. Hyslop, B. G. Nickerson, O. K. Ward, R. Harland, E. Ashby, and W. Stewart. "The Cascade Vulnerability Problem," *Journal of Computer Security* **2**(4) pp. 279–290 (1993).

924. A. D. Householder, G. Wassermann, A. Manion, and C. King. *The CERT Guide to Coordinated Vulnerability Disclosure*, Special Report CMU/SEI-2017-SR-022, Software Engineering Institute, Carnegie Mellon University, Pittsburgh, PA, USA (Aug. 2017).

925. R. Housley and T. Polk. *Planning for PKI: Best Practices Guide for Deploying Public Key Infrastructures*, John Wiley & Sons, Inc., New York, NY, USA (2001).

926. M. Howard and D. LeBlanc. *Writing Secure Code*, Microsoft Press (2003).

927. M. Howard, D. LeBlanc, and J. Viega. *24 Deadly Sins of Software Security: Programming Flaws and How to Fix Them*, McGraw-Hill, New York, NY, USA (2009).

928. W. Hsieh, M. Fiuczynk, C. Garrett, S. Savage, D. Becker, and B. Bershad. "Language Support for Extensible Operating Systems," *Proceedings of the Workshop on Compiler Support for System Software* pp. 127–133 (Feb. 1996).

929. N. Htoo-Mosher, R. Nasser, N. Zunic, and J. Straw. "E4 ITSEC Evaluation of PR/SM on ES/9000 Processors," *Proceedings of the 19th National Information Systems Security Conference* pp. 1–11 (Oct. 1996).

930. W.-M. Hu. "Lattice Scheduling and Covert Channels," *Proceedings of the 1992 IEEE Symposium on Research in Security and Privacy* pp. 52–61 (May 1992).

931. W.-M. Hu. "Reducing Timing Channels with Fuzzy Time," *Journal of Computer Security* **1**(3-4) pp. 233–254 (1992).

932. M. Huber, B. Taubmann, S. Wessel, H. P. Reiser, and G. Sigl. "A Flexible Framework for Mobile Device Forensics Based on Cold Boot Attacks," *EURASIP Journal on Information Security* **2016**(1) (Aug. 2016).

933. J. Hughes. "Certificate Inter-Operability — White Paper," *Computers & Security* **18**(3) pp. 221–230 (1999).

934. J. Hughes. "The Realities of PKI Inter-Operability," *Proceedings of the Secure Networking — CQRE [Secure] '99 International Exhibition and Congress* (*Lecture Notes in Computer Science* **1740**) pp. 127–132 (Nov. 1999).

935. C. Humphries, N. Prigent, C. Bidan, and F. Majorczyk. "ELVIS: Extensible Log VISualization," *Proceedings of the Tenth Workshop on Visualization for Cyber Security* pp. 9–16 (Oct. 2013).

936. J. Hunker, C. Gates, and M. Bishop. "Attribution Requirements for Next Generation Internets," *Proceedings of the 2011 IEEE International Conference on Technologies for Homeland Security* pp. 345–350 (Nov. 2011).

937. M. Huth and M. Ryan. *Logic in Computer Science: Modeling and Reasoning about Systems*, Cambridge University Press, Cambridge, UK (2004).

938. G. Iachello and K. Rannenberg. "Protection Profiles for Remailer Mixes," *Proceedings of the International Workshop on Design Issues in Anonymity and Unobservability* (*Lecture Notes in Computer Science* **2009**) pp. 181–230 (July 2001).

939. C. I'Anson and C. Mitchell. "Security Defects in CCITT Recommendation X.509—The Directory Authentication Framework," *ACM SIGCOMM Computer Communications Review* **20**(2) pp. 30–34 (Apr. 1990).

940. N. Idika and B. Bhargava. "Extending Attack Graph-Based Security Metrics and Aggregating Their Application," *IEEE Transactions on Dependable and Secure Computing* **9**(1) pp. 75–85 (Jan. 2012).

941. V. M. Igure and R. D. Williams. "Taxonomies of Attacks and Vulnerabilities in Computer Systems," *IEEE Communications Surveys & Tutorials* **10**(1) pp. 6–19 (Apr. 2008).

942. K. Ilgun, R. A. Kemmerer, and P. Porras. "State Transition Analysis: A Rule-Based Intrusion Detection Approach," *IEEE Transactions on Software Engineering* **21**(3) pp. 181–199 (Mar. 1995).

943. J. K. Iliffe and J. G. Jodeit. "A Dynamic Storage Allocation Scheme," *The Computer Journal* **5**(3) pp. 200–209 (1962).

944. P. G. Inglestat and M. A. Sasse. "The True Cost of Unusable Password Policies: Password Use in the Wild," *Proceedings of the 2010 SIGCHI Conference on Human Factors in Computing Systems* pp. 383–392 (Apr. 2010).

945. K. Ingols, R. Lippmann, and K. Piwowarski. "Practical Attack Graph Generation for Network Defense," *Proceedings of the 22nd Annual Computer Security Applications Conference* pp. 121–130 (Dec. 2006).

946. D. Irani, K. Webb, Steve amd Li, and C. Pu. "Modeling Unintended Personal-Information Leakage from Multiple Online Social Networks," *IEEE Internet Computing* **15**(3) pp. 13–19 (May 2011).

947. C. E. Irvine and D. Volpano. "A Practical Tool for Developing Trusted Applications," *Proceedings of the 11th Annual Computer Security Applications Conference* pp. 190–195 (Dec. 1995).

948. H. R. Isa, W. R. Shockley, and C. E. Irvine. "A Multi-Threading Architecture for Multilevel Secure Transaction Processing," *Proceedings of the 1999 IEEE Symposium on Security and Privacy* pp. 166–180 (May 1999).

949. D. K. Isenor and S. G. Zaky. "Fingerprint Identification Using Graph Matching," *Pattern Recognition* **19**(2) pp. 113–122 (1986).

950. N. Isogai, T. Matsunaka, and A. Miyaji. "Optimized χ^2-Attack Against RC6," *Proceedings of the First International Conference on Applied Cryptography and Network Security* (*Lecture Notes in Computer Science* **2846**) pp. 16–32 (Oct. 2003).

951. H. Israel. "Computer Viruses: Myth or Reality?" *Proceedings of the Tenth National Computer Security Conference* pp. 226–230 (Sep. 1987).

952. T. Iwata, K. Ohashi, and K. Minematsu. "Breaking and Repairing GCM Security Proofs," *Advances in Cryptology — CRYPTO 2012* (*Lecture Notes in Computer Science* **7417**) pp. 31–49 (Aug. 2012).

953. T. Jaeger, A. Prakash, J. Liedtke, and N. Islam. "Flexible Control of Downloaded Executable Content," *ACM Transactions on Information and System Security* **2**(2) pp. 177–228 (May 1999).

954. T. Jaeger, R. Sailer, and X. Zhang. "Analyzing Integrity Protection in the SELinux Example Policy," *Proceedings of the 12th USENIX Security Symposium* pp. 59–74 (Aug. 2003).

955. T. Jager, J. Schwenk, and J. Somorovsky. "On the Security of TLS 1.3 and QUIC Against Weaknesses in PKCS#1 V1.5 Encryption," *Proceedings of the 22nd ACM SIGSAC Conference on Computer and Communications Security* pp. 1185–1196 (Oct. 2015).

956. A. K. Jain, K. Nandakumar, and A. Ross. "50 Years of Biometric Research: Accomplishments, Challenges, and Opportunities," *Pattern Recognition Letters* **79** pp. 80–105 (Aug. 2016).

957. A. K. Jain, A. Ross, and S. Prabhakar. "An Introduction to Biometric Recognition," *IEEE Transactions on Circuits and Systems for Video Technology* **14**(1) pp. 4–20 (Jan. 2004).

958. S. Jajodia, P. Samarati, and V. S. Subrahmanian. "A Logical Language for Expressing Authorizations," *Proceedings of the 1997 IEEE Symposium on Security and Privacy* pp. 31–42 (May 1997).

959. S. Jajodia and R. Sandhu. "Towards a Multilevel Secure Relational Data Model," *Proceedings of the 1991 ACM SIGMOD International Conference on Management of Data* pp. 50–59 (May 1991).

960. M. Jakobsson, E. Shriver, B. K. Hillyer, and A. Juels. "A Practical Secure Physical Random Bit Generator," *Proceedings of the Fifth ACM Conference on Computer and Communications Security* pp. 103–111 (Nov. 1998).

961. P. A. Jamkhedkar and G. L. Heileman. "Digital Rights Management Architectures," *Computers & Electrical Engineering* **35**(2) pp. 376–394 (Mar. 2009).

962. S. Jana, D. E. Porter, and V. Shmatikov. "TxBox: Building Secure, Efficient Sandboxes with System Transactions," *Proceedings of the 2011 IEEE Symposium on Security and Privacy* pp. 329–344 (May 2011).

963. R. Jansen, F. Tschorsch, A. Johnson, and B. Scheuermann. "The Sniper Attack: Anonymously Deanonymizing and Disabling the Tor Network," *Proceedings of the 2014 Symposium on Network and Distributed System Security* pp. 24:1–24:15 (Feb. 2014).

964. B. Javadi, D. Kondo, J.-M. Vincent, and D. P. Anderson. "Discovering Statistical Models of Availability in Large Distributed Systems: An Empirical Study of SETI@home," *IEEE Transactions on Parallel and Distributed Systems* **22**(11) pp. 1896–1903 (Nov. 2011).

965. H. S. Javitz and A. Valdes. "The SRI IDES Statistical Anomaly Detector," *Proceedings of the 1991 IEEE Symposium on Research in Security and Privacy* pp. 316–326 (May 1991).

966. K. Jensen and N. Wirth. *PASCAL User Manual and Report*, Springer-Verlag Berlin Heidelberg, Berlin, Germany (1975).

967. L. Jia, J. Aljuraidan, E. Fragkaki, L. Bauer, M. Stroucken, K. Fukushima, S. Kiyomoto, and Y. Miyake. "Run-Time Enforcement of Information-Flow Properties on Android," *Proceedings of the 18th European Symposium on Research in Computer Security* (*Lecture Notes in Computer Science*) pp. 775–792 (Sep. 2013).

968. A. Johnson and P. Syverson. "More Anonymous Onion Routing Through Trust," *Proceedings of the 22nd Computer Security Foundations Workshop* (July 2009).

969. D. M. Johnson and F. J. Thayer. "Security and the Composition of Machines," *Proceedings of the First Computer Security Foundations Workshop* pp. 72–89 (June 1988).

970. H. L. Johnson and M. L. De Vilbiss. "Use of the Trusted Computer System Evaluation Criteria (TCSEC) for Complex, Evolving, Multipolicy Systems," *Proceedings of the 16th National Computer Security Conference* pp. 137–145 (Sep. 1993).

971. A. K. Jones and R. J. Lipton. "The Enforcement of Security Policies for Computation," *Proceedings of the Fifth ACM Symposium on Operating Systems Principles* pp. 197–206 (Nov. 1975).

972. A. K. Jones, R. J. Lipton, and L. Snyder. "A Linear Time Algorithm for Deciding Security," *Proceedings of the 17th Annual Symposium on Foundations of Computer Science* pp. 33–41 (Oct. 1976).

973. D. W. Jones. "Auditing Elections," *Communications of the ACM* **47**(10) pp. 46–50 (Oct. 2004).

974. J. Jonsson. "On the Security of CTR + CBC-MAC," *Proceedings of the Ninth International Workshop on Selected Areas in Cryptography* (*Lecture Notes in Computer Science* **2595**) pp. 76–93 (2002).

975. A. Jøsang, R. Ismail, and C. Boyd. "A Survey of Trust and Reputation Systems for Online Service Provision," *Decision Support Systems* **43**(2) pp. 618–644 (Mar. 2007).

976. M. Joseph. "Towards the Elimination of the Effects of Malicious Logic: Fault Tolerance Approaches," *Proceedings of the Tenth National Computer Security Conference* pp. 238–244 (Sep. 1987).

977. M. K. Joseph and A. Avižienis. "A Fault Tolerant Approach to Computer Viruses," *Proceedings of the 1988 IEEE Symposium on Security and Privacy* pp. 52–58 (Apr. 1988).

978. J. B. D. Joshi, E. Bertino, U. Latif, and A. Ghafoor. "A Generalized Temporal Role-Based Access Control Model," *IEEE Transactions on Knowledge and Data Engineering* **17**(1) pp. 4–23 (Jan. 2005).

979. J. Joshi, A. Ghafoor, W. Aref, and E. H. Spafford. "Digital Government Security Infrastructure Design Challenges," *IEEE Computer* **34**(2) pp. 66–72 (Feb. 2001).

980. A. Joux. "Authentication Failures in NIST version of GCM," Comments on the Draft GCM Specification, Gaithersburg, MD, USA (Apr. 2006)

981. N. Jovanovic, C. Kruegel, and E. Kirda. "Static Analysis for Detecting Taint-Style Vulnerabilities in Web Applications," *Journal of Computer Security* **18**(5) pp. 861–907 (2010).

982. R. Joyce and G. Gupta. "Identity Authentication Based on Keystroke Latencies," *Communications of the ACM* **33**(2) pp. 168–176 (Feb. 1990).

983. R. Jung, J.-H. Jourdan, R. Kerbbers, and D. Dryer. "RustBelt: Securing the Foundations of the Rust Programming Language," *Proceedings of the ACM on Programming Languages* **2**(POPL) pp. 66:1–66:34 (Jan. 2018).

984. J. E. Juni and R. Ponto. "Computer-Virus Infection of a Medical Diagnostic Computer," *New England Journal of Medicine* **320**(12) pp. 811–812 (Mar. 1989).

985. F. Kafka. *The Trial*, edited by R. Robinson, Oxford University Press, New York, NY, USA (Oct. 2009).

986. L. Kagal, T. Finin, and A. Joshi. "A Policy Language for a Pervasive Computing Environment," *Proceedings of the IEEE Fourth International Workshop on Policies for Distributed Systems and Networks* pp. 63–74 (June 2003).

987. C. Kahn. "Incentives to Help Stop Floods," *Proceedings of the 2000 Workshop on New Security Paradigms* pp. 127–132 (Sep. 2000).

988. D. Kahn. *The Codebreakers: The Story of Secret Writing*, The Macmillan Company, New York, NY, USA (1967).

989. D. Kahn. *Seizing the Enigma: The Race to Break the German U-Boats Codes, 1939–1943*, Houghton Mifflin, New York, NY, USA (1991).

990. D. Kahn. *The Codebreakers: The Comprehensive History of Secret Communication from Ancient Times to the Internet*, Scribner, New York, NY, USA (1996).

991. K. C. Kahn, W. M. Corwin, T. D. Dennis, H. D'Hooge, D. E. Hubka, L. A. Hutchins, J. T. Montague, and F. J. Pollack. "iMAX: A Multiprocessor Operating System for an Object-Based Computer," *Proceedings of the Eighth ACM Symposium on Operating Systems Principles* pp. 127–136 (Dec. 1981).

992. R. Y. Kain. *Advanced Computer Architecture: A Systems Design Approach*, Prentice Hall, Upper Saddle River, NJ, USA (1995).

993. R. Y. Kain and C. E. Landwehr. "On Access Checking in Capability-Based Systems," *Proceedings of the 1986 IEEE Symposium on Security and Privacy* pp. 95–100 (Apr. 1986).

994. T. Kalsi. *Practical Linux Security Cookbook*, Packt Publishing Ltd., Birmingham, UK (2016).

995. S. Kamara, S. Fahmy, E. E. Schultz, F. Kerschbaum, and M. Frantzen. "Analysis of Vulnerabilities in Internet Firewalls," *Computers & Security* **22**(3) pp. 214–232 (Apr. 2003).

996. A. Kaminsky, M. Kurdziel, and S. Radziszowski. "An Overview of Cryptanalysis Research for the Advanced Encryption Standard," *Proceedings of the 2010 Military Communications Conference* pp. 1310–1316 (Oct. 2010).

997. S. D. Kamvar, M. T. Schlosser, and H. Garcia-Molina. "The Eigentrust Algorithm for Reputation Management in P2P Networks," *Proceedings of the 12th International World Wide Web Conference* pp. 640–651 (May 2003).

998. M. H. Kang, A. P. Moore, and I. S. Moskowitz. "Design and Assurance Strategy for the NRL Pump," *IEEE Computer* **31**(4) pp. 56–64 (Apr. 1998).

999. M. H. Kang and I. S. Moskowitz. "A Pump for Rapid, Reliable, Secure Communication," *Proceedings of the First ACM Conference on Computer and Communications Security* pp. 119–129 (Nov. 1993).

1000. M. H. Kang, I. S. Moskowitz, and S. Chincheck. "The Pump: A Decade of Covert Fun," *Proceedings of the 21st Annual Computer Security Applications Conference* pp. 360–366 (Dec. 2005).

1001. M. H. Kang, I. S. Moskowitz, and D. C. Lee. "A Network Version of the Pump," *Proceedings of the 1995 IEEE Symposium on Security and Privacy* pp. 144–154 (May 1995).

1002. M. H. Kang, I. S. Moskowitz, and D. C. Lee. "A Network Pump," *IEEE Transactions on Software Engineering* **22**(5) pp. 329–338 (May 1996).

1003. L. Kanies. "ISconf: Theory, Practice, and Beyond," *Proceedings of the 17th Large Installation Systems Administration Conference* pp. 115–123 (Oct. 2003).

1004. H. Kannan, M. Dalton, and C. Kozyrakis. "Decoupling Dynamic Information Flow Tracking with a Dedicated Coprocessor," *Proceedings of the 2009 IEEE/IFIP International Conference on Dependable Systems and Networks* pp. 105–114 (June 2009).

1005. B. Kantor. *BSD Rlogin*, RFC 1282 (Dec. 1991).

1006. P. A. Karger. "Limiting the Damage Potential of Discretionary Trojan Horses," *Proceedings of the 1987 IEEE Symposium on Security and Privacy* pp. 32–37 (Apr. 1987).

1007. P. A. Karger and A. J. Herbert. "An Augmented Capability Architecture to Support Lattice Security and Traceability of Access," *Proceedings of the 1984 IEEE Symposium on Security and Privacy* pp. 2–12 (Apr. 1984).

1008. P. A. Karger and R. R. Schell. *Multics Security Evaluation: Vulnerability Analysis*, Technical Report ESD-TR-73-193, Vol. II, Electronic Systems Division, Hanscom Air Force Base, Hanscom Air Force Base, MA 01730 (June 1974).

1009. P. A. Karger and J. C. Wray. "Storage Channels in Disk Arm Optimization," *Proceedings of the 1991 IEEE Symposium on Research in Security and Privacy* pp. 52–61 (May 1991).

1010. P. A. Karger, M. E. Zurko, D. W. Bonin, A. H. Mason, and C. E. Kahn. "A VMM Security Kernel for the VAX Architecture," *Proceedings of the 1990 IEEE Symposium on Research in Security and Privacy* pp. 2–19 (May 1990).

1011. M. Kassner. "Anatomy of the Target Breach: Missed Opportunities and Lessons Learned," *ZDNet* (Feb. 2015).

1012. C. Kaufman, P. Hoffman, Y. Nir, and P. Eronen. *Internet Key Exchange Protocol Version 2 (IKEv2)*, RFC 7296 (Oct. 2014).

1013. C. Kaufman, R. Perlman, and M. Speciner. *Network Security: Private Communications in a Public World*, Prentice Hall, Inc, Upper Saddle River, NJ, USA (2002).

1014. M. Kaufmann and J. S. Moore. "An Industrial Strength Theorem Prover for a Logic Based on Common Lisp," *IEEE Transactions on Software Engineering* **23**(4) pp. 203–213 (Apr. 1997).

1015. Y. Kawatsura. *Secure Electronic Transaction (SET) Supplement for the V1.0 Internet Open Trading Protocol (IOTP)*, RFC 3538 (June 2003).

1016. K. Kaynar and F. Sivrijaya. "Distributed Attack Graph Generation," *IEEE Transactions on Dependable and Secure Computing* **13**(5) pp. 519–532 (Sep. 2015).

1017. G. Kedem and Y. Ishihara. "Brute Force Attack on UNIX Passwords with SIMD Computer," *Proceedings of the Eighth USENIX UNIX Security Symposium* (Aug. 1999).

1018. M. Keith, B. Shao, and P. J. Steinbart. "The Usability of Passphrases for Authentication: An Empirical Field Study," *International Journal of Human-Computer Studies* **65**(1) pp. 17–28 (Jan. 2007).

1019. M. Keith, B. Shao, and P. J. Steinbart. "A Behavioral Analysis of Passphrase Design and Effectiveness," *Journal of the Association for Information Systems* **10**(2) pp. 63–89 (Feb. 2009).

1020. P. G. Kelley, S. Komanduri, M. L. Mazurek, R. Shay, T. Vidas, L. Bauer, N. Christin, L. F. Cranor, and J. López. "Guess Again (and Again and Again): Measuring Password Strength by Simulating Password-Cracking Algorithms," *Proceedings of the 2012 IEEE Symposium on Security and Privacy* pp. 523–537 (May 2012).

1021. J. Kelsey, T. Kohno, and B. Schneier. "Amplified Boomerang Attacks Against Reduced-Round MARS and Serpent," *Proceedings of the Seventh International Workshop on Fast Software Encryption* (*Lecture Notes in Computer Science* **1978**) pp. 13–23 (2000).

1022. J. Kelsey and B. Schneier. "MARS Attacks! Preliminary Cryptanalysis of Reduced-Round MARS Variants," *Proceedings of the Third AES Candidate Conference* pp. 169–185 (Apr. 2000).

1023. J. Kelsey, B. Schneier, and D. Wagner. "Related-Key Cryptanalysis of 3-WAY, Biham-DES, CAST, DES-X, NewDES, RC2, and TEA," *Proceedings of the First International Conference on Information and Communications Security* (*Lecture Notes in Computer Science* **1334**) pp. 233–246 (1997).

1024. R. A. Kemmerer. "A Practical Approach to Identifying Storage and Timing Channels," *Proceedings of the 1982 IEEE Symposium on Security and Privacy* pp. 66–73 (Apr. 1982).

1025. R. A. Kemmerer. "Shared Resource Matrix Methodology: An Approach to Identifying Storage and Timing Channels," *ACM Transactions on Computer Systems* **1**(3) pp. 256–277 (Aug. 1983).

1026. R. A. Kemmerer. "Analyzing Encryption Protocols Using Formal Verification Techniques," *IEEE Journal on Selected Areas in Communication* **7**(4) pp. 448–457 (May 1989).

1027. R. A. Kemmerer. "A Practical Approach to Identifying Storage and Timing Channels: Twenty Years Later," *Proceedings of the 18th Annual Computer Security Applications Conference* pp. 109–118 (Dec. 2002).

1028. R. A. Kemmerer and P. Porras. "Covert Flow Trees: A Visual Approach to Analyzing Covert Storage Channels," *IEEE Transactions on Software Engineering* **17**(11) pp. 1166–1185 (Nov. 1991).

1029. R. A. Kemmerer and G. Vigna. "Intrusion Detection: A Brief History and Overview," *IEEE Computer* **35**(4) pp. supl27–supl30 (Apr. 2002).

1030. R. Kemmerer, C. Meadows, and J. Millen. "Three Systems for Cryptographic Protocol Analysis," *Journal of Cryptology* **7**(2) pp. 79–130 (June 1994).

1031. D. Kennedy, J. O'Gorman, D. Kearns, and M. Aharoni. *Metasploit: The Penetration Tester's Guide*, No Starch Press, San Francisco, CA, USA (2011).

1032. S. Kent. "Comments on 'Security Problems in the TCP/IP Protocol Suite,'" *ACM SIGCOMM Computer Communications Review* **19**(3) pp. 10–19 (July 1989).

1033. S. Kent. *Privacy Enhancement for Internet Electronic Mail: Part II: Certificate-Based Key Management*, RFC 1422 (Feb. 1993).

1034. S. Kent. *IP Authentication Header*, RFC 4302 (Dec. 2005).

1035. S. Kent. *IP Encapsulating Security Payload (ESP)*, RFC 4303 (Dec. 2005).

1036. S. Kent and K. Seo. *Security Architecture for the Internet Protocol*, RFC 4301 (Dec. 2005).

1037. S. T. Kent. "Encryption-Based Protection Protocols for Interactive User-Computer Communication over Physically Unsecured Channels," Master's Thesis, Dept. of Electrical Engineering and Computer Science, Massachusetts Institute of Technology, Cambridge, MA, USA (1976).

1038. J. O. Kephart and W. C. Arnold. "Automatic Extraction of Computer Virus Signatures," *Proceedings of the 4th Virus Bulletin International Conference* pp. 178–184 (1994).

1039. B. Kernighan and P. J. Plauger. *The Elements of Programming Style*, McGraw-Hill, New York, NY USA (1978).

1040. B. W. Kernighan and R. Pike. *The Practice of Programming*, Addison-Wesley, Reading, MA, USA (1999).

1041. B. W. Kernighan and P. J. Plaugher. *Software Tools*, Addison-Wesley, Reading, MA, USA (1976).

1042. A. D. Keromytis and V. Prevelakis. "Designing Firewalls: A Survey," Chapter 3 in *Network Security: Current Status and Future Directions*, edited by C. Douligeris and D. N. Serpanos, IEEE, Washington, DC, USA pp. 33–50 (2007).

1043. K. Keus, W. Kurth, and D. Loevenich. "Quality Assurance in the ITSEC-Evaluation Environment in Germany," *Proceedings of the 16th National Computer Security Conference* pp. 324–333 (Sep. 1993).

1044. K. Keus and K.-W. Schröder. "Measuring Correctness and Effectiveness: A New Approach Using Process Evaluation," *Proceedings of the 18th National Computer Security Conference* pp. 366–373 (Oct. 1995).

1045. D. Kewley, R. Fink, J. Lowry, and M. Dean. "Dynamic Approaches to Thwart Adversary Intelligence Gathering," *Proceedings of the 2001 DARPA Information Survivability Conference and Exposition II* pp. 176–185 (June 2001).

1046. S. Khan, A. Gani, A. W. A. Wahab, M. A. Bagiwa, M. Shiraz, S. U. Khan, R. Buyya, and A. Y. Zomaya. "Cloud Log Forensics: Foundations, State of the Art, and Future Directions," *ACM Computing Surveys* **49**(1) pp. 7:1–7:42 (July 2016).

1047. A. Kharraz, W. Robertson, D. Balzarotti, L. Bilge, and E. Kirda. "Cutting the Gordian Knot: A Look Under the Hood of Ransomware Attacks," *Proceedings of the 12th International Conference for Detection of Intrusion and Malware, and Vulnerability Assessment* (*Lecture Notes in Computer Science* **9148**) pp. 3–24 (July 2015).

1048. S. Khazaei and W. Meier. "New Directions in Cryptanalysis of Self-Synchronizing Stream Ciphers," *Proceedings of the Ninth International Conference on Cryptology in India: Progress in Cryptology — INDOCRYPT 2008* (*Lecture Notes in Computer Science* **5365**) pp. 15–26 (2008).

1049. H. Khurana, R. Bobba, T. Yardley, P. Agarwal, and E. Heine. "Design Principles for Power Grid Cyber-Infrastructure Authentication Protocols," *Proceedings of the 43rd Hawaii International Conference on System Sciences* pp. 1–10 (Jan. 2010).

1050. H. Khurana, M. Hadley, N. Lu, and D. A. Frincke. "Smart-Grid Security Issues," *IEEE Security & Privacy* **8**(1) pp. 81–85 (Jan. 2010).

1051. C. Kil, J. Jun, C. Bookholt, J. Xu, and P. Ning. "Address Space Layout Permutation (ASLP): Towards Fine-Grained Randomization of Commodity Software," *Proceedings of the 22nd Annual Computer Security Applications Conference* pp. 339-348 (Dec. 2006).

1052. S. Kiljan, K. Simoens, D. D. Cock, M. V. Eekelen, and H. Vranken. "A Survey of Authentication and Communications Security in Online Banking," *ACM Computing Surveys* **49**(4) pp. 61:1–61:35 (Feb. 2017).

1053. G. H. Kim and E. H. Spafford. "The Design and Implementation of Tripwire: A File System Integrity Checker," *Proceedings of the Second ACM Conference on Computer and Communications Security* pp. 18–29 (10.1145/191177.191183 1994).

1054. J. Kim, A. Biryukov, B. Preneel, and S. Hong. "On the Security of HMAC and NMAC Based on HAVAL, MD4, MD5, SHA-0 and SHA-1 (Extended Abstract)," *Proceedings of the 5th International Conference on Security and Cryptography for Networks* (*Lecture Notes in Computer Science* **4116**) pp. 242–256 (Sep. 2006).

1055. T. Kim and N. Zeldovich. "Practical and Effective Sandboxing for Non-Root Users," *Proceedings of the 2008 USENIX Annual Technical Conference* pp. 139–144 (June 2008).

1056. Y. Kim, R. Daly, J. Kim, C. Fallin, J. H. Lee, D. Lee, C. Wilkerson, K. Lai, and O. Mutlu. "Flipping Bits in Memory Without Accessing Them: An Experimental Study of DRAM Disturbance Errors," *ACM SIGARCH Computer Architecture News* **42**(3) pp. 361–372 (June 2014).

1057. Y. Kim, W. C. Lau, M. C. Chuah, and H. J. Chao. "PacketScore: A Statistics-Based Packet Filtering Scheme Against Distributed Denial-of-Service Attacks," *IEEE Transactions on Dependable and Secure Computing* **3**(2) pp. 141–155 (Apr. 2006).

1058. S. T. King, J. Tucek, A. Cozzie, C. Grier, W. Jiang, and Y. Zhou. "Designing and Implementing Malicious Hardware," *Proceedings of the First USENIX Workshop on Large-Scale Exploits and Emergent Threats* (Apr. 2008).

1059. J. Kirby, Jr. and C. Archer, Myla an Heitmeyer. "SCR: A Practical Approach to Building a High Assurance COMSEC System," *Proceedings of the 15th Annual Computer Security Applications Conference* pp. 109–118 (Dec. 1999).

1060. J. Kissell. *Mac Security Bible*, Wiley Publishing, Inc., Indianapolis, IN, USA (2010).

1061. A. Kleen. "Syncookies Implementation for the Linux Kernel," linux/net/ipv4/syncookies.c (1997).

1062. D. Klein. "A Capability Based Protection Mechanism Under Unix," *Proceedings of the Winter 1985 USENIX Technical Conference* pp. 152–159 (Jan. 1985).

1063. D. Klein. "Foiling the Cracker: A Survey of, and Improvements to, Password Security," *Proceedings of the Second UNIX Security Workshop* pp. 5–14 (Aug. 1990).

1064. G. Klein, J. Andronick, K. Elphinstone, T. Murray, T. Sewell, R. Kolanski, and G. Heiser. "Comprehensive Formal Verification of an OS Microkernel," *ACM Transactions on Computer Systems* **32**(1) pp. 2:1–2:70 (Feb. 2014).

1065. G. Klein, K. Elphinstone, G. Heiser, J. Andronick, D. Cock, P. Derrin, D. Elkaduwe, K. Engelhardt, R. Kolanski, M. Norrish, T. Sewell, H. Tuch, and S. Winwood. "seL4: Formal Verification of an OS Kernel," *Proceedings of the 22nd Symposium on Operating Systems Principles* pp. 207–220 (Oct. 2009).

1066. G. Klein, H. Rogge, F. Schneider, J. Toelle, M. Jahnke, and S. Karsch. "Response Initiation in Distributed Intrusion Response Systems for Tactical MANETs," *Proceedings of the 2010 European Conference on Computer Network Detection* pp. 55–62 (Oct. 2010).

1067. E. Kleiner and T. Newcomb. "On the Decidability of the Safety Problem for Access Control Policies," *Electronic Notes in Theoretical Computer Science* **185** pp. 107–120 (July 2007).

1068. J. C. Klensin. *Simple Mail Transfer Protocol*, RFC 2821 (Apr. 2001).

1069. J. C. Klensin. *Role of the Domain Name System (DNS)*, RFC 3467 (Feb. 2003).

1070. J. C. Klensin, P. Faltstrom, and C. Karp. *IAB – IDN Next Steps*, RFC 4690 (Sep. 2006).

1071. J. C. Knight and N. G. Leveson. "An Experimental Evaluation of the Assumption of Independence in Multiversion Programming," *IEEE Transactions on Software Engineering* **SE-12**(1) pp. 96–109 (Jan. 1986).

1072. J. C. Knight and N. G. Leveson. "A Reply to the Criticisms of the Knight & Leveson Experiment," *ACM SIGSOFT Software Engineering Notes* **15**(1) pp. 24–35 (Jan. 1990).

1073. P. Knight and C. Lewis. "Layer 2 and 3 Virtual Private Networks: Taxonomy, Technology, and Standardization Efforts," *IEEE Communications Magazine* **42**(6) pp. 121–131 (June 2004).

1074. L. R. Knudsen. "Truncated and Higher Order Differentials," *Proceedings of the Second International Workshop on Fast Software Encryption* (*Lecture Notes in Computer Science* **1008**) pp. 196–211 (Dec. 1994).

1075. L. R. Knudsen and V. Rijmen. "Weaknesses in LOKI97," *Proceedings of the Second AES Candidate Conference* (Mar. 1999).

1076. D. E. Knuth. *The Art of Computer Programming, Volume 2: Seminumerical Algorithms*, Addison-Wesley, Reading, MA, USA (1998).

1077. C. Ko, G. Fink, and K. Levitt. "Automated Detection of Vulnerabilities in Privileged Programs by Execution Monitoring," *Proceedings of the Tenth Annual Computer Security Applications Conference* pp. 134–144 (Dec. 1994).

1078. C. Ko, T. Fraser, L. Badger, and D. Kilpatrick. "Detecting and Countering System Intrusions Using Software Wrappers," *Proceedings of the Ninth USENIX Security Symposium* (Aug. 2000).

1079. C. Ko, M. Ruschitzka, and K. Levitt. "Execution Monitoring of Security-Critical Programs in Distributed Systems: A Specification-Based Approach," *Proceedings of the 1997 IEEE Symposium on Security and Privacy* pp. 175–187 (May 1997).

1080. H.-P. Ko. "Security Properties of Ring Brackets," *Proceedings of the Second Computer Security Foundations Workshop* pp. 41–46 (June 1989).

1081. A. H. Koblitz, N. Koblitz, and A. Menezes. "Elliptic Curve Cryptography: The Serpentine Course of a Paradigm Shift," *Journal of Number Theory* **131**(5) pp. 781–814 (May 2011).

1082. N. Koblitz. "Elliptic Curve Cryptosystems," *Mathematics of Computation* **48**(117) pp. 203–209 (Jan. 1987).

1083. M. Koch, L. V. Mancini, and F. Parisi-Presicce. "Decidability of Safety in Graph-Based Models for Access Control," *Proceedings of the Seventh European Symposium on Research in Computer Security* (*Lecture Notes in Computer Science* **2502**) pp. 229–244 (Oct. 2002).

1084. P. C. Kocher. "Timing Attacks on Implementations of Diffie-Hellman, RSA, DSS, and Other Systems," *Advances in Cryptology — CRYPTO '96* (*Lecture Notes in Computer Science*) pp. 104–113 (Aug. 1996).

1085. K. Kochetkova. "Tricky Locky Ransomware Robs American Hospitals," *Kaspersky Lab Daily* (Mar. 25, 2016)

1086. R. H. Koenen, J. Lacy, M. Mackay, and S. Mitchell. "The Long March to Interoperable Digital Rights Management," *Proceedings of the IEEE* **92**(6) pp. 883–897 (June 2004).

1087. L. M. Kohnfelder. *Towards a Practical Public-Key Cryptosystem*, Bachelor's Thesis, Massachusetts Institute of Technology, Cambridge, MA, USA (May 1978).

1088. T. Kohno, A. Stubblefield, A. D. Rubin, and D. S. Wallach. "Analysis of an Electronic Voting System," *Proceedings of the 2004 IEEE Symposium on Security and Privacy* pp. 27–40 (May 2004).

1089. H. Koike and K. Ohno. "SnortView: Visualization System of Snort Logs," *Proceedings of the 2004 ACM Workshop on Visualization and Data Mining for Computer Security* pp. 143–147 (Oct. 2004).

1090. C. Kolias, G. Kambourakis, A. Stavrou, and J. Voas. "DDoS in the IoT: Mirai and Other Botnets," *IEEE Computer* **50**(7) pp. 80–84 (July 2017).

1091. S. Kondakci. "Epidemic State Analysis of Computers Under Malware Attacks," *Simulation Modeling Practice and Theory* **16**(5) pp. 571–584 (May 2008).

1092. A. G. Konheim. *Cryptography: A Primer*, John Wiley & Sons, Inc., New York, NY, USA (1981).

1093. A. G. Konheim. *Computer Security and Cryptography*, Wiley Interscience, New York, NY, USA (2007).

1094. B. Kordy, S. Mauw, S. Radomirović, and P. Schweitzer. "Attack-Defense Trees," *Journal of Logic and Computation* **24**(1) pp. 55–87 (Feb. 2014).

1095. Y. Korff, P. Hope, and B. Potter. *Mastering FreeBSD and OpenBSD Security*, O'Reilly Media, Inc., Sebastopol, CA, USA (2005).

1096. K. Koscher, Czeskis, F. Roesner, S. Patel, T. Kohno, S. Checkoway, D. McCoy, B. Kantor, D. Anderson, H. Shacham, and S. Savage. "Experimental Security Analysis of a Modern Automobile," *Proceedings of the 2010 IEEE Symposium on Security and Privacy* pp. 447–462 (May 2010).

1097. K. Kothari and M. Wright. "Mimic: An Active Covert Channel That Evades Regularity-Based Detection," *Computer Networks* **57**(3) pp. 647–657 (Feb. 2013).

1098. S. M. Kramer. "On Incorporating Access Control Lists into the UNIX Operating System," *Proceedings of the UNIX Security Workshop* pp. 38–48 (Aug. 1988).

1099. K. Kratkiewicz and R. Lippmann. "A Taxonomy of Buffer Overflows for Evaluating Static and Dynamic Software Testing Tools," *Proceedings of the 2005 NIST Workshop on Software Security Assurance Tools, Techniques, and Metrics* (Nov. 2005).

1100. H. Krawczyk. "How to Predict Congruential Generators," *Journal of Algorithms* **13**(4) pp. 527–545 (Dec. 1992).

1101. H. Krawczyk. "The Order of Encryption and Authentication for Protecting Communications (or: How Secure Is SSL?)," *Advances in Cryptology — CRYPTO 2001* (*Lecture Notes in Computer Science* **2139**) pp. 310–331 (Aug. 2001).

1102. H. Krawczyk, M. Bellare, and R. Canetti. *HMAC: Keyed-Hashing for Message Authentication*, RFC 2104 (Feb. 1997).

1103. H. Krawczyk and P. Eronen. *HMAC-Based Extract-and-Expand Key Derivation Function (HKDF)*, RFC 5869 (June 2010).

1104. K. Krombholz, H. Hobel, M. Huber, and E. Weippl. "Advanced Social Engineering Attacks," *Journal of Information Security and Applications* **22** pp. 113–122 (June 2015).

1105. I. V. Krsul. *Software Vulnerability Analysis*, Technical Report 98-09, COAST, Purdue University, West Lafayette, IN, USA (May 1998).

1106. I. V. Krsul and E. H. Spafford. "Authorship Analysis: Identifying the Author of a Program," *Proceedings of the 18th National Computer Security Conference* pp. 514–524 (Oct. 1995).

1107. C. Kruegel, E. Kirda, D. Mutz, W. Robertson, and G. Vigna. "Automating Mimicry Attacks Using Static Binary Analysis," *Proceedings of the 15th USENIX Security Symposium* pp. 161–176 (July 2005).

1108. C. Kruegel, D. Mutz, W. Robertson, and F. Valeur. "Bayesian Event Classification for Intrusion Detection," *Proceedings of the 19th Annual Computer Security Applications Conference* pp. 14–23 (Dec. 2003).

1109. C. Kruegel, W. Robertson, and G. Vigna. "Detecting Kernel-Level Rootkits Through Binary Analysis," *Proceedings of the 20th Annual Computer Security Applications Conference* pp. 91–100 (Dec. 2004).

1110. A. S. Kubesch and S. Wicker. "Digital Rights Management: The Cost to Consumers," *Proceedings of the IEEE* **103**(5) pp. 726–733 (May 2015).

1111. D. R. Kuhn. "Mutual Exclusion of Roles as a Means of Implementing Separation of Duty in Role-Based Access Control Systems," *Proceedings of the Second ACM Workshop on Role-Based Access Control* pp. 23–30 (Nov. 1997).

1112. R. Kumar, P. Jovanovic, W. Burleson, and I. Polian. "Parametric Trojans for Fault-Injection Attacks on Cryptographic Hardware," *Proceedings of the 2014 Workshop on Fault Diagnosis and Tolerance in Cryptography* pp. 18–28 (Sep. 2014).

1113. S. Kumar and E. H. Spafford. "A Pattern Matching Model for Misuse Intrusion Detection," *Proceedings of the 17th National Computer Security Conference* pp. 11–21 (Oct. 1994).

1114. C. Kuo, S. Romanosky, and L. F. Cranor. "Human Selection of Mnemonic Phrase-Based Passwords," *Proceedings of the Second Symposium on Usable Privacy and Security* pp. 67–78 (July 2006).

1115. J. A. Kupsch and B. P. Miller. "Manual vs. Automated Vulnerability Assessment: A Case Study," *Proceedings of the First International Workshop on Managing Insider Security Threats* pp. 83–97 (June 2009).

1116. D. Kushner. "The Real Story of Stuxnet," *IEEE Spectrum* **50**(3) pp. 48–53 (Mar. 2013).

1117. R. Küsters, T. Truderung, B. Beckert, D. Bruns, M. Kirsten, and M. Mohr. "A Hybrid Approach for Proving Noninterference of Java Programs," *Proceedings of the 28th Computer Security Foundations Symposium* pp. 305–319 (July 2015).

1118. U. Kuter and J. Golbeck. "Using Probabilistic Confidence Models for Trust Inference in Web-Based Social Networks," *ACM Transactions on Internet Technologies* **10**(2) pp. 8:1–8:23 (May 2010).

1119. A. Kwon, M. AlSabah, D. Lazar, M. Dacier, and S. Devadas. "Circuit Fingerprinting Attacks: Passive Deanonymization of Tor Hidden Services," *Proceedings of the 24th USENIX Security Symposium* pp. 287–302 (Aug. 2015).

1120. U. Lah and J. R. Lewis. "How Expertise Affects a Digital-Rights-Management-Sharing Application's Usability," *IEEE Software* **33**(3) pp. 76–82 (May 2016).

1121. H. Lai, F. Ganjeizadeh, P. K. Jayachandran, and P. Ozcan. "A Statistical Analysis of the Effects of Scrum and Kanban on Software Development Projects," *Robotics and Computer-Integrated Manufacturing* **43** pp. 59–67 (Feb. 2017).

1122. J. Lai and W. Kou. "Self-Generated-Certificate Public Key Encryption Without Pairing," *Proceedings of the 10th International Conference on Practice and Theory in Public-Key Cryptography* (*Lecture Notes in Computer Science* **4450**) pp. 476–489 (Apr. 2007).

1123. N. Lai and T. Grey. "Strengthening Discretionary Access Controls to Inhibit Trojan Horses and Computer Viruses," *Proceedings of the 1988 Summer USENIX Conference* pp. 275–286 (June 1988).

1124. X. Lai and J. L. Massey. "A Proposal for a New Block Encryption Standard," *Advances in Cryptology — EUROCRYPT '90* (*Lecture Notes in Computer Science* **473**) pp. 389–404 (1991).

1125. X. Lai, J. L. Massey, and S. Murphy. "Markov Ciphers and Differential Cryptanalysis," *Advances in Cryptology — EUROCRYPT '91* (*Lecture Notes in Computer Science* **547**) pp. 17–38 (Apr. 1991).

1126. K. Lakkaraju and A. Slagell. "Evaluating the Utility of Anonymized Network Traces for Intrusion Detection," *Proceedings of the Fourth International Conference on Security and Privacy in Communication Networks* pp. 17:1–17:8 (Sep. 2008).

1127. K. Lakshminarayanan, D. Adkins, A. Perrig, and I. Stoica. "Securing User-Controlled Routing Infrastructures," *IEEE/ACM Transactions on Networking* **16**(3) pp. 549–561 (June 2008).

1128. B. A. LaMacchia and A. M. Odlyzko. "Computation of Discrete Logarithms in Prime Fields," *Designs, Codes and Cryptography* **1**(1) pp. 47–62 (1991).

1129. L. Lamport. "Time, Clocks, and the Ordering of Events in a Distributed System," *Communications of the ACM* **21**(7) pp. 558–565 (July 1978).

1130. L. Lamport. "Password Authentication with Insecure Communication," *Communications of the ACM* **24**(11) pp. 770–772 (Nov. 1981).

1131. B. W. Lampson. "A Note on the Confinement Problem," *Communications of the ACM* **16**(10) pp. 613–615 (Oct. 1973).

1132. B. W. Lampson. "Protection," *ACM SIGOPS Operating Systems Review* **8**(1) pp. 18–24 (Jan. 1974).

1133. C. E. Landwehr. "Formal Models for Computer Security," *ACM Computing Surveys* **13**(3) pp. 247–278 (Sep. 1981).

1134. C. E. Landwehr, A. R. Bull, J. P. McDermott, and W. S. Choi. "A Taxonomy of Computer Program Security Flaws," *ACM Computing Surveys* **26**(3) pp. 211–254 (Sep. 1994).

1135. C. E. Landwehr and D. M. Goldschlag. "Security Issues in Networks with Internet Access," *Proceedings of the IEEE* **85**(12) pp. 2034–2051 (Dec. 1997).

1136. C. E. Landwehr, C. L. Heitmeyer, and J. McLean. "A Security Model for Military Message Systems," *ACM Transactions on Computer Systems* **2**(3) pp. 198–222 (Aug. 1984).

1137. R. Langner. "Stuxnet: Dissecting a Cyberwarfare Weapon," *IEEE Security & Privacy* **9**(3) pp. 49–51 (May 2011).

1138. L. J. LaPadula. "The 'Basic Security Theorem' of Bell and LaPadula Revisited," *unpublished* (Apr. 1988); handout from the *First Computer Security Foundations Workshop*.

1139. M. V. Larsen and F. Gont. *Port Randomization Recommendations*, RFC 6056 (Jan. 2011).

1140. B. Lau and V. Svajcer. "Measuring Virtual Machine Detection in Malware Using DSD Tracer," *Journal in Computer Virology* **6**(3) pp. 181–195 (Aug. 2010).

1141. L. Laudan. *The Book of Risks: Fascinating Facts About the Chances We Take Every Day*, John Wiley and Sons, New York, NY, USA (1994).

1142. B. Laurie, G. Sisson, R. Arends, and D. Blacka. *DNS Security (DNSSEC) Hashed Authenticated Denial of Existence*, RFC 5155 (Mar. 2008).

1143. G. Lawton. "Biometrics: A New Era in Security," *IEEE Computer* **31**(8) pp. 16–18 (Aug. 1998).

1144. G. Lawton. "On the Trail of the Conficker Worm," *IEEE Computer* **42**(6) pp. 19–22 (June 2009).

1145. F. Leder and T. Werner. *Know Your Enemy: Containing Conficker*, Technical Report, The Honeynet Project (Apr. 2009).

1146. H. C. J. Lee and V. L. L. Thing. "Port Hopping for Resilient Networks," *Proceedings of the 60th IEEE Vehicular Technology Conference* pp. 3291–3295 (Sep. 2004).

1147. J. K. Lee and Y. M. Kim. "Lessons Learned from Practical Independent Verification and Validation Based on IEEE 1012," *Journal of Software Engineering and Applications* **5** pp. 810–815 (Oct. 2012).

1148. T. M. P. Lee. "Using Mandatory Integrity to Enforce 'Commercial' Security," *Proceedings of the 1988 IEEE Symposium on Security and Privacy* pp. 140–146 (Apr. 1988).

1149. X. Lee, W. Mao, E. Chen, N.-W. Hsu, and J. C. Klensin. *Registration and Administration Recommendations for Chinese Domain Names*, RFC 4713 (Oct. 2006).

1150. J. Lemon. "Resisting SYN Flood DoS Attacks with a SYN Cache," *Proceedings of the BSDCon 2002 Conference* (Feb. 2002).

1151. A. K. Lenstra, J. P. Hughes, M. Augier, J. W. Bos, T. Kleinjung, and C. Wachter. "Public Keys," *Advances in Cryptology — CRYPTO 2012* (*Lecture Notes in Computer Science* **7417**) pp. 626–642 (Aug. 2012).

1152. A. K. Lenstra, J. P. Hughes, M. Augier, J. W. Bos, T. Kleinjung, and C. Wachter. *Ron Was Wrong, Whit Is Right*, Cryptology ePrint Archive Report 2012/064, International Association for Cryptologic Research (Feb. 2012).

1153. P. Leong and C. Tham. "UNIX Password Encryption Considered Insecure," *Proceedings of the 1991 Winter USENIX Conference* pp. 269–279 (Jan. 1991).

1154. M. Lepinski and S. Kent. *An Infrastructure to Support Secure Internet Routing*, RFC 6480 (Feb. 2012).

1155. N. G. Leveson. *Safeware: System Safety and Computers*, ACM Press, New York, NY, USA (1995).

1156. N. G. Leveson. "Software Challenges in Achieving Space Safety," *Journal of the British Interplanetary Society* **62** pp. 265–272 (July 2009).

1157. A. Levi, M. U. Caglayan, and C. K. Koc. "Use of Nested Certificates for Efficient, Dynamic, and Trust Preserving Public Key Infrastructure," *ACM Transactions on Information and System Security* **7**(1) pp. 21–59 (Feb. 2004).

1158. J. G. Levine, J. B. Grizzard, and H. L. Owen. "Detecting and Categorizing Kernel-Level Rootkits to Aid Future Detection," *IEEE Security & Privacy* **4**(1) pp. 24–32 (Jan. 2006).

1159. P. H. Lewis. "TECHNOLOGY: ON THE NET; An Intel Computer Security Expert Runs Afoul of the Law. So Much for the 'Hacker Ethic'?" *The New York Times* p. D5 (Nov. 27, 1995).

1160. W. Ley. *Watchers of the Skies: An Informal History of Astronomy from Babylon to the Space Age*, Viking Press, New York, NY, USA (1966).

1161. J. Leyden. "First Trojan Using the Sony DRM Spotted," *The Register* (Nov. 10, 2005).

1162. K.-S. Lhee and S. J. Chapin. "Detection of File-Based Race Conditions," *International Journal of Information Security* **4**(1/2) pp. 105–119 (2005).

1163. H. Li and M. Singhal. "Trust Management in Distributed Systems," *IEEE Computer* **40**(2) pp. 45–53 (Feb. 2007).

1164. N. Li. "Local Names in SPKI/SDSI," *Proceedings of the 13th Computer Security Foundations Workshop* pp. 2–15 (July 2000).

1165. N. Li, T. Li, and S. Venkatasubramanian. "t-Closeness: Privacy Beyond k-Anonymity and ℓ-Diversity," *Proceedings of the IEEE 23rd International Conference on Data Engineering* pp. 106–115 (Apr. 2007).

1166. N. Li and M. V. Tripunitara. "On Safety in Discretionary Access Control," *Proceedings of the 2005 IEEE Symposium on Security and Privacy* pp. 96–109 (May 2005).

1167. N. Li, M. V. Tripunitara, and Z. Bizri. "On Mutually Exclusive Roles and Separation-of-Duty," *ACM Transactions on Information and System Security* **10**(2) pp. 5:1–5:36 (May 2007).

1168. P. Li, D. Gao, and M. K. Reiter. "Mitigating Access-Driven Timing Channels in Clouds using StopWatch," *Proceedings of the 43rd Annual IEEE/IFIP International Conference on Dependable Systems and Networks* pp. 1–12 (June 2013).

1169. P. Li and S. Zdancewic. "Encoding Information Flow in Haskell," *Proceedings of the 19th Computer Security Foundations Workshop* pp. 16–27 (July 2006).

1170. Q. Li and B.-H. Juang. "Speaker Verification Using Verbal Information Verification for Automatic Enrolment," *Proceedings of the 1998 IEEE International Conference on Acoustics, Speech and Signal Processing* pp. 133–136 (May 1998).

1171. Q. Li, B.-H. Juang, Q. Zhou, and C.-H. Lee. "Automatic Verbal Information Verification for User Authentication," *IEEE Transactions on Speech an Audio Processing* **8**(5) pp. 585–596 (Sep. 2000).

1172. Q. Li, B.-H. Juang, Q. Zhou, and F. K. Soong. "Recent Advancements in Automatic Speaker Authentication," *IEEE Robotics & Automation Magazine* **6**(1) pp. 24–34 (Mar. 1999).

1173. Y. Li, J. M. McCune, J. Newsome, A. Perrig, B. Baker, and W. Drewry. "MiniBox: A Two-Way Sandbox for x86 Native Code," *Proceedings of the 2014 USENIX Annual Technical Conference* pp. 409–420 (June 2014).

1174. Z. Li and W. Wang. "Rethinking About Type-Flaw Attacks," *Proceedings of the 2010 IEEE Global Communications Conference* pp. 1–5 (Dec. 2010).

1175. V. R. Liao, Yihua amd Vemuri. "Use of K-Nearest Neighbor Classifier for Intrusion Detection," *Computers & Security* **21**(5) pp. 439–448 (Oct. 2002).

1176. H. Lin, A. Slagell, C. Di Martino, Z. Kalbarczyk, and R. K. Iyer. "Adapting Bro into SCADA: Building a Specification-Based Intrusion Detection System for the DNP3 Protocol," *Proceedings of the Eighth Annual Cyber Security and Information Intelligence Research Workshop* pp. 5:1–5:4 (Jan. 2013).

1177. H.-Y. Lin and L. Harn. "A Generalized Secret Sharing Scheme with Cheater Detection," *Advances in Cryptology — ASIACRYPT '91* (*Lecture Notes in Computer Science* **739**) pp. 149–158 (Nov. 1991).

1178. S.-H. Lin, S.-Y. Kung, and L.-J. Lin. "Face Recognition/Detection by Probabilistic Decision-Based Neural Network," *IEEE Transactions on Neural Networks* **8**(1) pp. 114–132 (Jan. 1997).

1179. T. Y. Lin. "Chinese Wall Security Policy—An Aggressive Model," *Proceedings of the Fifth Annual Computer Security Applications Conference* pp. 282–289 (Dec. 1989).

1180. T. Y. Lin. "Chinese Wall Security Policy Models: Information Flows and Confining Trojan Horses," *Proceedings of the IFIP TC11/WG11.3 17th Annual Working Conference on Data and Applications Security* (*IFIP International Federation for Information Processing* **142**) pp. 275–287 (Aug. 2003).

1181. T. Y. Lin. "Chinese Wall Security Policy—Revisited: A Short Proof," *Proceedings of the 2007 IEEE International Conference on Systems, Man and Cybernetics* (Oct. 2007).

1182. O. Linda, T. Vollmer, and M. Manic. "Neural Network Based Intrusion Detection System for Critical Infrastructures," *Proceedings of the 2009 International Joint Conference on Neural Networks* pp. 1827–1834 (June 2009).

1183. R. R. Linde. "Operating System Penetration," *Proceedings of the AFIPS '75 National Computer Conference* pp. 361–268 (May 1975).

1184. R. R. Linde, C. Weissman, and C. E. Fox. "The ADEPT-50 Time Sharing System," *Proceedings of the AFIPS '69 Fall Joint Computer Conference* pp. 39–50 (Nov. 1969).

1185. T. Lindholm, F. Yellin, G. Bracha, and A. Buckley. *The Java Virtual Machine Specification*, Addison-Wesley, Boston, MA, USA (May 2014).

1186. U. Lindqvist and E. Jonsson. "How to Systematically Classify Computer Security Intrusions," *Proceedings of the 1997 IEEE Symposium on Security and Privacy* pp. 154–163 (May 1997).

1187. U. Lindqvist, T. Olovsson, and E. Jonsson. "An Analysis of a Secure System Based on Trusted Components," *Proceedings of the 11th Annual Conference on Computer Assurance* pp. 213–223 (Aug. 1996).

1188. Z. Ling, J. Luo, W. Yu, X. Fu, W. Jia, and W. Zhao. "Protocol-Level Attacks Against Tor," *Computer Networks* **57**(4) pp. 869–886 (Mar. 2013).

1189. J. Linn. *Privacy Enhancement for Internet Electronic Mail: Part I: Message Encryption and Authentication Procedures*, RFC 1421 (Feb. 1993).

1190. J. Linn and M. Nyström. "Attribute Certification: An Enabling Technology for Delegation and Role-Based Controls in Distributed Environments," *Proceedings of the Fourth ACM Workshop on Role-Based Access Controls* pp. 121–130 (Oct. 1999).

1191. S. Lipner. "Twenty Years of Evaluation Criteria and Commercial Technology," *Proceedings of the 1999 IEEE Symposium on Security and Privacy* pp. 111–112 (May 1999).

1192. S. B. Lipner. "A Comment on the Confinement Problem," *Proceedings of the Fifth ACM Symposium on Operating Systems Principles* pp. 192–196 (Dec. 1975).

1193. S. B. Lipner. "Non-Discretionary Controls for Commercial Applications," *Proceedings of the 1982 IEEE Symposium on Security and Privacy* pp. 2–10 (Apr. 1982).

1194. R. Lippmann, J. W. Haines, D. J. Fried, J. Korba, and K. Das. "The 1999 DARPA Off-Line Intrusion Detection Evaluation," *Computer Networks* **34**(4) pp. 579–595 (Oct. 2000).

1195. R. P. Lippmann, D. J. Fried, I. Graf, J. W. Haines, K. R. Kendall, D. McClung, D. Weber, S. E. Webster, D. Wyschogrod, R. K. Cunningham, and M. A. Zissman. "Evaluating Intrusion Detection Systems: The 1998 DARPA Off-line Intrusion Detection Evaluation," *Proceedings of the 2000 DARPA Information Survivability Conference and Exposition* (Jan. 2000).

1196. R. J. Lipton and T. A. Budd. "On Classes of Protection Systems," in [531], pp. 281–291.

1197. R. J. Lipton and L. Snyder. "A Linear Time Algorithm for Deciding Subject Security," *Journal of the ACM* **24**(3) pp. 455–464 (July 1977).

1198. A. Liska and T. Gallo. *Ransomware: Defending Against Digital Extortion*, O'Reilly Media, Sebastopol, CA, USA (2016).

1199. J. Littman. *The Watchman: The Twisted Life and Crimes of Serial Hacker Kevin Poulsen*, Little, Brown and Company, Boston, MA, USA (1997).

1200. A. X. Liu. "Firewall Policy Verification and Troubleshooting," *Computer Networks* **53**(16) pp. 2800–2809 (Nov. 2009).

1201. V. B. Livshits and M. S. Lam. "Finding Security Vulnerabilities in Java Applications with Static Analysis," *Proceedings of the 15th USENIX Security Symposium* pp. 271–286 (July 2005).

1202. J. Lobo, R. Bhatia, and S. Naqvi. "A Policy Description Language," *Proceedings of the 16th National Conference on Artificial Intelligence* pp. 291–298 (July 1999).

1203. M. Lochter and J. Merkle. *Elliptic Curve Cryptography (ECC) Brainpool Standard: Curves and Curve Generation*, RFC 5639 (Mar. 2010).

1204. S. W. Lodin and C. L. Schuba. "Firewalls Fend Off Invasions from the Net," *IEEE Spectrum* **35**(2) pp. 26–34 (Feb. 1998).

1205. B. W. Long. "Formal Verification of Type Flaw Attacks in Security Protocols," *Proceedings of the Tenth Asia-Pacific Software Engineering Conference* pp. 415–424 (Dec. 2003).

1206. J. Long and J. Wiles. *No-Tech Hacking: A Guide to Social Engineering, Dumpster Diving, and Shoulder Surfing*, Syngress Publishing, Inc., Burlington, MA, USA (2008).

1207. D. Longley and S. Rigby. "An Automatic Search for Security Flaws in Key Management Schemes," *Computers & Security* **11**(1) pp. 75–89 (Mar. 1992).

1208. L. López and J. Carracedo. "Hierarchical Organization of Certification Authorities for Secure Environments," *Proceedings of the 1997 Symposium on Network and Distributed System Security* pp. 112–121 (Feb. 1997).

1209. H. Lu, J. Rose, Y. Liu, A. Awad, and L. Hou. "Combining Mouse and Eye Movement Biometrics for User Authentication," in *Combining Mouse and Eye Movement Biometrics for User Authentication*, edited by I. Traoré, A. Awad, and I. Woungang, Springer, Berlin, Germany pp. 55–71 (2017).

1210. H. Lu, J. Vaidya, and V. Atluri. "An Optimization Framework for Role Mining," *Journal of Computer Security* **22**(1) pp. 1–31 (Jan. 2014).

1211. J. Lu, O. Dunkelman, N. Keller, and J. Kim. "New Impossible Differential Attacks on AES," *Proceedings of the Ninth International Conference on Cryptology in India: Progress in Cryptology — INDOCRYPT 2008* (*Lecture Notes in Computer Science* **5365**) pp. 279–293 (Dec. 2008).

1212. L. Lu, Z. Li, Z. Wu, W. Lee, and G. Jiang. "CHEX: Statically Vetting Android Apps for Component Hijacking Vulnerabilities," *Proceedings of the 19th ACM SIGSAC Conference on Computer and Communications Security* pp. 229–240 (Nov. 2012).

1213. M. W. Lucas. *PGP & GPG: Email for the Practical Paranoid*, No Starch Press, San Francisco, CA, USA (Apr. 2006).

1214. M. W. Lucas. *Sudo Mastery: User Access Control for Real People*, CreateSpace Independent Publishing Platform, Scotts Valley, CA, USA (2013).

1215. S. Lucks. "Attacking Triple Encryption," *Proceedings of the Fifth International Workshop on Fast Software Encryption* (*Lecture Notes in Computer Science*) pp. 239–253 (Mar. 1998).

1216. M. A. Ludwig. *The Giant Black Book of Computer Viruses*, American Eagle Publishers, Phoenix, AZ, USA (2009).

1217. A. Lumini and L. Nanni. "Overview of the Combination of Biometric Matchers," *Information Fusion* **33** pp. 71–85 (Jan. 2017).

1218. E. Lundin and E. Jonsson. "Anomaly-Based Intrusion Detection: Privacy Concerns and Other Problems," *Computer Networks* **34**(4) pp. 623–640 (Oct. 2000).

1219. T. F. Lunt and R. Jagannathan. "A Prototype Real-Time Intrusion-Detection Expert System," *Proceedings of the 1988 IEEE Symposium on Security and Privacy* pp. 59–66 (Apr. 1988).

1220. X. Luo, E. W. W. Chan, and R. K. C. Chang. "Detecting Pulsing Denial-of-Service Attacks with Nondeterministic Attack Intervals," *EURASIP Journal on Advances in Signal Processing* **2009** (Mar. 2009).

1221. X. Luo and R. K. C. Chang. "On a New Class of Pulsing Denial-of-Service Attacks and the Defense," *Proceedings of the 2005 Symposium on Network and Distributed System Security* (Feb. 2005).

1222. E. Lupu, N. Sloman, N. Dulay, and N. Damianou. "Ponder: Realizing Enterprise Viewpoint Concepts," *Proceedings of the Fourth International Enterprise Distributed Object Computing Conference* pp. 66–75 (Sep. 2000).

1223. R. R. Lutz. "Analyzing Software Requirements Errors in Safety-Critical, Embedded Systems," *Proceedings of the 1993 IEEEE International Symposium on Requirements Engineering* pp. 126–133 (Jan. 1993).

1224. R. R. Lutz and I. C. Mikulski. "Requirements Discovery During the Testing of Safety-Critical Software," *Proceedings of the 25th International Conference on Software Engineering* pp. 578–583 (May 2003).

1225. L. Lymberopoulos, E. Lupu, and M. Sloman. "PONDER Policy Implementation and Validation in a CIM and Differentiated Services Framework," *Proceedings of the 2004 IEEE/IFIP Network Operations and Management Symposium* pp. 31–44 (Apr. 2004).

1226. G. F. Lyon. *Nmap Network Scanning*, Insecure.Com, Sunnyvale, CA, USA (2008).

1227. D. Ma and G. Tsudik. "A New Approach to Secure Logging," *ACM Transactions on Storage* **5**(1) pp. 2:1–2:21 (Mar. 2009).

1228. A. Machanavajjhala, D. Kifer, J. Gehrke, and M. Venkitasubramaniam. "ℓ-Diversity: Privacy Beyond k-Anonymity," *ACM Transactions on Knowledge Discovery from Data* **1**(1) pp. 3:1–3:52 (Mar. 2007).

1229. P. MacKenzie, S. Patel, and R. Swaminathan. "Password-Authenticated Key Exchange Based on RSA," *International Journal of Information Security* **9**(6) pp. 387–410 (Dec. 2010).

1230. A. Mackie, J. Roculan, R. Russell, and M. Van Velzen. *NIMDA Worm Analysis, Version 2*, Incident Analysis Report, SecurityFocus, San Mateo, CA, USA (Sep. 2001).

1231. J. Madden, B. McMillin, and A. Sinha. "Environmental Obfuscation of a Cyber Physical System — Vehicle Example," *Proceedings of the 34th Annual IEEE Computer Software and Application Conference Workshops* pp. 176–181 (July 2010).

1232. A. Madhavapeddy and D. J. Scott. "Unikernels: The Rise of the Virtual Library Operating System," *Communications of the ACM* **57**(1) pp. 61–69 (Jan. 2014).

1233. F. Maggi, S. Zanero, and V. Iozzo. "Seeing the Invisible: Forensic Uses of Anomaly Detection and Machine Learning," *ACM SIGOPS Operating Systems Review* **42**(3) pp. 51–58 (Apr. 2008).

1234. S. Maguire. *Writing Solid Code*, Braughler Books (2013).

1235. A. Mahimkar and V. Shmatikov. "Game-Based Analysis of Denial-of-Service Prevention Protocols," *Proceedings of the 18th Computer Security Foundations Workshop* pp. 287–301 (June 2005).

1236. M. V. Mahoney and P. K. Chan. "An Analysis of the 1999 DARPA/Lincoln Laboratory Evaluation Data for Network Anomaly Detection," *Proceedings of the Sixth International Workshop on Recent Advances in Intrusion Detection* (*Lecture Notes in Computer Science* **2820**) pp. 220–237 (2003).

1237. W. H. Maisel and T. Kohno. "Improving the Security and Privacy of Implantable Medical Devices," *New England Journal of Medicine* **362** pp. 1164–1166 (Apr. 2010).

1238. D. Malkhi and M. K. Reiter. "Secure Execution of Java Applets Using a Remote Playground," *IEEE Transactions on Software Engineering* **26**(12) pp. 1197–1209 (Dec. 2000).

1239. P. K. Manadhata and J. M. Wing. "An Attack Surface Metric," *IEEE Transactions on Software Engineering* **37**(3) pp. 371–386 (May 2011).

1240. S. Mangard. "Hardware Countermeasures against DPA — A Statistical Analysis of Their Effectiveness," *Topics in Cryptology — The Cryptographers' Track at the RSA Conference 2004* (*Lecture Notes in Computer Science* **2964**) pp. 222–235 (Feb. 2004).

1241. J. Manico and A. Detlefsen. *Iron-Clad Java: Building Secure Web Applications*, McGraw-Hill Education, New York, NY, USA (2014).

1242. R. Manley, P. Magrath, and D. Gregg. "Code Generation for Hardware Accelerated AES," *Proceedings of the 21st International Conference on Application-Specific Systems Architectures and Processors* pp. 345–348 (July 2010).

1243. D. E. Mann and S. M. Christey. "Towards a Common Enumeration of Vulnerabilities," *Proceedings of the Second Workshop on Research with Vulnerability Databases* (Jan. 1999).

1244. I. Mann. *Hacking the Human: Social Engineering Techniques and Security Countermeasures*, Gower Publishing Co., Burlington, VT, USA (2008).

1245. F. Mansmann, T. Göbel, and W. Cheswick. "Visual Analysis of Complex Firewall Configurations," *Proceedings of the Ninth International Symposium on Visualization for Cyber Security* pp. 1–8 (Oct. 2012).

1246. H. Mantel. "On the Composition of Secure Systems," *Proceedings of the 2002 IEEE Symposium on Security and Privacy* pp. 88–101 (May 2002).

1247. H. Mantel and H. Sudbrock. "Comparing Countermeasures against Interrupt-Related Covert Channels in an Information-Theoretic Framework," *Proceedings of the 20th Computer Security Foundations Workshop* (July 2007).

1248. W. Mao. *Modern Cryptography: Theory and Practice*, Pearson Education, Upper Saddle River, NJ, USA (2004).

1249. E. Marasco and A. Ross. "A Survey on Antispoofing Schemes for Fingerprint Recognition Systems," *ACM Computing Surveys* **47**(2) pp. 28:1–28:36 (Jan. 2015).

1250. N. B. Margolin, B. N. Levine, J. D. Miller, and M. Wright. "Economic Incentives for Protecting Digital Rights Online," *Electronic Commerce Research and Applications* **10**(5) pp. 553–564 (Sep. 2011).

1251. C. Mariño, M. G. Penedo, M. Penas, M. J. Carreira, and F. Gonzalez. "A Novel Method for Person Authentication using Retinal Images," *Pattern Analysis and Applications* **9**(1) p. 21 (May 2006).

1252. S. Marinovic, N. Dulay, and M. Sloman. "Rumpole: An Introspective Break-Glass Access Control Language," *ACM Transactions on Information and System Security* **17**(1) pp. 2:1–2:32 (Aug. 2014).

1253. T. Markham and C. Williams. "Key Recovery Header for IPSEC," *Computers & Security* **19**(1) pp. 86–90 (Jan. 2000).

1254. M. Marlinspike and T. Perrin. *The X3DH Key Agreement Protocol* (Nov. 2016).

1255. K. Martin and I. S. Moskowitz. "Noisy Timing Channels with Binary Inputs and Outputs," *Proceedings of the Eighth International Workshop on Information Hiding* (*Lecture Notes in Computer Science* **4437**) pp. 124–144 (July 2006).

1256. R. A. Martin, S. M. Christey, and J. Jarzombek. "The Case for Common Flaw Enumeration," *Proceedings of the 2006 NIST Workshop on Software Security Assurance Tools, Techniques, and Metrics* (*NIST Special Publication 500-265*) pp. 29–35 (Feb. 2006).

1257. R. C. Martin. *Clean Code: A Handbook of Agile Software Craftsmanship*, Prentice Hall, Inc., Upper Saddle River, NJ, USA (2009).

1258. D. M. Martin Jr., S. Rajagopalan, and A. D. Rubin. "Blocking Java Applets at the Firewall," *Proceedings of the 1997 Symposium on Network and Distributed System Security* pp. 16–26 (Feb. 1997).

1259. N. Matloff and P. J. Salzman. *The Art of Debugging with GDB, DDD, and Eclipse*, No Starch Press, San Francisco, CA, USA (Sep. 2008).

1260. A. A. Matos. "Non-Disclosure for Distributed Mobile Code," *Proceedings of the 25th International Conference on Foundations of Software Technology and Theoretical Computer Science* (*Lecture Notes in Computer Science* **3821**) pp. 177–188 (Dec. 2005).

1261. M. Matsui. "Linear Cryptanalysis Method for DES Cipher," *Advances in Cryptology — EUROCRYPT '93* (*Lecture Notes in Computer Science* **765**) pp. 386–397 (May 1993).

1262. M. Matsui. "The First Experimental Cryptanalysis of the Data Encryption Standard," *Advances in Cryptology — CRYPTO '94* (*Lecture Notes in Computer Science* **839**) pp. 1–11 (1994).

1263. M. Matsumoto, S. Kitamura, and M. Sato. "High Assurance Technologies for Autonomous Decentralized Train Control System," *Proceedings of the Sixth IEEE International Symposium on High Assurance Systems Engineering* pp. 220–227 (Oct. 2001).

1264. J. Mattsson and M. Westerlund. "Authentication Key Recovery on Galois/Counter Mode (GCM)," *Progress in Cryptology — AFRICACRYPT 2016* (*Lecture Notes in Computer Science* **9646**) pp. 127–143 (Apr. 2016).

1265. S. M. Matyas and C. H. Meyer. "Generation, Distribution, and Installaton of Cryptographic Keys," *IBM Systems Journal* **17**(2) pp. 126–137 (Aug. 1978).

1266. S. Mauw and M. Oostdijk. "Foundations of Attack Trees," *Proceedings of the Eighth International Conference on Information Security and Cryptology* (*Lecture Notes in Computer Science* **3935**) pp. 186–198 (Dec. 2005).

1267. A. Maximov. "Two Linear Distinguishing Attacks on VMPC and RC4A and Weakness of RC4 Family of Stream Ciphers," *Proceedings of the 12th International Workshop on Fast Software Encryption* (*Lecture Notes in Computer Science* **3557**) pp. 329–345 (Feb. 2005).

1268. A. Maximov and A. Biryukov. "Two Trivial Attacks on Trivium," *Proceedings of the 14th International Workshop on Selected Areas in Cryptography* (*Lecture Notes in Computer Science* **4876**) pp. 36–55 (Aug. 2007).

1269. A. Maximov and D. Khovratovich. "New State Recovery Attack on RC4," *Advances in Cryptology — CRYPTO 2008* (*Lecture Notes in Computer Science* **5157**) pp. 297–316 (Aug. 2008).

1270. R. A. Maxion and K. M. C. Tan. "Benchmarking Anomaly-Based Detection Systems," *Proceedings of the 2000 International Conference on Dependable Systems and Networks* pp. 623–630 (June 2000).

1271. A. Mayer, A. Wool, and E. Ziskind. "Fang: A Firewall Analysis Engine," *Proceedings of the 2000 IEEE Symposium on Security and Privacy* pp. 177–187 (May 2000).

1272. P. Maymounkov and D. Mazières. "Kademlia: A Peer-to-Peer Information System Based on the XOR Metric," *Proceedings of the First International Workshop on Peer-to-Peer Systems* (*Lecture Notes in Computer Science* **2429**) pp. 53–65 (Mar. 2002).

1273. D. Mazières and M. F. Kaashoek. "The Design, Implementation and Operation of an Email Pseudonym Server," *Proceedings of the Fifth ACM Conference on Computer and Communications Security* pp. 27–36 (Oct. 1998).

1274. P. Mazzoleni, B. Crispo, S. Sivasubramanian, and E. Bertino. "XACML Policy Integration Algorithms," *ACM Transactions on Information and System Security* **11**(1) pp. 4:1–4:29 (Feb. 2008).

1275. S. McCanne and V. Jacobson. "The BSD Packet Filter: A New Architecture for User-Level Packet Capture," *Proceedings of the 1993 Winter USENIX Conference* (Jan. 1993).

1276. C. J. McCollum, J. R. Messing, and L. Notargiacomo. "Beyond the Pale of MAC and DAC - Defining New Forms of Access Control," *Proceedings of the 1990 IEEE Symposium on Research in Security and Privacy* pp. 190–200 (May 1990).

1277. S. McConnell. *Code Complete: A Practical Handbook of Software Construction*, Microsoft Press, Redmond, WA, USA (2004).

1278. D. McCullagh. "DVD Lawyers Make Secret Public," *Wired* (Jan. 26, 2000).

1279. D. McCullough. "Specifications for Multi-Level Security and a Hook-Up," *Proceedings of the 1987 IEEE Symposium on Security and Privacy* pp. 161–166 (Apr. 1987).

1280. D. McCullough. "Noninterference and the Composability of Security Properties," *Proceedings of the 1988 IEEE Symposium on Security and Privacy* pp. 177–186 (Apr. 1988).

1281. P. McDaniel and A. Prakash. "Methods and Limitations of Security Policy Reconciliation," *ACM Transactions on Information and System Security* **9**(3) pp. 259–291 (Aug. 2006).

1282. J. A. McDermid and Q. Shi. "Secure Composition of Systems," *Proceedings of the Eighth Annual Computer Security Applications Conference* pp. 112–122 (Nov. 1992).

1283. J. McDermott and C. Fox. "Using Abuse Case Models for Security Requirements Analysis," *Proceedings of the 15th Annual Computer Security Applications Conference* pp. 55–64 (Dec. 1999).

1284. J. P. McDermott. "Attack Net Penetration Testing," *Proceedings of the 2000 Workshop on New Security Paradigms* pp. 15–21 (2000).

1285. D. L. McDonald, R. J. Atkinson, and C. Metz. "One Time Passwords In Everything (OPIE): Experiences with Building and Using Stronger Authentication," *Proceedings of the Fifth USENIX UNIX Security Symposium* (June 1995).

1286. G. McGraw. "Software Assurance for Security," *IEEE Computer* **32**(4) pp. 103–105 (Apr. 1999).

1287. G. McGraw. *Software Security: Building Security In*, Addison-Wesley, Upper Saddle River, NJ, USA (2006).

1288. S. E. McGregor, E. A. Watkins, M. N. Al-Ameen, K. Caine, and F. Roesner. "When the Weakest Link is Strong: Secure Collaboration in the Case of the Panama Papers," *Proceedings of the 26th USENIX Security Symposium* pp. 505–522 (Aug. 2017).

1289. D. A. McGrew and J. Viega. "The Galois/Counter Mode of Operation (GCM)," Submission to NIST (Jan. 2004)

1290. D. A. McGrew and J. Viega. "The Security and Performance of the Galois/Counter Mode (GCM) of Operation," *Proceedings of the Fifth International Conference on Cryptology in India: Progress in Cryptology — INDOCRYPT 2004* (*Lecture Notes in Computer Science*) pp. 343–355 (Dec. 2004).

1291. J. McHugh. "Testing Intrusion Detection Systems: A Critique of the 1998 and 1999 DARPA Intrusion Detection System Evaluations as Performed by Lincoln Laboratory," *ACM Transactions on Information and System Security* **3**(4) pp. 262–294 (Nov. 2000).

1292. J. McHugh. "An Information Flow Tool for Gypsy," *Proceedings of the 17th Annual Computer Security Applications Conference* pp. 191–201 (Dec. 2001).

1293. M. D. McIlroy. "Virology 101," *Computing Systems* **2**(2) pp. 173–181 (Spring 1989).

1294. M. K. McKusick, K. Bostic, M. J. Marels, and J. S. Quarterman. *The Design and Implementation of the 4.4BSD Operating System*, Addison-Wesley, Reading, MA, USA (May 1996).

1295. S. McLaughlin, D. Podkuiko, S. Miadzvezhanka, A. Delozier, and P. McDaniel. "Multi-Vendor Penetration Testing in the Advanced Metering Infrastructure," *Proceedings of the 26th Annual Computer Security Applications Conference* pp. 107–116 (Dec. 2010).

1296. J. McLean. "A Comment on the 'Basic Security Theorem' of Bell and LaPadula," *Information Processing Letters* **20**(2) pp. 67–70 (Feb. 1985).

1297. J. McLean. "Reasoning about Security Models," *Proceedings of the 1987 IEEE Symposium on Security and Privacy* pp. 123–131 (Apr. 1987).

1298. J. McLean. "Proving Noninterference and Functional Correctness Using Traces," *Journal of Computer Security* **1**(1) pp. 37–57 (1992).

1299. J. McLean. "A General Theory of Composition for a Class of 'Possibilistic' Properties," *IEEE Transactions on Software Engineering* **22**(1) pp. 53–67 (Jan. 1996).

1300. J. McLean. "Is the Trusted Computing Base Concept Fundamentally Flawed?" *Proceedings of the 1997 IEEE Symposium on Security and Privacy* p. 2 (May 1997).

1301. J. McLean. "Twenty Years of Formal Methods," *Proceedings of the 1999 IEEE Symposium on Security and Privacy* pp. 113–114 (May 1999).

1302. D. McNutt. "Role-Based System Administration or Who, What, Where, and How," *Proceedings of the Seventh USENIX Systems Administration Conference* pp. 107–112 (Nov. 1993).

1303. W. S. McPhee. "Operating System Integrity in OS/VS2," *IBM Systems Journal* **13**(3) pp. 230–252 (1974).

1304. F. McSherry and R. Mahajan. "Differentially-Private Network Trace Analysis," *ACM SIGCOMM Computer Communications Review* **40**(4) pp. 123–134 (Aug. 2010).

1305. C. Meadows. "The Integrity Lock Architecture and Its Application to Message Systems: Reducing Covert Channels," *Proceedings of the 1987 IEEE Symposium on Security and Privacy* pp. 212–218 (Apr. 1987).

1306. C. Meadows. "Extending the Brewer-Nash Model to a Multilevel Context," *Proceedings of the 1990 IEEE Symposium on Research in Security and Privacy* pp. 95–102 (May 1990).

1307. C. Meadows. "The NRL Protocol Analyzer: An Overview," *Journal of Logic Programming* **26**(2) pp. 113–131 (Feb. 1996).

1308. C. Meadows. "A Representation of Protocol Attacks for Risk Assessment," in *A Representation of Protocol Attacks for Risk Assessment*, edited by R. N. Wright and P. G. Neumann (*DIMACS Series in Discrete Mathematics and Theoretical Computer Science* **38**), American Mathematical Society, Providence, RI, USA pp. 1–10 (1998).

1309. C. Meadows. "Analysis of the Internet Key Exchange Protocol Using the NRL Protocol Analyzer," *Proceedings of the 1999 IEEE Symposium on Security and Privacy* pp. 216–231 (May 1999).

1310. C. Meadows. "A Formal Framework and Evaluation Method for Network Denial of Service," *Proceedings of the 12th Computer Security Foundations Workshop* pp. 4–13 (June 1999).

1311. C. Meadows. "A Procedure for Verifying Security Against Type Confusion Attacks," *Proceedings of the 16th Computer Security Foundations Workshop* pp. 62–72 (June 2003).

1312. C. A. Meadows. "Analyzing the Needham-Schroeder Public Key Protocol: A Comparison of Two Approaches," *Proceedings of the Fourth European Symposium on Research in Computer Security* (*Lecture Notes in Computer Science* **1146**) pp. 351–364 (Sep. 1996).

1313. B. D. Medlin, K. Corley, and B. A. Romaniello. "Passwords Selected by Hospital Employees: An Investigative Study," *International Journal of Advanced Computer Science and Applications* **2**(11) pp. 77–81 (Nov. 2011).

1314. G. Medvinsky and B. C. Neuman. "NetCash: A Design for Practical Electronic Currency on the Internet," *Proceedings of the First ACM Conference on Computer and Communications Security* pp. 102–106 (1993).

1315. T. Melham. "Integrating Model Checking and Theorem Proving in a Reflective Functional Language," *Proceedings of the 2004 International Conference on Integrated Formal Methods* (*Lecture Notes in Computer Science* **2999**) pp. 36–39 (2004).

1316. P. Mell and T. Grance. *The NIST Definition of Cloud Computing*, Special Publication 800-145, National Institute of Standards and Technology, Gaithersburg, MD, USA (Sep. 2011).

1317. F. Mendel, T. Nad, and M. Schläffer. "Improving Local Collisions: New Attacks on Reduced SHA-256," *Advances in Cryptology — EUROCRYPT 2013* (*Lecture Notes in Computer Science* **7881**) pp. 262–278 (May 2013).

1318. A. J. Menezes, P. C. van Oorschot, and S. A. Vanstone. *Handbook of Applied Cryptography*, CRC Press, Boca Raton, FL, USA (1996).

1319. W. Meng, D. S. Wong, S. Furnell, and J. Zhou. "Surveying the Development of Biometric User Authentication on Mobile Phones," *IEEE Communications Surveys & Tutorials* **17**(3) pp. 1268–1293 (Third Quarter 2015).

1320. C. G. Menk III. "System Security Engineering Capability Maturity Model and Evaluations: Partners Within the Assurance Framework," *Proceedings of the 19th National Information Systems Security Conference* pp. 76–88 (Oct. 1996).

1321. R. Mercuri. "A Better Ballot Box?" *IEEE Spectrum* **39**(10) pp. 46–50 (Oct. 2002).

1322. R. C. Merkle. "Protocols for Public Key Cryptosystems," *Proceedings of the 1980 IEEE Symposium on Security and Privacy* pp. 122–134 (Apr. 1980).

1323. R. C. Merkle. "Fast Software Encryption Functions," *Advances in Cryptology — CRYPTO '90 (Lecture Notes in Computer Science* **537**) pp. 477–501 (1991).

1324. R. C. Merkle and M. E. Hellman. "Hiding Information and Signatures in Trapdoor Knapsacks," *IEEE Transactions on Information Theory* **24**(5) pp. 525–530 (Sep. 1978).

1325. R. C. Merkle and M. E. Hellman. "On the Security of Multiple Encryption," *Communications of the ACM* **24**(7) pp. 465–467 (July 1981).

1326. T. S. Messerges, E. A. Dabbish, and R. H. Sloan. "Investigations of Power Analysis Attacks on Smartcards," *Proceedings of the First USENIX Workshop on Smartcard Technology* pp. 151–161 (May 1999).

1327. C. H. Meyer. "Ciperext/Plaintext and Ciphertext/Key Dependence vs. Number of Rounds for the Data Encryption Standard," *Proceedings of the AFIPS '78 National Computer Conference* pp. 1119–1126 (June 1978).

1328. G. Meyer. *The PPP Encryption Control Protocol (ECP)*, RFC 1968 (June 1996).

1329. S. L. Mhlaba. "The Efficacy of International Regulation of Transborder Data Flows: The Case for the Clipper Chip," *Government Information Quarterly* **12**(4) pp. 353–366 (1995).

1330. G. G. Michaelson and M. R. Prior. *Naming Guidelines for the AARNet X.500*, RFC 1562 (Dec. 1993).

1331. C. Michel and L. Mé. "ADeLe: An Attack Description Language for Knowledge-Based Intrusion Detection," *Proceedings of the 16th IFIP International Information Security Conference (IFIP Advances in Information and Communication Technology* **65**) pp. 353–368 (June 2001).

1332. Microsoft. *Vulnerability in Server Service Could Allow Remote Code Execution (958644)*, Microsoft Security Bulletin MS08-67, Microsoft Corp., Redmond, WA, USA (Oct. 2008).

1333. G. L. Milán, M. G. Pérez, G. M. Pérez, and A. F. G. Skarmeta. "PKI-Based Trust Management in Inter-Domain Scenarios," *Computers & Security* **29**(2) pp. 278–290 (Mar. 2010).

1334. A. Milenkoski, M. Vieira, S. Kounev, A. Avritzer, and B. D. Payne. "Evaluating Computer Intrusion Detection Systems: A Survey of Common Practices," *ACM Computing Surveys* **48**(1) pp. 12:1–12:41 (Sep. 2015).

1335. J. Millen. "20 Years of Covert Channel Modeling and Analysis," *Proceedings of the 1999 IEEE Symposium on Security and Privacy* pp. 113–114 (May 1999).

1336. J. K. Millen. "The Interrogator: A Tool for Cryptographic Protocol Security," *Proceedings of the 1984 IEEE Symposium on Security and Privacy* pp. 134–141 (Apr. 1984).

1337. J. K. Millen. "Covert Channel Capacity," *Proceedings of the 1987 IEEE Symposium on Security and Privacy* pp. 60–66 (Apr. 1987).

1338. J. K. Millen. "A Resource Allocation Model for Denial of Service," *Proceedings of the 1992 IEEE Symposium on Research in Security and Privacy* pp. 137–147 (May 1992).

1339. J. K. Millen. "Unwinding Forward Correctability," *Journal of Computer Security* **3**(1) pp. 35–54 (1994/1995).

1340. J. K. Millen. "The Interrogator Model," *Proceedings of the 1995 IEEE Symposium on Security and Privacy* pp. 251–260 (May 1995).

1341. J. K. Millen, S. C. Clark, and S. B. Freedman. "The Interrogator: Protocol Security Analysis," *IEEE Transactions on Software Engineering* **13**(2) pp. 274–288 (Feb. 1987).

1342. J. K. Millen and M. W. Schwartz. "The Cascading Problem for Interconnected Networks," *Proceedings of the Fourth Annual Computer Security Applications Conference* pp. 269–274 (Dec. 1988).

1343. B. Miller. "Vital Signs of Identity," *IEEE Spectrum* **31**(2) pp. 22–30 (Feb. 1994).

1344. B. P. Miller, G. Cooksey, and F. Moore. "An Empirical Study of the Robustness of MacOS Applications Using Random Testing," *ACM SIGOPS Operating Systems Review* **41**(1) pp. 78–86 (Jan. 2007).

1345. B. P. Miller, L. Fredriksen, and B. So. "An Empirical Study of the Reliability of UNIX Utilities," *Communications of the ACM* **33**(12) pp. 32–44 (Dec. 1990).

1346. B. P. Miller, D. Koski, C. P. Lee, V. Maganty, R. Murthy, A. Natarajan, and J. Steidl. *Fuzz Revisited: A Re-examination of the Reliability of UNIX Utilities and Services*, Technical Report, Computer Sciences Department, University of Wisconsin, Madison, WI, USA (Oct. 1995).

1347. D. V. Miller and R. W. Baldwin. "Access Control by Boolean Expression Evaluation," *Proceedings of the Fifth Annual Computer Security Applications Conference* pp. 131–139 (Dec. 1989).

1348. G. A. Miller. "The Magical Number Seven, Plus or Minus Two: Some Limits on Our Capacity for Processing Information," *Psychological Review* **63**(2) pp. 81–97 (Mar. 1956).

1349. M. S. Miller and J. S. Shapiro. "Paradigm Regained: Abstraction Mechanisms for Access Control," *Proceedings of the 8th Asian Computer Science Conference* (*Lecture Notes in Computer Science* **2896**) pp. 224–242 (Dec. 2003).

1350. T. Miller. Analysis of the KNARK Rootkit. (Mar. 2001).

1351. V. S. Miller. "Use of Elliptic Curves in Cryptography," *Advances in Cryptology — CRYPTO '85* (*Lecture Notes in Computer Science* **218**) pp. 417–426 (Aug. 1985).

1352. M. Minsky. *Computation: Finite and Infinite Machines*, Prentice Hall, Inc., Englewood Cliffs, NJ, USA (June 1967).

1353. N. Minsky. "The Principle of Attenuation of Privileges and its Ramifications," in [531], pp. 255–277.

1354. N. H. Minsky. "Selective and Locally Controlled Transport of Privileges," *ACM Transactions on Programming Languages and Systems* **6**(4) pp. 573–602 (Oct. 1984).

1355. J. Mirkovic and P. Reiher. "D-WARD: A Source-End Defense against Flooding Denial-of-Service Attacks," *IEEE Transactions on Dependable and Secure Computing* **2**(3) pp. 216–232 (July 2005).

1356. J. Mirkovic, P. Reiher, S. Fahmy, R. Thomas, A. Hussain, S. Schwab, and C. Ko. "Measuring Denial of Service," *Proceedings of the Second ACM Workshop on Quality of Protection* pp. 53–58 (Oct. 2006).

1357. J. Mišić and V. B. Mišić. "Implementation of Security Policy for Clinical Information Systems over Wireless Sensor Networks," *Ad Hoc Networks* **5**(1) pp. 134–144 (Jan. 2007).

1358. S. Mister and S. E. Tavares. "Cryptanalysis of RC4-like Ciphers," *Proceedings of the Fifth International Workshop on Selected Areas in Cryptography* (*Lecture Notes in Computer Science* **1556**) pp. 131–143 (Aug. 1998).

1359. MIT Kerberos Team. Kerberos Version 4 End of Life Announcement. (Oct. 2006).

1360. J. C. Mitchell, V. Shmatikov, and U. Stern. "Finite-State Analysis of SSL 3.0," *Proceedings of the Seventh USENIX UNIX Security Symposium* (Jan. 1998).

1361. R. Mitchell and I.-R. Chen. "A Survey of Intrusion Detection in Wireless Network Applications," *Computer Communications* **42** pp. 1–23 (Apr. 2014).

1362. R. Mitchell and I.-R. Chen. "A Survey of Intrusion Detection Techniques for Cyber-Physical Systems," *ACM Computing Surveys* **46**(4) pp. 55:1–55:29 (Apr. 2014).

1363. K. D. Mitnick and W. L. Simon. *The Art of Deception: Controlling the Human Element of Security*, Wiley Publishing, Inc., Indianapolis, IN, USA (2002).

1364. S. Miyaguchi. "The FEAL Cipher Family," *Advances in Cryptology — CRYPTO '90* (*Lecture Notes in Computer Science* **537**) pp. 628–638 (1990).

1365. P. Mockapetris. *Domain Names — Concepts and Facilities*, RFC 1034 (Nov. 1987).

1366. P. Mockapetris. *Domain Names — Implementation and Specification*, RFC 1035 (Nov. 1987).

1367. J. C. Mogul, R. F. Rashid, and M. J. Accetta. "The Packet Filter: An Efficient Mechanism for User-Level Network Code," *Proceedings of the Eleventh ACM Symposium on Operating Systems Principles* pp. 39–51 (Dec. 1987).

1368. S. P. Mohanty. "A Secure Digital Camera Architecture for Integrated Real-Time Digital Rights Management," *Journal of Systems Architecture* **55**(10–12) pp. 468–480 (Oct. 2009).

1369. V. Molak (*ed*). *Fundamentals of Risk Analysis and Risk Management*, CRC Press, Boca Raton, FL, USA (1996).

1370. B. Möller, T. Duong, and K. Kotowicz. *This POODLE Bites: Exploiting the SSL 3.0 Fallback*, Technical Report, Google, Mountain View, CA, USA (Sep. 2014).

1371. I. Monga, E. Pouyoul, and C. Guok. "Software-Defined Networking for Big-Data Science - Architectural Models from Campus to the WAN," *Proceedings of the 2012 SC Companion: High Performance Computing, Networking Storage and Analysis* pp. 1629–1635 (Nov. 2012).

1372. F. Monrose, M. K. Reiter, Q. Li, and S. Wetzel. "Cryptographic Key Generation from Voice," *Proceedings of the 2001 IEEE Symposium on Security and Privacy* pp. 202–213 (May 2001).

1373. F. Monrose and A. Rubin. "Authentication via Keystroke Dynamics," *Proceedings of the Fourth ACM Conference on Computer and Communications Security* pp. 48–56 (Oct. 1997).

1374. R. Montanari, C. Stefanelli, and N. Dulay. "Flexible Security Policies for Mobile Agent Systems," *Microprocessors and Microsystems* **25**(2) pp. 93–99 (Apr. 2001).

1375. A. P. Moore and C. N. Payne, Jr.. "Increasing Assurance with Literate Programming Techniques," *Proceedings of the 11th Annual Conference on Computer Assurance* pp. 187–198 (June 1996).

1376. D. Moore, C. Shannon, and k. claffy. "Code-Red: A Case Study on the Spread and Victims of an Internet Worm," *Proceedings of the 2nd ACM SIGCOMM Workshop on Internet Measurment* pp. 273–284 (2002).

1377. J. H. Moore. "Protocol Failures in Cryptosystems," *Proceedings of the IEEE* **76**(5) pp. 594–602 (May 1988).

1378. A. Moradi, O. Mischke, and T. Eisenbarth. "Correlation-Enhanced Power Analysis Collision Attack," *Proceedings of the 12th International Workshop on Crptographic Hardware and Embedded Systems* (*Lecture Notes in Computer Science* **6225**) pp. 125–139 (Aug. 2010).

1379. M. Moriconi, X. Qian, R. A. Riemenschneider, and L. Gong. "Secure Software Architectures," *Proceedings of the 1997 IEEE Symposium on Security and Privacy* pp. 84–93 (May 1997).

1380. R. Morris and K. Thompson. "Password Security: A Case History," *Communications of the ACM* **22**(11) pp. 594–597 (Nov. 1979).

1381. P. Morrissey, N. P. Smart, and B. Warinschi. "A Modular Security Analysis of the TLS Handshake Protocol," *Advances in Cryptology — ASIACRYPT 2008* (*Lecture Notes in Computer Science* **5350**) pp. 55–73 (Dec. 2008).

1382. S. I. Moses. "Measuring The Robustness of Forensic Tools' Ability to Detect Data Hiding Techniques," Master's Thesis, Brigham Young University, Provo, UT (June 2017).

1383. I. S. Moskowitz. "Variable Noise Effects upon a Simple Timing Channel," *Proceedings of the 1991 IEEE Symposium on Research in Security and Privacy* pp. 362–372 (May 1991).

1384. I. S. Moskowitz, S. J. Greenwald, and M. H. Kang. "An Analysis of the Timed Z-Channel," *IEEE Transactions on Information Theory* **44**(7) pp. 3162–3168 (Nov. 1998).

1385. I. S. Moskowitz and M. H. Kang. "An Insecurity Flow Model," *Proceedings of the 1997 Workshop on New Security Paradigms* pp. 61–74 (Sep. 1997).

1386. I. S. Moskowitz and A. R. Miller. "Simple Timing Channels," *Proceedings of the 1984 IEEE Symposium on Security and Privacy* pp. 56–64 (May 1984).

1387. S. Motiee, K. Hawkey, and K. Beznosov. "Do Windows Users Follow the Principle of Least Privilege? Investigating User Account Control Practices," *Proceedings of the Sixth Symposium on Usable Privacy and Security* pp. 1:1–1:13 (July 2010).

1388. M. Motoyama, K. Levchenko, C. Kanich, D. McCoy, G. M. Voelker, and S. Savage. "Re: CAPTCHAs – Understanding CAPTCHA-Solving Services in an Economic Context," *Proceedings of the 19th USENIX Security Symposium* (Aug. 2010).

1389. R. Motwani, R. Panigrahy, V. Saraswat, and S. Ventkatasubramanian. "On the Decidability of Accessibility Problems (Extended Abstract)," *Proceedings of the 32nd Annual ACM Symposium on Theory of Computing* pp. 306–315 (May 2000).

1390. D. M'Raihi, M. Bellare, F. Hoornaert, D. Naccache, and O. Ranen. *HOTP: An HMAC-Based One-Time Password Algorithm*, RFC 4226 (Dec. 2005).

1391. D. M'Raihi, S. Machani, M. Pei, and J. Rydell. *TOTP: Time-Based One-Time Password Algorithm*, RFC 6238 (May 2011).

1392. L. Muñoz González, D. Sgandurra, A. Paudice, and E. C. Lupu. "Efficient Attack Graph Analysis Through Approximate Inference," *ACM Transactions on Privacy and Security* **20**(3) pp. 10:1–10:30 (Aug. 2017).

1393. J. P. Mueller. *Security for Web Developers Using Javascript, HTML, and CSS*, O'Reilly Media, Inc., Sebastopol, CA, USA (2016).

1394. L. Mui and E. Pearce. *X Windows System Administrator's Guide* **8**, O'Reilly Media, Inc., Sebastopol, CA, USA (1992).

1395. S. Mukkamala, G. Janoski, and A. Sung. "Intrusion Detection Using Neural Networks and Support Vector Machines," *Proceedings of the 2002 International Joint Conference on Neural Networks* pp. 1702–1707 (May 2002).

1396. D. K. Mulligan and A. K. Perzanowski. "The Magnificence of the Disaster: Reconstructing the Sony BMG Rootkit Incident," *Berkeley Technology Law Journal* **22**(3) pp. 1157–1232 (Summer 2007).

1397. C. Mulliner. "Privacy Leaks in Mobile Phone Internet Access," *Proceedings of the 14th International Conference on Intelligence in Next Generation Networks* pp. 1–6 (Oct. 2010).

1398. C. S. Mullins. *DB2 Developer's Guide: A Solutions-Oriented Approach to Learning the Foundation and Capabilities of DB2 for z/OS*, Sixth Edition, IBM Press, Boston, MA, USA (2012).

1399. D. Mulyono and H. S. Jinn. "A Study of Finger Vein Biometric for Personal Identification," *Proceedings of the IEEE International Symposium on Biometrics and Security Technologies* pp. 1–8 (Apr. 2008).

1400. C. Muñoz. "Formal Methods in Air Traffic Management: The Case of Unmanned Aircraft Systems (Invited Lecture)," *Proceedings of the 12th International Colloquium on Theoretical Aspects of Computing* (*Lecture Notes in Computer Science* **9399**) pp. 58–62 (2015).

1401. R. Munroe. "Password Strength," *xkcd* 936 (Aug. 2011).

1402. S. J. Murdoch and R. Anderson. "Verified by Visa and MasterCard SecureCode: Or, How Not to Design Authentication," *Proceedings of the Fourteenth International Conference on Financial Cryptography and Data Security* (*Lecture Notes in Computer Science* **6052**) pp. 336–342 (Jan. 2010).

1403. S. J. Murdoch, S. Drimer, R. Anderson, and M. Bond. "Chip and PIN is Broken," *Proceedings of the 2000 IEEE Symposium on Security and Privacy* pp. 443–446 (May 2010).

1404. S. Murphy. "The Cryptanalysis of FEAL-4 with 20 Chosen Plaintexts," *Journal of Cryptology* **2**(3) pp. 145–154 (Jan. 1990).

1405. W. H. Murray. "The Application of Epidemiology to Computer Viruses," *Computers & Security* **7**(2) pp. 139–145 (Apr. 1988).

1406. D. Mutz, G. Vigna, and R. Kemmerer. "An Experience Developing an IDS Stimulator for the Black-Box Testing of Network Intrusion Detection Systems," *Proceedings of the 19th Annual Computer Security Applications Conference* pp. 1–10 (Dec. 2003).

1407. A. C. Myers. "JFlow: Practical Mostly-Static Information Flow Control," *Proceedings of the 26th ACM SIGPLAN-SIGACT Symposium on Principles of Programming Languages* pp. 228–241 (1999).

1408. A. C. Myers. "Programming with Explicit Security Policies," *Proceedings of the 14th European Symposium on Programming* (*Lecture Notes in Computer Science* **3444**) pp. 1–4 (Apr. 2005).

1409. A. C. Myers and B. Liskov. "A Decentralized Model for Information Flow Control," *Proceedings of the 16th ACM Symposium on Operating Systems Principles* pp. 129–142 (Oct. 1997).

1410. A. C. Myers and B. Liskov. "Complete, Safe Information Flow with Decentralized Labels," *Proceedings of the 1998 IEEE Symposium on Security and Privacy* pp. 186–197 (May 1998).

1411. A. C. Myers and B. Liskov. "Protecting Privacy Using the Decentralized Label Model," *ACM Transactions on Software Engineering and Methodology* **9**(4) pp. 410–442 (Oct. 2000).

1412. A. C. Myers, A. Sabelfeld, and S. Zdancewic. "Enforcing Robust Declassification and Qualified Robustness," *Journal of Computer Security* **14**(2) pp. 157–196 (2006).

1413. C. Nachenberg. "Computer Virus-Antivirus Coevolution," *Communications of the ACM* **40**(1) pp. 46–51 (Jan. 1997).

1414. A. Nadeem and M. P. Howarth. "A Survey of MANET Intrusion Detection and Prevention Approaches for Network Layer Attacks," *IEEE Communications Surveys & Tutorials* **15**(4) pp. 2027–2045 (Fourth Quarter 2013).

1415. M. Naehrig, K. Lauter, and V. Vaikuntanathan. "Can Homomorphic Encryption Be Practical?," *Proceedings of the Third ACM Workshop on Cloud Computing Security* pp. 113–124 (Oct. 2011).

1416. V. Naessens, B. De Decker, and L. Demuynck. "Accountable Anonymous E-Mail," *Proceedings of the IFIP TC11 20th International Information Security Conference: Security and Privacy in the Age of Ubiquitous Computing* pp. 3–18 (May 2005).

1417. H. Nahari and R. L. Krutz. *Web Commerce Security: Design and Development*, John Wiley & Sons, Inc., New York, NY, USA (2011).

1418. J. Nakahara Jr.. "A Linear Analysis of Blowfish and Khufu," *Proceedings of the Third International Conference on Information Security Practice and Experience* (*Lecture Notes in Computer Science* **4464**) pp. 20–32 (May 2007).

1419. S. Nakamoto. "Bitcoin: A Peer-to-Peer Electronic Cash System," *unpublished* (2008)

1420. A. Narayanan and J. Clark. "Bitcoin's Academic Pedigree," *Communications of the ACM* **60**(12) pp. 36–45 (Dec. 2017).

1421. A. Narayanan and V. Shmatikov. "Fast Dictionary Attacks on Passwords Using Time-Space Tradeoff," *Proceedings of the 12th ACM Conference on Computer and Communications Security* pp. 364–372 (Nov. 2005).

1422. A. Narayanan and V. Shmatikov. "Robust De-anonymization of Large Sparse Datasets," *Proceedings of the 2008 IEEE Symposium on Security and Privacy* pp. 111–125 (May 2008).

1423. A. Narayanan and V. Shmatikov. "De-Anonymizing Social Networks," *Proceedings of the 2009 IEEE Symposium on Security and Privacy* pp. 173–187 (May 2009).

1424. M. J. Nash and R. J. Kennett. "Security Policy in a Complex Logistics Procurement," *Proceedings of the Ninth Annual Computer Security Applications Conference* pp. 46–53 (Dec. 1993).

1425. M. J. Nash and K. R. Poland. "Some Conundrums Concerning Separation of Duty," *Proceedings of the 1990 IEEE Symposium on Research in Security and Privacy* pp. 201–207 (May 1990).

1426. R. Natella, D. Cotroneo, and H. S. Madeira. "Assessing Dependability with Software Fault Injection: A Survey," *ACM Computing Surveys* **48**(3) pp. 44:1–44:55 (Feb. 2016).

1427. D. Naylor, A. Finamore, I. Leontiadis, Y. Grunenberger, M. Mellia, M. Munafò, K. Papagiannaki, and P. Steenkiste. "The Cost of the 'S' in HTTPS," *Proceedings of the 10th ACM International on Conference on Emerging Networking Experiments and Technologies* pp. 133–140 (Dec. 2014).

1428. NCA. "Mass Ransomware Spamming Event Targeting UK Computer Users," UK National Crime Agency Alert (Nov. 2013)

1429. V. Neagoe and M. Bishop. "Inconsistency in Deception for Defense," *Proceedings of the 2006 Workshop on New Security Paradigms* pp. 31–38 (Sep. 2006).

1430. R. W. Neal. "CryptoLocker Virus: New Malware Holds Computers For Ransom, Demands $300 Within 100 Hours and Threatens to Encrypt Hard Drive," *International Business Times* (Oct. 21, 2013).

1431. G. C. Necula. "Proof-Carrying Code," *Proceedings of the 24th ACM SIGPLAN-SIGACT Symposium on Principles of Programming Languages* pp. 106–119 (Jan. 1997).

1432. G. C. Necula and P. Lee. "Safe Kernel Extensions Without Run-Time Checking," *Proceedings of the Second USENIX Symposium on Operating Systems Design and Implementation* (Oct. 1996).

1433. G. C. Necula and P. Lee. "The Design and Implementation of a Certifying Compiler," *Proceedings of the 1998 ACM SIGPLAN Conference on Programming Language Design and Implementation* pp. 333–344 (Jan. 1998).

1434. G. C. Necula, S. McPeak, and W. Weimer. "CCured: Type-Safe Retrofitting of Legacy Code," *Proceedings of the 29th ACM SIGPLAN-SIGACT Symposium on Principles of Programming Languages* pp. 128–139 (Jan. 2002).

1435. R. M. Needham and M. D. Schroeder. "Using Encryption for Authentication in Large Networks of Computers," *Communications of the ACM* **21**(12) pp. 993–999 (Dec. 1978).

1436. R. M. Needham and M. D. Schroeder. "Authentication Revisited," *ACM SIGOPS Operating Systems Review* **21**(1) p. 7 (Jan. 1987).

1437. R. M. Needham and R. D. H. Walker. "The Cambridge CAP Computer and Its Protection System," *Proceedings of the Fifth ACM Symposium on Operating Systems Principles* pp. 1–10 (Nov. 1977).

1438. E. Nemeth, G. Snyder, H. T. R., and B. Whaley. *Unix and Linux System Administration Handbook*, Prentice Hall, Inc., Upper Saddle River, NJ, USA (2011).

1439. S. Nepal, W. Sherchan, and C. Paris. "STrust: A Trust Model for Social Networks," *Proceedings of the 10th IEEE International Conference on Trust, Security and Privacy in Computing and Communications* pp. 841–846 (Nov. 2011).

1440. B. C. Neuman and S. G. Stubblebine. "A Note on the Use of Timestamps as Nonces," *ACM SIGOPS Operating Systems Review* **27**(2) pp. 10–14 (Apr. 1993).

1441. B. C. Neuman and T. Ts'o. "Kerberos: An Authentication Service for Open Network Systems," *IEEE Communications Magazine* **32**(9) pp. 191–202 (Sep. 1994).

1442. B. C. Neuman, T. Yu, S. Hartman, and K. Raeburn. *The Kerberos Network Authentication Service (V5)*, RFC 4120 (July 2005).

1443. P. Neumann. "Computer System Security Evaluation," *Proceedings of the AFIPS '78 National Computer Conference* pp. 1087–1095 (June 1978).

1444. P. Neumann. *Computer-Related Risks*, ACM Press, New York, NY, USA (1994).

1445. P. G. Neumann. "Rainbows and Arrows: How the Security Criteria Address Computer Misuse," *Proceedings of the 13th National Computer Security Conference* pp. 414–4223 (Oct. 1990).

1446. P. G. Neumann. "Security Criteria for Electronic Voting," *Proceedings of the 16th National Computer Security Conference* pp. 478–482 (Sep. 1993).

1447. P. G. Neumann, R. S. Boyer, R. J. Feiertag, K. N. Levitt, and L. Robinson. *A Provably Secure Operating System: The System, Its Applications, and Proofs*, Report CSL-116, Computer Science Laboratory, SRI International, Menlo Park, CA, USA (May 1980).

1448. P. G. Neumann and R. J. Feiertag. "PSOS Revisited," *Proceedings of the 19th Annual Computer Security Applications Conference* pp. 1–9 (Dec. 2003).

1449. P. G. Neumann, R. J. Feiertag, K. N. Levitt, and L. Robinson. "Software Development and Proofs of Multi-Level Security," *Proceedings of the Second International Conference on Software Engineering* pp. 421–428 (Oct. 1976).

1450. P. G. Neumann, L. Robinson, K. N. Levitt, R. S. Boyer, and A. R. Saxena. *A Provably Secure Operating System*, Technical Report, Stanford Research Institute, Menlo Park, CA, USA (June 1975).

1451. J. Newman. *The World of Mathematics: A Small Library of the Literature of Mathematics from A'h-mosé the Scribe to Albert Einstein*, Simon and Schuster, New York, NY, USA (1956).

1452. J. S. Newman and S. M. Wander. "The Knowledge Path to Mission Success: Overview of the NSAS PBMA-KMS," *Proceedings of the 2002 Annual Reliability and Maintainability Symposium* pp. 601–606 (Jan. 2002).

1453. J. Newsome, B. Karp, and D. Song. "Polygraph: Automatically Generating Signatures for Polymorphic Worms," *Proceedings of the 2005 IEEE Symposium on Security and Privacy* pp. 226–241 (May 2005).

1454. J. Nieh and O. C. Leonard. "Examining VMware," *Dr. Dobb's Journal* **25**(8) pp. 70–76 (Aug. 2000).

1455. E. Nikolaropoulos. "Testing Safety-Critical Software," *Hewlett-Packard Journal* **48**(3) pp. 89–94 (June 1997).

1456. E. Nissim. *Fortinet Single Sign On Stack Overflow*, Advisory CORE-2015-0006, Core Security, Roswell, GA, USA (Mar. 2015).

1457. L. Nizer. *The Jury Returns*, Pocket Books, New York, NY, USA (Mar. 1968).

1458. P. Noce. "Notes on Computer Security: Art and Science," private communication (Dec. 2012)

1459. N. A. Nordbotten. "XML and Web Services Security Standards," *IEEE Communications Surveys and Tutorials* **11**(3) pp. 4–21 (Third Quarter 2009).

1460. S. Northcutt. *Computer Security Incident Handling: Step-by-Step (Version 2.3.1)*, SANS Institute, Bethesda, MD, USA (Mar. 2003).

1461. L. Notargiacomo, B. T. Blaustein, and C. T. McCollum. "Merging Models: Integrity, Dynamic Separation of Duty and Trusted Data Management," *Journal of Computer Security* **3**(2–3) pp. 207–230 (1995).

1462. B. Nowicki. *NFS: Network File System*, RFC 1094 (Mar. 1989).

1463. M. Nyanchama and S. Osborn. "Role-Based Security, Object Oriented Databases and Separation of Duty," *SIGMOD Record* **22**(4) pp. 45–51 (Dec. 1993).

1464. G. Nychis, V. Sekar, D. G. Andersen, H. Kim, and H. Zhang. "An Empirical Evaluation of Entropy-Based Traffic Anomaly Detection," *Proceedings of the Eighth ACM SIGCOMM Conference on Internet Measurement* pp. 151–156 (Oct. 2008).

1465. C. Oakes. "DVD Hackers Hit with Lawsuit," *Wired* (Dec. 28, 1999).

1466. D. O'Brien. "Recognizing and Recovering from Rootkit Attacks," *SysAdmin* **5**(11) pp. 8–20 (Nov. 1996).

1467. R. O'Brien and C. Rogers. "Developing Applications on LOCK," *Proceedings of the 14th National Computer Security Conference* pp. 147–156 (Oct. 1991).

1468. D. Octeau, P. McDaniel, S. Jha, A. Bartel, E. Bodden, J. Klein, and Y. Le Traon. "Effective Inter-Component Communication Mapping in Android with *Epicc*: An Essential Step Towards Holistic Security Analysis," *Proceedings of the 22nd USENIX Security Symposium* pp. 543–558 (Aug. 2013).

1469. P. Oechslin. "Making a Faster Cryptanalytic Time-Memory Trade-Off," *Advances in Cryptology — CRYPTO 2003* (*Lecture Notes in Computer Science* **2729**) pp. 617–630 (August 2003).

1470. S. Oh and S. Park. "Task-Role-Based Access Control Model," *Information Systems* **28**(6) pp. 533–562 (Sep. 2003).

1471. S. Oh and R. Sandhu. "A Model for Role Administration Using Organization Structure," *Proceedings of the Seventh ACM Symposium on Access Control Models and Technologies* pp. 155–162 (June 2002).

1472. T. Okamoto and K. Ohta. "Universal Electronic Cash," *Advances in Cryptology — CRYPTO '91* (*Lecture Notes in Computer Science* **576**) pp. 324–337 (Aug. 1992).

1473. M. Oliva and F. Saltor. "Integrating Multilevel Security Policies in Multilevel Federated Database Systems," *Proceedings of the IFIP TC11 / WG11.3 Fourteenth Annual Working Conference on Database Security* (*IFIP Advances in Information and Communication Technology* **73**) pp. 135–147 (Aug. 2002).

1474. S. O'Melia and A. J. Elbirt. "Instruction Set Extensions for Enhancing the Performance of Symmetric-Key Cryptography," *Proceedings of the 24th Annual Computer Security Applications Conference* pp. 465–474 (Dec. 2008).

1475. R. Oppliger. "Security at the Internet Layer," *IEEE Computer* **31**(9) pp. 43–47 (Sep. 1998).

1476. Oracle. *Oracle VM VirtualBox User Manual*, Technical Report, Oracle Corp., Redwood Shores, CA, USA (2016).

1477. E. Organick. *The Multics System: An Examination of Its Structure*, MIT Press, Boston, MA, USA (1972).

1478. E. Organick. *Computer System Organization: The B5700/B6700 Series*, Academic Press, Orlando, FL, USA (1973).

1479. H. Orman. *The OAKLEY Key Determination Protocol*, RFC 2412 (Nov. 1998).

1480. E. Osterweil, D. Massey, and L. Zhang. "Deploying and Monitoring DNS Security (DNSSEC)," *Proceedings of the 25th Annual Computer Security Applications Conference* pp. 429–438 (Dec. 2009).

1481. D. Otway and O. Rees. "Efficient and Timely Mutual Authentication," *ACM SIGOPS Operating Systems Review* **21**(1) pp. 8–10 (Jan. 1987).

1482. X. Ou, W. F. Boyer, and M. A. McQueen. "A Scalable Approach to Attack Graph Generation," *Proceedings of the 13th ACM Conference on Computer and Communications Security* pp. 336–345 (Oct. 2006).

1483. OWASP. *OWASP Top 10 - 2017: The Ten Most Critical Web Application Security Risks*, The Open Web Application Security Project (2017).

1484. W. A. Owens, K. W. Dam, and H. S. Lin (*ed*). *Technology, Policy, Law, and Ethics Regarding U.S. Acquisition and Use of Cyberattack Capabilities*, The National Academies Press, Washington, DC, USA (2009).

1485. S. Owre, J. M. Rushby, and N. Shankar. "PVS: A Prototype Verification System," *Proceedings of the 11th International Conference on Automated Deduction* (*Lecture Notes in Computer Science* **607**) pp. 748–752 (June 1992).

1486. C. Paar and J. Pelzl. *Understanding Cryptography: A Textbook for Students and Practitioners*, Springer, Heidelberg, Germany (2010).

1487. J. Page. "An Assured Pipeline Integrity Scheme for Virus Protection," *Proceedings of the 12th National Computer Security Conference* pp. 378–388 (Oct. 1989).

1488. P. Paillier. "Public-Key Cryptosystems Based on Composite Degree Residuosity Classes," *Advances in Cryptology — EUROCRYPT '99* (*Lecture Notes in Computer Science*) pp. 223–238 (May 1999).

1489. M. Pala and S. W. Smith. "Finding the PKI Needles in the Internet Haystack," *Journal of Computer Security* **18**(3) pp. 397–420 (2010).

1490. R. Pang, M. Allman, V. Paxson, and J. Lee. "The Devil and Packet Trace Anonymization," *ACM SIGCOMM Computer Communications Review* **36**(1) pp. 29–38 (2006).

1491. R. Pang, V. Paxson, R. Sommer, and L. Peterson. "Binpac: A Yacc for Writing Application Protocol Parsers," *Proceedings of the Sixth ACM SIGCOMM Conference on Internet Measurement* pp. 289–300 (Oct. 2006).

1492. J. S. Park, B. Montrose, and J. N. Froscher. "Tools for Information Security Assurance Arguments," *Proceedings of the 2001 DARPA Information Survivability Conference and Exposition II* pp. 287–296 (June 2001).

1493. J. S. Park and R. Sandhu. "Binding Identities and Attributes Using Digitally Signed Certificates," *Proceedings of the 16th Annual Computer Security Applications Conference* pp. 120–127 (Dec. 2000).

1494. S. K. Park and K. W. Miller. "Random Number Generators: Good Ones Are Hard to Find," *Communications of the ACM* **31**(10) pp. 1192–1201 (Oct. 1988).

1495. S. Park, H. Park, Y. Won, J. Lee, and S. Kent. *Traceable Anonymous Certificate*, RFC 5636 (Aug. 2009).

1496. D. Parker. *Crime by Computer*, Charles Scribner's Sons, New York, NY, USA (1976).

1497. M. Parks. "Target Offers $10 Million Settlement in Data Breach Lawsuit," *NPR* (Mar. 19, 2015).

1498. S. Parsons, K. Atkinson, Z. Li, P. McBurney, E. Sklar, M. Singh, K. Haigh, K. Levitt, and J. Rowe. "Argument Schemes for Reasoning about Trust," *Argumentation & Computation* **5**(2-3) pp. 160–190 (May 2014).

1499. E. Pasalic. "On Guess and Determine Cryptanalysis of LSFR-Based Stream Ciphers," *IEEE Transactions on Information Theory* **55**(7) pp. 3398–3406 (July 2009).

1500. B. Pawlowski, S. Shepler, C. Beame, B. Callaghan, M. Eisler, D. Noveck, D. Robinson, and R. Thurlow. "The NFS Version 4 Protocol," *Proceedings of the Second International Conference on System Administration and Networking* (May 2000).

1501. V. Paxson. "Bro: A System for Detecting Network Intruders in Real-Time," *Computer Networks* **31**(23-24) pp. 2435–2463 (Dec. 1999).

1502. A. Peacock, X. Ke, and M. Wilkerson. "Typing Patterns: A Key to User Identification," *IEEE Security & Privacy* **2**(5) pp. 40–47 (Sep. 2004).

1503. M. Pearce, S. Zeadally, and R. Hunt. "Virtualization: Issues, Security Threats, and Solutions," *ACM Computing Surveys* **45**(2) pp. 17:1–17:39 (Feb. 2013).

1504. S. Peisert. "A Model of Forensic Analysis Using Goal-Oriented Logging," Ph.D. Dissertation, Department of Computer Science and Engineering, University of California at San Diego, La Jolla, CA, USA (Mar. 2007).

1505. S. Peisert, W. Barnett, E. Dart, J. Cuff, R. L. Grossman, E. Balas, A. Berman, A. Shankar, and B. Tierney. "The Medical Science DMZ," *Journal of the American Medical Informatics Association* (May 2016).

1506. S. Peisert, M. Bishop, S. Karin, and K. Marzullo. "Principles-Driven Forensic Analysis," *Proceedings of the 2005 Workshop on New Security Paradigms* pp. 85–93 (Oct. 2005).

1507. S. Peisert, M. Bishop, S. Karin, and K. Marzullo. "Analysis of Computer Intrusions Using Sequences of Function Calls," *IEEE Transactions on Dependable and Secure Computing* **4**(2) pp. 137–150 (Apr. 2007).

1508. S. Peisert, M. Bishop, and K. Marzullo. "Computer Forensics *in Forensis*," *SIGOPS Operating Systems Review* **42**(3) pp. 112–122 (Apr. 2008).

1509. S. Peisert, M. Bishop, and A. Yasinsac. "Vote Selling, Voter Anonymity, and Forensic Logging of Electronic Voting Machines," *Proceedings of the 42nd Annual Hawaii International Conference on System Sciences* pp. 1–10 (Jan. 2009).

1510. S. Peisert, E. Talbot, and T. Kroeger. "Principles of Authentication," *Proceedings of the 2013 Workshop on New Security Paradigms* pp. 47–56 (Sep. 2013).

1511. T. Peng, C. Leckie, and K. Ramamohanarao. "Survey of Network-Based Defense Mechanisms Countering the DoS and DDoS Problems," *ACM Computing Surveys* **39**(1) pp. 3:1–3:42 (Apr. 2007).

1512. D. Penn. *Identity Theft Secrets: Exposing the Tricks of the Trade!*, iUniverse Publishing, Bloomington, IN, USA (2011).

1513. H. Perl, S. Dechand, M. Smith, D. Arp, F. Yamaguchi, K. Rieck, S. Fahl, and Y. Acar. "VCCFinder: Finding Potential Vulnerabilities in Open-Source Projects to Assist Code Audits," *Proceedings of the 22nd ACM SIGSAC Conference on Computer and Communications Security* pp. 426–437 (Oct. 2015).

1514. R. Perlman. "An Overview of PKI Trust Models," *IEEE Network* **13**(6) pp. 38–43 (Nov. 1999).

1515. N. Perlroth. "Apple Updates iOS to Patch a Security Hole Used to Spy on Dissidents," *The New York Times* p. B2 (Aug. 25, 2016).

1516. T. Perrin and M. Marlinspike. "The Double Ratchet Algorithm," *Signal Messenger* (Nov. 2016).

1517. D. S. Peterson, M. Bishop, and R. Pandey. "A Flexible Containment Mechanism for Executing Untrusted Code," *Proceedings of the 11th USENIX Security Symposium* pp. 207–225 (Aug. 2002).

1518. I. Peterson. *Fatal Defects: Chasing Killer Computer Bugs*, Vintage Books, New York, NY, USA (Apr. 1996).

1519. Z. N. J. Peterson, R. Burns, G. Ateniese, and S. Bono. "Design and Implementation of Verifiable Audit Trails for a Versioning File System," *Procedings of the Fifth USENIX Conference on File and Storage Technologies* pp. 93–106 (Feb. 2007).

1520. S. Petrović and A. Fúster-Sabater. "An Improved Cryptanalysis of the A5/2 Algorithm for Mobile Communications," *Proceedings of the 2002 IASTED International Conference Communication Systems and Networks* pp. 437–442 (Sep. 2002).

1521. C. P. Pfleeger. "Comparison of Trusted Systems Evaluation Criteria," *Proceedings of the Fifth Annual Conference on Computer Assurance, Systems Integrity, Software Safety and Process Security* pp. 135–143 (June 1990).

1522. V.-H. Pham and M. Dacier. "Honeypot Traces Forensics: The Observation Viewpoint Matters," *Proceedings of the Third International Conference on Network and System Security* pp. 365–372 (Oct. 2009).

1523. R. C.-W. Phan. "Cryptanalysis of Full Skipjack Block Cipher," *Electronics Letters* **38**(2) pp. 69–71 (Jan. 2002).

1524. C. Phillips and L. P. Swiler. "A Graph-Based System for Network-Vulnerability Analysis," *Proceedings of the 1998 Workshop on New Security Paradigms* pp. 71–79 (1998).

1525. J. Picciotto. "The Design of an Effective Auditing Subsystem," *Proceedings of the 1987 IEEE Symposium on Security and Privacy* pp. 13–22 (Apr. 1987).

1526. E. Pinheiro, W.-D. Weber, and L. A. Barroso. "Failure Trends in a Large Disk Drive Population," *Procedings of the Fifth USENIX Conference on File and Storage Technologies* pp. 17–28 (Feb. 2007).

1527. D. Pogue. *Windows 10: The Missing Manual*, O'Reilly Media, Sebastopol, CA, USA (2015).

1528. G. S. Poh, J.-J. Chin, W.-C. Yau, K.-K. R. Choo, and M. S. Mohamad. "Searchable Symmetric Encryption: Designs and Challenges," *ACM Computing Surveys* **50**(3) pp. 40:1–40:37 (Oct. 2017).

1529. W. T. Polk. "Approximating Clark-Wilson Access Triples with Basic UNIX Commands," *Proceedings of the Fourth USENIX UNIX Security Symposium* pp. 145–154 (Oct. 1993).

1530. W. T. Polk, N. E. Hastings, and A. Malpani. "Public Key Infrastructures That Satisfy Security Goals," *IEEE Internet Computing* **7**(4) pp. 60–67 (July 2003).

1531. M. Pomonis, T. Petsios, K. Jee, M. Polychronakis, and A. D. Keromytis. "IntFlow: Improving the Accuracy of Arithmetic Error Detection Using Information Flow Tracking," *Proceedings of the 30th Annual Computer Security Applications Conference* pp. 416–425 (Dec. 2014).

1532. G. J. Popek and R. P. Goldberg. "Formal Requirements for Virtualizable Third Generation Architectures," *Communications of the ACM* **17**(7) pp. 412–421 (July 1974).

1533. G. J. Popek and B. J. Walker. *The LOCUS Distributed System Architecture*, The MIT Press, Cambridge, MA, USA (1985).

1534. A. Popov. *Prohibiting RC4 Cipher Suites*, RFC 7465 (Feb. 2015).

1535. P. Porras, H. Saïdi, and V. Yegneswaran. "A Foray into Conficker's Logic and Rendezvous Points," *Proceedings of the Second USENIX Workshop on Large-Scale Exploits and Emergent Threats* pp. 7:1–7:9 (Apr. 2009).

1536. D. E. Porter, S. Boyd-Wickizer, J. Howell, R. Olinsky, and G. C. Hunt. "Rethinking the Library OS from the Top Down," *Proceedings of the 16th International Conference on Architectural Support for Programming Languages and Operating Systems* pp. 291–304 (Mar. 2011).

1537. J. B. Postel. *Transmission Control Protocol*, RFC 793 (Sep. 1981).

1538. J. B. Postel. *Simple Mail Transfer Protocol*, RFC 821 (Aug. 1982).

1539. J. B. Postel and J. Reynolds. *File Transfer Protocol (FTP)*, RFC 959 (Oct. 1985).

1540. D. Povey. "Optimistic Security: A New Access Control Paradigm," *Proceedings of the 1999 Workshop on New Security Paradigms* pp. 40–45 (Sep. 1999).

1541. E. J. Powanda and J. W. Genovese. "Configuring a Trusted System Using the TNI," *Proceedings of the Fourth Annual Computer Security Applications Conference* pp. 256–261 (Sep. 1988).

1542. S. Pozo, A. J. Varela-Vaca, and R. M. Gasca. "AFPL2, An Abstract Language for Firewall ACLs with NAT Support," *Proceedings of the Second International Conference on Dependability* pp. 52–59 (June 2009).

1543. M. M. Pozzo and T. E. Gray. "A Model for the Containment of Computer Viruses," *Proceedings of the AIAA/ASIS/DODCI Second Aerospace Computer Security Conference* pp. 11–18 (Dec. 1986).

1544. M. M. Pozzo and T. E. Gray. "An Approach to Containing Computer Viruses," *Computers & Security* **6**(4) pp. 321–331 (Aug. 1987).

1545. D. Price. "Pentium FDIV Flaw—Lessons Learned," *IEEE Micro* **15**(2) pp. 86–88 (Apr. 1995).

1546. G. Proctor and C. Cid. "On Weak Keys and Forgery Attacks Against Polynomial-Based MAC Schemes," *Journal of Cryptology* **28**(4) pp. 769–795 (Oct. 2015).

1547. N. Proctor. "The Restricted Access Processor: An Example of Formal Verification," *Proceedings of the 1985 IEEE Symposium on Security and Privacy* pp. 49–53 (Apr. 1985).

1548. P. E. Proctor. *The Practical Intrusion Detection Handbook*, Prentice Hall, Englewood Cliffs, NJ, USA (2001).

1549. E. Prouff, M. Rivain, and R. Bevan. "Statistical Analysis of Second Order Differential Power Analysis," *IEEE Transactions on Computers* **58**(6) pp. 799–811 (June 2009).

1550. T. H. Ptacek and T. N. Newsham. *Insertion, Evasion, and Denial of Service: Eluding Network Intrusion Detection*, Technical Report, Secure Networks, Inc. (Jan. 1998).

1551. N. J. Puketza, K. Zhang, M. Chung, B. Mukherjee, and R. A. Olsson. "A Methodology for Testing Intrusion Detection Systems," *IEEE Transactions on Software Engineering* **22**(10) pp. 719–729 (Oct. 1996).

1552. E. Rader, R. Wash, and B. Brooks. "Stories as Informal Lessons about Security," *Proceedings of the 11th Symposium on Usable Privacy and Security* pp. 6:1–6:17 (July 2012).

1553. T. Raffetseder, C. Kruegel, and E. Kirda. "Detecting System Emulators," *Proceedings of the 10th International Conference on Information Security* (*Lecture Notes in Computer Science* **4779**) pp. 1–18 (Oct. 2007).

1554. M. Raihan and M. Zulkernine. "AsmLSec: An Extension of Abstract State Machine Language for Attack Scenario Specification," *Proceedings of the 2007 International Conference on Availability, Reliability and Security* pp. 775–782 (Apr. 2007).

1555. F. Raja, K. Hawkey, S. Hsu, K.-L. C. Wang, and K. Beznosov. "A Brick Wall, a Locked Door, and a Bandit: A Physical Security Metaphor for Firewall Warnings," *Proceedings of the Seventh Symposium on Usable Privacy and Security* pp. 1:1–1:20 (July 2011).

1556. S. A. Rajunas, N. Hardy, A. C. Bomberger, W. S. Frantz, and C. R. Landau. "Security in KeyKOS," *Proceedings of the 1986 IEEE Symposium on Security and Privacy* pp. 78–85 (Apr. 1986).

1557. R. Ramachandra and C. Busch. "Presentation Attack Detection Methods for Face Recognition Systems: A Comprehensive Survey," *ACM Computing Surveys* **50**(1) pp. 8:1–8:37 (Mar. 2017).

1558. K. Ramachandran and B. Sikdar. "Modeling Malware Propagation in Gnutella Type Peer-to-Peer Networks," *Proceedings of the 20th International Parallel and Distributed Processing System* (Apr. 2006).

1559. K. Ramachandran and B. Sikdar. "Modeling Malware Propagation in Networks of Smart Cell Phones with Spatial Dynamics," *Proceedings of the 26th IEEE International Conference on Computer Communications* pp. 2516–2520 (May 2007).

1560. M. Ramadas, S. Ostermann, and B. Tjaden. "Detecting Anomalous Network Traffic with Self-Organizing Maps," *Proceedings of the Sixth International Workshop on Recent Advances in Intrusion Detection* (*Lecture Notes in Computer Science* **2820**) pp. 36–54 (2003).

1561. K. Raman, S. Baumes, K. Beets, and C. Ness. "Computer Security Handbook," Chapter 19 in *Social Engineering and Low-Tech Attacks*, edited by S. Bosworth, M. E. Kabay, and E. Whyte, John Wiley & Sons, Inc., Hoboken, NJ, USA pp. 19:1–19:22 (2009).

1562. R. Ramaswamy and T. Wolf. "High-Speed Prefix-Preserving IP Address Anonymization for Passive Measurement Systems," *IEEE/ACM Transactions on Networking* **15**(1) pp. 26–39 (Feb. 2007).

1563. S. Ramaswamy, R. Rastogi, and K. Shim. "Efficient Algorithms for Mining Outliers from Large Data Sets," *Proceedings of the 2000 ACM SIGMOD International Conference on Management of Data* pp. 427–438 (May 2000).

1564. B. Ramsdell and S. Turner. *Secure/Multipurpose Internet Mail Extensions (S/MIME) Version 3.2 Certificate Handling*, RFC 5750 (Jan. 2010).

1565. B. Ramsdell and S. Turner. *Secure/Multipurpose Internet Mail Extensions (S/MIME) Version 3.2 Message Specification*, RFC 5751 (Jan. 2010).

1566. K. N. Rao. "Security Audit for Embedded Avionics Systems," *Proceedings of the Fifth Annual Computer Security Applications Conference* pp. 78–84 (Dec. 1989).

1567. N. K. Ratha, J. H. Connell, and R. M. Bolle. "Enhancing Security and Privacy in Biometrics-Based Authentication Systems," *IBM Systems Journal* **40**(3) pp. 614–634 (2001).

1568. N. K. Ratha, J. H. Connell, and R. M. Bolle. "Biometrics Break-Ins and Band-Aids," *Pattern Recognition Letters* **24**(13) pp. 2105–2113 (Sep. 2003).

1569. C. Rathgeb and A. Uhl. "A Survey on Biometric Cryptosystems and Cancelable Biometrics," *EURASIP Journal on Information Security* **2011**(1) pp. 1–25 (Sep. 2011).

1570. B. Rathore, M. Brunner, M. Dilaj, O. Herrera, P. Brunati, R. K. Subramaniam, S. Raman, and U. Chavan. *Information Systems Security Assessment Framework (ISSAF)*, Draft 0.2.1A, Open Information Systems Security Group, London, UK (May 2006).

1571. M. Raya and J.-P. Hubaux. "Securing Vehicular Ad Hoc Networks," *Journal of Computer Security* **15**(1) pp. 39–68 (2007).

1572. F. Raynal, Y. Berthier, P. Biondi, and D. Kaminsky. "Honeypot Forensics Part I: Analyzing the Network," *IEEE Security & Privacy* **2**(4) pp. 72–78 (July 2004).

1573. F. Raynal, Y. Berthier, P. Biondi, and D. Kaminsky. "Honeypot Forensics Part II: Analyzing the Compromised Host," *IEEE Security & Privacy* **2**(5) pp. 77–80 (Sep. 2004).

1574. D. R. Redell and R. S. Fabry. "Selective Revocation and Capabilities," *Proceedings of the International Workshop on Protection in Operating Systems* pp. 197–209 (Aug. 1974).

1575. J. Reeds. "'Cracking' a Random Number Generator," *Cryptologia* **1**(1) pp. 20–26 (Jan. 1977).

1576. B. Reid. "Viewpoint: Reflections on Some Recent Widespread Computer Break-Ins," *Communications of the ACM* **30**(2) pp. 103–105 (Feb. 1987).

1577. K. Reinholtz and K. Patel. "Testing Autonomous Systems for Deep Space Exploration," *IEEE Aerospace and Electronic Systems Magazine* **23**(9) pp. 22–27 (Sep. 2008).

1578. R. P. Reitman. "A Mechanism for Information Control in Parallel Systems," *Proceedings of the Seventh ACM Symposium on Operating Systems Principles* pp. 55–63 (Dec. 1979).

1579. S. Rekhis and N. Boudriga. "A System for Formal Digital Forensic Investigation Aware of Anti-Forensic Attacks," *IEEE Transactions on Information Forensics and Security* **7**(2) pp. 635–650 (Apr. 2012).

1580. Y. Rekhter, R. G. Moskowitz, D. Karrenberg, G. J. de Groot, and E. Lear. *Address Allocation for Private Internets*, RFC 1918 (Feb. 1996).

1581. E. Rescorla. *SSL and TLS: Designing and Building Secure Systems*, Addison-Wesley, Boston, MA, USA (2001).

1582. S. S. Response. *Regin: Top-Tier Espionage Tool Enables Stealthy Surveillance, Version 1.1*, Technical Report, Symantec, Mountain View, CA, USA (Aug. 2015).

1583. K. Revett, H. Jahankhani, S. T. de Magalhães, and H. M. D. Santos. "A Survey of User Authentication Based on Mouse Dynamics," *Proceedings of the Fourth International Conference on Global E-Security* pp. 210–219 (June 2008).

1584. Y.-J. Rhee and T.-Y. Kim. "Practical Solutions to Key Recovery Based on PKI in IP Security," *Proceedings of the 21st International Conference on Computer Safety, Reliability and Security* (*Lecture Notes in Computer Science* **2434**) pp. 103–114 (Sep. 2002).

1585. C. Ribeiro, A. Zúquete, P. Ferreira, and P. Guedes. "SPL: An Access Control Language for Security Policies with Complex Constraints," *Proceedings of the 2001 Symposium on Network and Distributed System Security* (Feb. 2001).

1586. T. Rid and B. Buchanan. "Attributing Cyber Attacks," *The Journal of Strategic Studies* **38**(1-2) pp. 4–37 (2015).

1587. T. Riechmann and F. J. Hauck. "Meta Objects for Access Control: Extending Capability-Based Security," *Proceedings of the 1997 Workshop on New Security Paradigms* pp. 17–22 (Sep. 1997).

1588. R. Riley, X. Jiang, and D. Xu. "Multi-Aspect Profiling of Kernel Rootkit Behavior," *Proceedings of the Fourth ACM European Conference on Computer Systems* pp. 47–60 (Mar. 2009).

1589. E. Rissanen. *eXtensible Access Control Markup Language (XACML) Version 3.0 Plus Errata 01*, OASIS Standard, OASIS (July 2017).

1590. T. C. Ristenpart. "Time Stamp Synchronization of Distributed Sensor Logs: Impossibility Results and Approximation Algorithms," Master's Thesis, Dept. of Computer Science, University of California at Davis, Davis, CA, USA (2005).

1591. D. M. Ritchie. "On the Security of UNIX," in *UNIX System Manager's Manual*, USENIX Association, Berkeley, CA, USA pp. 17:1–17:3 (1979).

1592. D. M. Ritchie. "Joy of Reproduction," *USENET net.lang.c*, message bnews.research.314 (Nov. 1982)

1593. R. Rivest. *The MD4 Message-Digest Algorithm*, RFC 1320 (Apr. 1992).

1594. R. Rivest. *The MD5 Message-Digest Algorithm*, RFC 1321 (Apr. 1992).

1595. R. L. Rivest. "On the Notion of 'Software Independence' in Voting Systems," *Philosophical Transactions of the Royal Society A* **366**(1881) pp. 3759–3767 (Oct. 2008).

1596. R. L. Rivest and B. Lampson. *SDSI — A Simple Distributed Security Infrastructure* (Oct. 1996).

1597. R. L. Rivest, M. J. B. Robshaw, R. Sidney, and Y. L. Yin. "The RC6™ Block Cipher," *unpublished* (Aug. 1998).

1598. R. L. Rivest, A. Shamir, and L. Adleman. "A Method for Obtaining Digital Signatures and Public-Key Cryptosystems," *Communications of the ACM* **21**(2) pp. 120–126 (Feb. 1978).

1599. A. Roberts. "ORCON Creep: Information Sharing and the Threat to Government Accountability," *Government Information Quarterly* **21**(3) pp. 249–267 (2004).

1600. J. Rochlis and M. Eichin. "With Microscope and Tweezers: The Worm from MIT's Perspective," *Communications of the ACM* **32**(6) pp. 689–698 (June 1989).

1601. M. Roesch. "Snort—Lightweight Intrusion Detection for Networks," *Proceedings of the 13th Systems Administration Conference* pp. 229–238 (Nov. 1999).

1602. P. Rogaway. "Authenticated-Encryption with Associated-Data," *Proceedings of the Ninth ACM Conference on Computer and Communications Security* pp. 98–107 (Nov. 2002).

1603. R. Roman, P. Najera, and X. Lopez. "Securing the Internet of Things," *IEEE Computer* **44**(9) pp. 51–58 (Sep. 2011).

1604. L. Romano, A. Mazzeo, and N. Mazzocca. "SECURE: A Simulation Tool for PKI Design," *Proceedings of the Secure Networking — CQRE [Secure] '99 International Exhibition and Congress* (*Lecture Notes in Computer Science* **1740**) pp. 17–29 (Nov. 1999).

1605. A. W. Roscoe. "Modelling and Verifying Key-Exchange Protocols Using CSP and FDR," *Proceedings of the Eighth Computer Security Foundations Workshop* pp. 98–107 (June 1995).

1606. A. W. Roscoe, J. C. P. Woodcock, and L. Wulf. "Non-Interference Through Determinism," *Journal of Computer Security* **4**(1) pp. 27–53 (1996).

1607. K. H. Rosen. *Elementary Number Theory and Its Applications*, Addison-Wesley, Boston, MA, USA (2011).

1608. J. Rosenberg. *Name Assumptions*, RFC 4367 (Feb. 2006).

1609. T. Rosenblum and T. Garfinkel. "Virtual Machine Monitors: Current Technology and Future Trends," *IEEE Computer* **38**(5) pp. 39–47 (May 2005).

1610. G. Rosenzweig. *The Practical Guide To Mac Security*, CreateSpace Independent Publishing Platform, Scotts Valley, CA, USA (2017).

1611. N. C. Rowe. "Designing Good Deceptions in Defense of Information Systems," *Proceedings of the 20th Annual Computer Security Applications Conference* pp. 418–427 (Dec. 2004).

1612. N. C. Rowe. "A Model of Deception During Cyber-Attacks on Information Systems," *Proceedings of the First IEEE Symposium on Multi-Agent Security and Survivability* pp. 21–30 (Aug. 2004).

1613. F. B. Rowlett. *The Story of Magic: Memoirs of an American Cryptologic Pioneer*, Aegean Park Press, Walnut Creek, CA, USA (1998).

1614. H. A. Rowley, S. Baluja, and T. Kanade. "Neural Network-Based Face Detection," *IEEE Transactions on Pattern Analysis and Machine Intelligence* **20**(1) pp. 23–38 (Jan. 1998).

1615. A. Roy, D. S. Kim, and K. S. Trivedi. "Attack Countermeasure Trees (CT: Towards Unifying the Constructs of Attack and Defense Trees," *Security and Communication Networks* **5**(8) pp. 929–943 (Aug. 2012).

1616. W. W. Royce. "Managing the Development of Large Software Systens," *1970 WESTCON Technical Papers* pp. 1–9 (Aug. 1970).

1617. M. Rubia, J. C. Cruellas, and M. Medina. "The DEDICA Project: The Solution to the Interoperability Problems between the X.509 and EDIFACT Public Key Infrastructures," *Proceedings of the Secure Networking — CQRE [Secure] '99 International Exhibition and Congress* (*Lecture Notes in Computer Science* **1740**) pp. 17–29 (Nov. 1999).

1618. C. Rubin. "UNIX System V with B2 Security," *Proceedings of the 13th National Computer Security Conference* pp. 1–9 (Oct. 1990).

1619. R. A. Rueppel. "Stream Ciphers," in *Contemporary Cryptology:The Science of Information Integrity*, edited by G. J. Simmons, IEEE Press, Piscataway, NJ, USA pp. 65–134 (1992).

1620. M. C. Ruiz, D. Cazorla, F. Cuartero, and J. J. Pardo. "A Formal Specification and Performance Evaluation of the Purchase Phase in the SET Protocol," *Proceedings of the Seventh International Symposium on Symbolic and Numerical Algorithms for Scientific Computing* pp. 239–244 (Sep. 2005).

1621. N. Rump. "Can Digital Rights Management Be Standardized?" *IEEE Signal Processing Magazine* **21**(2) pp. 63–70 (Mar. 2004).

1622. S. Ruoti, J. Andersen, S. Heidbrink, M. O'Neill, E. Vaziripour, J. Wu, D. Zappala, and K. Seamons. "We're on the Same Page: A Usability Study of Secure Email Using Pairs of Novice Users," *Proceedings of the 2016 SIGCHI Conference on Human Factors in Computing Systems* pp. 4298–4308 (May 2016).

1623. S. Ruoti, J. Andersen, T. Hendershot, D. Zappala, and K. Seamons. "Private Webmail 2.0: Simple and Easy-to-Use Secure Email," *Proceedings of the 29th Annual Symposium on User Interface Software and Technology* pp. 461–472 (Oct. 2016).

1624. S. Ruoti, J. Andersen, D. Zappala, and K. Seamons. "Why Johnny Still, Still Can't Encrypt: Evaluating the Usability of a Modern PGP Client," *Computing Research Repository* (abs/1510.08555v2 [cs.CR]) (Mar. 2016).

1625. J. Rushby. *Noninterference, Transitivity, and Channel-Control Security Policies*, Technical Report CSL-92-2, SRI International, Menlo Park, CA, USA (May 2005).

1626. M. Russinovich. More on Sony: Dangerous Decloaking Patch, EULAs and Phoning Home," Microsoft Technet Blog (Nov. 2005)

1627. M. Russinovich. Sony, Rootkits and Digital Rights Management Gone Too Far," Microsoft Technet Blog (Oct. 2005)

1628. M. Russinovich and A. Margosis. *Troubleshooting with the Windows Sysinternals Tools*, Microsoft Press, Redmond, WA, USA (2016).

1629. A. Russo and A. Sabelfeld. "Dynamic vs. Static Flow-Sensitive Security Analysis," *Proceedings of the 23rd Computer Security Foundations Symposium* pp. 186–199 (July 2010).

1630. O. Ruwase and M. S. Lam. "A Practical Dynamic Buffer Overflow Detector," *Proceedings of the 2004 Symposium on Network and Distributed System Security* pp. 159–169 (Feb. 2004).

1631. M.-J. O. Saarinen. "Cycling Attacks on GCM, GHASH and Other Polynomial MACs and Hashes," *Proceedings of the 19th International Workshop on Fast Software Encryption* (*Lecture Notes in Computer Science* **7549**) pp. 216–225 (Mar. 2012).

1632. A. Sabelfeld and A. C. Myers. "Language-Based Information-Flow Security," *IEEE Journal on Selected Areas in Communication* **21**(1) pp. 5–19 (Jan. 2003).

1633. A. Sabelfeld and A. C. Myers. "A Model for Delimited Information Release," *Proceedings of the Second Mext-NSF-JSPS International Symposium on Software Security* (*Lecture Notes in Computer Science* **3233**) pp. 174–191 (Nov. 2004).

1634. A. Sabelfeld and D. Sands. "Probabilistic Noninterference for Multi-Threaded Programs," *Proceedings of the 13th Computer Security Foundations Workshop* pp. 200–214 (July 2000).

1635. A. Sabelfeld and D. Sands. "Declassification: Dimensions and Principles," *Journal of Computer Security* **17**(5) pp. 517–548 (2009).

1636. M. Sabhnani and G. Serpen. "Why Machine Learning Algorithms Fail in Misuse Detection on KDD Intrusion Detection Data Set," *Intelligent Data Analysis* **8**(4) pp. 403–415 (2004).

1637. T. L. Sadler. *Cybersecurity for Everyone: Securing Your Home or Small Business Network*, Signalman Publishing, Kissimmee, FL, USA (2015).

1638. J. Sajaniemi. "Modeling Spreadsheet Audit: A Rigorous Approach to Automatic Visualization," *Journal of Visual Languages & Computing* **11**(1) pp. 49–82 (Feb. 2000).

1639. S. Sakane, K. Kamada, S. Zrelli, and M. Ishiyama. *Problem Statement on the Cross-Realm Operation of Kerberos*, RFC 5868 (May 2010).

1640. R. G. Saltman. "Accuracy, Integrity and Security in Computerized Vote-Tallying," *Communications of the ACM* **31**(10) pp. 1184–1191 (Oct. 1988).

1641. J. Saltzer. "Protection and the Control of Information Sharing in Multics," *Communications of the ACM* **17**(7) pp. 388–402 (July 1974).

1642. J. H. Saltzer. *On the Naming and Binding of Network Destinations*, RFC 1498 (Aug. 1993).

1643. J. H. Saltzer and M. F. Kaashoek. *Principles of Computer System Design*, Morgan Kaufmann Publishers, Burlington, MA, USA (2009).

1644. J. H. Saltzer and M. D. Schroeder. "The Protection of Information in Computer Systems," *Proceedings of the IEEE* **63**(9) pp. 1278–1308 (Sep. 1975).

1645. A. Samal and P. A. Iyengar. "Automatic Recognition and Analysis of Human Faces and Facial Expressions: A Survey," *Pattern Recognition* **25**(1) pp. 65–77 (Jan. 1992).

1646. V. Samar. "Unified Login with Pluggable Authentication Modules (PAM)," *Proceedings of the Third ACM Conference on Computer and Communications Security* pp. 1–10 (Mar. 1996).

1647. M.-B. Samekh. "Lessons Learned from Flame, Three Years Later," *Securelist*, Kaspersky Labs, Moscow, Russian Federation (May 29, 2015).

1648. P. Samuelson. "DRM {and, or, vs.} the Law," *Communications of the ACM* **46**(4) pp. 41–45 (Apr. 2003).

1649. S. K. Sanadhya and P. Sarkar. "New Collision Attacks against Up to 24-Step SHA-2," *Proceedings of the Ninth International Conference on Cryptology in India: Progress in Cryptology — INDOCRYPT 2008* (*Lecture Notes in Computer Science* **5365**) pp. 91–103 (Dec. 2008).

1650. C. Sanders and J. Smith. *Applied Network Security Monitoring: Collection, Detection, and Analysis*, Syngress Press, Waltham, MA, USA (2014).

1651. R. Sandhu. "Expressive Power of the Schematic Protection Model (Extended Abstract)," *Proceedings of the First Computer Security Foundations Workshop* pp. 188–193 (June 1988).

1652. R. Sandhu. "Transformation of Access Rights," *Proceedings of the 1989 IEEE Symposium on Security and Privacy* pp. 259–268 (May 1989).

1653. R. Sandhu and G.-J. Ahn. "Decentralized Group Hierarchies in UNIX: An Experiment and Lessons Learned," *Proceedings of the 21st National Information Systems Security Conference* pp. 486–502 (Oct. 1998).

1654. R. Sandhu, V. Bhamidipati, and Q. Munawer. "The ARBAC97 Model for Role-Based Administration of Roles," *ACM Transactions on Information and System Security* **2**(1) pp. 105–135 (Feb. 1999).

1655. R. Sandhu, E. J. Coyne, H. L. Feinstein, and C. E. Youman. "Role-Based Access Control Models," *IEEE Computer* **29**(2) pp. 38–47 (Feb. 1996).

1656. R. S. Sandhu. "Analysis of Acyclic Attenuating Systems for the SSR Protection Model," *Proceedings of the 1985 IEEE Symposium on Security and Privacy* pp. 197–206 (Apr. 1985).

1657. R. S. Sandhu. "The Schematic Protection Model: Its Definitions and Analysis for Acyclic Attenuating Schemes," *Journal of the ACM* **35**(2) pp. 404–432 (Apr. 1988).

1658. R. S. Sandhu. "The Demand Operation in the Schematic Protection Model," *Information Processing Letters* **32**(4) pp. 213–219 (Sep. 1989).

1659. R. S. Sandhu. "Expressive Power of the Schematic Protection Model," *Journal of Computer Security* **1**(1) pp. 59–98 (1992).

1660. R. S. Sandhu. "The Typed Access Matrix Model," *Proceedings of the 1992 IEEE Symposium on Research in Security and Privacy* pp. 122–136 (May 1992).

1661. R. S. Sandhu. "Undecidability of Safety for the Schematic Protection Model with Cyclic Creates," *Journal of Computer and System Sciences* **44**(1) pp. 141–159 (Feb. 1992).

1662. R. S. Sandhu and S. Ganta. "On Testing for Absence of Rights in Access Control Models," *Proceedings of the Sixth Computer Security Foundations Workshop* pp. 109–118 (June 1993).

1663. R. S. Sandhu and S. Ganta. "On the Minimality of Testing for Rights in Transformation Models," *Proceedings of the 1994 IEEE Symposium on Research in Security and Privacy* pp. 230–241 (May 1994).

1664. R. S. Sandhu and G. S. Suri. "Non-Monotonic Transformation of Access Rights," *Proceedings of the 1992 IEEE Symposium on Research in Security and Privacy* pp. 148–161 (May 1992).

1665. S. Santesson, A. Malpani, S. Galperin, and C. Adams. *X.509 Internet Public Key Infrastructure Online Certificate Status Protocol - OCSP*, RFC 6960 (June 2013).

1666. S. T. Sarasamma, Q. A. Zhu, and J. Huff. "Hierarchical Kohonen Net for Anomaly Detection in Network Security," *IEEE Transactions on Systems, Man, and Cybernetics, Part B (Cybernetics)* **35**(2) pp. 302–312 (Apr. 2005).

1667. A. Sarkar, S. Köhler, B. Ludäscher, and M. Bishop. "Insider Attack Identification and Prevention Using a Declarative Approach," *IEEE Systems Journal* **PP**(99) pp. 1–12 (Oct. 2015).

1668. C. Satizábal, R. Páez, and J. Forné. "PKI Trust Relationships: From a Hybrid Architecture to a Hierarchical Model," *Proceedings of the First International Conference on Availability, Reliability and Security* (Apr. 2006).

1669. S. Savage, D. Wetherall, A. Karlin, and T. Anderson. "Practical Network Support for IP Traceback," *ACM SIGCOMM Computer Communications Review* **30**(4) pp. 295–306 (Oct. 2000).

1670. O. S. Saydjari, J. M. Beckman, and J. R. Leaman. "LOCK Trek: Navigating Uncharted Space," *Proceedings of the 1989 IEEE Symposium on Security and Privacy* pp. 167–175 (May 1989).

1671. O. S. Saydjari, J. M. Beckman, and J. R. Leamon. "Locking Computers Securely," *Proceedings of the Tenth National Computer Security Conference* pp. 129–141 (Sep. 1987).

1672. K. Scarfone and P. Mell. *Guide to Intrusion Detection and Prevention System (IDPS)*, Special Publication 800-94, National Institute of Standards and Technology, Gaithersburg, MD, USA (Feb. 2007).

1673. K. Scarfone, S. Murugiah, A. Cody, and A. Orebaugh. *Technical Guide to Information Security Testing and Assessment*, specpub 800-115, Computer Security Division, Information Technology Laboratory, National Institute of Standards and Technology, Gaithersburg, MD, USA (Sep. 2008).

1674. A. Schaad, J. Moffett, and J. Jacob. "The Role-Based Access Control System of a European Bank: A Case Study and Discussion," *Proceedings of the Sixth ACM Symposium on Access Control Models and Technologies* pp. 3–9 (May 2001).

1675. M. Schaefer, B. Gold, R. Linde, and J. Scheid. "Program Confinement in KVM/370," *Proceedings of the 1977 ACM Annual Conference* pp. 404–410 (1977).

1676. B. Schatz. "BodySnatcher: Towards Reliable Volatile Memory Acquisition by Software," *Digital Investigation* **4**(S) pp. 126–134 (Sep. 2007).

1677. R. R. Schell, T. F. Tao, and M. Heckman. "Designing the GEMSOS Security Kernel for Security and Performance," *Proceedings of the Eighth National Computer Security Conference* pp. 108–119 (Oct. 1985).

1678. K. Scheurer. "The Clipper Chip: Cryptography Technology and the Constitution—The Government's Answer to Encryption "Chips" Away at Constitutional Rights," *Rutgers Computer and Technology Law Journal* **21**(1) pp. 263–292 (1995).

1679. M. Schmid, F. Hill, and A. K. Ghosh. "Protecting Data from Malicious Software," *Proceedings of the 18th Annual Computer Security Applications Conference* (Dec. 2002).

1680. D. Schnackenberg, K. Djahandari, and D. Sterne. "Infrastructure for Intrusion Detection and Response," *Proceedings of the 2000 DARPA Information Survivability Conference and Exposition* pp. 3–11 (Jan. 2000).

1681. F. B. Schneider. "Implementing Fault-Tolerant Services Using the State Machine Approach: A Tutorial," *ACM Computing Surveys* **22**(4) pp. 299–319 (Dec. 1990).

1682. F. B. Schneider. "Enforceable Security Policies," *ACM Transactions on Information and System Security* **3**(1) pp. 30–50 (Feb. 2000).

1683. B. Schneier. "Description of a New Variable-Length Key, 64-Bit Block Cipher (Blowfish)," *Proceedings of the Cambridge Security Workshop on Fast Software Encryption* (*Lecture Notes in Computer Science* **809**) pp. 191–204 (Dec. 1993).

1684. B. Schneier. *Applied Cryptography: Protocols, Algorithms, and Source Code in C*, John Wiley & Sons, New York, NY, USA (1996).

1685. B. Schneier. "Attack Trees," *Dr. Dobb's Journal* pp. 21–29 (Dec. 1999).

1686. B. Schneier. "Inside Risks: The Uses and Abuses of Biometrics," *Communications of the ACM* **42**(8) p. 136 (Aug. 1999).

1687. B. Schneier. *Secrets and Lies: Digital Security in a Networked World*, Wiley Publishing, Inc., Indianapolis, IN, USA (2004).

1688. B. Schneier. "Sony's DRM Rootkit: The Real Story," *Schneier on Security* (Nov. 17, 2005).

1689. B. Schneier and J. Kelsey. "Secure Audit Logs to Support Computer Forensics," *ACM Transactions on Information and System Security* **2**(2) pp. 159–176 (May 1999).

1690. B. Schneier, J. Kelsey, D. Whiting, D. Wagner, C. Hall, and N. Ferguson. "Twofish: A 128-Bit Block Cipher," *unpublished* (June 1998).

1691. B. Schneier, J. Kelsey, D. Whiting, D. Wagner, C. Hall, and N. Ferguson. *The Twofish Encryption Algorithm: A 128-Bit Block Cipher*, John Wiley & Sons, New York, NY, USA (1999).

1692. E. Schreck and W. Ertel. "Disk Drive Generates High Speed Real Random Numbers," *Microsystem Technologies* **11**(8–10) pp. 616–622 (Aug. 2005).

1693. B. Schroeder and G. A. Gibson. "Understanding Disk Failure Rates: What Does an MTTF of 1,000,000 Hours Mean to You?" *ACM Transactions on Storage* **3**(3) pp. 8:1–8:31 (Oct. 2007).

1694. C. L. Schuba. *Addressing Weaknesses in the Domain Name System Protocol*, COAST TR 95-04, COAST Laboratory, Department of Computer Sciences, Purdue University, West Lafayette, IN 47907 (Aug. 1993).

1695. C. L. Schuba, I. V. Krsul, M. G. Kuhn, E. H. Spafford, A. Sundara, and D. Zamboni. "Analysis of a Denial of Service Attack on TCP," *Proceedings of the 1997 IEEE Symposium on Security and Privacy* pp. 208–223 (May 1997).

1696. C. L. Schuba and E. H. Spafford. "A Reference Model for Firewall Technology," *Proceedings of the 13th Annual Computer Security Applications Conference* pp. 133–145 (Dec. 1997).

1697. A. Schulter, K. Vieira, C. Westphall, C. Westphall, and S. Abderrahim. "Intrusion Detection for Computational Grids," *Proceedings of the 2008 New Technologies, Mobility and Security Conference and Workshops* pp. 1–5 (Nov. 2008).

1698. M. G. Schultz, E. Eskin, E. Zadok, and S. J. Stolfo. "Data Mining Methods for Detection of New Malicious Executables," *Proceedings of the 2001 IEEE Symposium on Security and Privacy* pp. 38–49 (May 2001).

1699. T. Schürmann and P. Grassberger. "Entropy Estimation of Symbol Sequences," *Chaos* **6**(3) pp. 414–427 (Sep. 1996).

1700. K. Schwaber and J. Sutherland. *The Scrum Guide: The Definitive Guide to Scrum: The Rules of the Game*, Technical Report, Scrum, Inc. (July 2013).

1701. E. J. Schwartz, T. Avgerinos, and D. Brumley. "All You Ever Wanted to Know about Dynamic Taint Analysis and Forward Symbolic Execution (But Might Have Been Afraid to Ask)," *Proceedings of the 2010 IEEE Symposium on Security and Privacy* pp. 317–331 (May 2010).

1702. K. L. Scott. "Overview of the Privacy Act of 1974," U. S. Department of Justice Office of Privacy and Civil Liberties, Washington DC, USA (2015).

1703. R. Scott. "Wide-Open Encryption Design Offers Flexible Implementations," *Cryptologia* **9**(1) pp. 75–91 (1985).

1704. R. C. Seacord. *Secure Coding in C and C++*, Addison-Wesley, Upper Saddle River, NJ, USA (2013).

1705. J. Seberry and J. Pieprzyk. *Cryptography: An Introduction to Computer Security*, Prentice Hall, Inc, Englewood Cliffs, NJ, USA (1990).

1706. D. Seeley. "Password Cracking: A Game of Wits," *Communications of the ACM* **32**(6) pp. 700–703 (June 1989).

1707. D. Seeley. "A Tour of the Worm," *Proceedings of the 1989 Winter USENIX Conference* pp. 287–304 (Jan. 1989).

1708. R. Seggelman, M. Tuexen, and M. G. Williams. *Transport Layer Security (TLS) and Datagram Transport Layer Security (DTLS) Heartbeat Extension*, RFC 6520 (Feb. 2012).

1709. D. Sehr, R. Muth, C. Biffle, V. Khimenko, E. Pasko, K. Schimpf, B. Yee, and B. Chen. "Adapting Software Fault Isolation to Contemporary CPU Architectures," *Proceedings of the 19th USENIX Security Symposium* pp. 1–12 (Aug. 2010).

1710. K. F. Seiden and J. P. Melanson. "The Auditing Facility for a VMM Security Kernel," *Proceedings of the 1990 IEEE Symposium on Research in Security and Privacy* pp. 262–277 (May 1990).

1711. R. Sekar, A. Gupta, J. Frullo, T. Shanbhag, A. Tiwari, H. Yang, and S. Zhou. "Specification-Based Anomaly Detection: A New Approach for Detecting Network Intrusions," *Proceedings of the Ninth ACM Conference on Computer and Communications Security* pp. 265–274 (Nov. 2002).

1712. A. Serjantov, R. Dingledine, and P. Syverson. "From a Trickle to a Flood: Active Attacks on Several Mix Types," *Proceedings of the Fifth International Workshop on Information Hiding* (*Lecture Notes in Computer Science* **2578**) pp. 36–52 (Oct. 2002).

1713. J. Sermersheim. *Lightweight Directory Access Protocol (LDAP): The Protocol*, RFC 4511 (June 2006).

1714. G. Serrao. "Rating Network Components," *Proceedings of the 18th National Computer Security Conference* pp. 344–355 (Oct. 1995).

1715. C. Servin and M. Ceberio. "Cascade Vulnerability Problem Simulator Tool," *Proceedings of the 2008 International Conference on Modeling, Simulation and Visualization Methods* pp. 227–231 (July 2008).

1716. C. Servin, M. Ceberio, E. Freudenthal, and S. Bistarelli. "An Optimization Approach Using Soft Constraints for the Cascade Vulnerability Problem," *Proceedngs of the 2007 Annual Meeting of the North American Fuzzy Information Processing Society* pp. 372–377 (June 2007).

1717. H. Shacham. "The Geometry of Innocent Flesh on the Bone: Return-Into-Libc Without Function Calls (On the x86)," *Proceedings of the 14th ACM Conference on Computer and Communications Security* pp. 552–561 (2007).

1718. H. Shacham, M. Page, B. Pfaff, E.-J. Goh, N. Modadugu, and D. Boneh. "On the Effectiveness of Address-Space Randomizaton," *Proceedings of the 11th ACM Conference on Computer and Communications Security* pp. 298–307 (Oct. 2004).

1719. G. Shah, A. Molina, and M. Blaze. "Keyboards and Covert Channels," *Proceedings of the 15th USENIX Security Symposium* pp. 59–75 (July 2006).

1720. N. Shahmehri, A. Mammar, E. Montes de Oca, D. Byers, A. Cavalli, S. Ardi, and W. Jimenez. "An Advanced Approach for Modeling and Detecting Software Vulnerabilities," *Information and Security Technology* **54**(9) pp. 997–1013 (Sep. 2012).

1721. H. R. Shahriari and R. Jalili. "Vulnerability Take Grant (VTG): An Efficient Approach to Analyze Network Vulnerabilities," *Computers & Security* **26**(5) pp. 349–360 (Aug. 2007).

1722. A. Shamir. "How to Share a Secret," *Communications of the ACM* **22**(11) pp. 612–613 (Nov. 1979).

1723. A. Shamir. "A Polynomial Time Algorithm for Breaking the Basic Merkle-Hellman Cryptosystem," *Proceedings of the 23rd Annual Symposium on Foundations of Computer Science* pp. 145–152 (Nov. 1982).

1724. A. Shamir. "Identity-Based Cryptosystems and Signature Schemes," *Advances in Cryptology — CRYPTO '84* (*Lecture Notes in Computer Science* **196**) pp. 47–53 (Aug. 1984).

1725. C. E. Shannon. "A Mathematical Theory of Communication," *Bell System Technical Journal* **27**(3) pp. 379–423 (July 1948).

1726. C. E. Shannon. "A Mathematical Theory of Communicaton," *Bell System Technical Journal* **27**(4) pp. 623–656 (Oct. 1948).

1727. C. E. Shannon. "Communication Theory of Secrecy Systems," *Bell System Technical Journal* **28**(4) pp. 656–715 (Oct. 1949).

1728. C. E. Shannon. "Prediction and Entropy of Printed English," *Bell System Technical Journal* **30**(1) pp. 50–64 (Jan. 1951).

1729. J. S. Shapiro and N. Hardy. "EROS: A Principle-Driven Operating System from the Ground Up," *IEEE Software* **19**(1) pp. 26–33 (Jan. 2002).

1730. J. S. Shapiro, J. M. Smith, and D. J. Farber. "EROS: A Fast Capability System," *Proceedings of the 17th ACM Symposium on Operating Systems Principles* pp. 170–185 (Dec. 1999).

1731. C. Shen, Z. Cai, X. Guan, Y. Du, and R. A. Maxion. "User Authentication Through Mouse Dynamics," *IEEE Transactions on Information Forensics and Security* **8**(1) pp. 16–30 (Jan. 2013).

1732. O. Sheyner, J. Haines, S. Jha, R. Lippmann, and J. M. Wing. "Automated Generation and Analysis of Attack Graphs," *Proceedings of the 2002 IEEE Symposium on Security and Privacy* pp. 273–284 (May 2002).

1733. S.-P. Shieh and V. D. Gligor. "Detecting Illicit Leakage of Information in Operating Systems," *Journal of Computer Security* **4**(2-3) pp. 123–148 (1996).

1734. C. Shiflett. *Essential PHP Security*, O'Reilly Media, Sebastopol, CA, USA (2005).

1735. A. Shimizu and S. Miyaguchi. "Fast Data Encipherment Algorithm FEAL," *Advances in Cryptology — CRYPTO '87* (*Lecture Notes in Computer Science* **304**) pp. 267–278 (1987).

1736. T. Shimomura and J. Markoff. *Takedown: The Pursuit and Capture of Kevin Mitnick, America's Most Wanted Computer Outlaw—By the Man Who Did It*, Hyperion, New York, NY, USA (1996).

1737. T. Shimoyama, M. Takenaka, and T. Koshiba. "Multiple Linear Cryptanalysis of a Reduced Round RC6," *Proceedings of the Ninth International Workshop on Fast Software Encryption* (*Lecture Notes in Computer Science* **2365**) pp. 76–88 (Feb. 2002).

1738. H. Shiravi, Ali amd Shiravi, M. Tavallaee, and A. A. Ghorbani. "Toward Developing a Systematic Approach to Generate Benchmark Datasets for Intrusion Detection," *Computers & Security* **31**(3) pp. 357–374 (May 2012).

1739. R. Shirey. *Internet Security Glossary, Version 2*, RFC 4949 (Aug. 2007).

1740. J. F. Shoch. "Inter-Network Naming, Addressing, and Routing," *Proceedings of Compcon Fall '78, Computer Communications Networks* pp. 72–79 (Sep. 1978).

1741. J. F. Shoch and J. A. Hupp. "The 'Worm' Programs—Early Experience with a Distributed Computation," *Communications of the ACM* **25**(3) pp. 172–180 (Mar. 1982).

1742. T. G. Shoriak. "SSL/TLS Protocol Enablement for Key Recovery," *Computers & Security* **19**(1) pp. 100–104 (Jan. 2000).

1743. A. Shostack and A. Stewart. *The New School of Information Security*, Addison-Wesley, Boston, MA, USA (2008).

1744. R. Shu, P. Wang, S. A. Gorski III, B. Andow, A. Nadkarni, L. Deshotels, J. Gionta, W. Enck, and X. Gu. "A Study of Security Isolation Techniques," *ACM Computing Surveys* **49**(3) pp. 50:1–50:37 (Oct. 2016).

1745. X. Shu, K. Tan, A. Ciambrone, and D. D. Yao. "Breaking the Target: An Analysis of Target Data Breach and Lessons Learned," *Computing Research Repository* (arXiv:1701.04940 [cs.CR]) (Jan. 2017).

1746. W. O. Sibert. "Auditing in a Distributed System: SunOS MLS Audit Trails," *Proceedings of the 11th National Computer Security Conference* pp. 82–90 (Oct. 1988).

1747. D. P. Sidhu and M. Gasser. "A Multilevel Secure Local Area Network," *Proceedings of the 1982 IEEE Symposium on Security and Privacy* pp. 137–143 (Apr. 1982).

1748. A. Silberschatz, P. S. Galvin, and G. Gagne. *Operating System Concepts*, John H. Wiley & Sons, Inc., Hoboken, NJ, USA (2013).

1749. G. J. Simmons. "How to (Really) Share a Secret," *Advances in Cryptology — CRYPTO '88* (*Lecture Notes in Computer Science* **403**) pp. 390–448 (Aug. 1988).

1750. G. J. Simmons. "Prepositioned Shared Secret and/or Shared Control Schemes," *Advances in Cryptology — EUROCRYPT '89* (*Lecture Notes in Computer Science* **434**) pp. 436–467 (Apr. 1989).

1751. G. J. Simmons. "Geometric Shared Secret and/or Shared Control Schemes," *Advances in Cryptology — CRYPTO '90* (*Lecture Notes in Computer Science* **537**) pp. 216–241 (Aug. 1990).

1752. G. J. Simmons and D. Holdridge. "Forward Search as a Cryptanalytic Tool Against a Public Key Privacy Channel," *Proceedings of the 1982 IEEE Symposium on Security and Privacy* pp. 117–128 (Apr. 1982).

1753. G. J. Simmons and C. Meadows. "The Role of Trust in Information Integrity Protocols," *Journal of Computer Security* **3**(1) pp. 71–84 (1995).

1754. R. T. Simon and M. E. Zurko. "Separation of Duty in Role-Based Environments," *Proceedings of the Tenth Computer Security Foundations Workshop* pp. 183–194 (June 1997).

1755. L. Simpson, M. Hendricksen, and W.-S. Yap. "Improved Cryptanalysis of the Common Scrambling Algorithm Stream Cipher," *Proceedings of the 14th Australasian Conference on Information Security and Privacy* (*Lecture Notes in Computer Science* **5594**) pp. 108–121 (July 2009).

1756. G. Sindre and A. L. Opdahl. "Eliciting Security Requirements with Misuse Cases," *Requirements Engineering* **10**(1) pp. 34–44 (Jan. 2005).

1757. L. Singaravelu, C. Pu, H. Härtig, and C. Helmuth. "Reducing TCB Complexity for Security-Sensitive Applications: Three Case Studies," *Proceedings of the First ACM SIGOPS/EuroSys European Conference on Computer Systems* pp. 161–174 (Apr. 2006).

1758. S. Singh, C. Estan, G. Varghese, and S. Savage. "Automated Worm Fingerprinting," *Proceedings of the Sixth Symposium on Operating System Design and Implementation* pp. 45–60 (Dec. 2004).

1759. A. Sinkov. *Elementary Cryptanalysis: A Mathematical Approach*, Mathematical Association of America, Washington, DC, USA (2009).

1760. S. Sivarajan. *Getting Started with Windows Server Security*, Packt Publishing Ltd., Birmingham, UK (2015).

1761. sKyWIper Analysis Team. *sKyWIper a.k.a. Flame a.k.a. Flamer: A Complex Malware for Targeted Attacks*, Technical Report v1.05 (May 31, 2012), Laboratory of Cryptography and System Security (CrySyS Lab), Budapest University of Technology and Economics, Budapest, Hungary (May 2012).

1762. N. J. Slamecka and P. Graf. "The Generation Effect: Delineation of a Phenomenon," *Journal of Experimental Psychology: Human Learning and Memory* **4**(6) pp. 592–604 (Nov. 1978).

1763. M. Slatalla and J. Quittner. *Masters of Deception: The Gang That Ruled Cyberspace*, HarperPerennial, New York, NY, USA (1995).

1764. S. E. Smaha. "Haystack: An Intrusion Detection System," *Proceedings of the Fourth Annual Computer Security Applications Conference* pp. 37–44 (Sep. 1988).

1765. M. Smart, G. R. Malan, and F. Jahanian. "Defeating TCP/IP Stack Fingerprinting," *Proceedings of the Ninth USENIX Security Symposium* (Aug. 2000).

1766. G. Smith and D. Volpano. "Secure Information Flow in a Multi-Threaded Imperative Language," *Proceedings of the 25th ACM SIGPLAN-SIGACT Symposium on Principles of Programming Languages* pp. 355–364 (Jan. 1998).

1767. K. Smith and M. Winslett. "Entity Modeling in the MLS Relational Model," *Proceedings of the 18th International Conference on Very Large Data Bases* pp. 199–210 (Aug. 1992).

1768. R. E. Smith. "Constructing a High Assurance Mail Guard," *Proceedings of the 17th National Computer Security Conference* pp. 247–253 (Oct. 1994).

1769. R. E. Smith. "Cost Profile of a Highly Assured, Secure Operating System," *ACM Transactions on Information and System Security* **4**(1) pp. 72–101 (Feb. 2001).

1770. S. L. Smith. "Authenticating Users by Word Association," *Computers & Security* **6**(6) pp. 464–470 (Dec. 1987).

1771. T. Smith. "User Definable Domains as a Mechanism for Implementing the Least Privilege Principle," *Proceedings of the Ninth National Computer Security Conference* pp. 143–148 (Sep. 1986).

1772. J. C. Snader. *VPNs Illustrated: Tunnels, VPNs, and IPsec: Tunnels, VPNs, and IPsec*, Addison-Wesley, Boston, MA, USA (2006).

1773. S. R. Snapp, J. Brentano, G. V. Dias, T. L. Goan, T. Grance, L. T. Heberlein, C.-L. Ho, K. N. Levitt, B. Mukherjee, D. L. Mansur, K. L. Pon, and S. E. Smaha. "A System for Distributed Intrusion Detection," *Proceedings of Compcon Spring '91* pp. 170–176 (Feb. 1991).

1774. S. R. Snapp, J. Brentano, G. V. Dias, T. L. Goan, L. T. Heberlein, C.-L. Ho, K. N. Levitt, B. Mukherjee, S. E. Smaha, T. Grance, D. M. Teal, and D. L. Mansur. "DIDS (Distributed Intrusion Detection System)—Motivation, Architecture, and an Early Prototype," *Proceedings of the 14th National Computer Security Conference* pp. 167–176 (Oct. 1991).

1775. B. Snow. "We Need Assurance!" *Proceedings of the 21st Annual Computer Security Applications Conference* pp. 7–17 (Dec. 2005).

1776. B. D. Snow. "The Future Is Not Assured—But It Should Be," *Proceedings of the 1999 IEEE Symposium on Security and Privacy* pp. 240–241 (May 1999).

1777. L. Snyder. "Theft and Conspiracy in the Take-Grant Protection Model," *Journal of Computer and System Sciences* **23**(3) pp. 333–347 (Dec. 1981).

1778. M. Sobirey, S. Fischer-Hübner, and K. Rannenberg. "Pseudonymous Audit for Privacy Enhanced Intrusion Detection," *Proceedings of the IFIP TC11 13th International Conference on Information Security* pp. 151–163 (May 1997).

1779. K. Sohr, M. Droiuneaud, G.-J. Ahn, and M. Gogolla. "Analyzing and Managing Role-Based Access Control Policies," *IEEE Transactions on Knowledge and Data Engineering* **20**(7) pp. 924–939 (July 2008).

1780. H. Soleimany, A. Sharifi, and M. Aref. "Improved Related-Key Boomerang Cryptanalysis of AES-256," *Proceedings of the 2010 International Conference on Information Science and Applications* pp. 1–7 (Apr. 2010).

1781. M. G. Solomon. *Security Strategies in Windows Platforms and Applications*, Jones and Bartlett Learning, Burlington, MA. USA (2014).

1782. D. J. Solove. *The Future of Reputation: Gossip, Rumor, and Privacy on the Internet*, Yale University Press, New Haven, CT, USA (2008).

1783. A. Somayaji and S. Forrest. "Automated Response Using System-Call Delays," *Proceedings of the Ninth USENIX Security Symposium* (Aug. 2000).

1784. R. Sommer. *The Bro Network Intrusion Detection System* (Dec. 2007).

1785. R. Sommer and V. Paxson. "Outside the Closed World: On Using Machine Learning for Network Intrusion Detection," *Proceedings of the 2010 IEEE Symposium on Security and Privacy* pp. 305–316 (May 2010).

1786. J. Sommers, V. Yegneswaran, and P. Barford. *Toward Comprehensive Traffic Generation for Online IDS Evaluation*, Technical Report 1525, Department of Computer Sciences, University of Wisconsin-Madison, Madison, WI, USA (Feb. 2006).

1787. I. Sommerville. *Software Engineering*, Addison-Wesley Publishing Company, Boston, MA, USA (2001).

1788. S. H. Son, C. Chaney, and N. P. Thomlinson. "Partial Security Policies to Support Timeliness in Secure Real-Time Databases," *Proceedings of the 1998 IEEE Symposium on Security and Privacy* pp. 136–147 (May 1998).

1789. W. Song, T. Kim, H. C. Kim, J. H. Choi, H.-J. Kong, and S.-R. Lee. "A Finger-Vein Verification System Using Mean Curvature," *Pattern Recognition Letters* **32**(11) pp. 1541–1547 (Aug. 2011).

1790. Sophos. "Troj/Arhiveus-A," Sophos Threat Center: Threat Analysis: Viruses and Spyware, Sophos, Santa Clara, CA, USA (May 2006).

1791. A. Sorkin. "Lucifer, a Cryptographic Algorithm," *Cryptologia* **8**(1) pp. 22–42 (1984).

1792. M. Soshi, M. Maekawa, and E. Okamoto. "The Dynamic-Typed Access Matrix Model and Decidability of the Safety Problem," *IEICE Transactions on Fundamentals of Electronics, Communications and Computer Sciences* **E87-A**(1) pp. 190–203 (Jan. 2004).

1793. M. Soucarros, C. Canovas-Dumas, J. Clédière, P. Elbaz-Vincent, and D. Réal. "Influence of the Temperature on True Random Number Generators," *Proceedings of the 2011 IEEE International Symposium on Hardware-Oriented Security and Trust* pp. 24–27 (June 2011).

1794. M. Souppaya and K. Scarfone. *Guide to Malware Incident Prevention and Handling for Desktops and Laptops*, Special Publication 800-145 Revision 1x, National Institute of Standards and Technology, Gaithersburg, MD, USA (July 2013).

1795. W. Soyinka. *Linux Administration: A Beginner's Guide, Seventh Edition*, McGraw-Hill Education (2015).

1796. E. H. Spafford. "Crisis and Aftermath," *Communications of the ACM* **32**(6) pp. 678–687 (June 1989).

1797. E. H. Spafford. "The Internet Worm Program: An Analysis," *ACM SIGCOMM Computer Communications Review* **19**(1) pp. 17–57 (Jan. 1989).

1798. E. H. Spafford. "Observations on Reusable Password Choices," *Proceedings of the Third USENIX Security Symposium* pp. 299–312 (Sep. 1992).

1799. E. H. Spafford. "OPUS: Preventing Weak Password Choices," *Computers & Security* **11**(3) pp. 273–278 (May 1992).

1800. E. H. Spafford, K. A. Heaphy, and D. J. Ferbrache. *A Computer Virus Primer*, Technical Report CSD-TR-935, Dept. of Computer Science, Purdue University, West Lafayette, IN, USA (Nov. 1989).

1801. E. H. Spafford and S. Weeber. "Software Forensics: Can We Track Code to Its Authors?," *Proceedings of the 15th National Computer Security Conference* pp. 641–650 (Oct. 1992).

1802. S. M. Specht and R. B. Lee. "Distributed Denial of Service: Taxonomies of Attacks, Tools and Countermeasures," *Proceedings of the ISCA 17th International Conference on Parallel and Distributed Computing Systems* pp. 543–550 (Sep. 2004).

1803. R. J. Spillman. *Classical and Contemporary Cryptology*, Pearson Education, Upper Saddle River, NJ, USA (2005).

1804. L. Spitzner. "The Honeynet Project: Trapping the Hackers," *IEEE Security & Privacy* **1**(2) pp. 15–23 (Mar. 2003).

1805. L. Spitzner. "Honeypots: Catching the Insider Threat," *Proceedings of the 19th Annual Computer Security Applications Conference* pp. 170–179 (Dec. 2003).

1806. P. Srisuresh and K. B. Egevang. *Traditional IP Network Address Translator (Traditional NAT)*, RFC 3022 (Jan. 2001).

1807. M. C. St. Johns. *Identification Protocol*, RFC 1413 (Feb. 1993).

1808. F. Stajano and P. Wilson. "Understanding Scam Victims: Seven Principles for Systems Security," *Communications of the ACM* **54**(3) pp. 70–75 (Mar. 2011).

1809. W. Stallings. *Network Security Essentials: Applications and Standards*, Pearson, Boston, MA, USA (2017).

1810. R. Stallman. "The Right to Read," *Communications of the ACM* **40**(2) pp. 85–87 (Feb. 1997).

1811. R. M. Stallman, R. Pesch, and S. Shebs. *Debugging with GDB — Reference Manual* **1**, Samurai Media Limited, Wickford, UK (Oct. 2015).

1812. R. M. Stallman, R. Pesch, and S. Shebs. *Debugging with GDB — Reference Manual* **2**, Samurai Media Limited, Wickford, UK (Oct. 2015).

1813. M. C. Stamm and K. J. Ray Liu. "Anti-Forensics of Digital Image Compression," *IEEE Transactions on Information Forensics and Security* **6**(3) pp. 1050–1065 (Sep. 2011).

1814. F.-X. Standaert, T. G. Malkin, and M. Yung. "A Unified Framework for the Analysis of Side-Channel Key Recovery Attacks," *Advances in Cryptology — EUROCRYPT 2009* (*Lecture Notes in Computer Science* **5479**) pp. 443–461 (Apr. 2009).

1815. F.-X. Standaert, G. Rouvroy, J.-J. Quisquater, and J.-D. Legat. "Efficient Implementation of Rijndael Encryption in Reconfigurable Hardware: Improvements and Design Tradeoffs," *Proceedings of the 5th International Workshop on Cryptographic Hardware and Embedded Systems* (*Lecture Notes in Computer Science* **2779**) pp. 334–350 (2003).

1816. S. Staniford-Chen, S. Cheung, R. Crawford, M. Dilger, J. Frank, J. Hoagland, K. Levitt, C. Wee, R. Yip, and D. Zerkle. "GrIDS—A Graph Based Intrusion Detection System for Large Networks," *Proceedings of the 19th National Information Systems Security Conference* pp. 361–370 (Oct. 1996).

1817. S. Staniford-Chen and L. T. Heberlein. "Holding Intruders Accountable on the Internet," *Proceedings of the 1995 IEEE Symposium on Security and Privacy* pp. 39–49 (May 1995).

1818. M. Starr. "Fridge Caught Sending Spam Emails in Botnet Attack," *CNET* (Jan. 19, 2014).

1819. A. M. Stavely. *Toward Zero Defect Programming*, Addison-Wesley, Reading, MA, USA (1999).

1820. stealth. "Kernel Rootkit Experiences," *Phrack* **11**(61) article 14 (Aug. 2003).

1821. J. G. Steiner, B. C. Neuman, and J. I. Schiller. "Kerberos: An Authentication Service for Open Network Systems," *Proceedings of the 1988 Winter USENIX Conference* pp. 191–202 (Winter 1988).

1822. B. Sterling. *The Hacker Crackdown: Law And Disorder on the Electronic Frontier*, Bantam Books, New York, NY, USA (1993).

1823. D. F. Sterne. "On the Buzzword 'Security Policy,'" *Proceedings of the 1991 IEEE Symposium on Research in Security and Privacy* pp. 219–230 (May 1991).

1824. F. A. Stevenson. "Cryptanalysis of Contents Scrambling System," *unpublished* (Nov. 1999).

1825. H. G. Stiegler. "A Structure for Access Control Lists," *Software: Practice and Experience* **9**(10) pp. 813–819 (Oct. 1979).

1826. D. R. Stinson. *Cryptography: Theory and Practice*, Chapman and Hall/CRC, Boca Raton, FL, USA (2006).

1827. E. Stobert and R. Biddle. "Memory Retrieval and Graphical Passwords," *Proceedings of the Ninth Symposium on Usable Privacy and Security* pp. 15:1–15:14 (July 2013).

1828. S. J. Stolfo, M. Ben Salem, and A. D. Keromytis. "Fog Computing: Mitigating Insider Data Theft Attacks in the Cloud," *Proceedings of the 2012 IEEE Symposium on Security and Privacy Workshops* pp. 125–128 (May 2012).

1829. C. Stoll. "Stalking the Wily Hacker," *Communications of the ACM* **31**(5) pp. 484–497 (May 1988).

1830. C. Stoll. "An Epidemiology of Viruses and Network Worms," *Proceedings of the 12th National Computer Security Conference* pp. 369–377 (Oct. 1989).

1831. C. Stoll. *The Cuckoo's Egg: Tracking a Spy Through the Maze of Computer Espionage*, Pocket Books, New York, NY, USA (2005).

1832. G. N. Stone, B. Lundy, and G. G. Xie. "Network Policy Languages: A Survey and a New Approach," *IEEE Network* **15**(1) pp. 10–21 (Jan. 2001).

1833. B. Stone-Gross, M. Cova, L. Cavallaro, B. Gilbert, M. Szydlowski, R. Kemmerer, C. Kruegel, and G. Vigna. "Your Botnet Is My Botnet: Analysis of a Botnet Takeover," *Proceedings of the 16th ACM Conference on Computer and Communications Security* pp. 635–647 (Nov. 2009).

1834. B. Stone-Gross, M. Cova, B. Gilbert, R. Kemmerer, C. Kruegel, and G. Vigna. "Analysis of a Botnet Takeover," *IEEE Security & Privacy* **9**(1) pp. 64–72 (Jan. 2011).

1835. J. Straw. "The Draft Federal Criteria and the ITSEC: Progress Towards Alignment," *Proceedings of the 16th National Computer Security Conference* pp. 311–323 (Sep. 1993).

1836. T. Strazzere and T. Wyatt. *Geinimi Trojan Technical Teardown*, Technical Report, Lookout Mobile Security, San Francisco, CA, USA (Jan. 2011).

1837. G. Stringhini, C. Kruegel, and G. Vigna. "Detecting Spammers on Social Networks," *Proceedings of the 26th Annual Computer Security Applications Conference* pp. 1–9 (Dec. 2010).

1838. E. Strother. "Denial of Service Protection — The Nozzle," *Proceedings of the 16th Annual Computer Security Applications Conference* pp. 32–41 (Dec. 2000).

1839. J. D. Strunk, G. R. Goodson, M. L. Scheinholtz, C. A. N. Soules, and G. R. Ganger. "Self-Securing Storage: Protecting Data in Compromised System," *Proceedings of the Fourth Symposium on Operating System Design & Implementation* (Oct. 2000).

1840. P. Su and M. Bishop. *How to Encrypt /usr/dict/words in About a Second*, Technical Report PCS-TR92-182, Dept. of Mathematics and Computer Science, Dartmouth College, Hanover, NH, USA (1992).

1841. L. Sun, T. Ebringer, and S. Boztas. "An Automatic Anti-Anti-VMware Technique Applicable for Multi-Stage Packed Malware," *Proceedings of the Third International Conference on Malicious and Unwanted Software* pp. 17–23 (Oct. 2008).

1842. D. Sutherland. "A Model of Information," *Proceedings of the Ninth National Computer Security Conference* pp. 175–183 (Sep. 1986).

1843. H. Sutter and A. Alexandrescu. *C++ Coding Standards*, Addison-Wesley, Boston, MA, USA (2005).

1844. L. Sweeney. *Uniqueness of Simple Demographics in the U.S. Population*, Technical Report Data Privacy Working Paper 3, Laboratory for International Data Privacy, Carnegie Mellon University, Pittsburgh, PA, USA (2000).

1845. L. Sweeney. "k-Anonymity: A Model for Protecting Privacy," *International Journal of Uncertainty, Fuzziness and Knowledge-Based Systems* **10**(5) pp. 557–570 (Oct. 2002).

1846. Symantec. *Ransomware and Businesses 2016*, ISTR Special Report, Symantec, Mountain View, CA, USA (Aug. 2016).

1847. P. Syverson. "Limitations on Design Principles for Public Key Protocols," *Proceedings of the 1996 IEEE Symposium on Security and Privacy* pp. 62–72 (May 1996).

1848. P. F. Syverson, M. G. Reed, and D. M. Goldschlag. "Private Web Browsing," *Journal of Computer Security* **5**(3) pp. 237–248 (Sep. 1997).

1849. J. Szczepanski, E. Wajnryb, J. M. Amigó, M. V. Sanchez-Vives, and M. Slater. "Biometric Random Number Generators," *Computers & Security* **23**(1) pp. 77–84 (Feb. 2004).

1850. P. Szor. *The Art of Computer Virus Research and Defense*, Addison-Wesley, Boston, MA, USA (Feb. 2005).

1851. H. Takabi, J. B. D. Joshi, and G.-J. Ahn. "Security and Privacy Challenges in Cloud Computing Environments," *IEEE Security & Privacy* **8**(6) pp. 24–31 (Nov. 2010).

1852. T. Takada and H. Koike. "MieLog: A Highly Interactive Visual Log Browser Using Information Visualization and Statistical Analysis," *Proceedings of the 16th Systems Administration Conference* pp. 133–144 (Nov. 2002).

1853. T. Takada and H. Koike. "Tudumi: Information Visualization System for Monitoring and Auditing Computer Logs," *Proceedings of the Sixth International Conference on Information Visualisation* pp. 570-576 (July 2002).

1854. L. Tam, M. Glassman, and M. Vandenwauver. "The Psychology of Password Management: A Tradeoff between Security and Convenience," *Behaviour & Information Technology* **29**(3) pp. 233–244 (May 2010).

1855. K. M. C. Tan and R. A. Maxion. "'Why 6?' Defining the Operational Limits of stide, an Anomaly-Based Intrusion Detector," *Proceedings of the 2002 IEEE Symposium on Security and Privacy* pp. 181–201 (May 2002).

1856. A. S. Tanenbaum. *Modern Operating Systems*, Pearson, Boston, MA, USA (2001).

1857. A. S. Tanenbaum and H. Bos. *Modern Operating Systems*, Pearson Education, Inc., Upper Saddle River, NJ, USA (2014).

1858. A. S. Tanenbaum, R. van Renesse, H. van Staveren, G. J. Sharp, and S. J. Mullender. "Experiences with the Amoeba Distributed Operating System," *Communications of the ACM* **33**(12) pp. 46–63 (Dec. 1990).

1859. A. S. Tanenbaum and D. J. Wetherall. *Computer Networks*, Prentice Hall, Inc, Upper Saddle River, NJ, USA (2011).

1860. J. J. Tardo and K. Alagappan. "SPX: Global Authentication Using Public Key Certificates," *Proceedings of the 1991 IEEE Symposium on Research in Security and Privacy* pp. 232–244 (May 1991).

1861. M. Tavallaee, E. Bagheri, W. Lu, and A. A. Ghorbani. "A Detailed Analysis of the KDD CUP 99 Data Set," *Proceedings of the 2009 IEEE Symposium on Computational Intelligence for Security and Defense Applications* pp. 1–6 (July 2009).

1862. T. Taylor. "Comparison Paper Between the Bell and LaPadula Model and the SRI Model," *Proceedings of the 1984 IEEE Symposium on Security and Privacy* pp. 195–202 (Apr. 1984).

1863. PaX Team. "Address Space Layout Randomization," *unpublished* (July 2001).

1864. V. Teja, P. Banerjee, N. N. Sharma, and R. K. Mittal. "Quantum Cryptography: State-of-Art, Challenges and Future Perspectives," *Proceedings of the Seventh International Conference on Nanotechnology* pp. 1296–1301 (Aug. 2007).

1865. S. J. Templeton and K. Levitt. "A Requires/Provides Model for Computer Attacks," *Proceedings of the 2000 Workshop on New Security Paradigms* pp. 31–38 (Sep. 2000).

1866. H. S. Teng, K. Chen, and S. C.-Y. Lu. "Adaptive Real-Time Anomaly Detection Using Inductively Generated Sequential Patterns," *Proceedings of the 1990 IEEE Symposium on Research in Security and Privacy* pp. 278–284 (May 1990).

1867. A. B. Teoh, D. C. Ngo, and A. Goh. "Personalised Cryptographic Key Generation Based on FaceHashing," *Computers & Security* **23**(7) pp. 606–614 (Oct. 2004).

1868. C. J. Testa, B. D. Wilner, and V. D. Gligor. "Trusted RUBIX Architecture and Policy Model Interpretation," *Proceedings of the Eighth Annual Computer Security Applications Conference* pp. 97–110 (Nov. 1992).

1869. The RAND Corporation. *A Million Random Digits with 100,000 Normal Deviates*, Free Press Publishers, Glencoe, IL, USA (1955).

1870. H. Thimbleby, S. Anderson, and P. Cairns. "A Framework for Modelling Trojans and Computer Virus Infection," *The Computer Journal* **41**(7) pp. 444–458 (Jan. 1998).

1871. C. Thomas, V. Sharma, and N. Balakrishnan. "Usefulness of DARPA Dataset for Intrusion Detection System Evaluation," *Proceedings of the 2008 Conference on Data Mining, Intrusion Detection, Information Assurance, and Data Networks Security* pp. 69730G:1–69730G:8 (Mar. 2008).

1872. R. K. Thomas and R. Sandhu. "Towards a Task-Based Paradigm for Flexible and Adaptable Access Control in Distributed Applications," *Proceedings of the 1992–1993 Workshop on New Security Paradigms* pp. 138–142 (1993).

1873. V. Thomas and N. Jyoti. "Combating File Infectors on Corporate Networks," *Proceedings of the Third International Conference on Malicious and Unwanted Software* pp. 85–91 (Oct. 2008).

1874. H. H. Thompson. "Application Penetration Testing," *IEEE Security & Privacy* **3**(1) pp. 66–69 (Feb. 2005).

1875. K. Thompson. "Reflections on Trusting Trust," *Communications of the ACM* **27**(8) pp. 761–763 (Aug. 1984).

1876. M. Thompson, N. Evans, and V. Kisekka. "Multiple OS Rotational Environment: An Implemented Moving Target Defense," *Proceedings of the Seventh International Symposium on Resilient Control Systems* (Aug. 2014).

1877. D. Thomsen. "Sidewinder: Combining Type Enforcement and Unix," *Proceedings of the 11th Annual Computer Security Applications Conference* pp. 14–20 (Dec. 1995).

1878. O. Thonnard and M. Dacier. "A Strategic Analysis of Spam Botnets Operations," *Proceedings of the Eighth Annual Collaboration, Electronic Messaging, Anti-Abuse and Spam Conference* pp. 162–171 (Sep. 2011).

1879. J. Thorpe, M. Al-Badawi, B. MacRae, and A. Salehi-Abari. "The Presentation Effect on Graphical Passwords," *Proceedings of the 2014 SIGCHI Conference on Human Factors in Computing Systems* pp. 2947–2950 (Apr. 2014).

1880. B. Thurasingham. "Security Issues for Federated Database Systems," *Computers & Security* **13**(6) pp. 509–525 (Dec. 1994).

1881. C. Timberg, G. Witte, and E. Nakashima. "Malware, Described in Leaked NSA Documents, Cripples Computers Worldwide," *The Washington Post* (May 12, 2017).

1882. A. H. Toderici and M. Stamp. "Chi-Square Distance and Metamorphic Virus Detection," *Journal of Computer Virology and Hacking Techniques* **9**(1) pp. 1–14 (Feb. 2013).

1883. T. Tokita, T. Sorimachi, and M. Matsui. "Linear Cryptanalysis of LOKI and s^2DES," *Advances in Cryptology— Proceedings of ASIACRYPT '94 (Lecture Notes in Computer Science* **917**) pp. 293–303 (1995).

1884. M. Tompa and H. Woll. "How to Share a Secret With Cheaters," *Journal of Cryptology* **1**(3) pp. 133–138 (Oct. 1989).

1885. G. Tonti, J. M. Bradshaw, R. Jeffers, R. Montanari, N. Suri, and A. Uszok. "Semantic Web Languages for Policy Representation and Reasoning: A Comparison of KAoS, Rei, and Ponder," *Proceedings of the Second International Semantic Web Conference* (*Lecture Notes in Computer Science* **2870**) pp. 419–437 (Oct. 2003).

1886. T. Tran, R. Pelizzi, and R. Sekar. "JaTE: Transparent and Efficient JavaScript Confinement," *Proceedings of the 31st Annual Computer Security Applications Conference* pp. 151–160 (Dec. 2015).

1887. W. Trappe and L. C. Washington. *Introduction to Cryptography with Coding Theory*, Prentice Hall, Inc, Upper Saddle River, NJ, USA (2006).

1888. M. V. Tripunitara and N. Li. *The Foundational Work of Harrison-Ruzzo-Ullman Revisited*, Technical Report 2006-33, CERIAS, Purdue University, West Lafayette, IN, USA (Sep. 2006).

1889. M. V. Tripunitara and N. Li. "A Theory for Comparing the Expressive Power of Access Control Models," *Journal of Computer Security* **15**(2) pp. 231–272 (2007).

1890. M. V. Tripunitara and N. Li. "The Foundational Work of Harrison-Ruzzo-Ullman Revisited," *IEEE Transactions on Dependable and Secure Computing* **10**(1) pp. 28–39 (Jan. 2013).

1891. K. Trivedi, G. Ciardo, B. Dasarathy, M. Grottke, A. Rindos, and B. Varshaw. "Achieving and Assuring High Availability," *Proceedings of the 2008 International Symposium on Parallel and Distributed Processing* (Apr. 2008).

1892. E. Tromer and R. Schuster. "DroidDisintegrator: Intra-Application Information Flow Control in Android Apps," *Proceedings of the 11th ACM Asia Conference on Computer and Communications Security* pp. 401–412 (May 2016).

1893. J. T. Trostle. "Modelling a Fuzzy Time System," *Proceedings of the 1993 IEEE Symposium on Research in Security and Privacy* pp. 82–89 (May 1993).

1894. D. Tsafrir, T. Hertz, D. Wagner, and D. Da Silva. "Portably Solving File Races with Hardness Amplification," *ACM Transactions on Storage* **4**(3) pp. 9:1–9:30 (Nov. 2008).

1895. C.-F. Tsai and C.-Y. Lin. "A Triangle Area Based Nearest Neighbors Approach to Intrusion Detection," *Pattern Recognition* **43**(1) pp. 222–229 (Jan. 2010).

1896. C.-R. Tsai and V. D. Gligor. "A Bandwidth Computation Model for Covert Storage Channels and Its Applications," *Proceedings of the 1988 IEEE Symposium on Security and Privacy* pp. 108–121 (Apr. 1988).

1897. C.-R. Tsai, V. D. Gligor, and C. S. Chandersekaran. "A Formal Method for the Identification of Covert Storage Channels in Source Code," *Proceedings of the 1987 IEEE Symposium on Security and Privacy* (Apr. 1987).

1898. J. J. O. Tsai, A. Liu, E. Juan, and A. Sahay. "Knowledge-Based Software Architectures: Acquisition, Specification, and Verification," *IEEE Transactions on Knowledge and Data Engineering* **11**(1) pp. 187–201 (Jan. 1999).

1899. T.-C. Tsai, A. Russo, and J. Hughes. "A Library for Secure Multi-Threaded Information Flow in Haskell," *Proceedings of the 20th Computer Security Foundations Workshop* pp. 187–202 (July 2007).

1900. C.-Y. Tseng, P. Balasubramanyam, C. Ko, R. Limprasittiporn, J. Rowe, and K. Levitt. "A Specification-Based Intrusion Detection System for AODV," *Proceedings of the First ACM Workshop on Security of Ad Hoc and Sensor Networks* pp. 125–134 (2003).

1901. K. Tsipenyuk, B. Chess, and G. McGraw. "Seven Pernicious Kingdoms: A Taxonomy of Software Security Errors," *IEEE Security & Privacy* **3**(6) pp. 81–84 (Nov. 2005).

1902. W. Tuchman. "Hellman Presents No Shortcut Solutions to DES," *IEEE Spectrum* **16**(7) pp. 40–41 (July 1979).

1903. W. Tuchman. "A Brief History of the Data Encryption Standard" in *Internet Besieged: Countering Cyberspace Scofflaws*, edited by D. E. Denning and P. J. Denning, Addison-Wesley, Reading, MA, USA pp. 275–280 (1998).

1904. W. L. Tuchman and C. Meyer. "Efficacy of the Data Encryption Standard," *Proceedings of Compcon Fall '78* pp. 340–347 (Sep. 1978).

1905. K. J. Turner. *Using Formal Description Techniques: An Introduction to Estelle, Lotos, and SDL*, John Wiley & Sons, Inc., New York, NY, USA (1993).

1906. S. Turner. "Transport Layer Security," *IEEE Internet Computing* **18**(6) pp. 60–63 (Nov. 2014).

1907. K. Twidle, N. Dulay, E. Lupu, and M. Sloman. "Ponder2: A Policy System for Autonomous Pervasive Environments," *Proceedings of the Fifth International Conference on Autonomic and Autonomous Systems* pp. 330–335 (Apr. 2009).

1908. R. Uhlig, G. Neiger, D. Rodgers, A. L. Santoni, F. C. M. Martins, A. V. Anderson, S. B. Bennett, A. Kägi, F. H. Leung, and L. Smith. "Intel Virtualization Technology," *IEEE Computer* **36**(5) pp. 48–56 (May 2005).

1909. L. Ullman. *Effortless E-Commerce with PHP and MySQL*, New Riders, San Francisco, CA, USA (2013).

1910. N. Unger, S. Dechand, J. Bonneau, S. Fahl, H. Perl, I. Goldberg, and M. Smith. "SoK: Secure Messaging," *Proceedings of the 2015 IEEE Symposium on Security and Privacy* pp. 232–249 (May 2015).

1911. T. E. Uribe and S. Cheung. "Automatic Analysis of Firewall and Network Intrusion Detection System Configurations," *Journal of Computer Security* **15**(6) pp. 691–715 (2007).

1912. US-CERT. *Indicators Associated with WannaCry Ransomware*, ALERT TA17-132A, US-CERT, Pittsburg, PA, USA (May 2017).

1913. B. Uscilowski. *Mobile Adware and Malware Analysis*, White Paper, Symantec Corporation, Mountain View, CA, USA (Oct. 2013).

1914. A. Uszok, J. Bradshaw, R. Jeffers, N. Suri, P. Hayes, M. Breedy, L. Bunch, M. Johnson, S. Kulkarni, and J. Lott. "KAoS Policy and Domain Services: Toward a Description-Logic Approach to Policy Representation, Deconfliction, and Enforcement," *Proceedings of the Fourth IEEE International Workshop on Policies for Distributed Systems and Networks* pp. 93–96 (June 2003).

1915. A. Uszok, J. M. Bradshaw, and R. Jeffers. "KAoS: A Policy and Domain Services Framework for Grid Computing and Semantic Web Services," *Proceedings of the Second International Conference on Trust Management* (*Lecture Notes in Computer Science* **2995**) pp. 16–26 (Mar. 2004).

1916. J. Vaidya, V. Atluri, and Q. Guo. "The Role Mining Problem: A Formal Perspective," *ACM Transactions on Information and System Security* **13**(3) pp. 27:1–27:31 (July 2010).

1917. J. Vaidya, V. Atluri, and J. Warner. "RoleMiner: Mining Roles Using Subset Enumeration," *Proceedings of the 13th ACM Conference on Computer and Communications Security* pp. 144–153 (Oct. 2006).

1918. G. Valenzise, M. Tagliasacchi, and S. Tubaro. "Revealing the Traces of JPEG Compression Anti-Forensics," *IEEE Transactions on Information Forensics and Security* **8**(2) pp. 335–349 (Feb. 2013).

1919. R. van der Meyden and C. Zhang. "A Comparison of Semantic Models for Noninterference," *Theoretical Computer Science* **411**(47) pp. 4123–4147 (Oct. 2010).

1920. T. van der Putte and J. Keuning. "Biometrical Fingerprint Recognition: Don't Get Your Fingers Burned," *Proceedings of the Fourth Smart Card Research and Advanced Application Conference* (*IFIP Advances in Information and Communication Technology* **52**) pp. 289–303 (Sep. 2000).

1921. M. van Dijk, C. Gentry, S. Halevi, and V. Vaikuntanathan. "Fully Homomorphic Encryption over the Integers," *Advances in Cryptology — EUROCRYPT 2010* (*Lecture Notes in Computer Science* **6110**) pp. 24–43 (May 2010).

1922. W. van Eck. "Electromagnetic Radiation from Video Display Units: An Eavesdropping Risk?" *Computers & Security* **4**(4) pp. 269–286 (Dec. 1985).

1923. P. C. van Oorschot and M. J. Wiener. "A Known-Plaintext Attack on Two-Key Triple Encryption," *Advances in Cryptology — CRYPTO '90* (*Lecture Notes in Computer Science* **473**) pp. 318–325 (May 1990).

1924. P. van Oorschot and C. Herley. "A Research Agenda Acknowledging the Persistence of Passwords," *IEEE Security & Privacy* **10**(1) pp. 28–36 (Jan. 2012).

1925. J. Vanegue. "The Weird Machines in Proof-Carrying Code," *Proceedings of the 2014 IEEE Security and Privacy Workshops* pp. 209–213 (May 2014).

1926. E. Vasquez-Fernandez and D. Gonzalez-Jiminez. "Face Recognition for Authentication on Mobile Devices," *Image and Vision Computing* **55**(1) pp. 31–33 (Nov. 2016).

1927. W. Venema. "TCP Wrapper: Network Monitoring, Access Control, and Booby Traps," *Proceedings of the Third USENIX Security Symposium* pp. 85–92 (July 1992).

1928. B. R. Venkatraman and R. E. Newman-Wolfe. "Capacity Estimation and Auditability of Network Covert Channels," *Proceedings of the 1995 IEEE Symposium on Security and Privacy* pp. 186–198 (May 1995).

1929. E. R. Verheul. "Selecting Secure Passwords," *Topics in Cryptology — CT-RSA 2007: The Cryptographers' Track at the RSA Conference* (*Lecture Notes in Computer Science* **4377**) pp. 49–66 (Feb. 2007).

1930. J. Viega. *The Myths of Security: What the Computer Security Industry Doesn't Want You to Know*, O'Reilly Media, Inc., Sebastopol, CA, USA (2009).

1931. J. Viega, J. T. Bloch, Y. Kohno, and G. McGraw. "ITS4: A Static Vulnerability Scanner for C and C++ Code," *Proceedings of the 16th Annual Computer Security Applications Conference* pp. 257–267 (Dec. 2000).

1932. J. Viega and G. McGraw. *Building Secure Software: How to Avoid Security Problems the Right Way*, Addison-Wesley, Boston, MA (2002).

1933. J. Viega, G. McGraw, T. Mutdosch, and E. W. Felten. "Statically Scanning Java Code: Finding Security Vulnerabilities," *IEEE Software* **17**(5) pp. 68–74 (Sep. 2000).

1934. J. Viega and D. A. McGrew. "The Security and Performance of the Galois/Counter Mode (GCM) of Operation," *Proceedings of the Fifth International Conference on Cryptology in India: Progress in Cryptology — INDOCRYPT 2004* (*Lecture Notes in Computer Science* **3348**) pp. 343–355 (Dec. 2004).

1935. J. Viega and M. Messier. *Secure Programming Cookbook for C and C++*, O'Reilly Media, Inc., Sebastopol, CA, USA (2003).

1936. Virgil. *The Aeneid*, Penguin Classics, New York, NY, USA (Dec. 2010).

1937. S. Visram, W. Artner, and P. Marsden. "Safety Case for the NERC Air Traffic Control System," *Proceedings of the 16th International Conference on Computer Safety, Reliability and Security* pp. 345–361 (Oct. 1997).

1938. P. Vixie. "DNS and BIND Security Issues," *Proceedings of the Fifth USENIX UNIX Security Symposium* pp. 209–216 (June 1995).

1939. J. Voas, A. Ghosh, G. McGraw, F. Charron, and K. Miller. "Defining an Adaptive Software Security Metric from a Dynamic Software Failure Tolerance Measure," *Proceedings of the 11th Annual Conference on Computer Assurance* pp. 250–263 (June 1996).

1940. J. M. Voas and A. K. Ghosh. "Software Fault Injection for Survivability," *Proceedings of the 2000 DARPA Information Survivability Conference and Exposition* pp. 338–346 (Jan. 2000).

1941. J. M. Voas, A. K. Ghosh, F. Charron, and L. Kassab. "Reducing Uncertainty About Common-Mode Failures," *Proceedings of the Eighth International Symposium on Software Reliability Engineering* pp. 308–319 (Nov. 1997).

1942. C. Vogt. "PUMA—A Capability-Based Architecture to Support Security and Fault Tolerance," *Proceedings of the 1990 International Workshop on Computer Architectures to Support Security and Persistance of Information* pp. 217–228 (May 1990).

1943. P. Vogt, F. Nentwich, N. Jovanovic, E. Kirda, C. Kruegel, and G. Vigna. "Cross-Site Scripting Prevention with Dynamic Data Tainting and Static Analysis," *Proceedings of the 2007 Symposium on Network and Distributed System Security* (Feb. 2007).

1944. M. Völp, C.-J. Hamann, and H. Härtig. "Avoiding Timing Channels in Fixed-Priority Schedulers," *Proceedings of the Third ACM Symposium on Information, Computer and Communications Security* pp. 44–55 (2008).

1945. D. Volpano, C. Irvine, and G. Smith. "A Sound Type System for Secure Flow Analysis," *Journal of Computer Security* **4**(2-3) pp. 167–187 (1996).

1946. L. von Ahn, M. Blum, N. J. Hopper, and J. Langford. "CAPTCHA: Using Hard AI Problems for Security," *Advances in Cryptology — EUROCRYPT 2003* pp. 294–311 (May 2003).

1947. S. von Solms and D. Naccache. "On Blind Signatures and Perfect Crimes," *Computers & Security* **11**(6) pp. 581–583 (Oct. 1992).

1948. J. Voris, N. Boggs, and S. J. Stolfo. "Lost in Translation: Improving Decoy Documents via Automated Translation," *Proceedings of the 2012 IEEE Symposium on Security and Privacy Workshops* pp. 129–133 (May 2012).

1949. V. L. Voydock and S. T. Kent. "Security Mechanisms in High-Level Network Protocols," *ACM Computing Surveys* **15**(2) pp. 135–171 (June 1983).

1950. D. Wagner. "The Boomerang Attack," *Proceedings of the Sixth International Workshop on Fast Software Encryption* pp. 156–170 (Mar. 1999).

1951. D. Wagner. "Voting Systems Audit Log Study," Technical Report, Office of the California Secretary of State, Sacramento, CA, USA (June 2010).

1952. D. Wagner, J. S. Foster, E. Brewer, and A. Aiken. "A First Step Towards Automated Detection of Buffer Overrun Vulnerabilities," *Proceedings of the 2001 Symposium on Network and Distributed System Security* pp. 3–17 (Feb. 2000).

1953. D. Wagner and B. Schneier. "Analysis of the SSL 3.0 Protocol," *Proceedings of the Second USENIX Workshop on Electronic Commerce* (Nov. 1996).

1954. D. Wagner and P. Soto. "Mimicry Attacks on Host-Based Intrusion Detection Systems," *Proceedings of the Ninth ACM Conference on Computer and Communications Security* pp. 255–264 (Nov. 2002).

1955. S. S. Wagstaff Jr. *The Joy of Factoring* **68**, American Mathematical Society, Providence, RI, USA (2013).

1956. R. Wahbe, S. Lucco, T. E. Anderson, and S. L. Graham. "Efficient Software-Based Fault Isolation," *Proceedings of the 14th ACM Symposium on Operating Systems Principles* pp. 203–216 (Dec. 1993).

1957. M. Waidner and B. Pfitzmann. "The Dining Cryptographers in the Disco: Unconditional Sender and Recipient Untraceability with Computationally Secure Serviceability," *Advances in Cryptology — EUROCRYPT '89* (*Lecture Notes in Computer Science* **434**) p. 690 (Apr. 1990).

1958. T. Walcott and M. Bishop. "Traducement: A Model for Record Security," *ACM Transactions on Information and System Security* **7**(4) pp. 576–590 (Nov. 2004).

1959. K. M. Walker, D. F. Sterne, M. L. Badger, M. J. Petkac, D. L. Shermann, and K. A. Oostendorp. "Confining Root Programs with Domain and Type Enforcement (DTE)," *Proceedings of the Sixth USENIX UNIX Security Symposium* (July 1996).

1960. S. T. Walker, S. B. Lipner, C. M. Ellison, and D. M. Balenson. "Commercial Key Recovery," *Communications of the ACM* **39**(3) pp. 41–47 (Mar. 1996).

1961. F. E. Walter, S. Battison, and F. Schweitzer. "A Model of a Trust-Based Recommendation System on a Social Network," *Autonomous Agents and Multi-Agent Systems* **16**(1) pp. 57–74 (Feb. 2008).

1962. D. Wang, L. Zhang, N. Ma, and X. Li. "Two Secret Sharing Schemes Based on Boolean Operations," *Pattern Recognition* **40**(10) pp. 2776–2785 (Oct. 2007).

1963. H. Wang, S. Jha, M. Livny, and P. D. McDaniel. "Security Policy Reconciliation in Distributed Computing Environments," *Proceedings of the Fifth IEEE International Workshop on Policies for Distributed Systems and Networks* pp. 137–145 (June 2004).

1964. J. Wang, F. Zhang, K. Sun, and A. Stavrou. "Firmware-Assisted Memory Acquisition and Analysis Tools for Digital Forensics," *Proceedings of the Sixth International Workshop on Systematic Approaches to Digital Forensic Engineering* (May 2011).

1965. L. Wang, K. Ohta, and N. Kunihiro. "New Key-Recovery Attacks on HMAC/NMAC-MD4 and NMAC-MD5," *Advances in Cryptology — EUROCRYPT 2008* (*Lecture Notes in Computer Science* **4965**) pp. 237–253 (Apr. 2008).

1966. Q. Wang, C. Wang, K. Ren, W. Lou, and J. Li. "Enabling Public Auditability and Data Dynamics for Storage Security in Cloud Computing," *IEEE Transactions on Parallel and Distributed Systems* **22**(5) pp. 847–859 (May 2010).

1967. W. Wang and Z. Lu. "Cyber Security in the Smart Grid: Survey and Challenges," *Computer Networks* **57**(5) pp. 1344–1371 (Apr. 2013).

1968. X. Wang, T. DeMartini, B. Wragg, M. Paramasivam, and C. Barlas. "The MPEG-21 Rights Expression Language and Rights Data Dictionary," *IEEE Transactions on Multimedia* **7**(3) pp. 408–417 (June 2005).

1969. X. Wang, G. Lao, T. DeMartini, H. Reddy, M. Nguyen, and E. Valenzuela. "XrML – eXtensible Rights Markup Language," *Proceedings of the 2002 ACM Workshop on XML Security* pp. 71–79 (Nov. 2002).

1970. X. Wang and M. K. Reiter. "Defending Against Denial-of-Service Attacks with Puzzle Auctions (Extended Abstract)," *Proceedings of the 2003 IEEE Symposium on Security and Privacy* pp. 78–92 (May 2003).

1971. X. Wang, Y. L. Yin, and H. Yu. "Finding Collisions in the Full SHA-1," *Advances in Cryptology — CRYPTO 2005* (*Lecture Notes in Computer Science* **3621**) pp. 17–36 (Aug. 2005).

1972. X. Wang and H. Yu. "How to Break MD5 and Other Hash Functions," *Advances in Cryptology — EUROCRYPT 2005* (*Lecture Notes in Computer Science* **3494**) pp. 19–35 (May 2005).

1973. X. Wang, N. Zeldovich, and M. F. Kaashoek. "Retroactive Auditing," *Proceedings of the Second Asia-Pacific Workshop on Systems* pp. 9:1–9:5 (July 2011).

1974. Z. Wang and R. B. Lee. "Capacity Estimation of Non-Synchronous Covert Channels," *Proceedings of the 25th IEEE International Conference on Distributed Computing Systems Workshops* (June 2005).

1975. R. Wash. "Folk Models of Home Computer Security," *Proceedings of the Sixth Symposium on Usable Privacy and Security* pp. 11:1–11:6 (July 2010).

1976. R. Wash and E. Rader. "Too Much Knowledge? Security Beliefs and Protective Behaviors Among United States Internet Users," *Proceedings of the 11th Symposium on Usable Privacy and Security* pp. 309–325 (July 2015).

1977. G. Wassermann and Z. Su. "Static Detection of Cross-Site Scripting Vulnerabilities," *Proceedings of the 30th International Conference on Software Engineering* pp. 171–180 (2008).

1978. B. Waters, A. Juels, J. A. Halderman, and E. W. Felten. "New Client Puzzle Outsourcing Techniques for DoS Resistance," *Proceedings of the 11th ACM Conference on Computer and Communications Security* pp. 246–256 (Oct. 2004).

1979. D. Watson. "Honeynets: A Tool for Counterintelligence in Online Security," *Network Security* **2007**(1) pp. 4–8 (Jan. 2007).

1980. J. Watson. "VirtualBox: Bits and Bytes Masquerading as Machines," *Linux Journal* (166) (Feb. 2008).

1981. P. Watson. "A Multi-Level Security Model for Partitioning Workflows over Federated Clouds," *Proceedings of the IEEE Third International Conference on Cloud Computing Technology and Science* pp. 180–188 (Nov. 2011).

1982. R. N. M. Watson. "TrustedBSD: Adding Trusted Operating System Features to FreeBSD," *Proceedings of the FREENIX Track: 2001 USENIX Annual Technical Conference* pp. 15–28 (2001).

1983. R. N. M. Watson, J. Anderson, B. Laurie, and K. Kennaway. "Capsicum: Practical Capabilities for UNIX," *Proceedings of the 19th USENIX Security Symposium* (Aug. 2010).

1984. R. N. M. Watson, J. Woodruff, P. G. Neumann, S. W. Moore, J. Anderson, D. Chisnall, N. Dave, B. Davis, K. Gudka, B. Laurie, S. J. Murdoch, R. Norton, M. Roe, S. Son, and M. Vadera. "CHERI: A Hybrid Capability-System Architecture for Scalable Software Compartmentalization," *Proceedings of the 2015 IEEE Symposium on Security and Privacy* pp. 20–37 (May 2015).

1985. M. A. Wayne, E. R. Jeffrey, G. M. Akselrod, and P. G. Kwiat. "Photon Arrival Time Quantum Random Number Generation," *Journal of Modern Optics* **56**(4) pp. 516–522 (Feb. 2009).

1986. C. Wee. "LAFS: A Logging and Auditing File System," *Proceedings of the 11th Annual Computer Security Applications Conference* pp. 231–240 (Dec. 1995).

1987. F. Wei, S. Roy, X. Ou, and Robby. "Amandroid: A Precise and General Inter-component Data Flow Analysis Framework for Security Vetting of Android Apps," *Proceedings of the 2014 ACM SIGSAC Conference on Computer and Communications Security* pp. 1329–1341 (Nov. 2014).

1988. J. Wei and C. Pu. "TOCTTOU Vulnerabilities in UNIX-Style File Systems: An Anatomical Study," *Proceedings of the 4th USENIX Conference on File and Storage Technologies* pp. 155–167 (Dec. 2005).

1989. M. Weir, S. Aggarwal, M. Collins, and H. Stern. "Testing Metrics for Password Creation Policies by Attacking Large Sets of Revealed Passwords," *Proceedings of the 17th ACM Conference on Computer and Communications Security* pp. 162–175 (Oct. 2010).

1990. M. Weir, S. Aggarwal, B. de Medeiros, and B. Glodek. "Password Cracking Using Probabilistic Context-Free Grammars," *Proceedings of the 2009 IEEE Symposium on Security and Privacy* pp. 391–405 (May 2009).

1991. M. Weiser. "Program Slicing," *IEEE Transactions on Software Engineering* **SE-10**(4) pp. 352–357 (July 1984).

1992. C. Weissman. "Security Controls in the ADEPT-50 Time-Sharing System," *Proceedings of the AFIPS '69 Fall Joint Computer Conference* pp. 119–133 (Nov. 1969).

1993. C. Weissman. "Essay 11: Penetration Testing" in [10], pp. 269–296.

1994. C. Weissman. *Security Penetration Testing Guideline: A Chapter of the Handbook for the Computer Security Certification of Trusted Systems*, Technical Memorandum 5540:082A, Naval Research Laboratory, Washington, DC, USA (Jan. 1995).

1995. C. Weissman. "MLS-PCA: A High Assurance Security Architecture for Future Avionics," *Proceedings of the 19th Annual Computer Security Applications Conference* pp. 2–12 (Dec. 2003).

1996. S. Wendzel, S. Zander, B. Fechner, and C. Herdin. "Pattern-Based Survey and Categorization of Network Covert Channel Techniques," *ACM Computing Surveys* **47**(3) pp. 50:1–50:26 (Apr. 2015).

1997. M. M. Wenzel. "Isabelle/Isar — A Versatile Environment for Human-Readable Formal Proof Documents," Ph.D. Dissertation, Informatics Institute, Technical University of Munich, Munich, Germany (Jan. 2002).

1998. R. West. "The Psychology of Security," *Communications of the ACM* **51**(4) pp. 34–40 (Apr. 2008).

1999. D. Wetherall. "Active Network Vision and Reality: Lessons from a Capsule-Based System," *Proceedings of the 2002 DARPA Active Networks Conference and Exposition* pp. 25–40 (May 2002).

2000. D. A. Wheeler. "Secure Programming HOWTO, Version 3.72," *unpublished* (2015).

2001. D. Whiting, R. Housley, and N. Ferguson. *Counter with CBC-MAC (CCM)*, RFC 3610 (Sep. 2003).

2002. A. Whitten and J. D. Tygar. "Why Johnny Can't Encrypt: A Usability Evaluation of PGP 5.0," *Proceedings of the Eighth USENIX UNIX Security Symposium* pp. 169–184 (Aug. 1999).

2003. D. R. Wichers, D. M. Cook, R. A. Olsson, J. Crossley, P. Kerchen, K. N. Levitt, and R. Lo. "PACLs: An Access Control List Approach to Anti-Viral Security," *Proceedings of the 13th National Computer Security Conference* pp. 340–349 (Oct. 1990).

2004. D. J. M. Wiemer. "Wiemer-Murray Domain Security Policy Model for International Interoperability," *Proceedings of the 21st National Information Systems Security Conference* pp. 526–536 (Oct. 1998).

2005. R. P. Wildes. "Iris Recognition: An Emerging Biometric Technology," *Proceedings of the IEEE* **85**(9) pp. 1348–1363 (Sep. 1997).

2006. M. V. Wilkes. *Time-Sharing Computer Systems*, Elsevier Science Inc., New York, NY, USA (1975).

2007. A. L. Wilkinson, D. H. Anderson, D. P. Chang, L. H. Hin, A. J. Mayo, I. T. Viney, R. Williams, and W. Wright. "A Penetration Analysis of a Burroughs Large System," *ACM SIGOPS Operating Systems Review* **15**(1) pp. 14–25 (Jan. 1981).

2008. J. R. Williams and K. Ferriaolo. "P^{3}I — Protection Profile Process Improvement," *Proceedings of the 22nd National Information Systems Security Conference* pp. 175–188 (Oct. 1999).

2009. S. P. Wilson, J. A. McDermid, P. M. Kirkham, C. H. Pygott, and D. J. Tombs. "Computer Based Support for Standards and Processes in Safety Critical Systems," *Proceedings of the 16th International Conference on Computer Safety, Reliability and Security* pp. 197–209 (Sep. 1997).

2010. J. M. Wing. "A Symbiotic Relationship Between Formal Methods and Security," *Proceedings of the 1998 Computer Security, Dependability and Assurance: From Needs to Solutions* pp. 26–38 (July 1998).

2011. I. Winkler. "The Non-Technical Threat to Computing Systems," *Computing Systems* **9**(1) pp. 3–14 (Winter 1996).

2012. H. B. Winkler-Parenty. "SYBASE: The Trusted Subject DBMS," *Proceedings of the 13th National Computer Security Conference* pp. 589–593 (Oct. 1990).

2013. R. Winton. "Hollywood Hospital Pays $17,000 in Bitcoin to Hackers; FBI Investigating," *Los Angeles Times* (Feb. 18, 2016).

2014. Wireshark. *Adb: Malformed Packet and Buffer Overflow*, Bug 14460, Wireshark (Feb. 2018).

2015. S. Wiseman. "A Secure Capability Computer System," *Proceedings of the 1986 IEEE Symposium on Security and Privacy* pp. 86–94 (Apr. 1986).

2016. S. Wiseman. "Preventing Viruses in Computer Systems," *Computers & Security* **8**(5) pp. 427–432 (Aug. 1989).

2017. T. Y. C. Woo and S. S. Lam. "Authentication for Distributed Systems," *IEEE Computer* **25**(1) pp. 39–52 (Jan. 1992).

2018. T. Y. C. Woo and S. S. Lam. "'Authentication' Revisited," *IEEE Computer* **25**(3) p. 10 (Mar. 1992).

2019. C. C. Wood. "Principles of Secure Information System Design," *Computers & Security* **9**(1) pp. 13–24 (Feb. 1990).

2020. C. C. Wood. "Principles of Secure Information Design with Groupware Examples," *Computers & Security* **12**(7) pp. 663–678 (Nov. 1993).

2021. C. C. Wood. *Information Security Policies Made Easy*, Information Shield, Sugar Land, TX, USA (2015).

2022. J. Woodruff, R. N. M. Watson, D. Chisnall, S. W. Moore, J. Anderson, B. Davis, B. Laurie, P. G. Neumann, R. Norton, and M. Roe. "The CHERI Capability Model: Revisiting RISC in an Age of Risk," *Proceedings of the 41st ACM/IEEE Annual International Symposium on Computer Architecture* pp. 457–468 (June 2014).

2023. B. Woodward. *The Secret Man: The Story of Watergate's Deep Throat*, Simon & Schuster, New York, NY, USA (2005).

2024. A. Wool. "A Quantitative Study of Firewall Configuration Errors," *IEEE Computer* **37**(6) pp. 62–67 (June 2004).

2025. J. C. Wray. "An Analysis of Covert Timing Channels," *Proceedings of the 1991 IEEE Symposium on Research in Security and Privacy* pp. 2–6 (May 1991).

2026. A. Wright. "Hacking Cars," *Communications of the ACM* **54**(11) pp. 18–19 (Nov. 2011).

2027. H. Wu and B. Preneel. "Cryptanalysis of the Stream Cipher ABC v2," *Proceedings of the 13th International Workshop on Selected Areas in Cryptography* (*Lecture Notes in Computer Science* **4356**) pp. 56–66 (Aug. 2006).

2028. H. Wu and B. Preneel. "Differential Cryptanalysis of the Stream Ciphers Py, Py6 and Pypy," *Advances in Cryptology — EUROCRYPT 2007* (*Lecture Notes in Computer Science* **4515**) pp. 276–290 (May 2007).

2029. S. X. Wu and W. Banzhaf. "The Use of Computational Intelligence in Intrusion Detection Systems: A Review," *Applied Soft Computing* **10**(1) pp. 1–35 (Jan. 2010).

2030. W. Wulf, E. Cohen, W. Corwin, A. Jones, R. Levin, C. Pierson, and F. Pollack. "HYDRA: The Kernel of a Multiprocessor Operating System," *Communications of the ACM* **17**(6) pp. 337–345 (June 1974).

2031. W. C. A. Wungaards and B. J. Overeinder. "Securing DNS: Extending DNS Servers with a DNSSEC Validator," *IEEE Security & Privacy* **7**(5) pp. 36–43 (Sep. 2009).

2032. X501. *Information Technology—Open Systems Interconnection—The Directory: Models*, Recommendation X.501, ITU-T (Nov. 2008).

2033. M. Xia, L. Gong, Y. Lyu, Z. Qi, and X. Liu. "Effective Real-Time Android Application Auditing," *Proceedings of the 2015 IEEE Symposium on Security and Privacy* pp. 899–914 (May 2015).

2034. Y. Xie and A. Aiken. "Static Detection of Security Vulnerabilities in Scripting Languages," *Proceedings of the 15th USENIX Security Symposium* pp. 179–192 (Aug. 2006).

2035. Y. Xie and S.-Z. Yu. "Monitoring the Application-Layer DDoS Attacks for Popular Websites," *IEEE/ACM Transactions on Networking* **17**(1) pp. 15–25 (Feb. 2009).

2036. L. Xiong and L. Liu. "PeerTrust: Supporting Reputation-Based Trust for Peer-to-Peer Electronic Communities," *IEEE Transactions on Knowledge and Data Engineering* **16**(7) pp. 843–857 (July 2004).

2037. K. Xu, H. Xiong, C. Wu, D. Stefan, and D. Yao. "Data-Provenance Verification for Secure Hosts," *IEEE Transactions on Dependable and Secure Computing* **9**(2) pp. 173–183 (Mar. 2012).

2038. R. Xu, H. Saïdi, and R. Andreson. "Aurasium: Practical Policy Enforcement for Android Applications," *Proceedings of the 21st USENIX Security Symposium* pp. 539–552 (Aug. 2012).

2039. Y. Xu, M. Bailey, F. Jahanian, K. Joshi, M. Hiltunen, and R. Schlichting. "An Exploration of L2 Cache Covert Channels in Virtualized Environments," *Proceedings of the Third ACM Workshop on Cloud Computing Security* pp. 29–40 (Oct. 2011).

2040. F. Yamaguchi, N. Golde, D. Arp, and K. Rieck. "Modeling and Discovering Vulnerabilities with Code Property Graphs," *Proceedings of the 2014 IEEE Symposium on Security and Privacy* pp. 590–604 (May 2014).

2041. R. V. Yampolskiy. "Analyzing User Password Selection Behavior for Reduction of Password Space," *Proceedings of the 40th Annual IEEE International Carnahan Conferences Security Technology* pp. 109–115 (Oct. 2006).

2042. J. Yan and A. S. El Ahmad. "Usability of CAPTCHAs or Usability Issues in CAPTCHA Design," *Proceedings of the Fourth Symposium on Usable Privacy and Security* pp. 44–52 (July 2008).

2043. K. Yang, M. Hicks, Q. Dong, T. Austin, and D. Sylvester. "A2: Analog Malicious Hardware," *Proceedings of the 2016 IEEE Symposium on Security and Privacy* pp. 18–37 (May 2016).

2044. X. Yang, D. Wetherall, and T. Anderson. "TVA: A DoS-Limiting Network Architecture," *IEEE/ACM Transactions on Networking* **16**(6) pp. 1267–1280 (Dec. 2008).

2045. Y. Yang, K. McLaughlin, T. Littler, S. Sezer, B. Pranggono, and H. F. Wang. "Intrusion Detection System for IEC 60870-5-104 Based SCADA Networks," *Proceedings of the 2013 IEEE Power and Energy Society General Meeting* pp. 1–5 (July 2013).

2046. D. Yaozu, L. Shaofan, M. Asit, N. Jun, T. Kun, X. Xuefei, Y. Fred, and Y. Wilfred. "Extending Xen with Intel Virtualization Technology," *Intel Technology Journal* **10**(3) pp. 193–203 (Aug. 2006).

2047. W.-S. Yap, S. L. Yeo, S.-H. Heng, and M. Henricksen. "Security Anaysis of GCM for Communication," *Security and Communication Networks* **7**(5) pp. 854–864 (May 2014).

2048. Y. Yarom and K. Falkner. "FLUSH+RELOAD: A High Resolution, Low Noise, L3 Cache Side-Channel Attack," *Proceedings of the 23rd USENIX Security Symposium* pp. 719–732 (Aug. 2014).

2049. A. Yasinsac and J. Childs. "Formal Analysis of Modern Security Protocols," *Information Sciences* **171**(1–3) pp. 189–211 (Mar. 2005).

2050. B. Yee, D. Sehr, G. Dardyk, J. B. Chen, R. Muth, T. Ormandy, S. Okasaka, N. Narula, and N. Fullagar. "Native Client: A Sandbox for Portable, Untrusted x86 Native Code," *Proceedings of the 2009 IEEE Symposium on Security and Privacy* pp. 79–93 (May 2009).

2051. K.-P. Yee. "User Interaction Design for Secure Systems," *Proceedings of the Fourth International Conference on Information and Communications Security* (*Lecture Notes in Computer Science* **2513**) pp. 278–290 (Dec. 2002).

2052. I.-L. Yen and R. Paul. "Key Applications for High-Assurance Systems," *IEEE Computer* **31**(4) pp. 35–36 (Apr. 1998).

2053. T. Yetiser. *Polymorphic Viruses: Implementation, Detection, and Protection*, Technical Report, VDS Advanced Research Group, Baltimore, MD, USA (Jan. 1993).

2054. H. Yin, C. Bockisch, and M. Aksit. "A Fine-Grained Debugger for Aspect-Oriented Programming," *Proceedings of the Eleventh Annual International Conference on Aspect-Oriented Software Development* pp. 59–70 (2012).

2055. H. Yin, D. Song, M. Egele, C. Kruegel, and E. Kirda. "Panorama: Capturing System-wide Information Flow for Malware Detection and Analysis," *Proceedings of the 14th ACM Conference on Computer and Communications Security* pp. 116–127 (Oct. 2007).

2056. H. Yin and H. Wang. "Building an Application-Aware IPsec Policy System," *IEEE/ACM Transactions on Networking* **15**(6) pp. 1502–1513 (Dec. 2007).

2057. V. L. Yisa, M. Baba, and E. T. Olaniyi. "A Review of Top Open Source Password Cracking Tools," *Proceedings of the 2016 International Conference on Information and Communication Technology and Its Applications* pp. 134–138 (Nov. 2016).

2058. T. Ylönen. "SSH—Secure Login Connections over the Internet," *Proceedings of the Sixth USENIX UNIX Security Symposium* pp. 37–42 (July 1996).

2059. T. Ylönen and C. Lonvick. *The Secure Shell (SSH) Protocol Architecture*, RFC 4251 (Jan. 2006).

2060. J. Yoo, E. Jee, and S. Cha. "Formal Modeling and Verification of Safety-Critical Software," *IEEE Software* **26**(3) pp. 42–49 (May 2009).

2061. K. Yoshio, Y. Yoshiaki, and T. Hidekazu. "An Improvement to a Decentralized Management Method for Uniquely Accessible Attribute Information," *Proceedings of the 2009 International Conference on Availability, Reliability and Security* pp. 984–989 (Mar. 2009).

2062. P. Yosifovich, A. Ionescu, M. E. Russinovich, and D. A. Solomon. *Windows Internals, Part 1: System Architecture, Processes, Threads, Memory Management, and More*, Microsoft Press, Redmond, WA, USA (2017).

2063. A. Young and M. Yung. "Cryptovirology: Extortion-Based Security Threats and Countermeasures," *Proceedings of the 1996 IEEE Symposium on Security and Privacy* pp. 129–139 (May 1996).

2064. C. Young. "Taxonomy of Computer Virus Defense Mechanisms," *Proceedings of the Tenth National Computer Security Conference* pp. 220–225 (Sep. 1987).

2065. C.-F. Yu and V. D. Gligor. "A Formal Specification and Verification Method for the Prevention of Denial of Service," *Proceedings of the 1988 IEEE Symposium on Security and Privacy* pp. 187–202 (Apr. 1988).

2066. C.-F. Yu and V. D. Gligor. "A Specification and Verification Method for Preventing Denial of Service," *IEEE Transactions on Software Engineering* **16**(6) pp. 581–592 (June 1990).

2067. T. Yu, S. Hartman, and K. Raeburn. "The Perils of Unauthenticated Encryption: Kerberos Version 4," *Proceedings of the 2004 Symposium on Network and Distributed System Security* (Feb. 2004).

2068. Y. Yu and W. Rodeheffer, Tom anbd Chen. "RaceTrack: Efficient Detection of Data Race Conditions via Adaptive Tracking," *Proceedings of the 20th ACM Symposium on Operating Systems Principles* pp. 221–234 (Dec. 2005).

2069. E. Yuan and J. Tong. "Attributed Based Access Control (ABAC) for Web Services," *Proceedings of the 2005 IEEE International Conference on Web Services* (July 2005).

2070. L. Yuan, J. Mai, Z. Su, H. Chen, C.-N. Chuah, and P. Mohapatra. "FIREMAN: A Toolkit for FIREwall Modeling and ANalysis," *Proceedings of the 2006 IEEE Symposium on Security and Privacy* pp. 213–228 (May 2006).

2071. R. Yuan and W. T. Strayer. *Virtual Private Networks: Technologies and Solutions*, Addison-Wesley, Boston, MA, USA (2001).

2072. J. Yuill, F. Wu, J. Settle, F. Gong, R. Forno, M. Huang, and J. Asbery. "Intrusion-Detection for Incident-Response, Using a Military Battlefield-Intelligence Process," *Computer Networks* **34**(4) pp. 671–697 (Oct. 2000).

2073. J. Yuill, M. Zappe, D. E. Denning, and F. Feer. "Honeyfiles: Deceptive Files for Intrusion Detection," *Proceedings of the Fifth Annual IEEE SMC Informaton Assurance Workshop* pp. 116–122 (June 2004).

2074. A. L. Yuille, P. W. Hallinan, and D. S. Cohen. "Feature Extraction from Faces Using Deformable Templates," *International Journal of Computer Vision* **8**(2) pp. 99–111 (Aug. 1992).

2075. A. Zakinthinos and E. S. Lee. "The Composability of Non-Interference," *Journal of Computer Security* **3**(4) pp. 269–281 (1995).

2076. D. Zamboni. *Learning CFEngine 3*, O'Reilly Media, Sebastopol, CA, USA (2012).

2077. S. Zander, G. Armitage, and P. Branch. "A Survey of Covert Channels and Countermeasures in Computer Network Protocols," *IEEE Communications Surveys & Tutorials* **9**(3) pp. 44–57 (Third Quarter 2007).

2078. P. Zave and M. Jackson. "Four Dark Corners of Requirements Engineering," *ACM Transactions on Software Engineering and Methodology* **6**(1) pp. 1–30 (Jan. 1997).

2079. S. Zawoad, A. K. Dutta, and R. Hasan. "SecLaaS: Secure Logging-as-a-Service for Cloud Forensics," *Proceedings of the Eighth ACM SIGSAC Symposium on Information, Computer and Communications Security* pp. 219–230 (May 2013).

2080. S. Zdancewic and A. C. Myers. "Robust Declassification," *Proceedings of the 14th Computer Security Foundations Workshop* pp. 15–23 (June 2001).

2081. K. D. Zeilenga. *COSINE LDAP/X.500 Schema*, RFC 4524 (June 2006).

2082. K. D. Zeilenga. *Lightweight Directory Access Protocol (LDAP): Directory Information Models*, RFC 4512 (June 2006).

2083. K. Zetter. "Palin E-Mail Hacker Says It Was Easy," *Wired* (Sep. 18, 2008).

2084. K. Zetter. "Researchers Uncover RSA Phishing Attack, Hiding in Plain Sight," *Wired* (Aug. 26, 2011).

2085. C. C. Zhang, M. Winslett, and C. A. Gunter. "On the Safety and Efficiency of Firewall Policy Deployment," *Proceedings of the 2007 IEEE Symposium on Security and Privacy* pp. 33–50 (May 2007).

2086. C. Zhang, T. Wang, T. Wei, Y. Chen, and W. Zou. "IntPatch: Automatically Fix Integer-Overflow-to-Buffer-Overflow Vulnerability at Compile-Time," *Proceedings of the 15th European Symposium on Research in Computer Security* (*Lecture Notes in Computer Science* **6345**) pp. 71–86 (Sep. 2010).

2087. D. Zhang, W.-K. Kong, J. You, and M. Wong. "Online Palmprint Identification," *IEEE Transactions on Pattern Analysis and Machine Intelligence* **25**(9) pp. 1041–1050 (Sep. 2003).

2088. D. Zhang, K. Ramamohanarao, R. Zhang, and S. Versteeg. "Efficient Graph Based Approach to Large Scale Role Engineering," *Transactions on Data Privacy* **7**(1) pp. 1–26 (2014).

2089. F. Zhang, A. Kondoro, and S. Muftic. "Location-Based Authentication and Authorization Using Smart Phones," *Proceedings of the 2012 IEEE International Conference on Trust, Security and Privacy in Computing and Communications* pp. 1285–1292 (June 2012).

2090. L. Zhang and A. C. Myers. "End-to-End Availability Policies and Noninterference," *Proceedings of the 18th Computer Security Foundations Workshop* pp. 272–286 (June 2005).

2091. L. Zhang, S. Tan, J. Yang, and Y. Chen. "VoiceLive: A Phoneme Localization Based Liveness Detection for Voice Authentication on Smartphones," *Proceedings of the 23rd ACM SIGSAC Conference on Computer and Communications Security* pp. 1080–1091 (Oct. 2016).

2092. X. Zhang, Y. Li, and D. Nalla. "An Attribute-Based Access Control Matrix Model," *Proceedings of the 2005 ACM Symposium on Applied Computing* pp. 359–363 (Mar. 2005).

2093. Y. Zhang, F. Monrose, and M. K. Reiter. "The Security of Modern Password Expiration: An Algorithmic Framework and Empirical Analysis," *Proceedings of the 17th ACM Conference on Computer and Communications Security* pp. 176–186 (Oct. 2010).

2094. G. Zheng, W. Li, and C. Zhan. "Cryptographic Key Generation from Biometric Data Using Lattice Mapping," *Proceedings of the 18th International Conference on Pattern Recognition* pp. 513–516 (Aug. 2006).

2095. Y. Zheng. "Digital Signcryption or How to Achieve Cost(Signature & Encryption) $\ll$ Cost(Signature) + Cost(Encryption)," *Advances in Cryptology — CRYPTO '97* (*Lecture Notes in Computer Science* **1294**) pp. 165–179 (Aug. 1997).

2096. Y. Zheng, J. Pieprzyk, and J. Seberry. "HAVAL—A One-Way Hashing Algorithm with Variable Length of Output," *Advances in Cryptology—AUSCRYPT '92* (*Lecture Notes in Computer Science* **718**) pp. 83–104 (Dec. 1992).

2097. Y. Zhou, X. Wang, Y. Chen, and Z. Wang. "ARMlock: Hardware-Based Fault Isolation for ARM," *Proceedings of the 21st ACM SIGSAC Conference on Computer and Communications Security* pp. 558–569 (Nov. 2014).

2098. H. Zhu, P. A. V. Hall, and J. H. R. May. "Software Unit Test Coverage and Adequacy," *ACM Computing Surveys* **29**(4) pp. 366–427 (Dec. 1997).

2099. L. Zhu, K. Jaganathan, and K. Lauter. *Elliptic Curve Cryptography (ECC) Support for Public Key Cryptography for Initial Authentication in Kerberos (PKINIT)*, RFC 5349 (Sep. 2008).

2100. L. Zhu, K. Jaganathan, and N. Williams. *Online Certificate Status Protocol (OCSP) Support for Public Key Cryptography for Initial Authentication in Kerberos (PKINIT)*, RFC 4557 (June 2006).

2101. L. Zhu and B. Tung. *Public Key Cryptography for Initial Authentication in Kerberos (PKINIT)*, RFC 4556 (June 2006).

2102. M. Zhu, Z. Hu, and P. Liu. "Reinforcement Learning Algorithms for Adaptive Cyber Defense Against Heartbleed," *Proceedings of the First ACM Workshop on Moving Target Defense* pp. 51–58 (Nov. 2014).

2103. Y. Zhu, X. Fu, B. Graham, R. Bettati, and W. Zhao. "On Flow Correlation Attacks and Countermeasures in Mix Networks," *Proceedings of the Fourth International Workshop on Privacy Enhancing Technologies* (*Lecture Notes in Computer Science* **3424**) pp. 207–225 (2004).

2104. X. Zi, L. Yao, X. Jiang, L. Pan, and J. Li. "Evaluating the Transmission Rate of Covert Timing Channels in a Network," *Computer Networks* **55**(12) pp. 2760–2771 (Aug. 2011).

2105. C.-N. Ziegler and G. Lausen. "Spreading Activation Models for Trust Propagation," *Proceedings of the 2004 IEEE International Conference on e-Technology, e-Commerce and e-Service* pp. 83–97 (Mar. 2004).

2106. D. P. Zimmerman. *The Finger User Information Protocol*, RFC 1288 (Dec. 1991).

2107. P. Zimmermann, A. Johnson, and J. Callas. *ZRTP: Media Path Key Agreement for Unicast Secure RTP*, RFC 6189 (Apr. 2011).

2108. D. Zissis and D. Lekkas. "Addressing Cloud Computing Security Issues," *Future Generation Computer Systems* **28**(3) pp. 583–592 (Mar. 2012).

2109. C. C. Zou, W. Gong, and D. Towsley. "Code Red Worm Propagation Modeling and Analysis," *Proceedings of the Ninth ACM Conference on Computer and Communications Security* pp. 138–147 (Nov. 2002).

2110. Z. Zuo and M. Zhou. "Some Further Theoretical Results about Computer Viruses," *The Computer Journal* **47**(6) pp. 627–633 (Jan. 2004).

2111. J. Zurawski. "The Science DMZ — Introduction and Architecture," Presentation at Operating Innovative Networks (Oct. 2013)

2112. M. E. Zurko and R. T. Simon. "User-Centered Security," *Proceedings of the 1996 Workshop on New Security Paradigms* pp. 27–33 (Sep. 1996).

2113. M. Zviran and W. J. Haga. "Cognitive Passwords: The Key to Easy Access Control," *Computers & Security* **9**(8) pp. 723–736 (Dec. 1990).

2114. *About Touch ID Advanced Security Technology*, Apple, Cupertino, CA, USA (Sep. 2017).

2115. Acceptable Use Policy, Section 310-23, Exhibit A, UC Davis Policy and Procedure Manual, Office of the Chancellor and Provost, University of California at Davis (Sep. 2013).

2116. *Advanced Encryption Standard*, FIPS PUB 197, National Institute of Standards and Technology, Gaithersburg, MD, USA (Nov. 2001).

2117. *AMD64 Architecture Programmer's Manual Volume 2: System Programming*, Number 24593 Rev. 3.23, Advanced Micro Devices, Sunnyvale, CA, USA (May 2013).

2118. *Arrangement on the Recognition of Common Criteria Certificates in the Field of Information Technology Security*, Technical Report, Common Criteria (July 2014).

2119. *Article 17: Right to Erasure ('Right to be Forgotten')*, Regulation (EU) 2016/679 of the European Parliament and of the Council (Apr. 2016)

2120. *Buffer Overflow in Kerberos Administration Daemon*, CERT Advisory CA-2002-29, CERT, Pittsburg, PA (Oct. 2002).

2121. *Buffer Overflow in Sendmail*, CERT Advisory CA-2003-25, CERT, Pittsburg, PA, USA (Oct. 2003).

2122. *Bundesamt für Sicherheit in der Informationstechnik*, Common Criteria (2017).

2123. California Elections Code, Division 19. Certification of Voting Systems. Chapter 3. Certification of Voting Systems. Article 1. Procedures for Certification of Voting Systems.

2124. *The Canadian Trusted Computer Product Evaluation Criteria, Version 3.0e*, Report, Canadian System Security Centre, Ottowa, ON, Canada (Jan. 1993).

2125. *CapROS: The Capability-based Reliable Operating System* (2016).

2126. *Cisco IOS Security Command Reference*, Cisco Systems, Inc., San Jose, CA, USA (Apr. 2011).

2127. *The Common Criteria*, Common Criteria (Apr. 2017).

2128. *Common Criteria: Certified Products*, Common Criteria (Dec. 2017).

2129. *Common Criteria for Information Technology Security Evaluation Version 3.1, Revision 5, Part 1: Introduction and General Model*, Technical Report CCMB-2017-04-001, Common Criteria (Apr. 2017).

2130. *Common Criteria for Information Technology Security Evaluation Version 3.1, Revision 5, Part 2: Security Functional Components*, Technical Report CCMB-2017-04-002, Common Criteria (Apr. 2017).

2131. *Common Criteria for Information Technology Security Evaluation Version 3.1, Revision 5, Part 3: Security Assurance Components*, Technical Report CCMB-2017-04-003, Common Criteria (Apr. 2017).

2132. *Common Criteria: Other Publications*, Common Criteria (Apr. 2017).

2133. *Common Methodology for Information Technology Security Evaluation Version 3.1, Revision 5: Evaluation Methodology*, Technical Report CCMB-2017-04-004, Common Criteria (Apr. 2017).

2134. *Common Vulnerabilities and Exposures*, The MITRE Corporation, Bedford, MA, USA (Mar. 2017).

2135. *Common Vulnerabilities and Exposures: CVE-1999-0965*, The MITRE Corporation, Bedford, MA, USA (Jan. 2000).

2136. *Common Vulnerabilities and Exposures: CVE-2016-3706*, The MITRE Corporation, Bedford, MA, USA (Mar. 2016).

2137. *Common Weakness Enumeration*, The MITRE Corporation, Bedford, MA, USA (Jan. 2017).

2138. *Communications and Technology Electronic Communications—Allowable Use*, Section 310-23, UC Davis Policy and Procedure Manual, Office of the Chancellor and Provost, University of California at Davis, Davis, CA, USA (Sep. 2013).

2139. *Communications Security Establishment, Government of Canada*, Common Criteria (July 2015).

2140. *Creating and Using Oracle Solaris Zones*, Number E54752, Oracle, Inc., Redwood City, CA, USA (Oct. 2017).

2141. *Cryptographic Algorithm Validation Program*, National Institute for Standards and Technology, Gaithersburg, MD, USA (Sep. 2017).

2142. *Cryptographic Module Validation Program*, National Institute for Standards and Technology, Gaithersburg, MD, USA (Sep. 2017).

2143. *CryptoLocker Ransomware Infections*, Alert TA13-309A, US-CERT, Pittsburg, PA, USA (Nov. 2013).

2144. *CSEC-The Swedish Certification Body for IT Security*, Common Criteria (Nov. 2017).

2145. *CWE Glossary*, The MITRE Corporation, Bedford, MA, USA (Jan. 2017).

2146. *Data Encryption Standard*, FIPS PUB 46, National Bureau of Standards, Gaithersburg, MD, USA (Jan. 1977).

2147. *DES Modes of Operation*, FIPS PUB 81, National Bureau of Standards, Gaithersburg, MD, USA (Dec. 1980).

2148. *Digital Signature Standard (DSS)*, FIPS PUB 186-4, National Institute of Standards and Technology, Gaithersburg, MD, USA (July 2013).

2149. *DNS Amplification Attacks*, Alert TA13-088A, US-CERT, Pittsburg, PA, USA (Oct. 2016).

2150. *Electronic Communications Policy*, University of California Office of the President, Oakland, CA, USA (Aug. 2005).

2151. *Electronic Mail Policy*, University of California Office of the President, Oakland, CA, USA (Mar. 1998).

2152. *Escrowed Encryption Standard (EES)*, FIPS PUB 185, National Institute of Standards and Technology, Gaithersburg, MD, USA (Feb. 1994).

2153. *The Evolution of the CWE Development and Research Views*, The MITRE Corporation, Bedford, MA, USA (Sep. 2008).

2154. *External Interface Guide to SET Secure Electronic Transaction* (Sep. 1997).

2155. *Federal Criteria for Information Technology Security, Version 1.0*, Technical Report, National Institute of Standards and Technology and National Security Agency, Gaithersburg, MD, USA (1992).

2156. *File Formats: priv_desc(4): Descriptions of Defined Privileges*, Sun Microsystems, Inc., Palo Alto, CA, USA (Sep. 1999).

2157. Financial Services Act of 1986, §48(2)(h), cited in [292].

2158. *FORTEZZA Cryptologic Interface Programmers Guide*, Technical Report Revision 1.52, National Security Agency, Ft. George G. Meade, MD, USA (Nov. 1995).

2159. *FORTEZZA Message Security Protocol Software Interface Control Document*, Technical Report Version 3.01, National Security Agency, Ft. George G. Meade, MD, USA (Nov. 1995).

2160. *Ghostscript Vulnerability*, CERT Advisory CA-1995-10, CERT, Pittsburg, PA, USA (Aug. 1995).

2161. *Good Practice Guide on Vulnerability Disclosure*, Catalogue Number TP-01-15-893-EN-N, European Union Agency for Network and Information Security, Heraklion, Greece (Nov. 2015).

2162. *Google 2-Step Verification*, Google, Mountain View, CA, USA.

2163. *A Guide to Understanding Audit in Trusted Systems*, Report NCSC-TG-001, Department of Defense, Washington, DC, USA (July 1987).

2164. *A Guide to Understanding Covert Channel Analysis of Trusted Systems*, Report NCSC-TG-030, Department of Defense, Washington, DC, USA (Nov. 1993).

2165. *Guidelines for Smart Grid Security*, Special Publication 7628 Revision 1, National Institute of Standards and Technology, Gaithersburg, MD, USA (Sep. 2014).

2166. *The Haskell Programming Language* (Dec. 2013).

2167. *HP-UX Security Vulnerability in sendmail*, CIAC Information Bulletin J-040, U.S. Department of Energy Computer Incident Advisory Capability, Livermore, CA, USA (Apr. 1999).

2168. *iAPX 432 General Data Processor Architecture Reference Manual*, Order Number 171860-004, Intel Corp., Santa Clara, CA, USA (1983).

2169. *Information about the PC CYBORG (AIDS) Trojan Horse*, CIAC Information Bulletin A-10, CIAC, Livermore, CA, USA (Dec. 1989).

2170. *Information Technology – Security Techniques – Security Requirements for Cryptographic Modules*, Standard ISO/IEC 19790:2006, International Organization for Standardization, Geneva, Switzerland (Mar. 2006).

2171. *Information Technology – Security Techniques – Security Requirements for Cryptographic Modules*, Standard ISO/IEC 19790:2012, International Organization for Standardization, Geneva, Switzerland (Aug. 2012).

2172. *Information Technology – Security Techniques – Systems Security Engineering — Capability Maturity Model® (SSE-CMM®)*, Standard ISO/IEC 21827:2008, International Organization for Standardization, Geneva, Switzerland (Oct. 2008).

2173. *Information Technology – Security Techniques – Test Requirements for Cryptographic Modules*, Standard ISO/IEC 24759:2008, International Organization for Standardization, Geneva, Switzerland (Feb. 2008).

2174. *Information Technology – Security Techniques – Test Requirements for Cryptographic Modules*, Standard ISO/IEC 24759:2014, International Organization for Standardization, Geneva, Switzerland (Feb. 2014).

2175. *Information Technology – Security Techniques – Test Requirements for Cryptographic Modules*, Standard ISO/IEC 24759:2017, International Organization for Standardization, Geneva, Switzerland (Feb. 2017).

2176. *Information Technology—Open Systems Interconnection—The Directory: Public-Key and Attribute Certificate Frameworks*, Recommendation X.509, ITU-T (Nov. 2008).

2177. *Information Technology Security Evaluation Criteria (ITSEC)*, Technical Report, Commission of the European Communities, Brussels, Belgium (1991).

2178. *Intel 64 and IA-32 Architectures Software Developer's Manual, Volume 3 (3A, 3B & 3C): System Programming Guide*, Order Number 325384-044US, Intel Corporation, Santa Clara, CA, USA (Aug. 2012).

2179. *Intel 64 and IA-32 Architectures Software Developer's Manual Volume 3A: System Programming Guide, Part 1*, Order Number 253668-060US, Intel Corporation, Santa Clara, CA, USA (Sep. 2016).

2180. *Intel Itanium Architecture Software Developer's Manual Volume 2: System Architecture*, Document Number 245318-005, Intel Corporation, Santa Clara, CA, USA (May 2010).

2181. *Internet Movie Database*.

2182. *IP Denial-of-Service Attacks*, CERT Advisory CA-1997-28, CERT, Pittsburg, PA, USA (Dec. 1997).

2183. *IT-Security Criteria: Criteria for the Evaluation of Trustworthiness of IT Systems*, Technical Report, German Information Security Agency, Bonn, Germany (June 1989).

2184. "Locky Ransomware Strain Led Kentucky Hospital to an 'Internal State of Emergency,'" Trend Micro Security News, Trend Micro, Irving, TX, USA (Mar. 24, 2016).

2185. "Mac_biba – Biba Data Integrity Policy," *FreeBSD Manual Pages for FreeBSD 11.1-RELEASE and Ports* (Jan. 2008).

2186. *Managing Security on the DG/UX System*, Number 093-7011389-04, Data General Corporation, Westboro, MA, USA (Nov. 1996).

2187. *Microsoft PlayReady Content Protection Technology*, White Paper, Microsoft Corp., Redmond, WA, USA (Apr. 2015).

2188. *Microsoft PlayReady Developing PlayReady Clients*, White Paper, Microsoft Corp., Redmond, WA, USA (Apr. 2015).

2189. *Microsoft PlayReady Protecting Premium Live TV Services with PlayReady*, White Paper, Microsoft Corp., Redmond, WA, USA (Apr. 2015).

2190. *MIME Conversion Buffer Overflow in Sendmail Versions 8.8.3 and 8.8.4*, CERT Advisory CA-1997-05, CERT, Pittsburg, PA, USA (Jan. 1997).

2191. *Multiple SunOS Vulnerabilities Patched*, CERT Advisory CA-1992-15, CERT, Pittsburgh, PA, USA (July 1992).

2192. *Nagios XI — Log Monitoring with Swatchdog*, Technical Report, Nagios Enterprises, LLC, St. Paul, MN, USA (Feb. 2017).

2193. *National Information Assurance Partnership*, Common Criteria (2017).

2194. *NIST Framework and Roadmap for Smart Grid Interoperability Standards, Release 3.0*, Special Publication 1108r3, National Institute of Standards and Technology, Gaithersburg, MD, USA (Sep. 2014).

2195. *NSA Releases Fortezza Algorithms*, Press Release, National Security Agency, Ft. George G. Meade, MD, USA (June 1998).

2196. *NSTISSP #11 FAQs* (Mar. 2005).

2197. *The OCaml Programming Language* (2018).

2198. *On the Protection of Individuals with Regard to the Processing of Personal Data and on the Free Movement of Such Data*, Directive 95/46/EC of the European Parliament and of the Council (Oct. 1995).

2199. *On the Protection of Natural Persons with Regard to the Processing of Personal Data by Competent Authorities for the Purposes of the Prevention, Investigation, Detection or Prosecution of Criminal Offences or the Execution of Criminal Penalties, and on the Free Movement of Such Data, and Repealing Council Framework Decision 2008/977/JHA*, Directive (EU) 2016/680 of the European Parliament and of the Council (Apr. 2016)

2200. *OpenLDAP Software 2.4 Administrator's Guide*, The OpenLDAP Project, Minden, NV, USA (Feb. 2016).

2201. *Overview of Red Team Reports*, Technical Report, Office of the California Secretary of State, Sacramento CA, USA (July 2007).

2202. *Password Management Guideline*, Technical Report CSC-STD-002-85, Department of Defense (Apr. 1985).

2203. *PDP-11 04/34/45/55 Processor Handbook*, Digital Equipment Corporation, Maynard, MA, USA (1976).

2204. *Penetration Testing Execution Standard* (Jan. 2012).

2205. *Privacy Act of 1974*, 5 U.S.C. §552a (2012).

2206. *Proceedings of a Workshop on Deterring Cyberattacks: Informing Strategies and Developing Options for U.S. Policy*, The National Academies Press, Washington, DC, USA (2010).

2207. *A Proposed Interpretation of the TCSEC for Virtual Machine Monitor Architectures*, Report, Trusted Information Systems, Inc., Glenwood, MD, USA (May 1990).

2208. *Ransomware and Recent Variants*, Alert TA16-091A, US-CERT, Pittsburg, PA, USA (Mar. 2016).

2209. *rpc.ypupdated Vulnerability*, CERT Advisory CA-1995-17, CERT, Pittsburg, PA, USA (Dec. 1995).

2210. *RSA SecurID Hardware Token Data Sheet*, RSA Data Security, Inc., Bedford, MA, USA (Oct. 2015).

2211. *RSA SecurID Hardware Token Technical Specifications*, RSA Data Security, Inc., Bedford, MA, USA (Oct. 2015).

2212. *The Rust Programming Language* (Dec. 2017).

2213. *Secure Hash Standard (SHS)*, FIPS PUB 180, National Institute of Standards and Technology, Gaithersburg, MD, USA (May 1993).

2214. *Secure Hash Standard (SHS)*, FIPS PUB 180-3, National Institute of Standards and Technology, Gaithersburg, MD, USA (Aug. 2015).

2215. *Securities and Investment Board Rules*, Chapter III, Part 5:08, cited in [292].

2216. *Security Configuration Guide: Access Control Lists, Cisco IOS XE Release 3S*, Cisco Systems, Inc., San Jose, CA, USA (2015).

2217. *Security Requirements for Cryptographic Modules*, FIPOS PUB 140-2, National Institute of Standards and Technology, Gaithersburg, MD, USA (May 2001).

2218. *Security Updates Available for Adobe Acrobat and Reader*, Adobe Security Bulletin APSB17-01, Adobe Systems, Inc., San Jose, CA, USA (Jan. 2017).

2219. *Sendmail Daemon Mode Vulnerability*, CERT Advisory CA-1996-24, CERT, Pittsburg, PA, USA (Nov. 1996).

2220. *Sendmail Group Permissions Vulnerability*, CERT Advisory CA-1996-25, CERT, Pittsburg, PA, USA (Dec. 1996).

2221. *Sendmail: Information Disclosure*, Gentoo Security Advisory GLSA 201412-32, Gentoo Security (Dec. 2014).

2222. *Sendmail prescan() Buffer Overflow Vulnerability*, Vulnerability Note VU#784980, US-CERT, Pittsburg, PA, USA (Sep. 2003).

2223. *Sendmail Signal I/O Race Condition*, Vulnerability Note VU#834865, US-CERT, Pittsburg, PA, USA (Mar. 2006).

2224. *Sendmail v5 Vulnerability*, CERT Advisory CA-1995-08, CERT, Pittsburg, PA, USA (Aug. 1995).

2225. *Sendmail Vulnerabilities*, CERT Advisory CA-1996-20, CERT, Pittsburg, PA,USA (Sep. 1996).

2226. *SET Secure Electronic Transaction Specification Book 1: Business Description, Version 1.0* (May 1997).

2227. *SET Secure Electronic Transaction Specification Book 2: Programmer's Guide, Version 1.0* (May 1997).

2228. *SET Secure Electronic Transaction Specification Book 3: Formal Protocol Definition, Version 1.0* (May 1997).

2229. *SHA-3 Standard: Permutation-Based Hash and Extendable-Output Functions*, FIPS PUB 202, National Institute of Standards and Technology, Gaithersburg, MD, USA (Aug. 2015).

2230. *SKIPJACK and KEA Algorithm Specifications, Version 2.0*, Technical Report, National Institute of Standards and Technology, Gaithersburg, MD, USA (May 1998).

2231. *Standards for Efficient Cryptography 2 (SEC 2): Recommended Elliptic Curve Domain Paramneters, Version 2.0*, Technical Report, Certicom Research (Jan. 2010).

2232. *Sun 4.1.X Loadmodule Vulnerability*, CERT Advisory CA-1995-12, CERT, Pittsburg, PA (Oct. 1995).

2233. *SunSHIELD Basic Security Module Guide*, Part Number 806-1789-10, Sun Microsystems, Inc., Palo Alto, CA, USA (Feb. 2000).

2234. *Symantec Decomposer Engine Multiple Parsing Vulnerabilities*, Security Advisory SYM16-010, Symantec, Inc., Mountain View, CA, USA (June 2016).

2235. *System Administration Guide: Security Services*, Part No. E27224-10, Oracle Corp., Redwood City, CA, USA (Jan. 2013).

2236. *Systems Security Engineering Capability Maturity Model (SSE-CMM) Model Description Document, Version 2.0*, Technical Report, Booz Allen & Hamilton, McLean, VA, USA (Apr. 1999).

2237. *Target: 40 Million Credit Cards Compromised*, CNN, Atlanta, GA, USA (Dec. 19, 2013).

2238. *Trojan Horse Version of TCP Wrappers*, CERT Advisory CA-1999-01, CERT, Pittsburg, PA (Jan. 1999).

2239. *Trusted Computer System Evaluation Criteria*, Technical Report DoD 5200.28-STD, Department of Defense (Dec. 1985).

2240. *Trusted Database Management System Interpretation*, Report NCSC-TG-021, Department of Defense, Washington, DC, USA (Apr. 1991).

2241. *Trusted Extensions Configuration and Administration*, Number E36840, Oracle, Inc., Redwood City, CA, USA (July 2014).

2242. *Trusted Network Interpretation*, Report NCSC-TG-005, Department of Defense, Washington, DC, USA (July 1987).

2243. *Trusted Platform Module Library Specification, Family "2.0", Level 00, Revision 01.38*, Technical Report, Trusted Computing Group, Beaverton, OR, USA (Sep. 2016).

2244. *Trusted Solaris Administrator's Procedures*, Number 805-8120-10, Sun Microsystems, Inc., Palo Alto, CA, USA (Dec. 2000).

2245. *Trusted Solaris Developer's Guide*, Manual Number 805-8116-10, Sun Microsystems, Inc., Palo Alto, CA, USA (Dec. 2000).

2246. *Trusted Solaris User's Guide*, Number 805-8115-10, Sun Microsystems, Inc., Palo Alto, CA, USA (Dec. 2000).

2247. *Unauthentic "Microsoft Corporation" Certificates*, CERT Advisory CA-2001-04, CERT, Pittsburg, PA, USA (Mar. 2001).

2248. *UNICOS Security Administration Reference Manual*, Cray Research, Inc., Mendota Heights, MN, USA (1989).

2249. *Virus Bulletin Archives*, Virus Bulletin, Abingdon, UK (2014).

2250. *Vulnerabilities Equities Policy and Process for the United States Government*, Charter, The White House, United States Government, Washington, DC, USA (Nov. 2017).

2251. *W32.Duqu: The Precursor to the Next Stuxnet*, Technical Report, Symantec Corporation, Mountain View, CA, USA (Oct. 2011).

2252. *WhatsApp Encryption Overview*, Technical White Paper, WhatsApp, Inc., Mountain View, CA, USA (Apr. 2016).

2253. *Windows Firewall Blocks Some Programs After You Install Windows XP SP3*, Microsoft Windows Technical Support Article 842242, Microsoft Corp., Redmond, WA, USA (Nov. 2007).

2254. *Writeable /etc/utmp Vulnerability*, CERT Advisory CA-1994-06, CERT, Pittsburg, PA, USA (Mar. 1994).

2255. *xterm Logfile Vulnerability*, CIAC Information Bulletin E-04, U.S. Department of Energy Computer Incident Advisory Capability, Livermore, CA, USA (Nov. 1993).

2256. *z/OS V2R1.0 Security Server RACF Command Language Reference*, IBM z/OS V2R1 SA23-2292-00, IBM Corporation, Poughkeepsie, NY, USA (2013).

Index

CREDITS

Cover: Captiva55/Shutterstock

Preface: "[Hortensio:] Madam, before you touch the . . . . And there it is in writing, fairly drawn." Shakespeare, *The Taming of the Shrew*, III, i, 62–68.

About the Author: Author photo by Holly O. Bishop.

Chapter 1: "[Antonio:] Whereof what's past is prologue, what to come / In yours and my discharge." Shakespeare, *The Tempest*, II, i, 257–258.

Chapter 2: "[Grandpre:] Description cannot suit itself in words / To demonstrate the life of such a battle / In life so lifeless as it shows itself." Shakespeare, *The Life of Henry the Fifth*, IV, ii, 53–55.

Chapter 2: "procedure cannot . . . the caller cannot". P. J. Denning. "Fault Tolerant Operating Systems," ACM Computing Surveys 8(4) pp. 359–389 (Dec. 1976).

Chapter 2: "privileges should not . . . system to another". N. Minsky. "The Principle of Attenuation of Privileges and its Ramifications," in [531], pp. 255–277.

Chapter 2: "System Program (ISP): . . . which users log in". S. B. Lipner. "Non-Discretionary Controls for Commercial Applications," Proceedings of the 1982 IEEE Symposium on Security and Privacy pp. 2–10 (Apr. 1982).

Chapter 2: "The system must . . . unauthorized recipients." R. H. Koenen, J. Lacy, M. Mackay, and S. Mitchell. "The Long March to Interoperable Digital Rights Management," Proceedings of the IEEE 92(6) pp. 883–897 (June 2004).

Chapter 3: "[Maria:] Ay, but you must confine yourself within the modest limits of order." Shakespeare, *Twelfth Night*, I, iii, 8–9.

Chapter 4: "[Portia:] Of a strange nature is the suit . . . [To Antonio.] You stand within his danger, do you not?" Shakespeare, *The Merchant of Venice*, IV, i, 177–180.

Chapter 4: "procedures shall include information on . . . authorized users, procedures for . . . network monitoring practices". Electronic Communications Policy University of California, 18, 2005.

Chapter 4: "any transfer of signals, writings, images . . . several electronic communications systems." M. Abadi and C. Fournet. "Access Control Based on Execution History," Proceedings of the 2003 Symposium on Network and Distributed System Security pp. 107–121 (Feb. 2003). URL: https://www.isoc.org/isoc/conferences/ndss/03/proceedings/papers/7.pdf

Chapter 5: "[Shepherd:] Sir, there lies such secrets . . . hour, if I may come to the speech of him." Shakespeare, *The Winter's Tale*, IV, iv, 785–788.

Chapter 5: "value of the [Basic Security Theorem] . . . security model for which it does not hold". J. McLean. "A Comment on the 'Basic Security Theorem' of Bell and LaPadula," Information Processing Letters 20(2) pp. 67–70 (Feb. 1985). DOI: 10.1016/0020-0190(85)90065-1

Chapter 6: "[Isabella:] Some one with child by him? . . . By vain, though apt affection." Shakespeare, *Measure for Measure*, I, iv, 45–48.

Chapter 7: "[Lady Macbeth:] Alack, . . . their daggers ready; He could not miss 'em . . ." Shakespeare, *Macbeth*, II, ii, 10–13.

Chapter 8: "[Juliet:] Come, vial. . . . No, no! this shall forbid it, lie thou there". Shakespeare, *The Tragedy of Romeo and Juliet*, IV, iii, 20–22.

Chapter 9: "[Goneril:] Combine together against the enemy, For those domestic poor particulars Are not to question here". Shakespeare, *The Tragedy of King Lear*, V, i, 29–31.

Chapter 10: "[York:] Then, York, be still awhile, till time do serve: Watch thou and wake when others be asleep, To pry into the secrets of the state". Shakespeare, *The Second Part of King Henry the Sixth*, I, i, 249–260.

Chapter 11: "[Valentine:] Why then, I would resort to her . . . What lets but one may enter at her window?" Shakespeare, *The Two Gentlemen of Verona*, III, i, 110–113.

Chapter 11: "must provide a user with the ability to display a full certification path for any certificate employed in PEM upon demand". S. Kent. Privacy Enhancement for Internet Electronic Mail: Part II: Certificate-Based Key Management, RFC 1422 (Feb. 1993). DOI: 10.17487/RFC1422

Chapter 11: "Private keys can be easily computed . . . key without knowing *s*." A. Shamir. "Identity-Based Cryptosystems and Signature Schemes," Advances in Cryptology — CRYPTO '84 (Lecture Notes in Computer Science 196) pp. 47–53 (Aug. 1984). DOI: 10.1007/3-540-39568-7_5

Chapter 11: "An end entity certificate is one issued to entities . . . that begins a certificate chain." D. Cooper, S. Santesson, S. Farrell, S. Boeyen, R. Housley, and T. Polk. Internet X.509 Public Key Infrastructure Certificate and Certificate Revocation List (CRL) Profile, RFC 5280 (May 2008). DOI: 10.17487/RFC5280

Chapter 11: "Version. This is either 3 or 4. Version 3 . . . cryptosystem identifed in field 4." J. Callas, L. Donnerhacke, H. Finney, D. Shaw, and R. Thayer. OpenPGP Message Format, RFC 4880 (Nov. 2007). DOI: 10.17487/RFC4880

Chapter 11: "Alice → Cathy . . . $\{k_{session}\}$kBob". B. Schneier. Applied Cryptography: Protocols, Algorithms, and Source Code in C, John Wiley & Sons, New York, NY, USA (1996).

Chapter 11: "Alice → Cathy . . . Bob : $\{r_2-1\}k_{session}$". R. M. Needham and M. D. Schroeder. "Using Encryption for Authentication in Large Networks of Computers," Communications of the ACM 21(12) pp. 993–999 (Dec. 1978).

Chapter 12: "[Iago:] So will I turn her virtue into pitch, And out of her own goodness make the net / That shall enmesh them all". Shakespeare, *The Tragedy of Othello*, II, iii, 361–363.

Chapter 12, Figure 12–5: Adapted from D. A. McGrew and J. Viega. The Galois/Counter Mode of Operation (GCM)," Submission to NIST (Jan. 2004) URL: http://csrc.nist.gov/CryptoToolkit/modes/proposedmodes/gcm/gcm-spec.pdf

Chapter 13: "[Antipholus of Syracuse:] To me she speaks; ... I'll entertain the offer'd fallacy". Shakespeare, *The Comedy of Errors*, II, ii, 185–190.

Chapter 13: "And where is that band who ... free and the home of the brave." "The Star-Spangled Banner," National Museum of American History.

Chapter 13: "It must always be invoked ... guessed passwords to be accepted." M. Bishop and D. V. Klein. "Improving System Security via Proactive Password Checking," Computers & Security 14(3) pp. 233–249 (Apr. 1995).

Chapter 13: "The set A of authentication information is ... the authentication and complementary information." M. Bishop. "Password Management," Proceedings of Compcon Spring '91 pp. 167–169 (Feb. 1991). DOI: 10.1109/CM-PCON.1991.128801

Chapter 14: "[Falstaff:] If I had a thousand sons, the first human principle I would teach them should be, to forswear thin potations and to addict themselves to sack". Shakespeare, *The Second Part of King Henry the Fourth*, IV, iii, 133–136.

Chapter 15: "[Aemelia:] Most mighty duke, behold a man ... am Dromio: pray, let me stay". Shakespeare, *The Comedy of Errors*, V, i, 332–338.

Chapter 15: "Generic certification of a user ... correctly identifies the principal." J. Callas, L. Donnerhacke, H. Finney, D. Shaw, and R. Thayer. OpenPGP Message Format, RFC 4880 (Nov. 2007).

Chapter 15: "They that can give up essential liberty to obtain a little temporary safety deserve neither liberty nor safety". J. Bartlett Familiar Quotations, Little, Brown and Co., Boston, MA (1901).

Chapter 15: "right to be let ... by civilized men". L. J. Brandeis. Olmstead et al. v. United States, 277 US 438 (June 1927).

Chapter 16: "[Cassio:] Why, no. The day had broke / Before we parted. I ha' made bold, Iago, / To send in to your wife. My suit to her / Is that she will to virtuous Desdemona / Procure me some access". Shakespeare, *The Tragedy of Othello*, III, i, 32–36.

Chapter 17: "[Bottom:] Masters, I am to discourse ... Athenian. I will tell you every thing, right as it fell out." Shakespeare, *A Midsummer Night's Dream*, IV, ii, 30–33.

Chapter 18: "[Troilus:] This is the monstruosity in love ... and the act a slave to limit". Shakespeare, *Troilus and Cressida*, III, ii, 82–84.

Chapter 18: "The coordinator sends a message ... and then acts accordingly." O. L. Costich and I. S. Moskowita. "Analysis of a Storage Channel in the Two Phase Commit Protocol," Proceedings of the Fourth Computer Security Foundations Workshop pp. 201–208 (June 1991). DOI: 10.1109/CSFW.1991.151587

Chapter 19: "[Bottom:] Not a whit: ... weaver: this will put them out of fear". Shakespeare, *A Midsummer Night's Dream*, III, i, 17–23.

Chapter 19: "Requirements definitions, omissions ... faulty upgrades, and decommissions". P. Neumann, Computer-Related Risks, ACM Press, New York, NY (1994). ISBN: 978-0-201-55805-0

Chapter 19: "Individuals and Interactions more than processes and tools ... more than following a plan". K. Beck, M. Beedle, A. van Bennekum, A. Cockburn, W. Cunningham, M. Fowler, J. Grenning, J. Highsmith, A. Hunt, R. Jeffries, J. Kern, B. Marick, R. C. Martin, S. Mellor, K. Schwaber, J. Sutherland, and D. Thomas. Manifesto for Agile Software Development. URL: agilemanifesto.org

Chapter 20: "[Lord Bardolph:] When we mean to build, ... or at last desist / To build at all?" Shakespeare, *King Henry IV*, Part II, I, iii, 41–48.

Chapter 21: "[Petruchio:] And, for an entrance to my entertainment ... His name is Licio, born in Mantua". Shakespeare, *The Taming of the Shrew*, II, i, 54–60.

Chapter 21: "The information being returned by a specific function ... than the level of the state variable." T. Taylor. "Comparison Paper Between the Bell and LaPadula Model and the SRI Model," Proceedings of the 1984 IEEE Symposium on Security and Privacy pp. 195–202 (Apr. 1984). DOI: 10.1109/SP.1984.10021

Chapter 22: "[Leonato:] O! she tore the letter into a thousand ... yea, though I love him, I should." Shakespeare, *Much Ado About Nothing*, II, iii, 156–161.

Chapter 22, Figure 22–2: K. Ferraiolo, L. Gallagher, and V. Thompson. "Building a Case for Assurance from Process," Proceedings of the 21st National Information Systems Security Conference pp. 719–729 (Oct. 1998).

Chapter 23: "[Titus Andronicus:] Ah!, ... How Troy was burnt and he made miserable?" Shakespeare, *The Tragedy of Titus Andronicus*, III, ii, 26–28.

Chapter 24: "[MacBeth:] I pull in resolution and begin. ... Dunsinane. Arm, arm, and out!" Shakespeare, *The Tragedy of Macbeth*, V, v, 42–46.

Chapter 24: "Incomplete parameter validation. ... Exploitable logic error." R. P. Abbott, J. S. Chin, J. E. Donnelley, W. L. Konigsford, S. Tokubo, and D. A. Webb. Security Analysis and Enhancements of Computer Operating Systems, NBSIR 76-1041, ICET, National Bureau of Standards, Washington, DC (Apr. 1976). URL: http://nvlpubs.ni

Chapter 24: "Example: The entry for the xterm race condition in Section 24.3.1". Common Vulnerabilities and Exposures: CVE-1999-0965 (Jan. 2000). http://cve.mitre.org/cgi-bin/cvename.cgi?name=CVE-1999-0965

Chapter 24: "A buffer overflow in a function in the GNU C library has the following entry". Common Vulnerabilities and Exposures: CVE-2016-3706 (Mar. 2016). URL: https://cve.mitre.org/cgi-bin/cvename.cgi?name=CVE-2016-3706

Chapter 24: "A category entry is an entry ... specific language or technology." CWE Glossary (Jan. 2017). URL: http://cwe.mitre.org/documents/glossary/index.html

Chapter 24: "Class describes a weakness ... language, system, or technology". The Evolution of the CWE Development and Research Views (Sep. 2008). URL: http://cwe.mitre.org/documents/views/view-evolution.html

Chapter 24: "System flaws that cause a large . . . . A system (i.e., TCB) is largely . . . specific set of design properties." S. Gupta and V. D. Gligor. "Towards a Theory of Penetration-Resistant Systems and Its Applications," Proceedings of the Fourth Computer Security Foundations Workshop pp. 62–78 (June 1991).

Chapter 24: "COMSEC is the communications security class . . . SPECSEC is the spectrum security class". P. Herzon. OSSTMM 3: Open Source Security Testing Methodology Manual, Technical Report, Institute for Security and Open Methodologies, New York, NY, USA (Dec. 2010). URL: http://www.isecom.org/mirror/OSSTMM.3.pdf

Chapter 24: "In the planning phase, the testers and . . . and how to mitigate these problems." K. Scarfone, S. Murugiah, A. Cody, and A. Orebaugh. Technical Guide to Information Security Testing and Assessment, specpub 800-115, Computer Security Division, Information Technology Laboratory, National Institute of Standards and Technology, Gaithersburg, MD, USA (Sep. 2008). DOI: 10.6028/NIST.SP.800-115

Chapter 24, Figure 24–11: S. Gupta and V. D. Gligor. "Experience with a Penetration Analysis Method and Tool," Proceedings of the 15th National Computer Security Conference pp. 165–183 (Oct. 1992), Figure 11(a), p. 178–9.

Chapter 25: "[Lady Macbeth:] Your servants ever / Have theirs . . . pleasure, / Still to return your own." Shakespeare, *The Tragedy of Macbeth*, I, vi, 27–30.

Chapter 25: "Text display shows the logs in a textual . . . is the locality of the technique." J. A. Hoagland, C. Wee, and K. Levitt. Audit Log-Analysis Using the Visual Audit Browser Toolkit, Technical Report CSE-95-11, Dept. of Computer Science, University of California at Davis, Davis, CA, USA (Sep. 1995). URL: http://www.cs.ucdavis.edu/research/tech-reports/1995/CSE-95-11.pdf

Chapter 25: "Simple sanitization, in which . . . as in information-tracking and format sanitization". E. A. Fisch, G. B. White, and U. W. Pooch. "The Design of an Audit Trail Analysis Tool," Proceedings of the Tenth Annual Computer Security Applications Conference pp. 126–132 (Dec. 1994). DOI: 10.1109/CSAC.1994.367314

Chapter 26: "[Hippolyta:] How chance Moonshine . . . passion ends the play." Shakespeare, *A Midsummer Night's Dream*, V, i, 320–323.

Chapter 26: "event can represent a single . . . resulting in a single, observable record". S. Kumar and E. H. Spafford. "A Pattern Matching Model for Misuse intrusion Detection," Proceedings of the 17th National Computer Security Conference pp. 11–21 (Oct.1994).

Chapter 27: "[Romeo:] Courage, man; the hurt cannot be much . . . and you shall find me a grave man." Shakespeare, *The Tragedy of Romeo and Juliet*, III, i, 98–101.

Chapter 27: "The thumbprint should take as . . . little to compute and compare." S. Staniford-Chen and L. T. Heberlein. "Holding Intruders Accountable on the Internet," Proceedings of the 1995 IEEE Symposium on Security and Privacy pp. 39–49 (May 1995). DOI: 10.1109/SECPRI.1995.398921

Chapter 27: "Publication. As above, the . . . constituency or other CSIRTs". N. Brownlee and E. Guttman. Expectations for Computer Security Incident Response, RFC 2350 (June 1998). DOI: 10.17487/RFC2350

Chapter 27: "Consider the entire system . . . presented in an understandable way". S. Peisert, M. Bishop, S. Karin, and K. Marzullo. "Principles-Driven Forensic Analysis," Proceedings of the 2005 Workshop on New Security Paradigms pp. 85–93 (Oct. 2005). DOI: 10.1145/1146269.1146291

Chapter 28: "[John of Gaunt:] . . . less happier lands". Shakespeare, *The Tragedy of King Richard the Second*, II, i, 43–49.

Chapter 28: "a model for enabling . . . service provider interaction". P. Mell and T. Grance. The NIST Definition of Cloud Computing, Special Publication 800-145, National Institute of Standards and Technology, Gaithersburg, MD (Sep. 2011). DOI: 10.6028/NIST.SP.800-145

Chapter 29: "[Imogen:] To your . . . me, beseech ye." Shakespeare, *Cymbeline*, II, ii, 8–10.

Chapter 29: "[p]rogrammer convenience is the antithesis of security". B. Reid. "Viewpoint: Reflections on Some Recent Widespread Computer Break-Ins," Communications of the ACM 30(2) pp. 103–105 (Feb. 1987). DOI: 10.1145/12527.315716

Chapter 30: "[Cominius:] Away! The . . . upon you yet." Shakespeare, *Coriolanus*, III, ii, 138–141.

Chapter 30: "He took his . . . awhile in thought". Lewis Carroll, Through the Looking-glass, and what Alice Found There, Macmillan and Co., London, 1882.

Chapter 31: "[Clown:] What is . . . a thousand tenants". Shakespeare, *Hamlet*, V, i, 42–45.

Chapter 31: "significant rates of failure". B. P. Miller, D. Koski, C. P. Lee, V. Maganty, R. Murthy, A. Natarajan, and J. Steidl. Fuzz Revisited: A Re-examination of the Reliability of UNIX Utilities and Services, Technical Report, Computer Sciences Department, University of Wisconsin, Madison, WI.

Appendix F, Figure F–10: Adapted from Advanced Encryption Standard, FIPS PUB 197, National Institute of Standards and Technology, Gaithersburg, MD (Nov. 2001). DOI: 10.6028/NIST.FIPS.197 p. 15, Figure 5

Appendix F, Figure F–13: Adapted from Advanced Encryption Standard, FIPS PUB 197, National Institute of Standards and Technology, Gaithersburg, MD (Nov. 2001). DOI: 10.6028/NIST.FIPS.197 p. 21, Figure 12

Appendix F, Figure F–14: Adapted from Advanced Encryption Standard, FIPS PUB 197, National Institute of Standards and Technology, Gaithersburg, MD (Nov. 2001). DOI: 10.6028/NIST.FIPS.197 Section A.2

Appendix F, Figure F–15: Adapted from Advanced Encryption Standard, FIPS PUB 197, National Institute of Standards and Technology, Gaithersburg, MD (Nov. 2001). DOI: 10.6028/NIST.FIPS.197 p. 20, Figure 11

Appendix F, Figure F–16: Adapted from Figure 15, Advanced Encryption Standard, FIPS PUB 197, National Institute of Standards and Technology, Gaithersburg, MD (Nov. 2001). DOI: 10.6028/NIST.FIPS.197 p. 25

Appendix F, Figure F–17: Adapted from Advanced Encryption Standard, FIPS PUB 197, National Institute of Standards and Technology, Gaithersburg, MD (Nov. 2001). DOI: 10.6028/NIST.FIPS.197 p. 25 Figure 15

Photo by izusek/gettyimages

Register Your Product at informit.com/register

Assess additional benefits and **save 35%** on your next purchase

- Automatically receive a coupon for 35% off your next purchase, valid for 30 days. Look for your code in your InformIT cart or the Manage Codes section of your account page.

- Download available product updates.

- Access bonus material if available.*

- Check the box to hear from us and receive exclusive offers on new editions and related products.

*Registration benefits vary by product. Benefits will be listed on your account page under Registered Products.

InformIT.com—The Trusted Technology Learning Source

InformIT is the online home of information technology brands at Pearson, the world's foremost education company. At InformIT.com, you can:

- Shop our books, eBooks, software, and video training
- Take advantage of our special offers and promotions (informit.com/promotions)
- Sign up for special offers and content newsletter (informit.com/newsletters)
- Access thousands of free chapters and video lessons

Connect with InformIT—Visit informit.com/community

the trusted technology learning source

Addison-Wesley · Adobe Press · Cisco Press · Microsoft Press · Pearson IT Certification · Prentice Hall · Que · Sams · Peachpit Press

P Pearson